PROSECUTION AND ADJUDICATION

FIFTH EDITION

by

FRANK W. MILLER
James Carr Professor Emeritus of Criminal Jurisprudence,
Washington University

ROBERT O. DAWSON
Bryant Smith Chair in Law,
University of Texas

GEORGE E. DIX
A. W. Walker Centennial Chair in Law,
University of Texas

RAYMOND I. PARNAS
Professor of Law Emeritus,
University of California, Davis

NEW YORK, NEW YORK
FOUNDATION PRESS
2000

Reprinted from
Miller, Dawson, Dix and Parnas'
Cases and Materials on Criminal Justice Administration
(Fifth Edition)
Pages 1 to 7, 603 to 1297

COPYRIGHT © 2000 By FOUNDATION PRESS
         11 Penn Plaza, Tenth Floor
         New York, NY 10001
         Phone Toll Free 1-877-888-1330
         Fax (212) 760-8705
         fdpress.com

ISBN 1-56662-987-X

TEXT IS PRINTED ON 10% POST
CONSUMER RECYCLED PAPER

PREFACE

This volume is a complete extract of the Introduction and Chapters 11 through 26 of Miller, Dawson, Dix, and Parnas, Criminal Justice Administration (Fifth Edition, 2000).

These materials deal with the formal processing of a serious criminal case through the judicial system. They are designed for discussion of the numerous issues posed by local statute, court rules and case law as well as the impact of actual or possible federal constitutional requirements upon this local law. In addition, they raise basic questions concerning the manner in which discretionary decisions are and should be made in the criminal justice system and how—if at all—the system should be structured so as to assure that discretion is best exercised.

Our intention is to avoid limiting discussion to arguments which might be made on behalf of defendants or the prosecution in criminal litigation, and to encourage consideration of how the criminal justice system might best be structured so as to achieve accuracy and other objectives. Reasonable resolution of any specific issue requires consideration of the criminal justice process as a whole, how it actually functions, and the relationship of issues under consideration to others that may or are being raised. We believe these materials enable informed discussion with this broad perspective.

Footnotes retained from material reprinted have been renumbered. Footnotes added by the editors have been identified by number. Footnotes and textual citations to authority have been deleted from principal opinions without specific indication of the omissions. Editors' footnotes are indicated by letters. We have noted omitted opinions in principal cases only when, in our view, the existence of such opinions is useful in understanding the procedural or precedential significance of the opinion reprinted.

FRANK W. MILLER
ROBERT O. DAWSON
GEORGE E. DIX
RAYMOND I. PARNAS

March, 2000

*

SUMMARY OF CONTENTS

TABLE OF CONTENTS

TABLE OF CASES

Principal cases are in bold type. Non-principal cases are in roman type. References are to Pages.

PROSECUTION AND ADJUDICATION

*

INTRODUCTION: THE CRIMINAL JUSTICE PROCESS

Analysis

NATIONAL ADVISORY COMMISSION ON CRIMINAL JUSTICE STANDARDS AND GOALS, COURTS 11–15 (1973)

* * *

ARREST

The first formal contact of an accused with the criminal justice system is likely to be an arrest by a police officer. In most cases, the arrest will be made upon the police officer's own evaluation that there is sufficient basis for believing that a crime had been committed by the accused. However, the arrest may be made pursuant to a warrant; in this case, the police officer or some other person will have submitted the evidence against the accused to a judicial officer, who determines whether the evidence is sufficient to justify an arrest. In some situations, the accused may have no formal contact with the law until he has been indicted by a grand jury. Following such an indictment, a court order may be issued authorizing police officers to take the accused into custody. But these are exceptional situations. Ordinarily, the arrest is made without any court order and the court's contact with the accused comes only after the arrest.

* * *

INITIAL JUDICIAL APPEARANCE

In all jurisdictions, a police officer or other person making an arrest must bring the arrested person before a judge within a short period of time. It is at this initial appearance that most accused have their first contact with the courts. This initial appearance is usually before a lower court—a justice of the peace or a magistrate. * * * Often by the time of the initial appearance, the prosecution will have prepared a formal document called a complaint, which charges the defendant with a specific crime.

At the initial appearance, several things may occur. First, the defendant will be informed of the charges against him, usually by means of the complaint. Second, he will be informed of his rights, including his constitutional privilege against self-incrimination. Third, if the case is one in which the accused will be provided with an attorney at State expense, the mechanical process of assigning the attorney at least may begin at this stage. Fourth, unless the defendant is convicted of an offense at this point, arrangements may be made concerning the release of the defendant before further proceedings. This may take the traditional form of setting bail, that is, establishment of an amount of security the defendant himself or a professional bondsman whom he may hire must deposit with the court (or

1

assume the obligation to pay) to assure that the defendant does appear for later proceedings. Pre-trial release, in some jurisdictions, also may take the form of being released on one's own recognizance, that is, release simply upon the defendant's promise to appear at a later time. * * *

Merits of the Case begin

In addition to these matters collateral to the issue of guilt, it is at the initial appearance that judicial inquiry into the merits of the case begins. If the charge is one the lower court has authority to try, the defendant may be asked how he pleads. If he pleads guilty, he may be convicted at this point. If he pleads not guilty, a trial date may be set and trial held later in this court.

However, if the charge is more serious, the court must give the defendant the opportunity for a judicial evaluation to determine whether there is enough evidence to justify putting him to trial in the higher court. In this type of case, the judge at the initial appearance ordinarily will ask the defendant whether he wants a preliminary hearing. If the defendant does, the matter generally is continued, or postponed to give both the prosecution and the defense time to prepare their cases.

Preliminary Hearing

The matter will be taken up again later in the lower court at the preliminary hearing. At this proceeding, the prosecutor introduces evidence to try to prove the defendant's guilt. He need not convince the court of the defendant's guilt beyond a reasonable doubt, but need only establish that there is enough evidence from which an average person (juror) could conclude that the defendant was guilty of the crime charged. If this evidence is produced, the court may find that the prosecution has established probable cause to believe the defendant guilty.

At this preliminary hearing the defendant may cross-examine witnesses produced by the prosecution and present evidence himself. If the court finds at the end of the preliminary hearing that probable cause does not exist, it dismisses the complaint. This does not ordinarily prevent the prosecution from bringing another charge, however. If the court finds that probable cause does exist, it orders that the defendant be bound over to the next step in the prosecution. As a practical matter, the preliminary hearing also serves the function of giving the defendant and his attorney a look at the case the prosecution will produce at trial. It gives a defense attorney the opportunity to cross-examine witnesses he later will have to confront. This informal previewing function may be more valuable to defendants than the theoretical function of the preliminary hearing.

FILING OF FORMAL CRIMINAL CHARGE

Grand Jury

Generally, it is following the decision of the lower court to bind over a defendant that the formal criminal charge is made in the court that would try the case if it goes to formal trial. If no grand jury action is to be taken, this is a simple step consisting of the prosecutor's filing a document called an information. But in many jurisdictions the involvement of the grand jury makes the process more complex. There, the decision at the preliminary hearing simply is to bind the defendant over for consideration by the grand jury. In these areas, the prosecutor then must go before the grand jury and again present his evidence. Only if the grand jury determines that there is probable cause does it act. Its action—consisting of issuing a document called an indictment—constitutes the formal charging of the defendant. If it does not find probable cause, it takes no action and the prosecution is dismissed.

In some jurisdictions, it is not necessary to have both a grand jury inquiry and a preliminary hearing. In most Federal jurisdictions, for example, if a defendant has been indicted by a grand jury he no longer has a right to a preliminary hearing, on the theory that he is entitled to only one determination as to whether probable cause exists.

Although the defendant is entitled to participate in the preliminary hearing, he has no right to take part in a grand jury inquiry. Traditionally, he has not been able to ascertain what went on in front of the grand jury, although increasingly the law has given him the right, after the fact, to know.

Participation of Δ

Following the formal charge—whether it has been by indictment or information—any of a variety of matters that require resolution may arise. The defendant's competency to stand trial may be in issue. This requires the court to resolve the question of whether the defendant is too ill mentally or otherwise impaired to participate meaningfully in his trial. If he is sufficiently impaired, trial must be postponed until he regains his competency.

competency

The defendant also may challenge the validity of the indictment or information or the means by which they were issued. For example, he may assert that those acts with which he is charged do not constitute a crime under the laws of the jurisdiction. Or, if he was indicted by a grand jury, he may assert 'that the grand jury was selected in a manner not consistent with State or Federal law and, therefore, that the indictment is invalid.

Challenges to Indictment

A defendant also may—and in some jurisdictions must—raise, before trial, challenges to the admissibility of certain evidence, especially evidence seized by police officers in a search or statements obtained from him by interrogation. In view of the rapid growth of legal doctrine governing the admissibility of statements of defendants and evidence obtained by police search and seizure, resolution of the issues raised by defendants' challenges to the admissibility of such evidence may be more complex and time-consuming than anything involved in determining guilt or innocence.

Challenges to Admissibility of Evidence

* * *

ARRAIGNMENT

In view of the potential complexity of pretrial matters, much of the significant activity in a criminal prosecution already may have occurred at the time the defendant makes his first formal appearance before the court that is to try him. This first appearance—the arraignment—is the point at which he is asked to plead to the charge. He need not plead, in which case a plea of not guilty automatically is entered for him. If he pleads guilty, the law requires that certain precautions be taken to assure that this plea is made validly. Generally, the trial judge accepting the plea first must inquire of the defendant whether he understands the charge against him and the penalties that may be imposed. The judge also must assure himself that there is some reasonable basis in the facts of the case for the plea. This

First Appearance

may involve requiring the prosecution to present some of its evidence to assure the court that there is evidence tending to establish guilt.

TRIAL

Unless the defendant enters a guilty plea, the full adversary process is put into motion. The prosecution now must establish to a jury or a judge the guilt of the defendant beyond a reasonable doubt. If the defendant elects to have the case tried by a jury, much effort is expended on the selection of a jury. Prospective jurors are questioned to ascertain whether they might be biased and what their views on numerous matters might be. Both sides have the right to have a potential juror rejected on the ground that he may be biased. In addition, both have the right to reject a limited number of potential jurors without having to state any reason. When the jury has been selected and convened, both sides may make opening statements explaining what they intend to prove or disprove.

The prosecution presents its evidence first, and the defendant has the option of making no case and relying upon the prosecution's inability to establish guilt beyond a reasonable doubt. He also has the option of presenting evidence tending to disprove the prosecution's case or tending to prove additional facts constituting a defense under applicable law. Throughout, however, the burden remains upon the prosecution. Procedurally, this is effectuated by defense motions to dismiss, which often are made after the prosecution's case has been presented and after all of the evidence is in. These motions in effect assert that the prosecution's case is so weak that no reasonable jury could conclude beyond a reasonable doubt that the defendant was guilty. If the judge grants the motion, he is in effect determining that no jury could reasonably return a verdict of guilty. This not only results in a dismissal of the prosecution but also prevents the prosecution from bringing another charge for the same crime.

After the evidence is in and defense motions are disposed of, the jury is instructed on the applicable law. Often both defense and prosecution lawyers submit instructions which they ask the court to read to the jury, and the court chooses from those and others it composes itself. It is in the formulation of these instructions that many issues regarding the definition of the applicable law arise and must be resolved. After—or sometimes before—the instructions are read, both sides present formal arguments to the jury. The jury then retires for its deliberations.

Generally, the jury may return only one of two verdicts: guilty or not guilty. A verdict of not guilty may be misleading; it may mean not that the jury believed that the defendant was not guilty but rather that the jury determined that the prosecution had not established guilt by the criterion—beyond a reasonable doubt—the law imposes. If the insanity defense has been raised, the jury may be told it should specify if insanity is the reason for acquittal; otherwise, there is no need for explanation. If a guilty verdict is returned, the court formally enters a judgment of conviction unless there is a legally sufficient reason for not doing so.

The defendant may attack his conviction, usually by making a motion to set aside the verdict and order a new trial. In his attack, he may argue that evidence was improperly admitted during the trial, that the evidence was so weak that no reasonable jury could have found that it established guilt beyond a reasonable doubt, or that there is newly discovered evidence which, had it been available at the time of trial, would have changed the result. If the court grants a motion raising one of these arguments, the effect generally is not to acquit the defendant but merely to require the holding of a new trial.

SENTENCING

Sentencing then follows. (If the court has accepted a plea of guilty, this step follows acceptance of the plea.) In an increasing number of jurisdictions, an investigation called the presentence report is conducted by professional probation officers. This involves investigation of the offense, the offender and his background, and any other matters of potential value to the sentencing judge. Following submission of the report to the court, the defendant is given the opportunity to comment upon the appropriateness of sentencing. In some jurisdictions, this has developed into a more extensive court hearing on sentencing issues, with the defendant given the opportunity to present evidence as well as argument for leniency. Sentencing itself generally is the responsibility of the judge, although in some jurisdictions juries retain that authority.

APPEAL

Following the conclusion of the proceeding in the trial court, the matter shifts to the appellate courts. In some jurisdictions, a defendant who is convicted of a minor offense in a lower court has the right to a new trial (trial de novo) in a higher court. But in most situations—and in all cases involving serious offenses—the right to appeal is limited to the right to have an appellate court examine the record of the trial proceedings for error. If error is found, the appellate court either may take definitive action—such as ordering that the prosecution be dismissed—or it may set aside the conviction and remand the case for a new trial. The latter gives the prosecution the opportunity to obtain a valid conviction. Generally, a time limit is placed upon the period during which an appeal may be taken.

COLLATERAL ATTACK

Even if no appeal is taken or the conviction is upheld, the courts' participation in the criminal justice process is not necessarily ended. To some extent, a convicted defendant who has either exhausted his appeal rights or declined to exercise them within the appropriate time limits can seek further relief by means of collateral attack upon the conviction. This method involves a procedure collateral to the standard process of conviction and appeal.

Traditionally this relief was sought by applying for a writ of habeas corpus on the ground that the conviction under which the applicant was held was invalid. Many jurisdictions have found this vehicle too cumbersome for modern problems and have developed special procedures for collateral attacks. * * *

A general view of The Criminal Justice System

This chart seeks to present a simple yet comprehensive view of the movement of cases through the criminal justice system. Procedures in individual jurisdictions may vary from the pattern shown here. The differing weights of line indicate the relative volumes of cases disposed of at various points in the system, but this is only suggestive since no nationwide data of this sort exists.

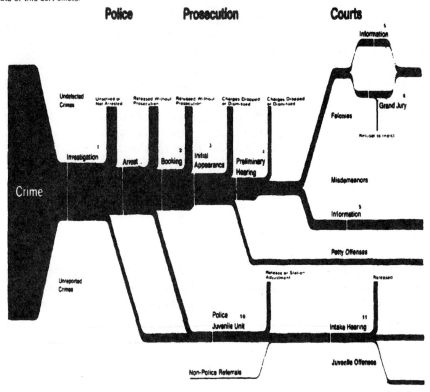

1 May continue until trial.

2 Administrative record of arrest. First step at which temporary release on bail may be available.

3 Before magistrate, commissioner, or justice of peace. Formal notice of charge, advice of rights. Bail set. Summary trials for petty offenses usually conducted here without further processing.

4 Preliminary testing of evidence against defendant. Charge may be reduced. No separate preliminary hearing for misdemeanors in some systems.

5 Charge filed by prosecutor on basis of information submitted by police or citizens. Alternative to grand jury indictment, often used in felonies, almost always in misdemeanors.

6 Reviews whether Government evidence sufficient to justify trial. Some States have no grand jury system; others seldom use it.

Source: The President's Commission on Law Enforcement and Administration of Justice, The Challenge of Crime in a Free Society (1967).

Corrections

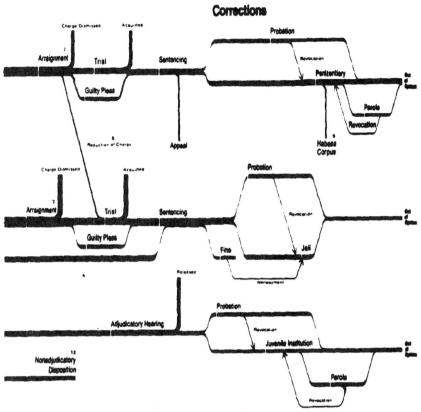

7 Appearance for plea; defendant elects trial by judge or jury (if available); counsel for indigent usually appointed here in felonies. Often not at all in other cases.

8 Charge may be reduced at any time prior to trial in return for plea of guilty or for other reasons.

9 Challenge on constitutional grounds to legality of detention. May be sought at any point in process.

10 Police often hold informal hearings, dismiss or adjust many cases without further processing.

11 Probation officer decides desirability of further court action.

12 Welfare agency, social services, counselling, medical care, etc., for cases where adjudicatory handling not needed.

PART TWO

Prosecution and Adjudication

*

CHAPTER 11

THE INITIAL APPEARANCE AND DETENTION

Analysis

Under Fed.R.Crim.Proc. 5(a) (reprinted in this Chapter), as well as under similar provisions in virtually all states, a person who is arrested must be "presented" before a judicial officer without substantial delay. Generally, this will be the defendant's first court appearance in connection with the prosecution; hence, it is frequently called the initial appearance. Depending upon local requirements and practice, a "complaint" may have been filed before the defendant's presentation "charging" the defendant with an offense. In felony and potentially in serious misdemeanor prosecutions, this complaint serves only the interim function of formalizing the charge until an indictment or information is filed. In some misdemeanor procedures, however, the complaint is the only formal charge in the case. Frequently, the initial appearance will be before a "lower" court judge who—if the charge is a serious one—lacks jurisdiction to adjudicate the defendant's guilt or innocence. In addition, the initial appearance takes place soon after apprehension. The defendant may not yet be represented by an attorney, or if an attorney is involved, the defendant and counsel may not yet be prepared to address matters relating to the case.

For these reasons, the functions of the initial appearance are quite limited. The defendant will generally be told of the charges and warned of the right to refrain from self-incrimination. Arrangements may be made (or begun) for appointment of counsel if the defendant asserts indigency, pretrial release or detention (see Chapter 12), and for a preliminary hearing (see Chapter 13). The principal case in this Chapter concerns a defendant's right to a judicial determination of "probable cause." This right which may be implemented by expanding the functions of the initial appearance to include the probable cause determination.

FEDERAL RULES OF CRIMINAL PROCEDURE

Rule 5. Initial Appearance Before the Magistrate Judge

(a) **In General.** Except as otherwise provided in this rule, an officer making an arrest under a warrant issued upon a complaint or any person making an arrest without a warrant shall take the arrested person without unnecessary delay before the nearest available federal magistrate judge or, if a federal magistrate judge is not reasonably available, before a state or local judicial officer authorized by 18 U.S.C. § 3041. If a person arrested without a warrant is brought before a magistrate judge, a complaint, satisfying the probable cause requirements of Rule 4(a), shall be promptly filed. When a person, arrested with or without a warrant or given a summons, appears initially before the magistrate judge, the magistrate judge shall proceed in accordance with the applicable subdivisions of this rule. * * *

(b) Misdemeanors and Other Petty Offenses. If the charge against the defendant is a misdemeanor [punishable by not more than one year in prison][a] or other petty offense [punishable by not more than six months' incarceration or a fine of not more than $5,000][b] triable by a United States magistrate judge under 18 U.S.C. § 3401, the magistrate judge shall proceed in accordance with Rule 58.

(c) Offenses not Triable by the United States Magistrate Judge. If the charge against the defendant is not triable by the United States magistrate judge, the defendant shall not be called upon to plead. The magistrate judge shall inform the defendant of the complaint against the defendant and of any affidavit filed therewith, of the defendant's right to retain counsel or to request the assignment of counsel if the defendant is unable to obtain counsel, and of the general circumstances under which the defendant may secure pretrial release. The magistrate judge shall inform the defendant that the defendant is not required to make a statement and that any statement made by the defendant may be used against the defendant. The magistrate judge shall also inform the defendant of the right to a preliminary examination. The magistrate judge shall allow the defendant reasonable time and opportunity to consult counsel and shall detain or conditionally release the defendant as provided by statute or in these rules.

A defendant is entitled to a preliminary examination, unless waived, when charged with any offense, other than a petty offense, which is to be tried by a judge of the district court. If the defendant waives preliminary examination, the magistrate judge shall forthwith hold the defendant to answer in the district court. If the defendant does not waive the preliminary examination, the magistrate judge shall schedule a preliminary examination. Such examination shall be held within a reasonable time but in any event not later than 10 days following the initial appearance if the defendant is in custody and no later than 20 days if the defendant is not in custody, provided, however, that the preliminary examination shall not be held if the defendant is indicted or if an information against the defendant is filed in district court before the date set for the preliminary examination. With the consent of the defendant and upon a showing of good cause, taking into account the public interest in the prompt disposition of criminal cases, time limits specified in this subdivision may be extended one or more times by a federal magistrate judge. In the absence of such consent by the defendant, time limits may be extended by a judge of the United States

a.   18 U.S.C. § 1.   b.   18 U.S.C. § 1.

only upon a showing that extraordinary circumstances exist and that delay is indispensable to the interests of justice.

Gerstein v. Pugh

Supreme Court of the United States, 1975.
420 U.S. 103, 95 S.Ct. 854, 43 L.Ed.2d 54.

■ MR. JUSTICE POWELL delivered the opinion of the Court.

The issue in this case is whether a person arrested under a prosecutor's information is constitutionally entitled to a judicial determination of probable cause for pretrial restraint of liberty.

issue

I.

In March 1971 respondents Pugh and Henderson were arrested in Dade County, Florida. Each was charged with several offenses under a prosecutor's information. Pugh was denied bail because one of the charges against him carried a potential life sentence, and Henderson remained in custody because he was unable to post a $4,500 bond.

In Florida, indictments are required only for prosecution of capital offenses. Prosecutors may charge all other crimes by information, without a prior preliminary hearing and without obtaining leave of court. Fla.Rule Crim.Proc. 3.140(a). At the time respondents were arrested, a Florida rule seemed to authorize adversary preliminary hearings to test probable cause for detention in all cases. Fla.Rule Crim.Proc. 1.122 (amended 1972). But the Florida courts had held that the filing of an information foreclosed the suspect's right to a preliminary hearing. They had also held that habeas corpus could not be used, except perhaps in exceptional circumstances, to test the probable cause for detention under an information. See Sullivan v. State ex rel. McCrory, 49 So.2d 794, 797 (Fla.1951). The only possible methods for obtaining a judicial determination of probable cause were a special statute allowing a preliminary hearing after 30 days, Fla.Stat.Ann. § 907.045 (1973), and arraignment, which the District Court found was often delayed a month or more after arrest. Pugh v. Rainwater, 332 F.Supp. 1107, 1110 (S.D.Fla.1971). As a result, a person charged by information could be detained for a substantial period solely on the decision of a prosecutor.

Respondents Pugh and Henderson filed a class action against Dade County officials in the Federal District Court claiming a constitutional right to a judicial hearing on the issue of probable cause and requesting declaratory and injunctive relief. Respondents Turner and Faulk, also in custody under informations, subsequently intervened. Petitioner Gerstein, the State Attorney for Dade County, was one of several defendants.

After an initial delay while the Florida legislature considered a bill that would have afforded preliminary hearings to persons charged by information, the District Court granted the relief sought. Pugh v. Rainwater, supra. The court certified the case as a class action under Fed.Rule Civ.Proc. 23(b)(2), and held that the Fourth and Fourteenth Amendments give all arrested persons charged by information a right to a judicial hearing on the question of probable cause. The District Court ordered the Dade County defendants to give the named plaintiffs an immediate preliminary hearing to determine probable cause for further detention. It also ordered them to submit a plan providing preliminary hearings in all cases instituted by information.

The defendants submitted a plan authored by Sheriff E. Wilson Purdy, and the District Court adopted it with modifications. The final order prescribed a detailed post-arrest procedure. 336 F.Supp. 490. Upon arrest the accused would be taken before a magistrate for a "first appearance hearing." The magistrate would explain the charges, advise the accused of his rights, appoint counsel if he was indigent, and proceed with a probable cause determination unless either the prosecutor or the accused was unprepared. If either requested more time, the magistrate would set the date for a "preliminary hearing," to be held within four days if the accused was in custody and within 10 days if he had been released pending trial. The order provided sanctions for failure to hold the hearings at prescribed times. At the "preliminary hearing" the accused would be entitled to counsel, and he would be allowed to confront and cross-examine adverse witnesses, to summon favorable witnesses, and to have a transcript made on request. If the magistrate found no probable cause, the accused would be discharged. He then could not be charged with the same offense by complaint or information, but only by indictment returned within 30 days.

The Court of Appeals for the Fifth Circuit stayed the District Court's order pending appeal, but while the case was awaiting decision, the Dade County judiciary voluntarily adopted a similar procedure of its own. Upon learning of this development, the Court of Appeals remanded the case for specific findings on the constitutionality of the new Dade County system. Before the District Court issued its findings, however, the Florida Supreme Court amended the procedural rules governing preliminary hearings state-wide, and the parties agreed that the District Court should direct its inquiry to the new rules rather than the Dade County procedures.

Under the amended rules every arrested person must be taken before a judicial officer within 24 hours. Fla.Rule Crim.Proc. 3.–130(b). This "first appearance" is similar to the "first appearance hearing" ordered by the District Court in all respects but the crucial one: the magistrate does not make a determination of probable cause. The rule amendments also changed the procedure for preliminary hearings, restricting them to felony charges and codifying the rule that no hearings are available to persons charged by information or indictment. Rule 3.131; see In re Rule 3.131(b), Florida Rules of Criminal Procedure, 289 So.2d 3 (Fla.1974).

In a supplemental opinion the District Court held that the amended rules had not answered the basic constitutional objection, since a defendant charged by information still could be detained pending trial without a judicial determination of probable cause. 355 F.Supp. 1286. Reaffirming its original ruling, the District Court declared that the continuation of this practice was unconstitutional. The Court of Appeals affirmed, 483 F.2d 778, modifying the District Court's decree in minor particulars and suggesting that the form of preliminary hearing provided by the amended Florida rules would be acceptable, as long as it was provided to all defendants in custody pending trial. Id., at 788–789.

State Attorney Gerstein petitioned for review, and we granted certiorari because of the importance of the issue. 414 U.S. 1062, 94 S.Ct. 567, 38 L.Ed.2d 467. We affirm in part and reverse in part.

II.

As framed by the proceedings below, this case presents two issues: whether a person arrested and held for trial on an information is entitled to a judicial determination of probable cause for detention, and if so, whether the adversary hearing ordered by the District Court and approved by the Court of Appeals is required by the Constitution.

a.

Both the standards and procedures for arrest and detention have been derived from the Fourth Amendment and its common-law antecedents. The standard for arrest is probable cause, defined in terms of facts and circumstances "sufficient to warrant a prudent man in believing that the [suspect] had committed or was committing an offense." Beck v. Ohio, 379 U.S. 89, 91, 85 S.Ct. 223, 225, 13 L.Ed.2d 142 (1964). * * *

To implement the Fourth Amendment's protection against unfounded invasions of liberty and privacy, the Court has required that the existence of probable cause be decided by a neutral and detached magistrate whenever possible. The classic statement of this principle appears in Johnson v. United States, 333 U.S. 10, 13–14, 68 S.Ct. 367, 369, 92 L.Ed. 436 (1948):

> "The point of the Fourth Amendment, which often is not grasped by zealous officers, is not that it denies law enforcement the support of the usual inferences which reasonable men draw from evidence. Its protection consists in requiring that those inferences be drawn by a neutral and detached magistrate instead of being judged by the officer engaged in the often competitive enterprise of ferreting out crime."

Maximum protection of individual rights could be assured by requiring a magistrate's review of the factual justification prior to any arrest, but such a requirement would constitute an intolerable handicap for legitimate law enforcement. * * *

Under this practical compromise, a policeman's on-the-scene assessment of probable cause provides legal justification for arresting a person suspected of crime, and for a brief period of detention to take the administrative steps incident to arrest. Once the suspect is in custody, however, the reasons that justify dispensing with the magistrate's neutral judgment evaporate. There no longer is any danger that the suspect will escape or commit further crimes while the police submit their evidence to a magistrate. And, while the State's reasons for taking summary action subside, the suspect's need for a neutral determination of probable cause increases significantly. The consequences of prolonged detention may be more serious than the interference occasioned by arrest. Pretrial confinement may imperil the suspect's job, interrupt his source of income, and impair his family relationships. See R. Goldfarb, Ransom 32–91 (1965); L. Katz,

Justice Is the Crime 51–62 (1972). Even pretrial release may be accompanied by burdensome conditions that effect a significant restraint on liberty. When the stakes are this high, the detached judgment of a neutral magistrate is essential if the Fourth Amendment is to furnish meaningful protection from unfounded interference with liberty. Accordingly, we hold that the Fourth Amendment requires a judicial determination of probable cause as a prerequisite to extended restraint on liberty following arrest.

* * *

B.

Under the Florida procedures challenged here, a person arrested without a warrant and charged by information may be jailed or subjected to other restraints pending trial without any opportunity for a probable cause determination.[1] Petitioner defends this practice on the ground that the prosecutor's decision to file an information is itself a determination of probable cause that furnishes sufficient reason to detain a defendant pending trial. Although a conscientious decision that the evidence warrants prosecution affords a measure of protection against unfounded detention, we do not think prosecutorial judgment standing alone meets the requirements of the Fourth Amendment. Indeed, we think the Court's previous decisions compel disapproval of the Florida procedure. In Albrecht v. United States, 273 U.S. 1, 5, 47 S.Ct. 250, 251, 71 L.Ed. 505 (1927), the Court held that an arrest warrant issued solely upon a United States Attorney's information was invalid because the accompanying affidavits were defective. Although the Court's opinion did not explicitly state that the prosecutor's official oath could not furnish probable cause, that conclusion was implicit in the judgment that the arrest was illegal under the Fourth Amendment.[2] * * *

In holding that the prosecutor's assessment of probable cause is not sufficient alone to justify restraint on liberty pending trial, we do not imply that the accused is entitled to judicial oversight or review of the decision to prosecute. Instead, we adhere to the Court's prior holding that a judicial hearing is not prerequisite to prosecution by information. Nor do we retreat from the established rule that illegal arrest or detention does not void a subsequent conviction. Thus, as the Court of Appeals noted below, although a suspect who is presently detained may challenge the probable cause for that confinement, a conviction will not be vacated on the ground

---

1. A person arrested under a warrant would have received a prior judicial determination of probable cause. Under Fla.Rule Crim.Proc. 3.120, a warrant may be issued upon a sworn complaint that states facts showing that the suspect has committed a crime. The magistrate may also take testimony under oath to determine if there is reasonable ground to believe the complaint is true.

2. By contrast, the Court has held that an indictment, "fair upon its face," and returned by a "properly constituted grand jury" conclusively determines the existence of probable cause and requires issuance of an arrest warrant without further inquiry. Ex parte United States, 287 U.S. 241, 250, 53 S.Ct. 129, 131, 77 L.Ed. 283 (1932). The willingness to let a grand jury's judgment substitute for that of a neutral and detached magistrate is attributable to the grand jury's relationship to the courts and its historical role of protecting individuals from unjust prosecution.

that the defendant was detained pending trial without a determination of probable cause. * * *

III.

Both the District Court and the Court of Appeals held that the determination of probable cause must be accompanied by the full panoply of adversary safeguards—counsel, confrontation, cross-examination, and compulsory process for witnesses. A full preliminary hearing of this sort is modeled after the procedure used in many States to determine whether the evidence justifies going to trial under an information or presenting the case to a grand jury. The standard of proof required of the prosecution is usually referred to as "probable cause," but in some jurisdictions it may approach a prima facie case of guilt. When the hearing takes this form, adversary procedures are customarily employed. The importance of the issue to both the State and the accused justifies the presentation of witnesses and full exploration of their testimony on cross-examination. This kind of hearing also requires appointment of counsel for indigent defendants. And, as the hearing assumes increased importance and the procedures become more complex, the likelihood that it can be held promptly after arrest diminishes.

These adversary safeguards are not essential for the probable cause determination required by the Fourth Amendment. The sole issue is whether there is probable cause for detaining the arrested person pending further proceedings. This issue can be determined reliably without an adversary hearing. The standard is the same as that for arrest.[3] That standard—probable cause to believe the suspect has committed a crime—traditionally has been decided by a magistrate in a nonadversary proceeding on hearsay and written testimony, and the Court has approved these informal modes of proof.

* * *

The use of an informal procedure is justified not only by the lesser consequences of a probable cause determination but also by the nature of the determination itself. It does not require the fine resolution of conflicting evidence that a reasonable-doubt or even a preponderance standard demands, and credibility determinations are seldom crucial in deciding whether the evidence supports a reasonable belief in guilt. See F. Miller, Prosecution: The Decision to Charge a Suspect with a Crime 64–109 (1969). This is not to say that confrontation and cross-examination might not enhance the reliability of probable cause determinations in some cases. In most cases, however, their value would be too slight to justify holding, as a matter of constitutional principle, that these formalities and safeguards

3. Because the standards are identical, ordinarily there is no need for further investigation before the probable cause determination can be made.

"Presumably, whomever the police arrest they must arrest on 'probable cause.' It is not the function of the police to arrest, as it were, at large and to use an interrogating process at police headquarters in order to determine whom they should charge before a committing magistrate on 'probable cause.'" Mallory v. United States, 354 U.S. 449, 456, 77 S.Ct. 1356, 1360, 1 L.Ed.2d 1479 (1957).

designed for trial must also be employed in making the Fourth Amendment determination of probable cause.[4]

Because of its limited function and its nonadversary character, the probable cause determination is not a "critical stage" in the prosecution that would require appointed counsel. The Court has identified as "critical stages" those pretrial procedures that would impair defense on the merits if the accused is required to proceed without counsel. Coleman v. Alabama, 399 U.S. 1, 90 S.Ct. 1999, 26 L.Ed.2d 387 (1970); United States v. Wade, 388 U.S. 218, 226–227, 87 S.Ct. 1926, 1931–1932, 18 L.Ed.2d 1149 (1967). In Coleman v. Alabama, where the Court held that a preliminary hearing was a critical stage of an Alabama prosecution, the majority and concurring opinions identified two critical factors that distinguish the Alabama preliminary hearing from the probable cause determination required by the Fourth Amendment. First, under Alabama law the function of the preliminary hearing was to determine whether the evidence justified charging the suspect with an offense. A finding of no probable cause could mean that he would not be tried at all. The Fourth Amendment probable cause determination is addressed only to pretrial custody. To be sure, pretrial custody may affect to some extent the defendant's ability to assist in preparation of his defense, but this does not present the high probability of substantial harm identified as controlling in *Wade* and *Coleman*. Second, Alabama allowed the suspect to confront and cross-examine prosecution witnesses at the preliminary hearing. The Court noted that the suspect's defense on the merits could be compromised if he had no legal assistance for exploring or preserving the witnesses' testimony. This consideration does not apply when the prosecution is not required to produce witnesses for cross-examination.

Although we conclude that the Constitution does not require an adversary determination of probable cause, we recognize that state systems of criminal procedure vary widely. There is no single preferred pretrial procedure, and the nature of the probable cause determination usually will be shaped to accord with a State's pretrial procedure viewed as a whole. While we limit our holding to the precise requirement of the Fourth Amendment, we recognize the desirability of flexibility and experimentation by the States. It may be found desirable, for example, to make the probable cause determination at the suspect's first appearance before a judicial officer,[5] or the determination may be incorporated into the procedure for setting bail or fixing other conditions of pretrial release. In some States, existing procedures may satisfy the requirement of the Fourth Amendment. Others may require only minor adjustment, such as accelera-

---

4. Criminal justice is already overburdened by the volume of cases and the complexities of our system. The processing of misdemeanors, in particular, and the early stages of prosecution generally are marked by delays that can seriously affect the quality of justice. A constitutional doctrine requiring adversary hearings for all persons detained pending trial could exacerbate the problem of pretrial delay.

5. Several States already authorize a determination of probable cause at this stage or immediately thereafter. This Court has interpreted the Federal Rules of Criminal Procedure to require a determination of probable cause at the first appearance. Jaben v. United States, 381 U.S. 214, 218, 85 S.Ct. 1365, 1367, 14 L.Ed.2d 345 (1965); Mallory v. United States, 354 U.S. 449, 454, 77 S.Ct. 1356, 1359, 1 L.Ed.2d 1479 (1957).

tion of existing preliminary hearings. Current proposals for criminal procedure reform suggest other ways of testing probable cause for detention.[6] Whatever procedure a State may adopt, it must provide a fair and reliable determination of probable cause as a condition for any significant pretrial restraint on liberty,[7] and this determination must be made by a judicial officer either before or promptly after arrest.

IV.

We agree with the Court of Appeals that the Fourth Amendment requires a timely judicial determination of probable cause as a prerequisite to detention, and we accordingly affirm that much of the judgment. As we do not agree that the Fourth Amendment requires the adversary hearing outlined in the District Court's decree, we reverse in part and remand to the Court of Appeals for further proceedings consistent with this opinion.

Holding

Affirmed in part, reversed in part, and remanded.

■ MR. JUSTICE STEWART, with whom MR. JUSTICE DOUGLAS, MR. JUSTICE BRENNAN, and MR. JUSTICE MARSHALL join, concurring.

I concur in Parts I and II of the Court's opinion, since the Constitution clearly requires at least a timely judicial determination of probable cause as a prerequisite to pretrial detention. Because Florida does not provide all defendants in custody pending trial with a fair and reliable determination

---

6. Under the Uniform Rules of Criminal Procedure (Proposed Final Draft 1974), a person arrested without a warrant is entitled, "without unnecessary delay," to a first appearance before a magistrate and a determination that grounds exist for issuance of an arrest warrant. The determination may be made on affidavits or testimony, in the presence of the accused. Rule 311. Persons who remain in custody for inability to qualify for pretrial release are offered another opportunity for a probable cause determination at the detention hearing, held no more than five days after arrest. This is an adversary hearing, and the parties may summon witnesses, but reliable hearsay evidence may be considered. Rule 344.

The A.L.I. Model Code of Pre-arraignment Procedure (Tent.Draft No. 5, 1972, and Tent.Draft No. 5A, 1973) also provides a first appearance, at which a warrantless arrest must be supported by a reasonably detailed written statement of facts. § 310. The magistrate may make a determination of probable cause to hold the accused, but he is not required to do so and the accused may request an attorney for an "adjourned session" of the first appearance to be held within 2 "court days." At that session, the magistrate makes a determination of probable cause upon a combination of written and live testimony:

"The arrested person may present written and testimonial evidence and arguments for his discharge and the state may present additional written and testimonial evidence and arguments that there is reasonable cause to believe that he has committed the crime of which he is accused. The state's submission may be made by means of affidavits, and no witnesses shall be required to appear unless the court, in the light of the evidence and arguments submitted by the parties, determines that there is a basis for believing that the appearance of one or more witnesses for whom the arrested person seeks subpoenas might lead to a finding that there is no reasonable cause." § 310.2(2) (Tent.Draft No. 5A, 1973).

7. Because the probable cause determination is not a constitutional prerequisite to the charging decision, it is required only for those suspects who suffer restraints on liberty other than the condition that they appear for trial. There are many kinds of pretrial release and many degrees of conditional liberty. We cannot define specifically those that would require a prior probable cause determination, but the key factor is significant restraint on liberty.

of probable cause for their detention, the respondents and the members of the class they represent are entitled to declaratory and injunctive relief.

Having determined that Florida's current pretrial detention procedures are constitutionally inadequate, I think it is unnecessary to go further by way of dicta. In particular, I would not, in the abstract, attempt to specify those procedural protections that constitutionally need *not* be accorded incarcerated suspects awaiting trial.

* * *

NOTES

1.   Under the Court's opinion, is there any reason why a judge could not make the *Gerstein* determination of probable cause by obtaining information over the telephone or by email?

2.   **How quick is "promptly?"** *Gerstein* held that a judicial determination of probable cause must be made "either before or promptly after arrest." The opinion did not, however, define "promptly." In County of Riverside v. McLaughlin, 500 U.S. 44, 111 S.Ct. 1661, 114 L.Ed.2d 49 (1991), the respondent, by federal class action, challenged a practice in Riverside County, California in which persons arrested without a warrant received a judicial determination of probable cause at the arraignment or first appearance before the magistrate. The arraignment occurred within 2 days of arrest, excluding weekends and holidays. Thus, one arrested late in the week might be held as long as 5 days before probable cause was determined by the magistrate; in the case of the Thanksgiving holiday, a 7–day delay was possible. The United States District Court issued an injunction requiring that determinations of probable cause be made within 36 hours of warrantless arrests, absent exigent circumstances. This order was affirmed by the United States Court of Appeals. McLaughlin v. County of Riverside, 888 F.2d 1276 (9th Cir.1989), cert. granted 498 U.S. 808, 111 S.Ct. 40, 112 L.Ed.2d 16 (1990).

The Supreme Court, in an opinion by Justice O'Connor, vacated the judgment of the Court of Appeals. The Ninth Circuit had erroneously interpreted *Gerstein* to require a determination of probable cause as soon as the administrative steps incident to arrest—fingerprinting, photographing, searching—were completed. This did not sufficiently allow for variations in state procedures and in particular did not take into account the need in some states to combine the *Gerstein* determination with the initial appearance before the magistrate. The Court concluded that "a jurisdiction that provides judicial determinations of probable cause within 48 hours of arrest will, as a general matter, comply with the promptness requirement of *Gerstein*." 111 S.Ct. at 1670. A determination may not be prompt, however, even if within the 48 hour guideline if it was delayed unreasonably, such as a delay to gather additional evidence to justify the arrest, a delay motivated by ill will against the arrestee, or a delay for delay's sake. Conversely, if the determination is made later than 48 hours after arrest, the burden is upon the government to justify it by showing "the existence of a bona fide emergency or other extraordinary circumstance." 111 S.Ct. at 1670. The Court made it clear that a desire to combine the probable cause determination with other pretrial proceedings will not justify delay beyond 48 hours, nor will intervening weekends.

Justice Marshall, joined by Justices Blackmun and Stevens, dissented, agreeing with the Court of Appeals that a *Gerstein* determination is required as soon as the administrative steps incident to arrest are completed. Justice Scalia dissented on the ground that any delay beyond 24 hours should create a presumption of unreasonableness requiring governmental rebuttal. This, he believed, was required by the historical common law requirement of prompt presentation to the magistrate following arrest.

3. **What remedy is there for a violation?** In Powell v. Nevada, 511 U.S. 79, 114 S.Ct. 1280, 128 L.Ed.2d 1 (1994), Petitioner was arrested without a warrant and held for four days before being presented to a magistrate. At his trial for murder, a statement made by Petitioner on the fourth day after his arrest was introduced into evidence. The Nevada Supreme Court held that the 48 hour rule of *McLaughlin* did not apply because Petitioner's prosecution began before *McLaughlin* was decided. The Supreme Court vacated that judgment on the ground that *McLaughlin* applies to all cases not yet final when the rule was announced. However, the Court noted Petitioner does not necessarily have to be re-tried because the Nevada Supreme Court had not considered the question what remedy is appropriate for a *McLaughlin* violation, which is a question the Supreme Court has not yet decided.

What remedies would be appropriate? Could they ever include excluding a statement made during a period of detention in violation of *McLaughlin's* requirement of presentment and judicial determination of probable cause within 48 hours?

CHAPTER 12

BAIL AND PREVENTIVE DETENTION

Analysis

EDITORS' INTRODUCTION: THE MONEY BAIL SYSTEM

American pretrial release practice and theory has been dramatically affected by an assumption that exclusive reliance can be placed on so-called money bail. Because the Supreme Court has left unclear the content of the Eighth Amendment as well as its application to the States, bail and pretrial release law has tended to be largely state law. Traditionally, state law—and often state constitutional law—has provided that except for certain suspects charged with crimes carrying the death penalty all defendants are bailable and all have a right to be free from excessive bail. In 1682, Pennsylvania provided by its Constitution that "all Prisoners shall be Bailable by Sufficient Sureties, unless for capital Offenses, where proof is evident or the presumption great." This was widely copied in state constitutions subsequently adopted elsewhere. See Carbone, Seeing Through the Emperor's New Clothes: Rediscovery of Basic Principles in the Administration of Bail, 34 Syracuse L.Rev. 517, 533–34 (1983). Moreover, courts have widely assumed that the sole legitimate function of bail is to provide reasonable assurance that the defendant will appear for trial and that bail must be set only with reference to the amount necessary to achieve this purpose.

The leading case addressing excessive bail is Stack v. Boyle, 342 U.S. 1, 72 S.Ct. 1, 96 L.Ed. 3 (1951). The twelve defendants were charged with conspiracy to advocate the violent overthrow of the United States government and bail was set at $50,000 each. Addressing their claim that this was excessive under the Eighth Amendment, the Supreme Court reasoned:

> [T]he modern practice of requiring a bail bond or the deposit of a sum of money subject to forfeiture serves as additional assurance of the presence of an accused. Bail set at a figure higher than an amount

reasonably calculated to fulfill this purpose is "excessive" under the Eighth Amendment.

Since the function of bail is limited, the fixing of bail for any individual defendant must be based upon standards relevant to the purpose of assuring the presence of that defendant. The traditional standards as expressed in the Federal Rules of Criminal Procedure [which provide that the amount is to be such as will insure the presence of the defendant "having regard to the nature and circumstances of the offense charged, the weight of the evidence against him, the financial ability of the defendant to give bail and the character of the defendant."] are to be applied in each case to each defendant.

342 U.S. at 5, 72 S.Ct. at 3–4, 96 L.Ed. at 6–7. Turning to the case before it, the Court noted that upon conviction the defendants would be subject to not more than five years' confinement and a fine of not more than $10,000. There was agreement that the $50,000 amount was much higher than was usually set in cases where the crime charged carried similar penalties. The Government urged that the Court consider the likelihood that the defendants owed allegiance to a foreign government and thus would be likely to flee. But the Court responded:

If bail in an amount greater than that usually fixed for serious charges of crimes is required in the case of any of the petitioners, that is a matter to which evidence should be directed in a hearing so that the constitutional rights of each petitioner may be preserved. In the absence of such a showing, we are of the opinion that the fixing of bail before trial in these cases cannot be squared with the statutory and constitutional standards for admission to bail.

342 U.S. at 5, 72 S.Ct. at 4, 96 L.Ed. at 7.

Despite the theory, however, empirical evidence showed that the pretrial release system was working in a manner that raised serious questions. Among the classic published works that influenced the movement toward reform were D. Freed and P. Wald, Bail in the United States: 1964 (1964); R. Goldfarb, Ransom: A Critique of the American Bail System (1965); C. Foote, The Coming Constitutional Crisis in Bail, 113 U.Pa.L.Rev. 959, 1125 (1965). Bail tended to be set, these studies established, largely on the basis of the charged offense, sometimes according to formalized "schedules." As a result, affluent defendants were able to secure release despite realistic concerns regarding the likelihood of their appearance for trial. Indigent defendants, on the other hand, were often detained because of their inability to make bail despite reason to believe they would appear for trial. Moreover, if there was a fear that a suspect would commit additional offenses prior to trial, bail was often set at an amount the suspect would be unable to meet without regard to his likelihood of appearance. Thus pretrial preventive detention was informally accomplished.

Concern also focused upon the impact of extensive pretrial detention of largely indigent defendants. The financial burden on society of maintaining the local jails necessary for this purpose, of course, was a consideration. In addition, the loss of liberty experienced by the defendants themselves was a significant concern. Families were denied the financial and other support that would be provided by the defendant. Evidence that detained suspects were sometimes sentenced to no imprisonment following conviction suggested that the burden upon offenders of awaiting trial sometimes exceeded that of being convicted.

Another important issue was whether pretrial detention tended to affect the outcome of cases. Detained defendants, of course, are less able than their released counterparts to assist counsel in preparing a defense or engaging in investigatory efforts in anticipation of trial. They are less able to make amends with victims and thus encourage the dropping of charges. Detention often results in loss of employment and community contacts, so following conviction a defendant who has been detained pending trial may present a less appealing case for probation or a short period of imprisonment than a convicted defendant who has been in the community pending trial. Whatever the causes, evidence suggested that pretrial detention tended to increase the risk of a defendant being convicted and of receiving a more severe sentence upon conviction. The classic study was Rankin, The Effect of Pretrial Detention, 39 N.Y.U.L.Rev. 641 (1964).

Many of those pushing for reform in the system urged that the problems of the bail system were largely attributable to, or at least increased by, the involvement of professional bondsmen. Such bondsmen agree for a fee—often approximately 10% of the face amount of the bail—to act as surety for the defendant. If the defendant appears as required, the bondsman's obligation is discharged; the defendant, of course, does not receive his fee back. If the defendant does not appear, the bondsman is liable for the face amount of bond, although he might escape or reduce liability by locating the defendant and presenting him to authorities.

In many localities, a defendant's ability to secure pretrial release depended upon his ability to find a bondsman able and willing to become a surety. A bondsman may require, as a condition to acting as surety, that the defendant or his family provide some sort of security to the bondsman. Thus the bondsmen and their practices and policies greatly affected the availability of pretrial release. In Pannell v. United States, 320 F.2d 698, 115 U.S.App.D.C. 379 (D.C.Cir.1963), Judge Skelly Wright commented:

> [T]he professional bondsman system as used in this District is odious. The effect of such a system is that the professional bondsmen hold the keys to the jail in their pockets. They determine for whom they will act as surety—who in their judgment is a good risk. The bad risks, in the bondsmen's judgment, *and the ones who are unable to pay the bondsmen's fees,* remain in jail. The court * * * [is] relegated to the relatively unimportant chore of fixing the amount of bail.

320 F.2d at 699 (Wright, J., concurring) (emphasis in original). During pretrial release, a bondsman could decide for whatever reasons seemed sufficient to him to "get off the risk." He could physically detain the defendant, present him to authorities, and—while the defendant remained incarcerated pending trial—thus escape any further risk of liability. If the defendant failed to appear, the bondsman had the authority to seek him out and take him into custody. Studies suggested that this broad authority of the bondsman was often abused in ways that gave defendants little or no practical recourse.

Involvement of the bondsman complicated the task of implementing the theoretical purpose of bail. Under approaches such as that discussed in Stack v. Boyle, the bailsetting task is to determine the likelihood of the defendant's appearance without regard to bail and then, if that is insufficient, to set bail in an amount that adds a sufficient financial incentive to appear to increase the likelihood of appearance to an acceptable level. But if bail was met by employing a professional bondsman, it was the bondsman who stood to lose by the defendant's nonappearance. This, of course, affected the manner in which even according to theory the bail amount should be determined. Chief Judge David Bazelon commented in *Pannell,* supra:

> It is frequently urged that eligibility for release and the amount of bond are intimately related, because the higher the bail the less "likelihood [there is] of [the defendant] fleeing or going into hiding." This argument presupposes that [a defendant] with higher bail has a more substantial stake and therefore a greater incentive not to flee. This may be true if no professional bondsman is involved. But if one is, it is he and not the court who determines [the defendant's] real stake. Under present practice the bondsman ordinarily makes the decision whether or not to require collateral for the bond. If he does, then [the defendant's] stake may be related to the amount of the bond. If he does not, then [the defendant] has no real financial stake in complying with the conditions of the bond, regardless of the amount, since the fee paid for the bond is not refundable under any circumstances. Hence the court does not decide—or even know—whether a higher bond for a particular applicant means that he has a greater stake.

320 F.2d at 701–02, 115 U.S.App.D.C. 379, 382 (Bazelon, C.J., concurring in part and dissenting in part).

The role of bondsmen in the system can, of course, be defended. They may perform a valuable role for which they are no more than adequately compensated. A bondsman who stands to lose a substantial amount by a defendant's nonappearance may take steps to assure that appearance, as by providing simple reminders when the appearance date approaches. In locating and apprehending defendants who have failed to appear, bondsmen are arguably performing a valuable function upon which overburdened law enforcement agencies cannot afford to spend time. See generally, Goldfarb, supra, at 119–25. On a less formal level, the involvement of a professional bondsman may enable a judge to "share" responsibility for a defendant's release and provide a buffer against any repercussions. The availability of bondsmen may result in the pretrial release of at least some defendants who would not otherwise be released. See Toborg, Bail Bondsmen and Criminal Court, 8 Justice System J. 141, 143–44 (1983).

Reform in the pretrial release system can be divided into two stages. The first, covered in Section A of this Chapter, took place primarily in the 1960's and consisted of modification of the criminal justice system's traditional exclusive reliance upon cash bail and professional bondsmen. The second, addressed in Section B of this Chapter, is currently underway and consists of providing mechanisms for the protection of society from those accused who pose significant dangers of committing further offenses if released pending trial.

A.   THE MOVEMENT AWAY FROM MONEY BAIL

During the 1960's, a strong movement developed that emphasized the need for bail decisions to be made individually with regard for the characteristics of particular defendants and for less reliance to be placed on money bail in general and bail bonds, requiring a surety, in particular.

Much of the impetus for these reforms came from programs based upon the Vera Foundation's Manhattan Bail Project begun in 1961. These programs involved personal interviews with arrested defendants, verification of information indicating that the defendants had ties to the community or otherwise suggesting that they would appear for further proceedings, and the recommendation of many of the defendants for release simply upon their own promise to appear for trial—release on their own recognizance, often referred to as "OR" or "ROR." Experience tended to show that those released after such preliminary screening did not fail to appear more significantly than defendants released under traditional bail procedures. Further:

> In order to study the influence of its own recommendations, Vera initiated the project with the use of an experimental control procedure. Out of all defendants believed by the project to be qualified for release, half were in fact recommended to the court, while the other half were placed in a control group, and their recommendations withheld. In the project's first year, 59% of its parole recommendations were followed by the court, compared to only 16% paroled in the control group. In short, recommendations based on facts nearly quadrupled the rate of releases.
>
> The subsequent case histories of defendants in both groups were thereafter analyzed. They showed that 60% of the recommended parolees had either been acquitted or had their cases dismissed, compared with only 23% of the control group. Moreover, of the 40% who were found guilty out of the parole group, only one out of six was sentenced to prison. In contrast, 96% of those convicted in the control group were sentenced to serve a jail term.

P.   Freed and P. Wald, Bail in the United States: 1964, 61–63 (1964).

In terms of the tendency of released defendants to appear, the studies are inconclusive. In contrast to the earliest reports of the Vera Foundation, some studies suggest that a larger percentage of those released on their own recognizance—as compared with those released on money bail—fail to appear for trial. C. Eskridge, Pretrial Release Programming—Issues and Trends (1983), reports on the many studies made and concludes:

> From the data now available, it appears that [pretrial release] programs in general are able to ensure the appearance of an accused individual for the appointed court hearings at least as well as the

traditional money bail system, and probably a bit better due to the screening ability of [pretrial release] programs.

Id., at 99–100.

The reform movement resulted in a number of changes. Some jurisdictions adopted the approach at issue in the principal case in this section. Others opted for increased availability of nonbail release often coupled with a "presumption" that a defendant is appropriate for release on his own recognizance. Perhaps the most influential legislation was the Bail Reform Act of 1966, which provided for release of suspects awaiting trial in federal court. These provisions, as amended by the Bail Reform Act of 1984 (discussed in more detail in the next section) are codified in 18 U.S.C.A. § 3142:

(b) Release on Personal Recognizance or Unsecured Appearance Bond.—The judicial officer shall order the pretrial release of the person on his personal recognizance, or upon execution of an unsecured appearance bond in an amount specified by the court, subject to the condition that the person not commit a Federal, State, or local crime during the period of his release, unless the judicial officer determines that such release will not reasonably assure the appearance of the person as required or will endanger the safety of any other person or the community.

(c) Release on Conditions.—(1) If the judicial officer determines that the release described in subsection (b) will not reasonably assure the appearance of the person as required or will endanger the safety of any other person or the community, he shall order the pretrial release of the person—

(A) subject to the condition that the person not commit a Federal, State, or local crime during the period of release; and

(B) subject to the least restrictive further condition, or combination of conditions, that he determines will reasonably assure the appearance of the person as required and the safety of any other person and the community, which may include the condition that the person—

(i) remain in the custody of a designated person, who agrees to assume supervision and to report any violation of a release condition to the court, if the designated person is able reasonably to assure the judicial officer that the person will appear as required and will not pose a danger to the safety of any other person or the community;

(ii) maintain employment, or, if unemployed, actively seek employment;

(iii) maintain or commence an educational program;

(iv) abide by specified restrictions on his personal associations, place of abode, or travel;

(v) avoid all contact with an alleged victim of the crime and with a potential witness who may testify concerning the offense;

(vi) report on a regular basis to a designated law enforcement agency, pretrial services agency, or other agency;

(vii) comply with a specified curfew;

(viii) refrain from possessing a firearm, destructive device, or other dangerous weapon;

(ix) refrain from excessive use of alcohol, or any use of a narcotic drug or other controlled substance * * * without a prescription by a licensed medical practitioner;

(x) undergo available medical, psychological, or psychiatric treatment, including treatment for drug or alcohol dependency, and remain in a specified institution if required for that purpose;

(xi) execute an agreement to forfeit upon failing to appear as required, property of a sufficient unencumbered value, including money, as is reasonably necessary to assure the appearance of the person as required, and shall provide the court with proof of ownership and the value of the property along with information regarding existing encumbrances as the judicial office may require;

(xii) execute a bail bond with solvent sureties; who will execute an agreement to forfeit in such amount as is reasonably necessary to assure appearance of the person as required and shall provide the court with information regarding the value of the assets and liabilities of the surety if other than an approved surety and the nature and extent of encumbrances against the surety's property; such surety shall have a net worth which shall have sufficient unencumbered value to pay the amount of the bail bond;

(xiii) return to custody for specified hours following release for employment, schooling, or other limited purposes; and

(xiv) satisfy any other condition that is reasonably necessary to assure the appearance of the person as required and to assure the safety of any other person and the community.

(2) The judicial officer may not impose a financial condition that results in the pretrial detention of the person.

(3) The judicial officer may at any time amend his order to impose additional or different conditions of release.

The 1966 statute assumed that the only relevant consideration was the assurance of the defendant's appearance at trial; denial of release on recognizance or on an unsecured bond and the imposition of conditions on release was authorized only upon determinations that this was necessary to assure the defendant's appearance. The 1984 statute provided for consideration of "the safety of any other person and the community." It also added a significant number of conditions that might be imposed upon pretrial release.

Some courts compelled reform on the basis of federal constitutional requirements. In Allen v. Burke, 1981 WL 15186, 29 Crim.L.Rep. (BNA) 2297 (June 4, 1981), award of attorneys' fees upheld, 690 F.2d 376 (4th Cir.1982), affirmed *sub nom.* Pulliam v. Allen, 466 U.S. 522, 104 S.Ct. 1970, 80 L.Ed.2d 565 (1984), for example, the federal district court ruled unconstitutional certain Virginia statutes and the practices under them in Culpepper County which allowed pretrial detention of those arrested for minor offenses:

> This court believes there is a constitutional right not to be jailed solely for failure to make bond on an offense for which no incarceration is authorized by the state. It offends basic notions of fairness to subject a pretrial detainee, clothed with the presumption of innocence, to a greater punishment than he could receive after being found guilty, solely because of inability to pay a money bond. The liberty interest at stake here is an important one. Freedom from bodily restraint and punishment without due process by the state is one of the more basic guarantees of the constitution.

1981 WL 15186, *2.

Other courts have been motivated by a concern that equal protection may be violated by a pretrial release system that offers pretrial liberty only to those with the resources to buy it. Equal protection, then, may bar the pretrial incarceration of an indigent defendant whose appearance for trial could reasonably be assured by other alternatives. See Pugh v. Rainwater, 572 F.2d 1053 (5th Cir.1978) (en banc), vacating 557 F.2d 1189 (5th Cir.1977).

Constitutional considerations may require further refinements in the process. In Van Atta v. Scott, 27 Cal.3d 424, 166 Cal.Rptr. 149, 613 P.2d 210 (1980), the California Supreme Court held that the state and federal requirements of due process imposed certain procedural requirements upon the process of deciding whether to grant a defendant ROR release. At the hearing, the prosecution must bear the burden of proof concerning the defendant's likelihood of appearing at future court proceedings, as to the defendant's record of nonappearances at prior court hearings, and as to the severity of the sentence the defendant faces if convicted. The detainee, however, may be required to bear the burden of producing evidence concerning ties to the community that suggest he will appear. In addition, the court refused to find a constitutional requirement that a statement of reasons be given when OR release is denied.

Schilb v. Kuebel

Supreme Court of the United States, 1971.
404 U.S. 357, 92 S.Ct. 479, 30 L.Ed.2d 502.

■ MR. JUSTICE BLACKMUN delivered the opinion of the Court.

John Schilb, of Belleville, Illinois, was arrested on January 16, 1969, and charged (a) with leaving the scene of an automobile accident and (b) with obstructing traffic. In order to gain his liberty pending trial, and in accord with the Illinois bail statutes hereinafter described, Schilb deposited

$75 in cash with the clerk of the court. This amount was 10% of the aggregate bail fixed on the two charges ($500 on the first and $250 on the second). At his ensuing trial Schilb was acquitted of the charge of leaving the scene, but was convicted of traffic obstruction. When he paid his fine, the amount Schilb had deposited was returned to him decreased, however, by $7.50 retained as "bail bond costs" by the court clerk pursuant to the statute. The amount so retained was 1% of the specified bail and 10% of the amount actually deposited.

Schilb, by this purported state class action against the court clerk, the county, and the county treasurer, attacks the statutory 1% charge on Fourteenth Amendment due process and equal protection grounds. The Circuit Court of St. Clair County upheld the statute and dismissed the complaint. The Supreme Court of Illinois affirmed, with two justices dissenting.

I

The Illinois bail statutes compose Article 110 of the State's Code of Criminal Procedure of 1963, made effective January 1, 1964. This Code complemented Illinois' then new and revised Criminal Code of 1961, made effective January 1, 1962. The work of revision of the theretofore existing statutes was that of a Joint Committee of the Illinois State and Chicago Bar Associations. See 1 Ill.Rev.Stat.1963, p. 1629.

Prior to 1964 the professional bail bondsman system with all its abuses was in full and odorous bloom in Illinois. Under that system the bail bondsman customarily collected the maximum fee (10% of the amount of the bond) permitted by statute, and retained that entire amount even though the accused fully satisfied the conditions of the bond. Payment of this substantial "premium" was required of the good risk as well as of the bad. The results were that a heavy and irretrievable burden fell upon the accused, to the excellent profit of the bondsman, and that professional bondsmen, and not the courts, exercised significant control over the actual workings of the bail system.

One of the stated purposes of the new bail provisions in the 1963 Code was to rectify this offensive situation. The purpose appears to have been accomplished. It is said that the bail bondsman abruptly disappeared in Illinois "due primarily to the success of the ten percent bail deposit provision." Boyle, Bail Under the Judicial Article, 17 De Paul L.Rev. 267, 272 (1968). * * *

II

Article 110 of the 1963 Code, as it read at the time Schilb was arrested and charged, provided that an eligible accused could obtain pretrial release in one of three ways:

(1) Under § 110–2 he may be released on his personal recognizance.

(2) Under § 110–7 he may execute a bail bond and deposit with the clerk cash equal to only 10% of the bail or $25, whichever is the greater. When bail is made in this way and the conditions of the bond have been performed, the clerk returns to the accused 90% of the sum

deposited. The remaining 10% (1% of the bail) is retained by the clerk "as bail bond costs."

(3) Under § 110–8 he may execute a bail bond and secure it by a deposit with the clerk of the full amount of the bail in cash, or in stocks and bonds authorized for trust funds in Illinois, or by unencumbered nonexempt Illinois real estate worth double the amount of the bail. When bail is made in this way and the conditions of the bond have been performed, the clerk returns the deposit of cash or stocks or bonds, or releases the real estate, as the case may be, without charge or retention of any amount.

In each case bail is fixed by a judicial officer. Section 110–5 prescribes factors to be considered in fixing the amount of bail. Under § 110–6 either the State or the defendant may apply to the court for an increase or for a reduction in the amount of bail or for alteration of the bond's conditions.

The choice between § 110–7 and § 110–8 is reserved to the accused.

The thinking and intentions of the Joint Committee revisers are apparent from the Committee's comments * * *[1]

The parties have stipulated that when bail in a particular case is fixed, the judge's "discretion in such respect is not guided by statute, rule of court or any definite, fixed standard; various and divers judges in fact fix the amount of bail for the same types of offenses at various and divers amounts, without relationship as to guilt or innocence of the particular defendant in a criminal charge, and without relationship of the particular offense charged and the bail fixed." They have also stipulated, "The actual cost of administering the provisions of said Sections 110–7 and 110–8 are substantially the same but there may probably be a slightly greater cost in the administration of Section 110–8."

III

The Court more than once has said that state legislative reform by way of classification is not to be invalidated merely because the legislature moves one step at a time. * * *

Bail, of course, is basic to our system of law, and the Eighth Amendment's proscription of excessive bail has been assumed to have application to the States through the Fourteenth Amendment. But we are not at all concerned here with any fundamental right to bail or with any Eighth

---

1. " * * * The provisions of sections 110–7 and 110–8 were designed to severely restrict the activities of professional bail bondsmen and to reduce the cost of liberty to arrested persons awaiting trial. * * * " P. 298.

"The committee realized full well the many arguments advanced in opposition to changing the present system. We were not impressed with any of them. If a person can pay a professional bondsman ten per cent of the bail amount as a fee, he can deposit it with the clerk. At the present time he re-

ceives nothing back from the bondsman if he appears for trial; his ten per cent fee is gone. Under the provisions of [§ 110–7(f)] he gets back ninety per cent of the amount deposited if he appears. The ten per cent of the deposit retained by the county will offset in monetary amount the costs of handling bail bonds (which must be done now anyway), and any loss resulting from the occasional bail jumper where the professional bondsman might now forfeit the amount of the bail. * * * " P. 300.

* * *

Amendment-Fourteenth Amendment question of bail excessiveness. Our concern, instead, is with the 1% cost-retention provision. This smacks of administrative detail and of procedure and is hardly to be classified as a "fundamental" right or as based upon any suspect criterion. The applicable measure, therefore, must be the traditional one: Is the distinction drawn by the statutes invidious and without rational basis?

IV

With this background, we turn to the appellants' primary argument. It is threefold: (1) that the 1% retention charge under § 110–7(f) is imposed on only one segment of the class gaining pretrial release; (2) that it is imposed on the poor and nonaffluent and not on the rich and affluent; and (3) that its imposition with respect to an accused found innocent amounts to a court cost assessed against the not-guilty person.

We are compelled to note preliminarily that the attack on the Illinois bail statutes, in a very distinct sense, is paradoxical. The benefits of the new system, as compared with the old, are conceded. And the appellants recognize that under the pre-1964 system Schilb's particular bail bond cost would have been 10% of his bail, or $75; that this premium price for his pretrial freedom, once paid, was irretrievable; and that, if he could not have raised the $75, he would have been consigned to jail until his trial. Thus, under the old system the cost of Schilb's pretrial freedom was $75, but under the new it was only $7.50. While acknowledging this obvious benefit of the statutory reform, Schilb and his coappellants decry the classification the statutes make and present the usual argument that the legislation must be struck down because it does not reform enough.

A. It is true that no charge is made to the accused who is released on his personal recognizance. We are advised, however, that this was also true under the old (pre-1964) system and that "Illinois has never charged people out on recognizance." Thus, the burden on the State with respect to a personal recognizance is no more under the new system than what the State had assumed under the old. Also, with a recognizance, there is nothing the State holds for safekeeping, with resulting responsibility and additional paperwork. All this provides a rational basis for distinguishing between the personal recognizance and the deposit situations.

There is also, however, no retention charge to the accused who deposits the full amount of cash bail or securities or real estate. Yet the administrative cost attendant upon the 10% deposit and that upon the full deposit are, by the stipulation, "substantially the same" with, indeed, any higher cost incurred with respect to the full deposit.

This perhaps is a more tenuous distinction, but we cannot conclude that it is constitutionally vulnerable. One who deposits securities or encumbers his real estate precludes the use of that property for other purposes. And one who deposits the full amount of his bail in cash is dispossessed of a productive asset throughout the period of the deposit; presumably, at least, its interim possession by the State accrues to the benefit of the State. Further, the State's protection against the expenses that inevitably are incurred when bail is jumped is greater when 100% cash or securities or real estate is deposited or obligated than when only 10% of the bail amount is advanced. The Joint Committee's and the State Legislature's decision in balancing these opposing considerations in the way that they did cannot be described as lacking in rationality to the point where equal protection considerations require that they be struck down.

* * *

B.   The poor-man-affluent-man argument centers, of course, in Griffin v. Illinois, 351 U.S. 12, 76 S.Ct. 585, 100 L.Ed. 891 (1956), and in the many later cases that "reaffirm allegiance to the basic command that justice be applied equally to all persons." Williams v. Illinois, 399 U.S. 235, 241, 90 S.Ct. 2018, 2022, 26 L.Ed.2d 586 (1970).

In no way do we withdraw today from the *Griffin* principle. That remains steadfast. But it is by no means certain, as the appellants suggest, that the 10% deposit provision under § 110–7 is a provision for the benefit of the poor and the less affluent and that the full-deposit provision of § 110–8 is one for the rich and the more affluent. It should be obvious that the poor man's real hope and avenue for relief is the personal recognizance provision of § 110–2. We do not presume to say, as the appellants in their brief intimate, that § 110–2 is not utilized by Illinois judges and made available for the poor and the less affluent.

Neither is it assured, as the appellants also suggest, that the affluent will take advantage of the full-deposit provision of § 110–8, with no retention charge, and that the less affluent are relegated to the 10% deposit provision of § 110–7 and the 1% retention charge. The record is silent, but the flow indeed may be the other way. The affluent, more aware of and more experienced in the marketplace, may see the advantage, in these days of high interest rates, in retaining the use of 90% of the bail amount. A 5% or greater return on this 90% in a short period of time more than offsets the 1% retention charge. In other words, it is by no means clear that the route of § 110–8 is more attractive to the affluent defendant than the § 110–7 route. The situation, therefore, wholly apart from the fact that appellant Schilb himself has not pleaded indigency, is not one where we may assume that the Illinois plan works to deny relief to the poor man merely because of his poverty.

C.   The court-cost argument is that the person found innocent but already "put to the expense, disgrace and anguish of a trial" is "then assessed a cost for exercising his right to release pending trial." Giaccio v. Pennsylvania, 382 U.S. 399, 86 S.Ct. 518, 15 L.Ed.2d 447 (1966), is cited. *Giaccio* was a holding that an ancient Pennsylvania statute that permitted the jury to impose court costs upon an acquitted defendant, in order to offset the expenses of prosecution, violated the Due Process Clause because of vagueness and the absence of any standards preventing the arbitrary imposition of costs. The Court thus did not reach the merits, although Mr. Justice Stewart and Mr. Justice Fortas, each separately concurring, 382 U.S., at 405, 86 S.Ct., at 522, felt that the very imposition of costs upon an acquitted defendant was violative of due process.

Giaccio is not dispositive precedent for the appellants here. Certainly § 110–7 is not subject to attack for vagueness or for lack of standards. Neither is it a vehicle for the imposition of costs of prosecution as was the

Pennsylvania statute. Instead, § 110–7 authorizes retention of the 1% as "bail bond costs." This is what that description implies, namely, an administrative cost imposed upon all those, guilty and innocent alike, who seek the benefit of § 110–7. This conclusion is supported by the presence of the long-established Illinois rule against the imposition of costs of prosecution upon an acquittal or discharged criminal defendant and by the Illinois court's own determination that the charge under § 110–7(f) is an administrative fee and not a cost of prosecution imposed under Ill.Rev.Stat., c. 38, § 180–3 (1969), only upon the convicted defendant.

* * *

VI

We refrain from nullifying this Illinois statute that, with its companion sections, has brought reform and needed relief to the State's bail system. The judgment of the Supreme Court of Illinois is affirmed.

Affirmed.

■ MR. JUSTICE MARSHALL, concurring.

* * *

In the evolving struggle for meaningful bail reform I cannot find the present Illinois move towards that objective to be unconstitutional.

■ MR. JUSTICE DOUGLAS, dissenting.

* * *

Some costs are the unavoidable consequences of a system of government which is required to proceed against its citizens in a public trial in an adversary proceeding. Yet I see no basis for saying that an accused must bear the costs incurred by the Government in its unsuccessful prosecution of him. * * * I would conclude, with Justices Stewart and Fortas in *Giaccio* [v. Pennsylvania, 382 U.S. 399, 86 S.Ct. 518, 15 L.Ed.2d 447] that [the imposition of costs upon acquitted defendants] violates due process. * * * The costs of administering the bail system occur, by definition, only during the course of criminal prosecutions. They are as much an element of the costs of conducting criminal cases as the prosecutor's salary * * *.

■ MR. JUSTICE STEWART, with whom MR. JUSTICE BRENNAN concurs, dissenting.

* * *

It is clear that not every person accused of a crime is free to choose to be released on his own recognizance. Yet those who are fortunate enough to be so released need pay no costs whatsoever. * * * A[n] * * * attempt to distinguish between those released on their own recognizance and those who deposit 10% turns on the idea that the members of the former class are more "worthy" of the benefit they receive and therefore may rationally be required to pay less. But while the criteria used by judges to determine release on one's own recognizance—e.g., length of residence in the jurisdiction, marital status, employment record, or past criminal record—are obviously relevant to the recognizance decision, they are not rationally related to the decision to impose purely administrative costs, especially when such costs are at least as great for those released on their own recognizance as for those required to post bond. * * * I think the imposition of administrative costs on only one class of persons seeking pretrial release violates the Equal Protection Clause of the Fourteenth Amendment. * * *

NOTES

1. **Court appearance incentives.** Other legal incentives can be created to encourage defendants released before trial to appear and to avoid violating conditions of their release. Many of these are illustrated by federal statutory provisions enacted as part of the Bail Reform Act of 1984. A violation of the conditions of a release order can lead to a revocation of pretrial release; this is considered in the next section. It can also serve as the basis for a prosecution for contempt of court. 18 U.S.C.A. § 3148(c).

Nonappearance can be made a criminal offense. Under 18 U.S.C.A. § 3146, a person released pursuant to the Act commits a criminal offense if he knowingly fails to appear before a court as required by the conditions of his release. Further:

> It is an affirmative defense to a prosecution under this section that uncontrollable circumstances prevented the person from appearing * * *, and that the person did not contribute to the creation of such circumstances in reckless disregard of the requirement that he appear * * *, and that he appeared * * * as soon as such circumstances ceased to exist.

18 U.S.C.A. § 3146(c). The penalty for the offense is determined by the penalty attached to the offense with which the person was charged before release. If the charged offense, for example, was a felony punishable by five to fifteen years of imprisonment, failure to appear is punishable by imprisonment for not more than five years, a fine of not more than $10,000, or both. A term of imprisonment imposed for failure to appear is to be consecutive "to the term of imprisonment for any other offense." 18 U.S.C.A. § 3146(b)(2).

Are these provisions likely to stimulate an appearance by a defendant who is not otherwise motivated to appear?

2. **Deterring the commission of offenses while released.** The Bail Act of 1984 also provides that if a person is convicted of an offense committed while released pursuant to the chapter, he is to receive a penalty in addition to the penalty prescribed for the offense of which he is convicted. If the offense of which he is convicted is a felony, the additional penalty is to be a term of imprisonment of not more than ten years. This additional term of imprisonment is to be consecutive to any other sentence of imprisonment. 18 U.S.C.A. § 3147. Is this likely to cause a released person otherwise inclined to commit an offense to avoid that offense?

3. **Avoiding detention by use of field release citations.** It is often urged that increased use by police of citations in lieu of arrests is a major method of addressing pretrial detention problems, especially in misdemeanor situations. Such a practice avoids the detention in the first place thus eliminating the need for a formal release procedure. It accomplishes the objectives of release more quickly than other methods and, since no additional personnel need be employed, may be less expensive than many alternatives. Provision can be made for officers in the field to issue citations to some persons rather than making a "stationhouse arrest." Further, since there may sometimes be reasons for requiring a stationhouse appearance, provision may also be made for release of other offenders on a citation after their appearance at the police station. See W. Thomas, Bail Reform in America

258 (1976) ("Citations should provide for the release of the majority of misdemeanants and many felony defendants as well.").

4.   **Effect of the bail reform movement on the criminal justice system.** In regard to the impact of the reform efforts, M. Feeley, Foreword to R. Flemming, Punishment Before Trial (1982), states:

> This movement has been one of the few clear successes in criminal justice reform during the past two decades. Today throughout the United States arrestees are much more likely to be released than they were twenty-five years ago. Many are now routinely released on their promise to appear. While money bail continues to exist and point up the contradictions inherent in our commitment to equal administration of the law, on average the amounts required are lower than before. No one seriously denies that the bail reform movement has had a significant impact.

Id., at xi. W. Thomas, Bail Reform in America 251–52 (1976) suggests that the major success of the bail reform movement may have been "the education and enlightenment of judges as to the importance of the bail decision, the need to consider individual factors in the setting of bail, and the consequences of pretrial detention."

On the other hand, in only a few jurisdictions have reforms eliminated the participation of professional bondsmen in the pretrial release process. See Toborg, Bailbondsmen and Criminal Courts, 8 Justice System J. 141 (1983).

B.   THE MOVEMENT FOR PREVENTIVE PRETRIAL DETENTION AND THE BAIL REFORM ACT OF 1984

Recent years have seen a growing demand for formal recognition in the pretrial release system of the community's interest in being protected from the commission of crimes by defendants awaiting trial. In a number of jurisdictions, this interest has been accommodated to some extent in pretrial release provisions. But federal legislation has paved the way for explicit and relatively complex provisions for pretrial detention. In 1971, defendants in the District of Columbia were subject to detention under a federal statute applicable only to that jurisdiction. See D.C.Code 1981, § 23–1322. The Bail Reform Act of 1984, however, created a system of preventive detention for the entire federal criminal justice system. Detention of a defendant is authorized, in some situations, as an initial matter, and in others as a consequence of a showing that the defendant has violated the conditions of a pretrial release.

State Provisions for Accommodating Community Protection

State pretrial detention statutes quite often provide for some consideration of the likelihood that a defendant will commit further offenses while on pretrial release. But they differ widely in the showing required and in the significance that is given to it. Some insert the defendant's demonstrated "dangerousness" as a factor to be considered in making pretrial release decisions which, in theory at least, are to turn upon the need to assure the defendant's appearance for trial. Under South Dakota law, for example, whether to release a defendant on unsecured release and what conditions to put upon release are to depend upon what is necessary to assure appearance for trial. S.D. Codified Laws 23A-43-2, 23A-43-3. As a result of a 1980 amendment, however, the factors to be considered in determining what conditions of release to impose now include "the risk that [the defendant] will * * * pose a danger to any person or to the community." Id., at 23A-43-4.

Some jurisdictions authorize the imposition of special conditions of release on defendants identified as posing special risks. Arkansas, for example, authorizes the judicial officer to consider whether "there exists a danger that the defendant will commit a serious crime" and, upon determining that such a risk exists, to impose certain conditions upon the defendant's release. These may include directions that the defendant not go to certain areas, not possess dangerous weapons or engage in certain activities, and a requirement that the defendant report to and remain under the supervision of an officer of the court. Ark.R.Crim.P. 9.3. Upon a showing that a defendant has willfully violated reasonable conditions of release, the release may be "revoke[d]." Id., at 9.5(c).

Other provisions authorize preventive detention as an initial matter. As was noted above, state constitutions have typically provided that defendants charged with crimes carrying the death penalty are not entitled to bail, at least when "the proof is evident or the presumption great." Other state constitutions make further exceptions. The Arizona Constitution, for example, specifies that the following (in addition to those charged with a capital offense) are not bailable:

> 2. Felony offenses committed when the person charged is already admitted to bail on a separate felony charge and where the proof is evident or the presumption great as to the present charge.

> 3. Felony offenses if the person charged poses a substantial danger to any other person or the community, if no conditions of release which may be imposed will reasonably assure the safety of the other person or the community and if the proof is evident or the presumption great as to the present charge.

Ariz.R.S. Const. Art. 2, § 22.

The procedures for invoking these provisions differs greatly among jurisdictions. The matter may be entrusted entirely to the discretion of the judge or specific factual matters may have to be proved beyond a reasonable doubt. A specific hearing on the risk posed by the defendant may or may not be required. Limits on the duration of any detention permitted may or may not be imposed. State provisions are thoroughly addressed in B. Gottlieb, The Pretrial Processing of "Dangerous" Defendants: A Comparative Analysis of State Laws (1984). Relevant state laws are digested in B. Gottlieb and P. Rosen, Public Danger as a Factor in Pretrial Release— Digest of State Laws (1985).

Bail Reform Act of 1984: Initial Detention

Under federal legislation, a judicial officer before whom an arrested person is presented may release the person on his personal recognizance or upon an unsecured appearance bond or may release him under one or more conditions. In addition, temporary detention is authorized if the arrestee is determined to be on pretrial release in connection with another offense, probation, or parole, or if the arrestee is determined to be neither a resident nor an alien lawfully admitted for permanent residence and, in either case, the person may flee or pose a danger to any other person or the community. If, after ten days, the appropriate court, parole, probation or immigration official fails to take the person into custody, the person is to be processed in accordance with the standard provisions of the statute. 18 U.S.C.A. § 3142(d).

Most importantly, however, the judicial officer is directed to order the person detained pending trial if, after a detention hearing:

> the judicial officer finds that no conditions or combination of conditions will reasonably assure the appearance of the person as required and the safety of any other person and the community * * *

18 U.S.C.A. § 3142(e). Detention proceedings can, of course, be before the district judge. But a United States magistrate is a judicial officer within the meaning of the statute, and therefore pretrial detention can be ordered by such magistrates. 28 U.S.C.A. § 636(a)(2).

When Detention Hearing Held. Whether a detention hearing needs to be held depends upon the category of the case and who seeks such a hearing. The judicial officer is directed to hold a hearing:

> (1) upon motion of the attorney for the Government, [in a case] that involves—

> > (A) a crime of violence;

> > (B) an offense for which the maximum sentence is life imprisonment or death;

> > (C) an offense for which a maximum term of imprisonment of ten years or more is prescribed in the Controlled Substances Act * * *, the Controlled Substances Import and Export Act * * *, the Maritime Drug Law Enforcement Act * * * or [uses a firearm during specified felonies, conspires to commit certain offenses outside the United States or commits certain acts of terrorism]; or

> > (D) any felony if the person has been convicted of two or more offenses described in subparagraphs (A) through (C) of this paragraph, or two or more State or local offenses that would have been offenses described in subparagraphs (A) through (C) of this paragraph if a circumstance giving rise to Federal jurisdiction had existed, or a combination of such offenses * * *.

18 U.S.C.A. § 3142(f). A hearing is also to be held:

> (2) upon motion of the attorney for the Government or upon the judicial officer's own motion, in a case that involves—

> > (A) a serious risk that the person will flee; or

> > (B) a serious risk that the person will obstruct or attempt to obstruct justice, or threaten, injure, or intimidate, or attempted to threaten, injure, or intimidate a prospective witness or juror.

18 U.S.C.A. § 3142(f). The hearing is to be held immediately upon the person's first appearance before the judicial officer unless a continuance is

sought. Except for good cause, a continuance granted at the request of the defendant cannot exceed five days and a continuance granted at the request of the Government cannot exceed three days. 18 U.S.C.A. § 3142(f).

Procedure At Detention Hearing. With regard to the procedural details of the hearing, the statute provides:

> At the hearing, the person has the right to be represented by counsel, and, if he is financially unable to obtain adequate representation, to have counsel appointed. The person shall be afforded an opportunity to testify, to present witnesses, to cross-examine witnesses who appear at the hearing, and to present information by proffer or otherwise. The rules concerning admissibility of evidence in criminal trials do not apply to the presentation and consideration of information at the hearing. The facts that the judicial officer uses to support a finding * * * that no condition or combination of conditions will reasonably assure the safety of any other person and the community shall be supported by clear and convincing evidence. The person may be detained pending completion of the hearing.

18 U.S.C.A. § 3142(f).

Making of the Detention Decision. In determining whether there are conditions of release that will assure the defendant's appearance and the safety of others and the community, the judicial officer is to take into account available information concerning:

> (1) the nature and circumstances of the offense charged, including whether the offense is a crime of violence or involves a narcotic drug;

> (2) the weight of the evidence against the person;

> (3) the history and characteristics of the person, including—

> > (A) the person's character, physical and mental condition, family ties, employment, financial resources, length of residence in the community, community ties, past conduct, history relating to drug or alcohol abuse, criminal history, and record concerning appearance at court proceedings; and

> > (B) whether, at the time of the current offense or arrest, the person was on probation, or parole, or on other release pending trial, sentencing, appeal, or completion of sentence for an offense under Federal, State, or local law; and

> (4) the nature and seriousness of the danger to any person or the community that would be posed by the person's release. In considering the conditions of release * * *, the judicial officer may upon his own motion, or shall upon the motion of the Government, conduct an inquiry into the source of the property to be designated for potential forfeiture or offered as collateral to secure a bond, and shall decline to accept the designation, or the use as collateral, of property that, because of its source, will not reasonably assure the appearance of the person as required.

18 U.S.C.A. § 3142(g).

Presumptions. The making of the detention decision is aided by certain presumptions. In those situations identified above as ones in which a detention hearing is to be held on motion of the Government, 18 U.S.C.A. § 3142(f)(1), a rebuttable presumption arises that no conditions will assure the safety of others and the community if the judge finds:

(1) the person has been convicted of a Federal offense that is described in subsection (f)(1) of this section, or of a State or local offense that would have been an offense described in subsection (f)(1) of this section if a circumstance giving rise to Federal jurisdiction had existed;

(2) the offense described in paragraph (1) of this subsection was committed while the person was on release pending trial for a Federal, State, or local offense; and

(3) a period of not more than five years has elapsed since the date of conviction, or the release of the person from imprisonment, for the offense described in paragraph (1) of this subsection, whichever is later.

In addition, the statute provides further:

Subject to rebuttal by the person, it shall be presumed that no condition or combination of conditions will reasonably assure the appearance of the person as required and the safety of the community if the judicial officer finds that there is probable cause to believe that the person committed an offense for which a maximum term of imprisonment of ten years or more is prescribed in the Controlled Substances Act * * *, the Controlled Substances Import and Export Act * * *, the Maritime Drug Law Enforcement Act * * * or [uses a firearm during specified felonies, conspires to commit certain offenses outside the United States or commits certain acts of terrorism].

18 U.S.C.A. § 3142(e).

Terms of Detention Order. In a detention order, the judicial officer is directed to:

(1) include written findings of fact and a written statement of the reasons for the detention;

(2) direct that the person be committed to the custody of the Attorney General for confinement in a corrections facility separate, to the extent practicable, from persons awaiting or serving sentences or being held in custody pending appeal;

(3) direct that the person be afforded reasonable opportunity for private consultation with counsel; and

(4) direct that, on order of a court of the United States or on request of an attorney for the Government, the person in charge of the corrections facility in which the person is confined deliver the person to a United States marshal for the purpose of an appearance in connection with a court proceeding.

In addition, the statute provides:

The judicial officer may, by subsequent order, permit the temporary release of the person, in the custody of a United States marshal or another appropriate person, to the extent that the judicial officer determines such release to be necessary for the preparation of the person's defense or for another compelling reason.

18 U.S.C.A. § 3142(i).

Review. If a detention order is issued by a magistrate, the defendant may secure review of this by the judge. Review is obtained by filing with the court a motion for revocation or amendment of the order. 18 U.S.C.A. § 3145(b). On the other hand, if a magistrate orders a defendant released, an attorney for the Government may obtain review of this decision by filing with the court a motion for revocation of the order. 18 U.S.C.A. § 3145(a)(1).

Appellate review is also available. A detained defendant may take an interlocutory appeal to the appropriate Court of Appeals from a detention order or a decision denying revocation of a detention order. 18 U.S.C.A. § 3145(c). The Government is also entitled to appeal from an order releasing a defendant or a decision denying a motion to revoke an order granting release. 18 U.S.C.A. §§ 3145(c), 3731.

Bail Reform Act of 1984: Detention Upon Violation of Release Conditions

In contrast with those provisions authorizing preventive detention of a defendant as an initial matter, other provisions of the federal statute address the consequences of a showing that the defendant violated the conditions of a pretrial release. An attorney for the Government may initiate the process by filing a motion with the district court. A warrant may then be issued for the person's arrest and the person is to be brought before a judicial officer. If the officer finds that there are conditions of release that will assure that the person will not flee and will not be dangerous to others or to the community and that the person will abide by these conditions, the officer can again release the defendant and is authorized to amend the conditions of release to impose any additional conditions regarded as necessary.

On the other hand, the appearance may also result in the revocation of release and the person's pretrial detention:

The judicial officer shall enter an order of revocation and detention if, after a hearing, the judicial officer—

(1) finds that there is—

(A) probable cause to believe that the person has committed a Federal, State, or local crime while on release; or

(B) clear and convincing evidence that the person has violated any other condition of his release; and

(2) finds that—

(A) based on the factors set forth in section 3142(g) [discussed above], there is no condition or combination of conditions of release that will assure that the person will not

> flee or pose a danger to the safety of any other person or the
> community; or
>
>> (B) the person is unlikely to abide by any condition or
>> combination of conditions of release.

Again, the judicial officer's task is aided by a presumption:

> If there is probable cause to believe that, while on release, the person
> committed a Federal, State, or local felony, a rebuttable presumption
> arises that no condition or combination of conditions will assure that
> the person will not pose a danger to the safety of any other person or
> the community.

18 U.S.C.A. § 3148(b).

United States v. Salerno

Supreme Court of the United States, 1987.
481 U.S. 739, 107 S.Ct. 2095, 95 L.Ed.2d 697.

■ CHIEF JUSTICE REHNQUIST delivered the opinion of the Court.

The Bail Reform Act of 1984 allows a federal court to detain an
arrestee pending trial if the government demonstrates by clear and convincing evidence after an adversary hearing that no release conditions "will
reasonably assure * * * the safety of any other person and the community." The United States Court of Appeals for the Second Circuit struck down
this provision of the Act as facially unconstitutional, because, in that
court's words, this type of pretrial detention violates "substantive due
process." We granted certiorari because of a conflict among the Courts of
Appeals regarding the validity of the Act. We hold that, as against the facial
attack mounted by these respondents, the Act fully comports with constitutional requirements. We therefore reverse.

I

Responding to "the alarming problem of crimes committed by persons
on release," S.Rep. No. 98–225, p. 3 (1983), U.S.Code Cong. & Admin.News
1984, pp. 3182, 3185, Congress formulated the Bail Reform Act of 1984, 18
U.S.C. § 3141 et seq. (1982 ed., Supp. III), as the solution to a bail crisis in
the federal courts. The Act represents the National Legislature's considered
response to numerous perceived deficiencies in the federal bail process. By
providing for sweeping changes in both the way federal courts consider bail
applications and the circumstances under which bail is granted, Congress
hoped to "give the courts adequate authority to make release decisions that
give appropriate recognition to the danger a person may pose to others if
released." S.Rep. No. 98–225, p. 3, U.S.Code Cong. & Admin.News 1984, p.
3185.

To this end, § 3141(a) of the Act requires a judicial officer to determine whether an arrestee shall be detained. Section 3142(e) provides that
"[i]f, after a hearing pursuant to the provisions of subsection (f), the
judicial officer finds that no condition or combination of conditions will
reasonably assure the appearance of the person as required and the safety
of any other person and the community, he shall order the detention of the

person prior to trial." Section 3142(f) provides the arrestee with a number of procedural safeguards. He may request the presence of counsel at the detention hearing, he may testify and present witnesses in his behalf, as well as proffer evidence, and he may cross-examine other witnesses appearing at the hearing. If the judicial officer finds that no conditions of pretrial release can reasonably assure the safety of other persons and the community, he must state his findings of fact in writing, § 3142(i), and support his conclusion with "clear and convincing evidence," § 3142(f).

The judicial officer is not given unbridled discretion in making the detention determination. Congress has specified the considerations relevant to that decision. These factors include the nature and seriousness of the charges, the substantiality of the government's evidence against the arrestee, the arrestee's background and characteristics, and the nature and seriousness of the danger posed by the suspect's release, § 3142(g). Should a judicial officer order detention, the detainee is entitled to expedited appellate review of the detention order. §§ 3145(b), (c).

Respondents Anthony Salerno and Vincent Cafaro were arrested on March 21, 1986, after being charged in a 29–count indictment alleging various Racketeer Influenced and Corrupt Organizations Act (RICO) violations, mail and wire fraud offenses, extortion, and various criminal gambling violations. The RICO counts alleged 35 acts of racketeering activity, including fraud, extortion, gambling, and conspiracy to commit murder. At respondents' arraignment, the Government moved to have Salerno and Cafaro detained pursuant to § 3142(e), on the ground that no condition of release would assure the safety of the community or any person. The District Court held a hearing at which the Government made a detailed proffer of evidence. The Government's case showed that Salerno was the "boss" of the Genovese Crime Family of La Cosa Nostra and that Cafaro was a "captain" in the Genovese Family. According to the Government's proffer, based in large part on conversations intercepted by a court-ordered wiretap, the two respondents had participated in wide-ranging conspiracies to aid their illegitimate enterprises through violent means. The Government also offered the testimony of two of its trial witnesses, who would assert that Salerno personally participated in two murder conspiracies. Salerno opposed the motion for detention, challenging the credibility of the Government's witnesses. He offered the testimony of several character witnesses as well as a letter from his doctor stating that he was suffering from a serious medical condition. Cafaro presented no evidence at the hearing, but instead characterized the wiretap conversations as merely "tough talk."

The District Court granted the Government's detention motion, concluding that the Government had established by clear and convincing evidence that no condition or combination of conditions of release would ensure the safety of the community or any person:

"The activities of a criminal organization such as the Genovese Family do not cease with the arrest of its principals and their release on even the most stringent of bail conditions. The illegal businesses, in place for many years, require constant attention and protection, or they will fail. Under these circumstances, this court recognizes a strong incentive on the part of its leadership to continue business as usual. When business as usual involves threats, beatings, and murder, the present danger such people pose in the community is self-evident." 631 F.Supp. 1364, 1375 (S.D.N.Y.1986).

Respondents appealed, contending that to the extent that the Bail Reform Act permits pretrial detention on the ground that the arrestee is likely to commit future crimes, it is unconstitutional on its face. Over a dissent, the United States Court of Appeals for the Second Circuit agreed. 794 F.2d 64 (1986). Although the court agreed that pretrial detention could be imposed if the defendants were likely to intimidate witnesses or otherwise jeopardize the trial process, it found "§ 3142(e)'s authorization of pretrial detention [on the ground of future dangerousness] repugnant to the concept of substantive due process, which we believe prohibits the total deprivation of liberty simply as a means of preventing future crimes." Id., at 71–72. The court concluded that the Government could not, consistent with due process, detain persons who had not been accused of any crime merely because they were thought to present a danger to the community. Id., at 72, quoting United States v. Melendez–Carrion, 790 F.2d 984, 1000–1001 (C.A.2 1986) (opinion of Newman, J.). It reasoned that our criminal law system holds persons accountable for past actions, not anticipated future actions. Although a court could detain an arrestee who threatened to flee before trial, such detention would be permissible because it would serve the basic objective of a criminal system—bringing the accused to trial. The court distinguished our decision in Gerstein v. Pugh, 420 U.S. 103, 95 S.Ct. 854, 43 L.Ed.2d 54 (1975), in which we upheld police detention pursuant to arrest. The court construed Gerstein as limiting such detention to the "'administrative steps incident to arrest.'" 794 F.2d, at 74, quoting Gerstein, 420 U.S., at 114, 95 S.Ct. at 863. The Court of Appeals also found our decision in Schall v. Martin, 467 U.S. 253, 104 S.Ct. 2403, 81 L.Ed.2d 207 (1984), upholding postarrest pretrial detention of juveniles, inapposite because juveniles have a lesser interest in liberty than do adults. The dissenting judge concluded that on its face, the Bail Reform Act adequately balanced the Federal Government's compelling interests in public safety against the detainee's liberty interests.

II

A facial challenge to a legislative Act is, of course, the most difficult challenge to mount successfully, since the challenger must establish that no set of circumstances exists under which the Act would be valid. The fact that the Bail Reform Act might operate unconstitutionally under some conceivable set of circumstances is insufficient to render it wholly invalid, since we have not recognized an "overbreadth" doctrine outside the limited context of the First Amendment. We think respondents have failed to shoulder their heavy burden to demonstrate that the Act is "facially" unconstitutional.

Respondents present two grounds for invalidating the Bail Reform Act's provisions permitting pretrial detention on the basis of future dangerousness. First, they rely upon the Court of Appeals' conclusion that the Act exceeds the limitations placed upon the Federal Government by the Due

Process Clause of the Fifth Amendment. Second, they contend that the Act contravenes the Eighth Amendment's proscription against excessive bail. We treat these contentions in turn.

A

The Due Process Clause of the Fifth Amendment provides that "No person shall * * * be deprived of life, liberty, or property, without due process of law. * * * "This Court has held that the Due Process Clause protects individuals against two types of government action. So-called "substantive due process" prevents the government from engaging in conduct that "shocks the conscience." Rochin v. California, 342 U.S. 165, 172, 72 S.Ct. 205, 209, 96 L.Ed. 183 (1952), or interferes with rights "implicit in the concept of ordered liberty," Palko v. Connecticut, 302 U.S. 319, 325–326, 58 S.Ct. 149, 152, 82 L.Ed. 288 (1937). When government action depriving a person of life, liberty, or property survives substantive due process scrutiny, it must still be implemented in a fair manner. Mathews v. Eldridge, 424 U.S. 319, 335, 96 S.Ct. 893, 903, 47 L.Ed.2d 18 (1976). This requirement has traditionally been referred to as "procedural" due process.

Respondents first argue that the Act violates substantive due process because the pretrial detention it authorizes constitutes impermissible punishment before trial. See Bell v. Wolfish, 441 U.S. 520, 535, and n. 16, 99 S.Ct. 1861, 1872, and n. 16, 60 L.Ed.2d 447 (1979). The Government, however, has never argued that pretrial detention could be upheld if it were "punishment." The Court of Appeals assumed that pretrial detention under the Bail Reform Act is regulatory, not penal, and we agree that it is.

As an initial matter, the mere fact that a person is detained does not inexorably lead to the conclusion that the government has imposed punishment. To determine whether a restriction on liberty constitutes impermissible punishment or permissible regulation, we first look to legislative intent. Schall v. Martin, 467 U.S., at 269, 104 S.Ct., at 2412. Unless Congress expressly intended to impose punitive restrictions, the punitive/regulatory distinction turns on " 'whether an alternative purpose to which [the restriction] may rationally be connected is assignable for it, and whether it appears excessive in relation to the alternative purpose assigned [to it].' "Ibid., quoting Kennedy v. Mendoza–Martinez, 372 U.S. 144, 168–169, 83 S.Ct. 554, 567–568, 9 L.Ed.2d 644 (1963).

We conclude that the detention imposed by the Act falls on the regulatory side of the dichotomy. The legislative history of the Bail Reform Act clearly indicates that Congress did not formulate the pretrial detention provisions as punishment for dangerous individuals. Congress instead perceived pretrial detention as a potential solution to a pressing societal problem. There is no doubt that preventing danger to the community is a legitimate regulatory goal.

Nor are the incidents of pretrial detention excessive in relation to the regulatory goal Congress sought to achieve. The Bail Reform Act carefully limits the circumstances under which detention may be sought to the most serious of crimes. See 18 U.S.C. § 3142(f) (detention hearings available if case involves crimes of violence, offenses for which the sentence is life imprisonment or death, serious drug offenses, or certain repeat offenders). The arrestee is entitled to a prompt detention hearing, ibid. and the maximum length of pretrial detention is limited by the stringent time limitations of the Speedy Trial Act.[2] See 18 U.S.C. § 3161 et seq. (1982 ed. and Supp. III). Moreover, as in Schall v. Martin, the conditions of confinement envisioned by the Act "appear to reflect the regulatory purposes relied upon by the government". 467 U.S., at 270, 104 S.Ct., at 2413. As in Schall, the statute at issue here requires that detainees be housed in a "facility separate, to the extent practicable, from persons awaiting or serving sentences or being held in custody pending appeal." 18 U.S.C. § 3142(i)(2). We conclude, therefore, that the pretrial detention contemplated by the Bail Reform Act is regulatory in nature, and does not constitute punishment before trial in violation of the Due Process Clause.

The Court of Appeals nevertheless concluded that "the Due Process Clause prohibits pretrial detention on the ground of danger to the community as a regulatory measure, without regard to the duration of the detention." 794 F.2d, at 71. Respondents characterize the Due Process Clause as erecting an impenetrable "wall" in this area that "no governmental interest—rational, important, compelling or otherwise—may surmount."

We do not think the Clause lays down any such categorical imperative. We have repeatedly held that the government's regulatory interest in community safety can, in appropriate circumstances, outweigh an individual's liberty interest. For example, in times of war or insurrection, when society's interest is at its peak, the government may detain individuals whom the government believes to be dangerous. See Ludecke v. Watkins, 335 U.S. 160, 68 S.Ct. 1429, 92 L.Ed. 1881 (1948) (approving unreviewable Executive power to detain enemy aliens in time of war); Moyer v. Peabody, 212 U.S. 78, 84–85, 29 S.Ct. 235, 236–237, 53 L.Ed. 410 (1909) (rejecting due process claim of individual jailed without probable cause by Governor in time of insurrection). Even outside the exigencies of war, we have found that sufficiently compelling governmental interests can justify detention of dangerous persons. Thus, we have found no absolute constitutional barrier to detention of potentially dangerous resident aliens pending deportation proceedings. Carlson v. Landon, 342 U.S. 524, 537–542, 72 S.Ct. 525, 532–535, 96 L.Ed. 547 (1952); Wong Wing v. United States, 163 U.S. 228, 16 S.Ct. 977, 41 L.Ed. 140 (1896). We have also held that the government may detain mentally unstable individuals who present a danger to the public, Addington v. Texas, 441 U.S. 418, 99 S.Ct. 1804, 60 L.Ed.2d 323 (1979), and dangerous defendants who become incompetent to stand trial, Jackson v. Indiana, 406 U.S. 715, 731–739, 92 S.Ct. 1845, 1854–1858, 32 L.Ed.2d 435 (1972); Greenwood v. United States, 350 U.S. 366, 76 S.Ct. 410, 100 L.Ed. 412 (1956). We have approved of postarrest regulatory detention of juveniles when they present a continuing danger to the community. *Schall v. Martin,* supra. Even competent adults may face substantial liberty restrictions as a result of the operation of our criminal justice system. If the

---

2. We intimate no view as to the point at which detention in a particular case might become excessively prolonged, and therefore punitive, in relation to Congress' regulatory goal.

police suspect an individual of a crime, they may arrest and hold him until a neutral magistrate determines whether probable cause exists. Gerstein v. Pugh, 420 U.S. 103, 95 S.Ct. 854, 43 L.Ed.2d 54 (1975). Finally, respondents concede and the Court of Appeals noted that an arrestee may be incarcerated until trial if he presents a risk of flight, see Bell v. Wolfish, 441 U.S., at 534, 99 S.Ct., at 1871, or a danger to witnesses.

Respondents characterize all of these cases as exceptions to the "general rule" of substantive due process that the government may not detain a person prior to a judgment of guilt in a criminal trial. Such a "general rule" may freely be conceded, but we think that these cases show a sufficient number of exceptions to the rule that the congressional action challenged here can hardly be characterized as totally novel. Given the well-established authority of the government, in special circumstances, to restrain individuals' liberty prior to or even without criminal trial and conviction, we think that the present statute providing for pretrial detention on the basis of dangerousness must be evaluated in precisely the same manner that we evaluated the laws in the cases discussed above.

The government's interest in preventing crime by arrestees is both legitimate and compelling. In *Schall,* supra, we recognized the strength of the State's interest in preventing juvenile crime. This general concern with crime prevention is no less compelling when the suspects are adults. Indeed, "[t]he harm suffered by the victim of a crime is not dependent upon the age of the perpetrator." Schall v. Martin, 467 U.S., at 264–265, 104 S.Ct., at 2410. The Bail Reform Act of 1984 responds to an even more particularized governmental interest than the interest we sustained in *Schall.* The statute we upheld in *Schall* permitted pretrial detention of any juvenile arrested on any charge after a showing that the individual might commit some undefined further crimes. The Bail Reform Act, in contrast, narrowly focuses on a particularly acute problem in which the government interests are overwhelming. The Act operates only on individuals who have been arrested for a specific category of extremely serious offenses. 18 U.S.C. § 3142(f). Congress specifically found that these individuals are far more likely to be responsible for dangerous acts in the community after arrest. See S.Rep. No. 98–225, pp. 6–7. Nor is the Act by any means a scattershot attempt to incapacitate those who are merely suspected of these serious crimes. The government must first of all demonstrate probable cause to believe that the charged crime has been committed by the arrestee, but that is not enough. In a full-blown adversary hearing, the government must convince a neutral decisionmaker by clear and convincing evidence that no conditions of release can reasonably assure the safety of the community or any person. 18 U.S.C. § 3142(f). While the government's general interest in preventing crime is compelling, even this interest is heightened when the government musters convincing proof that the arrestee, already indicted or held to answer for a serious crime, presents a demonstrable danger to the community. Under these narrow circumstances, society's interest in crime prevention is at its greatest.

On the other side of the scale, of course, is the individual's strong interest in liberty. We do not minimize the importance and fundamental nature of this right. But, as our cases hold, this right may, in circumstances where the government's interest is sufficiently weighty, be subordinated to the greater needs of society. We think that Congress' careful delineation of the circumstances under which detention will be permitted satisfies this standard. When the government proves by clear and convincing evidence that an arrestee presents an identified and articulable threat to an individual or the community, we believe that, consistent with the Due Process Clause, a court may disable the arrestee from executing that threat. Under these circumstances, we cannot categorically state that pretrial detention "offends some principle of justice so rooted in the traditions and conscience of our people as to be ranked as fundamental." Snyder v. Massachusetts, 291 U.S. 97, 105, 54 S.Ct. 330, 332, 78 L.Ed. 674 (1934).

Finally, we may dispose briefly of respondents' facial challenge to the procedures of the Bail Reform Act. To sustain them against such a challenge, we need only find them "adequate to authorize the pretrial detention of at least some [persons] charged with crimes." Schall, supra, 467 U.S., at 264, 104 S.Ct., at 2409, whether or not they might be insufficient in some particular circumstances. We think they pass that test. As we stated in Schall, "there is nothing inherently unattainable about a prediction of future criminal conduct." Id., at 278, 104 S.Ct., at 2417; see Jurek v. Texas, 428 U.S. 262, 274, 96 S.Ct. 2950, 2957, 49 L.Ed.2d 929 (1976) (opinion of STEWART, POWELL, and STEVENS, JJ.); id., at 279, 96 S.Ct., at 2959–2960 (WHITE, J., concurring in judgment).

Under the Bail Reform Act, the procedures by which a judicial officer evaluates the likelihood of future dangerousness are specifically designed to further the accuracy of that determination. Detainees have a right to counsel at the detention hearing, 18 U.S.C. § 3142(f). They may testify in their own behalf, present information by proffer or otherwise, and cross-examine witnesses who appear at the hearing. Ibid. The judicial officer charged with the responsibility of determining the appropriateness of detention is guided by statutorily enumerated factors, which include the nature and the circumstances of the charges, the weight of the evidence, the history and characteristics of the putative offender, and the danger of the community, § 3142(g). The government must prove its case by clear and convincing evidence, § 3142(f). Finally, the judicial officer must include written findings of fact and a written statement of reasons for a decision to detain, § 3142(i). The Act's review provisions, § 3145(c), provide for immediate appellate review of the detention decision.

We think these extensive safeguards suffice to repel a facial challenge. The protections are more exacting than those we found sufficient in the juvenile context, see Schall, 467 U.S., at 275–281, 104 S.Ct., at 2415–2418, and they far exceed what we found necessary to effect limited postarrest detention in Gerstein v. Pugh, 420 U.S. 103, 95 S.Ct. 854, 43 L.Ed.2d 54 (1975). Given the legitimate and compelling regulatory purpose of the Act and the procedural protections it offers, we conclude that the Act is not facially invalid under the Due Process Clause of the Fifth Amendment.

B

Respondents also contend that the Bail Reform Act violates the Excessive Bail Clause of the Eighth Amendment. The Court of Appeals did not address this issue because it found that the Act violates the Due Process Clause. We think that the Act survives a challenge founded upon the Eighth Amendment.

The Eighth Amendment addresses pretrial release by providing merely that "Excessive bail shall not be required." This Clause, of course, says nothing about whether bail shall be available at all. Respondents nevertheless contend that this Clause grants them a right to bail calculated solely upon considerations of flight. They rely on Stack v. Boyle, 342 U.S. 1, 5, 72 S.Ct. 1, 3, 96 L.Ed. 3 (1951), in which the Court stated that "Bail set at a figure higher than an amount reasonably calculated [to ensure the defendant's presence at trial] is 'excessive' under the Eighth Amendment." In respondents' view, since the Bail Reform Act allows a court essentially to set bail at an infinite amount for reasons not related to the risk of flight, it violates the Excessive Bail Clause. Respondents concede that the right to bail they have discovered in the Eighth Amendment is not absolute. A court may, for example, refuse bail in capital cases. And, as the Court of Appeals noted and respondents admit, a court may refuse bail when the defendant presents a threat to the judicial process by intimidating witnesses. Brief for Respondents 21–22. Respondents characterize these exceptions as consistent with what they claim to be the sole purpose of bail—to ensure integrity of the judicial process.

While we agree that a primary function of bail is to safeguard the courts' role in adjudicating the guilt or innocence of defendants, we reject the proposition that the Eighth Amendment categorically prohibits the government from pursuing other admittedly compelling interests through regulation of pretrial release. The above quoted dicta in *Stack v. Boyle* is far too slender a reed on which to rest this argument. The Court in *Stack* had no occasion to consider whether the Excessive Bail Clause requires courts to admit all defendants to bail, because the statute before the Court in that case in fact allowed the defendants to be bailed. Thus, the Court had to determine only whether bail, admittedly available in that case, was excessive if set at a sum greater than that necessary to ensure the arrestees' presence at trial.

The holding of *Stack* is illuminated by the Court's holding just four months later in Carlson v. Landon, 342 U.S. 524, 72 S.Ct. 525, 96 L.Ed. 547 (1952). In that case, remarkably similar to the present action, the detainees had been arrested and held without bail pending a determination of deportability. The Attorney General refused to release the individuals, "on the ground that there was reasonable cause to believe that [their] release would be prejudicial to the public interest and *would endanger the welfare and safety of the United States.*" Id., at 529, 72 S.Ct., at 528–529 (emphasis added). The detainees brought the same challenge that respondents bring to us today: the Eighth Amendment required them to be admitted to bail. The Court squarely rejected this proposition:

"The bail clause was lifted with slight changes from the English Bill of Rights Act. In England that clause has never been thought to accord a right to bail in all cases, but merely to provide that bail shall not be excessive in those cases where it is proper to grant bail. When this clause was carried over into our Bill of Rights, nothing was said that indicated any different concept. The Eighth Amendment has not prevented Congress from defining the classes of cases in which bail shall be allowed in this country. Thus, in criminal cases bail is not compulsory where the punishment may be death. Indeed, the very language of the Amendment fails to say all arrests must be bailable." Id., at 545–546, 72 S.Ct., at 536–537 (footnotes omitted).

Carlson v. Landon was a civil case, and we need not decide today whether the Excessive Bail Clause speaks at all to Congress' power to define the classes of criminal arrestees who shall be admitted to bail. For even if we were to conclude that the Eighth Amendment imposes some substantive limitations on the National Legislature's powers in this area, we would still hold that the Bail Reform Act is valid. Nothing in the text of the Bail Clause limits permissible government considerations solely to questions of flight. The only arguable substantive limitation of the Bail Clause is that the government's proposed conditions of release or detention not be "excessive" in light of the perceived evil. Of course, to determine whether the government's response is excessive, we must compare that response against the interest the government seeks to protect by means of that response. Thus, when the government has admitted that its only interest is in preventing flight, bail must be set by a court at a sum designed to ensure that goal, and no more. *Stack v. Boyle,* supra. We believe that when Congress has mandated detention on the basis of a compelling interest other than prevention of flight, as it has here, the Eighth Amendment does not require release on bail.

III

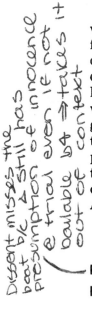

Dissent misses the boat b/c it still has presumption of innocence @ trial even if not bailable b4 → takes it out of context

In our society liberty is the norm, and detention prior to trial or without trial is the carefully limited exception. We hold that the provisions for pretrial detention in the Bail Reform Act of 1984 fall within that carefully limited exception. The Act authorizes the detention prior to trial of arrestees charged with serious felonies who are found after an adversary hearing to pose a threat to the safety of individuals or to the community which no condition of release can dispel. The numerous procedural safeguards detailed above must attend this adversary hearing. We are unwilling to say that this congressional determination, based as it is upon that primary concern of every government—a concern for the safety and indeed the lives of its citizens—on its face violates either the Due Process Clause of the Fifth Amendment or the Excessive Bail Clause of the Eighth Amendment.

The judgment of the Court of Appeals is therefore

Reversed.

■ JUSTICE MARSHALL, with whom JUSTICE BRENNAN joins, dissenting [omitted].

■ JUSTICE STEVENS, dissenting [omitted].

NOTES

1. **Applying the 8th Amendment to the States.** In Hunt v. Roth, 648 F.2d 1148 (8th Cir.1981), vacated as moot sub nom. Murphy v. Hunt, 455 U.S. 478, 102

S.Ct. 1181, 71 L.Ed.2d 353 (1982), Hunt had been charged in the Nebraska courts with forcible sexual assault as well as several other nonsexual felonies. He was denied bail under Article 1, Section 9 of the Nebraska Constitution, which provides for denial of bail to persons charged with "sexual offenses involving penetration by force or against the will of the victim, * * * where the proof is evident or the presumption great." He sought habeas corpus and declaratory relief in federal court on the ground that his pretrial detention violated his federal constitutional rights. The district court dismissed his claims but, on appeal, the Eighth Circuit reversed the dismissal of his claim for declaratory relief.

First, the Court of Appeals noted the absence of definitive authority as to whether the Eighth Amendment prohibition against excessive bail is incorporated into the Fourteenth Amendment and thus binding on the states. Noting that bail is basic to America's system of laws and related to the presumption of innocence, the court held that the excessive bail clause is incorporated into the Fourteenth Amendment. 648 F.2d at 1155–56. Second, it rejected the argument that the excessive bail clause does not address when pretrial release may be denied altogether:

> If the eighth amendment has any meaning beyond sheer rhetoric, the constitutional prohibition against excessive bail necessarily implies that unreasonable denial of bail is likewise prohibited. Logic defies any other resolution of the question.

Id. at 1157. Finally, testing the Nebraska provision under this approach, it concluded that the state constitutional section violated the eighth amendment:

> Under the challenged state procedures, bail *must* be denied to every person charged with "sexual offenses involving penetration by force or against the will of the victim" where the "proof is evident or the presumption great." Once the charge is made and it is determined that the proof is evident, no other relevant factor is weighed and no standards relevant to the purpose of assuring the presence of the defendant are considered. No discretion is vested in any judicial officer to grant or to deny bail. * * * [T]here exists a strong argument that bail may be denied without encroaching on constitutional concerns where a judicial officer weighs all the appropriate factors and makes a reasoned judgment that the defendant's past record demonstrates that bail will not reasonably assure his or her appearance or, arguendo, that he or she, because of the overall record and circumstances, poses a threat to the community. The fatal flaw in the Nebraska constitutional amendment is that the state has created an irrebuttable presumption that every individual charged with this particular offense is incapable of assuring his appearance by conditioning it upon reasonable bail or is too dangerous to be granted release. The constitutional protections involved are too fundamental to foreclose by arbitrary state decree. The state may be free to consider the nature of the charge and the degree of proof in granting or denying bail but it cannot give these factors conclusive force. * * *

Id. at 1162–65. (emphasis added) The Supreme Court, however, found that Hunt's conviction mooted his challenge to denial of pretrial bail and vacated the judgment of the Court of Appeals. Murphy v. Hunt, 455 U.S. 478, 102 S.Ct. 1181, 71 L.Ed.2d 353 (1982) (per curiam).

2. **Remedy for violation of the requirement of a prompt detention hearing.** The respondent in United States v. Montalvo–Murillo, 495 U.S. 711, 110 S.Ct. 2072, 109 L.Ed.2d 720 (1990) was arrested on federal drug violations. He was not provided a detention hearing at his first judicial appearance as required by 18 U.S.C.A. § 3142(f). The District Court and Court of Appeals took the position that although respondent should be detained under statutory criteria, he was required to be released because of the failure to comply with the requirement of a prompt

hearing. Respondent was released, fled and was at large at the time of the Supreme Court's decision. The Supreme Court reversed in an opinion by Justice Kennedy. The statute does not require release as a remedy for failure to hold a detention hearing in a timely fashion.

> We find nothing in the statute to justify denying the Government an opportunity to prove that the person is dangerous or a risk of flight once the statutory time for hearing has passed. We do not agree that we should, or can, invent a remedy to satisfy some perceived need to coerce the courts and the Government into complying with the statutory time limits. Magistrates and district judges can be presumed to insist upon compliance with the law without the threat that we must embarrass the system by releasing a suspect certain to flee from justice, as this one did in such a deft and prompt manner. The district court, the court of appeals, and this Court remain open to order immediate release of anyone detained in violation of the statute. Whatever other remedies may exist for detention without a timely hearing or for conduct that is aggravated or intentional, a matter not before us here, we hold that once the Government discovers that the time limits have expired, it may ask for a prompt detention hearing and make its case to detain based upon the requirements set forth in the statute.

495 U.S. at 721, 110 S.Ct. at 2079, 109 L.Ed.2d at 732. Justice Stevens, joined by Justices Brennan and Marshall, dissented.

United States v. Jessup

United States Court of Appeals, First Circuit, 1985.
757 F.2d 378.

■ BREYER, CIRCUIT JUDGE.

This appeal challenges the constitutionality of a provision of the Bail Reform Act of 1984, 18 U.S.C. § 3141 et seq., that requires judicial officers making bail decisions to apply a rebuttable presumption that one charged with a serious drug offense will likely flee before trial. 18 U.S.C. § 3142(e). We find that Congress has acted within the Constitution's prescribed limits in creating this rebuttable presumption and that the magistrate and district court have acted within their lawful authority in applying it, and related statutory provisions, to the appellant Mark Jessup. We affirm the district court's decision to deny him bail and to hold him in custody pending his trial.

I

The Bail Reform Act of 1984 ("the Act") makes it, in one respect, harder and, in another respect, easier for judicial officers to order pretrial detention of those accused of crimes. It makes it harder by specifying explicitly what was implicit in prior law, namely that magistrates and judges cannot impose any "financial condition" that will result in detention. § 3142(c). High money bail cannot be used as a device to keep a defendant in custody before trial. The Act makes detention easier by broadening the category of persons whom the officer can order detained. And, the Act specifies that a judicial officer shall order detention if he finds that no condition or combination of conditions [attaching to release] will reasonably assure the appearance of the person as required and the safety of any other person and the community * * *.

§ 3142(e). The Act sets forth procedures to be used in applying this standard. It provides a list of factors that the officer is to weigh when doing so § 3142(g); and it creates several "rebuttable presumptions" that the officer is to use when applying the basic standard.

This case concerns one of the "rebuttable presumptions" that the Act creates. It states

> Subject to rebuttal by the person, it shall be presumed that no condition or combination of conditions will reasonably assure the appearance of the person as required and the safety of the community if the judicial officer finds that there is probable cause to believe that the person committed an offense for which a maximum term of imprisonment of ten years or more is prescribed in the Controlled Substances Act (21 U.S.C. 801 et seq.) * * *.

§ 3142(e).

The magistrate here used the presumption in deciding to detain appellant Jessup. The magistrate found that Jessup posed a threat to the safety of the community in that, if released, he might continue to commit crimes. The magistrate also found that, if released, there was a substantial risk that Jessup would flee. In particular, the magistrate stated

> I am equally of the view that the defendant has not rebutted the presumption that no nonfinancial conditions or combination of nonfinancial conditions of release would reasonably assure his presence. The defendant is charged with a serious crime and the Government's evidence is strong. The defendant has been in this state for only two years; he has no family or relatives living here. In all the circumstances, I do not believe the fact that the defendant is engaged to a Massachusetts resident would deter him from fleeing the jurisdiction in view of the seriousness of the crime charged and the strength of the evidence against him.

Given this alternative basis for the magistrate's decision, we need not consider the Act's "dangerousness" provisions or the magistrate's "dangerousness" finding. It is well established that the government can keep a defendant in custody to secure his presence at trial. See Stack v. Boyle, 342 U.S. 1, 4, 72 S.Ct. 1, 3, 96 L.Ed. 3 (1951) ("The right to release before trial is conditioned upon the accused's giving adequate assurance that he will stand trial and submit to sentence if found guilty."); United States v. Abrahams, 575 F.2d 3, 8 (1st Cir.) (holding that bail may be denied in exceptional circumstances where financial condition of release cannot reasonably assure presence of defendant at trial), cert. denied, 439 U.S. 821, 99 S.Ct. 85, 58 L.Ed.2d 112 (1978). Thus the constitutional issue presented here is whether the government can use the Act's rebuttable presumption in doing so.

II

Before turning to the constitutional question, we must first decide what the rebuttable presumption means. What kind of burden is it designed to impose upon a defendant? Or, to cast the question in terms traditionally used in the law of evidence, does it impose a "burden of persuasion" or only a "burden of production"? See generally C. McCormick, *Evidence* § 342 et seq. (2d ed. 1972). If the former, the alleged drug offender would have to *prove* he would not flee—i.e., he would have to *persuade* the judicial officer on the point. If the latter, he would only have to introduce a certain amount of evidence contrary to the presumed fact; no change in the burden of persuasion is effected. Where the burden of persuasion lies may make a practical difference to a magistrate or judge genuinely uncertain on the basis of what the parties have presented.

The United States Attorney here suggests that Congress meant the presumption to shift the burden of persuasion to the defendant. And he cites a district court case, in support of this view. In two other cases, however, it has been held that Congress did not intend to shift the burden of persuasion to the defendant but intended to impose only a burden of production. We believe the latter interpretation is correct.

Our reasons for believing that the burden of persuasion does not shift include the following. First, we are chary of interpreting ambiguous language to mandate pretrial confinement where evidence before a magistrate is indeterminate. Although pretrial confinement to prevent flight is not punishment, but rather one of various restrictions on the freedom of an accused person aimed at facilitating trial, see Bell v. Wolfish, 441 U.S. 520, 535–39, 99 S.Ct. 1861, 1871–74, 60 L.Ed.2d 447 (1979), it is still a most severe restriction requiring clear cause.

Second, the Senate Judiciary Committee Report explaining the new presumption, while arguably ambiguous, does not suggest that Congress meant to impose a burden of persuasion on the defendant. To understand the relevance of the Report's description, one must realize that § 3142(e) creates not only the drug offender presumptions already mentioned (concerning "flight" and "danger") but it also creates a rebuttable presumption that one previously convicted of having committed a crime while free on bail is sufficiently "dangerous" to warrant detention. The Report describes both of these presumptions in the same place. It says that the object of this last presumption is to shift the burden

> to the defendant *to establish a basis for concluding* that there are conditions of release sufficient to assure that he will not again engage in dangerous criminal activity pending his trial.

S.Rep. No. 225, 98th Cong., 1st Sess. 19 (1983), U.S.Code Cong. & Admin.News 1984, pp. 1, 22 (emphasis added). The position of this sentence in the Report, its language, and the nature of the language of the statutory presumption all suggest that the words "establish a basis for concluding" aptly describe the intended effect of both § 3142(e) presumptions. And, these words do not say that the burden of persuasion shifts to the defendant, nor do they imply that it is up to the defendant to persuade the judicial officer.

Third, a later section in the Act, § 3148(b), establishes another similar presumption, this time in respect to a person who is released on bail (or the equivalent) and *then* commits a crime. The Act requires that such a person be brought back before the magistrate, who will consider whether to revoke his bail and detain him. The Act tells the magistrate that, if he finds probable cause to believe the person committed another crime while on release, he is to presume (subject to rebuttal) that detention is necessary to protect the community from still further crimes. That is to say, the Act applies a rebuttable presumption of "dangerousness." In describing the presumption, the Committee Report states that

> the establishment of probable cause to believe that the defendant has committed a serious crime while on release constitutes compelling evidence that the defendant poses a danger to the community, and, once such probable cause is established, it is appropriate that the burden rest on the defendant *to come forward with evidence* indicating that this conclusion is not warranted in his case.

S.Rep., supra, at 36 (emphasis added), U.S.Code Cong. & Admin.News 1984, p. 39. This language ("come forward with evidence") is traditionally used to suggest a shift in the burden of production, not of persuasion. (Compare, for example, the language used by the congressional Conference Committee which, in preparing the Federal Rules of Evidence, noted that a

> presumption shifts to the party against whom it is directed the burden of *going forward with evidence* to meet or rebut the presumption, but it does not shift to that party the burden of persuasion on the existence of the presumed fact).

Fed.R.Evid. 301, Notes of Conference Committee (emphasis added). The Act then does not impose a burden of persuasion even upon a defendant found likely to have just committed a crime while on bail. It would be anomalous to interpret the Act as imposing such a burden on those who committed such crimes in the past or on those charged with drug offenses, since they, if anything, present less risky cases.

Fourth, an examination of a related section of the Act, § 3143, shows that Congress knew how to create a 'burden of persuasion' when it wanted to do so. Section 3143 creates a presumption that a defendant who has been convicted of a crime may not be released pending his appeal or sentencing unless he shows "by clear and convincing evidence that [he] is not likely to flee or pose a danger to the safety of any other person or the community." § 3143(a), (b). (This provision differs from the Bail Reform Act of 1966, in which even convicted defendants were presumptively entitled to the same opportunity for release on bail as defendants who had not already been convicted. See 18 U.S.C. former § 3148.) The Judiciary Committee Report notes that

> The Committee intends that in overcoming the presumption in favor of detention [in § 3143] *the burden of proof* rests with the defendant.

S.Rep., supra, at 27 (emphasis added), U.S.Code Cong. & Admin.News 1984, p. 30. Congress could have used language similar to that of § 3143, or Report language similar to that just quoted, if it had intended § 3142(e) to impose a similar burden of persuasion. The absence of such language, and the proximity of §§ 3142 and 3143, reinforces our conclusion that § 3142 was meant to impose only a burden of production.

The government's strongest argument to the contrary rests upon two propositions:

(a) Congress did not intend to create a set of presumptions with little or no practical effect; and

(b) a 'burden of production' presumption would have little practical effect.

We agree with the first part of the argument: Congress did intend the presumption to have a practical effect. This can be seen in the Report's discussion of the § 3142(e) presumptions, which says that in the circumstances that trigger the presumption (a serious drug offense charge; past commission of a crime on bail), a *"strong probability arises* that no form of conditional release will be adequate." S.Rep., supra, at 19 (emphasis added), U.S.Code Cong. & Admin.News 1984, p. 22. In respect to the § 3148(b) presumption, the Report adds that

the establishment of probable cause to believe that the defendant has committed a serious crime while on release constitutes *compelling evidence* that the defendant poses a danger to the community.

Id. at 36 (emphasis added), U.S.Code Cong. & Admin.News 1984, p. 39.

We do not agree, however, with the second part of the argument. It is true that, under the prevailing judicial view, a "burden of production" presumption is a "bursting bubble." See C. McCormick, *Evidence* § 345 at 821 (2d ed. 1972) ("bursting bubble" theory is "the most widely followed theory of presumptions in American law"); Legille v. Dann, 544 F.2d 1, 6 (D.C.Cir.1976) (same). Under this theory, the presumption requires the 'presumed against' party to introduce evidence, but, once he does so, the presumption "bursts" and totally disappears, allowing the judge (or jury) to decide the question without reference to the presumption. Since a defendant can always provide the magistrate with *some* reason to believe him a good risk, a "bursting bubble" approach might render the presumption virtually meaningless, contrary to Congress's clear intent.

Nonetheless, Congress does not *have* to make a "bursting bubble" of each "burden of production" presumption. We believe that here it has *not* done so; rather, it has created a "burden of production" presumption that *does* have significant practical impact. That is to say, the Report's language, together with the history of the Act (with its emphasis on the importance of the presumption), indicates to us that Congress meant to impose a "burden of production" presumption, but it did not intend to make that presumption a "bursting bubble."

We are led to this conclusion in part by the strain of legal thought which has marked out a "middle ground" for some presumptions—holding that they neither shift the burden of persuasion nor "burst" once contrary evidence is presented. See Morgan, Instructing the Jury upon Presumptions and Burdens of Proof, 47 Harv.L.Rev. 59, 82–83 (1933); 21 C. Wright & K. Graham, *Federal Practice and Procedure (Evidence)* § 5122 at 566 (noting that while courts pay "lip service" to "bursting bubble" approach, "most of them [have] felt compelled to deviate from the 'bursting bubble' theory at one time or another in order to give greater effect to presumptions"); see generally Hecht & Pinzler, Rebutting Presumptions: Order Out of Chaos, 58 B.U.L.Rev. 527 (1978). Under this view, to remove the presumption entirely from a case once conflicting evidence has been presented could undercut the legislative purpose in creating the presumption (say, an intent to have courts follow the legislature's assessment of probabilities or the furtherance of some other specific public policy). The House Judiciary Committee adopted exactly this sort of "intermediate position" in its Report on Fed.R.Evid. 301. The Committee Report said that the 'bursting bubble' approach gave presumptions "too slight an effect," and proposed a version of Fed.R.Evid. 301 under which presumptions would "not vanish upon the introduction of contradicting evidence" but would remain available "to be considered by the jury." See Fed.R.Evid. 301 and accompanying committee reports; Hearings on Proposed Rules of Evidence Before the Subcommittee on Criminal Justice of the House Comm. on the Judiciary (Supp.), 93d Cong., 1st Sess., ser. 2, at 364 (Comm.Print 1973). A number of courts have also adopted this 'middle ground' view of presumptions. See, e.g., Montgomery County Fire Board v. Fisher, 53 Md.App. 435, 454 A.2d 394, 400 (1983) (statutory presumption that firefighter's heart disease is job related "does not disappear like the bursting bubble upon generation of a jury issue; rather it remains in the case as one of the elements to be considered"); Wright v. State Accident Insurance Fund, 289 Or. 323, 613 P.2d 755, 759–60 (1980) (same presumption) ("If there is opposing evidence, the trier of fact must weigh the evidence, giving the presumption the value of evidence, and determine upon which side the evidence preponderates."); Starr v. Campos, 134 Ariz. 254, 655 P.2d 794, 796 (1982) (jury weighs blood alcohol intoxication presumption along with other evidence); Walker v. Butterworth, 599 F.2d 1074, 1078 (1st Cir.1979) (sanity presumption carries evidentiary value).

The case for a "middle ground" position is particularly strong in this setting of a detention hearing, where the procedures are informal and there is no jury. In such a setting, there is no occasion for the presumption to play its traditional practical role in the judge's decision about whether to direct a verdict (if no evidence is produced) or whether, instead, to send an issue to the jury. In a detention hearing there is no jury. Thus a "bursting bubble" approach would call on the judge (or magistrate) to consider the presumption and then, if it is met with contrary evidence, to erase the presumption from his mind—not a task that is psychologically easy to accomplish.

Moreover, here the Act's history suggests a relatively obvious way to apply this presumption along the lines of the House Judiciary Committee's "intermediate position"—giving it some weight, without shifting the burden of persuasion. Congress investigated a general problem, the problem of drug offenders and flight. After hearing evidence, Congress concluded that "flight to avoid prosecution is particularly high among persons charged with major drug offenses." S.Rep., supra, at 20, U.S.Code Cong. & Admin.News 1984, p. 23. It found that "drug traffickers often have established ties outside the United States * * * [and] have both the resources and foreign contacts to escape to other countries * * *." Id. Congress then wrote its drug offender/flight presumption. These facts suggest that Congress intended magistrates and judges, who typically focus only upon the particular cases before them, to take account of the more general facts that

Congress found. In order to "rebut" the presumption, the defendant must produce some evidence; and the magistrate or judge should then still keep in mind the fact that Congress has found that offenders, as a general rule, pose *special* risks of flight. The magistrate or judge should incorporate that fact and finding among the other special factors that Congress has told him to weigh when making his bail decision. See § 3142(g) (judicial officer shall weigh, among other things, "nature of circumstances of offense," "weight of evidence," "history and characteristics of the person including * * * character, physical and mental condition, family history * * *, past conduct * * *," and so forth). Congress did not precisely describe just how a magistrate will weigh the presumption, along with (or against) other § 3142(g) factors. But the same can be said of each of the several § 3142(g) factors. It is not unusual for Congress to instruct a magistrate or judge conscientiously to weigh several different factors without specifying precise weights for each. See, e.g., Criminal Fine Enforcement Act of 1984, 18 U.S.C. § 3622.

Finally, the most common criticism of the "intermediate position" is that it will confuse a jury; the jury will not understand how to weigh a presumption against direct evidence. See Senate Judiciary Committee Notes on Fed.R.Evid. 301; C. McCormick, *Handbook of the Law of Evidence* § 345 at 825 & n. 60 (1972). This criticism has less weight in the context of a detention hearing, where no jury is involved, and the magistrate or judge is used to the process of weighing several competing factors.

Since the presumption is but one factor among many, its continued consideration by the magistrate does not impose a burden of persuasion upon the defendant. And, since Congress seeks only consideration of the general drug offender/flight problem, the magistrate or judge may still conclude that what is true in general is not true in the particular case before him. He is free to do so, and to release the defendant, as long as the defendant has presented some evidence and the magistrate or judge has evaluated all of the evidence with Congress's view of the general problem in mind. It is worth nothing that the Act requires that all detention orders "include written findings of fact and *a written statement of the reasons for the detention.*" § 3142(i)(1) (emphasis added). Thus, the defendant is protected from a weighing of factors that is arbitrary, or not in keeping with the Act.

In sum, the congressional report language about the presumption's nature and effect, the unsuitability of a "bursting bubble" presumption in an informal, nonjury hearing, and the availability of a "middle way," lead us to reject the government's "burden of persuasion" argument. Insofar as a magistrate or judge previously shared Congress's views about the general nature of the drug offender/flight problem, use of the new presumption might not make much difference. But, insofar as the magistrate or judge did not previously share those views, the presumption will have a significant practical effect. And this, we think, is what Congress intended.

III

We turn now to Jessup's claim that use of the drug offender/flight presumption is unconstitutional because it deprives him of his "liberty

* * * without due process of law." U.S. Constitution, Amendment V. In deciding whether this presumption makes Jessup's bail procedures constitutionally unfair, we shall ask 1) whether the presumption represents a reasonable congressional response to a problem of legitimate legislative concern, and 2) whether the presumption increases the risk of an erroneous deprivation of liberty—i.e., will it likely increase the risk that magistrates will release or detain the wrong people? See Schall v. Martin, __ U.S. __, 104 S.Ct. 2403, 2409, 81 L.Ed.2d 207 (1984); Mathews v. Eldridge, 424 U.S. 319, 335, 96 S.Ct. 893, 903, 47 L.Ed.2d 18 (1976) (determining procedural fairness by examining private interests, governmental interests, and risk of error).

The first question must be answered, on the record before us, in the government's favor. The government's interest in securing the appearance of a defendant at trial has been held important enough to warrant pretrial detention where there is a significant risk of flight.

Moreover, Congress held hearings and heard considerable evidence that drug offenders posed a special risk of "flight." It described this evidence, and the problems revealed as follows:

> the Committee received testimony that flight to avoid prosecution is particularly high among persons charged with major drug offenses. Because of the extremely lucrative nature of drug trafficking, and the fact that drug traffickers often have established substantial ties outside the United States from whence most dangerous drugs are imported into the country, these persons have both the resources and foreign contacts to escape to other countries with relative ease in order to avoid prosecution for offenses punishable by lengthy prison sentences. Even the prospect of forfeiture of bond in the hundreds of thousands of dollars has proven to be ineffective in assuring the appearance of major drug traffickers. In view of these factors, the Committee has provided in section 3142(e) that in a case in which there is probable cause to believe that the person has committed a grave drug offense, a rebuta- ble [sic] presumption arises that no condition or combination of conditions will reasonably assure the appearance of the person and the safety of the community.

* * *

The rationale for the use of financial conditions of release is that the prospect of forfeiture of the amount of a bond or of property used as collateral to secure release is sufficient to deter flight. However, when the proceeds of crime are used to post bond, this rationale no longer holds true. In recent years, there has been an increasing incidence of defendants, particularly those engaged in highly lucrative criminal activities such as drug trafficking, who are able to make extraordinarily high money bonds, posting bail and then fleeing the country. Among such defendants, forfeiture of bond is simply a cost of doing business, and it appears that there is a growing practice of reserving a portion of crime income to cover this cost of avoiding prosecution.

S.Rep., supra, at 20, 23–24 (citations omitted), U.S.Code Cong. & Admin.News 1984, pp. 23, 26, 27. The evidence that was presented in congressional hearings on this subject gave Congress, at the least, a substantial basis for reaching these conclusions. See, e.g., "Bail Reform," Hearings Before the Subcommittee on the Constitution of the Senate Judiciary Committee, 97th Cong., 1st Sess., Sept. 17, Oct. 21, 1981 at 67, 70 (graphs 1, 2) (Comm.Print 1982) (suggesting that in ten districts studied, drug offenders account for about *one-sixth* of all crimes charged but about *one-half* of all bail jumpers). See also sources collected in Appendix B. The drug offender/flight presumption seems a reasonable response to this general problem, requiring that a charged drug offender produce some evidence that he does not present a special risk and then requiring the magistrate to review the matter with Congress's general findings in mind.

Jessup, and a defendant in a related case, United States v. Lepere, No. 85–1012 (1st Cir., argued Feb. 4, 1985), attack the presumption in part by challenging the underlying congressional conclusions—by arguing that the evidence does not show a serious, special drug offender/flight problem. The Supreme Court, however, has cautioned us to give "significant weight" to the "capacity of Congress to amass the stuff of actual experience and cull conclusions from it." Usery v. Turner Elkhorn Mining, 428 U.S. 1, 28, 96 S.Ct. 2882, 2898, 49 L.Ed.2d 752 (1976). We cannot here reevaluate the statistical studies or other evidence presented at congressional hearings. To do so would invite potentially endless, unresolvable scholarly argument. (Statistical assumptions are almost always open to plausible attack.) And, doing so would overlook the fact that factual judgments in Congress (as elsewhere) often rest, less upon the gathering of numbers, than upon instinctive evaluation of the views of those with practical experience in the field—views that may reach the legislative ear both informally and formally. Given Congress's constitutional authority and practical fact-gathering power—a power far greater than that of courts—we are not persuaded that Congress's conclusions concerning the drug offender/flight problem are without substantial basis in fact, or that Congress's solution is unreasonable. And, we conclude that the government's interest in the presumption is a strong and legitimate one.

We also find that the presumption does not significantly increase the risk of an "erroneous deprivation" of liberty. Mathews v. Eldridge, 424 U.S. at 324–25, 96 S.Ct. at 897–98. The presumption shifts the burden of production, not the burden of persuasion. It applies only where there is probable cause to believe a person is guilty of a serious crime. The defendant can provide argument and evidence suggesting that he is not involved in the "highly lucrative" drug operations at the center of congressional concern. The Act further specifically provides a defendant with a hearing at which he

> has the right to be represented by counsel, and, if he is financially unable to obtain adequate representation, to have counsel appointed for him. The person shall be afforded an opportunity to testify, to present witnesses on his own behalf, to cross-examine witnesses who appear at the hearing, and to present information by proffer and otherwise.

> § 3142(f)(2)(B). Although the magistrate will keep the presumption in mind in making a decision, he will do so only as a reminder of

Congress's findings. Given the Act's procedural protections, the fact that the presumption does not shift the burden of persuasion, and the presumption's relation to Congress's factfinding powers, we cannot say that it promotes *less,* rather than *more,* accurate decisionmaking. Given the legitimate governmental interest in securing a defendant's appearance at trial, the presumption's restrictions on the defendant's liberty are constitutionally permissible.

Jessup's strongest argument to the contrary rests upon Leary v. United States, 395 U.S. 6, 89 S.Ct. 1532, 23 L.Ed.2d 57 (1969), which he cites for the proposition that a presumption in a criminal case is invalid unless there is "substantial assurance that the presumed fact is more likely than not to flow from the proved fact on which it is made to depend." Id. at 36, 89 S.Ct. at 1548. No one claims, he adds, that despite money bail and other release conditions, drug offenders are *more likely than not* to run away. We note, however, that the *Leary* Court applied this standard to a presumption in the context of a full blown criminal trial, where the presumption was used to establish an important element of the crime that was charged. Here, on the other hand, we deal with a presumption that is applied to a preliminary hearing, where decisions must be made quickly and where the purpose is not to punish but to increase the likelihood that the trial will go forward. It is well established that the constitutional guarantees at such hearings are less protective of defendants than at trial. * * * The Constitution does not require as great a degree of certainty for charging or for securing the presence at trial of one charged as for convicting that person at a criminal trial. In this context then, the substantial basis of information underlying 'drug offender/flight' conclusions is sufficient to meet the Constitution's requirement of adequate support for a presumption. We reject Jessup's claim that more support is necessary.

We do not consider the government's claim that a still lesser test ("some rational connection," see Usery v. Turner Elkhorn Mining, 428 U.S. at 28, 96 S.Ct. at 2898) is all that the presumptions need satisfy. This lesser standard, applied by the Supreme Court typically in cases involving economic regulation, see id., may be insufficient here, where personal liberty is at stake.

Finally, Jessup contends that the real purpose of the presumption is not to detain those likely to flee but rather to impose extra punishment upon alleged drug offenders. In deciding whether this is, in fact, its purpose, we must ask whether there is "an alternative purpose" with which the presumption is "rationally * * * connected * * * [and to which it is] assignable," and whether the presumption is "excessive in relation to the alternative purpose assigned." Bell v. Wolfish, 441 U.S. 520, 538, 99 S.Ct. 1861, 1873, 60 L.Ed.2d 447 (1979) (quoting Kennedy v. Mendoza–Martinez, 372 U.S. 144, 168–69, 83 S.Ct. 554, 567–68, 9 L.Ed.2d 644 (1963)). Here, the "alternative purpose" is obvious, namely Congress's stated object: preventing pretrial flight. For reasons previously given, the presumption does not impose an excessive burden in respect to this purpose. We find no legal basis for viewing the presumption as imposing "punishment." For these reasons, we believe the presumption, as we have interpreted it, is constitutional.

IV

Assuming the presumption's constitutionality, Jessup still claims his detention is unlawful for several reasons. First, he says that he is not the sort of drug offender (*i.e.*, one with important foreign connections) that Congress had in mind when it created the presumption; therefore, the magistrate should not have applied the presumption to him. The conclusion of this argument, however, does not follow from its premise. The presumption applies to Jessup for he fits within its terms. The Act allows him to present all the special features of his case directly to the magistrate. The less those features resemble the congressional paradigm, the less weight the magistrate will likely give to Congress's concern for flight. The individual characteristics of a case and the precise weight to be given the presumption are matters for a magistrate to take into account within the framework of factors set out in § 3142. In other words, Jessup's argument goes not to the applicability of the presumption but rather to the weight that should properly be accorded it.

Second, Jessup argues that the evidence was insufficient for the magistrate to conclude that "no condition or combination of conditions [attached to release] will reasonably assure * * * [his] appearance as required." § 3142(e). Giving appropriate weight to the scope of the magistrate's power to draw conclusions from the evidence presented, see C. Wright, *Federal Practice and Procedure: Criminal 2d* § 722 at 160 (1982) ("An order concerning release prior to conviction is to be affirmed if it is supported by the proceedings below"),[a] we find the evidence sufficient. On October 29, 1984, the magistrate had before him testimony of a DEA agent, Joseph O'Keefe, and the sworn statement of another DEA agent, Stephen Assarian, that Jessup and a codefendant had met with Assarian to arrange for the sale to Assarian of two kilograms of cocaine. Jessup and the codefendant later met with Assarian to consummate the arrangement, and Jessup showed Assarian the cocaine. Assarian and other DEA agents then arrested Jessup and his codefendant. The magistrate found this evidence adequate to establish 'probable cause' that Jessup committed the drug offense with which he was charged.

The magistrate then considered several factors weighing against release: 1) the offense charged was serious; 2) the offense was within Congress's definition of "dangerous federal offenses"; 3) the weight of the evidence against Jessup was strong (in particular, the evidence suggested to the magistrate that Jessup was a "trusted cohort" of his codefendant, who allegedly had been involved in cocaine dealing for some time); 4) Jessup had no relatives in Massachusetts; 5) Jessup had lived in Massachusetts for only two years; and 6) Jessup had been unemployed for six months before his arrest.

The magistrate also considered several factors weighing in favor of Jessup's release. They included 1) Jessup was engaged to a Massachusetts

---

a. Subsequently, in United States v. O'Brien, 895 F.2d 810 (1st Cir.1990), the court abandoned the "supported by the proceedings below" standard as based on the prior statute and substituted a more intru- sive review standard which it characterized as providing "independent review all detention decisions, giving deference to the determination of the district court." 895 F.2d at 814.

resident; 2) Jessup had a job offer (from his codefendant's brother); and 3) Jessup had no prior criminal record. (The United States Attorney has recently brought to our attention information suggesting that Jessup in fact has a prior criminal record; we have, however, conducted our review of the magistrate's decision on the basis of the record before the magistrate, and we have not considered this new information.)

The magistrate initially thought that several conditions, including posting of the $25,000 bond that Jessup's counsel suggested, *might* prove sufficient to guarantee Jessup's appearance. Reserving decision, the magistrate asked counsel to explain the source of the $25,000, see § 3142(g)(4), since Jessup had earlier said that he was indigent. Counsel then responded that Jessup could not raise the $25,000, and that Jessup should be released without the posting of a money bond. At that point, the magistrate concluded that no combination of *non*financial conditions would prove sufficient to assure both Jessup's "appearance" and the "safety of * * * the community."

As previously mentioned, the magistrate's decision rests adequately on the "appearance" ground alone. We believe that the magistrate could reasonably conclude from the facts we have listed that the serious charges, the strong evidence, the lack of Massachusetts connections, the possibility of prior involvement, and the lack of any monetary incentive to return would together create too great a risk of flight. We therefore conclude that the magistrate acted within his lawful powers.

Third, Jessup argues that, since the magistrate would have released him had he been able to post $25,000 bail, he must release him anyway. Otherwise, says Jessup, the magistrate violates the next to last sentence in § 3142(c) which says that

> The judicial officer may not impose a financial condition that results in the pretrial detention of the person.

In a literal sense, Jessup's failure to meet the "financial condition," while a necessary condition for Jessup's detention, is not in fact its relevant cause. Rather, Jessup is confined because *both* 1) he cannot raise the $25,000, *and* 2) no other set of conditions is sufficient to guarantee his appearance. That the quoted sentence from the Act does not foreclose detention in these circumstances is made very clear by the Senate Report, which states

> * * * section 3142(c) provides that a judicial officer may not impose a financial condition of release that results in the pretrial detention of the defendant. The purpose of this provision is to preclude the sub rosa use of money bond to detain dangerous defendants. However, its application does not necessarily require the release of a person who says he is unable to meet a financial condition of release which the judge has determined is the only form of conditional release that will assure the person's future appearance. Thus, for example, if a judicial officer determines that a $50,000 bond is the only means, short of detention, of assuring the appearance of a defendant who poses a serious risk of flight, and the defendant asserts that, despite the judicial officer's finding to the contrary, he cannot meet the bond, the judicial officer may reconsider the amount of the bond. If he still

concludes that the initial amount is reasonable and necessary then it would appear that there is no available condition of release that will assure the defendant's appearance.

S.Rep., supra, at 16, U.S.Code Cong. & Admin.News 1984, p. 19. This Report language is perfectly consistent with the basic purpose of the Act— to detain those who present serious risks of flight or danger *but not* to detain those who simply cannot afford a bail bond. See id. at 9–11.

Fourth, we note Jessup's argument that the $25,000 bond which the magistrate considered setting was constitutionally "excessive." He claims that it was too high because it prevented his release. He has been detained, however, not because he cannot raise the money, but because without the money, the risk of flight is too great. And, as we have previously indicated, it is well established that pretrial detention is constitutionally permissible for such a purpose.

Finally, we have asked ourselves whether it is fair to Jessup to affirm the detention order on the basis of an interpretation of the presumption that the magistrate might not have followed. We now hold that the presumption shifts the burden of production not persuasion and that once the defendant produces evidence, the magistrate will keep in mind Congress's general factual view about special drug offender risks, using it where appropriate along with the factors set out in § 3142(g) to judge the risk of flight in the particular case. Did the magistrate here use the presumption more strongly to Jessup's disadvantage? Having reviewed the magistrate's findings, we think not. The magistrate wrote that Jessup "has not rebutted" the presumption; but he also goes on to consider "all the circumstances" and then states his belief that Jessup would not be deterred from fleeing. Nothing in the record suggests the magistrate believed Jessup had to shoulder a "burden of persuasion" or that his decision turned upon that point. Of course, Jessup remains free to ask the magistrate for reconsideration of his detention order, a fact that allows Jessup a remedy if we have misread the magistrate's decision.

For these reasons, the judgment below is

Affirmed.

NOTES

1. **Release on bail after conviction.** Once a defendant has been convicted, the availability of release has traditionally been more limited than in the pretrial situation. The Supreme Court has held that there is no federal constitutional right to bail after conviction and pending appeal. McKane v. Durston, 153 U.S. 684, 14 S.Ct. 913, 38 L.Ed. 867 (1894). Statutory provisions vary widely. Illinois simply authorizes the court to "order that the original bail stand as bail pending appeal or deny, increase or reduce bail." Ill.—S.H.A. ch. 38, ¶ 110–7(d). New York provides that the factors relevant to pretrial release are also to be applied during appeal, except that instead of considering the weight of the evidence and the likelihood of conviction the court is to consider "the merit or lack of merit of the appeal." New York—McKinney's Crim.Proc.Law § 510.30(2)(a)(vii). Further:

Where the principal is a defendant-appellant in a pending appeal from a judgment of conviction, the court must also consider the likelihood of ultimate reversal of the judgment. A determination that the appeal is palpably without merit alone justifies, but does not require, a denial of the application [for bail], regardless of any determination made with respect to [other] factors * * *.

Id. at § 510.30(2)(b). Some provisions are considerably stricter. An Arizona statute provides:

A person shall not be continued at large on bail or be admitted to bail after conviction of a felony offense for which the person has received a sentence of imprisonment except when the * * * court * * * is satisfied upon investigation that the person in custody is in such physical condition that continued confinement would endanger his life.

Ariz.Rev.Stat. § 13–3961.01.

United States v. Miller, 753 F.2d 19 (3d Cir.1985), summarized the applicable provision of the Bail Reform Act of 1984, 18 U.S.C.A. § 3143(b), as follows:

[T]he defendant now has the burden of proving if s/he seeks bail pending appeal [by the defendant and] the court must find:

(1) that the defendant is not likely to flee or pose a danger to the safety of any other person or the community if released;

(2) that the appeal is not for purposes of delay;

(3) that the appeal raises a substantial question of fact or law; and

(4) that if that substantial question is determined favorably to defendant on appeal, that decision is likely to result in reversal or an order for a new trial of all counts on which imprisonment has been imposed.

753 F.2d at 24. Comparing these requirements with those under prior law, i.e., the Bail Reform Act of 1966, the court continued:

Under the new act, after first making the findings as to flight, danger, and delay, a court must determine that the question raised on appeal is a "substantial" one, i.e., it must find that the significant question at issue is one which is either novel, which has not been decided by controlling precedent, or which is fairly doubtful. This represents a marked change in the inquiry into the merits in the context of a bail determination, since the 1966 act only required the court to determine whether the issue was "frivolous" * * *.

Id. at 23.

2. **Post-conviction detention criteria.** The Supreme Court addressed the criteria that may be employed in deciding whether a state prisoner whose conviction has been invalidated by a United States District Court on federal habeas should be detained or released pending appeal by the state in Hilton v. Braunskill, 481 U.S. 770, 107 S.Ct. 2113, 95 L.Ed.2d 724 (1987). The Chief Justice, writing for the Court, identified the criteria:

[T]he possibility of flight should be taken into consideration * * *. We also think that, if the state establishes that there is a risk that the prisoner will pose a danger to the public if released, the court may take that factor into consideration in determining whether or not to enlarge him. The state's interest in continuing custody and rehabilitation pending a final determination of the case on appeal is also a factor to be considered; it will be strongest where the remaining portion of the sentence to be served is long, and weakest where there is little of the sentence remaining to be served.

The interest of the habeas petitioner in release pending appeal, always substantial, will be strongest where the factors mentioned in the preceding paragraph are weakest. The balance may depend to a large extent upon determination of the state's prospects of success in its appeal.

481 U.S. at 777, 107 S.Ct. at 2119–20, 95 L.Ed.2d at 733–34. The Court also distinguished the position of the successful habeas petitioner from that of the pretrial detainee:

> [A] successful habeas petitioner is in a considerably less favorable position than a pretrial arrestee * * * to challenge his continued detention pending appeal. Unlike a pretrial arrestee, a state habeas petitioner has been adjudged guilty beyond a reasonable doubt by a judge or jury, and this adjudication of guilt has been upheld by the appellate courts of the state. Although the decision of a district court granting habeas relief will have held that the judgment of conviction is constitutionally infirm, that determination itself may be overturned on appeal before the state must retry the petitioner. This being the case, we do not agree that the Due Process Clause prohibits a court from considering, along with the other factors that we previously described, the dangerousness of a habeas petitioner as part of its decision whether to release the petitioner pending appeal.

481 U.S. at 779, 107 S.Ct. at 2120, 95 L.Ed.2d at 734–35.

CHAPTER 13

DISCRETION TO PROSECUTE

Analysis

Prosecutors exercise very broad discretion in deciding whether to bring formal charges against individuals suspected of crimes. They use this discretion to screen some suspects out of the criminal justice system altogether, to divert others to community programs outside the system, to bargain for information and guilty pleas, and to prosecute some defendants fully. In the day-to-day decision-making process, prosecutors make their decisions relatively free of control, although they may be influenced by the desires and opinions of the public, the police and other government officials.

This Chapter deals with part of the charging process in criminal cases. In felony or other serious cases, the law usually provides for participation in the charging process by agencies outside the office of the public prosecutor—an examining magistrate in a preliminary examination or a body of lay persons assembled into a grand jury, or both. How those agencies function is the subject of the next Chapter. The charging process does not end when the prosecutor has made the initial decisions as to whether to charge, how many charges to bring, and how serious the charges will be. Those initial decisions are constantly reviewed as the case progresses through the courts. The practice of plea bargaining frequently requires the prosecutor to change the initial charging decision in the case in order to induce the defendant to waive trial and enter a plea of guilty. That part of prosecutorial discretion relating directly to plea bargaining is considered in Chapter 22.

This Chapter focuses upon the initial charging decisions made by prosecutors and upon controls, other than the preliminary examination and the grand jury, upon prosecutorial discretion in making those initial decisions.

A. THE PROSECUTOR'S CHARGING DECISIONS

In deciding whether to bring formal charges against a suspect, a prosecutor considers a variety of factors including the strength of the evidence, the suspect's background and characteristics, the costs and benefits of obtaining a conviction and the attitude of the community toward the offense the suspect is believed to have committed. Prosecutors screen a substantial number of suspects out of the criminal justice system. Department of Justice statistics for the years 1974 through 1978 reveal that an average of no more than twenty-five percent of the criminal cases brought to the attention of the 94 United States Attorneys ended in formal prosecution. The rates of prosecution varied greatly from offense to offense. A relatively high percentage of weapons control cases, controlled substance offenses, postal offenses, immigration cases, and cases of fraud against the government are formally prosecuted, while relatively few embezzlement, counterfeiting and forgery cases, escape cases, and stolen property cases end in formal prosecution. Frase, The Decision to File Federal Criminal Charges: A Quantitative Study of Prosecutorial Discretion, 47 U.Chi.L.Rev. 246, 252–53 (1980).

which cases get prosecuted?

The same study focused on prosecution practices by the United States Attorney for the Northern District of Illinois and on the reasons given when prosecution is declined. In forty-four percent of the cases declined the attorneys cited the minor nature of the offense as a reason for the declination. They cited the availability of state prosecution in twenty-six percent of the cases they declined; insufficiency of the evidence in twenty-two percent of the cases; and the characteristics of the defendant in twenty-one percent. Less frequently cited reasons for declining prosecution included the unavailability of the parties and the adequacy of civil or administrative remedies.

Why, according to DA's?

The National Advisory Commission on Criminal Justice Standards in its 1973 Report on Courts advocated open recognition of the "need to halt formal or informal action concerning some individuals who become involved in the criminal justice system." Criteria similar to those discussed above were set out, and a procedure established to encourage their uniform application. Among other things, the Commission recommended that the approval of the prosecutor be obtained before formal proceedings are begun; that the screening decision be made by an experienced prosecutor; that written guidelines should be formulated; that if screening occurs, it should be accompanied by a written statement of reasons.

The Commission recognized the essentially discretionary character of the screening decision but took different positions on whether negative and positive decisions should be subject to judicial review. A decision to prosecute would not be subject to review (except of course on evidence sufficiency grounds), nor would a failure to follow guidelines provide a basis for an attack. A decision not to prosecute would be subject to review at the instance of the police or the private complainant, but the standard for review would be merely whether the decision "was so unreasonable as to constitute an abuse of discretion."

Reviewing the decision to prosecute

Just as the prosecutor enjoys broad discretion in deciding whether to charge at all, he exercises broad discretion in choosing the specific charges to bring against a defendant. He may decide to charge a defendant suspected of several serious offenses with all those offenses, with only one serious offense, or with a single lesser offense. Courts recognize and accept this exercise of discretion by prosecutors. The Supreme Court has long held

Choosing among charges?

"that when an act violates more than one criminal statute, the Government may prosecute under either so long as it does not discriminate against any class of defendants." United States v. Batchelder, 442 U.S. 114, 123–24, 99 S.Ct. 2198, 2204, 60 L.Ed.2d 755, 764 (1979).

In choosing the charge the prosecutor considers many of the same factors he considers in deciding whether to charge at all—the defendant's background, the seriousness of his conduct, the desires of the public, the press, and the victim, and the strength of the evidence. But at this stage the prosecutor considers additional factors as well. He may decide to bring less than the most serious charge the evidence will support because he considers the minimum sentence under that charge too serious in relation to the defendant's conduct. Or the prosecutor may bring less than the most serious charge against a defendant because he believes that a jury would be more likely to convict the defendant on a lesser charge. Prosecutors often agree to bring a lesser charge in return for a defendant's guilty plea.

A prosecutor may also use his discretion to prosecute fully a defendant who, under normal circumstances, would not be charged at all or would be charged with a lesser offense. The decision to charge fully is often made in response to pressures from the police, the press, or the public. If a victim of a crime insists on full prosecution, prosecutors often agree. Prosecutors occasionally bring charges in response to requests from the suspects themselves. For example, in winter months in large cities habitual drunks or vagrants often request housing in the local jail. Some prosecutors oblige them by bringing serious charges against them so that they may be housed and fed for the duration of the cold weather. Prosecutors occasionally charge suspects with violation of statutes that are normally unenforced so that the suspects may be detained while investigation into other offenses proceeds. Finally, prosecutors may bring charges against defendants who were acquitted of previous charges or who received what is perceived as an inadequate sentence on a previous conviction.

Pathos.

In the recent past, it was not uncommon for prosecutors to use the threat of formal prosecution to persuade or compel suspects to comply with conditions set by the prosecutor. This kind of informal alternative to prosecution is being replaced, or at least supplemented, by formal pretrial diversion programs.

Threat of prosecution

Pretrial diversion is the pretrial suspension of formal criminal proceedings against a defendant for a specified period during which he is required to participate in a program that may include supervision, counseling, training, and psychological and medical treatment. If the defendant successfully completes the program, the charges against him may be dismissed. If he fails to complete the program in a satisfactory manner, his case is returned to the system for conventional resolution by plea, trial, or dismissal.

Pretrial Diversion

The 1967 report of the President's Commission on Law Enforcement and Administration of Justice, *The Challenge of Crime in a Free Society*, furnished the original impetus for the development of pretrial diversion programs. The report recommended that procedures be developed to identify and divert to community-based programs those offenders who are in need of treatment and for whom full criminal disposition is not required.

Within one year of this report three pilot programs had been established, and by 1975 cities and counties in at least thirty-five states had programs in operation or in the planning stage. In a number of states, the operation of pretrial diversion programs is regulated by statute or rule.

Most of the statutes set out basic criteria for determining the threshold eligibility of defendants for admission to pretrial diversion programs. These criteria include factors such as the age of the defendant, the crime with which he is charged, and his prior record. In addition, most of the statutes provide that the defendant must waive his right to a speedy trial and his right to be tried within the applicable statute of limitations. Arkansas conditions a defendant's admission to a pretrial diversion program on his pleading guilty.

Pretrial Diversion Statutes

The statutes typically specify the point in the prosecution process at which an application for admission to pretrial diversion may be initiated. They also specify whether the judge or the prosecutor makes the ultimate decision regarding diversion as well as the procedures the decision maker must follow. Several statutes prescribe procedures by which the defendant may challenge the denial of his application for admission to a program. Provisions for revocation of diversionary status are common to all the statutes, and several statutes establish mandatory procedures for revocation. Most statutes provide for automatic dismissal of charges if a defendant successfully completes his program, but a few provide only that charges *may* be dismissed if a defendant successfully completes his program.

Timing

In addition, some of the statutes specifically provide that the defendant has a right to notice of the terms, conditions and consequences of pretrial diversion. A few provide that a defendant has the right to consult his attorney before he consents to participation. Other provisions concern the expungement of the divertee's record, inadmissibility in a later criminal trial of information disclosed during the diversion process, and limits on the duration of diversion.

Notice

The benefits of pretrial diversion are, theoretically, various and extensive. Defendants benefit through participation because they avoid the stigma and possible imprisonment that often accompany conviction and they receive needed counseling, training, or treatment. The community benefits because defendants who participate in programs theoretically have a lower rate of recidivism than defendants processed through conventional criminal justice channels. The community benefits also because the cost of diversion is less than that of conventional prosecution. The criminal justice system itself benefits because diversion diminishes the caseloads of courts and prosecutors while permitting them to maintain a degree of control over the conduct of divertees. Thus the resources of the system are available to deal more effectively with serious crimes.

Benefits

Although the goals and purposes of diversion programs are laudable, the various legal issues created by them have not been fully resolved. The imposition of conditions and supervision on defendants who have not been convicted of crimes raises due process issues. Due process issues also arise in connection with the decisions to admit a defendant to a diversion program or to revoke the diversionary status of a defendant already

Probs.

admitted. Equal protection issues may arise from diversion eligibility requirements and from regional unavailability of diversion. Finally, the allocation of the power to make diversion decisions to either the court or the prosecutor creates separation of powers issues.

Occasionally, a prosecutor agrees with one whom he has charged with a criminal offense to dismiss the criminal charges in exchange for a waiver of any civil claim that may arise from the arrest and prosecution. The First Circuit held all such agreements invalid in Rumery v. Town of Newton, 778 F.2d 66 (1st Cir.1985), rev'd, 480 U.S. 386, 107 S.Ct. 1187, 94 L.Ed.2d 405 (1987), finding them to be inherently coercive to the defendant and finding a risk that criminal charges would be manufactured in defense to potential civil rights claims. The Supreme Court, in an opinion authored by Justice Powell, reversed. Rumery was arrested on witness tampering charges. His attorney negotiated an agreement with the prosecutor that those charges would be dismissed in exchange for Rumery's agreement not to bring civil suit for his arrest and prosecution. Rumery, free on bail, conferred at length with his attorney and signed the agreement. Charges were dismissed. Later, he brought civil suit under 42 U.S.C. § 1983, but the case was dismissed when the agreement was presented as a defense. Although the Supreme Court conceded that an offer of such an agreement could be coercive, this one was not. The idea originated with Rumery's attorney and the agreement was drafted by him. Rumery was not in custody and thought about the matter at length before signing it. Further, the person whom Rumery allegedly intimidated, who had brought sexual assault charges against Rumery's friend, had indicated a strong aversion to testifying in either a criminal or a civil case. The agreement served the important public purpose of saving her from the trauma of testifying, perhaps twice, in court. Justice O'Connor concurred in the judgment, but emphasized that the burden should be upon the government to prove in a civil suit that the release-dismissal agreement was voluntarily signed:

> Many factors may bear on whether a release was voluntary and not the product of overreaching, some of which come readily to mind. The knowledge and experience of the criminal defendant and the circumstances of the execution of the release, including, importantly, whether the defendant was counseled, are clearly relevant. The nature of the criminal charges that are pending is also important, for the greater the charge, the greater the coercive effect. The existence of a legitimate criminal justice objective for obtaining the release will support its validity. And, importantly, the possibility of abuse is clearly mitigated if the release-dismissal agreement is executed under judicial supervision.

480 U.S. at 401–02, 107 S.Ct. at 1197, 94 L.Ed.2d at 421–22. Justice Stevens, joined by Justices Brennan, Marshall and Blackmun, dissented and expressed the view that the prosecutor was placed in a conflict of interest between his public duty to prosecute criminal offenses and his desire to protect the police and municipality from possible civil suit. This conflict should ordinarily result in the invalidation of such release-dismissal agreements.

B. LIMITS ON PROSECUTORIAL DISCRETION

Although the prosecutor's discretion in making initial charging decisions is substantial, there are some limits upon it. The preliminary examination and the grand jury, the subjects of the next Chapter, are intended to assure that there is sufficient evidence to bring serious charges and in practice sometimes also serve to review the wisdom of bringing charges even when there is sufficient evidence to do so. This section deals with other controls over prosecutorial discretion. Following a consideration of whether a prosecutor's *failure* to make an affirmative charging decision is subject to sanction—or indeed can be reversed, the section focuses mainly upon whether the decision to charge violated the suspect's right to equal protection of the laws.

Compelling prosecutor(?)

In Peek v. Mitchell, 419 F.2d 575 (6th Cir.1970), plaintiffs sought injunctive relief against both federal and state prosecuting officials (as well as other state officials) to compel them to prosecute known civil rights violators. The court held that separation of powers considerations prevented the court from interfering with federal attorneys' control over criminal prosecutions, and that state officials were immune from even injunctive sanctions in the absence of any arbitrary or discriminatory actions.

Civil Rights implicated

Are there circumstances in which the refusal of state officials to initiate criminal proceedings violates the civil rights of the victim of the offense? In Leeke v. Timmerman, 454 U.S. 83, 102 S.Ct. 69, 70 L.Ed.2d 65 (1981), respondents sought damages for a conspiracy to violate their civil rights. Respondents were prison inmates who contended that guards used unnecessary force against them during a prison uprising. They presented information to a state magistrate in an effort to have arrest warrants issued for state criminal violations. The magistrate indicated he believed probable cause for issuance of the warrants existed. As a result of a meeting of the warden, the legal advisor of the corrections department and the local prosecutor, the latter requested that the magistrate not issue warrants. None was issued. Respondents filed a civil rights action and were awarded damages against the warden and the legal advisor. The Court of Appeals affirmed the judgment but the Supreme Court reversed. In a per curiam opinion, the Court reaffirmed the position it had taken in an earlier case that "a private citizen lacks a judicially cognizable interest in the prosecution or nonprosecution of another." 454 U.S. at 85–86, 102 S.Ct. at 70, 70 L.Ed.2d at 68. The Court extended this principle to include the transmittal of information that leads to a decision not to initiate the criminal process: "Just as respondents were able to present arguments as to why an arrest warrant should issue, a [prosecutor] must be able to present arguments as to why an arrest warrant should not issue." 454 U.S. at 87, 102 S.Ct. at 71, 70 L.Ed.2d at 68. Justice Brennan, joined by Justices Marshall and Blackmun, dissenting from summary reversal, characterized the conduct of the petitioners as the "deprivation of [respondents'] constitutional right of access to the courts, assured by the First and Fourteenth Amendments." 454 U.S. at 89, 102 S.Ct. at 72, 70 L.Ed.2d at 70.

NO

[Dissent says yes]

Wayte v. United States

Supreme Court of the United States, 1985.
470 U.S. 598, 105 S.Ct. 1524, 84 L.Ed.2d 547.

■ JUSTICE POWELL delivered the opinion of the Court.

The question presented is whether a passive enforcement policy under which the Government prosecutes only those who report themselves as having violated the law, or who are reported by others, violates the First and Fifth Amendments.

Issue

I

On July 2, 1980, pursuant to his authority under § 3 of the Military Selective Service Act, 62 Stat. 605, as amended, 50 U.S.C.App. § 453, the President issued Presidential Proclamation No. 4771, 3 CFR 82 (1981). This proclamation directed male citizens and certain male residents born during 1960 to register with the Selective Service System during the week of July 21, 1980. Petitioner fell within that class but did not register. Instead, he wrote several letters to Government officials, including the President, stating that he had not registered and did not intend to do so.

Petitioner's letters were added to a Selective Service file of young men who advised that they had failed to register or who were reported by others as having failed to register. For reasons we discuss, Selective Service adopted a policy of passive enforcement under which it would investigate and prosecute only the cases of nonregistration contained in this file. In furtherance of this policy, Selective Service sent a letter on June 17, 1981 to each reported violator who had not registered and for whom it had an address. The letter explained the duty to register, stated that Selective Service had information that the person was required to register but had not done so, requested that he either comply with the law by filling out an enclosed registration card or explain why he was not subject to registration, and warned that a violation could result in criminal prosecution and specified penalties. Petitioner received a copy of this letter but did not respond.

On July 20, 1981, Selective Service transmitted to the Department of Justice, for investigation and potential prosecution, the names of petitioner and 133 other young men identified under its passive enforcement system—all of whom had not registered in response to the Service's June letter. At two later dates, it referred the names of 152 more young men similarly identified. After screening out the names of those who appeared not to be in the class required to register, the Department of Justice referred the remaining names to the Federal Bureau of Investigation for additional inquiry and to the United States Attorneys for the districts in which the nonregistrants resided. Petitioner's name was one of those referred.

Pursuant to Department of Justice policy, those referred were not immediately prosecuted. Instead, the appropriate United States Attorney was required to notify identified nonregistrants by registered mail that, unless they registered within a specified time, prosecution would be considered. In addition, an FBI agent was usually sent to interview the nonregistrant before prosecution was instituted. This effort to persuade nonregistrants to change their minds became known as the "beg" policy. Under it, young men who registered late were not prosecuted, while those who never registered were investigated further by the Government. Pursuant to the "beg" policy, the United States Attorney for the Central District of California sent petitioner a letter on October 15, 1981 urging him to register or face possible prosecution. Again petitioner failed to respond.

On December 9, 1981, the Department of Justice instructed all United States Attorneys not to begin seeking indictments against nonregistrants until further notice. On January 7, 1982, the President announced a grace period to afford nonregistrants a further opportunity to register without penalty. This grace period extended until February 28, 1982. Petitioner still did not register.

Over the next few months, the Department decided to begin prosecuting those young men who, despite the grace period and "beg" policy, continued to refuse to register. It recognized that under the passive enforcement system those prosecuted were "liable to be vocal proponents of nonregistration" or persons "with religious or moral objections." Memorandum of March 17, 1982 from Lawrence Lippe, Chief General Litigation and Legal Advice Section, Criminal Division, Department of Justice, to D. Lowell Jensen, Assistant Attorney General, Criminal Division, App. 301. It also recognized that prosecutions would "undoubtedly result in allegations that the [case was] brought in retribution for the nonregistrant's exercise of his first amendment rights." The Department was advised, however, that Selective Service could not develop a more "active" enforcement system for quite some time. Because of this, the Department decided to begin seeking indictments under the passive system without further delay. On May 21, 1982, United States Attorneys were notified to begin prosecution of nonregistrants. On June 28, 1982, FBI agents interviewed petitioner and he continued to refuse to register. Accordingly, on July 22, 1982, an indictment was returned against him for knowingly and willfully failing to register with the Selective Service in violation of sections 3 and 12(a) of the Military Selective Service Act, 62 Stat. 605 and 622, as amended, 50 U.S.C.App. §§ 453 and 462(a). This was one of the first indictments returned against any individual under the passive policy.

II

Petitioner moved to dismiss the indictment on the ground of selective prosecution. He contended that he and the other indicted nonregistrants[1] were "vocal" opponents of the registration program who had been impermissibly targeted (out of an estimated 674,000 nonregistrants) for prosecution on the basis of their exercise of First Amendment rights. After a hearing, the District Court for the Central District of California granted

1.   The record indicates that only 13 of the 286 young men Selective Service referred to the Department of Justice had been indicted at the time the District Court considered this case. As of March 31, 1984, three more men had been indicted. The approximately 270 not indicted either registered, were found not to be subject to registration requirements, could not be found, or were under continuing investigation. The record does not indicate how many fell into each category.

petitioner's broad request for discovery and directed the Government to produce certain documents and make certain officials available to testify. The Government produced some documents and agreed to make some Government officials available but, citing executive privilege, it withheld other documents and testimony. On October 29, 1982, the District Court ordered the Government to produce the disputed documents and witness. The Government declined to comply and on November 5, 1982 asked the District Court to dismiss the indictment in order to allow an appeal challenging the discovery order. Petitioner asked for dismissal on several grounds, including discriminatory prosecution.

On November 15, 1982, the District Court dismissed the indictment on the ground that the Government had failed to rebut petitioner's prima facie case of selective prosecution. Following precedents of the Court of Appeals for the Ninth Circuit, the District Court found that in order to establish a prima facie case petitioner had to prove that (i) others similarly situated generally had not been prosecuted for conduct similar to petitioner's and (ii) the Government's discriminatory selection was based on impermissible grounds such as race, religion, or exercise of First Amendment rights. 549 F.Supp. 1376, 1380 (C.D.Cal.1982). Petitioner satisfied the first requirement, the District Court held, because he had shown that all those prosecuted were "vocal" nonregistrants[2] and because "[t]he inference is strong that the Government could have located non-vocal non-registrants, but chose not to." The District Court found the second requirement satisfied for three reasons. First, the passive enforcement program was " 'inherently suspect' " because " 'it focuse[d] upon the vocal offender * * * [and was] vulnerable to the charge that those chosen for prosecution [were] being punished for their expression of ideas, a constitutionally protected right.' " Ibid., quoting United States v. Steele, 461 F.2d 1148, 1152 (C.A.9 1972). Second, the Government's awareness that a disproportionate number of vocal nonregistrants would be prosecuted under the passive enforcement system indicated that petitioner was prosecuted because of his exercise of First Amendment rights. Finally, the involvement of high Government officials in the prosecution decisions "strongly suggest[ed] impermissible selective prosecution." The District Court then held that the Government had failed to rebut the prima facie case.

The Court of Appeals reversed. Applying the same test, it found the first requirement satisfied but not the second. The first was satisfied by petitioner's showing that out of the estimated 674,000 nonregistrants the 13 indicted had all been vocal nonregistrants. 710 F.2d 1385, 1387 (C.A.9 1983). As to the second requirement, the Court of Appeals held that petitioner had to show that the Government focused its investigation on him *because of* his protest activities. Petitioner's evidence, however, showed only that the Government was aware that the passive enforcement system would result in prosecutions primarily of two types of men—religious and oral objectors and vocal objectors—and that the Government recognized

---

2. This term is misleading insofar as it suggests that all those indicted had made public statements opposing registration. In some cases, the only statement made by the nonregistrant prior to indictment was his letter to the Government declaring his refusal to register.

that the latter type would probably make claims of selective prosecution. Finding no evidence of impermissible governmental motivation, the court held that the District Court's finding of a prima facie case of selective prosecution was clearly erroneous. The Court of Appeals also found two legitimate explanations for the Government's passive enforcement system: (i) the identities of nonreported nonregistrants were not known, and (ii) nonregistrants who expressed their refusal to register made clear their willful violation of the law.

III

In our criminal justice system, the Government retains "broad discretion" as to whom to prosecute. United States v. Goodwin, 457 U.S. 368, 380, n. 11, 102 S.Ct. 2485, 2492, n. 11, 73 L.Ed.2d 74 (1982); accord, Marshall v. Jerrico, Inc., 446 U.S. 238, 248, 100 S.Ct. 1610, 1616, 64 L.Ed.2d 182 (1980). "[S]o long as the prosecutor has probable cause to believe that the accused committed an offense defined by statute, the decision whether or not to prosecute, and what charge to file or bring before a grand jury, generally rests entirely in his discretion." Bordenkircher v. Hayes, 434 U.S. 357, 364, 98 S.Ct. 663, 668, 54 L.Ed.2d 604 (1978). This broad discretion rests largely on the recognition that the decision to prosecute is particularly ill-suited to judicial review. Such factors as the strength of the case, the prosecution's general deterrence value, the Government's enforcement priorities, and the case's relationship to the Government's overall enforcement plan are not readily susceptible to the kind of analysis the courts are competent to undertake. Judicial supervision in this area, moreover, entails systemic costs of particular concern. Examining the basis of a prosecution delays the criminal proceeding, threatens to chill law enforcement by subjecting the prosecutor's motives and decisionmaking to outside inquiry, and may undermine prosecutorial effectiveness by revealing the Government's enforcement policy. All these are substantial concerns that make the courts properly hesitant to examine the decision whether to prosecute.

As we have noted in a slightly different context, however, although prosecutorial discretion is broad, it is not " 'unfettered.' Selectivity in the enforcement of criminal laws is * * * subject to constitutional constraints." United States v. Batchelder, 442 U.S. 114, 125, 99 S.Ct. 2198, 2205, 60 L.Ed.2d 755 (1979) (footnote omitted). In particular, the decision to prosecute may not be " 'deliberately based upon an unjustifiable standard such as race, religion, or other arbitrary classification,' " Bordenkircher v. Hayes, supra, 434 U.S., at 364, 98 S.Ct., at 668, quoting Oyler v. Boles, 368 U.S. 448, 456, 82 S.Ct. 501, 505, 7 L.Ed.2d 446 (1962), including the exercise of protected statutory and constitutional rights, see United States v. Goodwin, supra, 457 U.S., at 372, 102 S.Ct., at 2488.

It is appropriate to judge selective prosecution claims according to ordinary equal protection standards. See Oyler v. Boles, supra. Under our prior cases, these standards require petitioner to show both that the passive enforcement system had a discriminatory effect and that it was motivated by a discriminatory purpose. Personnel Administrator of Mass. v. Feeney, 442 U.S. 256, 99 S.Ct. 2282, 60 L.Ed.2d 870 (1979); Arlington

Heights v. Metropolitan Housing Development Corp., 429 U.S. 252, 97 S.Ct. 555, 50 L.Ed.2d 450 (1977); Washington v. Davis, 426 U.S. 229, 96 S.Ct. 2040, 48 L.Ed.2d 597 (1976). All petitioner has shown here is that those eventually prosecuted, along with many not prosecuted, reported themselves as having violated the law. He has not shown that the enforcement policy selected nonregistrants for prosecution on the basis of their speech. Indeed, he could not have done so given the way the "beg" policy was carried out. The Government did not prosecute those who reported themselves but later registered. Nor did it prosecute those who protested registration but did not report themselves or were not reported by others. In fact, the Government did not even investigate those who wrote letters to Selective Service criticizing registration unless their letters stated affirmatively that they had refused to comply with the law. The Government, on the other hand, did prosecute people who reported themselves or were reported by others but who did not publicly protest. These facts demonstrate that the Government treated all reported nonregistrants similarly. It did not subject vocal nonregistrants to any special burden. Indeed, those prosecuted in effect selected themselves for prosecution by refusing to register after being reported and warned by the Government.

Even if the passive policy had a discriminatory effect, petitioner has not shown that the Government intended such a result. The evidence he presented demonstrated only that the Government was aware that the passive enforcement policy would result in prosecution of vocal objectors and that they would probably make selective prosecution claims. As we have noted, however, " '[d]iscriminatory purpose' * * * implies more than * * * intent as awareness of consequences. It implies that the decisionmaker * * * selected or reaffirmed a particular course of action at least in part 'because of,' not merely 'in spite of,' its adverse effects upon an identifiable group." Personnel Administrator of Mass. v. Feeney, supra, 442 U.S., at 279, 99 S.Ct., at 2296 (footnotes and citations omitted). In the present case, petitioner has not shown that the Government prosecuted him *because of* his protest activities. Absent such a showing, his claim of selective prosecution fails.

IV

Petitioner also challenges the passive enforcement policy directly on First Amendment grounds. In particular, he claims that "[e]ven though the [Government's passive] enforcement policy did not overtly punish protected speech as such, it inevitably created a content-based regulatory system with a concomitantly disparate, content-based impact on nonregistrants."[3] This

---

3. As an initial matter, we note doubt that petitioner has demonstrated injury to his First Amendment rights. The Government's "beg" policy removed most, if not all, of any burden passive enforcement placed on free expression. Because of this policy, nonregistrants could protest registration and still avoid any danger of prosecution. By simply registering after they had reported themselves to the Selective Service, nonregistrants satisfied their obligation and could thereafter continue to protest registration. No matter how strong their protest, registration immunized them from prosecution. Strictly speaking, then, the passive enforcement system penalized continued violation of the Military Selective Service Act, not speech. The only right it burdened was the asserted "right" not to register, a "right" without foundation either in the Constitution or the history of

Court has held that when, as here, " 'speech' and 'nonspeech' elements are combined in the same course of conduct, a sufficiently important governmental interest in regulating the nonspeech element can justify incidental limitations on First Amendment freedoms." United States v. O'Brien, 391 U.S. 367, 376, 88 S.Ct. 1673, 1678, 20 L.Ed.2d 672 (1968). Government regulation is justified

> "if it is within the constitutional power of the Government; if it furthers an important or substantial governmental interest; if the governmental interest is unrelated to the suppression of free expression; and if the incidental restriction on alleged First Amendment freedoms is no greater than is essential to the furtherance of that interest." Id., at 377, 88 S.Ct., at 1679.

* * *

There can be no doubt that the passive enforcement policy meets the second condition. Few interests can be more compelling than a nation's need to ensure its own security. It is well to remember that freedom as we know it has been suppressed in many countries. Unless a society has the capability and will to defend itself from the aggressions of others, constitutional protections of any sort have little meaning. Recognizing this fact, the Framers listed "provid[ing] for the common defence," U.S. Const., Preamble, as a motivating purpose for the Constitution and granted Congress the power to "provide for the common Defence and general Welfare of the United States," Art. I, § 8, cl. 1. See also The Federalist Nos. 4, 24, and 25. This Court, moreover, has long held that the power "to raise and support armies . . . is broad and sweeping," United States v. O'Brien, supra, 391 U.S., at 377, 88 S.Ct., at 1679; accord Lichter v. United States, 334 U.S. 742, 755–758, 68 S.Ct. 1294, 1301–1303, 92 L.Ed. 1694 (1948); Selective Draft Law Cases, 245 U.S. 366, 38 S.Ct. 159, 62 L.Ed. 349 (1918), and that the "power . . . to classify and conscript manpower for military service is 'beyond question,' " United States v. O'Brien, supra, 391 U.S., at 377, 88 S.Ct., at 1679, quoting Lichter v. United States, supra, 334 U.S., at 756, 68 S.Ct., at 1302; accord Selective Draft Law Cases, supra. With these principles in mind, the three reasons the Government offers in defense of this particular enforcement policy are sufficiently compelling to satisfy the second *O'Brien* requirement—as to either those who reported themselves or those who were reported by others.

First, by relying on reports of nonregistration, the Government was able to identify and prosecute violators without further delay. Although it still was necessary to investigate those reported to make sure that they were required to register and had not, the Government did not have to search actively for the names of these likely violators. Such a search would have been difficult and costly at that time. Indeed, it would be a costly step in any "active" prosecution system involving thousands of nonregistrants. The passive enforcement program thus promoted prosecutorial efficiency. Second, the letters written to Selective Service provided strong, perhaps

our country. See Selective Draft Law Cases, 245 U.S. 366, 38 S.Ct. 159, 62 L.Ed.2d 349 (1918).

conclusive evidence of the nonregistrant's intent not to comply—one of the elements of the offense. Third, prosecuting visible nonregistrants was thought to be an effective way to promote general deterrence, especially since failing to proceed against publicly known offenders would encourage others to violate the law.

The passive enforcement policy also meets the final requirement of the *O'Brien* test, for it placed no more limitation on speech than was necessary to ensure registration for the national defense. Passive enforcement not only did not subject "vocal" nonregistrants to any special burden, but also was intended to be only an interim enforcement system. Although Selective Service was engaged in developing an active enforcement program when it investigated petitioner, it had by then found no practicable way of obtaining the names and current addresses of likely nonregistrants.[4] Eventually, it obtained them by matching state driver's license records with Social Security files. It took some time, however, to obtain the necessary authorizations and to set up this system. Passive enforcement was the only effective interim solution available to carry out the Government's compelling interest.

We think it important to note as a final matter how far the implications of petitioner's First Amendment argument would extend. Strictly speaking, his argument does not concern passive enforcement but self-reporting. The concerns he identifies would apply to all nonregistrants who report themselves even if the Selective Service engaged only in active enforcement. For example, a nonregistrant who wrote a letter informing Selective Service of his failure to register could, when prosecuted under an active system, claim that the Selective Service was prosecuting him only because of his "protest." Just as in this case, he could have some justification for believing that his letter had focused inquiry upon him. Prosecution in either context would equally "burden" his exercise of First Amendment rights. Under the petitioner's view, then, the Government could not constitutionally prosecute a self-reporter—even in an active enforcement system—unless perhaps it could prove that it would have prosecuted him without his letter. On principle, such a view would allow any criminal to obtain immunity from prosecution simply by reporting himself and claiming that he did so in order to "protest" the law. The First Amendment confers no such immunity from prosecution.

First Amendment Analysis. [handwritten marginal note]

V

We conclude that the Government's passive enforcement system together with its "beg" policy violated neither the First nor Fifth Amendments. Accordingly, we affirm the judgment of the Court of Appeals.

Holding [handwritten marginal note]

It is so ordered.

■ JUSTICE MARSHALL, with whom JUSTICE BRENNAN joins, dissenting [omitted].

---

4. Selective Service had tried to use Social Security records but found that the addresses there were hopelessly stale. And under the law, 26 U.S.C. § 6103, it could gain no useful access to IRS records—the only other recognized federal source of generally accurate information.

NOTES

1. Suppose the person selected for prosecution presents evidence that his selection was based on protests in a more public manner, for example participation in draft-counseling during the Vietnam War? See United States v. Falk, 479 F.2d 616 (7th Cir.1973).

2. Is it proper to prosecute a person suspected of crime "A" merely because he is believed to have committed crime "B"? See United States v. Choate, 619 F.2d 21 (9th Cir.1980). Would it matter whether the person had previously been convicted of crime "B"?

3. **Disclosure of information to advance a selective prosecution claim.** The Court in United States v. Armstrong, 517 U.S. 456, 116 S.Ct. 1480, 134 L.Ed.2d 687 (1996), addressed the question of what showing must be made of selective prosecution in order to warrant a trial court ordering disclosure of records of prosecutorial decisions as possible evidence to substantiate the claim. The Court, in an opinion by The Chief Justice, addressed the preliminary showing that is needed to advance an equal protection/selective prosecution claim. Respondent had been charged with a "crack" cocaine offense. He sought to show that only African–Americans had been charged with that offense. While respondent presented some evidence that African–Americans had been charged with that offense and that few whites had been charged, he failed to show that the government had declined to charge whites under circumstances in which African–Americans had been charged. The Court held that the absence of such a showing of discrimination among those potential defendants who are "similarly situated" precluded the District Court from ordering the wide-ranging discovery involved in this case.

4. **Charging the same conduct as a felony or a misdemeanor.** Some state courts have found a violation of both their state constitutions and the equal protection clause of the fourteenth amendment when a prosecutor has discretion to charge the same conduct either as a felony or a misdemeanor. See, e.g., Olsen v. Delmore, 48 Wash.2d 545, 295 P.2d 324 (1956). To what extent do cases like *Olsen* survive the *Batchelder* case?

In United States v. Batchelder, 442 U.S. 114, 99 S.Ct. 2198, 60 L.Ed.2d 755 (1979), respondent, a previously convicted felon, was convicted of receiving a firearm that had travelled in interstate commerce. The judge imposed the maximum sentence of five years in prison. The Court of Appeals held that because another statute prohibited precisely the same conduct and provided for a maximum sentence of two years, Congress intended to limit punishment for such conduct to two years. After concluding there was no Congressional intent to limit punishment to the lesser term, Justice Marshall for the Court addressed the constitutional issues raised by the co-existence of the two provisions:

> More importantly, there is no appreciable difference between the discretion a prosecutor exercises when deciding whether to charge under one of two statutes with different elements and the discretion he exercises when choosing one of two statutes with identical elements. In the former situation, once he determines that the proof will support conviction under either statute, his decision is indistinguishable from the one he faces in the latter context. The prosecutor may be influenced by the penalties available upon conviction, but this fact, standing alone, does not give rise to a violation of the Equal Protection or Due Process Clause. (citations omitted) Just as a defendant has no constitutional right to elect which of two applicable federal statutes shall be the basis of his indictment and prosecution neither is he entitled to choose the penalty scheme under which he will be sentenced.

Approaching the problem of prosecutorial discretion from a slightly differ-ent perspective, the Court of Appeals postulated that the statutes might impermissibly delegate to the Executive Branch the Legislature's responsibility to fix criminal penalties. We do not agree. The provisions at issue plainly demarcate the range of penalties that prosecutors and judges may seek and impose. In light of that specificity, the power that Congress has delegated to those officials is no broader than the authority they routinely exercise in enforcing the criminal laws. Having informed the courts, prosecutors and defendants of the permissible punishment alternatives available under each Title, Congress has fulfilled its duty.

442 U.S. at 125–26, 99 S.Ct. at 2205, 60 L.Ed.2d at 765–66.

5. **Restrictions on pretrial diversion eligibility.** Several state pretrial diversion statutes limit admission to diversion programs to certain classes of defendants. Several statutes provide that only first offenders or suspects charged with non-violent crimes are eligible for diversion. In Massachusetts only defendants between the ages of seventeen and twenty-one are eligible Mass.Gen.Laws Ann. ch. 276A § 2 (West 1999). In addition, most of the statutes direct the prosecutor or the court to consider various other factors in deciding to admit a defendant to pretrial diversion. These factors include the defendant's background, his attitudes, his family and employment situation, the seriousness of his offense, and his amenability to rehabilitation. Do any of these eligibility requirements create equal protection problems? Should the validity of the requirements be judged by the rational relationship or the compelling state interest test?

In United States v. Smith, 354 A.2d 510 (D.C.App.1976), the court found acceptable the prosecutor's practice of refusing to admit to the informal diversion program any defendant who chose to litigate any issues in his case. In this case the defendant was denied admission to the diversion program after he had moved unsuccessfully for a dismissal of the charges on the ground that the punishment prescribed by the statute for his offense violated the eighth amendment.

In Cleveland v. State, 417 So.2d 653 (Fla.1982), the court held that a pretrial diversion decision is not subject to judicial review:

The state attorney has complete discretion in making the decision to charge and prosecute. In State v. Jogan, 388 So.2d 322 (Fla. 3d DCA 1980), for example, the trial judge dismissed the information against the defendant conditioned on the defendant's enlistment in the military. The district court reversed and remanded holding that the decision to prosecute or nolle prosequi is a pretrial posture vested solely in the state attorney's discretion. The court felt that the state attorney alone had the right to nolle prosequi a defendant conditioned upon his entry into the military. The trial court has great latitude in post-trial proceedings and thus forms the necessary check and balance.

The pretrial diversion is essentially a conditional decision not to prosecute similar to the nolle prosequi situation postulated by *Jogan*. It is a pretrial decision and does not divest the state attorney of the right to institute proceedings if the conditions are not met. The pretrial intervention program is merely an alternative to prosecution and should remain in the prosecutor's discretion. See Commonwealth v. Kindness, 247 Pa.Super. 99, 371 A.2d 1346 (1977). Two factors in the statutory scheme which create the pretrial interven-tion program support the determination that each party concerned has total discretion to refuse to consent. First, section 944.025(2) requires consent of the administrator of the program, victim, judge, and state attorney, but fails to provide for *any* form of review. In addition, section 944.025(4), Florida Statutes, allows the state attorney to continue prosecution if defendant is not fulfilling his obligations under the program or if the public interest requires. The fact that the state attorney has this discretion to reinstate prosecution is consistent with the view that the pretrial diversion consent by the state attorney is a prosecutorial function.

Finally, defendant's reliance on comparable programs in other states is misplaced. The California program statutorily provides for trial court review. See People v. Superior Court, 11 Cal.3d 59, 520 P.2d 405, 113 Cal.Rptr. 21 (1974). Other programs were created by court rule and are, therefore, subject to court review of the diversion decision. Florida's program was statutorily created and does not expressly provide for judicial review.

We hold that the pretrial diversion decision of the state attorney is prosecutorial in nature and, thus, is not subject to judicial review. * * *

Id. at 654.

6. **Restrictions on termination of pretrial diversion supervision.** Would a prosecutorial decision to terminate diversion be subject to judicial review? In United States v. Hicks, 693 F.2d 32 (5th Cir.1982), the court upheld a speedy trial waiver which was a condition to admission to a pretrial diversion program:

> The government argues that the district court did not have the power to review the decision to terminate appellant from the program. It argues that the court would be participating in the decision to charge. Weaving the argument from the strands of prosecutorial discretion and separation of powers, it seeks to insulate the pretrial diversion program from any and all judicial review.

> That would take us too far. The court below, in holding this hearing, was not participating in the decision to charge. The diversion agreement is a contract. The government sought to hold the accused to his side of the bargain, i.e. the waiver of his speedy trial rights. The court was entitled to hear evidence on the violations to make sure that the government had lived up to its side of the bargain.

> The court is also charged with the responsibility for safeguarding the constitutional rights of the accused. An apt analogy is the plea bargain. Like pretrial diversion, the plea bargain is an agreement between the prosecutor and the accused. The court has a duty to supervise this process and insure that the defendant's plea is voluntary and that he is informed of his constitutional rights. United States v. Adams, 566 F.2d 962, 966 (5th Cir.1978); Fed.R.Crim.P. 11. In Santobello v. New York, 404 U.S. 257, 92 S.Ct. 495, 30 L.Ed.2d 427 (1971), the Supreme Court dealt with a plea bargain in which the prosecutor failed to keep a commitment regarding sentence recommendation. The court remanded the plea to the state courts for reconsideration. The Court stated

>> This phase of the process of criminal justice, and the adjudicative element inherent in accepting a plea of guilty, must be attended by safeguards to insure the defendant what is reasonably due in the circumstances. Those circumstances will vary, but a constant factor is that when a plea rests in any significant degree on a promise or agreement of the prosecutor, so that it can be said to be part of the indictment or consideration, such promise must be fulfilled.

> Id. at 263, 92 S.Ct. at 499. While we acknowledge that no "adjudicative element" is present in the pretrial diversion context, we think the analogy sufficiently persuasive to defeat the government's argument that the court lacks jurisdiction to hold a hearing. Our holding is of a limited nature. We do not decide that the court is required to hold a hearing prior to termination of the agreement, with or without request by defendant. We simply hold that in this case the court was entitled to decide whether defendant should be held to his waiver of speedy trial.

Effect of the Agreement and Waiver

The trial court found that the defendant had violated the terms of his agreement. The government presented appellant's probation officer Maples at the hearing. He testified that Hicks violated several conditions of his probation. First, Hicks failed to inform the office when he got a job. Second, Hicks moved without reporting his new address. Third, Maples testified that Hicks used abusive language in the probation office after Maples requested that Hicks not behave rudely in handing in his reports (said to violate the condition requiring Hicks to follow his probation officer's instructions). The findings of fact are not clearly erroneous.[5]

We think that the government is entitled to hold the defendant to strict compliance with the terms of the agreement. It could be argued that the violations here were not substantial. In United States v. Reed, 573 F.2d 1020, 1024 (8th Cir.1978), the court stated

> The decision to revoke probation should not merely be a reflexive reaction to an accumulation of technical violations of the conditions imposed upon the offender. That approach would be inconsistent with and detrimental to the goals of the probation program:
>
> > While presumably it would be inappropriate for a field agent *never* to revoke, the whole thrust of the probation-parole movement is to keep men in the community, working with adjustment problems there, and using revocation only as a last resort when treatment has failed or is about to fail. [Citations omitted]
>
> Rather, probation should be revoked only in those instances in which the offender's behavior demonstrates that he or she "cannot be counted on to avoid antisocial activity." Morrissey v. Brewer, supra, 408 U.S. at 479, 92 S.Ct. at 2599.

See *Lacey,* 661 F.2d at 1022. There are important differences, however, between pretrial diversion and probation. First, the defendant has no right to be placed in the program. The government has given the defendant a benefit in allowing him to forego the burdens attendant upon a criminal prosecution. In exchange, it may properly require strict compliance with the diversion conditions. Second, the standard for violation in *Reed* is promulgated pursuant to the court's supervisory powers of the probation system. See United States v. Feinberg, 631 F.2d 388, 391 (5th Cir.1980). The courts have no similar powers over the pretrial diversion program. Lastly, in probation the government has already

---

5. Our review in this area may be limited. In probation revocation, this court has stated

> The evidence to support a revocation need not establish guilt beyond a reasonable doubt; all that is required is that the evidence of the facts reasonably satisfy the judge that the conduct of the probationer violates the conditions of probation. The district court has broad discretion with regard to the revocation of probation, and its actions will not be disturbed in the absence of a clear showing of an abuse of that discretion.

United States v. Lacey, 661 F.2d 1021, 1022 (5th Cir.1981), cert. denied, 456 U.S. 961, 102 S.Ct. 2036, 72 L.Ed.2d 484 (1982). Of course, probation is court supervised. In reviewing revocations of parole, this court has applied an arbitrary and capricious standard. Thompson v. United States, Federal Prison Industries, 492 F.2d 1082 (5th Cir.1974); Sexton v. United States, 429 F.2d 1300 (5th Cir.1970). Since pretrial diversion is a program administered by the Justice Department, considerations of separation of powers and prosecutorial discretion might mandate an even more limited standard of review. However, this is an issue that this court need not address since no error was committed by whatever standard we review the decision.

obtained a judicial determination of the accused's guilt. Thus, society's interest in convicting the accused has been achieved. Procedural bars to ending probation or parole are more appropriate because the immediate result of probation revocation is imprisonment. In pretrial diversion, there has been no determination of guilt. Strict compliance may be required in order to safeguard the public's interest in seeing criminals punished for their antisocial behavior.

Having upheld the government's decision to terminate Hicks from the program, it follows that Hicks can be held to his waiver of his speedy trial rights.

Id. at 33–35.

CHAPTER 14

THE PRELIMINARY EXAMINATION AND THE GRAND JURY

Analysis

Despite the almost unlimited discretion granted the prosecutor concerning the decision to charge (see Chapter 13), virtually all jurisdictions impose a pretrial screening device in serious cases between the prosecutor's decision to charge and trial on that charge. This may limit the filing of charges, the progress of charges to the trial process, or both. The two major devices used are the preliminary examination or hearing and the grand jury. Both involve scrutiny of the sufficiency of evidence to support actual or proposed charges and sometimes—although perhaps without formal authorization—of the wisdom of bringing the charges.

The preliminary examination, the subject of the first section of this Chapter, is frequently held in a "lower" court that lacks jurisdiction to try the case on its merits. The proceeding is to some extent an adversary one and the presiding judge's function is to determine the existence of "probable cause" to believe the defendant guilty. If probable cause is found to exist, the defendant is "bound over" for further proceedings.

The grand jury also performs a screening function when called upon to consider charges against a particular person. This should be distinguished from the grand jury's investigatory function, addressed in Chapter 9. When the grand jury's screening function is performed, it has the effect of determining the actual charge. If the grand jury finds the evidence sufficient to establish probable cause, it returns an indictment which is filed in the court with jurisdiction over the offense and becomes the charging document in the case.

Among the important questions raised by the variations in preliminary screening devices is the desirable or perhaps constitutionally necessary relationship among the preliminary examination, the process of grand jury indictment, and the bringing of formal charges. The Fifth Amendment to the United States Constitution requires that a prosecution in federal court for an "infamous crime," meaning one for which imprisonment might exceed one year, must be based upon a grand jury indictment. One accused of a serious federal crime, then, has a right before formal charging to screening by a grand jury.

But the federal Constitution imposes few if any requirements upon the states. In Hurtado v. California, 110 U.S. 516, 4 S.Ct. 111, 28 L.Ed. 232 (1884), the Supreme Court held that the Fourteenth Amendment requirement of due process does not require indictment by a grand jury. Stressing the need for federal constitutional requirements to accommodate development in the law, it reasoned:

> [W]e are unable to say that the substitution for ... indictment by a grand jury of the proceeding by information after examination and commitment by a magistrate, certifying to the probable guilt of the defendant, with the right on his part to the aid of counsel, and to the cross-examination of the witnesses produced for the prosecution, is not due process of law. It ... carefully considers and guards the substantial interest of the prisoner.

110 U.S. at 538, 4 S.Ct. at 122, 28 L.Ed. at 239. Later, however, the Court further held that when the information process has been substituted for grand jury indictment, a preliminary examination is not constitutionally required. In Lem Woon v. Oregon, 229 U.S. 586, 33 S.Ct. 783, 57 L.Ed. 1340 (1913), the plaintiff in error urged that due process was violated by his trial and conviction of murder because under Oregon law at the time no preliminary examination or commitment by a magistrate was required for the prosecutor to charge the offense. The Court rejected this, regarding the matter as disposed of by *Hurtado*:

> [S]ince ... the "due process of law" clause does not require the state to adopt the institution and procedure of a grand jury, we are unable to see upon what theory it can be held that an examination, or the opportunity for one, prior to the formal accusation by the district attorney is obligatory upon the states.

229 U.S. at 590, 33 S.Ct. at 784, 57 L.Ed. at 1342. Does this follow? The language from *Hurtado* suggests that the procedure upheld there was an acceptable alternative to grand jury indictment only because it provided for a meaningful "examination and commitment by a magistrate" before charges could be filed.

The absence of significant federal constitutional requirements here, however, does not resolve the questions of local criminal justice policy, which include whether any formal screening of charges should be provided and, if so, how that should be done.

The Uniform Rules of Criminal Procedure suggest a third method of effectuating pretrial screening. Under Rule 481, a defendant is authorized to move in the trial court for a pretrial judgment of acquittal. If the motion appears meritorious on its face, depositions, statements, and other matters are to be produced before the trial court which is then to rule on the motion. If the motion is granted, it constitutes an acquittal except that the prosecution may appeal. Underlying the position of the Uniform Rules is the assumption that neither the preliminary examination nor the grand jury, even if modified, hold adequate promise of being screening devices of maximum effectiveness and efficiency. In considering the following materials, consider also the extent to which the nontraditional alternative suggested in the Uniform Rules might be more appropriate than either of the traditional vehicles utilized for pretrial screening.

A. THE PRELIMINARY EXAMINATION

The preliminary examination or hearing varies tremendously among American jurisdictions, both in procedure and in function. Perhaps some of this is due to its history. Originally, the examination was a device used for gathering information by taking testimony from witnesses and for restraining the suspect—by committing him to jail or requiring him to post bail—pending prosecution. In this context, it served primarily the interests of the prosecution in assuring the suspect's availability for later formal charges and trial. See Anderson, The Preliminary Hearing—Better Alternatives or More of the Same, 35 Mo.L.Rev. 281, 284 (1970). As concern for the interests of suspects grew, however, the preliminary examination became more significant as a vehicle for requiring the prosecution to make a preliminary showing of the suspect's guilt before the suspect would be put to the deprivation of liberty (or the expense of posting bail) pending the consideration of formal charges by the grand jury. *Id.*, at 285. At this stage, it served primarily as a means of protecting suspects' interest in liberty until formal charges could be brought. Since grand juries were sometimes convened quite infrequently, this was not an insignificant matter. Months could pass between a suspect's arrest and the convening of the next grand jury that might indict him.

In a manner that has not been well documented or studied, the preliminary examination evolved in many jurisdictions into a means of limiting not merely the prosecution's ability to detain the defendant pending formal charges but, in addition, its ability under some circumstances to charge the defendant at all. See C. Whitebread, Criminal Procedure 332 (1980). It is likely that this accompanied the abandonment of grand jury indictment in favor of charging by information. L. Orfield, Criminal Procedure From Arrest to Appeal 52 (1947); Dession, From Indictment to Information—Implications of the Shift, 42 Yale L.J. 163, 170 (1932). As the notes in this section make clear, however, in many jurisdictions today the preliminary examination serves as a device for screening charges as well as for inquiring into the justification for restraint of the suspect. The difference between these two functions is not always drawn and may be of little practical significance today.

In any case, the preliminary examination—perhaps in part because of its flexibility—lends itself to serving other and often informal functions. Where prosecutors have the option of proceeding by either indictment or information and thus of going through one or the other of the traditional screening devices, their responses may be informative on the actual significance of the alternative screening devices. An empirical study addressed the use of preliminary hearings and grand juries in a jurisdiction—Arizona—that permits charges to be brought either by grand jury indictment or by an information filed by the prosecutor. D. Emerson and N. Ames, The Role of the Grand Jury and the Preliminary Hearing in Pretrial Screening (U.S. Dept. of Justice, 1984). The state's two large cities, the report noted, had developed different practices for charging major cases. One relied heavily upon grand jury indictment; the other utilized primarily the information option which, under state law, entitled the defendant to a preliminary hearing. One prosecutor identified those considerations indicating that a preliminary hearing would be desirable from the prosecution's perspective:

— a need existed to have a witness's testimony preserved for possible later use, a process most readily accomplished by having the witness testify at a preliminary hearing;

— confusion and uncertainty existed concerning the events, which might be clarified by witnesses' testimony at a preliminary hearing;

— a need existed to secure an additional identification of the defendant by the victim;

— some doubt existed as to the victim's interest in pursuing the prosecution and the preliminary hearing would serve to confirm that interest; and

— the victim's willingness to testify was in doubt and this could be resolved by determining whether the witness was willing to participate in a preliminary hearing.

Id., at 24.

In the city relying heavily upon non-grand jury charging, only a small percent of cases actually involved a preliminary hearing. This was because the hearing was not held in most cases. *Id.*, at 22. Sometimes this waiver was in return for some specific benefit, such as release on the defendant's own recognizance or some advantageous scheduling. *Id.*, at 26. Where preliminary hearings were held, defendants seldom introduced or offered evidence. Defense counsel explained that they seldom hoped to obtain a finding of no probable cause so that such action was unlikely to be of any help. Further, putting defense witnesses on the stand at this stage might provide the prosecution with information concerning the defense strategy and might make the witness subject to future impeachment should the case go to trial. *Id.*, at 60. But defense counsel often cross examined the prosecution's witnesses, suggesting that the opportunity for informal discovery was often taken. *Id.*, at 59.

The report noted that preliminary hearings in practice tend to serve a variety of functions other than that of screening out cases in which the prosecution has failed to show probable cause. One was to provide the defense with discovery, including an opportunity to probe state witnesses for information that might later serve as the basis for attacking the admissibility of evidence on search and seizure grounds. *Id.*, at 72. In addition, it permitted the preservation of evidence in a form that under local evidence law would permit its use at trial. This was perceived as valuable for several reasons. It often removed any incentive for the defendant or others to harass the witness. When the witness was young and likely to forget the events (or at least some details) before trial, the preserved testimony was likely to be better than the witness' trial testimony. *Id.*, at 73. The transcript of the preliminary hearing also was often valuable in impeaching witnesses who later testified at trial. *Id.*

In addition, the preliminary hearing served as a means of reviewing the conditions of pretrial release. Bail amounts or conditions were sometimes addressed in a more adversary environment than previously. As noted above, defendants' waivers of scheduled preliminary hearings were sometimes rewarded in this context. *Id.*, at 145–46.

The preliminary hearing also served as a means for encouraging plea negotiations, in large part because it constitutes the first formal opportunity for the parties to meet face-to-face. Often, cases scheduled for preliminary hearings were resolved by agreements to plead guilty to misdemeanors in the lower court or to waive the preliminary hearing and to plead guilty to a felony offense in the trial court. *Id.*, at 146.

Comparing the two cities, the report noted that neither practice resulted in formal screening out of a significant number of cases. *Id.*, at 146. Because of the tendency to rely on the testimony of police officers alone in grand jury proceedings and the opportunity for cross examination in preliminary hearings, the study concluded that "the preliminary hearing does appear to be a slightly more rigorous mechanism for determining probable cause." *Id.*, at 148.

FEDERAL RULES OF CRIMINAL PROCEDURE

Rule 5.1 Preliminary Examination

(a) Probable Cause Finding. If from the evidence it appears that there is probable cause to believe that an offense has been committed and that the defendant committed it, the federal magistrate judge shall forthwith hold the defendant to answer in district court. The finding of probable cause may be based upon hearsay evidence in whole or in part. The defendant may cross-examine adverse witnesses and may introduce evidence. Objections to evidence on the ground that it was acquired by unlawful means are not properly made at the preliminary examination. Motions to suppress must be made to the trial court as provided in Rule 12.

(b) Discharge of Defendant. If from the evidence it appears that there is no probable cause to believe that an offense has been committed or that the defendant committed it, the federal magistrate judge shall dismiss the complaint and discharge the defendant. The discharge of the defendant shall not preclude the government from instituting a subsequent prosecution for the same offense.

* * *

Coleman v. Alabama

Supreme Court of the United States, 1970.
399 U.S. 1, 90 S.Ct. 1999, 26 L.Ed.2d 387.

■ MR. JUSTICE BRENNAN announced the judgment of the Court and delivered the following opinion.

* * *

II.

This Court has held that a person accused of crime "requires the guiding hand of counsel at every step in the proceedings against him," Powell v. Alabama, 287 U.S. 45, 69, 53 S.Ct. 55, 64, 77 L.Ed. 158 (1932), and that that constitutional principle is not limited to the presence of counsel at trial. "It is central to that principle that in addition to counsel's presence at trial, the accused is guaranteed that he need not stand alone against the State at any stage of the prosecution, formal or informal, in court or out, where counsel's absence might derogate from the accused's right to a fair trial." United States v. Wade, [388 U.S. 218, 226, 87 S.Ct. 1926, 1932, 18 L.Ed.2d 1149 (1967)]. Accordingly, "the principle of Powell v. Alabama and succeeding cases requires that we scrutinize *any* pretrial confrontation of the accused to determine whether the presence of his counsel is necessary to preserve the defendant's basic right to a fair trial as affected by his right meaningfully to cross-examine the witnesses against him and to have effective assistance of counsel at the trial itself. It calls upon us to analyze whether potential substantial prejudice to defendant's rights inheres in the particular confrontation and the ability of counsel to help avoid that prejudice." Id., at 227, 87 S.Ct. at 1932. Applying this test, the Court has held that "critical stages" include the pretrial type of arraignment where certain rights may be sacrificed or lost, Hamilton v. Alabama, 368 U.S. 52, 54, 82 S.Ct. 157, 158–159, 7 L.Ed.2d 114 (1961), see White v. Maryland, 373 U.S. 59, 83 S.Ct. 1050, 10 L.Ed.2d 193 (1963), and the pretrial lineup, United States v. Wade, supra; Gilbert v. California, supra. Cf. Miranda v. Arizona, 384 U.S. 436, 86 S.Ct. 1602, 16 L.Ed.2d 694 (1966), where the Court held that the privilege against compulsory self-incrimination includes a right to counsel at a pretrial custodial interrogation. See also Massiah v. United States, 377 U.S. 201, 84 S.Ct. 1199, 12 L.Ed.2d 246 (1964).

The preliminary hearing is not a required step in an Alabama prosecution. The prosecutor may seek an indictment directly from the grand jury without a preliminary hearing. The opinion of the Alabama Court of Appeals in this case instructs us that under Alabama law the sole purposes of a preliminary hearing are to determine whether there is sufficient evidence against the accused to warrant presenting his case to the grand jury and if so to fix bail if the offense is bailable. 44 Ala.App., at 433, 211 So.2d 917; 211 So.2d, at 920. See Code of Alabama, Tit. 15, §§ 139, 140, 151. The court continued:

> "At the preliminary hearing ... the accused is not required to advance any defenses, and failure to do so does not preclude him from availing himself of every defense he may have upon the trial of the case. Also Pointer v. State of Texas [380 U.S. 400, 85 S.Ct. 1065, 13 L.Ed.2d 923 (1965)] bars the admission of testimony given at a pretrial proceeding where the accused did not have the benefit of cross-examination by and through counsel. Thus, nothing occurring at the preliminary hearing in the absence of counsel can substantially prejudice the rights of the accused on trial." 44 Ala.App., at 433, 211 So.2d, at 921.

This Court is of course bound by this construction of the governing Alabama law. However, from the fact that in cases where the accused has no lawyer at the hearing the Alabama courts prohibit the State's use at trial of anything that occurred at the hearing, it does not follow that the Alabama preliminary hearing is not a "critical stage" of the State's criminal process. The determination whether the hearing is a "critical stage" requiring the provision of counsel depends, as noted, upon an analysis "whether potential substantial prejudice to defendant's rights inheres in the ... confrontation and the ability of counsel to help avoid that prejudice." United States v. Wade, supra, 388 U.S. at 227, 87 S.Ct. at 1932. Plainly the guiding hand of counsel at the preliminary hearing is essential to protect the indigent accused against an erroneous or improper prosecution. First, the lawyer's skilled examination and cross-examination of witnesses may expose fatal weaknesses in the State's case, that may lead the magistrate to refuse to bind the accused over. Second, in any event, the skilled interrogation of witnesses by an experienced lawyer can fashion a vital impeachment tool for use in cross-examination of the State's witnesses at the trial, or preserve testimony favorable to the accused of a witness who does not appear at the trial. Third, trained counsel can more effectively discover the case the State has against his client and make possible the preparation of a proper defense to meet that case at the trial. Fourth, counsel can also be influential at the preliminary hearing in making effective arguments for the accused on such matters as the necessity for an early psychiatric examination or bail.

The inability of the indigent accused on his own to realize these advantages of a lawyer's assistance compels the conclusion that the Alabama preliminary hearing is a "critical stage" of the State's criminal process at which the accused is "as much entitled to such aid [of counsel] ... as at the trial itself." Powell v. Alabama, supra, 287 U.S. at 57, 53 S.Ct. at 60.

III.

There remains, then, the question of the relief to which petitioners are entitled. The trial transcript indicates that the prohibition against use by the State at trial of anything that occurred at the preliminary hearing was scrupulously observed. Cf. White v. Maryland, supra. But on the record it cannot be said whether or not petitioners were otherwise prejudiced by the absence of counsel at the preliminary hearing. That inquiry in the first instance should more properly be made by the Alabama courts. The test to be applied is whether the denial of counsel at the preliminary hearing was harmless error under Chapman v. California, 386 U.S. 18, 87 S.Ct. 824, 17 L.Ed.2d 705 (1967).

We accordingly vacate the petitioners' convictions and remand the case to the Alabama courts for such proceedings not inconsistent with this opinion as they may deem appropriate to determine whether such denial of counsel was harmless error, and therefore whether the convictions should be reinstated or a new trial ordered.

It is so ordered.

Convictions vacated and case remanded with directions.

* * *

Myers v. Commonwealth

Supreme Judicial Court of Massachusetts, 1973.
363 Mass. 843, 298 N.E.2d 819.

■ TAURO, CHIEF JUSTICE.

This is a petition for a writ of certiorari and related relief brought under G.L. c. 211, § 3, asking the court to exercise its supervisory power "to correct and prevent errors and abuses" in probable cause hearings conducted in the District Courts of the Commonwealth. The petitioner asks us to vacate a finding of probable cause in the Municipal Court of the Roxbury District and remand the case to that court for a new probable cause hearing consistent with the requirements of G.L. c. 276, § 38, which he alleges were violated in his initial preliminary hearing. ...

The pertinent facts may be summarized briefly. On February 23, 1973, a preliminary examination was held pursuant to G.L. c. 276, § 38, before a judge of the Municipal Court to determine whether there was probable cause to support the prosecution of the petitioner on charges of rape, assault by means of a dangerous weapon, breaking and entering at night, and breaking and entering at night and committing rape of a person lawfully therein. At that probable cause hearing, only the complaining witness was called to testify on behalf of the Commonwealth. At the end of direct examination the petitioner's counsel began his cross-examination of the witness. When the petitioner's counsel questioned the complaining witness about her alleged belief in witchcraft, the judge stated that he had heard enough testimony to find probable cause which made further cross-examination by the petitioner's counsel unnecessary. The petitioner's counsel stated to the court that he wished to complete his cross-examination of the complaining witness, and introduce further evidence in the defendant's behalf. The judge repeated his finding of probable cause and terminated the hearing. The question before us is whether the judge's finding of probable cause before the petitioner had an opportunity to complete cross-examination of the complaining witness and to present relevant testimony and witnesses in his own behalf violated the petitioner's "substantive rights."

1. The rules governing the conduct of preliminary hearings in the Commonwealth are summarily set forth in G.L. c. 276, § 38, "The court or justice before whom a person is taken upon a charge of crime shall, as soon as may be, examine on oath the complainant and the witnesses for the prosecution, in the presence of the defendant, relative to any material matter connected with such charge. ... *[T]he witnesses for the prisoner, if any, shall be examined on oath, and he may be assisted by counsel in such examination and in the cross examination of the witnesses in support of the prosecution*" (emphasis supplied). The Commonwealth contends that this statute should not be interpreted as granting the defendant an absolute "inflexible" right to cross-examine prosecution witnesses and present testimony in his own behalf at the preliminary hearing because the examining

magistrate has the discretion to find probable cause after listening only to the witnesses for the prosecution. The petitioner argues that c. 276, § 38, grants defendants at such hearings *mandatory* fundamental procedural rights to confront their accusers and present testimony in their own behalf.

The petitioner's construction of the statute is supported by its express mandatory terms ("witnesses for the prisoner if any, *shall* be examined" [emphasis supplied]). "It is difficult to see how language could have been framed which would more clearly and categorically impose an absolute obligation." However, "[t]he word 'shall' as used in statutes ... is not of inflexible signification and not infrequently is construed as permissive or directory in order to effectuate a legislative purpose."

Therefore, the controversy before us as to the proper statutory construction of c. 276, § 38, cannot be resolved without examining the purposes (and procedure) of a probable cause hearing in order to determine which construction of the statute best effectuates those purposes.

2. The judge's chief task at a preliminary hearing is to determine whether the defendant should be bound over for trial in the Superior Court. Defendants are held for trial only if the examining magistrate finds (1) "that a crime has been committed" *and* (2) "that there is probable cause to believe the prisoner guilty." These two requirements are designed to establish an effective bind-over standard which distinguishes between groundless or unsupported charges and meritorious prosecutions. Thus, the preliminary hearing's primary function is to screen out at this early but critical stage of the criminal process those cases that should not go to trial thereby sparing individuals from being held for trial, and from being unjustifiably prosecuted.

The United States Supreme Court recognized the importance of the preliminary hearing's screening function in Coleman v. Alabama, 399 U.S. 1, 90 S.Ct. 1999, 26 L.Ed.2d 387, where the court held that Alabama's preliminary hearing is a "critical stage" of the State's criminal process at which the accused is entitled to the aid of counsel. ...

Since the examining magistrate's chief task is to determine whether there is sufficient credible evidence to proceed to trial which justifies binding the defendant over, his determination of probable cause to bind over is somewhat analogous in function to the trial court's ruling on a motion for a directed verdict as to whether there is sufficient evidence to send the case to the jury. Unfortunately since this court has never defined the quantum of evidence needed to satisfy probable cause to bind over, some District Court judges have equated probable cause to bind over with probable cause for arrest (and search).

In finding probable cause to arrest, the examining magistrate has determined only that at the time *of the arrest* (or at the time when the warrant for arrest is requested), the "facts and circumstances within ... [the officers'] knowledge and of which they had reasonably trustworthy information were sufficient to warrant a prudent man in believing that the defendant had committed or was committing an offence." Commonwealth v. Stevens, Mass., 283 N.E.2d 673. ...

... [T]here is a "large difference" between probable cause to arrest [or search] and probable cause to bind over, "and therefore a like difference in the quanta and modes of proof required to establish them." Brinegar v. United States, [338 U.S. 160, 69 S.Ct. 1302, 93 L.Ed. 1879]. A judicial finding of probable cause to arrest validates only the initial decision to arrest the suspect, not the decision made later in the criminal process to hold the defendant for trial. Since many valid arrests are based on reliable hearsay information which could not be introduced at the defendant's trial, probable cause to arrest does not automatically mean that the Commonwealth has sufficient competent legal evidence to justify the costs both to the defendant and to the Commonwealth of a full trial. Therefore the standard of probable cause to bind over must require a greater quantum of legally competent[1] evidence than the probable cause to arrest finding to insure that the preliminary hearing's screening standard is defined in a way that effectuates its purpose.

Since the examining magistrate's determination of the minimum quantum of evidence required to find probable cause to bind over is somewhat analogous in function to the court's ruling on a motion for a directed verdict at trial as to whether there is sufficient evidence to warrant submission of the case to the jury, we have decided to adopt a "directed verdict" rule in defining the minimum quantum of credible evidence necessary to support a bind-over determination. The examining magistrate should view the case as if it were a trial and he were required to rule on whether there is enough credible evidence to send the case to the jury. Thus, the magistrate should dismiss the complaint when, on the evidence presented, a trial court would be bound to acquit as a matter of law. The minimum quantum of evidence required by this bind-over standard is more than that for probable cause for arrest but less than would "prove the defendant's guilt beyond a reasonable doubt."

3. We must construe G.L. c. 276, § 38, in a manner which effectuates its primary purpose of screening out "an erroneous or improper prosecution," Coleman v. Alabama, 399 U.S. at 9, 90 S.Ct. 1999. ... The Commonwealth's interpretation of the statute fails....

The Commonwealth argues that once a prima facie showing of probable cause has been made by prosecution testimony, the examining magistrate can end the hearing before the defendant's attorney has had an opportunity to make a complete cross-examination of the prosecution witness or to present an affirmative defence. We fail to see how such a limited procedure could possibly effectuate the hearing's primary function of screening out cases that should not go to trial. To require such minimal proof of probable cause would render the hearing, in many instances, an

---

1. Since the primary objective of the probable cause hearing is to screen out those cases where the *legally admissible* evidence of the defendant's guilt would be insufficient to warrant submission of the case to a jury if it had gone to trial, the rules of evidence at the preliminary hearing should in general be the same rules that are applicable at the criminal trial. ... Unlike a finding of probable cause for arrest which can be based solely on reliable hearsay testimony, probable cause to hold the defendant for trial must be based on competent testimony which would be admissible at trial. Compare Federal Rule 5.1 Preliminary Examination. If it appears that added exceptions to the hearsay rule are desirable to insure an effective probable cause hearing, specific rules may be developed....

empty ritual with a foregone conclusion. If the examining magistrate could simply rest his finding of probable cause on the ipse dixit of the prosecution, there would be little need for defence counsel's presence, let alone the defendant's.

* * *

The primary function of the probable cause hearing of screening out "an erroneous or improper prosecution," Coleman v. Alabama, 399 U.S., supra, at 9, 90 S.Ct. 1999, can only be effectuated by an adversary hearing where the defendant is given a meaningful opportunity to challenge the credibility of the prosecution's witnesses and to raise any affirmative defences he may have. . . .

The facts of the instant case provide an excellent illustration of this point. The only witness at the petitioner's probable cause hearing was the complaining witness who repeated her accusation that the petitioner had raped her. If the petitioner had been afforded his statutory rights, he would have introduced testimony challenging the complaining witness's credibility and supporting his defence of a consensual sexual relationship.[2] The examining magistrate could not have possibly made an informed judgment on the question of whether there was sufficient credible evidence of the defendant's guilt to support a bind over until he had considered all of this evidence.

In some cases, the evidence introduced in behalf of the defendant will do no more than raise a conflict which can best be resolved by a jury at the actual trial where the Commonwealth must prove the defendant's guilt beyond a reasonable doubt. But, in other cases, the evidence elicited by defence counsel on cross-examination or from the testimony of defence witnesses or from other evidence may lead the examining magistrate to disbelieve the prosecution's witnesses and discharge the defendant for lack of probable cause.

* * *

4. In view of our interpretation of the statute, c. 276, § 38, we need not decide the petitioner's contention that the due process requirements of the United States Constitution mandate that the defendant in a probable cause hearing shall have the right to cross-examine prosecution witnesses and present testimony in his own defence. . . .[3]

2. If permitted, the petitioner's counsel would have introduced in evidence a psychiatric evaluation of the prosecutrix which noted that she "has a hysterical neurosis, a condition in which people might make up stories and then half believe them themselves. I would question the veracity of her statements." Defence counsel also wished to introduce a "medical report on the prosecutrix which shows that she received no abdominal injury, no pelvic trauma and that a vaginal discharge test for spermatozoa performed by a physician at the Boston City Hospital the morning of the alleged rape indicated no spermatozoa."

3. Moreover, the Commonwealth's interpretation would permit a procedure that would be subject to serious challenge on equal protection grounds. Past experience indicates that most District Court judges permit defendants (if they so desire) to present testimony in their own behalf at probable cause hearings. The Commonwealth's interpretation of the statute, which gives defendants a right to do so only at the trial court's discretion, would create a situation where

Our analysis of the purposes (and procedure) of the probable cause hearing leads us to conclude that the defendant must be given the opportunity to cross-examine his accusers and present testimony in his own behalf in order to insure that the hearing's vital screening function will be effectuated. Therefore, we hold that c. 276, § 38, grants defendants mandatory statutory rights to cross-examine prosecution witnesses and present testimony in their own behalf *before* the examining magistrate determines whether there is sufficient legally admissible evidence of the defendant's guilt to justify binding him over for trial.

5. The Commonwealth argues in its brief that granting defendants inflexible statutory rights to cross-examine witnesses against them and to present testimony in their own behalf would transform the preliminary hearing into a full-blown trial with disastrous results to a criminal justice system that is already overburdened. However, past experience indicates that trial strategy usually prevents such a result as both the prosecution and the defence wish to withhold as much of their case as possible.

"[N]ormally defense counsel will be more concerned at the preliminary with exploring rather than destroying the prosecution's case. If they were aware of the defects in testimony capable of attack on cross-examination, most lawyers would prefer to save the attack for trial rather than tip their hand at this early stage." Graham & Letwin, 18 U.C.L.A.Law Rev. 916, 926. For the same reasons, defence tactics usually mitigate against putting the defendant on the stand or presenting exculpatory testimony at the preliminary hearing unless defence counsel believes his evidence is compelling enough to overcome the prosecution's case.

In those instances where the defendant does choose to exercise his statutory rights, the examining magistrate at the hearing has the same broad discretion as a trial judge in limiting the scope of cross-examination to relevant issues in dispute. However, the judge at a preliminary hearing should allow reasonable latitude to the scope of the defendant's cross-examination of prosecution witnesses in order to effectuate the ancillary discovery and impeachment functions of the hearing noted in the *Coleman* . . . [case]. . . .

Since the summary manner in which the petitioner's probable cause hearing was conducted denied the petitioner his statutory right to cross-examine witnesses and present evidence before the issue of probable cause was determined, the petitioner must be given a new preliminary hearing to determine whether there is probable cause to hold him on the charges pending against him. Therefore, . . . the original probable cause finding is vacated and the case is remanded to the Municipal Court of the Roxbury District for a new preliminary hearing to be conducted in accordance with the requirements of c. 276, § 38.

So ordered.

some defendants would be afforded a full adversary hearing upon demand while others received summary hearings in which probable cause findings rested on the unchallenged ipse dixit of prosecution witnesses. Certainly, such a discrepancy in the type of probable cause hearing afforded defendants similarly situated would raise a serious constitutional question as to whether those defendants, who received summary hearings, were being denied the equal protection of the law.

NOTES

1. **Admissibility requirements.** Other courts (and legislatures) have disagreed that the bindover decision must be made on admissible evidence. In State v. Morrissey, 295 N.W.2d 307 (N.D.1980), for example, the court reasoned that probable cause in the bindover context has the same meaning as it does in the arrest situation and this meaning demands that hearsay may be relied upon in determining whether it exists. The Colorado court has held that hearsay is admissible, People v. Szloboda, 44 Colo.App. 164, 620 P.2d 36 (1980), but has also held that exclusive reliance on "hearsay-upon-hearsay" in binding a defendant over for trial is not permissible. Maestas v. District Court, 189 Colo. 443, 541 P.2d 889 (1975). See also, State v. Anderson, 612 P.2d 778 (Utah 1980), holding that given the defendant's confrontation rights at a preliminary hearing, it was error to allow the state to present the "testimony" of its main witness by affidavit.

2. **Discovery functions.** The Massachusetts court stated that the scope of cross-examination permitted a defendant at the preliminary hearing should be such as to further the defendant's interest in discovery. But other courts have suggested that discovery is not a permissible basis for defense questions and questioning may be cut off if it proceeds beyond challenging probable cause and into discovery. See Coleman v. Burnett, 155 U.S.App.D.C. 302, 315–17, 477 F.2d 1187, 1200–02 (D.C.Cir.1973). Questioning may also be cut off if it goes beyond what under local standards are the proper issues in the preliminary. See State v. Russo, 101 Wis.2d 206, 303 N.W.2d 846 (1981). A major factor limiting the discovery value of the preliminary hearing is the absence of any requirement that the prosecution produce any particular evidence. The prosecution has almost if not complete discretion as to how to establish probable cause. In People v. Blackman, 91 Ill.App.3d 130, 46 Ill.Dec. 524, 414 N.E.2d 246 (1980), the judge presiding over the preliminary hearing, at the request of the defense, required the state to produce two specific witnesses. Finding this error, the appellate court stressed the state's ability to use hearsay to establish probable cause and its discretion as to what to produce to meet its burden.

3. **Defense witnesses.** Footnote 2 in *Myers,* supra, as well as dicta in *Myers'* text, indicates that in addition to a normal right to cross-examine prosecution witnesses, the suspect would have a similar right to call witnesses of his own. The problem arose in State v. Rud, 359 N.W.2d 573 (Minn.1984). The suspect wished to call his alleged child abuse victims to determine the exact times and locations of the claimed incidents of abuse, so that he could call alibi witnesses. Although it was unnecessary to pass on the general question of the suspect's right to call witnesses, the court held that he could not call the child abuse victims because he did not and could not claim that their testimony would lead directly to dismissal. And see Fed.R.Crim.P. 5.1(a), supra, for the general position.

4. **Defenses.** To what extent, if any, should the judge presiding over a preliminary hearing be concerned with "defensive" matters, such as self-defense, entrapment, etc.? Drawing the line between probable cause and matters that should be left for trial on the merits is not an easy one. See People v. Johnson, 618 P.2d 262 (Colo.1980), a theft prosecution in which a major question was whether the defendant's use of the money at issue was authorized by a contract. The Colorado Supreme Court held that the construction of the contract was a matter for trial on guilt or innocence, not for consideration at the preliminary hearing.

5. **Effect of a finding of no probable cause.** What if the preliminary hearing judge refuses to bind a defendant over? In most jurisdictions, this will not preclude the prosecution from securing an indictment and prosecuting the defendant. People v. Uhlemann, 9 Cal.3d 662, 108 Cal.Rptr. 657, 511 P.2d 609 (1973); People v. Anderson, 92 Ill.App.3d 849, 48 Ill.Dec. 183, 416 N.E.2d 78 (1981). The

PART 2 PROSECUTION AND ADJUDICATION

effect of a refusal to bind over upon the prosecution's ability to charge the defendant by means of an information is less settled. In State v. Thomas, 529 S.W.2d 379 (Mo.1975) the court adopted what it described as the "prevailing general rule," which permits the state to seek an indictment but not to charge the defendant by information. Jones v. State, 481 P.2d 169 (Okla.Crim.App.1971) held that the preliminary hearing judge's action would be binding upon the prosecution, whether it sought to proceed by indictment or information, unless the prosecution produced additional evidence or established good cause justifying a second preliminary hearing. But some courts have found no bar to a second charge and a second preliminary hearing on that charge. State v. Bloomer, 197 Kan. 668, 421 P.2d 58 (1966); Thomas v. Justice Court, 538 P.2d 42 (Wyo.1975). Other courts have apparently regarded the preliminary hearing judge's decision as binding upon the prosecution, but see no problem in filing charges (and having a second preliminary hearing) before another judge with authority to hold such a hearing. State v. Maki, 291 Minn. 427, 192 N.W.2d 811 (1971); Commonwealth v. Hetherington, 460 Pa. 17, 331 A.2d 205 (1975).

Gilboy, Prosecutors' Discretionary Use of the Grand Jury to Initiate or to Reinitiate Prosecution, 1984 Am.B.Found.Res.J. 1, studying homicide cases actually initiated in Cook County, Illinois, over a 39 month period, found: (a) although re-initiated cases showed a lower rate of conviction, one half of them, nevertheless, resulted in convictions; (b) defendants in re-initiated cases were more likely to demand trials and were more likely to seek bench trials than did defendants with initial probable cause findings. Is it important that in every case which went to the grand jury first the prosecutor's request for an indictment was met, that the re-initiated cases all fell into a group in which there had been a prior no probable cause finding at a preliminary examination, that re-initiation always was before a grand jury, and that no grand jury refused to indict after a no probable cause finding at a preliminary examination? In considering this question, see infra note 6.

A related matter concerns the ability of the preliminary hearing judge to control the charge upon which the defendant is ultimately tried, especially where the prosecutor—following the bindover decision—elects to file an information. In some jurisdictions, a prosecutor who proceeds on an information is limited to the offense for which the defendant was bound over. State v. McCrary, 97 N.M. 306, 639 P.2d 593 (App. 1982). But in others, the preliminary hearing is limited to determining whether there is probable cause to believe that the defendant committed some felony. If this determination is made, the preliminary hearing judge has no authority to bind over on a specific charge. See State ex rel. Thomas v. Crouch, 603 S.W.2d 532 (Mo.1980), appeal dismissed for want of a substantial federal question 451 U.S. 901, 101 S.Ct. 1965, 68 L.Ed.2d 289 (1981) (prosecutor could file capital murder indictment although preliminary hearing judge bound over only for second degree murder). In State v. Hooper, 101 Wis.2d 517, 305 N.W.2d 110 (1981), the court held that once a defendant was bound over at a preliminary hearing, the prosecutor's choice as to a specific charge is subject to attack only for abuse of discretion.

6. **Choosing a preliminary or grand jury.** The Oregon Supreme Court in State v. Freeland, 295 Or. 367, 667 P.2d 509 (1983), held that although a grant of discretion to the prosecutor to initiate prosecution by information—with its accompanying preliminary—or by indictment, was not per se unconstitutional, the prosecutor's choice must be based on permissible criteria consistently applied in order that similarly situated defendants were offered preliminaries. Greater efficiency and dispatch by using the grand jury was found to be a permissible criterion in State v. Eells, 72 Or.App. 492, 696 P.2d 564 (1985).

In another part of her study, Gilboy, supra, found that the grand jury was initially used in only twenty per cent of the cases and that it was the preferred method for "stronger cases". The reasons given for choosing the grand jury route included avoiding witness intimidation, quickly resolving highly publicized cases, saving court time, and, in some instances, making it more convenient for witnesses. The preliminary examination route was preferred when there was an unusually high risk that a witness would be unavailable at a later stage and to test the strength of the state's case. There was some concern expressed that if the preliminary were used too infrequently, a bill, regularly introduced in the Illinois Legislature to require the preliminary in all cases, would pass.

7. **Post-indictment preliminaries.** In most jurisdictions, a defendant against whom an indictment has been returned has no right to a preliminary hearing. This is based upon the ground that both the indictment process and the preliminary hearing are to determine probable cause and there is no legitimate function served by two such determinations. E.g., United States v. Simon, 510 F.Supp. 232 (E.D.Pa.1981); King v. Venters, 595 S.W.2d 714 (Ky.1980); State *ex rel.* Rowe v. Ferguson, 165 W.Va. 183, 268 S.E.2d 45 (1980). But in State v. Holmes, 388 So.2d 722 (La.1980), the court held that whether to hold a preliminary hearing for an indicted defendant was discretionary with the trial court. And in Hawkins v. Superior Court, 22 Cal.3d 584, 150 Cal.Rptr. 435, 586 P.2d 916 (1978) the California Supreme Court held that the state constitutional requirement of equal protection entitled indicted defendants to a preliminary hearing. After reviewing the benefits which the Supreme Court in Coleman v. Alabama found to flow from the preliminary hearing, the court emphasized the prosecution's control over the alternative grand jury process and reasoned:

> These benefits to the defense which inhere in an adversarial preliminary hearing are either completely denied to a defendant charged in a secret, nonadversarial grand jury proceeding, or ultimately realized by such a defendant only to a limited extent. It cannot be seriously argued that an indicted defendant enjoys a comparable opportunity to discover the state's case and develop evidence because he later obtains a transcript of grand jury proceedings. Such a transcript will invariably reflect only what the prosecutor permits it to reflect; it is certainly no substitute for the possibility of developing further evidence through a probing cross examination of prosecution witnesses—a possibility foreclosed with the denial of an adversarial proceeding. There is no other effective means for the defense to compel the cooperation of a hostile witness; in the unlikely event that all the prosecution witnesses agree to submit to defense interviews, the defense must still incur unnecessary expense and hardship which may be substantial.

22 Cal.3d at 589, 150 Cal.Rptr. at 438, 586 P.2d at 919. By denying indicted defendants access to these advantages which are afforded those charged by information, the court concluded, the state was denying equal protection. Other courts, however, have responded to similar arguments by characterizing these advantages of a preliminary hearing as incidental and unintended side-effects and as of minimal importance given other ways to achieve them. In State ex rel. Rowe v. Ferguson, supra, for example, the court concluded that liberalized discovery for criminal defendants has greatly reduced the importance of the discovery function of the preliminary hearing.

8. **Reform of the California preliminary.** The California preliminary hearing or examination was dramatically changed by an initiative measure—Proposition 115 or the "Crime Victims Justice Reform Act"—adopted in 1990 by the voters of that state. The measure affected both statutory and constitutional provisions. Perhaps the purpose of the changes is best reflected in section 866(b) of the California Penal Code as amended by the measure:

It is the purpose of a preliminary examination to establish whether there exists probable cause to believe that the defendant has committed a felony. The examination shall not be used for purposes of discovery.

Moreover, the availability of preliminary examinations was reduced by providing in article I, section 14.1 of the California Constitution: "If a felony is prosecuted by indictment, there shall be no postindictment preliminary hearing."

To implement the voters' obvious desire to reduce the impact of preliminary examinations upon crime victims, article I, section 30(b) of the Constitution was amended by Proposition 115 to add the following:

In order to protect victims and witnesses in criminal cases, hearsay evidence shall be admissible at preliminary hearings, as prescribed by the Legislature or by the people through the initiative process.

This was effectuated by amendment of Section 872(b) of the Penal Code to provide:

Notwithstanding Section 1200 of the Evidence Code [the hearsay rule], the finding of probable cause may be based in whole or in part upon the sworn testimony of a law enforcement officer relating the statements of declarants made out of court offered for the truth of the matter asserted. Any law enforcement officer testifying as to hearsay statements shall either have five years of law enforcement experience or have completed a training course certified by the Commission on Peace Officer Standards and Training which includes training in the investigation and reporting of cases and testifying at preliminary hearings.

Section 1203 of California's Evidence Code requires that hearsay declarants be made available for cross-examination. The 1990 initiative enacted section 1203.1, which provides:

Section 1203 is not applicable if the hearsay statement is offered at a preliminary examination, as provided in Section 872 of the Penal Code.

A defendant's right to call witnesses at the preliminary examination was also limited by amendment of Penal Code section 866(a) to provide:

Upon the request of the prosecuting attorney, the magistrate shall require an offer of proof from the defense as to the testimony expected from [a defense] witness. The magistrate shall not permit the testimony of any defense witness unless the offer of proof discloses to the satisfaction of the magistrate, in his or her discretion, that the testimony of that witness, if believed, would be reasonably likely to establish an affirmative defense, negate an element of a crime charged, or impeach the testimony of a prosecution witness or the statement of a declarant testified to by a prosecution witness.

As the California Supreme Court commented in Whitman v. Superior Court (People), 54 Cal.3d 1063, 2 Cal.Rptr.2d 160, 820 P.2d 262 (1991):

[Section 866, as amended by the initiative] marks a sharp contrast to this court's previous expansive concept of the preliminary hearing as a discovery and trial preparation device, allowing counsel the opportunity to "fashion" their impeachment tools for use in cross-examination at trial, to preserve testimony favorable to the defense, and to provide the defense "with valuable information about the case against the accused, enhancing its ability to evaluate the desirability of entering a plea or to prepare for trial."

54 Cal.3d at 1081, 2 Cal.Rptr.2d at 170, 820 P.2d at 272, quoting from Hawkins v. Superior Court, 22 Cal.3d 584, 588, 150 Cal.Rptr. 435, 438, 586 P.2d 916, 919 (1978), discussed in note 7, supra.

The California Supreme Court recognized that the enactment of article I, section 14.1 of the California Constitution negated its earlier holding in *Hawkins* that the state Equal Protection Clause gave an indicted felony defendant a right to a preliminary examination. It also held that granting preliminary examinations to only nonindicted defendants does not violate the Equal Protection Clause of the Fourteenth Amendment. Bowens v. Superior Court (People), 1 Cal.4th 36, 2 Cal.Rptr.2d 376, 820 P.2d 600 (1991).

In *Whitman,* supra, the court turned to the effect of the constitutional and statutory provisions permitting hearsay to be used by the prosecution. In *Whitman,* the only witness at the defendant's preliminary examination was a "reader" police officer, that is, an officer with the experience required by section 872(b) but who had no direct, personal knowledge of the offense or the investigation and simply read the report of the investigating officers. The voters' intention, held the court, was not to permit use of this sort of hearsay:

> Properly construed, Proposition 115 does not authorize a finding of probable cause based on the testimony of a noninvestigating officer or "reader" merely reciting the police report of an investigating officer. We believe the probable intent of the framers of the measure was to allow a properly qualified investigating officer to relate out-of-court statements by crime victims or witnesses, including other law enforcement personnel, without requiring the victims' or witnesses' presence in court. The testifying officer, however, must not be a mere reader but must have sufficient knowledge of the crime or the circumstances under which the out-of-court statement was made so as to meaningfully assist the magistrate in assessing the reliability of the statement.

54 Cal.3d at 1072–73, 2 Cal.Rptr.2d at 164–65, 820 P.2d at 266–67.

For a general discussion, see Berend, Proposition 115 Preliminary Hearings: Sacrificing Reliability on the Altar of Expediency, 23 Pac.L.J. 1131 (1992).

B. THE GRAND JURY

The second major vehicle for pretrial screening is the grand jury. Whether the grand jury can or does perform an acceptable screening function is disputed. Among the concerns that can be raised as to the ability of the grand jury to function effectively are its dependence upon the prosecution for information, investigatory assistance, and legal advice, and the potential difficulty which lay jurors may experience in resolving the sometimes complex legal issues that even probable cause determinations raise. For a vigorous presentation of the view that grand juries are no more than alter egos of prosecutors, see Antell, The Modern Grand Jury: Benighted Supergovernment, 51 A.B.A.J. 153 (1965).

Unless the grand jury is to be abandoned as a pretrial screening tool, however, consideration should be given to the manner in which its function is to be structured. This is the major concern of the present section. In addition, however, attention needs to be paid to the manner in which those requirements imposed will be enforced. Traditionally, this was sought to be accomplished in part by rigidly requiring the prosecution to prove at trial those matters alleged in the indictment and limiting the ability of the prosecution and trial court to change or "amend" an indictment. A defendant's right to indictment, it was reasoned, demanded that he be tried on precisely the charge returned by the grand jury. If amendment of the indictment was permitted, the defendant might be tried and convicted of a version of the offense on which the grand jury never passed.

Modern rules of procedure and proof have strayed away from this approach. The trend was illustrated by United States v. Miller, 471 U.S. 130, 105 S.Ct. 1811, 85 L.Ed.2d 99 (1985). Miller was indicted by a federal grand jury for mail fraud. The indictment alleged that he used the mails to make a fraudulent claim to his insurance company concerning losses allegedly resulting from a burglary. Specifically, the indictment alleged that he fraudulently represented to his insurer that the losses were incurred in a scheme to which he had not consented and that he fraudulently represented the value of the property taken. Under the substantive criminal law, using the mails to obtain insurance proceeds and fraudulently misrepresenting the amount of the loss was sufficient to constitute the crime. At trial, the Government sought unsuccessfully to have struck from the indictment the allegations that Miller consented in advance to the removal of the property and that he misrepresented this in the claim sent through the mails. Its evidence showed that Miller did fraudulently exaggerate the amount of his loss; the Government did not prove his prior consent to the taking of the property and any misrepresentation concerning that. In a sense, there was what has traditionally been called a "variance between the pleading and the proof." The Government's evidence proved the defendant committed the offense charged; it proved that, however, in a way varying from the allegations in the indictment because not all of the allegations made by the grand jury were proved by the trial evidence. The jury convicted Miller. On appeal, the Court of Appeals—taking a traditional approach—held that to permit Miller's conviction on the basis of proof of some but not all of the allegations in the indictment violated his Fifth Amendment right to grand jury indictment. The grand jury, it reasoned, may well have declined to indict him on the theory that the only fraud involved was an exaggeration of the losses incurred. He was convicted of an offense, the Court of Appeals concluded, for which he had not been indicted. 715 F.2d 1360 (9th Cir.1983), modified 728 F.2d 1269 (9th Cir.1984).

The Supreme Court reversed the Court of Appeals and upheld the conviction. It reaffirmed that the right to indictment means that new allegations cannot be added to an indictment except by the grand jury. Moreover, a defendant cannot be convicted on the basis of evidence proving matters not alleged in an indictment. But it rejected the argument that the Fifth Amendment bars convicting a defendant on the basis of facts which constitute the offense but are less than the total facts alleged in the indictment. The Government proved Miller's guilt and it did so by proving only facts alleged in the indictment. It failed to prove some facts alleged in the indictment but these allegations were "in no way essential to the offense on which the jury convicted" and could be regarded as "surplusage" and ignored. 471 U.S. at 145, 105 S.Ct. at 1820, 85 L.Ed.2d at 111.

In *Miller,* is it possible that if the presentation to the grand jury had involved only evidence that Miller had exaggerated the amount of his losses, the grand jury might have refused to indict because of deficiencies in the evidence that the exaggeration was fraudulent or because in its judgment such an exaggeration, even if fraudulent, should not be treated as a serious criminal offense? If so, perhaps the decision in *Miller* reflects the Supreme Court's view that the right to indictment does not include the right to have the grand jury scrutinize the sufficiency of the evidence on each of several alternative ways the accused may have committed the crime. Perhaps it reflects a view that the right to indictment does not include the right to have the grand jury consider, if the evidence establishes probable cause, whether as a matter of prosecutorial judgment charges should be pursued. Or maybe it reflects a view that whatever the content of the Fifth Amendment right to indictment, this right should not be enforced by restricting the Government in its trial proof.

Alleged discrimination in the selection of grand jurors raises issues closely resembling those presented by the petit jury selection process. These issues are therefore considered in Chapter 23 in connection with the right to trial by jury.

Costello v. United States

Supreme Court of the United States, 1956.
350 U.S. 359, 76 S.Ct. 406, 100 L.Ed. 397.

■ MR. JUSTICE BLACK delivered the opinion of the Court.

We granted certiorari in this case to consider a single question: " 'May a defendant be required to stand trial and a conviction be sustained where only hearsay evidence was presented to the grand jury which indicted him?' " 350 U.S. 819, 76 S.Ct. 48.

Petitioner, Frank Costello, was indicted for wilfully attempting to evade payment of income taxes due the United States for the years 1947, 1948 and 1949. The charge was that petitioner falsely and fraudulently reported less income than he and his wife actually received during the taxable years in question. Petitioner promptly filed a motion for inspection of the minutes of the grand jury and for a dismissal of the indictment. His motion was based on an affidavit stating that he was firmly convinced there could have been no legal or competent evidence before the grand jury which indicted him since he had reported all his income and paid all taxes due. The motion was denied. At the trial which followed the Government offered evidence designed to show increases in Costello's net worth in an attempt to prove that he had received more income during the years in question than he had reported. To establish its case the Government called and examined 144 witnesses and introduced 368 exhibits. All of the testimony and documents related to business transactions and expenditures by petitioner and his wife. The prosecution concluded its case by calling three government agents. Their investigations had produced the evidence used against petitioner at the trial. They were allowed to summarize the vast amount of evidence already heard and to introduce computations showing, if correct, that petitioner and his wife had received far greater income than they had reported. We have held such summarizations admissible in a "net worth" case like this. United States v. Johnson, 319 U.S. 503, 63 S.Ct. 1233, 87 L.Ed. 1546.

Counsel for petitioner asked each government witness at the trial whether he had appeared before the grand jury which returned the indictment. This cross-examination developed the fact that the three investigating officers had been the only witnesses before the grand jury. After the Government concluded its case, petitioner again moved to dismiss the indictment on the ground that the only evidence before the grand jury was "hearsay," since the three officers had no firsthand knowledge of the transactions upon which their computations were based. Nevertheless the trial court again refused to dismiss the indictment, and petitioner was convicted. The Court of Appeals affirmed, holding that the indictment was valid even though the sole evidence before the grand jury was hearsay. Petitioner here urges: (1) that an indictment based solely on hearsay evidence violates that part of the Fifth Amendment providing that "No person shall be held to answer for a capital, or otherwise infamous crime, unless on a presentment or indictment of a Grand Jury . . ." and (2) that if the Fifth Amendment does not invalidate an indictment based solely on hearsay we should now lay down such a rule for the guidance of federal courts. See McNabb v. United States, 318 U.S. 332, 340–341, 63 S.Ct. 608, 612–613, 87 L.Ed. 819.

The Fifth Amendment provides that federal prosecutions for capital or otherwise infamous crimes must be instituted by presentments or indictments of grand juries. But neither the Fifth Amendment nor any other constitutional provision prescribes the kind of evidence upon which grand juries must act. The grand jury is an English institution, brought to this country by the early colonists and incorporated in the Constitution by the Founders. There is every reason to believe that our constitutional grand jury was intended to operate substantially like its English progenitor. The basic purpose of the English grand jury was to provide a fair method for instituting criminal proceedings against persons believed to have committed crimes. Grand jurors were selected from the body of the people and their work was not hampered by rigid procedural or evidential rules. In fact, grand jurors could act on their own knowledge and were free to make their presentments or indictments on such information as they deemed satisfactory. Despite its broad power to institute criminal proceedings the grand jury grew in popular favor with the years. It acquired an independence in England free from control by the Crown or judges. Its adoption in our Constitution as the sole method for preferring charges in serious criminal cases shows the high place it held as an instrument of justice. And in this country as in England of old the grand jury has convened as a body of laymen, free from technical rules, acting in secret, pledged to indict no one because of prejudice and to free no one because of special favor. As late as 1927 an English historian could say that English grand juries were still free to act on their own knowledge if they pleased to do so. And in 1852 Mr. Justice Nelson on circuit could say "No case has been cited, nor have we been able to find any, furnishing an authority for looking into and revising the judgment of the grand jury upon the evidence, for the purpose of determining whether or not the finding was founded upon sufficient proof. . . ." United States v. Reed, 27 Fed.Cas. pages 727, 738, No. 16,134.

In Holt v. United States, 218 U.S. 245, 31 S.Ct. 2, 4, 54 L.Ed. 1021, this Court had to decide whether an indictment should be quashed because supported in part by incompetent evidence. Aside from the incompetent evidence "there was very little evidence against the accused." The Court refused to hold that such an indictment should be quashed, pointing out that "The abuses of criminal practice would be enhanced if indictments could be upset on such a ground." 218 U.S. at page 248, 31 S.Ct. at page 4. The same thing is true where as here all the evidence before the grand jury was in the nature of "hearsay." If indictments were to be held open to challenge on the ground that there was inadequate or incompetent evidence before the grand jury, the resulting delay would be great indeed. The result of such a rule would be that before trial on the merits a defendant could always insist on a kind of preliminary trial to determine the competency and adequacy of the evidence before the grand jury. This is not required by the Fifth Amendment. An indictment returned by a legally constituted and unbiased grand jury, like an information drawn by the prosecutor, if valid on its face, is enough to call for trial of the charge on the merits. The Fifth Amendment requires nothing more.

Petitioner urges that this Court should exercise its power to supervise the administration of justice in federal courts and establish a rule permitting defendants to challenge indictments on the ground that they are not supported by adequate or competent evidence. No persuasive reasons are advanced for establishing such a rule. It would run counter to the whole history of the grand jury institution, in which laymen conduct their inquiries unfettered by technical rules. Neither justice nor the concept of a fair trial requires such a change. In a trial on the merits, defendants are entitled to a strict observance of all the rules designed to bring about a fair verdict. Defendants are not entitled, however, to a rule which would result in interminable delay but add nothing to the assurance of a fair trial.

Affirmed.

■ MR. JUSTICE CLARK and MR. JUSTICE HARLAN took no part in the consideration or decision of this case.

■ MR. JUSTICE BURTON, concurring.

I agree with the denial of the motion to quash the indictment. In my view, however, this case does not justify the breadth of the declarations made by the Court. I assume that this Court would not preclude an examination of grand-jury action to ascertain the existence of bias or prejudice in an indictment. Likewise, it seems to me that if it is shown that the grand jury had before it no substantial or rationally persuasive evidence upon which to base its indictment, that indictment should be quashed. To hold a person to answer to such an empty indictment for a capital or otherwise infamous federal crime robs the Fifth Amendment of much of its protective value to the private citizen.

* * *

NOTES

1. **Disclosing to the grand jury that testimony is hearsay.** Despite the principal case, some lower federal courts have been disturbed by what they view as excessive reliance upon hearsay before the grand jury. Concern has often focused on

whether the prosecutor deceived the grand jury by not disclosing the hearsay nature of the evidence or otherwise. In response to that concern, the Ninth Circuit has held that deliberate use of perjured testimony before a grand jury by the prosecution constitutes misconduct invalidating the indictment. See United States v. Samango, 607 F.2d 877 (9th Cir.1979). A leading case, United States v. Estepa, 471 F.2d 1132 (2d Cir.1972), involves an indictment returned on the basis of the testimony of a single police officer, who testified concerning a number of incidents in a manner not making clear that he lacked first-hand knowledge of these matters. The Second Circuit noted that it had "previously condemned the casual attitude with respect to the presentation of evidence to a grand jury manifested by the decision of the Assistant United States Attorney to rely on the testimony of the law enforcement officer who knew least, rather than subject the other officers, or himself, to some minor inconvenience...." 471 F.2d at 1135. Summarizing its position, the court stated:

> We have been willing to allow ample ... latitude in the needless use of hearsay, subject to only two provisos—that the prosecutor does not deceive grand jurors as to "the shoddy merchandise they are getting so they can seek something better if they wish," or that the case does not involve "a high probability that with eyewitness rather than hearsay testimony the grand jury would not have indicted."

471 F.2d at 1137. Because the government violated the first of these two provisos, the conviction was reversed and the case remanded with instructions to the District Court to dismiss the indictment without prejudice to the right of the government to seek another indictment.

Other circuits have disapproved of the *Estepa* position. United States v. Barone, 584 F.2d 118, 125 (6th Cir.1978) (court is "not disposed" to follow *Estepa,* but no need to reach issue because no deception of grand jury); United States v. Chanen, 549 F.2d 1306, 1311 (9th Cir.1977). Even in the Second Circuit, *Estepa* has been distinguished where deception was absent. Thus it was found inapplicable in United States v. James, 609 F.2d 36, 49 (2d Cir.1979), cert. denied 445 U.S. 905, 100 S.Ct. 1082, 63 L.Ed.2d 321 (1980), where substantial non-hearsay evidence was presented to the grand jury and the prosecutor told the grand jury that much of the evidence it had received was hearsay and that it could have those witnesses with first-hand knowledge of the matters brought before it if the grand jury wished. In a few jurisdictions, hearsay may not be relied upon by the grand jury. See People v. Jackson, 18 N.Y.2d 516, 277 N.Y.S.2d 263, 223 N.E.2d 790 (1966), holding that a confession of a codefendant implicating the defendant could not be considered by the grand jury.

2. **Illegally-obtained evidence.** Does or should it make any difference that the grand jury considered evidence that would under the Constitution be inadmissible at trial? In United States v. Calandra, 414 U.S. 338, 94 S.Ct. 613, 38 L.Ed.2d 561 (1974) the federal District Court granted Calandra's motion to suppress certain evidence on the ground that it had been seized in violation of Calandra's Fourth Amendment rights. It further ordered that Calandra need not answer questions which it was anticipated would be asked him by a grand jury investigating the matter if those questions were based on the suppressed evidence. Reversing, a majority of the Supreme Court, in an opinion by Justice Powell, explained:

> In deciding whether to extend the exclusionary rule to grand jury proceedings, we must weigh the potential injury to the historic role and functions of the grand jury against the potential benefits of the rule as applied in this context. It is evident that this extension of the exclusionary rule would seriously impede the grand jury. Because the grand jury does not finally adjudicate guilt or innocence, it has traditionally been allowed to pursue its

investigative and accusatorial functions unimpeded by the evidentiary and procedural restrictions applicable to a criminal trial. Permitting witnesses to invoke the exclusionary rule before a grand jury would precipitate adjudication of issues hitherto reserved for the trial on the merits and would delay and disrupt grand jury proceedings. Suppression hearings would halt the orderly progress of an investigation and might necessitate extended litigation of issues only tangentially related to the grand jury's primary objective. The probable result would be "protracted interruptions of grand jury proceedings." Gelbard v. United States, 408 U.S. 41, 70, 92 S.Ct. 2357, 2372, 33 L.Ed.2d 179 (1972) (White, J., concurring), effectively transforming them into preliminary trials on the merits. In some cases the delay might be fatal to the enforcement of the criminal law. . . . In sum, we believe that allowing a grand jury witness to invoke the exclusionary rule would unduly interfere with the effective and expeditious discharge of the grand jury's duties.

Against this potential damage to the role and functions of the grand jury, we must weigh the benefits to be derived from this proposed extension of the exclusionary rule. Suppression of the use of illegally seized evidence against the search victim in a criminal trial is thought to be an important method of effectuating the Fourth Amendment. But it does not follow that the Fourth Amendment requires adoption of every proposal that might deter police misconduct.

* * *

Any incremental deterrent effect which might be achieved by extending the rule to grand jury proceedings is uncertain at best. Whatever deterrence of police misconduct may result from the exclusion of illegally seized evidence from criminal trials, it is unrealistic to assume that application of the rule to grand jury proceedings would significantly further that goal. Such an extension would deter only police investigation consciously directed toward the discovery of evidence solely for use in a grand jury investigation. The incentive to disregard the requirement of the Fourth Amendment solely to obtain an indictment from a grand jury is substantially negated by the inadmissibility of the illegally seized evidence in a subsequent criminal prosecution of the search victim. For the most part, a prosecutor would be unlikely to request an indictment where a conviction could not be obtained. We therefore decline to embrace a view that would achieve a speculative and undoubtedly minimal advance in the deterrence of police misconduct at the expense of substantially impeding the role of the grand jury.

414 U.S. at 349–52, 94 S.Ct. at 620–22, 38 L.Ed.2d at 572–73. In Gelbard v. United States, supra, the Court held that the statutory exclusionary provision of the federal "wiretap" statute, 18 U.S.C. § 2515, entitled a grand jury witness to decline to answer questions that were the product of electronic surveillance conducted in violation of the statute. But the majority carefully distinguished the issue that would be presented by an effort to challenge an indictment as the product of a violation of the federal statute and noted evidence of Congressional intent to leave undisturbed by the statute the longstanding rule prohibiting attacks on indictments because of presentation of tainted evidence to the indicting grand jury. 408 U.S. at 60, 92 S.Ct. at 2367, 33 L.Ed.2d at 193–94. In re Ellsberg, 446 F.2d 954 (1st Cir.1971) held that the federal statute did not require dismissal of an indictment because the grand jury had considered evidence obtained in violation of the statute. But in State v. Mayes, 284 Md. 625, 399 A.2d 597 (1979) the Maryland court construed a state statute modeled on the federal act as mandating dismissal of an indictment because the grand jury considered evidence obtained in violation of the statute.

3. **Judicial review of indictment for probable cause.** In a few jurisdictions, the trial court is authorized to review the evidence supporting an indictment and to dismiss any indictment found unsupported by sufficient evidence. Colo.Rev. Stat. § 16–5–204(4)(k)(West 1998); N.Y.Crim.Proc.Law §§ 210.20, 210.30 (McKinney 1979). Describing the function of the trial court under the Colorado statute, the Colorado Supreme Court has stated:

> [T]he district court function in conducting the review of the grand jury record ... is much like the role of the court at a preliminary hearing and ... the same rule applies in determining the existence or absence of probable cause. The court must draw all inferences in favor of the prosecution and when there is a conflict in the testimony a question of fact exists for determination at trial.

People v. Summers, 197 Colo. 445, 447, 593 P.2d 969, 970 (1979). Bayless, Grand Jury Reform: The Colorado Experience, 67 A.B.A.J. 568, 572 (1981), commenting on practice under the Colorado statute, states that about 10 percent of indictments reviewed under the section have been dismissed. All but one of the dismissals, however, were followed by successful reindictments; in the remaining case, the grand jury had indicted against the recommendation of the prosecutor and no reindictment was sought.

4. **Exculpatory evidence.** Does a prosecutor have a duty to present exculpatory evidence to a grand jury? In Johnson v. Superior Court, 15 Cal.3d 248, 124 Cal.Rptr. 32, 539 P.2d 792 (1975) the California Supreme Court held that "when a district attorney seeking an indictment is aware of evidence reasonably tending to negate guilt, he is obligated ... to inform the grand jury of its nature and existence, so that the grand jury may exercise its power ... to order the evidence produced." 15 Cal.3d at 255, 124 Cal.Rptr. at 36, 539 P.2d at 796. But the court relied heavily upon Cal.Penal Code § 939.7, which provides that whenever a grand jury "has reason to believe that other evidence within its reach will explain away the charge, it shall order the evidence to be produced."

The Supreme Court considered federal prosecutors' duty to present exculpatory evidence to grand juries in United States v. Williams, 504 U.S. 36, 112 S.Ct. 1735, 118 L.Ed.2d 352 (1992). The Tenth Circuit had held, pursuant to what it regarded as the federal courts' "supervisory power," that federal prosecutors in possession of "substantial exculpatory evidence" concerning a suspect under consideration by a grand jury had a duty to present that evidence to the grand jury. Finding on the facts of *Williams* that the Government violated this duty and that there was at least a grave doubt as to whether the grand jury's decision to indict Williams was free from substantial influence by this violation, the lower courts required that Williams' indictment be dismissed. The Supreme Court reversed, and disapproved the Tenth Circuit's position. Federal grand juries, Justice Scalia explained for the Court, are "functionally independe[nt]" from the judicial branch, and therefore the federal judiciary has at most very limited supervisory power to fashion rules of procedure for grand jury proceedings. This limited power does not include the authority to promulgate rules that would "reshap[e] the grand jury institution." A rule requiring prosecutors to present exculpatory as well as incriminating evidence to grand juries would "alter the grand jury's historical role, transforming it from an accusatory to an adjudicatory body." The target of a grand jury investigation has no right to tender his "defense" to the grand jury. A grand jury can clearly refuse to hear exculpatory evidence. Federal courts cannot scrutinize the evidentiary support for a grand jury's decision to indict. Imposing upon a prosecutor a legal obligation to present to the grand jury exculpatory evidence in his possession would be incompatible with these aspects of the grand jury. If the courts will not review the evidentiary support for the grand jury's decision, for example, there is no sense in those same courts scrutinizing the prosecutor's presentation to the grand jury.

Moreover, a target could "circumnavigate the system by delivering [his exculpatory evidence] to the prosecutor, whereupon it would have to be passed on to the grand jury * * *." The requirement applied to the case below by the Tenth Circuit, then, was beyond the authority of that court to develop pursuant to its inherent supervisory authority. Williams had not contended, Justice Scalia noted, that the Fifth Amendment itself compelled a rule requiring prosecutorial disclosure of exculpatory evidence to grand juries.

Four members of the Court dissented in an opinion by Justice Stevens. Grand juries, he reasoned, are subject to the control of the courts. The Supreme Court therefore has authority to create and enforce limited rules applicable in grand jury proceedings. Rules prohibiting prosecutorial misconduct are within this authority. Grand juries serve in part to protect citizens against arbitrary and oppressive governmental action. Prohibitions against prosecutorial misconduct—such as misleading grand juries—do not alter the traditional role of grand juries but merely assure their ability to perform one of their traditional functions. The nature of a grand jury proceeding precludes a rule requiring prosecutors to ferret out and present all evidence bearing on a suspect's guilt or innocence.

> But that does not mean that the prosecutor may mislead the grand jury into believing that there is probable cause to indict by withholding clear evidence to the contrary. I thus agree with the Department of Justice that "when a prosecutor conducting a grand jury inquiry is personally aware of substantial evidence which directly negates the guilt of a subject of the investigation, the prosecutor must present or otherwise disclose such evidence to the grand jury before seeking an indictment against such a person." U.S. Dept. of Justice, United States Attorneys' Manual, Title 9, ch. 11, par. 9–11.233, 88 (1988).

504 U.S. at 69–70, 112 S.Ct. at 1754, 118 L.Ed.2d at 379 (Stevens, J., dissenting). To enforce this, he concluded, the federal courts have the power to dismiss indictments because the prosecutor violated this duty.

5.   **Target's right to appear before grand jury.** Several jurisdictions, in an apparent effort to improve the screening role of the grand jury, have given persons against whom an indictment is being considered a right to appear before the grand jury. N.M.Stat.Ann. § 31–6–11(B) provides:

> The target shall be notified of his target status and be given an opportunity to testify, if he desires to do so, unless the prosecutor determines that notification may result in flight, endanger other persons, obstruct justice, or the prosecutor is unable with reasonable diligence to notify such person.

This, of course, must be distinguished from the ability of an investigating grand jury to require a target to appear and the rights of such a target when compelled to appear; these are presented in Chapter 9, supra. Would one who is notified of his target status under this section be well-advised to seek an opportunity to appear before the grand jury? Bayless, Grand Jury Reform: The Colorado Experience, 67 A.B.A.J. 568, 570 (1981) notes that voluntary appearances by targets before the grand jury are rare under the Colorado statute.

6.   **Record of grand jury proceedings.** Jurisdictions vary widely in regard to the information kept on grand jury proceedings and concerning defendants' access to what information is kept. Rule 6(e)(1) of the Federal Rules of Criminal Procedure provides:

> All proceedings, except when the grand jury is deliberating or voting, shall be recorded stenographically or by an electronic recording device. An unintentional failure of any recording to reproduce all or any portion of the proceeding shall not affect the validity of the prosecution. The recording or reporter's notes or any transcript prepared therefrom shall remain in the custody or control of

the attorney for the government unless otherwise ordered by the court in a particular case.

Grand jurors, government attorneys, court reporters, and others—but not witnesses—are barred by Rule 6(e)(2) from disclosing matters occurring before a grand jury. Rule 6(e)(3)(B)(ii) permits disclosure of matters occurring before a grand jury:

> when permitted by a court at the request of the defendant, upon a showing that grounds may exist for a motion to dismiss the indictment because of matters occurring before the grand jury.

How does a defendant make such a showing without access to the information establishing what happened before the grand jury?

Some jurisdictions not only require that information be compiled but also that it be disclosed to the defense. Rule 12.8 of the Arizona Rules of Criminal Procedure, for example, requires that, within 20 days of the return of an indictment, a transcript of the court reporter's notes of the grand jury proceedings (except the deliberations) and the foreman's record of the votes on indictments be filed with the court and made available to the defense and the prosecution.

7. **Presence of persons who are not witnesses.** Rule 6(d) of the Federal Rules of Criminal Procedure provides that only specified persons, including "the witness under examination" may be present during grand jury proceedings. What legal consequences should ensue from failure to comply with that restriction? In United States v. Mechanik, 475 U.S. 66, 106 S.Ct. 938, 89 L.Ed.2d 50 (1986), two Government witnesses were present while each testified before the grand jury. Despite the exercise of diligence, defendants did not learn of this until after the trial had begun, when the information was disclosed as part of Jencks Act materials. The District Court overruled a motion to dismiss the indictment, but the Court of Appeals reversed on the ground that a violation of Rule 6(d) requires automatic reversal of any subsequent conviction. The Supreme Court, in an opinion authored by Justice Rehnquist, reversed. Expressly offering no opinion as to what the consequences of a violation should be when it is brought to the attention of the trial court before trial begins, the Court concluded that the subsequent convictions of the defendants rendered the violation harmless:

> The error involving Rule 6(d) in these cases had the theoretical potential to affect the grand jury's determination whether to indict these particular defendants for the offenses with which they were charged. But the petit jury's subsequent guilty verdict not only means that there was probable cause to believe that the defendants were guilty as charged, but that they are in fact guilty as charged beyond a reasonable doubt. Measured by the petit jury's verdict, then, any error in the grand jury proceedings connected with the charging decision was harmless beyond a reasonable doubt.

475 U.S. at 70, 106 S.Ct. at 941–42, 89 L.Ed.2d at 56.

Chief Justice Burger concurred on the ground the case should be controlled by Costello v. United States. Is there any practical difference between Justice Burger's position and that of the Court as applied to a violation brought to the attention of the District Court before trial begins?

Justice O'Connor, joined by Justices Brennan and Blackmun, concurred in the judgment on the ground that the test of harm should be whether the violation had a detrimental impact on the grand jury proceedings themselves. She argued that "the remedy of dismissal of the indictment is appropriate if it is established that the violation substantially influenced the grand jury's decision to indict, or if there is grave doubt as to whether it had such effect." 475 U.S. at 78, 106 S.Ct. at 945, 89 L.Ed.2d at 61. The Court's position, she complained, encourages trial courts to delay their rulings on motions to dismiss until after the jury's verdict. If the jury acquits, the question is moot and if it convicts any violation is harmless. Justice Marshall dissented on the ground, among others, that the Court's position renders Rule 6(d) "almost unenforceable."

8. **Prosecutorial misconduct before grand jury.** In Bank of Nova Scotia v. United States, 487 U.S. 250, 108 S.Ct. 2369, 101 L.Ed.2d 228 (1988), the Court considered the standard by which instances of prosecutorial misconduct before the grand jury should be assessed when a motion to dismiss an indictment is presented to the trial court before the trial begins. The indictment in this case was dismissed for various violations of Rule 6 of the Federal Rules of Criminal Procedure. The Court of Appeals reversed the dismissal and the Supreme Court, in an opinion by Justice Kennedy, affirmed. In the context of pretrial motions to dismiss, the Court adopted the standard proposed by Justice O'Connor in her concurring opinion in United States v. Mechanik that dismissal is appropriate "if it is established that the violation substantially influenced the grand jury's decision to indict" or if there is "grave doubt" that the decision to indict was free from the substantial influence of the violation. The Court concluded there was no evidence that the Rule 6 violations had any effect on the grand jury's decision to indict, in short, that the defendant was prejudiced in any fashion by the violations. Justice Marshall dissented, as he had in *Mechanik,* on the ground that "Rule 6 violations can be deterred and redressed effectively only by a *per se* rule of dismissal."

Under the combined effects of *Mechanik* and *Bank of Nova Scotia* what should an appellate court do if a trial court refuses to rule on a motion to dismiss filed before trial and the defendant is convicted at trial?

Petitioner in Midland Asphalt Corp. v. United States, 489 U.S. 794, 109 S.Ct. 1494, 103 L.Ed.2d 879 (1989) moved in the District Court for dismissal of an indictment because of a violation of Rule 6(e) prohibiting public disclosure of matters that occurred before a grand jury. The District Court denied the motion and the Court of Appeals dismissed the appeal on the ground it was interlocutory. The Supreme Court, in an unanimous opinion by Justice Scalia, affirmed the dismissal. The Court rejected the argument that the harmless error doctrine of United States v. Mechanik required provision of an interlocutory appeal since appeal after conviction was effectively eliminated. It also distinguished Abney v. United States in which it had provided for interlocutory appeal from trial court double jeopardy rulings. Finally, it rejected the argument that the Grand Jury Clause of the Fifth Amendment required interlocutory appeal in this situation: "Only a defect so fundamental that it causes the grand jury no longer to be a grand jury, or the indictment no longer to be an indictment, gives rise to the constitutional right not to be tried. An isolated breach of the traditional secrecy requirements does not do so." 489 U.S. at 802, 109 S.Ct. at 1500, 103 L.Ed.2d at 890.

CHAPTER 15

RIGHT TO A SPEEDY TRIAL

Analysis

Delay in administering the criminal justice system is, of course, a matter of major concern. It raises a number of matters of legal significance, some constitutional, others of statutory dimensions. The major—but not the only—federal constitutional provision addressing delay is the Sixth Amendment's speedy trial guarantee, made applicable to the states through the Fourteenth Amendment's Due Process clause. Klopfer v. North Carolina, 386 U.S. 213, 87 S.Ct. 988, 18 L.Ed.2d 1 (1967). Section A of this Chapter addresses the protections given both state and federal court defendants by this provision.

Delay issues have also been addressed by legislation. Congress responded to problems arising in the processing of federal criminal cases with the Federal Speedy Trial Act of 1974. A number of states have enacted similar legislation, some of it modeled in significant ways after the federal act. Section B of this Chapter addresses these statutes by focusing upon the Federal Speedy Trial Act and problems in its implementation.

A. SIXTH AMENDMENT SPEEDY TRIAL GUARANTEE

Barker v. Wingo

Supreme Court of the United States, 1972.
407 U.S. 514, 92 S.Ct. 2182, 33 L.Ed.2d 101.

■ MR. JUSTICE POWELL delivered the opinion of the Court.

Although a speedy trial is guaranteed the accused by the Sixth Amendment to the Constitution, this Court has dealt with that right on infrequent occasions. . . .

. . . [I]n none of these cases have we attempted to set out the criteria by which the speedy trial right is to be judged. 398 U.S., at 40–41, 90 S.Ct. at 1570. This case compels us to make such an attempt.

I.

On July 20, 1958, in Christian County, Kentucky, an elderly couple was beaten to death by intruders wielding an iron tire tool. Two suspects, Silas Manning and Willie Barker, the petitioner, were arrested shortly thereafter. The grand jury indicted them on September 15. Counsel was appointed on September 17, and Barker's trial was set for October 21. The Commonwealth had a stronger case against Manning, and it believed that Barker could not be convicted unless Manning testified against him. Manning was naturally unwilling to incriminate himself. Accordingly, on October 23, the day Silas Manning was brought to trial, the Commonwealth sought and obtained the first of what was to be a series of 16 continuances of Barker's trial. Barker made no objection. By first convicting Manning, the Commonwealth would remove possible problems of self-incrimination and would be able to assure his testimony against Barker.

The Commonwealth encountered more than a few difficulties in its prosecution of Manning. The first trial ended in a hung jury. A second trial resulted in a conviction, but the Kentucky Court of Appeals reversed because of the admission of evidence obtained by an illegal search. Manning v. Commonwealth, 328 S.W.2d 421 (1959). At his third trial, Manning was again convicted, and the Court of Appeals again reversed because the trial court had not granted a change of venue. Manning v. Commonwealth, 346 S.W.2d 755 (1960). A fourth trial resulted in a hung jury. Finally, after five trials, Manning was convicted, in March 1962, of murdering one victim, and after a sixth trial, in December 1962, he was convicted of murdering the other.

Manning Prosecution =

The Christian County Circuit Court holds three terms each year—in February, June, and September. Barker's initial trial was to take place in the September term of 1958. The first continuance postponed it until the February 1959 term. The second continuance was granted for one month only. Every term thereafter for as long as the Manning prosecutions were in process, the Commonwealth routinely moved to continue Barker's case to the next term. When the case was continued from the June 1959 term until the following September, Barker, having spent 10 months in jail, obtained his release by posting a $5,000 bond. He thereafter remained free in the community until his trial. Barker made no objection, through his counsel, to the first 11 continuances.

Barker Prosecution =

When on February 12, 1962, the Commonwealth moved for the twelfth time to continue the case until the following term, Barker's counsel filed a motion to dismiss the indictment. The motion to dismiss was denied two weeks later, and the Commonwealth's motion for a continuance was granted. The Commonwealth was granted further continuances in June 1962 and September 1962, to which Barker did not object.

In February 1963, the first term of court following Manning's final conviction, the Commonwealth moved to set Barker's trial for March 19. But on the day scheduled for trial, it again moved for a continuance until the June term. It gave as its reason the illness of the ex-sheriff who was the chief investigating officer in the case. To this continuance, Barker objected unsuccessfully.

The witness was still unable to testify in June, and the trial which had been set for June 19, was continued again until the September term over Barker's objection. This time the court announced that the case would be dismissed for lack of prosecution if it were not tried during the next term. The final trial date was set for October 9, 1963. On that date, Barker again moved to dismiss the indictment, and this time specified that his right to a speedy trial had been violated. The motion was denied; the trial commenced with Manning as the chief prosecution witness; Barker was convicted and given a life sentence.

Barker appealed his conviction to the Kentucky Court of Appeals, relying in part on his speedy trial claim. The court affirmed. Barker v. Commonwealth, 385 S.W.2d 671 (1964). In February 1970 Barker petitioned for habeas corpus in the United States District Court for the Western District of Kentucky. Although the District Court rejected the petition without holding a hearing, the court granted petitioner leave to appeal *in forma pauperis* and a certificate of probable cause to appeal. On appeal, the Court of Appeals for the Sixth Circuit affirmed the District Court. 442 F.2d 1141 (1971). It ruled that Barker had waived his speedy trial claim for the entire period before February 1963, the date on which the court believed he had first objected to the delay by filing a motion to dismiss. In this belief the court was mistaken, for the record reveals that the motion was filed in February 1962. The Commonwealth so conceded at oral argument before this Court. The court held further that the remaining period after the date on which Barker first raised his claim and before his trial—which it thought was only eight months but which was actually 20 months—was not unduly long. In addition, the court held that Barker had shown no resulting prejudice, and that the illness of the ex-sheriff was a valid justification for the delay. We granted Barker's petition for certiorari. 404 U.S. 1037, 92 S.Ct. 719, 30 L.Ed.2d 729 (1972).

II.

The right to a speedy trial is generically different from any of the other rights enshrined in the Constitution for the protection of the accused. In addition to the general concern that all accused persons be treated according to decent and fair procedures, there is a societal interest in providing a speedy trial which exists separate from, and at times in opposition to the interests of the accused. The inability of courts to provide a prompt trial has contributed to a large backlog of cases in urban courts which, among other things, enables defendants to negotiate more effectively for pleas of guilty to lesser offenses and otherwise manipulate the system. In addition, persons released on bond for lengthy periods awaiting trial have an opportunity to commit other crimes. It must be of little comfort to the residents of Christian County, Kentucky, to know that Barker was at large on bail for over four years while accused of a vicious and brutal murder of which he was ultimately convicted. Moreover, the longer an accused is free awaiting trial, the more tempting becomes his opportunity to jump bail and escape. Finally, delay between arrest and punishment may have a detrimental effect on rehabilitation.[1]

1. "[I]t is desirable that punishment   should follow offence as closely as possible;

If an accused cannot make bail, he is generally confined, as was Barker for 10 months, in a local jail. This contributes to the overcrowding and generally deplorable state of those institutions. Lengthy exposure to these conditions "has a destructive effect on human character and makes the rehabilitation of the individual offender much more difficult." At times the result may even be violent rioting. Finally, lengthy pretrial detention is costly. The cost of maintaining a prisoner in jail varies from $3 to $9 per day, and this amounts to millions across the Nation. In addition, society loses wages which might have been earned, and it must often support families of incarcerated breadwinners.

A second difference between the right to speedy trial and the accused's other constitutional rights is that deprivation of the right may work to the accused's advantage. Delay is not an uncommon defense tactic. As the time between the commission of the crime and trial lengthens, witnesses may become unavailable or their memories may fade. If the witnesses support the prosecution, its case will be weakened, sometimes seriously so. And it is the prosecution which carries the burden of proof. Thus, unlike the right to counsel or the right to be free from compelled self-incrimination, deprivation of the right to speedy trial does not *per se* prejudice the accused's ability to defend himself.

Finally, and perhaps most importantly, the right to speedy trial is a more vague concept than other procedural rights. It is, for example, impossible to determine with precision when the right has been denied. We cannot definitely say how long is too long in a system where justice is supposed to be swift but deliberate. As a consequence, there is no fixed point in the criminal process when the State can put the defendant to the choice of either exercising or waiving the right to a speedy trial. If, for example, the State moves for a 60–day continuance, granting that continuance is not a violation of the right to speedy trial unless the circumstances of the case are such that further delay would endanger the values the right protects. It is impossible to do more than generalize about when those circumstances exist. There is nothing comparable to the point in the process when a defendant exercises or waives his right to counsel or his right to a jury trial. Thus, as we recognized in **Beavers v. Haubert,** [198 U.S. 77, 25 S.Ct. 573, 49 L.Ed.2d 950 (1905)] any inquiry into a speedy trial claim necessitates a functional analysis of the right in the particular context of the case:

> "The right of a speedy trial is necessarily relative. It is consistent with delays and depends upon circumstances. It secures rights to a defendant. It does not preclude the rights of public justice." 198 U.S., at 87, 25 S.Ct. at 576, 49 L.Ed. 950.

The amorphous quality of the right also leads to the unsatisfactorily severe remedy of dismissal of the indictment when the right has been deprived. This is indeed a serious consequence because it means that a defendant who may be guilty of a serious crime will go free, without having

for its impression upon the minds of men is weakened by distance, and, besides, distance adds to the uncertainty of punishment, by affording new chances of escape." J. Bentham, The Theory of Legislation 326 (Ogden ed. 1931).

been tried. Such a remedy is more serious than an exclusionary rule or a reversal for a new trial, but it is the only possible remedy.

III.

Perhaps because the speedy trial right is so slippery, two rigid approaches are urged upon us as ways of eliminating some of the uncertainty which courts experience in protecting the right. The first suggestion is that we hold that the Constitution requires a criminal defendant to be offered a trial within a specified time period. The result of such a ruling would have the virtue of clarifying when the right is infringed and of simplifying courts' application of it. Recognizing this, some legislatures have enacted laws, and some courts have adopted procedural rules which more narrowly define the right. The United States Court of Appeals for the Second Circuit has promulgated rules for the district courts in that Circuit establishing that the government must be ready for trial within six months of the date of arrest, except in unusual circumstances, or the charge will be dismissed. This type of rule is also recommended by the American Bar Association.

But such a result would require this Court to engage in legislative or rulemaking activity, rather than in the adjudicative process to which we should confine our efforts. We do not establish procedural rules for the States, except when mandated by the Constitution. We find no constitutional basis for holding that the speedy trial right can be quantified into a specified number of days or months. The States, of course, are free to prescribe a reasonable period consistent with constitutional standards, but our approach must be less precise.

The second suggested alternative would restrict consideration of the right to those cases in which the accused has demanded a speedy trial. Most States have recognized what is loosely referred to as the "demand rule," although eight States reject it. It is not clear, however, precisely what is meant by that term. Although every federal court of appeals that has considered the question has endorsed some kind of demand rule, some have regarded the rule within the concept of waiver, whereas others have viewed it as a factor to be weighed in assessing whether there has been a deprivation of the speedy trial right. We shall refer to the former approach as the demand-waiver doctrine. The demand-waiver doctrine provides that a defendant waives any consideration of his right to speedy trial for any period prior to which he has not demanded a trial. Under this rigid approach, a prior demand is a necessary condition to the consideration of the speedy trial right. This essentially was the approach the Sixth Circuit took below.

Such an approach, by presuming waiver of a fundamental right from inaction, is inconsistent with this Court's pronouncements on waiver of constitutional rights. The Court has defined waiver as "an intentional relinquishment or abandonment of a known right or privilege." Johnson v. Zerbst, 304 U.S. 458, 464, 58 S.Ct. 1019, 1023, 82 L.Ed. 1461 (1938). Courts should "indulge every reasonable presumption against waiver," Aetna Ins. Co. v. Kennedy, 301 U.S. 389, 393, 57 S.Ct. 809, 812, 81 L.Ed. 1177 (1937), and they should "not presume acquiescence in the loss of fundamental rights," Ohio Bell Tel. Co. v. Public Utilities Comm'n, 301 U.S. 292, 307, 57

S.Ct. 724, 731, 81 L.Ed. 1093 (1937). In Carnley v. Cochran, 369 U.S. 506, 82 S.Ct. 884, 8 L.Ed.2d 70 (1962), we held:

> "Presuming waiver from a silent record is impermissible. The record must show, or there must be an allegation and evidence which show, that an accused was offered counsel but intelligently and understandably rejected the offer. Anything less is not waiver." Id., at 516, 82 S.Ct., at 890.

The Court has ruled similarly with respect to waiver of other rights designed to protect the accused.

In excepting the right to speedy trial from the rule of waiver we have applied to other fundamental rights, courts that have applied the demand-waiver rule have relied on the assumption that delay usually works for the benefit of the accused and on the absence of any readily ascertainable time in the criminal process for a defendant to be given the choice of exercising or waiving his right. But it is not necessarily true that delay benefits the defendant. There are cases in which delay appreciably harms the defendant's ability to defend himself. Moreover, a defendant confined to jail prior to trial is obviously disadvantaged by delay as is a defendant released on bail but unable to lead a normal life because of community suspicion and his own anxiety.

The nature of the speedy trial right does make it impossible to pinpoint a precise time in the process when the right must be asserted or waived, but that fact does not argue for placing the burden of protecting the right solely on defendants. A defendant has no duty to bring himself to trial; the State has that duty as well as the duty of insuring that the trial is consistent with due process. Moreover, for the reasons earlier expressed, society has a particular interest in bringing swift prosecutions, and society's representatives are the ones who should protect that interest.

It is also noteworthy that such a rigid view of the demand-waiver rule places defense counsel in an awkward position. Unless he demands a trial early and often, he is in danger of frustrating his client's right. If counsel is willing to tolerate some delay because he finds it reasonable and helpful in preparing his own case, he may be unable to obtain a speedy trial for his client at the end of that time. Since under the demand-waiver rule no time runs until the demand is made, the government will have whatever time is otherwise reasonable to bring the defendant to trial after a demand has been made. Thus, if the first demand is made three months after arrest in a jurisdiction which prescribes a six-month rule, the prosecution will have a total of nine months—which may be wholly unreasonable under the circumstances. The result in practice is likely to be either an automatic, *pro forma* demand made immediately after appointment of counsel or delays which but for the demand-waiver rule, would not be tolerated. Such a result is not consistent with the interests of defendants, society, or the Constitution.

We reject, therefore, the rule that a defendant who fails to demand a speedy trial forever waives his right. This does not mean, however, that the defendant has no responsibility to assert his right. We think the better rule is that the defendant's assertion of or failure to assert his right to a speedy trial is one of the factors to be considered in an inquiry into the deprivation of the right. Such a formulation avoids the rigidities of the demand-waiver rule and the resulting possible unfairness in its application. It allows the trial court to exercise a judicial discretion based on the circumstances, including due consideration of any applicable formal procedural rule. It would permit, for example, a court to attach a different weight to a situation in which the defendant knowingly fails to object from a situation in which his attorney acquiesces in long delay without adequately informing his client, or from a situation in which no counsel is appointed. It would also allow a court to weigh the frequency and force of the objections as opposed to attaching significant weight to a purely *pro forma* objection.

In ruling that a defendant has some responsibility to assert a speedy trial claim, we do not depart from our holdings in other cases concerning the waiver of fundamental rights, in which we have placed the entire responsibility on the prosecution to show that the claimed waiver was knowingly and voluntarily made. Such cases have involved rights which must be exercised or waived at a specific time or under clearly identifiable circumstances, such as the rights to plead not guilty, to demand a jury trial, to exercise the privilege against self-incrimination, and to have the assistance of counsel. We have shown above that the right to a speedy trial is unique in its uncertainty as to when and under what circumstances it must be asserted or may be deemed waived. But the rule we announce today, which comports with constitutional principles, places the primary burden on the courts and the prosecutors to assure that cases are brought to trial. We hardly need add that if delay is attributable to the defendant, then his waiver may be given effect under standard waiver doctrine, the demand rule aside.

We, therefore, reject both of the inflexible approaches—the fixed-time period because it goes further than the Constitution requires; the demand-waiver rule because it is insensitive to a right which we have deemed fundamental. The approach we accept is a balancing test, in which the conduct of both the prosecution and the defendant are weighed.[2]

IV.

A balancing test necessarily compels courts to approach speedy trial cases on an *ad hoc* basis. We can do little more than identify some of the factors which courts should assess in determining whether a particular defendant has been deprived of his right. Though some might express them in different ways, we identify four such factors: Length of delay, the reason for the delay, the defendant's assertion of his right, and prejudice to the defendant.

The length of the delay is to some extent a triggering mechanism. Until there is some delay which is presumptively prejudicial, there is no necessity for inquiry into the other factors that go into the balance. Nevertheless, because of the imprecision of the right to speedy trial, the length of delay that will provoke such an inquiry is necessarily dependent

---

2. Nothing we have said should be interpreted as disapproving a presumptive rule adopted by a court in the exercise of its supervisory powers which establishes a fixed time period within which cases must normally be brought. . . .

upon the peculiar circumstances of the case.[3] To take but one example, the delay that can be tolerated for an ordinary street crime is considerably less than for a serious, complex conspiracy charge.

Closely related to length of delay is the reason the government assigns to justify the delay. Here, too, different weights should be assigned to different reasons. A deliberate attempt to delay the trial in order to hamper the defense should be weighted heavily against the government.[4] A more neutral reason such as negligence or overcrowded courts should be weighted less heavily but nevertheless should be considered since the ultimate responsibility for such circumstances must rest with the government rather than with the defendant. Finally, a valid reason, such as a missing witness, should serve to justify appropriate delay.

We have already discussed the third factor, the defendant's responsibility to assert his right. Whether and how a defendant asserts his right is closely related to the other factors we have mentioned. The strength of his efforts will be affected by the length of the delay, to some extent by the reason for the delay, and most particularly by the personal prejudice, which is not always readily identifiable, that he experiences. The more serious the deprivation, the more likely a defendant is to complain. The defendant's assertion of his speedy trial right, then, is entitled to strong evidentiary weight in determining whether the defendant is being deprived of the right. We emphasize that failure to assert the right will make it difficult for a defendant to prove that he was denied a speedy trial.

A fourth factor is prejudice to the defendant. Prejudice, of course, should be assessed in the light of the interests of defendants which the speedy trial right was designed to protect. This Court has identified three such interests: (i) to prevent oppressive pretrial incarceration; (ii) to minimize anxiety and concern of the accused; and (iii) to limit the possibility that the defense will be impaired.[5] Of these, the most serious is the last, because the inability of a defendant adequately to prepare his case skews the fairness of the entire system. If witnesses die or disappear during a delay, the prejudice is obvious. There is also prejudice if defense witnesses are unable to recall accurately events of the distant past. Loss of memory, however, is not always reflected in the record because what has been forgotten can rarely be shown.

We have discussed previously the societal disadvantages of lengthy pretrial incarceration, but obviously the disadvantages for the accused who cannot obtain his release are even more serious. The time spent in jail awaiting trial has a detrimental impact on the individual. It often means

---

3. For example, the First Circuit thought a delay of nine months overly long, absent a good reason, in a case that depended on eyewitness testimony. United States v. Butler, 426 F.2d 1275, 1277 (1970).

4. We have indicated on previous occasions that it is improper for the prosecution intentionally to delay "to gain some tactical advantage over [defendants] or to harass them." United States v. Marion, 404 U.S. 307, 325, 92 S.Ct. 455, 466, 30 L.Ed.2d 468 (1971).

5. In Klopfer v. North Carolina, 386 U.S. 213, 221–222, 87 S.Ct. 988, 992–993, 18 L.Ed.2d 1 (1967), we indicated that a defendant awaiting trial on bond might be subjected to public scorn, deprived of employment, and chilled in the exercise of his right to speak for, associate with, and participate in unpopular political causes.

loss of a job; it disrupts family life; and it enforces idleness. Most jails offer little or no recreational or rehabilitative programs. The time spent in jail is simply dead time. Moreover, if a defendant is locked up, he is hindered in his ability to gather evidence, contact witnesses, or otherwise prepare his defense. Imposing those consequences on anyone who has not yet been convicted is serious. It is especially unfortunate to impose them on those persons who are ultimately found to be innocent. Finally, even if an accused is not incarcerated prior to trial, he is still disadvantaged by restraints on his liberty and by living under a cloud of anxiety, suspicion, and often hostility. . . .

We regard none of the four factors identified above as either a necessary or sufficient condition to the finding of a deprivation of the right of speedy trial. Rather, they are related factors and must be considered together with such other circumstances as may be relevant. In sum, these factors have no talismanic qualities; courts must still engage in a difficult and sensitive balancing process. But, because we are dealing with a fundamental right of the accused, this process must be carried out with full recognition that the accused's interest in a speedy trial is specifically affirmed in the Constitution.

V.

The difficulty of the task of balancing these factors is illustrated by this case, which we consider to be close. It is clear that the length of delay between arrest and trial—well over five years—was extraordinary. Only seven months of that period can be attributed to a strong excuse, the illness of the ex-sheriff who was in charge of the investigation. Perhaps some delay would have been permissible under ordinary circumstances, so that Manning could be utilized as a witness in Barker's trial, but more than four years was too long a period, particularly since a good part of that period was attributable to the Commonwealth's failure or inability to try Manning under circumstances that comported with due process.

Two counterbalancing factors, however, outweigh these deficiencies. The first is that prejudice was minimal. Of course, Barker was prejudiced to some extent by living for over four years under a cloud of suspicion and anxiety. Moreover, although he was released on bond for most of the period, he did spend 10 months in jail before trial. But there is no claim that any of Barker's witnesses died or otherwise became unavailable owing to the delay. The trial transcript indicates only two very minor lapses of memory—one on the part of a prosecution witness—which were in no way significant to the outcome.

More important than the absence of serious prejudice, is the fact that Barker did not want a speedy trial. Counsel was appointed for Barker immediately after his indictment and represented him throughout the period. No question is raised as to the competency of such counsel. Despite the fact that counsel had notice of the motions for continuances, the record shows no action whatever taken between October 21, 1958, and February 12, 1962, that could be construed as the assertion of the speedy trial right. On the latter date, in response to another motion for continuance, Barker moved to dismiss the indictment. The record does not show on what ground this motion was based, although it is clear that no alternative motion was made for an immediate trial. Instead the record strongly suggests that while he hoped to take advantage of the delay in which he had acquiesced, and thereby obtain a dismissal of the charges, he definitely did not want to be tried. Counsel conceded as much at oral argument:

> "Your honor, I would concede that Willie Mae Barker probably—I don't know this for a fact—probably did not want to be tried. I don't think any man wants to be tried. And I don't consider this a liability on his behalf. I don't blame him." Tr. of Oral Arg. 39.

The probable reason for Barker's attitude was that he was gambling on Manning's acquittal. The evidence was not very strong against Manning, as the reversals and hung juries suggest, and Barker undoubtedly thought that if Manning were acquitted, he would never be tried. Counsel also conceded this:

> "Now, it's true that the reason for this delay was the Commonwealth of Kentucky's desire to secure the testimony of the accomplice, Silas Manning. And it's true that if Silas Manning were never convicted, Willie Mae Barker would never have been convicted. We concede this." Id., at 15.

That Barker was gambling on Manning's acquittal is also suggested by his failure, following the *pro forma* motion to dismiss filed in February 1962, to object to the Commonwealth's next two motions for continuances. Indeed, it was not until March 1963, after Manning's convictions were final, that Barker, having lost his gamble, began to object to further continuances. At that time, the Commonwealth's excuse was the illness of the ex-sheriff, which Barker has conceded justified the further delay.

We do not hold that there may never be a situation in which an indictment may be dismissed on speedy trial grounds where the defendant has failed to object to continuances. There may be a situation in which the defendant was represented by incompetent counsel, was severely prejudiced, or even cases in which the continuances were granted *ex parte*. But barring extraordinary circumstances, we would be reluctant indeed to rule that a defendant was denied this constitutional right on a record that strongly indicates as does this one, that the defendant did not want a speedy trial. We hold, therefore, that Barker was not deprived of his due process right to a speedy trial.

The judgment of the Court of Appeals is affirmed.

Affirmed.

MR. JUSTICE WHITE, with whom MR. JUSTICE BRENNAN joins, concurring.

* * *

[M]any defendants will believe that time is on their side and will prefer to suffer whatever disadvantages delay may entail. But, for those who desire an early trial, these personal factors should prevail if the only countervailing considerations offered by the State are those connected with crowded dockets and prosecutorial case loads. A defendant desiring a speedy trial, therefore, should have it within some reasonable time; and only special circumstances presenting a more pressing public need with respect to the case itself should suffice to justify delay. Only if such special considerations are in the case and if they outweigh the inevitable personal prejudice resulting from delay would it be necessary to consider whether there has been or would be prejudice to the defense at trial. . . .

Of course, cases will differ among themselves as to the allowable time between charge and trial so as to permit prosecution and defense adequately to prepare their case. But unreasonable delay in run-of-the-mill criminal cases cannot be justified by simply asserting that the public resources provided by the State's criminal-justice system are limited and that each case must await its turn. As the Court points out, this approach also subverts the State's own goals in seeking to enforce its criminal laws.

NOTES

1. **When the right to a speedy trial begins.** In United States v. Marion, 404 U.S. 307, 92 S.Ct. 455, 30 L.Ed.2d 468 (1971), the Supreme Court held that the Sixth Amendment's speedy trial protection does not begin until "either a formal indictment or information or else the actual restraints imposed by arrest and holding to answer a criminal charge." 404 U.S. at 320, 92 S.Ct. at 463, 30 L.Ed.2d at 479. Only after arrest or charge, reasoned the Court, does the defendant face the major evils that are the concern of the constitutional provision: loss of liberty, disruption of employment, drain on financial resources, curtailment of associations, public obloquy and anxiety. Earlier delay, the Court acknowledged, may interfere with a defendant's eventual ability to defend himself against criminal charges. But this possibility of prejudice does not warrant extending the protection of the speedy trial clause to pre-charge or pre-arrest situations. The Court did comment that some constitutional protection against pre-arrest or charge delay did exist. "[T]he Government concedes," it noted, "that the Due Process Clause . . . would require dismissal of the indictment if it were shown at trial that the pre-indictment delay in this case caused substantial prejudice to appellees' rights to a fair trial and that the delay was an intentional device to gain tactical advantage over the accused." 404 U.S. at 324, 92 S.Ct. at 465, 30 L.Ed.2d at 481. Since the appellees had relied entirely upon the possibility of prejudice at trial and had made no effort to show either actual prejudice or a delay intended to secure tactical advantage for the Government, the Court found no need to "determine when and in what circumstances actual prejudice resulting from pre-accusation delays requires the dismissal of the prosecution." Id.

2. **Prejudice to the defense.** The question how the fourth *Barker* factor—prejudice to the defense—should be analyzed was addressed by the Court in Doggett v. United States, 505 U.S. 647, 112 S.Ct. 2686, 120 L.Ed.2d 520 (1992). In 1980, Doggett was indicted on a federal drug conspiracy charge. When officers sought to arrest him three weeks later, they were told by his mother that he had left for Colombia four days earlier. The arrest warrant was entered on various law enforcement computer databases, including NCIC, but no further steps of substance were taken to apprehend him. In 1982, Doggett returned to the United States, married, earned a college degree, found a steady job as a computer operations manager, lived openly under his own name, and stayed within the law. In 1988, federal marshals ran a credit check on several thousand persons wanted on arrest warrants and discovered Doggett's whereabouts. He was promptly located and arrested. Doggett filed a motion to dismiss the indictment for speedy trial violation.

The United States District Court denied Doggett's speedy trial claim. He entered a conditional plea of guilty and appealed. The Eleventh Circuit affirmed the conviction. The United States Supreme Court, in an opinion by Justice Souter, reversed.

The length of the delay was well over the presumptively prejudicial one year delay. As to the reason for the delay, the government was negligent in failing to apprehend him at least during the 6 year period when he was living openly under his own name in the United States. As to prompt assertion of the right to a speedy trial, Doggett claimed that he did not know of the indictment until his arrest in 1988 and in the stipulation entered with the guilty plea, the government conceded it had no contradictory information.

As to prejudice from the delay, Doggett was unable to show that his defense was prejudiced from lost exculpatory evidence. However, "excessive delay presumptively compromises the reliability of a trial in ways that neither party can prove or, for that matter, identify." If the government had used diligence in apprehending Doggett, he would have been required to show actual prejudice to prevail. On the other hand, if Doggett could have shown intentional delay by the government to obtain a tactical advantage, no showing of prejudice at all would have been required of him. The delay here was neither, but was negligent. The Court concluded,

> Although negligence is obviously to be weighed more lightly than a deliberate intent to harm the accused's defense, it still falls on the wrong side of the divide between acceptable and unacceptable reasons for delaying a criminal prosecution once it has begun. And such is the nature of the prejudice presumed that the weight we assign to official negligence compounds over time as the presumption of evidentiary prejudice grows. Thus, our toleration of such negligence varies inversely with its protractedness * * * and its consequent threat to the fairness of the accused's trial. Condoning prolonged and unjustifiable delays in prosecution would both penalize many defendants for the state's fault and simply encourage the government to gamble with the interests of criminal suspects assigned a low prosecutorial priority. The Government, indeed, can hardly complain too loudly, for persistent neglect in concluding a criminal prosecution indicates an uncommonly feeble interest in bringing an accused to justice; the more weight the Government attaches to securing a conviction, the harder it will try to get it.

> [T]o warrant granting relief, negligence unaccompanied by particularized trial prejudice must have lasted longer than negligence demonstrably causing such prejudice * * *. When the Government's negligence * * * causes delay six times as long as that generally sufficient to trigger judicial review * * * and when the presumption of prejudice, albeit unspecified, is neither extenuated, as by the defendant's acquiescence, * * * nor persuasively rebutted, the defendant is entitled to relief.

505 U.S. at 657–58, 112 S.Ct. at 2693–94, 120 L.Ed.2d at 531–32. Justice O'Connor, dissenting, characterized the harm to Doggett from the delay as "speculative." She also noted that the delay harmed the Government's ability to discharge its burden of proof. Justice Thomas, joined by The Chief Justice and Justice Scalia, dissented on the ground that the Sixth Amendment guarantee of a speedy trial does not protect against prejudice to the defense.

3. **What counts as delay?** If charges are filed, dismissed, and later reinstated, should the period between the dismissal and reinstatement count in determining whether the constitutional right to a speedy trial has been violated? In United States v. MacDonald, 456 U.S. 1, 102 S.Ct. 1497, 71 L.Ed.2d 696 (1982) the respondent, a military officer, was charged by military authorities with the murder of his wife and two daughters. Six months later, these charges were dismissed. Over five years later, MacDonald was indicted by civilian authorities for the murders and convicted. The Court of Appeals reversed the convictions on the ground his right to

a speedy trial had been violated. The Supreme Court, in an opinion authored by the Chief Justice, reversed. The majority likened the circumstances when charges have been dismissed to those before any charges have been filed. As in United States v. Marion, then, the speedy trial protection has no applicability during that time period: "[T]he Speedy Trial Clause has no application after the Government, acting in good faith, formally drops charges. Any undue delay after charges are dismissed, like any delay before charges are filed, must be scrutinized under the Due Process Clause, not the Speedy Trial Clause." 456 U.S. at 7, 102 S.Ct. at 1501, 71 L.Ed.2d at 703. The majority minimized the role of the speedy trial provision in preventing prejudice to the defense from pre-trial delay:

> The Sixth Amendment right to a speedy trial is ... not primarily intended to prevent prejudice to the defense caused by passage of time; that interest is protected primarily by the Due Process Clause and by statutes of limitations. The speedy trial guarantee is designed to minimize the possibility of lengthy incarceration prior to trial, to reduce the lesser, but nevertheless substantial, impairment of liberty imposed on an accused while released on bail, and to shorten the disruption of life caused by arrest and the presence of unresolved criminal charges.

456 U.S. at 8, 102 S.Ct. at 1502, 71 L.Ed.2d at 704. Justice Marshall, in a dissent joined in by Justices Brennan and Blackmun, argued that the speedy trial provision should be applied during the time charges are dismissed and that under the majority opinion "the government could indefinitely delay a second prosecution for no reason, or even in bad faith, if the defendant is unable to show actual prejudice at trial." 456 U.S. at 21, 102 S.Ct. at 1508, 71 L.Ed.2d at 712. Justice Stevens agreed with the approach of the dissenters but on these facts would not have found the respondent's speedy trial rights had been violated.

4. **Justification for delay.** In United States v. Loud Hawk, 474 U.S. 302, 106 S.Ct. 648, 88 L.Ed.2d 640 (1986), the District Court dismissed the indictment with prejudice, from which the Government appealed. After a delay of over 46 months, during which the appellate and subsequent trial court processes worked their way, respondents stood re-indicted before the District Court, the appellate courts having ruled for the Government. Respondents claimed their re-indictment was vindictive, a position supported as to one respondent and rejected as to others by the District Court. Both sides appealed from this decision, and the Government ultimately prevailed. During pendency of these appeals, respondents were released on their own recognizances. Back again before the District Court, respondents successfully claimed their rights to a speedy trial had been violated and the indictments were dismissed. At this point 90 months had passed from the time of respondents' arrests and initial charges. The Government appealed to the Court of Appeals, this time unsuccessfully. The United States Supreme Court, in an opinion authored by Justice Powell, reversed the decision of the Court of Appeals.

The first round of appeals, during which time respondents were not charged with any offenses, do not count against the Government under *MacDonald* because respondents were not incarcerated or subjected to other substantial restrictions on their liberty during that period. The pendency of appellate processes designed to test the correctness of the trial court's dismissal of charges does not take this case from the effect of *MacDonald*. As to the appeals and cross-appeals on the question of vindictive prosecution, the Court concluded the Government's position was so strong that delay to effectuate its appeal was justified. The respondent's appellate claim as to vindictive prosecution, by contrast, was "so lacking in merit that the time consumed by this appeal should not weigh in support of respondents' speedy trial claim." 475 U.S. at 317, 106 S.Ct. at 657, 88 L.Ed.2d at 655. Justice Marshall, joined by Justices Brennan, Blackmun, and Stevens, dissented.

5. **Persons incarcerated in other cases.** Persons already incarcerated pursuant to a conviction for a different offense present a special problem, which is aggravated when the pending charge and the offense of which the person has been convicted arise in different jurisdictions. In Smith v. Hooey, 393 U.S. 374, 89 S.Ct. 575, 21 L.Ed.2d 607 (1969), the Supreme Court held that the right of speedy trial applied to Texas state charges against Smith, who was serving a sentence in a federal correctional institution. Repeated demands by Smith that he be tried on the state indictment were ignored for six years. Holding that the Sixth Amendment right to speedy trial applied to the case, the Court reasoned:

[T]his constitutional guarantee has universally been thought essential to protect at least three basic demands of criminal justice in the Anglo–American legal system: "[1] to prevent undue and oppressive incarceration prior to trial, [2] to minimize anxiety and concern accompanying public accusation and [3] to limit the possibilities that long delay will impair the ability of an accused to defend himself." United States v. Ewell, 383 U.S. 116, 120, 86 S.Ct. 773, 776, 15 L.Ed.2d 627. These demands are both aggravated and compounded in the case of an accused who is imprisoned by another jurisdiction.

At first blush it might appear that a man already in prison under a lawful sentence is hardly in a position to suffer from "undue and oppressive incarceration prior to trial." But the fact is that delay in bringing such a person to trial on a pending charge may ultimately result in as much oppression as is suffered by one who is jailed without bail upon an untried charge. First, the possibility that the defendant already in prison might receive a sentence at least partially concurrent with the one he is serving may be forever lost if trial of the pending charge is postponed. Secondly, under procedures now widely practiced, the duration of his present imprisonment may be increased, and the conditions under which he must serve his sentence greatly worsened, by the pendency of another criminal charge outstanding against him.

And while it might be argued that a person already in prison would be less likely than others to be affected by "anxiety and concern accompanying public accusation," there is reason to believe that an outstanding untried charge (of which even a convict may, of course, be innocent) can have fully as depressive an effect upon a prisoner as upon a person who is at large. . . .

Finally, it is self-evident that "the possibilities that long delay will impair the ability of an accused to defend himself" are markedly increased when the accused is incarcerated in another jurisdiction. Confined in a prison, perhaps far from the place where the offense covered by the outstanding charge allegedly took place, his ability to confer with potential defense witnesses, or even to keep track of their whereabouts, is obviously impaired. And, while "evidence and witnesses disappear, memories fade, and events lose their perspective," a man isolated in prison is powerless to exert his own investigative efforts to mitigate these erosive effects of the passage of time.

* * *

[W]e hold today that the Sixth Amendment right to a speedy trial may not be dispensed with . . . lightly. . . . Upon the petitioner's demand, Texas had a constitutional duty to make a diligent good-faith effort to bring him before the Harris County court for trial.

393 U.S. at 378–83, 89 S.Ct. at 577–79, 21 L.Ed.2d at 611–14. See also Dickey v. Florida, 398 U.S. 30, 90 S.Ct. 1564, 26 L.Ed.2d 26 (1970). If a jurisdiction, despite "diligent, good-faith effort," was unsuccessful in securing a defendant for trial in this context, would delay be excused?

6. **Interstate Agreement on Detainers.** The Sixth Amendment issues discussed by Smith v. Hooey are also dealt with by the Interstate Agreement on Detainers, enacted by the United States and 48 states. Under the Agreement, a prisoner in one member state has a right to be tried by another member state "within one hundred and eighty days after he shall have caused to be delivered" to the state filing the charges a demand for a speedy trial. Failure to observe the time requirement results in dismissal of the charges with prejudice. In Fex v. Michigan, 507 U.S. 43, 113 S.Ct. 1085, 122 L.Ed.2d 406 (1993), the Supreme Court, in an opinion by Justice Scalia, held that the 180 day time period begins to run from the time the demand is received by the court and prosecutor in the State in which the charges had been filed, rather than from the time the prisoner gave the demand to his warden for transmittal. The opinion, based largely on textual analysis, also concluded that the burdens of non-deliverance of the demand or of delay in deliverance under the Court's interpretation were less than the burdens imposed on society should the petitioner's position be adopted. The latter might result in preclusion of prosecution in a case in which the prosecutor had received no timely notice of demand or even no notice at all of demand. Justice Blackmun, joined by Justice Stevens, dissented.

7. **Remedy for violation of speedy trial right.** The appropriate judicial response to a finding that prompt disposition requirements have been violated is a difficult issue. In Strunk v. United States, 412 U.S. 434, 93 S.Ct. 2260, 37 L.Ed.2d 56 (1973), the Court of Appeals had found an unjustified delay of 259 days between indictment and trial, during which time petitioner had been incarcerated serving a sentence on another conviction. But rather than order dismissal of the charge, it remanded the case with directions to the trial court to credit the defendant's sentence for a time equal to the improper delay. The Supreme Court unanimously reversed, commenting:

The Court of Appeals [stated]:

"The remedy for a violation of this constitutional right has traditionally been the dismissal of the indictment or the vacation of the sentence. Perhaps the severity of that remedy has caused courts to be extremely hesitant in finding a failure to afford a speedy trial. Be that as it may, we know of no reason why less drastic relief may not be granted in appropriate cases. Here no question is raised about the sufficiency of evidence showing defendant's guilt, and, as we have said, he makes no claim of having been prejudiced in presenting his defense. In these circumstances, the vacation of the sentence and a dismissal of the indictment would seem inappropriate. Rather, we think the proper remedy is to remand the case to the district court with direction to enter an order instructing the Attorney General to credit the defendant with the period of time elapsing between the return of the indictment and the date of the arraignment. ..." 467 F.2d, at 973.

It is correct, as the Court of Appeals noted, that *Barker* [v. Wingo, 407 U.S. 514, 92 S.Ct. 2182, 33 L.Ed.2d 101 (1972)] prescribes "flexible" standards based on practical considerations. However, that aspect of the holding in *Barker* was directed at the process of determining *whether* a denial of speedy trial had occurred; it did not deal with the remedy for denial of this right. By definition, such denial is unlike some of the other guarantees of the Sixth Amendment. For example, failure to afford a public trial, an impartial jury, notice of charges, or compulsory service can ordinarily be cured by providing those guaranteed rights in a new trial. The speedy trial guarantee recognizes that a prolonged delay may subject the accused to an emotional stress that can be presumed to result in the ordinary person from uncertainties in the prospect of facing public trial or of receiving a sentence longer than, or consecutive to, the one he is presently serving—uncertainties that a prompt trial removes. Smith v. Hooey, 393 U.S., at 379, 89 S.Ct., at 577, 578; United States v. Ewell, 383 U.S. 116, 120, 86 S.Ct. 773, 776, 15 L.Ed.2d 627 (1966). We recognize, as the Court did in Smith v. Hooey, that the stress from a delayed trial may be less on a prisoner already confined, whose family ties and employment have been interrupted, but other factors such as the prospect of rehabilitation may also be affected adversely. The remedy chosen by the Court of Appeals does not deal with these difficulties.

The Government's reliance on *Barker* to support the remedy fashioned by the Court of Appeals is further undermined when we examine the Court's opinion in that case as a whole. It is true that *Barker* described dismissal of an indictment for denial of a speedy trial as an "unsatisfactorily severe remedy." Indeed, in practice, "it means that a defendant who may be guilty of a serious crime will go free, without having been tried." 407 U.S., at 522, 92 S.Ct., at 2188, 407 U.S. 514, 33 L.Ed.2d 101. But such severe remedies are not unique in the application of constitutional standards. In light of the policies which underlie the right to a speedy trial, dismissal must remain, as *Barker* noted, "the only possible remedy."

412 U.S. at 438–40, 93 S.Ct. at 2263, 37 L.Ed.2d at 60–61. Was the Court correct in its conclusion that the policies of the right to speedy trial demand that dismissal with prejudice always be the remedy for violation of that right?

B.   FEDERAL SPEEDY TRIAL ACT

EDITORS' INTRODUCTION: OUTLINE OF THE STATUTE

Unlike the Court, which refuses to prescribe specific time limitations for the right to a speedy trial, Congress in the Speedy Trial Act, 18 U.S.C.A. §§ 3161–74 (West 1999), requires that an indictment or information be presented within 30 days from arrest or issuance of a summons, with a 30 day extension if no grand jury is in session. If a defendant pleads not guilty he must be brought to trial within 70 days, but not less than 30 days, from the filing date of the information or indictment, or from the date he appeared before a judicial officer of the court in which the charge is pending, whichever date last occurs. In computing this time period, § 3161(h) of the Act specifically excludes any period of delay resulting from: other proceedings concerning the defendant; deferment to allow defendant to demonstrate his good conduct; absence or unavailability of defendant or an essential witness; defendant's mental or physical inability to stand trial; treatment of defendant pursuant to section 2902 of title 28 U.S.C.A. (civil commitment and rehabilitation of narcotics addicts); dismissal of previous information or indictment, upon motion of the attorney for the government, and subsequent filing of charges for the same offense; and a continuance granted by a judge on his findings that the ends of justice will be best served. The time period for a defendant who enters a guilty or nolo contendere plea and who subsequently withdraws it begins when the order for withdrawal of the plea becomes final.

Failure to comply with section 3161 requires dismissal of (1) the charge—if an information or indictment is not filed within the time limit—or (2) the indictment or information—if defendant is not brought to trial within the time limit. Under section 3162, the court has discretion to dismiss the charges with or without prejudice; in doing so, the court considers: "the seriousness of the offense; the facts and circumstances of the case which led to the dismissal; and the impact of a reprosecution on the administration of this chapter and on the administration of justice." 18 U.S.C.A. § 3162(a)(1)(West 1999). But, the right to dismissal is considered waived if the defendant fails to move for dismissal prior to trial or enters a plea of guilty or nolo contendere. Additionally, the Act provides for monetary and disciplinary sanctions against any counsel for the defense or government attorney who: (a) knowingly allows the case to be set for trial without disclosing that a necessary witness would be unavailable for trial; (b) files a frivolous motion solely to delay the proceedings; (c) knowingly gives false information to obtain a continuance; or (d) willfully fails to proceed to trial without justification.

Finally, the Act unequivocally states: "no provision of this chapter shall be interpreted as a bar to any claim of denial of speedy trial as required by amendment VI of the Constitution." 18 U.S.C.A. § 3173(West 1999).

The federal statute and similar state provisions sometimes modeled after it are subject to the objection that they violate federal and state constitutional provisions mandating separation of judicial and legislative powers. In United States v. Howard, 440 F.Supp. 1106 (D.Md.1977), *aff'd on other grounds*, 590 F.2d 564 (4th Cir.1979), for example, the court held that the time within which the judiciary must act on matters *sub curia* is a matter that must remain within the control of the courts. Since the federal statute attempts to interfere with the judiciary's exclusive authority in this area, it is unconstitutional. The same judge again held the statute unconstitutional in United States v. Brainer, 515 F.Supp. 627 (D.Md.1981), rev'd, 691 F.2d 691 (4th Cir.1982). Elaborating on its conclusion, the court stated:

> A major constitutional shortcoming of the Speedy Trial Act is that it diminishes the independence and flexibility of the ... judicial power without adequately taking account of all the interests involved. The right of defendants and society, to assure that criminal trials are achieved as expeditiously as possible is only one area of concern affected by the far-reaching provisions of the Speedy Trial Act. Other societal interests are implicated.... The ability of the criminal justice system to operate effectively and efficiently has been severely impeded by the Speedy Trial Act. Resources are misdirected, unnecessary severances required, cases proceed to trial inadequately prepared, and in some indeterminate number of cases, indictments against guilty persons dismissed.

515 F.Supp. at 637. The Supreme Court of Ohio, however, upheld its state speedy trial statute against similar arguments, primarily on the ground that the statute represented legislative implementation of a constitutional imperative. State v. Pachay, 64 Ohio St.2d 218, 416 N.E.2d 589 (1980).

United States v. Taylor

Supreme Court of the United States, 1988.
487 U.S. 326, 108 S.Ct. 2413, 101 L.Ed.2d 297.

■ JUSTICE BLACKMUN delivered the opinion of the Court.

This case requires us to consider the bounds of a district court's discretion to choose between dismissal with and without prejudice, as a remedy for a violation of the Speedy Trial Act of 1974, as amended, 18 U.S.C. § 3161 et seq. (1982 ed. and Supp. IV) (Act).

I

On July 25, 1984, respondent Larry Lee Taylor was indicted by a federal grand jury on charges of conspiracy to distribute cocaine and possession of 400 grams of cocaine with intent to distribute. His trial was scheduled to commence in the United States District Court for the Western District of Washington in Seattle on November 19, 1984, the day prior to the expiration of the 70–day period within which the Act requires the Government to bring an indicted individual to trial. See 18 U.S.C. § 3161(c)(1). Respondent failed to appear for trial, and a bench warrant was issued for his arrest. On February 5, 1985, respondent was arrested by local police officers in San Mateo County, Cal., on state charges that subsequently were dismissed. Respondent's return to Seattle for his federal trial was delayed for a number of reasons, some related to his being required to testify as a defense witness in a federal narcotics prosecution then pending in San Francisco, and others involving slow processing, the convenience of the United States Marshals service, and what the District Court would later describe as the "lackadaisical" attitude on the part of the Government. On April 24, 1985, while respondent was back in San Francisco to testify at a retrial of the narcotics prosecution, a federal grand jury in Seattle issued a superseding indictment against respondent, adding a failure-to-appear charge based on his nonappearance at the scheduled November 19, 1984, trial.

Upon his return to Seattle, respondent moved to dismiss all charges against him, alleging that the Speedy Trial Act had been violated. The District Court rejected the Government's argument that because respondent had failed to appear for trial, the 70–day speedy trial clock began anew when respondent was arrested on February 5, 1985. After considering the time between respondent's nonappearance on November 19, 1984, and the issuance of the superseding indictment on April 24, 1985, the court determined that the time respondent was at large, or testifying in the San Francisco prosecution, or being held on state charges, as well as some reasonable time for transporting him to Seattle, were excludable under 18 U.S.C. § 3161(h). The District Court concluded, however, that, despite these time exclusions, 15 nonexcludable days had passed, that the clock thus had expired 14 days before the superseding indictment, and that dismissal of the original indictment therefore was mandated. App. to Pet. for Cert. 27a–29a.[6]

---

6. The 15 nonexcludable days included the 6 days between the end of the federal trial in San Francisco at which respondent was testifying and the date on which state charges against respondent were dropped; the 5 additional days after the state charges were dropped that it took the United States Marshals Service to bring respondent before a federal magistrate on the federal bench warrant; and 4 days beyond the 10 days provided for by 18 U.S.C. § 3161(h)(1)(H) that the Marshals Service took to transport respondent back to Seattle.

The District Court found that, although respondent was charged with serious offenses, there was "no excuse for the government's lackadaisical behavior in this case." Id., at 30a. The court observed that some of the Government's explanations for the various nonexcludable delays were inconsistent; that the Marshals Service failed to produce respondent expeditiously when requested to do so by a San Mateo County judge; and that even after the state charges were dropped, respondent was not immediately brought before a federal magistrate on the fugitive warrant. The District Court also noted that after an order issued to bring respondent back to Seattle for trial, the Government responded, but without "dispatch," accommodating the Marshals Service's interest in moving several prisoners at once instead of moving respondent within the time period provided for by the Act. It said:

> "[T]he court concludes that the administration of the [Act] and of justice would be seriously impaired if the court were not to respond sternly to the instant violation. If the government's behavior in this case were to be tacitly condoned by dismissing the indictment without prejudice, then the [Speedy Trial Act] would become a hollow guarantee." Id., at 30a–31a.

The court dismissed the original counts with prejudice to reprosecution.[7]

A divided panel of the United States Court of Appeals for the Ninth Circuit affirmed. 821 F.2d 1377 (1987). The full panel agreed with the District Court's holding that respondent's failure to appear for trial on November 19, 1984, should not restart the speedy trial clock, and confirmed the District Court's calculation of 15 nonexcludable days between respondent's flight and the issuance of the superseding indictment. Id., at 1383–1385.

Applying an abuse of discretion standard, the Court of Appeals reviewed the District Court's discussion of its decision to dismiss the drug charges with prejudice. Characterizing the lower court's purpose as sending "a strong message to the government" that the Act must be "observed," even with respect to recaptured fugitives, the majority concluded: "Under the peculiar circumstances of this case, we see no need to disturb that ruling on appeal. The district court acted within the bounds of its discretion." Id., at 1386.

The third judge concurred with the finding of a Speedy Trial Act violation, but concluded that the District Court abused its discretion in barring reprosecution. After reviewing the chronology and disputing whether, as a factual matter, the Government had failed to act reasonably, he felt that "none of the delay shown in this case—although admittedly nonexcludable under the statute—was of such studied, deliberate, and callous nature as to justify dismissal with prejudice." Id., at 1387.

7. The District Court rejected respondent's motion to dismiss the failure-to-appear charge, finding that after subtracting the various time periods held excludable, the Government had not violated the 30-day arrest-to-indictment provision of § 3161(b). See App. to Pet. for Cert. 31a–32a. Respondent eventually entered a plea of guilty to this charge and was sentenced to five years' imprisonment.

On the Government's petition, which suggested that further guidance was needed with respect to the application of the Speedy Trial Act's remedy provision, § 3162, we granted certiorari.

II

A

Neither party has asked this Court to review the lower courts' decision that a violation of the Act actually occurred. And the statute admits no ambiguity in its requirement that when such a violation has been demonstrated, "the information or indictment shall be dismissed on motion of the defendant." § 3162(a)(2). The only question before us, therefore, is whether the District Court abused its discretion under the Act in dismissing the indictment with prejudice rather than permitting reprosecution. In relevant part, the Act's remedy provision, § 3162(a)(2), instructs:

> "If a defendant is not brought to trial within the time limit required by section 3161(c) as extended by 3161(h), the information or indictment shall be dismissed on motion of the defendant. ...In determining whether to dismiss the case with or without prejudice, the court shall consider, among others, each of the following factors: the seriousness of the offense; the facts and circumstances of the case which led to the dismissal; and the impact of a reprosecution on the administration of this chapter and on the administration of justice."

As is plain from this language, courts are not free simply to exercise their equitable powers in fashioning an appropriate remedy, but, in order to proceed under the Act, must consider at least the three specified factors. Because Congress employed somewhat broad and open-ended language, we turn briefly to the legislative history of the Act for some additional indication of how the contemplated choice of remedy should be made.

[After reviewing the Act's legislative history, the Court concluded its thrust was] that the decision to dismiss with or without prejudice was left to the guided discretion of the district court, and that neither remedy was given priority.

B

Consistent with the prevailing view, the Court of Appeals stated that it would review the dismissal with prejudice under an abuse of discretion standard. The court did not, however, articulate what that standard required.

This Court previously has recognized—even with respect to another statute the legislative history of which indicated that courts were to have "wide discretion exercising their equitable powers," 118 Cong.Rec. 7168 (1972), quoted in Albemarle Paper Co. v. Moody, 422 U.S. 405, 421, 95 S.Ct. 2362, 2373, 45 L.Ed.2d 280 (1975)—that "discretionary choices are not left to a court's 'inclination, but to its judgment; and its judgment is to be guided by sound legal principles.'" Id., at 416, 95 S.Ct., at 2371, quoting United States v. Burr, 25 F.Cas. 30, 35 (No. 14692D) (CC Va.1807) (Marshall, C.J.). Thus, a decision calling for the exercise of judicial discretion "hardly means that it is unfettered by meaningful standards or shielded from thorough appellate review." Albemarle Paper Co., 422 U.S., at 416, 95 S.Ct., at 2371.

Whether discretion has been abused depends, of course, on the bounds of that discretion and the principles that guide its exercise. Had Congress merely committed the choice of remedy to the discretion of district courts, without specifying factors to be considered, a district court would be expected to consider "all relevant public and private interest factors," and to balance those factors reasonably. Piper Aircraft Co. v. Reyno, 454 U.S. 235, 257, 102 S.Ct. 252, 266, 70 L.Ed.2d 419 (1981). Appellate review of that determination necessarily would be limited, with the absence of legislatively identified standards or priorities.

In the Speedy Trial Act, however, Congress specifically and clearly instructed that courts "*shall consider,* among others, *each of the following factors,*" § 3162(a)(2) (emphasis added), and thereby put in place meaningful standards to guide appellate review. Although the role of an appellate court is not to substitute its judgment for that of the trial court, review must serve to ensure that the purposes of the Act and the legislative compromise it reflects are given effect. Where, as here, Congress has declared that a decision will be governed by consideration of particular factors, a district court must carefully consider those factors as applied to the particular case and, whatever its decision, clearly articulate their effect in order to permit meaningful appellate review. Only then can an appellate court ascertain whether a district court has ignored or slighted a factor that Congress has deemed pertinent to the choice of remedy, thereby failing to act within the limits prescribed by Congress.

Factual findings of a district court are, of course, entitled to substantial deference and will be reversed only for clear error. Anderson v. Bessemer City, 470 U.S. 564, 105 S.Ct. 1504, 84 L.Ed.2d 518 (1985). A judgment that must be arrived at by considering and applying statutory criteria, however, constitutes the application of law to fact and requires the reviewing court to undertake more substantive scrutiny to ensure that the judgment is supported in terms of the factors identified in the statute. Nevertheless, when the statutory factors are properly considered, and supporting factual findings are not clearly in error, the district court's judgment of how opposing considerations balance should not lightly be disturbed.

III

Because the District Court did not fully explicate its reasons for dismissing with prejudice the substantive drug charges against respondent, we are left to speculate in response to some of the parties' arguments pro and con. Respondent, for example, argues that the District Court may have taken into account the fact that respondent's codefendant had been sentenced on the same charges to three years' imprisonment, and that by dismissing the drug charges but sentencing respondent to five years' imprisonment on the failure-to-appear charge, it would be possible to effect substantial justice while sending at the same time "a strong message" to the Marshals Service and the local United States Attorney. See Tr. of Oral Arg. 29, 32. There are several problems with that line of reasoning, not the least of which is that the District Court did not articulate it. To the extent that respondent is suggesting that his codefendant's 3–year sentence implies that the offenses with which both were charged were not "serious," his argument is directly at odds with the District Court's statement expressly to the contrary: "there is no question that the drug violations with which [respondent] is charged are serious," App. to Pet. for Cert. 30a. We have no reason to doubt the court's conclusion in that regard. Moreover, at the time the District Court decided to dismiss the drug charges against respondent, he had not yet entered a plea to the failure-to-appear charge, so that the court could not be certain that any opportunity would arise to take the drug violations into account in sentencing.[8]

With regard to the second factor that the statute requires a court to consider, that is, the circumstances of the case leading to dismissal, we find it difficult to know what to make of the District Court's characterization of the Government's conduct as "lackadaisical." We do not dispute that a truly neglectful attitude on the part of the Government reasonably could be factored against it in a court's consideration of this issue, but the District Court gave no indication of the foundation for its conclusion. The court's discussion following that statement merely recounted the Speedy Trial Act violations, and chastised the Government for failing to make "any particular show of concern," or to "respon[d] with dispatch." App. to Pet. for Cert. 30a. The District Court did not find that the Government acted in bad faith with respect to respondent; neither did the court discover any pattern of neglect by the local United States Attorney, or evidence of what the Court of Appeals' majority later termed "the government's apparent antipathy toward a recaptured fugitive." 821 F.2d, at 1386; see also Tr. of Oral Arg. 34–35. Any such finding, suggesting something more than an isolated unwitting violation, would clearly have altered the balance. Instead, the extent of the District Court's explanation for its determination that "the second factor, ... tends strongly to support the conclusion that the dismissal must be with prejudice," was that there was "no excuse" for the Government's conduct. App. to Pet. for Cert. 30a.

Then there is the fact of respondent's failure to appear. The Government was prepared to go to trial on the 69th day of the indictment-to-trial period, and it was respondent, not the prosecution, who prevented the trial from going forward in a timely fashion. Respondent argues that he has

---

8. Even more important, respondent had not entered a guilty plea to, or been convicted of, the drug charges. It would have been highly improper—and we shall not presume the District Court assumed such unbridled discretion—to sentence respondent with undue harshness on one count, on the basis of the Court's untested and unsubstantiated assumption of what the facts might have been shown to be with regard to the drug charges, see Tr. of Oral Arg. 29–30, without the sort of inquiry conducted, in another context, under Fed.Rule Crim.Proc. 32. Although we realize it could be tempting to wrap up the "equities" in a single package and, with the best of intentions, effect what could be regarded as an essentially just result, we could not condone an approach that would violate the rights of defendants and misapply the Speedy Trial Act in the hope that the errors would balance out in the end. Contrary to the dissent's suggestion, see post, at 3–4, we do not question here the wisdom of Congress' decision to assess different penalties for failure to appear depending on the severity of the underlying charge. What we cannot countenance is a decision to punish someone more severely than would otherwise have been considered appropriate for the charged offense, solely for the reason that other charges had been dismissed under the Speedy Trial Act.

been charged separately and punished for his failure to appear for trial, that all the time he was at large has been excluded from the speedy trial calculation, and that the District Court therefore was correct in not considering his flight as a factor in deciding whether to bar reprosecution. Respondent also observes that the Court of Appeals held, and the Government does not dispute here, that respondent's failure to appear for a trial scheduled with only one day remaining in the indictment-to-trial period does not restart the full 70–day speedy trial clock. See 821 F.2d, at 1380–1383. That respondent's flight does not restart the clock, however, goes only to whether there has been a violation of the Act, and not to what the appropriate remedy should be. Respondent's culpable conduct and, in particular, his responsibility for the failure to meet the timely trial schedule in the first instance are certainly relevant as "circumstances of the case which led to the dismissal," § 3162(a)(2), and weigh heavily in favor of permitting reprosecution. These factors, however, were considered by neither the District Court nor the Court of Appeals' majority.

Petitioner argues that the District Court failed to consider that the delay caused by the Government's unexcused conduct was brief, and that there was no consequential prejudice to respondent. The length of delay, a measure of the seriousness of the speedy trial violation, in some ways is closely related to the issue of the prejudice to the defendant. The longer the delay, the greater the presumptive or actual prejudice to the defendant, in terms of his ability to prepare for trial or the restrictions on his liberty:

> "[I]nordinate delay between public charge and trial, ... wholly aside from possible prejudice to a defense on the merits, may 'seriously interfere with the defendant's liberty, whether he is free on bail or not, and ... may disrupt his employment, drain his financial resources, curtail his associations, subject him to public obloquy, and create anxiety in him, his family and his friends.' "Barker v. Wingo, 407 U.S. 514, 537, 92 S.Ct. 2182, 2195, 33 L.Ed.2d 101 (1972) (WHITE, J., concurring), quoting United States v. Marion, 404 U.S. 307, 320, 92 S.Ct. 455, 463, 30 L.Ed.2d 468 (1971).

The District Court found the Act's 70–day indictment-to-trial period here was exceeded by 14 nonexcludable days, but made no finding of prejudice. Indeed, the Court of Appeals concluded that the delay, "although not wholly insubstantial, was not so great as to mandate dismissal with prejudice." 821 F.2d, at 1385. That court also found that there was no prejudice to respondent's trial preparation. Ibid. And, as respondent was being held to answer not only for the drug charges but also on a valid bench warrant issued after he did not appear, neither does there seem to have been any additional restrictions or burdens on his liberty as a result of the speedy trial violation.[9] Thus, although the absence of prejudice is not dispositive, in this case it is another consideration in favor of permitting reprosecution.

9. We do not decide that as a matter of law there could never be any prejudice to a defendant whose speedy trial rights were violated, but who was also being held on other charges. Because "prejudice" may take many forms, such determinations must be made on a case-by-case basis in the light of the facts.

The District Court's decision to dismiss with prejudice rested largely on its conclusion that the alternative would tacitly condone the Government's behavior, and that a stern response was appropriate in order to vindicate the guarantees of the Speedy Trial Act. We certainly encourage district courts to take seriously their responsibility to consider the "impact of a reprosecution on the administration" of justice and of the Speedy Trial Act, § 3162(a)(2). It is self-evident that dismissal with prejudice always sends a stronger message than dismissal without prejudice, and is more likely to induce salutary changes in procedures, reducing pretrial delays. See Brief for United States 31. Nonetheless, the Act does not require dismissal with prejudice for every violation. Dismissal without prejudice is not a toothless sanction: it forces the Government to obtain a new indictment if it decides to reprosecute, and it exposes the prosecution to dismissal on statute of limitations grounds. Given the burdens borne by the prosecution and the effect of delay on the Government's ability to meet those burdens, substantial delay well may make reprosecution, even if permitted, unlikely. If the greater deterrent effect of barring reprosecution could alone support a decision to dismiss with prejudice, the consideration of the other factors identified in § 3162(a)(2) would be superfluous, and all violations would warrant barring reprosecution.

Perhaps there was more to the District Court's decision than meets the eye. It is always difficult to review a cold appellate record and acquire a full understanding of all the facts, nuances, and attitudes that influence a trial judge's decisionmaking, and we undertake such close review with reluctance. That is why the administration of the Speedy Trial Act and the necessity for thorough appellate review require that a district court carefully express its decision whether or not to bar reprosecution in terms of the guidelines specified by Congress. When the decision whether to bar reprosecution is analyzed in the framework established by the Act, it is evident from the record before us that the District Court abused its discretion in this case. The court did not explain how it factored in the seriousness of the offenses with which respondent stood charged. The District Court relied heavily on its unexplained characterization of the Government conduct as "lackadaisical," while failing to consider other relevant facts and circumstances leading to dismissal. Seemingly ignored were the brevity of the delay and the consequential lack of prejudice to respondent, as well as respondent's own illicit contribution to the delay. At bottom, the District Court appears to have decided to dismiss with prejudice in this case in order to send a strong message to the Government that unexcused delays will not be tolerated. That factor alone, by definition implicated in almost every Speedy Trial Act case, does not suffice to justify barring reprosecution in light of all the other circumstances present.

IV

Ordinarily, a trial court is endowed with great discretion to make decisions concerning trial schedules and to respond to abuse and delay where appropriate. The Speedy Trial Act, however, confines the exercise of that discretion more narrowly, mandating dismissal of the indictment upon violation of precise time limits, and specifying criteria to consider in deciding whether to bar reprosecution. The District Court failed to consider all the factors relevant to the choice of a remedy under the Act. What factors it did rely on were unsupported by factual findings or evidence in the record. We conclude that the District Court abused its discretion under the Act, and that the Court of Appeals erred in holding otherwise. Accordingly, the judgment of the Court of Appeals is reversed.

It is so ordered.

───────

■ JUSTICE WHITE, concurring.

I join the Court's opinion, agreeing that when a defendant, through deliberate misconduct, interferes with compliance with the Speedy Trial Act and a violation of the Act then occurs, dismissal with prejudice should not be ordered unless the violation is caused by Government conduct that is much more serious than is revealed by this record.

───────

■ JUSTICE SCALIA, concurring in part [omitted].

───────

■ JUSTICE STEVENS, with whom JUSTICE BRENNAN and JUSTICE MARSHALL, join, dissenting [omitted].

NOTES

1. **Periods excluded from the statute.** The federal statute permits the trial judge to exclude certain periods of time from consideration in the analysis required by the Act:

(8)(A) Any period of delay resulting from a continuance granted by any judge on his own motion or at the request of the defendant or his counsel or at the request of the attorney for the Government, if the judge granted such continuance on the basis of his findings that the ends of justice served by taking such action outweigh the best interest of the public and the defendant in a speedy trial. No such period of delay resulting from a continuance granted by the court in accordance with this paragraph shall be excludable under this subsection unless the court sets forth, in the record of the case, either orally or in writing, its reasons for finding that the ends of justice served by the granting of such continuance outweigh the best interests of the public and the defendant in a speedy trial.

(B) The factors, among others, which a judge shall consider in determining whether to grant a continuance under subparagraph (A) of this paragraph in any case are as follows:

(i) Whether the failure to grant such a continuance in the proceeding would be likely to make a continuation of such proceeding impossible, or result in a miscarriage of justice.

(ii) Whether the case is so unusual or so complex, due to the number of defendants, the nature of the prosecution, or the existence of novel questions of fact or law, that it is unreasonable to expect adequate preparation for pretrial proceedings or for the trial itself within the time limits established by this section.

(iii) Whether, in a case in which arrest precedes indictment, delay in the filing of the indictment is caused because the arrest occurs at a time such that it is unreasonable to expect return and filing of the indictment within the period specified in section 3161(b), or because the facts upon which the grand jury must base its determination are unusual or complex.

(iv) Whether the failure to grant such a continuance in a case which, taken as a whole, is not so unusual or so complex as to fall within clause (ii), would deny the defendant reasonable time to obtain counsel, would unreasonably deny the defendant or the Government continuity of counsel, or would deny counsel for the defendant or the attorney for the Government the reasonable time necessary for effective preparation, taking into account the exercise of due diligence.

(C) No continuance under paragraph (8)(A) of this subsection shall be granted because of general congestion of the court's calendar, or lack of diligent preparation or failure to obtain available witnesses on the part of the attorney for the Government.

18 U.S.C.A. § 3161(h)(West 1999). Are these provisions so broad that a decision by a District Judge to exclude a given period is virtually unreviewable?

2. **Professional responsibility obligations.** Standard 4–1.2 of the American Bar Association Standards for Criminal Justice states that counsel for defendants should not seek to delay by using procedural devices when there is no legitimate basis for doing so. In a study devoted to counsel's awareness of and compliance with this standard, the conclusion was drawn that because the lawyers interviewed believed their first obligation is to their clients rather than to the court, they frequently ignored the standard and used procedural devices for purposes of delay. See J. Jones, The Compliance of [a Major] Public Defender's Office With The American Bar Association Standards for The Administration of Criminal Justice (undated) (paper on file with the University of Texas School of Law Criminal Justice Project).

CHAPTER 16

COMPETENCY TO STAND TRIAL

Analysis

There is universal agreement that it is a violation of due process as well as the nonconstitutional procedural law of virtually all jurisdictions to try a defendant who is "incompetent." Despite the pervasive federal constitutional aspects of the matter, however, United States Supreme Court caselaw has tended to deal with the procedural aspects of the inquiry into competency and disposition of incompetent defendants rather than with the ultimate question of competency.

What is widely-regarded as the constitutionally-required criteria for evaluating defendants' competency were stated in the per curiam decision in Dusky v. United States, 362 U.S. 402, 80 S.Ct. 788, 4 L.Ed.2d 824 (1960). After accepting the Solicitor General's suggestion that the record failed to support the trial judge's finding of competency, the Court remanded for a new hearing on the matter. It then commented:

> We ... agree with the suggestion of the Solicitor General that it is not enough for the district judge to find that "the defendant [is] oriented to time and place and [has] some recollection of events," but that the "test must be whether he has sufficient present ability to consult with his lawyer with a reasonable degree of rational understanding—and whether he has a rational as well as factual understanding of the proceedings against him."

362 U.S. at 402, 80 S.Ct. at 788–89, 4 L.Ed.2d at 825. Whether this language deserves the prominence it has assumed can be questioned. It is contained in a per curiam decision, handed down before the full constitutional ramifications of competency were developed, and was taken—perhaps uncritically—from a confession of error by the government. Moreover, it arguably contains substantial ambiguity. What is required for a client to consult with his lawyer "with a reasonable degree of rational understanding?" Must the defendant be able to participate effectively in the trial (as by testifying to his version of the events) as well as to discuss them with the attorney? While the so-called *Dusky* standard makes clear that the defendant must "understand" the proceedings as well as be able to consult

with his lawyer, is it clear what "a rational as well as factual" understanding involves?

The Supreme Court has also suggested that the criteria for determining competency may shift depending upon various characteristics of the proceedings. In Westbrook v. Arizona, 384 U.S. 150, 86 S.Ct. 1320, 16 L.Ed.2d 429 (1966), an apparently adequate determination had been made that the defendant was competent to stand trial in a general sense. He had also, however, waived his right to representation by counsel and had undertaken to represent himself. The Court held that a separate inquiry into his competency to waive his constitutional right to the assistance of counsel and to proceed to conduct his own defense might be necessary and remanded for consideration of this question. It did not address what standard should be applied if such an inquiry were found necessary. But in Massey v. Moore, 348 U.S. 105, 108, 75 S.Ct. 145, 147, 99 L.Ed. 135, 138 (1954) the Court had commented, "One might not be insane in the sense of being incapable of standing trial and yet lack the capacity to stand trial without benefit of counsel." On remand in *Westbrook,* the state appellate court directed a further examination of the defendant designed to address, as separate inquiries, his ability to understand the proceedings, his ability to assist in his defense, and his ability "to intelligently and competently waive his constitutional right to the assistance of counsel and conduct his own defense." State v. Westbrook, 101 Ariz. 206, 417 P.2d 530 (1966).

The Court returned to the criteria for determining competency in Godinez v. Moran, 509 U.S. 389, 113 S.Ct. 2680, 125 L.Ed.2d 321 (1993). Godinez shot and killed a bartender and a bar patron and then removed the bar's cash register. Nine days later, he shot and killed his former wife and then shot himself in the abdomen and slit his own wrists. Nevertheless, he survived and was charged with three counts of first degree murder. Two psychiatrists examined him. On the basis of their reports the trial judge found Godinez competent to stand trial. Godinez first pleaded not guilty, but then told the court that he wished to discharge his attorneys, represent himself, and plead guilty. After making a variety of inquiries of him, the court accepted both his waiver of counsel and his plea of guilty. Godinez was subsequently sentenced to death. Several years later, he filed a petition for post-conviction relief in the state court, which held a hearing and determined that he had been competent to represent himself. In subsequent federal habeas litigation, however, the Court of Appeals for the Ninth Circuit held the determinations that Godinez was competent did not adequately protect his federal constitutional rights. *Westbrook,* the court concluded, means that the competency of a defendant who waives counsel or pleads guilty must be determined by a higher standard than *Dusky* directs for assessing the competency of defendants who go to trial. A defendant who waives counsel or pleads guilty is competent, it reasoned, only if he has "the capacity for 'reasoned choice' among the alternatives available to him." Since no determination that Godinez had this capacity was made, his conviction and death sentence were held constitutionally invalid.

The Supreme Court reversed, reasoning that the Ninth Circuit had read too much into *Westbrook.* Justice Thomas explained the Court's position:

[A]ll criminal defendants—not merely those who plead guilty—may be required to make important decisions once criminal proceedings have been initiated. And while the decision to plead guilty is undeniably a profound one, it is no more complicated than the sum total of decisions that a defendant may be called upon to make during the course of a trial. * * * This being so, we can conceive of no basis for demanding a higher level of competence for those defendants who choose to plead guilty. If the *Dusky* standard is adequate for defendants who plead not guilty, it is necessarily adequate for those who plead guilty.

Nor do we think that a defendant who waives his right to the assistance of counsel must be more competent than a defendant who does not, since there is no reason to believe that the decision to waive counsel requires an appreciably higher level of mental functioning than the decision to waive other constitutional rights. * * *

Requiring that a criminal defendant be competent has a modest aim: It seeks to ensure that he has the capacity to understand the proceedings and to assist counsel. While psychiatrists and scholars may find it useful to classify the various kinds and degrees of competence, and while States are free to adopt competency standards that are more elaborate than the *Dusky* formulation, the Due Process Clause does not impose these additional requirements.

509 U.S. at 398–402, 113 S.Ct. at 2686–88, 125 L.Ed.2d at 332–34. *Westbrook,* Justice Thomas commented, simply means that in some cases trial judges are obligated to both inquire into the defendants' competency using the *Dusky* standard and satisfy themselves that the defendants' waivers are both knowing and voluntary.

Justice Blackmun, joined by Justice Stevens, dissented. The competency of defendants such as Godinez, who seek to proceed without counsel, must be determined by a standard that demands that they have the capacity to appreciate their position and to make a rational choice regarding representation, he argued. *Dusky's* test, he concluded, does not assure this:

[T]he standard for competence to stand trial is specifically designed to measure a defendant's ability to "consult with counsel" and to "assist in preparing his defense." A finding that a defendant is competent to stand trial establishes only that he is capable of aiding his attorney in making the critical decisions required at trial or in plea negotiations. The reliability or even relevance of such a finding vanishes when its basic premise—that counsel will be present—ceases to exist. The question is no longer whether the defendant can proceed with an attorney, but whether he can proceed alone and uncounselled. I do not believe we place an excessive burden upon a trial court by requiring it to conduct a specific inquiry into that question at the juncture when a defendant whose competency has already been questioned seeks to waive counsel and represent himself.

509 U.S. at 412–13, 113 S.Ct. at 2693–94, 125 L.Ed.2d at 341 (Blackmun, J., dissenting).

A.   THE DUTY TO INQUIRE INTO COMPETENCY

The procedural significance of the due process bar against trying or convicting an incompetent defendant is increased because of the trial judge's duty, established in the principal case of this section, to inquire without request into a defendant's competency under certain circumstances. Consider whether the caselaw provides an adequate standard for use by trial judges in deciding when such an inquiry is necessary. Consider also the type of inquiry required. Is an examination by psychiatrists or other mental health professionals required? Is a full hearing (perhaps before a jury) ever necessary and, if so, when?

Use this case also to apply the *Dusky* standard discussed in the introduction to this Chapter. Do the criteria set out in the Court's language in *Dusky* provide adequate guidance in assessing Robinson's competency? If only the evidence brought to the attention of the judge was available upon further inquiry, should—or must—Robinson be found incompetent to stand trial?

Pate v. Robinson

Supreme Court of the United States, 1966.
383 U.S. 375, 86 S.Ct. 836, 15 L.Ed.2d 815.

■ MR. JUSTICE CLARK delivered the opinion of the Court.

In 1959 respondent Robinson was convicted of the murder of his common-law wife, Flossie May Ward, and was sentenced to imprisonment for life. Being an indigent he was defended by court-appointed counsel. It was conceded at trial that Robinson shot and killed Flossie May, but his counsel claimed that he was insane at the time of the shooting and raised the issue of his incompetence to stand trial. On writ of error to the Supreme Court of Illinois it was asserted that the trial court's rejection of these contentions deprived Robinson of due process of law under the Fourteenth Amendment. His conviction was affirmed, the court finding that no hearing on mental capacity to stand trial had been requested, that the evidence failed to raise sufficient doubt as to his competence to require the trial court to conduct a hearing on its own motion, and further that the evidence did not raise a "reasonable doubt" as to his sanity at the time of the offense. . . .

We have concluded that Robinson was constitutionally entitled to a hearing on the issue of his competence to stand trial. Since we do not think there could be a meaningful hearing on that issue at this late date, we direct that the District Court, after affording the State another opportunity to put Robinson to trial on its charges within a reasonable time, order him discharged. Accordingly, we affirm the decision of the Court of Appeals in this respect, except insofar as it contemplated a hearing in the District Court on Robinson's competence. Our disposition makes it unnecessary to reach the other reasons given by the Court of Appeals for reversal.

I.

The State concedes that the conviction of an accused person while he is legally incompetent violates due process, Bishop v. United States, 350 U.S. 961, 76 S.Ct. 440, 100 L.Ed. 835 (1956), and that state procedures must be adequate to protect this right. It insists, however, that Robinson intelligently waived this issue by his failure to request a hearing on his competence at the trial; and further, that on the basis of the evidence before the trial judge no duty rested upon him to order a hearing *sua sponte*. A determination of these claims necessitates a detailed discussion of the conduct of the trial and the evidence touching upon the question of Robinson's competence at that time.

The uncontradicted testimony of four witnesses called by the defense revealed that Robinson had a long history of disturbed behavior. His mother testified that when he was between seven and eight years of age a brick dropped from a third floor hit Robinson on the head. "He blacked out and the blood run from his head like a faucet." Thereafter "he acted a little peculiar." The blow knocked him "cockeyed" and his mother took him to a specialist "to correct the crossness of his eyes." He also suffered headaches during his childhood, apparently stemming from the same event. His conduct became noticeably erratic about 1946 or 1947 when he was visiting his mother on a furlough from the Army. While Robinson was sitting and talking with a guest, "he jumped up and run to a bar and kicked a hole in the bar and he run up in the front." His mother asked "what on earth was wrong with him and he just stared at [her], and paced the floor with both hands in his pockets." On other occasions he appeared in a daze, with a "glare in his eyes," and would not speak or respond to questions. In 1951, a few years after his discharge from the service, he "lost his mind and was pacing the floor saying something was after him." This incident occurred at the home of his aunt, Helen Calhoun. Disturbed by Robinson's conduct, Mrs. Calhoun called his mother about six o'clock in the morning, and she "went to see about him." Robinson tried to prevent Mrs. Calhoun from opening the door, saying "that someone was going to shoot him or someone was going to come in after him." His mother testified that, after gaining admittance, "I went to him and hugged him to ask him what was wrong and he went to pushing me back, telling me to get back, somebody was going to shoot him, somebody was going to shoot him." Upon being questioned as to Robinson's facial expression at the time, the mother stated that he "had that starey look and seemed to be just a little foamy at the mouth." A policeman was finally called. He put Robinson, his mother and aunt in a cab which drove them to Hines Hospital. On the way Robinson tried to jump from the cab, and upon arrival at the hospital he was so violent that he had to be strapped in a wheel chair. He then was taken in an ambulance to the County Psychopathic Hospital, from which he was transferred to the Kankakee State Hospital. The medical records there recited:

> "The reason for admission: The patient was admitted to this hospital on the 5th day of June, 1952, from the Hines Hospital. Patient began presenting symptoms of mental illness about a year ago at which

time he came to his mother's house. He requested money and when it was refused, he suddenly kicked a hole in her bar.

* * *

"Was drinking and went to the Psychopathic Hospital. He imagined he heard voices, voices of men and women and he also saw things. He saw a little bit of everything. He saw animals, snakes and elephants and this lasted for about two days. He went to Hines. They sent him to the Psychopathic Hospital. The voices threatened him. He imagined someone was outside with a pistol aimed at him. He was very, very scared and he tried to call the police and his aunt then called the police. He thought he was going to be harmed. And he says this all seems very foolish to him now. Patient is friendly and tries to cooperate.

* * *

"He went through an acute toxic episode from which he has some insight. He had been drinking heavily. I am wondering possibly he isn't schizophrenic. I think he has recovered from this condition. I have seen the wife and she is in a pathetic state. I have no objection to giving him a try."

After his release from the state hospital Robinson's irrational episodes became more serious. His grandfather testified that while Robinson was working with him as a painter's assistant, "all at once, he would come down [from the ladder] and walk on out and never say where he is going and whatnot and he would be out two or three hours, and at times he would be in a daze and when he comes out, he comes back just as fresh. He just says he didn't do anything. I noticed that he wasn't at all himself." The grandfather also related that one night when Robinson was staying at his house Robinson and his wife had a "ruckus," which caused his wife to flee to the grandfather's bedroom. Robinson first tried to kick down the door. He then grabbed all of his wife's clothes from their room and threw them out in the yard, intending to set them on fire. Robinson got so unruly that the grandfather called the police to lock him up.

In 1953 Robinson, then separated from his wife, brought their 18–month-old son to Mrs. Calhoun's home and asked permission to stay there for a couple of days. She observed that he was highly nervous, prancing about and staring wildly. While she was at work the next day Robinson shot and killed his son and attempted suicide by shooting himself in the head. It appeared that after Robinson shot his son, he went to a nearby park and tried to take his life again by jumping into a lagoon. By his mother's description, he "was wandering around" the park, and walked up to a policeman and "asked him for a cigarette." It was stipulated that he went to the South Park Station on March 10, 1953, and said that he wanted to confess to a crime. When he removed his hat the police saw that he had shot himself in the head. They took him to the hospital for treatment of his wound.

Robinson served almost four years in prison for killing his son, being released in September 1956. A few months thereafter he began to live with Flossie May Ward at her home. In the summer of 1957 or 1958 Robinson "jumped on" his mother's brother-in-law and "beat him up terrible." She went to the police station and swore out a warrant for his arrest. She described his abnormalities and told the officers that Robinson "seemed to have a disturbed mind." She asked the police "to pick him up so I can have him put away." Later she went back to see why they had not taken him into custody because of "the way he was fighting around in the street, people were beating him up." She made another complaint a month or so before Robinson killed Flossie May Ward. However, no warrant was ever served on him.

The killing occurred about 10:30 p.m. at a small barbecue house where Flossie May Ward worked. At that time there were 10 customers in the restaurant, six of them sitting at the counter. It appears from the record that Robinson entered the restaurant with a gun in his hand. As he approached the counter, Flossie May said, "Don't start nothing tonight." After staring at her for about a minute, he walked to the rear of the room and, with the use of his hand, leaped over the counter. He then rushed back toward the front of the restaurant, past two other employees working behind the counter, and fired once or twice at Flossie May. She jumped over the counter and ran out the front door with Robinson in pursuit. She was found dead on the sidewalk. Robinson never spoke a word during the three-to-four minute episode.

Subsequently Robinson went to the apartment of a friend, Mr. Moore, who summoned the police. When three officers, two in uniform, arrived, Robinson was standing in the hall approximately half way between the elevator and the apartment. Unaware of his identity, the officers walked past him and went to the door of the apartment. Mrs. Moore answered the door and told them that Robinson had left a short time earlier. As the officers turned around they saw Robinson still standing where they had first observed him. Robinson made no attempt to avoid being arrested. When asked his address he gave several evasive answers. He also denied knowing anything about the killing.

Four defense witnesses expressed the opinion that Robinson was insane. In rebuttal the State introduced only a stipulation that Dr. William H. Haines, Director of the Behavior Clinic of the Criminal Court of Cook County would, if present, testify that in his opinion Robinson knew the nature of the charges against him and was able to cooperate with counsel when he examined him two or three months before trial. However, since the stipulation did not include a finding of sanity the prosecutor advised the court that "we should have Dr. Haines' testimony as to his opinion whether this man is sane or insane. It is possible that the man might be insane and know the nature or the charge or be able to cooperate with his counsel. I think it should be in evidence, your Honor, that Dr. Haines' opinion is that this defendant was sane when he was examined." However, the court told the prosecutor, "You have enough in the record now. I don't think you need Dr. Haines." In his summation defense counsel emphasized "our defense is clear. . . . It is as to the sanity of the defendant at the time of the crime and also as to the present time." The court, after closing argument by the defense, found Robinson guilty and sentenced him to prison for his natural life.

II.

The State insists that Robinson deliberately waived the defense of his competence to stand trial by failing to demand a sanity hearing as provided by Illinois law. But it is contradictory to argue that a defendant may be incompetent, and yet knowingly or intelligently "waive" his right to have the court determine his capacity to stand trial. See Taylor v. United States, 282 F.2d 16, 23 (C.A.8th Cir.1960). In any event, the record shows that counsel throughout the proceedings insisted that Robinson's present sanity was very much in issue. He made a point to elicit Mrs. Robinson's opinion of Robinson's "present sanity." And in his argument to the judge, he asserted that Robinson "should be found not guilty and presently insane on the basis of the testimony that we have heard." Moreover, the prosecutor himself suggested at trial that "we should have Dr. Haines' testimony as to his opinion whether this man is sane or insane." With this record we cannot say that Robinson waived the defense of incompetence to stand trial.

We believe that the evidence introduced on Robinson's behalf entitled him to a hearing on this issue. The court's failure to make such inquiry thus deprived Robinson of his constitutional right to a fair trial. See Thomas v. Cunningham, 313 F.2d 934 (C.A.4th Cir.1963). Illinois jealously guards this right. Where the evidence raises a *"bona fide* doubt" as to a defendant's competence to stand trial, the judge on his own motion must impanel a jury and conduct a sanity hearing pursuant to Ill.Rev.Stat., c. 38, § 104–2 (1963). People v. Shrake, 25 Ill.2d 141, 182 N.E.2d 754 (1962). The Supreme Court of Illinois held that the evidence here was not sufficient to require a hearing in light of the mental alertness and understanding displayed in Robinson's "colloquies" with the trial judge. 22 Ill.2d, at 168, 174 N.E.2d, at 823. But this reasoning offers no justification for ignoring the uncontradicted testimony of Robinson's history of pronounced irrational behavior. While Robinson's demeanor at trial might be relevant to the ultimate decision as to his sanity, it cannot be relied upon to dispense with a hearing on that very issue. Cf. Bishop v. United States, 350 U.S. 961, 76 S.Ct. 440, 100 L.Ed. 835 (1956), reversing, 96 U.S.App.D.C. 117, 120, 223 F.2d 582, 585 (1955). Likewise, the stipulation of Dr. Haines' testimony was some evidence of Robinson's ability to assist in his defense. But, as the state prosecutor seemingly admitted, on the facts presented to the trial court it could not properly have been deemed dispositive on the issue of Robinson's competence.

III.

Having determined that Robinson's constitutional rights were abridged by his failure to receive an adequate hearing on his competence to stand trial, we direct that the writ of habeas corpus must issue and Robinson be discharged, unless the State gives him a new trial within a reasonable time. ...It has been pressed upon us that it would be sufficient for the state court to hold a limited hearing as to Robinson's mental competence at the time he was tried in 1959. If he were found competent, the judgment against him would stand. But we have previously emphasized the difficulty of retrospectively determining an accused's competence to stand trial.

Dusky v. United States, 362 U.S. 402, 80 S.Ct. 788, 4 L.Ed.2d 824 (1960). The jury would not be able to observe the subject of their inquiry, and expert witnesses would have to testify solely from information contained in the printed record. That Robinson's hearing would be held six years after the fact aggravates these difficulties. This need for concurrent determination distinguishes the present case from Jackson v. Denno, 378 U.S. 368, 84 S.Ct. 1774, 12 L.Ed.2d 908 (1964), where we held that on remand the State could discharge its constitutional obligation by giving the accused a separate hearing on the voluntariness of his confession.

If the State elects to retry Robinson, it will of course be open to him to raise the question of his competence to stand trial at that time and to request a special hearing thereon. In the event a sufficient doubt exists as to his present competence such a hearing must be held. If found competent to stand trial, Robinson would have the usual defenses available to an accused.

The case is remanded to the District Court for action consistent with this opinion. It is so ordered.

Case remanded to District Court with directions.

■ MR. JUSTICE HARLAN, whom MR. JUSTICE BLACK joins, dissenting. [omitted].

NOTES

1. **Duty to inquire mid-trial.** Defendant was charged with participating along with four others in the rape and sexual abuse of his wife. At trial, defendant's wife testified that he would sometimes roll down the stairs when he did not get his way or was worried, that she had initially declined to prosecute because she believed defendant needed psychiatric care, but she had changed her mind after talking with a psychiatrist and following defendant's efforts to choke her to death the Sunday evening prior to trial. On the morning of the second day of trial, defendant's lawyer announced that defendant had shot himself in the abdomen. Could trial proceed without further inquiry into defendant's competence to stand trial? See Drope v. Missouri, 420 U.S. 162, 95 S.Ct. 896, 43 L.Ed.2d 103 (1975) (no).

2. **Rights concerning psychiatric examination.** The inquiry into a defendant's competence to stand trial mandated in some situations by *Robinson* will often involve a psychiatric interview. In Estelle v. Smith, 451 U.S. 454, 101 S.Ct. 1866, 68 L.Ed.2d 359 (1981), the Court stated:

> A criminal defendant, who neither initiates a psychiatric evaluation nor attempts to introduce any psychiatric evidence, may not be compelled to respond to a psychiatrist if his statements can be used against him at a capital sentencing proceeding.

451 U.S. at 468, 101 S.Ct. at 1876, 68 L.Ed.2d at 372. But the Court explained that a defendant who was warned about his Fifth Amendment right not to have interview disclosures so used could voluntarily consent to the interview. And in the absence of consent:

> If, upon being adequately warned, [Smith] had indicated that he would not answer [the psychiatrist's] questions, the validly ordered competency examina-

tion nevertheless could have proceeded upon the condition that the results would be applied solely for that purpose.

451 U.S. at 468, 101 S.Ct. at 1876, 68 L.Ed.2d at 372–73.

Finally, the Court held that failure to notify Smith's already appointed attorney that the psychiatric examination would encompass matters relevant to sentencing denied Smith his Sixth Amendment right to counsel. 451 U.S. at 470–71, 101 S.Ct. at 1877, 68 L.Ed.2d at 374.

In Powell v. Texas, 492 U.S. 680, 109 S.Ct. 3146, 106 L.Ed.2d 551 (1989) (per curiam), the defendant had been interviewed by two psychiatrists who later testified at the sentencing stage of his capital murder trial in support of the prosecution's contention that Powell was dangerous. The state court had concluded that even if the interviews violated Powell's Fifth and Sixth Amendment rights, he had waived the right to object to the testimony by introducing psychiatric testimony in support of an insanity defense at trial. Reversing, the Supreme Court acknowledged some support in its decisions for the proposition that introduction of evidence in support of an insanity defense waives Fifth Amendment objections, at least to the use of testimony offered at the guilt stage of the trial to rebut the defense. But it held that this rationale did not also support a waiver of the Sixth Amendment right with regard to evidence offered on the sentencing issue of dangerousness:

> While it may be unfair to the State to permit the defendant to use psychiatric testimony without allowing the State to rebut that testimony, it certainly is not unfair to require the State to provide counsel with notice before examining the defendant concerning future dangerousness.

492 U.S. at 685, 109 S.Ct. at 3150, 106 L.Ed.2d at 556. Since the psychiatrists had interviewed Powell in violation of his Sixth Amendment right to counsel, the use of their testimony on the dangerousness sentencing issue was impermissible.

3. **Burden of proof.** Constitutional limits upon the allocation and nature of the burden of proof regarding competency to stand trial were addressed in Medina v. California, 505 U.S. 437, 112 S.Ct. 2572, 120 L.Ed.2d 353 (1992). Medina had been charged with first degree murder and defense counsel asked for an inquiry into his competency to stand trial. Under California procedure, the issue was tried to a jury. The jury was instructed that a defendant is presumed competent and that Medina had the burden of proving his incompetency by a preponderance of the evidence. After the jury found Medina competent, trial proceeded, he was convicted, and the death penalty was assessed. Before the Supreme Court, he argued that the California presumption of competency and California's requirement that he prove competency by a preponderance of the evidence offended due process.

The appropriate standard, Justice Kennedy explained for the Court, is that applied in Patterson v. New York, 432 U.S. 197, 97 S.Ct. 2319, 53 L.Ed.2d 281 (1977), discussed on pages 1004–06 of the text. Substantial deference must be given to legislative judgments, and a legislative decision does not violate due process unless it offends a "principle of justice so rooted in the traditions and conscience of our people as to be ranked as fundamental."

Applying that standard, the majority found no due process violation. There is no settled tradition as to the proper allocation of the burden of proof on competency, and "[c]ontemporary practice" of the states and the federal government is varied. Placement of the burden on the defendant does not "transgress[ ] any recognized principle of 'fundamental fairness' in operation." Medina argued that "psychiatry is an inexact science," and placing on him the burden of proof requires that he bear the risk of being required to stand trial as a result of an erroneous finding of competency. Rejecting this, the Court reasoned that defense counsel will often have the best access to information and evidence, even if the defendant's ability to participate is impaired. Justice Kennedy explained:

> The Due Process Clause does not * * * require a State to adopt one procedure over another on the basis that it may produce results more favorable to the accused. * * * [I]t is enough that the State affords the criminal defendant on whose behalf a plea of incompetence is asserted a reasonable opportunity to demonstrate that he is not competent to stand trial.

505 U.S. at 451, 112 S.Ct. at 2580, 120 L.Ed.2d at 367.

Justice Blackmun, joined by Justice Stevens, dissented:

> [T]he Due Process clause does not simply forbid the State from trying and convicting a person who is incompetent. It also demands adequate *anticipatory, protective procedures* to minimize the risk that an incompetent person will be convicted. * * * In my view, [the majority's approach] introduces a systematic and unacceptably high risk that persons will be tried and convicted who are unable to follow or participate in the proceedings determining their fate.

505 U.S. at 458–64, 112 S.Ct. at 2584–87, 120 L.Ed.2d at 371–76. He found three reasons why the majority's reliance upon defense counsel's access to information and evidence was inappropriate:

> First, while the defendant is in custody, the State itself obviously has the most direct, unfettered access to him and is in the best position to observe his behavior. * * *
>
> Second, a competency determination is primarily a medical and psychiatric determination * * * [I]t is the experts and not the lawyers who are credited as the "best-informed," and most able to gauge a defendant's ability to understand and participate in the legal proceedings affecting him.
>
> Third, * * * [defense counsel's] view will likely have no outlet in, or effect on, the competency determination. Unlike the testimony of medical specialists or lay witnesses, the testimony of defense counsel is far more likely to be discounted by the factfinder as self-interested and biased. Defense counsel may also be discouraged in the first place from testifying for fear of abrogating an ethical responsibility or the attorney-client privilege.

505 U.S. at 465–66, 112 S.Ct. at 2588, 120 L.Ed.2d at 376–77.

But in Cooper v. Oklahoma, 517 U.S. 348, 116 S.Ct. 1373, 134 L.Ed.2d 498 (1996), the Court held that due process bars placing upon a defendant the burden of proving he is incompetent by clear and convincing evidence. Common law tradition and the law of most modern jurisdictions, Justice Stevens noted for the Court, require only proof by a preponderance of the evidence. Moreover, the defendant's fundamental right to be tried only while competent outweighs the State's interests:

> For the defendant, the consequences of an erroneous determination of competency are dire. Because he lacks the ability to communicate effectively with counsel, he may be unable to exercise other "rights deemed essential to a fair trial." * * * With the assistance of counsel, the defendant also is called upon to make myriad smaller decisions concerning the course of the defense. The importance of these rights and decisions demonstrates that an erroneous determination of competence threatens a "fundamental component of our criminal justice system."
>
> By comparison to the defendant's interest, the injury to the State of the opposite error—a conclusion that the defendant is incompetent when he is in fact malingering—is modest. To be sure, such an error imposes an expense on the State treasury and frustrates the State's interest in the prompt disposition

of criminal charges. But the error is subject to correction in subsequent proceeding and the State may detain the incompetent defendant * * *.

[W]e perceive no sound basis for allocating to the criminal defendant the large share of the risk which accompanies a clear and convincing evidence standard. * * * While important state interests are unquestionably at stake, * * * the defendant's fundamental right to be tried only while competent outweighs the State's interests in the efficient operation of its criminal justice system.

517 U.S. at 364–67, 116 S.Ct. at 1381–83, 134 L.Ed.2d at 512–14.

B. PROCESSING OF INCOMPETENT DEFENDANTS

The manner in which a defendant determined incompetent to stand trial may be processed is, of course, a matter of some moment. In part, this is because the matter bears upon issues concerning the competency process. If a defendant found incompetent can, on that basis alone, be detained in a treatment or care facility for a prolonged period of time, perhaps a persuasive argument can be made that even a possibly-incompetent defendant should be able to "waive" inquiry into competency. The principal case in this section develops the federal constitutional limits upon the manner in which the states may deal with defendants incompetent to stand trial.

Jackson v. Indiana

Supreme Court of the United States, 1972.
406 U.S. 715, 92 S.Ct. 1845, 32 L.Ed.2d 435.

■ MR. JUSTICE BLACKMUN delivered the opinion of the Court.

We are here concerned with the constitutionality of certain aspects of Indiana's system for pretrial commitment of one accused of crime.

Petitioner, Theon Jackson, is a mentally defective deaf mute with a mental level of a pre-school child. He cannot read, write, or otherwise communicate except through limited sign language. In May 1968, at age 27, he was charged in the Criminal Court of Marion County, Indiana, with separate robberies of two women. The offenses were alleged to have occurred the preceding July. The first involved property (a purse and its contents) of the value of four dollars. The second concerned five dollars in money. The record sheds no light on these charges since, upon receipt of not guilty pleas from Jackson, the trial court set in motion the Indiana procedures for determining his competency to stand trial. Ind.Ann.Stat. § 9–1706a (Supp.1971), now Ind.Code 35–5–3–2 (1971).

As the statute requires, the court appointed two psychiatrists to examine Jackson. A competency hearing was subsequently held at which petitioner was represented by counsel. The court received the examining doctors' joint written report and oral testimony from them and from a deaf school interpreter through whom they had attempted to communicate with petitioner. The report concluded that Jackson's almost nonexistent communication skill, together with his lack of hearing and his mental deficiency, left him unable to understand the nature of the charges against him or to participate in his defense. One doctor testified that it was extremely unlikely that petitioner could ever learn to read or write and questioned whether petitioner even had the ability to develop any proficiency in sign language. He believed that the interpreter had not been able to communicate with petitioner to any great extent and testified that petitioner's "prognosis appears rather dim." The other doctor testified that even if Jackson were not a deaf mute, he would be incompetent to stand trial, and doubted whether petitioner had sufficient intelligence ever to develop the necessary communication skills. The interpreter testified that Indiana had no facilities that could help someone as badly off as Jackson to learn minimal communication skills.

On this evidence, the trial court found that Jackson "lack[ed] comprehension sufficient to make his defense," § 9–1706a, and ordered him committed to the Indiana Department of Mental Health until such time as that Department should certify to the court that "the defendant is sane."

* * *

Equal Protection

Because the evidence established little likelihood of improvement in petitioner's condition, he argues that commitment under § 9–1706a in his case amounted to a commitment for life. This deprived him of equal protection, he contends, because, absent the criminal charges pending against him, the State would have had to proceed under other statutes generally applicable to all other citizens: either the commitment procedures for feeble-minded persons, or those for mentally ill persons. . . .

In Baxstrom v. Herold, 383 U.S. 107, 86 S.Ct. 760, 15 L.Ed.2d 620 (1966), the Court held that a state prisoner civilly committed at the end of his prison sentence on the finding of a surrogate was denied equal protection when he was deprived of a jury trial that the State made generally available to all other persons civilly committed. Rejecting the State's argument that Baxstrom's conviction and sentence constituted adequate justification for the difference in procedures, the Court said that "there is no conceivable basis for distinguishing the commitment of a person who is nearing the end of a penal term from all other civil commitments." . . . The Court also held that Baxstrom was denied equal protection by commitment to an institution maintained by the state corrections department for "dangerously mentally ill" persons, without a judicial determination of his "dangerous propensities" afforded all others so committed.

If criminal conviction and imposition of sentence are insufficient to justify less procedural and substantive protection against indefinite commitment than that generally available to all others, the mere filing of criminal charges surely cannot suffice. . . .

Respondent argues, however, that because the record fails to establish affirmatively that Jackson will never improve, his commitment "until sane" is not really an indeterminate one. It is only temporary, pending possible change in his condition. Thus, presumably, it cannot be judged against commitments under other state statutes that are truly indeterminate. The State relies on the lack of "exactitude" with which psychiatry can predict the future course of mental illness. . . .

Were the State's factual premise that Jackson's commitment is only temporary a valid one, this might well be a different case. But the record does not support that premise. . . .

We note also that neither the Indiana statute nor state practice make the likelihood of the defendant's improvement a relevant factor. The State did not seek to make any such showing, and the record clearly establishes that the chances of Jackson's ever meeting the competency standards of § 9–1706a are at best minimal, if not nonexistent. The record also rebuts any contention that the commitment could contribute to Jackson's improvement. Jackson's § 9–1706a commitment is permanent in practical effect.

We therefore must turn to the question whether, because of the pendency of the criminal charges which triggered the State's invocation of § 9–1706a, Jackson was deprived of substantial rights to which he would have been entitled under either of the other two state commitment statutes. *Baxstrom* held that the State cannot withhold from a few the procedural protections or the substantive requirements for commitment that are available to all others. In this case commitment procedures under all three statutes appear substantially similar: notice, examination by two doctors, and a full judicial hearing at which the individual is represented by counsel and can cross-examine witnesses and introduce evidence. Under each of the three statutes, the commitment determination is made by the court alone, and appellate review is available.

In contrast, however, what the State must show to commit a defendant under § 9–1706a, and the circumstances under which an individual so committed may be released, are substantially different from the standards under the other two statutes.

Under § 9–1706a, the State needed to show only Jackson's inability to stand trial. We are unable to say that, on the record before us, Indiana could have civilly committed him as mentally ill under § 22–1209 or committed him as feeble-minded under § 22–1907. The former requires at least (1) a showing of mental illness and (2) a showing that the individual is in need of "care, treatment, training or detention." § 22–1201(1). Whether Jackson's mental deficiency would meet the first test is unclear; neither examining physician addressed himself to this. Furthermore, it is problematical whether commitment for "treatment" or "training" would be appropriate since the record establishes that none is available for Jackson's condition at any state institution. The record also fails to establish that Jackson is in need of custodial care or "detention." He has been employed at times, and there is no evidence that the care he long received at home has become inadequate. The statute appears to require an independent showing of dangerousness ("requires . . . detention in the interest of the welfare of such person or . . . others . . . :"). Insofar as it may require such a showing, the pending criminal charges are insufficient to establish it, and no other supporting evidence was introduced. For the same reasons, we cannot say that this record would support a feeble-mindedness commitment under § 22–1907 on the ground that Jackson is "unable properly to care for [himself]." § 22–1801.

More important, an individual committed as feeble-minded is eligible for release when his condition "justifies it," § 22–1814, and an individual civilly committed as mentally ill when the "superintendent or administrator shall discharge such person *or* [when] cured of such illness." § 22–1223 (emphasis supplied). Thus in either case release is appropriate when the individual no longer requires the custodial care or treatment or detention which occasioned the commitment, or when the department of mental health believes release would be in his best interests. The evidence available concerning Jackson's past employment and home care strongly suggests that under these standards he might be eligible for release at almost any time, even if he did not improve. On the other hand, by the terms of his present § 9–1706a commitment, he will not be entitled to release at all absent an unlikely substantial change for the better in his condition.

Baxstrom did not deal with the standard for release, but its rationale is applicable here. The harm to the individual is just as great if the State, without reasonable justification, can apply standards making his commitment a permanent one when standards generally applicable to all others afford him a substantial opportunity for early release.

As we noted above, we cannot conclude that pending criminal charges provide a greater justification for different treatment than conviction and sentence. Consequently, we hold that by subjecting Jackson to a more lenient commitment standard and to a more stringent standard of release than those generally applicable to all others not charged with offenses, and by thus condemning him in effect to permanent institutionalization without the showing required for commitment or the opportunity for release afforded by § 22–1209 or § 22–1907, Indiana deprived petitioner of equal protection of the laws under the Fourteenth Amendment.[1]

---

1. Petitioner also argues that the incompetency commitment deprived him of the right to be assigned to a special "institution for feeble-minded persons" to which he would have been statutorily directed by a § 22–1907 commitment. The State maintains two such institutions. The Indiana Supreme Court thought ..., considering Jackson's condition, his incompetency commitment can still culminate in assignment to a special facility. The State, in argument, went one step further. It contended that in practice the assignment process under all three statutes is identical: the individual is remanded to the central state authority, which assigns him to an appropriate institution regardless of how he was committed.

. . .

Moreover, nothing in the record demonstrates that different or better treatment is available at a special institution than at the general facilities for the mentally ill. We are not faced here, as we were in *Baxstrom*, with commitment to a distinctly penal or maximum security institution designed for dangerous inmates and not administered by the general state mental health authorities. Therefore, we cannot say that by virtue of his incompetency commitment Jackson has been denied an assignment or appropriate treatment to which those not charged with crimes would generally be entitled.

Similarly, Jackson's incompetency commitment did not deprive him of privileges such as furloughs to which he claims a feeble-mindedness commitment would entitle him. The statutes relate such privileges to particular institutions, not to the method of commitment. Thus patients assigned to the Muscatatuck institution are entitled to furloughs regardless of the statute under which they were committed; and persons committed as feeble-minded would not be entitled to furloughs if assigned to a general mental institution.

Due Process

For reasons closely related to those discussed . . . above, we also hold that Indiana's indefinite commitment of a criminal defendant solely on account of his incompetency to stand trial does not square with the Fourteenth Amendment's guarantee of due process.

* * *

The federal statute, 18 U.S.C.A. §§ 4244 to 4246, is not dissimilar to the Indiana law. It provides that a defendant found incompetent to stand trial may be committed "until the accused shall be mentally competent to stand trial or until the pending charges against him are disposed of according to law." § 4246. . . .

Since Greenwood [v. United States, 350 U.S. 366, 76 S.Ct. 410, 100 L.Ed. 412 (1956)] federal courts without exception have found improper any straightforward application of §§ 4244 and 4246 to a defendant whose chance of attaining competency to stand trial is slim, thus effecting an indefinite commitment on the grounds of incompetency alone. . . .

These decisions have imposed a "rule of reasonableness" upon §§ 4244 and 4246. Without a finding of dangerousness, one committed thereunder can be held only for a "reasonable period of time" necessary to determine whether there is a substantial chance of his attaining the capacity to stand trial in the foreseeable future. If the chances are slight, or if the defendant does not in fact improve, then he must be released or granted a §§ 4247–4248 hearing. Some States appear to commit indefinitely a defendant found incompetent to stand trial until he recovers competency. Other States require a finding of dangerousness to support such a commitment or provide forms of parole. New York has recently enacted legislation mandating release of incompetent defendants charged with misdemeanors after 90 days of commitment, and release and dismissal of charges against those accused of felonies after they have been committed for two-thirds of the maximum potential prison sentence. The practice of automatic commitment with release conditioned solely upon attainment of competence has been decried on both policy and constitutional grounds. Recommendations for changes made by commentators and study committees have included incorporation into pretrial commitment procedures of the equivalent of the federal "rule of reason," a requirement of a finding of dangerousness or of full-scale civil commitment, periodic review by court or mental health administrative personnel of the defendant's condition and progress, and provisions for ultimately dropping charges if the defendant does not improve. One source of this criticism is undoubtedly the empirical data available which tends to show that many defendants committed before trial are never tried, and that those defendants committed pursuant to ordinary civil proceedings are, on the average, released sooner than defendants automatically committed solely on account of their incapacity to stand trial. Related to these statistics are substantial doubts about whether the rationale for pretrial commitment—that care or treatment will aid the accused in attaining competency—is empirically valid given the state of most of our mental institutions. However, very few courts appear to have addressed the problem directly in the state context.

* * *

The States have traditionally exercised broad power to commit persons found to be mentally ill. The substantive limitations on the exercise of this power and the procedures for invoking it vary drastically among the States. The particular fashion in which the power is exercised—for instance, through various forms of civil commitment, defective delinquency laws, sexual psychopath laws, commitment of persons acquitted by reason of insanity—reflects different combinations of distinct bases for commitment sought to be vindicated. The bases that have been articulated include dangerousness to self, dangerousness to others, and the need for care or treatment or training. Considering the number of persons affected, it is perhaps remarkable that the substantive constitutional limitations on this power have not been more frequently litigated.

We need not address these broad questions here. It is clear that Jackson's commitment rests on proceedings that did not purport to bring into play, indeed did not even consider relevant, *any* of the articulated bases for exercise of Indiana's power of indefinite commitment. The state statutes contain at least two alternative methods for invoking this power. But Jackson was not afforded any "formal commitment proceedings addressed to [his] ability to function in society," or to society's interest in his restraint, or to the State's ability to aid him in attaining competency through custodial care or compulsory treatment, the ostensible purpose of the commitment. At the least, due process requires that the nature and duration of commitment bear some reasonable relation to the purpose for which the individual is committed.

We hold, consequently, that a person charged by a State with a criminal offense who is committed solely on account of his incapacity to proceed to trial cannot be held more than the reasonable period of time necessary to determine whether there is a substantial probability that he will attain that capacity in the foreseeable future. If it is determined that this is not the case, then the State must either institute the customary civil commitment proceeding that would be required to commit indefinitely any other citizen, or release the defendant. Furthermore, even if it is determined that the defendant probably soon will be able to stand trial, his continued commitment must be justified by progress toward that goal. In light of differing state facilities and procedures and a lack of evidence in this record, we do not think it appropriate for us to attempt to prescribe arbitrary time limits. We note, however, that petitioner Jackson has now been confined for three and one-half years on a record that sufficiently establishes the lack of a substantial probability that he will ever be able to participate fully in a trial.

These conclusions make it unnecessary for us to reach petitioner's Eighth–Fourteenth Amendment claim.

Disposition of the Charges

Petitioner also urges that fundamental fairness requires that the charges against him now be dismissed. The thrust of his argument is that the record amply establishes his lack of criminal responsibility at the time the crimes are alleged to have been committed. The Indiana court did not discuss this question. Apparently it believed that by reason of Jackson's incompetency commitment the State was entitled to hold the charges pending indefinitely. On this record, Jackson's claim is a substantial one. For a number of reasons, however, we believe the issue is not sufficiently ripe for ultimate decision by us at this time.

A.   Petitioner argues that he has already made out a complete insanity defense. Jackson's criminal responsibility at the time of the alleged offenses, however, is a distinct issue from his competency to stand trial. The competency hearing below was not directed to criminal responsibility, and evidence relevant to it was presented only incidentally. Thus, in any event, we would have to remand for further consideration of Jackson's condition in the light of Indiana's law of criminal responsibility.

B.   Dismissal of charges against an incompetent accused has usually been thought to be justified on grounds not squarely presented here: particularly, the Sixth–Fourteenth Amendment right to a speedy trial, or the denial of due process inherent in holding pending criminal charges indefinitely over the head of one who will never have a chance to prove his innocence. Jackson did not present the Sixth–Fourteenth Amendment issue to the state courts. Nor did the highest state court rule on the due process issue, if indeed it was presented to that court in precisely the above-described form. We think, in light of our holdings [above] that the Indiana courts should have the first opportunity to determine these issues.

C.   Both courts and commentators have noted the desirability of permitting some proceedings to go forward despite the defendant's incompetency. For instance, § 4.06(3) of the Model Penal Code would permit an incompetent accused's attorney to contest any issue "susceptible of fair determination prior to trial and without the personal participation of the defendant." An alternative draft of § 4.06(4) of the Model Penal Code would also permit an evidentiary hearing at which certain defenses, not including lack of criminal responsibility, could be raised by defense counsel on the basis of which the court might quash the indictment. Some States have statutory provisions permitting pretrial motions to be made or even allowing the incompetent defendant a trial at which to establish his innocence, without permitting a conviction. We do not read this Court's previous decisions to preclude the States from allowing at a minimum, an incompetent defendant to raise certain defenses such as insufficiency of the indictment, or make certain pretrial motions, through counsel. Of course, if the Indiana courts conclude that Jackson was almost certainly not capable of criminal responsibility when the offenses were committed, dismissal of the charges might be warranted. But even if this is not the case, Jackson may have other good defenses that could sustain dismissal or acquittal and which might now be asserted. We do not know if Indiana would approve procedures such as those mentioned here, but these possibilities will be open on remand.

Reversed and remanded.

NOTES

1. **Incompetency during initial phases of the case.** What is the proper procedure when a defendant who is allegedly incompetent to stand trial is presented before a magistrate for an initial appearance or a preliminary examination? Compare Flint v. Sater, 374 P.2d 929 (Okla.Crim.App.1962) with State v. McCredden, 33 Wis.2d 661, 148 N.W.2d 33 (1967). In the latter case the court suggested:

> [W]e conclude that the proper procedure to be followed by the circuit court, where a defendant is bound over by the magistrate to determine the issue of insanity, is to hold a hearing to establish whether it is probable that he committed the felony charged in the information. The information should first be filed but no plea thereto should be required. If the defendant is without counsel, counsel should be provided with the right to cross-examine the state's witnesses and to call witnesses on behalf of the defendant. At the conclusion of this hearing a finding should be made on the issue of probable guilt. If this finding is in the affirmative then the court shall proceed to determine the insanity issue. If on the other hand the finding is that the state has failed to prove the probability that the defendant has committed the felony charged in the information, or all the felonies charged if there is more than one, the defendant should be discharged subject to the right of the court to temporarily detain him so as to permit civil proceedings to be instituted ... to determine his mental competency.

33 Wis.2d at 669–70, 148 N.W.2d at 37–38.

2. **Effect of incompetency on pretrial release.** What effect should a defendant's potential incompetency have upon his right to pretrial release? May bail be revoked for purposes of hospitalizing him? Could this be justified if a psychiatric examination could be conducted on an out-patient basis? If a defendant is found incompetent, may bail be revoked or denied on the ground that he is dangerous to others? See United States v. Curry, 410 F.2d 1372 (4th Cir.1969).

3. **Forcing defendants to take medication.** If a defendant is determined to be incompetent to stand trial because of a mental illness, under what circumstances may the defendant be forced to take medication that may sufficiently reduce his symptoms to render him competent to stand trial? Whether federal constitutional considerations limit the states' ability to so medicate incompetent defendants seemed to be at issue in Riggins v. Nevada, 504 U.S. 127, 112 S.Ct. 1810, 118 L.Ed.2d 479 (1992). Riggins, charged with murder, was found incompetent to stand trial and then was treated with Mellaril, a powerful antipsychotic medication. He received 800 milligrams of the drug each day. Riggins was subsequently found to be competent and trial was scheduled. He moved to terminate his treatment with the Mellaril, contending that continued treatment infringed upon his freedom. He also argued that his continued treatment would affect his demeanor and mental state during trial and thus would interfere with his ability to offer an insanity defense, since it would deprive him of the ability to show the jurors his "true mental state." The trial court denied the motion. Riggins was tried, and testified in his own defense. The jury—rejecting his insanity defense—convicted him and set his punishment at death.

The Supreme Court held that even assuming that Riggins' treatment with the Mellaril was "medically appropriate," on the facts of the case this treatment denied Riggins a full and fair trial under Fourteenth Amendment due process. In Washington v. Harper, 494 U.S. 210, 110 S.Ct. 1028, 108 L.Ed.2d 178 (1990), the Court had held that the Fourteenth Amendment's due process clause limits a state's ability to involuntarily treat a prison inmate with antipsychotic drugs because such forcible medication "represents a substantial interference with that person's liberty." 494

U.S. at 229, 110 S.Ct. at 1041, 108 L.Ed.2d at 203. Justice O'Connor explained for the *Riggins* Court:

> Under *Harper,* forcing antipsychotic drugs on a convicted prisoner is impermissible absent a finding of overriding justification and a determination of medical appropriateness. The Fourteenth Amendment affords at least as much protection to persons the State detains for trial. * * * Thus, once Riggins moved to terminate administration of antipsychotic medication, the State became obligated to establish the need for Mellaril and the medical appropriateness of the drug.
>
> Although we have not had occasion to develop substantive standards for judging forced administration of such drugs in the trial or pretrial settings, Nevada certainly would have satisfied due process if the prosecution had demonstrated, and the District Court had found, that treatment with antipsychotic medication was medically appropriate and, considering less intrusive alternatives, essential for sake of Riggins' own safety or the safety of others.... Similarly, the State might have been able to justify medically appropriate, involuntary treatment with the drug by establishing that it could not obtain an adjudication of Riggins' guilt or innocence by using less intrusive means.... We note that during the * * * hearing [in the state court] Riggins did not contend that he had the right to be tried without Mellaril if its discontinuation rendered him incompetent.... The question whether a competent criminal defendant may refuse antipsychotic medication if cessation of medication would render him incompetent at trial is not before us.

504 U.S. at 135–36, 112 S.Ct. at 1815, 118 L.Ed.2d at 489–90.

The trial court had not made the findings that due process required.

> This error may well have impaired the constitutionally protected trial rights Riggins invokes. At the hearing to consider terminating medication, [one expert] suggested that the dosage administered to Riggins * * * could make him "uptight." [Another expert] testified that a patient taking 800 milligrams of Mellaril each day might suffer from drowsiness or confusion. It is clearly possible that such side effects had an impact upon not just Riggins' outward appearance, but also the contents of his testimony on direct or cross examination, his ability to follow the proceedings, or the substance of his communication with counsel.

504 U.S. at 137, 112 S.Ct. at 1816, 118 L.Ed.2d at 490. Requiring Riggins to demonstrate actual prejudice, the Court concluded, would lead to speculation and thus the demonstration of "a strong possibility that Riggins' defense was impaired due to the administration of Mellaril" required that relief be granted. The constitutional error was not "cured" by Riggins' ability at trial to present expert testimony to the jury regarding the effects upon his demeanor of the Mellaril he was taking. This could not have had any impact upon the possibility that the drug affected Riggins' own testimony, his interaction with counsel, or his comprehension. "[A]n unacceptable risk of prejudice remained." 504 U.S. at 138, 112 S.Ct. at 1816, 118 L.Ed.2d at 491.

Justice Kennedy concurred in the judgment of the Court but wrote separately to express his view on the issue not reached by the Court. He reviewed the possible side effects of antipsychotic medications such as the Mellaril administered to Riggins and their possible effects upon defendants at trial. Insofar as the medication inhibits defendants' ability to react and respond to the proceedings and to demonstrate remorse and compassion, he observed, the drug may result in especially acute prejudice during the sentencing stage and in a capital case "may * * * be determinative of whether the offender lives or dies." He then concluded:

In my view elementary protections against state intrusion require the State in every case to make a showing that there is no significant risk that the medication will impair or alter in any material way the defendant's capacity or willingness to react to the testimony at trial or to assist his counsel. Based on my understanding of the medical literature, I have substantial reservations that the State can make that showing. * * *

If the State cannot render the defendant competent without involuntary medication, then it must resort to civil commitment, if appropriate, unless the defendant becomes competent through other means. If the defendant cannot be tried without his behavior and demeanor being affected in this substantial way by involuntary treatment, in my view the Constitution requires that society bear this cost in order to preserve the integrity of the trial process.

504 U.S. at 141–45, 112 S.Ct. at 1818–20, 118 L.Ed.2d at 493–96 (Kennedy, J. concurring in the judgment).

Justice Thomas, joined in part by Justice Scalia, dissented, arguing that Riggins failed to establish that he was actually forced to take the Mellaril and that even if he was forced to take it, he failed to demonstrate that this deprived him of a ''fair'' trial. 504 U.S. at 147, 112 S.Ct. at 1821, 118 L.Ed.2d at 497.

CHAPTER 17

DISCOVERY AND DISCLOSURE

Analysis

EDITORS' INTRODUCTION: ISSUES UNDER MODERN DISCOVERY PROVISIONS

The rights of the parties to criminal litigation to notice concerning the theories or evidence that will be relied upon by their opponents and to access to statements and physical evidence in the possession of those opponents is a relatively recent development in criminal procedure. Prior to the promulgation of Fed.R.Crim.P. 16 in 1946, no right to such discovery existed in federal litigation; even that early version of Rule 16 conferred only limited disclosure duties. But a strong movement, led judicially by United States Supreme Court Justice Brennan as a (then) member of the New Jersey Supreme Court and by Justice Traynor of the California Supreme Court, has resulted in increasingly broad formal discovery requirements. These requirements are the subject of the present Chapter.

Some discovery rights have developed as a matter of constitutional mandate, but most have their basis in legislation or court rule. Some courts, however, have found an inherent power to compel discovery even in the absence of statutory or rule authority. Thus in United States v. Nobles, 422 U.S. 225, 234–36, 95 S.Ct. 2160, 2168–69, 45 L.Ed.2d 141, 151–52 (1975), the Supreme Court held that the federal judiciary has such inherent power to compel some disclosure, at least during trial, by the defendant as well as by the prosecution.

Various model formulations have been developed, including Fed. R.Crim.P. 16, the Uniform Rules of Criminal Procedure drafted by the Conference of Commissioners on Uniform State Laws, the American Law Institute's Model Code of Pre-arraignment Procedure, the Standards of the National Association of Prosecuting Attorneys, and the National Advisory

Commission's volume on Courts. Perhaps the most influential formulation, however, has been the American Bar Association's Standards Relating to Discovery and Procedure Before Trial (Approved Draft, 1970), revised in 1978, II Standards for Criminal Justice, Standard 11–1.1 et seq. (1980) (the "ABA Standards"). By 1975, 22 states had substantially implemented these Standards through court rule, legislation, or judicial adoption. Robinson, The ABA Standards for Criminal Justice: What They Mean to the Criminal Defense Attorney, 1 Nat.J.Crim.Def. 3 (1975).

Basic Consideration

The ABA Standards, which advocate broad discovery, suggest that such discovery will further the expeditious and fair disposition of criminal charges by encouraging thorough preparation by both sides and by aiding early recognition and disposition of constitutional, collateral, and procedural issues. In addition, discovery is seen as minimizing inequities among similarly situated defendants and as increasing the likelihood that the decision as to which plea to enter will be an informed judgment. See ABA Standards, Standard 1.1. The arguments against discovery were summarized by the Iowa Supreme Court in State v. Eads, 166 N.W.2d 766 (Iowa 1969):

> (1) It would afford the defendant increased opportunity to produce perjured testimony and to fabricate evidence to meet the State's case; (2) witnesses would be subject to bribe, threat and intimidation; (3) since the State cannot compel the defendant to disclose his evidence, disclosure by the State would afford the defendant an unreasonable advantage at trial; and (4) disclosure is unnecessary in any event because of the other sources of information which defendant has under existing law.

166 N.W.2d at 769.

Types of "Discovery"

Discussions concerning discovery generally involve several significantly different procedural matters that can usefully be distinguished. First, discovery may involve notice. Under the Federal Rules of Criminal Procedure, for example, a defendant must give pretrial notice concerning the intention to raise insanity or similar defenses, Fed.R.Crim.P. 12.2, or alibi, Fed.R.Crim.P. 12.1. Uniform Rules of Criminal Procedure 422 would require the prosecution to give the defense notice as to whether any evidence the prosecution intends to use was obtained by search, wiretap, lineup, or voice identification. It also requires notice concerning whether any confession or admission by the defendant, or evidence obtained by use of such confession or admission, will be offered.

A second type of discovery consists of one party's right of access to evidence in the possession of another party. Fed.R.Crim.P. 16(a)(1)(C), for example, gives a defendant the right to "inspect and copy or photograph" certain physical evidence in the possession of the government. A third category consists of a right to have certain items provided by the other party. Fed.R.Crim.P. 16(a)(1)(B) requires that upon request the government furnish the defendant with a copy of the defendant's criminal record.

Finally, a defendant may be obligated to participate in a procedure designed to develop certain evidence. Uniform Rules of Criminal Procedure 434, for example, would require a defendant under some circumstances to participate in a lineup, submit handwriting samples, and similarly cooperate in other nontestimonial procedures.

The timing of discovery must also be considered. As a general rule, a defendant's right to disclosure—especially of the statements of prosecution witnesses—during trial is broader than the right to pretrial access to them. But pretrial access to information may be of substantially greater value in preparing a defense or in deciding to accept an offered plea bargain rather than to mount any defense at all.

Implementation

There are wide variations as to the manner in which discovery is implemented. First, the duty to grant discovery may arise in several ways. A party may have a duty to provide discovery without request; Uniform Rules of Criminal Procedure 422 would impose upon the prosecution the duty to provide the notice discussed above without regard to any request by the defense. Or, the duty may depend upon request; the government's duty to give a defendant access to physical evidence under Fed.R.Crim.P. 16, discussed above, arises only upon defense request. In other situations, the duty arises only upon entry of a court order. The defendant's duty to participate in nontestimonial procedures under Uniform Rules of Criminal Procedure 434, for example, arises only when the court, upon motion by the prosecutor, orders such participation.

If issues arise as to whether discovery requirements have been adequately complied with, provisions are sometimes made for the court to consider certain evidence *in camera*, that is, without the presence of the parties, and to grant relief only if this consideration indicates that discovery is appropriate. Fed.R.Crim.Proc. 16(d)(1). If a party believes that only part of a document or similar item is subject to discovery, some procedures permit the party to excise the other portions of it, perhaps indicating on the copy furnished the opponent that an excision has been made. Uniform Rules of Criminal Procedure 421(b)(4).

A party who believes that otherwise required discovery is, for some special reason, inappropriate in the situation presented is sometimes authorized to apply to the court for an order denying or restricting disclosure or perhaps limiting further dissemination of the information by the party to whom it is disclosed. Fed.R.Crim.P. 16(d)(1), for example, provides:

> Upon a sufficient showing the court may at any time order that the discovery or inspection be denied, restricted, or deferred, or make such other order as is appropriate.

The duty to disclose is generally a continuing duty, so that if information not previously available is later developed the party has a responsibility to communicate it to the opponent. Fed.R.Crim.P. 16(c) provides:

> If, prior to or during trial a party discovers additional evidence or material previously requested or ordered, which is subject to discovery or inspection under this rule, he shall promptly notify the other party

or his attorney or the court of the existence of the additional evidence or material.

Work Product Exception

Work product of the lawyers in the case and perhaps their agents or investigators is often exempted from discovery. Fed.R.Crim.P. 16(a)(2), (b)(2). But there are wide variations as to what constitutes work product. The major question is whether factual information developed by lawyers or investigators is protected from disclosure. ABA Standard 11–2.6(b) limits the work product exception to "legal research" and "records, correspondence, reports or memoranda to the extent that they contain the opinions, theories or conclusions of the prosecuting attorneys or members of his legal staff." Uniform Rules of Criminal Procedure 421(b)(1) contains an identical provision. In United States v. Nobles, 422 U.S. 225, 95 S.Ct. 2160, 45 L.Ed.2d 141 (1975) the Supreme Court found no need to delineate the scope of the work product doctrine as a bar to disclosure at trial and specifically no need to determine whether it protected from disclosure to the government portions of a report by a defense investigator to defense counsel.

Sanctions

Trial judges are generally given broad discretion to fashion appropriate remedies for noncompliance with discovery requirements. Fed.R.Crim.P. 16(d)(2), for example, provides:

> the court may order [a] party to permit the discovery or inspection, grant a continuance, or prohibit the party from introducing evidence not disclosed, or it may enter such other order as it deems just under the circumstances.

Some formulations specifically authorize the trial judge, upon finding prosecutorial noncompliance with discovery requirements, to—among other options—consider dismissal of the prosecution. Uniform Rules of Criminal Procedure 421(e). This drastic remedy may not be favored. In People v. Zamora, 28 Cal.3d 88, 615 P.2d 1361, 167 Cal.Rptr. 573 (1980) defendant asserted excessive force as a defense to a charge of battery upon two police officers; the files concerning these officers, which may have indicated they were violence-prone, had been destroyed. Holding that the appropriate remedy was not dismissal of the charges, the court indicated that the jury should be told of the destruction of the records and that they could infer from this destruction that the records would have shown that the officers were prone to excessive force.

* * *

The Court dealt with the issue of precluding a defense witness from testifying as a discovery sanction in Taylor v. Illinois, 484 U.S. 400, 108 S.Ct. 646, 98 L.Ed.2d 798 (1988). Preparatory to Taylor's trial for attempted murder, his attorney was ordered to disclose to the prosecutor "the names and last known addresses of persons he intends to call as witnesses" as well as any statements they may have given the defense. The names of two defense witnesses were provided pursuant to this order. On the second day of trial, defense counsel sought to amend his witness list to include

Alfred Wormley, explaining to the court that he had not been included earlier because he did not know his whereabouts. The court reserved ruling on the motion until he heard Wormley's testimony. The next day, counsel appeared in court with Wormley, whose testimony was presented to the court outside the presence of the jury as an offer of proof. On cross-examination, Wormley acknowledged that he had been interviewed in his own home by defense counsel the preceding week. The trial court, expressing doubts about the veracity of Wormley's proposed testimony, precluded the defense from calling him to the stand. Following his conviction and its affirmance by the appellate court system, petitioner argued before the United States Supreme Court that precluding a defense witness from testifying as a sanction for a discovery violation was absolutely prohibited by the Compulsory Process Clause of the Sixth Amendment. The Court rejected that position:

> The principle that undergirds the defendant's right to present exculpatory evidence is also the source of essential limitations on the right. The adversary process could not function effectively without adherence to rules of procedure that govern the orderly presentation of facts and arguments to provide each party with a fair opportunity to assemble and submit evidence to contradict or explain the opponent's case. The trial processes would be a shambles if either party had an absolute right to control the time and content of his witnesses' testimony. ... The State's interest in the orderly conduct of a criminal trial is sufficient to justify the imposition and enforcement of firm, though not always inflexible, rules relating to the identification and presentation of evidence.

484 U.S. at 410–11, 108 S.Ct. at 653, 98 L.Ed.2d at 811–12. The Court also acknowledged that there are sanctions available that are less drastic than witness preclusion, such as granting the State a continuance or a mistrial or even holding the defendant or his attorney in contempt. The Court suggested that the preclusion sanction is appropriate in cases, such as this one, in which the violation is deliberate and engaged in to gain a tactical advantage over the opponent and is also appropriate in situations such as this in which the truthfulness of the proposed testimony of the witness is suspect. Justice Brennan, joined by Justices Marshall and Blackmun, dissented, taking the position that preclusion is permitted by the Compulsory Process Clause only when the defendant was personally involved in the discovery violation.

hmm... I kind of agree

Informal Practice

Even in those jurisdictions that have limited formal rights of discovery, local practice is often such that defense lawyers are given access to much or all of the prosecution's case in advance. Prosecutors provide such discovery in the belief that such a practice induces the disposition of cases by pleas of guilty because it shows defense counsel the strength of the government's case against his or her client. A major problem with this "open file" practice, however, is that defense lawyers' access to the prosecution's files may depend upon such matters as their experience and personal relationships with prosecuting attorneys. Thus the client of a defense lawyer who finds himself in the unusual situation of being denied access to the prosecution's files may be materially prejudiced because of considerations unrelated to the merits of his case or the interests of the criminal justice system. The absence of formal discovery rights, of course, precludes efforts to seek judicial redress. See Comment, In Search of the Adversary System—The Cooperative Practices of Private Criminal Defense Attorneys, 50 Tex.L.Rev. 60 (1971).

This Chapter considers separately issues raised by prosecutorial disclosure to the defense and defense disclosure to the prosecution. Both areas involve constitutional as well as other considerations.

A.   PROSECUTORIAL DISCLOSURE

FEDERAL RULES OF CRIMINAL PROCEDURE

Rule 16. Discovery and Inspection

(a) Disclosure of Evidence by the Government.

(1) Information Subject to Disclosure.

(A) *Statement of Defendant.* Upon request of a defendant the government shall disclose to the defendant and make available for inspection, copying, or photographing: any relevant written or recorded statements made by the defendant, or copies thereof, within the possession, custody or control of the government, the existence of which is known, or by the exercise of due diligence may become known, to the attorney for the government; that portion of any written record containing the substance of any relevant oral statement made by the defendant whether before or after arrest in response to interrogation by any person then known to the defendant to be a government agent; and recorded testimony of the defendant before a grand jury which relates to the offense charged. The government shall also disclose to the defendant the substance of any other relevant oral statement made by the defendant whether before or after arrest in response to interrogation by any person then known by the defendant to be a government agent if the government intends to use that statement at trial. * * *

(B) *Defendant's Prior Record.* Upon request of the defendant, the government shall furnish to the defendant such copy of his prior criminal record, if any, as is within the possession, custody, or control of the government, the existence of which is known, or by the exercise of due diligence may become known, to the attorney for the government.

(C) *Documents and Tangible Objects.* Upon request of the defendant the government shall permit the defendant to inspect and copy or photograph books, papers, documents, photographs, tangible objects, buildings or places, or copies or portions thereof, which are within the possession, custody or control of the government, and which are material to the preparation of his defense or are intended for use by the government as evidence in chief at the trial, or were obtained from or belong to the defendant.

(D) *Reports of Examinations and Tests.* Upon request of a defendant the government shall permit the defendant to inspect and copy or photograph any results or reports of physical or mental examinations, and of scientific tests or experiments, or copies thereof, which are within the possession, custody, or control of the government, the existence of which is known, or by the exercise of due diligence may become known, to the attorney for the government, and which are material to the preparation of the defense or are intended for use by the government as evidence in chief at the trial.

(E) Expert Witnesses. At the defendant's request, the government shall disclose to the defendant a written summary of testimony that the government intends to use under Rules 702 [Testimony by Experts], 703 [Bases of Opinion Testimony by Experts], or 705 [Disclosure of Facts or Data Underlying Expert Opinion] of the Federal Rules of Evidence during its case-in-chief at trial. If the government requests discovery [summary of testimony defendant intends to use under Rules 702, 703 or 705] under subdivision (b)(1)(C)(ii) [when the defendant has given notice of intent to present expert testimony on defendant's mental condition] of this rule and the defendant complies, the government shall, at the defendant's request, disclose to the defendant a written summary of testimony the government intends to use under Rules 702, 703, or 705 as evidence at trial on the issue of the defendant's mental condition. The summary provided under this subdivision shall describe the witnesses' opinions, the bases and the reasons for those opinions, and the witnesses' qualifications.

NOTE

In United States v. Armstrong, 517 U.S. 456, 116 S.Ct. 1480, 134 L.Ed.2d 687 (1996), the Court addressed the question of the scope of a defendant's right to discovery of documents or other tangible objects under Rule 16(a)(1)(C), particularly the meaning of "material to the preparation of his defense". The Court, through The Chief Justice, held that only material that is relevant to defeating the government's case-in-chief is discoverable under this provision. The respondent had requested discovery of prosecutorial records concerning the race of the defendants charged in an effort to make out a claim of selective prosecution. Under the Court's interpretation of Rule 16, he was not entitled to receive such material. Justices Souter, Ginsburg, Breyer and Stevens, all writing separately, disagreed with this holding or emphasized its limited application to selective prosecution claims.

1. CONSTITUTIONAL OBLIGATIONS

United States v. Bagley

Supreme Court of the United States, 1985.
473 U.S. 667, 105 S.Ct. 3375, 87 L.Ed.2d 481.

■ JUSTICE BLACKMUN announced the judgment of the Court and delivered an opinion of the Court except as to Part III.

In **Brady v. Maryland,** 373 U.S. 83, 87, 83 S.Ct. 1194, 1196, 10 L.Ed.2d 215 (1963), this Court held that "the suppression by the prosecution of evidence favorable to an accused upon request violates due process where the evidence is material either to guilt or punishment." The issue in the present case concerns the standard of materiality to be applied in determining whether a conviction should be reversed because the prosecutor failed to disclose requested evidence that could have been used to impeach Government witnesses.

I

In October 1977, respondent Hughes Anderson Bagley was indicted in the Western District of Washington on 15 charges of violating federal narcotics and firearms statutes. On November 18, 24 days before trial, respondent filed a discovery motion. The sixth paragraph of that motion requested:

> "The names and addresses of witnesses that the government intends to call at trial. Also the prior criminal records of witnesses, and any deals, promises or inducements made to witnesses in exchange for their testimony." App. 18.[1]

The Government's two principal witnesses at the trial were James F. O'Connor and Donald E. Mitchell. O'Connor and Mitchell were state law-enforcement officers employed by the Milwaukee Railroad as private security guards. Between April and June 1977, they assisted the federal Bureau of Alcohol, Tobacco and Firearms (ATF) in conducting an undercover investigation of respondent.

The Government's response to the discovery motion did not disclose that any "deals, promises or inducements" had been made to O'Connor or Mitchell. In apparent reply to a request in the motion's ninth paragraph for "[c]opies of all Jencks Act material,"[2] the Government produced a series of affidavits that O'Connor and Mitchell had signed between April 12 and May 4, 1977, while the undercover investigation was in progress. These affidavits recounted in detail the undercover dealings that O'Connor and Mitchell were having at the time with respondent. Each affidavit concluded with the statement, "I made this statement freely and voluntarily without any threats or rewards, or promises of reward having been made to me in return for it."

Respondent waived his right to a jury trial and was tried before the court in December 1977. At the trial, O'Connor and Mitchell testified about both the firearms and the narcotics charges. On December 23, the court

---

1. In addition, ¶ 10(b) of the motion requested "[p]romises or representations made to any persons the government intends to call as witnesses at trial, including but not limited to promises of no prosecution, immunity, lesser sentence, etc.," and ¶ 11 requested "[a]ll information which would establish the reliability of the Milwaukee Railroad Employees in this case, whose testimony formed the basis for the search warrant." App. 18–19.

2. The Jencks Act, 18 U.S.C. § 3500, requires the prosecutor to disclose, after direct examination of a Government witness and on the defendant's motion, any statement of the witness in the Government's possession that relates to the subject matter of the witness' testimony.

found respondent guilty on the narcotics charges, but not guilty on the firearms charges.

In mid–1980, respondent filed requests for information pursuant to the Freedom of Information Act and to the Privacy Act of 1974, 5 U.S.C. §§ 552 and 552a. He received in response copies of ATF form contracts that O'Connor and Mitchell had signed on May 3, 1977. Each form was entitled "Contract for Purchase of Information and Payment of Lump Sum Therefor." The printed portion of the form stated that the vendor "will provide" information to ATF and that "upon receipt of such information by the Regional Director, Bureau of Alcohol, Tobacco and Firearms, or his representative, and upon the accomplishment of the objective sought to be obtained by the use of such information to the satisfaction of said Regional Director, the United States will pay to said vendor a sum commensurate with services and information rendered." Each form contained the following typewritten description of services:

> "That he will provide information regarding T–I and other violations committed by Hughes A. Bagley, Jr.; that he will purchase evidence for ATF; that he will cut [sic] in an undercover capacity for ATF; that he will assist ATF in gathering of evidence and testify against the violator in federal court."

The figure "$300.00" was handwritten in each form on a line entitled "Sum to Be Paid to Vendor."

Because these contracts had not been disclosed to respondent in response to his pretrial discovery motion,[3] respondent moved under 28 U.S.C. § 2255 to vacate his sentence. He alleged that the Government's failure to disclose the contracts, which he could have used to impeach O'Connor and Mitchell, violated his right to due process under Brady v. Maryland, supra.

The motion came before the same District Judge who had presided at respondent's bench trial. An evidentiary hearing was held before a Magistrate. The Magistrate found that the printed form contracts were blank when O'Connor and Mitchell signed them and were not signed by an ATF representative until after the trial. He also found that on January 4, 1978, following the trial and decision in respondent's case, ATF made payments of $300 to both O'Connor and Mitchell pursuant to the contracts.[4] Although the ATF case agent who dealt with O'Connor and Mitchell testified that these payments were compensation for expenses, the Magistrate found that this characterization was not borne out by the record. There was no documentation for expenses in these amounts; Mitchell testified that his payment was not for expenses, and the ATF forms authorizing the payments treated them as rewards.

3. The Assistant United States Attorney who prosecuted respondent stated in stipulated testimony that he had not known that the contracts existed and that he would have furnished them to respondent had he known of them.

4. The Magistrate found, too, that ATF paid O'Connor and Mitchell, respectively, $90 and $80 in April and May 1977 before trial, but concluded that these payments were intended to reimburse O'Connor and Mitchell for expenses, and would not have provided a basis for impeaching O'Connor's and Mitchell's trial testimony. The District Court adopted this finding and conclusion.

The District Court adopted each of the Magistrate's findings except for the last one to the effect that "[n]either O'Connor nor Mitchell expected to receive the payment of $300 or any payment from the United States for their testimony." Instead, the court found that it was "probable" that O'Connor and Mitchell expected to receive compensation, in addition to their expenses, for their assistance, "though perhaps not for their testimony." The District Court also expressly rejected the Magistrate's conclusion that:

> "Because neither witness was promised or expected payment for his testimony, the United States did not withhold, during pretrial discovery, information as to any 'deals, promises or inducements' to these witnesses. Nor did the United States suppress evidence favorable to the defendant, in violation of Brady v. Maryland, 373 U.S. 83, 83 S.Ct. 1194, 10 L.Ed.2d 215 (1963)."

The District Court found beyond a reasonable doubt, however, that had the existence of the agreements been disclosed to it during trial, the disclosure would have had no effect upon its finding that the Government had proved beyond a reasonable doubt that respondent was guilty of the offenses for which he had been convicted. The District Court reasoned: Almost all of the testimony of both witnesses was devoted to the firearms charges in the indictment. Respondent, however, was acquitted on those charges. The testimony of O'Connor and Mitchell concerning the narcotics charges was relatively very brief. On cross-examination, respondent's counsel did not seek to discredit their testimony as to the facts of distribution but rather sought to show that the controlled substances in question came from supplies that had been prescribed for respondent's personal use. The answers of O'Connor and Mitchell to this line of cross-examination tended to be favorable to respondent. Thus, the claimed impeachment evidence would not have been helpful to respondent and would not have affected the outcome of the trial. Accordingly, the District Court denied respondent's motion to vacate his sentence.

The United States Court of Appeals for the Ninth Circuit reversed. Bagley v. Lumpkin, 719 F.2d 1462 (1983). The Court of Appeals began by noting that, according to precedent in the Circuit, prosecutorial failure to respond to a specific *Brady* request is properly analyzed as error, and a resulting conviction must be reversed unless the error is harmless beyond a reasonable doubt. The court noted that the District Judge who had presided over the bench trial concluded beyond a reasonable doubt that disclosure of the ATF agreement would not have affected the outcome. The Court of Appeals, however, stated that it "disagree[d]" with this conclusion. In particular, it disagreed with the Government's—and the District Court's—premise that the testimony of O'Connor and Mitchell was exculpatory on the narcotics charges, and that respondent therefore would not have sought to impeach "his own witness."

The Court of Appeals apparently based its reversal, however, on the theory that the Government's failure to disclose the requested *Brady* information that respondent could have used to conduct an effective cross-examination impaired respondent's right to confront adverse witnesses. The court noted: "In Davis v. Alaska, ... the Supreme Court held that the

Ct. of App. reverse conviction

denial of the 'right of *effective* cross-examination' was ' "constitutional error of the first magnitude" ' requiring automatic reversal." 719 F.2d, at 1464 (quoting Davis v. Alaska, 415 U.S. 308, 318, 94 S.Ct. 1105, 1111, 39 L.Ed.2d 347 (1974)) (emphasis added by Court of Appeals). In the last sentence of its opinion, the Court of Appeals concluded: "we hold that the government's failure to provide requested *Brady* information to Bagley so that he could effectively cross-examine two important government witnesses requires an automatic reversal."

We granted certiorari, 469 U.S. 1016, 105 S.Ct. 427, 83 L.Ed.2d 354 (1984), and we now reverse.

II

The holding in Brady v. Maryland requires disclosure only of evidence that is both favorable to the accused and "material either to guilt or punishment." 373 U.S., at 87, 83 S.Ct. at 1197. See also Moore v. Illinois, 408 U.S. 786, 794–795, 92 S.Ct. 2562, 2567–2568, 33 L.Ed.2d 706, (1972). The Court explained in United States v. Agurs, 427 U.S. 97, 104, 96 S.Ct. 2392, 2398, 49 L.Ed.2d 342 (1976): "A fair analysis of the holding in *Brady* indicates that implicit in the requirement of materiality is a concern that the suppressed evidence might have affected the outcome of the trial." The evidence suppressed in *Brady* would have been admissible only on the issue of punishment and not on the issue of guilt, and therefore could have affected only Brady's sentence and not his conviction. Accordingly, the Court affirmed the lower court's restriction of Brady's new trial to the issue of punishment.

The *Brady* rule is based on the requirement of due process. Its purpose is not to displace the adversary system as the primary means by which truth is uncovered, but to ensure that a miscarriage of justice does not occur. Thus, the prosecutor is not required to deliver his entire file to defense counsel, but only to disclose evidence favorable to the accused that, if suppressed, would deprive the defendant of a fair trial:

"For unless the omission deprived the defendant of a fair trial, there was no constitutional violation requiring that the verdict be set aside; and absent a constitutional violation, there was no breach of the prosecutor's constitutional duty to disclose. . . .

" . . . But to reiterate a critical point, the prosecutor will not have violated his constitutional duty of disclosure unless his omission is of sufficient significance to result in the denial of the defendant's right to a fair trial." 427 U.S., at 108, 96 S.Ct. at 2400.

In *Brady* and *Agurs,* the prosecutor failed to disclose exculpatory evidence. In the present case, the prosecutor failed to disclose evidence that the defense might have used to impeach the Government's witnesses by showing bias or interest. Impeachment evidence, however, as well as exculpatory evidence, falls within the *Brady* rule. See Giglio v. United States, 405 U.S. 150, 154, 92 S.Ct. 763, 766, 31 L.Ed.2d 104 (1972). Such evidence is "evidence favorable to an accused," *Brady,* 373 U.S. at 87, 83 S.Ct. at 1196, so that, if disclosed and used effectively, it may make the difference between conviction and acquittal. Cf. Napue v. Illinois, 360 U.S.

264, 269, 79 S.Ct. 1173, 1177, 3 L.Ed.2d 1217 (1959) ("The jury's estimate of the truthfulness and reliability of a given witness may well be determinative of guilt or innocence, and it is upon such subtle factors as the possible interest of the witness in testifying falsely that a defendant's life or liberty may depend").

The Court of Appeals treated impeachment evidence as constitutionally different from exculpatory evidence. According to that court, failure to disclose impeachment evidence is "even more egregious" than failure to disclose exculpatory evidence "because it threatens the defendant's right to confront adverse witnesses." 719 F.2d, at 1464. Relying on Davis v. Alaska, 415 U.S. 308, 94 S.Ct. 1105, 39 L.Ed.2d 347 (1974), the Court of Appeals held that the Government's failure to disclose requested impeachment evidence that the defense could use to conduct an effective cross-examination of important prosecution witnesses constitutes " 'constitutional error of the first magnitude' " requiring automatic reversal. 719 F.2d, at 1464 (quoting Davis v. Alaska, supra, at 318, 94 S.Ct. at 1111).

This Court has rejected any such distinction between impeachment evidence and exculpatory evidence. In Giglio v. United States, supra, the Government failed to disclose impeachment evidence similar to the evidence at issue in the present case, that is, a promise made to the key government witness that he would not be prosecuted if he testified for the Government. This Court said:

> "When the 'reliability of a given witness may well be determinative of guilt or innocence,' nondisclosure of evidence affecting credibility falls within the general rule [of *Brady*]. We do not, however, automatically require a new trial whenever 'a combing of the prosecutors' files after the trial has disclosed evidence possibly useful to the defense but not likely to have changed the verdict....' A finding of materiality of the evidence is required under *Brady*. ... A new trial is required if 'the false testimony could ... in any reasonable likelihood have affected the judgment of the jury....' " 405 U.S., at 154, 92 S.Ct. at 766 (citations omitted).

Thus, the Court of Appeals' holding is inconsistent with our precedents.

Moreover, the court's reliance on Davis v. Alaska for its "automatic reversal" rule is misplaced. In *Davis,* the defense sought to cross-examine a crucial prosecution witness concerning his probationary status as a juvenile delinquent. The defense intended by this cross-examination to show that the witness might have made a faulty identification of the defendant in order to shift suspicion away from himself or because he feared that his probationary status would be jeopardized if he did not satisfactorily assist the police and prosecutor in obtaining a conviction. Pursuant to a state rule of procedure and a state statute making juvenile adjudications inadmissible, the trial judge prohibited the defense from conducting the cross-examination. This Court reversed the defendant's conviction, ruling that the direct restriction on the scope of cross-examination denied the defendant "the right of effective cross-examination" which "would be constitutional error of the first magnitude and no amount of showing of want of prejudice would cure it. Brookhart v. Janis, 384 U.S. 1, 3, 86 S.Ct. 1245,

1246, 16 L.Ed.2d 314." 415 U.S., at 318, 94 S.Ct. at 1111 (quoting Smith v. Illinois, 390 U.S. 129, 131, 88 S.Ct. 748, 750, 19 L.Ed.2d 956 (1968)).

The present case, in contrast does not involve any direct restriction on the scope of cross-examination. The defense was free to cross-examine the witnesses on any relevant subject, including possible bias or interest resulting from inducements made by the Government. The constitutional error, if any, in this case was the Government's failure to assist the defense by disclosing information that might have been helpful in conducting the cross-examination. As discussed above, such suppression of evidence amounts to a constitutional violation only if it deprives the defendant of a fair trial. Consistent with "our overriding concern with the justice of the finding of guilt," United States v. Agurs, 427 U.S., at 112, 96 S.Ct. at 2401, a constitutional error occurs, and the conviction must be reversed, only if the evidence is material in the sense that its suppression undermines confidence in the outcome of the trial.

III

A

It remains to determine the standard of materiality applicable to the nondisclosed evidence at issue in this case. Our starting point is the framework for evaluating the materiality of *Brady* evidence established in United States v. Agurs. The Court in *Agurs* distinguished three situations involving the discovery, after trial, of information favorable to the accused that had been known to the prosecution but unknown to the defense. The first situation was the prosecutor's knowing use of perjured testimony or, equivalently, the prosecutor's knowing failure to disclose that testimony used to convict the defendant was false. The Court noted the well-established rule that "a conviction obtained by the knowing use of perjured testimony is fundamentally unfair, and must be set aside if there is any reasonable likelihood that the false testimony could have affected the judgment of the jury." 427 U.S., at 103, 96 S.Ct. at 2397 (footnote omitted). Although this rule is stated in terms that treat the knowing use of perjured testimony as error subject to harmless-error review, it may as easily be stated as a materiality standard under which the fact that testimony is perjured is considered material unless failure to disclose it would be harmless beyond a reasonable doubt. The Court in *Agurs* justified this standard of materiality on the ground that the knowing use of perjured testimony involves prosecutorial misconduct and, more importantly, involves "a corruption of the truth-seeking function of the trial process."

At the other extreme is the situation in *Agurs* itself, where the defendant does not make a *Brady* request and the prosecutor fails to disclose certain evidence favorable to the accused. The Court rejected a harmless-error rule in that situation, because under that rule every nondisclosure is treated as error, thus imposing on the prosecutor a constitutional duty to deliver his entire file to defense counsel. At the same time, the Court rejected a standard that would require the defendant to demonstrate that the evidence if disclosed probably would have resulted in acquittal. Id., at 111, 96 S.Ct. at 2401. The Court reasoned: "If the standard applied to the usual motion for a new trial based on newly discovered evidence were the same when the evidence was in the State's possession as when it was found in a neutral source, there would be no special significance to the prosecutor's obligation to serve the cause of justice." Ibid. The standard of materiality applicable in the absence of a specific *Brady* request is therefore stricter than the harmless-error standard but more lenient to the defense than the newly discovered evidence standard.

D req. & P ③
dn make
responsive ev.
com

The third situation identified by the Court in *Agurs* is where the defense makes a specific request and the prosecutor fails to disclose responsive evidence. The Court did not define the standard of materiality applicable in this situation, but suggested that the standard might be more lenient to the defense than in the situation in which the defense makes no request or only a general request. Id., at 106, 96 S.Ct. at 2398. The Court also noted: "When the prosecutor receives a specific and relevant request, the failure to make any response is seldom, if ever, excusable."

The Court has relied on and reformulated the *Agurs* standard for the materiality of undisclosed evidence in two subsequent cases arising outside the *Brady* context. In neither case did the Court's discussion of the *Agurs* standard distinguish among the three situations described in *Agurs*. In United States v. Valenzuela–Bernal, 458 U.S. 858, 874, 102 S.Ct. 3440, 3450, 73 L.Ed.2d 1193 (1982), the Court held that due process is violated when testimony is made unavailable to the defense by Government deportation of witnesses "only if there is a reasonable likelihood that the testimony could have affected the judgment of the trier of fact." And in Strickland v. Washington, 466 U.S. 668, 104 S.Ct. 2052, 80 L.Ed.2d 674 (1984), the Court held that a new trial must be granted when evidence is not introduced because of the incompetence of counsel only if "there is a reasonable probability that, but for counsel's unprofessional errors, the result of the proceeding would have been different." Id., at 694, 104 S.Ct. at 2068. The *Strickland* Court defined a "reasonable probability" as "a probability sufficient to undermine confidence in the outcome."

We find the *Strickland* formulation of the *Agurs* test for materiality sufficiently flexible to cover the "no request," "general request," and "specific request" cases of prosecutorial failure to disclose evidence favorable to the accused: The evidence is material only if there is a reasonable probability that, had the evidence been disclosed to the defense, the result of the proceeding would have been different. A "reasonable probability" is a probability sufficient to undermine confidence in the outcome.

The Government suggests that a materiality standard more favorable to the defendant reasonably might be adopted in specific request cases. The Government notes that an incomplete response to a specific request not only deprives the defense of certain evidence, but has the effect of representing to the defense that the evidence does not exist. In reliance on this misleading representation, the defense might abandon lines of independent investigation, defenses, or trial strategies that it otherwise would have pursued.

We agree that the prosecutor's failure to respond fully to a *Brady* request may impair the adversary process in this manner. And the more specifically the defense requests certain evidence, thus putting the prosecutor on notice of its value, the more reasonable it is for the defense to assume from the nondisclosure that the evidence does not exist, and to make pretrial and trial decisions on the basis of this assumption. This possibility of impairment does not necessitate a different standard of materiality, however, for under the *Strickland* formulation the reviewing court may consider directly any adverse effect that the prosecutor's failure to respond might have had on the preparation or presentation of the defendant's case. The reviewing court should assess the possibility that such effect might have occurred in light of the totality of the circumstances and with an awareness of the difficulty of reconstructing in a post-trial proceeding the course that the defense and the trial would have taken had the defense not been misled by the prosecutor's incomplete response.

B

In the present case, we think that there is a significant likelihood that the prosecutor's response to respondent's discovery motion misleadingly induced defense counsel to believe that O'Connor and Mitchell could not be impeached on the basis of bias or interest arising from inducements offered by the Government. Defense counsel asked the prosecutor to disclose any inducements that had been made to witnesses, and the prosecutor failed to disclose that the possibility of a reward had been held out to O'Connor and Mitchell if the information they supplied led to "the accomplishment of the objective sought to be obtained . . . to the satisfaction of [the Government]." This possibility of a reward gave O'Connor and Mitchell a direct, personal stake in respondent's conviction. The fact that the stake was not guaranteed through a promise or binding contract, but was expressly contingent on the Government's satisfaction with the end result, served only to strengthen any incentive to testify falsely in order to secure a conviction. Moreover, the prosecutor disclosed affidavits that stated that O'Connor and Mitchell received no promises of reward in return for providing information in the affidavits implicating respondent in criminal activity. In fact, O'Connor and Mitchell signed the last of these affidavits the very day after they signed the ATF contracts. While petitioner is technically correct that the blank contracts did not constitute a "promise of reward," the natural effect of these affidavits would be misleadingly to induce defense counsel to believe that O'Connor and Mitchell provided the information in the affidavits, and ultimately their testimony at trial recounting the same information, without any "inducements."

The District Court, nonetheless, found beyond a reasonable doubt that, had the information that the Government held out the possibility of reward to its witnesses been disclosed, the result of the criminal prosecution would not have been different. If this finding were sustained by the Court of Appeals, the information would be immaterial even under the standard of materiality applicable to the prosecutor's knowing use of perjured testimony. Although the express holding of the Court of Appeals was that the nondisclosure in this case required automatic reversal, the Court of Appeals also stated that it "disagreed" with the District Court's finding of harmless error. In particular, the Court of Appeals appears to have disagreed with the factual premise on which this finding expressly was based. The District Court reasoned that O'Connor's and Mitchell's testimony was exculpatory on the narcotics charges. The Court of Appeals, however, concluded, after reviewing the record, that O'Connor's and Mitchell's testimony was in fact inculpatory on those charges. 719 F.2d, at 1464, n. 1. Accordingly, we reverse the judgment of the Court of Appeals and remand the case to that court for a determination whether there is a reasonable probability that, had the inducement offered by the Government to O'Connor and Mitchell been disclosed to the defense, the result of the trial would have been different.

It is so ordered.

■ JUSTICE POWELL took no part in the decision of this case.

■ JUSTICE WHITE, with whom THE CHIEF JUSTICE and JUSTICE REHNQUIST join, concurring in part and concurring in the judgment. [omitted].

■ JUSTICE MARSHALL, with whom JUSTICE BRENNAN joins, dissenting. [omitted].

* * *

■ JUSTICE STEVENS, dissenting.

This case involves a straightforward application of the rule announced in Brady v. Maryland, 373 U.S. 83, 83 S.Ct. 1194, 10 L.Ed.2d 215 (1963), a case involving nondisclosure of material evidence by the prosecution in response to a specific request from the defense. I agree that the Court of Appeals misdescribed that rule, but I respectfully dissent from the Court's unwarranted decision to rewrite the rule itself.

* * *

The question in *Agurs* was whether the *Brady* rule should be *extended,* to cover a case in which there had been neither perjury nor a specific request—that is, whether the prosecution has some constitutional duty to search its files and disclose automatically, or in response to a general request, all evidence that "might have helped the defense, or might have affected the outcome." 427 U.S., at 110, 96 S.Ct. at 2400. Such evidence would, of course, be covered by the *Brady* formulation if it were specifically requested. We noted in *Agurs,* however, that because there had been no specific defense request for the later-discovered evidence, there was no notice to the prosecution that the defense did not already have that evidence or that it considered the evidence to be of particular value. Id., at 106–107, 96 S.Ct. at 2398–2399. Consequently, we stated that in the absence of a request the prosecution has a constitutional duty to volunteer only "obviously exculpatory evidence." Id., at 107. Because this constitutional duty to disclose is *different* from the duty described in *Brady,* it is not surprising that we developed a different standard of materiality in the *Agurs* context. Necessarily describing the "inevitably imprecise" standard in terms appropriate to post-trial review, we held that no constitutional violation occurs in the absence of a specific request unless "the omitted evidence creates a reasonable doubt that did not otherwise exist." Id., at 108, 112, 96 S.Ct. at 2399, 2402.

What the Court ignores with regard to *Agurs* is that its analysis was restricted entirely to the general or no-request context. The "standard of materiality" we fashioned for the purpose of determining whether a prosecutor's failure to *volunteer* exculpatory evidence amounted to constitutional error was and is unnecessary with regard to the two categories of prosecutorial suppression already covered by the *Brady* rule. The specific situation in *Agurs,* as well as the circumstances of United States v. Valenzuela-Burnal, 458 U.S. 858, 102 S.Ct. 3440, 73 L.Ed.2d 1193 (1982) and Strickland v. Washington, 466 U.S. 668, 104 S.Ct. 2052, 80 L.Ed.2d 674 (1984), simply fall "outside the *Brady* context."

But the *Brady* rule itself unquestionably applies to this case, because the Government failed to disclose favorable evidence that was clearly responsive to the defendant's specific request. Bagley's conviction therefore must be set aside if the suppressed evidence was "material"—and it obviously was—and if there is "any reasonable likelihood" that it could have affected the judgment of the trier of fact. ...

The Court, however, today sets out a reformulation of the *Brady* rule in which I have no such confidence. Even though the prosecution suppressed evidence that was specifically requested, apparently the Court of Appeals may now reverse only if there is a "reasonable probability" that the suppressed evidence "would" have altered "the result of the trial." According to the Court this single rule is "sufficiently flexible" to cover specific as well as general or no-request instances of nondisclosure, because, at least in the view of Justice Blackmun and Justice O'Connor, a reviewing court can "consider directly" under this standard the more threatening effect that nondisclosure in response to a specific defense request will generally have on the truth-seeking function of the adversary process. (Opinion of Justice Blackmun).

I cannot agree. The Court's approach stretches the concept of "materiality" beyond any recognizable scope, transforming it from merely an evidentiary concept as used in *Brady* and *Agurs,* which required that material evidence be admissible and probative of guilt or innocence in the context of a specific request, into a result-focused standard that seems to include an independent weight in favor of affirming convictions despite evidentiary suppression. Evidence favorable to an accused and relevant to the dispositive issue of guilt apparently may still be found not "material," and hence suppressible by prosecutors prior to trial, unless there is a reasonable probability that its use would result in an acquittal. Justice Marshall rightly criticizes the incentives such a standard creates for prosecutors "to gamble, to play the odds, and to take a chance that evidence will later turn out not to have been potentially dispositive."

Moreover, the Court's analysis reduces the significance of deliberate prosecutorial suppression of potentially exculpatory evidence to that merely of one of numerous factors that "may" be considered by a reviewing court. This is not faithful to our statement in *Agurs* that "[w]hen the prosecutor receives a specific and relevant request, the failure to make any response is seldom, if ever, excusable." 427 U.S., at 106, 96 S.Ct. at 2399. Such suppression is far more serious than mere nondisclosure of evidence in which the defense has expressed no particular interest. A reviewing court should attach great significance to silence in the face of a specific request, when responsive evidence is later shown to have been in the Government's possession. Such silence actively misleads in the same way as would an affirmative representation that exculpatory evidence does not exist when, in fact, it does (i.e., perjury)—indeed, the two situations are aptly described as "sides of a single coin." Babcock, Fair Play; Evidence Favorable to An Accused and Effective Assistance of Counsel, 34 Stan.L.Rev. 1133, 1151 (1982).

Accordingly, although I agree that the judgment of the Court of Appeals should be vacated and that the case should be remanded for further proceedings, I disagree with the Court's statement of the correct standard to be applied. I therefore respectfully dissent from the judgment that the case be remanded for determination under the Court's new standard.

NOTES

1. **Is there a duty to preserve evidence?** Are police under a constitutional obligation to preserve evidence that might prove useful to a defendant in the trial of a criminal charge? In California v. Trombetta, 467 U.S. 479, 104 S.Ct. 2528, 81 L.Ed.2d 413 (1984), the respondent was arrested for driving while intoxicated. He provided police with a sample of his breath which was analyzed by an intoxilyzer machine. The readout from the machine was admitted at trial under a presumption of intoxication law. The California Court of Appeal reversed the conviction on the ground it was a violation of due process for the police not to preserve a sample of respondent's breath, using available means, to permit defense testing. The Supreme Court, on petition of the State of California, reversed the Court of Appeal. Justice Marshall, writing for a unanimous Court, noted that the Court has

> never squarely addressed the Government's duty to take affirmative steps to preserve evidence on behalf of criminal defendants. The absence of doctrinal development in this area reflects, in part, the difficulty of developing rules to deal with evidence destroyed through prosecutorial neglect or oversight. Whenever potentially exculpatory evidence is permanently lost, courts face the treacherous task of divining the import of materials whose contents is unknown and, very often, disputed.... Moreover, fashioning remedies for the illegal destruction of evidence can pose troubling choices. In nondisclosure cases, a court can grant the defendant a new trial at which the previously suppressed evidence may be introduced. But, when evidence has been destroyed in violation of the Constitution, the court must choose between barring further prosecution or suppressing ... the State's most probative evidence.

467 U.S. at 486–87, 104 S.Ct. at 2533, 81 L.Ed.2d at 420. Justice Marshall noted that California officials acted in good faith and in accordance with their normal practices. There is no claim of official animus toward the respondent or of a conscious effort to suppress exculpatory evidence.

> Whatever duty the Constitution imposes on the States to preserve evidence, that duty must be limited to evidence that might be expected to play a significant role in the suspect's defense. To meet this standard of constitutional materiality, see United States v. Agurs ..., evidence must both possess an exculpatory value that was apparent before the evidence was destroyed, and also be of such a nature that the defendant would be unable to obtain comparable evidence by other reasonably available means.

467 U.S. at 488–89, 104 S.Ct. at 2534, 81 L.Ed.2d at 422. Finally, Justice Marshall observed that the chances are extremely remote that any preserved breath sample would have been exculpatory.

The Court returned to the issue in Arizona v. Youngblood, 488 U.S. 51, 109 S.Ct. 333, 102 L.Ed.2d 281 (1988). During investigation of a sexual assault upon a ten-year old child, officers collected the victim's clothing, which contained stains made by the assailant's semen, but did not freeze or refrigerate it. At trial, Youngblood's principal defense was that the victim's identification was in error. Expert testimony was introduced that had the victim's clothing been frozen or refrigerated, tests could have been done that would have exonerated Youngblood, assuming he was in fact not the assailant. The state appellate courts held the resulting conviction invalid, but the Supreme Court reversed. The likelihood that the unpreserved evidence would have exonerated the defendant, Chief Justice Rehnquist noted for the Court, was greater in *Youngblood* than in *Trombetta,* but the prosecution had not attempted to make any use of the materials in its own case. Despite this, the Court held that "unless a criminal defendant can show bad faith on the part of the police, failure to preserve potentially useful evidence does not constitute a denial of due process." The requirement of bad faith, it explained,

> both limits the extent of the police's obligation to preserve evidence to reasonable bounds and confines it to that class of cases where the interests of justice most clearly require it, i.e., those cases in which the police themselves by their conduct indicate that the evidence could form a basis for exonerating the defendant.

488 U.S. at 58, 109 S.Ct. at 337, 102 L.Ed.2d at 289. While the officers here may have been negligent, there was "no suggestion" of bad faith. The Court also disapproved a suggestion by the lower court that the police were constitutionally deficient for failing to conduct the tests themselves:

> The situation here is no different than a prosecution for drunk driving that rests on police observation alone; the defendant is free to argue to the finder of fact that a breathalyzer test might have been exculpatory, but the police do not have a constitutional duty to perform any particular tests.

488 U.S. at 59, 109 S.Ct. at 338, 102 L.Ed.2d at 290. Justice Stevens concurred in the judgment, but declined to adopt an absolute requirement of bad faith. 488 U.S. at 59, 109 S.Ct. at 338, 102 L.Ed.2d at 290–91 (Stevens, J., concurring in the judgment). Justice Blackmun, joined by Justices Brennan and Marshall, dissented:

> [W]here no comparable evidence is likely to be available to the defendant, police must preserve physical evidence of a type that they reasonably should know has the potential, if tested, to reveal immutable characteristics of the criminal, and hence to exculpate a defendant charged with the crime.

488 U.S. at 69, 109 S.Ct. at 343, 102 L.Ed.2d at 297 (Blackmun, J., dissenting).

2. **Information in the possession of others.** What information in the possession of persons other than the prosecutors actually trying the case must be disclosed under the Due Process standard? In Giglio v. United States, 405 U.S. 150, 92 S.Ct. 763, 31 L.Ed.2d 104 (1972) certain information concerning a promise made to a witness was in the possession of an Assistant United States Attorney who had been involved in Giglio's prosecution at an early stage. When questioned at trial, the witness denied having been promised anything for his testimony. The Assistant United States Attorney who tried the case was unaware of the promise. Nevertheless, the Supreme Court found a violation of Due Process. A prosecutor's office is an "entity," the Court reasoned, and the lawyers involved in a case have a responsibility to pass along information to lawyers who subsequently assume responsibility for the case.

3. **Timing of disclosure.** When must disclosure required by Due Process occur? In United States v. McPartlin, 595 F.2d 1321 (7th Cir.1979), defendants appealed a conviction on the ground that withholding evidence favorable to them

until the beginning of the trial violated their due process rights under *Brady.* The court stated:

> There is nothing in *Brady* or *Agurs* to require that such disclosures be made before trial,.... Thus, even though evidence might be material or might create a reasonable doubt as to guilt, Due Process, albeit requiring eventual disclosure, does not require that in all instances this disclosure must occur before trial.
>
> The appropriate standard to be applied in a case such as this is whether the disclosure came so late as to prevent the defendant from receiving a fair trial.

595 F.2d at 1346. The court reasoned:

> The concern of *Agurs* and *Brady* is whether the suppression of exculpatory material until after trial requires that a new trial be given so that this evidence may be considered. The Court in *Agurs* characterized the situations to which the *Brady* principles apply as those involving "the discovery, *after trial,* of information which had been known to the prosecution but unknown to the defense." 427 U.S. at 103, 96 S.Ct. at 2397 (emphasis supplied). Indeed the standard developed in *Agurs* can only sensibly be applied to the suppression of evidence throughout the trial: "if the *omitted* evidence creates a reasonable doubt that did not otherwise exist, constitutional error has been committed." Id. at 112, 96 S.Ct. at 2402 (emphasis supplied).

Id. Similar views have been expressed by other circuits.

4. **Materiality.** *Bagley*'s materiality standard was addressed in some detail in Kyles v. Whitley, 514 U.S. 419, 115 S.Ct. 1555, 131 L.Ed.2d 490 (1995). Kyles sought federal habeas corpus relief from his Louisiana conviction and death sentence on the ground that the prosecution had failed to disclose a number of exculpatory matters. Discussing the federal constitutional law to be applied to Kyles' contention, the Court explained:

> Four aspects of materiality under *Bagley* bear emphasis. Although the constitutional duty is triggered by the potential impact of favorable but undisclosed evidence, a showing of materiality does not require demonstration by a preponderance that disclosure of the suppressed evidence would have resulted ultimately in the defendant's acquittal (whether based on the presence of reasonable doubt or acceptance of an explanation for the crime that does not inculpate the defendant). *Bagley*'s touchstone of materiality is a "reasonable probability" of a different result, and the adjective is important. The question is not whether the defendant would more likely than not have received a different verdict with the evidence, but whether in its absence he received a fair trial, understood as a trial resulting in a verdict worthy of confidence. A "reasonable probability" of a different result is accordingly shown when the Government's evidentiary suppression "undermines confidence in the outcome of the trial." *Bagley,* 473 U.S., at 678, 105 S.Ct., at 3381.
>
> The second aspect of *Bagley* materiality bearing emphasis here is that it is not a sufficiency of evidence test. A defendant need not demonstrate that after discounting the inculpatory evidence in light of the undisclosed evidence, there would not have been enough left to convict. The possibility of an acquittal on a criminal charge does not imply an insufficient evidentiary basis to convict. One does not show a *Brady* violation by demonstrating that some of the inculpatory evidence should have been excluded, but by showing that the favorable evidence could reasonably be taken to put the whole case in such a different light as to undermine confidence in the verdict.

*[handwritten marginal note: *Not probable acquittal]*

*[handwritten marginal note: *Not legal insufficiency]*

Third, we note that * * * once a reviewing court applying *Bagley* has found constitutional error there is no need for further harmless-error review. Assuming arguendo that a harmless error enquiry were to apply, a *Bagley* error could not be treated as harmless, since "a reasonable probability that, had the evidence been disclosed to the defense, the result of the proceeding would have been different," necessarily entails the conclusion that the suppression must have had " 'substantial and injurious effect or influence in determining the jury's verdict,' " Brecht v. Abrahamson, 507 U.S. 619, 113 S.Ct. 1710, 1712, 123 L.Ed.2d 353 (1993) [(setting out the standard of harmlessness generally to be applied in habeas cases)], quoting Kotteakos v. United States, 328 U.S. 750, 776, 66 S.Ct. 1239, 1253, 90 L.Ed. 1557 (1946). * * *

The fourth and final aspect of *Bagley* materiality to be stressed here is its definition in terms of suppressed evidence considered collectively, not item-by-item. * * * [T]he Constitution is not violated every time the government fails or chooses not to disclose evidence that might prove helpful to the defense. We have never held that the Constitution demands an open file policy (however such a policy might work out in practice), and the rule in *Bagley* (and, hence, in *Brady*) requires less of the prosecution than the ABA Standards for Criminal Justice, which call generally for prosecutorial disclosures of any evidence tending to exculpate or mitigate.

While the definition of *Bagley* materiality in terms of the cumulative effect of suppression must accordingly be seen as leaving the government with a degree of discretion, it must also be understood as imposing a corresponding burden. On the one side, showing that the prosecution knew of an item of favorable evidence unknown to the defense does not amount to a *Brady* violation, without more. But the prosecution, which alone can know what is undisclosed, must be assigned the consequent responsibility to gauge the likely net effect of all such evidence and make disclosure when the point of "reasonable probability" is reached. This in turn means that the individual prosecutor has a duty to learn of any favorable evidence known to the others acting on the government's behalf in the case, including the police. But whether the prosecutor succeeds or fails in meeting this obligation (whether, that is, a failure to disclose is in good faith or bad faith), the prosecution's responsibility for failing to disclose known, favorable evidence rising to a material level of importance is inescapable.

The State of Louisiana would prefer an even more lenient rule. It pleads that some of the favorable evidence in issue here was not disclosed even to the prosecutor until after trial, and it suggested below that it should not be held accountable under *Bagley* and *Brady* for evidence known only to police investigators and not to the prosecutor. To accommodate the State in this manner would, however, amount to a serious change of course from the *Brady* line of cases. In the State's favor it may be said that no one doubts that police investigators sometimes fail to inform a prosecutor of all they know. But neither is there any serious doubt that "procedures and regulations can be established to carry [the prosecutor's] burden and to insure communication of all relevant information on each case to every lawyer who deals with it." Giglio v. United States, 405 U.S. 150, 154, 92 S.Ct. 763, 766, 31 L.Ed.2d 104 (1972). Since, then, the prosecutor has the means to discharge the government's *Brady* responsibility if he will, any argument for excusing a prosecutor from disclosing what he does not happen to know about boils down to a plea to substitute the police for the prosecutor, and even for the courts themselves, as the final arbiters of the government's obligation to ensure fair trials.

Short of doing that, we were asked at oral argument to raise the threshold of materiality because the *Bagley* standard "makes it difficult ... to know" from the "perspective [of the prosecutor at] trial ... exactly what might become important later on." The State asks for "a certain amount of leeway in making a judgment call" as to the disclosure of any given piece of evidence.

Uncertainty about the degree of further "leeway" that might satisfy the State's request for a "certain amount" of it is the least of the reasons to deny the request. At bottom, what the State fails to recognize is that, with or without more leeway, the prosecution cannot be subject to any disclosure obligation without at some point having the responsibility to determine when it must act. Indeed, even if due process were thought to be violated by every failure to disclose an item of exculpatory or impeachment evidence (leaving harmless error as the government's only fallback), the prosecutor would still be forced to make judgment calls about what would count as favorable evidence, owing to the very fact that the character of a piece of evidence as favorable will often turn on the context of the existing or potential evidentiary record. Since the prosecutor would have to exercise some judgment even if the State were subject to this most stringent disclosure obligation, it is hard to find merit in the State's complaint over the responsibility for judgment under the existing system, which does not tax the prosecutor with error for any failure to disclose, absent a further showing of materiality. Unless, indeed, the adversary system of prosecution is to descend to a gladiatorial level unmitigated by any prosecutorial obligation for the sake of truth, the government simply cannot avoid responsibility for knowing when the suppression of evidence has come to portend such an effect on a trial's outcome as to destroy confidence in its result.

This means, naturally, that a prosecutor anxious about tacking too close to the wind will disclose a favorable piece of evidence. This is as it should be. Such disclosure will serve to justify trust in the prosecutor as "the representative ... of a sovereignty ... whose interest ... in a criminal prosecution is not that it shall win a case, but that justice shall be done." Berger v. United States, 295 U.S. 78, 88, 55 S.Ct. 629, 633, 79 L.Ed. 1314 (1935). And it will tend to preserve the criminal trial, as distinct from the prosecutor's private deliberations, as the chosen forum for ascertaining the truth about criminal accusations. The prudence of the careful prosecutor should not therefore be discouraged.

514 U.S. at 434–40, 115 S.Ct. at 1565–69, 131 L.Ed.2d at 506–10.

In the course of concluding that on the complicated facts before it the nondisclosed information at issue was material under *Bagley,* the Court commented that undisclosed information that would have permitted "the effective impeachment of one eyewitness can call for a new trial even though the attack does not extend directly to others." 514 U.S. at 445, 115 S.Ct. at 1571, 131 L.Ed.2d at 513. This, Justice Scalia observed in dissent, "is the major contribution of today's opinion to *Brady* litigation." "[W]ith our endorsement," he continued, "it will surely be trolled past appellate courts in all future failure to disclose cases." 514 U.S. at 469, 115 S.Ct. at 1582, 131 L.Ed.2d at 528 (Scalia, J., dissenting). He disagreed with the majority's comments on the merits of the matter:

The weakening of one witness's testimony does not weaken the unconnected testimony of another witness; and to entertain the possibility that the jury will give it such an effect is incompatible with the whole idea of a materiality standard, which presumes that the incriminating evidence that would have been destroyed by proper disclosure can be logically separated from the incriminating evidence that would have remained unaffected.

514 U.S. at 469, 115 S.Ct. at 1583, 131 L.Ed.2d at 528.

The Court returned to *Bagley* materiality in Wood v. Bartholomew, 516 U.S. 1, 116 S.Ct. 7, 133 L.Ed.2d 1 (1995)(per curiam). At Bartholomew's state trial for premeditated murder, his brother Rodney testified that Bartholomew had told him before the events that he planned to rob the target laundromat and leave no witnesses. Prosecutors failed to disclose to the defense that before trial Rodney had taken a lie detector test and his negative answers to several questions (had he assisted the defendant in the robbery and had he and the defendant been in laundromat together) indicated deception to the examiner. The federal appeals court considering Bartholomew's request for federal habeas corpus relief had erred, the Supreme Court concluded, in finding that this information was "material" under *Bagley*. Evidence of the result of the test results was itself inadmissible. The lower court's conclusion that defense counsel, had he been given this information, would have discovered admissible evidence indicating innocence was "based on mere speculation, in violation of the standards [the Supreme Court has] established." Bartholomew's contention that had defense counsel been given this information he would have deposed Rodney before trial and thus have been able to more effectively cross-examine Rodney at trial was similarly insufficient; defense counsel sought to minimize his cross-examination of Rodney and unsuccessful efforts in the federal habeas proceeding to use the lie detector results in eliciting contradictions or admissions from Rodney suggest defense counsel would have fared no better before trial. A finding of materiality, the Court stressed, must be based on "more than speculation with slight support * * *." 516 U.S. at 8, 116 S.Ct. at 11, 133 L.Ed.2d at 8.

+778 n.2

2.   STATUTORY CONSIDERATIONS

Apart from possible constitutional limits, a number of significant issues regarding prosecutorial disclosure exist. Some concern the extent to which it is desirable to provide for such discovery. Other and obviously related ones deal with the construction of statutes and court rules authorizing disclosure. Much of the controversy concerns defense access to the prior statements of prosecution witnesses. This is the subject of the principal case in this subsection.

People v. Bassett

Supreme Court of Illinois, 1974.
56 Ill.2d 285, 307 N.E.2d 359.

■ DAVIS, JUSTICE.

[In the course of a prison riot hostages were taken and three guards killed. Defendants were convicted of murder.]

It is urged that the prosecution had in its possession various statements, made by witnesses for the People, which should have been turned over to the defense in accordance with People v. Wolff (1960), 19 Ill.2d 318, 167 N.E.2d 197. This question is now controlled by Supreme Court Rule 412, which was not effective at the time of this trial.

. . . Section (a)(i) of Supreme Court Rule 412 provides that upon written motion of defense counsel the State shall disclose to defense counsel the following material and information within its possession and control:

"(i) the names and last known addresses of persons whom the State intends to call as witnesses, together with their relevant written or recorded statements, memoranda containing substantially verbatim reports of their oral statements, and a list of memoranda reporting or summarizing their oral statements. Upon written motion of defense counsel memoranda reporting or summarizing oral statements shall be examined by the court *in camera* and if found to be substantially verbatim reports of oral statements shall be disclosed to defense counsel." 50 Ill.2d R. 412.

Wolff concerned testimony given by a People's witness who testified on cross-examination that he had made a statement to the police, but couldn't recall if it had been written down. Defense counsel then asked if the statement had ever been shown to the witness, the State objected on the ground that defense counsel was assuming the existence of the statement, and the objection was sustained. In *Wolff*, at page 327, 167 N.E.2d at page 201, this court stated:

"... where no privilege exists, and where the relevancy and competency of a statement or report has been established, the trial judge shall order the document delivered directly to the accused for his inspection and use for impeachment purposes. However, if the prosecution claims that any document ordered to be produced contains matter which does not relate to the testimony of the witness sought to be impeached, the trial judge will inspect the document and may, at his discretion, delete unrelated matters before delivery is made to the accused."

The instant case concerns interviews by State personnel with at least 800 to 900 inmates of Menard Penitentiary. The procedure followed according to the prosecuting attorneys, was that notes would be taken on yellow paper during the interview but these would not be verbatim notes. After all the interviews were completed, these notes were transcribed onto white cards, allegedly containing a narrative of what the prosecutor expected to prove by each witness. The prosecution claims that no attempt was made to obtain the signatures of those being interviewed and no such "formal statement" was produced.

It must be conceded that the representatives of the People who conducted these interviews sought to take notes that would be of some use in the preparation and trial of the case; and that when assistant Attorney General Crain or others transcribed these original "rough notes" into "narrative" form on white cards, it was done in such a manner as to make these cards useful at trial. It would seem that these cards would be useless unless they accurately summarized the point the People wished to be proved by any given witness.

There is also testimony that these cards were used in discussing a prospective witness's testimony before trial, and that at the discussion the witness thought he was being told what he had said in his initial interview. He did not say that what was read to him from the card was word for word what he had previously stated, but that it accurately reflected the substance of what he had told the interviewer.

In this case the defense could not prove the existence of the original notes, for they had been destroyed by the prosecution. The defense was then faced with showing that the white cards being used by Crain were verbatim or substantially verbatim copies of the witnesses' earlier remarks. Crain stated repeatedly and strenuously that no verbatim or substantially verbatim statements existed. The truth or falsity of this statement depends upon one's conception of the rationale behind the *Wolff* case and later decisions.

In People v. Sumner (1969), 43 Ill.2d 228, 235, 252 N.E.2d 534, 538, we stated:

> "Curtis's statement should also have been given to the defendant. This court in People v. Wolff, 19 Ill.2d 318, 167 N.E.2d 197, expressly adopted the Federal rule first announced in Jencks v. United States, 353 U.S. 657, 77 S.Ct. 1007, 1 L.Ed.2d 1103, and later made part of a Federal statute (18 U.S.C. sec. 3500) that where the relevancy and competency of a statement or report has been established, and no privilege exists, the trial court, on appropriate demand, shall order the statement or report delivered directly to the accused for his inspection and possible use for impeachment purposes. (19 Ill.2d at 327, 167 N.E.2d 197; see also People v. Cagle, 41 Ill.2d 528, 532, 244 N.E.2d 200.) It was expressly recognized in *Wolff* that once a statement is shown to contain pertinent material, only the defense should be permitted to determine whether it may be useful for impeachment."

This decision precludes the trial court from examining the statement to determine if it is in fact impeaching.

Sumner outlines the proper approach to the problem, and the application of that rationale to the instant case requires that the white cards used by the People's attorneys at trial should have been made available to the defense for impeachment purposes. It must be noted that there may be some problem here in determining what is or is not the substance of the statement by the witness.

The prosecution admittedly had recorded information on white cards of such a nature as to be useful in its examination of the witnesses. The prosecutor had not personally interviewed all of the witnesses, and he could not possibly keep over 800 interviews straight in his mind, even if he had. These cards, by their very nature, had to be a reproduction in one form or another of what the witness said when interviewed earlier. As such, that portion of the material which can fairly be said to be the witness's statement must be turned over to the defense so that they may determine its worth as impeachment material. In the event the prosecutor claims that validly protected work product is also contained in the statement, the trial judge can review the material *in camera* for the limited purpose of excising the work-product material.

The defense here has laid as good a foundation for the admission of this evidence as is possible, and should have been provided the white cards for examination, subject to the People's right to have work product deleted therefrom. The People argue that the destruction of the rough notes taken during interviews of witnesses does not warrant the striking of the witnesses' testimony, absent a showing of bad faith on the part of the State. We agree with that general proposition, but inasmuch as we have held that the white cards should have been made available to the defense, the issue of the destruction of the original rough notes loses its relevance.

■ UNDERWOOD, CHIEF JUSTICE (dissenting):

* * *

If the majority's reason for requiring production of the summaries is that the "yellow sheets" upon which the original "rough notes" were written have been destroyed by the State, it would, in my opinion, be far preferable to simply say so. As matters now stand, Rule 412 and our earlier decisions require statements to be verbatim or substantially so before their production may be ordered; the majority opinion appears to eliminate that requirement. The answers to questions which arise in almost every criminal case ought not to be left by this court in such a confusing state.

NOTES

1. **Witness lists.** Whether pretrial disclosure to the defense of the identities of prosecution witnesses is desirable remains disputed. The model discovery provisions favor disclosure. ABA Standard 11–2.1(a)(1); Uniform Rules of Criminal Procedure 421(a). But Fed.R.Crim.P. 16 does not provide for this. A 1975 proposed revision would have required the government, upon request, to furnish the defense with a written list of witnesses the government intends to call at trial. This was rejected by Congress. Federal Rules of Criminal Procedure Amendments Act of 1975, 89 Stat. 370 (1975). The House Conference Report indicates that concerns regarding discouragement of witnesses and improper contacts designed to influence the testimony of witnesses were responsible for the legislative action. H. Conf. Report No. 94–414, 94th Cong., 1st Sess. (1975), reprinted in [1975] U.S.Code Cong. & Ad.News 713, 716. In capital cases, however, a federal statute requires a prosecutor to provide the defense with a list of prosecution witnesses at least three days before trial. 18 U.S.C.A. § 3432.

2. **Jencks material.** Disclosure of a prosecution witness's statements after the witness has testified is widely regarded as a matter distinguishable from pretrial disclosure and is more generally available. The rule requiring such disclosure is commonly referred to as the Jencks rule, after Jencks v. United States, 353 U.S. 657, 77 S.Ct. 1007, 1 L.Ed.2d 1103 (1957) in which the Court first recognized a right to such disclosure in federal criminal prosecutions. The basic provision governing such disclosure in federal litigation is Rule 26.2 of the Federal Rules of Criminal Procedure:

> (a) Motion for Production. After a witness other than the defendant has testified on direct examination, the court, on motion of a party who did not call the witness, shall order the attorney for the government or the defendant and the defendant's attorney, as the case may be, to produce, for the examination and use of the moving party, any statement of the witness that is in their possession and that relates to the subject matter concerning which the witness has testified.

> (b) Production of Entire Statement. If the entire contents of the statement relate to the subject matter concerning which the witness has testified, the court shall order that the statement be delivered to the moving party.

(c) Production of Excised Statement. If the other party claims that the statement contains privileged information or matter that does not relate to the subject matter concerning which the witness has testified, the court shall order that it be delivered to the court in camera. Upon inspection, the court shall excise the portions of the statement that are privileged or that do not relate to the subject matter concerning which the witness has testified, and shall order that the statement, with such material excised, be delivered to the moving party. Any portion of the statement that is withheld from the defendant over the defendant's objection must be preserved by the attorney for the government, and, if the defendant appeals a conviction, must be made available to the appellate court for the purpose of determining the correctness of the decision to excise the portion of the statement.

(d) Recess for Examination of Statement. Upon delivery of the statement to the moving party, the court, upon application of that party, may recess the proceedings so that counsel may examine the statement and prepare to use it in the proceedings.

(e) Sanction for Failure to Produce Statement. If the other party elects not to comply with an order to deliver a statement to the moving party, the court shall order that the testimony of the witness be stricken from the record and that the trial proceed, or, if it is the attorney for the government who elects not to comply, shall declare a mistrial if required by the interest of justice.

(f) Definition. As used in this rule, a "statement" of a witness means:

(1) a written statement made by the witness that is signed or otherwise adopted or approved by the witness;

(2) a substantially verbatim recital of an oral statement made by the witness that is recorded contemporaneously with the making of the oral statement and that is contained in a stenographic, mechanical, electrical, or other recording or a transcription thereof; or

(3) a statement, however taken or recorded, or a transcription thereof, made by the witness to a grand jury.

(g) Scope of Rule. This rule applies at a suppression hearing conducted under Rule 12, at trial under this rule, and to the extent specified:

(1) in Rule 32(c)(2) at sentencing;

(2) in Rule 32.1(c) at a hearing to revoke or modify probation or supervised release;

(3) in Rule 46(i) at a detention hearing;

(4) in Rule 8 of the Rules Governing Proceedings under 28 U.S.C. § 2255; and

(5) in Rule 5.1 at a preliminary examination.

3. **Police reports.** Should police reports be subject to pretrial discovery? Consider State v. Eads, 166 N.W.2d 766, 769 (Iowa 1969) holding that the trial court abused its discretion in ordering disclosure of such a report. Suppose a police report or similar document quotes directly the words of persons interviewed. Does that make them—or at least portions of them—"statements" of those persons and subject to discovery if the governing court rule or statute makes statements of such persons discoverable? See State v. Latimore, 284 So.2d 423, 425 (Fla.App.1973), holding that "police and other investigation reports *which do not quote [a person whose statement is subject to disclosure] directly and are never signed or shown to that person* are not statements within [the discovery rule] and thus are not subject to discovery thereunder." (emphasis supplied)

B. DISCLOSURE BY THE DEFENSE

EDITORS' INTRODUCTION: DEFENSE DISCLOSURE PROVISIONS

As defendants' rights to discovery from the prosecution increased, a parallel trend developed requiring at least certain discovery by the prosecution from the defendant. Generally, however, even in those jurisdictions that provide for defense disclosure, the prosecution is required to disclose more than it is entitled to obtain from the defense.

Perhaps the most widely-provided form of disclosure required of the defense concerns the intention to raise certain defenses. The federal provisions are typical. Fed.R.Crim.P. 12.1 requires the defense, upon written demand of the government, to provide the government with pretrial written notice of intent to offer a defense of alibi. This notice is to state the specific place or places at which the defendant will claim to have been at the time of the alleged offense and the names and addresses of those witnesses upon whom the defense will rely in an effort to establish this alibi. Fed.R.Crim.P. 12.2 requires the defense, without any demand by the government, to notify the government in writing before trial of the defense intention to rely upon the defense of insanity at trial or to introduce expert testimony bearing upon the issue of whether the defendant had the mental state required for the offense charged.

Some jurisdictions go further. Ariz.R.Crim.P. 15.2(b) requires notice by the defendant of all defenses as to which the defense will introduce evidence at trial, "including but not limited to, alibi, insanity, self-defense, entrapment, impotency, marriage, insufficiency of a prior conviction, mistaken identity, and good character." The notice is to include specification concerning the persons, including the defendant, who will be called as witnesses at trial in support of each defense. The first version of the ABA Standards contained a similar provision. Standards Relating to Discovery and Procedure Before Trial, Standard 3.3 (Approved Draft, 1970). In 1978, however, these were revised to require notice only regarding alibi and defenses involving mental impairments. II Standards for Criminal Justice, Standard 11–3.3 (1980). The commentary suggests some difficulty in interpreting how literally "any defense" in the original formulation was to be taken. In addition, it notes that disclosure should be limited to those defenses that tend to require special preparation by the prosecution or that are likely to generate midtrial delays if pretrial notice is not given. Alibi and insanity, it concludes, are defenses "generally considered" to have these characteristics. Id., at 11.55.

Provision is also sometimes made for prosecution access to physical items in the possession of the defense. Fed.R.Crim.P. 16(b)(1), for example, provides:

(1) Information Subject to Disclosure.

(A) *Documents and Tangible Objects.* If the defendant requests disclosure under subdivision (a)(1)(C) or (D) [providing for inspection and copying of documents, tangible objects, and reports of examinations and tests, see page 758, supra] of this rule, upon compliance with such request of the government, the defendant, on request of the government shall permit the government to inspect and copy or photograph books, papers, documents, photographs, tangible objects, or copies or portions thereof, which are within the possession, custody, or control of the defendant and which the defendant intends to introduce as evidence in chief at the trial.

(B) *Reports of Examinations and Tests.* If the defendant requests disclosure under subdivision (a)(1)(C) or (D) of this rule, upon compliance with such request by the government, the defendant, on request of the government, shall permit the government to inspect and copy or photograph any results or reports of physical or mental examinations and of scientific tests or experiments made in connection with the particular case, or copies thereof, within the possession or control of the defendant, which the defendant intends to introduce as evidence in chief at the trial or which were prepared by a witness whom the defendant intends to call at the trial when the results or reports relate to his testimony.

(C) Expert Witnesses. Under the following circumstances, the defendant shall, at the government's request, disclose to the government a written summary of testimony that the defendant intends to use under Rules 702, 703, or 705 of the Federal Rules of Evidence at trial: (i) if the defendant requests disclosure under subdivision (a)(1)(E) of this rule and the government complies, or (ii) if the defendant has given notice under Rule 12.2(b) of an intent to present expert testimony on the defendant's mental condition. This summary shall describe the witnesses' opinion, the bases and reasons for those opinions, and the witnesses' qualifications.

A major consideration is the extent to which a defendant's duty to disclose or provide access should be conditioned upon the defendant's exercise of his right to discovery against the prosecution. It is, of course, under Fed.R.Crim.P. 16(b)(1), above. The ABA's advisory committee urged unconditional discovery:

> If disclosures to the accused promotes finality, orderliness, and efficiency in prosecution generally, these gains should not depend upon the possible capricious willingness of the accused to make reciprocal discovery. ... Certainly, the usual reasons for denying disclosure to the accused—dangers of "perjury or intimidation of witnesses—are not alleviated by forcing the defendant to make discovery, nor are they heightened by his failure to disclose."

Standards Relating to Discovery and Procedure Before Trial, Commentary to § 1.2, p. 45 (Approved Draft 1970). The first version of the ABA Standards provided for independent discovery. ABA Standards 3.1, 3.2, 3.3 (Approved Draft 1970). In the 1978 revision, defense disclosure of reports or statements which the defense intends to use at trial was made conditional upon the defendant's having invoked his discovery rights, following the pattern of Fed.R.Crim.P. 16(b)(1). No explanation was offered. II Standards for Criminal Justice, Standard 11-3.2 (1980). The Advisory Committee on the Federal Rules noted that making the government's right to discovery conditional may minimize the risk that government discovery will be viewed as an infringement of the defendant's constitutional rights. Committee on Rules of Practice and Procedure of the Judicial Conference of the United States, Preliminary Draft of Proposed Amendments to Rules of Criminal Procedure for the United States District Courts, 48 F.R.D. 546, 607 (1970).

The major—but not only—constitutional concern regarding defense disclosure is whether such requirements violate defendant's privilege against compelled self-incrimination. In Williams v. Florida, 399 U.S. 78, 90 S.Ct. 1893, 26 L.Ed.2d 446 (1970), the Court considered Florida's requirement that a defendant intending to claim alibi give the state pretrial notice of this intention and furnish the prosecution with information as to the place the defendant will claim to have been and with the names and addresses of alibi witnesses the defense plans to use. Nothing in the Fifth Amendment, the Court reasoned, would preclude a trial court from granting a continuance at trial upon the State's request after an alibi witness had testified. Nor would the State be precluded from using this continuance to locate or develop rebuttal evidence and using this when trial continued. The Florida rule, it concluded, did essentially the same thing:

> At most, the rule only compelled petitioner to accelerate the timing of his disclosure, forcing him to divulge at an earlier date information that the petitioner from the beginning planned to divulge at trial. Nothing in the Fifth Amendment entitles a defendant as a matter of constitutional right to await the end of the State's case before announcing the nature of his defense, any more than it entitles him to await the jury's verdict on the State's case-in-chief before deciding whether or not to take the stand himself.

399 U.S. at 85, 90 S.Ct. at 1898, 26 L.Ed.2d at 452. Justice Black, dissenting, argued that a defendant who complied with the requirement and later decided not to present the alibi defense might suffer an infringement of Fifth Amendment interests under the Florida rule:

> Necessarily the defendant will have given the prosecutor the names of persons who may have some knowledge about the defendant himself or his activities. Necessarily the prosecutor will have every incentive to question these persons fully, and in doing so he may discover new leads or evidence. Undoubtedly, there will be situations in which the State will seek to use such information—information it would probably never have obtained but for the defendant's coerced cooperation.

399 U.S. at 110, 90 S.Ct. at 1911, 26 L.Ed.2d at 482. Justice Black's approach had been earlier accepted by the California Supreme Court, which had held that a defendant could not be compelled to disclose prior to trial the names, addresses and expected testimony of defense witnesses. Prudhomme v. Superior Court, 2 Cal.3d 320, 466 P.2d 673, 85 Cal.Rptr. 129 (1970). The California court did, however, indicate that disclosure could be required concerning witnesses who would be produced concerning a particular defense and perhaps other categories of witnesses "from which a court could attempt to determine [disclosure's] incriminating effect." 2 Cal.3d at 326, 466 P.2d at 677, 85 Cal.Rptr. at 133.

The Florida rule at issue in *Williams* required that after defense disclosure of intent to offer an alibi, the State notify the defense of any witnesses it intends to offer in rebuttal to the alibi. In Wardius v. Oregon, 412 U.S. 470, 93 S.Ct. 2208, 37 L.Ed.2d 82 (1973) the Court struck down as violative of Due Process the Oregon notice-of-alibi rule which imposed no such reciprocal duty on the state:

> [I]n the absence of a strong showing of state interests to the contrary, discovery must be a two-way street. The State may not insist that trials be run as a "search for truth" so far as defense witnesses are concerned, while maintaining "poker game" secrecy for its own witnesses. It is fundamentally unfair to require a defendant to divulge the details of his own case while at the same time subjecting him to the hazard of surprise concerning refutation of the very pieces of evidence which he disclosed to the State.

412 U.S. at 475–76, 93 S.Ct. at 2212–13, 37 L.Ed.2d at 88.

In Brooks v. Tennessee, 406 U.S. 605, 92 S.Ct. 1891, 32 L.Ed.2d 358 (1972), the Court held invalid a state statute requiring that if a defendant testifies in his own defense this must be done before any other defense testimony is taken. Emphasizing that a defendant might not be able to assess at the end of the State's case the extent to which his own testimony would be useful or necessary to his defense, the Court held the requirement an impermissible burden on the defendant's privilege against self-incrimination and a violation of the due process right to "the guiding hand of counsel." Would a requirement that the defendant disclose before trial whether or not he will testify in his defense be subject to the same objection?

United States v. Nobles

Supreme Court of the United States, 1975.
422 U.S. 225, 95 S.Ct. 2160, 45 L.Ed.2d 141.

■ Mr. Justice Powell delivered the opinion of the Court.

In a criminal trial, defense counsel sought to impeach the credibility of key prosecution witnesses by testimony of a defense investigator regarding statements previously obtained from the witnesses by the investigator. The question presented here is whether in these circumstances a federal trial court may compel the defense to reveal the relevant portions of the investigator's report for the prosecution's use in cross-examining him. The U.S. Court of Appeals for the Ninth Circuit concluded that it cannot. 510 F.2d 146. We granted certiorari, 419 U.S. 1119, 95 S.Ct. 801, 42 L.Ed.2d 819 (1975), and now reverse.

I.

Respondent was tried and convicted on charges arising from an armed robbery of a federally insured bank. The only significant evidence linking him to the crime was the identification testimony of two witnesses, a bank teller and a salesman who was in the bank during the robbery. Respondent offered an alibi but, as the Court of Appeals recognized, 510 F.2d, at 150, his strongest defense centered around attempts to discredit these eyewitnesses. Defense efforts to impeach them gave rise to the events that lead to this decision.

In the course of preparing respondent's defense, an investigator for the defense interviewed both witnesses and preserved the essence of those conversations in a written report. When the witnesses testified for the prosecution, respondent's counsel relied on the report in conducting their cross-examination. Counsel asked the bank teller whether he recalled having told the investigator that he had seen only the back of the man he identified as respondent. The witness replied that he did not remember making such a statement. He was allowed, despite defense counsel's initial objection, to refresh his recollection by referring to a portion of the investigator's report. The prosecutor also was allowed to see briefly the relevant portion of the report. The witness thereafter testified that although the report indicated that he told the investigator he had seen only respondent's back, he in fact had seen more than that and continued to insist that respondent was the bank robber.

The other witness acknowledged on cross-examination that he too had spoken to the defense investigator. Respondent's counsel twice inquired whether he told the investigator that "all blacks looked alike" to him, and in each instance the witness denied having made such a statement. The prosecution again sought inspection of the relevant portion of the investigator's report, and respondent's counsel again objected. The court declined to order disclosure at that time, but ruled that it would be required if the investigator testified as to the witnesses' alleged statements from the witness stand. The court further advised that it would examine the investigator's report *in camera* and would excise all reference to matters not relevant to the precise statements at issue.

After the prosecution completed its case, respondent called the investigator as a defense witness. The court reiterated that a copy of the report, inspected and edited *in camera*, would have to be submitted to Government counsel at the completion of the investigator's impeachment testimony. When respondent's counsel stated that he did not intend to produce the report, the court ruled that the investigator would not be allowed to testify about his interviews with the witnesses.

The Court of Appeals for the Ninth Circuit, . . . found that the Fifth Amendment prohibited the disclosure condition imposed in this case. . . . [W]e think the court erred.

* * *

The Court of Appeals concluded that the Fifth Amendment renders criminal discovery "basically a one-way street." 501 F.2d, at 154. Like many generalizations in constitutional law, this one is too broad. The relationship between the accused's Fifth Amendment rights and the prosecution's ability to discover materials at trial must be identified in a more discriminating manner.

The Fifth Amendment privilege against compulsory self-incrimination is an "intimate and personal one," which protects "a private inner sanctum of individual feeling and thought and proscribes state intrusion to exact self-condemnation." Couch v. United States, 409 U.S. 322, 327, 93 S.Ct. 611, 615, 34 L.Ed.2d 548 (1973). As we noted in Couch, 409 U.S., at 328, "the privilege is a *personal* privilege: it adheres basically to the person, not to information that may incriminate him."

In this instance disclosure of the relevant portions of the defense investigator's report would not impinge on the fundamental values protected by the Fifth Amendment. The court's order was limited to statements allegedly made by third parties who were available as witnesses to both the prosecution and the defense. Respondent did not prepare the report, and there is no suggestion that the portions subject to the disclosure order reflected any information that he conveyed to the investigator. The fact that these statements of third parties were elicited by a defense investigator on respondent's behalf does not convert them into respondent's personal communications. Requiring their production from the investigator therefore would not in any sense compel respondent to be a witness against himself or extort communications from him.

We thus conclude that the Fifth Amendment privilege against compulsory self-incrimination, being personal to the defendant, does not extend to the testimony or statements of third parties called as witnesses at trial. The Court of Appeals' reliance on this constitutional guarantee as a bar to the disclosure here ordered was misplaced.

* * *

The court's preclusion sanction was an entirely proper method of assuring compliance with its order. Respondent's argument that this ruling deprived him of the Sixth Amendment rights to compulsory process and cross-examination misconceives the issue. The District Court did not bar the investigator's testimony. It merely prevented respondent from presenting to the jury a partial view of the credibility issue by adducing the investigator's testimony and thereafter refusing to disclose the contemporaneous report that might offer further critical insights. The Sixth Amendment does not confer the right to present testimony free from the legitimate demands of the adversarial system; one cannot invoke the Sixth Amendment as a justification for presenting what might have been a half-truth. Deciding, as we do, that it was within the court's discretion to assure that the jury would hear the full testimony of the investigator rather than a truncated portion favorable to respondent, we think it would be artificial indeed to deprive the court of the power to effectuate that judgment. Nor do we find constitutional significance in the fact that the court in this instance was able to exclude the testimony in advance rather than receive it in evidence and thereafter charge the jury to disregard it when respondent's counsel refused, as he said he would, to produce the report.

NOTES

1. **Notice of defense evidence.** The respondent in Michigan v. Lucas, 500 U.S. 145, 111 S.Ct. 1743, 114 L.Ed.2d 205 (1991) was charged with the rape of his former girlfriend. Under Michigan's rape shield law, evidence of the victim's prior sexual conduct was made inadmissible, subject to an exception for prior sexual acts between the defendant and the victim. For the exception to apply, the defendant

was required to give notice of intent to present such evidence and an offer of proof within 10 days of his arraignment. The trial court would then conduct an in camera hearing to determine whether the proposed evidence would be admitted. Lucas failed to give the statutory notice but wished at trial to introduce his own testimony that he and the victim had had sexual intercourse prior to the incident on trial. The trial court refused to permit this testimony for failure to comply with the rape shield statute. The Michigan Court of Appeals reversed Lucas' conviction on the ground that as applied to prior sexual relations between the defendant and the victim the notice provision serves no useful purpose. The Supreme Court, in an opinion by Justice O'Connor, reversed the Court of Appeals. The Court found that the notice requirement

> permits a prosecutor to interview persons who know the parties and otherwise investigate whether such a prior relationship actually existed. When a prior sexual relationship is conceded, the notice-and-hearing procedure allows a court to determine in advance of trial whether evidence of the relationship "is material to a fact at issue in the case" and whether "its inflammatory or prejudicial nature outweigh[s] its probative value." [Quoting from the Michigan statute.]

500 U.S. at 150, 111 S.Ct. at 1747, 114 L.Ed.2d at 212. Citing United States v. Nobles and Taylor v. Illinois, the Court held that the Michigan Court of Appeals

> erred in adopting a *per se* rule that Michigan's notice-and-hearing requirement violates the Sixth Amendment in all cases where it is used to preclude evidence of past sexual conduct between a rape victim and a defendant. The Sixth Amendment is not so rigid. The notice-and-hearing requirement serves legitimate state interests in protecting against surprise, harassment, and undue delay. Failure to comply with this requirement may in some cases justify even the severe sanction of preclusion.

500 U.S. at 152, 111 S.Ct. at 1748, 114 L.Ed.2d at 214. The Court remanded the case to the Michigan court to determine whether the state statute authorized preclusion and, if so, whether on these particular facts preclusion would violate the Sixth Amendment. Justice Stevens, joined by Justice Marshall, dissented. Justice Blackmun filed a concurring opinion.

2. **Reciprocal discovery in California.** In 1990, California voters approved an initiative measure—the Crime Victims Justice Reform Act or Proposition 115— that made numerous changes in the state's criminal justice system, often thus "overruling" decisions of the California Supreme Court. Among the changes made were modifications of discovery. Article I of the California Constitution was amended to add Section 30, which provides in part:

> (c) In order to provide for fair and speedy trials, discovery in criminal cases shall be reciprocal in nature, as prescribed by the Legislature or by the people through the initiative process.

The initiative measure also added a new Chapter to the Penal Code. This chapter mandates discovery by both the defendant and the prosecution. With regard to disclosure by the defense, Section 1054.3 provides:

> The defendant and his or her attorney shall disclose to the prosecuting attorney:

> (a) The names and addresses of persons, other than the defendant, he or she intends to call as witnesses at trial, together with any relevant written or recorded statements of those persons, or reports of the statements of those persons, including any reports or statements of experts made in connection with the case, and including the results of physical or mental examinations,

scientific tests, experiments, or comparisons which the defendant intends to offer in evidence at the trial.

(b) Any real evidence which the defendant intends to offer in evidence at the trial.

Under section 1054.6, neither the defendant nor the prosecutor is required to disclose any materials or information which are work product as defined in section 2018 of the Code of Civil Procedure. Section 2018(c) defines "work product" as "[a]ny writing that reflects an attorney's impressions, conclusions, opinions, or legal research or theories * * *."

CHAPTER 18

RIGHT TO AN IMPARTIAL TRIAL

Analysis

EDITORS' INTRODUCTION: CHANGE OF VENUE AND OF JUDGE

Defendants and society in general both have an important interest in having "fair" trials, in the sense that the trials result in accurate determinations as to whether there was proof beyond a reasonable doubt of the defendants' guilt. This interest may be endangered by any of a number of circumstances. Among those most frequently claimed, however, are incompetence of the trial judge, bias or partiality of the trial judge or members of the trial jury, consideration by the trial jury or judge of information other than evidence admitted at trial, and the presence of disruptive factors that prevent the judge or jury from carefully and objectively evaluating the sufficiency of the evidence produced by the prosecution to prove guilt. Assuring that trials are not affected by such circumstances is, of course, primarily a nonconstitutional matter of local procedure. But it is also clear that dangers to fairness may violate the general requirement of due process or more specific federal constitutional rights that are, in part at least, designed to assure trial accuracy.

Some of these rights are addressed elsewhere in this book. The prohibition against trying an incompetent defendant, for example, considered in Chapter 16, is in part based upon the fear that a trial conducted without the defendant's participation will result in error. Those aspects of the right to jury trial that involve a defendant's right to a verdict joined by an adequate number of a jury of adequate size and to participate in selecting that jury—addressed in Chapter 23—also, of course, are based in large part upon the need to assure accuracy. The present Chapter presents several additional matters related to the fairness of the trial process.

There are several aspects of nonconstitutional procedure that are designed to deal with the problems raised in the principal case contained in this Chapter. These procedures need to be examined as background for consideration of that case.

Change of Venue

Venue in criminal proceedings generally lies in the locality (often the county) in which the conduct constituting the crime was committed. But American jurisdictions generally have procedures for changing the location of a trial when there is sufficient reason to believe that trial in the locality provided by general venue rules would be "unfair." Uniform Rules of Criminal Procedure Rule 462 is a useful example of such a provision:

Rule 462. [Transfer of Prosecution]

(a) *For Prejudice in the [County].* Upon motion of the defendant [or the prosecuting attorney] conforming to Rule 451, [or upon its own motion,] the court shall transfer the prosecution as to the defendant to another [county] if satisfied that there is a reasonable likelihood that a fair and impartial trial cannot be had in the [county] in which it is pending. The motion may be supported by qualified public opinion surveys or opinion testimony offered by individuals. A showing of actual prejudice is not required. It is not a ground for a denial of the motion that one transfer has already been granted.

(b) *Transfer in Other Cases.* For the convenience of parties or witnesses and in the interest of justice, the court upon motion of the defendant may transfer the prosecution as to him to another [county].

(c) *Disposition.* A motion for transfer made before the jury is impaneled shall be disposed of before impaneling. If a motion for transfer is permitted to be made, or if reconsideration or review of a prior denial is sought, after impaneling, the fact that the jury satisfies legal requirements is not controlling if it appears there is a reasonable likelihood that a fair and impartial trial cannot be had in the [county] in which the prosecution is pending.

(d) *Claim not Precluded.* A claim that a prosecution should have been transferred is not precluded by a waiver of the right to trial by jury or by a failure to exercise all available peremptory challenges.

Unlike some state provisions, the Uniform Rule does not require that a motion for transfer or change of venue be accompanied by sworn statements that a fair trial cannot be had in the locality. It makes optional a provision for motion by the prosecutor, which is part of many state provisions. By requiring that the trial judge determine only that there is a "reasonable likelihood" that a fair trial cannot be had in the locality, the Uniform Rule apparently uses a less restrictive standard than is applied in many jurisdictions, which require a finding that in fact a fair trial cannot be had in the locality.

Change or Substitution of Judge

Local procedures also often provide for proceedings to determine whether the case should be heard before a judge other than the one initially designated to hear it. There is substantial variation among the provisions. The Uniform Rules of Criminal Procedure provide as follows:

Rule 741. [Substitution of Judge]

(a) *On Demand.* A defendant may obtain a substitution of the judge before whom a trial or other proceeding is to be conducted by filing a demand therefor, but if trial has commenced before a judge no demand may be filed as to him. A defendant may not file more than one demand in a case. If there are two or more defendants, a defendant may not file a demand, if another defendant has filed a demand, unless a motion for severance of defendants has been denied. The demand shall be signed by the defendant or his counsel, and shall be filed at least [ten days] before the time set for commencement of trial and at least [three days] before the time set for any other proceeding, but it may be filed within [one day] after the defendant ascertains or should have ascertained the judge who is to preside at the trial or proceeding.

(b) *On Own Motion.* A judge on his own motion may disqualify himself from presiding over a trial or other proceeding.

(c) *For Cause.* A judge may not preside over a trial or other proceeding if upon motion of a party it appears that he is disqualified for a cause provided [by law or by the Code of Judicial Conduct]. The motion to disqualify shall be heard before another judge regularly sitting in the same court or a judge designated by [the appropriate assigning authority], and, unless otherwise ordered by that judge for cause, shall be made at least [ten days] before the time set for commencement of trial and at least [three days] before the time set for any other proceeding, but it may be made within [one day] after the party ascertains or should have ascertained the judge who is to preside at the trial or proceeding.

Probably the major variation among provisions for change of judge is the split as to whether at least one change should be available upon simple request and without inquiry into possible causes, such as bias. The arguments for providing a right to such a change of judge include claims that inquiries into the existence of bias invite delay, detract from the dignity and public image of the courts, strain the relationships between counsel and the judge, and often arouse such resentment that if the effort to establish grounds for disqualification fails the procedure may well assure the impossibility of a fair trial. Moreover, it is claimed, lawyers can be relied upon to use restraint in exercising the right to an automatic change of judge. See Staff Report, Disqualification of Judges for Prejudice or Bias—Common Law Evolution, Current Status, and the Oregon Experience, 48 Ore.L.Rev. 311, 401 (1969). But given the likely basis for a motion for automatic change of judge, perhaps judges will react to such motions much the same as they would react to specified and supported assertions concerning their alleged biases or inadequacies.

Murphy v. Florida

Supreme Court of the United States, 1975.
421 U.S. 794, 95 S.Ct. 2031, 44 L.Ed.2d 589.

■ MR. JUSTICE MARSHALL delivered the opinion of the Court.

The question presented by this case is whether the petitioner was denied a fair trial because members of the jury had learned from news accounts about a prior felony conviction or certain facts about the crime with which he was charged. Under the circumstances of this case, we find that petitioner has not been denied due process, and we therefore affirm the judgment below.

I.

Petitioner was convicted in the Dade County, Florida, Criminal Court in 1970 of breaking and entering a home, while armed, with intent to commit robbery, and of assault with intent to commit robbery. The charges stemmed from the January 1968 robbery of a Miami Beach home and petitioner's apprehension, with three others, while fleeing from the scene.

The robbery and petitioner's arrest received extensive press coverage because petitioner had been much in the news before. He had first made himself notorious for his part in the 1964 theft of the Star of India sapphire from a museum in New York. His flamboyant life style made him a continuing subject of press interest; he was generally referred to—at least in the media—as "Murph the Surf."

Before the date set for petitioner's trial on the instant charges, he was indicted on two counts of murder in Broward County, Florida. Thereafter the Dade County court declared petitioner mentally incompetent to stand trial; he was committed to a hospital and the prosecutor *nolle prossed* the robbery indictment. In August 1968 he was indicted by a federal grand jury for conspiring to transport stolen securities in interstate commerce. After petitioner was adjudged competent for trial, he was convicted on one count of murder in Broward County (March 1969) and pleaded guilty to one count of the federal indictment involving stolen securities (December 1969). The indictment for robbery was refiled in August 1969 and came to trial one year later.

The events of 1968 and 1969 drew extensive press coverage. Each new case against petitioner was considered newsworthy, not only in Dade County but elsewhere as well. The record in this case contains scores of articles reporting on petitioner's trials and tribulations during this period; many purportedly relate statements that petitioner or his attorney made to reporters.

Jury selection in the present case began in August 1970. Seventy-eight jurors were questioned. Of these, 30 were excused for miscellaneous personal reasons; 20 were excused peremptorily by the defense or prosecution; 20 were excused by the court as having prejudged petitioner; and the remaining eight served as the jury and two alternates. Petitioner's motions to dismiss the chosen jurors, on the ground that they were aware that he had previously been convicted of either the 1964 Star of India theft or the Broward County murder, were denied, as was his renewed motion for a change of venue based on allegedly prejudicial pretrial publicity.

At trial, petitioner did not testify or put on any evidence; assertedly in protest of the selected jury, he did not cross-examine any of the State's witnesses. He was convicted on both counts, and after an unsuccessful appeal he sought habeas corpus relief in the District Court for the Southern District of Florida.

The District Court denied petitioner relief, D.C.Fla., 363 F.Supp. 1224, and the Court of Appeals for the Fifth Circuit affirmed. 495 F.2d 553 (1974). We granted certiorari, 419 U.S. 1088, 95 S.Ct. 677, 42 L.Ed.2d 680 (1974) in order to resolve the apparent conflict between the decision below and that of the Third Circuit in United States ex rel. Doggett v. Yeager, 472

F.2d 229 (1973), over the applicability of Marshall v. United States, 360 U.S. 310, 79 S.Ct. 1171, 3 L.Ed.2d 1250 (1959), to state criminal proceedings.

II.

The defendant in *Marshall* was convicted of dispensing certain drugs without a prescription. In the course of the trial seven of the jurors were exposed to various news accounts relating that Marshall had previously been convicted of forgery, that he and his wife had been arrested for other narcotics offenses, and that he had for some time practiced medicine without a license. After interviewing the jurors, however, the trial judge denied a motion for a mistrial, relying on the jurors' assurances that they could maintain impartiality in spite of the news articles.

Noting that the jurors had been exposed to information with a high potential for prejudice, this Court reversed the conviction. It did so, however, expressly "[i]n the exercise of [its] supervisory power to formulate and apply proper standards for enforcement of the criminal law in the federal courts," and not as a matter of constitutional compulsion. 360 U.S., at 313, 79 S.Ct. at 1173.

In the face of so clear a statement, it cannot be maintained that *Marshall* was a constitutional ruling now applicable, through the Fourteenth Amendment, to the States. Petitioner argues, nonetheless that more recent decisions of this Court have applied to state cases the principle underlying the *Marshall* decision: that persons who have learned from news sources of a defendant's prior criminal record are presumed to be prejudiced. We cannot agree that *Marshall* has any application beyond the federal courts.

Petitioner relies principally upon Irvin v. Dowd, 366 U.S. 717, 81 S.Ct. 1639, 6 L.Ed.2d 751 (1961), Rideau v. Louisiana, 373 U.S. 723, 83 S.Ct. 1417, 10 L.Ed.2d 663 (1963), Estes v. Texas, 381 U.S. 532, 85 S.Ct. 1628, 14 L.Ed.2d 543 (1965), and Sheppard v. Maxwell, 384 U.S. 333, 86 S.Ct. 1507, 16 L.Ed.2d 600 (1966). In each of these cases, this Court overturned a state court conviction obtained in a trial atmosphere that had been utterly corrupted by press coverage.

In Irvin v. Dowd the rural community in which the trial was held had been subjected to a barrage of inflammatory publicity immediately prior to trial, including information on the defendant's prior convictions, his confession to 24 burglaries and six murders including the one for which he was tried, and his unaccepted offer to plead guilty in order to avoid the death sentence. As a result, eight of the 12 jurors had formed an opinion that the defendant was guilty before the trial began; some went "so far as to say that it would take evidence to overcome their belief" in his guilt. In these circumstances, the Court readily found actual prejudice against the petitioner to a degree that rendered a fair trial impossible.

Prejudice was presumed in the circumstances under which the trials in *Rideau, Estes,* and *Sheppard* were held. In those cases the influence of the news media, either in the community at large or in the courtroom itself, pervaded the proceedings. In *Rideau* the defendant had "confessed" under police interrogation to the murder of which he stood convicted. A 20–minute film of his confession was broadcast three times by a television station in the community where the crime and the trial took place. In reversing, the Court did not examine the *voir dire* for evidence of actual prejudice because it considered the trial under review "but a hollow formality"—the real trial had occurred when tens of thousand of people, in a community of 150,000 had seen and heard the defendant admit his guilt to the cameras.

The trial in *Estes* had been conducted in a circus atmosphere, due in large part to the intrusions of the press, which was allowed to sit within the bar of the court and to overrun it with television equipment. Similarly, *Sheppard* arose from a trial infected not only by a background of extremely inflammatory publicity but also by a courthouse given over to accommodate the public appetite for carnival. The proceedings in these cases were entirely lacking in the solemnity and sobriety to which a defendant is entitled in a system that subscribes to any notion of fairness and rejects the verdict of a mob. They cannot be made to stand for the proposition that juror exposure to information about a state defendant's prior convictions or to news accounts of the crime with which he is charged alone presumptively deprives the defendant of due process. To resolve this case, we must turn, therefore, to any indications in the totality of circumstances that petitioner's trial was not fundamentally fair.

III.

The constitutional standard of fairness requires that a defendant have "a panel of impartial, 'indifferent' jurors." Irvin v. Dowd, supra, 366 U.S., at 722, 81 S.Ct. at 1642. Qualified jurors need not, however, be totally ignorant of the facts and issues involved.

> "To hold that the mere existence of any preconceived notion as to the guilt or innocence of an accused, without more, is sufficient to rebut the presumption of a prospective juror's impartiality would be to establish an impossible standard. It is sufficient if the juror can lay aside his impression or opinion and render a verdict based on the evidence presented in court." Id., at 723, 81 S.Ct. at 1642.

At the same time, the juror's assurances that he is equal to this task cannot be dispositive of the accused's rights, and it remains open to the defendant to demonstrate "the actual existence of such an opinion in the mind of the juror as will raise the presumption of partiality." Ibid.

The *voir dire* in this case indicates no such hostility to petitioner by the jurors who served in his trial as to suggest a partiality that could not be laid aside. Some of the jurors had a vague recollection of the robbery with which petitioner was charged and each had some knowledge of petitioner's past crimes, but none betrayed any belief in the relevance of petitioner's past to the present case. Indeed, four of the six jurors volunteered their views of its irrelevance, and one suggested that people who have been in trouble before are too often singled out for suspicion of each new crime—a predisposition that could only operate in petitioner's favor.

In the entire *voir dire* transcript furnished to us, there is only one colloquy on which petitioner can base even a colorable claim of partiality by a juror. In response to a leading and hypothetical question, presupposing a two-or three-week presentation of evidence against petitioner and his failure to put on any defense, one juror conceded that his prior impression of petitioner would dispose him to convict. We cannot attach great significance to this statement, however, in light of the leading nature of counsel's questions and the juror's other testimony indicating that he had no deep impression of petitioner at all.

The juror testified that he did not keep up with current events and, in fact, had never heard of petitioner until he arrived in the room for prospective jurors where some veniremen were discussing him. He did not know that petitioner was "a convicted jewel thief" even then; it was petitioner's counsel who informed him of this fact. And he volunteered that petitioner's murder conviction, of which he had just heard, would not be relevant to his guilt or innocence in the present case, since "[w]e are not trying him for murder."

Even these indicia of impartiality might be disregarded in a case where the general atmosphere in the community or courtroom is sufficiently inflammatory, but the circumstances surrounding petitioner's trial are not at all of that variety. Petitioner attempts to portray them as inflammatory by reference to the publicity to which the community was exposed. The District Court found, however, that the news articles concerning petitioner had appeared almost entirely during the period between December 1967 and January 1969, the latter date being seven months before the jury in this case was selected. 363 F.Supp., at 1228. They were, moreover, largely factual in nature. Compare Beck v. Washington, 369 U.S. 541, 82 S.Ct. 955, 8 L.Ed.2d 98 (1962), with Sheppard v. Maxwell, supra.

The length to which the trial court must go in order to select jurors who appear to be impartial is another factor relevant in evaluating those jurors' assurances of impartiality. In a community where most veniremen will admit to a disqualifying prejudice, the reliability of the others' protestations may be drawn into question; for it is then more probable that they are part of a community deeply hostile to the accused, and more likely that they may unwittingly have been influenced by it. In Irvin v. Dowd, for example, the Court noted that 90% of those examined on the point were inclined to believe in the accused's guilt, and the court had excused for this cause 268 of the 430 veniremen. In the present case, by contrast, 20 of the 78 persons questioned were excused because they indicated an opinion as to petitioner's guilt. This may indeed be 20 more than would occur in the trial of a totally obscure person, but it by no means suggests a community with sentiment so poisoned against petitioner as to impeach the indifference of jurors who displayed no hostile animus of their own.

In sum, we are unable to conclude, in the circumstances presented in this case, that petitioner did not receive a fair trial. Petitioner has failed to show that the setting of the trial was inherently prejudicial or that the jury selection process of which he complains permits an inference of actual prejudice. The judgment of the Court of Appeals must therefore be affirmed.

■ MR. JUSTICE BRENNAN, dissenting.

I dissent. Irvin v. Dowd, 366 U.S. 717, 81 S.Ct. 1639, 6 L.Ed.2d 751 (1961), requires reversal of this conviction. As in that case, petitioner here was denied a fair trial. The risk that taint of widespread publicity regarding his criminal background, known to all members of the jury, infected the jury's deliberations is apparent, the trial court made no attempt to prevent discussion of the case or petitioner's previous criminal exploits among the prospective jurors, and one juror freely admitted that he was predisposed to convict petitioner.

* * *

Others who ultimately served as jurors revealed similar prejudice toward petitioner on *voir dire.* One juror conceded that it would be difficult, during deliberations, to put out of his mind that petitioner was a convicted criminal. He also admitted that he did not "hold a convicted felon in the same regard as another person who has never been convicted of a felony," and admitted further that he had termed petitioner a "menace."

A third juror testified that she knew from several sources that petitioner was a convicted murderer, and was aware that the community regarded petitioner as a criminal who "should be put away." She disclaimed having a fixed opinion about the result she would reach, but acknowledged that the fact that petitioner was a convicted criminal would probably influence her verdict.

* * *

Still another juror testified that the comments of venire members in discussing the case had made him "sick to [his] stomach." He testified that one venireman had said that petitioner was "thoroughly rotten," and that another had said, "Hang him, he's guilty."

Moreover, the Court ignores the crucial significance of the fact that at no time before or during this daily buildup of prejudice against Murphy did the trial judge instruct the prospective jurors not to discuss the case among themselves. Indeed the trial judge took no steps to insulate the jurors from media coverage of the case or from the many news articles that discussed petitioner's last criminal exploits.

It is of no moment that several jurors ultimately testified that they would try to exclude from their deliberations their knowledge of petitioner's past misdeeds and of his community reputation. *Irvin* held in like circumstances that little weight could be attached to such self-serving protestations....

On the record of this *voir dire,* therefore, the conclusion is to me inescapable that the attitude of the entire venire toward Murphy reflected the "then current community pattern of thought as indicated by the popular news media," id., at 725, 81 S.Ct. at 1644, and was infected with the taint of the view that he was a "criminal" guilty of notorious offenses, including that for which he was on trial. It is a plain case, from a review of the entire *voir dire,* where "the extent and nature of the publicity had caused such a buildup of prejudice that excluding the preconception of guilt from the deliberations would be too difficult for the jury to be honestly found impartial." Bloeth v. Denno, 2 Cir., 313 F.2d 364 (1963). In my view, the denial of a change of venue was therefore prejudicial error, and I would reverse the conviction.

NOTES

1. **Intensity of publicity.** The effects of pretrial publicity on the impartiality of the trial jury was at issue in Patton v. Yount, 467 U.S. 1025, 104 S.Ct. 2885, 81 L.Ed.2d 847 (1984). In 1966, respondent, a high school math teacher, was tried for the murder of an 18–year old female student in a rural Pennsylvania community. Written and oral confessions to the offense were admitted in evidence; he was convicted but the Pennsylvania Supreme Court ordered a new trial because the confessions had been unlawfully obtained. Prior to his second trial in 1970 in the same community, respondent moved for a change of venue, which was denied. Local publicity was intense at the time of the offense, the first trial, the reversal of the conviction and before jury selection in the second trial began. After his conviction in the second trial and after affirmance by state appellate courts, respondent filed a petition for habeas corpus in federal district court claiming prejudicial pretrial publicity. The district court denied relief, but the Third Circuit reversed on the basis of Irvin v. Dowd. The Supreme Court, in an opinion by Justice Powell, reversed:

> [Irvin v. Dowd] held that adverse pretrial publicity can create such a presumption of prejudice in a community that the jurors' claims that they can be impartial should not be believed. . . . In *Irvin,* the Court observed that it was during the six or seven months immediately preceding trial that "a barrage of newspaper headlines, articles, cartoons and pictures was unleashed against [the defendant]." . . . In this case, the extensive adverse publicity and the community's sense of outrage were at their height prior to Yount's first trial in 1966. The jury selection for Yount's second trial, at issue here, did not occur until four years later, at a time when prejudicial publicity was greatly diminished and community sentiment had softened. In these circumstances, we hold that the trial court did not commit manifest error in finding that the jury as a whole was impartial.

467 U.S. at 1031, 104 S.Ct. at 2889, 81 L.Ed.2d at 854. Justice Marshall did not participate; Justice Stevens, joined by Justice Brennan, dissented.

2. **Questioning panelists about publicity.** The issue in Mu'Min v. Virginia, 500 U.S. 415, 111 S.Ct. 1899, 114 L.Ed.2d 493 (1991) was whether the Sixth and Fourteenth Amendments right to an impartial jury was violated by the refusal of the trial court to question members of the jury panel about the content of pretrial publicity they had acknowledged receiving concerning the case and the defendant. Mu'Min was charged with a murder committed when he escaped from a prison work detail. Publicity was extensive and included the fact that he was already serving a prison sentence for murder, that he had been six times rejected for parole, details of the murder for which he was serving the prison sentence, and indications that he had confessed to the murder with which he was now charged. Twenty-six prospective jurors appeared for voir dire. Sixteen acknowledged they had read or heard about the case. One of the 16 was excused for cause when he stated he could not be impartial in light of the publicity. Further voir dire was conducted in panels of 4 persons. Each person stated that he or she could be impartial and would wait until the entire case was presented before forming an opinion about defendant's guilt or innocence. Defense counsel asked the trial court to question members of the panel who had heard about the case as to the content of the information they had received. The trial court refused this request. Of the 12 persons who were the jury,

8 had read or heard something about the case. Mu'Min was convicted and received the death penalty. The Supreme Court, in an opinion by Chief Justice Rehnquist, held that the trial court's actions did not violate the 6th and 14th Amendments. The Court acknowledged that questioning concerning content would have enabled petitioner to exercise peremptory challenges more intelligently, but refused to make such questions a constitutional requirement because under Ross v. Oklahoma, 487 U.S. 81, 108 S.Ct. 2273, 101 L.Ed.2d 80 (1988) peremptory challenges are not required by the Constitution. Petitioner's reliance on Irvin v. Dowd is misplaced since in that case 8 of 12 jurors had formed an opinion from pretrial publicity as to guilt, while in this case although 8 of 12 had heard of the case none expressed an opinion as to guilt.

> Had the trial court in this case been confronted with the "wave of public passion" engendered by pretrial publicity that occurred in connection with Irvin's trial, the Due Process Clause of the Fourteenth Amendment might well have required more extensive examination of potential jurors than it undertook here. But the showings are not comparable; the cases differ both in the kind of community in which the coverage took place and in the extent of media coverage. Unlike the community involved in *Irvin*, the county in which petitioner was tried, Prince William, had a population in 1988 of 182,537, and this was one of nine murders committed in the county that year. It is a part of the metropolitan Washington statistical area, which has a population of over 3 million, and in which, unfortunately, hundreds of murders are committed each year. In *Irvin*, news accounts included details of the defendant's confessions to 24 burglaries and six murders, including the one for which he was tried, as well as his unaccepted offer to plead guilty in order to avoid the death sentence. They contained numerous opinions as to his guilt, as well as opinions about the appropriate punishment. While news reports about Mu'Min were not favorable, they did not contain the same sort of damaging information. Much of the pretrial publicity was aimed at the Department of Corrections and the criminal justice system in general, criticizing the furlough and work release programs that made this and other crimes possible. Any killing that ultimately results in a charge of capital murder will engender considerable media coverage, and this one may have engendered more than most because of its occurrence during the 1988 Presidential campaign, when a similar crime committed by a Massachusetts inmate became a subject of national debate. But, while the pretrial publicity in this case appears to have been substantial, it was not of the same kind or extent as that found to exist in *Irvin*.

500 U.S. at 429–30, 111 S.Ct. at 1907, 114 L.Ed.2d at 508.

Justice Marshall, joined by Justices Blackmun and Stevens, dissented. Justice Kennedy dissented because "a juror's acknowledgement of exposure to pretrial publicity initiates a duty to assess that individual juror's ability to be impartial." That duty was not discharged in this case:

> The questions were asked of groups, and individual jurors attested to their own impartiality by saying nothing. I would hold * * * that when a juror admits exposure to pretrial publicity about a case, the court must conduct a sufficient colloquy with the individual juror to make an assessment of the juror's ability to be impartial. The trial judge should have substantial discretion in conducting the *voir dire*, but, in my judgment, findings of impartiality must be based on something more than the mere silence of the individual in response to questions asked *en masse*.

500 U.S. at 452, 111 S.Ct. at 1919, 114 L.Ed.2d at 523.

3. **Public access to trial proceedings.** The extent to which some or all of the problems presented in *Murphy* may be attacked by barring the public, the press,

or both from the trial was reduced by Richmond Newspapers, Inc. v. Virginia, 448 U.S. 555, 100 S.Ct. 2814, 65 L.Ed.2d 973 (1980), in which a majority of the Supreme Court concluded that the First Amendment creates a right in the public—and apparently in the representatives of the press—to attend a criminal trial. When and how this might be limited was not addressed; there was no opinion of the Court. In the case, the judge presiding over the state murder trial of one Stevenson, with the agreement of both the defense and the prosecution, closed the trial. Defense counsel specifically voiced concern regarding "difficulty with information between jurors," that information might be published inaccurately and seen by jurors, and that "this is a small community." The trial judge also observed that having people in the courtroom is "distracting to the jury." All members of the court except Justice Powell (who did not participate) and Justice Rehnquist (who dissented) agreed that under the circumstances presented the state trial judge's action was constitutionally unacceptable.

In Globe Newspaper Co. v. Superior Court for the County of Norfolk, 457 U.S. 596, 102 S.Ct. 2613, 73 L.Ed.2d 248 (1982) the appellant newspaper had been excluded from a criminal trial under a Massachusetts statute that had been construed to mandate the exclusion of the public from any trial involving specified sex offenses against persons under the age of 18. The United States Supreme Court, in an opinion by Justice Brennan, relying on *Richmond Newspapers, Inc.*, held that the statute violated the newspaper's First Amendment right of access to the courtroom. The Commonwealth argued that the statute furthered two compelling interests in avoiding the trauma of young persons testifying publicly about intimate events and in encouraging them to come forward to testify in the trial. The Court agreed that the first interest advanced was compelling but denied that it justified a mandatory closure rule, since "the circumstances of the particular case may affect the significance of the interest.... Among the factors to be weighed are the minor victim's age, psychological maturity, and understanding, the nature of the crime, the desires of the victim, and the interests of parents and relatives." 457 U.S. at 608, 102 S.Ct. at 2621, 73 L.Ed.2d at 257–59. As to the second interest advanced, the Court noted that much of the argument could be advanced for all victims of crime and that the statute did not prohibit the press from publishing details of the victim's testimony gained from other sources. The Court noted that "in individual cases, and under appropriate circumstances, the First Amendment does not necessarily stand as a bar to the exclusion from the courtroom of the press and general public during the testimony of minor sex-offense victims." 457 U.S. at 611, n. 27, 102 S.Ct. at 2622, n. 27, 73 L.Ed.2d at 259–60, n. 27.

4. **Public access to pretrial proceedings.** Apparently a trial judge has somewhat more flexibility in closing at least some pretrial proceedings. In Gannett Co., Inc. v. DePasquale, 443 U.S. 368, 99 S.Ct. 2898, 61 L.Ed.2d 608 (1979) the trial judge granted the defense motion that the public and the press be excluded from a pretrial hearing on the admissibility of the defendant's confession. Finding no constitutional error, a majority of the Court stressed that closure was only temporary, since the press and the public were given full opportunity to scrutinize and publicize a transcript of the suppression hearing as soon as the danger of prejudice to the defendant was over. Moreover, the trial judge had considered the interest in the press and the public in having access to the proceedings but—and apparently reasonably, in the view of the majority—concluded that this was outweighed by the defendant's need for a fair trial. 443 U.S. at 392–93, 99 S.Ct. at 2912, 61 L.Ed.2d at 629.

The Court considered the closure of a suppression hearing over defendant's Sixth Amendment public trial objection in Waller v. Georgia, 467 U.S. 39, 104 S.Ct. 2210, 81 L.Ed.2d 31 (1984). Waller was prosecuted for various gambling violations. After the jury was selected, the trial court conducted a hearing on a motion to suppress evidence obtained as a result of a court-ordered wiretap. The State moved to close the hearing to the public on the ground that under Georgia law unnecessary publication of the wiretap fruits might make the evidence inadmissible against others and that the privacy interests of others would be invaded by a public hearing. The trial court closed the hearing which lasted seven days; only two and one-half hours of the hearing were devoted to playing tapes of the intercepted telephone conversations.

The Supreme Court, in an opinion for an unanimous Court authored by Justice Powell, held that the defendant's right to a public trial extended to suppression hearings, as well as to the trial itself. It also held that closure of a suppression hearing over Sixth Amendment objection must meet the First Amendment standards set out in *Press-Enterprise*. The trial court's closure order was unjustified:

> [T]he State's proffer was not specific as to whose privacy interests might be infringed, how they would be infringed, what portions of the tapes might infringe them, and what portion of the evidence consisted of the tapes. ... The court did not consider alternatives to immediate closure of the entire hearing: directing the government to provide more detail about its need for closure, *in camera* if necessary, and closing only those parts of the hearing that jeopardized the interests advanced. As it turned out, of course, the closure was far more extensive than necessary.

467 U.S. at 48–49, 104 S.Ct. at 2216–17, 81 L.Ed.2d at 40. As to remedy, the Court held it was not necessary to award a new trial but instead remanded the case for a new suppression hearing: "A new trial need be held only if a new, public suppression hearing results in the suppression of material evidence not suppressed at the first trial, or in some other material change in the positions of the parties." 467 U.S. at 40, 104 S.Ct. at 2212, 81 L.Ed.2d at 41.

The Court considered the applicability of the First Amendment right of access to criminal proceedings to preliminary hearings in Press–Enterprise Co. v. Superior Court, 478 U.S. 1, 106 S.Ct. 2735, 92 L.Ed.2d 1 (1986). The trial court had, with defendant's consent, closed a preliminary hearing to the press and public. Defendant was charged with 12 counts of murder. The preliminary hearing lasted for 41 days and concluded with a finding of probable cause on all charges. Petitioner attempted unsuccessfully in the California courts to obtain a transcript of the preliminary hearing. The California Supreme Court held there is no First Amendment right of access to preliminary hearings. The United States Supreme Court, in an opinion by Chief Justice Burger, reversed. Preliminary hearings have traditionally been open to the public and in many cases they are the only adversarial proceedings in a case because of the large percentage of pleas of guilty following full preliminaries. When a request for closure of a preliminary is based upon the right of the accused to a fair trial, closure is permissible under the First Amendment

> only if specific findings are made demonstrating that first, there is a substantial probability that the defendant's right to a fair trial will be prejudiced by publicity that closure would prevent and, second, reasonable alternatives to closure cannot adequately protect the defendant's fair trial rights.

478 U.S. at 14, 106 S.Ct. at 2743, 92 L.Ed.2d at 13–14. Because the California Supreme Court failed to apply this standard, its judgment was reversed. Justice Stevens, joined in part by Justice Rehnquist, dissented.

5. **Closing jury selection to the public.** Are there circumstances in which a trial judge would be justified in closing all or parts of jury selection proceedings to the press and public? In Press–Enterprise Company v. Superior Court, 464 U.S. 501, 104 S.Ct. 819, 78 L.Ed.2d 629 (1984), the petitioner newspaper moved that jury selection proceedings in a rape/murder trial be open to the press. The trial court

ruled that only that portion of the proceedings involving a general explanation of the case to the jury panel would be open and that the portion involving individual questioning of members of the panel would be closed. Thus, all but three days of the six week jury selection proceeding was closed. After the jury was selected, the newspaper moved for release of a complete transcript of the proceedings, but this too was denied. The California state courts upheld the trial court but the Supreme Court, in an opinion authored by the Chief Justice, vacated and remanded the case.

The Chief Justice noted that historically criminal trials, including jury selection proceedings, have been open to the public. He characterized criminal trials as having a "presumption of openness" which may be overcome "only by an overriding interest based on findings that closure is essential to preserve higher values and is narrowly tailored to serve that interest." 464 U.S. at 510, 104 S.Ct. at 824, 78 L.Ed.2d at 638. The California courts attempted to justify closure on the ground that it would promote candor by members of the jury panel in responding to the often probing questions by counsel and it was needed to protect the privacy of members of the panel. The Chief found neither argument persuasive. The trial court's closure order was too broad. It did not consider alternatives to the sweeping closure order. When a prospective juror indicates a desire for private discussion of a question, that desire can be accommodated by examining the person *in camera* but on the record with counsel present. The privacy interest of members of the panel cannot justify refusal to release a transcript of the proceedings to the press after the jury has been selected, but in certain circumstances it might justify excising a portion of the transcript or preserving the anonymity of certain members of the panel. The trial court did not make the necessary findings and its order was too broad in light of the arguments advanced in support of it. Justices Blackmun and Stevens concurred in separate opinions. Justice Marshall concurred in the judgment of the Court.

6. **Restricting the contents of published reports.** Another method of dealing with at least some of the problems raised in *Murphy* is to limit dissemination of information by the press, without denying it access to the information. But the acceptability of this approach was limited in Nebraska Press Ass'n v. Stuart, 427 U.S. 539, 96 S.Ct. 2791, 49 L.Ed.2d 683 (1976). The trial judge had issued a so-called "gag order," which—as ultimately modified by the Nebraska Supreme Court—prohibited the reporting of the existence and nature of any confessions or admissions made by the defendant to law enforcement officers, of any confessions or admissions made to any third parties, except members of the press, and of any other facts "strongly implicative" of the defendant. The majority of the court declined to hold that such orders were prohibited under any circumstances, but it examined the justification of the order before it under a presumption of invalidity attaching to prior restraint of the press:

> [W]e must examine the evidence before the trial judge when the order was entered to determine (a) the nature and extent of pretrial news coverage; (b) whether other measures would be likely to mitigate the effect of unrestrained pretrial publicity; and (c) how effectively a restraining order would operate to prevent the threatened danger. The precise terms of the restraining order are also important. We must then consider whether the record supports the entry of a prior restraint on publication, one of the most extraordinary remedies known to our jurisprudence.

427 U.S. at 562, 96 S.Ct. at 2804, 49 L.Ed.2d at 699. Its review of the record led the majority to conclude that there was insufficient evidence that further publicity would so distort the views of potential jurors that twelve satisfactory jurors could not be found. No adequate basis was presented for concluding that means other than pretrial restraint of the press would not sufficiently mitigate the effects of

publicity so as to make the prior restraint unnecessary. Moreover, given the fact that the events took place in a community of 850 persons, the record did not establish with sufficient clarity that the restraining order would in fact serve its intended purpose. That portion of the order prohibiting the reporting of "information strongly implicative of the accused" was held impermissibly vague and broad, and the order was also held fatally broad insofar as it prohibited the reporting of evidence produced at open court at the defendant's preliminary hearing. 427 U.S. at 565–70, 96 S.Ct. at 2804–07, 49 L.Ed.2d at 701–04. Justice Brennan, joined by Justices Stewart and Marshall, concurred in the judgment but urged that prior restraint of the press could never be used to safeguard a defendant's right to a fair trial. 427 U.S. at 604, 96 S.Ct. at 2824, 49 L.Ed.2d at 724.

7. **Controlling publicity through bar discipline.** The Supreme Court considered the constitutionality under the First Amendment of the use of bar disciplinary rules to restrict attorneys in making pre-trial comments concerning a case in Gentile v. State Bar of Nevada, 501 U.S. 1030, 111 S.Ct. 2720, 115 L.Ed.2d 888 (1991). The Supreme Court of Nevada had promulgated bar disciplinary rule 177 (almost identical to ABA Model Rule of Professional Conduct 3.6) concerning trial publicity:

1. A lawyer shall not make an extrajudicial statement that a reasonable person would expect to be disseminated by means of public communication if the lawyer knows or reasonably should know that it will have a substantial likelihood of materially prejudicing an adjudicative proceeding.

2. A statement referred to in subsection 1 ordinarily is likely to have such an effect when it refers to a civil matter triable to a jury, a criminal matter, or any other proceeding that could result in incarceration, and the statement relates to:

(a) the character, credibility, reputation or criminal record of a party, suspect in a criminal investigation or witness, or the identity of a witness, or the expected testimony of a party or witness;

(b) in a criminal case or proceeding that could result in incarceration, the possibility of a plea of guilty to the offense or the existence or contents of any confession, admission, or statement given by a defendant or suspect or that person's refusal or failure to make a statement;

(c) the performance or results of any examination or test or the refusal or failure of a person to submit to an examination or test, or the identity or nature of physical evidence expected to be presented;

(d) any opinion as to the guilt or innocence of a defendant or suspect in a criminal case or proceeding that could result in incarceration;

(e) information the lawyer knows or reasonably should know is likely to be inadmissible as evidence in a trial and would if disclosed create a substantial risk of prejudicing an impartial trial; or

(f) the fact that a defendant has been charged with a crime, unless there is included therein a statement explaining that the charge is merely an accusation and that the defendant is presumed innocent until and unless proven guilty.

3. Notwithstanding subsection 1 and 2(a-f), a lawyer involved in the investigation or litigation of a matter may state without elaboration:

(a) the general nature of the claim or defense; * * *

Gentile, a Las Vegas criminal defense attorney, called a press conference shortly after his client was arrested and charged with offenses arising out of four kilograms of cocaine and almost $300,000 in travelers' checks that were missing from a safety deposit box. The box had been used by police in an undercover operation and was part of a business—Western Vault Corporation—owned by petitioner's client. There was extensive local publicity concerning the case before and after the arrest and charge. Petitioner examined the rules of discipline before calling the press conference and refused to answer several questions at the conference on grounds to do so would violate those rules. At the conference petitioner stated that his client was innocent, that the likely thief was a police detective (whom he named) and that others who claimed to be victims of similar losses were rug dealers or convicted money launderers, who were working with police wrongfully to accuse his client. At trial six months later, petitioner's client was acquitted of all charges. The Nevada Bar then brought disciplinary proceedings, which resulted in the Nevada Supreme Court ultimately issuing a private reprimand against petitioner for violation of Rule 177. The United States Supreme Court reversed. The Court held, through Justice Kennedy, that the rules as interpreted by the Nevada Supreme Court, were void for vagueness. Petitioner was misled by the "safe harbor" provision of Rule 177(3)(a) into believing that his conduct at the press conference was protected from bar discipline:

> A lawyer seeking to avail himself of Rule 177(3)'s protection must guess at its contours. The right to explain the "general" nature of the defense without "elaboration" provides insufficient guidance because "general" and "elaboration" are both classic terms of degree. In the context before us, these terms have no settled usage or tradition of interpretation in law. The lawyer has no principle for determining when his remarks pass from the safe harbor of the general to the forbidden sea of the elaborated.

501 U.S. at 1048–49, 111 S.Ct. at 2731, 115 L.Ed.2d at 906–07. Then Justice Kennedy, writing for himself and Justices Marshall, Blackmun and Stevens, concluded that the Rule as applied in this case violated the First Amendment because this is pure political speech and the same standards should be used to determine whether petitioner's speech was protected by the First Amendment as any other person's. While the standard of the rule—"substantial likelihood of materially prejudicing an adjudicative proceeding"—is acceptable under the First Amendment, its application to the facts of this case violated petitioner's First Amendment rights. Chief Justice Rehnquist, writing for the Court, held that lawyers can be held to a lesser standard of First Amendment protection than other persons:

> Lawyers representing clients in pending cases are key participants in the criminal justice system, and the State may demand some adherence to the precepts of that system in regulating their speech as well as their conduct * * *. Because lawyers have special access to information through discovery and client communications, their extrajudicial statements pose a threat to the fairness of a pending proceeding since lawyers' statements are likely to be received as especially authoritative * * *. We agree with the majority of the States that the "substantial likelihood of material prejudice" standard constitutes a constitutionally permissible balance between the First Amendment rights of attorneys in pending cases and the state's interest in fair trials.

501 U.S. at 1074–75, 111 S.Ct. at 2744–45, 115 L.Ed.2d at 923. Chief Justice Rehnquist, writing for himself and for Justices White, Scalia and Souter, concluded that Rule 177 as applied in this case should not be held void for vagueness. Justice O'Connor, while joining in Justice Kennedy's opinion that the Rule was as applied void for vagueness, emphasized her belief that lawyers may be judged by lower First Amendment standards than other persons because "lawyers are officers of the court and, as such, may legitimately be subject to ethical precepts that keep them from engaging in what otherwise might be constitutionally protected speech."

8. **Televising trials.** The Supreme Court's action in Estes v. Texas, discussed in *Murphy,* has been interpreted as a holding that televising a trial is inherently a denial of due process. Estes v. Texas, 381 U.S. 532, 552, 85 S.Ct. 1628, 1637, 14 L.Ed.2d 543, 555 (1965) (Warren, C.J., concurring). But this reading of *Estes* was rejected in Chandler v. Florida, 449 U.S. 560, 101 S.Ct. 802, 66 L.Ed.2d 740 (1981). In *Chandler,* a television camera had covered one afternoon of defendants' trial in state court for conspiracy, grand larceny, and possession of burglary tools. This was done pursuant to recently-revised Canon 3A(7) of the Florida Code of Judicial Conduct, permitting electronic media and still photography coverage of judicial proceedings in accordance with guidelines promulgated by the Florida Supreme Court. Treating the issue as one of first impression, the Court rejected the argument that broadcast coverage is prohibited as a matter of federal constitutional law. The Court noted the danger that coverage may impair the ability of jurors to decide the issue of guilt or innocence uninfluenced by extraneous matters. But the risk of such prejudice, the Court concluded, does not justify an absolute constitutional ban on all broadcast coverage. 449 U.S. at 575, 101 S.Ct. at 810, 66 L.Ed.2d at 752. Turning to the possibility that the coverage of the particular case before it may have constituted a denial of due process, the majority reasoned:

> [A] defendant has the right on review to show that the media's coverage of his case—printed or broadcast—compromised the ability of the jury to judge him fairly. Alternatively, a defendant might show that broadcast coverage of his particular case had an adverse impact on the trial participants sufficient to constitute a denial of due process. Neither showing was made in this case.

> To demonstrate prejudice in a specific case a defendant must show something more than juror awareness that the trial is such as to attract the attention of broadcasters. No doubt the presence of a camera in the courtroom made the jurors aware that the trial was thought to be of sufficient interest to the public to warrant coverage. * * * But the appellants have not attempted to show with any specificity that the presence of cameras impaired the ability of the jurors to decide the case on only the evidence before them or that their trial was affected adversely by the impact on any of the participants of the presence of cameras and the prospect of broadcast.

449 U.S. at 581, 101 S.Ct. at 813, 66 L.Ed.2d at 755–56.

9. **Proving juror prejudice.** When a defendant urges that his trial was rendered unfair by the bias of a particular juror, to what extent must the defendant show "actual bias?" In Smith v. Phillips, 455 U.S. 209, 102 S.Ct. 940, 71 L.Ed.2d 78 (1982), Phillips had been convicted of murder and attempted murder in a New York court after a jury trial. He subsequently sought federal habeas corpus relief. Information developed after trial showed that one of the trial jurors, during the trial, applied for and actively pursued employment with the prosecutor's office as an investigator. Phillips urged that this juror's participation in the guilt-determining process deprived him of a fair trial. The federal District Court found insufficient evidence to establish that the juror was actually biased in favor of the prosecution but found "imputed bias" on the ground that an average person in the juror's position would believe that a guilty verdict would improve the consideration given to his employment application. Relief was granted, and this was affirmed on appeal to the United States Court of Appeals for the Second Circuit. The Supreme Court, over the dissent of Justice Marshall joined by Justices Brennan and Stevens, reversed. Rejecting Phillips' argument that actual bias is so difficult to prove that it should not be the standard for determining whether the right to a fair trial has been violated, Justice Rehnquist explained for the Court that "the remedy for allegations of juror partiality is a hearing at which the defendant has the opportunity to prove actual bias." 455 U.S. at 215, 102 S.Ct. at 945, 71 L.Ed.2d at 85. Phillips

was given such a hearing and failed to make the requisite showing of actual bias. Justice O'Connor concurred, but wrote separately to express her understanding that in some circumstances a post-conviction hearing on the existence of actual bias may not be adequate to remedy a claim of juror bias and to suggest that the Court's opinion does not foreclose the use of "implied bias" in such appropriate situations. 455 U.S. at 221, 102 S.Ct. at 948, 71 L.Ed.2d at 89.

10. **Determining juror bias.** The manner in which the trial court handled information about possible juror bias was the subject of Rushen v. Spain, 464 U.S. 114, 104 S.Ct. 453, 78 L.Ed.2d 267 (1983). Respondent was on trial for murder and other offenses. The State attempted to show that the crimes were the product of a conspiracy by the Black Panther Party and that respondent was a member of the Party. During the trial, evidence was introduced that one Pratt, identified as a member of the Black Panther Party, had murdered a Santa Monica woman in 1968. This triggered the memory of juror Fagan that the woman who had been murdered had been a very close friend of hers. She twice approached the trial judge *ex parte* to explain her personal acquaintance with the murder victim and to express the concern that she would cry if evidence of the murder were presented further in the trial. On each occasion, she assured the trial judge that this fact would not affect her disposition of the case. The trial judge did not record these conversations or reveal them to the parties. After respondent was convicted, his attorney learned of these events and a hearing was conducted to determine whether a new trial should be granted. The trial court concluded it should not and this was approved by the California Court of Appeal. On a petition for writ of habeas corpus, a federal District Court concluded that the *ex parte* communications between Ms. Fagan and the trial judge violated the respondent's right to be present during all critical stages of the proceedings and his right to be represented by counsel. This was affirmed by the Ninth Circuit on the ground that an unrecorded *ex parte* communication between a trial judge and juror can never be harmless error.

The Supreme Court without oral argument, reversed the Ninth Circuit. The *per curiam* opinion, citing Smith v. Phillips, concluded that the error of the trial judge was harmless beyond a reasonable doubt and that the post-verdict hearing conducted by the trial court was sufficient to protect the respondent's rights. The Court noted

> There is scarcely a lengthy trial in which one or more jurors does not have occasion to speak to the trial judge about something, whether it relates to a matter of personal comfort or to some aspect of the trial. The lower federal courts' conclusion that an unrecorded *ex parte* communication between trial judge and juror can never be harmless error ignores these day-to-day realities of courtroom life and undermines society's interest in the administration of criminal justice.

464 U.S. at 140, 104 S.Ct. at 466, 78 L.Ed.2d at 273. Justice Stevens concurred in the judgment. He would find that a violation of the right to counsel can never be harmless error but that that right was not violated in this case. Instead, he would characterize the issue involved here as whether the due process right "to notice and an opportunity to be heard in a meaningful manner and at a meaningful time [was violated] by the trial judge's failure to notify the defense of a fact raising a question about a juror's partiality." 464 U.S. at 126, 104 S.Ct. at 460, 78 L.Ed.2d at 278. He concluded that while the trial judge should have promptly notified the defense of the juror communication, failure to do so did not violate due process. Justices Marshall and Blackmun dissented.

11. **Impartial judge.** An impartial trial also includes the right to an "unbiased judge." In Tumey v. Ohio, 273 U.S. 510, 47 S.Ct. 437, 71 L.Ed. 749 (1927), the Court held that a trial before a mayor who personally received fees and costs levied

by him against prohibition law violators violated the Fourteenth Amendment's Due Process Clause. In Dugan v. Ohio, 277 U.S. 61, 48 S.Ct. 439, 72 L.Ed. 784 (1928), however, the Court distinguished *Tumey* on the grounds that (1) in *Dugan* the mayor had only limited executive responsibility and (2) the fines collected went not to the mayor but to the city. Therefore, due process was not denied.

In Ward v. Village of Monroeville, 409 U.S. 57, 93 S.Ct. 80, 34 L.Ed.2d 267 (1972), the mayor had wide executive powers in a municipality a substantial part of whose income was derived from fines imposed by the mayor in ordinance violation and traffic cases. The Court found a violation of due process even though the mayor received no personal benefit, and even though a defendant was entitled to trial de novo as of right. With regard to the latter, the Court said:

> Respondent also argues that any unfairness at the trial level can be corrected on appeal and trial *de novo* in the County Court of Common Pleas. We disagree. This "procedural safeguard" does not guarantee a fair trial in the mayor's court; there is nothing to suggest that the incentive to convict would be diminished by the possibility of reversal on appeal. Nor, in any event, may the State's trial court procedure be deemed constitutionally acceptable simply because the State eventually offers a defendant an impartial adjudication. Petitioner is entitled to a neutral and detached judge in the first instance.

409 U.S. at 61–62, 93 S.Ct. at 83–84, 34 L.Ed.2d at 271. And, in a footnote, the Court added:

> The question presented on this record is the constitutionality of the Mayor's participation in the adjudication and punishment of a defendant in a litigated case where he elects to contest the charges against him. We intimate no view that it would be unconstitutional to permit a mayor or similar official to serve in essentially a ministerial capacity in a traffic or ordinance violation case to accept a free and voluntary plea of guilty or *nolo contendere,* a forfeiture of collateral, or the like.

409 U.S. at 62, 93 S.Ct. at 84, 34 L.Ed.2d at 271.

12. **Judicial impartiality in contempt proceedings.** A defendant's federal constitutional right to an unbiased judge has been most extensively developed in a series of cases involving citation of a defendant or defense lawyer for contempt of court on the basis of conduct during trial. In some situations, at least where the judge does not immediately adjudge the defendant guilty of contempt, due process requires that contempt proceedings be held before a judge other than the one who presided over the trial at which the alleged contempt occurred. This is so where the alleged contempt consists of a highly personal attack upon the judge, as in Mayberry v. Pennsylvania, 400 U.S. 455, 91 S.Ct. 499, 27 L.Ed.2d 532 (1971), where the defendant called the trial judge, among other things, a "fool" and a "dirty tyranical old dog." It is also so where the trial judge is so provoked and embroiled in controversy that either there is actual bias or a sufficient likelihood or appearance of bias. Taylor v. Hayes, 418 U.S. 488, 94 S.Ct. 2697, 41 L.Ed.2d 897 (1974). In *Taylor,* before sentencing the defendant the trial judge made a statement concerning defense counsel, whom he was to hold in contempt. In this statement, he described counsel as not "a lawyer" and as having put on the worst "display" the judge had seen. Further, the judge refused to permit counsel to respond, threatened to gag him, sentenced him to four and one-half years in jail, disbarred him from practice in the court, and denied bond pending appeal. Given this evidence that "marked personal feelings were present on both sides," the Supreme Court held that determination of the contempt charges by the trial judge violated due process. See also, Johnson v. Mississippi, 403 U.S. 212, 91 S.Ct. 1778, 29 L.Ed.2d 423 (1971) (due process violated by trial of contempt charges before trial judge, given affidavits of two lawyers that judge's grand jury charges revealed deep prejudice against civil

rights lawyers, and evidence that immediately before adjudication of contempt judge was losing party in counsel's civil rights suit). The implications of this line of cases are not entirely clear. Given the practical situation, it appears certain that where the trial judge properly cites for contempt immediately after the contemptuous conduct, due process does not require a different judge. But are there constitutional limitations upon the situations in which such immediate action is permissible? To what extent do these cases provide support for the proposition that bias (or the likelihood or appearance of bias) on the part of the judge presiding over a criminal trial on charges other than contempt violates due process? Does it make any difference whether the case is being tried to a jury?

13. **Judicial recusal.** The Supreme Court addressed the scope of the federal recusal of judges statute in Liteky v. United States, 510 U.S. 540, 114 S.Ct. 1147, 127 L.Ed.2d 474 (1994). Petitioners were charged with destruction of government property, which involved a political protest at a military base. One of the Petitioners had previously been tried before the same judge on a similar charge. Based on the judge's actions in the previous trial, Petitioners made a motion to have the judge recused under 28 U.S.C. § 455(a), which requires a federal judge to "disqualify himself in any proceeding in which his impartiality might reasonably be questioned." The motion was denied and the Petitioners were convicted. The Court of Appeals affirmed on the ground that "matters arising out of the course of judicial proceedings are not a proper basis for recusal." The Supreme Court, in an opinion for the Court by Justice Scalia, affirmed.

The position taken by the Court of Appeals goes too far. A judge can acquire a bias or prejudice from information obtained in judicial proceedings that make him or her unfit to sit further in the case. As to what constitutes a "bias or prejudice,"

> Not all unfavorable disposition towards an individual (or his case) is properly described by those terms. One would not say, for example, that world opinion is biased or prejudiced against Adolf Hitler. The words connote a favorable or unfavorable disposition or opinion that is somehow wrongful or inappropriate, either because it is undeserved, or because it rests upon knowledge that the subject ought not to possess (for example, a criminal juror who has been biased or prejudiced by receipt of inadmissible evidence concerning the defendant's prior criminal activities), or because it is excessive in degree (for example, a criminal juror who is so inflamed by properly admitted evidence of a defendant's prior criminal activities that he will vote guilty regardless of the facts).

510 U.S. at 550, 114 S.Ct. at 1155, 127 L.Ed.2d at 488. As applied to a judge,

> The judge who presides at a trial may, upon completion of the evidence, be exceedingly ill disposed towards the defendant, who has been shown to be a thoroughly reprehensible person. But the judge is not thereby recusable for bias or prejudice, since his knowledge and the opinion it produced were properly and necessarily acquired in the course of the proceedings, and are indeed sometimes (as in a bench trial) necessary to completion of the judge's task. As Judge Jerome Frank pithily put it: "Impartiality is not gullibility. Disinterestedness does not mean child-like innocence. If the judge did not form judgments of the actors in those court-house dramas called trials, he could never render decisions." * * * Also not subject to deprecatory characterization as "bias" or "prejudice" are opinions held by judges as a result of what they learned in earlier proceedings. It has long been regarded as normal and proper for a judge to sit in the same case upon its remand, and to sin in successive trials involving the same defendant.

510 U.S. at 550, 114 S.Ct. at 1155, 127 L.Ed.2d at 488. The reasons invoked by Petitioners—rulings and comments by the judge during the previous trial—are insufficient to require recusal under the statute: "All occurred in the course of

judicial proceedings, and neither (1) relied upon knowledge acquired outside such proceedings nor (2) displayed deepseated and unequivocal antagonism that would render fair judgment impossible." 510 U.S. at 556, 114 S.Ct. at 1158, 127 L.Ed.2d at 491–92. Justice Kennedy, joined by Justices Blackmun, Stevens and Souter, concurred in the judgment and criticized the majority for requiring too great a showing of unfairness in order to mandate recusal.

14. **Right to a law-trained judge.** A defendant's right to a "law-trained" judge was addressed in North v. Russell, 427 U.S. 328, 96 S.Ct. 2709, 49 L.Ed.2d 534 (1976). At issue were the validity of trials conducted by Kentucky nonlawyer judges in police courts located in the state's less populous counties. These courts have jurisdiction over criminal cases punishable by a fine of no more than $500, imprisonment for no longer than twelve months, or both. A defendant convicted in police court, whether on a plea of guilty or after a trial, has a right to appeal to a circuit court, presided over by a lawyer-judge, and a trial *de novo* in that court. North urged that the constitutional right to representation in cases resulting in incarceration would be meaningless without a lawyer-judge to understand the arguments of counsel; the increased complexity of both substantive and procedural criminal law, he further argued, requires that judges be lawyers so as to be able to rule accurately on complicated issues that arise even in some simple misdemeanor cases. The majority of the Court declined to decide whether a defendant could be convicted and imprisoned after a proceeding in which the only trial afforded is conducted by a lay judge. Under Kentucky procedure, a defendant is entitled to a trial *de novo* before a law-trained circuit judge, and by pleading guilty in police court a defendant can in effect bypass the police court and secure an initial trial before the circuit court. This, it concluded, satisfies due process. The majority assumed that Kentucky police court judges inform defendants of their right to representation by counsel (where it applies), of their right to a trial *de novo* in circuit court, and of the procedural steps necessary to secure that trial *de novo*. Justice Stewart, joined by Justice Marshall, dissented, urging that in a trial resulting in imprisonment before a nonlawyer judge the constitutional right to the assistance of counsel becomes a "hollow mockery." He found the majority's reliance upon defendants' right to a trial *de novo* in circuit court unpersuasive because there was no evidence that defendants are informed of this right, implementing it requires multiple court appearances, delay and a financial burden, and a trial *de novo* practice would turn "what should be a solemn court proceeding ... into nothing more than a sham." 427 U.S. at 346, 96 S.Ct. at 2717–18, 49 L.Ed.2d at 545–46.

CHAPTER 19

JOINDER AND SEVERANCE OF CHARGES AND DEFENDANTS

Analysis

The simplest structure for the trial of a criminal case is the trial of a single charge against a single defendant. Many criminal trials fit that model. The laws in most jurisdictions, however, permit the prosecutor to depart from that model, either by bringing a multiplicity of charges or by charging more than one defendant or by both. The rationale for permitting departure from the one charge/one defendant model is to increase the efficiency of the system of adjudication by trial. The danger in such practices is that a defendant's right to a fair trial may be jeopardized because of the multiplicity of charges brought or because he is being tried with one or more codefendants. The laws permitting such proceedings contemplate a two-step structure for determining the scope of the trial: an initial decision whether to join charges and/or defendants in a single proceeding and a decision made by the trial court whether, assuming joinder was authorized by law, one or more of the charges or defendants should be severed from the trial.

The joinder and severance provisions of the Federal Rules of Criminal Procedure provide a useful starting place. Rule 8 provides:

(a) *Joinder of Offenses.* Two or more offenses may be charged in the same indictment or information in a separate count for each offense if the offenses charged, whether felonies or misdemeanors or both, are of the same or similar character or are based on the same act or transaction or on two or more acts or transactions connected together or constituting parts of a common scheme or plan.

(b) *Joinder of Defendants.* Two or more defendants may be charged in the same indictment or information if they are alleged to have participated in the same act or transaction or in the same series of acts or transactions constituting an offense or offenses. Such defendants may be charged in one or more counts together or separately and all of the defendants need not be charged in each count.

Rule 13 authorizes the trial court to consolidate two or more indictments or informations for trial "if the offenses, and the defendants if there is more than one, could have been joined in a single indictment or information."

Rule 14 authorizes the trial court to grant relief from prejudicial joinder of charges or defendants:

> If it appears that a defendant or the government is prejudiced by a joinder of offenses or of defendants in an indictment or information or by such joinder for trial together, the court may order an election or separate trials of counts, grant a severance of defendants or provide whatever other relief justice requires. In ruling on a motion by a defendant for severance the court may order the attorney for the government to deliver to the court for inspection *in camera* any statements or confessions made by the defendants which the government intends to introduce in evidence at the trial.

A.   JOINDER AND SEVERANCE OF CHARGES

Under what circumstances is it appropriate to adjudicate more than one criminal charge in the same trial? What gains in efficiency are achieved by permitting multiplicity of charges? What risks to a fair adjudication of guilt or innocence are created by such a procedure? Are there, or should there be, limitations on the number and complexity of charges that can be brought to trial at one time?

Bringing multiple charges against the same defendant, whether in a single proceeding or in sequential proceedings, can raise difficult double jeopardy questions. Those questions are considered in Chapter 20 in context with other double jeopardy issues. In this Section, the limits, if any, that should be placed on multiplicity of charges apart from jeopardy considerations are examined.

United States v. Foutz

United States Court of Appeals, Fourth Circuit, 1976.
540 F.2d 733.

■ WINTER, CIRCUIT JUDGE.

Pembrick Edward Foutz, Jr. was convicted by a jury of twice robbing the Kensington, Maryland, branch of the Bank of Bethesda, in violation of 18 U.S.C.A. §§ 2 and 2113(a), (b), (d), and (f). Although the two robberies took place two and one-half months apart, Foutz was tried for both offenses in one proceeding; his motion for relief from prejudicial joinder under Fed.R.Crim.P. 14 was denied by the district court. On appeal, Foutz argues that the district judge abused his discretion by not granting a severance. He claims that prejudice arose from the fact that the same jury heard evidence of both crimes, whereas had he been tried separately for each robbery, evidence of one offense would not have been admissible at the trial for the other. We agree, and reverse and remand for new, separate trials for each robbery.

I.

On December 30, 1974, a lone black male, armed with a handgun, robbed the Bank of Bethesda at Kensington, Maryland. He entered through the front door, vaulted the tellers' counter at teller position number two, and took money from two tellers' drawers. He left through the same door and walked up a side street. The robber wore a turtleneck sweater pulled up over his mouth and a beret-type hat. Two bank employees testified that Foutz appeared similar to the robber. No fingerprints of Foutz were found at the scene, and the photographs taken by the bank surveillance camera were apparently not helpful in identification. The defense presented as an alibi witness a Washington police cadet who testified with considerable certainty and specificity that Foutz was with her in Washington at the time of the robbery.

On March 13, 1975, the same bank was robbed by a group of three black males. They entered by the front door. One robber, allegedly Foutz, stood near the door holding a handgun on the bank employees. He wore a wide-brimmed hat and may have had on a turtleneck sweater. The other two robbers vaulted the tellers' counter near position number two and took money from several tellers' drawers. All three robbers then escaped down the same side street used by the lone gunman in the previous robbery. There they were observed entering an automobile which was shown to be registered to Foutz. Two bank employees testified that Foutz resembled the robber who stood near the door and held the gun. So far as the record reveals, no fingerprints were found, and apparently the surveillance photographs did not depict the robber alleged to be Foutz. The defense presented an alibi witness who was unable to account for Foutz' whereabouts at the time of the robbery.

Foutz was charged with both robberies in one indictment, as permitted by Fed.R.Crim.P. 8(a), since the offenses were of the "same or similar character." He then made a timely motion for a severance under Rule 14, alleging that he would be prejudiced by a joint trial. The motion was denied. The jury returned a verdict of guilty of both robberies. A motion for a new trial on the grounds of prejudicial joinder was denied. Foutz was sentenced to twenty-five years, imprisonment for each offense, the sentences to run concurrently.

II.

Rule 14 provides that a severance may be granted "[i]f it appears that a defendant or the government is prejudiced by a joinder of offenses.... " The granting of a severance under Rule 14 is committed to the discretion of the district court. ... In this case, we believe it was an abuse of that discretion not to grant a severance.

We begin our analysis with Rule 8 which permits joinder under three circumstances: (1) if the offenses "are of the same or similar character"; (2) if they "are based on the same act or transaction"; or (3) if they are based "on two or more acts or transactions connected together or constituting parts of a common scheme or plan." In the instant case, joinder was initially permissible only because the offenses were of the same or similar character. When two or more offenses are joined for trial solely on this theory, three sources of prejudice are possible which may justify the granting of a severance under Rule 14: (1) the jury may confuse and cumulate the evidence, and convict the defendant of one or both crimes when it would not convict him of either if it could keep the evidence properly segregated;[1] (2) the defendant may be confounded in presenting defenses, as where he desires to assert his privilege against self-incrimination with respect to one crime but not the other;[2] or (3) the jury may conclude that the defendant is guilty of one crime and then find him guilty of the other because of his criminal disposition. As we view the record, we are concerned here with the latter form of prejudice.

While to the layman's mind a defendant's criminal disposition is logically relevant to his guilt or innocence of a specific crime, the law regards the inference from general to specific criminality so weak, and the danger of prejudice so great, that it attempts to prevent conviction on account of a defendant's bad character. Thus, evidence of "other crimes" which is relevant only to prove a criminal disposition is universally acknowledged to be inadmissible.

One inevitable consequence of a joint trial is that the jury will be aware of evidence of one crime while considering the defendant's guilt or innocence of another. If the rationale of the "other crimes" rule is correct, it would seem that some degree of prejudice is necessarily created by permitting the jury to hear evidence of both crimes.

Although the law does not allow consideration of other crimes as evidence of a defendant's criminal disposition, evidence of other crimes is admissible for certain other purposes because its probative value is then thought to outweigh its prejudicial effect. In those instances where evidence of one crime is admissible at a separate trial for another, it follows that a defendant will not suffer any additional prejudice if the two offenses are tried together.[3]

When offenses are joined under Rule 8 on the ground that they "are based on the same act or transaction or on two or more acts or transactions connected together or constituting parts of a common scheme or plan," it is manifest that evidence of one offense would ordinarily be admissible at a separate trial for the other. When offenses are joined because they "are of

---

1. See Drew v. United States, 118 U.S.App.D.C. 11, 331 F.2d 85, 88 (1964); 1 Wright, Federal Practice and Procedure § 222 at 437.

2. See Cross v. United States, 118 U.S.App.D.C. 324, 335 F.2d 987, 989–90 (1964); 8 Moore's Federal Practice ¶ 14.03 at 14–11 to 14–14.1.

3. This standard does not require that every item of evidence relating to one offense be admissible in a separate trial for the other,

but rather looks in a broader sense to whether the rules relating to "other crimes" evidence have been satisfied. And, at least in the case of non-violent crimes, it is ordinarily the fact of the defendant's having engaged in prior or subsequent criminal conduct that is likely to be damaging in the eyes of the jury rather than the details of its commission. Baker v. United States, 131 U.S.App.D.C. 7, 401 F.2d 958, 975 (1968) (footnote omitted).

the same or similar character," however, admissibility at separate trials is not so clear.

In this case, the government argues that evidence of one bank robbery would have been admissible at a trial for the other in order to prove the identity of the perpetrator, under the so-called "handiwork" or "signature" exception to the other crimes rule. Under this exception, if the prosecution can produce evidence tending to show that the defendant committed the "other crime," and if that crime was committed in a manner so similar to that of the offense for which the defendant is being tried that it is highly probable that the same person committed both crimes, then evidence of the "other crime" is admissible to prove that the defendant committed the offense with which he is charged. The government's proof, especially that showing the use of Foutz' automobile by the robbers, tended to identify Foutz as one of the perpetrators of the second robbery. Thus, if the two robberies were committed in a sufficiently similar manner, evidence of the second robbery would have been admissible at a separate trial for the first, and untoward prejudice could not inhere in joinder.

We do not think that the two robberies were so similar as to warrant the inference that they were perpetrated by the same individual. The same bank was robbed twice; beyond this, the differences between the crimes are more striking than the similarities, and such similarities as do exist "all fit into an obvious tactical pattern which would suggest itself to almost anyone disposed to commit a depredation of this sort." Drew v. United States, 331 F.2d at 93 (robbery of two High's ice cream stores by negroes wearing sunglasses); see United States v. Carter, 154 U.S.App.D.C. 238, 475 F.2d 349 (1973) (two robberies by a man wearing a fur coat and a fur hat; held insufficient similarity).

The first robbery was committed by a single black male; the second by three such persons. In both instances, access to the bank was through the front door, hardly a remarkable congruity. In the first robbery, the gunman vaulted the counter at teller position number two; in the second, the two "bag" men vaulted the counter at the same point. This apparent similarity loses most of its significance, however, because, under the government's theory of the case, Foutz was not one of the men who vaulted the counter in the second robbery, but was stationed near the door with a gun trained on the bank employees. In the first crime, the robber was described as wearing a turtleneck sweater and a beret-type hat; the person claimed to have been Foutz in the second robbery was described as wearing a wide-brimmed hat and perhaps a turtleneck. This possible, limited similarity of apparel is less than compelling. The first robber was last seen walking down a side street; the trio in the second crime fled in a getaway car which had been parked on the same street. Thus as far as the evidence revealed, the locomotive method of escape was different in each case; and use of a side street instead of a main thoroughfare in fleeing the site of a crime is not a uniquely ingenious stroke of criminal artistry.

We conclude that evidence showing that Foutz was one of the perpetrators of the March 13, 1975 robbery would not have been admitted to prove his identity as the perpetrator of the December 30, 1974 crime, had he been tried separately for that offense. We therefore conclude that Foutz was sufficiently prejudiced by the district court's denial of Foutz' motion for severance to constitute that denial an abuse of discretion requiring reversal.[4]

III.

The government urges that any prejudice resulting from the joint trial of the two robberies was cured by the court's limiting instructions which required the jury to consider each offense and the evidence thereof separately. It is said that where the evidence is "simple and distinct," the jury can be trusted to segregate the evidence properly. This position finds some support in the cases. See United States v. Adams, 434 F.2d 756, 758–59 (2 Cir.1970); Drew v. United States, 331 F.2d at 91–92 (dictum); United States v. Lotsch, 102 F.2d 35, 36 (2 Cir.), cert. denied, 307 U.S. 622, 59 S.Ct. 793, 83 L.Ed. 1500 (1939).[5]

While the law often permits the jury to hear evidence admissible for one purpose but not for another, and presumes that the jury will follow a limiting instruction, this practice is justified by practical considerations of trial convenience and expedition. When offenses are initially joined on the ground that they "are of the same or similar character," and evidence of one offense would not be admissible at a separate trial for the other, the saving of time effected by a joint trial is minimal. "Ordinarily, the only time saved by such joinder is the selection of one jury rather than two. Except for character witnesses, the evidence will usually be entirely separate." 8 Moore's Federal Practice ¶ 8.05[2] at 8–19 (footnotes omitted); see 1 Wright, Federal Practice and Procedure § 143 at 318; . . . . Thus, the only real convenience served by permitting joint trial of unrelated offenses against the wishes of the defendant may be the convenience of the prosecution in securing a conviction.

We therefore reject the government's argument. The reasons for the rule which the government invokes are largely inapplicable and the prejudice to the defendant, arising from the weakness of the government's one case and strength of the other, so marked that we cannot presume that the jury adhered to limiting instructions and properly "segregate[d] [the] evidence into separate intellectual boxes," Bruton v. United States, 391 U.S. 123, 131, 88 S.Ct. 1620, 1625, 20 L.Ed.2d 476 (1968), quoting People v.

---

4. Our conclusion finds support in the ABA Project on Minimum Standards for Criminal Justice, Standards Relating to Joinder and Severance at 291. Section 2.2(a) provides:

Whenever two or more offenses have been joined for trial solely on the ground that they are of the same or similar character, the defendant shall have a right to a severance of the offenses.

See also 8 Moore's Federal Practice ¶ 8.05[2] at 8.22 ("a persuasive argument [has been made] for generally barring joinder of similar offenses, except perhaps where they would be independently admissible as prior similar acts"); 1 Wright, Federal Prac-

tice and Procedure § 143 at 317–18 ("It may fairly be asked, however, whether such joinder should ever be allowed."); . . . .

5. The "simple and distinct" test articulated in *Drew* may well be an appropriate standard for measuring the danger of prejudice resulting from the jury's confusing and cumulating the evidence. It does not address itself, however, to the graver mischief possible where the jury, while limiting its consideration of the evidence to the crime to which it relates, properly finds the defendant guilty of one crime but considers that finding probative of his guilt of another.

Aranda, 63 Cal.2d 518, 528–29, 47 Cal.Rptr. 353, 359–60, 407 P.2d 265, 271–72.

IV.

Other factors are sometimes said to mitigate the prejudice flowing from joinder of unrelated offenses. In United States v. Clayton, [450 F.2d 16, 19 (1st Cir.1971), cert. denied 405 U.S. 975, 92 S.Ct. 1200, 31 L.Ed.2d 250 (1972)] the First Circuit relied on the fact that the defendant received concurrent sentences (as did Foutz) in upholding the district court's refusal to grant a severance. We are unpersuaded by this reasoning. Even if it could be concluded with the requisite degree of certainty that the defendant would have been convicted of at least one of the offenses in separate trials, conviction of two crimes instead of one may postpone parole eligibility or result in other serious consequences for the defendant. Thus, while concurrent sentencing may ameliorate the prejudicial effect of a joint trial, it cannot cure it completely.

It has also been said that where evidence of *both* crimes is overwhelming, no prejudice inheres in a joint trial. Cf. United States v. Clayton, 450 F.2d at 19 (evidence on both charges "strong"; "this was not an instance where a weak evidentiary case and a strong one were joined in the hope that an overlapping consideration of the evidence would lead to convictions on both"). The rule is inapplicable here.

We have no doubt that the government proved enough of a case against Foutz with respect to the March 13, 1975 robbery based principally on the positive identification of his automobile as the getaway car, to permit, but not require, the jury to find him guilty. In contrast, the only evidence of Foutz' involvement in the December 30, 1974 robbery, aside from its putative similarity to the later crime, was the testimony of two witnesses that Foutz' appearance was "similar" to that of the robber; and opposed to this testimony was an unusually strong alibi. We think it highly probable that a jury ignorant of the second crime and Foutz' alleged participation therein would have acquitted him of the earlier robbery. There is thus a strong likelihood that the jury found Foutz guilty of the second robbery, and then concluded that since he had once robbed the bank, it was plausible that he had done so before. Since we cannot say that the government's case with respect to the March 13, 1975 robbery was indefensible, it is possible that the jury found him guilty of that crime under the rationale that with so much smoke there must be fire. Had the two offenses not been joined for trial, these "spillovers" could not have occurred, and Foutz might well have been acquitted of the first crime; possibly of both.[6]

We thus conclude that Foutz' convictions of both offenses must be reversed and he must be afforded new, separate trials.

* * *

Reversed and Remanded.

---

6. Joinder of similar offenses remains proper where evidence of one crime could be admitted at a separate trial for the other.

NOTES

1. **Harmfulness of misjoinder.** The question whether a misjoinder of offenses can ever be harmless error was presented in United States v. Lane, 474 U.S. 438, 106 S.Ct. 725, 88 L.Ed.2d 814 (1986). James Lane was indicted in count one for mail fraud in connection with the arson of a restaurant, while he and his son, Dennis, were indicted in counts two through four with mail fraud in connection with the arson of a duplex. Respondents unsuccessfully sought severance of count one from the remaining counts on the ground they were misjoined under Rule 8(b). On appeal from conviction on all counts, the Court of Appeals held there was a misjoinder and that it was *per se* harmful and required reversal of the convictions. The Supreme Court, in an opinion authored by Chief Justice Burger, reversed. The Circuits were divided on whether misjoinder can ever be harmless error. The Supreme Court had held in Chapman v. California, 386 U.S. 18, 87 S.Ct. 824, 17 L.Ed.2d 705 (1967) that even errors of constitutional magnitude (which misjoinder is not) can be harmless. Federal Rules of Criminal Procedure Rule 52(a) directs that errors that do not "affect substantial rights shall be disregarded." The Court in *Lane* held that Rule 8(b) misjoinder requires reversal only if it "results in actual prejudice because it 'had substantial and injurious effect or influence in determining the jury's verdict.' " 474 U.S. at 449, 106 S.Ct. at 732, 88 L.Ed.2d at 826. Because of the overwhelming evidence of guilt, the careful limiting instructions of the trial court to the jury and the likelihood that evidence of the count one offense would have been admissible on the question of intent in a separate trial of counts two through four, the misjoinder was harmless. Justices Brennan, Blackmun, Stevens and Marshall dissented.

2. **Defendant's rights to testify and to remain silent.** What should happen when two charges are joined for trial and the defendant expresses a desire to testify in defense of one charge but to remain silent with respect to the other? In Cross v. United States, 335 F.2d 987, 118 U.S.App.D.C. 324 (D.C.Cir.1964) defendant was charged with robbery of a church rectory in Count I of the indictment and with robbery of a tourist home in Count II. The alleged offenses occurred about two months apart. He filed a motion to sever the charges and for a separate trial on each; the trial court denied the motion. At the trial, Cross expressed a desire to testify in his defense of Count II but to remain silent as to Count I. The trial court took the position that he was permitted to take the stand or not but if he elected to testify he could be cross-examined as to both counts. Cross testified:

> His testimony on Count II was that he was a victim and not a cohort of the armed robbers who entered the tourist home behind him. This testimony, which met the Government's case directly, was so convincing that the jury believed it despite the prosecutor's efforts at cross-examination and impeachment. On Count I, however, his denial was plainly evasive and unconvincing. He testified that he had been drinking heavily and did not know his whereabouts at the time of the church robbery. On cross-examination he was open to questioning concerning his generally tawdry way of life and his prior convictions.

335 F.2d at 990, 118 U.S.App.D.C. at 327. The jury acquitted Cross on Count II but returned a verdict of guilty on Count I. On appeal, the District of Columbia Circuit reversed and remanded for a new trial:

> Prejudice may develop when an accused wishes to testify on one but not the other of two joined offenses which are clearly distinct in time, place and evidence. His decision whether to testify will reflect a balancing of several factors with respect to each count: the evidence against him, the availability of defense evidence other than his testimony, the plausibility and substantiality of his testimony, the possible effects of demeanor, impeachment, and cross-

examination. But if the two charges are joined for trial, it is not possible for him to weigh these factors separately as to each count. If he testifies on one count, he runs the risk that any adverse effects will influence the jury's consideration of the other count. Thus he bears the risk on both counts, although he may benefit on only one. Moreover, a defendant's silence on one count would be damaging in the face of his express denial of the other. Thus he may be coerced into testifying on the count upon which he wished to remain silent. It is not necessary to decide whether this invades his constitutional right to remain silent, since we think it constitutes prejudice within the meaning of Rule 14.

... Cross had ample reason not to testify on Count I and would not have done so if that count had been tried separately. In a separate trial of that count the jury would not have heard his admissions of prior convictions and unsavory activities; nor would he have been under duress to offer dubious testimony on that count in order to avoid the damaging implication of testifying on only one of the two joined counts. Since the joinder embarrassed and confounded Cross in making his defense, the joinder was prejudicial within the meaning of Rule 14.

335 F.2d at 989–91, 118 U.S.App.D.C. at 326–28.

B.   JOINDER AND SEVERANCE OF DEFENDANTS

This Section focuses upon the considerations that should permit or prohibit the joining together for trial of two or more defendants who are charged with the same offense or with offenses arising out of the same course of conduct. The related problems raised by the representation of two or more jointly charged defendants by the same defense attorney are considered in Chapter 24, "Effective Assistance of Counsel."

Schaffer v. United States

Supreme Court of the United States, 1960.
362 U.S. 511, 80 S.Ct. 945, 4 L.Ed.2d 921.

■ MR. JUSTICE CLARK delivered the opinion of the Court.

Involved here are questions concerning joinder of defendants under Rule 8(b) of the Federal Rules of Criminal Procedure, 18 U.S.C.A. ....

The indictment charged transportation in interstate commerce of goods known to have been stolen and having a value in excess of $5,000. It contained three substantive counts. Count 1 charged the two Schaffers (petitioners in No. 111) and the three Stracuzzas (defendants below, who either pleaded guilty or had the charges against them *nolle prossed* at trial) with transporting stolen ladies' and children's wearing apparel from New York to Pennsylvania. Count 2 charged petitioner Marco and the Stracuzzas with a similar movement of stolen goods from New York to West Virginia. Count 3 charged petitioner Karp and the Stracuzzas with like shipments from New York to Massachusetts. The fourth and final count of the indictment charged all of these parties with a conspiracy to commit the substantive offenses charged in the first three counts. The petitioners here were tried on the indictment simultaneously in a single trial. On motion of petitioners for acquittal at the close of the Government's case, the court dismissed the conspiracy count for failure of proof. This motion was denied, however, as to the substantive counts, the court finding that no prejudice would result from the joint trial. Upon submission of the substantive counts to the jury on a detailed charge, each petitioner was found guilty and thereafter fined and sentenced to prison. The Court of Appeals affirmed the convictions, likewise finding that no prejudice existed by reason of the joint trial. 266 F.2d 435. We granted certiorari. 361 U.S. 809, 80 S.Ct. 58, 4 L.Ed.2d 58.

* * *

We first consider the question of joinder of defendants under Rule 8(b) of the Federal Rules of Criminal Procedure. It is clear that the initial joinder of the petitioners was permissible under that Rule, which allows the joinder of defendants "in the same indictment ... if they are alleged to have participated in the same act or transaction or in the same series of acts or transactions constituting an offense or offenses." It cannot be denied that the petitioners were so charged in the indictment. The problem remaining is whether, after dismissal of the conspiracy count before submission of the cases to the jury, a severance should have been ordered under Rule 14 of the Federal Rules of Criminal Procedure. This Rule requires a separate trial if "it appears that a defendant or the government is prejudiced by a joinder of offenses or of defendants in an indictment or information or by such joinder for trial together.... " Under the circumstances here, we think there was no such prejudice.

It is admitted that the three Stracuzzas were the common center of the scheme to transport the stolen goods. The four petitioners here participated in some steps of the transactions in the stolen goods, although each was involved with separate interstate shipments. The separate substantive charges of the indictment employed almost identical language and alleged violations of the same criminal statute during the same period and in the same manner. This made proof of the over-all operation of the scheme competent as to all counts. The variations in the proof related to the specific shipments proven against each petitioner. This proof was related to each petitioner separately and proven as to each by different witnesses. It included entirely separate invoices and other exhibits, all of which were first clearly identified as applying only to a specific petitioner and were so received and shown to the jury under painstaking instructions to that effect. In short, the proof was carefully compartmentalized as to each petitioner. The propriety of the joinder prior to the failure of proof of conspiracy was not assailed. When the Government rested, however, the petitioners filed their motion for dismissal and it was sustained as to the conspiracy count. The petitioners then pressed for acquittal on the remaining counts, and the court decided that the evidence was sufficient on the substantive counts. The case was submitted to the jury on each of these counts, and under a charge which was characterized by petitioners' counsel as being "extremely fair." This charge meticulously set out separately the evidence as to each of the petitioners and admonished the jury that they were "not to take into consideration any proof against one defendant and apply it by inference or otherwise to any other defendant."

Petitioners contend that prejudice would nevertheless be implicit in a continuation of the joint trial after dismissal of the conspiracy count. They say that the resulting prejudice could not be cured by any cautionary instructions, and that therefore the trial judge was left with no discretion. Petitioners overlook, however, that the joinder was authorized under Rule 8(b) and that subsequent severance was controlled by Rule 14, which provides for separate trials where "it appears that a defendant ... is prejudiced ... by such joinder for trial.... " It appears that not only was no prejudice shown, but both the trial court and the Court of Appeals affirmatively found that none was present. We cannot say to the contrary on this record. Nor can we fashion a hard-and-fast formula that, when a conspiracy count fails, joinder is error as a matter of law. We do emphasize, however, that, in such a situation, the trial judge has a continuing duty at all stages of the trial to grant a severance if prejudice does appear. And where, as here, the charge which originally justified joinder turns out to lack the support of sufficient evidence, a trial judge should be particularly sensitive to the possibility of such prejudice. However, the petitioners here not only failed to show any prejudice that would call Rule 14 into operation but even failed to request a new trial. Instead they relied entirely on their motions for acquittal. Moreover, the judge was acutely aware of the possibility of prejudice and was strict in his charge—not only as to the testimony the jury was not to consider, but also as to that evidence which was available in the consideration of the guilt of each petitioner separately under the respective substantive counts. The terms of Rule 8(b) having been met and no prejudice under Rule 14 having been shown, there was no misjoinder.

* * *

The judgments are therefore affirmed.

Affirmed.

■ MR. JUSTICE DOUGLAS, with whom THE CHIEF JUSTICE, MR. JUSTICE BLACK, and MR. JUSTICE BRENNAN concur, dissenting.

* * *

... There must somehow be a nexus between the several transactions charged against the several defendants, lest proof of distinct transactions blend to the prejudice of some defendants. The evidence concerning these petitioners was not in any proper sense of the words evidence concerning "the same series of acts or transactions" constituting an offense. The Schaffers had nothing to do with Karp's shipments to Massachusetts nor Marco's shipments to West Virginia; nor did the latter two have anything to do with Schaffers' shipments to Pennsylvania. The only possible connection between these disparate transactions was the fact that each petitioner dealt with the Stracuzzas, who were the brains of these deals. But that was a happenstance which did not make petitioners any the less strangers to each other. The Pennsylvania, Massachusetts, and West Virginia shipments had nothing in common except that they were all from the house of Stracuzza. Yet customers of one shop, engaged in an illegal enterprise, do not become participants "in the same series of acts or transactions," unless somehow or other what each does is connected up with the others or has some relation to them.

It is said that the joinder was proper if participation "in the same series" of transactions was "alleged" in the indictment. Such an allegation, to be sure, saves the indictment from attack at the preliminary stages. Yet once it becomes apparent during the trial that the defendants have not participated "in the same series" of transactions, it would make a mockery of Rule 8(b) to hold that the allegation alone, now known to be false, is enough to continue the joint trial.

... It is not enough to say that evidence of the guilt of each of the present petitioners may have been clear. Reasons for severance are founded on the principle that evidence against one person may not be used against a codefendant whose crime is unrelated to the others. Instructions can be given the jury and admonitions can be made explicit that the line between the various defendants must be kept separate. The district judge conscientiously made that effort here. But where, as here, there is no nexus between the several crimes, the mounting proof of the guilt of one is likely to affect another. There is no sure way to protect against it except by separate trials, especially where, as here, the several defendants, though unconnected, commit the crimes charged by dealing with one person, one house, one establishment. By a joint trial of such separate offenses, a subtle bond is likely to be created between the several defendants though they have never met nor acted in unison; prejudice within the meaning of Rule 14 is implicit.

* * *

NOTES

1. **Circumstances mandating severance.** What are some of the circumstances that should require a trial court to sever the cases of defendants joined for trial? Should it be sufficient that one defendant in testifying in his own behalf intends to incriminate a codefendant? See People v. Braune, 363 Ill. 551, 2 N.E.2d 839 (1936). That one defendant chooses to represent himself while the co-defendant is represented by counsel? See United States v. Sacco, 563 F.2d 552 (2d Cir.1977). That one defendant intends to testify while another does not? See United States v. Shuford, 454 F.2d 772 (4th Cir.1971). That the attorney for the testifying defendant intends to comment to the jury on the failure of a codefendant to testify? See De Luna v. United States, 308 F.2d 140 (5th Cir.1962). That one defendant intends to testify as to a joint alibi with a codefendant, an alibi which the co-defendant wishes his attorney to disavow to the jury? See United States v. Gambrill, 449 F.2d 1148, 146 U.S.App.D.C. 72 (D.C.Cir.1971). That one defendant would testify in favor of a co-defendant in a severed trial but intends not to testify in his own trial? See Byrd v. Wainwright, 428 F.2d 1017 (5th Cir.1970). That one defendant has a prior criminal record that will be admissible in evidence while the other does not? See Hardin v. Commonwealth, 437 S.W.2d 931 (Ky.App. 1968). See, generally, Dawson, Joint Trials of Defendants in Criminal Cases: An Analysis of Efficiencies and Prejudices, 77 Mich.L.Rev. 1379 (1979).

2. **Antagonistic defenses.** The Supreme Court considered the issue when severance of defendants is required because of mutually antagonistic defenses in Zafiro v. United States, 506 U.S. 534, 113 S.Ct. 933, 122 L.Ed.2d 317 (1993).

Defendants Garcia and Soto were confronted by government agents while carrying a box up the stairs of an apartment building. They dropped the box and ran into an apartment. The box contained 55 pounds of cocaine. In the apartment, agents found two other persons, Zafiro and Martinez. A search of the apartment revealed a suitcase with 16 pounds of cocaine, a small quantity of heroin and 4 pounds of marijuana. Next to the suitcase was a sack containing over $20,000 in cash. All four were charged with various drug offenses. Each moved for severance from the other defendants. Soto claimed he knew nothing about what was in the box he and Garcia were carrying. Garcia claimed the box belonged to Soto and that Garcia was ignorant of its contents. Zafiro, whose apartment it was, claimed she knew nothing of the drugs in the suitcase, which belonged to her boyfriend, Martinez. Martinez' position was that he was just visiting his girlfriend and had no idea she was involved in distributing drugs. The District Court denied severance and a joint trial resulted in the conviction of each defendant. The Court of Appeals affirmed the convictions over the claim that severance was required because of the nature of the defenses presented at the trial.

The Supreme Court, in an opinion by Justice O'Connor, affirmed. Asserting there is a preference in the federal system for joint trials of defendants who are indicted together, the Court rejected the argument that severance is mandated whenever mutually antagonistic defenses are asserted. Rather,

> a district court should grant a severance under Rule 14 only if there is a serious risk that a joint trial would compromise a specific trial right of one of the defendants, or prevent the jury from making a reliable judgment about guilt or innocence. Such a risk might occur when evidence that the jury should not consider against a defendant and that would not be admissible if a defendant were tried alone is admitted against a codefendant. For example, evidence of a codefendant's wrongdoing in some circumstances erroneously could lead a jury to conclude that a defendant was guilty. When many defendants are tried together in a complex case and they have markedly different degrees of culpability, this risk of prejudice is heightened. Evidence that is probative of a defendant's guilt but technically admissible only against a codefendant also might present a risk of prejudice * * *. Conversely, a defendant might suffer prejudice if essential exculpatory evidence that would be available to a defendant tried alone were unavailable in a joint trial.

506 U.S. at 539, 113 S.Ct. at 938, 122 L.Ed.2d at 325. The Court concluded that the District Court's instructions to the jury to consider each defendant's fate individually were sufficient protection on these facts. Justice Stevens concurred in the judgment, noting that the defenses asserted in this case were not truly mutually antagonistic in that it was possible to believe one defense without also believing that the other defendant was for that reason guilty.

3. **Accusatory confessions.** In Bruton v. United States, 391 U.S. 123, 88 S.Ct. 1620, 20 L.Ed.2d 476 (1968) petitioner was jointly tried with one Evans for armed postal robbery. In the trial, a postal inspector testified that Evans had confessed guilt to him and had named Bruton as his partner in the offense. Evans did not testify and the trial court instructed the jury that it could not consider Evans' confession as evidence against Bruton. The Supreme Court concluded that the procedure employed violated Bruton's right to confrontation of witnesses:

> Not every admission of inadmissible hearsay or other evidence can be considered to be reversible error unavoidable through limiting instructions; instances occur in almost every trial where inadmissible evidence creeps in, usually inadvertently. "A defendant is entitled to a fair trial but not a perfect one." Lutwak v. United States, 344 U.S. 604, 619, 73 S.Ct. 481, 490, 97 L.Ed. 593; see Hopt v. People of Utah, 120 U.S. 430, 438, 7 S.Ct. 614, 617, 30 L.Ed. 708; cf.

Fed.Rule Crim.Proc. 52(a). It is not unreasonable to conclude that in many such cases the jury can and will follow the trial judge's instructions to disregard such information. Nevertheless, ... there are some contexts in which the risk that the jury will not, or cannot, follow instructions is so great, and the consequences of failure so vital to the defendant, that the practical and human limitations of the jury system cannot be ignored. Such a context is presented here, where the powerfully incriminating extrajudicial statements of a codefendant, who stands accused side-by-side with the defendant, are deliberately spread before the jury in a joint trial. Not only are the incriminations devastating to the defendant but their credibility is inevitably suspect, a fact recognized when accomplices do take the stand and the jury is instructed to weigh their testimony carefully given the recognized motivation to shift blame onto others. The unreliability of such evidence is intolerably compounded when the alleged accomplice, as here, does not testify and cannot be tested by cross-examination. It was against such threats to a fair trial that the Confrontation Clause was directed.

391 U.S. at 135–36, 88 S.Ct. 1627–28, 20 L.Ed.2d at 484–85.

4. **Redacting accusatory confessions.** The Supreme Court considered the validity of editing a co-defendant's confession to eliminate references to the defendant (redaction) in Richardson v. Marsh, 481 U.S. 200, 107 S.Ct. 1702, 95 L.Ed.2d 176 (1987). Marsh was being jointly tried with one Williams for two murders committed during a robbery. Williams had confessed to police, and had stated that Marsh and Martin (a fugitive at the time of trial) had knowingly participated in the offenses with him. Williams' confession was edited by the trial court to eliminate all references not only to Marsh but to the participation by any party in the offense other than Martin. Williams' confession recounted a conversation between Williams and Martin while driving to the scene of the offense with Marsh, in which Martin stated he would kill the victims after the robbery. As so edited, it was introduced in his joint trial with Marsh. Williams did not testify, but Marsh did. She admitted presence at the scene of the offenses, but denied she knew a robbery was to occur, stating she did not hear the conversation in the car between Williams and Martin because she was in the back seat next to a radio speaker. One of the surviving victims testified that Marsh admitted Williams into her home and prevented her and her son from escaping during the robbery. The trial court instructed the jury that it could not consider Williams' confession against Marsh. In federal habeas corpus, the Sixth Circuit held that the redaction was ineffectual because other evidence linked Marsh with the offense and created an unacceptable risk the jury considered the confession in its context as evidence against Marsh in violation of the Confrontation Clause. The Supreme Court, in an opinion authored by Justice Scalia, reversed the Court of Appeals. Because the co-defendant's confession in *Bruton* named Bruton as a participant in the offense, the risk was unacceptable that the jury would be unable to follow the trial court's instruction not to consider it against him.

By contrast, in this case the confession was not incriminating on its face, and became so only when linked with evidence introduced later at trial (the defendant's own testimony).

Where the necessity of such linkage is involved, it is a less valid generalization that the jury will not likely obey the instruction to disregard the evidence. Specific testimony that "the defendant helped me commit the crime" is more vivid than inferential incrimination, and hence more difficult to thrust out of mind. Moreover, with regard to such an explicit statement the only issue is, plain and simply, whether the jury can possibly be expected to forget it in assessing the defendant's guilt; whereas with regard to inferential incrimination the judge's instruction may well be successful in dissuading the jury from entering onto the path of inference in the first place, so that there is no incrimination to forget. In short, while it may not always be simple for the members of a jury to obey the instruction that they disregard an incriminating inference, there does not exist the overwhelming probability of their inability to do so that is the foundation of *Bruton's* exception to the general rule [that juries follow instructions].

481 U.S. at 208, 107 S.Ct. at 1707–08, 95 L.Ed.2d at 186. The Court held that "the Confrontation Clause is not violated by the admission of a nontestifying codefendant's confession with a proper limiting instruction when, as here, the confession is redacted to eliminate not only the defendant's name, but any references to her existence." 481 U.S. at 211, 107 S.Ct. at 1709, 95 L.Ed.2d at 188. Finally, the Court noted that it expressed "no opinion on the admissibility of a confession in which the defendant's name has been replaced with a symbol or neutral pronoun." 481 U.S. at 211, n. 5, 107 S.Ct. at 1709, n. 5, 95 L.Ed.2d at 188, n. 5. Justice Stevens, joined by Justices Brennan and Marshall, dissented.

The petitioner in Gray v. Maryland, 523 U.S. 185, 118 S.Ct. 1151, 140 L.Ed.2d 294 (1998) was convicted of involuntary manslaughter in a joint trial with one Bell. At the trial, Bell's custodial confession was read which detailed his, Gray's and a deceased third person's role along with unnamed others in the assault and killing of Stacey. Gray's and the other person's names were deleted and replaced with blank spaces or the word "deleted." As read to the jury, part of the confession was as follows:

Question: Who was in the group that beat Stacey?

Answer: Me, deleted, deleted, and a few other guys.

Immediately after the redacted confession was read to the jury, the prosecutor asked the detective "after he gave you that information, you subsequently were able to arrest Mr. Kevin Gray; is that correct?" To which he responded, "That's correct." The written statement admitted into evidence and shown to the jury replaced Gray's and the deceased co-actor's name with "deleted" or a blank space set apart by commas: ", ,". The trial court instructed the jury that the confession was evidence only against Bell, who had not testified. Gray testified and denied participation in the offense. Although the Maryland Court of Appeals reversed the conviction on *Bruton* grounds, the Maryland high court reversed the Court of Appeals. The United States Supreme Court, in an opinion by Justice Breyer, vacated the conviction and remanded, holding that *Bruton* not Richardson v. Marsh controlled this case.

The five-judge majority distinguished *Richardson* on the ground that the confession in that case was redacted to eliminate any reference to Richardson or any other third person at all, while in this case the redaction clearly referenced two other persons, and that the jury would likely decide that Gray was one of the "deleted" persons. The majority opinion provided this explanation of possible jury behavior:

Consider a simplified but typical example, a confession that reads "I, Bob Smith, along with Sam Jones, robbed the bank." To replace the words "Sam Jones" with an obvious blank will not likely fool anyone. A juror somewhat familiar with criminal law would know immediately that the blank, in the phrase "I, Bob Smith, along with , robbed the bank," refers to defendant Jones. A juror who does not know the law and who therefore wonders to whom the blank might refer need only lift his eyes to Jones, sitting at counsel table, to find what will seem the obvious answer, at least if the juror hears the judge's instruction not to consider the confession as evidence against Jones, for that instruction will provide an obvious reason for the blank. A more sophisticated juror, wondering if the blank refers to someone else, might also wonder how, if it did, the prosecutor could argue the confession is reliable, for the prosecutor, after all, has been arguing that Jones, not someone else, helped Smith commit the crime.

523 U.S. at 198, 118 S.Ct. at 1155, 140 L.Ed.2d at 301. Justice Scalia, joined by The Chief Justice, Justice Kennedy and Justice Thomas, dissented on the ground *Richardson* controls this case. Justice Scalia objected to any redaction beyond the obvious deletion of names:

> For inchoate offenses—conspiracy in particular—redaction to delete all references to a confederate would often render the confession nonsensical. If the question was "Who agreed to beat Stacey?", and the answer was "Me and Kevin," we might redact the answer to "Me and [deleted]," or perhaps to "Me and somebody else," but surely not to just "Me"—for that would no longer be a confession to the conspiracy charge, but rather the foundation for an insanity defense. To my knowledge we have never before endorsed—and to my strong belief we should not endorse—the redaction of a statement by some means other than the deletion of certain words, with the fact of the deletion shown. The risk to the integrity of our system (not to mention the increase in its complexity) posed by the approval of such free-lance editing seems to me infinitely greater than the risk posed by the entirely honest reproduction that the Court disapproves.

523 U.S. at 203–04, 118 S.Ct. at 1160, 140 L.Ed.2d at 307–08.

CHAPTER 20

DOUBLE JEOPARDY

Analysis

EDITORS' INTRODUCTION: THE INTERESTS PROTECTED

The Fifth Amendment, after providing that no person is to be held to answer for an infamous crime except on presentation or indictment by a grand jury, continues, "nor shall any person be subject for the same offense to be twice put in jeopardy of life or limb.... " This prohibition against double jeopardy was held binding on the states in Benton v. Maryland, 395 U.S. 784, 89 S.Ct. 2056, 23 L.Ed.2d 707 (1969), overruling Palko v. Connecticut, 302 U.S. 319, 58 S.Ct. 149, 82 L.Ed. 288 (1937):

> The fundamental nature of the guarantee against double jeopardy can hardly be doubted. Its origin can be traced to Greek and Roman times, and it became established in the common law of England long before this Nation's independence. ...Today, every state incorporates some form of the prohibition in its constitution or common law. As this court put it in Green v. United States, 355 U.S. 184, 187–88, 78 S.Ct. 221, 223, 2 L.Ed.2d 199, 204 (1957), "[t]he underlying idea, one that is

deeply ingrained in at least the Anglo–American system of jurisprudence, is that the State with all its resources and power should not be allowed to make repeated attempts to convict an individual for an alleged offense, thereby subjecting him to embarrassment, expense and ordeal and compelling him to live in a continuing state of anxiety and insecurity, as well as enhancing the possibility that even though innocent he may be found guilty."

395 U.S. at 795–96, 89 S.Ct. at 2063, 23 L.Ed.2d at 716–17.

The interests furthered by the prohibition against double jeopardy may be more complex than the language from *Green* indicates. Clearly, the prohibition recognizes and implements an interest in finality. Once put into jeopardy, a defendant has a legitimate interest in having to defend that proceeding but that proceeding only. As the *Green* language suggests, this may be because repeated trials create an unacceptable risk that an innocent defendant will be convicted. But as that same language suggests, this interest seems also to be based upon an independent notion that "fairness" to defendants demands that the government limit itself to one effort to establish a defendant's guilt.

It is also possible that the prohibition protects against multiple punishment. Commentators and courts have traditionally regarded this as an established part of the basis for double jeopardy doctrine. See Westen and Drubel, supra at 84, 106–22. But Whalen v. United States, 445 U.S. 684, 100 S.Ct. 1432, 63 L.Ed.2d 715 (1980), discussed below, suggests that the Court may not regard the prohibition as addressing the propriety of multiple punishment where only a single proceeding is involved.

Double jeopardy issues arise in a variety of procedural contexts. But there are a number of matters sufficiently general to warrant preliminary discussion.

Raising and Resolving Double Jeopardy Issues

Under common law pleading practice, former acquittal and former conviction were pleas in bar and "a mass of learning grew up concerning those pleas both with respect to the manner in which they could be proved and the circumstances under which they were available." L. Orfield, Criminal Procedure from Arrest to Appeal 268 (1947). The procedure for assertion of a claim of former jeopardy differs among jurisdictions under modern law, but the matter is usually one that is to be raised and resolved prior to the trial on the merits. Id. at 306; Fed.R.Crim.Proc., Rule 12. In a number of jurisdictions, however, if a claim of former jeopardy raises a question of fact, this is to be submitted to the jury along with guilt-innocence issues. Kite v. State, 506 P.2d 946 (Okla.Crim.App.1973). Apparently there is no right to a jury determination of such fact issues in the federal courts, and the determination of the merits of a claim of former jeopardy is to be made by the trial judge. United States v. Young, 503 F.2d 1072 (3d Cir.1974).

In Abney v. United States, 431 U.S. 651, 97 S.Ct. 2034, 52 L.Ed.2d 651 (1977), the defendant in a federal criminal prosecution had filed a motion to dismiss on double jeopardy grounds. The District Court denied the motion and Abney sought to take an interlocutory appeal under 28 U.S.C.A. § 1291, which authorizes appeal from all "final decisions" of the district courts. The Supreme Court held that the district court's order denying the motion to dismiss was a final order within the meaning of the statute. It was a complete and—for trial purposes—final rejection of the claim. Moreover, it concerned a claim collateral to, and separable from, the issue of guilt or innocence. Further:

> [T]he rights conferred on a criminal accused by the Double Jeopardy Clause would be significantly undermined if appellate review of double jeopardy claims were postponed until after conviction and sentence. ...[T]his court has long recognized that the Double Jeopardy Clause protects an individual against more than being subjected to double punishments. It is a guarantee against being twice put to *trial* for the same offense. ...It thus protects interests wholly unrelated to the propriety of any subsequent conviction. ...Obviously, these aspects of the guarantee's protections would be lost if the accused were forced to "run the gauntlet" a second time before an appeal could be taken; even if the accused is acquitted, or, if convicted, has his conviction ultimately reversed on double jeopardy grounds, he has still been forced to endure a trial that the Double Jeopardy Clause was designed to prohibit. Consequently, if a criminal defendant is to avoid *exposure* to double jeopardy and thereby enjoy the full protection of the Clause, his double jeopardy challenge to the indictment must be reviewable before that subsequent exposure occurs.

431 U.S. at 660–62, 97 S.Ct. at 2040–41, 52 L.Ed.2d at 660–61 (emphasis in original). Is it possible that inherent in the Double Jeopardy Clause is a right to interlocutory appellate review of a rejection of a double jeopardy claim? In *Abney,* the Court "approached" the question of statutory construction before it with the principle in mind that there is no constitutional right to appeal. 431 U.S. at 656, 97 S.Ct. at 2038, 52 L.Ed.2d at 657–58. Perhaps if a state chooses to make appellate review of double jeopardy claims available to defendants, it is constitutionally necessary that such review be available on an interlocutory basis.

Abney, then, suggests the desirability and perhaps the constitutional necessity of pretrial resolution of double jeopardy claims. In interesting contrast is Illinois v. Vitale, 447 U.S. 410, 100 S.Ct. 2260, 65 L.Ed.2d 228 (1980). An automobile driven by Vitale struck two small children; both died as a result of the accident. At the scene, a traffic citation was issued charging Vitale with failing to reduce speed in violation of § 11–601(a) of the Illinois Vehicle Code, which provides that "[s]peed must be decreased as necessary to avoid colliding with any person.... " Vitale was convicted of the violation and a fine of $15 was imposed. The next day, a petition was filed in juvenile court alleging that Vitale "without lawful justification while recklessly driving a motor vehicle" caused the death of the two children killed in the accident, and thereby committed involuntary manslaughter. The relevant part of the Illinois Criminal Code, Ill.Rev.Stat.1973 ch. 38, § 9–3, provided that "[a] person who kills an individual without lawful justification commits involuntary manslaughter if his acts ... which cause the death are such as are likely to cause death or great bodily harm to some individual, and he performs them recklessly." A motion to dismiss was filed on the ground that the manslaughter prosecution was violative of double jeopardy. The Illinois courts ultimately held that the motion should have been granted because "failing to reduce speed" was a lesser included offense of involuntary manslaughter and the conviction for the former barred prosecution for the latter. In re Vitale, 71 Ill.2d 229, 375 N.E.2d 87, 16 Ill.Dec. 456 (1978).

The Supreme Court reversed and remanded. Justice White, speaking for a majority of the Court, concluded that under Illinois law proof of involuntary manslaughter may not always require proof of failure to slow. The "acts ... likely to cause death or great bodily injury [performed] recklessly," required by the manslaughter statute, might but need not always involve failing to decrease speed to avoid a collision with a person. If, as a matter of Illinois law, a careless failure to slow is *always* a necessary element of involuntary manslaughter, then the *trial* on the manslaughter charge would be barred. But "the mere possibility that the State will seek to rely on [the failure to slow] to establish an element of its manslaughter case would not be sufficient to bar the latter prosecution," the majority concluded. If, however, the State at trial actually proved the failure to slow as a necessary element of its manslaughter charge, or if before trial it conceded that it planned to do so, Vitale's claim of double jeopardy "would be substantial." 447 U.S. at 419–20, 100 S.Ct. at 2266–67, 65 L.Ed.2d at 238.

Justice Stevens, joined by Justices Brennan, Stewart, and Marshall, dissented. He urged that the majority's implication that the State may go to trial before Vitale is entitled to a determination concerning his claim of double jeopardy violates "the vital interest in avoiding a second trial" emphasized in *Abney:*

> If a defendant is entitled to have an appellate court rule on his double jeopardy claim in advance of trial, he is surely entitled to a definitive ruling by the trial court in advance of trial. Since the State has not provided [Vitale] with notice of any basis for the prosecution that does not depend upon proving, for the second time, a careless failure to reduce speed, I would not require [him] to stand trial again.

447 U.S. at 427–28, 100 S.Ct. at 2271, 65 L.Ed.2d at 242–43.

The ramifications of *Vitale* are not clear. Two offenses may have such a relationship that one is a "necessarily included offense" of the other; this relationship exists only if, given the abstract definitions of the two offenses, proof of one always and necessarily involves proof of the other. The *Vitale* dicta indicate that where this relationship exists, a second trial is barred, i.e., a defendant is entitled to a pretrial determination that an asserted claim of double jeopardy is meritorious. But situations where this "necessarily included offense" relationship does not exist may be such that in its proof of one crime the government will in fact rely upon all of the facts used in a prior proceeding to establish guilt of another. In such cases, one of the offenses is an "included offense" of the other, although not a *necessarily* included one. *Vitale* seems to hold that in such situations a defendant's claim of double jeopardy need not be resolved prior to trial unless the government "concedes" that it will rely upon proof of the included offense at trial. Where no such concession is made, a defendant's claim of double jeopardy need not be resolved until during or after trial, when the trial court can determine whether or not the government is relying on proof of the included offense. Is this consistent with the policy interests stressed in *Abney?*

It does not appear that Vitale made any efforts before trial to require the government to specify what evidence it would rely upon in its efforts to prove him guilty of manslaughter. Suppose Vitale had moved for greater specification in the allegations and had urged that such greater specificity was essential to vindicating his interest in having any valid double jeopardy claim determined in his favor before he was required to "run the gauntlet" a second time. Under *Abney,* would he be constitutionally entitled to such greater specificity? As a matter of sound procedural policy, should defendants be entitled to such pretrial specificity of the proof that will be relied upon by the government at trial?

Attachment of Jeopardy

One proceeding does not bar a subsequent prosecution unless jeopardy attached in the first proceeding. Unless jeopardy attached, the disposition of the case cannot conceivably be regarded as an acquittal or a conviction and the absence of a reasonable basis for terminating it will not preclude the government from starting anew. Therefore, it is of major importance to identify the point in a criminal proceeding at which jeopardy attaches. The matter was addressed in Crist v. Bretz, 437 U.S. 28, 98 S.Ct. 2156, 57 L.Ed.2d 24 (1978). Defendants' first prosecution had been terminated after a jury was empaneled and sworn but before any witnesses were called by the state. In a subsequent trial, their double jeopardy objection was overruled on the ground that jeopardy had not attached in the first proceeding. The Supreme Court held this to be constitutional error. The time when jeopardy attaches in a jury trial "serves as the lynchpin for all double jeopardy jurisprudence," the majority noted, and consequently the traditional federal rule—that jeopardy attaches in a jury trial when the jury is empaneled and sworn—is an integral part of the constitutional guarantee against double jeopardy and is binding on the states. 437 U.S. at 38, 98 S.Ct. at 2162, 57 L.Ed.2d at 33. In a bench trial, the federal rule has been that jeopardy attaches when the court begins to hear evidence, i.e., when the first witness is sworn. Serfass v. United States, 420 U.S. 377, 388, 95 S.Ct. 1055, 1062, 43 L.Ed.2d 265, 274 (1975). *Bretz* strongly suggests this rule will be regarded a part of the federal constitutional standard and also binding on the states.

"Separate Sovereignties" Exception

The Supreme Court has repeatedly held that successive prosecutions based on the same conduct are permissible if they are brought by separate and distinct "sovereignties." Whether the first prosecution resulted in acquittal or conviction is apparently of no consequence. Thus trial in a state court does not bar trial in federal court on the basis of the same conduct. Bartkus v. Illinois, 359 U.S. 121, 79 S.Ct. 676, 3 L.Ed.2d 684 (1959); Abbate v. United States, 359 U.S. 187, 79 S.Ct. 666, 3 L.Ed.2d 729

(1959). Conceptually, the Court has reasoned that two offenses are involved, one under the law of each of the two sovereignties, and thus the prohibition against multiple jeopardy for the "same" offense is not violated. See United States v. Wheeler, 435 U.S. 313, 317, 98 S.Ct. 1079, 1082–83, 55 L.Ed.2d 303, 309 (1978). The policy justification for the exception, the Court has stressed, is that each sovereignty has an interest independent of the interest of the other in punishing the conduct. To permit one sovereignty to frustrate the interest of the other by initiating prosecution first would unacceptably deprive the other sovereignty of its right to enforce its own laws. United States v. Wheeler, supra, 435 U.S. at 317–18, 98 S.Ct. at 1083, 55 L.Ed.2d at 309.

A limitation upon the exception is the requirement that the two prosecutions be brought by entities that are in fact separate sovereignties. The federal government and a state government or its subdivision are separate sovereignties. Abbate v. United States, supra. But a state and its municipalities are not, and successive prosecutions by a municipality and then the state itself violates double jeopardy. Waller v. Florida, 397 U.S. 387, 90 S.Ct. 1184, 25 L.Ed.2d 435 (1970). The United States Government and an Indian tribe, however, are separate sovereignties. United States v. Wheeler, supra. Two prosecuting authorities are separate sovereignties under this requirement if the power of each to punish the conduct at issue is "inherent." If one prosecuting authority is merely exercising authority delegated by the other, the two authorities are not separate sovereignties and successive prosecutions are barred. United States v. Wheeler, supra.

In Heath v. Alabama, 474 U.S. 82, 106 S.Ct. 433, 88 L.Ed.2d 387 (1985), the Court applied the doctrine of separate sovereignties to the prosecution of petitioner by Alabama for committing murder during a kidnapping after he had been convicted in Georgia for the same homicide. In an opinion for the Court, Justice O'Connor concluded that Alabama and Georgia were separate sovereignties under the *Wheeler* test and that the same conduct could, therefore, form the basis of a criminal prosecution by each. The petitioner had argued the Court should adopt a balancing test and permit multiple prosecutions in this situation only if "allowing only one entity to exercise jurisdiction over the defendant will interfere with the unvindicated interests of the second entity and that multiple prosecutions therefore are necessary for the satisfaction of the legitimate interests of both entities." 474 U.S. at 92, 106 S.Ct. at 439, 88 L.Ed.2d at 396. The Court rejected this argument:

> A State's interest in vindicating its sovereign authority through enforcement of its laws by definition can never be satisfied by another State's enforcement of *its* own laws. Just as the Federal Government has the right to decide that a state prosecution has not vindicated a violation of the "peace and dignity" of the Federal Government, a State must be entitled to decide that a prosecution by another State has not satisfied its legitimate sovereign interest.

474 U.S. at 93, 106 S.Ct. at 440, 88 L.Ed.2d at 397. Justices Brennan and Marshall dissented.

In 1959, the United States Attorney General acknowledged that the government's ability to prosecute following state proceedings could, if applied indiscriminately and with bad judgment, cause considerable hardship. As a result, he promulgated a department policy of bringing federal prosecution after a state trial for the same act or acts only where "the reasons are compelling." Further, no such federal case is to be tried without approval by an Assistant Attorney General, who should bring the case to the attention of the Attorney General before granting approval. See 27 U.S.Law Week 2509 (April 7, 1959). This policy, and the related Justice Department policy of prosecuting together different offenses arising out of the same transaction, came to be known as the "Petite Policy," after Petite v. United States, 361 U.S. 529, 80 S.Ct. 450, 4 L.Ed.2d 490 (1960). In *Petite*, the Supreme Court, at the request of the government, directed dismissal of a federal prosecution which the government determined to have been brought in violation of its policy announced in 1959.

The roles of the courts and the Justice Department in the enforcement of the *Petite* policy were raised in Rinaldi v. United States, 434 U.S. 22, 98 S.Ct. 81, 54 L.Ed.2d 207 (1977). Rinaldi and several companions participated in a plot to rob safe-deposit boxes in a Miami hotel. In February, 1973, they were charged with state offenses based on this activity and, one month later, federal indictments were returned based on the same conduct. In May, Rinaldi was convicted of the state charges and sentenced to six years imprisonment. Nevertheless, the federal prosecution proceeded to trial. Later, it appeared that this was because a Justice Department official (not the appropriate Assistant Attorney General) feared the state conviction would be reversed on appeal. In violation of the *Petite* policy, no approval was obtained from the appropriate Assistant United States Attorney General; it is not clear whether such approval would have been granted had it been sought. Rinaldi was tried and convicted of the federal charges and received a twelve-year prison term. The government then moved to dismiss the prosecution because of the violation of the *Petite* policy. The motive for this is not entirely clear. On oral argument before the Fifth Circuit, counsel for the government indicated that dismissal was sought at this time because Rinaldi's state conviction had been affirmed by the state's intermediate appellate court (although it had not yet been considered by the state's highest appellate tribunal) and therefore its integrity was sufficiently assured. But the Solicitor General subsequently took the position that dismissal was sought only because it was discovered at this time by the Assistant Attorney General in charge of enforcement of the *Petite* policy that the prior authorization required by the policy had not been obtained.

The federal district court denied the motion to dismiss. United States v. Washington, 390 F.Supp. 842 (S.D.Fla.1975). This was affirmed on appeal to penalize the government's bad faith attempt to manipulate judicial time and resources through a "capricious, inconsistent application" of the *Petite* policy. In re Washington, 544 F.2d 203 (5th Cir.1976) (en banc). The court commented that it could not understand how Rinaldi might have been unfairly harmed by this, since he was convicted in an apparently fair trial and still retained the right to appeal his conviction. 544 F.2d at 209.

The Supreme Court reversed, and directed dismissal of the case. The majority found that the government's motion to dismiss was made without bad faith, and was not tainted by any bad faith that might have existed earlier in the case. The record was entirely consistent with the Government's argument that the Assistant Attorney General in charge of enforcement of the *Petite* policy was unaware of its violation until shortly before the filing of the motion to dismiss. The purpose of the *Petite* policy is to protect individuals from unfairness associated with needless multiple prosecutions; "the defendant, therefore, should receive the benefit of the policy whenever its application is urged by the government." 434 U.S. at 31, 98 S.Ct. at 86, 54 L.Ed.2d at 215. Turning to the intermediate appellate court's conclusion that denial of the motion for dismissal was justified by the need to deter misconduct by prosecutors, the majority responded, "we fail to see how rewarding those responsible for the *Petite* policy violation with a conviction serves to deter prosecutorial misconduct." 434 U.S. at 31 n. 17, 86 S.Ct. at 86 n. 17, 54 L.Ed.2d at 215 n. 17. If the government were to pursue federal prosecution on the sole basis that the state conviction might fall on appeal, the Court commented, this "would indeed mark a departure from the *Petite* policy." 434 U.S. at 30 n. 16, 98 S.Ct. at 86 n. 16, 54 L.Ed.2d at 214 n. 16.

Suppose the defendant but not the government urges that nonprosecution is dictated by the *Petite* policy? Should a federal trial judge consider what result is dictated by the policy, or should the government's interpretation of the policy be conclusive? In *Rinaldi,* the district judge commented that the federal sentences were more severe than those imposed in the state proceedings, 390 F.Supp. at 844, suggesting that he may have regarded the low penalties in the state proceeding as a "compelling reason", under the *Petite* policy, rendering federal prosecution appropriate. Could the dismissal have been denied on this basis, or is the determination as to the adequacy of the sentence imposed in the state proceeding solely within the prerogative of the government?

Government Appeal

The limits placed by double jeopardy upon the ability of the government to appeal in criminal proceedings presents a number of difficult problems. For many years, the existence of statutory limitations upon such appeals made it unnecessary for the federal courts to reach constitutional questions. But in 1970, Congress amended the Criminal Appeals Act, 18 U.S.C.A. § 3731, so as to authorize government appeals in federal prosecutions wherever this was permitted by the Constitution. See United States v. Wilson, 420 U.S. 332, 337, 95 S.Ct. 1013, 1019, 43 L.Ed.2d 232, 238 (1975). This has required the Court to discuss the impact of the double jeopardy clause upon governmental appeals in a number of post–1970 decisions.

The leading brief for virtually unlimited governmental appeals was authored by Justice Holmes, dissenting in Kepner v. United States, 195 U.S. 100, 134–37, 24 S.Ct. 797, 806–07, 49 L.Ed. 114, 126–28 (1904). A defendant is not placed in jeopardy more than once, he reasoned, as long as both (or all) trials are part of the same cause. The system of appellate review that Justice Holmes' "continuing jeopardy" concept would permit was characterized by the Court in United States v. Wilson, supra, as having "symmetry to recommend it" and as avoiding release of some defendants who have benefited from instructions or evidentiary rulings unduly favorable to them. But the Court rejected it, as it had before, explaining that such a system

> would allow the prosecutor to seek to persuade a second trier of fact of the defendant's guilt after having failed with the first; it would permit him to re-examine the weaknesses in his first presentation in order to strengthen the second; and it would disserve the defendant's legitimate interest in the finality of a verdict of acquittal.

420 U.S. at 352, 95 S.Ct. at 1026, 43 L.Ed.2d at 246–47.

But the Court has also rejected the notion that double jeopardy should bar any appeal from a ruling in favor of the defendant or any termination of the proceeding in the defendant's favor. In *Wilson,* after the jury had returned a verdict of guilty, the trial judge granted a defense motion to dismiss on the ground that the proceedings were brought in violation of the defendant's Due Process rights. In making this determination, the trial judge relied in part upon the evidence produced at trial and apparently upon what this evidence showed concerning the impact of the delay upon the defendant's ability fairly to challenge the government's case. Opposing the government's efforts to appeal the trial judge's ruling, Wilson urged that double jeopardy bars appeal of any order discharging a defendant when that order is based on facts outside of the indictment. The majority in *Wilson* rejected this argument and held that the double jeopardy bar against government appeals applies only when there is a danger of subjecting the defendant to a second trial for the same offense. Explaining, the Court stated:

> Although review of any ruling of law discharging a defendant obviously enhances the likelihood of conviction and subjects him to continuing expense and anxiety, a defendant has no legitimate claim to benefit from an error of law when that error could be corrected without subjecting him to a second trial before a second trier of fact.

420 U.S. at 345, 95 S.Ct. at 1023, 43 L.Ed.2d at 242–43. Where the government could, on appeal, be granted relief without subjecting the defendant to a second trial, double jeopardy is not violated by the appeal. Should the government win on the merits in *Wilson,* the appellate court could simply remand the case with directions to the trial judge to enter judgment on the jury verdict. Since no retrial would be necessary to grant the government relief should it win, appeal by the government is permissible.

Several procedural consequences of this position articulated in *Wilson* are clear from the caselaw. The government may appeal from a ruling made before jeopardy attaches; since no trial has been held, there is no danger of a second trial following a governmental victory on appeal. United States v. Sanford, 429 U.S. 14, 97 S.Ct. 20, 50 L.Ed.2d 17 (1976); Serfass v. United States, 420 U.S. 377, 95 S.Ct. 1055, 43 L.Ed.2d 265 (1975).

If the defendant prevails on appeal in a system with several tiers of appellate tribunals, the government may seek further review of the intermediate court's ruling. The intermediate court can be reversed without subjecting the defendant to a second trial. Forman v. United States, 361

U.S. 416, 80 S.Ct. 481, 4 L.Ed.2d 412 (1960). At least some post-verdict actions by the trial judge can be appealed, because the appellate court can reverse and remand with directions to reinstate the verdict already returned in the previously-held trial. United States v. Morrison, 429 U.S. 1, 97 S.Ct. 24, 50 L.Ed.2d 1 (1976) (government could appeal trial judge's ruling, made after a finding of guilty at a nonjury trial, that the marijuana which was the subject of the charge should be suppressed and that the trial court would "take appropriate action consistent with" this ruling—apparently acquitting the defendant—if the ruling was not appealed or if it was affirmed on appeal); United States v. Wilson, supra.

On the other hand, it is clear that the government cannot appeal from an acquittal. Fong Foo v. United States, 369 U.S. 141, 82 S.Ct. 671, 7 L.Ed.2d 629 (1962) (Court of Appeals erred in granting writ of mandamus ordering trial judge to retry defendants after trial judge had erroneously directed jury to return verdict of acquittal and entered formal judgment of acquittal). In United States v. Martin Linen Supply Co., 430 U.S. 564, 97 S.Ct. 1349, 51 L.Ed.2d 642 (1977), the jury in defendants' criminal contempt trial could not agree on a verdict and was discharged. As was permitted by Rule 29(c) of the Federal Rules of Criminal Procedure, defendants then made a timely motion for judgments of acquittal which was granted by the trial judge. The government sought to appeal; the Supreme Court held that appeal was barred. The judgments entered by the trial court were acquittals "in substance as well as form" 430 U.S. at 572, 97 S.Ct. at 1355, 51 L.Ed.2d at 651, and the application of double jeopardy should not be affected by the timing of the trial judge in entering a judgment of acquittal. 430 U.S. at 575, 97 S.Ct. at 1356, 51 L.Ed.2d at 653. Further, the Court noted:

> a successful governmental appeal reversing the judgments of acquittal would necessitate another trial, or, at least, "further proceedings of some sort, devoted to the resolution of factual issues going to the elements of the offense charged. . . ." United States v. Jenkins, 420 U.S. 358, 370, 95 S.Ct. 1006, 1013, 43 L.Ed.2d 250, 259 (1975).

430 U.S. at 570, 97 S.Ct. at 1354, 51 L.Ed.2d at 650.

But some matters remain unclear. May the government appeal from a post-verdict judgment of acquittal where the jury has returned a verdict of guilty? Unlike the situation at issue in *Martin Linen Supply Co.*, such cases would permit the government to be granted relief—an order directing the trial judge to enter judgment of conviction on the jury verdict—without another trial and perhaps even without "further proceedings of some sort, devoted to the resolution of factual issues going to the elements of offenses charged." On the other hand, perhaps an acquittal—as long as it is an acquittal "in substance as well as form"—is insulated from appellate review even if the government could be granted relief without the necessity for a new trial. Consider this in relation to section (A), "Former Acquittal." Another problem is presented by pre-verdict "dismissals" that may or may not involve acquittals on the merits; these are the subject of subsection (C)(2).

In any case, the availability of appellate review seems clearly a separate aspect of double jeopardy law. While this is nowhere spelled out, the decisions strongly suggest that prosecution appeals might be permissible in some situations where double jeopardy would bar the government from simply starting over with a new proceeding. Exactly when the government has—or constitutionally can have—the option of appeal but not of starting prosecution anew is an interesting problem.

———

Because of the interplay among a variety of procedural issues, effective categorization of double jeopardy cases is a difficult task. It is useful, however, to distinguish the decisions according to the outcome in the first proceeding: acquittal, conviction, or termination in some other way— usually by the trial judge's declaration of a mistrial—that involves neither acquittal nor conviction. The first three sections of this chapter follow this distinction.

But in regard to each of these areas, it is important to consider the extent to which the prohibition does or should preclude another trial on a charge related to that on which the first proceeding was held but which is "technically" not for the same crime. In addition, consideration must be given to the extent to which double jeopardy has application to situations in which there have not been multiple proceedings. Among these issues are the limits which the doctrine places upon appeal by the prosecution and upon conviction, punishment, or both for several related offenses in the course of the same prosecution.

The final section of this chapter deals with the limitations the Double Jeopardy Clause places on the ability of the government to pursue both criminal prosecution and civil forfeiture of property used in the commission of the same criminal offense.

A.   FORMER ACQUITTAL

Given the policies underlying the Double Jeopardy provision, a situation involving a previous acquittal presents what is probably the strongest case for rigorous application of the doctrine. Perhaps the most important issue in administering this aspect of Double Jeopardy is defining what constitutes an "acquittal."

Burks v. United States

Supreme Court of the United States, 1978.
437 U.S. 1, 98 S.Ct. 2141, 57 L.Ed.2d 1.

■ MR. CHIEF JUSTICE BURGER delivered the opinion of the Court.

We granted certiorari to resolve the question of whether an accused may be subjected to a second trial when conviction in a prior trial was reversed by an appellate court solely for lack of sufficient evidence to sustain the jury's verdict.

I.

Petitioner Burks was tried in the United States District Court for the crime of robbing a federally insured bank by use of a dangerous weapon, a violation of 18 U.S.C.A. § 2113(d). Burks' principal defense was insanity. To prove this claim petitioner produced three expert witnesses who testified, albeit with differing diagnoses of his mental condition, that he suffered from a mental illness at the time of the robbery, which rendered him substantially incapable of conforming his conduct to the requirements of the law. In rebuttal the Government offered the testimony of two experts, one of whom testified that although petitioner possessed a character disorder, he was not mentally ill. The other prosecution witness acknowledged a character disorder in petitioner, but gave a rather ambiguous answer to the question of whether Burks had been capable of conforming his conduct to the law. Lay witnesses also testified for the Government, expressing their opinion that petitioner appeared to be capable of normal functioning and was sane at the time of the alleged offense.

Before the case was submitted to the jury, the court denied a motion for a judgment of acquittal. The jury found Burks guilty as charged. Thereafter, he filed a timely motion for a new trial, maintaining, among other things, "that the evidence was insufficient to support the verdict." The motion was denied by the District Court, which concluded that petitioner's challenge to the sufficiency of the evidence was "utterly without merit."[1]

On appeal petitioner narrowed the issues by admitting the affirmative factual elements of the charge against him, leaving only his claim concerning criminal responsibility to be resolved. With respect to this point, the Court of Appeals agreed with petitioner's claim that the evidence was insufficient to support the verdict and reversed his conviction. . . .

. . . [T]he Court of Appeals, rather than terminating the case against petitioner, remanded to the District Court "for a determination of whether a directed verdict of acquittal should be entered or a new trial ordered." Indicating that the District Court should choose the appropriate course "from a balancing of the equities," the court explicitly adopted the procedures utilized by the Fifth Circuit in United States v. Bass, 490 F.2d 846, 852–853 (1974), "as a guide" to be used on remand:

> "[W]e reverse and remand the case to the district court where the defendant will be entitled to a directed verdict of acquittal unless the government presents sufficient additional evidence to carry its burden on the issue of defendant's sanity. As we noted earlier, the question of sufficiency of the evidence to make an issue for the jury on the defense of insanity is a question of law to be decided by the trial judge. . . . If the district court sitting without the presence of the jury, is satisfied by the government's presentation, it may order a new trial. . . . Even if the government presents additional evidence, the district judge may refuse to order a new trial if he finds from the record that the prosecution

---

1. Petitioner did not file a post-trial motion for judgment of acquittal, which he was entitled to do under Fed.Rule Crim.Proc. 29(c).

had the opportunity fully to develop its case or in fact did so at the first trial."

The Court of Appeals assumed it had the power to order this "balancing" remedy by virtue of the fact that Burks had explicitly requested a new trial. . . .

II.

* * *

. . . [At least one proposition emerged from our decisions in this area]: a defendant who *requests* a new trial as one avenue of relief may be required to stand trial again, even when his conviction was reversed due to failure of proof at the first trial. Given that petitioner here appealed from a denial of a motion for a new trial—although he had moved for acquittal during trial—our prior cases would seem to indicate that the Court of Appeals had power to remand on the terms it ordered. To reach a different result will require a departure from those holdings.

III.

It is unquestionably true that the Court of Appeals' decision "represente[d] a resolution, correct or not, of some or all of the factual elements of the offense charged." United States v. Martin Linen Supply Co., 430 U.S. 564, 571, 97 S.Ct. 1349, 1355, 51 L.Ed.2d 642 (1977). By deciding that the government had failed to come forward with sufficient proof of petitioner's capacity to be responsible for criminal acts, that court was clearly saying that Burks' criminal culpability had not been established. If the District Court had so held in the first instance, as the reviewing court said it should have done, a judgment of acquittal would have been entered and, of course petitioner could not be retried for the same offense. Consequently, . . . it should make no difference that the reviewing court, rather than the trial court, determined the evidence to be insufficient. The appellate decision unmistakably meant that the District Court had erred in failing to grant a judgment of acquittal. To hold otherwise would create a purely arbitrary distinction between those in petitioner's position and others who would enjoy the benefit of a correct decision by the District Court.

The Double Jeopardy Clause forbids a second trial for the purpose of affording the prosecution another opportunity to supply evidence which it failed to muster in the first proceeding. This is central to the objective of the prohibition against successive trials. . . .

Nonetheless, . . . our past holdings do not appear consistent with what we believe the Double Jeopardy Clause commands. A close reexamination of those precedents, however, persuades us that they have not properly construed the Clause, and accordingly should no longer be followed.

* * *

[Ball v. United States, 163 U.S. 662, 16 S.Ct. 1192, 41 L.Ed. 300 (1896)] came before the Court twice, the first occasion being on writ of error from federal convictions for murder. On this initial review, those defendants who had been found guilty obtained a reversal of their convictions due to a fatally defective indictment. On remand after appeal, the trial court dismissed the flawed indictment and proceeded to retry the defendants on a new indictment. They were again convicted and the defendants came once more to this Court, arguing that their second trial was barred because of former jeopardy. The Court rejected this plea in a brief statement:

> "[A] defendant, who procures a judgment against him upon an indictment to be set aside, may be tried anew upon the same indictment, or upon another indictment, for the same offence of which he had been convicted." . . .

The reversal in *Ball* was therefore based not on insufficiency of evidence, but rather on trial error, i.e., failure to dismiss a faulty indictment. . . .

We have no doubt that *Ball* was correct in allowing a new trial to rectify *trial error*. . . .

Various rationales have been advanced to support the policy of allowing retrial to correct trial error, but in our view the most reasonable justification is that advanced in [United States v. Tateo, 377 U.S. 463, 466, 84 S.Ct. 1587, 1589, 12 L.Ed.2d 448, 451 (1964)]:

> "It would be a high price indeed for society to pay were every accused granted immunity from punishment because of any defect sufficient to constitute reversible error in the proceedings leading to conviction."

In short, reversal for trial error, as distinguished from evidentiary insufficiency, does not constitute a decision to the effect that the government has failed to prove its case. As such, it implies nothing with respect to the guilt or innocence of the defendant. Rather, it is a determination that a defendant has been convicted through a judicial process which is defective in some fundamental respect, e.g., incorrect receipt or rejection of evidence, incorrect instructions, or prosecutorial misconduct. When this occurs, the accused has a strong interest in obtaining a fair re-adjudication of his guilt free from error, just as society maintains a valid concern for insuring that the guilty are punished. See Note, Double Jeopardy: A New Trial After Appellate Reversal for Insufficient Evidence, 31 U.Chi.L.Rev. 365, 370 (1964).

The same cannot be said when a defendant's conviction has been overturned due to a failure of proof at trial, in which case the prosecution cannot complain of prejudice, for it has been given one fair opportunity to offer whatever proof it could assemble.[2] Moreover, such an appellate reversal means that the Government's case was so lacking that it should not have even been *submitted* to the jury. Since we necessarily afford absolute finality to a jury's *verdict* of acquittal—no matter how erroneous its decision—it is difficult to conceive how society has any greater interest in retrying a defendant when, on review, it is decided as a matter of law that the jury could not properly have returned a verdict of guilty.

* * *

2. It has been suggested, for example, that an appeal from a conviction amounts to a "waiver" of former jeopardy protections . . ., or that the appeal somehow continues the jeopardy which attached at the first trial. . . .

In our view it makes no difference that a defendant has sought a new trial as one of his remedies, or even as the sole remedy. It cannot be meaningfully said that a person "waives" his right to a judgment of acquittal by moving for a new trial. ... Since we hold today that the Double Jeopardy Clause precludes a second trial once the reviewing court has found the evidence legally insufficient, the only "just" remedy available for that court is the direction of a judgment of acquittal. To the extent that our prior decisions suggest that by moving for a new trial, a defendant waives his right to a judgment of acquittal on the basis of evidentiary insufficiency those cases are overruled.

Accordingly, the judgment of the Court of Appeals is reversed, and the case remanded for proceedings consistent with this opinion.

Reversed and remanded.

NOTES

1. **Trial judge finding of evidence insufficiency.** Suppose the trial court rather than an appellate tribunal determines that the evidence suggesting guilt is in some sense deficient. Does *Burks* bar another trial of the defendant? The Supreme Court commented on the matter in Hudson v. Louisiana, 450 U.S. 40, 101 S.Ct. 970, 67 L.Ed.2d 30 (1981). Hudson was convicted of murder in a jury trial; after verdict, the trial judge granted a defense motion for a new trial, made on the ground that the jury's verdict was contrary to the evidence. Hudson was retried, the state's evidence included testimony not presented at the first trial, and the jury convicted. Habeas corpus relief was sought in state courts on the basis that the second trial violated Hudson's rights under the Double Jeopardy clause. The Louisiana Supreme Court found no violation of *Burks,* reasoning that the trial judge, in granting a new trial, had found insufficient evidence to support the verdict rather than no evidence. *Burks,* it concluded, is limited to situations "where, *as a matter of law,* a reviewing court has determined that in a prior trial there was *no evidence* of the crime charged or an essential element thereof." State v. Hudson, 373 So.2d 1294 (La. 1979). A unanimous Supreme Court, speaking through Justice Powell, reversed. The record was clear, Justice Powell observed, that the state trial judge granted a new trial because the evidence was legally insufficient to support the verdict. "Nothing in *Burks* suggests ...," he continued, "that double jeopardy protections are violated only when the prosecution has adduced no evidence at all of the crime or an element thereof." 450 U.S. at 43, 101 S.Ct. at 972, 67 L.Ed.2d at 34. The Louisiana Supreme Court had not, Justice Powell commented, found it significant that the trial judge rather than an appellate court made the determination that the evidence was insufficient and the State had not contested this conclusion. 450 U.S. at 44 n. 6, 101 S.Ct. at 973 n. 6, 67 L.Ed.2d at 35 n. 6.

The State had argued that under state law the trial judge had the authority to function as a "13th juror" and in this capacity to grant a new trial because he entertained personal doubts as to the verdict. Further, it urged that the new trial in the case before the Court was granted pursuant to this authority and that *Burks* does not apply to a new trial granted for this reason because the trial judge's action was not based upon a determination that the state failed to meet its burden of proof at trial. The Court rejected this argument on the ground that the record established that the new trial was granted because the trial judge determined that the state failed to prove its case as a matter of law and thus was not acting as a "13th juror." But it continued:

We do not decide whether the Double Jeopardy Clause would have barred Louisiana from retrying [Hudson] if the trial judge had granted a new trial in [his "13th juror"] capacity, for that is not the case before us. We note, however, that *Burks* precludes retrial where the State has failed as a matter of law to prove its case despite a fair opportunity to do so. By definition, a new trial ordered by a trial judge acting as a "13th juror" is not such a case. Thus, nothing in *Burks* precludes retrial in such a case.

450 U.S. at 44 n. 5, 101 S.Ct. at 973 n. 5, 67 L.Ed.2d at 34–35 n. 5.

2. **Appellate court reversal on the weight of the evidence.** In Tibbs v. Florida, 457 U.S. 31, 102 S.Ct. 2211, 72 L.Ed.2d 652 (1982) the Court developed further the distinction suggested by the "13th juror" concept in *Hudson*. Defendant was convicted of murder and rape. On appeal, the Florida Supreme Court found that while the evidence was sufficient under federal standards to support the conviction, the verdict was against "the weight of the evidence." It reversed and remanded for a new trial. On re-prosecution, the Florida Supreme Court held that double jeopardy did not prevent re-prosecution when the reversal was because the verdict was against the weight of the evidence, rather than for evidence insufficiency. The Supreme Court, in an opinion authored by Justice O'Connor, affirmed. The Court advanced the following distinction:

[A] conviction rests upon insufficient evidence when, even after viewing the evidence in the light most favorable to the prosecution, no rational factfinder could have found the defendant guilty beyond a reasonable doubt. A reversal based on the weight of the evidence, on the other hand, draws the appellate court into questions of credibility. The "weight of the evidence" refers to "a determination [by] the trier of fact that a greater amount of credible evidence supports one side of an issue or cause than the other."

457 U.S. at 37, 102 S.Ct. at 2216, 72 L.Ed.2d at 658–59. The Court concluded that "an appellate court's disagreement with the jurors' weighing of the evidence does not require the special deference accorded verdicts of acquittal" which is the justification for the prohibition on re-prosecution following reversal for evidence insufficiency. 457 U.S. at 42, 102 S.Ct. at 2218, 72 L.Ed.2d at 662–63. Justice White, in a dissent joined in by Justices Brennan, Marshall and Blackmun, expressed concern that the Court's position would undermine *Burks* in that appellate courts might be tempted to characterize insufficiency reversals as being because the verdict was against the weight of the evidence to permit re-prosecution.

3. **Appeals resulting in trials *de novo*.** It is quite common in the United States for less serious criminal offenses to be prosecuted under a two-tier system. The first trial is not in a court of record. If the defendant is acquitted, that concludes the prosecution. If the defendant is convicted, he is entitled to appeal to a higher court, but since there is no record "below" the appeal results in a trial *de novo*, that is, in an entirely new trial rather than a review of the correctness of the first trial.

Suppose a defendant is convicted in the first trial of a two-tier system and asserts his right to a trial *de novo*. If he believes that there was insufficient evidence of guilt below, is he entitled to a determination of that issue before proceeding to the trial *de novo*? The respondent in Justices of Boston Municipal Court v. Lydon, 466 U.S. 294, 104 S.Ct. 1805, 80 L.Ed.2d 311 (1984) was charged with possessing burglary implements with intent to steal. Under Massachusetts law, he could insist upon a jury trial and if convicted pursue normal appellate remedies on the record of the trial. He could instead elect a bench trial and if convicted obtain a trial *de novo* before a judge or jury; if convicted in the trial *de novo*, normal appellate remedies would then become available. He chose the latter course of action and was convicted in the first trial, receiving a sentence of two years' imprisonment. After appealing for the trial *de novo,* he was released on his personal recognizance and moved to dismiss the prosecution on the ground there was no evidence introduced in the trial that he intended to steal and that a second trial was barred under *Burks.* This claim was rejected by the trial *de novo* court and by the Massachusetts Supreme Judicial Court. Respondent then sought habeas corpus relief in Federal District Court, which concluded that under *Burks* a second trial was foreclosed if the evidence against respondent at the bench trial was insufficient and that it was. The Court of Appeals affirmed.

The Supreme Court, in an opinion authored by Justice White, reversed. Respondent, like the petitioner Burks, was placed in jeopardy by the trial but, unlike Burks, jeopardy had not terminated at the time respondent demanded the *de novo* court review the sufficiency of the evidence:

> In this case, the Commonwealth is not attempting to impose multiple punishments for a single offense. Nor is it making another attempt to convict Lydon after acquittal. It is satisfied with the results of the bench trial and would have abided the results of a jury trial had Lydon taken that initial course. The conceptual difficulty for Lydon is that he has not been acquitted; he simply maintains that he ought to have been. . . .

> The Double Jeopardy Clause is not an absolute bar to successive trials. The general rule is that the Clause does not bar reprosecution of a defendant whose conviction is overturned on appeal. . . .[I]mplicit in the . . . rule permitting retrial after reversal of a conviction is the concept of "continuing jeopardy. . . . " Interests supporting the continuing jeopardy principle involve fairness to society, lack of finality, and limited waiver. . . .Acquittals, unlike convictions, terminate the initial jeopardy. . . .In *Burks* . . . we recognized that an unreversed determination by a reviewing court that the evidence was legally insufficient likewise served to terminate the initial jeopardy.

> We assume, without deciding, that jeopardy attached at the swearing of the first witness at Lydon's bench trial. The question then is whether jeopardy has now terminated. Lydon's double jeopardy argument requires an affirmative answer to that question, but he fails to identify any stage of the state proceedings that can be held to have terminated jeopardy. Unlike Burks, who could rest his claim upon the appellate court's determination of insufficiency, Lydon is faced with the unreversed determination of the bench-trial judge, contrary to Lydon's assertion, that the prosecution had met its burden of proof.

466 U.S. at 307–09, 104 S.Ct. at 1813–14, 80 L.Ed.2d at 324–25. Does Justice White's position mean that an appellate court has no constitutional obligation to determine whether the evidence below was sufficient? What would have been the status of the case if the *de novo* court judge had determined that the evidence was insufficient?

Justice Brennan, joined by Justice Marshall, concurred in the judgment. Justice O'Connor concurred in the judgment on the ground that respondent, released on personal recognizance, was not in custody and could not, therefore, invoke the habeas jurisdiction of the Federal District Court. Justice Powell, joined by The Chief Justice, concurred in the judgment and in all of the Court's opinion except that part holding that respondent was in custody for federal habeas jurisdiction purposes. Justice Stevens concurred in the judgment in a separate opinion.

4. **The requirement of a termination of proceedings.** The Court considered a related double jeopardy question in Richardson v. United States, 468 U.S. 317, 104 S.Ct. 3081, 82 L.Ed.2d 242 (1984). Petitioner was charged with three counts of federal narcotics violations. At trial, the jury acquitted him of one count but was unable to reach verdicts on the remaining counts. The trial court declared a

mistrial and denied post-trial motions for judgments of acquittal. Before the second trial was scheduled to begin, petitioner moved for dismissal on the grounds there was insufficient evidence in the first trial to submit the case to the jury and that retrial should be barred under *Burks*. The trial court denied the motion and petitioner took an immediate appeal. The Court of Appeals dismissed the appeal on the ground the trial court's order was not a collateral order permitting interlocutory appeal under *Abney*. The Supreme Court, in an opinion by Justice Rehnquist, held that the order was appealable under *Abney*. However, the Court then concluded that the petitioner had no double jeopardy claim to submit to an appellate court in an interlocutory appeal or otherwise. *Burks* held that when an appellate court finds the evidence was insufficient to support a conviction, double jeopardy precludes reprosecution for the same offense. Here, however, no court, trial or appellate, has determined that the government presented insufficient evidence at the first trial. The Court has held since *Perez* and *Logan* that double jeopardy does not preclude reprosecution for the same offense when there was a "manifest necessity" for declaring a mistrial, such as a genuinely hung jury:

> We think that the principles governing our decision in *Burks,* and the principles governing our decisions in the hung jury cases, are readily reconciled when we recognize that the protection of the Double Jeopardy Clause by its terms applies only if there has been some event, such as an acquittal, which terminates the original jeopardy. . . . Since jeopardy attached here when the jury was sworn . . . petitioner's argument necessarily assumes that the judicial declaration of a mistrial was an event which terminated jeopardy in his case and which allowed him to assert a valid claim of double jeopardy.

> But this proposition is irreconcilable with cases such as *Perez* and *Logan,* and we hold on the authority of these cases that the failure of a jury to reach a verdict is not an event which terminates jeopardy. . . . The Government, like the defendant, is entitled to resolution of the case by verdict from the jury, and jeopardy does not terminate when the jury is discharged because it is unable to agree. Regardless of the sufficiency of the evidence at petitioner's first trial, he has no valid double jeopardy claim to prevent his retrial.

468 U.S. at 325–26, 104 S.Ct. at 3086, 82 L.Ed.2d at 250–51. Justice Brennan, joined by Justice Marshall, concurred in that part of the Court's opinion holding that an interlocutory appeal is available, but dissented from the remainder of the opinion. He argued that the majority "improperly ignores the realities of the defendant's situation and relies instead on a formalistic concept of 'continuing jeopardy.' " 468 U.S. at 327, 104 S.Ct. at 3087, 82 L.Ed.2d at 252. Justice Stevens dissented on the ground that an interlocutory appeal should not be available in these circumstances.

5. **Jurisdictional deficiencies in proceedings.** Courts have sometimes stated that if the charging instrument in a criminal proceeding is so defective that any conviction on it would necessarily be invalid, an acquittal in that proceeding does not bar a second proceeding. E.g., Thompson v. State, 527 S.W.2d 888 (Tex.Cr.App.1975). This position was rejected as a statement of federal constitutional law in Benton v. Maryland, 395 U.S. 784, 89 S.Ct. 2056, 23 L.Ed.2d 707 (1969). The state urged that Benton's acquittal in the first proceeding did not bar retrial, because the indictment was void and no jeopardy attaches under such a defective indictment. Characterizing the state's position as an effort to use its own error to deprive Benton of the benefit of acquittal, the Court held that the indictment must be viewed as at worst only voidable at the defendant's option. An acquittal on such an indictment cannot, over the defendant's objection, be set aside. 395 U.S. at 796–97, 89 S.Ct. at 2063–64, 23 L.Ed.2d at 717–18.

6. **Appeals from post-verdict judgments of acquittal.** Suppose a jury returns a verdict of guilty and the trial judge then grants a post-verdict motion for judgment of acquittal. See, e.g., Fed.R.Crim.Pro.Rule 29(c). Does—and should—the government have a right to appeal that ruling? Several courts have held that appeal is permitted. United States v. Steed, 646 F.2d 136 (4th Cir.1981); United States v. Dreitzler, 577 F.2d 539 (9th Cir.1978), cert. denied 440 U.S. 921, 99 S.Ct. 1246, 59 L.Ed.2d 473 (1979); United States v. Boyd, 566 F.2d 929 (5th Cir.1978). In United States v. Jenkins, 420 U.S. 358, 365, 95 S.Ct. 1006, 1011, 43 L.Ed.2d 250, 256 (1975), the Court assumed such an appeal would be proper. In United States v. Scott, 437 U.S. 82, 98 S.Ct. 2187, 57 L.Ed.2d 65 (1978), overruling the specific holding of *Jenkins,* the Court noted that post-*Jenkins* decisions never explicitly repudiated this assumption. 437 U.S. at 91 n. 7, 98 S.Ct. at 2193 n. 7, 57 L.Ed.2d at 74 n. 7.

Federal Rules of Criminal Procedure Rule 29(b), as amended in 1994, permits the trial judge to reserve ruling on a motion for judgment of acquittal:

> The court may reserve decision on a motion for judgment of acquittal, proceed with the trial (where the motion is made before the close of all the evidence), submit the case to the jury and decide the motion either before the jury returns a verdict or after it returns a verdict of guilty or is discharged without having returned a verdict. If the court reserves decision, it must decide the motion on the basis of the evidence at the time the ruling was reserved.

7. **What is the same offense for prior acquittal purposes?** Suppose the government sought to prosecute the defendant for a different offense but one that was related in its commission to that of which the defendant was acquitted? What is the criterion for determining whether this second proceeding would be for the "same offense" for double jeopardy purposes? The next section considers the issue in the context of prior convictions and addresses the so-called "*Blockburger* Rule" as a standard for resolving the question of whether two different crimes are the "same" for prior conviction purposes. It has been widely assumed that the same standard applied where the prior proceeding resulted in acquittal. E.g., Sanabria v. United States, 437 U.S. 54, 70 n. 24, 98 S.Ct. 2170, 2182 n. 24, 57 L.Ed.2d 43, 57 n. 24 (1978). After examining this approach as applied to prior conviction situations, consider whether there are any justifications for using a different standard when the first proceeding resulted in acquittal.

A conviction of a lesser included offense constitutes an implied acquittal of the more serious offense for Double Jeopardy purposes. In Green v. United States, 355 U.S. 184, 78 S.Ct. 221, 2 L.Ed.2d 199 (1957), Green was charged with first degree murder but the jury—as the trial judge's instructions permitted—returned a verdict of guilty of second degree murder. Following reversal of this conviction on appeal, Green was retried for first degree murder. Finding this in violation of the prohibition against Double Jeopardy, the Court concluded that the first trial must be given the same effect as would have been required had the jury returned a verdict which expressly read, "We find the defendant not guilty of murder in the first degree but guilty of murder in the second degree." 355 U.S. at 191, 78 S.Ct. at 225, 2 L.Ed.2d at 206.

8. **Jeopardy in non-capital punishment decisions.** When, if ever, is the imposition of a sentence less than the statutory maximum for the crime at issue an "acquittal" of any more severe punishment for Double Jeopardy purposes? Generally, sentencing has not been regarded as having this Double Jeopardy effect. North Carolina v. Pearce, 395 U.S. 711, 89 S.Ct. 2072, 23 L.Ed.2d 656 (1969). The traditional approach was followed and defended in United States v. DiFrancesco, 449 U.S. 117, 101 S.Ct. 426, 66 L.Ed.2d 328 (1980). Following DiFrancesco's conviction for various racketeering offenses, the government sought to have him

sentenced to the special increased term provided by 18 U.S.C.A. § 3575 for "dangerous special offenders." After determining that DiFrancesco was within the statute, the trial judge imposed the special term but made it concurrent with other sentences already imposed. The government sought to appeal on the ground that the decision to make the dangerous offender term concurrent was an abuse of discretion. But the Court of Appeals for the Second Circuit dismissed the appeal as barred by Double Jeopardy. By a 5-to-4 vote, the Supreme Court reversed. Refusing to accord a criminal sentence the same finality and conclusiveness given to an acquittal, Justice Blackmun reasoned for the majority that the considerations underlying the prohibition against Double Jeopardy—the need to avoid undue embarrassment, expense, anxiety and security and the risk of erroneous conviction—do not apply:

> This limited appeal does not involve a retrial or approximate the ordeal of a trial on the basic issue of guilt or innocence. . . . [T]he appeal is to be taken promptly and is essentially on the record of the sentencing court. The defendant, of course, is charged with knowledge of the statute and its appeal provisions, and has no expectation of finality in his sentence until the appeal has expired. To be sure, the appeal may prolong the period of any anxiety that may exist, but it does so only for the finite period provided by the statute. The appeal is no more of an ordeal than any Government appeal . . . from the dismissal of an indictment or information. The defendant's primary concern and anxiety obviously relates to the determination of innocence or guilt, and that already is behind him. The defendant is subjected to no risk of being harassed and then convicted, although innocent. Furthermore, a sentence is characteristically determined in large part on the basis of information, such as the presentence report, developed outside the courtroom. It is purely a judicial determination, and much that goes into it is the result of inquiry that is nonadversarial in nature.

449 U.S. at 136, 101 S.Ct. at 437, 66 L.Ed.2d at 345–46. Justice Brennan, joined by Justices White, Marshall, and Stevens, dissented, urging that imposition of a less-than-maximum sentence be regarded as analogous to acquittal. He characterized the majority's distinction between acquittals and sentences as resting upon a faulty understanding of the import to the defendant of sentencing:

> [M]ost defendants are more concerned with how much time they must spend in prison than with whether their record shows a conviction. . . . [C]learly, the defendant does not breathe a sigh of relief once he has been found guilty. Indeed, an overwhelming number of criminal defendants are willing to enter plea bargains in order to keep their time in prison as brief as possible. Surely, the Court cannot believe . . . that the sentencing phase is merely incidental and that defendants do not suffer acute anxiety. To the convicted defendant, the sentencing phase is certainly as critical as the guilt-innocence phase.

449 U.S. at 149, 101 S.Ct. at 444, 66 L.Ed.2d at 354.

Respondent in Pennsylvania v. Goldhammer, 474 U.S. 28, 106 S.Ct. 353, 88 L.Ed.2d 183 (1985) had been convicted of 56 counts of forgery and 56 counts of theft. He was sentenced to a five year prison sentence on one theft count and to five years' probation on one of the forgery counts. Sentences on the remaining counts were suspended. On appeal he successfully argued that 34 of the theft counts, including the one on which he had received the prison sentence, were barred from prosecution under the statute of limitations. The Commonwealth sought a ruling from the Pennsylvania Supreme Court remanding the case to the trial court for resentencing on the remaining 22 theft counts, but that court refused on the ground to do so would violate double jeopardy. The United States Supreme Court, in a per curiam opinion, reversed on the ground that resentencing in these circumstances was governed by *DiFrancesco* and was not prohibited by the Fifth Amendment.

9. **Jeopardy in capital punishment decisions.** A different approach to capital sentencing was taken, however, in Bullington v. Missouri, 451 U.S. 430, 101 S.Ct. 1852, 68 L.Ed.2d 270 (1981). Under the Missouri capital sentencing procedure, a separate sentencing hearing must be held before the jury which convicted the defendant of capital murder. The jury must determine whether the state has proven any of the ten listed aggravating circumstances beyond a reasonable doubt, whether those aggravating circumstances that have been proven warrant imposition of the death penalty, and whether there are any mitigating circumstances that outweigh the aggravating circumstances. A unanimous decision to impose death is required. Bullington was convicted of capital murder and, after the required sentencing hearing, a sentence of life imprisonment was imposed. A new trial was granted by the trial judge, however, on the basis that exclusion of women from the trial jury violated Bullington's Sixth and Fourteenth Amendment rights. Before the beginning of the second trial, the state announced it would seek the death penalty. The Missouri Supreme Court declined to bar this, concluding that the Double Jeopardy Clause did not preclude imposition of the death penalty should Bullington be convicted of capital murder on the retrial. The Supreme Court reversed. Holding that Double Jeopardy barred the imposition of the death penalty at Bullington's second trial, Justice Blackmun reasoned for the majority that the rationale for the general sentencing rule is that the usual unstructured sentencing proceeding renders it impossible to conclude that a sentence less than the maximum constitutes a decision that the state has failed to prove its case for a more severe penalty. But under a structured sentencing proceeding such as that before the Court, the decision to impose life imprisonment rather than death can reliably be said to reflect a conclusion by the trier of fact that despite a fair opportunity the state has failed to prove its case for imposition of death. Moreover, the reasons for giving an acquittal on guilt or innocence finality apply:

> The "embarrassment, expense and ordeal" and the "anxiety and insecurity" faced by a defendant at the penalty phase of a Missouri capital murder trial surely are at least equivalent to that faced by any defendant at the guilt phase of a criminal trial. The "unacceptably high risk that the [prosecution], with its superior resources, would wear down a defendant," ... thereby leading to an erroneously imposed death sentence, would exist if the State were to have a further opportunity to convince a jury to impose the ultimate punishment.

451 U.S. at 445, 101 S.Ct. at 1861, 68 L.Ed.2d at 283.

In Arizona v. Rumsey, 467 U.S. 203, 104 S.Ct. 2305, 81 L.Ed.2d 164 (1984), the respondent was convicted of capital murder committed during an armed robbery. Under Arizona law, the trial judge, not the jury, has sentencing authority in capital cases. The trial judge was authorized to impose the death penalty only if after a hearing he found the presence of at least one aggravating circumstance from a statutory list of seven possibilities. The trial judge interpreted the provision defining as an aggravating circumstance committing murder "as consideration for the receipt, or in expectation of the receipt, of anything of pecuniary value" to apply only to murder-for-hire, not to a murder committed during a robbery or theft. Accordingly, a sentence of life imprisonment was imposed. Respondent appealed another point to the Arizona Supreme Court and State filed a cross-appeal. The court denied respondent's claim, but ruled that the trial judge had misconstrued the aggravating circumstance statute—that it did include murder committed during robbery or theft. It remanded the penalty portion of the case for a new hearing. At the new hearing, the trial court imposed the death penalty. Respondent appealed again to the Arizona Supreme Court, this time claiming that imposition of the death penalty violated his right against twice being placed in jeopardy. The court agreed and the State sought and obtained a writ of certiorari from the United States Supreme Court.

The Court, in an opinion by Justice O'Connor, held that *Bullington* was violated by imposition of the death penalty:

> That the sentencer in Arizona is the trial judge rather than the jury does not render the sentencing proceeding any less like a trial. . . . Nor does the availability of appellate review, including reweighing of aggravating and mitigating circumstances, make the appellate process part of a single continuing sentencing proceedings. The Supreme Court of Arizona noted that its role is strictly that of an appellate court, not a trial court. Indeed, no appeal need be taken if life imprisonment is imposed, and the appellate reweighing can work only to the defendant's advantage. . . .

> In making its findings, the trial court relied on a misconstruction of the statute defining the pecuniary gain aggravating circumstances. Reliance on an error of law, however, does not change the double jeopardy effects of a judgment that amounts to an acquittal on the merits. . . .

> [United States v. Wilson, discussed on p. 822 of the Casebook, is not applicable.] By contrast, in respondent's initial capital sentencing, there was only one decisionmaker and only one set of findings of fact, all favorable to respondent. The trial court "acquitted" respondent of the death penalty, and there was no verdict of "guilty" for the appellate court to reinstate.

467 U.S. at 210–12, 104 S.Ct. at 2309–10, 81 L.Ed.2d at 171–72.

Justice Rehnquist, joined by Justice White, dissented:

In no sense can it be meaningfully argued that the State failed to "prove" its case—the existence of at least one aggravating circumstance. It is hard to see how there has been an "implied acquittal" of a statutory aggravating circumstance when the record explicitly establishes the factual basis that such an aggravating circumstance existed. But for the trial judge's erroneous construction of governing state law, the judge would have been required to impose the death penalty.

> If, as a matter of state law, the Arizona Supreme Court had simply corrected the erroneous sentence itself without remanding, there could be no argument that *Bullington* would prevent the imposition of the death sentence. That much was made clear in our decision in United States v. Wilson. . . .

467 U.S. at 214, 104 S.Ct. at 2311, 81 L.Ed.2d at 173.

The Arizona death penalty scheme came under further Supreme Court review in Poland v. Arizona, 476 U.S. 147, 106 S.Ct. 1749, 90 L.Ed.2d 123 (1986). The trial court sentenced petitioners to death for the murders of two Purolator guards committed during a robbery. It found as an aggravating circumstance that the killings were "especially heinous, cruel, or depraved" but found that the pecuniary gain aggravating circumstance in issue in Arizona v. Rumsey was not present because it interpreted that circumstance to require proof of a murder for hire. On appeal, the Arizona Supreme Court reversed and remanded for a new trial for trial error. It also found that the aggravating circumstance that the killings were "heinous, cruel or depraved" was not supported by the evidence. However, it further concluded that the trial court had misunderstood the law in limiting the *Rumsey* circumstance to murders for hire, and that it applies to murder during robbery. It explicitly stated the death penalty could be imposed upon proper proof following a new trial. Following conviction on remand, petitioners were again sentenced to death. The trial court found that both the pecuniary gain and heinous manner circumstances were proved. The Arizona Supreme Court found again the evidence insufficient to support the heinous manner circumstance but sufficient to support that dealing with pecuniary gain. It rejected petitioners' argument that Double Jeopardy precluded imposition of the death penalty in light of the earlier finding of insufficiency to support the heinous manner circumstance. The United States Supreme Court, in an opinion authored by Justice White, affirmed. Unlike in *Rumsey,* at no point did either the trial or appellate courts conclude that the State had failed to prove its case for the death penalty. The Arizona Supreme Court did conclude that the State had failed to prove the heinous manner circumstance, but also found that the trial court had misconstrued the reach of the pecuniary gain circumstance and clearly intended to authorize the death penalty upon appropriate proof during remand. There is a difference between aggravating circumstances and the verdict of death. The death penalty can be imposed by the trial court only if at least one aggravating circumstance is shown and it is not outweighed by any mitigating circumstance. Here, the trial court, unlike in *Rumsey,* concluded that the death penalty was appropriate and the Arizona Supreme Court did not reject that ultimate conclusion:

> The defendant may argue on appeal that the evidence presented at his sentencing hearing was as a matter of law insufficient to support the aggravating circumstances on which his death sentence was based, but the Double Jeopardy Clause does not require the reviewing court, if it sustains that claim, to ignore evidence in the record supporting another aggravating circumstance which the sentencer has erroneously rejected. Such a rule would have the odd and unacceptable result of requiring a reviewing court to enter a death penalty "acquittal" even though that court is of the view that the State has "proved its case."

476 U.S. at 157, 106 S.Ct. at 1756, 90 L.Ed.2d at 133. Justice Marshall, joined by Justices Brennan and Blackmun, dissented.

In Spaziano v. Florida, 468 U.S. 447, 104 S.Ct. 3154, 82 L.Ed.2d 340 (1984), the petitioner was convicted of capital murder. Under Florida law, the trial jury heard evidence relevant to punishment and recommended to the trial court that a sentence of life imprisonment be imposed. The trial court, as authorized by state law, ordered and received a presentence report concerning petitioner. The court then imposed a sentence of death. The Supreme Court, in an opinion by Justice Blackmun, upheld the Florida procedure. The Court concluded there is no Sixth Amendment right to a jury determination of the question of life or death for a person convicted of a capital offense. Since Florida law validly provided that the role of the jury was advisory only, there was no double jeopardy objection to the trial judge imposing a death sentence in the face of a jury recommendation of life.

The petitioner in Schiro v. Farley, 510 U.S. 222, 114 S.Ct. 783, 127 L.Ed.2d 47 (1994) was charged in count one with knowingly killing another, in count two with killing another while committing rape and in count three with killing another while committing deviate conduct. The State sought the death penalty on counts two and three. The jury returned a verdict of guilty on count two and left the remaining verdict sheets blank. Under Indiana law, imposition of the death penalty requires the State to prove at the penalty phase of the proceedings the existence of at least one of nine aggravating circumstances, including that the defendant *intentionally* killed the victim while committing or attempting to commit rape. Although the jury recommended against the death penalty, the trial judge rejected that recommendation on the ground that the aggravating circumstance of intentional killing during rape had been shown. On direct appeals and in federal habeas, Petitioner unsuccessfully argued that the double jeopardy clause prohibited finding in the penalty phase that he had intentionally killed during rape because he had been acquitted of that theory by the jury in the guilt/innocence phase. He also argued the State was collaterally estopped from attempting to show intentional murder as an aggravating circumstance.

The Supreme Court, in an opinion authored by Justice O'Connor, affirmed denial of habeas relief. The Court rejected Petitioner's prior acquittal claim on the ground the guilt/innocence and penalty phases were part of a single trial. It distinguished *Bullington,*

> This case is manifestly different. Neither the prohibition against a successive trial on the issue of guilt, nor the *Bullington* prohibition against a second capital sentencing proceeding, is implicated here—the State did not reprosecute Schiro for intentional murder, nor did it force him to submit to a second death penalty hearing. It simply conducted a single sentencing hearing in the course of a single prosecution. The state is entitled to "one fair opportunity" to prosecute a defendant * * * and that opportunity extends not only to prosecution at the guilt phase, but also to present evidence at an ensuing sentencing proceeding.

510 U.S. at 231, 114 S.Ct. at 790, 127 L.Ed.2d at 58.

The Court refused to decide whether the constitutional principle of collateral estoppel (*Ashe v. Swenson,* later this chapter) could apply to preclude a penalty phase verdict based upon a guilt/innocence phase finding. It concluded that Petitioner had failed to prove the threshold requirement that he had obtained a favorable finding from the jury at guilt innocence on the issue of intentional killing. The three counts were independent of each other; one was not a lesser included offense of another. The jury was not instructed to consider the counts in any particular order. The question of intent to kill was not disputed during the guilt/innocence phase.

10. **"Acquittals" in non-capital sentencing proceedings.** Does *Bullington* apply to non-capital sentencing proceedings? The petitioner in Monge v. California, 524 U.S. 721, 118 S.Ct. 2246, 141 L.Ed.2d 615, 1998 WL 336328 (1998) was charged with using a minor to sell marijuana, sale or transportation of marijuana and possession of marijuana. The State notified petitioner it would seek to prove two sentence enhancement allegations: that petitioner had a prior conviction for assault and that he had served a prison sentence on that conviction. Under California's three strikes law, proof of those allegations could result in more than doubling the sentence. The petitioner was convicted of all three charges and the trial court in a hearing without a jury found that he had been convicted of an assault and that under California law it was a "serious felony" because a dangerous weapon (a stick) was used in commission of the offense. The court also found he had been imprisoned for that offense. The trial court imposed an eleven year sentence. On appeal, the Court of Appeal reversed on the ground there was no evidence in the record that a dangerous weapon had been used in the assault offense. The court refused to permit the State the opportunity to prove its allegations in a new sentencing hearing on the ground such an opportunity was precluded by the Double Jeopardy Clause under *Bullington.*

The California Supreme Court reversed the Court of Appeals, holding that *Bullington* is confined to capital offense proceedings. The Supreme Court, in an opinion by Justice O'Connor, affirmed. The Court characterized *Bullington* as being an exception to the general rule that double jeopardy principles do not apply to the sentencing phase of cases. That exception was created because of the unique characteristics of capital cases:

> The penalty phase of a capital trial is undertaken to assess the gravity of a particular offense and to determine whether it warrants the ultimate punish-

ment; it is in many respects a continuation of the trial on guilt or innocence of capital murder.

524 U.S. at __, 118 S.Ct. at 2252, 141 L.Ed.2d at 626. Justice Scalia, joined by Justices Souter and Ginsburg, dissented. He argued that the sentence enhancements in this case are really elements of the offense with which petitioner had been charged and as elements are entitled to Double Jeopardy Clause protection the same as other elements of the offense:

> Suppose that a State repealed all of the violent crimes in its criminal code and replaced them with only one offense, 'knowingly causing injury to another,' bearing a penalty of 30 days in prison, but subject to a series of 'sentencing enhancements' authorizing additional punishment up to life imprisonment or death on the basis of various levels of mens rea, severity of injury, and other surrounding circumstances. Could the state then grant the defendant a jury trial, with requirement of proof beyond a reasonable doubt, solely on the question whether he 'knowingly cause[d] injury to another,' but leave it for the judge to determine by a preponderance of the evidence whether the defendant acted intentionally or accidentally, whether he used a deadly weapon, and whether the victim ultimately died from the injury the defendant inflicted?

524 U.S. at __, 118 S.Ct. at 2255, 141 L.Ed.2d at 630. Justice Stevens dissented separately on the ground that the preclusion of re-prosecution imposed by Burks v. United States (earlier this chapter) should be applied to the failure to prove that the assault was a serious felony in this case.

11. **What evidence is considered in determining whether there has been a sentencing "acquittal?"** The respondent in Lockhart v. Nelson, 488 U.S. 33, 109 S.Ct. 285, 102 L.Ed.2d 265 (1988), entered a plea of guilty to burglary. The State then introduced evidence of four prior felony convictions. Under Arkansas law, this permitted the imposition of a sentence of between 20 and 40 years. At his sentencing hearing, respondent stated that he believed that one of those convictions had been the subject of a gubernatorial pardon, which would have made that conviction not eligible for use to enhance punishment. When the prosecutor suggested that respondent was confusing a pardon with a commutation of sentence, respondent agreed that was the case. There was, therefore, no defense objection to the admission of that conviction into evidence. After unsuccessful appeals in the state courts, a federal District Court determined that respondent had in fact been pardoned for the prior conviction in question and set aside the sentence. When the State announced its intention to replace the pardoned conviction with another one it had not previously used, the District Court held that double jeopardy principles precluded the State from attempting to resentence respondent as an habitual offender on the burglary charge. The Eighth Circuit affirmed.

The Supreme Court, in an opinion by the Chief Justice, reversed. The majority characterized the question as whether a court should consider all the evidence or only all the admissible evidence in determining whether the evidence at trial was sufficient. It concluded that all the evidence admitted must be considered, including any improperly admitted evidence:

> It is quite clear from our opinion in *Burks* that a reviewing court must consider all of the evidence admitted by the trial court in deciding whether retrial is permissible under the Double Jeopardy Clause—indeed, that was the *ratio decidendi of Burks*.... The basis for the *Burks* exception to the general rule [permitting re-trial after appellate reversal] is that a reversal for insufficiency of the evidence should be treated no differently than a trial court's granting a judgment of acquittal at the close of all the evidence. A trial court in passing on such a motion considers all of the evidence it has admitted, and to make the

analogy complete it must be this same quantum of evidence which is considered by the reviewing court.

488 U.S. at 40–42, 109 S.Ct. at 291, 102 L.Ed.2d at 274. The majority further noted that if the respondent had offered evidence at the sentencing hearing of the pardon, "the trial judge would presumably have allowed the prosecutor an opportunity to offer evidence of another prior conviction to support the habitual offender charge." 488 U.S. at 42, 109 S.Ct. at 291, 102 L.Ed.2d at 274. The majority viewed its decision as doing only what the trial judge would have done had the matter been properly raised there.

Justice Marshall, joined by Justices Brennan and Blackmun, dissented:

If, in seeking to prove Nelson's four prior convictions, the State had offered documented evidence to prove three valid prior convictions and a blank piece of paper to prove a fourth, no one would doubt that Arkansas had produced insufficient evidence and that the Double Jeopardy Clause barred retrial. There is no constitutionally significant difference between that hypothetical and this case.

488 U.S. at 46, 109 S.Ct. at 294, 102 L.Ed.2d at 277. Justice Marshall also argued that whether improperly admitted evidence should be considered in assessing evidence sufficiency might be made to depend upon why the evidence was admissible. Unreliable evidence, such as inadmissible hearsay, might not be counted, while evidence that should have been excluded under a Fourth Amendment exclusionary rule might be counted.

Ashe v. Swenson

Supreme Court of the United States, 1970.
397 U.S. 436, 90 S.Ct. 1189, 25 L.Ed.2d 469.

■ MR. JUSTICE STEWART delivered the opinion of the Court.

In Benton v. Maryland, 395 U.S. 784, 89 S.Ct. 2056, 23 L.Ed.2d 707, the Court held that the Fifth Amendment guarantee against double jeopardy is enforceable against the States through the Fourteenth Amendment. The question in this case is whether the State of Missouri violated that guarantee when it prosecuted the petitioner a second time for armed robbery in the circumstances here presented.

Sometime in the early hours of the morning of January 10, 1960, six men were engaged in a poker game in the basement of the home of John Gladson at Lee's Summit, Missouri. Suddenly three or four masked men, armed with a shotgun and pistols, broke into the basement and robbed each of the poker players of money and various articles of personal property. The robbers—and it has never been clear whether there were three or four of them—then fled in a car belonging to one of the victims of the robbery. Shortly thereafter the stolen car was discovered in a field, and later that morning three men were arrested by a state trooper while they were walking on a highway not far from where the abandoned car had been found. The petitioner was arrested by another officer some distance away.

The four were subsequently charged with seven separate offenses—the armed robbery of each of the six poker players and the theft of the car. In May 1960 the petitioner went to trial on the charge of robbing Donald Knight, one of the participants in the poker game. At the trial the State called Knight and three of his fellow poker players as prosecution witnesses. Each of them described the circumstances of the holdup and itemized his own individual losses. The proof that an armed robbery had occurred and that personal property had been taken from Knight as well as from each of the others was unassailable. The testimony of the four victims in this regard was consistent both internally and with that of the others. But the State's evidence that the petitioner had been one of the robbers was weak. Two of the witnesses thought that there had been only three robbers altogether, and could not identify the petitioner as one of them. Another of the victims, who was the petitioner's uncle by marriage, said that at the "patrol station" he had positively identified each of the other three men accused of the holdup, but could say only that the petitioner's voice "sounded very much like" that of one of the robbers. The fourth participant in the poker game did identify the petitioner, but only by his "size and height, and his actions."

The cross-examination of these witnesses was brief, and it was aimed primarily at exposing the weakness of their identification testimony. Defense counsel made no attempt to question their testimony regarding the holdup itself or their claims as to their losses. Knight testified without contradiction that the robbers had stolen from him his watch, $250 in cash, and about $500 in checks. His billfold, which had been found by the police in the possession of one of the three other men accused of the robbery, was admitted in evidence. The defense offered no testimony and waived final argument.

The trial judge instructed the jury that if it found that the petitioner was one of the participants in the armed robbery, the theft of "any money" from Knight would sustain a conviction. He also instructed the jury that if the petitioner was one of the robbers, he was guilty under the law even if he had not personally robbed Knight. The jury—though not instructed to elaborate upon its verdict—found the petitioner "not guilty due to insufficient evidence."

Six weeks later the petitioner was brought to trial again, this time for the robbery of another participant in the poker game, a man named Roberts. The petitioner filed a motion to dismiss, based on his previous acquittal. The motion was overruled, and the second trial began. The witnesses were for the most part the same, though this time their testimony was substantially stronger on the issue of the petitioner's identity. For example, two witnesses who at the first trial had been wholly unable to identify the petitioner as one of the robbers, now testified that his features, size, and mannerisms matched those of one of their assailants. Another witness who before had identified the petitioner only by his size and actions now also remembered him by the unusual sound of his voice. The State further refined its case at the second trial by declining to call one of the participants in the poker game whose identification testimony at the first trial had been conspicuously negative. The case went to the jury on instructions virtually identical to those given at the first trial. This time the jury found the petitioner guilty, and he was sentenced to a 35–year term in the state penitentiary.

* * *

... The question is ... whether collateral estoppel ... is a part of the Fifth Amendment's guarantee against double jeopardy. ... "Collateral estoppel" is an awkward phrase, but it stands for an extremely important principle in our adversary system of justice. It means simply that when an issue of ultimate fact has once been determined by a valid and final judgment, that issue cannot again be litigated between the same parties in any future lawsuit. Although first developed in civil litigation, collateral estoppel has been an established rule of federal criminal law at least since this Court's decision more than 50 years ago in United States v. Oppenheimer, 242 U.S. 85, 37 S.Ct. 68, 61 L.Ed. 161. ... The federal decisions have made clear that the rule of collateral estoppel in criminal cases is not to be applied with the hypertechnical and archaic approach of a 19th century pleading book, but with realism and rationality. Where a previous judgment of acquittal was based upon a general verdict, as is usually the case, this approach requires a court to "examine the record of a prior proceeding, taking into account the pleadings, evidence, charge, and other relevant matter, and conclude whether a rational jury could have grounded its verdict upon an issue other than that which the defendant seeks to foreclose from consideration." The inquiry "must be set in a practical frame and viewed with an eye to all the circumstances of the proceedings." Sealfon v. United States, 332 U.S. 575, 579, 68 S.Ct. 237, 240. Any test more technically restrictive would, of course, simply amount to a rejection of the rule of collateral estoppel in criminal proceedings, at least in every case where the first judgment was based upon a general verdict of acquittal.

Straightforward application of the federal rule to the present case can lead to but one conclusion. For the record is utterly devoid of any indication that the first jury could rationally have found that an armed robbery had not occurred, or that Knight had not been a victim of that robbery. The single rationally conceivable issue in dispute before the jury was whether the petitioner had been one of the robbers. And the jury by its verdict found that he had not. The federal rule of law, therefore, would make a second prosecution for the robbery of Roberts wholly impermissible.

The ultimate question to be determined, then, in the light of Benton v. Maryland, supra, is whether this established rule of federal law is embodied in the Fifth Amendment guarantee against double jeopardy. We do not hesitate to hold that it is. For whatever else that constitutional guarantee may embrace, it surely protects a man who has been acquitted from having to "run the gantlet" a second time. Green v. United States, 355 U.S. 184, 190, 78 S.Ct. 221, 225, 2 L.Ed.2d 199.

The question is not whether Missouri could validly charge the petitioner with six separate offenses for the robbery of the six poker players. It is not whether he could have received a total of six punishments if he had been convicted in a single trial of robbing the six victims. It is simply whether, after a jury determined by its verdict that the petitioner was not one of the robbers, the State could constitutionally hale him before a new jury to litigate that issue again.

After the first jury had acquitted the petitioner of robbing Knight, Missouri could certainly not have brought him to trial again upon that charge. Once a jury had determined upon conflicting testimony that there was at least a reasonable doubt that the petitioner was one of the robbers, the State could not present the same or different identification evidence in a second prosecution for the robbery of Knight in the hope that a different jury might find that evidence more convincing.The situation is constitutionally no different here, even though the second trial related to another victim of the same robbery. For the name of the victim, in the circumstances of this case, had no bearing whatever upon the issue of whether the petitioner was one of the robbers.

In this case the State in its brief has frankly conceded that following the petitioner's acquittal, it treated the first trial as no more than a dry run for the second prosecution: "No doubt the prosecutor felt the state had a provable case on the first charge and, when he lost, he did what every good attorney would do—he refined his presentation in light of the turn of events at the first trial." But this is precisely what the constitutional guarantee forbids.

The judgment is reversed, and the case is remanded to the Court of Appeals for the Eighth Circuit for further proceedings consistent with this opinion.

It is so ordered.

Reversed and remanded.

■ MR. JUSTICE BRENNAN, whom MR. JUSTICE DOUGLAS and MR. JUSTICE MARSHALL join, concurring [omitted].

■ MR. CHIEF JUSTICE BURGER, dissenting [omitted].

NOTES

1. **Mutuality of collateral estoppel.** In Simpson v. Florida, 403 U.S. 384, 91 S.Ct. 1801, 29 L.Ed.2d 549 (1971) (per curiam), the defendant was acquitted of the robbery of a store manager. This was on retrial; the first trial resulted in a conviction which was overturned on appeal. He was then tried and convicted for the robbery of a customer. The state courts upheld the conviction, reasoning that the conviction in the first trial gave rise to a "double collateral estoppel," which precluded Simpson from contending—for *Ashe* collateral estoppel purposes—that the state failed to prove his identity as the perpetrator of both robberies. The Supreme Court reversed. Rejecting the rationale of the state court's holding, the Court declared that mutuality is not an ingredient of collateral estoppel as embodied in *Ashe*. In Harris v. Washington, 404 U.S. 55, 92 S.Ct. 183, 30 L.Ed.2d 212 (1971) (per curiam), the defendant's acquittal in the first trial followed the trial judge's exclusion of certain evidence offered by the state. He was later convicted of a crime against another victim of the same incident at a trial at which the evidence was admitted. On appeal from this conviction, the state court held that the evidence was properly admitted and collateral estoppel did not apply because the state's evidence had been improperly excluded at the first trial, Harris' identity as the perpetrator had not been "fully litigated," and *Ashe* did not apply. The Supreme Court reversed, holding that *Ashe* governed, "irrespective of whether the jury considered all relevant evidence [in the first proceeding], and irrespective of the good faith of the State in bringing successive prosecutions." 404 U.S. at 56–57, 92 S.Ct. at 184, 30 L.Ed.2d at 215.

2. **Acquittal of the principal and conviction of the accessory.** The Court has assumed that the collateral estoppel aspect of double jeopardy has no application if the second prosecution involves a different defendant than the first. In Standefer v. United States, 447 U.S. 10, 100 S.Ct. 1999, 64 L.Ed.2d 689 (1980), Standefer was charged with aiding and abetting a revenue official in accepting unauthorized compensation. Before Standefer's trial, the alleged principal—the revenue official—was tried and acquitted of the charges against him. Nevertheless, Standefer was tried and convicted. Affirming the conviction, the Court noted, "Nothing in the Double Jeopardy Clause or the Due Process Clause forecloses putting [Standefer] on trial as an aider and abettor simply because another jury has determined that his principal was not guilty of the offenses charged." 447 U.S. at 22 n. 16, 100 S.Ct. at 2007 n. 16, 64 L.Ed.2d at 699 n. 16.

A somewhat related issue was raised in Harris v. Rivera, 454 U.S. 339, 102 S.Ct. 460, 70 L.Ed.2d 530 (1981) (per curiam). Rivera, his wife Cynthia Humdy, and Earl Robinson were jointly tried in a bench trial for a number of offenses related to a robbery incident; the state's evidence showed that Humdy had been apprehended outside of the apartment in which the robbery had taken place and Rivera and Robinson had been found inside the apartment. Robinson testified in his own defense; Rivera and Humdy did not. The trial judge acquitted Robinson of all charges but convicted Rivera and Humdy of robbery, larceny and burglary. In subsequent federal habeas corpus litigation, the Court of Appeals for the Second Circuit held that there was an apparent inconsistency between the trial judge's verdicts acquitting Robinson and convicting Rivera and, in the absence of an adequate explanation for this apparent inconsistency in the record, this inconsistency violated Rivera's federal constitutional rights. The Supreme Court reversed. Rivera noted the Court's decisions finding no defect in inconsistent jury verdicts, but urged that these decisions rested upon the jury's unreviewable power to acquit and were therefore distinguishable. The Court acknowledged that the inconsistencies between the two verdicts may have been the result of consideration of impermissible factors, such as the failure of Rivera to testify at trial. But it noted that there were also other explanations, including the possibility that the judge's observations in the courtroom created reasonable doubt as to Robinson's guilt that the judge might not have been able to articulate in a convincing manner. "We are not persuaded," the Court concluded, "that an apparent inconsistency in a trial judge's verdict gives rise to an inference of irregularity in his finding of guilt that is sufficiently strong to overcome the well-established presumption that the judge adhered to basic rules of procedure." 454 U.S. at 346–47, 102 S.Ct. at 465, 70 L.Ed.2d at 536. It then continued:

> The question that [Rivera] has standing to raise is whether his trial was fairly conducted. ...Apart from the acquittal of Robinson, this record discloses no constitutional error. Even assuming that this acquittal was logically inconsistent with the conviction of [Rivera], [Rivera], who was found guilty beyond a reasonable doubt after a fair trial, has no constitutional ground to complain that Robinson was acquitted.

454 U.S. at 348, 102 S.Ct. at 465–66, 70 L.Ed.2d at 537.

3. **Inconsistent verdicts.** The Court further addressed the question of inconsistent jury verdicts in United States v. Powell, 469 U.S. 57, 105 S.Ct. 471, 83 L.Ed.2d 461 (1984). Respondent was charged with certain drug offenses and with facilitating through communication facilities those same offenses. The jury acquitted her of the "predicate" drug offenses but found her guilty of the "compound" facilitating offenses. The Ninth Circuit held this necessitated setting aside the convictions for the compound offenses. The Court, in an opinion authored by Justice Rehnquist, reversed:

> [I]nconsistent verdicts—even verdicts that acquit on a predicate offense while convicting on the compound offense—should not necessarily be interpreted as a windfall to the Government at the defendant's expense. It is equally possible that the jury, convinced of guilt, properly reached its conclusion on the compound offense, and then through mistake, compromise, or lenity, arrived at an inconsistent conclusion on the lesser offense. But in such situations the Government has no recourse if it wishes to correct the jury's error; the Government is precluded from appealing or otherwise upsetting such an acquittal by the Constitution's Double Jeopardy Clause.

469 U.S. at 65, 105 S.Ct. at 476–77, 83 L.Ed.2d at 468. The Court also rejected the respondent's argument that principles of collateral estoppel should apply in this situation:

> [T]he argument necessarily assumes that the acquittal on the predicate offense was proper—the one the jury "really meant." This, of course, is not necessarily correct; all we know is that the verdicts are inconsistent. The Government could just as easily—and erroneously—argue that since the jury convicted on the compound offense the evidence on the predicate offense must have been sufficient. The problem is that the same jury reached inconsistent results; once that is established principles of collateral estoppel—which are predicated on the assumption that the jury acted rationally and found certain facts in reaching its verdict—are no longer useful.

469 U.S. at 68, 105 S.Ct. at 478, 83 L.Ed.2d at 470–71.

4. **Other offense evidence and former acquittal.** The petitioner in Dowling v. United States, 493 U.S. 342, 110 S.Ct. 668, 107 L.Ed.2d 708 (1990) was on trial for bank robbery. At that trial, the government was permitted under Rule 404(b) of the Federal Rules of Evidence to introduce the testimony of a witness who claimed that two weeks after the bank robbery Dowling had entered her dwelling and robbed her. This evidence was introduced to assist in proving that Dowling was the perpetrator of the bank robbery. However, Dowling had previously been acquitted of all charges by a jury in the dwelling robbery case. The trial judge instructed the jury in the bank robbery trial that Dowling had been acquitted in the previous case. The jury in the bank robbery trial returned a verdict of guilty. The Court of Appeals upheld the conviction. In the Supreme Court, Dowling made the claim that exclusion of the evidence of the dwelling robbery was required by the collateral estoppel principle of Ashe v. Swenson. The Supreme Court, in an opinion by Justice White, rejected this argument. Collateral estoppel is not applicable because a lower burden of proof is available to the government in showing in the bank robbery trial that Dowling committed the dwelling robbery than was required to convict him of the dwelling robbery. In the bank robbery trial, it did not have to show Dowling's guilt of the dwelling robbery by proof beyond a reasonable doubt; it had only to introduce evidence from which the jury could reasonably conclude that the act occurred and that the defendant was the actor. This is similar to the forfeiture cases discussed in Note 5 supra. Therefore, there is no inconsistency between the jury acquittal in the dwelling robbery case (establishing a reasonable doubt of guilt in that case) and proof by a lower standard of the same conduct in the bank robbery trial. However, Justice White continued, even if the principle of collateral estoppel were applicable, the burden is upon the criminal defendant to prove why the first jury acquitted him. Dowling failed to show that the only rational basis for the dwelling robbery jury's acquittal was a reasonable doubt that Dowling was the robber. Justice Brennan, joined by Justices Marshall and Stevens, dissented.

B.   MULTIPLE CONVICTIONS

When the defendant claims a former conviction rather than a former acquittal, it is arguable that somewhat different concerns are raised. Should application of the Double Jeopardy clause be any different in a former conviction situation? Should it make any difference if the "prior" conviction took place in the same prosecution as the conviction which the defendant is seeking to prevent?

Brown v. Ohio

Supreme Court of the United States, 1977.
432 U.S. 161, 97 S.Ct. 2221, 53 L.Ed.2d 187.

■ MR. JUSTICE POWELL delivered the opinion of the Court.

The question in this case is whether the Double Jeopardy Clause of the Fifth Amendment bars prosecution and punishment for the crime of stealing an automobile following prosecution and punishment for the lesser included offense of operating the same vehicle without the owner's consent.

I.

On November 29, 1973, the petitioner, Nathaniel Brown, stole a 1965 Chevrolet from a parking lot in East Cleveland, Ohio. Nine days later, on December 8, 1973, Brown was caught driving the car in Wickliffe, Ohio. The Wickliffe police charged him with "joyriding"—taking or operating the car without the owner's consent—in violation of Ohio Rev.Code § 4549.04(D).[3] The complaint charged that "on or about December 8, 1973, ... Nathaniel H. Brown did unlawfully and purposely take, drive or operate a certain motor vehicle to wit; a 1965 Chevrolet ... without the consent of the owner one Gloria Ingram. ..."Brown pled guilty to this charge and was sentenced to 30 days in jail and a $100 fine.

Upon his release from jail on January 8, 1974, Brown was returned to East Cleveland to face further charges, and on February 5 he was indicted by the Cuyahoga County grand jury. The indictment was in two counts, the first charging the theft of the car "on or about the 29th day of November 1973," in violation of Ohio Rev.Code § 4549.04(A),[4] and the second charging joyriding on the same date in violation of § 4549.04(D). A bill of particulars filed by the prosecuting attorney specified that

> "on or about the 29th day of November, 1973, ... Nathaniel Brown unlawfully did steal a Chevrolet motor vehicle, and take, drive or

3. Section 4549.04(D) provided at the time: "No person shall purposely take, operate, or keep any motor vehicle without the consent of its owner." A violation was punishable as a misdemeanor. Section 4549.04 was repealed effective January 1, 1974.

4. Section 4549.04(A) provided: "No person shall steal any motor vehicle." A violation was punishable as a felony.

operate such vehicle without the consent of the owner, Gloria Ingram.... "

Brown objected to both counts of the indictment on the basis of former jeopardy.

On March 18, 1974, at a pretrial hearing in the Cuyahoga County Court of Common Pleas, Brown pled guilty to the auto theft charge on the understanding that the court would consider his claim of former jeopardy on a motion to withdraw the plea.[5] Upon submission of the motion, the court overruled Brown's double jeopardy objections. The court sentenced Brown to six months in jail but suspended the sentence and placed Brown on probation for one year.

The Ohio Court of Appeals affirmed. It held that under Ohio law the misdemeanor of joyriding was included in the felony of auto theft:

> "Every element of the crime of operating a motor vehicle without the consent of the owner is also an element of the crime of auto theft. 'The difference between the crime of stealing a motor vehicle, and operating a motor vehicle without the consent of the owner is that conviction for stealing requires proof of an intent on the part of the thief to *permanently* deprive the owner of possession.' ... [T]he crime of operating a motor vehicle without the consent of the owner is a lesser included offense of auto theft.... "

Although this analysis led the court to agree with Brown that "for purposes of double jeopardy the two prosecutions involve the same statutory offense," it nonetheless held the second prosecution permissible:

> "The two prosecutions are based on two separate acts of the appellant, one which occurred on November 29th and one which occurred on December 8th. Since appellant has not shown that both prosecutions are based on the same act or transaction, the second prosecution is not barred by the double jeopardy clause."

The Ohio Supreme Court denied leave to appeal.

We granted certiorari to consider Brown's double jeopardy claim, 429 U.S. 893 (1976), and we now reverse.

II.

The Double Jeopardy Clause of the Fifth Amendment, applicable to the States through the Fourteenth, provides that no person shall "be subject for the same offence to be twice put in jeopardy of life or limb." It has long been understood that separate statutory crimes need not be identical—either in constituent elements or in actual proof—in order to be the same within the meaning of the constitutional prohibition. 1 Bishop's New Criminal Law § 1051 (1892); Comment, Twice in Jeopardy, 75 Yale L.J. 262, 268–269 (1965). The principal question in this case is whether auto theft and joyriding, a greater and lesser included offense under Ohio law, constitute the "same offense" under the Double Jeopardy Clause.

---

5. The joyriding count of the indict-   ment was *nol-prossed*.

Res judicata
— 3rd protection
CMl v. Hunter?

The Double Jeopardy Clause "protects against a second prosecution for the same offense after acquittal. It protects against a second prosecution for the same offense after conviction. And it protects against multiple punishments for the same offense." North Carolina v. Pearce, 395 U.S. 711, 717, 89 S.Ct. 2072, 2076, 23 L.Ed.2d 656 (1969). Where consecutive sentences are imposed at a single criminal trial, the role of the constitutional guarantee is limited to assuring that the court does not exceed its legislative authorization by imposing multiple punishments for the same offense. Where successive prosecutions are at stake, the guarantee serves "a constitutional policy of finality for the defendant's benefit." United States v. Jorn, 400 U.S. 470, 479, 91 S.Ct. 547, 554, 27 L.Ed.2d 543 (1971) (plurality opinion). That policy protects the accused from attempts to relitigate the facts underlying a prior acquittal and from attempts to secure additional punishment after a prior conviction and sentence.

The established test for determining whether two offenses are sufficiently distinguishable to permit the imposition of cumulative punishment was stated in Blockburger v. United States, 284 U.S. 299, 304, 52 S.Ct. 180, 182, 76 L.Ed. 306 (1932):

> "The applicable rule is that where the same act or transaction constitutes a violation of two distinct statutory provisions, the test to be applied to determine whether there are two offenses or only one, is whether each provision requires proof of a fact which the other does not. ...."

This test emphasizes the elements of the two crimes. "If each requires proof that the other does not, the *Blockburger* test would be satisfied, notwithstanding a substantial overlap in the proof offered to establish the crimes. ..." Iannelli v. United States, 420 U.S. 770, 785 n. 17, 95 S.Ct. 1284, 1293, 43 L.Ed.2d 616 (1975).

If two offenses are the same under this test for purposes of barring consecutive sentences at a single trial, they necessarily will be the same for purposes of barring successive prosecutions. Where the judge is forbidden to impose cumulative punishment for two crimes at the end of a single proceeding, the prosecutor is forbidden to strive for the same result in successive proceedings. Unless "each statute requires proof of an additional fact which the other does not," Morey v. Commonwealth, 108 Mass. 433, 434 (1871), the Double Jeopardy Clause prohibits successive prosecutions as well as cumulative punishment.

We are mindful that the Ohio courts "have the final authority to interpret that State's legislation." Garner v. Louisiana, 368 U.S. 157, 169, 82 S.Ct. 248, 254, 7 L.Ed.2d 207 (1961). Here the Ohio Court of Appeals has authoritatively defined the elements of the two Ohio crimes: joyriding consists of taking or operating a vehicle without the owner's consent, and auto theft consists of joyriding with the intent permanently to deprive the owner of possession. Joyriding is the lesser included offense. The prosecutor who has established joyriding need only prove the requisite intent in order to establish auto theft; the prosecutor who has established auto theft necessarily has established joyriding as well.

Applying the *Blockburger* test, we agree with the Ohio Court of Appeals that joyriding and auto theft, as defined by that court, constitute "the same statutory offense" within the meaning of the Double Jeopardy Clause. For it is clearly *not* the case that "each statute requires proof of an additional fact which the other does not." 284 U.S., at 304, 52 S.Ct., at 182. As is invariably true of a greater and lesser included offense, the lesser offense—joyriding—requires no proof beyond that which is required for conviction of the greater—auto theft. The greater offense is therefore by definition the "same" for purposes of double jeopardy as any lesser offense included in it.

This conclusion merely restates what has been this Court's understanding of the Double Jeopardy Clause at least since In re Nielsen was decided in 1889. In that case the Court endorsed the rule that

> "where . . . a person has been tried and convicted for a crime which has various incidents included in it, he cannot be a second time tried for one of those incidents without being twice put in jeopardy for the same offence." 131 U.S., at 188, 9 S.Ct., at 675.

Although in this formulation the conviction of the greater precedes the conviction of the lesser, the opinion makes it clear that the sequence is immaterial. . . .

III.

After correctly holding that joyriding and auto theft are the same offense under the Double Jeopardy Clause, the Ohio Court of Appeals nevertheless concluded that Nathaniel Brown could be convicted of both crimes because the charges against him focused on different parts of his 9-day joyride. We hold a different view. The Double Jeopardy Clause is not such a fragile guarantee that prosecutors can avoid its limitations by the simple expedient of dividing a single crime into a series of temporal or spatial units. The applicable Ohio statutes, as written and as construed in this case, make the theft and operation of a single car a single offense. Although the Wickliffe and East Cleveland authorities may have had different perspectives on Brown's offense, it was still only one offense under Ohio Law.[6] Accordingly, the specification of different dates in the two charges on which Brown was convicted cannot alter the fact that he was placed twice in jeopardy for the same offense in violation of the Fifth and Fourteenth Amendments.

Reversed.

The concurring opinion of MR. JUSTICE BRENNAN, in which MR. JUSTICE MARSHALL joined, is omitted.

---

6. We would have a different case if the Ohio Legislature had provided that joyriding is a separate offense for each day in which a motor vehicle is operated without the owner's consent. We also would have a different case if in sustaining Brown's second conviction the Ohio courts had construed the joyriding statute to have that effect. We then would have to decide whether the state courts' construction, applied retroactively in this case, was such "an unforeseeable judicial enlargement of a criminal statute" as to violate due process.

The dissenting opinion of MR. JUSTICE BLACKMUN, with whom THE CHIEF JUSTICE and MR. JUSTICE REHNQUIST, joined, is omitted.

NOTES

1. **Greater and lesser offenses.** In Harris v. Oklahoma, 433 U.S. 682, 97 S.Ct. 2912, 53 L.Ed.2d 1054 (1977) (per curiam), Harris had been a participant in a robbery resulting in the shooting death of the victim. He was first convicted of felony murder; in a second trial he was convicted of the robbery. Citing *Brown* but not *Blockburger*, the Court held the robbery conviction invalid. "When as here, conviction of a greater crime, murder, cannot be had without conviction of the lesser crime, robbery with firearms, the Double Jeopardy Clause bars prosecution for the lesser crime after conviction of the greater one." 433 U.S. at 682, 97 S.Ct. at 2913, 53 L.Ed.2d at 1056. But in Jeffers v. United States, 432 U.S. 137, 97 S.Ct. 2207, 53 L.Ed.2d 168 (1977), the Court split 4 to 4 on whether a defendant could be prosecuted for a greater offense after conviction for a lesser included offense where, at the trial for the lesser offense, the defendant had affirmatively sought separate trials on the two offenses.

In Morris v. Mathews, 475 U.S. 237, 106 S.Ct. 1032, 89 L.Ed.2d 187 (1986), respondent entered a plea of guilty to aggravated robbery and received a prison sentence of 7 to 25 years. Later, he was charged with aggravated murder, which under Ohio law was defined as a purposeful killing during flight from aggravated robbery. His contention that jeopardy precluded his prosecution because he had already been convicted of the aggravated robbery alleged in the aggravated murder indictment was overruled. He was convicted of aggravated murder and received a sentence of life imprisonment. The Ohio appellate courts denied relief but the United States Supreme Court remanded for further consideration in light of Illinois v. Vitale. On re-consideration, the Ohio court held that respondent could not be convicted of aggravated murder, but could be convicted of murder and modified the conviction to murder and the sentence to a term of 15 years to life. Being denied further relief on direct appeal, respondent filed a petition for writ of habeas corpus in federal District Court contending he was entitled to an entirely new trial, which was denied. The Sixth Circuit granted relief on the ground that although jeopardy did not bar a conviction for murder, that such a conviction could not stand if there was a "reasonable possibility" that respondent had been prejudiced by being prosecuted for aggravated murder. It found that evidence of the robbery had been admitted in the aggravated murder trial that would not have been admitted in a murder trial and that the jury may have been prejudiced by that evidence. The Supreme Court, in an opinion authored by Justice White, reversed. The Court of Appeals had applied an incorrect standard. The standard, derived from Strickland v. Washington (Casebook chapter 24), should be whether the defendant can "demonstrate a reasonable probability that he would not have been convicted of the non-jeopardy-barred offense absent the presence of the jeopardy-barred offense," that he must show that "but for the improper inclusion of the jeopardy-barred charge, the result of the proceeding probably would have been different." 475 U.S. at 247, 106 S.Ct. at 1038, 89 L.Ed.2d at 197. Respondent has not met that standard. Justice Blackmun, joined by Justice Powell, concurred in the judgment on the ground the Court of Appeals had correctly stated the standard, but that it was incorrect in concluding it had been met on the facts of this case. Justice Marshall, dissenting, agreed with the statement of the standard made by the Court of Appeals, but unlike Justice Blackmun, concluded that the respondent had met the standard. Justice Brennan agreed with Justice Marshall on this point.

2. **Continuing criminal enterprise and target offense.** In Garrett v. U.S., 471 U.S. 773, 105 S.Ct. 2407, 85 L.Ed.2d 764 (1985), Garrett entered a plea of guilty to the offense of importation of marijuana and received a five-year prison sentence. Later, he was indicted for engaging in a continuing criminal enterprise, which requires proof that the defendant in concert with 5 or more others, and occupying a position of organizer, supervisor or other position of management, engaged in a continuing series of felony violations of the law from which he obtained substantial income or resources. One of the three violations alleged against the defendant in this case was the importation of marijuana charge to which he had already plead guilty. His motions to dismiss the continuing criminal enterprise indictment on the ground he had already been convicted of a lesser included offense of that charge were denied by the trial court. He was convicted of engaging in a continuing criminal enterprise and received a sentence of 40 years to run consecutively to the 5 year sentence he had received earlier. The Court of Appeals affirmed the conviction and sentence over double jeopardy claims and the Supreme Court, in an opinion authored by Justice Rehnquist, affirmed.

The first inquiry is to determine whether Congress intended for the offense of continuing criminal enterprise to be separate from any constituent offenses that may be also alleged. The legislative intent is clear that Congress desired the continuing criminal enterprise offense to be separate. Garrett claimed his case is controlled by Brown v. Ohio, but the Court distinguished *Brown* on the ground that some of the conduct alleged against Garrett in the continuing criminal enterprise case had not even occurred at the time of the marijuana importation case:

> Obviously the conduct in which Garrett was charged with engaging in the Florida indictment [for continuing criminal enterprise], when compared with that with which he was charged in the Washington indictment [for importation of marijuana] does not lend itself to the simple analogy of a single course of conduct—stealing a car—comprising a lesser included misdemeanor within a felony. Here the continuing criminal enterprise was alleged to have spanned more than five years; the acts charged in the Washington indictment were alleged to have occurred on single days in 1979 and 1980, respectively. Whenever it was during the five-and-one-half-year period alleged in the indictment that Garrett committed the first of the three predicate offenses required to form the basis for a continuing criminal enterprise prosecution, it could not then have been said with any certainty that he would necessarily go ahead and commit the other violations required to render him liable on a continuing criminal enterprise charge. Every minute that Nathaniel Brown drove or possessed the stolen automobile he was simultaneously committing both the lesser included misdemeanor and the greater felony, but the same simply is not true of Garrett.

471 U.S. at 788–89, 105 S.Ct. at 2416, 85 L.Ed.2d at 777–78. The Court then likened this case to Diaz v. United States, 223 U.S. 442, 32 S.Ct. 250, 56 L.Ed. 500 (1912) in which a defendant plead guilty to assault and after the victim later died was convicted of homicide. The Diaz Court had said, "At the time of the trial for the [assault] the death had not ensued, and not until it did ensue was the homicide committed. Then, and not before, was it possible to put the accused in jeopardy for that offense." Justices Stevens, Brennan and Marshall dissented.

Missouri v. Hunter

Supreme Court of the United States, 1983.
459 U.S. 359, 103 S.Ct. 673, 74 L.Ed.2d 535.

■ CHIEF JUSTICE BURGER delivered the opinion of the court.

We granted certiorari to consider whether the prosecution and conviction of a criminal defendant in a single trial on both a charge of "armed criminal action" and a charge of first degree robbery—the underlying felony—violates the Double Jeopardy Clause of the Fifth Amendment.

I

On the evening of November 24, 1978, respondent and two accomplices entered an A & P supermarket in Kansas City, Missouri. Respondent entered the store manager's office and ordered the manager, at gun point, to open two safes. While the manager was complying with the demands of the robbers, respondent struck him twice with the butt of his revolver. While the robbery was in progress, an employee who drove in front of the store observed the robbery and went to a nearby bank to alert an off-duty police officer. That officer arrived at the front of the store and ordered the three men to stop. Respondent fired a shot at the officer and the officer returned the fire but the trio escaped.

Respondent and his accomplices were apprehended. In addition to being positively identified by the store manager and the police officer at trial and in a line-up, respondent made an oral and written confession which was admitted in evidence. At his trial, respondent offered no direct evidence and was convicted of robbery in the first degree, armed criminal action and assault with malice.

Missouri's statute proscribing robbery in the first degree, Mo.Ann.Stat. App. § 560.120 (Vernon 1979), provides:

> "Every person who shall be convicted of feloniously taking the property of another from his person, or in his presence, and against his will, by violence to his person, or by putting him in fear of some immediate injury to his person; or who shall be convicted of feloniously taking the property of another from the person of his wife, servant, clerk or agent, in charge thereof, and against the will of such wife, servant, clerk or agent by violence to the person of such wife, servant, clerk or agent, or by putting him or her in fear of some immediate injury to his or her person, shall be adjudged guilty of robbery in the first degree."

Mo.Ann.Stat.App. § 560.135 (Vernon 1979) prescribes the punishment for robbery in the first degree and provides in pertinent part:

> "Every person convicted of robbery in the first degree by means of a dangerous and deadly weapon and every person convicted of robbery in the first degree by any other means shall be punished by imprisonment by the division of corrections for not less than five years. . . ."

Mo.Stat.App. § 559.225 (Vernon 1979) proscribes armed criminal action and provides in pertinent part:

> "[A]ny person who commits any felony under the laws of this state by, with, or through the use, assistance, or aid of a dangerous or deadly weapon is also guilty of the crime of armed criminal action and, upon conviction, shall be punished by imprisonment by the division of corrections for a term of not less than three years. The punishment imposed pursuant to this subsection shall be in addition to any punishment provided by law for the crime committed by, with, or

through the use, assistance, or aid of a dangerous or deadly weapon. No person convicted under this subsection shall be eligible for parole, probation, conditional release or suspended imposition or execution of sentence for a period of three calendar years."

Pursuant to these statutes respondent was sentenced to concurrent terms of (a) ten years' imprisonment for the robbery; (b) 15 years for armed criminal action; and (c) to a consecutive term of five years' imprisonment for assault, for a total of 20 years.

On appeal to the Missouri Court of Appeals, respondent claimed that his sentence for both robbery in the first degree and armed criminal action violated the Double Jeopardy Clause of the Fifth Amendment of the United States Constitution made applicable to the states by the Fourteenth Amendment. The Missouri Court of Appeals agreed and reversed respondent's conviction and 15–year sentence for armed criminal action. 622 S.W.2d 374 (1981). The Court of Appeals relied entirely upon the holding of the Missouri Supreme Court opinions in State v. Haggard, 619 S.W.2d 44 (Mo.1981); Sours v. State, 593 S.W.2d 208 (Mo.), vacated sub nom. Missouri v. Sours, 446 U.S. 962, 100 S.Ct. 2935, 64 L.Ed.2d 820 (1980) (*Sours I*); and Sours v. State, 603 S.W.2d 592 (1980), cert. denied, 449 U.S. 1131, 101 S.Ct. 953, 67 L.Ed.2d 118 (1981) (*Sours II*). The State's timely alternative motion for rehearing or transfer to the Missouri Supreme Court was denied by the Court of Appeals on September 15, 1981. The Missouri Supreme Court denied review on November 10, 1981.

We granted certiorari, 456 U.S. 914, 102 S.Ct. 1767, 72 L.Ed.2d 173 (1982), and we vacate and remand.

II

The Missouri Supreme Court first adopted its challenged approach to the Double Jeopardy issue now before us in *Sours I,* supra. In that case, as here, the defendant was convicted and sentenced separately for robbery in the first degree and armed criminal action based on the robbery. The Missouri Supreme Court concluded that under the test announced in Blockburger v. United States, 284 U.S. 299, 52 S.Ct. 180, 76 L.Ed. 306 (1932), armed criminal action and any underlying offense are the "same offense" under the Fifth Amendment's Double Jeopardy Clause. That court acknowledged that the Missouri legislature had expressed its clear intent that a defendant should be subject to conviction and sentence under the armed criminal action statute in addition to any conviction and sentence for the underlying felony. 593 S.W.2d, at 216. The court nevertheless held that the Double Jeopardy Clause "prohibits imposing punishment for both armed criminal action and for the underlying felony." Id., at 223. It then set aside the defendant's conviction for armed criminal action.

When the State sought review here in *Sours I,* we remanded the case for reconsideration in light of our holding in Whalen v. United States, 445 U.S. 684, 100 S.Ct. 1432, 63 L.Ed.2d 715 (1980). Missouri v. Sours, 446 U.S. 962, 100 S.Ct. 2935, 64 L.Ed.2d 820 (1980). On remand, in *Sours II,* supra, the Missouri Supreme Court adhered to its previous ruling that armed criminal action and the underlying felony are the "same offense" and that the Double Jeopardy Clause bars separate punishment of a defendant for each offense, notwithstanding the acknowledged intent of the legislature to impose two separate punishments for the two defined offenses.

Most recently, in State v. Haggard, supra, the Missouri Supreme Court reexamined its decisions in *Sours I,* supra, and *Sours II,* supra, in light of our 1981 holding in Albernaz v. United States, 450 U.S. 333, 101 S.Ct. 1137, 67 L.Ed.2d 275 (1981). The Missouri court, however, remained unpersuaded, stating:

> "Until such time as the Supreme Court of the United States declares clearly and unequivocally that the Double Jeopardy Clause of the Fifth Amendment of the United States Constitution does not apply to the legislative branch of government, we cannot do other than what we perceive to be our duty to refuse to enforce multiple punishments for the same offense arising out of a single transaction." 619 S.W.2d, at 51.

This view manifests a misreading of our cases on the meaning of the Double Jeopardy Clause of the Fifth Amendment; we need hardly go so far as suggested to decide that a legislature constitutionally can prescribe cumulative punishments for violation of its first degree robbery statute and its armed criminal action statute.

III

The Double Jeopardy Clause is cast explicitly in terms of being "twice put in jeopardy." We have consistently interpreted it " 'to protect an individual from being subjected to the hazards of trial and possible conviction more than once for an alleged offense.' " Burks v. United States, 437 U.S. 1, 11, 98 S.Ct. 2141, 2147, 57 L.Ed.2d 1 (1978), quoting Green v. United States, 355 U.S. 184, 187, 78 S.Ct. 221, 223, 2 L.Ed.2d 199 (1957). Because respondent has been subjected to only one trial, it is not contended that his right to be free from multiple trials for the same offense has been violated. Rather, the Missouri court vacated respondent's conviction for armed criminal action because of the statements of this Court that the Double Jeopardy Clause also "protects against multiple punishments for the same offense." North Carolina v. Pearce, 395 U.S. 711, 717, 89 S.Ct. 2072, 2076, 23 L.Ed.2d 656 (1969). Particularly in light of recent precedents of this Court, it is clear that the Missouri Supreme Court has misperceived the nature of the Double Jeopardy Clause's protection against multiple punishments. With respect to cumulative sentences imposed in a single trial, the Double Jeopardy Clause does no more than prevent the sentencing court from prescribing greater punishment than the legislature intended.

In Whalen v. United States, 445 U.S. 684, 100 S.Ct. 1432, 63 L.Ed.2d 715 (1980), we addressed the question whether cumulative punishments for the offenses of rape and of killing the same victim in the perpetration of the crime of rape was contrary to federal statutory and constitutional law. A divided Court relied on Blockburger v. United States, 284 U.S. 299, 52 S.Ct. 180, 76 L.Ed. 306 (1932), in holding that the two statutes in controversy proscribed the "same" offense. The opinion in *Blockburger* stated:

"The applicable rule is that where the same act or transaction constitutes a violation of two distinct statutory provisions, the test to be applied to determine whether there are two offenses or only one, is whether each provision requires proof of a fact which the other does not." 284 U.S., at 304, 52 S.Ct., at 182.

In *Whalen* we also noted that *Blockburger* established a rule of statutory construction in these terms:

"The assumption underlying the rule is that Congress *ordinarily* does not intend to punish the same offense under two different statutes. Accordingly, where two statutory provisions proscribe the 'same offense,' they are construed not to authorize cumulative punishments *in the absence of a clear indication of contrary legislative intent.*" 445 U.S., at 691–692, 100 S.Ct., at 1437–1438 (emphasis added).

We went on to emphasize the qualification on that rule:

"[W]here the offenses are the same ... cumulative sentences are not permitted, *unless elsewhere specially authorized by Congress.*" Id., at 693, 100 S.Ct., at 1438 (emphasis added).

It is clear, therefore, that the result in *Whalen* turned on the fact that the Court saw no "clear indication of contrary legislative intent." Accordingly, under the rule of statutory construction, we held that cumulative punishment could not be imposed under the two statutes.

In Albernaz v. United States, 450 U.S. 333, 101 S.Ct. 1137, 67 L.Ed.2d 275 (1981), we addressed the issue whether a defendant could be cumulatively punished in a single trial for conspiracy to import marihuana and conspiracy to distribute marihuana. There, in contrast to *Whalen,* we concluded that the two statutes did not proscribe the "same" offense in the sense that " 'each provision requires proof of a fact [that] the other does not.' "450 U.S. 339, 101 S.Ct. at 1142, quoting *Blockburger,* supra, 284 U.S., at 304, 52 S.Ct., at 182. We might well have stopped at that point and upheld the petitioners' cumulative punishments under the challenged statute since cumulative punishment can presumptively be assessed after conviction for two offenses that are not the "same" under *Blockburger.* See, e.g., American Tobacco Co. v. United States, 328 U.S. 781, 66 S.Ct. 1125, 90 L.Ed. 1575 (1946). However, we went on to state that because:

"The *Blockburger* test is a 'rule of statutory construction,' and because it serves as a means of discerning congressional purpose *the rule should not be controlling where, for example, there is a clear indication of contrary legislative intent.*" Albernaz v. United States, supra, 450 U.S., at 340, 101 S.Ct., at 1143 (emphasis added).

We found "[n]othing ... in the legislative history which ... discloses an intent contrary to the presumption which should be accorded to these statutes after application of the *Blockburger* test." Ibid. We concluded our discussion of the impact of clear legislative intent on the *Whalen* rule of statutory construction with this language:

[T]he question of what punishments are constitutionally permissible is no different from the question of what punishment the Legislative Branch intended to be imposed. *Where Congress intended, as it did here, to impose multiple punishments, imposition of such sentences does not violate the Constitution.* Id., at 344, 101 S.Ct., at 1145 (emphasis added) (footnote omitted).

Here, the Missouri Supreme Court has construed the two statutes at issue as defining the same crime. In addition, the Missouri Supreme Court has recognized that the legislature intended that punishment for violations of the statutes be cumulative. We are bound to accept the Missouri court's construction of that State's statutes. See O'Brien v. Skinner, 414 U.S. 524, 531, 94 S.Ct. 740, 743, 38 L.Ed.2d 702 (1974). However, we are not bound by the Missouri Supreme Court's legal conclusion that these two statutes violate the Double Jeopardy Clause, and we reject its legal conclusion.

Our analysis and reasoning in *Whalen* and *Albernaz* lead inescapably to the conclusion that simply because two criminal statutes may be construed to proscribe the same conduct under the *Blockburger* test does not mean that the Double Jeopardy Clause precludes the imposition, in a single trial, of cumulative punishments pursuant to those statutes. The rule of statutory construction noted in *Whalen* is not a constitutional rule requiring courts to negate clearly expressed legislative intent. Thus far, we have utilized that rule only to limit a federal court's power to impose convictions and punishments when the will of Congress is not clear. Here, the Missouri Legislature has made its intent crystal clear. Legislatures, not courts, prescribe the scope of punishments.

Where, as here, a legislature specifically authorizes cumulative punishment under two statutes, regardless of whether those two statutes prescribe the "same" conduct under *Blockburger,* a court's task of statutory construction is at an end and the prosecutor may seek and the trial court or jury may impose cumulative punishment under such statutes in a single trial.

Accordingly, the judgment of the Court of Appeals of Missouri, Western District, is vacated and the case is remanded for further proceedings not inconsistent with this opinion.

So ordered.

■ JUSTICE MARSHALL, with whom JUSTICE STEVENS joins, dissenting. [Omitted].

NOTES

1. **Simultaneous trial of multiple offenses.** The respondent in Ohio v. Johnson, 467 U.S. 493, 104 S.Ct. 2536, 81 L.Ed.2d 425 (1984) was charged with murder, involuntary manslaughter, aggravated robbery and grand theft, all arising out of the same occurrence. At his arraignment before the trial court, respondent offered to plead guilty to involuntary manslaughter, which under Ohio law was a lesser included offense of murder, and to theft, which was a lesser included offense of robbery. Over objection by the prosecutor, the trial court accepted the pleas of guilty. It then dismissed the murder and robbery charges on the ground that further prosecution of them would violate respondent's rights under double jeopardy. The Ohio appellate courts affirmed the action of the trial court. The Supreme Court, in an opinion by Justice Rehnquist, reversed.

Respondent's jeopardy interests in avoiding cumulative punishments for the same offense are defined by Missouri v. Hunter. Thus, it is ultimately a question of legislative intent:

> We accept, as we must, the Ohio Supreme Court's determination that the Ohio legislature did not intend cumulative punishment for the two pairs of crimes involved here. But before respondent can ever be punished for the offenses of murder and aggravated robbery he will first have to be found guilty of those offenses. The trial court's dismissal of these more serious charges did more than simply prevent the imposition of cumulative punishments; it halted completely the proceedings that ultimately would have led to a verdict of guilt or innocence on these more serious charges. Presumably the trial court, in the event of a guilty verdict on the more serious offenses, will have to confront the question of cumulative punishments as a matter of state law, but because of that court's ruling preventing even the trial of the more serious offenses that stage of the prosecution was never reached. While the Double Jeopardy Clause may protect a defendant against cumulative punishments for convictions on the same offense, the Clause does not prohibit the State from prosecuting respondent for such multiple offenses in a single prosecution.

467 U.S. at 499–500, 104 S.Ct. at 2541, 81 L.Ed.2d at 433. Respondent also argued that the trial court's action was required by Brown v. Ohio because the guilty pleas constituted prior convictions of lesser included offenses:

> Respondent's argument is apparently based on the assumption that trial proceedings, like amoebae, are capable of being infinitely subdivided, so that a determination of guilt and punishment on one count of a multi-count indictment immediately raises a double jeopardy bar to continued prosecution of any remaining counts that are greater or lesser included offenses of the charge just concluded. We have never held that, and decline to hold it now. . . .
>
> No interest of respondent protected by the Double Jeopardy Clause is implicated by continuing prosecution on the remaining charges brought in the indictment. Here respondent offered only to resolve part of the charges against him, while the State objected to disposing of any of the counts against respondent without a trial. Respondent has not been exposed to conviction on the charges to which he pleaded not guilty, nor has the State had the opportunity to marshal its evidence and resources more than once or to hone its presentation of its case through a trial. The acceptance of a guilty plea to lesser included offenses while charges on the greater offenses remain pending, moreover, has none of the implications of an "implied acquittal" which results from a verdict convicting a defendant on lesser included offenses rendered by a jury charged to consider both greater and lesser included offenses.

467 U.S. at 501–02, 104 S.Ct. at 2542, 81 L.Ed.2d at 434. Justice Stevens, joined by Justice Marshall, dissenting, took the position that a conviction based on a plea of guilty has the same legal effect as a conviction based on a jury's verdict and respondent should receive the benefits of prior conviction protection.

2. ***Blockburger* and simultaneous prosecution.** In several cases, the Court addressed the application of the *Blockburger* test to multiple convictions in the same trial. In United States v. Woodward, 469 U.S. 105, 105 S.Ct. 611, 83 L.Ed.2d 518 (1985), the respondent had been convicted of both failing to report he was bringing more than $5,000 into the United States and of willfully making a false statement to a government agency. Both convictions were predicated on the same act: answering "no" to the customs question whether he had more than $5,000 in his possession. The Ninth Circuit had held that *Blockburger,* as a test of Congressional intent, precluded multiple convictions, but the Court, *per curiam,* reversed. Proof of the currency violation does not necessarily include proof of the

false statement violation, since "a traveler who enters the country and passes through customs prepared to answer questions truthfully, but is never asked whether he is carrying over $5,000 in currency, might nonetheless be subject to conviction [under the currency statute but would not have violated the false statement statute]." 469 U.S. at 108, 105 S.Ct. at 612, 83 L.Ed.2d at 521.

In Ball v. United States, 470 U.S. 856, 105 S.Ct. 1668, 84 L.Ed.2d 740 (1985) the petitioner was convicted of being a convicted felon who had received a weapon that had travelled in interstate commerce and of being a convicted felon who had possessed a weapon that had travelled in interstate commerce. Both convictions were based on his possession of the same firearm. The Court, in an opinion authored by the Chief Justice, held that *Blockburger* had been violated because "proof of illegal receipt of a firearm *necessarily* includes proof of illegal possession of that weapon." 470 U.S. at 862, 105 S.Ct. at 1672, 84 L.Ed.2d at 746. Further, the fact that sentences on the two convictions in this case were made to run concurrently does not cure the harm:

> The second conviction, whose concomitant sentence is served concurrently, does not evaporate simply because of the concurrence of the sentence. The separate *conviction*, apart from the concurrent sentence, has potential adverse collateral consequences that may not be ignored. For example, the presence of two convictions on the record may delay the defendant's eligibility for parole or result in an increased sentence under a recidivist statute for a future offense. Moreover, the second conviction may be used to impeach the defendant's credibility and certainly carries the societal stigma accompanying any criminal conviction. ... Thus, the second conviction, even if it results in no greater sentence, is an impermissible punishment.

470 U.S. at 864–65, 105 S.Ct. at 1673, 84 L.Ed.2d at 748. The Court emphasized, however, that the Government is still permitted to charge and seek to prove both violations in the same trial. And the trial court is authorized to submit both charges to the jury. Should the jury return verdicts of guilty on each charge, however, the trial court must then exercise discretion to vacate the conviction on one of the charges and impose sentence on the other.

The Petitioner in Rutledge v. United States, 517 U.S. 292, 116 S.Ct. 1241, 134 L.Ed.2d 419 (1996) was convicted of conspiracy to distribute controlled substances and of conducting a continuing criminal enterprise to distribute controlled substances. The convictions occurred in the same trial and Petitioner received a life sentence without parole for each offense. Sentences were made to run concurrently.

The Second Circuit rejected the claim that the conspiracy offense was a lesser included offense of the continuing criminal enterprise offense, but the Supreme Court, in a unanimous opinion by Justice Stevens, reversed.

The offense of continuing criminal enterprise requires that the defendant act in concert with five or more others with respect to whom the defendant occupies a leadership position. The Court concluded that acting in concert implies an agreement and that in this case the same agreement was being prosecuted as conspiracy and as continuing criminal enterprise. The continuing criminal enterprise offense requires proof of several facts not required under the conspiracy offense, but the reverse is not true. Since the agreement is implicit in the requirement that the defendant act in concert with others, conspiracy requires proof of no fact not required by continuing criminal enterprise. It is, then, a lesser included offense of continuing criminal enterprise.

Therefore, there is a presumption that the Double Jeopardy Clause prohibits convictions for both offenses in the same trial, unless legislative intent can be found to authorize multiple convictions and punishment. There is no suggestion that

Congress intended for a single agreement to be punishable both as a conspiracy and as continuing criminal enterprise. Therefore, the Double Jeopardy Clause prohibits convictions for both offenses.

3. **Remedy for double jeopardy violation in simultaneous prosecution.** The respondent in Jones v. Thomas, 491 U.S. 376, 109 S.Ct. 2522, 105 L.Ed.2d 322 (1989) was convicted in the same trial of both felony murder and the underlying felony of attempted robbery. He received a 15 year sentence for attempted robbery and a consecutive life sentence for felony murder. After he had served the 15 year sentence, the United States Court of Appeals held that he was entitled to immediate release because the imposition of both sentences violated double jeopardy protections. The Supreme Court, in an opinion by Justice Kennedy, held that gubernatorial commutation of the 15 year sentence to time already served and crediting the time served to the life sentence was adequate to remedy the double jeopardy violation:

> Double jeopardy is an area of the law filled with technical rules, and the protections it affords defendants might at times be perceived as technicalities. This is irrelevant where the ancient and important principles embodied in the Double Jeopardy Clause are implicated ... But neither the Double Jeopardy Clause nor any other constitutional provision exists to provide unjustified windfalls. The Missouri court's alteration of respondent's sentence to a single term for felony murder with credit for time served provided suitable protection of his double jeopardy rights.

491 U.S. at 387, 109 S.Ct. at 2529, 105 L.Ed.2d at 335. Justice Scalia, joined by Justices Stevens, Brennan and Marshall, dissented.

4. **Prosecution for offense already "used" in sentencing.** Does the Double Jeopardy Clause prohibition against multiple punishments for the same offense prohibit prosecution for an offense the underlying conduct of which has already been taken into account under federal Sentencing Guidelines as "relevant conduct" in the sentence for a previous conviction? The petitioner in Witte v. United States, 515 U.S. 389, 115 S.Ct. 2199, 132 L.Ed.2d 351 (1995) was convicted of a marijuana offense. Conspiracy to commit a cocaine offense was taken into account as relevant conduct by the court in selecting the sentence in the marijuana case. Later, petitioner was indicted for the cocaine offense and interposed a claim of double jeopardy. The District Court upheld the claim but the Fifth Circuit reversed. The Supreme Court, in an opinion by Justice O'Connor, affirmed. It held that consideration of the defendant character at sentencing, as evidenced in part by prior criminal conduct, is not punishment for that conduct but only for the offense for which he is being sentenced. Accordingly, as in the case of repeat offender statutes that enhance punishment for prior criminal convictions, multiple punishment for the same offense does not occur when unadjudicated criminal conduct is taken into account in sentencing for conviction of a different offense. The Sentencing Guidelines further protect against "double counting" by providing for concurrent sentences should the petitioner be found guilty of the cocaine charge, because it was previously taken into account as "relevant conduct" in the marijuana case.

5. **Using conduct at sentencing for which defendant had been acquitted.** May a United States District Court take into account as relevant conduct at sentencing acts for which the defendant has been tried and acquitted by a jury? The United States Supreme Court, in a *per curiam* reversal of the Ninth Circuit, held in United States v. Watts, 519 U.S. 148, 117 S.Ct. 633, 136 L.Ed.2d 554 (1997) that a District Court may under federal statutory and Sentencing Commission provisions take such acts into account despite the acquittal. As to the Double Jeopardy Clause issue, the Court held that the jury acquittal did not constitute a finding that the defendant did not do the acts charged, but rather constituted only a conclusion that

the government had failed to prove beyond a reasonable doubt that the defendant engaged in the charged conduct. So long as the government subsequently at sentencing proves by a preponderance of the evidence that the defendant did engage in that conduct and that it is relevant to sentencing for an offense for which the defendant stands convicted, there is no Double Jeopardy preclusion to considering the conduct by the sentencing court. Justice Stevens dissented.

United States v. Dixon

Supreme Court of the United States, 1993.
509 U.S. 688, 113 S.Ct. 2849, 125 L.Ed.2d 556.

■ JUSTICE SCALIA announced the judgment of the Court and delivered the opinion of the Court with respect to Parts I, II, and IV, and an opinion with respect to Parts III and V, in which JUSTICE KENNEDY joins.

In both of these cases, respondents were tried for criminal contempt of court for violating court orders that prohibited them from engaging in conduct that was later the subject of a criminal prosecution. We consider whether the subsequent criminal prosecutions are barred by the Double Jeopardy Clause.

I

Respondent Alvin Dixon was arrested for second-degree murder and was released on bond. Consistent with the District of Columbia's bail law authorizing the judicial officer to impose any condition that "will reasonably assure the appearance of the person for trial or the safety of any other person or the community," D.C.Code Ann. § 23–1321(a) (1989), Dixon's release form specified that he was not to commit "any criminal offense," and warned that any violation of the conditions of release would subject him "to revocation of release, an order of detention, and prosecution for contempt of court." See § 23–1329(a) (authorizing those sanctions).

While awaiting trial, Dixon was arrested and indicted for possession of cocaine with intent to distribute, in violation of D.C.Code Ann. § 33–541(a)(1) (1988). The court issued an order requiring Dixon to show cause why he should not be held in contempt or have the terms of his pretrial release modified. At the show-cause hearing, four police officers testified to facts surrounding the alleged drug offense; Dixon's counsel cross-examined these witnesses and introduced other evidence. The court concluded that the Government had established " 'beyond a reasonable doubt that [Dixon] was in possession of drugs and that those drugs were possessed with the intent to distribute.' " 598 A.2d 724, 728 (D.C.1991). The court therefore found Dixon guilty of criminal contempt under § 23–1329(c), which allows contempt sanctions after expedited proceedings without a jury and "in accordance with principles applicable to proceedings for criminal contempt." For his contempt, Dixon was sentenced to 180 days in jail. D.C.Code § 23–1329(c) (maximum penalty of six months' imprisonment and $1000 fine). He later moved to dismiss the cocaine indictment on double jeopardy grounds; the trial court granted the motion.

Respondent Michael Foster's route to this Court is similar. Based on Foster's alleged physical attacks upon her in the past, Foster's estranged wife Ana obtained a civil protection order (CPO) in Superior Court of the District of Columbia. See D.C.Code Ann. § 16–1005(c) (1989) (CPO may be issued upon a showing of good cause to believe that the subject "has committed or is threatening an intrafamily offense"). The order, to which Foster consented, required that he not " 'molest, assault, or in any manner threaten or physically abuse' " Ana Foster; a separate order, not implicated here, sought to protect her mother. 598 A.2d, at 725–726.

Over the course of eight months, Ana Foster filed three separate motions to have her husband held in contempt for numerous violations of the CPO. Of the 16 alleged episodes, the only charges relevant here are three separate instances of threats (on November 12, 1987, and March 26 and May 17, 1988) and two assaults (on November 6, 1987, and May 21, 1988), in the most serious of which Foster "threw [his wife] down basement stairs, kicking her body[,] . . . pushed her head into the floor causing head injuries, [and Ana Foster] lost consciousness." 598 A.2d, at 726.

After issuing a notice of hearing and ordering Foster to appear, the court held a 3-day bench trial. Counsel for Ana Foster and her mother prosecuted the action; the United States was not represented at trial, although the United States Attorney was apparently aware of the action, as was the court aware of a separate grand jury proceeding on some of the alleged criminal conduct. As to the assault charges, the court stated that Ana Foster would have "to prove as an element, first that there was a Civil Protection Order, and then [that] . . . the assault as defined by the criminal code, in fact occurred." At the close of the plaintiffs' case, the court granted Foster's motion for acquittal on various counts, including the alleged threats on November 12 and May 17. Foster then took the stand and generally denied the allegations. The court found Foster guilty beyond a reasonable doubt of four counts of criminal contempt (three violations of Ana Foster's CPO, and one violation of the CPO obtained by her mother), including the November 6, 1987 and May 21, 1988 assaults, but acquitted him on other counts, including the March 26 alleged threats. He was sentenced to an aggregate 600 days' imprisonment. See § 16–1005(f) (authorizing contempt punishment); Sup.Ct. of D.C. Intrafamily Rules 7(c), 12(e) (maximum punishment of six months' imprisonment and $300 fine).

The United States Attorney's Office later obtained an indictment charging Foster with simple assault on or about November 6, 1987 (Count I, violation of § 22–504); threatening to injure another on or about November 12, 1987, and March 26 and May 17, 1988 (Counts II–IV, violation of § 22–2307); and assault with intent to kill on or about May 21, 1988 (Count V, violation of § 22–501). App. 43–44. Ana Foster was the complainant in all counts; the first and last counts were based on the events for which Foster had been held in contempt, and the other three were based on the alleged events for which Foster was acquitted of contempt. Like Dixon, Foster filed a motion to dismiss, claiming a double jeopardy bar to all counts, and also collateral estoppel as to Counts II–IV. The trial court denied the double-jeopardy claim and did not rule on the collateral-estoppel assertion.

The Government appealed the double jeopardy ruling in *Dixon,* and Foster appealed the trial court's denial of his motion. The District of

Columbia Court of Appeals consolidated the two cases, reheard them en banc, and, relying on our recent decision in Grady v. Corbin, 495 U.S. 508 (1990), ruled that both subsequent prosecutions were barred by the Double Jeopardy Clause. 598 A.2d, at 725. In its petition for certiorari, the Government presented the sole question "[w]hether the Double Jeopardy Clause bars prosecution of a defendant on substantive criminal charges based upon the same conduct for which he previously has been held in criminal contempt of court." We granted certiorari, 503 U.S. 1004 (1992).

II

To place these cases in context, one must understand that they are the consequence of an historically anomalous use of the contempt power. In both *Dixon* and *Foster,* a court issued an order directing a particular individual not to commit criminal offenses. (In Dixon's case, the court incorporated the entire criminal code; in Foster's case, the criminal offense of simple assault.) That could not have occurred at common law, or in the 19th–century American judicial system.

* * *

The Double Jeopardy Clause, whose application to this new context we are called upon to consider, provides that no person shall "be subject for the same offence to be twice put in jeopardy of life or limb." U.S. Const., Amdt. 5. This protection applies both to successive punishments and to successive prosecutions for the same criminal offense. See North Carolina v. Pearce, 395 U.S. 711 (1969). It is well established that criminal contempt, at least the sort enforced through nonsummary proceedings, is "a crime in the ordinary sense." *Bloom,* supra, at 201. Accord, New Orleans v. The Steamship Co., 20 Wall. 387, 392 (1874).

We have held that constitutional protections for criminal defendants other than the double jeopardy provision apply in nonsummary criminal contempt prosecutions just as they do in other criminal prosecutions. See, e.g., Gompers v. Bucks Stove & Range Co., 221 U.S. 418, 444 (1911) (presumption of innocence, proof beyond a reasonable doubt, and guarantee against self-incrimination); Cooke v. United States, 267 U.S. 517, 537 (1925) (notice of charges, assistance of counsel, and right to present a defense); In re Oliver, 333 U.S. 257, 278 (1948) (public trial). We think it obvious, and today hold, that the protection of the Double Jeopardy Clause likewise attaches. Accord, Menna v. New York, 423 U.S. 61 (1975) (*per curiam*); Colombo v. New York, 405 U.S. 9 (1972) (*per curiam*).

In both the multiple punishment and multiple prosecution contexts, this Court has concluded that where the two offenses for which the defendant is punished or tried cannot survive the "same-elements" test, the double jeopardy bar applies. See, e.g., Brown v. Ohio, 432 U.S. 161, 168–169 (1977); Blockburger v. United States, 284 U.S. 299, 304 (1932) (multiple punishment); Gavieres v. United States, 220 U.S. 338, 342 (1911) (successive prosecutions). The same-elements test, sometimes referred to as the *"Blockburger* "test, inquires whether each offense contains an element not contained in the other; if not, they are the "same offence" and double jeopardy bars additional punishment and successive prosecution. In a case such as *Yancy,* for example, in which the contempt prosecution was for disruption of judicial business, the same-elements test would not bar subsequent prosecution for the criminal assault that was part of the disruption, because the contempt offense did not require the element of criminal conduct, and the criminal offense did not require the element of disrupting judicial business.[7]

We recently held in *Grady* that in addition to passing the *Blockburger* test, a subsequent prosecution must satisfy a "same-conduct" test to avoid the double jeopardy bar. The *Grady* test provides that, "if, to establish an essential element of an offense charged in that prosecution, the government will prove conduct that constitutes an offense for which the defendant has already been prosecuted," a second prosecution may not be had.

A

The first question before us today is whether *Blockburger* analysis permits subsequent prosecution in this new criminal contempt context, where judicial order has prohibited criminal act. If it does, we must then proceed to consider whether *Grady* also permits it.

We begin with *Dixon.* The statute applicable in Dixon's contempt prosecution provides that "[a] person who has been conditionally released ... and who has violated a condition of release shall be subject to ... prosecution for contempt of court." § 23–1329(a). Obviously, Dixon could not commit an "offence" under this provision until an order setting out conditions was issued. The statute by itself imposes no legal obligation on anyone. Dixon's cocaine possession, although an offense under D.C.Code Ann. § 33–541(a) (1988 and Supp. 1992), was not an offense under § 23–1329 until a judge incorporated the statutory drug offense into his release order.

In this situation, in which the contempt sanction is imposed for violating the order through commission of the incorporated drug offense, the later attempt to prosecute Dixon for the drug offense resembles the situation that produced our judgment of double jeopardy in Harris v. Oklahoma, 433 U.S. 682 (1977) (*per curiam*). There we held that a subsequent prosecution for robbery with a firearm was barred by the Double Jeopardy Clause, because the defendant had already been tried for felony-murder based on the same underlying felony. We have described our terse *per curiam* in *Harris* as standing for the proposition that, for double jeopardy purposes, "the crime generally described as felony murder" is not "a separate offense distinct from its various elements." Illinois v. Vitale, 447 U.S. 410, 420–421 (1980). Accord, Whalen v. United States, 445 U.S. 684, 694 (1980). So too here, the "crime" of violating a condition of release cannot be abstracted from the "element" of the violated condition. The *Dixon* court order incorporated the entire governing criminal code in the same manner as the *Harris* felony-murder statute incorporated the several

---

7. State v. Yancy, 4 N.C. 133 (1814), it should be noted, involved what is today called summary contempt. We have not held, and do not mean by this example to decide, that the double-jeopardy guarantee applies to such proceedings.

enumerated felonies. Here, as in *Harris,* the underlying substantive criminal offense is "a species of lesser-included offense." *Vitale,* supra, at 420. Accord, *Whalen,* supra.

* * *

* * * Because Dixon's drug offense did not include any element not contained in his previous contempt offense, his subsequent prosecution violates the Double Jeopardy Clause.

The foregoing analysis obviously applies as well to Count I of the indictment against Foster, charging assault in violation of § 22–504, based on the same event that was the subject of his prior contempt conviction for violating the provision of the CPO forbidding him to commit simple assault under § 22–504. The subsequent prosecution for assault fails the *Blockburger* test, and is barred.

B

The remaining four counts in *Foster,* assault with intent to kill (Count V; § 22–501) and threats to injure or kidnap (Counts II–IV; § 22–2307), are not barred under *Blockburger.* As to Count V: Foster's conduct on May 21, 1988 was found to violate the Family Division's order that he not "molest, assault, or in any manner threaten or physically abuse" his wife. At the contempt hearing, the court stated that Ana Foster's attorney, who prosecuted the contempt, would have to prove first, knowledge of a CPO, and second, a willful violation of one of its conditions, here simple assault as defined by the criminal code. On the basis of the same episode, Foster was then indicted for violation of § 22–501, which proscribes assault with intent to kill. Under governing law, that offense requires proof of specific intent to kill; simple assault does not. See Logan v. United States, 483 A.2d 664, 672–673 (D.C.1984). Similarly, the contempt offense required proof of knowledge of the CPO, which assault with intent to kill does not. Applying the *Blockburger* elements test, the result is clear: These crimes were different offenses and the subsequent prosecution did not violate the Double Jeopardy Clause.

Counts II, III, and IV of Foster's indictment are likewise not barred. These charged Foster under § 22–2307 (forbidding anyone to "threate[n] . . . to kidnap any person or to injure the person of another or physically damage the property of any person") for his alleged threats on three separate dates. Foster's contempt prosecution included charges that, on the same dates, he violated the CPO provision ordering that he not "in any manner threaten" Ana Foster. Conviction of the contempt required willful violation of the CPO—which conviction under § 22–2307 did not; and conviction under § 22–2307 required that the threat be a threat to kidnap, to inflict bodily injury, or to damage property—which conviction of the contempt (for violating the CPO provision that Foster not "in any manner threaten") did not. Each offense therefore contained a separate element, and the *Blockburger* test for double jeopardy was not met.

IV

Having found that at least some of the counts at issue here are not barred by the *Blockburger* test, we must consider whether they are barred by the new, additional double jeopardy test we announced three Terms ago in *Grady v. Corbin*. They undoubtedly are, since *Grady* prohibits "a subsequent prosecution if, to establish an essential element of an offense charged in that prosecution [here, assault as an element of assault with intent to kill, or threatening as an element of threatening bodily injury], the government will prove conduct that constitutes an offense for which the defendant has already been prosecuted [here, the assault and the threatening, which conduct constituted the offense of violating the CPO]." 495 U.S., at 510.

We have concluded, however, that *Grady* must be overruled. Unlike *Blockburger* analysis, whose definition of what prevents two crimes from being the "same offence," U.S. Const., Amdt. 5, has deep historical roots and has been accepted in numerous precedents of this Court, *Grady* lacks constitutional roots. The "same-conduct" rule it announced is wholly inconsistent with earlier Supreme Court precedent and with the clear common-law understanding of double jeopardy. See, e.g., Gavieres v. United States, 220 U.S., at 345 (in subsequent prosecution, "[w]hile it is true that the conduct of the accused was one and the same, two offenses resulted, each of which had an element not embraced in the other"). We need not discuss the many proofs of these statements, which were set forth at length in the *Grady* dissent. See 495 U.S., at 526 (Scalia, J., dissenting).

* * *

But *Grady* was not only wrong in principle; it has already proved unstable in application. Less than two years after it came down, in United States v. Felix, 503 U.S. 378 (1992), we were forced to recognize a large exception to it. There we concluded that a subsequent prosecution for conspiracy to manufacture, possess, and distribute methamphetamine was not barred by a previous conviction for attempt to manufacture the same substance. We offered as a justification for avoiding a "literal" (i.e., faithful) reading of *Grady* "longstanding authority" to the effect that prosecution for conspiracy is not precluded by prior prosecution for the substantive offense. Of course the very existence of such a large and longstanding "exception" to the *Grady* rule gave cause for concern that the rule was not an accurate expression of the law. This "past practice" excuse is not available to support the ignoring of *Grady* in the present case, since there is no Supreme Court precedent even discussing this fairly new breed of successive prosecution (criminal contempt for violation of a court order prohibiting a crime, followed by prosecution for the crime itself).

A hypothetical based on the facts in *Harris* reinforces the conclusion that *Grady* is a continuing source of confusion and must be overruled. Suppose the State first tries the defendant for felony-murder, based on robbery, and then indicts the defendant for robbery with a firearm in the same incident. Absent *Grady*, our cases provide a clear answer to the double-jeopardy claim in this situation. Under *Blockburger*, the second prosecution is not barred—as it clearly was not barred at common law, as a famous case establishes. In King v. Vandercomb, 2 Leach. 708, 717, 168 Eng.Rep. 455, 460 (K.B.1796), the government abandoned, midtrial, prosecution of defendant for burglary by breaking and entering and stealing goods, because it turned out that no property had been removed on the date of the alleged burglary. The defendant was then prosecuted for burglary by breaking and entering with intent to steal. That second prosecution was allowed, because "these two offences are so distinct in their nature, that evidence of one of them will not support an indictment for the other." Ibid. Accord, English and American cases cited in *Grady*, 495 U.S., at 532–535 (Scalia, J., dissenting).

Having encountered today yet another situation in which the pre-*Grady* understanding of the Double Jeopardy Clause allows a second trial, though the "same-conduct" test would not, we think it time to acknowledge what is now, three years after *Grady*, compellingly clear: the case was a mistake. We do not lightly reconsider a precedent, but, because *Grady* contradicted an "unbroken line of decisions," contained "less than accurate" historical analysis, and has produced "confusion," we do so here. Solorio v. United States, 483 U.S. 435, 439, 442, 450 (1987). Although *stare decisis* is the "preferred course" in constitutional adjudication, "when governing decisions are unworkable or are badly reasoned, 'this Court has never felt constrained to follow precedent.'" Payne v. Tennessee, 501 U.S. 808 (1991) (quoting Smith v. Allwright, 321 U.S. 649, 665 (1944), and collecting examples). We would mock *stare decisis* and only add chaos to our double jeopardy jurisprudence by pretending that *Grady* survives when it does not. We therefore accept the Government's invitation to overrule *Grady*, and Counts II, III, IV, and V of Foster's subsequent prosecution are not barred.[8]

V

Dixon's subsequent prosecution, as well as Count I of Foster's subsequent prosecution, violate the Double Jeopardy Clause.[9] For the reasons set forth in Part IV, the other Counts of Foster's subsequent prosecution do not violate the Double Jeopardy Clause.[10] The judgment of the District of Columbia Court of Appeals is affirmed in part and reversed in part, and the case is remanded for proceedings not inconsistent with this opinion.

It is so ordered.

■ CHIEF JUSTICE REHNQUIST, with whom JUSTICE O'CONNOR and JUSTICE THOMAS join, concurring in part and dissenting in part.

Respondent Alvin Dixon possessed cocaine with intent to distribute it. For that he was held in contempt of court for violating a condition of his bail release. He was later criminally charged for the same conduct with possession with intent to distribute cocaine. Respondent Michael Foster assaulted and threatened his estranged wife. For that he was held in contempt of court for violating a civil protection order entered in a domestic relations proceeding. He was later criminally charged for the same conduct with assault, threatening to injure another, and assault with intent to kill.

---

8. We do not address the motion to dismiss the threat counts based on collateral estoppel, see *Ashe v. Swenson*, supra, because neither lower court ruled on that issue.

9. Justices White, Stevens, and Souter concur in this portion of the judgment.

10. Justice Blackmun concurs only in the judgment with respect to this portion.

The Court today concludes that the Double Jeopardy Clause prohibits the subsequent prosecutions of Foster for assault and Dixon for possession with intent to distribute cocaine, but does not prohibit the subsequent prosecutions of Foster for threatening to injure another or for assault with intent to kill. After finding that at least some of the charges here are not prohibited by the "same-elements" test set out in Blockburger v. United States, 284 U.S. 299, 304 (1932), the Court goes on to consider whether there is a double-jeopardy bar under the "same-conduct" test set out in Grady v. Corbin, 495 U.S. 508, 510 (1990), and determines that there is. However, because the same-conduct test is inconsistent with the text and history of the Double Jeopardy Clause, was a departure from our earlier precedents, and has proven difficult to apply, the Court concludes that *Grady* must be overruled. I do not join Part III of Justice Scalia's opinion because I think that none of the criminal prosecutions in this case were barred under *Blockburger*. I must then confront the expanded version of double jeopardy embodied in *Grady*. For the reasons set forth in the *Grady* dissent, supra, at 526 (Scalia, J., dissenting), and in Part IV of the Court's opinion, I, too, think that *Grady* must be overruled. I therefore join Parts I, II, and IV of the Court's opinion, and write separately to express my disagreement with Justice Scalia's application of *Blockburger* in Part III.

In my view, *Blockburger*'s same-elements test requires us to focus not on the terms of the particular court orders involved, but on the elements of contempt of court in the ordinary sense. Relying on Harris v. Oklahoma, 433 U.S. 682 (1977), a three-paragraph *per curiam* in an unargued case, Justice Scalia concludes otherwise today, and thus incorrectly finds in Part III–A of his opinion that the subsequent prosecutions of Dixon for drug distribution and of Foster for assault violated the Double Jeopardy Clause. In so doing, Justice Scalia rejects the traditional view—shared by every federal court of appeals and state supreme court that addressed the issue prior to *Grady*—that, as a general matter, double jeopardy does not bar a subsequent prosecution based on conduct for which a defendant has been held in criminal contempt. I cannot subscribe to a reading of *Harris* that upsets this previously well-settled principle of law. Because the generic crime of contempt of court has different elements than the substantive criminal charges in this case, I believe that they are separate offenses under *Blockburger*. I would therefore limit *Harris* to the context in which it arose: where the crimes in question are analogous to greater and lesser included offenses. The crimes at issue here bear no such resemblance.

* * *

In sum, I think that the substantive criminal prosecutions in this case, which followed convictions for criminal contempt, did not violate the Double Jeopardy Clause, at least before our decision in *Grady*. Under *Grady*, "the Double Jeopardy Clause bars a subsequent prosecution if, to establish an essential element of an offense charged in that prosecution, the government will prove conduct that constitutes an offense for which the defendant has already been prosecuted." 495 U.S., at 510. As the Court points out, this case undoubtedly falls within that expansive formulation: To secure convictions on the substantive criminal charges in this case, the Government will have to prove conduct that was the basis for the contempt convictions. Forced, then, to confront *Grady,* I join the Court in overruling that decision.

■ JUSTICE WHITE, with whom JUSTICE STEVENS joins, and with whom JUSTICE SOUTER joins as to Part I, concurring in the judgment in part and dissenting in part.

I am convinced that the Double Jeopardy Clause bars prosecution for an offense if the defendant already has been held in contempt for its commission. Therefore, I agree with the Court's conclusion that both Dixon's prosecution for possession with intent to distribute cocaine and Foster's prosecution for simple assault were prohibited. In my view, however, Justice Scalia's opinion gives short shrift to the arguments raised by the United States. I also am uncomfortable with the reasoning underlying this holding, in particular the application of Blockburger v. United States, 284 U.S. 299 (1932), to the facts of this case, a reasoning that betrays an overly technical interpretation of the Constitution. As a result, I concur only in the judgment in Part III–A.

The mischief in Justice Scalia's approach is far more apparent in the second portion of today's decision. Constrained by his narrow reading of the Double Jeopardy Clause, he asserts that the fate of Foster's remaining counts depends on Grady v. Corbin, 495 U.S. 508 (1990), which the Court then chooses to overrule. I do not agree. Resolution of the question presented by Foster's case no more requires reliance on *Grady* than it points to reasons for reversing that decision. Rather, as I construe the Clause, double jeopardy principles compel equal treatment of *all* of Foster's counts. I dissent from the Court's holding to the contrary. Inasmuch as *Grady* has been dragged into this case, however, I agree with Justice Blackmun and Justice Souter that it should not be overruled. From this aspect of the Court's opinion as well, I dissent.

* * *

II

If, as the Court agrees, the Double Jeopardy Clause cannot be ignored in this context, my view is that the subsequent prosecutions in both *Dixon* and *Foster* were impermissible as to *all* counts. I reach this conclusion because the offenses at issue in the contempt proceedings were either identical to, or lesser included offenses of, those charged in the subsequent prosecutions. Justice Scalia's contrary conclusion as to some of Foster's counts, which he reaches by exclusive focus on the formal elements of the relevant crimes, is divorced from the purposes of the constitutional provision he purports to apply. Moreover, the results to which this approach would lead are indefensible.

A

The contempt orders in *Foster* and *Dixon* referred in one case to the District's laws regarding assaults and threats, and, in the other, to the criminal code in its entirety. The prohibitions imposed by the court orders, in other words, duplicated those already in place by virtue of the criminal statutes. Aside from differences in the sanctions inflicted, the distinction between being punished for violation of the criminal laws and being punished for violation of the court orders, therefore, is simply this: Whereas in the former case "the entire population" is subject to prosecution, in the latter such authority extends only to "those particular persons whose legal obligations result from their earlier participation in proceedings before the court." *Young,* 481 U.S., at 800, n. 10. But the *offenses* that are to be sanctioned in either proceeding must be similar, since the contempt orders incorporated, in full or in part, the criminal code.

Thus, in this case, the offense for which Dixon was held in contempt was possession with intent to distribute drugs. Since he previously had been indicted for precisely the same offense, the double jeopardy bar should apply. In Foster's contempt proceeding, he was acquitted with respect to threats allegedly made on November 12, 1987, and March 26 and May 17, 1988. He was found in contempt of court for having committed the following offenses: Assaulting his wife on November 6, 1987, and May 21, 1988, and threatening her on September 17, 1987. 598 A.2d, at 727; App. 42. The subsequent indictment charged Foster with simple assault on November 6, 1987 (Count I); threatening to injure another on or about November 12, 1987, and March 26 and May 17, 1988 (Counts II, III, and IV); and assault with intent to kill on or about May 21, 1988 (Count V). All of the offenses for which Foster was either convicted or acquitted in the contempt proceeding were similar to, or lesser included offenses of, those charged in the subsequent indictment. Because "the Fifth Amendment forbids successive prosecution ... for a greater and lesser included offense," Brown v. Ohio, 432 U.S. 161, 169 (1977); see also *Grafton,* 206 U.S., at 349–351, the second set of trials should be barred in their entirety.

B

Professing strict adherence to *Blockburger's* so-called "same elements" test, see *Blockburger v. United States,* 284 U.S. 299 (1932), Justice Scalia opts for a more circuitous approach. The elements of the crime of contempt, he reasons, in this instance are (1) the existence and knowledge of a court, or CPO; and (2) commission of the underlying substantive offense. Where the criminal conduct that forms the basis of the contempt order is identical to that charged in the subsequent trial, Justice Scalia concludes, *Blockburger* forbids retrial. All elements of Foster's simple assault offense being included in his previous contempt offense, prosecution on that ground is precluded. The same is true of Dixon's drug offense. I agree with this conclusion, though would reach it rather differently: Because in a successive prosecution case the risk is that a person will have to defend himself more than once against the same charge, I would have put to the side the CPO (which, as it were, triggered the court's authority to punish the defendant for acts already punishable under the criminal laws) and compared the substantive offenses of which respondents stood accused in both prosecutions.

The significance of our disaccord is far more manifest where an element is added to the second prosecution. Under Justice Scalia's view, the double jeopardy barrier is then removed because each offense demands proof of an element the other does not: Foster's conviction for contempt requires proof of the existence and knowledge of a CPO, which conviction for assault with intent to kill does not; his conviction for assault with intent to kill requires proof of an intent to kill, which the contempt conviction did not. Finally, though he was acquitted in the contempt proceedings with respect to the alleged November 12, March 26, and May 17 threats, his conviction under the threat charge in the subsequent trial required the additional proof that the threat be to kidnap, to inflict bodily injury, or to damage property. As to these counts, and absent any collateral estoppel problem, Justice Scalia finds that the Constitution does not prohibit retrial.

The distinction drawn by Justice Scalia is predicated on a reading of the Double Jeopardy Clause that is abstracted from the purposes the constitutional provision is designed to promote. To focus on the statutory elements of a crime makes sense where *cumulative* punishment is at stake, for there the aim simply is to uncover legislative intent. The *Blockburger* inquiry, accordingly, serves as a means to determine this intent, as our cases have recognized. See Missouri v. Hunter, 459 U.S., at 368. But, as Justice Souter shows, adherence to legislative will has very little to do with the important interests advanced by double jeopardy safeguards against *successive* prosecutions. The central purpose of the Double Jeopardy Clause being to protect against vexatious multiple prosecutions, see *Hunter,* supra, at 365; United States v. Wilson, 420 U.S., at 343, these interests go well beyond the prevention of unauthorized punishment. The same-elements test is an inadequate safeguard, for it leaves the constitutional guarantee at the mercy of a legislature's decision to modify statutory definitions. Significantly, therefore, this Court has applied an inflexible version of the same-elements test only once, in 1911, in a successive prosecution case, see Gavieres v. United States, 220 U.S. 338 (1911), and has since noted that "[t]he *Blockburger* test is not the only standard for determining whether successive prosecutions impermissibly involve the same offense." *Brown,* 432 U.S., at 166–167, n. 6. Rather, "[e]ven if two offenses are sufficiently different to permit the imposition of consecutive sentences, successive prosecutions will be barred in some circumstances where the second prosecution requires the relitigation of factual issues already resolved by the first." Ibid.

Take the example of Count V in *Foster:* For all intents and purposes, the offense for which he was convicted in the contempt proceeding was his assault against his wife. The majority, its eyes fixed on the rigid elements-test, would have his fate turn on whether his subsequent prosecution charges "simple assault" or "assault with intent to kill." Yet, because the crime of "simple assault" is included within the crime of "assault with intent to kill," the reasons that bar retrial under the first hypothesis are equally present under the second: These include principles of finality, see *United States v. Wilson,* supra, at 343; protecting Foster from "embarrassment" and "expense," Green v. United States, 355 U.S., at 187; and preventing the government from gradually fine-tuning its strategy, thereby minimizing exposure to a mistaken conviction. Id., at 188. See also Tibbs v. Florida, 457 U.S. 31, 41 (1982); Arizona v. Washington, 434 U.S. 497, 503–504 (1978); supra, at 5.

Analysis of the threat charges (Counts II–IV) makes the point more clearly still. In the contempt proceeding, it will be recalled, Foster was acquitted of the—arguably lesser-included—offense of threatening "in any manner." As we have stated,

> "the law attaches particular significance to an acquittal. To permit a second trial after an acquittal, however mistaken the acquittal might have been, would present an unacceptably high risk that the Government, with its vastly superior resources, might wear down the defendant so that 'even though innocent he may be found guilty.' " United States v. Scott, 437 U.S. 82, 91 (1978) (citation omitted).

To allow the government to proceed on the threat counts would present precisely the risk of erroneous conviction the Clause seeks to avoid. That the prosecution had to establish the existence of the CPO in the first trial, in short, does not in any way modify the prejudice potentially caused to a defendant by consecutive trials.

To respond, as the majority appears to do, that concerns relating to the defendant's interests against repeat trials are "unjustified" because prosecutors "have little to gain and much to lose" from bringing successive prosecutions and because "the Government must be deterred from abusive, repeated prosecutions of a single offender for similar offenses by the sheer press of other demands upon prosecutorial and judicial resources," ante, at 21–22, n. 15, is to get things exactly backwards. The majority's prophesies might be correct, and double jeopardy might be a problem that will simply take care of itself. Not so, however, according to the Constitution, whose firm prohibition against double jeopardy cannot be satisfied by wishful thinking.

C

* * *

III

Once it is agreed that the Double Jeopardy Clause applies in this context, the Clause, properly construed, both governs this case and disposes of the distinction between Foster's charges upon which Justice Scalia relies. I therefore see little need to draw *Grady* into this dispute. In any event, the United States itself has not attempted to distinguish between *Dixon* and *Foster* or between the charges of "assault" on the one hand and, on the other, "assault with intent to kill" and "threat to injure another." The issue was not raised before the Court of Appeals or considered by it, and it was neither presented in the petition for certiorari nor briefed by either party. Under these circumstances, it is injudicious to address this matter. See, e.g., Mazer v. Stein, 347 U.S. 201, 206, n. 5 (1954); Adickes v. S.H. Kress & Co., 398 U.S. 144, 147, n. 2 (1970).

The majority nonetheless has chosen to consider *Grady* anew and to overrule it. I agree with Justice Blackmun and Justice Souter that such a course is both unwarranted and unwise. Hence, I dissent from the judgment overruling *Grady*.

IV

Believing that the Double Jeopardy Clause bars Foster's and Dixon's successive prosecutions on all counts, I would affirm the judgment of the District of Columbia Court of Appeals. I concur in the judgment of the Court in Part III–A which holds that Dixon's subsequent prosecution and Count I of Foster's subsequent prosecution were barred. I disagree with Justice Scalia's application of *Blockburger* in Part III–B. From Part IV of the opinion, in which the majority decides to overrule *Grady,* I dissent.

■ JUSTICE BLACKMUN, concurring in the judgment in part and dissenting in part.

I cannot agree that contempt of court is the "same offence" under the Double Jeopardy Clause as either assault with intent to kill or possession of cocaine with intent to distribute it. I write separately to emphasize two interrelated points.

I

I agree with Justice Souter that "the *Blockburger* test is not the exclusive standard for determining whether the rule against successive prosecutions applies in a given case." I also share both his and Justice White's dismay that the Court so cavalierly has overruled a precedent that is barely three years old and that has proved neither unworkable nor unsound. I continue to believe that Grady v. Corbin, 495 U.S. 508 (1990), was correctly decided, and that the Double Jeopardy Clause prohibits a subsequent criminal prosecution where the proof required to convict on the later offense would require proving conduct that constitutes an offense for which a defendant already has been prosecuted.

* * *

II

Contempt is one of the very few mechanisms available to a trial court to vindicate the authority of its orders. I fear that the Court's willingness to overlook the unique interests served by contempt proceedings not only will jeopardize the ability of trial courts to control those defendants under their supervision but will undermine their ability to respond effectively to unmistakable threats to their own authority and to those who have sought the court's protection.

This fact is poignantly stressed by the *amici:*

"[C]ontempt litigators and criminal prosecutors seek to further different interests. A battered woman seeks to enforce her private order to end the violence against her. In contrast, the criminal prosecutor is vindicating *society's* interest in enforcing its criminal law. The two interests are not the same, and to consider the contempt litigator and the criminal prosecutor as one and the same would be to adopt an absurd fiction" (emphasis in original). Brief for Ayuda et al. as *Amici Curiae* 20.

Finally, I cannot so easily distinguish between "summary" and "nonsummary" contempt proceedings, for the interests served in both are fundamentally similar. It is as much a "disruption of judicial process" to disobey a judge's conditional release order as it is to disturb a judge's courtroom. And the interests served in vindicating the authority of the court are fundamentally different from those served by the prosecution of violations of the substantive criminal law. Because I believe that neither Dixon nor Foster would be "subject for the same offence to be twice put in jeopardy of life or limb," U.S. Const., Amdt. 5, I would reverse the judgment of the District of Columbia Court of Appeals.

JUSTICE SOUTER, with whom JUSTICE STEVENS joins, concurring in the judgment in part and dissenting in part.

While I agree with the Court as far as it goes in holding that a citation for criminal contempt and an indictment for violating a substantive criminal statute may amount to charges of the "same offence" for purposes of the Double Jeopardy Clause, U.S. Const., Amdt. 5, I cannot join the Court in restricting the Clause's reach and dismembering the protection against successive prosecution that the Constitution was meant to provide. The Court has read our precedents so narrowly as to leave them bereft of the principles animating that protection, and has chosen to overrule the most recent of the relevant cases, Grady v. Corbin, 495 U.S. 508 (1990), decided three years ago. Because I think that *Grady* was correctly decided, amounting merely to an expression of just those animating principles, and because, even if the decision had been wrong in the first instance, there is no warrant for overruling it now, I respectfully dissent. I join Part I of Justice White's opinion, and I would hold, as he would, both the prosecution of Dixon and the prosecution of Foster under all the counts of the indictment against him to be barred by the Double Jeopardy Clause.

* * *

VIII

Grady simply applied a rule with roots in our cases going back well over 100 years. *Nielsen* held that the Double Jeopardy Clause bars successive prosecutions for more than one statutory offense where the charges comprise the same act, and *Harris,* as understood in *Vitale,* is properly read as standing for the same rule. Overruling *Grady* alone cannot remove this principle from our constitutional jurisprudence. Only by uprooting the entire sequence of cases, *Grady, Vitale, Harris,* and *Nielsen,* could this constitutional principle be undone. Because I would not do that, I would affirm the judgment of the Court of Appeals. I concur in the judgment of the Court in *Dixon* and with respect to Count I in *Foster,* but respectfully dissent from the disposition of the case with respect to Counts II–V in *Foster.*

C.   TERMINATION WITHOUT ACQUITTAL OR CONVICTION

EDITORS' INTRODUCTION: DEVELOPMENT OF JEOPARDY
PROTECTION AGAINST ABORTED PROSECUTIONS

English common law double jeopardy doctrine extended a bar to a subsequent trial only if the first trial resulted in either a conviction or acquittal. Early considerations of the Fifth Amendment guarantee of double jeopardy regarded the provision as similarly limited. See Crist v. Bretz, 437 U.S. 28, 33, 98 S.Ct. 2156, 2159, 57 L.Ed.2d 24, 30–31 (1978). In the 19th century, however, state courts began to merge the double jeopardy guarantees in the state and Federal constitutions with a distinguishable common law rule against discharge of a jury without a verdict. See Crist v. Bretz, supra, 437 U.S. at 40–49, 98 S.Ct. at 2163–68, 57 L.Ed.2d at 34–40 (Powell, J., dissenting). By the time of United States v. Perez, 22 U.S. 579, 6 L.Ed. 165, 9 Wheat. 579 (1824), the Court accepted the proposition that a defendant could be placed in jeopardy by a prosecution not culminating in a conviction or acquittal and this has remained an established part of double jeopardy jurisprudence. In Wade v. Hunter, 336 U.S. 684, 69 S.Ct. 834, 93 L.Ed. 974 (1949), this aspect of double jeopardy was referred to as a defendant's "valued right to have his trial completed by a particular tribunal." The policy underlying this expansion of double jeopardy was described by a state court as follows:

> If the judge can arbitrarily discharge and empanel juries until one is obtained that will render such a verdict as the state demands, or the attorney for the prosecution desires, and the only protection against such oppression is that a new trial may be ordered in the court trying him, or by the court of last resort, then of what value is [the] boasted right [to be free of double jeopardy]?

O'Brian v. Commonwealth, 72 Ky. (9 Bush.) 333, 339, 15 Am.Rep. 715, 720 (1873).

In United States v. Scott, 437 U.S. 82, 98 S.Ct. 2187, 57 L.Ed.2d 65 (1978), Justice Rehnquist, speaking for the Court, indicated that defendants' interest in avoiding multiple prosecutions even where no final determination of guilt or innocence had been made in the first proceeding may be raised in two different situations. These differ, he continued, in the nature of the action taken by the trial judge in the first proceeding. One situation exists when the trial judge grants a "mistrial." Mistrials may ordinarily be granted on the motion of either party or by the court on its own motion. In such situations, the trial judge contemplates that another prosecution will be brought, or at least that the government will have the opportunity to bring one. As Illinois v. Sommerville makes clear, however, in some situations the trial judge's expectations cannot constitutionally be fulfilled.

Another situation is presented, Justice Rehnquist asserted in *Scott,* when the trial judge "terminates the proceedings favorably to the defendant on a basis not related to factual guilt or innocence." The granting of a motion for such relief, he continued, "obviously contemplates that the proceedings will terminate then and there in favor of the defendant. The prosecution, if it wishes to reinstate the proceedings in the face of such a ruling, ordinarily must seek reversal of the decision of the trial court." 437 U.S. at 92–94, 98 S.Ct. at 2194–95, 57 L.Ed.2d at 75–76. Discussion of these situations is complicated by variations in terminology used in various jurisdictions. Most frequently these actions are labeled "dismissals." "Dismissal with prejudice" is intended to constitute a bar to subsequent proceedings, at least on the same charge. But trial judges sometimes grant a "dismissal without prejudice," which is clearly intended to permit the prosecution to begin anew its efforts to convict the defendant.

It is clear that the labels used by trial judges will not be conclusive and that trial court actions can, when offered in bar to a subsequent proceeding, be functionally characterized, at least to some extent. In Lee v. United States, 432 U.S. 23, 97 S.Ct. 2141, 53 L.Ed.2d 80 (1977), the defense moved for dismissal of the information on the ground that it failed to allege a necessary element of the offense charged. The trial judge granted the motion. When the state recharged the defendant with sufficient information, the dismissal of the first charge was offered in bar to the second proceeding. Holding that the defendant's plea of former jeopardy was properly rejected, the Supreme Court made clear that it was irrelevant that the trial judge in the first proceeding had labeled his action a "dismissal" of the information. The situation was one in which a mistrial could have been properly granted and was analyzed by the Court as if that was the action taken by the trial judge.

Because the Court in *Scott* clearly indicated that it viewed the situations distinguished in that case as involving different double jeopardy principles, this section divides the material accordingly.

1.   Mistrials

If a trial judge terminates a trial by declaring a mistrial, it is reasonably certain that the judge anticipates that this action will not bar a second trial on the same indictment or information. Despite this intent, however, double jeopardy bars further proceedings in certain circumstances.

Illinois v. Somerville

Supreme Court of the United States, 1973.
410 U.S. 458, 93 S.Ct. 1066, 35 L.Ed.2d 425.

■ Mr. Justice Rehnquist delivered the opinion of the Court.

We must here decide whether declaration of a mistrial over the defendant's objection, because the trial court concluded that the indictment was insufficient to charge a crime, necessarily prevents a State from subsequently trying the defendant under a valid indictment. We hold that the mistrial met the "manifest necessity" requirement of our cases, since the trial court could reasonably have concluded that the "ends of public justice" would be defeated by having allowed the trial to continue. Therefore, the Double Jeopardy Clause of the Fifth Amendment, made applicable to the States through the Due Process Clause of the Fourteenth Amendment, Benton v. Maryland, 395 U.S. 784, 89 S.Ct. 2056, 23 L.Ed.2d 707 (1969), did not bar retrial under a valid indictment.

I.

On March 19, 1964, respondent was indicted by an Illinois grand jury for the crime of theft. The case was called for trial and a jury impaneled and sworn on November 1, 1965. The following day, before any evidence had been presented, the prosecuting attorney realized that the indictment was fatally deficient under Illinois law because it did not allege that respondent intended to permanently deprive the owner of his property. Under the applicable Illinois criminal statute, such intent is a necessary element of the crime of theft, and failure to allege intent renders the indictment insufficient to charge a crime. But under the Illinois Constitution at that time, an indictment was the sole means by which a criminal proceeding such as this may be commenced against a defendant. Illinois further provides that only formal defects, of which this was not one, may be cured by amendment. The combined operation of these rules of Illinois procedure and substantive law meant that the defect in the indictment was "jurisdictional"; it could not be waived by the defendant's failure to object, and could be asserted on appeal or in a post-conviction proceeding to overturn a final judgment of conviction.

Faced with this situation, the Illinois trial court concluded that further proceedings under this defective indictment would be useless and granted the State's motion for a mistrial. On November 3, the grand jury handed down a second indictment alleging the requisite intent. Respondent was arraigned two weeks after the first trial was aborted, raised a claim of double jeopardy which was overruled, and the second trial commenced shortly thereafter. The jury returned a verdict of guilty, sentence was imposed, and the Illinois courts upheld the conviction. Respondent then sought federal habeas corpus, alleging that the conviction constituted double jeopardy contrary to the prohibition of the Fifth and Fourteenth Amendments. The Seventh Circuit ... held that respondent's petition for habeas corpus should have been granted because ... jeopardy had attached when the jury was impaneled and sworn, and a declaration of mistrial over respondent's objection precluded a retrial under a valid indictment. 447 F.2d 733 (1971). For the reasons stated below, we reverse that judgment.

II.

The fountainhead decision construing the Double Jeopardy Clause in the context of a declaration of a mistrial over a defendant's objection is United States v. Perez, 9 Wheat. 579 (1824). Mr. Justice Story, writing for a unanimous Court, set forth the standards for determining whether a retrial, following a declaration of a mistrial over a defendant's objection, constitutes double jeopardy within the meaning of the Fifth Amendment. In holding that the failure of the jury to agree on a verdict of either acquittal or conviction did not bar retrial of the defendant, Mr. Justice Story wrote:

"We think, that in all cases of this nature, the law has invested Courts of Justice with the authority to discharge a jury from giving any verdict, whenever, in their opinion, taking all the circumstances into consideration, there is a manifest necessity for the act, or the ends of public justice would otherwise be defeated. They are to exercise a sound discretion on the subject; and it is impossible to define all the circumstances, which would render it proper to interfere. To be sure, the power ought to be used with the greatest caution, under urgent circumstances, and for very plain and obvious causes; and, in capital cases especially, Courts should be extremely careful how they interfere with any of the chances of life, in favour of the prisoner. But, after all, they have the right to order the discharge; and the security which the public have for the faithful, sound, and conscientious exercise of this discretion, rests, in this, as in other cases, upon the responsibility of the Judges, under their oaths of office." Id., at 580.

This formulation, consistently adhered to by this Court in subsequent decisions, abjures the application of any mechanical formula by which to judge the propriety of declaring a mistrial in the varying and often unique situations arising during the course of a criminal trial. The broad discretion reserved to the trial judge in such circumstances has been consistently reiterated in decisions of this Court. . . .

In reviewing the propriety of the trial judge's exercise of his discretion, this Court, following the counsel of Mr. Justice Story, has scrutinized the action to determine whether, in the context of that particular trial, the declaration of a mistrial was dictated by "manifest necessity" or the "ends of public justice." The interests of the public in seeing that a criminal prosecution proceed to verdict, either of acquittal or conviction, need not be forsaken by the formulation or application of rigid rules that necessarily preclude the vindication of that interest. . . .

In United States v. Perez, supra, and Logan v. United States, 144 U.S. 263, 12 S.Ct. 617, 36 L.Ed. 429 (1892), this Court held that "manifest necessity" justified the discharge of juries unable to reach verdicts, and, therefore, the Double Jeopardy Clause did not bar retrial. In Simmons v. United States, 142 U.S. 148, 12 S.Ct. 171, 35 L.Ed. 968 (1891), a trial judge dismissed the jury, over defendant's objection, because one of the jurors had been acquainted with the defendant, and, therefore, was probably prejudiced against the Government; this Court held that the trial judge properly exercised his power "to prevent the defeat of the ends of public justice." Id., at 154, 12 S.Ct., at 172. In Thompson v. United States, 155 U.S. 271, 15 S.Ct. 73, 39 L.Ed. 146 (1894), a mistrial was declared after the trial judge learned that one of the jurors was disqualified, he having been a member of the grand jury that indicted the defendant. Similarly, in Lovato v. New Mexico, 242 U.S. 199, 37 S.Ct. 107, 61 L.Ed. 244 (1916), the defendant demurred to the indictment, his demurrer was overruled, and a jury sworn. The district attorney, realizing that the defendant had not pleaded to the indictment after the demurrer had been overruled, moved for the discharge of the jury and arraignment of the defendant for pleading; the jury was discharged, the defendant pleaded not guilty, the same jury was again impaneled, and a verdict of guilty rendered. In both of those cases this Court held that the Double Jeopardy Clause did not bar re-prosecution.

While virtually all of the cases turn on the particular facts and thus escape meaningful categorization, . . . it is possible to distill from them a general approach, premised on the "public justice" policy enunciated in United States v. Perez, to situations such as that presented by this case. A trial judge properly exercises his discretion to declare a mistrial if an impartial verdict cannot be reached, or if a verdict of conviction could be reached but would have to be reversed on appeal due to an obvious procedural error in the trial. If an error would make reversal on appeal a certainty, it would not serve "the ends of public justice" to require that the Government proceed with its proof when, if it succeeded before the jury, it would automatically be stripped of that success by an appellate court. This was substantially the situation in both Thompson v. United States, supra, and Lovato v. New Mexico, supra. While the declaration of a mistrial on the basis of a rule or a defective procedure that would lend itself to prosecutorial manipulation would involve an entirely different question, cf. Downum v. United States, [372 U.S. 734, 83 S.Ct. 1033, 10 L.Ed.2d 100 (1963)], such was not the situation in the above cases or in the instant case.

In Downum v. United States, the defendant was charged with six counts of mail theft, and forging and uttering stolen checks. A jury was selected and sworn in the morning, and instructed to return that afternoon. When the jury returned, the Government moved for the discharge of the jury on the ground that a key prosecution witness, for two of the six counts against defendant, was not present. The prosecution knew, prior to the selection and swearing of the jury, that this witness could not be found and had not been served with a subpoena. The trial judge discharged the jury over the defendant's motions to dismiss two counts for failure to prosecute and to continue the other four. This Court, in reversing the convictions on the ground of double jeopardy, emphasized that "[e]ach case must turn on its facts," 372 U.S., at 737, 83 S.Ct., at 1035 and held that the second prosecution constituted double jeopardy, because the absence of the witness and the reason therefor did not there justify, in terms of "manifest necessity," the declaration of a mistrial.

In United States v. Jorn, [400 U.S. 470, 91 S.Ct. 547, 27 L.Ed.2d 543 (1971)], the Government called a taxpayer witness in a prosecution for willfully assisting in the preparation of fraudulent income tax returns. Prior to his testimony, defense counsel suggested he be warned of his constitutional right against compulsory self-incrimination. The trial judge warned him of his rights, and the witness stated that he was willing to testify and that the Internal Revenue Service agent who first contacted him warned him of his rights. The trial judge, however, did not believe the witness' declaration that the IRS had so warned him, and refused to allow him to testify until after he had consulted with an attorney. After learning from the Government that the remaining four witnesses were "similarly situated," and after surmising that they, too, had not been properly informed of their rights, the trial judge declared a mistrial to give the witnesses the opportunity to consult with attorneys. In sustaining a plea in bar of double jeopardy to an attempted second trial of the defendant, the plurality opinion of the Court, emphasizing the importance to the defendant of proceeding before the first jury sworn, concluded:

"It is apparent from the record that no consideration was given to the possibility of a trial continuance; indeed, the trial judge acted so abruptly in discharging the jury that, had the prosecutor been disposed to suggest a continuance, or the defendant to object to the discharge of the jury, there would have been no opportunity to do so. When one examines the circumstances surrounding the discharge of this jury, it seems abundantly apparent that the trial judge made no effort to exercise a sound discretion to assure that, taking all the circumstances into account, there was a manifest necessity for the *sua sponte* declaration of this mistrial. United States v. Perez, 9 Wheat., at 580. Therefore, we must conclude that in the circumstances of this case, appellee's reprosecution would violate the double jeopardy provision of the Fifth Amendment." 400 U.S., at 487, 91 S.Ct., at 558.

III.

* * *

[R]espondent argues that our decision in United States v. Jorn, supra, which respondent interprets as narrowly limiting the circumstances in which a mistrial is manifestly necessary, requires affirmance. Emphasizing the " 'valued right to have his trial completed by a particular tribunal,' " United States v. Jorn, supra, at 484 of 400 U.S., at 557 of 91 S.Ct., . . . respondent contends that the circumstances did not justify depriving him of that right.

* * *

We believe that in light of the State's established rules of criminal procedure, the trial judge's declaration of a mistrial was not an abuse of discretion. . . .

In the instant case, the trial judge terminated the proceeding because a defect was found to exist in the indictment that was, as a matter of Illinois law, not curable by amendment. The Illinois courts have held that even after a judgment of conviction has become final, the defendant may be released on habeas corpus, because the defect in the indictment deprives the trial court of "jurisdiction." The rule prohibiting the amendment of all but formal defects in indictments is designed to implement the State's policy of preserving the right of each defendant to insist that a criminal prosecution against him be commenced by the action of a grand jury. The trial judge was faced with a situation similar to those in *Simmons, Lovato,* and *Thompson,* in which a procedural defect might or would preclude the public from either obtaining an impartial verdict or keeping a verdict of conviction if its evidence persuaded the jury. If a mistrial were constitutionally unavailable in situations such as this, the State's policy could only be implemented by conducting a second trial after verdict and reversal on appeal, thus wasting time, energy, and money for all concerned. Here, the trial judge's action was a rational determination designed to implement a legitimate state policy, with no suggestion that the implementation of that policy in this manner could be manipulated so as to prejudice the defendant. This situation is thus unlike *Downum,* where the mistrial entailed not only a delay for the defendant, but also operated as a post-jeopardy continuance to allow the prosecution an opportunity to strengthen its case. Here, the delay was minimal, and the mistrial was, under Illinois law, the only way in which a defect in the indictment could be corrected. Given the established standard of discretion . . ., we cannot say that the declaration of a mistrial was not required by "manifest necessity" or the "ends of public justice."

* * *

The determination by the trial court to abort a criminal proceeding where jeopardy has attached is not one to be lightly undertaken, since the interest of the defendant in having his fate determined by the jury first impaneled is itself a weighty one. United States v. Jorn, supra. Nor will the lack of demonstrable additional prejudice preclude the defendant's invocation of the double jeopardy bar in the absence of some important countervailing interest of proper judicial administration. Ibid. But where the declaration of a mistrial implements a reasonable state policy and aborts a proceeding that at best would have produced a verdict that could have been upset at will by one of the parties, the defendant's interest in proceeding to verdict is outweighed by the competing and equally legitimate demand for public justice. . . .

Reversed.

■ MR. JUSTICE WHITE, with whom MR. JUSTICE DOUGLAS and MR. JUSTICE BRENNAN join, dissenting.

* * *

There was not, in this case any more than in *Downum* and *Jorn*, "manifest necessity". . . . I cannot find "manifest necessity" for a mistrial to compensate for prosecutorial mistake. . . .

NOTES

1. **Deference to trial judge's assessment of need for mistrial.** At trial, defense counsel in the opening statement, told the jury that it would hear evidence that the state had purposefully withheld evidence from the defense at a preceding trial; there was apparently no basis for believing the state's earlier action intentional. At the state's request and over defense objection, a mistrial was declared. Could another trial be held? See Arizona v. Washington, 434 U.S. 497, 98 S.Ct. 824, 54 L.Ed.2d 717 (1978), permitting another trial and emphasizing that "the highest degree of respect" must be given the trial judge's assessment of the need for terminating the prior proceeding rather than pursuing some other method of dealing with the danger that juror bias may have been created by defense counsel's action. 434 U.S. at 511, 98 S.Ct. at 833, 54 L.Ed.2d at 732.

2. **Defense motion for mistrial.** Suppose defense counsel moves for the mistrial. In United States v. Dinitz, 424 U.S. 600, 96 S.Ct. 1075, 47 L.Ed.2d 267 (1976), Dinitz' lead counsel at his drug trial repeatedly failed to observe the trial judge's limitations on the subject matter of opening statements. The trial judge ejected counsel from the courthouse and offered Dinitz three alternatives: (a) a stay pending appeal of the order ejecting lead counsel; (b) continuation of the trial with Dinitz' other lawyers representing him; or (c) a declaration of mistrial permitting Dinitz to obtain another lead trial counsel. Dinitz moved for a mistrial. At a second proceeding held over his assertion of former jeopardy he was convicted. The Supreme Court affirmed. If a mistrial is declared on defense motion, the Court held, the "manifest necessity" standard need not be met for a second trial to be permissible:

Even when judicial or prosecutorial error prejudices a defendant's prospects of securing an acquittal, he may nonetheless desire "to go to the first jury and, perhaps, end the dispute then and there with an acquittal." United States v. Jorn, [400 U.S. 470,] 484, 91 S.Ct. [547,] 557, 27 L.Ed.2d [543,] 556 [1971]. Our prior decisions recognize the defendant's right to pursue this course in the absence of circumstances of manifest necessity requiring a *sua sponte* judicial declaration of mistrial. But it is evident that when judicial or prosecutorial error seriously prejudices a defendant, he may have little interest in completing the trial and obtaining a verdict from the first jury. The defendant may reasonably conclude that a continuation of the tainted proceeding would result in a conviction followed by a lengthy appeal and, if a reversal is secured, by a second prosecution. In such circumstances, a defendant's mistrial request has objectives not unlike the interests served by the Double Jeopardy Clause—the avoidance of the anxiety, expense and delay occasioned by multiple prosecutions. ...The important consideration, for purposes of the Double Jeopardy Clause, is that the defendant retain primary control over the course to be followed in the event of such error.

[To apply the manifest necessity standard to a defense motion for mistrial] undermines rather than furthers the protections of the Double Jeopardy Clause. In the event of severely prejudicial error a defendant might well consider an immediate new trial a preferable alternative to the prospect of a probable conviction followed by an appeal, a reversal of the conviction, and a later retrial. [Application of the manifest necessity standard], in effect, instructs trial judges to reject the most meritorious mistrial motion in the absence of manifest necessity and to require, instead, that the trial proceed to its conclusion despite a legitimate claim of seriously prejudicial error. ...

424 U.S. at 608–10, 96 S.Ct. at 1080–81, 47 L.Ed.2d at 274–76. Even if the trial judge may have overreacted in expelling defense counsel, the Court concluded, there was no evidence that this was done in bad faith to goad Dinitz into requesting a mistrial or to prejudice his prospects for an acquittal. Retrial, therefore, was not prohibited by double jeopardy, even though "manifest necessity" for the mistrial may not have existed.

3. **Prosecutorial misconduct.** The Court in Oregon v. Kennedy, 456 U.S. 667, 102 S.Ct. 2083, 72 L.Ed.2d 416 (1982) addressed the question of when, if ever, double jeopardy bars a re-prosecution when the first trial was terminated by a mistrial at the defendant's behest. Kennedy was being tried for theft of an oriental rug. The State called a rug dealer as an expert witness. On cross-examination, defendant elicited, to show bias, that the witness had once filed a criminal charge against the defendant. On re-direct, the prosecutor asked the witness, "Have you ever done business with the Kennedys?" When the witness responded, "No," the prosecutor asked, "Is that because he is a crook?" The defendant moved for a mistrial, which was granted by the trial court. On re-prosecution, he claimed his double jeopardy rights were infringed. Following conviction, the Oregon Court of Appeals reversed on the ground that the prosecutor had "overreached" in asking the question and that jeopardy barred re-prosecution despite the defendant's motion for mistrial.

The Supreme Court, in an opinion authored by Justice Rehnquist, reversed. The Court acknowledged that language in some of its prior opinions had provided support for the Oregon court's conclusion that jeopardy barred re-prosecution if the motion for mistrial was occasioned by "prosecutorial or judicial overreaching" or when "the error that prompted the mistrial is intended to provoke a mistrial or is motivated by bad faith or undertaken to harass or prejudice the defendant." 456 U.S. at 670, 102 S.Ct. at 2086, 72 L.Ed.2d at 420–21. The Court rejected those formulations of the standard and, instead, opted for limiting the standard to those circumstances in which the prosecutor "intended to provoke the defendant into moving for a mistrial." 456 U.S. at 679, 102 S.Ct. at 2091, 72 L.Ed.2d at 426–27. The Court gave the following as explanation for rejecting the broader standard:

The difficulty with the more general standards which would permit a broader exception than one merely based on intent is that they offer virtually no standards for their application. Every act on the part of a rational prosecutor during a trial is designed to "prejudice" the defendant by placing before the judge or jury evidence leading to a finding of his guilt. Given the complexity of the rules of evidence, it will be a rare trial of any complexity in which some proffered evidence by the prosecutor or by the defendant's attorney will not be found objectionable by the trial court. Most such objections are undoubtedly curable by simply refusing to allow the proffered evidence to be admitted, or in the case of a particular line of inquiry taken by counsel with a witness, by an admonition to desist from a particular line of inquiry.

. . .

By contrast, a standard that examines the intent of the prosecutor, though certainly not entirely free from practical difficulties, is a manageable standard to apply. It merely calls for the court to make a finding of fact. Inferring the existence or nonexistence of intent from objective facts and circumstances is a familiar process in our criminal justice system.

456 U.S. at 674–75, 102 S.Ct. at 2089, 72 L.Ed.2d at 424–25. Justice Stevens, concurring, would have applied an "overreaching" standard but would have concluded that the prosecutor's conduct in this case did not violate that standard.

4. **Hung juries.** The Supreme Court has, as it noted in *Somerville,* found no bar to retrial when the jury in the first proceeding was unable to arrive at a unanimous verdict and consequently a mistrial was declared. The propriety of this position was challenged in Findlater, Retrial After a Hung Jury: The Double Jeopardy Problem, 129 U.Pa.L.Rev. 701 (1981). She stresses that defendants whose first prosecutions result in hung juries "in all probability, have a higher percent of innocents among them than do accused in general." Id., at 735. Moreover, the first proceeding terminated for a reason that suggests to the prosecutor the need to make not only an error-free but also more effective and persuasive presentation in the second trial. Consequently, retrials present a significant risk of convictions of innocent defendants.

5. **Opportunity to comment regarding mistrial.** In 1993, the Supreme Court added the following rule to the Federal Rules of Criminal Procedure:

Rule 26.3 Mistrial

Before ordering a mistrial, the court shall provide an opportunity for the government and for each defendant to comment on the propriety of the order, including whether each party consents or objects to a mistrial, and to suggest any alternatives.

The Advisory Committee explained that the rule was in part a response to several recent appellate decisions barring retrial of defendants after mistrials found on appeal to have been the result of precipitous action by district judges, who had failed to solicit the view of the parties as to the need for a mistrial and feasibility of any alternative action. The Committee added:

The Committee regards the Rule as a balanced and modest procedural device which could benefit both the prosecution and the defense. * * * The Rule * * * ensures that the defendant has the opportunity to dissuade a judge from declaring a mistrial in a case where granting one would not be an abuse of discretion, but the defendant believes the prospects for a favorable outcome before that particular court or jury are stronger than they would be at a retrial.

Preliminary Draft of Proposed Amendments, Committee Note to Proposed Rule 26.3, 137 F.R.D. 417, 497 (1991).

2. DISMISSALS AND SIMILAR MATTERS

Trial courts sometimes "dismiss" a prosecution, but the precise procedural effect of this action is not always clear. Technically, dismissal renders the indictment or information a nullity and no further prosecution may be had on that charging instrument. But a superseding indictment or information may be obtained charging similar or identical offenses on the basis of the same events. See United States v. Holder, 399 F.Supp. 220, 226 (D.S.D.1975). Where a dismissal occurs after jeopardy has attached, it is quite likely that the trial judge regards the action as precluding the state from beginning anew. But it is often unclear whether this is because the applicable nonconstitutional procedural law attaches this effect to the dismissal or because it is assumed—rightly or wrongly—that double jeopardy requires this result.

United States v. Scott, reprinted in this section, raises the question of when the prosecution may appeal a dismissal or its equivalent and, if it wins, reprosecute the defendant for the same offense. But suppose appeal is unavailable or, for some reason, the prosecution does not wish to use the appeal process. Is it permissible in any cases where appeal would be allowed by double jeopardy for the state simply to begin again at the trial level, hoping perhaps to have a different judge hear the case or to persuade the same judge that the earlier dismissal was inappropriate?

It is important to distinguish from these situations the problem presented by dismissal of a case before jeopardy attaches. Double jeopardy, of course, does not bar prosecution. But there may be nonconstitutional procedural law that makes some such dismissals "with prejudice." In the federal system, a pre-jeopardy dismissal under Fed.R.Crim.P. 48(a) is generally "without prejudice" and the defendant can be reindicted. United States v. Pope, 574 F.2d 320, 327 (6th Cir.1978), cert. denied 439 U.S. 868, 99 S.Ct. 195, 58 L.Ed.2d 179 (1978). But there is authority for the proposition that a trial court may dismiss under the rule "with prejudice" if it finds the situation meriting this. See White v. United States, 377 F.2d 948, 126 U.S.App.D.C. 309 (D.C.Cir.1967). This is a result of nonconstitutional procedural law, however, not double jeopardy.

United States v. Scott

Supreme Court of the United States, 1978.
437 U.S. 82, 98 S.Ct. 2187, 57 L.Ed.2d 65.

■ MR. JUSTICE REHNQUIST delivered the opinion of the Court.

On March 5, 1975, respondent, a member of the police force in Muskegon, Mich., was charged in a three-count indictment with distribution of various narcotics. Both before his trial in the United States District Court for the Western District of Michigan, and twice during the trial, respondent moved to dismiss the two counts of the indictment which concerned transactions that took place during the preceding September, on the ground that his defense had been prejudiced by preindictment delay. At the close of all the evidence, the court granted respondent's motion. Although the court did not explain its reasons for dismissing the second count, it explicitly concluded that respondent had "presented sufficient proof of prejudice with respect to the first count." Pet. for Cert. 8a. The court submitted the third count to the jury which returned a verdict of not guilty.

The Government sought to appeal the dismissals of the first two counts to the United States Court of Appeals for the Sixth Circuit. That court, relying on our opinion in United States v. Jenkins, 420 U.S. 358, 95 S.Ct. 1006, 43 L.Ed.2d 250 (1975), concluded that any further prosecution of respondent was barred by the Double Jeopardy Clause of the Fifth Amendment, and therefore dismissed the appeal. 544 F.2d 903 (1976). The Government has sought review in this Court only with regard to the dismissal of the first count. We granted certiorari to give further consideration to the applicability of the Double Jeopardy Clause to Government appeals from orders granting defense motions to terminate a trial before verdict. We now reverse.

I.

* * *

We ... held in *Jenkins, supra,* 420 U.S., at 370, 95 S.Ct., at 1013, that, whether or not a dismissal of an indictment after jeopardy had attached amounted to an acquittal on the merits, the Government had no right to appeal, because "further proceedings of some sort, devoted to the resolution of factual issues going to the elements of the offense charged, would have been required upon reversal and remand."

If *Jenkins* is a correct statement of the law, the judgment of the Court of Appeals relying on that decision, as it was bound to do, would in all likelihood have to be affirmed. Yet, though our assessment of the history and meaning of the Double Jeopardy Clause in [United States v.] *Wilson* [420 U.S. 332, 95 S.Ct. 1013, 43 L.Ed.2d 232 (1975)], *Jenkins,* and Serfass v. United States, 420 U.S. 377, 95 S.Ct. 1055, 43 L.Ed.2d 265 (1975), occurred only three Terms ago, our vastly increased exposure to the various facets of the Double Jeopardy Clause has now convinced us that *Jenkins* was wrongly decided. It placed an unwarrantedly great emphasis on the defendant's right to have his guilt decided by the first jury empaneled to try him so as to include those cases where the defendant himself seeks to terminate the trial before verdict on grounds unrelated to factual guilt or innocence. We have therefore decided to overrule *Jenkins,* and thus to reverse the judgment of the Court of Appeals in this case.

* * *

IV.

Our decision in *Jenkins* was based upon our perceptions of the underlying purposes of the Double Jeopardy Clause ...:

> "The underlying idea, one that is deeply ingrained in at least the Anglo–American system of jurisprudence is that the State with all its resources and power should not be allowed to make repeated attempts to convict an individual for an alleged offense, thereby subjecting him to embarrassment, expense and ordeal and compelling him to live in a

continuing state of anxiety and insecurity. ...'' *Jenkins,* supra, 420 U.S., at 370, 95 S.Ct., at 1013, quoting *Green* [v. United States, 355 U.S. 184, 187, 78 S.Ct. 221, 223, 2 L.Ed.2d 199 (1957)].

Upon fuller consideration, we are now of the view that this language from *Green,* while entirely appropriate in the circumstances of that opinion, is not a principle which can be expanded to include situations in which the defendant is responsible for the second prosecution. It is quite true that the Government with all its resources and power should not be allowed to make repeated attempts to convict an individual for an alleged offense. This truth is expressed in the three common-law pleas of *autrefois acquit, autrefois convict,* and pardon, which lie at the core of the area protected by the Double Jeopardy Clause. As we have recognized in cases from [United States v.] *Ball* [163 U.S. 662, 16 S.Ct. 1192, 41 L.Ed. 300 (1896)] to Sanabria v. United States [437 U.S. 54, 98 S.Ct. 2170, 57 L.Ed.2d 43 (1978)], a defendant once acquitted may not be again subjected to trial without violating the Double Jeopardy Clause.

But that situation is obviously a far cry from the present case, where the Government was quite willing to continue with its production of evidence to show the defendant guilty before the jury first empaneled to try him, but the defendant elected to seek termination of the trial on grounds unrelated to guilt or innocence. This is scarcely a picture of an all-powerful state relentlessly pursuing a defendant who had either been found not guilty or who had at least insisted on having the issue of guilt submitted to the first trier of fact. It is instead a picture of a defendant who chooses to avoid conviction and imprisonment, not because of his assertion that the Government has failed to make out a case against him, but because of a legal claim that the Government's case against him must fail even though it might satisfy the trier of fact that he was guilty beyond a reasonable doubt.

We have previously noted that "the trial judge's characterization of his own action cannot control the classification of the action." [United States v. Jorn, 400 U.S. 470, 478 n. 7, 91 S.Ct. 547, 554 n. 7, 27 L.Ed.2d 543 (1971)] (opinion of Harlan, J.), citing United States v. Sisson, 399 U.S. 267, 290, 90 S.Ct. 2117, 2129, 26 L.Ed.2d 608 (1970). See also [United States v. Martin Linen Supply Co., 430 U.S. 564, 671, 97 S.Ct. 1349, 1354, 51 L.Ed.2d 642 (1977)]; *Wilson,* 420 U.S. at 336, 95 S.Ct., at 1018. Despite respondent's contentions, an appeal is not barred simply because a ruling in favor of a defendant "is based upon facts outside the face of the indictment," id., at 348, 95 S.Ct., at 1024 or because it "is granted on the ground ... that the defendant simply cannot be convicted of the offense charged," *Lee,* supra, at 30. Rather, a defendant is acquitted only when "the ruling of the judge, whatever its label, actually represents a resolution [in the defendant's favor], correct or not, of some or all of the factual elements of the offense charged." *Martin Linen,* 430 U.S., at 571, 97 S.Ct., at 1355. Where the court, before the jury returns a verdict, enters a judgment of acquittal pursuant to Fed.Rule Crim.Proc. 29, appeal will be barred only when "it is plain that the District Court ... evaluated the Government's evidence and determined that it was legally insufficient to support a conviction." Id., 420 U.S. at 572, 97 S.Ct., at 1355.

Our opinion in *Burks* [v. United States, 437 U.S. 1, 98 S.Ct. 2141, 57 L.Ed.2d 1 (1978)] necessarily holds that there has been a "failure of proof" ... requiring an acquittal when the Government does not submit sufficient evidence to rebut a defendant's essentially factual defense of insanity, though it may otherwise be entitled to have its case submitted to the jury. The defense of insanity, like the defense of entrapment, arises from "the notion that Congress could not have intended criminal punishment for a defendant who has committed all the elements of a proscribed offense," United States v. Russell, 411 U.S. 423, 435, 93 S.Ct. 1637, 1644, 36 L.Ed.2d 366 (1973), where other facts established to the satisfaction of the trier of fact provide a legally adequate justification for otherwise criminal acts. Such a factual finding does "necessarily establish the criminal defendant's lack of criminal culpability," post, (Brennan, J., dissenting), under the existing law; the fact that "the acquittal may result from erroneous evidentiary rulings or erroneous interpretations of governing legal principles," ibid, affects the accuracy of that determination, but it does not alter its essential character. By contrast, the dismissal of an indictment for preindictment delay represents a legal judgment that a defendant, although criminally culpable, may not be punished because of a supposed constitutional violation.

We think that in a case such as this the defendant, by deliberately choosing to seek termination of the proceedings against him on a basis unrelated to factual guilt or innocence of the offense of which he is accused, suffers no injury cognizable under the Double Jeopardy Clause if the Government is permitted to appeal from such a ruling of the trial court in favor of the defendant. We do not thereby adopt the doctrine of "waiver" of double jeopardy rejected in *Green,* supra. Rather, we conclude that the Double Jeopardy Clause, which guards against Government oppression, does not relieve a defendant from the consequences of his voluntary choice. In *Green,* the question of defendant's factual guilt or innocence of murder in the first degree was actually submitted to the jury as a trier of fact; in the present case, respondent successfully avoided such a submission of the first count of the indictment by persuading the trial court to dismiss it on a basis which did not depend on guilt or innocence. He was thus neither acquitted nor convicted, because he himself successfully undertook to persuade the trial court not to submit the issue of guilt or innocence to the jury which had been empaneled to try him.

The reason for treating a trial aborted on the initiative of the trial judge differently from a trial verdict reversed on appeal, for purposes of double jeopardy, is thus described in *Jorn,* supra, at 484 (opinion of Harlan, J.):

> "[I]n the first situation the defendant has not been deprived of his option to go to the first jury, and, perhaps, end the dispute then and there with an acquittal. On the other hand, where the judge, acting without the defendant's consent, aborts the proceeding, the defendant has been deprived of his 'valued right to have his trial completed by a particular tribunal.' "

We think the same reasoning applies in *pari passu* where the defendant, instead of obtaining a reversal of his conviction on appeal, obtains the termination of the proceedings against him in the trial court without any finding by a court or jury as to his guilt or innocence. He has not been "deprived" of his valued right to go to the first jury; only the public has been deprived of its valued right to "one complete opportunity to convict those who have violated its laws." Arizona v. Washington [434 U.S. 497, 98 S.Ct. 824, 54 L.Ed.2d 717 (1978).] No interest protected by the Double Jeopardy Clause is invaded when the Government is allowed to appeal and seek reversal of such a midtrial termination of the proceedings in a manner favorable to the defendant.[11]

It is obvious from what we have said that we believe we pressed too far in *Jenkins* the concept of the "defendant's valued right to have his trial completed by a particular tribunal." Wade v. Hunter, 336 U.S. 684, 689, 69 S.Ct. 834, 837, 93 L.Ed. 974 (1949). We now conclude that where the defendant himself seeks to have the trial terminated without any submission to either judge or jury as to his guilt or innocence, an appeal by the Government from his successful effort to do so is not barred by 18 U.S.C. § 3731.

* * *

The judgment of the Court of Appeals is therefore reversed, and the cause remanded for further proceedings.

_____

■ MR. JUSTICE BRENNAN, with whom MR. JUSTICE WHITE, MR. JUSTICE MARSHALL, and MR. JUSTICE STEVENS join, dissenting [omitted].

NOTE

Interpreting the meaning of the trial court's decision. In Smalis v. Pennsylvania, 476 U.S. 140, 106 S.Ct. 1745, 90 L.Ed.2d 116 (1986), petitioners, in a jury-waived trial for various arson-related offenses, filed a demurrer at the close of the Commonwealth's case. The trial court granted the demurrer with the comment that there was insufficient evidence to conclude the defendants were guilty beyond a reasonable doubt. The Commonwealth appealed this order and the Superior Court concluded the appeal was barred by jeopardy. The Pennsylvania Supreme Court,

---

11. We should point out that it is entirely possible for a trial court to reconcile the public interest in the Government's right to appeal from an erroneous conclusion of law with the defendant's interest in avoiding a second prosecution. In [United States v. Wilson, 420 U.S. 332, 95 S.Ct. 1013, 43 L.Ed.2d 232 (1975)], the court permitted the case to go to the jury, which returned a verdict of guilt, but it subsequently dismissed the indictment for preindictment delay on the basis of evidence adduced at trial. Most recently in United States v. Ceccolini, [435 U.S. 268, (1978)] we described similar action with approval: "The District Court had sensibly first made its finding on the factual question of guilt or innocence, and then ruled on the motion to suppress; a reversal of these rulings would require no further proceedings in the District Court, but merely a reinstatement of the finding of guilt." ...

We of course do not suggest that a midtrial dismissal of a prosecution, in response to a defense motion on grounds unrelated to guilt or innocence, is necessarily improper. Such rulings may be necessary to terminate proceedings marred by fundamental error. But where a defendant prevails on such a motion, he takes the risk that an appellate court will reverse the trial court.

relying on United States v. Scott, reversed on the ground that in ruling on a demurrer the trial court does not make a factual determination but rather a ruling of law as to whether "the evidence, if credited by the jury, is legally sufficient to warrant the conclusion that the defendant is guilty beyond a reasonable doubt." It remanded for consideration on the merits. The United States Supreme Court reversed in a unanimous decision. Justice White concluded that the action of the trial court was an acquittal under *Scott* since it was a determination that the Commonwealth's evidence was insufficient to establish factual guilt. That a state may characterize such a decision as a ruling on law rather than a determination of fact makes no difference for jeopardy purposes. Since an appellate ruling in the favor of the Commonwealth would require either a new trial or further proceedings in the trial court devoted to the resolution of factual issues going to the elements of the offense charged, the appeal itself is not permissible.

D. FORFEITURE OF PROPERTY ASSOCIATED WITH THE COMMISSION OF CRIMINAL OFFENSES

United States v. Ursery

Supreme Court of the United States, 1996.
518 U.S. 267, 116 S.Ct. 2135, 135 L.Ed.2d 549.

■ CHIEF JUSTICE REHNQUIST delivered the opinion of the Court.

In separate cases, the United States Court of Appeals for the Sixth Circuit and the United States Court of Appeals for the Ninth Circuit held that the Double Jeopardy Clause prohibits the Government from both punishing a defendant for a criminal offense and forfeiting his property for that same offense in a separate civil proceeding. We consolidated those cases for our review, and now reverse. These civil forfeitures (and civil forfeitures generally), we hold, do not constitute "punishment" for purposes of the Double Jeopardy Clause.

I

No. 95–345: Michigan Police found marijuana growing adjacent to respondent Guy Ursery's house, and discovered marijuana seeds, stems, stalks, and a growlight within the house. The United States instituted civil forfeiture proceedings against the house, alleging that the property was subject to forfeiture under 84 Stat. 1276, as amended, 21 U.S.C. § 881(a)(7) because it had been used for several years to facilitate the unlawful processing and distribution of a controlled substance. Ursery ultimately paid the United States $13,250 to settle the forfeiture claim in full. Shortly before the settlement was consummated, Ursery was indicted for manufacturing marijuana, in violation of § 841(a)(1). A jury found him guilty, and he was sentenced to 63 months in prison.

The Court of Appeals for the Sixth Circuit by a divided vote reversed Ursery's criminal conviction, holding that the conviction violated the Double Jeopardy Clause of the Fifth Amendment of the United States Constitution. 59 F.3d 568 (1995). The court based its conclusion in part upon its belief that our decisions in United States v. Halper, 490 U.S. 435, 109 S.Ct.

1892, 104 L.Ed.2d 487 (1989), and Austin v. United States, 509 U.S. 602, 113 S.Ct. 2801, 125 L.Ed.2d 488 (1993), meant that any civil forfeiture under § 881(a)(7) constitutes punishment for purposes of the Double Jeopardy Clause. Ursery, in the court's view, had therefore been "punished" in the forfeiture proceeding against his property, and could not be subsequently criminally tried for violation of 21 U.S.C. § 841(a)(1).

No. 95–346: Following a jury trial, Charles Wesley Arlt and James Wren were convicted of: conspiracy to aid and abet the manufacture of methamphetamine, in violation of 21 U.S.C. § 846; conspiracy to launder monetary instruments, in violation of 18 U.S.C. § 371; and numerous counts of money laundering, in violation of § 1956. The District Court sentenced Arlt to life in prison and a 10–year term of supervised release, and imposed a fine of $250,000. Wren was sentenced to life imprisonment and a 5–year term of supervised release.

Before the criminal trial had started, the United States had filed a civil in rem complaint against various property seized from, or titled to, Arlt and Wren, or Payback Mines, a corporation controlled by Arlt. The complaint alleged that each piece of property was subject to forfeiture both under 18 U.S.C. § 981(a)(1)(A), which provides that "[a]ny property . . . involved in a transaction or attempted transaction in violation of" § 1956 (the money-laundering statute) "is subject to forfeiture to the United States"; and under 21 U.S.C. § 881(a)(6), which provides for the forfeiture of (i) "[a]ll . . . things of value furnished or intended to be furnished by any person in exchange for" illegal drugs, (ii) "all proceeds traceable to such an exchange," and (iii) "all moneys, negotiable instruments, and securities used or intended to be used to facilitate" a federal drug felony. The parties agreed to defer litigation of the forfeiture action during the criminal prosecution. More than a year after the conclusion of the criminal trial, the District Court granted the Government's motion for summary judgment in the civil forfeiture proceeding.

Arlt and Wren appealed the decision in the forfeiture action, and the Court of Appeals for the Ninth Circuit reversed, holding that the forfeiture violated the Double Jeopardy Clause. 33 F.3d 1210 (1994). The court's decision was based in part upon the same view as that expressed by the Court of Appeals for the Sixth Circuit in Ursery's case—that our decisions in *Halper,* supra, and *Austin,* supra, meant that, as a categorical matter, forfeitures under § 981(a)(1)(A) and § 881(a)(6) always constitute "punishment."

We granted the Government's petition for certiorari in each of the two cases, and we now reverse. 511 U.S. 767, 114 S.Ct. 1937, 128 L.Ed.2d 767 (1994).

II

The Double Jeopardy Clause provides: "[N]or shall any person be subject for the same offence to be twice put in jeopardy of life or limb." U.S. Const., Amdt. 5. The Clause serves the function of preventing both "successive punishments and . . . successive prosecutions." United States v. Dixon, 509 U.S. 688, 696, 113 S.Ct. 2849, 2855, 125 L.Ed.2d 556 (1993), citing North Carolina v. Pearce, 395 U.S. 711, 89 S.Ct. 2072, 23 L.Ed.2d

656 (1969). The protection against multiple punishments prohibits the Government from " 'punishing twice, or attempting a second time to punish criminally for the same offense.' " Witte v. United States, 515 U.S. 389, 395, 115 S.Ct. 2199, 2204, 132 L.Ed.2d 351 (1995)(emphasis omitted), quoting Helvering v. Mitchell, 303 U.S. 391, 399, 58 S.Ct. 630, 633, 82 L.Ed. 917 (1938).

In the decisions that we review, the Courts of Appeals held that the civil forfeitures constituted "punishment," making them subject to the prohibitions of the Double Jeopardy Clause. The Government challenges that characterization of the forfeitures, arguing that the courts were wrong to conclude that civil forfeitures are punitive for double jeopardy purposes.

A

Since the earliest years of this Nation, Congress has authorized the Government to seek parallel in rem civil forfeiture actions and criminal prosecutions based upon the same underlying events. See, e.g., Act of July 31, 1789, ch. 5, § 12, 1 Stat. 39 (goods unloaded at night or without a permit subject to forfeiture and persons unloading subject to criminal prosecution); § 25, id., at 43 (persons convicted of buying or concealing illegally imported goods subject to both monetary fine and in rem forfeiture of the goods); § 34, id., at 46 (imposing criminal penalty and in rem forfeiture where person convicted of relanding goods entitled to drawback); see also The Palmyra, 12 Wheat. 1, 14–15, 6 L.Ed. 531 (1827)("Many cases exist, where there is both a forfeiture in rem and a personal penalty"); cf. Calero–Toledo v. Pearson Yacht Leasing Co., 416 U.S. 663, 683, 94 S.Ct. 2080, 2091–2092, 40 L.Ed.2d 452 (1974)(discussing adoption of forfeiture statutes by early Congresses). And, in a long line of cases, this Court has considered the application of the Double Jeopardy Clause to civil forfeitures, consistently concluding that the Clause does not apply to such actions because they do not impose punishment.

One of the first cases to consider the relationship between the Double Jeopardy Clause and civil forfeiture was Various Items of Personal Property v. United States, 282 U.S. 577, 51 S.Ct. 282, 75 L.Ed. 558 (1931). In Various Items, the Waterloo Distilling Corporation had been ordered to forfeit a distillery, warehouse, and denaturing plant, on the ground that the corporation had conducted its distilling business in violation of federal law. The Government conceded that the corporation had been convicted of criminal violations prior to the initiation of the forfeiture proceeding, and admitted that the criminal conviction had been based upon "the transactions set forth . . . as a basis for the forfeiture." Id., at 579, 51 S.Ct., at 283. Considering the corporation's argument that the forfeiture action violated the Double Jeopardy Clause, this Court unanimously held that the Clause was inapplicable to civil forfeiture actions:

"[This] forfeiture proceeding . . . is in rem. It is the property which is proceeded against, and, by resort to a legal fiction, held guilty and condemned as though it were conscious instead of inanimate and insentient. In a criminal prosecution it is the wrongdoer in person who is proceeded against, convicted, and punished. The forfeiture is no part of the punishment for the criminal offense. The provision of the Fifth Amendment to the

Constitution in respect of double jeopardy does not apply." Id., at 581, 51 S.Ct., at 284 (citations omitted; emphasis added).

In reaching its conclusion, the Court drew a sharp distinction between in rem civil forfeitures and in personam civil penalties such as fines: Though the latter could, in some circumstances, be punitive, the former could not. Ibid. Referring to a case that was decided the same day as Various Items, the Court made its point absolutely clear:

> In United States v. La Franca, [282 U.S.] 568 [51 S.Ct. 278, 75 L.Ed. 551 (1931)], we hold that, under § 5 of the Willis–Campbell Act, a civil action to recover taxes, which in fact are penalties, is punitive in character and barred by a prior conviction of the defendant for a criminal offense involving the same transactions. This, however, is not that case, but a proceeding in rem to forfeit property used in committing an offense.

Id., at 580, 51 S.Ct., at 283.

Had the Court in Various Items found that a civil forfeiture could constitute a "punishment" under the Fifth Amendment, its holding would have been quite remarkable. As that Court recognized, "[a]t common law, in many cases, the right of forfeiture did not attach until the offending person had been convicted and the record of conviction produced." Ibid. In other words, at common law, not only was it the case that a criminal conviction did not bar a civil forfeiture, but, in fact, the civil forfeiture could not be instituted unless a criminal conviction had already been obtained. Though this Court had held that common-law rule inapplicable where the right of forfeiture was "created by statute, in rem, cognizable on the revenue side of the exchequer," The Palmyra, supra, at 14, it never had suggested that the Constitution prohibited for statutory civil forfeiture what was required for common-law civil forfeiture. For the Various Items Court to have held that the forfeiture was prohibited by the prior criminal proceeding would have been directly contrary to the common-law rule, and would have called into question the constitutionality of forfeiture statutes thought constitutional for over a century. See United States v. Curtiss–Wright Export Corp., 299 U.S. 304, 327–328, 57 S.Ct. 216, 224–225, 81 L.Ed. 255 (1936)(Evidence of a longstanding legislative practice "goes a long way in the direction of proving the presence of unassailable grounds for the constitutionality of the practice").

Following its decision in Various Items, the Court did not consider another double jeopardy case involving a civil forfeiture for 40 years. Then, in One Lot Emerald Cut Stones v. United States, 409 U.S. 232, 93 S.Ct. 489, 34 L.Ed.2d 438 (1972)(per curiam), the Court's brief opinion reaffirmed the rule of Various Items. In *Emerald Cut Stones*, after having been acquitted of smuggling jewels into the United States, the owner of the jewels intervened in a proceeding to forfeit them as contraband. We rejected the owner's double jeopardy challenge to the forfeiture, holding that "[i]f for no other reason the forfeiture is not barred by the Double Jeopardy Clause of the Fifth Amendment because it involves neither two criminal trials nor two criminal punishments." 409 U.S., at 235, 93 S.Ct., at 492. Noting that the forfeiture provisions had been codified separately from parallel criminal provisions, the Court determined that the forfeiture clearly was "a civil sanction." Id., at 236, 93 S.Ct., at 492–493. The forfeitures were not criminal punishments because they did not impose a second in personam penalty for the criminal defendant's wrongdoing.

In our most recent decision considering whether a civil forfeiture constitutes punishment under the Double Jeopardy Clause, we again affirmed the rule of Various Items. In United States v. One Assortment of 89 Firearms, 465 U.S. 354, 104 S.Ct. 1099, 79 L.Ed.2d 361 (1984), the owner of the defendant weapons was acquitted of charges of dealing firearms without a license. The Government then brought a forfeiture action against the firearms under 18 U.S.C. § 924(d), alleging that they were used or were intended to be used in violation of federal law.

In another unanimous decision, we held that the forfeiture was not barred by the prior criminal proceeding. We began our analysis by stating the rule for our decision:

"Unless the forfeiture sanction was intended as punishment, so that the proceeding is essentially criminal in character, the Double Jeopardy Clause is not applicable. The question, then, is whether a § 924(d) forfeiture proceeding is intended to be, or by its nature necessarily is, criminal and punitive, or civil and remedial." *89 Firearms,* supra, at 362, 104 S.Ct., at 1105 (citations omitted).

Our inquiry proceeded in two stages. In the first stage, we looked to Congress' intent, and concluded that "Congress designed forfeiture under § 924(d) as a remedial civil sanction." 465 U.S., at 363, 104 S.Ct., at 1105. This conclusion was based upon several findings. First, noting that the forfeiture proceeding was in rem, we found it significant that "actions in rem have traditionally been viewed as civil proceedings, with jurisdiction dependent upon the seizure of a physical object." 89 Firearms, id., at 363, 104 S.Ct., at 1105, citing, Calero–Toledo v. Pearson Yacht Leasing Co., 416 U.S., at 684, 94 S.Ct., at 2092. Second, we found that the forfeiture provision, because it reached both weapons used in violation of federal law and those "intended to be used" in such a manner, reached a broader range of conduct than its criminal analogue. Third, we concluded that the civil forfeiture "further[ed] broad remedial aims," including both "discouraging unregulated commerce in firearms," and "removing from circulation firearms that have been used or intended for use outside regulated channels of commerce." *89 Firearms,* supra, at 364, 104 S.Ct., at 1105–1106.

In the second stage of our analysis, we looked to " 'whether the statutory scheme was so punitive either in purpose or effect as to negate' Congress' intention to establish a civil remedial mechanism," 465 U.S., at 365, 104 S.Ct., at 1106, quoting United States v. Ward, 448 U.S. 242, 248–249, 100 S.Ct. 2636, 2641, 65 L.Ed.2d 742 (1980). Considering several factors that we had used previously in order to determine whether a civil proceeding was so punitive as to require application of the full panoply of constitutional protections required in a criminal trial, see id., at 248, 100 S.Ct., at 2641, we found only one of those factors to be present in the § 924(d) forfeiture. By itself, however, the fact that the behavior proscribed by the forfeiture was already a crime proved insufficient to turn the forfeiture into a punishment subject to the Double Jeopardy Clause. Hence, we found that the petitioner had "failed to establish by the 'clearest proof' that Congress has provided a sanction so punitive as to 'transfor[m] what was clearly intended as a civil remedy into a criminal penalty.' " *89 Firearms,* supra, at 366, 104 S.Ct., at 1107, quoting Rex Trailer Co. v. United States, 350 U.S. 148, 154, 76 S.Ct. 219, 222, 100 L.Ed. 149 (1956). We concluded our decision by restating that civil forfeiture is "not an additional penalty for the commission of a criminal act, but rather is a separate civil sanction, remedial in nature." *89 Firearms,* supra, at 366, 104 S.Ct., at 1107.

B

Our cases reviewing civil forfeitures under the Double Jeopardy Clause adhere to a remarkably consistent theme. Though the two-part analytical construct employed in 89 Firearms was more refined, perhaps, than that we had used over 50 years earlier in Various Items, the conclusion was the same in each case: in rem civil forfeiture is a remedial civil sanction, distinct from potentially punitive in personam civil penalties such as fines, and does not constitute a punishment under the Double Jeopardy Clause. See Gore v. United States, 357 U.S. 386, 392, 78 S.Ct. 1280, 1284, 2 L.Ed.2d 1405 (1958)("In applying a provision like that of double jeopardy, which is rooted in history and is not an evolving concept ... a long course of adjudication in this Court carries impressive authority").

In the case that we currently review, the Court of Appeals for the Ninth Circuit recognized as much, concluding that after *89 Firearms,* "the law was clear that civil forfeitures did not constitute 'punishment' for double jeopardy purposes." 33 F.3d, at 1218. Nevertheless, that court read three of our decisions to have "abandoned" 89 Firearms and the oft-affirmed rule of Various Items. According to the Court of Appeals for the Ninth Circuit, through our decisions in United States v. Halper, 490 U.S. 435, 109 S.Ct. 1892, 104 L.Ed.2d 487 (1989), Austin v. United States, 509 U.S. 602, 113 S.Ct. 2801, 125 L.Ed.2d 488 (1993), and Department of Revenue of Mont. v. Kurth Ranch, 511 U.S. 767, 114 S.Ct. 1937, 128 L.Ed.2d 767 (1994), we "changed [our] collective mind," and "adopted a new test for determining whether a nominally civil sanction constitutes 'punishment' for double jeopardy purposes." 33 F.3d, at 1218–1219. The Court of Appeals for the Sixth Circuit shared the view of the Ninth Circuit, though it did not directly rely upon *Kurth Ranch.* We turn now to consider whether *Halper, Austin,* and *Kurth Ranch* accomplished the radical jurisprudential shift perceived by the Courts of Appeals.

In *Halper,* we considered "whether and under what circumstances a civil penalty may constitute 'punishment' for the purposes of double jeopardy analysis." *Halper,* supra, at 436, 109 S.Ct., at 1895. Based upon his submission of 65 inflated Medicare claims, each of which overcharged the Government by $9, Halper was criminally convicted of 65 counts of violating the false-claims statute, 18 U.S.C. § 287 (1982 ed.), as well as of 16 counts of mail fraud, and was sentenced to two years in prison and fined $5,000. Following that criminal conviction, the Government successfully brought a civil action against Halper under 31 U.S.C. § 3729 (1982 ed. and Supp. II). The District Court hearing the civil action determined that Halper was liable to the Government for over $130,000 under § 3729, which then provided for liability in the amount of $2,000 per violation, double the Government's actual damages, and court costs. The court concluded that imposing the full civil penalty would constitute a second punishment for Halper's already-punished criminal offense, however, and therefore reduced Halper's liability to double the actual damages suffered by the Government and the costs of the civil action. The Government directly appealed that decision to this Court.

This Court agreed with the District Court's analysis. We determined that our precedent had established no absolute and irrebuttable rule that a civil fine cannot be "punishment" under the Double Jeopardy Clause. Though it was well established that "a civil remedy does not rise to the level of 'punishment' merely because Congress provided for civil recovery in excess of the Government's actual damages," we found that our case law did "not foreclose the possibility that in a particular case a civil penalty ... may be so extreme and so divorced from the Government's damages and expenses as to constitute punishment." 490 U.S., at 442, 109 S.Ct., at 1898. Emphasizing the case-specific nature of our inquiry, id., at 448, 109 S.Ct., at 1901–1902, we compared the size of the fine imposed on Halper, $130,000, to the damages actually suffered by the Government as a result of Halper's actions, estimated by the District Court at $585. Noting that the fine was more than 220 times greater than the Government's damages, we agreed with the District Court that "Halper's $130,000 liability is sufficiently disproportionate that the sanction constitutes a second punishment in violation of double jeopardy." Id., at 452, 109 S.Ct., at 1904. We remanded to the District Court so that it could hear evidence regarding the Government's actual damages, and could then reduce Halper's liability to a nonpunitive level. Ibid.

In Austin, we considered whether a civil forfeiture could violate the Excessive Fines Clause of the Eighth Amendment to the Constitution, which provides that "[e]xcessive bail shall not be required, nor excessive fines imposed.... " U.S. Const., Amdt. 8. Aware that Austin had sold two grams of cocaine the previous day, police searched his mobile home and body shop. Their search revealed small amounts of marijuana and cocaine, a handgun, drug paraphernalia, and almost $5,000 in cash. Austin was charged with one count of possessing cocaine with intent to distribute, to which he pleaded guilty. The Government then initiated a civil forfeiture proceeding against Austin's mobile home and auto shop, contending that they had been "used" or were "intended for use" in the commission of a drug offense. See 21 U.S.C. §§ 881(a)(4) and (a)(7). Austin contested the forfeiture on the ground of the Excessive Fines Clause, but the District Court and the Court of Appeals held the forfeiture constitutional.

We limited our review to the question "whether the Excessive Fines Clause of the Eighth Amendment applies to forfeitures of property under 21 U.S.C. §§ 881(a)(4) and (a)(7)." Austin, supra, at 604, 113 S.Ct., at 2803. We began our analysis by rejecting the argument that the Excessive Fines Clause was limited solely to criminal proceedings: The relevant question was not whether a particular proceeding was criminal or civil, we determined, but rather was whether forfeiture under §§ 881(a)(4) and (a)(7) constituted "punishment" for the purposes of the Eighth Amendment.

Austin, supra, at 610, 113 S.Ct., at 2806. In an effort to answer that question, we briefly reviewed the history of civil forfeiture both in this country and in England, see id., at 611–618, 113 S.Ct., at 2806–2810, taking a categorical approach that contrasted sharply with Halper's case-specific approach to determining whether a civil penalty constitutes punishment. Ultimately, we concluded that "forfeiture under [§§ 881(a)(4) and (a)(7)] constitutes 'payment to a sovereign as punishment for some offense,' and, as such, is subject to the limitations of the Eighth Amendment's Excessive Fines Clause." Id., at 622, 113 S.Ct., at 2812.

In Department of Revenue of Mont. v. Kurth Ranch, 511 U.S. 767, 114 S.Ct. 1937, 128 L.Ed.2d 767 (1994), we considered whether a state tax imposed on marijuana was invalid under the Double Jeopardy Clause when the taxpayer had already been criminally convicted of owning the marijuana which was taxed. We first established that the fact that Montana had labeled the civil sanction a "tax" did not end our analysis. We then turned to consider whether the tax was so punitive as to constitute a punishment subject to the Double Jeopardy Clause. Several differences between the marijuana tax imposed by Montana and the typical revenue-raising tax were readily apparent. The Montana tax was unique in that it was conditioned on the commission of a crime and was imposed only after the taxpayer had been arrested: thus, only a person charged with a criminal offense was subject to the tax. We also noted that the taxpayer did not own or possess the taxed marijuana at the time that the tax was imposed. From these differences, we determined that the tax was motivated by a " 'penal and prohibitory intent rather than the gathering of revenue.' " Id., at ___, 114 S.Ct., at 1947. Concluding that the Montana tax proceeding "was the functional equivalent of a successive criminal prosecution," we affirmed the Court of Appeals' judgment barring the tax. Id., at ___, 114 S.Ct., at 1948.

We think that the Court of Appeals for the Sixth Circuit and the Court of Appeals for the Ninth Circuit misread Halper, Austin, and Kurth Ranch. None of those decisions purported to overrule the well-established teaching of Various Items, Emerald Cut Stones, and 89 Firearms. Halper involved not a civil forfeiture, but a civil penalty. That its rule was limited to the latter context is clear from the decision itself, from the historical distinction that we have drawn between civil forfeiture and civil penalties, and from the practical difficulty of applying Halper to a civil forfeiture.

In Halper, we emphasized that our decision was limited to the context of civil penalties: What we announce now is a rule for the rare case, the case such as the one before us, where a fixed-penalty provision subjects a prolific but small-gauge offender to a sanction overwhelmingly disproportionate to the damages he has caused. The rule is one of reason: Where a defendant previously has sustained a criminal penalty and the civil penalty sought in the subsequent proceeding bears no rational relation to the goal of compensating the Government for its loss, but rather appears to qualify as "punishment" in the plain meaning of the word, then the defendant is entitled to an accounting of the Government's damages and costs to determine if the penalty sought in fact constitutes a second punishment. 490 U.S., at 449–450, 109 S.Ct., at 1902.

The narrow focus of Halper followed from the distinction that we have drawn historically between civil forfeiture and civil penalties. Since at least Various Items, we have distinguished civil penalties such as fines from civil forfeiture proceedings that are in rem. While a "civil action to recover ... penalties, is punitive in character," and much like a criminal prosecution in that "it is the wrongdoer in person who is proceeded against ... and punished," in an in rem forfeiture proceeding, "it is the property which is proceeded against, and by resort to a legal fiction, held guilty and condemned." Various Items, 282 U.S., at 580–581, 51 S.Ct., at 283–284. Thus, though for Double Jeopardy purposes we have never balanced the value of property forfeited in a particular case against the harm suffered by the Government in that case, we have balanced the size of a particular civil penalty against the Government's harm. See, e.g., Rex Trailer Co. v. United States, 350 U.S. 148, 154, 76 S.Ct. 219, 222–223, 100 L.Ed. 149 (1956)(fines not "so unreasonable or excessive" as to transform a civil remedy into a criminal penalty); United States ex rel. Marcus v. Hess, 317 U.S. 537, 63 S.Ct. 379, 87 L.Ed. 443 (1943)(fine of $315,000 not so disproportionate to Government's harm of $101,500 as to transform the fine into punishment). Indeed, the rule set forth in Halper developed from the teaching of Rex Trailer and Hess. See Halper, supra, at 445–447, 109 S.Ct., at 1900–1901.

It is difficult to see how the rule of Halper could be applied to a civil forfeiture. Civil penalties are designed as a rough form of "liquidated damages" for the harms suffered by the Government as a result of a defendant's conduct. See Rex Trailer, supra, at 153–154, 76 S.Ct., at 222–223. The civil penalty involved in Halper, for example, provided for a fixed monetary penalty for each false claim count on which the defendant was convicted in the criminal proceeding. Whether a "fixed-penalty provision" that seeks to compensate the Government for harm it has suffered is "so extreme" and "so divorced" from the penalty's nonpunitive purpose of compensating the Government as to be a punishment may be determined by balancing the Government's harm against the size of the penalty. Civil forfeitures, in contrast to civil penalties, are designed to do more than simply compensate the Government. Forfeitures serve a variety of purposes, but are designed primarily to confiscate property used in violation of the law, and to require disgorgement of the fruits of illegal conduct. Though it may be possible to quantify the value of the property forfeited, it is virtually impossible to quantify, even approximately, the nonpunitive purposes served by a particular civil forfeiture. Hence, it is practically difficult to determine whether a particular forfeiture bears no rational relationship to the nonpunitive purposes of that forfeiture. Quite simply, the case-by-case balancing test set forth in Halper, in which a court must compare the harm suffered by the Government against the size of the penalty imposed, is inapplicable to civil forfeiture.

We recognized as much in Kurth Ranch. In that case, the Court expressly disclaimed reliance upon Halper, finding that its case-specific approach was impossible to apply outside the context of a fixed civil-penalty provision. Reviewing the Montana marijuana tax, we held that because "tax statutes serve a purpose quite different from civil penalties, ... Halper's method of determining whether the exaction was remedial or punitive simply does not work in the case of a tax statute." Kurth Ranch, supra, at ____, 114 S.Ct., at 1948 (internal quotation marks omitted); see also id., at ____, 114 S.Ct., at 1949–1950 (REHNQUIST, C.J., dissenting)(Halper inapplicable outside of " 'fixed-penalty provision[s]' "that are meant "to recover the costs incurred by the Government for bringing someone to book for some violation of law"). This is not to say that there is no occasion for analysis of the Government's harm. 89 Firearms makes clear the relevance of an evaluation of the harms alleged. The point is simply that Halper's case-specific approach is inapplicable to civil forfeitures.

In the cases that we review, the Courts of Appeals did not find Halper difficult to apply to civil forfeiture because they concluded that its case-by-case balancing approach had been supplanted in Austin by a categorical approach that found a civil sanction to be punitive if it could not "fairly be said solely to serve a remedial purpose." See Austin, 509 U.S., at 610, 113 S.Ct., at 2806; see also Halper, supra, at 448, 109 S.Ct., at 1901–1902. But Austin, it must be remembered, did not involve the Double Jeopardy Clause at all. Austin was decided solely under the Excessive Fines Clause of the Eighth Amendment, a constitutional provision which we never have understood as parallel to, or even related to, the Double Jeopardy Clause of the Fifth Amendment. The only discussion of the Double Jeopardy Clause contained in Austin appears in a footnote that acknowledges our decisions holding that "[t]he Double Jeopardy Clause has been held not to apply in civil forfeiture proceedings ... where the forfeiture could properly be characterized as remedial." Austin, supra, at 608, n. 4, 113 S.Ct., at 2804, n. 4. And in Austin we expressly recognized and approved our decisions in One Lot Emerald Cut Stones v. United States, 409 U.S. 232, 93 S.Ct. 489, 34 L.Ed.2d 438 (1972), and United States v. One Assortment of 89 Firearms, 465 U.S. 354, 104 S.Ct. 1099, 79 L.Ed.2d 361 (1984). See Austin, supra, at 608, n. 4, 113 S.Ct., at 2804, n. 4.

We acknowledged in Austin that our categorical approach under the Excessive Fines Clause was wholly distinct from the case-by-case approach of Halper, and we explained that the difference in approach was based in a significant difference between the purposes of our analysis under each constitutional provision. See Austin, supra, at 622, n. 14, 113 S.Ct., at 2812, n. 14. It is unnecessary in a case under the Excessive Fines Clause to inquire at a preliminary stage whether the civil sanction imposed in that particular case is totally inconsistent with any remedial goal. Because the second stage of inquiry under the Excessive Fines Clause asks whether the particular sanction in question is so large as to be "excessive," see Austin, 509 U.S., at 622–623, 113 S.Ct., at 2812–2813 (declining to establish criteria for excessiveness), a preliminary-stage inquiry that focused on the disproportionality of a particular sanction would be duplicative of the excessiveness analysis that would follow. See id., at 622, n. 14, 113 S.Ct., at 2812, n. 14 ("[I]t appears to make little practical difference whether the Excessive Fines Clause applies to all forfeitures ... or only to those that cannot be characterized as purely remedial," because the Excessive Fines Clause "prohibits only the imposition of 'excessive' fines, and a fine that serves purely remedial purposes cannot be considered 'excessive' in any event"). Forfeitures effected under 21 U.S.C. §§ 881(a)(4) and (a)(7) are subject to review for excessiveness under the Eighth Amendment after Austin; this does not mean, however, that those forfeitures are so punitive as to constitute punishment for the purposes of double jeopardy. The holding of Austin was limited to the Excessive Fines Clause of the Eighth Amendment, and we decline to import the analysis of Austin into our double jeopardy jurisprudence.

In sum, nothing in *Halper, Kurth Ranch,* or *Austin,* purported to replace our traditional understanding that civil forfeiture does not constitute punishment for the purpose of the Double Jeopardy Clause. Congress long has authorized the Government to bring parallel criminal proceedings and civil forfeiture proceedings, and this Court consistently has found civil forfeitures not to constitute punishment under the Double Jeopardy Clause. It would have been quite remarkable for this Court both to have held unconstitutional a well-established practice, and to have overruled a long line of precedent, without having even suggested that it was doing so. Halper dealt with in personam civil penalties under the Double Jeopardy Clause; Kurth Ranch with a tax proceeding under the Double Jeopardy Clause; and Austin with civil forfeitures under the Excessive Fines Clause. None of those cases dealt with the subject of this case: in rem civil forfeitures for purposes of the Double Jeopardy Clause.

C

We turn now to consider the forfeitures in these cases under the teaching of Various Items, Emerald Cut Stones, and 89 Firearms. Because it provides a useful analytical tool, we conduct our inquiry within the framework of the two-part test used in 89 Firearms. First, we ask whether Congress intended proceedings under 21 U.S.C. § 881, and 18 U.S.C. § 981, to be criminal or civil. Second, we turn to consider whether the proceedings are so punitive in fact as to "persuade us that the forfeiture proceeding[s] may not legitimately be viewed as civil in nature," despite Congress' intent. 89 Firearms, 465 U.S., at 366, 104 S.Ct., at 1107.

There is little doubt that Congress intended these forfeitures to be civil proceedings. As was the case in 89 Firearms, "Congress' intent in this regard is most clearly demonstrated by the procedural mechanisms it established for enforcing forfeitures under the statute[s]." 465 U.S., at 363, 104 S.Ct., at 1105. Both 21 U.S.C. § 881 and 18 U.S.C. § 981, which is entitled "Civil forfeiture," provide that the laws "relating to the seizure, summary and judicial forfeiture, and condemnation of property for violation of the customs laws ... shall apply to seizures and forfeitures incurred" under § 881 and § 981. See 21 U.S.C. § 881(d); 18 U.S.C. § 981(d). Because forfeiture proceedings under the customs laws are in rem, see 19 U.S.C. § 1602 et seq., it is clear that Congress intended that a forfeiture under § 881 or § 981, like the forfeiture reviewed in 89 Firearms, would be a proceeding in rem. Congress specifically structured these forfeitures to be impersonal by targeting the property itself. "In contrast to the in personam nature of criminal actions, actions in rem have traditionally been viewed as civil proceedings, with jurisdiction dependent upon seizure of a physical object." 89 Firearms, 465 U.S., at 363, 104 S.Ct., at 1105, citing Calero–Toledo, 416 U.S., at 684, 94 S.Ct., at 2092.

Other procedural mechanisms governing forfeitures under § 981 and § 881 also indicate that Congress intended such proceedings to be civil.

Forfeitures under either statute are governed by 19 U.S.C. § 1607, which provides that actual notice of the impending forfeiture is unnecessary when the Government cannot identify any party with an interest in the seized article, and by § 1609, which provides that seized property is subject to forfeiture through a summary administrative procedure if no party files a claim to the property. And 19 U.S.C. § 1615, which governs the burden of proof in forfeiture proceedings under § 881 and § 981, provides that once the Government has shown probable cause that the property is subject to forfeiture, then "the burden of proof shall lie upon [the] claimant." In sum, "[b]y creating such distinctly civil procedures for forfeitures under [§ 881 and § 981], Congress has 'indicate[d] clearly that it intended a civil, not a criminal sanction.'" 89 Firearms, supra, at 363, 104 S.Ct., at 1105, quoting Helvering v. Mitchell, 303 U.S., at 402, 58 S.Ct., at 634.

Moving to the second stage of our analysis, we find that there is little evidence, much less the " 'clearest proof' "that we require, see 89 Firearms, supra, at 365, 104 S.Ct., at 1106, quoting Ward, 448 U.S., at 249, 100 S.Ct., at 2641–2642, suggesting that forfeiture proceedings under 21 U.S.C. §§ 881(a)(6) and (a)(7), and 18 U.S.C. § 981(a)(1)(A), are so punitive in form and effect as to render them criminal despite Congress' intent to the contrary. The statutes involved in this case are, in most significant respects, indistinguishable from those reviewed, and held not to be punitive, in Various Items, Emerald Cut Stones, and 89 Firearms.

Most significant is that § 981(a)(1)(A), and §§ 881(a)(6) and (a)(7), while perhaps having certain punitive aspects, serve important nonpunitive goals. Title 21 U.S.C. § 881(a)(7), under which Ursery's property was forfeited, provides for the forfeiture of "all real property ... which is used or intended to be used, in any manner or part, to commit, or to facilitate the commission of" a federal drug felony. Requiring the forfeiture of property used to commit federal narcotics violations encourages property owners to take care in managing their property and ensures that they will not permit that property to be used for illegal purposes. See Bennis v. Michigan, 516 U.S. 442, 450, 116 S.Ct. 994, 1000, 134 L.Ed.2d 68 (1996)("Forfeiture of property prevents illegal uses ... by imposing an economic penalty, thereby rendering illegal behavior unprofitable"); 89 Firearms, supra, at 364 (forfeiture "discourages unregulated commerce in firearms"); Calero–Toledo, supra, at 687–688, 94 S.Ct., at 2094. In many circumstances, the forfeiture may abate a nuisance. See, e.g., United States v. 141st Street Corp., 911 F.2d 870 (C.A.2 1990)(forfeiting apartment building used to sell crack cocaine); see also Bennis, supra, at ___, 116 S.Ct., at 1000 (affirming application of Michigan statute abating car as a nuisance; forfeiture "prevent[s] further illicit use of" property); cf. 89 Firearms, supra, at 364, 104 S.Ct., at 1106 (forfeiture "remov[ed] from circulation firearms that have been used or intended for use" illegally); Emerald Cut Stones, 409 U.S., at 237, 93 S.Ct., at 493 (forfeiture "prevented forbidden merchandise from circulating in the United States").

The forfeiture of the property claimed by Arlt and Wren took place pursuant to 18 U.S.C. § 981(a)(1)(A), and 21 U.S.C. § 881(a)(6). Section 981(a)(1)(A) provides for the forfeiture of "any property" involved in illegal money-laundering transactions. Section 881(a)(6) provides for the forfeiture of "[a]ll ... things of value furnished or intended to be furnished by any person in exchange for" illegal drugs; "all proceeds traceable to such an exchange"; and "all moneys, negotiable instruments, and securities used or intended to be used to facilitate" a federal drug felony. The same remedial purposes served by § 881(a)(7) are served by § 881(a)(6) and § 981(a)(1)(A). Only one point merits separate discussion. To the extent that § 881(a)(6) applies to "proceeds" of illegal drug activity, it serves the additional nonpunitive goal of ensuring that persons do not profit from their illegal acts.

Other considerations that we have found relevant to the question whether a proceeding is criminal also tend to support a conclusion that § 981(a)(1)(A) and §§ 881(a)(6) and (a)(7) are civil proceedings. See Ward, supra, at 247–248, n. 7, 249, 100 S.Ct., at 2640–2641, n. 7, 2641–2642 (listing relevant factors and noting that they are neither exhaustive nor dispositive). First, in light of our decisions in Various Items, Emerald Cut Stones, and 89 Firearms, and the long tradition of federal statutes providing for a forfeiture proceeding following a criminal prosecution, it is absolutely clear that in rem civil forfeiture has not historically been regarded as punishment, as we have understood that term under the Double Jeopardy Clause. Second, there is no requirement in the statutes that we currently review that the Government demonstrate scienter in order to establish that the property is subject to forfeiture; indeed, the property may be subject to forfeiture even if no party files a claim to it and the Government never shows any connection between the property and a particular person. See 19 U.S.C. § 1609. Though both § 881(a) and § 981(a) contain an "innocent owner" exception, we do not think that such a provision, without more indication of an intent to punish, is relevant to the question whether a statute is punitive under the Double Jeopardy Clause. Third, though both statutes may fairly be said to serve the purpose of deterrence, we long have held that this purpose may serve civil as well as criminal goals. See, e.g., 89 Firearms, supra, at 364, 104 S.Ct., at 1105–1106; Calero–Toledo, supra, at 677–678, 94 S.Ct., at 2088–2089. We recently reaffirmed this conclusion in Bennis v. Michigan, supra, at __, 116 S.Ct., at 1000, where we held that "forfeiture ... serves a deterrent purpose distinct from any punitive purpose." Finally, though both statutes are tied to criminal activity, as was the case in 89 Firearms, this fact is insufficient to render the statutes punitive. See 89 Firearms, 465 U.S., at 365–366, 104 S.Ct., at 1106–1107. It is well settled that "Congress may impose both a criminal and a civil sanction in respect to the same act or omission," Helvering, 303 U.S., at 399, 58 S.Ct., at 633. By itself, the fact that a forfeiture statute has some connection to a criminal violation is far from the "clearest proof" necessary to show that a proceeding is criminal.

We hold that these in rem civil forfeitures are neither "punishment" nor criminal for purposes of the Double Jeopardy Clause. The judgments of the Court of Appeals for the Sixth Circuit, in No. 95–345, and of the Court of Appeals for the Ninth Circuit, in No. 95–346, are accordingly reversed.

It is so ordered.

■ JUSTICE KENNEDY, concurring.

I join the Court's opinion and add these further observations.

In Austin v. United States, 509 U.S. 602, 619–622, 113 S.Ct. 2801, 2810–2812, 125 L.Ed.2d 488 (1993), we described the civil in rem forfeiture provision of 21 U.S.C. § 881(a)(7) at issue here as punitive. In Libretti v. United States, 516 U.S. 29, 116 S.Ct. 356, 133 L.Ed.2d 271 (1995), we reviewed 21 U.S.C. § 853, which in almost identical terms provides for criminal forfeiture of property involved in or derived from drug crimes. We held that the "fundamental nature of criminal forfeiture" is punishment. 516 U.S. at ___, 116 S.Ct. at 364. Today the Court holds that the civil in rem forfeitures here are not punishment implicating the protections of the Double Jeopardy Clause. Ante, at ___–___. I write to explain why, in my view, our holding is consistent with both Austin and Libretti.

* * *

The key distinction is that the instrumentality-forfeiture statutes are not directed at those who carry out the crimes, but at owners who are culpable for the criminal misuse of the property. See Austin, supra, at 619, 113 S.Ct., at 2810–2811 (statutory "exemptions serve to focus the provisions on the culpability of the owner"). The theory is that the property, whether or not illegal or dangerous in nature, is hazardous in the hands of this owner because either he uses it to commit crimes, or allows others do so. The owner can be held accountable for the misuse of the property. Cf. One 1958 Plymouth Sedan, supra, at 699, 85 S.Ct., at 1250 ("There is nothing even remotely criminal in possessing an automobile. It is only the alleged use to which this particular automobile was put that subjects [the owner] to its possible loss.") The same rationale is at work in the statutory provisions enabling forfeiture of currency "used or intended to be used" to facilitate a criminal offense, § 881(a)(6). See also 18 U.S.C. § 981(a)(1)(A) (property involved in money-laundering transactions or attempts in violation of 18 U.S.C. § 1956). Since the punishment befalls any property holder who cannot claim statutory innocence, whether or not he committed any criminal acts, it is not a punishment for a person's criminal wrongdoing.

Forfeiture, then, punishes an owner by taking property involved in a crime, and it may happen that the owner is also the wrongdoer charged with a criminal offense. But the forfeiture is not a second in personam punishment for the offense, which is all the Double Jeopardy Clause prohibits. See ante, at ___ ("The forfeitures were not criminal punishments because they did not impose a second in personam penalty for the criminal defendant's wrongdoing."); One Lot Emerald Cut Stones v. United States, 409 U.S. 232, 235, 93 S.Ct. 489, 492, 34 L.Ed.2d 438 (1972)(per curiam)("the forfeiture is not barred by the Double Jeopardy Clause of the Fifth Amendment because it involves neither two criminal trials nor two criminal punishments").* * *

■ JUSTICE SCALIA, with whom JUSTICE THOMAS joins, concurring in the judgment.

In my view, the Double Jeopardy Clause prohibits successive prosecution, not successive punishment. See Department of Revenue of Mont. v. Kurth Ranch, 511 U.S. 767, 796–800, 802–804, 114 S.Ct. 1937, 1955–1957, 1958–1959, 128 L.Ed.2d 767 (1994)(SCALIA, J., dissenting). Civil forfeiture proceedings of the sort at issue here are not criminal prosecutions, even under the standard of Kennedy v. Mendoza–Martinez, 372 U.S. 144, 164, 83 S.Ct. 554, 565, 9 L.Ed.2d 644 (1963), and United States v. Ward, 448 U.S. 242, 248–251, 100 S.Ct. 2636, 2641–2643, 65 L.Ed.2d 742 (1980).

■ JUSTICE STEVENS, concurring in the judgment in part and dissenting in part.

The question the Court poses is whether civil forfeitures constitute "punishment" for purposes of the Double Jeopardy Clause. Because the numerous federal statutes authorizing forfeitures cover such a wide variety of situations, it is quite wrong to assume that there is only one answer to that question. For purposes of analysis it is useful to identify three different categories of property that are subject to seizure: proceeds, contraband, and property that has played a part in the commission of a crime. The facts of these two cases illustrate the point.

In No. 95–346 the Government has forfeited $405,089.23 in currency. Those funds are the proceeds of unlawful activity. They are not property that respondents have any right to retain. The forfeiture of such proceeds, like the confiscation of money stolen from a bank, does not punish respondents because it exacts no price in liberty or lawfully derived property from them. I agree that the forfeiture of such proceeds is not punitive and therefore I concur in the Court's disposition of No. 95–346.

None of the property seized in No. 95–345 constituted proceeds of illegal activity. Indeed, the facts of that case reveal a dramatically different situation. Respondent Ursery cultivated marijuana in a heavily wooded area not far from his home in Shiawassee County, Michigan. The illegal substance was consumed by members of his family, but there is no evidence, and no contention by the Government, that he sold any of it to third parties. Acting on the basis of the incorrect assumption that the marijuana plants were on respondent's property, Michigan police officers executed a warrant to search the premises. In his house they found marijuana seeds, stems, stalks, and a growlight. I presume those items were seized, and I have no difficulty concluding that such a seizure does not constitute punishment because respondent had no right to possess contraband. Accordingly, I agree with the Court's opinion insofar as it explains why the forfeiture of contraband does not constitute punishment for double jeopardy purposes.

The critical question presented in No. 95–345 arose, not out of the seizure of contraband by the Michigan police, but rather out of the decision by the United States Attorney to take respondent's home. There is no evidence that the house had been purchased with the proceeds of unlawful activity and the house itself was surely not contraband. Nonetheless, 21 U.S.C. § 881(a)(7) authorized the Government to seek forfeiture of respondent's residence because it had been used to facilitate the manufacture and distribution of marijuana. Respondent was then himself prosecuted for and convicted of manufacturing marijuana. In my opinion none of the reasons supporting the forfeiture of proceeds or contraband provides a sufficient basis for concluding that the confiscation of respondent's home was not punitive.

The Government has advanced four arguments in support of its position that the forfeiture of respondent's home under § 881(a)(7) followed by his prosecution under § 841(a)(1) did not violate the Double Jeopardy Clause: (1) the forfeiture was not punitive; (2) even if punitive, it was not a "jeopardy"; (3) even if both the forfeiture and the prosecution were jeopardizes, they were not based on the same offense under the rule of Blockburger v. United States, 284 U.S. 299, 52 S.Ct. 180, 76 L.Ed. 306 (1932); and (4) in all events, the two cases should be deemed to constitute a single proceeding for double jeopardy purposes. Because the Court addresses only the first of these arguments, I shall begin by explaining why both reason and precedent support the conclusion that the taking of respondent's home was unmistakably punitive in character. I shall then comment on the other three arguments.* * *

The applicability of collateral estoppel and double jeopardy principles to proceedings to forfeit property was the subject of United States v. One Assortment of 89 Firearms, 465 U.S. 354, 104 S.Ct. 1099, 79 L.Ed.2d 361 (1984). One Mulcahey was acquitted of engaging in the business of dealing in firearms without a license. The government then instituted a proceeding seeking forfeiture of the firearms involved under a statute authorizing forfeiture of firearms used or intended to be used in violation of federal law. Mulcahey interposed the defense of collateral estoppel and double jeopardy. The District Court rejected the defense, but the Fourth Circuit reversed, holding both defenses applicable. The Supreme Court, in an opinion authored by the Chief Justice for a unanimous Court, reversed the Court of Appeals.

The burden of proof in the forfeiture was on the government but was only by a preponderance of the evidence. That precluded applicability of the defense of collateral estoppel:

[A]n acquittal on criminal charges does not prove that the defendant is innocent; it merely proves the existence of a reasonable doubt as to his guilt.... [T]he jury verdict in the criminal action did not negate the possibility that preponderance of the evidence could show that Mulcahey was engaged in an unlawful firearms business. Mulcahey's acquittal ... therefore does not estop the government from proving in a civil proceeding that the firearms should be forfeited.... It is clear that the difference in the relative burdens of proof in the criminal and civil actions precludes the application of the doctrine of collateral estoppel.

465 U.S. at 361, 104 S.Ct. at 1104, 79 L.Ed.2d at 368.

As to Mulcahey's double jeopardy claim, that he had been acquitted of conduct that formed the basis of the forfeiture action, the Chief Justice reasoned that the claim must fail unless the forfeiture proceeding was "essentially criminal in character." That inquiry depends upon whether Congress intended the forfeiture sanction to be criminal and, even if it did not, whether the sanction was so punitive in effect that it should be regarded as criminal. An examination of the legislative history led the Chief Justice to the conclusion that the sanction was intended by Congress to be civil. Congress labeled the forfeiture proceeding a proceeding in rem, not in personam. The forfeiture proceeding plays an important role in furthering the prophylactic purposes of the 1968 gun control legislation by discouraging unregulated commerce in firearms and by removing from circulation firearms that have been used or intended for use outside regulated channels of commerce. Keeping potentially dangerous weapons out of the hands of unlicensed dealers is a goal plainly more remedial than punitive.

465 U.S. at 364, 104 S.Ct. at 1106, 79 L.Ed.2d at 369. As to the effect of the sanction, the fact that the basis for the forfeiture was also made a crime does not resolve the question since "Congress may impose both a criminal and a civil sanction for the same act or omission." Further, the overlap is not complete since the forfeiture sanction included firearms intended for use in violation of the law as well as those in fact so used. Therefore, the forfeiture proceeding is in purpose and effect remedial, not punitive, and double jeopardy does not apply.

NOTE

Civil monetary penalties. In Hudson v. United States, 522 U.S. 93, 118 S.Ct. 488, 139 L.Ed.2d 450 (1997), the Court abandoned the approach it had taken in *Halper* in favor of a more traditional manner of determining multiple punishment double jeopardy questions regarding the relationship between criminal prosecutions and civil monetary penalties. Petitioner was a banker. The United States Department of the Treasury assessed a civil money penalty of $16,000 against him and entered an order of debarment from further employment in the banking business. Later, Hudson was prosecuted for criminal charges arising out of the conduct that gave rise to the money penalties and debarment order. He claimed double jeopardy under *Halper*, which claim was ultimately rejected by the United States Court of Appeals on the ground the monetary penalty was not so disproportional to the proven damages to the government as to render it a punishment under *Halper*. The Supreme Court, in an opinion by The Chief Justice, affirmed the Court of Appeals, but on a much broader ground.

Stating that *Halper* marked the first time the Court had applied the Double Jeopardy Clause to a sanction without determining that it was criminal and that subsequent cases have shown its test to be unworkable, the Court substituted a two-step process to replace the remedial analysis of *Halper*. First, did the legislature intend the sanction to be civil or criminal. In this case, the Court believed the evidence was clear that the Congress intended the monetary penalty and debarment to be civil sanctions. Second, if the legislature intended to create a civil penalty, did it in fact do so. Here the test (which was used by the Court in *Ursery*) is whether there is the "clearest proof" the sanctions are "so punitive in form and effect as to render them criminal despite" legislative intent. In addressing that question, the Court used some of the factors listed in *Kennedy v. Mendoza–Martinez*, 372 U.S. 144, 83 S.Ct. 554, 9 L.Ed.2d 644 (1963), a case involving forfeiture of U.S. citizenship for absence from the country to evade military service. The factors, which are to be used to assess the statute on its face, not as applied, are (1) whether the sanction has historically been regarded as punishment—in this case they have not; (2) whether the sanction involved an affirmative disability or restraint—while petitioner is debarred from further participation in the banking industry, that does not approach imprisonment in severity; (3) whether the sanction comes into play only upon a finding of scienter—neither the monetary penalty nor the debarment require a knowing violation of the law; (4) whether the behavior to which it applies is already a crime—it is here but that is not sufficient to raise a jeopardy bar to multiple proceedings; and (5) whether the operation of the sanction will promote the traditional aims of punishment, retribution and deterrence—the mere presence of a deterrence function does not convert the monetary penalty and debarment into criminal sanctions.

The Chief Justice's opinion was joined in by Justices O'Conner, Scalia, Kennedy, and Thomas. Justice Scalia, joined by Justice Thomas, concurred in the opinion but would go further to hold that protection against multiple punishment is not a purpose of the Double Jeopardy Clause. Justice Souter concurred in the judgment and joined in "much of [the Court's] opinion" but disputed the soundness of the requirement that the criminal nature of the sanction must be established by the "clearest proof." Similarly, Justice Breyer, joined by Justice Ginsburg, concurred in the judgment but did not join the Court's opinion on the requirements of "clearest proof" and that the statute be evaluated only on its face. Justice Stevens, concurring in the judgment, would have applied *Blockburger* to this case rather than use it as a vehicle for re-evaluating *Halper*.

Can you imagine a nominally civil sanction that would be held to be criminal under the factors as they are applied in *Hudson*?

CHAPTER 21

PRETRIAL HEARINGS AND RELATED MATTERS

Analysis

EDITORS' INTRODUCTION: THE PROCEDURAL CONTEXT OF PRETRIAL HEARINGS

There are at least two major considerations that affect provisions governing pretrial motion practice in criminal cases. The first is the federal constitutional right to have certain matters decided by the trial judge out of the presence of the jury, a matter addressed in the principal case in this chapter. This, of course, does not address the need to determine the matter *pretrial;* where the right to have a matter decided by the judge applies, it can be respected by halting trial, sending the jury out of the courtroom, and conducting the required inquiry at that time. The second consideration, however, is the administrative convenience of determining before trial those matters that can be addressed without inquiry into the defendant's guilt or innocence. A procedure that accomplishes this avoids the necessity for trial interruptions and the waste of having jurors and others merely sit idly by while matters other than guilt-or-innocence are being litigated. In addition, pretrial resolution of such matters as the admissibility of crucial evidence may encourage the parties to settle the case—as by entering into a plea agreement—and thus may make a contested trial unnecessary.

Several aspects of what has become known as pretrial motion practice should be explored before the constitutional problems presented by the principal case are addressed.

OBLIGATION TO RAISE MATTERS PRETRIAL

In a large number of jurisdictions, a defendant is, as a general rule, obligated to raise certain matters before trial. For example, Uniform Rules of Criminal Procedure 451(c) provides:

Unless otherwise ordered by the court for cause shown, a party may assert the following only in a pretrial motion . . . :

(1) Defenses and objections based on defects in the institution of the prosecution, other than the lack of jurisdiction of the court over the person or subject matter which can be raised at any time;

(2) Defenses and objections based on defects in the [charging instrument];

(3) Requests regarding discovery ... ;

(4) Requests that potential testimony or other evidence should be suppressed ... ;

(5) Requests for joinder, dismissal, or severance [under the Rules relating to joinder and severance]; and

(6) Requests for transfer of prosecution....

See also, F.R.Crim.P. 12(f). The Uniform Rules contemplate that a matter may be raised later "for cause shown," and reasonable unawareness of the bases for raising a matter is clearly "cause." But the Uniform Rules, in another section, require the prosecution to provide the defense with pretrial notice of its intention to use certain evidence at trial, including any confession, admission or statement made by the defendant, evidence obtained as a result of any such confession, admission, or statement, a search or seizure, wiretap, or any form of electronic surveillance or eavesdropping, and evidence relating to a lineup, showup, picture or voice identification of the defendant. Uniform Rules of Criminal Procedure 422(a)(1). Such notice, of course, would generally justify requiring matters concerning such evidence to be raised before trial.

DETERMINATION OF MATTERS RAISED BY PRETRIAL MOTION

Uniform Rules of Criminal Procedure 451(e) states what is widely-accepted practice, i.e., that matters raised before trial are to be resolved before trial on the merits, except where the trial judge determines that pretrial resolution of the matter would be "impractical." Issues concerning the Sixth Amendment right to speedy trial, for example, may require consideration of the effect of the delay upon the defense's ability effectively to contest the prosecution's case. A pretrial motion to dismiss on such grounds, then, might reasonably be resolved only after some or all of the evidence bearing upon guilt or innocence has been produced.

APPEAL

If a trial judge resolves a pretrial matter (or any other) in favor of the defendant and the defendant is—perhaps as a result—later acquitted, double jeopardy bars the prosecution from obtaining appellate relief. Despite the general reluctance to provide for interlocutory appeals in criminal cases, therefore, a number of jurisdictions have given the prosecution a limited right to appeal before trial from adverse decisions on pretrial matters. In federal prosecutions, for example, 18 U.S.C.A. § 3731 provides as follows:

An appeal by the United States shall lie to a court of appeals from a decision or order of a district court suppressing or excluding evidence ..., not made after the defendant has been put in jeopardy and before the verdict or finding on an indictment or information, if the United States attorney certifies to the district court that the appeal is not taken for purposes of delay and that the evidence is a substantial proof of a fact material in the proceeding.

Defendants are usually not authorized to pursue interlocutory appeals, primarily because they have access to appellate courts through an appeal from any conviction that may follow a determination of a pretrial matter. The rule that a guilty plea "forfeits" the right to complain of many matters, however, may sometimes encourage defendants to demand a full trial on the merits only to preserve rulings on pretrial motions as possible errors on appeal. To deal with this situation, some jurisdictions have enacted provisions permitting a defendant who pleads guilty to appeal on the basis of rulings on pretrial matters. N.Y.Criminal Procedure Law § 710.70(2), for example, provides:

> An order finally denying a motion to suppress evidence may be reviewed upon an appeal from an ensuing judgment of conviction notwithstanding the fact that such judgment is entered upon a plea of guilty.

FEDERAL CONSTITUTIONAL RIGHT TO PRETRIAL RESOLUTION OF CERTAIN MATTERS

The due process requirement considered in the principal case in this chapter does not appear to address the right to a *pretrial* resolution of those matters it covers. There is, however, some basis for believing that federal constitutional considerations may, in some limited situations, demand that state procedure provide for resolution before trial of matters by both trial and appellate courts. See Abney v. United States, 431 U.S. 651, 97 S.Ct. 2034, 52 L.Ed.2d 651 (1977), discussed in Chapter 20. In United States v. MacDonald, 435 U.S. 850, 98 S.Ct. 1547, 56 L.Ed.2d 18 (1978), however, the Court held that an order denying a motion to dismiss made on Sixth Amendment speedy trial grounds was not an appealable order under the federal statute, implying, of course, that there is no federal constitutional right to an interlocutory appeal from such an order.

OMNIBUS HEARING PROPOSALS

Among proposals for giving pretrial motion practice more structure, in hopes of increasing efficiency as well as of assuring that all relevant matters are addressed, perhaps the most prominent is the suggestion of the American Bar Association's Project on Standards for Criminal Justice for an "omnibus hearing" in all cases in which a plea of not guilty is entered. A.B.A. Project on Standards for Criminal Justice, Standards Relating to Discovery and Procedure Before Trial §§ 5.2(b), 5.3 (Approved Draft 1970). Motions and similar requests should be made at or before this hearing. At the hearing, the trial court, using "an appropriate check-list form," is to assure that representation and discovery have been provided, rule on motions and other requests for relief or action, and ascertain whether there are any other procedural or constitutional issues which should be considered. Id., at § 5.3(a). Former Supreme Court Justice Tom C. Clark described the objective of the proposal as follows:

> The omnibus hearing ... is designed to facilitate the speedy and just disposition of cases. Trials may be eliminated or substantially shortened by the hearing, for prosecutors and defense counsel are encouraged to meet and lay all their cards on the table....
>
> The omnibus hearing is also designed to flush out constitutional issues as well as other questions in dispute and to resolve them before trial rather than in the middle of trial when the jury would have to cool its heels while the matter is settled. By using the omnibus hearing, the issues are considerably sharpened and narrowed when the trial begins, the proceedings are shortened, and the likelihood of a subsequent appeal is reduced.

Clark, The Omnibus Hearing in State and Federal Courts, 59 Cornell L.Rev. 761, 765 (1974). Some reports have indicated less optimism. See e.g., R. Nimmer, The Omnibus Hearing: An Experiment in Relieving Inefficiency, Unfairness and Judicial Delay (1971).

Watkins v. Sowders

Supreme Court of the United States, 1981.
449 U.S. 341, 101 S.Ct. 654, 66 L.Ed.2d 549.

■ JUSTICE STEWART delivered the opinion of the Court.

These cases, consolidated for argument and decision in the Court of Appeals and in this Court, present the question whether a state criminal trial court is constitutionally compelled to conduct a hearing outside the presence of the jury whenever a defendant contends that a witness' identification of him was arrived at improperly.

I.

A.

John Watkins, the petitioner in No. 79–5949, was convicted in a Kentucky court of attempting to rob a Louisville liquor store. On the night of January 11, 1975, four men entered the store, one of whom asked for a pack of cigarettes. Walter Smith, an employee of the store, turned around to get the cigarettes, and one of the men said, "This is a hold-up." Donald Goeing, a part-owner of the store, had been stocking a soft-drink cooler, and when he heard those words, he turned towards the robbers. The man who had spoken thereupon fired two shots at him, one striking him in his arm, the other in the region of his heart. The four men then fled.

That night Smith and Goeing described the gunman to the police. Two days later, the police in the presence of Smith conducted a lineup consisting of three men, one of whom was Watkins. Smith identified Watkins as the gunman. That same day, the police took Watkins to Goeing's hospital bed, and Goeing identified Watkins as the man who had shot him. Watkins was then charged with first-degree robbery and first-degree assault.

At the subsequent trial of Watkins, the prosecution called Smith and Goeing as witnesses. They both identified Watkins as Goeing's assailant but were not asked by the prosecution about the lineup or the showup. Watkins' counsel, however, cross-examined both men at some length about both the lineup and showup. The prosecution then called a police officer. He testified that he had taken Watkins to be identified at the hospital because "at that time there was some question as to whether or not Mr. Goeing was going to survive the incident." Watkins' counsel cross-examined the officer about both the showup and the lineup and through him introduced pictures of the lineup. For the defense, Watkins' counsel called two witnesses who said that they had been in a pool hall with Watkins at the time of the robbery and another witness who said he had been in the liquor store at the time of the robbery and had not seen Watkins. Finally, Watkins himself testified to his innocence.

On appeal, as he had at trial, counsel for Watkins argued that the trial court had a constitutional obligation to conduct a hearing outside the presence of the jury to determine whether the identification evidence was admissible. The Supreme Court of Kentucky rejected that argument. . . . The court [also] found that the identification procedures "fail[ed] to raise any impermissible suggestiveness" and that Watkins "was in no way prejudiced." Watkins v. Kentucky, 565 S.W.2d 630, 631.

Watkins then unsuccessfully sought a writ of habeas corpus in the United States District Court for the Western District of Kentucky.

* * *

The Court of Appeals for the Sixth Circuit affirmed the District Court's judgment and, like the District Court, ruled that a hearing on the admissibility of identification evidence need not be held outside the presence of the jury. Turning to the evidence itself, the court cited Stovall v. Denno, 388 U.S. 293, 87 S.Ct. 1967, 18 L.Ed.2d 1199, as authority for holding that "given the seriousness of the wounds to Donald Goeing, a showup was necessary in this case." Summitt v. Bordenkircher, 608 F.2d 247, 251. The federal appellate court also held that the lineup evidence had been constitutionally admissible at the state trial.

B.

James Summitt, the petitioner in No. 79–5951, was convicted in a Kentucky court of rape. Late on the night of July 20, 1974, the prosecutrix was forced into a car occupied by two men, driven to an isolated location, raped by one of the men, and then returned to her own car. The next day she reported the crime to the police, described the rapist, and looked through 12 volumes of photographs from police files, without identifying the man who had raped her. Two days later she was taken to another police station, where she examined more pictures. A police officer testified at the subsequent trial of Summitt that "after a short time she pointed to the defendant's picture and said, 'This is the man that raped me. There's no doubt about it, this is Jimbo, the man that raped me.'" In addition to the officer, the prosecutrix and her stepfather as witnesses for the prosecution described the prosecutrix's examination of the police photographs, and the prosecutrix testified that Summitt was the man who had raped her. There was extensive cross-examination.

The Supreme Court of Kentucky found "no error in the trial court's refusal to conduct a suppression hearing and no semblance of impermissible suggestiveness in the identification procedure." 550 S.W.2d 548, 550. Summitt then sought a writ of habeas corpus in the United States District Court for the Western District of Kentucky, but that court found no constitutional error. The Court of Appeals, as in the consolidated *Watkins* case, affirmed the judgment of the District Court, 608 F.2d 247.

We granted certiorari to consider the constitutional claim asserted by both petitioners throughout their state and federal court proceedings. 445 U.S. 962, 100 S.Ct. 1312, 63 L.Ed.2d 759.

II.

The issue before us is not, of course, whether a trial court acts prudently in holding a hearing out of the presence of the jury to determine the admissibility of identification evidence. The prudence of such a hearing has been emphasized by many decisions in the Courts of Appeals, most of which have in various ways admonished trial courts to use that procedure. The issue here, rather, is whether such a hearing is required by the Due Process Clause of the Fourteenth Amendment.

In urging an affirmative answer, the petitioners first cite cases holding that a defendant has a right to the presence of his counsel at a post-indictment lineup, e.g., United States v. Wade, 388 U.S. 218, 87 S.Ct. 1926, 18 L.Ed.2d 1149, and that an identification procedure, in the absence of a lineup, may be so defective as to deprive a defendant of due process of law, e.g., Stovall v. Denno, 388 U.S. 293, 87 S.Ct. 1967, 18 L.Ed.2d 1199. The petitioners then analogize their cases to Jackson v. Denno, 378 U.S. 368, 84 S.Ct. 1774, 12 L.Ed.2d 908, in which this Court enunciated a defendant's right "to have a fair hearing and a reliable determination on the issue of voluntariness," id., at 377, 84 S.Ct., at 1781, and in which the Court declared unconstitutional a New York procedure which gave the jury what was in practice unreviewable discretion to decide whether a confession was or was not voluntary.

The petitioners contend that Jackson v. Denno established a *per se* due process right to a hearing outside the presence of the jury whenever a question of the voluntariness of a confession is raised. If such a hearing is required where the voluntariness of a confession is at issue, it follows, the petitioners argue, that a similar hearing must also be required where the propriety of identification procedures has been questioned.

Even if it be assumed that Jackson v. Denno did establish the *per se* rule asserted,[1] the petitioners' argument must fail, because Jackson v. Denno is not analogous to the cases now before us. The Court in *Jackson* did reject the usual presumption that a jury can be relied upon to determine issues according to the trial judge's instructions, but the Court did so because of the peculiar problems the issue of the voluntariness of a

---

1. See Pinto v. Pierce, 389 U.S. 31, 32, 88 S.Ct. 192, 193, 19 L.Ed.2d 31:

"This Court has never ruled that all voluntariness hearings must be held outside the presence of the jury, regardless of the circumstances.... [B]ecause a disputed confession may be found involuntary and inadmissible by the judge, it would seem prudent to hold voluntariness hearings outside the presence of the jury.... In this case, however, the confession was held voluntary and admitted as evidence suitable for consideration by the jury."

confession presents. The Court pointed out that, while an involuntary confession is inadmissible in part because such a confession is likely to be unreliable, it is also inadmissible even if it is true, because of the " 'strongly felt attitude of our society that important human values are sacrificed where an agency of the government, in the course of securing a conviction, wrings a confession out of an accused against his will.' "378 U.S., at 385, 84 S.Ct., at 1785, quoting Blackburn v. Alabama, 361 U.S. 199, 206–207, 80 S.Ct. 274, 279, 4 L.Ed.2d 242. The Court concluded in *Jackson* that a jury "may find it difficult to understand the policy forbidding reliance upon a coerced, but true confession.... Objective consideration of the conflicting evidence concerning the circumstances of the confession becomes difficult and the [jury's] implicit findings become suspect." Id., 378 U.S., at 382, 84 S.Ct., at 1783.

Where identification evidence is at issue, however, no such special considerations justify a departure from the presumption that juries will follow instructions. It is the reliability of identification evidence that primarily determines its admissibility, Manson v. Brathwaite, 432 U.S. 98, 113–114, 97 S.Ct. 2243, 2252, 53 L.Ed.2d 140; United States ex rel. Kirby v. Sturges, 510 F.2d 397, 402–404 (C.A.7 1975) (Stevens, J.). And the proper evaluation of evidence under the instructions of the trial judge is the very task our system must assume juries can perform. Indeed, as the cases before us demonstrate, the *only* duty of a jury in cases in which identification evidence has been admitted will often be to assess the reliability of that evidence. Thus the Court's opinion in Manson v. Brathwaite approvingly quoted Judge Leventhal's statement that,

> " '[w]hile identification testimony is significant evidence, such testimony is still only evidence, and, unlike the presence of counsel, is not a factor that goes to the very heart'—the "integrity"—of the adversary process.

> " 'Counsel can both cross-examine the identification witnesses and argue in summation as to factors causing doubts as to the accuracy of the identification—including reference to both any suggestibility in the identification procedure and any countervailing testimony such as alibi.' " 432 U.S. 98, 114, n. 14, 97 S.Ct. 2243, 2253 n. 14, quoting Clemons v. United States, 133 U.S.App.D.C. 27, 48, 408 F.2d 1230, 1251 (1968) (concurring opinion) (footnote omitted).

The petitioners argue, however, that cross-examination is inadequate in cases such as these. They assert that the presence of the jury deterred their lawyers from cross-examining the witnesses vigorously and fully as to the possible improprieties of the pretrial identifications in these cases. The petitioners point to no specific instances in the trial when their counsel were thus deterred, and the record reveals that the cross-examination on the identity issues was, if not always effective, both active and extended. Nonetheless, the petitioners rely on a passage from United States v. Wade, supra, which referred to

> "the predicament in which Wade's counsel found himself—realizing that possible unfairness at the lineup may be the sole means of attack upon the unequivocal courtroom identification, and having to probe in the dark in an attempt to discover and reveal unfairness, while

bolstering the government witness' courtroom identification by bring-ing out and dwelling upon his prior identification." 388 U.S., at 241, 87 S.Ct., at 1939.

The petitioners, however, attribute undue significance to this passage. The "predicament" described in *Wade* was no more than part of the Court's demonstration that, if identification stemming from an improperly conducted lineup was to be excluded, a courtroom identification based on such a lineup logically had to be excluded as well.

A "predicament," if one chooses to call it that, is always presented when a lawyer decides on cross-examination to ask a question that may produce an answer unfavorable to his client. Yet, under our adversary system of justice, cross-examination has always been considered a most effective way to ascertain truth. We decline in these cases to hold that the Due Process Clause of the Fourteenth Amendment inevitably requires the abandonment of the time-honored process of cross-examination as the device best suited to determine the trustworthiness of testimonial evidence.

A judicial determination outside the presence of the jury of the admis-sibility of identification evidence may often be advisable. In some circum-stances, not presented here, such a determination may be constitutionally necessary. But it does not follow that the Constitution requires a *per se* rule compelling such a procedure in every case.

Accordingly, the judgments are

Affirmed.

■ JUSTICE BRENNAN, with whom JUSTICE MARSHALL joins, dissenting.

* * *

Any purported distinction between the instant cases and *Jackson* is plainly specious. In *Jackson,* this Court invalidated a New York State procedure whereby the jury was instructed first to determine the voluntari-ness of a defendant's confession and then to disregard the confession if it concluded that the confession was involuntary. *Jackson* struck down this practice and required first that the voluntariness of a confession be determined by the judge before its admission in evidence, and second that the jury not be allowed to consider an inadmissible confession. *Jackson* refused to rely on the curative effect of jury instructions where the trial judge had not applied " 'the exclusionary rules before permitting evidence to be submitted to the jury.' " 378 U.S., at 382, n. 10, 84 S.Ct., at 1783, n. 10, quoting Meltzer, Involuntary Confessions: The Allocation of Responsi-bility Between Judge and Jury, 21 U.Chi.L.Rev. 317, 327 (1954).

For purposes of the instant cases, three factors central to our decision in *Jackson* are apposite. First, *Jackson* stated, as the Court today notes, "that the Fourteenth Amendment forbids the use of involuntary confes-sions ... because of the probable unreliability of confessions that are obtained in a manner deemed coercive." Second, *Jackson* stated, as the Court today further notes, that involuntary confessions are inadmissible "because of the 'strongly felt attitude of our society that important human values are sacrificed where an agency of the government, in the course of securing a conviction, wrings a confession out of an accused against his will.' " Third, because of the sensitive nature of confession evidence, *Jackson* found that instructions were not adequate to assure that the jury would ignore involuntary confession evidence:

"Under the New York procedure, the fact of a defendant's confession is solidly implanted in the jury's mind, for it has not only heard the confession, but it has also been instructed to consider and judge its voluntariness and is in position to assess whether it is true or false. If it finds the confession involuntary, does the jury—indeed, can it—then disregard the confession in accordance with its instructions? If there are lingering doubts about the sufficiency of the other evidence, does the jury unconsciously lay them to rest by resort to the confession? Will uncertainty about the sufficiency of the other evidence to prove guilt beyond a reasonable doubt actually result in acquittal when the jury knows the defendant has given a truthful confession?" 378 U.S., at 388, 84 S.Ct., at 1786 (footnote omitted).

Similar considerations plainly require a hearing in the case of identification evidence. First, there can be little doubt that identification evidence is as potentially unreliable as confession evidence. Second, suggestive confrontation procedures which, in the totality of circumstances, create " 'a very substantial likelihood of irreparable misidentification,' "are as impermissible a police practice as the securing of a custodial confession determined, in the totality of the circumstances, to be involuntary. And third, because of the extraordinary impact of much eyewitness identification evidence, juries hearing such evidence will be no more able fully to ignore it upon instruction of the trial judge than will juries hearing confession evidence. To expect a jury to engage in the collective mental gymnastic of segregating and ignoring such testimony upon instruction is utterly unrealistic. The Court's bald assertion, therefore, that jury instructions are adequate to protect the accused, is as untrue for identification evidence as it is for involuntary confessions.

Nor can it be assumed, as the Court has, that cross-examination will protect the accused in this circumstance. That is no more true here than it was in *Jackson,* where the defendant was also allowed to cross-examine on the question of voluntariness. Cross-examination, of course, affects the weight and credibility given by the jury to evidence, but cross-examination is both an ineffective and a wrong tool for purging inadmissible identification evidence from the jurors' minds. It is an ineffective tool because all of the scientific evidence suggests that much eyewitness identification testimony has an unduly powerful effect on jurors. Thus, the jury is likely to give the erroneously admitted evidence substantial weight, however skillful the cross-examination. Cross-examination is also a wrong tool in the sense that jury instructions are the means normally employed to cure the erroneous introduction of evidence. At best, cross-examination might diminish the weight the jury accords to the inadmissible evidence. The likelihood is, however, that the jury would continue to give the improperly admitted evidence substantial weight, even if properly instructed to disregard it.

* * *

In the instant cases, the suggestiveness of the confrontation procedures was clearly shown, and equally clearly cross-examination in front of the jury was inadequate to test the reliability of the evidence because of the undoubted inhibiting effect on cross-examination from fear that rigorous questioning of hostile witnesses would strengthen the eyewitnesses' testimony and impress it upon the jury. In any event, the record is inadequate to decide that petitioners could not have succeeded in foreclosing admission of the evidence if they had been afforded a hearing out of the jury's presence in the first place. Accordingly, I would remand for such further proceedings as are necessary to give these petitioners "a fair hearing and a reliable determination," Jackson v. Denno, supra, 378 U.S., at 377, 84 S.Ct., at 1781, that the identification evidence in each trial was not erroneously admitted.

NOTES

1. **Magistrate-judge relationship in pretrial determinations.** What role should—or must—the trial judge play in resolving issues raised by attacks upon the admissibility of evidence? The Federal Magistrates Act, 28 U.S.C.A. § 631 et seq. authorizes a federal District Judge to designate a magistrate to conduct hearings on motions to suppress evidence and to submit to the judge proposed findings of fact and recommended dispositions of the motions. Any party may file objections. The judge is then to "make a de novo determination" of those portions of the recommendations or proposed findings to which objection has been made. The judge may receive further evidence.

In United States v. Raddatz, 447 U.S. 667, 100 S.Ct. 2406, 65 L.Ed.2d 424 (1980), the defendant filed a motion to suppress his confession, alleging that it was made in return for an agreement that certain federal charges would be dismissed. At a hearing before a magistrate, he testified that such a promise had been made; the federal agents involved in the investigation testified that no such promises had been made. The magistrate submitted a proposed finding that no promise to dismiss charges had been made and a recommendation that the motion be denied. Over the defendant's objections, the District Court accepted the magistrate's recommendation and denied the motion.

The Supreme Court affirmed. The statute, concluded the majority, does not require that the District Court conduct a de novo *hearing* on contested aspects of the magistrate's proposed conclusions. In making the de novo *determination* directed by the statute, the court may rely upon the transcript of the testimony taken before the magistrate. Further, this does not offend due process. Defendants' interests at stake in a suppression hearing are "of a lesser magnitude" than those involved in trial, and the process that is due in the former context is therefore less demanding and elaborate. Finally, since the ultimate decision remains with the District Court, the statute does not offend a defendant's right to a determination of the matter by an Article III judge.

Justice Marshall, joined by Justice Brennan, dissented, urging that due process requires that the District Court conduct an evidentiary hearing whenever there are case-dispositive issues that cannot be resolved on the basis of the record developed in the hearing before the magistrate. Further, where resolution of an issue depends—as it did in the instant case—upon the credibility of the witnesses, the record does not permit resolution of it. In explanation, Justice Marshall urged that resolution of such matters on the basis of an inadequate record creates "an intolerably high risk of error." Further, "as a matter of basic fairness, a person facing the prospect of grievous loss is entitled to relate his version of the facts to the official entrusted with judging its accuracy." 444 U.S. at 696, 100 S.Ct. at 2423, 65 L.Ed.2d at 446. In addition, Justice Marshall regarded the majority's approach as functionally entrusting decision on such matters to magistrates, in violation of defendants' Article III right to a determination of such matters by an Article III judge. Justice Stewart, joined by Justices Brennan and Marshall, dissented on the ground that the Federal Magistrates Act required the result reached by Justice Marshall on constitutional grounds. 447 U.S. at 689–90, 100 S.Ct. at 2419, 65 L.Ed.2d at 441–42. Justice Powell concurred in the majority's reading of the statute as conferring broad discretion on the district courts as to whether or not to rehear evidence in these cases. But he further dissented from the majority's unwillingness to find that in cases such as the one before the court where the outcome of the hearing depends entirely upon an assessment of the credibility of the witnesses that due process requires the court to rehear crucial witnesses. 447 U.S. at 686, 100 S.Ct. at 2418, 65 L.Ed.2d at 440.

2. **Applicability of rules of evidence to admissibility hearings.** Must—and should—the rules of evidence be applied in hearings on the admissibility of evidence challenged on constitutional grounds? In United States v. Matlock, 415 U.S. 164, 94 S.Ct. 988, 39 L.Ed.2d 242 (1974) the government, in an effort to establish that one Gayle Graff had authority to consent to a search of a bedroom, offered testimony that Graff had told officers before the search that she and the defendant occupied the bedroom at issue. The trial judge applied the hearsay rule and excluded the evidence. This was held to have been error. In such hearings, the Court concluded, the rules of evidence applicable in criminal trials do not operate with "full force" and there should be no automatic rule excluding all hearsay. On the facts of the case, there was no doubt that Graff had in fact made the statements. Nothing in the record suggested doubt as to their accuracy. Moreover, they constituted an admission of cohabitation out of wedlock by Graff (a crime in the jurisdiction) and therefore were admissions against her penal interest which carried their own "indicia of reliability." Graff had testified at the hearing and thus was available for cross-examination. Consequently, they should have been admitted and considered by the trial judge. 415 U.S. at 172–77, 94 S.Ct. at 994–96, 39 L.Ed.2d at 250–53. Lower courts have assumed that the rules of evidence do not apply at hearings on motions to suppress. E.g., United States v. Killebrew, 594 F.2d 1103 (6th Cir.1979), cert. denied 442 U.S. 933, 99 S.Ct. 2867, 61 L.Ed.2d 302.

3. **Burden of proof in admissibility hearings.** The burden of proof at hearings on the admissibility of evidence and similar matters is not entirely clear. In Lego v. Twomey, 404 U.S. 477, 92 S.Ct. 619, 30 L.Ed.2d 618 (1972) the Court held that in a hearing on the voluntariness of a confession, the prosecution must establish voluntariness by a preponderance of the evidence. Rejecting the argument that proof beyond a reasonable doubt should be required, the Court noted no indication that admissibility rulings have been unreliable or found "otherwise wanting" because not based on a standard requiring more than proof by a preponderance of the evidence. In Miranda v. Arizona, 384 U.S. 436, 475, 86 S.Ct. 1602, 1628, 16 L.Ed.2d 694, 724 (1966), the Court commented that when a confession is obtained during interrogation without the presence of an attorney, "a heavy burden" is placed on the government to demonstrate a knowing and intelligent waiver of the right to counsel and the privilege against self-incrimination.

In hearings on Fourth Amendment claims, the lower courts have tended to distribute the burden of proof variously, depending upon the specific issue. The defendant, as the moving party, has been held to have the burden of establishing that a "search" within Fourth Amendment meaning took place. United States v. Freeland, 562 F.2d 383 (6th Cir.1977), cert. denied 434 U.S. 957, 98 S.Ct. 484, 54 L.Ed.2d 315 (1977) (defendant had burden of showing sufficient governmental involvement in luggage examination to render it a "search"). Once a warrantless search has been demonstrated, other cases hold, the prosecution has the burden of establishing the "reasonableness" of the search. E.g., United States v. Lee, 541 F.2d 1145 (5th Cir.1976). Where the prosecution's theory is that the defendant consented to the search or seizure, some cases hold, the prosecution has the burden of proving an effective consent. United States v. Williams, 604 F.2d 1102 (8th Cir.1979). Where articulated consent is shown, however, and the defendant claims that it is ineffective because it was procured by fraud or misrepresentations, some cases hold that the defendant has the burden of showing that such fraud or misrepresentations existed. United States v. Meier, 607 F.2d 215 (8th Cir.1979), cert. denied 445 U.S. 966, 100 S.Ct. 1658, 64 L.Ed.2d 243 (1980). In United States v. Matlock, 415 U.S. 164, 177 n. 14, 94 S.Ct. 988, 996 n. 14, 39 L.Ed.2d 242, 253 n. 14 (1974) the Supreme Court found no occasion to consider whether the trial judge had erred in requiring the prosecution to prove a valid consent by the greater weight of the evidence. Where the prosecution claims that despite an unlawful search or seizure challenged evidence is nevertheless admissible because of an exception to the exclusionary rule (such as "dissipation of taint" or "inevitable legitimate discovery"), under other lower court decisions, the prosecution has the burden of proving the factual foundation for its claim. United States v. Brookins, 614 F.2d 1037 (5th Cir.1980).

4. **Trial use of admissibility hearing testimony.** When, if ever, may a defendant's testimony at a hearing out of the presence of the jury be used against the defendant on the trial of guilt or innocence? In Simmons v. United States, 390 U.S. 377, 88 S.Ct. 967, 19 L.Ed.2d 1247 (1968) the defendant was charged with robbery of a bank. Prior to trial, he filed a motion to suppress certain evidence (a gun holster, a sack similar to one used in the robbery, and coin cards and bill wrappers from the robbed bank) which had been seized in a search of a suitcase. In order to establish his "standing" to contest the search of the suitcase, he took the witness stand at the hearing on his motion and testified that the suitcase was similar to one he had owned and that clothing found in the suitcase was his. His motion was overruled; at trial, the government introduced against him his testimony at the suppression hearing, which tended to connect him with the evidence seized in the search. The Court of Appeals affirmed the resulting conviction, but the Supreme Court reversed:

> The rule adopted by the courts below does not merely impose upon a defendant a condition which may deter him from asserting a Fourth Amendment objection—it imposed a condition of a kind to which this Court has always been particularly sensitive. For a defendant who wishes to establish standing must do so at the risk that the words he utters may later be used to incriminate him. Those courts which have allowed the admission of testimony given to establish standing have reasoned that there is no violation of the Fifth Amendment's Self–Incrimination Clause because the testimony was voluntary. ...However, the assumption which underlies this reasoning is that the defendant has a choice: he may refuse to testify and give up the benefit. When this assumption is applied to a situation in which the "benefit" to be gained is that afforded by another provision of the Bill of Rights, an undeniable tension is created. Thus, in this case [the defendant] was obliged either to give up what he believed, with advice of counsel, to be a valid Fourth Amendment claim or, in legal effect, to waive his Fifth Amendment privilege against self-incrimination. In these circumstances, we find it intolerable that one constitutional right should have to be surrendered in order to assert another. We therefore hold that when a defendant testifies in support of a motion to suppress evidence on Fourth Amendment grounds, his testimony may not thereafter be admitted against him at trial on the issue of guilt unless he makes no objection.

390 U.S. at 393–94, 88 S.Ct. at 976, 19 L.Ed.2d at 1258–59. But suppose the defendant had taken the stand and testified at trial that neither the suitcase nor its contents belonged to him? Would his testimony at the motion to suppress have then been admissible to impeach his trial testimony? Consider Harris v. New York, 401 U.S. 222, 91 S.Ct. 643, 28 L.Ed.2d 1 (1971)(holding that a custodial statement that was inadmissible under Miranda v. Arizona in the State's case-in-chief at trial could if trustworthy be admitted on rebuttal to impeach defendant's contradictory testimony).

In United States v. Kahan, 415 U.S. 239, 94 S.Ct. 1179, 39 L.Ed.2d 297 (1974), Kahan, a former immigrations inspector, was charged with improperly receiving gratuities for official acts and with perjury. He requested appointment of an attorney and, at his arraignment, he responded to a direct question as to whether he had funds to employ an attorney by claiming indigency and without disclosing that he had access to and control over four savings accounts in which he had deposited approximately $27,000. At trial, evidence concerning his deposits in these accounts (which exceeded his reported income for the period) was admitted as tending to show that he had improperly received substantial money as charged in the indictment. The government was also permitted to show his statements to the court as to his lack of funds; these were admitted as false exculpatory statements indicating his awareness that the bank deposits were incriminating and as evidence of willfulness in making statements before the grand jury with knowledge of their falsity. He was convicted and the Supreme Court found no constitutional error:

> Even assuming that the *Simmons* principle [can be] appropriately extended to Sixth Amendment claims for appointed counsel . . . , a question which we do not now decide . . . , that principle cannot be applied to protect respondent here. *Simmons* barred the use of pretrial testimony at trial to prove its incriminating content. Here, by contrast, the incriminating component of respondent's pretrial statements derives not from their content, but from respondent's knowledge of their falsity. The truth of the matter was that respondent was not indigent, and did not have a right to appointment of counsel under the Sixth Amendment. We are not dealing, as was the Court in *Simmons,* with what was "believed" by the claimant to be a "valid" constitutional claim. . . . Respondent was not, therefore, faced with the type of intolerable choice *Simmons* sought to relieve. The protective shield of *Simmons* is not to be converted into a license for false representations on the issue of indigency free from the risk that the claimant will be held accountable for his falsehood. Cf. Harris v. New York, 401 U.S. 222, 226, 91 S.Ct. 643, 646, 28 L.Ed.2d 1 (1971).

415 U.S. at 243, 94 S.Ct. at 1181, 39 L.Ed.2d at 301.

5. **Relationship of voluntariness to reliability.** Can a confession be voluntary and unreliable? Is there a constitutional right to present to a jury evidence bearing on the reliability of a confession despite a trial court ruling that the confession is voluntary? In Crane v. Kentucky, 476 U.S. 683, 106 S.Ct. 2142, 90 L.Ed.2d 636 (1986), petitioner's confession was the principal evidence against him in his murder trial. The trial court had heard evidence at a pretrial hearing that the confession had been coerced but found it to have been voluntarily given. The 16–year–old petitioner had testified that he had been detained in a windowless room for a protracted period of time, that he had been surrounded by as many as six police officers during the questioning, that he had repeatedly requested and been denied permission to telephone his mother, and that he had been badgered into making a false confession. Several police officers testified in contradiction. At trial, the defense attempted to present to the jury the same evidence it had presented at the suppression hearing, but the trial court ruled the evidence inadmissible. Petitioner was convicted of murder and his conviction was affirmed by the Kentucky Supreme

Court. The United States Supreme Court, in an opinion authored by Justice O'Connor for a unanimous Court, reversed. Justice O'Connor stated,

> the circumstances surrounding the taking of a confession can be highly relevant to two separate inquiries, one legal and one factual. The manner in which a statement was extracted is, of course, relevant to the purely legal question of its voluntariness, a question most, but not all, States assign to the trial judge alone to resolve. . . . But the physical and psychological environment that yielded the confession can also be of substantial relevance to the ultimate factual issue of the defendant's guilt or innocence. Confessions, even those that have been found to be voluntary, are not conclusive of guilt. And, as with any other part of the prosecutor's case, a confession may be shown to be "insufficiently corroborated or otherwise . . . unworthy of belief." Lego v. Twomey. . . . Indeed, stripped of the power to describe to the jury the circumstances that prompted his confession, the defendant is effectively disabled from answering the one question every rational juror needs answered: If the defendant is innocent, why did he previously admit his guilt? Accordingly, regardless of whether the defendant marshaled the same evidence earlier in support of an unsuccessful motion to suppress, and entirely independent of any question of voluntariness, a defendant's case may stand or fall on his ability to convince the jury that the manner in which the confession was obtained casts doubt on its credibility.

476 U.S. at 688–89, 106 S.Ct. at 2145–46, 90 L.Ed.2d at 644. Excluding this evidence under the circumstances of this case deprived the petitioner of his constitutional right to be heard in his own defense.

CHAPTER 22

ADJUDICATION OF GUILT BY PLEA

Analysis

The vast majority of criminal convictions are based upon pleas of guilty and nolo contendere rather than contested proceedings culminating in a finding of guilt by a judge or jury. Probably 90% of convictions for serious offenses are obtained in this manner; if misdemeanors are included, the figure approaches 98%. See Newman, Reshape the Deal, 9 Trial 11 (May/June 1973).

For formal purposes of the criminal justice system, the difference between the guilty plea and the plea of nolo contendere is minimal. Both lead to conviction, and the requirements for entry of a guilty plea generally apply as well to the nolo plea. Technically, the nolo plea is not an admission of guilt but an indication of the defendant's willingness to give up the opportunity to contest the allegation. Therefore, traditionally it could not be used in later civil proceedings against the defendant as an admission. III ABA Standards for Criminal Justice 14–10. Nevertheless, some believe that there are sound reasons for limiting use of the nolo plea. A United States Department of Justice memorandum directs United States Attorneys to oppose entry of a plea of nolo contendere unless the Assistant Attorney General with supervisory responsibility over the subject matter has approved acceptance of the plea. U.S. Department of Justice, Materials Relating to Prosecutorial Discretion, 24 Crim.L.Rptr. 3001, 3006 (Nov. 22, 1978). In explanation, the memorandum quoted a prior departmental directive:

> One of the factors which has tended to breed contempt for federal law enforcement in recent times has been the practice of permitting as a matter of course in many criminal indictments the plea of nolo contendere.... Uncontrolled use of the plea has led to shockingly low sentences and insignificant fines which are no deterrent to crime....
> [A] person permitted to plead nolo contendere admits guilt for purposes of imposing punishment for his acts and yet, for all other purposes, and as far as the public is concerned, persists in his denial of wrongdoing. It is no wonder that the public regards consent to such a plea by the Government as an admission that it has only a technical case at most and that the whole proceeding was just a fiasco.

Id. The memo also notes that should the Government later seek civil sanctions against the defendant, use of the nolo plea might require the Government to expend valuable resources in proving the same facts as were at issue in the criminal case. Id. In examining the following materials, consider whether the same requirements should be applied to nolo pleas and pleas of guilty.

The issues concerning guilty pleas are pervasively influenced by the practice of plea bargaining, which is considered in the third section of this chapter. However, attention is initially addressed to two matters presented by all guilty pleas, whether the result of plea bargaining or not. First, the procedure necessary for entry of a plea and judgment of conviction is considered. Second, the effect of the plea upon the defendant's later ability to raise certain procedural issues related to the charge and conviction is explored.

A.   ENTRY OF THE PLEA OF GUILTY

EDITORS' INTRODUCTION: STRUCTURES FOR PLEA ACCEPTANCE

The procedural aspects for the acceptance of guilty and *nolo* pleas are increasingly covered by detailed statutory provisions. Many of these statutes are based upon several model formulations. See III American Bar Association Standards for Criminal Justice, Standards 14–1.1 et seq. (the "ABA Standards"); Uniform Rules of Criminal Procedure 444. Federal practice is governed primarily by Fed.R.Crim.P. 11, reprinted in this section. Several aspects of the largely-statutory framework in which pleas are entered require preliminary consideration here. However, a number of federal constitutional concerns are raised by the guilty plea process and convictions based upon pleas. These are the subject of the Supreme Court decisions discussed in this section. Because the major constitutional issues, regarding "voluntariness" for example, are created by plea bargaining, rather than plea acceptance, they are presented primarily in the final section of this chapter.

Entry of the Plea

Several aspects of the procedural requirements often imposed upon the plea acceptance process can be usefully distinguished. First, the trial judge is generally directed by "admonition requirements" to specifically inform the defendant of certain matters before the plea is accepted. Second, the judge may be required to inquire as to certain matters, such as the existence of a plea bargain and any promises that have been made to the defendant. Third, the judge may be required to make certain findings of fact relating to the voluntariness of the offered plea and similar matters before accepting it. This is closely related to the requirement of a "factual basis" for the plea, considered below. Fourth, it may be necessary that a formal record of the proceedings be made. ABA Standard 14–1.7, for example, would require a verbatim record of the proceedings, including the admonitions and the inquiries demanded of the trial judge.

The Supreme Court rigorously applied Rule 11 in McCarthy v. United States, 394 U.S. 459, 89 S.Ct. 1166, 22 L.Ed.2d 418 (1969). McCarthy pleaded guilty to willfully and knowingly attempting to evade federal tax payments. At sentencing, his attorney urged that his failure to pay the taxes had not been deliberate and was the result of negligent bookkeeping during a time when McCarthy had a drinking problem. The trial judge had not complied with Rule 11's requirement that he personally address the defendant and determine that he understand the nature of the charge. The Government argued that since McCarthy stated a desire to plead guilty and was informed of the consequences of his plea, the trial court could assume he understood the charges. Rejecting this, the Court explained:

> We cannot accept this argument which completely ignores the two purposes of Rule 11.... First, although the procedure embodied in Rule 11 has not been held to be constitutionally mandated, it is designed to assist the district judge in making the constitutionally required determination that a defendant's guilty plea is truly voluntary. Second, the Rule is intended to produce a complete record at the time the plea is entered of the factors relevant to this voluntariness determination. Thus, the more meticulously the Rule is adhered to, the more it tends to discourage, or at least to enable more expeditious disposition of, the numerous and often frivolous post-conviction attacks on the constitutional validity of guilty pleas.

... By personally interrogating the defendant, not only will the judge be better able to ascertain the plea's voluntariness, but he also will develop a more complete record to support his determination in a subsequent post-conviction attack.

These two purposes have their genesis in the nature of a guilty plea. A defendant who enters such a plea simultaneously waives several constitutional rights, including his privilege against compulsory self-incrimination, his right to trial by jury, and his right to confront his accusers. For this waiver to be valid under the Due Process Clause, it must be "an intentional relinquishment or abandonment of a known right or privilege." ... Consequently, if a defendant's guilty plea is not equally voluntary and knowing, it has been obtained in violation of due process and is therefore void. Moreover, because a guilty plea is an admission of all the elements of a formal criminal charge, it cannot be truly voluntary unless the defendant possesses an understanding of the law in relation to the facts.

Thus, in addition to directing the judge to inquire into the defendant's understanding of the nature of the charge and the consequences of his plea, Rule 11 also requires the judge to satisfy himself that there is a factual basis for the plea. The judge must determine "that the conduct which the defendant admits constitutes the offense charged in the indictment or information or an offense included therein to which the defendant has pleaded guilty." Requiring this examination of the relation between the law and the acts the defendant admits having committed is designed to "protect a defendant who is in the position of pleading voluntarily with an understanding of the nature of the charge but without realizing that his conduct does not actually fall within the charge."

To the extent that the district judge thus exposes the defendant's state of mind on the record through personal interrogation, he not only facilitates his own determination of a guilty plea's voluntariness, but he also facilitates that determination in any subsequent postconviction proceeding based upon a claim that the plea was involuntary. Both of these goals are undermined in proportion to the degree the district judge resorts to "assumptions" not based upon recorded responses to his inquiries. For this reason, we reject the Government's contention that Rule 11 can be complied with although the district judge does not personally inquire whether the defendant understood the nature of the charge.

394 U.S. at 465–67, 89 S.Ct. at 1170–71, 22 L.Ed.2d at 425–26.

The Court continued (in a footnote):

The nature of the inquiry required by Rule 11 must necessarily vary from case to case, and therefore, we do not establish any general guidelines other than those expressed in the Rule itself. As our discussion of the facts in this particular case suggests, however, where the charge encompasses lesser included offenses, personally addressing the defendant as to his understanding of the essential elements of the charge to which he pleads guilty would seem a necessary prerequisite to a determination that he understands the meaning of the charge. 394 U.S. at 467 n. 20, 89 S.Ct. at 1171 n. 20, 22 L.Ed.2d at 426 n. 20. As the cases in this section indicate, a major question in the guilty plea area is the extent, if any, to which the Supreme Court's construction of Rule 11 is also binding on the states as a matter of federal constitutional law. The Court purported to base its decision "solely upon our construction of Rule 11 and ... pursuant to our supervisory power over the lower federal courts" and not to reach any of the constitutional arguments urged by McCarthy. 394 U.S. at 464, 89 S.Ct. at 1169, 22 L.Ed.2d at 424. But the case clearly has constitutional ramifications.

Factual Basis

A number of statutory formulations, including Fed.R.Crim.P. 11(f), require the trial judge to determine that there is a "factual basis" for the plea. This amounts to a requirement that there be some evidence, albeit perhaps not evidence admissible under trial rules, that supports the conclusion that the defendant is in fact guilty. In effect, such a requirement precludes conviction upon the basis of a plea alone. Requiring a factual basis tends to assure that defendants who plead guilty are in fact guilty, thus preventing conviction of the innocent. Requiring a factual basis also assists the court in sentencing (see III Standards for Criminal Justice 14–34), and increases the quality of the contemporaneous record, which discourages later attacks upon the validity of the plea and conviction (or at least eases the task of resolving issues raised in such attacks).

Withdrawal of a Plea

In federal practice, withdrawal of a guilty plea is governed by Fed. R.Crim.P. 32(e):

* * *

> If a motion for withdrawal of a plea of guilty or nolo contendere is made before sentence is imposed [or] imposition of sentence is suspended ... the court may permit withdrawal of the plea upon a showing by the defendant of any fair and just reason. At any later time, a plea may be set aside only on direct appeal or by motion under 28 U.S.C.A. § 2255 [considered in Chapter 26].

The respondent in United States v. Hyde, 520 U.S. 670, 117 S.Ct. 1630, 137 L.Ed.2d 935 (1997) entered pleas of guilty to four counts of an eight count indictment. After appropriate Rule 11 inquiry, the District Court accepted the pleas of guilty but deferred a decision on whether to accept the plea bargain until receipt of the presentence report. Upon re-appearance in court for sentencing, Hyde attempted to withdraw his pleas of guilty, claiming they had been coerced. The District Court, after hearing evidence, concluded they had not been coerced, refused to permit Hyde to withdraw his pleas, and sentenced him in accordance with the plea agreement. The Ninth Circuit reversed on the ground that the absolute right to withdraw a plea for any reason prior to its acceptance by the court is extended to the time a plea bargain is accepted in plea bargained cases because the plea and the bargain are "inextricably bound up together." The Supreme Court, in a unanimous opinion authored by The Chief Justice, held that reading Rule 11 in conjunction with the provisions of Rule 32 require that the defendant show a "fair and just reason" for withdraw of a plea in a circumstance such as this one in which the withdrawal effort is made after the plea is accepted but before the District Court has decided whether to accept the plea agreement.

Later Attack

A conviction resting upon a plea of guilty or nolo contendere can be attacked in several ways. Within the time allotted for appeal, the defendant can seek appellate relief on the ground that the plea was not accepted in compliance with the applicable procedures. United States v. McCarthy, supra. Even if there has been compliance with these requirements, a defendant nevertheless may mount a collateral attack upon the conviction by showing that despite this compliance, the plea was coerced. Fontaine v. United States, 411 U.S. 213, 93 S.Ct. 1461, 36 L.Ed.2d 169 (1973) (per curiam). In *Fontaine,* the defendant stated in open court at the time his plea was accepted that his plea was voluntary. The government urged that this precluded him from later repudiating this statement and attempting to show in collateral attack that his plea was coerced. Rejecting this, the Court explained:

> The objective of Rule 11 of the Federal Rules of Criminal Procedure, of course, is to flush out and resolve all such issues, but like any procedural mechanism, its exercise is neither always perfect nor uniformly invulnerable to subsequent challenge calling for an opportunity to prove the allegations.

411 U.S. at 215, 93 S.Ct. at 1462, 36 L.Ed.2d at 172.

FEDERAL RULES OF CRIMINAL PROCEDURE

Rule 11. Pleas

(a) Alternatives.

(1) In General. A defendant may plead not guilty, guilty, or nolo contendere. If a defendant refuses to plead or if a defendant corporation fails to appear, the court shall enter a plea of not guilty.

(2) Conditional Pleas. With the approval of the court and the consent of the government, a defendant may enter a conditional plea of guilty or nolo contendere, reserving in writing the right, on appeal from the judgment, to review of the adverse determination of any specified pretrial motion. A defendant who prevails on appeal shall be allowed to withdraw the plea.

(b) Nolo Contendere. A defendant may plead nolo contendere only with the consent of the court. Such a plea shall be accepted by the court only after due consideration of the views of the parties and the interest of the public in the effective administration of justice.

(c) Advice to Defendant. Before accepting a plea of guilty or nolo contendere, the court must address the defendant personally in open court

and inform the defendant of, and determine that the defendant understands, the following:

(1) the nature of the charge to which the plea is offered, the
mandatory minimum penalty provided by law, if any, and the maximum possible penalty provided by law, including the effect of any
special parole or supervised release term, the fact that the court is
required to consider any applicable sentencing guidelines but may
depart from those guidelines under some circumstances, and, when
applicable, that the court may also order the defendant to make
restitution to any victim of the offense; and

(2) if the defendant is not represented by an attorney, that the
defendant has the right to be represented by an attorney at every stage
of the proceeding and, if necessary, one will be appointed to represent
the defendant; and

(3) that the defendant has the right to plead not guilty or to
persist in that plea if it has already been made, the right to be tried by
a jury and at that trial the right to the assistance of counsel, the right
to confront and cross-examine adverse witnesses, and the right against
compelled self-incrimination; and

(4) that if a plea of guilty or nolo contendere is accepted by the
court there will not be a further trial of any kind, so that by pleading
guilty or nolo contendere the defendant waives the right to a trial; and

(5) if the court intends to question the defendant under oath, on
the record, and in the presence of counsel about the offense to which
the defendant has pleaded, that the defendant's answers may later be
used against the defendant in a prosecution for perjury or false
statement; and

(6) the terms of any provision in a plea agreement waiving the
right to appeal or to collaterally attack the sentence.[a]

(d) Insuring That the Plea is Voluntary. The court shall not accept a
plea of guilty or nolo contendere without first, by addressing the defendant
personally in open court, determining that the plea is voluntary and not the
result of force or threats or of promises apart from a plea agreement. The
court shall also inquire as to whether the defendant's willingness to plead
guilty or nolo contendere results from prior discussions between the
attorney for the government and the defendant or the defendant's attorney.

---

a. This subsection was added effective
December 1, 1999. The Committee Note
states that this addition is made "to reflect
the increasing practice of including provisions in plea agreements which require the
defendant to waive certain appellate rights.
The increased use of such provisions is due in
part to the increasing number of direct appeals and collateral reviews challenging sentencing decisions. Given the increased use of
such provisions, the Committee believed it
was important to insure that first, a complete
records exists regarding any waiver provisions, and second, that the waiver was voluntarily and knowingly made by the defendant.
Although a number of federal courts have
approved the ability of a defendant to enter
into such waiver agreements, the Committee
takes no position on the underlying validity
of such waivers."

(e) Plea Agreement Procedure.

(1) In General. The attorney for the government and the attorney for the defendant or the defendant when acting pro se may engage in discussions with a view toward reaching an agreement that, upon the entering of a plea of guilty or nolo contendere to a charged offense or to a lesser or related offense, the attorney for the government will do any of the following:

(A) move for dismissal of other charges; or

(B) recommend or agree not to oppose the defendant's request for a particular sentence or sentencing range, or that a particular provision of the Sentencing Guidelines, or policy statement, or sentencing factor is or is not applicable to the case. Any such recommendation or request is not binding on the court;[b] or

(C) agree that a specific sentence or sentencing range is the appropriate disposition of the case or that a particular provision of the Sentencing Guidelines, or policy statement, or sentencing factor is or is not applicable to the case. Such a plea agreement is binding on the court once it is accepted by the court.[c]

The court shall not participate in any such discussions.

(2) Notice of Such Agreement. If a plea agreement has been reached by the parties, the court shall, on the record, require the disclosure of the agreement in open court or, on a showing of good cause, in camera, at the time the plea is offered. If the agreement is of the type specified in subdivision (e)(1)(A) or (C), the court may accept or reject the agreement, or may defer its decision as to the acceptance or rejection until there has been an opportunity to consider the presentence report. If the agreement is of the type specified in subdivision (e)(1)(B), the court shall advise the defendant that if the court does not accept the recommendation or request the defendant nevertheless has no right to withdraw the plea.

(3) Acceptance of a Plea Agreement. If the court accepts the plea agreement, the court shall inform the defendant that it will embody in the judgment and sentence the disposition provided for in the plea agreement.

(4) Rejection of a Plea Agreement. If the court rejects the plea agreement, the court shall, on the record, inform the parties of this fact, advise the defendant personally in open court or, on a showing of good cause, in camera, that the court is not bound by the plea agreement, afford the defendant the opportunity to then withdraw the plea, and advise the defendant that if the defendant persists in a guilty plea or plea of nolo contendere the disposition of the case may be less favorable to the defendant than that contemplated by the plea agreement.

(5) Time of Plea Agreement Procedure. Except for good cause shown, notification to the court of the existence of a plea agreement

b. This subsection was amended effective December 1, 1999 to include references to the Sentencing Guidelines.

c. This subsection was amended effective December 1, 1999 to include references to the Sentencing Guidelines.

shall be given at the arraignment or at such other time, prior to trial, as may be fixed by the court.

(6) Inadmissibility of Pleas, Plea Discussions, and Related Statements. Except as otherwise provided in this paragraph, evidence of the following is not, in any civil or criminal proceeding, admissible against the defendant who made the plea or was a participant in the plea discussions:

(A) a plea of guilty which was later withdrawn;

(B) a plea of nolo contendere;

(C) any statement made in the course of any proceedings under this rule regarding either of the foregoing pleas; or

(D) any statement made in the course of plea discussions with an attorney for the government which do not result in a plea of guilty or which result in a plea of guilty later withdrawn.

However, such a statement is admissible (i) in any proceeding wherein another statement made in the course of the same plea or plea discussions has been introduced and the statement ought in fairness be considered contemporaneously with it, or (ii) in a criminal proceeding for perjury or false statement if the statement was made by the defendant under oath, on the record, and in the presence of counsel.

(f) Determining Accuracy of Plea. Notwithstanding the acceptance of a plea of guilty, the court should not enter a judgment upon such plea without making such inquiry as shall satisfy it that there is a factual basis for the plea.

(g) Record of Proceedings. A verbatim record of the proceedings at which the defendant enters a plea shall be made and, if there is a plea of guilty or nolo contendere, the record shall include, without limitation, the court's advice to the defendant, the inquiry into the voluntariness of the plea including any plea agreement, and the inquiry into the accuracy of a guilty plea.

(h) Harmless Error. Any variance from the procedures required by this rule which does not affect substantial rights shall be disregarded.

NOTES

1. **Consequences of not complying with Rule 11.** Under what circumstances will a failure to comply with applicable procedural requirements for a guilty plea invalidate the plea (and the conviction) and thus give the defendant the opportunity to go to trial or to again plead guilty, at the defendant's option? In McCarthy v. U.S., 394 U.S. 459, 89 S.Ct. 1166, 22 L.Ed.2d 418 (1969), the Government urged that even if the record showed noncompliance with Fed. R.Crim.P. 11 it was entitled to an opportunity to demonstrate from other parts of the record that the plea was entered voluntarily and with an understanding of the charge. Further, it argued, if this could not be shown, the defendant was entitled to no more than a remand for an evidentiary hearing at which the voluntariness or understanding nature of the plea would be at issue. If at this hearing, the Government argued, it established by evidence outside of the record in the original guilty plea proceeding that the plea was understanding and voluntary, the defen-

dant's conviction should stand. It acknowledged, however, that the Government would have the burden of demonstrating that the plea was understanding and voluntary. The Court rejected this position and held that a defendant who demonstrates on direct appeal that his plea was accepted in violation of Rule 11 is entitled to have the conviction reversed and to plead anew. Explaining, the Court stated:

> From the defendant's perspective, the efficacy of shifting the burden of proof to the Government at a later voluntariness hearing is questionable. In meeting its burden, the Government will undoubtedly rely upon the defendant's statement that he desired to plead guilty and frequently a statement that the plea was not induced by any threats or promises. This prima facie case for voluntariness is likely to be treated as irrebuttable in cases such as this one, where the defendant's reply is limited to his own plaintive allegations that he did not understand the nature of the charge and therefore failed to assert a valid defense or to limit his guilty plea only to a lesser included offense. No matter how true these allegations may be, rarely, if ever, can a defendant corroborate them in a postplea voluntariness hearing.

> Rule 11 is designed to eliminate any need to resort to a later factfinding proceeding "in this highly subjective area." Heiden v. United States, [353 F.2d 53, 55 (9th Cir.1965)]. The Rule "contemplates that disputes as to the understanding of the defendant and the voluntariness of his action are to be eliminated at the outset.... " Ibid. ...There is no adequate substitute for demonstrating in the record at the time the plea is entered the defendant's understanding of the nature of the charge against him.

> · · ·

> We thus conclude that prejudice inheres in a failure to comply with Rule 11, for noncompliance deprives the defendant of the Rule's procedural safeguards that are designed to facilitate a more accurate determination of the voluntariness of his plea. ...[This] not only will insure that every accused is afforded those procedural safeguards, but also will help reduce the great waste of judicial resources required to process the frivolous attacks on guilty plea convictions that are encouraged, and are more difficult to dispose of, when the original record is inadequate. It is, therefore, not too much to require that, before sentencing defendants to years of imprisonment, district judges take the few minutes necessary to inform them of their rights and to determine whether they understand the action they are taking.

394 U.S. at 469–72, 89 S.Ct. at 1172–74, 22 L.Ed.2d at 427–28. Suppose, however, a trial judge erroneously understates the maximum prison term to which the defendant could be sentenced upon conviction of the crime to which he is offering to plead guilty. Following conviction, the judge sentences the defendant to a prison term shorter than the term which he mistakenly represented to the defendant as the maximum provided by statute. On appeal, is the defendant entitled to have the conviction reversed and to plead anew?

2. **Challenges in collateral proceedings.** If a convicted defendant seeks relief through collateral attack rather than on direct appeal, a more serious deviation from the procedural requirements for the taking of the plea may be required. In the United States v. Timmreck, 441 U.S. 780, 99 S.Ct. 2085, 60 L.Ed.2d 634 (1979), the defendant pleaded guilty to criminal conspiracy in federal District Court. The judge formally addressed him and complied with Rule 11 of the Federal Rules of Criminal Procedure, except that he failed to inform Timmreck that the applicable statute made a period of at least three years parole mandatory. Timmreck was informed that a sentence of 15 years imprisonment and a fine of $25,000 could be imposed. After accepting the plea, the trial judge sentenced Timmreck to

10 years imprisonment, a special parole term of 5 additional years, and a fine of $5,000. No appeal was taken. Two years later, Timmreck moved to vacate his sentence under 28 U.S.C.A. § 2255 on the ground the trial judge had violated Rule 11 by failing to inform him of the mandatory special parole term. Timmreck's lawyer testified that his normal practice was to inform his clients of the mandatory parole term but he could not recall whether he had given Timmreck this informa- tion. The District Court denied Timmreck's motion on the ground that since he received a sentence within the maximum as it was described to him no prejudice was suffered as the result of the violation of Rule 11. On appeal, however, the Court of Appeals ordered relief granted, reasoning that any violation of Rule 11 permits collateral attack upon the resulting conviction. A unanimous Supreme Court re- versed. After noting that the violation of Rule 11 was neither constitutional nor jurisdictional, it continued:

> Nor can any claim reasonably be made that the error here resulted in a "complete miscarriage of justice" or in a proceeding "inconsistent with the rudimentary demands of fair procedure." Respondent does not argue that he was actually unaware of the special parole term or that, if he had been properly advised by the trial judge, he would not have pleaded guilty. His only claim is of a technical violation of the rule. That claim could have been raised on direct appeal ... but was not.

441 U.S. at 784, 99 S.Ct. at 2087, 60 L.Ed.2d at 638. Finding it unnecessary to determine whether relief would be available in the context of "other aggravating circumstances," the Court held that a showing of only a failure to comply with the formal requirements of Rule 11 as was made by Timmreck did not entitle him to relief.

Several years later Rule 11(c)(1) was amended, as set out above, to specifically require the court to inform the defendant of "the effect of any special parole term." What is the effect of this amendment on *Timmreck?*

3. **Applicability to property forfeiture.** The petitioner in Libretti v. Unit- ed States, 516 U.S. 29, 116 S.Ct. 356, 133 L.Ed.2d 271 (1995) entered a plea of guilty to engaging in a continuing criminal enterprise. As part of the plea agree- ment, he consented to the forfeiture of property of a substantial value that the government believed had been used in, or acquired with the proceeds of, drug transactions. On appeal, Libretti claimed that the criminal forfeiture order was invalid because the District Court had failed to find as required by Rule 11 (f) that there was a factual basis for identifying the property as assets subject to criminal forfeiture. The Court, in an opinion by Justice O'Connor, rejected this claim on the ground that rather than being a criminal offense, "[f]orfeiture is an element of the sentence imposed *following* conviction or, as here, a plea of guilty, and thus falls outside the scope of Rule 11(f)." 516 U.S. at 38–39, 116 S.Ct. at 363, 133 L.Ed.2d at 362.

Boykin v. Alabama

Supreme Court of the United States, 1969.
395 U.S. 238, 89 S.Ct. 1709, 23 L.Ed.2d 274.

■ MR. JUSTICE DOUGLAS delivered the opinion of the Court.

In the Spring of 1966, within the period of a fortnight, a series of armed robberies occurred in Mobile, Alabama. The victims, in each case, were local shopkeepers open at night who were forced by a gunman to hand over money. While robbing one grocery store, the assailant fired his gun once, sending a bullet through a door into the ceiling. A few days earlier in a drugstore, the robber had allowed his gun to discharge in such a way that the bullet, on ricochet from the floor, struck a customer in the leg. Shortly thereafter, a local grand jury indicted petitioner, a 27–year-old Negro, on five counts of common-law robbery—an offense punishable in Alabama by death.

Before the matter came to trial, the court determined that petitioner was indigent and appointed counsel to represent him. Three days later, at his arraignment, petitioner pleaded guilty to all five indictments. So far as the record shows, the judge asked no questions of petitioner concerning his plea, and petitioner did not address the court.

Trial strategy may of course make a plea of guilty seem the desirable course. But the record is wholly silent on that point and throws no light on it.

Alabama provides that when a defendant pleads guilty, "the Court must cause the punishment to be determined by a jury" (except where it is required to be fixed by the court)…. The jury, upon deliberation, found petitioner guilty and sentenced him severally to die on each of the five indictments.

* * *

It was error, plain on the face of the record, for the trial judge to accept petitioner's guilty plea without an affirmative showing that it was intelligent and voluntary. …

A plea of guilty is more than a confession which admits that the accused did various acts; it is itself a conviction; nothing remains but to give judgment and determine punishment. Admissibility of a confession must be based on a "reliable determination on the voluntariness issue which satisfies the constitutional rights of the defendant." Jackson v. Denno, 378 U.S. 368, 387, 84 S.Ct. 1774, 1786, 12 L.Ed.2d 908. The requirement that the prosecution spread on the record the prerequisites of a valid waiver is no constitutional innovation. In Carnley v. Cochran, 369 U.S. 506, 516, 82 S.Ct. 884, 890, 8 L.Ed.2d 70, we dealt with a problem of waiver of the right to counsel, a Sixth Amendment right. We held: "Presuming waiver from a silent record is impermissible. The record must show, or there must be an allegation and evidence which show, that an accused was offered counsel but intelligently and understandingly rejected the offer. Anything less is not waiver."

We think that the same standard must be applied to determining whether a guilty plea is voluntarily made. For, as we have said, a plea of guilty is more than an admission of conduct; it is a conviction. Ignorance, incomprehension, coercion, terror, inducements, subtle or blatant threats might be a perfect cover-up of unconstitutionality. The question of an effective waiver of a federal constitutional right in a proceeding is of course governed by federal standards.

Several federal constitutional rights are involved in a waiver that takes place when a plea of guilty is entered in a state criminal trial. First is the privilege against compulsory self-incrimination guaranteed by the Fifth Amendment and applicable to the States by reason of the Fourteenth.

...Second is the right to trial by jury. Third, is the right to confront one's accusers. ...We cannot presume a waiver of these three important federal rights from a silent record.

What is at stake for an accused facing death or imprisonment demands utmost solicitude of which courts are capable in canvassing the matter with the accused to make sure he has a full understanding of what the plea connotes and of its consequence. When the judge discharges that function, he leaves a record adequate for any review that may be later sought ... and forestalls the spin-off of collateral proceedings that seek to probe murky memories.

* * *

Reversed.

■ MR. JUSTICE HARLAN, whom MR. JUSTICE BLACK joins, dissenting.

The Court today holds that petitioner Boykin was denied due process of law, and that his robbery convictions must be reversed outright, solely because "the record [is] inadequate to show that petitioner ... intelligently and knowingly pleaded guilty." ... The Court thus in effect fastens upon the States, as a matter of federal constitutional law, the rigid prophylactic requirements of Rule 11 of the Federal Rules of Criminal Procedure.

* * *

I would hold that petitioner Boykin is not entitled to outright reversal of his conviction simply because of the "inadequacy" of the record pertaining to his guilty plea. Further, I would not vacate the judgment below and remand for a state-court hearing on voluntariness. For even if it is assumed for the sake of argument that petitioner would be entitled to such a hearing if he had alleged that the plea was involuntary, a matter which I find it unnecessary to decide, the fact is that he has never made any such claim. Hence, I consider that petitioner's present arguments relating to his guilty plea entitle him to no federal relief.

NOTES

1. **What must the record show?** Must the record in a guilty plea case show, on its face, that the defendant was informed of his rights to trial by jury, confrontation of accusers, and silence? Compare People v. Jaworski, 387 Mich. 21, 194 N.W.2d 868 (1972) (both logic and language of *Boykin* "require that the defendant must be informed of these three rights, for without knowledge he cannot understandingly waive those rights") with Wilkins v. Erickson, 505 F.2d 761 (9th Cir.1974) ("*Boykin* does not require specific articulation of the ... three rights in a state proceeding").

2. **Proof of the absence of waivers.** The respondent in Parke v. Raley, 506 U.S. 20, 113 S.Ct. 517, 121 L.Ed.2d 391 (1992) challenged the admissibility of prior convictions under a Kentucky recidivist statute on the ground that the record in the prior cases did not show the waivers of constitutional rights required to be shown by *Boykin*. No stenographic record existed of the pleas of guilty upon which the convictions were based. The Sixth Circuit held, on federal habeas, that when no record exists the burden is upon the State to prove the validity of the plea and no presumption of regularity attaches to the judgment. It also held that the State must

make that showing by clear and convincing evidence. The Supreme Court, in an opinion by Justice O'Connor, reversed. The Court noted that with respect to convictions that are several years old, a missing or nonexistent record is "not atypical." Without evidence that governmental misconduct is responsible for the absence of a record, the state is permitted to presume that a conviction was obtained in compliance with *Boykin* based upon a judgment of conviction. Therefore, the burden of producing evidence as to noncompliance with *Boykin* may constitutionally be placed upon the criminal defendant. This is fair since often the criminal defendant has the best access to information concerning the circumstances of the acceptance of the plea. The Court also held that if the state is given the burden of persuasion as to compliance with *Boykin,* the Due Process Clause does not require a higher standard of persuasion than a preponderance of the evidence. Justice Blackmun concurred in the judgment on the understanding that the Kentucky statutory scheme was a sentencing provision only and did not create a separate criminal offense.

3. **Elements of the offense(s) charged.** Will the plea be invalidated as involuntary because the defendant has not been informed of every element of the crime to which he is pleading guilty? In Henderson v. Morgan, 426 U.S. 637, 96 S.Ct. 2253, 49 L.Ed.2d 108 (1976), the Supreme Court overturned a conviction on a plea entered under just such circumstances. The defendant was indicted on a charge of first-degree murder, pleaded guilty to second-degree murder, and was sentenced to imprisonment for 25 years to life. The Court said:

> When he was in seventh grade, respondent was committed to the Rome State School for Mental Defectives where he was classified as "retarded." He was released to become a farm laborer and ultimately went to work on Mrs. Francisco's farm. Following an argument, she threatened to return him to state custody. He then decided to abscond. During the night he entered Mrs. Francisco's bedroom with a knife, intending to collect his earned wages before leaving; she awoke, began to scream, and he stabbed her. He took a small amount of money, fled in her car, and became involved in an accident about 80 miles away. The knife was found in the glove compartment of her car. He was promptly arrested and made a statement to the police. He was then 19 years old and substantially below average intelligence.
>
> . . .
>
> Petitioner contends that the District Court applied an unrealistically rigid rule of law. Instead of testing the voluntariness of a plea by determining whether a ritualistic litany of the formal legal elements of an offense was read to the defendant, petitioner argues that the court should examine the totality of the circumstances and determine whether the substance of the charge, as opposed to its technical elements, was conveyed to the accused. We do not disagree with the thrust of petitioner's argument, but we are persuaded that even under the test which he espouses, this judgment finding respondent guilty of second-degree murder was defective.
>
> We assume, as petitioner argues, that the prosecutor had overwhelming evidence of guilt available. We also accept petitioner's characterization of the competence of respondent's counsel and of the wisdom of their advice to plead guilty to a charge of second-degree murder. Nevertheless, such a plea cannot support a judgment of guilty unless it was voluntary in a constitutional sense. And clearly the plea could not be voluntary in the sense that it constituted an intelligent admission that he committed the offense unless the defendant received "real notice of the true nature of the charge against him, the first and most universally recognized requirement of due process." Smith v. O'Grady, 312 U.S. 329, 334, 61 S.Ct. 572, 574, 85 L.Ed. 859 (1941).

The charge of second-degree murder was never formally made. Had it been made, it necessarily would have included a charge that respondent's assault was "committed with a design to effect the death of the person killed." That element of the offense might have been proved by the objective evidence even if respondent's actual state of mind was consistent with innocence or manslaughter. But even if such a design to effect death would almost inevitably have been inferred from evidence that respondent repeatedly stabbed Mrs. Francisco, it is nevertheless also true that a jury would not have been required to draw that inference. The jury would have been entitled to accept defense counsel's appraisal of the incident as involving only manslaughter in the first degree. Therefore, an admission by respondent that he killed Mrs. Francisco does not necessarily also admit that he was guilty of second-degree murder.

There is nothing in this record that can serve as a substitute for either a finding after trial, or a voluntary admission, that respondent had the requisite intent. Defense counsel did not purport to stipulate to that fact; they did not explain to him that his plea would be an admission of that fact; and he made no factual statement or admission necessarily implying that he had such intent. In these circumstances it is impossible to conclude that his plea to the unexplained charge of second-degree murder was voluntary.

Petitioner argues that affirmance of the Court of Appeals will invite countless collateral attacks on judgments entered on pleas of guilty, since frequently the record will not contain a complete enumeration of the elements of the offense to which an accused person pleads guilty.[1] We think petitioner's fears are exaggerated.

Normally the record contains either an explanation of the charge by the trial judge, or at least a representation by defense counsel that the nature of the offense has been explained to the accused. Moreover, even without such an express representation, it may be appropriate to presume that in most cases defense counsel routinely explain the nature of the offense in sufficient detail to give the accused notice of what he is being asked to admit. This case is unique because the trial judge found as a fact that the element of intent was not explained to respondent. Moreover, respondent's unusually low mental capacity provides a reasonable explanation for counsel's oversight; it also forecloses the conclusion that the error was harmless beyond a reasonable doubt, for it lends at least a modicum of credibility to defense counsel's appraisal of the homicide as a manslaughter rather than a murder.

426 U.S. at 641–47, 96 S.Ct. at 2256–59, 49 L.Ed.2d at 113–16.

B.   EFFECT OF A GUILTY PLEA ON LATER ASSERTION OF RIGHTS

The fact of a guilty plea greatly limits a defendant's ability to later attack his conviction on the basis of alleged errors, even errors of constitutional dimension. Some issues, however, "survive" a guilty plea and can later be raised on appeal or in collateral attack proceedings. Distinguishing the two types of errors is not an easy task.

---

1. There is no need in this case to decide whether notice of the true nature, or substance, of a charge always requires a description of every element of the offense; we assume it does not. Nevertheless, intent is such a critical element of the offense of second-degree murder that notice of that element is required.

Some matters are arguably no longer issues because of the effect of a guilty plea upon the procedure that leads to conviction. The prosecution may, for example, have in its possession evidence which, if challenged at trial, the trial court would have to exclude on constitutional or other grounds. If a defendant pleads guilty, however, that evidence may not be introduced at all and therefore a defendant may have no basis for claiming that his conviction rests upon it.

But more importantly, the fact of a plea of guilty or *nolo contendere* may serve to preclude a defendant from raising certain issues whether or not those are procedurally presented given the posture of the trial court proceedings. To some extent, a plea of guilty in state criminal proceedings bars later efforts to assert federal constitutional rights in a federal forum. This was assumed in two of the three cases making up the *Brady* trilogy, presented in the final section of this chapter.

The survival of issues was addressed directly in Tollett v. Henderson, 411 U.S. 258, 93 S.Ct. 1602, 36 L.Ed.2d 235 (1973). Henderson had pleaded guilty to murder in a Tennessee court; he was convicted and sentenced to a term of 99 years in prison. Twenty years later, he sought federal habeas corpus relief, urging that the grand jury which returned the indictment to which he had pled had been selected in a racially discriminatory manner. A majority of the Supreme Court, in an opinion by Justice Rehnquist, held that even if Henderson showed racial discrimination in the selection of the indicting grand jury, he would not, on that basis, be entitled to federal habeas corpus relief:

> [A] guilty plea represents a break in the chain of events which has preceded it in the criminal process. When a criminal defendant has solemnly admitted in open court that he is in fact guilty of the offense with which he is charged, he may not thereafter raise independent claims relating to the deprivation of constitutional rights that occurred prior to the entry of the guilty plea.

411 U.S. at 267, 93 S.Ct. at 1608, 36 L.Ed.2d at 243. As the later cases discussed in this section make clear, however, this is subject to at least some qualification. In addition, it is necessary to distinguish other attacks which a defendant may make. The alleged deprivation of constitutional (or other) rights can be urged to have had such an influence upon the plea as to render the plea itself invalid. Or, the advice of counsel (or lack of either counsel or advice) may be urged as a basis for finding the plea constitutionally infirm. These matters are considered later in this chapter.

Blackledge v. Perry

Supreme Court of the United States, 1974.
417 U.S. 21, 94 S.Ct. 2098, 40 L.Ed.2d 628.

■ MR. JUSTICE STEWART delivered the opinion of the Court.

While serving a term of imprisonment in a North Carolina penitentiary, the respondent Perry became involved in an altercation with another inmate. A warrant issued, charging Perry with the misdemeanor of assault with a deadly weapon, N.C.Gen.Stat. § 14–33(b)(1) (1969 ed.). Under North

Carolina law, the District Court Division of the General Court of Justice has exclusive jurisdiction for the trial of misdemeanors. N.C.Gen.Stat. § 7A–272. Following a trial without a jury in the District Court of Northampton County, Perry was convicted of this misdemeanor and given a six-month sentence, to be served after completion of the prison term he was then serving.

Perry then filed a notice of appeal to the Northampton County Superior Court. Under North Carolina law, a person convicted in the District Court has a right to a trial *de novo* in the Superior Court. N.C.Gen.Stat. §§ 7A–290, 15–177.1. The right to trial *de novo* is absolute, there being no need for the appellant to allege error in the original proceeding. When an appeal is taken, the statutory scheme provides that the slate is wiped clean; the prior conviction is annulled, and the prosecution and the defense begin anew in the Superior Court.

After the filing of the notice of appeal, but prior to the respondent's appearance for trial *de novo* in the Superior Court, the prosecutor obtained an indictment from a grand jury, charging Perry with the felony of assault with a deadly weapon with intent to kill inflicting serious bodily injury, N.C.Gen.Stat. § 14–32(a) (1969 ed.). The indictment covered the same conduct for which Perry had been tried and convicted in the District Court. Perry entered a plea of guilty to the indictment in the Superior Court, and was sentenced to a term of five to seven years in the penitentiary, to be served concurrently with the identical prison sentence he was then serving.

* * *

[T]he Due Process Clause is not offended by all possibilities of increased punishment upon retrial after appeal, but only by those that pose a realistic likelihood of "vindictiveness." ... [I]n the situation here the central figure is not the judge or the jury, but the prosecutor. The question is whether the opportunities for vindictiveness in this situation are such as to impel the conclusion that due process of law requires [a bar to the more serious charge.] We conclude that the answer must be in the affirmative.

A prosecutor clearly has a considerable stake in discouraging convicted misdemeanants from appealing and thus obtaining a trial *de novo* in the Superior Court, since such an appeal will clearly require increased expenditures of prosecutorial resources before the defendant's conviction becomes final, and may even result in a formerly convicted defendant going free. And, if the prosecutor has the means readily at hand to discourage such appeals—by "upping the ante" through a felony indictment whenever a convicted misdemeanant pursues his statutory appellate remedy—the State can insure that only the most hardy defendants will brave the hazards of a *de novo* trial.

* * *

A person convicted of an offense is entitled to pursue his statutory right to a trial *de novo*, without apprehension that the State will retaliate by substituting a more serious charge for the original one, thus subjecting him to a significantly increased potential period of incarceration. ...

The remaining question is whether, because of his guilty plea to the felony charge in the Superior Court, Perry is precluded from raising his constitutional claims in this federal habeas corpus proceeding. In contending that such is the case, the petitioner warden relies chiefly on this Court's decision last Term in Tollett v. Henderson, 411 U.S. 258, 93 S.Ct. 1602, 36 L.Ed.2d 235.

The precise issue presented in *Tollett* was "whether a state prisoner, pleading guilty with the advice of counsel, may later obtain release through federal habeas corpus by proving only that the indictment to which he pleaded was returned by an unconstitutionally selected grand jury." Id., at 260, 93 S.Ct. at 1604. The Court answered that question in the negative. . . .

While the petitioner's reliance upon the *Tollett* opinion is understandable, there is a fundamental distinction between this case and that one. Although the underlying claims presented in *Tollett* and the *Brady* trilogy were of constitutional dimension, none went to the very power of the State to bring the defendant into court to answer the charge brought against him. The defendants in McMann v. Richardson, for example, could surely have been brought to trial without the use of the allegedly coerced confessions, and even a tainted indictment of the sort alleged in *Tollett* could have been "cured" through a new indictment by a properly selected grand jury. In the case at hand, by contrast, the nature of the underlying constitutional infirmity is markedly different. Having chosen originally to proceed on the misdemeanor charges in the District Court, the State of North Carolina was, under the facts of this case, simply precluded by the Due Process Clause from calling upon the respondent to answer to the more serious charge in the Superior Court. Unlike the defendant in *Tollett,* Perry is not complaining of "antecedent constitutional violations" or of a "deprivation of constitutional rights that occurred prior to the entry of the guilty plea." Rather, the right that he asserts and that we today accept is the right not to be hailed into court at all upon the felony charge. The very initiation of the proceedings against him in the Superior Court thus operated to deny him due process of law.

The "practical result" dictated by the Due Process Clause in this case is that North Carolina simply could not permissibly require Perry to answer to the felony charge. That being so, it follows that his guilty plea did not foreclose him from attacking his conviction in the Superior Court proceedings through a federal writ of habeas corpus.

Accordingly, the judgment of the Court of Appeals for the Fourth Circuit is affirmed.

■ MR. JUSTICE REHNQUIST, dissenting.

* * *

II.

. . . I believe this case is governed by cases culminating in Tollett v. Henderson, 411 U.S. 258, 93 S.Ct. 1602, 36 L.Ed.2d 235 (1973). . . . The assertion by the Court that this reasoning is somehow inapplicable here because the claim goes "to the very power of the State to bring the defendant into court to answer the charge brought against him" is little other than a conclusion. Any difference between the issue resolved the other way in Tollett v. Henderson and the issue before us today is at most semantic. But the Court's "test" not only fails to distinguish *Henderson* [*Tollett*]; it also fails to provide any reasoned basis on which to approach such questions as whether a speedy trial claim is merged in a guilty plea. I believe the Court's departure today from the principles of *Henderson* [*Tollett*] and the cases preceding it must be recognized as a potentially major breach in the wall of certainty surrounding guilty pleas for which we have found constitutional sanction in those cases.

There is no indication in this record that respondent's guilty plea was the result of an agreement with the prosecutor. But the Court's basis for distinguishing the *Henderson* [*Tollett*] and *Brady* cases seems so insubstantial as to permit the doctrine of this case to apply to guilty pleas which have been obtained as a result of "plea bargains." In that event it will be not merely the State which stands to lose, but the accused defendant in the position of the respondent as well. Since the great majority of criminal cases are resolved by plea bargaining, defendants as a class have at least as great an interest in the finality of voluntary guilty pleas as do prosecutors. If that finality may be swept aside with the ease exhibited by the Court's approach today, prosecutors will have a reduced incentive to bargain, to the detriment of the many defendants for whom plea bargaining offers the only hope for ameliorating the consequences to them of a serious criminal charge.

* * *

■ MR. JUSTICE POWELL joins in Part II of this opinion.

Menna v. New York

Supreme Court of the United States, 1975.
423 U.S. 61, 96 S.Ct. 241, 46 L.Ed.2d 195.

PER CURIAM.

On November 7, 1968, after being granted immunity, petitioner refused to answer questions put to him before a duly convened Kings County, N.Y., Grand Jury which was investigating a murder conspiracy. On March 18, 1969, petitioner refused to obey a court order to return to testify before the same Grand Jury in connection with the same investigation. On that date, petitioner was adjudicated in contempt of court under Sec. 750 of the New York Judiciary Law for his failure to testify before the Grand Jury; and, on March 21, 1969, after declining an offer to purge his contempt, petitioner was sentenced to a flat 30-day term in civil jail. Petitioner served his sentence.

On June 10, 1970, petitioner was indicted for his refusal to answer questions before the Grand Jury on November 7, 1968. After asserting unsuccessfully that this indictment should be dismissed under the Double Jeopardy Clause of the Fifth Amendment to the United States Constitution, petitioner pleaded guilty to the indictment and was sentenced on his plea.

Petitioner appealed, claiming that the Double Jeopardy Clause precluded the State from haling him into court on the charge to which he had pleaded guilty.[2] The New York Court of Appeals affirmed the conviction, declining to address the double jeopardy claim on the merits. It held, relying, inter alia, on Tollett v. Henderson, 411 U.S. 258, 93 S.Ct. 1602, 36 L.Ed.2d 235 (1973), that the double jeopardy claim had been "waived" by petitioner's counseled plea of guilty.

We reverse. Where the State is precluded by the United States Constitution from haling a defendant into court on a charge, federal law requires that a conviction on that charge be set aside even if the conviction was entered pursuant to a counseled plea of guilty. Blackledge v. Perry, 417 U.S. 21, 30, 94 S.Ct. 2098, 2103, 40 L.Ed.2d 628 (1974).[3] The motion for leave to proceed in forma pauperis and the petition for certiorari are granted, and the case is remanded to the New York Court of Appeals for a determination of petitioner's double jeopardy claim on the merits, a claim on which we express no view.

NOTES

1. **Plead and appeal provisions.** One result of rules such as that applied in Tollett v. Henderson is that a defendant who wishes appellate review of a trial court ruling on matters such as motions to suppress evidence may have to go to trial despite no realistic expectation of any result other than conviction on the crime charged. This has led a number of jurisdictions to give a defendant access to appellate courts on direct appeal despite a plea of guilty, at least for purposes of raising certain issues. New York—McKinney's Crim.Pro.Law § 710.70(2), for example, provides that an order denying a motion to suppress evidence may be reviewed on appeal from a judgment of conviction, "notwithstanding the fact that such judgment of conviction is predicated upon a plea of guilty."

2. **Effect of state plead and appeal provisions on the availability of federal relief.** To what extent would the provisions of Rule 11(a)(2), set out at

2. The State concedes that petitioner's double jeopardy claim is a strong one on the merits. In light of the flat 30–day sentence imposed, the earlier conviction was a criminal conviction ...; and New York law supports the proposition that the earlier conviction was based, at least in part, on the failure to answer questions on November 7, 1968, and was thus for the same crime as the one charged in the instant indictment. ...

3. Neither Tollett v. Henderson, 411 U.S. 258, 93 S.Ct. 1602, 36 L.Ed.2d 235 (1973), nor our earlier cases on which it relied, e.g., Brady v. United States, 397 U.S. 742, 90 S.Ct. 1463, 25 L.Ed.2d 747 (1970), and McMann v. Richardson, 397 U.S. 759, 90 S.Ct. 1441, 25 L.Ed.2d 763 (1970), stand for the proposition that counseled guilty pleas inevitably "waive" all antecedent constitutional violations. If they did so hold, the New York Court of Appeals might be correct. However, in *Tollett* we emphasized that waiv-

er was not the basic ingredient of this line of cases,.... The point of these cases is that a counseled plea of guilty is an admission of factual guilt so reliable that, where voluntary and intelligent, it quite validly removes the issue of factual guilt from State's imposition of punishment. A guilty plea, therefore, simply renders irrelevant those constitutional violations not logically inconsistent with the valid establishment of factual guilt and which do not stand in the way of convictions, if factual guilt is validly established. Here, however, the claim is that the State may not convict petitioner no matter how validly his factual guilt is established. The guilty plea, therefore, does not bar the claim.

We do not hold that a double jeopardy claim may never be waived. We simply hold that a plea of guilty to a charge does not waive a claim that—judged on its face—the charge is one which the State may not constitutionally prosecute.

page 930 above, increase the availability of collateral relief? In Lefkowitz v. Newsome, 420 U.S. 283, 95 S.Ct. 886, 43 L.Ed.2d 196 (1975), Newsome, charged in New York state courts, had moved for suppression of certain evidence seized in connection with his arrest. He argued that his arrest was in violation of federal constitutional standards. His motion was denied. He then pleaded guilty and was convicted; on direct appeal, the New York appellate courts affirmed the conviction. Newsome next sought federal habeas corpus relief in federal District Court. This was opposed by the state on the ground that by pleading guilty he had lost the right to review of his constitutional claims through the federal habeas corpus route. The Supreme Court held, however, that in view of New York Crim.Pro.Law § 710.70(2) (discussed in Note 1, supra), Newsome was entitled to pursue federal habeas corpus remedies: "[W]hen state law permits a defendant to plead guilty without forfeiting his right to judicial review of specified constitutional issues, the defendant is not foreclosed from pursuing those constitutional claims in a federal habeas corpus proceeding." 420 U.S. at 293, 95 S.Ct. at 891–92, 43 L.Ed.2d at 204.

3. **Waiver of evidence sufficiency claims.** Respondents in United States v. Broce, 488 U.S. 563, 109 S.Ct. 757, 102 L.Ed.2d 927 (1989) entered pleas of guilty pursuant to an agreement with the government to two counts of conspiracy. Later, in collateral proceedings, they were permitted to show with evidence outside the record in their case that each conspiracy to which they had plead guilty was really part of a single, larger conspiracy. The District Court refused to set aside the convictions on the ground that respondents' pleas of guilty were admissions of the two conspiracies. The Court of Appeals held that under Blackledge v. Perry and Menna v. New York the pleas of guilty did not waive respondents' claim that only one conspiracy existed. The Supreme Court, in an opinion by Justice Kennedy, reversed. *Blackledge* and *Menna* are distinguishable because in them

> the determination that the second indictment could not go forward should have been made by the presiding judge at the time the plea was entered on the basis of the existing record.... The respondents here, in contrast, pleaded guilty to indictments that on their face described separate conspiracies. They cannot prove their claim by relying on those indictments and the existing record. Indeed ... they cannot prove their claim without contradicting those indictments, and that opportunity is foreclosed by the admissions inherent in their guilty pleas.

488 U.S. at 575–76, 109 S.Ct. at 765–66, 102 L.Ed.2d at 938.

C. PLEA BARGAINING

The entire subject of guilty pleas is influenced by the practice of plea bargaining, which is described in the first subsection that follows. Subsequent subsections address specific issues relating to structuring the guilty plea process to accommodate plea bargaining, determination of whether particular pleas offered pursuant to bargains are constitutionally or otherwise "acceptable," and possible abolition of plea bargaining entirely. While relatively few voices have called for efforts to completely abolish plea bargaining, more have suggested restricting the practice. For example, California's passage of "The Victim's Bill of Rights" initiative in 1982 prohibits plea bargaining at the felony trial court level except under specified circumstances. However, most "reform" has involved efforts at open recognition and regulation of the process. Fed.R.Crim.Pro. 11 is an example of this approach.

Plea bargaining takes a variety of forms. But a central question, in addition to the factual voluntariness of a plea entered pursuant to plea bargaining, is the acceptability of a process which results in sentence disparities between those who plead and those who go to trial. Even if it is acceptable for the sentencing judge to reward a guilty plea, it does not necessarily follow, of course, that it is also acceptable for the prosecutor to have the power (perhaps in cooperation with defense counsel) to achieve the same result. This may be a power that is acceptable, if at all, only if judicially exercised. But if it is inappropriate for a sentencing judge to reward a defendant's willingness to plead guilty, it seems to necessarily follow that it is also inappropriate to achieve this same objective by other methods, such as a reduction in charge at the option of the prosecutor.

The issue was addressed by the American Bar Association's Standards for Criminal Justice. The original formulation of those standards, approved in 1968, provided that a sentence in excess of that which would be justified by other purposes of the criminal law should not be imposed because the defendant has chosen to go to trial. Standards Relating to Pleas of Guilty, Standard 1.8(b) (Approved Draft, 1968). It also provided, however, that:

> It is proper for the court to grant charge and sentence concessions to defendants who enter a plea of guilty or nolo contendere when the interest of the public in the effective administration of criminal justice would thereby be served. Among the considerations which are appropriate in determining this question are:
>
> (i) that the defendant by his plea has aided in ensuring the prompt and certain application of correctional measures to him;
>
> * * *
>
> (vi) that the defendant by his plea has aided in avoiding delay (including delay due to crowded dockets) in the disposition of other cases and thereby has increased the probability of prompt and certain application of correctional measures to other offenders.

Id., Standard 1.8(a).

In 1979, however, the American Bar Association approved the following amended version of this standard:

> (a) The fact that a defendant has entered a plea of guilty or nolo contendere should not, by itself alone, be considered by the court as a mitigating factor in imposing sentence. It is proper for the court to grant charge and sentence concessions to defendants who enter a plea of guilty or nolo contendere when consistent with the protection of the public, the gravity of the offense, and the needs of the defendant, and when there is substantial evidence to establish that:
>
> (i) the defendant is genuinely contrite and has shown a willingness to assume responsibility for his or her conduct;
>
> (ii) the concessions will make possible alternative correctional measures which are better adapted to achieving protective, deterrent, or other purposes of correctional treatment, or will prevent undue harm to the defendant from the form of conviction;

(iii) the defendant, by making public trial unnecessary, has demonstrated genuine consideration for the victims of his or her criminal activity, by desiring either to make restitution or to prevent unseemly public scrutiny or embarrassment to them; or

(iv) the defendant has given or offered cooperation when such cooperation has resulted or may result in the successful prosecution of other offenders engaged in equally serious or more serious criminal conduct.

(b) The court should not impose upon a defendant any sentence in excess of that which would be justified by any of the protective, deterrent, or other purposes of the criminal law because the defendant has chosen to require the prosecution to prove guilt at trial rather than to enter a plea of guilty or nolo contendere.

III ABA Standards for Criminal Justice, Standard 14–1.8 (1980). Is there a significant difference between the two versions of the standard? If so, which is the more desirable? Which is most "practical?" Which is most consistent with the various constitutional rights involved? Is some other approach better? Consider the position(s) of the Standards in evaluating the following material.

1.   PRACTICES AND CONTROVERSIES

Newman, Reshape the Deal
9 Trial 11 (1973).*

The Negotiated Plea. Throwing oneself on the mercy of the court is one thing; arranging for charge and sentencing concession ahead of time is, or may be, a more complex and even more controversial issue. When the term "plea bargaining" is used, it rarely refers to simple mercy-of-the-court situations. What is generally meant is a prearraignment "deal" between the prosecution and the defense in which charges are dropped (in spite of sufficient evidence) or where specific sentence promises are made in exchange for the defendant's willingness to plead guilty. There is ample research today to indicate that plea negotiations are common, even routine, in many—perhaps all—jurisdictions in the country.

* * *

Plea Negotiation Practices. While research has shown plea bargaining to be common in courts across the land, there are variations in types of plea-agreements and in the actual procedures followed by prosecutors and defense in different jurisdictions. Part of this variation is the result of differences in criminal codes, especially sentencing provisions, from one place to another. In states with statutorily mandated sentences for certain crimes (20–to–life for armed robbery, for example), the only way a defendant can achieve sentence leniency is to have the charges lowered. In other

* Reprinted from Trial Magazine, 20 Garden St., Cambridge, Mass. (May/June 1973).

places, where indeterminate sentences are common and the judge has wide discretion to choose among types and lengths of sentences regardless of charge, reduction is less important than a pre-plea promise from the prosecutor to "recommend" probation or some other lenient penalty.

The way a typical bargaining session works is as follows: A defendant is apprehended and initially charged with armed robbery, an offense carrying a mandatory minimum prison term of 20 years. Either on his own or through counsel he indicates to the prosecutor a willingness to plead guilty to a lesser crime in order to avoid the mandatory sentence of the higher charge.

In some cases, though actually a settlement process, negotiation can be quite adversary in its own right. The defense counsel may indicate to the prosecutor that he thinks the state has no evidence against his client except possibly a charge of disorderly conduct. The prosecutor in turn may state that he is not only going to push the armed robbery charge but plans to level a special count of being a habitual offender unless the defendant cooperates. Defense counsel then offers to have his client plead guilty to petty larceny with the prosecutor countering by offering to reduce the charge to second degree robbery.

So it goes. Eventually an agreed upon lesser charge—burglary or grand larceny, for example—may result and the defendant will plead guilty, facing at most a substantially reduced prison sentence and at best perhaps probation.

If the defendant wishes to be placed on probation, he may push in negotiation for more than charge reduction. He may also ask the prosecuting attorney to promise that at sentencing the state will "recommend" probation if and when asked by the court. This is a customary (though not universal) practice.

A prosecutor's recommendation of probation is a strong factor in the defendant's favor although a weaker, and also a vigorously sought after promise, is for the prosecutor to make no recommendation at the time of sentencing or to agree "not to oppose" probation if requested by the defendant. After all, the offender knows that should the prosecutor arise at sentencing and recommend a long prison term (perhaps reading prior convictions into the record) it is highly likely that incarceration will result.

Therefore, in most jurisdictions, a preplea sentence promise by the prosecutor is a major concession, even though the district attorney has no official authority to actually impose sentence.

There are other considerations that occasionally arise in plea negotiation depending upon the particular defendant, the crime or crimes charged and the sentencing structure and practices of the jurisdiction in question.

For example, often a person arrested for one crime is subsequently charged with others. It is rare that a burglar is apprehended on his first attempt and, once nabbed, the police may "solve" 20 or 30 separate burglaries, all potential charges against the defendant. Theoretically he could be tried on each count and could receive consecutive sentences. If, for example, he were accused of ten burglaries, tried separately on each and convicted on only half yet got one to three on each (to be served consecutively) he would in effect face a five to fifteen-year sentence. Therefore he may seek to have charges joined into a single accusation, or have some of the counts dismissed if he is willing to plead to one or perhaps two.

Additionally, some offenders may be facing a habitual offender rap, which is normally filed as a separate indictment or information. In exchange for pleading to the crime as charged he may avoid such "supercharging" by the state. Then, too, some defendants are on parole or probation for prior convictions and may negotiate for revocation of the old sentence if the new charge is dismissed or sufficiently reduced.

There is even some "lateral" bargaining, primarily to modify the conviction label without affecting sentence at all. Some defendants are willing to plead guilty to serious crimes such as robbery to avoid conviction of certain sex crimes like rape or sodomy because, while the potential sentence may be longer, the label and its attendant consequences throughout the life of the defendant are considered to be a better deal.

Permutations and combinations of plea agreements are almost endless especially where multiple charges are involved, but the end result is always the same: The defendant is allowed to plead guilty to lesser offenses or receives a preadjudication sentence promise in exchange for his willingness to give up his right to trial.

Why Plea Bargain? Motivations of the guilty defendant in plea bargaining are readily discernible. He wishes to minimize both the sentence which follows conviction and the label which attaches to it. He also usually hopes to avoid publicity, not only for himself, but perhaps to protect his family and friends from likely notoriety if he demands trial. Occasionally he may wish to protect accomplices or confederates by taking the rap himself.

The bargaining motivations of the state are somewhat less readily discernible, though in every instance the bargained plea is much more efficient, cheaper and more certain than a contested case.

There are, however, other more subtle but no less important motivations on the part of the prosecutor and other state officials for engaging in plea negotiation and in fact encouraging it. Some of these are self-seeking, but others rest on a sincere attempt to individualize justice, to build equity into a system that otherwise would be too harsh in certain types of cases.

One of the self-seeking motivations on the part of the state is to avoid challenge not only of the amount of evidence but the ways it was obtained. In spite of all the current controversy about illegal searches, wiretaps, failure to give *Miranda* warnings and the like, such issues are really paramount only in cases where pretrial motions are denied and which go to trial.

A plea of guilty waives almost all defects in the state's case. The way evidence was obtained is never tested. Whether the *Miranda* warning was given or not is irrelevant in the case of the defendant who pleads guilty. The insanity defense, or entrapment, and other important procedural and substantive issues are mooted by the guilty plea.

In short, the guilty plea doesn't refine and hone the law, rather it avoids sticky questions of police practices, prosecutorial trial skills and even the adequacy of legislative sentencing provisions. Furthermore, in most cases the plea satisfies all interested parties. The defendant has his deal; the prosecutor has an assured conviction (for a trial, no matter how carefully prepared, is always an uncertainty given the vagaries of juries), the victim is theoretically satisfied by conviction of the perpetrator and correctional agencies receive an offender who has admitted his guilt. It is always a difficult task for correctional authorities who receive an offender who, though sentenced after a full jury trial, still protests his innocence. How does rehabilitation begin?

At any rate, given the absence of challenge to police methods at one end, and a confessed criminal received in prison at the other, there is more than simple overcrowding behind the state's willingness, to accept the plea. It is not only a quick and efficient way of processing defendants, it is a safe way, for pleading defendants do not rock the boat.

There are, however, a number of other state considerations underlying plea negotiation that are less self-seeking, and perhaps more consistent with a general desire to build equity into our criminal justice system, particularly in regard to sentencing.

It is common practice in many state legislatures (and in Congress as well) for very severe laws to be passed in the heat of anger or at the height of public indignation over what appears to be a serious crime wave. A few years ago about half the states adopted very harsh "sex psychopath" laws. In recent years a number of states have adopted severe sale-of-narcotic laws, mandating life imprisonment or even death to "pushers."

In passing such laws the drafters typically have in mind the worst offenders—the organized criminal or the professional dopefiend who sells heroin to school children or is otherwise the most vicious or professional violator. However, in the day-to-day operation of courts the types of sale-of-narcotics defendants who appear are rarely professional heroin pushers but are more likely to be young men or women who have sold a couple of pills or marijuana cigarettes to friends.

Technically they are guilty of sale of narcotics and in most cases there is little doubt that the evidence held by the state is sufficient to prove the charge. Yet confronted with these cases it is a rare prosecutor or trial judge who wishes to give a mandatory life sentence (sometimes nonparoleable) to an 18-year-old offender whose crime is selling a few reefers to a buddy. On the other hand the district attorney may be unwilling or reluctant to dismiss the case entirely so that the lesser charge of "possession" or some related crime may be offered as a desirable solution.

This motivation pattern for bargaining is an extension of traditional prosecutor's discretion but here instead of dismissing the case the prosecutor in effect sentences the defendant. The reason for this is the nature of criminal law itself. Legislation defining crimes and fixing penalties is necessarily general and broad and if the prosecutor and other court officials are confronted with individual cases which, while they technically fit the same statutory category, are readily distinguishable in terms of the actual harm they have done to victims or to the social order in general they can only achieve individualization of sentences by reducing charges. There are a number of such situations where charge reduction is used to individualize justice without really violating the legislative intent of proceeding against very serious criminals.

In addition to the avoidance of inappropriately excessive mandatory sentences, other motivations which have been identified are:

- reduction to avoid a criminal label which would imply in the public mind that the defendant was guilty of conduct which is really not consistent with the actions that form his criminal violation.

* * *

- where there is a crime involving codefendants of unequal culpability. This is simply a recognition of the prosecutor's discretion to distinguish what the legislatures cannot do; that is, to determine the degree of involvement in a single offense on the part of multiple persons involved in a crime.

An older, sophisticated armed robber who has as a look-out a young, inexperienced, clean-record accomplice may be convicted "on the nose" but his accomplice offered a lesser charge (perhaps attempted robbery or burglary) to balance culpability and consequences. The same thing occurs when there are other mitigating circumstances in the crime, such as the participation of the victim in the criminal activity itself as, for example, in certain forms of confidence games.

- where the therapeutic benefits of alternative sentences can best be achieved by charge reduction or by awarding probation when normally such would not be the case. This is indeed a mercy-of-the-court situation but one which ignores the other administrative advantages of negotiation.

This is an extension of sentencing discretion, with primary concern to place the defendant in the best correctional setting possible which might be precluded if he's convicted on the nose. A mandatory prison term for a good-risk young violator may be more damaging to the community in the long run than if he is given a break on his first sentence.

- reduction to support law enforcement efforts by rewarding informants, state witnesses and the like with lesser charges and sentences. This is sometimes called "trading the little ones for the big ones," but the fact remains that unless differential court leniency is shown major cases cannot be developed.

* * *

The prevailing attitude toward the process (until recently at least) on the part of many, including some appellate courts, is that there is something dirty about plea bargaining, something corruptive or potentially corruptive in negotiating with criminals for punishment less than could be levied if the full force of the law were used. While it is true that from one perspective plea negotiation does act to avoid legislative mandate, and, like the exercise of all administrative discretion, has the *potential* for corruption, another side of the coin is presented by equity decisions, by a conscientious attempt to introduce "justice" into individual cases.

National Advisory Commission on Criminal Justice Standards and Goals

Courts 47–48 (1973).

The Commission ... totally condemns plea bargaining as an institution. ... [I]t has concluded that [plea bargaining] exacts unacceptable costs from all concerned. Perhaps the major cost is that of reduced rationality in the processing of criminal defendants. Whether a defendant is convicted should depend upon the evidence available to convict him, and what disposition is made of a convicted offender should depend upon what action best serves rehabilitative and deterrent needs. The likelihood that these factors will control conviction and disposition is minimized in the inevitable "horsetrading" atmosphere of plea negotiation. Some defendants suffer from the resulting irrationality.

But the public's interest in disposition of cases to serve its interest in protection also suffers. ...

Another major cost involved in plea negotiation is the burden it inevitably places upon the exercise of the rights involved in trial—the rights to jury trial, to confront and cross-examine witnesses, to have the judge or jury convinced of guilt beyond a reasonable doubt, and similar matters. It is inherent in plea negotiation that leniency will be given in return for nonassertion of these rights.

* * *

[I]t is wholly unacceptable to add to [the inevitable costs of trial] the necessity of forfeiting a discount that could otherwise have been obtained. Probably the major individual victim of today's plea bargaining system is the defendant who exercises his right to trial and suffers a substantially more severe sentence than he would have received had he pleaded guilty.

By imposing a penalty upon the exercise of procedural rights in those cases in which there is a reasonable likelihood that the rights will be vindicated, the plea negotiation system creates a significant danger to the innocent. Many of the rights it discourages are rights designed to prevent the conviction of innocent defendants. To the extent these rights are rendered nonoperative by the plea negotiation system, innocent defendants are endangered. ...

NOTES

1. **Impact of defense counsel on plea bargaining.** Some studies have developed evidence that a lawyer's success in the plea bargaining process may depend not only upon the prosecutor's perception of the lawyer's skill and vigor but also upon the existence or nonexistence of a personal relationship between defense counsel and prosecutor. See Dear, Adversary Review: An Experiment in Performance Evaluation, 57 Den.L.J. 401, 416–17 (1980); White, A Proposal for Reform of the Plea Bargaining Process, 119 U.Pa.L.Rev. 439, 448 (1971). A defendant, then, may suffer by comparison with other defendants because of defense counsel's inability or unwillingness to develop such relationships. But does this distinguish plea bargaining from the trial process? Is a lawyer's personality likely to have no effect upon the judge or jury in a contested case?

2. **Pressures on defense counsel to plea bargain.** Alschuler, The Defense Attorney's Role in Plea Bargaining, 84 Yale L.J. 1179 (1975), explores the factors that may render lawyers susceptible to the pressures of the plea bargaining process. Privately-retained lawyers, he notes, often set a single fee at the outset of the case to cover the lawyer's work however the case may proceed. Once the lawyer has collected this fee, the lawyer has a strong financial interest in earning that fee as efficiently as possible. This can often be accomplished by pleading the client guilty. "[T]he guilty-plea system," Alschuler concludes, "subjects even honest and conscientious lawyers to temptations that have no place in a rational system of administering justice." Id., at 1199.

2. "VOLUNTARINESS" OF PLEAS AND RELATED MATTERS

a. BASIC VOLUNTARINESS CONSIDERATIONS

Challenges to the "voluntariness" (and thus the constitutional validity) of a guilty plea are not confined to situations in which the plea is the culmination of plea bargaining. But the effect of plea bargaining upon the validity of guilty pleas presents some of the most significant voluntariness issues. In 1970, the Supreme Court undertook to deal with plea bargaining and its effect upon guilty pleas when those pleas are challenged as violative of federal constitutional standards. Three cases decided together in May of 1970, Brady v. United States, 397 U.S. 742, 90 S.Ct. 1463, 25 L.Ed.2d 747 (1970), McMann v. Richardson, 397 U.S. 759, 90 S.Ct. 1441, 25 L.Ed.2d 763 (1970), and Parker v. North Carolina, 397 U.S. 790, 90 S.Ct. 1458, 25 L.Ed.2d 785 (1970)—the *Brady* trilogy—resulted. These constitute the foundation for federal constitutional doctrine in this area. Some aspects of these cases, of course, have important ramifications for pleas that are not related to plea agreements. For example, the issue of the impact of a coerced confession or other inadmissible "evidence" upon a subsequent plea of guilty, at issue in both *McMann* and *Parker,* can certainly arise in a nonbargain situation.

Brady v. United States

Supreme Court of the United States, 1970.
397 U.S. 742, 90 S.Ct. 1463, 25 L.Ed.2d 747.

■ MR. JUSTICE WHITE delivered the opinion of the Court.

In 1959, petitioner was charged with kidnaping in violation of 18 U.S.C.A. § 1201(a). Since the indictment charged that the victim of the kidnaping was not liberated unharmed, petitioner faced a maximum penalty of death if the verdict of the jury should so recommend. Petitioner, represented by competent counsel throughout, first elected to plead not guilty. Apparently because the trial judge was unwilling to try the case without a jury, petitioner made no serious attempt to reduce the possibility of a death penalty by waiving a jury trial. Upon learning that his codefendant, who had confessed to the authorities, would plead guilty and be available to testify against him, petitioner changed his plea to guilty. His plea was accepted after the trial judge twice questioned him as to the voluntariness of his plea. Petitioner was sentenced to 50 years' imprisonment, later reduced to 30.

In 1967, petitioner sought relief under 28 U.S.C.A. § 2255, claiming that his plea of guilty was not voluntarily given because § 1201(a) operated to coerce his plea. . . .

After a hearing, the District Court for the District of New Mexico denied relief. . . . The court held that § 1201(a) was constitutional and found that petitioner decided to plead guilty when he learned that his codefendant was going to plead guilty: petitioner pleaded guilty "by reason of other matters and not by reason of the statute" or because of any acts of the trial judge. The court concluded that "the plea was voluntarily and knowingly made."

The Court of Appeals for the Tenth Circuit affirmed, determining that the District Court's findings were supported by substantial evidence and specifically approving the finding that petitioner's plea of guilty was voluntary. 404 F.2d 601 (1968). We granted certiorari, 395 U.S. 976, 89 S.Ct. 2146, 23 L.Ed.2d 764 (1969), to consider the claim that the Court of Appeals was in error in not reaching a contrary result on the authority of this Court's decision in United States v. Jackson, 390 U.S. 570 (1968). We affirm.

I.

In United States v. Jackson, supra, the defendants were indicted under § 1201(a). The District Court dismissed the § 1201(a) count of the indictment, holding the statute unconstitutional because it permitted imposition of the death sentence only upon a jury's recommendation and thereby made the risk of death the price of a jury trial. This Court held the statute valid, except for the death penalty provision; with respect to the latter, the Court agreed with the trial court "that the death penalty provision . . . imposes an impermissible burden upon the exercise of a constitutional right. . . . " 390 U.S., at 572, 88 S.Ct., at 1211. The problem was to determine "whether the Constitution permits the establishment of such a death penalty, applicable only to those defendants who assert the right to contest their guilt before a jury." 390 U.S., at 581, 88 S.Ct., at 1216. The inevitable effect of the provision was said to be to discourage assertion of the Fifth Amendment right not to plead guilty and to deter exercise of the Sixth Amendment right to demand a jury trial. Because the legitimate goal of limiting the death penalty to cases in which a jury recommends it could be achieved without penalizing those defendants who plead not guilty and elect a jury trial, the death penalty provision "needlessly penalize[d] the assertion of a constitutional right," 390 U.S., at 583, 88 S.Ct., at 1217, and was therefore unconstitutional.

Since the "inevitable effect" of the death penalty provision of § 1201(a) was said by the Court to be the needless encouragement of pleas of guilty and waivers of jury trial, Brady contends that *Jackson* requires the invalidation of every plea of guilty entered under that section, at least when the fear of death is shown to have been a factor in the plea. Petitioner, however, has read far too much into the *Jackson* opinion.

The Court made it clear in *Jackson* that it was not holding § 1201(a) inherently coercive of guilty pleas: "the fact that the Federal Kidnaping Act tends to discourage defendants from insisting upon their innocence and demanding trial by jury hardly implies that every defendant who enters a guilty plea to a charge under the Act does so involuntarily." 390 U.S., at 583, 88 S.Ct., at 1218.

* * *

Plainly, it seems to us, *Jackson* ruled neither that all pleas of guilty encouraged by the fear of a possible death sentence are involuntary pleas nor that such encouraged pleas are invalid whether involuntary or not. *Jackson* prohibits the imposition of the death penalty under § 1201(a), but that decision neither fashioned a new standard for judging the validity of guilty pleas nor mandated a new application of the test theretofore fashioned by courts and since reiterated that guilty pleas are valid if both "voluntary" and "intelligent." See Boykin v. Alabama, 395 U.S. 238, 242, 89 S.Ct. 1709, 1711–1712, 23 L.Ed.2d 274 (1969).

That a guilty plea is a grave and solemn act to be accepted only with care and discernment has long been recognized. Central to the plea and the foundation for entering judgment against the defendant is the defendant's admission in open court that he committed the acts charged in the indictment. He thus stands as a witness against himself and he is shielded by the Fifth Amendment from being compelled to do so—hence the minimum requirement that his plea be the voluntary expression of his own choice. But the plea is more than an admission of past conduct; it is the defendant's consent that judgment of conviction may be entered without a trial—a waiver of his right to trial before a jury or a judge. Waivers of constitutional rights not only must be voluntary but must be knowing, intelligent acts done with sufficient awareness of the relevant circumstances and likely consequences. On neither score was Brady's plea of guilty invalid.

II.

The trial judge in 1959 found the plea voluntary before accepting it; the District Court in 1968, after an evidentiary hearing, found that the plea was voluntarily made; the Court of Appeals specifically approved the finding of voluntariness. We see no reason on this record to disturb the judgment of those courts. Petitioner, advised by competent counsel, tendered his plea after his codefendant, who had already given a confession, determined to plead guilty and became available to testify against petitioner. It was this development which the District Court found to have triggered Brady's guilty plea.

The voluntariness of Brady's plea can be determined only by considering all of the relevant circumstances surrounding it. One of these circumstances was the possibility of a heavier sentence following a guilty verdict after a trial. It may be that Brady, faced with a strong case against him and recognizing that his chances for acquittal were slight, preferred to plead guilty and thus limit the penalty to life imprisonment rather than to elect a jury trial which could result in a death penalty. But even if we assume that Brady would not have pleaded guilty except for the death penalty provision of § 1201(a), this assumption merely identifies the penalty provision as a "but for" cause of his plea. That the statute caused the plea in this sense does not necessarily prove that the plea was coerced and invalid as an involuntary act.

The State to some degree encourages pleas of guilty at every important step in the criminal process. For some people, their breach of a State's law is alone sufficient reason for surrendering themselves and accepting punishment. For others, apprehension and charge, both threatening acts by the Government, jar them into admitting their guilt. In still other cases, the post-indictment accumulation of evidence may convince the defendant and his counsel that a trial is not worth the agony and expense to the defendant and his family. All these pleas of guilty are valid in spite of the State's responsibility for some of the factors motivating the pleas; the pleas are no more improperly compelled than is the decision by a defendant at the close of the State's evidence at trial that he must take the stand or face certain conviction.

Of course, the agents of the State may not produce a plea by actual or threatened physical harm or by mental coercion overbearing the will of the defendant. But nothing of the sort is claimed in this case; nor is there evidence that Brady was so gripped by fear of the death penalty or hope of leniency that he did not or could not, with the help of counsel, rationally weigh the advantages of going to trial against the advantages of pleading guilty. Brady's claim is of a different sort: that it violates the Fifth Amendment to influence or encourage a guilty plea by opportunity or promise of leniency and that a guilty plea is coerced and invalid if influenced by the fear of a possibly higher penalty for the crime charged if a conviction is obtained after the State is put to its proof.

Insofar as the voluntariness of his plea is concerned, there is little to differentiate Brady from (1) the defendant, in a jurisdiction where the judge and jury have the same range of sentencing power, who pleads guilty because his lawyer advises him that the judge will very probably be more lenient than the jury; (2) the defendant, in a jurisdiction where the judge alone has sentencing power, who is advised by counsel that the judge is normally more lenient with defendants who plead guilty than with those who go to trial; (3) the defendant who is permitted by prosecutor and judge to plead guilty to a lesser offense included in the offense charged; and (4) the defendant who pleads guilty to certain counts with the understanding that other charges will be dropped. In each of these situations,[4] as in Brady's case, the defendant might never plead guilty absent the possibility or certainty that the plea will result in a lesser penalty than the sentence that could be imposed after a trial and a verdict of guilty. We decline to hold, however, that a guilty plea is compelled and invalid under the Fifth Amendment whenever motivated by the defendant's desire to accept the certainty or probability of a lesser penalty rather than face a wider range of

---

4. We here make no reference to the situation where the prosecutor or judge, or both, deliberately employ their charging and sentencing powers to induce a particular defendant to tender a plea of guilty. In Brady's case there is no claim that the prosecutor threatened prosecution on a charge not justified by the evidence or that the trial judge threatened Brady with a harsher sentence if convicted after trial in order to induce him to plead guilty.

possibilities extending from acquittal to conviction and a higher penalty authorized by law for the crime charged.

The issue we deal with is inherent in the criminal law and its administration because guilty pleas are not constitutionally forbidden, because the criminal law characteristically extends to judge or jury a range of choice in setting the sentence in individual cases, and because both the State and the defendant often find it advantageous to preclude the possibility of the maximum penalty authorized by law. For a defendant who sees slight possibility of acquittal, the advantages of pleading guilty and limiting the probable penalty are obvious—his exposure is reduced, the correctional processes can begin immediately, and the practical burdens of a trial are eliminated. For the State there are also advantages—the more promptly imposed punishment after an admission of guilt may more effectively attain the objectives of punishment; and with the avoidance of trial, scarce judicial and prosecutorial resources are conserved for those cases in which there is a substantial issue of the defendant's guilt or in which there is substantial doubt that the State can sustain its burden of proof. It is this mutuality of advantage which perhaps explains the fact that at present well over three-fourths of the criminal convictions in this country rest on pleas of guilty, a great many of them no doubt motivated at least in part by the hope or assurance of a lesser penalty than might be imposed if there were a guilty verdict after a trial to judge or jury.

Of course, that the prevalence of guilty pleas is explainable does not necessarily validate those pleas or the system which produces them. But we cannot hold that it is unconstitutional for the State to extend a benefit to a defendant who in turn extends a substantial benefit to the State and who demonstrates by his plea that he is ready and willing to admit his crime and to enter the correctional system in a frame of mind which affords hope for success in rehabilitation over a shorter period of time than might otherwise be necessary.

A contrary holding would require the States and Federal Government to forbid guilty pleas altogether, to provide a single invariable penalty for each crime defined by the statutes, or to place the sentencing function in a separate authority having no knowledge of the manner in which the conviction in each case was obtained. In any event, it would be necessary to forbid prosecutors and judges to accept guilty pleas to selected counts, to lesser included offenses, or to reduced charges. The Fifth Amendment does not reach so far.

Bram v. United States, 168 U.S. 532, 18 S.Ct. 183, 42 L.Ed. 568 (1897), held that the admissibility of a confession depended upon whether it was compelled within the meaning of the Fifth Amendment. To be admissible, a confession must be " 'free and voluntary: that is, must not be extracted by any sort of threats or violence, nor obtained by any direct or implied promises, however slight, nor by the exertion of any improper influence.' " 168 U.S., at 542–543, 18 S.Ct., at 187. More recently, Malloy v. Hogan, 378 U.S. 1, 84 S.Ct. 1489, 12 L.Ed.2d 653 (1964), carried forward the *Bram* definition of compulsion in the course of holding applicable to the States the Fifth Amendment privilege against compelled self-incrimination.

Bram is not inconsistent with our holding that Brady's plea was not compelled even though the law promised him a lesser maximum penalty if he did not go to trial. *Bram* dealt with a confession given by a defendant in custody, alone and unrepresented by counsel. In such circumstances, even a mild promise of leniency was deemed sufficient to bar the confession, not because the promise was an illegal act as such, but because defendants at such times are too sensitive to inducement and the possible impact on them too great to ignore and too difficult to assess. But *Bram* and its progeny did not hold that the possibly coercive impact of a promise of leniency could not be dissipated by the presence and advice of counsel, any more than Miranda v. Arizona, 384 U.S. 436, 86 S.Ct. 1602, 16 L.Ed.2d 694 (1966), held that the possibly coercive atmosphere of the police station could not be counteracted by the presence of counsel or other safeguards.

Brady's situation bears no resemblance to Bram's. Brady first pleaded not guilty; prior to changing his plea to guilty he was subjected to no threats or promises in face-to-face encounters with the authorities. He had competent counsel and full opportunity to assess the advantages and disadvantages of a trial as compared with those attending a plea of guilty; there was no hazard of an impulsive and improvident response to a seeming but unreal advantage. His plea of guilty was entered in open court and before a judge obviously sensitive to the requirements of the law with respect to guilty pleas. Brady's plea, unlike Bram's confession, was voluntary.

The standard as to the voluntariness of guilty pleas must be essentially that defined by Judge Tuttle of the Court of Appeals for the Fifth Circuit:

> " '[A] plea of guilty entered by one fully aware of the direct consequences, including the actual value of any commitments made to him by the court, prosecutor, or his own counsel, must stand unless induced by threats (or promises to discontinue improper harassment), misrepresentation (including unfulfilled or unfulfillable promises), or perhaps by promises that are by their nature improper as having no proper relationship to the prosecutor's business (e.g. bribes).' 242 F.2d at page 115."[5]

Under this standard, a plea of guilty is not invalid merely because entered to avoid the possibility of a death penalty.

III.

The record before us also supports the conclusion that Brady's plea was intelligently made. He was advised by competent counsel, he was made aware of the nature of the charge against him, and there was nothing to indicate that he was incompetent or otherwise not in control of his mental faculties; once his confederate had pleaded guilty and became available to testify, he chose to plead guilty, perhaps to ensure that he would face no more than life imprisonment or a term of years. Brady was aware of

---

5. Shelton v. United States, 246 F.2d 571, 572 n. 2 (C.A. 5th Cir.1957) (en banc), rev'd on confession of error on other grounds, 356 U.S. 26, 78 S.Ct. 563, 2 L.Ed.2d 579 (1958).

precisely what he was doing when he admitted that he had kidnapped the victim and had not released her unharmed.

It is true that Brady's counsel advised him that § 1201(a) empowered the jury to impose the death penalty and that nine years later in United States v. Jackson, supra, the Court held that the jury had no such power as long as the judge could impose only a lesser penalty if trial was to the court or there was a plea of guilty. But these facts do not require us to set aside Brady's conviction.

Often the decision to plead guilty is heavily influenced by the defendant's appraisal of the prosecution's case against him and by the apparent likelihood of securing leniency should a guilty plea be offered and accepted. Considerations like these frequently present imponderable questions for which there are no certain answers; judgments may be made that in the light of later events seem improvident, although they were perfectly sensible at the time. The rule that a plea must be intelligently made to be valid does not require that a plea be vulnerable to later attack if the defendant did not correctly assess every relevant factor entering into his decision. A defendant is not entitled to withdraw his plea merely because he discovers long after the plea has been accepted that his calculus misapprehended the quality of the State's case or the likely penalties attached to alternative courses of action. More particularly, absent misrepresentation or other impermissible conduct by state agents, a voluntary plea of guilty intelligently made in the light of the then applicable law does not become vulnerable because later judicial decisions indicate that the plea rested on a faulty premise. A plea of guilty triggered by the expectations of a competently counseled defendant that the State will have a strong case against him is not subject to later attack because the defendant's lawyer correctly advised him with respect to the then existing law as to possible penalties but later pronouncements of the courts, as in this case, hold that the maximum penalty for the crime in question was less than was reasonably assumed at the time the plea was entered.

The fact that Brady did not anticipate United States v. Jackson, supra, does not impugn the truth or reliability of his plea. We find no requirement in the Constitution that a defendant must be permitted to disown his solemn admissions in open court that he committed the act with which he is charged simply because it later develops that the State would have had a weaker case than the defendant had thought or that the maximum penalty then assumed applicable has been held inapplicable in subsequent judicial decisions.

This is not to say that guilty plea convictions hold no hazards for the innocent or that the methods of taking guilty pleas presently employed in this country are necessarily valid in all respects. This mode of conviction is no more foolproof than full trials to the court or to the jury. Accordingly, we take great precautions against unsound results, and we should continue to do so, whether conviction is by plea or by trial. We would have serious doubts about this case if the encouragement of guilty pleas by offers of leniency substantially increased the likelihood that defendants, advised by competent counsel, would falsely condemn themselves. But our view is to the contrary and is based on our expectations that courts will satisfy themselves that pleas of guilty are voluntarily and intelligently made by competent defendants with adequate advice of counsel and that there is nothing to question the accuracy and reliability of the defendants' admissions that they committed the crimes with which they are charged. In the case before us, nothing in the record impeaches Brady's plea or suggests that his admissions in open court were anything but the truth.

Although Brady's plea of guilty may well have been motivated in part by a desire to avoid a possible death penalty, we are convinced that his plea was voluntarily and intelligently made and we have no reason to doubt that his solemn admission of guilt was truthful.

Affirmed.

■ MR. JUSTICE BLACK, while adhering to his belief that United States v. Jackson, 390 U.S. 570, 88 S.Ct. 1209, 20 L.Ed.2d 138 was wrongly decided, concurs in the judgment and in substantially all of the opinion in this case.

* * *

[Mr. Justice Brennan, with whom Mr. Justice Douglas and Mr. Justice Marshall join, dissenting in Parker v. North Carolina, 397 U.S. 790, 90 S.Ct. 1474 (1970), which is omitted, and concurring in the result in Brady v. United States.]

In United States v. Jackson, 390 U.S. 570, 88 S.Ct. 1209, 20 L.Ed.2d 138 (1968), we held that the operative effect of the capital punishment provisions of the Federal Kidnaping Act was unconstitutionally "to discourage assertion of the Fifth Amendment right not to plead guilty and to deter exercise of the Sixth Amendment right to demand a jury trial." 390 U.S., at 581, 88 S.Ct., at 1216. The petitioners in these cases claim that they were the victims of the very vices we condemned in *Jackson*. Yet the Court paradoxically holds that each of the petitioners must be denied relief even if his allegations are substantiated. Indeed, the Court apparently holds that never, except perhaps in highly unrealistic hypothetical situations, will the constitutional defects identified in *Jackson* vitiate a guilty plea.[6] In so holding, the Court seriously undermines the rational underpinnings of *Jackson* and departs broadly from our prior approach to the determination of the voluntariness of guilty pleas and also confessions. This is merely one manifestation of a design to insulate all guilty pleas from subsequent attack no matter what influences induced them. I cannot acquiesce in this

---

6. The precise contours of the Court's theory, developed principally in Brady v. United States, are unclear. The Court initially states that "the possibility of a heavier sentence following a guilty verdict after a trial" is one of the "relevant circumstances" to be taken into account in determining the voluntariness of the guilty plea. ...Subsequently, however, after discussing its notion of voluntariness, the Court concludes that "a plea of guilty is not invalid merely because entered to avoid the possibility of a death penalty." ... Elsewhere the Court states that "there [is no] evidence that Brady was so gripped by fear of the death penalty or hope of leniency that he did not or could not, with the help of counsel, rationally weigh the advantages of going to trial against the advantages of pleading guilty." ... If the latter is what the Court deems to be the criterion of voluntariness, the holding is totally without precedent, for it has never been thought that an individual's mental state must border on temporary insanity before his confession or guilty plea can be found "involuntary."

wholesale retreat from the sound principles to which we have previously adhered.

* * *

There is some intimation in the Court's opinions in the instant cases that, at least with respect to guilty pleas, "involuntariness" covers *only* the narrow class of cases in which the defendant's will has been literally overborne. At other points, however, the Court apparently recognizes that the term "involuntary" has traditionally been applied to situations in which an individual, while perfectly capable of rational choice, has been confronted with factors that the government may not constitutionally inject into the decision-making process. ... [I]t has long been held that certain promises of leniency or threats of harsh treatment by the trial judge or the prosecutor unfairly burden or intrude upon the defendant's decision-making process. Even though the defendant is not necessarily rendered incapable of rational choice, his guilty plea nonetheless may be invalid.

Thus the legal concept of "involuntariness" has not been narrowly confined but refers to a surrender of constitutional rights influenced by considerations that the government cannot properly introduce. The critical question that divides the Court is what constitutes an impermissible factor, or, more narrowly in the context of these cases, whether the threat of the imposition of an unconstitutional death penalty is such a factor.

... [W]e have consistently taken great pains to insulate the accused from the more obvious and oppressive forms of physical coercion. Beyond this, in the analogous area of coerced confessions, for example, it has long been recognized that various psychological devices, some of a very subtle and sophisticated nature, may be employed to induce statements. Such influences have been condemned by this Court. ...

The Court's answer to the stringent criterion of voluntariness imposed by *Bram* and subsequent cases is that the availability of counsel to an accused effectively offsets the illicit influence upon him which threats or promises by the government may impose. Of course, the presence of counsel is a factor to be taken into account in any overall evaluation of the voluntariness of a confession or a guilty plea. However, it hardly follows that the support provided by counsel is sufficient by itself to insulate the accused from the effect of any threat or promise by the government.

It has frequently been held, for example, that a guilty plea induced by threats or promises by the trial judge is invalid because of the risk that the trial judge's impartiality will be compromised and because of the inherently unequal bargaining power of the judge and the accused. The assistance of counsel in this situation, of course, may improve a defendant's bargaining *ability,* but it does not alter the underlying inequality of *power.* Significantly, the Court explicitly refrains from expressing its views on that issue. ...This is an unfortunate omission, for judicial promises of leniency in return for a guilty plea provide a useful analogy to what has occurred in the instant cases. Here, the government has promised the accused, through the legislature, that he will receive a substantially reduced sentence if he pleads guilty. In fact, the legislature has simultaneously threatened the accused with the ultimate penalty—death—if he insists upon a jury trial and promised a penalty no greater than life imprisonment if he pleads guilty.

... In any particular case, therefore, the influence of this unconstitutional factor must necessarily be given weight in determining the voluntariness of a plea.

... [I]t is perfectly possible that a defendant pleaded guilty for reasons entirely unrelated to the penalty scheme, for example, because his guilt was clear or because he desired to spare himself and his family "the spectacle and expense of protracted courtroom proceedings." 390 U.S., at 584, 88 S.Ct., at 1217. The converse, however, is equally clear: not every defendant who pleaded guilty under the Act did so voluntarily, that is, uninfluenced by the highly coercive character of the penalty scheme. This much is merely the teaching of *Jackson.*

... Today the Court appears to distinguish sharply between a guilty plea that has been "encouraged" by the penalty scheme and one that has been entered "involuntarily."

* * *

Of course, whether in a given case the penalty scheme has actually exercised its pernicious influence so as to make a guilty plea involuntary can be decided only by consideration of the factors that actually motivated the defendant to enter his plea. If a particular defendant can demonstrate that the death penalty scheme exercised a significant influence upon his decision to plead guilty, then, under *Jackson,* he is entitled to reversal of the conviction based upon his illicitly produced plea.

* * *

We are dealing here with the legislative imposition of a markedly more severe penalty if a defendant asserts his right to a jury trial and a concomitant legislative promise of leniency if he pleads guilty. This is very different from the give-and-take negotiation common in plea bargaining between the prosecution and defense, which arguably possess relatively equal bargaining power. No such flexibility is built into the capital penalty scheme where the government's harsh terms with respect to punishment are stated in unalterable form.

Furthermore, the legislatively ordained penalty scheme may affect any defendant, even one with respect to whom plea bargaining is wholly inappropriate because his guilt is uncertain. Thus the penalty scheme presents a clear danger that the innocent, or those not clearly guilty, or those who insist upon their innocence, will be induced nevertheless to plead guilty. This hazard necessitates particularly sensitive scrutiny of the voluntariness of guilty pleas entered under this type of death penalty scheme.

The penalty schemes involved here are also distinguishable from most plea bargaining because they involve the imposition of death—the most severe and awesome penalty known to our law. This Court has recognized that capital cases are treated differently in some respects from noncapital cases. We have identified the threat of a death penalty as a factor to be given considerable weight in determining whether a defendant has deliberately waived his constitutional rights.

* * *

Parker comes here after denial of state post-conviction relief. The North Carolina courts have consistently taken the position that United States v. Jackson has no applicability to the former North Carolina capital punishment scheme. Thus, the merits of Parker's contention that his plea was motivated by the unconstitutional death penalty have not been considered by the state courts. I would, therefore, reverse the judgment of the North Carolina Court of Appeals and remand the *Parker* case to that court for proceedings not inconsistent with the principles elaborated herein.

* * *

An independent examination of the record in the instant case [*Brady*] convinces me that the conclusions of the lower courts are not clearly erroneous. Although Brady was aware that he faced a possible death sentence, there is no evidence that this factor alone played a significant role in his decision to enter a guilty plea. Rather, there is considerable evidence, which the District Court credited, that Brady's plea was triggered by the confession and plea decision of his codefendant and not by any substantial fear of the death penalty. Moreover, Brady's position is dependent in large measure upon his own assertions, years after the fact, that his plea was motivated by fear of the death penalty and thus rests largely upon his own credibility. For example, there is no indication, contemporaneous with the entry of the guilty plea, that Brady thought he was innocent and was pleading guilty merely to avoid possible execution. Furthermore, Brady's plea was accepted by a trial judge who manifested some sensitivity to the seriousness of a guilty plea and questioned Brady at length concerning his guilt and the voluntariness of the plea before it was finally accepted.

In view of the foregoing, I concur in the result reached by the Court in the *Brady* case.

NOTES

1. **Effect of illegally-obtained evidence on the validity of a guilty plea.** In both McMann v. Richardson and Parker v. North Carolina, the defendants urged that they had been coerced into giving police confessions and that their guilty pleas were the result of those confessions, i.e., "but for" the illegal coercion exerted upon them and the resulting confessions, they would not have pleaded guilty. A majority of the Court rejected this. Justice White, speaking for the Court in *McMann,* observed that the case did not involve "the situation where the circumstances that coerced the confession have abiding impact and also taint the plea. It is not disputed that in such cases a guilty plea is properly open to challenge." 397 U.S. at 767, 90 S.Ct. at 1447, 25 L.Ed.2d at 771. Emphasizing that the defendants in both cases were represented by counsel at the time they entered their plea, the majority held that a showing of a "but for" relationship between the coercion and the confession, on one hand, and the plea, on the other, was not sufficient. In explanation, Justice White stated in *McMann:*

> For the defendant who considers his confession involuntary and hence unusable against him at a trial, tendering a plea of guilty would seem a most improbable

alternative. The sensible course would be to contest his guilt, prevail on his confession claim at trial, on appeal, or, if necessary, in a collateral proceeding, and win acquittal, however guilty he might be. ... If he nevertheless pleads guilty the plea can hardly be blamed on the confession which in his view was inadmissible evidence and no proper part of the State's case. Since by hypothesis the evidence aside from the confession is weak and the defendant has no reasons of his own to plead, a guilty plea in such circumstances is nothing less than a refusal to present his federal claims to the state court in the first instance—a choice by the defendant to take the benefits, if any, of a plea of guilty and then to pursue his coerced-confession claim in collateral proceedings. Surely later allegations that the confession rendered his plea involuntary would appear incredible, and whether his plain bypass of state remedies was an intelligent act depends on whether he was so incompetently advised by counsel concerning the forum in which he should first present his federal claim that the Constitution will afford him another chance to plead.

A more credible explanation for a plea of guilty by a defendant who would go to trial except for his prior confession is his prediction that the law will permit his admissions to be used against him by the trier of fact. At least the probability of the State's being permitted to use the confession as evidence is sufficient to convince him that the State's case is too strong to contest and that a plea of guilty is the most advantageous course. Nothing in this train of events suggests that the defendant's plea, as distinguished from his confession, is an involuntary act. His later petition for collateral relief asserting that a *coerced* confession induced his plea is at most a claim that the admissibility of his confession was mistakenly assessed and that since he was erroneously advised, either under the then applicable law or under the law later announced, his plea was an unintelligent and voidable act. The Constitution, however, does not render pleas of guilty so vulnerable.

... [T]he decision to plead guilty before the evidence is in frequently involves the making of difficult judgments. All the pertinent facts normally cannot be known unless witnesses are examined and cross-examined in court. Even then the truth will often be in dispute. In the face of unavoidable uncertainty, the defendant and his counsel must make their best judgment as to the weight of the State's case. Counsel must predict how the facts, as he understands them, would be viewed by a court. If proved, would those facts convince a judge or jury of the defendant's guilt? On those facts would evidence seized without a warrant be admissible? Would the trier of fact on those facts find a confession voluntary and admissible? Questions like these cannot be answered with certitude; yet a decision to plead guilty must necessarily rest upon counsel's answers, uncertain as they may be. Waiving trial entails the inherent risk that the good-faith evaluations of a reasonably competent attorney will turn out to be mistaken either as to the facts or as to what a court's judgment might be on given facts.

That a guilty plea must be intelligently made is not a requirement that all advice offered by the defendant's lawyer withstand retrospective examination in a post-conviction hearing. Courts continue to have serious differences among themselves on the admissibility of evidence, both with respect to the proper standard by which the facts are to be judged and with respect to the application of that standard to particular facts. That this Court might hold a defendant's confession inadmissible in evidence, possibly by a divided vote, hardly justifies a conclusion that the defendant's attorney was incompetent or ineffective when he thought the admissibility of the confession sufficiently probable to advise a plea of guilty.

In our view a defendant's plea of guilty based on reasonably competent advice is an intelligent plea not open to attack on the ground that counsel may have misjudged the admissibility of the defendant's confession. Whether a plea of guilty is unintelligent and therefore vulnerable when motivated by a confession erroneously thought admissible in evidence depends as an initial matter, not on whether a court would retrospectively consider counsel's advice to be right or wrong, but on whether that advice was within the range of competence demanded of attorneys in criminal cases.

397 U.S. at 768–71, 90 S.Ct. at 1447–49, 25 L.Ed.2d at 772–73.

2. **Misunderstanding the deal.** The informality of plea bargaining has traditionally given rise to significant problems in determining whether a plea was sufficiently "intelligent" to meet constitutional or other standards. In Huffman v. State, 499 S.W.2d 565 (Mo.App.1973), for example, the defendant pleaded guilty to a reduced charge believing that his sentence would not exceed the two years' imprisonment recommended by the prosecution. No firm promises had been made to him, but he was advised by counsel and the prosecutor that although the judge need not follow the recommendation it was likely that the judge would do so. In denying relief to the defendant, the Missouri court explained:

> In State v. Rose, 440 S.W.2d 441 (Mo.1969), relied upon by appellant, the Missouri Supreme Court distinguished between the sort of things deemed misleading and those which are not when it said that there was a difference between "specific assurances and opinion or speculation based upon general court practice" and that a plea may be withdrawn for a defendant who reasonably relies on the former. . . . In the instant case there were no "positive representations" but only strongly expressed opinions by counsel and the prosecutor, always offered with the *caveat* that the trial court did not have to adopt the prosecutor's recommendation. . . . [A]ppellant had no reasonable basis to believe that a lesser sentence than he ultimately received was assured.

499 S.W.2d at 568. Suppose that defense counsel mistakenly believed that the prosecutor's recommendations would be binding on the court? See People v. Wright, 21 Ill.App.3d 301, 314 N.E.2d 733 (1974) (relief must be granted, because "a motion to withdraw a plea of guilty should be allowed upon a showing of misapprehension of the facts or law or of any misrepresentations by a person having apparent authority."). Suppose defense counsel misrepresents to the defendant that the court has committed itself to a given sentence? See Mosher v. Lavallee, 491 F.2d 1346 (2d Cir.1974) (where plea was stimulated by false statement to defendant by counsel that judge had promised given sentence relief, must be granted because of ineffective assistance of counsel).

Bordenkircher v. Hayes

Supreme Court of the United States, 1978.
434 U.S. 357, 98 S.Ct. 663, 54 L.Ed.2d 604.

■ Mr. Justice Stewart delivered the opinion of the Court.

The question in this case is whether the Due Process Clause of the Fourteenth Amendment is violated when a state prosecutor carries out a threat made during plea negotiations to reindict the accused on more serious charges if he does not plead guilty to the offense with which he was originally charged.

I.

The respondent, Paul Lewis Hayes, was indicted by a Fayette County, Ky., grand jury on a charge of uttering a forged instrument in the amount of $88.30, an offense then punishable by a term of two to 10 years in prison. Ky.Rev.Stat. § 434.130 (repealed 1974). After arraignment, Hayes, his retained counsel, and the Commonwealth's attorney met in the presence of the clerk of the court to discuss a possible plea agreement. During these conferences the prosecutor offered to recommend a sentence of five years in prison if Hayes would plead guilty to the indictment. He also said that if Hayes did not plead guilty and "save the court the inconvenience and necessity of a trial," he would return to the grand jury to seek an indictment under the Kentucky Habitual Criminal Act, then Ky.Rev.Stat. § 431.190 (repealed 1975), which would subject Hayes to a mandatory sentence of life imprisonment by reason of his two prior felony convictions. Hayes chose not to plead guilty, and the prosecutor did obtain an indictment charging him under the Habitual Criminal Act. It is not disputed that the recidivist charge was fully justified by the evidence, that the prosecutor was in possession of this evidence at the time of the original indictment, and that Hayes' refusal to plead guilty to the original charge was what led to his indictment under the habitual criminal statute.

A jury found Hayes guilty on the principal charge of uttering a forged instrument and, in a separate proceeding, further found that he had twice before been convicted of felonies. As required by the habitual offender statute, he was sentenced to a life term in the penitentiary. The Kentucky Court of Appeals rejected Hayes' constitutional objections to the enhanced sentence, holding in an unpublished opinion that imprisonment for life with the possibility of parole was constitutionally permissible in light of the previous felonies of which Hayes had been convicted, and that the prosecutor's decision to indict him as an habitual offender was a legitimate use of available leverage in the plea bargaining process.

On Hayes' petition for a federal writ of habeas corpus, the United States District Court for the Eastern District of Kentucky agreed that there had been no constitutional violation in the sentence or the indictment procedure, and denied the writ. The Court of Appeals for the Sixth Circuit reversed the District Court's judgment. . . .

It may be helpful to clarify at the outset the nature of the issue in this case. While the prosecutor did not actually obtain the recidivist indictment until after the plea conferences had ended, his intention to do so was clearly put forth at the outset of the plea negotiations. Hayes was thus fully informed of the true terms of the offer when he made his decision to plead not guilty. This is not a situation, therefore, where the prosecutor without notice brought an additional and more serious charge after plea negotiations relating only to the original indictment had ended with the defendant's insistence on pleading not guilty. As a practical matter, in short, this case would be no different if the grand jury had indicted Hayes as a recidivist from the outset, and the prosecutor had offered to drop that charge as part of the plea bargain.

* * *

This Court held in North Carolina v. Pearce, 395 U.S. 711, 725, 89 S.Ct. 2072, 2080, 23 L.Ed.2d 656, that the Due Process Clause of the Fourteenth Amendment "requires that vindictiveness against a defendant for having successfully attacked his first conviction must play no part in the sentence he receives after a new trial." The same principle was later applied to prohibit a prosecutor from reindicting a convicted misdemeanant on a felony charge after the defendant had invoked an appellate remedy, since in this situation there was also a "realistic likelihood of 'vindictiveness.' " Blackledge v. Perry [417 U.S. 21, at 27, 94 S.Ct. 2098, at 2102] [reprinted at page 907, supra].

In those cases the Court was dealing with the State's unilateral imposition of a penalty upon a defendant who had chosen to exercise a legal right to attack his original conviction—a situation "very different from the give-and-take negotiation common in plea bargaining between the prosecution and the defense, which arguably possess relatively equal bargaining power." The Court has emphasized that the due process violation in cases such as *Pearce* and *Perry* lay not in the possibility that a defendant might be deterred from the exercise of a legal right, but rather in the danger that the State might be retaliating against the accused for lawfully attacking his conviction. See Blackledge v. Perry, supra, 417 U.S., at 26–28, 94 S.Ct., at 2101–02.

To punish a person because he has done what the law plainly allows him to do is a due process violation of the most basic sort, and for an agent of the State to pursue a course of action whose objective is to penalize a person's reliance on his legal rights is "patently unconstitutional." But in the "give-and-take" of plea bargaining, there is no such element of punishment or retaliation so long as the accused is free to accept or reject the prosecution's offer.

Plea bargaining flows from "the mutuality of advantage" to defendants and prosecutors, each with his own reasons for wanting to avoid trial. Defendants advised by competent counsel and protected by other procedural safeguards are presumptively capable of intelligent choice in response to prosecutorial persuasion, and unlikely to be driven to false self-condemnation. Indeed, acceptance of the basic legitimacy of plea bargaining necessarily implies rejection of any notion that a guilty plea is involuntary in a constitutional sense simply because it is the end result of the bargaining process. By hypothesis, the plea may have been induced by promises of a recommendation of a lenient sentence or a reduction of charges, and thus by fear of the possibility of a greater penalty upon conviction after a trial.

While confronting a defendant with the risk of more severe punishment clearly may have a "discouraging effect on the defendant's assertion of his trial rights, the imposition of these difficult choices [is] an inevitable"—and permissible—"attribute of any legitimate system which tolerates and encourages the negotiation of pleas." It follows that, by tolerating and encouraging the negotiation of pleas, this Court has necessarily accepted as constitutionally legitimate the simple reality that the prosecutor's interest at the bargaining table is to persuade the defendant to forego his right to plead not guilty.

It is not disputed here that Hayes was properly chargeable under the recidivist statute, since he had in fact been convicted of two previous felonies. In our system, so long as the prosecutor has probable cause to believe that the accused committed an offense defined by statute, the decision whether or not to prosecute, and what charge to file or bring before a grand jury, generally rests entirely in his discretion.[7] Within the limits set by the legislature's constitutionally valid definition of chargeable offenses, "the conscious exercise of some selectivity in enforcement is not in itself a federal constitutional violation" so long as "the selection was [not] deliberately based upon an unjustifiable standard such as race, religion, or other arbitrary classification." To hold that the prosecutor's desire to induce a guilty plea is an "unjustifiable standard," which, like race or religion, may play no part in his charging decision, would contradict the very premises that underlie the concept of plea bargaining itself. Moreover, a rigid constitutional rule that would prohibit a prosecutor from acting forthrightly in his dealings with the defense could only invite unhealthy subterfuge that would drive the practice of plea bargaining back into the shadows from which it has so recently emerged.

There is no doubt that the breadth of discretion that our country's legal system vests in prosecuting attorneys carries with it the potential for both individual and institutional abuse. And broad though that discretion may be, there are undoubtedly constitutional limits upon its exercise. We hold only that the course of conduct engaged in by the prosecutor in this case, which no more than openly presented the defendant with the unpleasant alternatives of foregoing trial or facing charges on which he was plainly subject to prosecution, did not violate the Due Process Clause of the Fourteenth Amendment.

Accordingly, the judgment of the Court of Appeals is

Reversed.

■ MR. JUSTICE BLACKMUN, with whom MR. JUSTICE BRENNAN and MR. JUSTICE MARSHALL join, dissenting.

Prosecutorial vindictiveness, it seems to me, in the present narrow context, is the fact against which the Due Process Clause ought to protect. I perceive little difference between vindictiveness after what the Court describes ... as the exercise of a "legal right to attack his original conviction," and vindictiveness in the "give-and-take negotiation common in plea bargaining." Prosecutorial vindictiveness in any context is still prosecutorial vindictiveness. The Due Process Clause should protect an accused against it, however it asserts itself. The Court of Appeals rightly so held, and I would affirm the judgment.

It might be argued that it really makes little difference how this case, now that it is here, is decided. The Court's holding gives plea bargaining full sway despite vindictiveness. A contrary result, however, merely would prompt the aggressive prosecutor to bring the greater charge initially in

7. This case does not involve the constitutional implications of a prosecutor's offer during plea bargaining of adverse or lenient treatment for some person *other* than the accused, which might pose a greater danger of inducing a false guilty plea by skewing the assessment of the risks a defendant must consider.

every case, and only thereafter to bargain. The consequences to the accused would still be adverse, for then he would bargain against a greater charge, face the likelihood of increased bail, and run the risk that the court would be less inclined to accept a bargained plea. Nonetheless, it is far preferable to hold the prosecution to the charge it was originally content to bring and to justify in the eyes of its public.[8]

* * *

■ MR. JUSTICE POWELL, dissenting.

Although I agree with much of the Court's opinion, I am not satisfied that the result in this case is just or that the conduct of the plea bargaining met the requirements of due process.

* * *

It seems to me that the question to be asked under the circumstances is whether the prosecutor reasonably might have charged respondent under the Habitual Criminal Act in the first place. The deference that courts properly accord the exercise of a prosecutor's discretion perhaps would foreclose judicial criticism if the prosecutor originally had sought an indictment under that act, as unreasonable as it would have seemed.[9] But here

---

8. That prosecutors, without saying so, may sometimes bring charges more serious than they think appropriate for the ultimate disposition of a case, in order to gain bargaining leverage with a defendant, does not add support to today's decision, for this Court, in its approval of the advantages to be gained from plea negotiations, has never openly sanctioned such deliberate overcharging or taken such a cynical view of the bargaining process. Normally, of course, it is impossible to show that this is what the prosecutor is doing, and the courts necessarily have deferred to the prosecutor's exercise of discretion in initial charging decisions.

Even if overcharging is to be sanctioned, there are strong reasons of fairness why the charges should be presented at the beginning of the bargaining process, rather than as a filliped threat at the end. First, it means that a prosecutor is required to reach a charging decision without any knowledge of the particular defendant's willingness to plead guilty; hence the defendant who truly believes himself to be innocent, and wishes for that reason to go to trial, is not likely to be subject to quite such a devastating gamble since the prosecutor has fixed the incentives for the average case.

Second, it is healthful to keep charging practices visible to the general public, so that political bodies can judge whether the policy being followed is a fair one. Visibility is en-

hanced if the prosecutor is required to lay his cards on the table with an indictment of public record at the beginning of the bargaining process, rather than making use of unrecorded verbal warnings of more serious indictments yet to come.

Finally, I would question whether it is fair to pressure defendants to plead guilty by threat of reindictment on an enhanced charge for the same conduct when the defendant has no way of knowing whether the prosecutor would indeed be entitled to bring him to trial on the enhanced charge. Here, though there is no dispute that respondent met the then current definition of a habitual offender under Kentucky law, it is conceivable that a properly instructed Kentucky grand jury, in response to the same considerations that ultimately moved the Kentucky Legislature to amend the habitual offender statute, would have refused to subject respondent to such an onerous penalty for his forgery charge. There is no indication in the record that, once the new indictment was obtained, respondent was given another chance to plead guilty to the forged check charge in exchange for a five year sentence.

9. The majority suggests ... that this case cannot be distinguished from the case where the prosecutor initially obtains an indictment under an enhancement statute and later agrees to drop the enhancement charge in exchange for a guilty plea. I would agree the prosecutor evidently made a reasonable, responsible judgment not to subject an individual to a mandatory life sentence when his only new offense had societal implications as limited as those accompanying the uttering of a single $88 forged check and when the circumstances of his prior convictions confirmed the inappropriateness of applying the habitual criminal statute. I think it may be inferred that the prosecutor himself deemed it unreasonable and not in the public interest to put this defendant in jeopardy of a sentence of life imprisonment.

There may be situations in which a prosecutor would be fully justified in seeking a fresh indictment for a more serious offense. The most plausible justification might be that it would have been reasonable and in the public interest initially to have charged the defendant with the greater offense. In most cases a court could not know why the harsher indictment was sought, and an inquiry into the prosecutor's motive would neither be indicated nor likely to be fruitful. In those cases, I would agree with the majority that the situation would not differ materially from one in which the higher charge was brought at the outset. . . .

But this is not such a case. Here, any inquiry into the prosecutor's purpose is made unnecessary by his candid acknowledgement that he threatened to procure and in fact procured the habitual criminal indictment because of respondent's insistence on exercising his constitutional rights. We have stated in unequivocal terms, that "*Jackson* and *Pearce* are clear and subsequent cases have not diluted their force: if the only objective of a state practice is to discourage the assertion of constitutional rights it is 'patently unconstitutional.' " Chaffin v. Stynchcombe, 412 U.S. 17, 32 n. 20, 93 S.Ct. 1977, 1986, 36 L.Ed.2d 714 (1973). And in Brady v. United States, 397 U.S. 742, 90 S.Ct. 1463, 25 L.Ed.2d 747 (1970), we drew a distinction between the situation there approved and the "situation where the prosecutor or judge, or both, deliberately employ their charging and sentencing powers to induce a particular defendant to tender a plea of guilty." Id., at 751 n. 8, 90 S.Ct., at 1470.

The plea-bargaining process, as recognized by this Court, is essential to the functioning of the criminal-justice system. It normally affords genuine benefits to defendants as well as to society. And if the system is to work effectively, prosecutors must be accorded the widest discretion, within constitutional limits, in conducting bargaining. . . . This is especially true when a defendant is represented by counsel and presumably is fully advised of his rights. Only in the most exceptional case should a court conclude that the scales of the bargaining are so unevenly balanced as to arouse suspicion. In this case, the prosecutor's actions denied respondent due process because their admitted purpose was to discourage and then to penalize with unique severity his exercise of constitutional rights. Implementation of a

that these two situations would be alike *only if* it were assumed that the hypothetical prosecutor's decision to charge under the enhancement statute was occasioned not by consideration of the public interest but by a strategy to discourage the defendant from exercising his constitutional rights. In theory, I would condemn both practices. In practice, the hypothetical situation is largely unreviewable. The majority's view confuses the propriety of a particular exercise of prosecutorial discretion with its unreviewability. In the instant case, however, we have no problem of proof.

strategy calculated solely to deter the exercise of constitutional rights is not a constitutionally permissible exercise of discretion. I would affirm the opinion of the Court of Appeals on the facts of this case.

NOTES

1. **Statutory sentencing differentials.** Insofar as United States v. Jackson (discussed in Justice White's *Brady* opinion) prohibits imposition of a more severe penalty under a statutory scheme which penalizes exercise of the right to trial, has it survived the *Brady* trilogy and *Bordenkircher?* In Corbitt v. New Jersey, 439 U.S. 212, 99 S.Ct. 492, 58 L.Ed.2d 466 (1978), Corbitt was charged with first degree murder under New Jersey law. Under the applicable statutory provisions, if he was found guilty by a jury of that offense, a sentence of life imprisonment was mandatory. If a plea of no contest was accepted, however, the trial judge had discretion to sentence him to life imprisonment or to imprisonment for a term not to exceed thirty years. After a jury trial, Corbitt was convicted and received the mandatory sentence of life imprisonment. A majority of the Supreme Court rejected the argument that *Jackson* prohibited this. *Jackson,* Justice White reasoned for the majority, involved the death penalty, which is unique in its severity and irrevocability. Moreover, in *Corbitt* but not in *Jackson* an accused who pleaded not guilty (or no contest) could have received the same sentence as was mandated for conviction on a jury verdict. The choice which Corbitt faced under the New Jersey statutory scheme was not significantly different than the choices posed to the defendant by the prosecutor in *Bordenkircher.* The majority's language, however, leaves open the possibility that some statutory inducements to plead guilty may offend due process. "We hold only that a state may make due allowances for pleas in their sentencing decisions and that New Jersey has not exceeded its powers in this respect by its statutory provision extending the possibility of leniency to those who plead guilty in homicide cases." Further, "[W]e are unconvinced that the New Jersey statutory pattern exerts such a powerful influence to coerce inaccurate guilty pleas that it should be deemed constitutionally suspect." 439 U.S. at 225, 90 S.Ct. at 500, 58 L.Ed.2d at 478.

Justice Stewart, concurring in the judgment, found the distinction between statutory provisions for leniency and plea bargaining significant:

> It seems to me that there is a vast difference between the settlement of litigation through negotiation between counsel for the parties, and a state statute such as is involved in the present case. While a prosecuting attorney, acting as an advocate, necessarily must be able to settle an adversary criminal lawsuit through plea bargaining with his adversary a state legislature has a quite different function to perform. Could a state legislature provide that the penalty for every criminal offense to which a defendant pleads guilty is to be one-half the penalty to be imposed upon a defendant convicted of the same offense after a not guilty plea? I would suppose that such legislation would be clearly unconstitutional under United States v. Jackson.

439 U.S. at 227, 99 S.Ct. at 501–02, 58 L.Ed.2d at 479.

2. **Vindictive prosecution.** Should a "presumption of vindictiveness" apply to invalidate the bringing of more serious charges when a defendant has insisted on asserting rights to a jury trial on lesser charges? In United States v. Goodwin, 457 U.S. 368, 102 S.Ct. 2485, 73 L.Ed.2d 74 (1982), the defendant was charged with several misdemeanor offenses arising out of an assault upon a peace officer. The case was being handled by an attorney on loan from the Justice Department to the United States Attorney's office. Defendant insisted on a trial by jury, which resulted in transfer of the case from the federal Magistrate to the United States District

Court for trial. The case was also transferred to an Assistant United States Attorney for trial. He reviewed the facts and decided to file felony charges. On appeal from felony convictions, defendant contended that the prosecutorial action in this case violated the principles of Blackledge v. Perry. The Court of Appeals reversed the conviction on the ground that although there was no evidence of vindictiveness on the part of the prosecutor, a "presumption of vindictiveness" based on *Blackledge* should be applied in this case. The Supreme Court, in an opinion by Justice Stevens, reversed.

Justice Stevens distinguished *Blackledge* on the ground that it involved a re-trial of a case already tried and that is more likely to evoke prosecutorial vindictive-ness than is assertion of rights before trial by the defendant. Thus, this case is more like Bordenkircher v. Hayes. Since there was no evidence of actual vindictiveness, the reversal of the conviction would have to rest upon a presumption:

> There is good reason to be cautious before adopting an inflexible presump-tion of prosecutorial vindictiveness in a pretrial setting. In the course of preparing a case for trial, the prosecutor may uncover additional information that suggests a basis for further prosecution or he simply may come to realize that information possessed by the State has a broader significance. At this stage of the proceedings, the prosecutor's assessment of the proper extent of prosecu-tion may not have crystallized. In contrast, once a trial begins—and certainly by the time a conviction has been obtained—it is much more likely that the State has discovered and assessed all of the information against an accused and has made a determination, on the basis of that information, of the extent to which he should be prosecuted. Thus, a change in the charging decision made after an initial trial is completed is much more likely to be improperly motivated than is a pretrial decision.

457 U.S. at 381, 102 S.Ct. at 2492–93, 73 L.Ed.2d at 85–86. Justice Brennan, joined by Justice Marshall, dissented.

The Supreme Court applied the presumption of vindictiveness of *Blackledge* in Thigpen v. Roberts, 468 U.S. 27, 104 S.Ct. 2916, 82 L.Ed.2d 23 (1984). Following an accident in which he lost control of his vehicle and collided with another vehicle, killing a passenger in the other vehicle, respondent was charged with reckless driving, driving while his license was revoked, driving on the wrong side of the road and driving while intoxicated. He was convicted of those offenses before a justice of the peace and invoked his right to a trial de novo. While the cases were pending trial de novo he was indicted for involuntary manslaughter arising from the same accident. The State abandoned the misdemeanor charges and respondent was convicted of manslaughter. Ultimately, the Fifth Circuit set aside the manslaughter conviction on the ground it had been obtained in violation of respondent's right against double jeopardy. The Supreme Court, in an opinion by Justice White, affirmed the Court of Appeals on the ground that the manslaughter prosecution was vindictive under *Blackledge* and found it unnecessary to reach the double jeopardy question. The case was squarely controlled by *Blackledge* and the State made no effort to rebut the presumption of vindictiveness, but instead argued the inapplica-bility of that case. Justice Rehnquist dissented on the ground that the conviction was valid under the *Blockburger* test and that *Vitale* does not create a separate test for determining the same offense for jeopardy purposes. Justice O'Connor, joined by Justice Powell, dissented on the ground that jeopardy should be held not to attach to the first proceeding when the defendant has the absolute right to a trial *de novo*.

3. **Vindictive prosecution—interlocutory appeal.** If a defendant raises a question of prosecutorial vindictiveness prior to trial and the trial court rules against the claim, should he be entitled to take an interlocutory appeal on that issue? In United States v. Hollywood Motor Car Co., Inc., 458 U.S. 263, 102 S.Ct.

3081, 73 L.Ed.2d 754 (1982), the Supreme Court, in a per curiam opinion, held there should be no right of interlocutory appeal in that circumstance. Denial of a claim of prosecutorial vindictiveness, unlike a denial of a claim of double jeopardy (see Abney v. United States on p. 844 of Casebook) can be reviewed adequately by the appellate court following a conviction at trial. Any other decision would soon lead to piecemeal litigation:

> [T]here is a superficial plausibility to the contention that any claim, particularly a constitutional claim, that would be dispositive of the entire case if decided favorably to a criminal defendant, should be decided as quickly as possible in the course of the litigation. But if such a principle were to be applied ... the policy against piecemeal appeal in criminal cases would be swallowed by ever-multiplying exceptions.

458 U.S. at 270, 102 S.Ct. at 3085, 73 L.Ed.2d at 760. Justice Blackmun, joined by Justices Brennan and Marshall, dissented.

b.   TRIAL JUDGE PARTICIPATION

Frank v. Blackburn

United States Court of Appeals, Fifth Circuit (en banc), 1980.
646 F.2d 873, modified 646 F.2d 902 (5th Cir.1981).

■ FAY, CIRCUIT JUDGE.

A Louisiana state court jury convicted Jimmy Frank of armed robbery. A Louisiana state court judge sentenced him to thirty-three years in prison. In a petition for habeas corpus, Frank ... attacked the sentence on the ground that the trial judge impermissibly increased the term of confinement because Frank rejected a plea bargain offer and elected to stand trial. ...A majority of the en banc court now finds that no constitutional rights were violated in the conviction and sentencing of Jimmy Frank. ...

* * *

Jimmy Frank contends that because he elected to stand trial rather than plea bargain, his prison sentence on conviction was increased in violation of the fourteenth amendment. Once before the trial and once during a recess in the prosecution's case, the trial judge conducted a plea bargaining session in his chambers. Both the prosecutor and defense counsel participated in these sessions. On both occasions the judge, in response to a request from defense counsel, personally stated that he would sentence Frank to a period of twenty years confinement in return for a plea of guilty. Frank rejected both offers, stood trial, and was convicted by the jury, whereupon the judge imposed a sentence of thirty-three years in prison. Jimmy Frank alleges that the twenty year sentence offered in exchange for a guilty plea was increased by thirteen years after conviction solely to punish him for standing trial. ...

* * *

It should be emphasized that while Rule 11 requires the trial judge to play an active role in insuring that a defendant's guilty plea is voluntary, uncoerced, and made with knowledge of the consequences, the rule specifically prohibits the judge from assuming the role of an active negotiator in the plea bargaining process. See Fed.R.Crim.P. 11(e)(1). This prohibition against judicial participation in plea negotiations avoids the "chilling effect" such participation might have on a defendant's decision to either accept a plea bargain or go to trial. Several valid reasons for keeping the trial judge out of plea discussions have been noted:

> (1) judicial participation in the discussions can create the impression in the mind of the defendant that he would not receive a fair trial were he to go to trial before this judge; (2) judicial participation in the discussions makes it difficult for the judge objectively to determine the voluntariness of the plea when it is offered; (3) judicial participation to the extent of promising a certain sentence is inconsistent with the theory behind the use of the presentence investigation report; and (4) the risk of not going along with the disposition apparently desired by the judge may seem so great to the defendant that he will be induced to plead guilty even if innocent.

American Bar Association Project on Minimum Standards for Criminal Justice, Standards Relating To Pleas of Guilty, Commentary § 3.3(a).

* * *

A state court may not accept a guilty plea unless the defendant enters it voluntarily and with a complete understanding of the nature of the charge and the consequences of his plea. The general voluntary-intelligent standard for plea taking is rooted in the due process clauses of the Constitution and is therefore applicable in both state and federal courts. . . .

Because Rule 11 is not binding on the states, a federal court reviewing a state court plea bargain may only set aside a guilty plea or plea agreement which fails to satisfy due process. If a defendant understands the charges against him, understands the consequences of a guilty plea, and voluntarily chooses to plead guilty, without being coerced to do so, the guilty plea and any concomitant agreement will be upheld on federal review. . . .

* * *

We agree wholeheartedly with Frank's assertion that a defendant cannot be punished *simply* for exercising his constitutional right to stand trial. . . .

* * *

A panel of this court found that the record in this case demonstrated "that the judge lacked reason to increase defendant's sentence over what he proposed in the plea bargaining sessions. . . . With regard to the conduct of the defendant during the course of the robbery and his subsequent arrest, [the] testimony at the preliminary hearing was virtually identical with [the] testimony at trial. Thus, prior to the start of the trial itself, the judge had a virtually complete picture of the events on the night of the robbery." Frank v. Blackburn, 605 F.2d 910, 915 (5th Cir.1979). We find the panel's view of the record too narrow. While the general information in the hands of the judge at the time of plea bargaining may have been the same as at sentencing, we find persuasive the trial judge's assertion that "the Court had more graphic, descriptive and detailed evidence of the crime and the character of the individual at the time of sentencing." ...

* * *

Because the panel opinion placed special emphasis on the trial judge's *personal* involvement in the plea discussions in this case, we note that with respect to the responsibilities of the trial judge, the A.B.A. standards take the position that judicial participation in plea discussions is undesirable. See Pleas of Guilty § 3.3(a). Unlike Fed.R.Crim.P. 11, however, the standards recognize the propriety of procedures which, when requested by the parties and consented to by the trial judge, will also allow a greater degree of certainty when the proposed concessions involve the sentence or the dismissal of other charges before the court. Section 3.3(b) authorizes the trial judge to allow the prosecuting attorney and defense counsel to indicate to him in advance of the plea why they agree that certain concessions would be appropriate. The judge is then permitted to indicate whether he will concur in these concessions if the information in the presentence report is consistent with the representations made to him.

> This procedure, it must be emphasized, does not contemplate participation by the judge in the plea discussions. The judge only becomes involved after the parties have reached agreement, and thus there would appear to be little basis upon which the defendant or counsel could conclude that the judge is attempting to force a certain result upon the parties. Moreover, the judge does not initiate the conference; he is brought into the matter prior to tender of the plea only upon the request of the parties.

Pleas of Guilty, Commentary, § 3.3(b).

In the instant case, there is no record of the actual plea discussions which took place in the trial judge's chambers. The stipulation of the parties suggests, however, that it was defendant's counsel who asked the judge for a sentence proposal; presumably the prosecutor was willing to go along with the judge's proposal. Although we do not wholeheartedly approve of the plea proceedings which took place in the judge's chambers, we do not find the participation in this case to be constitutionally prohibited. ...

* * *

■ HILL, CIRCUIT JUDGE, with whom KRAVITCH, FRANK M. JOHNSON, JR., REAVLEY and THOMAS A. CLARK, CIRCUIT JUDGES, join, dissenting:

* * *

There is good reason for the exclusion of the court from plea bargain negotiation. Plea bargaining has been described as "give-and-take negotiation ... between the prosecution and defense, which arguably possess relatively equal bargaining power." Bordenkircher v. Hayes, 434 U.S. 357, 362, 98 S.Ct. 663, 667, 54 L.Ed.2d 604 (1978), quoting, Parker v. North

Carolina, 397 U.S. 790, 90 S.Ct. 1458, 25 L.Ed.2d 785 (1970) (opinion of Brennan, J.).

Equal bargaining power is essential to constitutionally valid plea bargaining. Indeed, the Supreme Court has stated that "plea bargaining flows from 'the mutuality of advantage' to defendants and prosecutors, each with his own reasons for wanting to avoid trial." Bordenkircher v. Hayes, 434 U.S. at 363, 98 S.Ct. at 668, quoting, Brady v. United States, 397 U.S. 742, 752, 90 S.Ct. 1463, 1471, 25 L.Ed.2d 747 (1970). Unless this mutual advantage exists the system breaks down; bargaining becomes coercion.

Of course, Jimmy Frank went to trial so there is no allegation of a coerced plea.[10] Coercing a plea, however, is only one way in which a trial judge may violate the Constitution by intruding into the plea bargaining process. Here, we are confronted with another. Specifically, we must decide under what circumstances a judge may impose a harsher penalty following conviction when he has previously "proposed" an appropriate sentence in exchange for a plea of guilty. I can come to no other conclusion but that North Carolina v. Pearce, 395 U.S. 711, 89 S.Ct. 2072, 23 L.Ed.2d 656 (1969) should control the outcome.

* * *

Several lessons emerge from [the] cases. First, under a *Pearce* analysis it is not necessary to demonstrate "actual retaliatory motivation." As previously discussed, that would be virtually impossible. Rather, the court should focus on the presence or absence of a "realistic likelihood of vindictiveness." In assessing such a likelihood, the Court has focused on those imposing the second sentence or taking the second action.

* * *

In the instant case the trial judge proposed a sentence of twenty years to defendant's counsel in exchange for a guilty plea. In so doing, he impaired his impartiality. In effect he became a third bargainer with a well-defined position. He had a "personal stake" in the process being resolved his way and therefore a "motivation to engage in self-vindication." Finally, he had an "institutional interest" in imposing punishment through the sentencing process to discourage what he may well have viewed as a meritless trial. In short, the very same indicia of vindictiveness that were present in *Pearce* are present here.

It should be made clear that I am not, as *Pearce* did not, presuming that the trial judge was vindictive. Rather, the "realistic likelihood" that he could have been compels the rule that he must affirmatively state his reasons for imposing a harsher sentence.

* * *

10. The facts of this case do not require us to determine to what extent a trial judge may constitutionally participate in the plea bargaining process. Here, it is enough to say that his participation has triggered the necessity for the constitutional protection announced in North Carolina v. Pearce, 395 U.S. 711, 89 S.Ct. 2072, 23 L.Ed.2d 656 (1969).

■ RUBIN, CIRCUIT JUDGE, with whom RANDALL, CIRCUIT JUDGE, joins, dissenting.

* * *

... A trial judge who joins in sentence bargaining enters the contest with infinitely greater bargaining power than the accused. He is seldom completely neutral: absent public interest in the trial of a particular case, it is in his interest to dispose of cases without trial and, thus, to clear his docket with minimal effort. If he may offer the defendant a deal in return for a guilty plea, and then, when this proffer is rejected, impose a greater sentence, without stated and justifiable reasons, he not only exerts coercive pressure on the accused but affects detrimentally the administration of justice in his court. The criminal defense cogniscenti will quickly learn that, when this judge's proffer is rejected, the defendant, if convicted, will pay a higher price. It is a denial of due process for the judge thus to stain his robes.

NOTES

1. **Acknowledgement of guilt.** On petition for rehearing, the court deleted the following sentence from its discussion concerning the justification for the thirty-three year sentence:

> Even if the trial provided no additional evidence of character, the mere fact that Jimmy Frank refused to acknowledge his guilt and showed no willingness to assume responsibility for his conduct may have led the judge to conclude that this defendant lacked potential for rehabilitation thus justifying the imposition of a greater sentence than that offered in exchange for a guilty plea.

646 F.2d 902 (5th Cir.1981) (on petition for rehearing). Judge Hill observed that the sentence was deleted "presumably ... because the Majority ... concluded that it does not state the law." 646 F.2d at 902 (Hill, J., dissenting).

2. **Right to know of likely sentence differential.** If disparity routinely exists between sentences upon plea or trial, should the defendant have the right to know before making his choice? In United States v. Harris, 635 F.2d 526 (6th Cir.1980), it was disclosed that the probation officer routinely gave a pretrial sentence recommendation to the prosecutor but not to the defense. In *Harris* the prosecutor disclosed to the defense that probation would recommend 3 years on a guilty plea and 5 years on a conviction upon trial. The Court upheld the conviction and sentence since the defendant chose to go to trial despite the sentence recommendation information; and there was no evidence in the record that the District Court was influenced by the pretrial recommendation of the probation officer when it sentenced appellant. As to the practice mentioned, despite its holding, the Court stated:

> Using the probation officer's recommendation to try to persuade the defendant to plead guilty involves the court in the plea bargaining process as the probation office is an arm of the court. While participation of the trial judge in plea negotiations may not amount to a constitutional violation which justifies overturning a guilty plea ..., Rule 11(e)(1), Fed.R.Crim.Pro., forbids the court from participating in plea negotiations. Under Rule 11, the judge's role is limited to acceptance or rejection of the plea agreement after a thorough review of the relevant factors; the judge should not participate in the plea bargaining

process. . . . Thus, the judge could not tell the defendant prior to accepting a guilty plea what sentence he would likely give should the plea be accepted. . . .

In the present case, the judge himself did not make any representations to the defendant. However, the probation officer who is an arm of the court did so. His recommendation has the weight of the court behind it. If the court puts its imprimatur on a plea offer, the defendant might be coerced into taking it, fearing rejection would mean the imposition of a greater sentence after trial or that he would not get a fair trial before the judge whom he has challenged. . . . The trial court must not penalize the defendant for exercising his constitutional right to plead not guilty and go to trial; whether or not the defendant exercises his right to trial must have no bearing on the sentence he receives. . . . By having the probation officer recommend one sentence for pleading guilty and another sentence for going to trial, the court will be seen as considering whether or not the defendant exercises his right to trial in determining the sentence and the defendant may well feel pressured to plead guilty. . . .

In the future, . . . District Judges should not disclose the probation officer's sentence recommendations to either the defendant or the attorney for the government prior to trial or the acceptance of a guilty or a nolo contendere plea, where the recommendation could in any way affect a defendant's decision to plead guilty or go to trial.

635 F.2d at 528–29.

c. PLEADING GUILTY WITHOUT ADMITTING GUILT

A plea of guilty usually constitutes an admission by the defendant that he has in fact committed a crime. Acceptance of the plea and sentencing then follow logically from the defendant's admission of guilt. Occasionally, however, a defendant pleads guilty but at the same time claims that he is innocent. In that case, a plea of guilty is patently not an admission of factual guilt, and the judge must decide whether the law allows the acceptance of a guilty plea under these circumstances.

North Carolina v. Alford

Supreme Court of the United States, 1970.
400 U.S. 25, 91 S.Ct. 160, 27 L.Ed.2d 162.

■ MR. JUSTICE WHITE delivered the opinion of the Court.

On December 2, 1963, Alford was indicted for first-degree murder, a capital offense under North Carolina law. The court appointed an attorney to represent him, and this attorney questioned all but one of the various witnesses who appellee said would substantiate his claim of innocence. The witnesses, however, did not support Alford's story but gave statements that strongly indicated his guilt. Faced with strong evidence of guilt and no substantial evidentiary support for the claim of innocence, Alford's attorney recommended that he plead guilty, but left the ultimate decision to Alford himself. The prosecutor agreed to accept a plea of guilty to a charge of second-degree murder, and on December 10, 1963, Alford pleaded guilty to the reduced charge.

Before the plea was finally accepted by the trial court, the court heard the sworn testimony of a police officer who summarized the State's case.

Two other witnesses besides Alford were also heard. Although there was no eyewitness to the crime, the testimony indicated that shortly before the killing Alford took his gun from his house, stated his intention to kill the victim and returned home with the declaration that he had carried out the killing. After the summary presentation of the State's case, Alford took the stand and testified that he had not committed the murder but that he was pleading guilty because he faced the threat of the death penalty if he did not do so. In response to the questions of his counsel, he acknowledged that his counsel had informed him of the difference between second-and first-degree murder and of his rights in case he chose to go to trial. The trial court then asked appellee if, in light of his denial of guilt, he still desired to plead guilty to second-degree murder and appellee answered, "Yes, sir. I plead guilty on—from the circumstances that he [Alford's attorney] told me." After eliciting information about Alford's prior criminal record, which was a long one, the trial court sentenced him to 30 years' imprisonment, the maximum penalty for second-degree murder.

* * *

Ordinarily, a judgment of conviction resting on a plea of guilty is justified by the defendant's admission that he committed the crime charged against him and his consent that judgment be entered without a trial of any kind. The plea usually subsumes both elements, and justifiably so, even though there is no separate, express admission by the defendant that he committed the particular acts claimed to constitute the crime charged in the indictment. Here Alford entered his plea but accompanied it with the statement that he had not shot the victim.

If Alford's statements were to be credited as sincere assertions of his innocence, there obviously existed a factual and legal dispute between him and the State. Without more, it might be argued that the conviction entered on his guilty plea was invalid, since his assertion of innocence negatived any admission of guilt, which, as we observed last Term in *Brady,* is normally "[c]entral to the plea and the foundation for entering judgment against the defendant. . . ."397 U.S. at 748.

In addition to Alford's statement, however, the court had heard an account of the events on the night of the murder, including information from Alford's acquaintances that he had departed from his home with his gun stating his intention to kill and that he had later declared that he had carried out his intention. Nor had Alford wavered in his desire to have the trial court determine his guilt without a jury trial. Although denying the charge against him, he nevertheless preferred the dispute between him and the State to be settled by the judge in the context of a guilty plea proceeding rather than by a formal trial. Thereupon, with the State's telling evidence and Alford's denial before it, the trial court proceeded to convict and sentence Alford for second-degree murder.

State and lower federal courts are divided upon whether a guilty plea can be accepted when it is accompanied by protestations of innocence and hence contains only a waiver of **trial** but no admission of guilt. . . .

* * *

Implicit in the *nolo contendere* cases is a recognition that the Constitution does not bar imposition of a prison-sentence upon an accused who is unwilling expressly to admit his guilt but who, faced with grim alternatives, is willing to waive his trial and accept the sentence.

These cases would be directly in point if Alford had simply insisted on his plea but refused to admit the crime. The fact that his plea was denominated a plea of guilty rather than a plea of *nolo contendere* is of no constitutional significance with respect to the issue now before us, for the Constitution is concerned with the practical consequences, not the formal categorizations of state law. ... Thus, while most pleas of guilty consist of both a waiver of trial and an express admission of guilt, the latter element is not a constitutional requisite to the imposition of criminal penalty. An individual accused of crime may voluntarily, knowingly, and understandingly consent to the imposition of a prison sentence even if he is unwilling or unable to admit his participation in the acts constituting the crime.

Nor can we perceive any material difference between a plea which refuses to admit commission of the criminal act and a plea containing a protestation of innocence when, as in the instant case, a defendant intelligently concludes that his interests require entry of a guilty plea and the record before the judge contains strong evidence of actual guilt. Here the State had a strong case of first-degree murder against Alford. Whether he realized or disbelieved his guilt, he insisted on his plea because in his view he had absolutely nothing to gain by a trial and much to gain by pleading. Because of the overwhelming evidence against him, a trial was precisely what neither Alford nor his attorney desired. Confronted with the choice between a trial for first-degree murder, on the one hand, and a plea of guilty to second-degree murder, on the other, Alford quite reasonably chose the latter and thereby limited the maximum penalty to a 30–year term. When his plea is viewed in light of the evidence against him, which substantially negated his claim of innocence and which further provided a means by which the judge could test whether the plea was being intelligently entered,[11] its validity cannot be seriously questioned. In view of the strong factual basis for the plea demonstrated by the State and Alford's clearly expressed desire to enter it despite his professed belief in his innocence, we hold that the trial judge did not commit constitutional error in accepting it.[12]

11. Because of the importance of protecting the innocent and of insuring that guilty pleas are a product of free and intelligent choice, various state and federal court decisions properly caution that pleas coupled with claims of innocence should not be accepted unless there is a factual basis for the plea, ...

In the federal courts, Rule 11 of the Criminal Rules expressly provides that a court "shall not enter a judgment upon a plea of guilty unless it is satisfied that there is a factual basis for the plea."

12. Our holding does not mean that a trial judge must accept every constitutionally valid guilty plea merely because a defendant wishes so to plead. A criminal defendant does not have an absolute right under the Constitution to have his guilty plea accepted by the court, although the States may by statute or otherwise confer such a right. Likewise, the States may bar their courts from accepting guilty pleas from any defendants who assert their innocence. Cf. Fed.Rule Crim.Proc. 11, which gives a trial judge discretion to "refuse to accept a plea of guilty. ..." We need not now delineate the scope of that discretion.

... Alford now argues in effect that the State should not have allowed him this choice but should have insisted on proving him guilty of murder in the first degree. The States in their wisdom may take this course by statute or otherwise and may prohibit the practice of accepting pleas to lesser included offenses under any circumstances. But this is not the mandate of the Fourteenth Amendment and the Bill of Rights. The prohibitions against involuntary or unintelligent pleas should not be relaxed, but neither should an exercise in arid logic render those constitutional guarantees counterproductive and put in jeopardy the very human values they were meant to preserve.

The Court of Appeals for the Fourth Circuit was in error to find Alford's plea of guilty invalid because it was made to avoid the possibility of the death penalty. That court's judgment directing the issuance of the writ of habeas corpus is vacated and the case is remanded to the Court of Appeals for further proceedings consistent with this opinion.

It is so ordered.

[The dissenting opinion of Mr. Justice Brennan, with whom Justices Douglas and Marshall joined, is omitted.]

NOTES

1. **Resistance to *Alford* pleas.** Despite *Alford,* Alschuler, The Defense Attorney's Role in Plea Bargaining, 84 Yale L.J. 1179, 1279–80 (1975), notes, many attorneys refuse to permit clients who deny guilt to plead guilty. In part, this is due to the reluctance of trial judges to accept so-called *Alford* pleas. Public defenders, he observes, appeared to be less willing than private attorneys to permit pleas of this sort, perhaps because public defenders are more vulnerable to post-conviction claims of ineffective assistance of counsel. But even lawyers with policies against *Alford* pleas often report exceptions. Some distinguished between "pro forma" and "bona fide" protestations of innocence, and refused to cooperate in *Alford* pleas only in the case of the latter. In addition, some saw no objection to an *Alford* plea if the client acknowledged the conduct constituting the crime but claimed a defense, such as self-defense, entrapment, or the like. Id., at 1281.

2. **Should there be a right to enter an *Alford* plea?** What, if any, right should a defendant have to enter an *Alford* plea? Alschuler, The Defense Attorney's Role in Plea Bargaining, 84 Yale L.J. 1179, 1301 (1975), points out that *Alford* itself poses no bar to judicial rejection of such pleas. This results, he argues, in some defendants being denied the benefits of a plea because they are unwilling to mouth the "magic words" acknowledging guilt and constitutes unjustified unequal treatment. One possible solution, he notes, is to continue to recognize judicial discretion to refuse such pleas, but to require the judge—if the defendant is ultimately convicted—to impose a sentence no more severe than would have been imposed if the *Alford* plea had been accepted. Id., at 1303–04.

3. ROLE OF THE TRIAL JUDGE IN ACCEPTING OR REJECTING THE PLEA

Once a defendant has decided to plead guilty, whether following plea bargaining or not, a judge must decide whether the plea is legally acceptable. This subsection deals with some of the issues involved in a judge's rejection of a negotiated plea.

United States v. Ammidown

United States Court of Appeals, District of Columbia Circuit, 1973.
497 F.2d 615, 162 U.S.App.D.C. 28.

■ LEVENTHAL, CIRCUIT JUDGE.

In this unusual case the trial judge rejected a plea bargain struck between the prosecution and the defense on the ground that the public interest required that the defendant be tried on a greater charge. Under the facts presented we hold that the trial judge exceeded his discretion and accordingly reverse.

I.

In a case of extraordinary notoriety, Robert L. Ammidown was charged with first degree murder and conspiracy to commit murder in the death of his wife. Ammidown admitted that a month previous he arranged to have her murdered. . . . At the last minute he changed his mind, ... [A]ccording to his written confession, Ammidown and an associate, Richard Anthony Lee, devised a plan whereby Lee would abduct Mrs. Ammidown and by threat to her life extort a sum of money to be used by Ammidown and Lee to make the down payment for a club on the Eastern Shore of Maryland. . . .

[A]t the prearranged spot, Lee jumped into Ammidown's car and directed him to drive to the East Capitol Street Bridge, where Lee dragged Mrs. Ammidown from the car and raped her, as planned, to impress Mrs. Ammidown "with the seriousness of the threat."

What then happened was that Lee killed Mrs. Ammidown. Ammidown did not confess to complicity in the murder.

Just prior to trial, the United States Attorney and Ammidown entered into this agreement: Ammidown would plead guilty to second degree murder, and the first degree murder charge would be dismissed. There was no agreement for the prosecutor to recommend sentence less than the maximum, life imprisonment. Ammidown, then aged 49, had no possibility of being even considered for parole for 15 years. Ammidown agreed to testify in the grand jury proceedings and impending trial of Lee, a much younger man, who was believed by the prosecution to be involved in another murder.

The trial judge, however, refused to approve the agreement and accept the lesser plea. With full understanding of the prosecutor's concern with the importance of Ammidown's agreement in connection with its successful prosecution of Lee, the court nonetheless decided that under Rule 11 of the Federal Rules of Criminal Procedure it had the discretion to refuse the plea when it found that the crime was so heinous and the evidence of guilt so overwhelming that the public interest would be ill-served by a judgment of second degree murder, which it referred to as a "tap on the wrist." Appellant then pleaded not guilty to first degree and second degree murder; at trial he was convicted of first degree murder and felony murder and sentenced to two terms of life imprisonment, to run consecutively.

Appellant now asserts that the failure of the trial court to accept his proffered plea of guilty to second degree murder constituted reversible error, and asks this court to remand with instructions to enter a judgment of second degree murder. The Government has decided that it could not in good conscience oppose the appellant; consequently, the position of the trial judge has been ably presented by . . . [counsel].

II.

[Despite the absence of any specific provision in Rule 11, the court concluded that the District Judge did have discretion to reject a plea based upon a bargain agreed to by both the government and the defense. Rule 11 now explicitly provides for this. In developing a foundation for the authority to reject the plea, the court noted that the functional effect of accepting the plea would be to dismiss the charge of first degree murder. Under Fed.R.Crim.P. 48(a), dismissal of an indictment requires leave of the court. Turning to the caselaw concerning the District Court's authority under Rule 48(a), the court noted that some decisions involve situations in which the defendant concurs in the government's motion to dismiss but the court is concerned whether dismissal would adequately protect the public. These decisions, the court concluded, contain some principles useful in addressing the manner in which the discretionary power to reject a bargained plea should be exercised. Editors.]

. . . [I]n the exercise of its responsibility, the court will not be content with a mere conclusory statement by the prosecutor that dismissal is in the public interest, but will require a statement of reasons and underlying factual basis. . . . [T]he court does not have primary responsibility, but rather the role of guarding against abuse of prosecutorial discretion. The rule contemplates exposure of the reasons for dismissal "in order to prevent abuse of the uncontrolled power of dismissal previously enjoyed by prosecutors," and in pursuance of this purpose "to gain the Court's favorable discretion, it should be satisfied that the reasons advanced for the proposed dismissal are substantial."

In this context, it may be helpful to note the considerations, other than protection of defendant, that have been taken into account by courts. If the reason is that the evidence is not sufficient to warrant prosecution, the court recognizes that the responsibility is on the prosecution and is satisfied "if there is a considered judgment," and an application made in good faith, unless it appears that the assigned reason for the dismissal has no basis in fact. In one case, a district court stated that a complete dismissal of charges against an individual, amply supported by the evidence, was not properly grounded in the consideration that the defendant corporation of which he was president would comply with ecology laws. Without commenting on that opinion as such, we note that it expressly recognized that a different consideration applies when the case is not entirely dismissed as to a defendant but he has received a substantial sentence for a phase of the same offense. And of course that is the situation that is involved when there is no dismissal simpliciter, but a plea of guilty to a lesser included offense like second degree murder.

Of particular significance to the case at bar is that even a court which would not accept an unexplained motion for dismissal determined, on reconsideration, that it was satisfied with the prosecutor's subsequent explanation that prejudice would likely be worked upon the Government in another criminal action.

C.

The third element of a plea bargain involving a plea to a lesser included offense, and indeed the most frequent motive behind it, is to circumscribe the judge's discretion in pronouncing sentence. See D. Newman, Conviction 105 (1966). The negotiated plea reduces the upper and lower limits of the range of sentence available to the judge. It is axiomatic that, within the limits imposed by the legislature, imposition of sentence is a matter for discretion of the trial judge. The prosecutor has no role beyond the advisory, and even that is frowned on in the District Court for the District of Columbia. We hesitate to say, therefore, that the United States Attorney and the defendant can by plea manipulate this traditional power of the judge without any recourse by the judge permitting him to forestall gross abuses of prosecutorial discretion.

D.

We have identified that both the District Judge and the United States Attorney have roles in the plea bargaining process. What is required is an effort to harmonize their responsibilities, and to suggest a standard for determining when judicial intervention may be proper.

We start with the presumption that the determination of the United States Attorney is to be followed in the overwhelming number of cases. He alone is in a position to evaluate the government's prosecution resources and the number of cases it is able to prosecute.

Where vigorous prosecution of one case threatens to undermine successful prosecution of another, it has traditionally been the prosecutor who determines which case will be pressed to conclusion, and his decision has been given great deference by the courts.

On the other hand, we do not think Rule 48(a) intends the trial court to serve merely as a rubber stamp for the prosecutor's decision. We agree that "the judge should be satisfied that the agreement adequately protects the public interest". Newman, supra, at 136; The Challenge of Crime in a Free Society: Report of the President's Commission on Law Enforcement & Administration of Justice 118 (1966).

We now state what, in our view, are the appropriate doctrines governing trial judges in considering whether to deny approval either to dismissals of cases outright or to the diluted dismissal—a guilty plea to a lesser included offense.

First, the trial judge must provide a reasoned exercise of discretion in order to justify a departure from the course agreed on by the prosecution and defense. This is not a matter of absolute judicial prerogative. The authority has been granted to the judge to assure protection of the public interest, and this in turn involves one or more of the following components: (a) fairness to the defense, such as protection against harassment; (b) fairness to the prosecution interest, as in avoiding a disposition that does not serve due and legitimate prosecutorial interests; (c) protection of the sentencing authority reserved to the judge. The judge's statement or opinion must identify the particular interest that leads him to require an unwilling defendant and prosecution to go to trial.

We now turn to the content of these components, and begin by passing any discussion of fairness to the defense, since it is not directly involved in the case at bar and it has already been identified in the precedent referred to earlier in this opinion. As to fairness to the prosecution interest, here we have a matter in which the primary responsibility, obviously, is that of the prosecuting attorney. The District Court cannot disapprove of his action on the ground of incompatibility with prosecutive responsibility unless the judge is in effect ruling that the prosecutor has abused his discretion. The requirement of judicial approval entitles the judge to obtain and evaluate the prosecutor's reasons. ...The judge may withhold approval if he finds that the prosecutor has failed to give consideration to factors that must be given consideration in the public interest, factors such as the deterrent aspects of the criminal law. However, trial judges are not free to withhold approval of guilty pleas on this basis merely because their conception of the public interest differs from that of the prosecuting attorney. The question is not what the judge would do if he were the prosecuting attorney, but whether he can say that the action of the prosecuting attorney is such a departure from sound prosecutorial principle as to mark it an abuse of prosecutorial discretion.

In like vein, we note that a judge is free to condemn the prosecutor's agreement as a trespass on judicial authority only in a blatant and extreme case. In ordinary circumstances, the change in grading of an offense presents no question of the kind of action that is reserved for the judiciary.

Applying these tests to the case at bar, we find the record establishes beyond all doubt that the United States Attorney considered, indeed agonized over, the public interest and concluded that it was best served by assuring a successful prosecution of Lee—"a young man ... a killer."

* * *

The trial judge was not free to disapprove this assessment by the prosecutor without both stating his reasons and determining that the prosecutor abused his discretion. Neither of these elements appears in the case at bar. The trial judge provided no statement of reasons, and such colloquy as appears indicates that the judge assumed that the correct test was what the judge independently considered best in the public interest.

When we come to the possible ground of intrusion on the sentencing function of the trial judge, we have a consideration that is interdependent of the other. That is to say, a dropping of an offense that might be taken as an intrusion on the judicial function if it were not shown to be related to a prosecutorial purpose takes on an entirely different coloration if it is explained to the judge that there was a prosecutorial purpose, an insufficiency of evidence, a doubt as to the admissibility of certain evidence under exclusionary rules, a need for evidence to bring another felon to justice, or other similar consideration.

III.

Because the trial judge did not provide a statement of reasons based on intrusion on the sentencing authority of the judge, it would be necessary to remand in any event. At the time the judge took the action appealed from, first degree murder was punishable by death, and second degree murder by a maximum of life imprisonment. We need not consider what kind of remand we might have provided if that kind of sentencing disparity were in effect at the present time. For the Supreme Court's decision in Furman v. Georgia, 408 U.S. 238, 92 S.Ct. 2726, 33 L.Ed.2d 346 (1972), has established the unavailability of the death sentence for appellant. We are required to accompany our reversal for lack of requisite findings with a disposition in the interest of justice, that takes into account current conditions.

The situation as it stands today is such that we cannot conceive that if the trial judge were required to provide a current reassessment of the problem in the light of the standards set forth in this opinion, he could justify his rejection of the first degree murder reversal and of the second degree murder plea as reflecting a sentence disparity so blatant as to constitute an intrusion upon the judicial domain. The life sentence is mandatory on a conviction for first degree murder, and discretionary with the court on a conviction for murder in the second degree. Parole is available after a minimum of 20 years in the case of first degree murder, and after a minimum of 15 years in the case of murder in the second degree. The difference is insufficient by itself to warrant judicial rejection of a properly bargained plea of guilty to murder in the second degree on the ground of undue interference with the sentencing domain of the judiciary.

Our duty as a court of appeals calls on us to reverse the action of the trial judge, but we think it only appropriate to accompany our action with an explicit statement that we are fully sensitive to his revulsion concerning this sordid crime. . . . If the decision were for the trial judge alone to make, his sentiment that the interest of justice called for trial on a charge of first degree murder would be conclusive. But our responsibility to apply the law calls on us to take into account both that a decision of the prosecutor was also involved and that substantial reasons undergirded his conclusion that the overriding public interest called for a certainty in the riddance of the hired gun.

For the reasons stated, the judgment and sentence on a conviction of murder in the first degree is vacated and the case remanded with instructions to accept appellant's plea of guilty to second degree murder.

NOTES

1. **Scope of judicial discretion to reject the deal.** Other courts have regarded the standard adopted in *Ammidown* as excessively deferential to the prosecution. In United States v. Bean, 564 F.2d 700 (5th Cir.1977), the court observed that to its knowledge, no other federal circuit had followed *Ammidown* in so drastically limiting the discretion of the judge. The *Bean* court held that in considering offered plea bargains, courts "may be governed by the same broad standards that apply in sentencing." 564 F.2d at 703. Therefore,

> A decision that a plea bargain will result in the defendant's receiving too light a sentence under the circumstances of the case is a sound reason for the judge's

refusing to accept the agreement. . . . Rule 11 does not compel a judge to impose an inappropriate sentence.

564 F.2d at 704.

2. **Accepting pleas over prosecutor's objection.** Does—or should—a trial court have the authority to permit a defendant to plead guilty to some but not all offenses charged or to a less serious offense than that charged if the prosecutor objects? See Genesee County Prosecutor v. Genesee Circuit Judge, 391 Michigan 115, 215 N.W.2d 145 (1974), holding that no such authority existed under Michigan law. If a trial judge accepts such a plea despite his lack of formal authority to do so, does double jeopardy permit the prosecution to obtain appellate relief and try the defendant on the greater charge (or all of the charges)?

4. THE NECESSITY OF RESPECTING A BARGAIN ONCE MADE

Changed circumstances or simple reconsideration may make a plea bargain less attractive to either the prosecutor or the defendant than it was when the bargain was initially reached. This subsection discusses the consequences of a party's failure to adhere to the agreed-upon bargain.

Santobello v. New York

Supreme Court of the United States, 1971.
404 U.S. 257, 92 S.Ct. 495, 30 L.Ed.2d 427.

■ MR. CHIEF JUSTICE BURGER delivered the opinion of the Court.

We granted certiorari in this case to determine whether the State's failure to keep a commitment concerning the sentence recommendation on a guilty plea required a new trial.

The facts are not in dispute. The State of New York indicted petitioner in 1969 on two felony counts, Promoting Gambling in the First Degree, and Possession of Gambling Records in the First Degree, N.Y. Penal Law, McKinney's Consol.Laws, c. 40, §§ 225.10, 225.20. Petitioner first entered a plea of not guilty to both counts. After negotiations, the Assistant District Attorney in charge of the case agreed to permit petitioner to plead guilty to a lesser-included offense, Possession of Gambling Records in the Second Degree, N.Y.Penal Law § 225.15, conviction of which would carry a maximum prison sentence of one year. The prosecutor agreed to make no recommendation as to the sentence.

On June 16, 1969, petitioner accordingly withdrew his plea of not guilty and entered a plea of guilty to the lesser charge. Petitioner represented to the sentencing judge that the plea was voluntary and that the facts of the case as described by the Assistant District Attorney, were true. The court accepted the plea and set a date for sentencing [which through a series of delays did not occur until January 9, 1970].

* * *

At this appearance, another prosecutor had replaced the prosecutor who had negotiated the plea. The new prosecutor recommended the maximum one-year sentence. In making this recommendation, he cited petitioner's criminal record and alleged links with organized crime. Defense counsel immediately objected on the ground that the State had promised petitioner before the plea was entered that there would be no sentence recommendation by the prosecution. He sought to adjourn the sentence hearing in order to have time to prepare proof of the first prosecutor's promise. The second prosecutor, apparently ignorant of his colleague's commitment, argued that there was nothing in the record to support petitioner's claim of a promise, but the State, in subsequent proceedings, has not contested that such a promise was made.

The sentencing judge ended discussion, with the following statement, quoting extensively from the pre-sentence report:

> "Mr. Aronstein [Defense Counsel], I am not at all influenced by what the District Attorney says, so that there is no need to adjourn the sentence, and there is no need to have any testimony. It doesn't make a particle of difference what the District Attorney says he will do, or what he doesn't do.

> "I have here, Mr. Aronstein, a probation report. I have here a history of a long, long serious criminal record. I have here a picture of the life history of this man. . . .

> " 'He is unamenable to supervision in the community. He is a professional criminal.' This is in quotes. 'And a recidivist. Institutionalization—'; that means, in plain language, just putting him away, 'is the only means of halting his anti-social activities,' and protecting you, your family, me, my family, protecting society. 'Institutionalization.' Plain language, put him behind bars.

> "Under the plea, I can only send him to the New York City Correctional Institution for men for one year, which I am hereby doing."

The judge then imposed the maximum sentence of one year.

* * *

This record represents another example of an unfortunate lapse in orderly prosecutorial procedures, in part, no doubt, because of the enormous increase in the workload of the often understaffed prosecutor's offices. The heavy workload may well explain these episodes, but it does not excuse them. The disposition of criminal charges by agreement between the prosecutor and the accused, sometimes loosely called "plea bargaining," is an essential component of the administration of justice. Properly administered, it is to be encouraged. If every criminal charge were subjected to a full-scale trial, the States and the Federal Government would need to multiply by many times the number of judges and court facilities.

Disposition of charges after plea discussions is not only an essential part of the process but a highly desirable part for many reasons. It leads to prompt and largely final disposition of most criminal cases; it avoids much of the corrosive impact of enforced idleness during pre-trial confinement for those who are denied release pending trial; it protects the public from those accused persons who are prone to continue criminal conduct even while on pre-trial release; and, by shortening the time between charge and disposition, it enhances whatever may be the rehabilitative prospects of the guilty when they are ultimately imprisoned.

However, all of these considerations presuppose fairness in securing agreement between an accused and a prosecutor. . . .

This phase of the process of criminal justice, and the adjudicative element inherent in accepting a plea of guilty, must be attended by safeguards to insure the defendant what is reasonably due in the circumstances. Those circumstances will vary, but a constant factor is that when a plea rests in any significant degree on a promise or agreement of the prosecutor, so that it can be said to be part of the inducement or consideration, such promise must be fulfilled.

On this record, petitioner "bargained" and negotiated for a particular plea in order to secure dismissal of more serious charges, but also on condition that no sentence recommendation would be made by the prosecutor. It is now conceded that the promise to abstain from a recommendation was made, and at this stage the prosecution is not in a good position to argue that its inadvertent breach of agreement is immaterial. The staff lawyers in a prosecutor's office have the burden of "letting the left hand know what the right hand is doing" or has done. That the breach of agreement was inadvertent does not lessen its impact.

We need not reach the question whether the sentencing judge would or would not have been influenced had he known all the details of the negotiations for the plea. He stated that the prosecutor's recommendation did not influence him and we have no reason to doubt that. Nevertheless, we conclude that the interests of justice and appropriate recognition of the duties of the prosecution in relation to promises made in the negotiation of pleas of guilty will be best served by remanding the case to the state courts for further consideration. The ultimate relief to which petitioner is entitled we leave to the discretion of the state court, which is in a better position to decide whether the circumstances of this case require only that there be specific performance of the agreement on the plea, in which case petitioner should be resentenced by a different judge, or whether, in the view of the state court, the circumstances require granting the relief sought by petitioner, i.e., the opportunity to withdraw his plea of guilty. We emphasize that this is in no sense to question the fairness of the sentencing judge; the fault here rests on the prosecutor, not on the sentencing judge.

The judgment is vacated and the case is remanded for reconsideration not inconsistent with this opinion.

■ MR. JUSTICE MARSHALL, with whom MR. JUSTICE BRENNAN and MR. JUSTICE STEWART join, concurring in part and dissenting in part.

I agree with much of the majority's opinion, but conclude that petitioner must be permitted to withdraw his guilty plea. This is the relief petitioner requested and, on the facts set out by the majority, it is a form of relief to which he is entitled.

* * *

United States v. Benchimol

Supreme Court of the United States, 1985.
471 U.S. 453, 105 S.Ct. 2103, 85 L.Ed.2d 462.

■ PER CURIAM.

In April 1976, respondent pleaded guilty in the United States District Court for the Northern District of California to an information charging him with one count of mail fraud in violation of 18 U.S.C. § 1341. Respondent pleaded pursuant to a plea bargain whereby the Government agreed to recommend probation on condition that restitution be made. The District Court disregarded the recommendation and sentenced respondent to six years of treatment and supervision under the Youth Corrections Act, 18 U.S.C. § 5010(b). He was released on parole after serving 18 months of his sentence, but a warrant for his arrest because of parole violation was issued in 1978, and he was eventually taken into custody on that warrant in October 1981. A few days before his arrest on this warrant, he filed a motion under Federal Rule of Criminal Procedure 32(d) and 28 U.S.C. § 2255 to withdraw his guilty plea or, in the alternative, to have his sentence vacated and be resentenced to the time already served. He claimed that the Government had failed to comply with its part of the plea bargain upon which his guilty plea was based.

The District Court that had received the guilty plea also heard respondent's application for collateral relief, and denied it. The Court of Appeals by a divided vote reversed that judgment, holding that: "[W]hen the government undertakes to recommend a sentence pursuant to a plea bargain, it has the duty to state its recommendation clearly to the sentencing judge and to express the justification for it." 738 F.2d 1001, 1002 (C.A.9 1984). . . . The Court of Appeals had this view of the facts:

> "Benchimol agreed to plead guilty. The government concedes that in exchange for the guilty plea it promised to recommend probation with restitution. However, at the sentencing hearing, the pre-sentence report incorrectly stated that the government would stand silent. Benchimol's counsel informed the court that the government instead recommended probation with restitution. The Assistant United States Attorney then stated: 'That is an accurate representation.' "Ibid.

The Court of Appeals concluded that the Government had breached its plea bargain because, although the Assistant United States Attorney concurred with defense counsel's statement that the Government recommended probation with restitution, it "made no effort to explain its reasons for agreeing to recommend a lenient sentence but rather left an impression with the court of less-than-enthusiastic support for leniency." Ibid.

We think this holding misconceives the effect of the relevant rules and of the applicable case law. Federal Rule of Criminal Procedure 11(e) provides an elaborate formula for the negotiation of plea bargains, which allows the attorney for the Government to agree to move for dismissal of other charges and to agree that a specific sentence is the appropriate disposition of the case. It also authorizes the Government attorney to make a recommendation for a particular sentence, or agree not to oppose the defendant's request for such a sentence, with the understanding that such recommendation or request shall not be binding upon the court.

It may well be that the Government in a particular case might commit itself to "enthusiastically" make a particular recommendation to the Court, and it may be that the Government in a particular case might agree to explain to the Court the reasons for the Government's making a particular recommendation. But respondent does not contend, nor did the Court of Appeals find, that the Government had in fact undertaken to do either of these things here. The Court of Appeals simply held that as a matter of law such an undertaking was to be implied from the Government's agreement to recommend a particular sentence. But our view of Rule 11(e) is that it speaks in terms of what the parties in fact agree to, and does not suggest that such implied-in-law terms as were read into this agreement by the Court of Appeals have any place under the Rule.

The Court of Appeals relied on cases such as United States v. Grandinetti, 564 F.2d 723 (C.A.5 1977), and United States v. Brown, 500 F.2d 375 (C.A.4 1974), for the conclusion it reached with respect to the requirement of "enthusiasm," but it appears to us that in each of these cases the Government attorney appearing personally in court at the time of the plea bargain expressed personal reservations about the agreement to which the Government had committed itself. This is quite a different proposition than an appellate determination from a transcript of the record made many years earlier that the Government attorney had "left an impression with the court of less-than-enthusiastic support for leniency." When the Government agrees pursuant to Rule 11(e) to make a recommendation with respect to sentence, it must carry out its part of the bargain by making the promised recommendation; but even if Rule 11(e) allows bargaining about degrees of enthusiasm, there appears to have been none here.

Rule 11(e) may well contemplate agreement by the Government in a particular case to state to the court its reasons for making the recommendation which it agrees to make. The Government suggests that spreading on the record its reasons for agreement to a plea bargain in a particular case—for example, that it did not wish to devote scarce resources to a trial of this particular defendant, or that it wished to avoid calling the victim as a witness—would frequently harm, rather than help, the defendant's quest for leniency. These may well be reasons why the defendant would not wish to exact such a commitment from the Government, but for purposes of this case it is enough that no such agreement was made in fact. Since Rule 11(e) speaks generally of the plea bargains that the parties make, it was error for the Court of Appeals to imply as a matter of law a term which the parties themselves did not agree upon.

For these reasons, we conclude that there was simply no default on the part of the Government in this case, to say nothing of a default remediable on collateral attack under 28 U.S.C. § 2255 or under Federal Rule of Criminal Procedure 32(d), as in effect before August 1, 1983. See Hill v. United States, 368 U.S. 424, 428, 82 S.Ct. 468, 471, 7 L.Ed.2d 417 (1962). The petition for certiorari is accordingly granted, and the judgment of the Court of Appeals is

Reversed. [The concurring opinion of JUSTICE STEVENS, and the dissenting opinion of JUSTICE BRENNAN with JUSTICE MARSHALL are omitted.]

NOTES

1. **Prosecutor's statements at sentencing.** Defendant agrees to plead guilty to one of several charges. In return, the prosecution agrees to dismiss other charges and to give no recommendation to the court as to sentencing or disposition of the case. In the presentence report, the probation officer recommends a suspended sentence and supervised probation. At the hearing on sentencing, the following exchange takes place:

> (The Court): Now, does the State want to say anything with regard to this disposition?
>
> (Mr. Howard [the prosecutor]): No, Your Honor. I agreed as part of our plea bargaining that I would not in this case make a recommendation to this Court. I would just state that I am not in full compliance with the recommendation of the Probation Officer, but I have not gone into it that fully.

Defendant is sentenced to five years' imprisonment. Was *Santobello* violated? See Miller v. State, 272 Md. 249, 322 A.2d 527 (1974) (over dissent, holding yes). Would *Benchimol* alter this result?

> Suppose that, at the sentencing hearing, the prosecutor makes the recommendation for three years as provided in the plea agreement. The following exchange then occurs:
>
> THE COURT: Why?
>
> PROSECUTOR: Well, Your Honor, that was part of the plea bargaining.
>
> THE COURT: Not because you believe in it?
>
> PROSECUTOR: Well, Your Honor, I do have some problems with that, anyhow, but that is the way I understand it.

Has *Santobello* been violated? See United States v. Brown, 500 F.2d 375 (4th Cir.1974), holding (over dissent) yes on the ground that "the consideration which induced defendant's guilty plea was not simply the prospect of a formal recitation of a possible sentence but rather the promise [of] ... sound advice, expressed with some degree of advocacy, of a government officer familiar both with the defendant and with his record and cognizant of his public duty as a prosecutor ... ". 500 F.2d at 377. Would *Benchimol* change this conclusion?

2. **Is an agreement binding before the plea is entered?** Once the prosecutor and defense attorney have arrived at a plea bargain, does the constitution preclude the prosecutor from reneging on the deal before the plea is entered? In Mabry v. Johnson, 467 U.S. 504, 104 S.Ct. 2543, 81 L.Ed.2d 437 (1984), respondent was serving a 21 year prison sentence for burglary. He was charged with murder. The prosecutor offered to recommend a sentence of 21 years to run concurrently with the burglary sentence in exchange for a plea of guilty to the murder. The defense attorney, after consulting with his client, communicated to the prosecutor that the offer was accepted. The prosecutor then informed defense counsel that he had mistakenly made the offer; he proposed instead to recommend a sentence of 21 years to be served consecutively to the burglary sentence in exchange for a plea of guilty. Defendant ultimately accepted this offer and plead guilty to the murder charge; he received a sentence of 21 years to be served consecutively to the burglary sentence. The Court of Appeals in federal habeas corpus proceedings set aside the murder conviction on the ground that defendant's due process rights had been violated by the prosecutor's withdrawal of his offer after it had been accepted

by the defense. The Supreme Court, in a unanimous opinion by Justice Stevens, reversed the Court of Appeals. Justice Stevens observed that "a plea bargain standing alone is without constitutional significance; in itself it is a mere executory agreement which, until embodied in the judgment of a court, does not deprive an accused of liberty or any other constitutionally protected interest." 467 U.S. at 507, 104 S.Ct. at 2546, 81 L.Ed.2d at 442. Justice Stevens then distinguished *Santobello:*

> Respondent's plea was in no sense induced by the prosecutor's withdrawn offer; unlike Santobello, who pleaded guilty thinking he had bargained for a specific prosecutorial sentencing recommendation which was not ultimately made, at the time respondent pleaded guilty he knew the prosecution would recommend a 21–year consecutive sentence ... [H]e pleaded guilty with the advice of competent counsel and with full awareness of the consequences—he knew that the prosecutor would recommend and that the judge could impose the sentence now under attack. Respondent's plea was thus in no sense the product of governmental deception; it rested on no "unfulfilled promises" and fully satisfied the test for voluntariness and intelligence.

467 U.S. at 510, 104 S.Ct. at 2548, 81 L.Ed.2d at 444. There was no evidence respondent had detrimentally relied upon the first plea agreement.

3. **Prosecutor's withdrawal of consent.** If the sentencing court decides to impose a lesser punishment than the agreement contemplates, should the prosecution be permitted to withdraw consent to the guilty plea? In People v. Farrar, 52 N.Y.2d 302, 437 N.Y.S.2d 961, 419 N.E.2d 864 (1981), the court characterized this opportunity as the counterpart of the defendant's right to withdraw the plea if the trial judge decides to impose a more severe sentence and held that the prosecution should have the opportunity:

> However justified the court's unwillingness to impose the negotiated sentence, fairness dictates that [the prosecution's option to withdraw consent] be left open. Of course, this is not to say that the People's application must be granted in all cases, for, among other things, prejudice to a defendant following a plea may prevent restoration to *status quo ante* and render vacatur of the plea inappropriate. Absent defendant's showing of such prejudice or other circumstances militating against vacatur, however, relief to the People would be proper.

52 N.Y.2d at 308, 437 N.Y.S.2d at 963, 419 N.E.2d at 866.

5. **Statements made during or after negotiation.** Under what, if any, circumstances are confessions made during plea negotiations later admissible? In Hutto v. Ross, 429 U.S. 28, 97 S.Ct. 202, 50 L.Ed.2d 194 (1976), the defendant and the prosecution had arrived at an agreement pursuant to which the defendant would plead guilty and the prosecution would recommend a fifteen year sentence with ten years suspended. When the prosecutor inquired concerning the defendant's willingness to make a statement concerning the crimes, defense counsel advised the defendant that the bargain did not require any such statement. Nevertheless, the defendant made a statement confessing to the offenses charged. Later, after the defendant withdrew from the agreement and demanded jury trial, this statement was introduced against him and he was convicted. The Supreme Court found no constitutional defect in the proceedings. Framing the issue as "whether a confession is *per se* inadmissible in a criminal trial because it was made subsequent to an agreed upon plea bargain that did not call for such a confession", it concluded:

> The existence of the bargain may well have entered into respondent's decision to give a statement, but counsel made it clear to respondent that he could enforce the terms of the plea bargain whether or not he confessed. The confession thus does not appear to have been the result of "any direct or

implied promises" or any coercion on the part of the prosecution, and was not involuntary.

429 U.S. at 30, 97 S.Ct. 203–04, 50 L.Ed.2d at 194. The Court specifically noted that the case did not involve the admissibility of statements made during the plea negotiation process. 429 U.S. at 30 n. 3, 97 S.Ct. at 203 n. 3, 50 L.Ed.2d at 197 n. 3.

6. **Waiving confidentiality of statements made during plea negotiations.** Federal Rules of Criminal Procedure 11(e)(6) provides that evidence of "any statement made in the course of plea discussions with an attorney for the government which do not result in a plea of guilty" are inadmissible in evidence. Can the defendant agree with the prosecutor to waive that exclusion as to statements that might be used to impeach later testimony in the event of a trial?

The respondent in United States v. Mezzanatto, 513 U.S. 196, 115 S.Ct. 797, 130 L.Ed.2d 697 (1995) made incriminatory statements during plea discussions with a prosecutor concerning his role in a drug distribution scheme. Before discussions began, he agreed to waive the protections of Rule 11(e) as to any statements he might make that could be used to impeach contradictory trial testimony. Plea discussions concluded without an agreement and the case went to trial. The government was permitted to impeach respondent's trial testimony with prior inconsistent statements he had made during the aborted plea discussions. The Ninth Circuit, viewing the exclusion as non-waivable, reversed the conviction. The Supreme Court, in an opinion by Justice Thomas, reversed the Ninth Circuit and reinstated the conviction.

The Court found nothing in the Rule to rebut the general presumption that legal rights can be waived by their intended beneficiary. Accordingly, it announced the rule that "absent some affirmative indication that the agreement was entered into unknowingly or involuntarily, an agreement to waive the exclusionary provisions of the plea-statement Rules is valid and enforceable." 513 U.S. at 210, 115 S.Ct. at 806, 130 L.Ed.2d at 710.

Justice Ginsburg concurred with the observation that an agreement to permit statements made during plea discussions to be admitted during the Government's case-in-chief might be dealt with differently on the ground admission would be inconsistent with Congress's intent to promote plea bargaining by the exclusionary provision.

7. **Remedies for post-plea entry agreement breach by defendant.** What remedies are available to the government when the defendant repudiates a plea bargain after he has pled guilty and been sentenced in accordance with its terms? The respondent in Ricketts v. Adamson, 483 U.S. 1, 107 S.Ct. 2680, 97 L.Ed.2d 1 (1987), was charged with first degree murder. As part of a plea agreement, he promised to testify against two others charged with the same offense in exchange for being permitted to plead guilty to second degree murder and receiving a negotiated prison sentence. He pled guilty, testified against the others, and was sentenced to the term he had negotiated. An appellate court reversed the convictions of the others and remanded for a new trial. Respondent refused to testify again against the others, taking the position that this contingency was not covered by the plea agreement. The State of Arizona obtained an order vacating the second degree murder conviction and sentence and re-instating the charge of first degree murder. Respondent was convicted under that charge and given the death penalty. His claim that this procedure was prohibited by the double jeopardy clause was accepted by the United States Court of Appeals, but the Supreme Court, in an opinion by Justice White, reversed. Respondent's interpretation of the plea agreement is untenable in view of his promise to "testify fully and completely in any Court, State or Federal, when requested by proper authorities against any and all parties involved in the murder of Don Bolles." The Court rejected the argument

that reinstatement of first degree murder charges was precluded because respondent had not explicitly waived double jeopardy protections in the plea agreement:

> The terms of the agreement could not be clearer: in the event of respondent's breach occasioned by a refusal to testify, the parties would be returned to the *status quo ante*, in which case respondent would have *no* double jeopardy defense to waive. And, an agreement specifying that charges may be *reinstated* given certain circumstances is, at least under the provisions of this plea agreement, *precisely* equivalent to an agreement waiving a double jeopardy defense.

483 U.S. at 10, 107 S.Ct. at 2685–86, 97 L.Ed.2d at 11–12. Justice Brennan, joined by Justices Marshall, Blackmun and Stevens, dissented.

5. EFFORTS TO ABOLISH PLEA BARGAINING

The National Advisory Commission on Criminal Justice Standards and Goals recommendation that plea bargaining should be prohibited no later than 1978 has not been followed nationwide. Some efforts to bar plea bargaining have been undertaken, however, and these provide some basis for believing that the traditional skepticism concerning the practicality of positions such as that of the Commission may be unwarranted.

Parnas and Atkins, Abolishing Plea Bargaining: A Proposal, 14 Crim. L.Bull. 101, 110–14 (1978), review reform efforts in the federal Southern District of California, Multnomah County, Oregon, and Maricopa County, Arizona and report conclusions somewhat similar to those in the report on the Alaska efforts, infra. But compare Callan, An Experience in Justice Without Plea Negotiation, 13 L. & Soc. 327 (1979), reporting on the practice in El Paso, Texas, and providing some support for those who fear that elimination of plea bargaining will produce a disruptive increase in contested cases. The state-wide experience in Alaska is discussed in RUBENSTEIN AND CLARK, CONCLUSIONS, in THE OFFICIAL PROHIBITION OF PLEA BARGAINING ON THE DISPOSITION OF FELONY CASES IN ALASKA CRIMINAL COURTS 219–29 (ALASKA JUDICIAL COUNCIL, 1978). The study concluded that there was considerable change in the system of plea bargaining as a result.

Parnas and Atkins, Abolishing Plea Bargaining: A Proposal, 14 Crim. L.Bull. 101 (1978), suggest that if plea bargaining is to be eliminated, the key to a workable system will be the appropriateness of the charge. Given the importance of the charging decision in a system without plea bargaining, they conclude that "there must be a control on [charging] beyond the district attorney's good faith and adherence to established criteria." Id., at 119. They propose a charge setting hearing before a judge. After considering the prosecutor's recommendation (which would carry great weight) and informally considering information concerning the matter, the judge would select an appropriate charge that would be binding during the remainder of the prosecution. If new information became available, a subsequent hearing to modify the charge might be granted under "exceptional circumstances." Id., at 119–20.

CALIFORNIA PENAL CODE (1982)

§ 1192.7. **[Limitation of plea bargaining.]** (a) Plea bargaining in any case in which the indictment or information charges any serious felony or any offense of driving while under the influence of alcohol, drugs, narcotics, or any other intoxicating substance, or any combination thereof, is prohibited, unless there is insufficient evidence to prove the people's case, or testimony of a material witness cannot be obtained, or a reduction or dismissal would not result in a substantial change in sentence.

(b) As used in this section "plea bargaining" means any bargaining, negotiation, or discussion between a criminal defendant, or his or her counsel, and a prosecuting attorney or judge, whereby the defendant agrees to plead guilty or nolo contendere, in exchange for any promises, commitments, concessions, assurances, or consideration by the prosecuting attorney or judge relating to any charge against the defendant or to the sentencing of the defendant.

(c) As used in this section "serious felony" means any of the following: (1) Murder or voluntary manslaughter; (2) mayhem; (3) rape; (4) sodomy by force, violence, duress, menace, or threat of great bodily harm; (5) oral copulation by force, violence, duress, menace, or threat of great bodily harm; (6) lewd acts on a child under the age of 14 years; (7) any felony punishable by death or imprisonment in the state prison for life; (8) any other felony in which the defendant inflicts great bodily injury on any person, other than an accomplice, or any felony in which the defendant uses a firearm; (9) attempted murder; (10) assault with intent to commit rape or robbery; (11) assault with a deadly weapon or instrument on a peace officer; (12) assault by a life prisoner on a noninmate; (13) assault with a deadly weapon by an inmate; (14) arson; (15) exploding a destructive device or any explosive with intent to injure; (16) exploding a destructive device or any explosive causing great bodily injury; (17) exploding a destructive device or any explosive with intent to murder; (18) burglary of a residence; (19) robbery; (20) kidnapping; (21) taking of a hostage by an inmate of a state prison; (22) attempt to commit a felony punishable by death or imprisonment in the state prison for life; (23) any felony in which the defendant personally used a dangerous or deadly weapon; (24) selling, furnishing, administering or providing heroin, cocaine, or phencyclidine (PCP) to a minor, (25) any attempt to commit a crime listed in this subdivision other than an assault.

(d) The provisions of this section shall not be amended by the Legislature except by statute passed in each house by rollcall vote entered in the journal two-thirds of the membership concurring, or by a statute that becomes effective only when approved by the electors.

NOTES

1. **The California provision in practice.** The California Penal Code provision has been construed in practice as permitting substantial plea bargaining. The prohibition applies to those cases—but only to those cases, it is urged—in which an indictment or information has been filed that "charges" one of the specified offenses. Felonies are often charged by information rather than indictment. A preliminary charge in the form of a complaint is filed in a lower court. No information is filed in the superior court—the court with general trial jurisdiction—unless a preliminary hearing has been held in the lower court or the defendant has waived this hearing. Substantial plea bargaining occurs during these early steps and

before an information is filed in superior court charging the offense. Is this consistent with the spirit which moved California voters to approve § 1192.7 by initiative in 1982?

2. For an extensive explication of alternatives to plea bargaining, see Alschuler, Implementing the Criminal Defendant's Right to Trial: Alternatives to the Plea Bargaining System, 50 U.Chi.L.Rev. 931 (1983).

CHAPTER 23

ADJUDICATION OF GUILT OR INNOCENCE BY TRIAL

Analysis

This Chapter considers very selectively some of the issues raised by the criminal trial as a method of adjudication of guilt or innocence. Four clusters of federal constitutional issues are discussed: the requirement of proof beyond a reasonable doubt, the right to trial by jury, the rights to confrontation, cross-examination and compulsory process, and the privilege against self-incrimination. The right to the effective assistance of counsel at trial is considered in Chapter 24.

A.   PROOF BEYOND A REASONABLE DOUBT

In In re Winship, 397 U.S. 358, 90 S.Ct. 1068, 25 L.Ed.2d 368 (1970), the Court held that the "beyond a reasonable doubt standard" was required in Juvenile Court at the trial stage of serious juvenile delinquency cases by Fourteenth Amendment Due Process. Also in that opinion, the Court made explicit for the first time that that standard was constitutionally mandated in adult criminal trials:

> The requirement that guilt of a criminal charge be established by proof beyond a reasonable doubt dates at least from our early years as a Nation. The "demand for a higher degree of persuasion in criminal cases was recurrently expressed from ancient times, [though] its crystallization into the formula 'beyond a reasonable doubt' seems to have occurred as late as 1798. It is now accepted in common law jurisdictions as the measure of persuasion by which the prosecution must convince the trier of all the essential elements of guilt." C. McCormick, Evidence § 321, pp. 681–682 (1954); see also 9 J. Wigmore, Evidence, § 2497 (3d ed. 1940). Although virtually unanimous adherence to the reasonable-doubt standard in common-law jurisdictions may not conclusively establish it as a requirement of due process, such adherence does "reflect a profound judgment about the way in which law should be enforced and justice administered." Duncan v. Louisiana, 391 U.S. 145, 155, 88 S.Ct. 1444, 1451, 20 L.Ed.2d 491 (1968).

> Expressions in many opinions of this Court indicate that it has long been assumed that proof of a criminal charge beyond a reasonable doubt is constitutionally required. . . . Mr. Justice Frankfurter stated that "[i]t is the duty of the Government to establish . . . guilt beyond a reasonable doubt. This notion—basic in our law and rightly one of the boasts of a free society—is a requirement and a safeguard of due process of law in the historic, procedural content of 'due process.'" Leland v. Oregon, supra, 343 U.S., at 802–803, 72 S.Ct., at 1009 (dissenting opinion). In a similar vein, the Court said in Brinegar v. United States, supra, 338 U.S., at 174, 69 S.Ct., at 1310, that "[g]uilt in a criminal case must be proved beyond a reasonable doubt and by evidence confined to that which long experience in the common-law tradition, to some extent embodied in the Constitution, has crystallized into rules of evidence consistent with that standard. These rules are historically grounded rights of our system, developed to safeguard men from dubious and unjust convictions, with resulting forfeitures of life, liberty and property." Davis v. United States, supra, 160 U.S., at 488, 16 S.Ct., at 358 stated that the requirement is implicit in "constitutions . . . [which] recognize the fundamental principles that are deemed essential for the protection of life and liberty." In *Davis* a murder conviction was reversed because the trial judge instructed the jury that it was their duty to convict when the evidence was equally balanced regarding the sanity of the accused. This Court said: "On the contrary, he is entitled to an acquittal of the specific crime charged, if upon all the evidence, there is reasonable doubt whether he was capable in law

of committing crime. ...No man should be deprived of his life under the forms of law unless the jurors who try him are able, upon their consciences, to say that the evidence before them ... is sufficient to show beyond a reasonable doubt the existence of every fact necessary to constitute the crime charged." Id., at 484, 493, 16 S.Ct., at 357, 360.

The reasonable-doubt standard plays a vital role in the American scheme of criminal procedure. It is a prime instrument for reducing the risk of convictions resting on factual error. The standard provides concrete substance for the presumption of innocence—that bedrock "axiomatic and elementary" principle whose "enforcement lies at the foundation of the administration of our criminal law." Coffin v. United States, supra, 156 U.S., at 453, 15 S.Ct., at 403. As the dissenters in the New York Court of Appeals observed, and we agree, "a person accused of a crime ... would be at a severe disadvantage, a disadvantage amounting to a lack of fundamental fairness, if he could be adjudged guilty and imprisoned for years on the strength of the same evidence as would suffice in a civil case." 24 N.Y.2d, at 205, 299 N.Y.S.2d, at 422, 247 N.E.2d, at 259.

The requirement of proof beyond a reasonable doubt has this vital role in our criminal procedure for cogent reasons. The accused during a criminal prosecution has at stake interest of immense importance, both because of the possibility that he may lose his liberty upon conviction and because of the certainty that he would be stigmatized by the conviction. Accordingly, a society that values the good name and freedom of every individual should not condemn a man for commission of a crime when there is reasonable doubt about his guilt. As we said in Speiser v. Randall, supra, 357 U.S., at 525–526, 78 S.Ct., at 1342: "There is always in litigation a margin of error, representing error in factfinding, which both parties must take into account. Where one party has at stake an interest of transcending value—as a criminal defendant his liberty—this margin of error is reduced as to him by the process of placing on the other party the burden of ... persuading the factfinder at the conclusion of the trial of his guilt beyond a reasonable doubt. Due process commands that no man shall lose his liberty unless the Government has borne the burden of ... convincing the factfinder of his guilt." To this end, the reasonable-doubt standard is indispensable, for it "impresses on the trier of fact the necessity of reaching a subjective state of certitude of the facts in issue." Dorsen & Reznick, In Re Gault and the Future of Juvenile Law, 1 Family Law Quarterly, No. 4, pp. 1, 26 (1967).

Moreover, use of the reasonable-doubt standard is indispensable to command the respect and confidence of the community in applications of the criminal law. It is critical that the moral force of the criminal law not be diluted by a standard of proof that leaves people in doubt whether innocent men are being condemned. It is also important in our free society that every individual going about his ordinary affairs have confidence that his government cannot adjudge him guilty of a criminal offense without convincing a proper factfinder of his guilt with utmost certainty.

Lest there remain any doubt about the constitutional stature of the reasonable-doubt standard, we explicitly hold that the Due Process Clause protects the accused against conviction except upon proof beyond a reasonable doubt of every fact necessary to constitute the crime with which he is charged.

397 U.S. at 361–64, 90 S.Ct. at 1071–73, 25 L.Ed.2d at 373–75. This section explores the ramifications of *Winship,* including those affecting the substantive definition of criminal offenses as well as others of a more procedural nature.

Mullaney v. Wilbur

Supreme Court of the United States, 1975.
421 U.S. 684, 95 S.Ct. 1881, 44 L.Ed.2d 508.

■ MR. JUSTICE POWELL delivered the opinion of the Court.

The State of Maine requires a defendant charged with murder to prove [by a "fair preponderance"] that he acted "in the heat of passion on sudden provocation" in order to reduce the homicide to manslaughter. We must decide whether this rule comports with the due process requirement, as defined in In re Winship, 397 U.S. 358, 364, 90 S.Ct. 1068, 1072, 25 L.Ed.2d 368 (1970), that the prosecution prove beyond a reasonable doubt every fact necessary to constitute the crime charged.

I.

* * *

[T]he jury found respondent guilty of murder.

Respondent appealed to the Maine Supreme Judicial Court, arguing that he had been denied due process because he was required to negate the element of malice aforethought by proving that he had acted in the heat of passion on sudden provocation. . . .

The Maine Supreme Judicial Court rejected this contention. . . .

Respondent next successfully petitioned for a writ of habeas corpus in federal district court. . . .

The Court of Appeals for the First Circuit affirmed . . .

* * *

Because of the importance of the issues presented, we . . . granted certiorari. . . . We now affirm.

* * *

III.

* * *

A.

Our analysis may be illuminated if this issue is placed in historical context.

* * *

[A]t common law the burden of proving heat of passion on sudden provocation appears to have rested on the defendant.

... [T]he large majority of States ... now require the prosecution to prove the absence of the heat of passion on sudden provocation beyond a reasonable doubt. See LaFave & Austin, Criminal Law 539–540 (1972).

This historical review establishes two important points. First, the fact at issue here—the presence or absence of the heat of passion on sudden provocation—has been, almost from the inception of the common law of homicide, the single most important factor in determining the degree of culpability attaching to an unlawful homicide. And, second, the clear trend has been toward requiring the prosecution to bear the ultimate burden of proving this fact. ...

B.

Petitioners, the warden of the Maine Prison and the State of Maine, argue that despite these considerations *Winship* should not be extended to the present case. They note that as a formal matter the absence of the heat of passion on sudden provocation is not a "fact necessary to constitute the *crime* "of felonious homicide in Maine. In re Winship, 397 U.S., at 364, 90 S.Ct., at 1073 (emphasis supplied). This distinction is relevant, according to petitioners, because in *Winship* the facts at issue were essential to establish criminality in the first instance whereas the fact in question here does not come into play until the jury already has determined that the defendant is guilty and may be punished at least for manslaughter. In this situation, petitioners maintain, the defendant's critical interests in liberty and reputation are no longer of paramount concern since, irrespective of the presence or absence of the heat of passion on sudden provocation, he is likely to lose his liberty and certain to be stigmatized. In short, petitioners would limit *Winship* to those facts which, if not proved, would wholly exonerate the defendant.

This analysis fails to recognize that the criminal law of Maine, like that of other jurisdictions, is concerned not only with guilt or innocence in the abstract but also with the degree of criminal culpability. Maine has chosen to distinguish those who kill in the heat of passion from those who kill in the absence of this factor. Because the former are less "blameworth[y]," they are subject to substantially less severe penalties. By drawing this distinction, while refusing to require the prosecution to establish beyond a reasonable doubt the fact upon which it turns, Maine denigrates the interests found critical in *Winship*.

The safeguards of due process are not rendered unavailing simply because a determination may already have been reached that would stigmatize the defendant and that might lead to a significant impairment of personal liberty. The fact remains that the consequences resulting from a verdict of murder, as compared with a verdict of manslaughter, differ significantly. ...

Moreover, if *Winship* were limited to those facts that constitute a crime as defined by state law, a State could undermine many of the interests that decision sought to protect without effecting any substantive change in its law. It would only be necessary to redefine the elements that comprise different crimes, characterizing them as factors that bear solely on the extent of punishment.[1] ...

Winship is concerned with substance rather than this kind of formalism.[2] The rationale of that case requires an analysis that looks to the "operation and effect of the law as applied and enforced by the state," and to the interests of both the State and the defendant as affected by the allocation of the burden of proof.

* * *

These interests are implicated to a greater degree in this case than they were in *Winship* itself. Petitioner there faced an 18–month sentence, with a maximum possible extension of an additional four and one-half years, 397 U.S., at 360, 90 S.Ct., at 1070, whereas respondent here faces a differential in sentencing ranging from a nominal fine to a mandatory life sentence. Both the stigma to the defendant and the community's confidence in the administration of the criminal law are also of greater consequence in this case, since the adjudication of delinquency involved in *Winship* was "benevolent" in intention, seeking to provide "a generously conceived program of compassionate treatment." In re Winship, 397 U.S., at 376, 90 S.Ct., at 1079 (Burger, C.J., dissenting).

Not only are the interests underlying *Winship* implicated to a greater degree in this case, but in one respect the protection afforded those interests is less here. In *Winship* the ultimate burden of persuasion remained with the prosecution, although the standard had been reduced to proof by a fair preponderance of the evidence. In this case, by contrast, the State has affirmatively shifted the burden of proof to the defendant. The result, in a case such as this one where the defendant is required to prove the critical fact in dispute, is to increase further the likelihood of an erroneous murder conviction. Such a result directly contravenes the principle articulated in Speiser v. Randall, 357 U.S. 513, 525–526, 78 S.Ct. 1332, 1342, 2 L.Ed.2d 1460 (1958):

> "[W]here one party has at stake an interest of transcending value—as a criminal defendant his liberty—th[e] margin of error is reduced as to him by the process of placing on the [prosecution] the burden ... of persuading the factfinder at the conclusion of the trial...."

* * *

1. Many States impose different statutory sentences on different degrees of assault. If *Winship* were limited to a State's definition of the elements of a crime, these States could define all assaults as a single offense and then require the defendant to disprove the elements of aggravation—e.g., intent to kill or intent to rob. But see State v. Ferris, 249 A.2d 523 (Me.1969) (prosecution must prove elements of aggravation in criminal assault case by proof beyond a reasonable doubt).

2. Indeed, in *Winship* itself the Court invalidated the burden of proof in a juvenile delinquency proceeding even though delinquency was not formally considered a "crime" under state law. 397 U.S. at 365–366, 90 S.Ct. at 1073–1074, id., at 373–374, 90 S.Ct. at 1077–1078 (Harlan, J., concurring).

C.

* * *

Nor is the requirement of proving a negative unique in our system of criminal jurisprudence.[3] Maine itself requires the prosecution to prove the absence of self-defense beyond a reasonable doubt. See State v. Millett, 273 A.2d 504 (1971).[4] Satisfying this burden imposes an obligation that, in all practical effect, is identical to the burden involved in negating the heat of passion on sudden provocation. Thus, we discern no unique hardship on the prosecution that would justify requiring the defendant to carry the burden of proving a fact so critical to criminal culpability.[5]

IV.

Maine law requires a defendant to establish by a preponderance of the evidence that he acted in the heat of passion on sudden provocation in order to reduce murder to manslaughter. Under this burden of proof a defendant can be given a life sentence when the evidence indicates that it is *as likely as not* that he deserves a significantly lesser sentence. This is an intolerable result in a society where, to paraphrase Mr. Justice Harlan, it is far worse to sentence one guilty only of manslaughter as a murderer than to sentence a murderer for the lesser crime of manslaughter. In re Winship, 397 U.S., at 372, 90 S.Ct., at 1076 (concurring opinion). We therefore hold

3. ... Many States do require the defendant to show that there is "some evidence" indicating that he acted in the heat of passion before requiring the prosecution to negate this element by proving the absence of passion beyond a reasonable doubt. Nothing in this opinion is intended to affect that requirement.

4. In *Millett* the Maine Supreme Judicial Court adopted the "majority rule" regarding proof of self-defense. The burden of producing "some evidence" on this issue rests with the defendant, but the ultimate burden of persuasion by proof beyond a reasonable doubt remains on the prosecution.

5. This conclusion is supported by consideration of a related line of cases. Generally in a criminal case the prosecution bears both the production burden and the persuasion burden. In some instances, however, it is aided by a presumption, see Davis v. United States, 160 U.S. 469, 16 S.Ct. 353, 40 L.Ed. 499 (1895) (presumption of sanity), or a permissible inference, see United States v. Gainey, 380 U.S. 63, 85 S.Ct. 754, 13 L.Ed.2d 658 (1965) (inference of knowledge from presence at an illegal still). These procedural devices require (in the case of a presumption) or permit (in the case of an inference) the trier of fact to conclude that the prosecution has met its burden of proof with respect to

the presumed or inferred fact by having satisfactorily established other facts. Thus, in effect they require the defendant to present some evidence contesting the otherwise presumed or inferred fact. See Barnes v. United States, 412 U.S. 837, 846 n. 11, 93 S.Ct. 2357, 37 L.Ed.2d 380 (1973). Since they shift the production burden to the defendant, these devices must satisfy certain due process requirements. See e.g., Barnes v. United States, supra; Turner v. United States, 396 U.S. 398, 90 S.Ct. 642, 24 L.Ed.2d 610 (1970).

In each of these cases, however, the ultimate burden of persuasion by proof beyond a reasonable doubt remained on the prosecution. See, e.g., Barnes v. United States, 412 U.S., at 845 n. 9, 93 S.Ct., at 2362; Davis v. United States, 160 U.S., at 484–488, 16 S.Ct., at 356–358. Shifting the burden of persuasion to the defendant obviously places an even greater strain upon him since he no longer need only present some evidence with respect to the fact at issue; he must affirmatively establish that fact. Accordingly, the Due Process Clause demands more exacting standards before the State may require a defendant to bear this ultimate burden of persuasion. See generally Ashford & Risinger, Presumptions, Assumptions and Due Process in Criminal Cases: A Theoretical Overview, 79 Yale L.J. 165 (1969).

that the Due Process Clause requires the prosecution to prove beyond a reasonable doubt the absence of the heat of passion on sudden provocation when the issue is properly presented in a homicide case. Accordingly, the judgment below is affirmed.

Affirmed.

■ Mr. Justice Rehnquist, with whom The Chief Justice joins, concurring.

* * *

I agree with the Court that In re Winship, 397 U.S. 358, 90 S.Ct. 1068, 25 L.Ed.2d 368 (1970), does require that the prosecution prove beyond a reasonable doubt every element which constitutes the crime charged against a defendant. I see no inconsistency between that holding and the holding of Leland v. Oregon, 343 U.S. 790, 72 S.Ct. 1002, 96 L.Ed. 1302 (1952). In the latter case this Court held that there was no constitutional requirement that the State shoulder the burden of proving the sanity of the defendant.

The Court noted in *Leland* that the issue of insanity as a defense to a criminal charge was considered by the jury only after it had found that all elements of the offense, including the *mens rea* if any required by state law, had been proven beyond a reasonable doubt. Id., at 792, 795, 72 S.Ct., at 1004–1005. Although as the state court's instructions in *Leland* recognized, id., at 794–795, 72 S.Ct., at 1005–1006, evidence relevant to insanity as defined by state law may also be relevant to whether the required *mens rea* was present, the existence or nonexistence of legal insanity bears no necessary relationship to the existence or nonexistence of the required mental elements of the crime. For this reason, Oregon's placement of the burden of proof on insanity on Leland, unlike Maine's redefinition of homicide in the instant case, did not effect an unconstitutional shift in the State's traditional burden of proof beyond a reasonable doubt of all necessary elements of the offense. Id., at 795, 72 S.Ct., at 1005. . . . Having once met that rigorous burden of proof that, for example, in a case such as this, the defendant not only killed a fellow human being, but did it with malice aforethought, the State could quite consistently with such a constitutional principle conclude that a defendant who sought to establish the defense of insanity, and thereby escape any punishment whatever for a heinous crime, should bear the laboring oar on such an issue.

NOTES

1. **Re-defining offense elements.** The significance of *Mullaney* may have been affected by Patterson v. New York, 432 U.S. 197, 97 S.Ct. 2319, 53 L.Ed.2d 281 (1977). Patterson had been charged with murder under a New York statute defining the crime as causing the death of another with the intent of causing the death of that person or a third individual. But under other provisions of the state's homicide statutes, if a defendant established, by a preponderance of the evidence, that an intentional killing was committed "under the influence of extreme emotional disturbance," he is to be convicted only of manslaughter. In an opinion by Justice White, a majority of the Supreme Court held that the New York scheme did not violate *Mullaney*. The New York scheme, the Court reasoned, was unlike the Maine

statute in that it did not presume any element of the offense of murder (i.e., lack of provocation) and place the burden on the defendant to rebut that presumption. The absence of extreme emotional disturbance is not an element of murder and therefore Leland v. Oregon (discussed in *Mullaney*) did not bar the state from placing the burden of proof on the defendant. Addressing the broader ramifications of the case, Justice White continued, "We . . . decline to adopt as a constitutional imperative, operative countrywide, that a State must disprove beyond a reasonable doubt every fact constituting any and all affirmative defenses related to the culpability of an accused." 432 U.S. at 210, 97 S.Ct. at 2327, 53 L.Ed.2d at 292. The Court acknowledged that some language in *Mullaney* might be read as requiring the prosecution to prove beyond a reasonable doubt any fact affecting the degree of criminal culpability. "The Court," Justice White commented, "did not intend *Mullaney* to have such far-reaching effect." 432 U.S. 215 n. 15, 97 S.Ct. at 2329 n. 15, 53 L.Ed.2d at 295 n. 15.

In Martin v. Ohio, 480 U.S. 228, 107 S.Ct. 1098, 94 L.Ed.2d 267 (1987), the defendant was convicted of aggravated murder in a trial in which she raised a claim of self-defense. Ohio law defined aggravated murder as a killing committed purposely and with prior calculation and design. It placed the burden upon the state to prove each element of aggravated murder beyond a reasonable doubt. Under Ohio law, self-defense was classified as an affirmative defense. The burden of producing evidence of self-defense was placed on the defendant and, once produced, the burden of persuasion was upon the defendant to prove self-defense by a preponderance of the evidence. The United States Supreme Court, in an opinion authored by Justice White, rejected the argument that the Ohio scheme violated *Mullaney*. Instead, it came within *Patterson:*

> The State did not exceed its authority in defining the crime of murder as purposely causing the death of another with prior calculation or design. It did not seek to shift to Martin the burden of proving any of those elements, and the jury's verdict reflects that none of her self-defense evidence raised a reasonable doubt about the state's proof that she purposefully killed with prior calculation and design. She nevertheless had the opportunity under state law and the instructions given to justify the killing and show herself to be blameless by proving that she acted in self-defense. The jury thought she had failed to do so, and Ohio is as entitled to punish Martin as one guilty of murder as New York was to punish Patterson.

480 U.S. at 233, 107 S.Ct. at 1102, 94 L.Ed.2d at 274. The Court noted that nothing in the trial court's instructions prevented the jury from using the evidence offered on self-defense to assist it in deciding whether the State carried its burden of proving that the killing was committed with prior calculation and design. Further, although only two states, Ohio and South Carolina, place the burden of persuasion on the defendant in cases of self-defense, the question of constitutionality "is not answered by cataloging the practices of other States. We are no more convinced that the Ohio practice of requiring self-defense to be proved by the defendant is unconstitutional than we are that the Constitution requires the prosecution to prove the sanity of a defendant who pleads not guilty by reason of insanity." 480 U.S. at 236, 107 S.Ct. at 1103, 94 L.Ed.2d at 276. Justice Powell, joined by Justices Brennan, Marshall, and Blackmun, dissented.

2. **Offense element or sentence enhancer?** In McMillan v. Pennsylvania, 477 U.S. 79, 106 S.Ct. 2411, 91 L.Ed.2d 67 (1986), the petitioners had been sentenced under a statutory scheme that required a minimum sentence of 5 years upon conviction of specified offenses if it is shown by a preponderance of the evidence at a sentencing hearing that the offender "visibly possessed a firearm" during the commission of the offense. The Pennsylvania Supreme Court rejected the

argument that permitting proof by a preponderance violated *Mullaney*. The United States Supreme Court, in an opinion by Justice Rehnquist, affirmed. *Mullaney,* as explicated in *Patterson,* does suggest there are certain constitutional minimum restrictions on the ability of the states to define the elements of criminal offenses to avoid the requirement that each be proved beyond a reasonable doubt, but this case does not reach those limits. While Pennsylvania could have made visible possession of a firearm an element of various other offenses, and would have been required to comply with *Mullaney* had it done so, instead

> [i]t simply took one factor that has always been considered by sentencing courts to bear on punishment—the instrumentality used in committing a violent felony—and dictated the precise weight to be given that factor if the instrumentality is a firearm. Pennsylvania's decision to do so has not transformed against its will a sentencing factor into an "element" of some hypothetical "offense."

477 U.S. at 89–90, 106 S.Ct. at 2418, 91 L.Ed.2d at 78–79. The Court also rejected the arguments that due process requires that there be proof by clear and convincing evidence and that there is a right to trial by jury on the question whether petitioners visibly possessed a firearm during the offense. Justice Stevens, dissenting, distinguished between the aggravating circumstances at issue in this case and the mitigating circumstances at issue in *Patterson.* He argued that,

> a state legislature may not dispense with the requirement of proof beyond a reasonable doubt for conduct that it targets for severe criminal penalties. Because the Pennsylvania statute challenged in this case describes conduct that the Pennsylvania legislature obviously intended to prohibit, and because it mandates lengthy incarceration for the same, I believe that the conduct so described is an element of the criminal offense to which the proof beyond a reasonable doubt requirement applies.

477 U.S. at 96, 106 S.Ct. at 2421, 91 L.Ed.2d at 83. Justice Stevens argued that we can rely upon the political process to guard against overzealous use of mitigating or exculpating circumstances to avoid the effects of *Mullaney.* For example, a legislature would not make it a criminal offense to be in a bank subject to an affirmative defense to be proved by the defendant that he was not robbing it. Justice Marshall, joined by Justices Brennan and Blackmun, dissenting, agreed with much of Justice Stevens' opinion but disapproved of his distinction between aggravating and mitigating circumstances and of his willingness to rely upon democratic processes to protect against *Mullaney*-abuse in the latter circumstance.

The petitioner in Jones v. United States, 526 U.S. 227, 119 S.Ct. 1215, 143 L.Ed.2d 311 (1999) was convicted under the federal carjacking statute, which made it a federal crime to steal a motor vehicle by use of a firearm. The offense was punishable by not more then 15 years imprisonment, but if serious bodily injury resulted by not more than 25 years and if death resulted by any number of years up to life. Jones was simply charged with committing carjacking with no allegation of serious bodily injury or death. After his conviction, the District Court, based on information about injuries to the victim contained in the presentence investigation report, imposed a sentence of 25 years. The Supreme Court, in an opinion by Justice Souter, held that the serious bodily injury must be plead and proved at trial to authorize the 25 year sentence since the fact is an element of the offense, not merely a sentence enhancement fact. The Court distinguished McMillan v. Pennsylvania on the ground that the provision in that case merely required the imposition of a minimum sentence upon showing of the enhancement fact and did not attempt to increase the maximum punishment otherwise authorized for the offense. The Court also distinguished Almendarez–Torres v. United States [Chapter 25 of this Supplement] on the ground of the history of treatment of prior convictions as a sentencing factor, not an element of a subsequent offense.

Finally, Justice Souter noted for the Court that adopting the position that the fact of serious bodily injury is merely a sentence enhancer would place the statute in constitutional jeopardy under due process and jury trial provisions, which is a further reason for interpreting it to create an element of the offense instead. Justice Stevens concurred on the ground that the due process and jury trial provisions of the Constitution forbid making serious bodily injury a sentence enhancement. Justice Scalia concurred on the ground that to do so would violate the right to trial by jury. Justice Kennedy, joined by The Chief Justice and Justices O'Connor and Breyer, dissented.

3. **Evidence sufficiency review as a constitutional requirement.** *Winship* has clearly directed increased attention at the sufficiency of the evidence to support a state conviction. Earlier, in Thompson v. City of Louisville, 362 U.S. 199, 80 S.Ct. 624, 4 L.Ed.2d 654 (1960), the Court held that a state conviction violated Due Process when there was "no evidence whatever" in the record supporting the finding of guilt. But in Jackson v. Virginia, 443 U.S. 307, 99 S.Ct. 2781, 61 L.Ed.2d 560 (1979), the Court held that in light of *Winship* greater scrutiny of the sufficiency of the evidence was warranted:

> After *Winship* the critical inquiry on review of the sufficiency of the evidence to support a criminal conviction must be not simply to determine whether the jury was properly instructed, but to determine whether the record evidence could reasonably support a finding of guilt beyond a reasonable doubt. But this inquiry does not require a court to "ask itself whether *it* believes that the evidence at the trial established guilt beyond a reasonable doubt." Instead, the relevant question is whether, after viewing the evidence in the light most favorable to the prosecution, *any* rational trier of fact could have found the essential elements of the crime beyond a reasonable doubt.

443 U.S. at 318–19, 99 S.Ct. at 2788–89, 61 L.Ed.2d at 573. On the facts of the case before it, the Court found sufficient circumstantial evidence that the petitioner acted with premeditation in killing the deceased to support the conviction.

4. **Burdens of production and persuasion.** Jury instructions may raise constitutional issues by classifying and allocating the burdens of going forward with the evidence and of proof. In Henderson v. Kibbe, 431 U.S. 145, 97 S.Ct. 1730, 52 L.Ed.2d 203 (1977), the defendant was charged with second degree murder. Prosecution evidence showed that he had abducted the highly-intoxicated victim, robbed him, and left him abandoned—without his glasses or warm clothing—on a rural, unlighted road. Another driver, traveling in excess of the posted speed limit, subsequently struck the victim and killed him. The controlling statute provided for liability of a defendant if, "under circumstances evincing a depraved indifference to human life, he recklessly engages in conduct which creates a grave risk of death to another person, and thereby causes the death of another person". Although there was substantial argument over whether the cause of the victim's death was the defendant's conduct or that of the driver, no instructions concerning the meaning of the statutory language—"thereby causes the death of another person"—were requested or given. Kibbe was convicted, but in later federal habeas corpus litigation the Second Circuit held that the failure to instruct the jury on causation created a high risk that the jury had not made a finding that the prosecution had proven causation by proof beyond a reasonable doubt. Consequently, the conviction violated In re Winship. The Supreme Court reversed, noting that a convicted person's burden of establishing that an erroneous instruction renders the conviction subject to collateral attack is especially heavy when no request for the instruction was made in the trial court. Although an instruction on causation would not have been cumulative of the instruction defining recklessness, the Court concluded, it was logical to assume that an instruction on causation would not have affected the

jury verdict. Would such an instruction have been constitutionally necessary had Kibbe specifically and vigorously demanded it at trial?

In Sandstrom v. Montana, 442 U.S. 510, 99 S.Ct. 2450, 61 L.Ed.2d 39 (1979), the petitioner was convicted of the offense of deliberate murder, which required proof that he intentionally caused the death of another. Petitioner had confessed to killing the victim but contended it was not done intentionally, and relied upon the testimony of mental health experts in support of his contention. Over his objection, the trial court instructed the jury without further elaboration that the "law presumes that a person intends the ordinary consequences of his voluntary acts." A unanimous Supreme Court held that the instruction violated the petitioner's rights under *Winship*. Proceeding on the basis that the relevant question is how a reasonable jury might understand such an instruction, the Court suggested four possible interpretations that it might have been given: as merely a permissible inference; as a statement that the burden of producing "some evidence" is upon the defendant but that the ultimate burden of persuasion remains upon the prosecution; as a statement that the burden of persuasion is upon the defendant; and as a conclusive presumption or rule of law that must control its deliberations on that issue. Since either of the latter two interpretations would violate petitioner's rights under *Winship* and since it cannot be said the jury did not employ one of them in reaching its verdict, the conviction was reversed.

In Francis v. Franklin, 471 U.S. 307, 105 S.Ct. 1965, 85 L.Ed.2d 344 (1985), Justice Brennan, for a 5–4 Court, found a denial of due process even when the *Sandstrom* instruction explicitly informed the jury that the presumption of intent was rebuttable and the entire jury charge contained several general instructions concerning the presumption of innocence and the States burden of proof beyond a reasonable doubt:

* * *

The analysis is straightforward. "The threshold inquiry in ascertaining the constitutional analysis applicable to this kind of jury instruction is to determine the nature of the presumption it describes." *Winship*, 442 U.S., at 514, 99 S.Ct., at 2454. The court must determine whether the challenged portion of the instruction creates a mandatory presumption . . . or merely a permissive inference . . .

Mandatory presumptions must be measured against the standards of *Winship* as elucidated in *Sandstrom*. Such presumptions violate the Due Process Clause if they relieve the State of the burden of persuasion on an element of an offense. . . . [6] A permissive inference does not relieve the State of its burden of persuasion because it still requires the State to convince the jury that the suggested conclusion should be inferred based on the predicate facts proven. Such inferences do not necessarily implicate the concerns of *Sandstrom*. A permissive inference violates the Due Process Clause only if the suggested conclusion is not one that reason and common sense justify in light of the proven facts before the jury. . . .

Analysis must focus initially on the specific language challenged, but the inquiry does not end there. If a specific portion of the jury charge, considered in isolation, could reasonably have been understood as creating a presumption that relieves the State of its burden of persuasion on an element of an offense, the potentially offending words must be considered in the context of the charge

6. We are not required to decide in this case whether a mandatory presumption that shifts only a burden of production to the defendant is consistent with the Due Process Clause, and we express no opinion on that question.

as a whole. Other instructions might explain the particular infirm language to the extent that a reasonable juror could not have considered the charge to have created an unconstitutional presumption. ...This analysis "requires careful attention to the words actually spoken to the jury ..., for whether a defendant has been accorded his constitutional rights depends upon the way in which a reasonable juror could have interpreted the instruction." *Sandstrom*, supra, 442 U.S., at 514, 99 S.Ct., at 2454.

* * *

As we explained in *Sandstrom*, general instructions on the State's burden of persuasion and the defendant's presumption of innocence are not "rhetorically inconsistent with a conclusive or burden-shifting presumption," because "[t]he jury could have interpreted the two sets of instructions as indicating that the presumption was a means by which proof beyond a reasonable doubt as to intent could be satisfied." 442 U.S., at 518–519, n. 7, 99 S.Ct., at 2456, n. 7.

* * *

Language that merely contradicts and does not explain a constitutionally infirm instruction will not suffice to absolve the infirmity. A reviewing court has no way of knowing which of the two irreconcilable instructions the jurors applied in reaching their verdict.[7]

471 U.S. at 313–22, 105 S.Ct. at 1971–75, 85 L.Ed.2d at 353–58.

5. **Harmless error.** When, if ever, may an instruction of the type condemned by *Sandstrom* and *Franklin* be considered harmless error?

In Rose v. Clark, 478 U.S. 570, 106 S.Ct. 3101, 92 L.Ed.2d 460 (1986), the trial court instructed the jury that malice is an element of murder and that all homicides are presumed to be malicious in the absence of evidence which would rebut that presumption. Respondent was found guilty of first-degree murder for one killing and of second-degree murder for the other. On federal habeas corpus, the District Court held that the trial court's instruction violated *Sandstrom*. This was affirmed by the Court of Appeals, which also held that the error could not be regarded as harmless because respondent had contested the issue of malice at the trial. The Supreme Court, in an opinion by Justice Powell, vacated and remanded. The Court concluded that the harmless error standard of Chapman v. California, discussed infra, applies. It made the generalization that

> if the defendant had counsel and was tried by an impartial adjudicator, there is a strong presumption that any other errors that may have occurred are subject to harmless error analysis. The thrust of the many constitutional rules governing the conduct of criminal trials is to ensure that those trials lead to fair and correct judgments. Where a reviewing court can find that the record developed at trial establishes guilt beyond a reasonable doubt, the interest in fairness had been satisfied and the judgment should be affirmed. As we have repeatedly

7. The Court today holds that contradictory instructions as to intent—one of which imparts to the jury an unconstitutional understanding of the allocation of burdens of persuasion—create a reasonable likelihood that a juror understood the instructions in an unconstitutional manner, unless other language in the charge *explains* the infirm language sufficiently to eliminate this possibility. If such a reasonable possibility of an unconstitutional understanding exists, "we have no way of knowing that [the defendant] was not convicted on the basis of the unconstitutional instruction." *Sandstrom*, 442 U.S., at 526, 99 S.Ct., at 2460. For this reason, it has been settled law since Stromburg v. California, 283 U.S. 359, 51 S.Ct. 532, 75 L.Ed. 1117 (1931), that when there exists a reasonable possibility that the jury relied on an unconstitutional understanding of the law in reaching a guilty verdict, that verdict must be set aside.

stated, "the Constitution entitles a criminal defendant to a fair trial, not a perfect one."

478 U.S. at 579, 106 S.Ct. at 3106, 92 L.Ed.2d at 471. Because the Court of Appeals did not consider whether the error here was harmless under *Chapman* the case was remanded with instructions to do so.

The Court further discussed harmless error in the context of burden-shifting jury instructions in Yates v. Evatt, 500 U.S. 391, 111 S.Ct. 1884, 114 L.Ed.2d 432 (1991). In Yates' murder trial, the court instructed the jury on the definition of murder, which included "malice" as an element. It further instructed the jury that malice is implied or presumed (1) from the willful, deliberate and intentional doing of an unlawful act and (2) from the use of a deadly weapon. The state supreme court found that these were mandatory presumptions, although rebuttable ones, and were, therefore, unconstitutional under *Sandstrom* and *Francis*. However, it found them to be harmless errors. The Supreme Court, in an opinion by Justice Souter, reversed. It established an approach to analyzing whether burden-shifting instructions were harmless under Chapman v. California (Casebook p. 1236) test of whether it appears "beyond a reasonable doubt that the error complained of did not contribute to the verdict obtained." The ultimate question is whether the "error [was] unimportant in relation to everything else the jury considered on the issue in question, as revealed by the record." The first step is to ask what evidence, based on the instructions and the record, the jury must have considered in reaching its verdict. The second step is to weigh the probative force of that evidence against the probative force of the invalid presumption. The standard is

> whether the force of the evidence presumably considered by the jury in accordance with the instructions is so overwhelming as to leave it beyond a reasonable doubt that the verdict resting on that evidence would have been the same in the absence of the presumption. It is only when the effect of the presumption is comparatively minimal to this degree that it can be said, in *Chapman's* words, that the presumption did not contribute to the verdict rendered.

500 U.S. at 405, 111 S.Ct. at 1893–94, 114 L.Ed.2d at 449. It then analyzed the evidence in light of that standard and concluded it could not find the errors harmless.

6. **Commenting on presumption of innocence.** Jury instructions play an important part in implementing or hindering the presumption of innocence, i.e. the requirement of proof beyond a reasonable doubt. What happens when the prosecution makes derogatory comments about the presumption of innocence and the court then refuses to give a jury instruction on the presumption?

Taylor v. Kentucky, 436 U.S. 478, 98 S.Ct. 1930, 56 L.Ed.2d 468 (1978), was a state prosecution for robbery. The only prosecution witness was the victim, who identified Taylor as the robber; Taylor testified to an alibi. In the opening statement, the prosecutor observed that the complaining witness had taken out a warrant against Taylor and that the grand jury had indicted Taylor. In the closing statement, the prosecutor stated that Taylor, "like any other defendant who's ever been tried who's in the penitentiary or in the reformatory today," had the presumption of innocence, and in the course of argument declared that "[o]ne of the first things defendants do after they rip someone off, they get rid of the evidence." Defense counsel asked the trial judge to instruct the jury that "[t]he law presumes a defendant to be innocent of a crime" and that the indictment, which had been read to the jury, was not evidence to be considered against the defendant. The trial judge refused these requests but did instruct the jury that the state had the burden of proving Taylor's guilt beyond a reasonable doubt. The Supreme Court reversed, finding that on the facts of Taylor's case due process was violated by the trial judge's refusal of the requested instruction on the presumption of innocence. Without holding that the prosecutor's comments and argument were reversible error or even improper, the Court found that they were relevant to the issue before it. The comments during opening argument invited the jury to draw inferences of guilt from the fact of arrest and indictment. The references during closing argument to Taylor's status as a defendant implied that all defendants are guilty and invited the jury to consider this in determining his guilt or innocence of the crime charged.

Consequently, the refusal of the requested instructions on presumption of innocence deprived Taylor of a fair trial.

However, in Kentucky v. Whorton, 441 U.S. 786, 99 S.Ct. 2088, 60 L.Ed.2d 640 (1979) (per curiam), where the Kentucky Supreme Court had held that failure to give the presumption of innocence instruction automatically required reversal of the respondent's conviction under *Taylor*, the Supreme Court reversed on the ground that *Taylor* should not be given such an expansive interpretation:

> [T]he failure to give a requested instruction on the presumption of innocence does not in and of itself violate the Constitution. Under *Taylor,* such a failure must be evaluated in light of the totality of the circumstances—including all the instructions to the jury, the arguments of counsel, whether the weight of the evidence was overwhelming, and other relevant factors—to determine whether the defendant received a constitutionally fair trial.

441 U.S. at 789, 99 S.Ct. at 2090, 60 L.Ed.2d at 643. Mr. Justice Stewart, joined by Justices Brennan and Marshall, dissented on the ground that failure to give the instruction upon request is always constitutional error. They would have vacated the judgment for consideration of whether the error was harmless. Compare Coffin v. United States, 156 U.S. 432, 460–61, 15 S.Ct. 394, 405–06, 39 L.Ed. 481, 493–94 (1895), holding that in federal criminal trials it is reversible error to refuse a request for a proper instruction on the presumption of innocence.

7. **Defining proof beyond a reasonable doubt.** Trial courts sometimes attempt to define reasonable doubt in jury instructions mandating use of the constitutional standard of proof beyond a reasonable doubt. In Cage v. Louisiana, 498 U.S. 39, 111 S.Ct. 328, 112 L.Ed.2d 339 (1990), the trial court had included the following in the jury instructions concerning the meaning of reasonable doubt:

> "This doubt, however, must be a reasonable one; that is one that is founded upon a real tangible substantial basis and not upon mere caprice and conjecture. *It must be such doubt as would give rise to a grave uncertainty,* raised in your mind by reasons on the unsatisfactory character of the evidence or lack thereof. A reasonable doubt is not a mere possible doubt. *It is an actual substantial doubt.* It is a doubt that a reasonable man can seriously entertain. What is required is not an absolute or mathematical certainty, but a *moral certainty.*"

498 U.S. at 40, 111 S.Ct. at 329, 112 L.Ed.2d at 342 (alteration in original). The Supreme Court, per curiam, found this instruction violated In re Winship,

> The charge * * * equated a reasonable doubt with a "grave uncertainty" and an "actual substantial doubt," and stated that what was required was a "moral certainty" that the defendant was guilty. It is plain to us that the words "substantial" and "grave," as they are commonly understood, suggest a higher degree of doubt than is required for acquittal under the reasonable doubt standard. When those statements are then considered with the reference to "moral certainty," rather than evidentiary certainty, it becomes clear that a reasonable juror could have interpreted the instruction to allow a finding of guilt based on a degree of proof below that required by the Due Process Clause.

498 U.S. at 41, 111 S.Ct. at 329–30, 112 L.Ed.2d at 342. What definition of reasonable doubt could a trial court give that would satisfy Due Process? Should a trial court refrain from giving the jury any definition at all? Is the trial court constitutionally required to give a definition? Is "proof beyond a reasonable doubt" a concept the jury can be expected to understand without elaboration?

The Court in Victor v. Nebraska, 511 U.S. 1, 114 S.Ct. 1239, 127 L.Ed.2d 583 (1994), in an opinion by Justice O'Connor, held that the instructions in that case and in Sandoval v. California did not violate due process. The instruction in Sandoval v. California defined reasonable doubt by using the words "moral evidence" and "moral certainty." Victor challenged the instruction in his case for using the terms "substantial doubt" and "strong probabilities" in defining the burden of proof. Unlike in Cage v. Louisiana, the Court concluded here that " 'taken as a whole, the instructions correctly conveyed the concept of reasonable doubt to the jury.' * * * There is no reasonable likelihood that the jurors who determined petitioners' guilt applied the instructions in a way that violated the Constitution." 511 U.S. at 22–23, 114 S.Ct. at 1251, 127 L.Ed.2d at 601.

A jury instruction on reasonable doubt that violates *Cage* cannot be harmless error, the Court held in Sullivan v. Louisiana, 508 U.S. 275, 113 S.Ct. 2078, 124 L.Ed.2d 182 (1993). The Fifth Amendment requirement of proof beyond a reasonable doubt and the Sixth Amendment requirement of a jury verdict are interrelated, Justice Scalia reasoned for the Court, and a verdict returned by a jury inaccurately instructed on reasonable doubt does not meet the Sixth Amendment jury trial requirement. As applied to harmless error situations, the Sixth Amendment jury trial guarantee demands that a reviewing court inquire as to what if any effect the error had upon the verdict actually returned in the case. It does not permit an inquiry into what effect the error might have upon some "reasonable" jury. If under *Cage* a jury has been misinstructed on the prosecution's burden of proof, all of the jury's findings are vitiated. There is, therefore, no verdict to use in a harmless error analysis.

> There being no jury verdict of guilty-beyond-a-reasonable-doubt, the question whether the *same* verdict of guilty-beyond-a-reasonable-doubt would have been rendered absent the constitutional error is utterly meaningless. There is no *object*, so to speak, upon which harmless-error scrutiny can operate. The most an appellate court can conclude is that a jury *would surely have found* [the defendant] guilty beyond a reasonable doubt—not that the jury's actual finding of guilty beyond a reasonable doubt *would surely not have been different* absent the constitutional error. That is not enough.

508 U.S. at 280, 113 S.Ct. at 2082, 124 L.Ed.2d at 189–90. Alternatively, the Court reasoned, the right to a jury verdict of guilty beyond a reasonable doubt is "a 'basic protectio[n]' whose precise effects are unmeasurable." Therefore, an instruction that violates this right is one of the "structural defects in the constitution of the trial mechanism, which defy analysis by 'harmless error' standards." Under Arizona v. Fulminante, 499 U.S. 279, 111 S.Ct. 1246, 113 L.Ed.2d 302 (1991), such defects cannot be harmless error.

8. **Witness credibility instructions.** Jury instructions pertaining to the credibility of witnesses also affect the burden of proof. In Cool v. United States, 409 U.S. 100, 93 S.Ct. 354, 34 L.Ed.2d 335 (1972), it was held constitutional error to instruct jurors that they should disregard the testimony of an alleged accomplice (called by the defense) unless they were convinced it was true beyond a reasonable doubt. Given the heavy reliance upon the testimony by the defense, the Court commented, the effect of the instruction was to shift to the defendant the burden of proving innocence by proof beyond a reasonable doubt. In Cupp v. Naughten, 414 U.S. 141, 94 S.Ct. 396, 38 L.Ed.2d 368 (1973), several eyewitnesses identified the

defendant as the perpetrator of the robbery charged and the defense produced no witnesses. In addition to instructing the jury on the prosecution's burden of proof, the trial judge told them:

> "Every witness is presumed to speak the truth. This presumption may be overcome by the manner in which the witness testifies, by the nature of his or her testimony, by evidence affecting his or her character, interest, or motives, by contradictory evidence, or by a presumption."

414 U.S. at 142, 94 S.Ct. at 398, 38 L.Ed.2d at 371. This was held not to invalidate the conviction.

9. **Trying defendant in jail clothes.** Other aspects of the conduct of a trial may also infringe upon the right to have the prosecution prove guilt beyond a reasonable doubt. In Estelle v. Williams, 425 U.S. 501, 96 S.Ct. 1691, 48 L.Ed.2d 126 (1976), the Court assumed that compelling a defendant to appear at trial in jail clothing would violate the right:

> [T]he accused's condition implicit in such distinctive, identifiable attire may affect a juror's judgment. The defendant's clothing is so likely to be a continuing influence throughout the trial that, not unlike placing a jury in the custody of deputy sheriffs who were also witnesses for the prosecution, an unacceptable risk is presented of impermissible factors coming into play.
>
> * * *
>
> That it may be more convenient for jail administrators ... provides no justification for the practice.

425 U.S. at 504–05, 96 S.Ct. at 1693, 48 L.Ed.2d at 131. But it also noted that in some situations a defendant might prefer to stand trial in jail garments, hoping by this to elicit sympathy from the jury. The constitutional prohibition, therefore, is against compelling a defendant to stand trial in identifiable prison clothing. Since the respondent in *Williams* had not objected before the trial judge to the unavailability of street clothing, the Court concluded, there was no showing of the compulsion necessary to establish a constitutional violation.

B.   RIGHT TO A TRIAL BY JURY

Historically, the right to trial by jury has been one of the unique attributes of adjudication of guilt or innocence by trial rather than plea. But implementation of that right in the modern context involves several complex problems. It is necessary to determine whether the right exists in all criminal prosecutions and, if not, where the line is to be drawn. Limits upon the composition of the jury must be defined. Finally, the appropriate size and vote required for a determination of guilt or innocence must be determined. These matters are the subject of this Section.

The Sixth Amendment right to jury trial and the Fifth Amendment right to proof beyond a reasonable doubt are "interrelated." Sullivan v. Louisiana, 508 U.S. 275, 278, 113 S.Ct. 2078, 2081, 124 L.Ed.2d 182, 188 (1993). Together, "these provisions require criminal convictions to rest upon a jury determination that the defendant is guilty of every element of the crime with which he is charged, beyond a reasonable doubt." United States v. Gaudin, 515 U.S. 506, 518, 115 S.Ct. 2310, 2313, 132 L.Ed.2d 444, 449 (1995). *Gaudin* presented the question whether there is an exception to this general rule for the materiality of the allegedly false statement in a perjury prosecution. At Gaudin's trial for making false statements on federal loan documents, the trial judge instructed the jury that the Government was required to prove that the alleged false statements were material but he added:

> [t]he issue of materiality ... is not submitted to you for your decision but rather is a matter for the decision of the court. You are instructed that the statements charged in the indictment are material statements.

Finding that this was error, the Court considered and rejected the Government's contention that case law indicating that materiality is a matter for the court rather than the jury created or reflected an exception to the general Fifth and Sixth Amendment rule:

> [W]e find nothing like a consistent historical tradition supporting the proposition that the element of materiality in perjury prosecutions is to be decided by the judge. Since that proposition is contrary to the uniform general understanding (and we think the only understanding consistent with principle) that the Fifth and Sixth Amendments require conviction by a jury of all elements of the crime, we must reject those cases that have embraced it. Though uniform postratification practice can shed light upon the meaning of an ambiguous constitutional provision, the practice here is not uniform, and the core meaning of the constitutional guarantees is unambiguous.

515 U.S. at 518–19, 115 S.Ct. at 2317–18, 132 L.Ed.2d at 455.

1. PROSECUTIONS TO WHICH THE RIGHT APPLIES

The Sixth Amendment grants the right to trial by jury to defendants in "all criminal prosecutions." The right to a jury in state criminal proceedings, however, is not specifically provided for in the Federal Constitution. The following case deals with that issue.

Duncan v. Louisiana

Supreme Court of the United States, 1968.
391 U.S. 145, 88 S.Ct. 1444, 20 L.Ed.2d 491.

■ MR. JUSTICE WHITE delivered the opinion of the Court.

Appellant, Gary Duncan, was convicted of simple battery.... Under Louisiana law simple battery is a misdemeanor, punishable by a maximum of two years' imprisonment and a $300 fine. Appellant sought trial by jury, but because the Louisiana Constitution grants jury trials only in cases in which capital punishment or imprisonment at hard labor may be imposed, the trial judge denied the request. Appellant was convicted and sentenced to serve 60 days in the parish prison and pay a fine of $150. Appellant sought review in the Supreme Court of Louisiana, asserting that the denial of jury trial violated rights guaranteed to him by the United States Constitution. The Supreme Court, finding "[n]o error of law in the ruling complained of," denied appellant a writ of certiorari. Pursuant to 28 U.S.C.A. § 1257(2) appellant sought review in this Court, alleging that the Sixth and Fourteenth Amendments to the United States Constitution secure the right to jury trial in state criminal prosecutions where a sentence as long as two years may be imposed. . . .

Appellant was 19 years of age when tried. While driving on Highway 23 in Plaquemines Parish on October 18, 1966, he saw two younger cousins engaged in a conversation by the side of the road with four white boys. Knowing his cousins, Negroes who had recently transferred to a formerly all-white high school, had reported the occurrence of racial incidents at the school, Duncan stopped the car, got out, and approached the six boys. At trial the white boys and a white onlooker testified, as did appellant and his cousins. The testimony was in dispute on many points, but the witnesses agreed that appellant and the white boys spoke to each other, that appellant encouraged his cousins to break off the encounter and enter his car and that appellant was about to enter the car himself for the purpose of driving away with his cousins. The whites testified that just before getting in the car appellant slapped Herman Landry, one of the white boys, on the elbow. The Negroes testified that appellant had not slapped Landry, but had merely touched him. The trial judge concluded that the State had proved beyond a reasonable doubt that Duncan had committed simple battery, and found him guilty.

I.

The Fourteenth Amendment denies the States the power to "deprive any person of life, liberty, or property, without due process of law." In resolving conflicting claims concerning the meaning of this spacious language, the Court has looked increasingly to the Bill of Rights for guidance; many of the rights guaranteed by the first eight Amendments to the Constitution have been held to be protected against state action by the Due Process Clause of the Fourteenth Amendment. . . .

The test for determining whether a right extended by the Fifth and Sixth Amendments with respect to federal criminal proceedings is also protected against state action by the Fourteenth Amendment has been phrased in a variety of ways in the opinions of this Court. The question has been asked whether a right is among those " 'fundamental principles of liberty and justice which lie at the base of all our civil and political institutions,' "; whether it is "basic in our system of jurisprudence,"; and whether it is "a fundamental right, essential to a fair trial". The claim before us is that the right to trial by jury guaranteed by the Sixth Amendment meets these tests. The position of Louisiana, on the other hand, is that the Constitution imposes upon the States no duty to give a jury trial in any criminal case, regardless of the seriousness of the crime or the size of the punishment which may be imposed. Because we believe that trial by jury in criminal cases is fundamental to the American scheme of justice, we hold that the Fourteenth Amendment guarantees a right of jury trial in all criminal cases which—were they to be tried in a federal court— would come within the Sixth Amendment's guarantee. Since we consider the appeal before us to be such a case, we hold that the Constitution was violated when appellant's demand for jury trial was refused.

The history of trial by jury in criminal cases has been frequently told. It is sufficient for present purposes to say that by the time our Constitution was written, jury trial in criminal cases had been in existence in England for several centuries and carried impressive credentials traced by many to Magna Carta.

* * *

Jury trial came to America with English colonists, and received strong support from them. Royal interference with the jury trial was deeply resented. Among the resolutions adopted by the First Congress of the American Colonies (the Stamp Act Congress) on October 19, 1765—resolutions deemed by their authors to state "the most essential rights and liberties of the colonists"—was the declaration:

"That trial by jury is the inherent and invaluable right of every British subject in these colonies." . . .

The Constitution itself, in Art. III, § 2, commanded:

"The Trial of all Crimes, except Cases of Impeachment, shall be by Jury; and such Trial shall be held in the State where the said Crimes shall have been committed."

Objections to the Constitution because of the absence of a bill of rights were met by the immediate submission and adoption of the Bill of Rights. Included was the Sixth Amendment which, among other things provided:

"In all criminal prosecutions, the accused shall enjoy the right to a speedy and public trial, by an impartial jury of the State and district wherein the crime shall have been committed."

The constitutions adopted by the original States guaranteed jury trial. Also, the constitution of every State entering the Union thereafter in one form or another protected the right to jury trial in criminal cases.

* * *

Jury trial continues to receive strong support. The laws of every State guarantee a right to jury trial in serious criminal cases; no State has dispensed with it; nor are there significant movements underway to do so. Indeed, the three most recent state constitutional revisions, in Maryland, Michigan, and New York, carefully preserved the right of the accused to have the judgment of a jury when tried for a serious crime.

* * *

The guarantees of jury trial in the Federal and State Constitutions reflect a profound judgment about the way in which law should be enforced and justice administered. A right to jury trial is granted to criminal defendants in order to prevent oppression by the Government. Those who wrote our constitutions knew from history and experience that it was necessary to protect against unfounded criminal charges brought to eliminate enemies and against judges too responsive to the voice of higher authority. The framers of the constitutions strove to create an independent judiciary but insisted upon further protection against arbitrary action. Providing an accused with the right to be tried by a jury of his peers gave him an inestimable safeguard against the corrupt or overzealous prosecutor and against the compliant, biased, or eccentric judge. If the defendant preferred the common-sense judgment of a jury to the more tutored but perhaps less sympathetic reaction of the single judge, he was to have it. Beyond this, the jury trial provisions in the Federal and State Constitutions reflect a fundamental decision about the exercise of official power—a reluctance to entrust plenary powers over the life and liberty of the citizen to one judge or to a group of judges. Fear of unchecked power, so typical of our State and Federal Governments in other respects, found expression in the criminal law in this insistence upon community participation in the determination of guilt or innocence. The deep commitment of the Nation to the right of jury trial in serious criminal cases as a defense against arbitrary law enforcement qualifies for protection under the Due Process Clause of the Fourteenth Amendment, and must therefore be respected by the States.

Of course jury trial has "its weaknesses and the potential for misuse." We are aware of the long debate, especially in this century, among those who write about the administration of justice, as to the wisdom of permitting untrained laymen to determine the facts in civil and criminal proceedings. Although the debate has been intense, with powerful voices on either side most of the controversy has centered on the jury in civil cases. Indeed, some of the severest critics of civil juries acknowledge that the arguments for criminal juries are much stronger. In addition, at the heart of the dispute have been express or implicit assertions that juries are incapable of adequately understanding evidence or determining issues of fact, and that they are unpredictable, quixotic, and little better than a roll of dice. Yet, the most recent and exhaustive study of the jury in criminal cases concluded that juries do understand the evidence and come to sound conclusions in most of the cases presented to them and that when juries differ with the result at which the judge would have arrived, it is usually because they are serving some of the very purposes for which they were created and for which they are now employed.[a]

The State of Louisiana urges that holding that the Fourteenth Amendment assures a right to jury trial will cast doubt on the integrity of every trial conducted without a jury. Plainly, this is not the import of our holding. Our conclusion is that in the American States, as in the federal judicial system, a general grant of jury trial for serious offenses is a fundamental right, essential for preventing miscarriages of justice and for assuring that fair trials are provided for all defendants. We would not assert, however, that every criminal trial—or any particular trial—held before a judge alone is unfair or that a defendant may never be as fairly treated by a judge as he would be by a jury. Thus we hold no constitutional doubts about the practices, common in both federal and state courts, of accepting waivers of jury trial and prosecuting petty crimes without extending a right to jury trial. However, the fact is that in most places more trials for serious crimes are to juries than to a court alone; a great many defendants prefer the judgment of a jury to that of a court. Even where defendants are satisfied with bench trials, the right to a jury trial very

---

a. H. Kalven, Jr. & H. Zeisel, The American Jury 4, n. 24 (1966).

likely serves its intended purpose of making judicial or prosecutorial unfairness less likely.

* * *

II

Louisiana's final contention is that even if it must grant jury trials in serious criminal cases, the conviction before us is valid and constitutional because here the petitioner was tried for simple battery and was sentenced to only 60 days in the parish prison. We are not persuaded. It is doubtless true that there is a category of petty crimes or offenses which is not subject to the Sixth Amendment jury trial provision and should not be subject to the Fourteenth Amendment jury trial requirement here applied to the States. Crimes carrying possible penalties up to six months do not require a jury trial if they otherwise qualify as petty offenses, Cheff v. Schnackenberg, 384 U.S. 373, 86 S.Ct. 1523, 16 L.Ed.2d 629 (1966). But the penalty authorized for a particular crime is of major relevance in determining whether it is serious or not and may in itself, if severe enough, subject the trial to the mandates of the Sixth Amendment. District of Columbia v. Clawans, 300 U.S. 617, 57 S.Ct. 660, 81 L.Ed. 843 (1937). The penalty authorized by the law of the locality may be taken "as a gauge of its social and ethical judgments," 300 U.S., at 628, 81 L.Ed. at 848, of the crime in question. In *Clawans* the defendant was jailed for 60 days, but it was the 90–day authorized punishment on which the Court focused in determining that the offense was not one for which the Constitution assured trial by jury. In the case before us the Legislature of Louisiana has made simple battery a criminal offense punishable by imprisonment for up to two years and a fine. The question, then, is whether a crime carrying such a penalty is an offense which Louisiana may insist on trying without a jury.

We think not. So-called petty offenses were tried without juries both in England and in the Colonies and have always been held to be exempt from the otherwise comprehensive language of the Sixth Amendment's jury trial provisions. There is no substantial evidence that the Framers intended to depart from this established common-law practice, and the possible consequences to defendants from convictions for petty offenses have been thought insufficient to outweigh the benefits to efficient law enforcement and simplified judicial administration resulting from the availability of speedy and inexpensive nonjury adjudications. These same considerations compel the same result under the Fourteenth Amendment. Of course the boundaries of the petty offense category have always been ill-defined, if not ambulatory. . . .

In determining whether the length of the authorized prison term or the seriousness of other punishment is enough in itself to require a jury trial, we are counseled by District of Columbia v. Clawans, supra, to refer to objective criteria, chiefly the existing laws and practices in the Nation. In the federal system, petty offenses are defined as those punishable by no more than six months in prison and a $500 fine. In 49 of the 50 States crimes subject to trial without a jury, which occasionally include simple battery, are punishable by no more than one year in jail. Moreover, in the late 18th century in America crimes triable without a jury were for the most part punishable by no more than a six-month prison term, although there appear to have been exceptions to this rule. We need not, however, settle in this case the exact location of the line between petty offenses and serious crimes. It is sufficient for our purposes to hold that a crime punishable by two years in prison is, based on past and contemporary standards in this country, a serious crime and not a petty offense.[8] Consequently, appellant was entitled to a jury trial and it was error to deny it.

The judgment below is reversed and the case is remanded for proceedings not inconsistent with this opinion.

NOTES

1. **Defining a "serious" offense.** The line between "serious" and "petty" offenses, left unsettled in *Duncan,* was drawn in Baldwin v. New York, 399 U.S. 66, 90 S.Ct. 1886, 26 L.Ed.2d 437 (1970). Baldwin, after unsuccessfully petitioning for a jury trial, was convicted of "jostling" (a misdemeanor designed to deal with pickpocketing) and sentenced to the maximum term allowable, one year. On appeal, he challenged the constitutionality of his conviction under the New York statute, which prohibited jury trials in the New York City Criminal Court where he was tried. The Supreme Court reversed. Justice White, in a plurality opinion joined by Justices Brennan and Marshall, concluded that "no offense can be deemed 'petty' for purposes of the right to trial by jury where imprisonment for more than six months is authorized." 399 U.S. at 69, 90 S.Ct. at 1888, 26 L.Ed.2d at 440. Responding to the concurring opinion of Justice Black, joined by Justice Douglas, which argued that the Sixth Amendment guarantees, much as its language suggests, a jury trial "in all criminal prosecutions," Justice White continued:

> One who is threatened with the possibility of imprisonment for six months may find little difference between the potential consequences which face him, and the consequences which faced appellant here. Indeed, the prospect of imprisonment for however short a time will seldom be viewed by the accused as a trivial or "petty" matter and may well result in quite serious repercussions affecting his career and his reputation. Where the accused cannot possibly face more than six months imprisonment, we have held that these disadvantages, onerous though they may be, may be outweighed by the benefits which result from speedy and inexpensive nonjury adjudications. We cannot, however, conclude that these administrative conveniences, in light of the practices which now exist in every one of the 50 States as well as in the federal courts, can similarly

8. It is argued that Cheff v. Schnackenberg, 384 U.S. 373, 86 S.Ct. 1523, 16 L.Ed.2d 629 (1966), interpreted the Sixth Amendment as meaning that to the extent that the length of punishment is a relevant criterion in distinguishing between serious crimes and petty offenses, the critical factor is not the length of sentence authorized but the length of the penalty actually imposed. In our view that case does not reach the situation where a legislative judgment as to the seriousness of the crime is imbedded in the statute in the form of an express authorization to impose a heavy penalty for the crime in question. *Cheff* involved criminal contempt, an offense applied to a wide range of conduct including conduct not so serious as to require jury trial absent a long sentence. In addition criminal contempt is unique in that legislative bodies frequently authorize punishment without stating the extent of the penalty which can be imposed. The contempt statute under which Cheff was prosecuted, 18 U.S.C.A. § 401, treated the extent of punishment as a matter to be determined by the forum court. It is therefore understandable that this Court in *Cheff* seized upon the penalty actually imposed as the best evidence of the seriousness of the offense for which Cheff was tried.

justify denying an accused the important right to trial by jury where the possible penalty exceeds six months' imprisonment.

399 U.S. at 73–74, 90 S.Ct. at 1890–91, 26 L.Ed.2d at 443.

The Supreme Court returned to the task of drawing a line to define the right to a trial by jury in Blanton v. City of North Las Vegas, 489 U.S. 538, 109 S.Ct. 1289, 103 L.Ed.2d 550 (1989). Petitioner was charged with driving under the influence of alcohol, which under Nevada law carried a maximum statutory penalty of 6 months' imprisonment and a $1,000 fine. One convicted of that offense would also automatically have his motor vehicle operator's license suspended for 90 days and would be required to attend at his own expense an alcohol education course. As an alternative to imprisonment, the trial court could order a person convicted of this offense to perform 48 hours of work for the community while dressed in "distinctive garb" which identifies him as a DUI offender. Petitioner claims that the combination of these penalties made the offense a non-petty one that carried with it the right of trial by jury. Justice Marshall, writing for a unanimous Court, disagreed:

> Although we did not hold in *Baldwin* that an offense carrying a maximum prison term of six months or less automatically qualifies as a "petty" offense, and decline to do so today, we do find it appropriate to presume for purposes of the Sixth Amendment that society views such an offense as "petty." A defendant is entitled to jury trial in such circumstances only if he can demonstrate that any additional statutory penalties, viewed in conjunction with the maximum authorized period of incarceration, are so severe that they clearly reflect a legislative determination that the offense in question is a "serious" one. This standard, albeit somewhat imprecise, should ensure the availability of a jury trial in the rare situation where a legislature packs an offense it deems "serious" with onerous penalties that nonetheless "do not puncture the 6–month incarceration line."

489 U.S. at 543, 109 S.Ct. at 1293, 103 L.Ed.2d at 556–57. The Court then examined the full package of penalties for the offense and concluded it remained a petty offense for Sixth Amendment purposes.

The offense at issue in United States v. Nachtigal, 507 U.S. 1, 113 S.Ct. 1072, 122 L.Ed.2d 374 (1993)(per curiam) was driving under the influence and carried a maximum punishment of six months' imprisonment and a $5,000 fine. Alternatively, the court could impose probation not to exceed five years and to impose numerous conditions to the probation. Under *Blanton*, the Supreme Court held, this was a petty offense for which jury trial was not available. The maximum term of imprisonment—six months—creates a presumption that the offense is a petty one and the additional penalties "are not sufficiently severe to overcome this presumption." The fine could be $4,000 greater than was permissible in *Blanton*, but that was not controlling. Nor was the probation alternative:

> Like a monetary penalty, the liberty infringement caused by a term of probation is far less intrusive than incarceration. The discretionary probation conditions do not alter this conclusion; while they obviously entail a greater infringement on liberty than probation without attendant conditions, they do not approximate the severe loss of liberty caused by imprisonment for more than six months.

507 U.S. at 5, 113 S.Ct. at 1074, 122 L.Ed.2d at 380.

Petitioner in Lewis v. United States, 518 U.S. 322, 116 S.Ct. 2163, 135 L.Ed.2d 590 (1996), a postal worker, was charged with two counts of obstructing the mail. Each count carried a possible sentence of not more than six months. The federal magistrate denied petitioner's request for a jury trial on the ground each count charged but a petty offense and stated that the total sentence on both counts would not in this case exceed six months. The United States Supreme Court, in an opinion by Justice O'Connor, approved. The nature of the offense is determined by each offense, not by the possible consecutive sentences that could be imposed. The government could have charged each count in a separate charging instrument and cumulative sentences following separate non-jury trials could have been imposed. Since there was no deprivation of the right to a jury trial, the effect of the magistrate's statement limiting liability to six months total punishment was not reached. Justice Kennedy, joined by Justice Breyer, concurred in the judgment on the ground that ordinarily a jury trial right should attach in this circumstance but that since the magistrate voluntarily limited petitioner's liability to a term not to exceed six months, the Sixth Amendment was not violated in this particular case. Justice Stevens, joined by Justice Ginsburg, dissented.

2. **Juvenile proceedings.** In McKeiver v. Pennsylvania, 403 U.S. 528, 91 S.Ct. 1976, 29 L.Ed.2d 647 (1971), the Supreme Court held that the due process clause of the Fourteenth Amendment does not provide a right to trial by jury in state juvenile court delinquency proceedings despite the fact that a juvenile could be deprived of liberty for years. In a separate opinion Justice Brennan stressed the need for a state to provide some alternate procedure such as public access to the hearing to provide due process protection to a juvenile "from oppression by the Government."

2. COMPOSITION OF THE JURY

All potential jurors, as determined by the governing law, constitute the jury pool. Those called from the pool for possible selection to a petit jury are termed the jury venire (or panel). Voir dire is the questioning of venirepersons, by defense counsel, the prosecutor, and/or the court itself, to select the petit jury. If the pool or venire is not drawn from a fair cross section of the community, i.e., if certain "cognizable" groups are excluded, successful constitutional attack may result. Although the petit jury itself need not consist of a fair cross section of the community, successful constitutional attack may be made if peremptory challenges are exercised in a discriminatory manner.

Powers v. Ohio
Supreme Court of the United States, 1991
499 U.S. 400, 111 S.Ct. 1364, 113 L.Ed.2d 411

■ JUSTICE KENNEDY delivered the opinion of the Court.

Jury service is an exercise of responsible citizenship by all members of the community, including those who otherwise might not have the opportunity to contribute to our civic life. Congress recognized this over a century ago in the Civil Rights Act of 1875, which made it a criminal offense to exclude persons from jury service on account of their race. See 18 U.S.C. § 243. In a trilogy of cases decided soon after enactment of this prohibition, our Court confirmed the validity of the statute, as well as the broader constitutional imperative of race neutrality in jury selection. In the many times we have confronted the issue since those cases, we have not questioned the premise that racial discrimination in the qualification or selection of jurors offends the dignity of persons and the integrity of the courts. Despite the clarity of these commands to eliminate the taint of racial discrimination in the administration of justice, allegations of bias in the jury selection process persist. In this case, petitioner alleges race discrimination in the prosecution's use of peremptory challenges. Invoking the Equal Protection Clause and federal statutory law, and relying upon well-established principles of standing, we hold that a criminal defendant may object to race-based exclusions of jurors effected through peremptory challenges whether or not the defendant and the excluded juror share the same races.

I

Petitioner Larry Joe Powers, a white man, was indicted in Franklin County, Ohio, on two counts of aggravated murder and one count of attempted aggravated murder. Each count also included a separate allegation that petitioner had a firearm while committing the offense. Powers pleaded not guilty and invoked his right to a jury trial.

In the jury selection process, Powers objected when the prosecutor exercised his first peremptory challenge to remove a black venireperson. Powers requested the trial court to compel the prosecutor to explain, on the record, his reasons for excluding a black person. The trial court denied the request and excused the juror. The State proceeded to use nine more peremptory challenges, six of which removed black venirepersons from the jury. Each time the prosecution challenged a black prospective juror, Powers renewed his objections, citing our decision in Batson v. Kentucky, 476 U.S. 79, 106 S.Ct. 1712, 90 L.Ed.2d 69 (1986). His objections were overruled. The record does not indicate that race was somehow implicated in the crime or the trial; nor does it reveal whether any black persons sat on petitioner's petit jury or if any of the nine jurors petitioner excused by peremptory challenges were black persons.

The empaneled jury convicted Powers on counts of murder, aggravated murder, and attempted aggravated murder, each with the firearm specifications, and the trial court sentenced him to a term of imprisonment of 53 years to life. Powers appealed his conviction to the Ohio Court of Appeals, contending that the prosecutor's discriminatory use of peremptories violated the Sixth Amendment's guarantee of a fair cross section in his petit jury, the Fourteenth Amendment's Equal Protection Clause, and Article I, §§ 10 and 16, of the Ohio Constitution. Powers contended that his own race was irrelevant to the right to object to the prosecution's peremptory challenges. The Court of Appeals affirmed the conviction, and the Supreme Court of Ohio dismissed Powers' appeal on the ground that it presented no substantial constitutional question.

Petitioner sought review before us, renewing his Sixth Amendment fair cross section and Fourteenth Amendment equal protection claims. While the petition for certiorari was pending, we decided Holland v. Illinois, 493 U.S. 474, 110 S.Ct. 803, 107 L.Ed.2d 905 (1990). In Holland it was alleged the prosecution had used its peremptory challenges to exclude from the jury members of a race other than the defendant's. We held the Sixth Amendment did not restrict the exclusion of a racial group at the peremptory challenge stage. Five members of the Court there said a defendant might be able to make the objection on equal protection grounds. After our decision in Holland, we granted Powers' petition for certiorari limited to the question whether, based on the Equal Protection Clause, a white defendant may object to the prosecution's peremptory challenges of black venirepersons. 493 U.S. 1068, 110 S.Ct. 1109, 107 L.Ed.2d 1017 (1990). We now reverse and remand.

II

For over a century, this Court has been unyielding in its position that a defendant is denied equal protection of the laws when tried before a jury from which members of his or her race have been excluded by the State's purposeful conduct. "The Equal Protection Clause guarantees the defendant that the State will not exclude members of his race from the jury venire on account of race, Strauder, [100 U.S.,] at 305 [25 L.Ed. 664], or on the false assumption that members of his race as a group are not qualified to serve as jurors, see Norris v. Alabama, 294 U.S. 587, 599 [55 S.Ct. 579, 584, 79 L.Ed. 1074] (1935); Neal v. Delaware, 103 U.S. 370, 397 [26 L.Ed. 567] (1880)." Batson, supra, 476 U.S., at 86, 106 S.Ct., at 1717 (footnote omitted). Although a defendant has no right to a "petit jury composed in whole or in part of persons of [the defendant's] own race," Strauder, 100 U.S., at 305, 25 L.Ed. 664, he or she does have the right to be tried by a jury whose members are selected by nondiscriminatory criteria.

We confronted the use of peremptory challenges as a device to exclude jurors because of their race for the first time in Swain v. Alabama, 380 U.S. 202, 85 S.Ct. 824, 13 L.Ed.2d 759 (1965). Swain involved a challenge to the so-called struck jury system, a procedure designed to allow both the prosecution and the defense a maximum number of peremptory challenges. The venire in noncapital cases started with about 35 potential jurors, from which the defense and the prosecution alternated with strikes until a petit panel of 12 jurors remained. The defendant in Swain, who was himself black, alleged that the prosecutor had used the struck jury system and its numerous peremptory challenges for the purpose of excluding black persons from his petit jury. In finding that no constitutional harm was alleged, the Court in Swain sought to reconcile the command of racial neutrality in jury selection with the utility, and the tradition, of peremptory challenges. The Court declined to permit an equal protection claim premised on a pattern of jury strikes in a particular case, but acknowledged that proof of systematic exclusion of black persons through the use of peremptories over a period of time might establish an equal protection violation. Id., at 222–228, 85 S.Ct., at 836–840.

We returned to the problem of a prosecutor's discriminatory use of peremptory challenges in Batson v. Kentucky. There, we considered a situation similar to the one before us today, but with one exception: Batson, the defendant who complained that black persons were being excluded from his petit jury, was himself black. During the voir dire examination of the venire for Batson's trial, the prosecutor used his peremptory challenges to strike all four black persons on the venire, resulting in a petit jury composed only of white persons. Batson's counsel moved without success to discharge the jury before it was empaneled on the ground that the prosecutor's removal of black venirepersons violated his rights under the Sixth and Fourteenth Amendments. Relying upon the Equal Protection Clause alone, we overruled Swain to the extent it foreclosed objections to the discriminatory use of peremptories in the course of a specific trial. 476 U.S., at 90–93, 106 S.Ct., at 1719–1721. In Batson we held that a defendant can raise an equal protection challenge to the use of peremptories at his own trial by showing that the prosecutor used them for the purpose of excluding members of the defendant's race. Id., at 96, 106 S.Ct., at 1722.

The State contends that our holding in the case now before us must be limited to the circumstances prevailing in Batson and that in equal protection analysis the race of the objecting defendant constitutes a relevant precondition for a Batson challenge. Because Powers is white, the State argues, he cannot object to the exclusion of black prospective jurors. This limitation on a defendant's right to object conforms neither with our accepted rules of standing to raise a constitutional claim nor with the substantive guarantees of the Equal Protection Clause and the policies underlying federal statutory law.

In Batson, we spoke of the harm caused when a defendant is tried by a tribunal from which members of his own race have been excluded. But we did not limit our discussion in Batson to that one aspect of the harm caused by the violation. Batson "was designed 'to serve multiple ends,' " only one of which was to protect individual defendants from discrimination in the selection of jurors. Allen v. Hardy, 478 U.S. 255, 259, 106 S.Ct. 2878, 2880, 92 L.Ed.2d 199 (1986) (per curiam) (quoting Brown v. Louisiana, 447 U.S. 323, 329, 100 S.Ct. 2214, 2220, 65 L.Ed.2d 159 (1980)). Batson recognized that a prosecutor's discriminatory use of peremptory challenges harms the excluded jurors and the community at large. 476 U.S., at 87, 106 S.Ct., at 1718.

The opportunity for ordinary citizens to participate in the administration of justice has long been recognized as one of the principal justifications for retaining the jury system. See Duncan v. Louisiana, 391 U.S. 145, 147–158, 88 S.Ct. 1444, 1446–1452, 20 L.Ed.2d 491 (1968). In Balzac v. Porto Rico, 258 U.S. 298, 42 S.Ct. 343, 66 L.Ed. 627 (1922), Chief Justice Taft wrote for the Court:

> "The jury system postulates a conscious duty of participation in the machinery of justice.... One of its greatest benefits is in the security it gives the people that they, as jurors actual or possible, being part of the judicial system of the country can prevent its arbitrary use or abuse." Id., at 310, 42 S.Ct., at 347.

And, over 150 years ago, Alexis de Tocqueville remarked:

> "[T]he institution of the jury raises the people itself, or at least a class of citizens, to the bench of judicial authority [and] invests the people, or that class of citizens, with the direction of society.
>
> . . . . .
>
> " ... The jury ... invests each citizen with a kind of magistracy; it makes them all feel the duties which they are bound to discharge towards society; and the part which they take in the Government. By

obliging men to turn their attention to affairs which are not exclusively their own, it rubs off that individual egotism which is the rust of society.

. . . . .

"I do not know whether the jury is useful to those who are in litigation; but I am certain it is highly beneficial to those who decide the litigation; and I look upon it as one of the most efficacious means for the education of the people which society can employ." 1 Democracy in America 334–337 (Schocken 1st ed. 1961).

Jury service preserves the democratic element of the law, as it guards the rights of the parties and ensures continued acceptance of the laws by all of the people. See Green v. United States, 356 U.S. 165, 215, 78 S.Ct. 632, 659, 2 L.Ed.2d 672 (1958) (Black, J., dissenting). It "affords ordinary citizens a valuable opportunity to participate in a process of government, an experience fostering, one hopes, a respect for law." Duncan, supra, 391 U.S., at 187, 88 S.Ct., at 1469 (Harlan, J., dissenting). Indeed, with the exception of voting, for most citizens the honor and privilege of jury duty is their most significant opportunity to participate in the democratic process.

While States may prescribe relevant qualifications for their jurors, see Carter v. Jury Comm'n of Greene County, 396 U.S. 320, 332, 90 S.Ct. 518, 524, 24 L.Ed.2d 549 (1970), a member of the community may not be excluded from jury service on account of his or her race. "Whether jury service be deemed a right, a privilege, or a duty, the State may no more extend it to some of its citizens and deny it to others on racial grounds than it may invidiously discriminate in the offering and withholding of the elective franchise." Carter, supra, 396 U.S., at 330, 90 S.Ct., at 523. Over a century ago, we recognized that:

"The very fact that [members of a particular race] are singled out and expressly denied . . . all right to participate in the administration of the law, as jurors, because of their color, though they are citizens, and may be in other respects fully qualified, is practically a brand upon them, affixed by the law, an assertion of their inferiority, and a stimulant to that race prejudice which is an impediment to securing to individuals of the race that equal justice which the law aims to secure to all others." Strauder, supra, 100 U.S., at 308.

Discrimination in the jury selection process is the subject of a federal criminal prohibition, and has been since Congress enacted the Civil Rights Act of 1875. The prohibition has been codified at 18 U.S.C. § 243, which provides:

"No citizen possessing all other qualifications which are or may be prescribed by law shall be disqualified for service as grand or petit juror in any court of the United States, or of any State on account of race, color, or previous condition of servitude; and whoever, being an officer or other person charged with any duty in the selection or summoning of jurors, excludes or fails to summon any citizen for such cause, shall be fined not more than $5,000."

In Peters v. Kiff, 407 U.S. 493, 92 S.Ct. 2163, 33 L.Ed.2d 83 (1972), Justice White spoke of "the strong statutory policy of § 243, which reflects the central concern of the Fourteenth Amendment." Id., at 507, 92 S.Ct., at 2170 (opinion concurring in judgment). The Court permitted a white defendant to challenge the systematic exclusion of black persons from grand and petit juries. While Peters did not produce a single majority opinion, six of the Justices agreed that racial discrimination in the jury selection process cannot be tolerated and that the race of the defendant has no relevance to his or her standing to raise the claim.

Racial discrimination in the selection of jurors in the context of an individual trial violates these same prohibitions. A State "may not draw up its jury lists pursuant to neutral procedures but then resort to discrimination at 'other stages in the selection process.'" Batson, 476 U.S., at 88, 106 S.Ct., at 1718 (quoting Avery v. Georgia, 345 U.S. 559, 562, 73 S.Ct. 891, 892, 97 L.Ed. 1244 (1953)). We so held in Batson, and reaffirmed that holding in Holland. See 493 U.S., at 479, 110 S.Ct., at 806–807. In Holland, the Court held that a defendant could not rely on the Sixth Amendment to object to the exclusion of members of any distinctive group at the peremptory challenge stage. We noted that the peremptory challenge procedure has acceptance in our legal tradition. See id., at 481, 110 S.Ct., at 808. On this reasoning we declined to permit an objection to the peremptory challenge of a juror on racial grounds as a Sixth Amendment matter. As the Holland Court made explicit, however, racial exclusion of prospective jurors violates the overriding command of the Equal Protection Clause, and "race-based exclusion is no more permissible at the individual petit jury stage than at the venire stage." Id., at 479, 110 S.Ct., at 807.

We hold that the Equal Protection Clause prohibits a prosecutor from using the State's peremptory challenges to exclude otherwise qualified and unbiased persons from the petit jury solely by reason of their race, a practice that forecloses a significant opportunity to participate in civic life. An individual juror does not have a right to sit on any particular petit jury, but he or she does possess the right not to be excluded from one on account of race.

It is suggested that no particular stigma or dishonor results if a prosecutor uses the raw fact of skin color to determine the objectivity or qualifications of a juror. We do not believe a victim of the classification would endorse this view; the assumption that no stigma or dishonor attaches contravenes accepted equal protection principles. Race cannot be a proxy for determining juror bias or competence. "A person's race simply 'is unrelated to his fitness as a juror.'" Batson, supra, 476 U.S., at 87, 106 S.Ct., at 1718 (quoting Thiel v. Southern Pacific Co., supra, 328 U.S., at 227, 66 S.Ct., at 989 (Frankfurter, J., dissenting)). We may not accept as a defense to racial discrimination the very stereotype the law condemns.

We reject as well the view that race-based peremptory challenges survive equal protection scrutiny because members of all races are subject to like treatment, which is to say that white jurors are subject to the same risk of peremptory challenges based on race as are all other jurors. The suggestion that racial classifications may survive when visited upon all persons is no more authoritative today than the case which advanced the theorem, Plessy v. Ferguson, 163 U.S. 537, 16 S.Ct. 1138, 41 L.Ed. 256 (1896). This idea has no place in our modern equal protection jurisprudence. It is axiomatic that racial classifications do not become legitimate on the assumption that all persons suffer them in equal degree. Loving v. Virginia, 388 U.S. 1, 87 S.Ct. 1817, 18 L.Ed.2d 1010 (1967).

III

We must consider whether a criminal defendant has standing to raise the equal protection rights of a juror excluded from service in violation of these principles. In the ordinary course, a litigant must assert his or her own legal rights and interests, and cannot rest a claim to relief on the legal rights or interests of third parties. Department of Labor v. Triplett, 494 U.S. 715, 720, 110 S.Ct. 1428, 1431, 108 L.Ed.2d 701 (1990); Singleton v. Wulff, 428 U.S. 106, 96 S.Ct. 2868, 49 L.Ed.2d 826 (1976). This fundamental restriction on our authority admits of certain, limited exceptions. We have recognized the right of litigants to bring actions on behalf of third parties, provided three important criteria are satisfied: The litigant must have suffered an "injury in fact," thus giving him or her a "sufficiently concrete interest" in the outcome of the issue in dispute, id., at 112, 96 S.Ct., at 2873; the litigant must have a close relation to the third party, id., at 113–114, 96 S.Ct., at 2873–2874; and there must exist some hindrance to the third party's ability to protect his or her own interests. Id., at 115–116, 96 S.Ct., at 2874–2875. These criteria have been satisfied in cases where we have permitted criminal defendants to challenge their convictions by raising the rights of third parties. See, e.g., Eisenstadt v. Baird, 405 U.S. 438, 92 S.Ct. 1029, 31 L.Ed.2d 349 (1972); Griswold v. Connecticut, 381 U.S. 479, 85 S.Ct. 1678, 14 L.Ed.2d 510 (1965); see also McGowan v. Maryland, 366 U.S. 420, 81 S.Ct. 1101, 6 L.Ed.2d 393 (1961). By similar reasoning, we have permitted litigants to raise third-party rights in order to prevent possible future prosecution. See, e.g., Doe v. Bolton, 410 U.S. 179, 93 S.Ct. 739, 35 L.Ed.2d 201 (1973).

The discriminatory use of peremptory challenges by the prosecution causes a criminal defendant cognizable injury, and the defendant has a concrete interest in challenging the practice. See Allen v. Hardy, 478 U.S., at 259, 106 S.Ct., at 2880 (recognizing a defendant's interest in "neutral jury selection procedures"). This is not because the individual jurors dismissed by the prosecution may have been predisposed to favor the defendant; if that were true, the jurors might have been excused for cause. Rather, it is because racial discrimination in the selection of jurors "casts doubt on the integrity of the judicial process," Rose v. Mitchell, 443 U.S. 545, 556, 99 S.Ct. 2993, 3000, 61 L.Ed.2d 739 (1979), and places the fairness of a criminal proceeding in doubt.

The jury acts as a vital check against the wrongful exercise of power by the State and its prosecutors. Batson, 476 U.S., at 86, 106 S.Ct., at 1717. The intrusion of racial discrimination into the jury selection process damages both the fact and the perception of this guarantee. "Jury selection is the primary means by which a court may enforce a defendant's right to be tried by a jury free from ethnic, racial, or political prejudice, Rosales–Lopez v. United States, 451 U.S. 182, 188 [101 S.Ct. 1629, 1634, 68 L.Ed.2d 22]

(1981); Ham v. South Carolina, 409 U.S. 524 [93 S.Ct. 848, 35 L.Ed.2d 46] (1973); Dennis v. United States, 339 U.S. 162 [70 S.Ct. 519, 94 L.Ed. 734] (1950), or predisposition about the defendant's culpability, Irvin v. Dowd, 366 U.S. 717 [81 S.Ct. 1639, 6 L.Ed.2d 751] (1961)." Gomez v. United States, 490 U.S. 858, 873, 109 S.Ct. 2237, 2246–2247, 104 L.Ed.2d 923 (1989). Active discrimination by a prosecutor during this process condones violations of the United States Constitution within the very institution entrusted with its enforcement, and so invites cynicism respecting the jury's neutrality and its obligation to adhere to the law. The cynicism may be aggravated if race is implicated in the trial, either in a direct way as with an alleged racial motivation of the defendant or a victim, or in some more subtle manner as by casting doubt upon the credibility or dignity of a witness, or even upon the standing or due regard of an attorney who appears in the cause.

Unlike the instances where a defendant seeks to object to the introduction of evidence obtained illegally from a third party, see, e.g., United States v. Payner, 447 U.S. 727, 100 S.Ct. 2439, 65 L.Ed.2d 468 (1980), here petitioner alleges that the primary constitutional violation occurred during the trial itself. A prosecutor's wrongful exclusion of a juror by a race-based peremptory challenge is a constitutional violation committed in open court at the outset of the proceedings. The overt wrong, often apparent to the entire jury panel, casts doubt over the obligation of the parties, the jury, and indeed the court to adhere to the law throughout the trial of the cause. The voir dire phase of the trial represents the "jurors' first introduction to the substantive factual and legal issues in a case." Gomez, supra, 490 U.S., at 874, 109 S.Ct., at 2247. The influence of the voir dire process may persist through the whole course of the trial proceedings. Ibid. If the defendant has no right to object to the prosecutor's improper exclusion of jurors, and if the trial court has no duty to make a prompt inquiry when the defendant shows, by adequate grounds, a likelihood of impropriety in the exercise of a challenge, there arise legitimate doubts that the jury has been chosen by proper means. The composition of the trier of fact itself is called in question, and the irregularity may pervade all the proceedings that follow.

The purpose of the jury system is to impress upon the criminal defendant and the community as a whole that a verdict of conviction or acquittal is given in accordance with the law by persons who are fair. The verdict will not be accepted or understood in these terms if the jury is chosen by unlawful means at the outset. Upon these considerations, we find that a criminal defendant suffers a real injury when the prosecutor excludes jurors at his or her own trial on account of race.

We noted in Singleton that in certain circumstances "the relationship between the litigant and the third party may be such that the former is fully, or very nearly, as effective a proponent of the right as the latter." 428 U.S., at 115, 96 S.Ct., at 2874. Here, the relation between petitioner and the excluded jurors is as close as, if not closer than, those we have recognized to convey third-party standing in our prior cases. See, e.g., Griswold v. Connecticut, supra (Planned Parenthood official and a licensed physician can raise the constitutional rights of contraceptive users with whom they had professional relationships); Craig, supra (licensed beer vendor has standing to raise the equal protection claim of a male customer challenging a statutory scheme prohibiting the sale of beer to males under the age of 21 and to females under the age of 18); Department of Labor v. Triplett, 494 U.S. 715, 110 S.Ct. 1428, 108 L.Ed.2d 701 (1990) (attorney may challenge an attorney's fees restriction by asserting the due process rights of the client). Voir dire permits a party to establish a relation, if not a bond of trust, with the jurors. This relation continues throughout the entire trial and may in some cases extend to the sentencing as well.

Both the excluded juror and the criminal defendant have a common interest in eliminating racial discrimination from the courtroom. A venireperson excluded from jury service because of race suffers a profound personal humiliation heightened by its public character. The rejected juror may lose confidence in the court and its verdicts, as may the defendant if his or her objections cannot be heard. This congruence of interests makes it necessary and appropriate for the defendant to raise the rights of the juror. And, there can be no doubt that petitioner will be a motivated, effective advocate for the excluded venirepersons' rights. Petitioner has much at stake in proving that his jury was improperly constituted due to an equal protection violation, for we have recognized that discrimination in the jury selection process may lead to the reversal of a conviction. See Batson, 476 U.S., at 100, 106 S.Ct., at 1725; Vasquez v. Hillery, 474 U.S. 254, 264, 106 S.Ct. 617, 623, 88 L.Ed.2d 598 (1986); Rose v. Mitchell, 443 U.S., at 551, 99 S.Ct., at 2997–2998; Cassell v. Texas, 339 U.S. 282, 70 S.Ct. 629, 94 L.Ed. 839 (1950). Thus, " 'there seems little loss in terms of effective advocacy from allowing [the assertion of this claim] by' the present jus tertii champion." Craig, supra, 429 U.S., at 194, 97 S.Ct., at 455 (quoting Singleton, 428 U.S., at 118, 96 S.Ct., at 2876).

The final inquiry in our third-party standing analysis involves the likelihood and ability of the third parties, the excluded venirepersons, to assert their own rights. See Singleton, supra, at 115–116, 96 S.Ct., at 2874–2875. We have held that individual jurors subjected to racial exclusion have the legal right to bring suit on their own behalf. Carter, 396 U.S., at 329–330, 90 S.Ct., at 523–524. As a practical matter, however, these challenges are rare. See Alschuler, The Supreme Court and the Jury: Voir Dire, Peremptory Challenges, and the Review of Jury Verdicts, 56 U.Chi.L.Rev. 153, 193–195 (1989). Indeed, it took nearly a century after the Fourteenth Amendment and the Civil Rights Act of 1875 came into being for the first such case to reach this Court. See Carter, supra, at 320, 90 S.Ct., at 518.

The barriers to a suit by an excluded juror are daunting. Potential jurors are not parties to the jury selection process and have no opportunity to be heard at the time of their exclusion. Nor can excluded jurors easily obtain declaratory or injunctive relief when discrimination occurs through an individual prosecutor's exercise of peremptory challenges. Unlike a challenge to systematic practices of the jury clerk and commissioners such as we considered in Carter, it would be difficult for an individual juror to show a likelihood that discrimination against him at the voir dire stage will recur. See Los Angeles v. Lyons, 461 U.S. 95, 105–110, 103 S.Ct. 1660, 1666–1670, 75 L.Ed.2d 675 (1983). And, there exist considerable practical barriers to suit by the excluded juror because of the small financial stake involved and the economic burdens of litigation. See Vasquez, supra, 474 U.S., at 262, n. 5, 106 S.Ct., at 623, n. 5; Rose v. Mitchell, supra, 443 U.S., at 558, 99 S.Ct., at 3001. The reality is that a juror dismissed because of race probably will leave the courtroom possessing little incentive to set in motion the arduous process needed to vindicate his own rights. See Barrows v. Jackson, 346 U.S. 249, 257, 73 S.Ct. 1031, 1035, 97 L.Ed. 1586 (1953).

We conclude that a defendant in a criminal case can raise the third-party equal protection claims of jurors excluded by the prosecution because of their race. In so doing, we once again decline "to reverse a course of decisions of long standing directed against racial discrimination in the administration of justice." Cassell v. Texas, supra, 339 U.S., at 290, 70 S.Ct., at 633 (Frankfurter, J., concurring in judgment). To bar petitioner's claim because his race differs from that of the excluded jurors would be to condone the arbitrary exclusion of citizens from the duty, honor, and privilege of jury service. In Holland and Batson, we spoke of the significant role peremptory challenges play in our trial procedures, but we noted also that the utility of the peremptory challenge system must be accommodated to the command of racial neutrality. Holland, 493 U.S., at 486–487, 110 S.Ct., at 810–811; Batson, supra, 476 U.S., at 98–99, 106 S.Ct., at 1723–1724.

The Fourteenth Amendment's mandate that race discrimination be eliminated from all official acts and proceedings of the State is most compelling in the judicial system. Rose v. Mitchell, supra, 443 U.S., at 555, 99 S.Ct., at 2999–3000. We have held, for example, that prosecutorial discretion cannot be exercised on the basis of race, Wayte v. United States, 470 U.S. 598, 608, 105 S.Ct. 1524, 1531, 84 L.Ed.2d 547 (1985), and that, where racial bias is likely to influence a jury, an inquiry must be made into such bias. Ristaino v. Ross, 424 U.S. 589, 596, 96 S.Ct. 1017, 1021, 47 L.Ed.2d 258 (1976); see also Turner v. Murray, 476 U.S. 28, 106 S.Ct. 1683, 90 L.Ed.2d 27 (1986). The statutory prohibition on discrimination in the selection of jurors, 18 U.S.C. § 243, enacted pursuant to the Fourteenth Amendment's Enabling Clause, makes race neutrality in jury selection a visible, and inevitable, measure of the judicial system's own commitment to the commands of the Constitution. The courts are under an affirmative duty to enforce the strong statutory and constitutional policies embodied in that prohibition. See Peters v. Kiff, 407 U.S., at 507, 92 S.Ct., at 2170–2171 (WHITE, J., concurring in judgment); see also id., at 505, 92 S.Ct., at 2169–2170 (opinion of MARSHALL, J.).

The emphasis in Batson on racial identity between the defendant and the excused prospective juror is not inconsistent with our holding today that race is irrelevant to a defendant's standing to object to the discriminatory use of peremptory challenges. Racial identity between the defendant and the excused person might in some cases be the explanation for the prosecution's adoption of the forbidden stereotype, and if the alleged race bias takes this form, it may provide one of the easier cases to establish both a prima facie case and a conclusive showing that wrongful discrimination has occurred. But to say that the race of the defendant may be relevant to discerning bias in some cases does not mean that it will be a factor in others, for race prejudice stems from various causes and may manifest itself in different forms.

It remains for the trial courts to develop rules, without unnecessary disruption of the jury selection process, to permit legitimate and well-founded objections to the use of peremptory challenges as a mask for race prejudice. In this case, the State concedes that, if we find the petitioner has standing to object to the prosecution's use of the peremptory challenges, the case should be remanded. We find that petitioner does have standing. The judgment is reversed, and the case is remanded for further proceedings not inconsistent with our opinion.

It is so ordered.

■ JUSTICE SCALIA, with whom the CHIEF JUSTICE joins, dissenting [omitted].

NOTES

1. **Civil suits.** Does *Batson* apply to civil suits between private parties? Petitioner in Edmonson v. Leesville Concrete Co., 500 U.S. 614, 111 S.Ct. 2077, 114 L.Ed.2d 660 (1991), a black construction worker, sued for injuries suffered on the work site. During jury selection, Leesville used 2 of its 3 peremptory challenges to remove blacks from the panel. The jury consisted of 11 whites and one black. The District Court rejected petitioner's *Batson* claim on the ground that decision applied only in criminal cases. The Supreme Court, in an opinion by Justice Kennedy, held that under Powers v. Ohio race-based use of strikes violates the excluded persons' equal protection rights. Although Leesville is a private party, its use of strikes was state action because strikes are authorized by law and can be used only in a court proceeding. The case was remanded for a determination whether petitioner had made a prima facie case of racial discrimination in the defendant's use of strikes. Justice O'Connor, joined by Chief Justice Rehnquist and Justice Scalia, dissented on the ground that the defendant's use of strikes did not constitute state action. Justice Scalia dissented separately, with the observation that the decision

> will not necessarily be a net help rather than hindrance to minority litigants in obtaining racially diverse juries. In criminal cases, *Batson v. Kentucky* already prevents the *prosecution* from using race-based strikes. The effect of today's decision (which logically must apply to criminal prosecutions) will be to prevent the *defendant* from doing so—so that the minority defendant can no longer seek to prevent an all-white jury, or to seat as many jurors of his own race as possible. To be sure, it is ordinarily more difficult to *prove* race-based strikes of white jurors, but defense counsel can generally be relied upon to do what we say the Constitution requires. So in criminal cases, today's decision represents a net loss to the minority litigant.

500 U.S. at 644, 111 S.Ct. at 2095, 114 L.Ed.2d at 689.

2. **Defense strikes.** *Batson* was held to apply to peremptory challenges by criminal defendants in Georgia v. McCollum, 505 U.S. 42, 112 S.Ct. 2348, 120 L.Ed.2d 33 (1992). The State filed a motion requesting an order from the trial court to preclude Respondent, who is white, from using strikes to eliminate African-Americans from his criminal jury in a trial in which the victims were African-American. The trial court denied this motion and the Georgia Supreme Court affirmed in an interlocutory appeal. The Supreme Court, in an opinion by Justice Blackmun, reversed and held that *Batson* applies to strikes used by criminal defendants:

"Be it at the hands of the State or the defense," if a court allows jurors to be excluded because of group bias, "[it] is [a] willing participant in a scheme that could only undermine the very foundation of our system of justice—our citizens' confidence in it." Just as public confidence in criminal justice is undermined by a conviction in a trial where racial discrimination has occurred in jury selection, so is public confidence undermined where a defendant, assisted by racially discriminatory peremptory strikes, obtains an acquittal.

505 U.S. at 49–50, 112 S.Ct. at 2354, 120 L.Ed.2d at 45. The Court then sought to distinguish cases in which criminal defendants have been held to have a constitutional right to question potential jurors about racial attitudes:

[A] defendant has the right to an impartial jury that can view him without racial animus, which so long has distorted our system of criminal justice. We have, accordingly, held that there should be a mechanism for removing those on the venire whom the defendant has specific reason to believe would be incapable of confronting and suppressing their racism. See Ham v. South Carolina, 409 U.S. 524, 526–527, 93 S.Ct. 848, 35 L.Ed.2d 46 (1973) * * *.

But there is a distinction between exercising a peremptory challenge to discriminate invidiously against jurors on account of race and exercising a peremptory challenge to remove an individual juror who harbors racial prejudice. This Court firmly has rejected the view that assumptions of partiality based on race provide a legitimate basis for disqualifying a person as an impartial juror.

505 U.S. at 58–59, 112 S.Ct. at 2358–59, 120 L.Ed.2d at 51. Justice Thomas concurred in the judgment with the comment, "I am certain that black criminal defendants will rue the day that this court ventured down this road that inexorably will lead to the elimination of peremptory strikes." 505 U.S. at 60, 112 S.Ct. at 2359–60, 120 L.Ed.2d at 52. Justice O'Connor dissented on the ground that there is no state action when a criminal defendant exercises a peremptory challenge.

3. **Gender-based strikes.** Does Batson apply to strikes based on gender? Petitioner in J.E.B. v. Alabama ex rel. T.B., 511 U.S. 127, 114 S.Ct. 1419, 128 L.Ed.2d 89 (1994) was the respondent in a paternity suit. The State used 9 of its 10 strikes to remove men from the jury panel, while Petitioner used 9 of his 10 strikes to remove women from the panel. The jury was composed entirely of women. Petitioner was adjudicated the father of the child and ordered to pay support. Before the Supreme Court, he claimed that the State's use of its strikes violated equal protection of the laws. The Court, in an opinion by Justice Blackmun, held that the State's use of strikes to remove men from the jury panel violated equal protection of the laws:

Discrimination in jury selection, whether based on race or on gender, causes harm to the litigants, the community, and the individual jurors who are wrongfully excluded from participation in the judicial process. The litigants are harmed by the risk that the prejudice which motivated the discriminatory selection of the jury will infect the entire proceedings * * *. The community is harmed by the State's participation in the perpetuation of invidious group stereotypes and the inevitable loss of confidence in our judicial system that state-sanctioned discrimination in the courtroom engenders.

511 U.S. at 140, 114 S.Ct. at 1427, 128 L.Ed.2d at 104. Justice O'Connor, concurring, would limit the equal protection principle to actions by the government. Justice Scalia, joined by The Chief Justice and Justice Thomas, dissented.

4. **Procedures for implementing Batson.** In Batson v. Kentucky, 476 U.S. 79, 106 S.Ct. 1712, 90 L.Ed.2d 69 (1986), Justice Powell established the following procedures for litigating Batson claims at the trial level:

[A] defendant may establish a prima facie case of purposeful discrimination in selection of the petit jury solely on evidence concerning the prosecutor's exercise of peremptory challenges at the defendant's trial. To establish such a case, the defendant first must show that he is a member of a cognizable racial group, and that the prosecutor has exercised peremptory challenges to remove from the venire members of the defendant's race. Second, the defendant is entitled to rely on the fact, as to which there can be no dispute, that peremptory challenges constitute a jury selection practice that permits "those to discriminate who are of a mind to discriminate." Finally, the defendant must show that these facts and any other relevant circumstances raise an inference that the prosecutor used that practice to exclude the veniremen from the petit jury on account of their race. This combination of factors in the empanelling of the petit jury, as in the selection of the venire, raises the necessary inference of purposeful discrimination.

In deciding whether the defendant has made the requisite showing, the trial court should consider all relevant circumstances. For example, a "pattern" of strikes against black jurors included in the particular venire might give rise to an inference of discrimination. Similarly, the prosecutor's questions and statements during *voir dire* examination and in exercising his challenges may support or refute an inference of discriminatory purpose. These examples are merely illustrative. We have confidence that trial judges, experienced in supervising *voir dire*, will be able to decide if the circumstances concerning the prosecutor's use of peremptory challenges creates a prima facie case of discrimination against black jurors.

Once the defendant makes a prima facie showing, the burden shifts to the State to come forward with a neutral explanation for challenging black jurors. Though this requirement imposes a limitation in some cases on the full peremptory character of the historic challenge, we emphasize that the prosecutor's explanation need not rise to the level justifying exercise of a challenge for cause. But the prosecutor may not rebut the defendant's prima facie case of discrimination by stating merely that he challenged jurors of the defendant's race on the assumption—or his intuitive judgment—that they would be partial to the defendant because of their shared race. Just as the Equal Protection Clause forbids the States to exclude black persons from the venire on the assumption that blacks as a group are unqualified to serve as jurors, so it forbids the States to strike black veniremen on the assumption that they will be biased in a particular case simply because the defendant is black. The core guarantee of equal protection, ensuring citizens that their State will not discriminate on account of race, would be meaningless were we to approve the exclusion of jurors on the basis of such assumptions, which arise solely from the jurors' race. Nor may the prosecutor rebut the defendant's case merely by denying that he had a discriminatory motive or "affirming his good faith in individual selections." If these general assertions were accepted as rebutting a defendant's prima facie case, the Equal Protection Clause "would be but a vain and illusory requirement." The prosecutor therefore must articulate a neutral explanation related to the particular case to be tried. The trial court then will have the duty to determine if the defendant has established purposeful discrimination.

476 U.S. at 96–98, 106 S.Ct. at 1723–24, 90 L.Ed.2d at 87–89.

5. **Language as a race-neutral reason.** In Hernandez v. New York, 500 U.S. 352, 111 S.Ct. 1859, 114 L.Ed.2d 395 (1991), the Court addressed the question what showing must be made to justify the use of peremptory challenges on racial groups. Hernandez, identified in the Supreme Court's opinion as a "Latino," was on

trial for attempted murder. The prosecutor used four peremptory challenges to exclude Latino potential jurors. A *Batson* claim was made with respect to two of those panel members. The prosecutor, without waiting for the trial court to rule on whether a *prima facie* showing had been made, volunteered that the reason he struck those two was that he was not persuaded they would be able to accept the official interpretation of Spanish language testimony because they were bilingual. This was based on their responses to that question on *voir dire* and their demeanor while responding. He added that since the defendant, victims, and all the civilian witnesses were Latino, he had no reason to exclude Latinos from the jury. The trial court found no *Batson* violation, which was upheld by the New York appellate courts on direct appeal from Hernandez' conviction. The United States Supreme Court, in a plurality opinion authored by Justice Kennedy and joined in by The Chief Justice and Justices White and Souter, affirmed. Because the prosecutor volunteered an explanation for his strikes, the question whether defendant had made a prima facie case of discrimination became moot. The prosecutor's neutral explanation—one based on something other than the race of the juror—was that

> the challenges rested neither on the intention to exclude Latino or bilingual jurors, nor on stereotypical assumptions about Latinos or bilinguals. The prosecutor's articulated basis for these challenges divided potential jurors into two classes: those whose conduct during *voir dire* would persuade him they might have difficulty in accepting the translator's rendition of Spanish-language testimony and those potential jurors who gave no such reason for doubt. Each category would include both Latinos and non-Latinos. While the prosecutor's criterion might well result in the disproportionate removal of prospective Latino jurors, that disproportionate impact does not turn the prosecutor's actions into a *per se* violation of the Equal Protection Clause.

500 U.S. at 361, 111 S.Ct. at 1867, 114 L.Ed.2d at 407. Once the prosecutor offered race-neutral explanations, the trial court was required to find whether the defendant had established purposeful discrimination. An appellate court can set aside such a finding only if it is clearly erroneous. Justice O'Connor, joined by Justice Scalia, concurred in the judgment, commenting,

> if, as in this case, the trial court believes the prosecutor's nonracial justification, and that finding is not clearly erroneous, that is the end of the matter. *Batson* does not require that a prosecutor justify a jury strike at the level of a for-cause challenge. It also does not require that the justification be unrelated to race. *Batson* requires only that the prosecutor's reason for striking a juror not *be* the juror's race.

500 U.S. at 375, 111 S.Ct. at 1875, 114 L.Ed.2d at 416. Justice Stevens, joined by Justice Marshall and in part by Justice Blackmun, dissented.

6. **Prosecutor's race-neutral explanation.** The Court refined somewhat the procedural steps in the trial litigation of a *Batson* claim in its *per curiam* opinion in Purkett v. Elem, 514 U.S. 765, 115 S.Ct. 1769, 131 L.Ed.2d 834 (1995). After the prosecutor struck two African–American panelists, respondent made a *Batson* objection. The prosecutor explained the strike of one panelist because he had long unkempt hair, a mustache and a goatee type beard. He explained striking the second panelist because he also had a mustache and goatee type beard. He added that those were the only members of the panel with facial hair. Further, the second panelist had once been the victim of a robbery with a sawed-off shotgun and the prosecutor expressed concern that he would not therefore regard the unarmed robbery being tried as robbery. The trial court overruled the *Batson* objection. On federal habeas following conviction, the Eighth Circuit found the trial court had not complied with *Batson* because the prosecutor's statement did not explain how the

objectionable features would affect each person's ability to perform duties as a juror in the case.

The Supreme Court reversed. *Batson* claims require a three step procedure in the trial court: (1) a prima facie case of discrimination by the claimant, (2) a neutral explanation for the strike in question by the party exercising the challenged strike, and (3) a showing of purposeful discrimination by the claimant. The Court of Appeals erroneously combined steps (2) and (3). Step (2) merely requires that the explanation be non-discriminatory. It does not require that the explanation must relate to trial strategy. Once a non-discriminatory explanation is provided, then the burden shifts to the *Batson* claimant to show purposeful discrimination. So long as the step (2) explanation is race-neutral, it doesn't matter that it is "silly or superstitious." Such an explanation may fail, but only at step (3) and only as part of the conclusion that the claimant has shown purposeful discrimination.

7. **Abolish peremptory challenges?** Although concurring in the reversal of the conviction in *Batson*, Justice Marshall stated:

> The decision today will not end the racial discrimination that peremptories inject into the jury-selection process. That goal can be accomplished only by eliminating peremptory challenges entirely.

* * *

Evidentiary analysis similar to that set out by the Court has been adopted as a matter of state law in States including Massachusetts and California. Cases from those jurisdictions illustrate the limitations of the approach. First, defendants cannot attack the discriminatory use of peremptory challenges at all unless the challenges are so flagrant as to establish a prima facie case. This means, in those States, that where only one or two black jurors survive the challenges for cause, the prosecutor need have no compunction about striking them from the jury because of their race. See Commonwealth v. Robinson, 382 Mass. 189, 195, 415 N.E.2d 805, 809–810 (1981) (no prima facie case of discrimination where defendant is black, prospective jurors include three blacks and one Puerto Rican, and prosecutor excludes one for cause and strikes the remainder peremptorily, producing all-white jury); People v. Rousseau, 129 Cal.App.3d 526, 536–537, 179 Cal.Rptr. 892, 897–898 (1982) (no prima facie case where prosecutor peremptorily strikes only two blacks on jury panel). Prosecutors are left free to discriminate against blacks in jury selection provided that they hold that discrimination to an "acceptable" level.

Second, when a defendant can establish a prima facie case, trial courts face the difficult burden of assessing prosecutors' motives. See King v. County of Nassau, 581 F.Supp. 493, 501–502 (E.D.N.Y.1984). Any prosecutor can easily assert facially neutral reasons for striking a juror, and trial courts are ill-equipped to second-guess those reasons. How is the court to treat a prosecutor's statement that he struck a juror because the juror had a son about the same age as defendant, see People v. Hall, 35 Cal.3d 161, 197 Cal.Rptr. 71, 672 P.2d 854 (1983), or seemed "uncommunicative," King, supra, at 498, or "never cracked a smile" and, therefore "did not possess the sensitivities necessary to realistically look at the issues and decide the facts in this case," Hall, supra, at 165, 197 Cal.Rptr. at 73, 672 P.2d, at 856? If such easily generated explanations are sufficient to discharge the prosecutor's obligation to justify his strikes on nonracial grounds, then the protection erected by the Court today may be illusory.

Nor is outright prevarication by prosecutors the only danger here. "[I]t is even possible that an attorney may lie to himself in an effort to convince himself that his motives are legal." King, supra, at 502. A prosecutor's own conscious or unconscious racism may lead him easily to the conclusion that a prospective black juror is "sullen," or "distant," a characterization that would not have come to his mind if a white juror had acted identically. A judge's own conscious or unconscious racism may lead him to accept such an explanation as well supported. As Justice Rehnquist concedes, prosecutors' peremptories are based on their "seat-of-the-pants instincts" as to how particular jurors will vote. Yet "seat-of-the-pants instincts" may often be just another term for racial prejudice. . . .

The inherent potential of peremptory challenges to distort the jury process by permitting the exclusion of jurors on racial grounds should ideally lead the Court to ban them entirely from the criminal justice system. . . .

Some authors have suggested that the courts should ban prosecutors' peremptories entirely, but should zealously guard the defendant's peremptory as "essential to the fairness of trial by jury," and "one of the most important of the rights secured to the accused." I would not find that an acceptable solution. Our criminal justice system "requires not only freedom from any bias against the accused, but also from any prejudice against his prosecution. Between him and the state the scales are to be evenly held." We can maintain that balance, not by permitting both prosecutor and defendant to engage in racial discrimination in jury selection, but by banning the use of peremptory challenges by prosecutors and by allowing the States to eliminate the defendant's peremptory as well.

476 U.S. at 102–08, 106 S.Ct. at 1726–29, 90 L.Ed.2d at 92–95 . .

8. **Systematic exclusion.** Prior to *Batson*, in the only Supreme Court opinion on the issue, Swain v. Alabama, 380 U.S. 202, 85 S.Ct. 824, 13 L.Ed.2d 759 (1965), the court found no violation of equal protection in a prosecutor's use of peremptory challenges to strike Blacks from the defendant's trial jury. Dictum concurred in by four Justices implied that a meritorious claim might be stated "when the prosecutor in a county, in case after case, whatever the circumstances, whatever the crime and whoever the defendant or the victim may be," removed every Black from every petit jury. 380 U.S. at 223, 85 S.Ct. at 837, 13 L.Ed.2d at 774.

9. **Statistical proof of systematic exclusion.** Systematic exclusion of cognizable groups from the jury venire has traditionally been proved by a showing of a statistical difference in the per cent of the group in the population and the per cent of the group on the venire. In Whitus v. Georgia, 385 U.S. 545, 87 S.Ct. 643, 17 L.Ed.2d 599 (1967), for example, it was shown that 27.1% of the taxpayers in the county and 42.6% of males over 21 in the county were Black. Of 33 prospective grand jurors drawn, 3 were Black; only one Black actually served on the grand jury. A venire of 90 persons was selected for the petit jury to try the defendants; only seven of these were Blacks, and no Black was actually accepted on the petit jury. Further, there was a showing that the jury lists had been made up from an earlier list compiled from tax returns which indicated clearly the taxpayer's race. This, the Court held, "constituted a prima facie case of purposeful discrimination" which was not overcome by testimony of the jury commissioners that no one was included or excluded from the list because of race.

In People v. Harris, 36 Cal.3d 36, 201 Cal.Rptr. 782, 679 P.2d 433 (1984), the California Supreme Court found that the defendant had made a prima facie showing of the systematic exclusion of Blacks and Hispanics from jury venires when voter registration lists were used as the sole source of the venires. The defendant had furnished statistics showing that significant percentages of Blacks and Hispanics did not register to vote, and thus were not included in jury venire selection.

10. **Permitting women to opt out of jury service.** In Duren v. Missouri, 439 U.S. 357, 99 S.Ct. 664, 58 L.Ed.2d 579 (1979), Duren had been convicted of murder and assault in a state court sitting in Jackson County, Missouri. Under Missouri law, any woman who requested not to serve was exempted from jury duty. Practice in Jackson County was to excuse any woman who failed to appear for jury service on the appointed day. Census figures indicated that 54% of the adult inhabitants of Jackson County were women; during the period in which Duren's jury was selected, only 14.5% of the persons on the jury venires were women. The Supreme Court reversed, reasoning that the above evidence established a prima facie violation of the Constitution's fair-cross-section requirement and that on the record the state had not justified this by showing that "a significant state interest [was] manifestly and primarily advanced by those aspects of the jury selection process [that resulted in the underrepresentation of women]." It explained:

> We recognize that a State may have an important interest in assuring that those members of the family responsible for the care of children are available to do so. An exemption appropriately tailored to this interest would, we think, survive a fair-cross-section challenge.

439 U.S. at 369, 99 S.Ct. at 671, 58 L.Ed.2d at 590. But the exemption provided by Missouri was not appropriately tailored to this interest.

What would be the holding under *Duren* if exfelons were excluded from serving as jurors by state law? Resident aliens? See Rubio v. Superior Court, 24 Cal.3d 93, 154 Cal.Rptr. 734, 593 P.2d 595 (1979) in which the court held that neither were "cognizable groups within the meaning of the representative cross-section rule."

11. **Exclusions from grand juries.** The prohibition against intentional exclusion of identifiable groups from the petit jury venire has also been enforced in the grand jury context. In Castaneda v. Partida, 430 U.S. 482, 97 S.Ct. 1272, 51 L.Ed.2d 498 (1977), the Court held that the petitioner had made a *prima facie* showing of discrimination against Mexican–Americans in the grand jury selection process. Since the state had made no effort to refute this showing, respondent's conviction had to fall.

The appropriateness of the remedy of reversal of a criminal conviction when discriminatory selection of grand jurors has been shown was the subject of the Court's decision in Vasquez v. Hillery, 474 U.S. 254, 106 S.Ct. 617, 88 L.Ed.2d 598 (1986). A majority of the Court rejected the argument that any deficiency in the selection of grand jurors was rendered harmless in light of respondent's conviction in an error-free trial.

The Court has also addressed the question of racial and gender discrimination in the selection of federal grand jury foremen in Hobby v. United States, 468 U.S. 339, 104 S.Ct. 3093, 82 L.Ed.2d 260 (1984). However, finding the functions of the federal grand jury foreman to be ministerial and clerical in nature, the Court stated that:

> [T]he role of the foreman of a federal grand jury is not so significant to the administration of justice that discrimination in the appointment of that office impugns the fundamental fairness of the process itself so as to undermine the integrity of the indictment.

468 U.S. at 345, 104 S.Ct. at 3097–98, 82 L.Ed.2d at 266.

However, the result might be different if the foreman had the power to veto an indictment as in Rose v. Mitchell, 443 U.S. 545, 99 S.Ct. 2993, 61 L.Ed.2d 739 (1979), although the Court concluded that a prima facie case of racial discrimination in foremen selection had not been established, even if none had been selected in 20 years.

Rose was further distinguished in *Hobby* because the defendants in *Rose* brought their claim as a denial of equal protection of the laws, whereas *Hobby* based his claim on fundamental fairness under the due process clause:

> *Rose* involved a claim brought by two Negro defendants under the Equal Protection Clause. As members of the class allegedly excluded from service as grand jury foremen, the *Rose* defendants had suffered the injuries of stigmatization and prejudice associated with racial discrimination. ...Petitioner [a white male], however, has alleged only that the exclusion of women and Negroes from the position of grand jury foremen violates his right to fundamental fairness under the Due Process Clause. ...[D]iscrimination in the selection of federal grand jury foremen cannot be said to have a significant impact upon the due process interests of criminal defendants. Thus, the nature of petitioner's alleged injury and the constitutional basis of his claim distinguish his circumstances from those of the defendants in *Rose*.

468 U.S. at 347, 104 S.Ct. at 3098, 82 L.Ed.2d at 267–68. Justice Marshall, joined by Justices Brennan and Stevens, dissented.

The Supreme Court in Campbell v. Louisiana, 523 U.S. 392, 118 S.Ct. 1419, 140 L.Ed.2d 551 (1998) held that the standing of a white person to challenge under the Equal Protection Clause discrimination against African Americans recognized by Powers v. Ohio in the context of trial jury formation applies also to the selection of grand jurors. Under Louisiana procedure, the trial judge selects the grand jury foreperson before the balance of the jurors are selected; the foreperson is a full voting member of the grand jury. Petitioner showed that in over 15 years in the Parish in issue no African American had ever served as grand jury foreperson, although twenty percent of the registered voters in the Parish are African American. The Court in an opinion by Justice Kennedy held that the same considerations that led the Court in *Powers* to extend standing also applied in the grand jury context. Justice Thomas, joined by Justice Scalia, dissented from the holding giving standing to the petitioner.

12. **Intentional inclusion of identifiable groups.** To what, if any, extent is the intentional *inclusion* of members of an identifiable group in jury venires permissible? See Brooks v. Beto, 366 F.2d 1 (5th Cir.1966), *cert. denied* 386 U.S. 975, 87 S.Ct. 1169, 18 L.Ed.2d 135 (1967), approving—in the circumstances of the case—the intentional inclusion of Blacks in the grand jury which indicted Brooks.

3.   THE JURY SIZE AND AGREEMENT REQUIRED

Juries traditionally have consisted of twelve jurors, and unanimity has been required for a verdict. But neither of these features was explicitly included in the United States Constitution, and both eventually came under close scrutiny. After an historical inquiry into the size and unanimity requirements, a fragmented Supreme Court rejected the argument that these commonly accepted notions are constitutionally required, as indicated in the materials in this Section.

Apodaca v. Oregon

Supreme Court of the United States, 1972.
406 U.S. 404, 92 S.Ct. 1628, 32 L.Ed.2d 184.

■ MR. JUSTICE WHITE announced the judgment of the Court in an opinion in which THE CHIEF JUSTICE, MR. JUSTICE BLACKMUN, and MR. JUSTICE REHNQUIST joined.

Robert Apodaca, Henry Morgan Cooper, Jr., and James Arnold Madden were convicted respectively of assault with a deadly weapon, burglary in a dwelling, and grand larceny before separate Oregon juries, all of which returned less than unanimous verdicts. The vote in the cases of Apodaca and Madden, was 11–1, while the vote in the case of Cooper was 10–2, the minimum requisite vote under Oregon law for sustaining a conviction. After convictions had been affirmed by the Oregon Court of Appeals, and review had been denied by the Supreme Court of Oregon, all three sought review in this Court upon a claim that conviction of crime by a less than unanimous jury violates the right to trial by jury in criminal cases specified by the Sixth Amendment and made applicable to the States by the Fourteenth. We granted certiorari to consider this claim, which we now find to be without merit.

In Williams v. Florida, 399 U.S. 78, 90 S.Ct. 1893, 26 L.Ed.2d 446 (1970), we had occasion to consider a related issue: whether the Sixth Amendment's right to trial by jury requires that all juries consist of 12 men. After considering the history of the 12–man requirement and the functions it performs in contemporary society, we concluded that it was not of constitutional stature. [In explanation, the Court said in Williams:

> . . . [The] essential feature of a jury obviously lies in the interposition between the accused and his accuser of the common-sense judgment of a group of laymen, and in the community participation and shared responsibility which results from that group's determination of guilt or innocence. The performance of this role is not a function of the particular number of the body which makes up the jury. To be sure, the number should probably be large enough to promote group deliberation, free from outside attempts at intimidation, and to provide a fair possibility for obtaining a representative cross section of the community. But we find little reason to think that these goals are in any meaningful sense less likely to be achieved when the jury numbers six, than when it numbers 12—particularly if the requirement of unanimity is retained. And, certainly the reliability of the jury as a factfinder hardly seems likely to be a function of its size.

> It might be suggested that the 12–man jury gives a defendant a greater advantage since he has more "chances" of finding a juror who will insist on acquittal and thus prevent conviction. But the advantage might just as easily belong to the State, which also needs only one juror out of twelve insisting on guilt to prevent acquittal. What few experiments have occurred—usually in the civil area—indicate that there is no discernible difference between the results reached by the two different-sized juries. In short, neither currently available evidence nor theory suggests that the 12–man jury is necessarily more advantageous to the defendant than a jury composed of fewer members.

399 U.S. at 100–01, 90 S.Ct. at 1906–07, 26 L.Ed.2d at 460–61. Editors.] We reach the same conclusion today with regard to the requirement of unanimity.

I.

Like the requirement that juries consist of 12 men, the requirement of unanimity arose during the Middle Ages and had become an accepted feature of the common-law jury by the 18th century. But, as we observed in *Williams,* "the relevant constitutional history, casts considerable doubt on the easy assumption ... that if a given feature existed in a jury at common law in 1789, then it was necessarily preserved in the Constitution." Id., at 92–93. The most salient fact in the scanty history of the Sixth Amendment, which we reviewed in full in *Williams,* is that, as it was introduced by James Madison in the House of Representatives, the proposed Amendment provided for trial

> "by an impartial jury of the freeholders of the vicinage, with the requisite of unanimity for conviction, of the right of challenge, and other accustomed requisites. ..." 1 Annuals of Cong. 435 (1789).

Although it passed the House with little alteration, this proposal ran into considerable opposition in the Senate,.... [T]he Amendment that ultimately emerged ... provided only for trial

> "by an impartial jury of the State and district wherein the crime shall have been committed, which district shall have been previously ascertained by law. ..."

As we observed in *Williams,* one can draw conflicting inferences from this legislative history. One possible inference is that Congress eliminated references to unanimity and to the other "accustomed requisites" of the jury because those requisites were thought already to be implicit in the very concept of jury. A contrary explanation, which we found in *Williams* to be the more plausible, is that the deletion was intended to have some substantive effect. See 399 U.S., at 96–97, 90 S.Ct., at 1903, 1904. Surely one fact that is absolutely clear from this history is that, after a proposal had been made to specify precisely which of the common-law requisites of the jury were to be preserved by the Constitution, the Framers explicitly rejected the proposal and instead left such specification to the future. As in *Williams,* we must accordingly consider .what is meant by the concept "jury" and determine whether a feature commonly associated with it is constitutionally required. And, as in *Williams,* our inability to divine "the intent of the Framers" when they eliminated references to the "accustomed requisites" requires that in determining what is meant by a jury we must turn to other than purely historical considerations.

II.

Our inquiry must focus upon the function served by the jury in contemporary society. As we said in *Duncan,* the purpose of trial by jury is to prevent oppression by the Government by providing a "safeguard against the corrupt or overzealous prosecutor and against the compliant, biased, or eccentric judge." Duncan v. Louisiana, supra, 391 U.S. at 156, 88 S.Ct. at 1451. "Given this purpose, the essential feature of a jury obviously lies in the interposition between the accused and his accuser of the commonsense judgment of a group of laymen. ..."Williams v. Florida, supra, 399 U.S. at 100, 90 S.Ct. at 1906. A requirement of unanimity, however, does not materially contribute to the exercise of this commonsense judgment. As we said in *Williams,* a jury will come to such a judgment as long as it consists of a group of laymen representative of a cross section of the community who have the duty and the opportunity to deliberate, free from outside attempts at intimidation, on the question of a defendant's guilt. In terms of this function we perceive no difference between juries required to act unanimously and those permitted to convict or acquit by votes of 10 to two or 11 to one. Requiring unanimity would obviously produce hung juries in some situations where nonunanimous juries will convict or acquit.[9] But in either case, the interest of the defendant in having the judgment of his peers interposed between himself and the officers of the State who prosecute and judge him is equally well served.

III.

Petitioners nevertheless argue that unanimity serves other purposes constitutionally essential to the continued operation of the jury system. Their principal contention is that a Sixth Amendment "jury trial" made mandatory on the States by virtue of the Due Process Clause of the Fourteenth Amendment, Duncan v. Louisiana, supra, should be held to require a unanimous jury verdict in order to give substance to the reasonable doubt standard otherwise mandated by the Due Process Clause. See In re Winship, 397 U.S. 358, 363–364 (1970).

We are quite sure, however, that the Sixth Amendment itself has never been held to require proof beyond a reasonable doubt in criminal cases. The reasonable doubt standard developed separately from both the jury trial and the unanimous verdict. As the Court noted in the *Winship* case, the rule requiring proof of crime beyond a reasonable doubt did not crystallize in this country until after the Constitution was adopted. And in that case, which held such a burden of proof to be constitutionally required, the Court purported to draw no support from the Sixth Amendment.

* * *

IV.

Petitioners also cite quite accurately a long line of decisions of this Court upholding the principle that the Fourteenth Amendment requires jury panels to reflect a cross section of the community. They then contend that unanimity is a necessary precondition for effective application of the cross section requirement, because a rule permitting less than unanimous verdicts will make it possible for convictions to occur without the acquiescence of minority elements within the community.

There are two flaws in this argument. One is petitioners' assumption that every distinct voice in the community has a right to be represented on every jury and a right to prevent conviction of a defendant in any case. All that the Constitution forbids, however, is systematic exclusion of identifiable segments of the community from jury panels and from the juries ultimately drawn from those panels; a defendant may not, for example, challenge the makeup of a jury merely because no members of his race are

9. The most complete statistical study of jury behavior has come to the conclusion that when juries are required to be unanimous, "the probability that an acquittal minority will hang the jury is about as great as that a guilty minority will hang it." H. Kalven & H. Zeisel, The American Jury 461 (1966).

on the jury, but must prove that his race has been systematically excluded. No group, in short, has the right to block convictions; it has only the right to participate in the overall legal processes by which criminal guilt and innocence are determined.

We also cannot accept petitioners' second assumption—that minority groups, even when they are represented on a jury, will not adequately represent the viewpoint of those groups simply because they may be outvoted in the final result. They will be present during all deliberations, and their views will be heard. We cannot assume that the majority of the jury will refuse to weigh the evidence and reach a decision upon rational grounds, just as it must now do in order to obtain unanimous verdicts, or that a majority will deprive a man of his liberty on the basis of prejudice when a minority is presenting a reasonable argument in favor of acquittal. We simply find no proof for the notion that a majority will disregard its instructions and cast its votes for guilt or innocence based on prejudice rather than the evidence.

We accordingly affirm the judgment of the Court of Appeals of Oregon.

It is so ordered.

Judgment affirmed.

■ MR. JUSTICE BLACKMUN, concurring.

I join the Court's opinion and judgment.... I add only the comment, which should be obvious and should not need saying, that in so doing I do not imply that I regard a State's split verdict system as a wise one. My vote means only that I cannot conclude that the system is constitutionally offensive. Were I a legislator, I would disfavor it as a matter of policy. Our task here, however, is not to pursue and strike down what happens to impress us as undesirable legislative policy.

I do not hesitate to say, either, that a system employing a 7–5 standard, rather than a 9–3 or 75% minimum, would afford me great difficulty. As Mr. Justice White points out "a substantial majority of the jury" are to be convinced. That is all that is before us in each of these cases.

■ MR. JUSTICE POWELL, concurring....

* * *

I concur in the plurality opinion ... insofar as it concludes that a defendant in a state court may constitutionally be convicted by less than a unanimous verdict, but I am not in accord with a major premise upon which that judgment is based. Its premise is that the concept of jury trial, as applicable to the States under the Fourteenth Amendment, must be identical in every detail to the concept required in federal courts by the Sixth Amendment. I do not think that all of the elements of jury trial within the meaning of the Sixth Amendment are necessarily embodied in or incorporated into the Due Process Clause of the Fourteenth Amendment. ...

In an unbroken line of cases reaching back into the late 1800's, the Justices of this Court have recognized, virtually without dissent, that unanimity is one of the indispensable features of *federal* jury trial. In these cases, the Court has presumed that unanimous verdicts are essential in federal jury trials, not because unanimity is necessarily fundamental to the function performed by the jury, but because that result is mandated by history. The reasoning which runs throughout this Court's Sixth Amendment precedents is that, in amending the Constitution to guarantee the right to jury trial, the Framers desired to preserve the jury safeguard as it was known to them at common law. At the time the Bill of Rights was adopted, unanimity had long been established as one of the attributes of a jury conviction at common law. It therefore seems to me, in accord both with history and precedent, that the Sixth Amendment requires a unanimous jury verdict to convict in a federal criminal trial.

But it is the Fourteenth Amendment, rather than the Sixth, which imposes upon the States the requirement that they provide jury trials to those accused of serious crimes. . . .

The question, therefore, which should be addressed in this case is whether unanimity is in fact so fundamental to the essentials of jury trial that this particular requirement of the Sixth Amendment is necessarily binding on the States under the Due Process Clause of the Fourteenth Amendment.

* * *

■ Mr. Justice Douglas, with whom Mr. Justice Brennan and Mr. Justice Marshall concur, dissenting.

* * *

I.

. . . [I]n cases dealing with juries it had always been assumed that a unanimous jury was required. Today the bases of those cases are discarded and two centuries of American history are shunted aside.

The result of today's decision is anomalous: though unanimous jury decisions are not required in state trials, they are constitutionally required in federal prosecutions. How can that be possible when both decisions stem from the Sixth Amendment?

* * *

II.

The plurality approves a procedure which diminishes the reliability of a jury. First, it eliminates the circumstances in which a minority of jurors (a) could have rationally persuaded the entire jury to acquit, or (b) while unable to persuade the majority to acquit, nonetheless could have convinced them to convict only on a lesser-included offense. Second, it permits prosecutors in Oregon and Louisiana to enjoy a conviction-acquittal ratio substantially greater than that ordinarily returned by unanimous juries.

The diminution of verdict reliability flows from the fact that nonunanimous juries need not debate and deliberate as fully as must unanimous juries. As soon as the requisite majority is attained, further consideration is not required either by Oregon or by Louisiana even though the dissident jurors might, if given the chance, be able to convince the majority. Such persuasion does in fact occasionally occur in States where the unanimous requirement applies: "In roughly one case in ten, the minority eventually succeeds in reversing an initial majority, and these may be cases of special importance."[10] One explanation for this phenomenon is that because jurors are often not permitted to take notes and because they have imperfect memories, the forensic process of forcing jurors to defend their conflicting recollections and conclusions flushes out many nuances which otherwise would go overlooked. This collective effort to piece together the puzzle of historical truth, however, is cut short as soon as the requisite majority is reached in Oregon and Louisiana. Indeed, if a necessary majority is immediately obtained, then no deliberation at all is required in these States. (There is a suggestion that this may have happened in the 10–2 verdict rendered in only 41 minutes in Apodaca's case.) To be sure, in jurisdictions other than these two States, initial majorities normally prevail in the end, but about a tenth of the time the rough and tumble of the juryroom operates to reverse completely their preliminary perception of guilt or innocence. The Court now extracts from the juryroom this automatic check against hasty factfinding by relieving jurors of the duty to hear out fully the dissenters.

It is said that there is no evidence that majority jurors will refuse to listen to dissenters whose votes are unneeded for conviction. Yet human experience teaches that polite and academic conversation is no substitute for the earnest and robust argument necessary to reach unanimity. As mentioned earlier, in Apodaca's case, whatever courtesy dialogue transpired could not have lasted more than 41 minutes. I fail to understand why the Court should lift from the States the burden of justifying so radical a departure from an accepted and applauded tradition and instead demand that these defendants document with empirical evidence what has always been thought to be too obvious for further study.

To be sure in Williams v. Florida, 399 U.S. 78, 88, 90 S.Ct. 1893, 1899, 26 L.Ed.2d 446, we held that a State could provide a jury less than 12 in number in criminal trial. We said "What few experiments have occurred— usually in the civil area—indicate that there is no discernible difference between the results reached by the two different-sized juries. In short, neither currently available evidence nor theory suggests that the 12–man jury is necessarily more advantageous to the defendant than a jury composed of fewer members." Id., at 101–102, 90 S.Ct. at 1906.

That rationale of *Williams* can have no application here. *Williams* requires that the change be neither more nor less advantageous to either the State or the defendant. It is said that such a showing is satisfied here since a 3:9 (Louisiana) or 2:10 (Oregon) verdict will result in acquittal. Yet experience shows that the less than unanimous jury overwhelmingly favors the States.

Moreover, even where an initial majority wins the dissent over to its side, the ultimate result in unanimous jury States may nonetheless reflect

---

10. H. Kalven & H. Zeisel, The American Jury 490 (1966). See also The American Jury: Notes For an English Controversy, 48 Chi. B.Rec. 195 (1967).

the reservations of uncertain jurors. I refer to many compromise verdicts on lesser-included offenses and lesser sentences. Thus, even though a minority may not be forceful enough to carry the day, their doubts may nonetheless cause a majority to exercise caution. Obviously, however, in Oregon and Louisiana, dissident jurors will not have the opportunity through full deliberation to temper the opposing faction's degree of certainty of guilt.

The new rule also has an impact on cases in which a unanimous jury would have neither voted to acquit nor to convict, but would have deadlocked. In unanimous jury States, this occurs about 5.6% of the time. Of these deadlocked juries, Kalven and Zeisel say that 56% contain either one, two, or three dissenters. In these latter cases, the majorities favor the prosecution 44% (of the 56%) but the defendant only 12% (of the 56%).[11] Thus, by eliminating these deadlocks, Louisiana wins 44 cases for every 12 that it loses, obtaining in this band of outcomes a substantially more favorable conviction ratio (3.67) than the unanimous jury ratio of slightly less than two guilty verdicts for every acquittal. H. Kalven & H. Zeisel, The American Jury 461, 488 (Table 159) (1966). By eliminating the one and two dissenting juror cases, Oregon does even better, gaining 4.25 convictions for every acquittal. While the statutes on their face deceptively appear to be neutral, the use of the nonunanimous jury stacks the truth-determining process against the accused. Thus, we take one step more away from the accusatorial system that has been our proud boast.

It is my belief that a unanimous jury is necessary if the great barricade known as proof beyond a reasonable doubt is to be maintained. ...

Today the Court approves a nine to three verdict. Would the Court relax the standard of reasonable doubt still further by resorting to eight to four verdicts or even a majority rule? Moreover, in light of today's holdings and that of Williams v. Florida, in the future would it invalidate three to two or even two to one convictions?

Is the next step the elimination of the presumption of innocence?

[The dissenting opinions of Mr. Justice Brennan (joined by Mr. Justice Marshall), Mr. Justice Stewart (joined by Mr. Justice Brennan and Mr. Justice Marshall), and Mr. Justice Marshall (joined by Mr. Justice Brennan) are omitted.]

NOTES

1. **But not one juror fewer than six.** In Ballew v. Georgia, 435 U.S. 223, 98 S.Ct. 1029, 55 L.Ed.2d 234 (1978), the Court concluded:

11. The American Jury, at 460, n. 3.

Last Vote of Deadlocked Juries

Vote for Conviction	Per Cent
11:1	24
10:2	10
9:3	10
8:4	6
7:5	13
6:6	13
5:7	8
4:8	4
3:9	4
2:10	8
1:11	–
	100%

Number of Juries in Sample—48.

[T]he purpose and functioning of the jury in a criminal trial is seriously impaired, and to a constitutional degree, by a reduction in size to below six members. ... [T]he assembled data raise substantial doubt about the reliability and appropriate representation of panels smaller than six. Because of the fundamental importance of the jury trial to the American system of criminal justice, any further reduction that promotes inaccurate and possibly biased decisionmaking, that causes untoward differences in verdicts, and that prevents juries from truly representing their communities, attains constitutional significance.

435 U.S. at 239, 98 S.Ct. at 1038–39, 55 L.Ed.2d at 246. In addition, the Court commented that reduction of jury size from six to five would result in only minimal savings in court time and financial costs.

2. **Six person juries must be unanimous.** In Burch v. Louisiana, 441 U.S. 130, 99 S.Ct. 1623, 60 L.Ed.2d 96 (1979), the Court, in an opinion by Justice Rehnquist, declared:

[M]uch the same reasons that led us in *Ballew* to decide that use of a five-member jury threatened the fairness of the proceeding and the proper role of the jury, lead us to conclude now that conviction for a nonpetty offense by only five members of a six-person jury presents a similar threat to preservation of the substance of the jury trial guarantee and justifies our requiring verdicts rendered by six-person juries to be unanimous. ...

[footnote 11: We, of course, intimate no view as to the constitutionality of nonunanimous verdicts rendered by juries comprised of more than six members.]

441 U.S. at 138 & n. 11, 99 S.Ct. at 1627–28 & n. 11, 60 L.Ed.2d at 103–04 & n. 11.

3. **Reducing size of juries after trial begins.** Rule 23(b) of the Federal Rules of Criminal Procedure provides:

Juries shall be of 12 but at any time before verdict the parties may stipulate in writing with the approval of the court that the jury shall consist of any number less than 12 or that a valid verdict may be returned by a jury of less than 12 should the court find it necessary to excuse one or more jurors for any just cause after trial commences. Even absent such stipulation, if the court finds it necessary to excuse a juror for just cause after the jury has retired to consider its verdict, in the discretion of the court a valid verdict may be returned by the remaining 11 jurors.

4. **Unanimity.** Rule 31 of the Federal Rules of Criminal Procedure provides that verdicts of federal juries in criminal cases must be unanimous.

5. **Agreement on a single legal theory of guilt.** Must the jury agree on a single legal theory of an offense when more than one have been charged and submitted to it? In Schad v. Arizona, 501 U.S. 624, 111 S.Ct. 2491, 115 L.Ed.2d 555 (1991), petitioner was charged with first-degree murder by premeditated killing and by killing in perpetration of robbery. There was evidence in support of each theory. The jury was instructed to return a verdict of not guilty, guilty of first-degree murder, or guilty of the lesser included offense of second degree murder, but was not required to agree upon which theory of first degree murder it found proved. The jury returned a verdict of guilty of first degree murder and the death sentence was imposed. Petitioner's contention that this procedure violated the Due Process Clause was rejected by the Court. In a plurality opinion by Justice Souter, joined by The Chief Justice and Justices O'Connor and Kennedy, the issue was characterized as whether under Arizona law first-degree murder is a single crime or whether premeditated murder and felony murder are separate crimes. Acknowledging that "nothing in our history suggests that the Due Process Clause would permit a State

to convict anyone under a charge of 'Crime' so generic that any combination of jury findings of embezzlement, reckless driving, murder, burglary, tax evasion, or littering, for example, would suffice for conviction," this is not such a case. The Arizona court has determined that there is only one offense of first-degree murder and the Supreme Court is not free to take a different view of Arizona law; the only question is whether the view taken by the Arizona court is constitutional. Both premeditated killing and felony-murder are simply different forms of *mens rea*. Historically, each has simply been a different way of defining the same criminal offense. Finally, felony murder can be regarded as the moral equivalent of premeditated killing. Justice Scalia, concurring, placed emphasis upon the historical roots of the Arizona practice:

> Submitting killing in the course of a robbery and premeditated killing to the jury under a single charge is not some novel composite that can be subjected to the indignity of "fundamental fairness" review. It was the norm when this country was founded, was the norm when the Fourteenth Amendment was adopted in 1868, and remains the norm today. Unless we are here to invent a Constitution rather than enforce one, it is impossible that a practice as old as the common law and still in existence in the vast majority of States does not provide that process which is "due."

501 U.S. at 651, 111 S.Ct. at 2507, 115 L.Ed.2d at 577–78. Justice White, joined by Justices Marshall, Blackmun and Stevens, dissenting, took issue with the plurality's characterization of the two legal theories as simply alternative *mens rea* for the offense of first degree murder:

> [I]t is entirely possible that half of the jury believed the defendant was guilty of premeditated murder and not guilty of felony murder/robbery, while half believed exactly the reverse.... [T]he plurality affirms this conviction without knowing that even a single element of either of the ways for proving first-degree murder, except the fact of a killing, has been found by a majority of the jury, let alone found unanimously by the jury as required by Arizona law. A defendant charged with first-degree murder is at least entitled to a verdict—something petitioner did not get in this case as long as the possibility exists that no more than six jurors voted for any one element of first-degree murder, except the fact of a killing.

501 U.S. at 655, 111 S.Ct. at 2509, 115 L.Ed.2d at 580.

The Court was asked in Richardson v. United States, 526 U.S. 813, 119 S.Ct. 1707, 143 L.Ed.2d 985 (1999) whether a jury is required to agree unanimously on each violation of federal drug law necessary to support the charge of a continuing criminal enterprise brought by the Government. Distinguishing Schad v. Arizona, the Court in an opinion by Justice Breyer held that unanimous agreement on each supporting violation (although not on each one alleged, since an excess might be alleged) was required. Each violation alleged is an element of the continuing criminal enterprise offense and a sufficient minimum number must be proved (assumed in the opinion to be three) to the unanimous agreement of the jury as to each. The violations here are criminal offenses, unlike the means alleged in *Schad* to commit the criminal offense of first degree murder.

6. **Evidence sufficiency when alternative legal theories are presented to the jury.** What should happen when theories are presented to a jury in the alternative, a general verdict of guilty is returned, and the evidence is insufficient to support one of those theories? Petitioner in Griffin v. United States, 502 U.S. 46, 112 S.Ct. 466, 116 L.Ed.2d 371 (1991) was charged with conspiracy to defraud the United States Government. Two objects of the conspiracy were charged: defrauding the Internal Revenue Service and defrauding the Drug Enforcement Administration. The jury was instructed to return a verdict of guilty if it found that petitioner

participated in either of the two objects of the conspiracy. The jury returned a general verdict of guilty. The Government conceded there was insufficient evidence that petitioner conspired to defraud the DEA. The Supreme Court, in an opinion by Justice Scalia, held that the verdict could stand despite the insufficiency of evidence.

The Court distinguished prior cases in which the theories submitted were based upon constitutionally protected conduct or in which the theories were not authorized by law. Evidence insufficiency is different:

> Jurors are not generally equipped to determine whether a particular theory of conviction submitted to them is contrary to law—whether, for example, the action in question is protected by the Constitution, is time barred, or fails to come within the statutory definition of the crime. When, therefore, jurors have been left the option of relying upon a legally inadequate theory, there is no reason to think that their own intelligence and expertise will save them from that error. Quite the opposite is true, however, when they have been left the option of relying upon a factually inadequate theory, since jurors *are* well equipped to analyze the evidence.

502 U.S. at 59, 112 S.Ct. at 474, 116 L.Ed.2d at 382–83.

C.   CONFRONTATION, CROSS-EXAMINATION AND COMPULSORY PROCESS TO OBTAIN WITNESSES

The Sixth Amendment provides, in part, that, "in all criminal prosecutions, the accused shall enjoy the right ... to be confronted with the witnesses against him [and the right] to have compulsory process for obtaining witnesses in his favor.... " The Fourteenth Amendment imposes upon the states both the requirement that the accused be afforded confrontation rights, Pointer v. Texas, 380 U.S. 400, 85 S.Ct. 1065, 13 L.Ed.2d 923 (1965), and compulsory process, Washington v. Texas, 388 U.S. 14, 87 S.Ct. 1920, 18 L.Ed.2d 1019 (1967). Despite the concise language of the constitutional provision, however, the rights have broad implications. In Faretta v. California, 422 U.S. 806, 95 S.Ct. 2525, 45 L.Ed.2d 562 (1975) the Court observed:

> The rights to notice, confrontation, and compulsory process, when taken together, guarantee that a criminal charge may be answered in a manner now considered fundamental to the fair administration of American justice—through the calling and interrogation of favorable witnesses, and the orderly introduction of evidence. In short, the [Sixth] Amendment constitutionalizes the right in an adversary criminal trial to make a defense as we know it.

422 U.S. at 818, 95 S.Ct. at 2532–33, 45 L.Ed.2d at 572.

1.   CONFRONTATION

Recently the Court has addressed a series of confrontation clause issues involving the tension between providing "a defense as we know it" and protecting victims of child abuse from traditional aspects of that defense.

In Coy v. Iowa, 487 U.S. 1012, 108 S.Ct. 2798, 101 L.Ed.2d 857 (1988), appellant was convicted of sex offenses against two 13 year old girls. At his trial, under authority of a state statute authorizing testimony in such cases by closed circuit television or from behind a screen, they testified behind a screen that enabled appellant to hear them and see them dimly but which prevented them from seeing him. The United States Supreme Court, in an opinion by Justice Scalia, concluded this procedure violated the Confrontation Clause:

> The perception that confrontation is essential to fairness has persisted over the centuries because there is much truth to it. A witness "may feel quite differently when he has to repeat his story looking at the man whom he will harm greatly by distorting or mistaking the facts. He can now understand what sort of human being that man is.... " It is always more difficult to tell a lie about a person "to his face" than "behind his back." In the former context, even if the lie is told, it will often be told less convincingly. The Confrontation Clause does not, of course, compel the witness to fix his eyes upon the defendant; he may studiously look elsewhere, but the trier of fact will draw its own conclusions. Thus the right to face-to-face confrontation serves much the same purposes as a less explicit component of the Confrontation Clause that we have had more frequent occasion to discuss—the right to cross-examine the accuser; both "ensur[e] the integrity of the fact-finding process.... " The State can hardly gainsay the profound effect upon a witness of standing in the presence of the person the witness accuses, since that is the very phenomenon it relies upon to establish the potential "trauma" that allegedly justified the extraordinary procedure in the present case. That face-to-face presence may, unfortunately, upset the truthful rape victim or abused child; but by the same token it may confound and undo the false accuser, or reveal the child coached by a malevolent adult. It is a truism that constitutional protections have costs.

487 U.S. at 1019–20, 108 S.Ct. at 2802, 101 L.Ed.2d at 866. The Court remanded the case for a determination whether the violation of appellant's confrontation rights was harmless beyond a reasonable doubt "on the basis of the remaining evidence." Justice O'Connor, joined by Justice White, concurred to emphasize that while the Confrontation Clause was violated by the procedures employed in this case, its command is not absolute. In a case in which there was a specific finding of necessity, supported by the evidence, she would permit a trial procedure that employed something other than face-to-face confrontation.

Another child abuse case two years after *Coy*, provided Justice O'Connor that opportunity. This time Justice Scalia dissented. That case, Maryland v. Craig, is the principal case in this section, which together with the notes provides an examination of the general parameters of these Sixth Amendment rights.

Maryland v. Craig

Supreme Court of the United States, 1990.
497 U.S. 836, 110 S.Ct. 3157, 111 L.Ed.2d 666.

■ JUSTICE O'CONNOR delivered the opinion of the Court.

This case requires us to decide whether the Confrontation Clause of the Sixth Amendment categorically prohibits a child witness in a child abuse case from testifying against a defendant at trial, outside the defendant's physical presence, by one-way closed circuit television.

I

In October 1986, a Howard County grand jury charged respondent, Sandra Ann Craig, with child abuse, first and second degree sexual offenses, perverted sexual practice, assault, and battery. The named victim in each count was Brooke Etze, a six-year-old child who, from August 1984 to June 1986, had attended a kindergarten and prekindergarten center owned and operated by Craig.

In March 1987, before the case went to trial, the State sought to invoke a Maryland statutory procedure that permits a judge to receive, by one-way closed circuit television, the testimony of a child witness who is alleged to be a victim of child abuse. To invoke the procedure, the trial judge must first "determin[e] that testimony by the child victim in the courtroom will result in the child suffering serious emotional distress such that the child cannot reasonably communicate." Md.Cts. & Jud.Proc.Code Ann. § 9–102(a)(1)(ii) (1989). Once the procedure is invoked, the child witness, prosecutor, and defense counsel withdraw to a separate room; the judge, jury, and defendant remain in the courtroom. The child witness is then examined and cross-examined in the separate room, while a video monitor records and displays the witness' testimony to those in the courtroom. During this time the witness cannot see the defendant. The defendant remains in electronic communication with defense counsel, and objections may be made and ruled on as if the witness were testifying in the courtroom.

In support of its motion invoking the one-way closed circuit television procedure, the State presented expert testimony that Brooke, as well as a number of other children who were alleged to have been sexually abused by Craig, would suffer "serious emotional distress such that [they could not] reasonably communicate," § 9–102(a)(1)(ii), if required to testify in the courtroom. ...Craig objected to the use of the procedure on Confrontation Clause grounds, but the trial court rejected that contention, concluding that although the statute "take[s] away the right of the defendant to be face to face with his or her accuser," the defendant retains the "essence of the right of confrontation," including the right to observe, cross-examine, and have the jury view the demeanor of the witness. ...The trial court further found that, "based upon the evidence presented ... the testimony of each of these children in a courtroom will result in each child suffering serious emotional distress ... such that each of these children cannot reasonably communicate." Id., at 66. The trial court then found Brooke and three other children competent to testify and accordingly permitted them to testify against Craig via the one-way closed circuit television procedure. The jury convicted Craig on all counts, ...

The Court of Appeals of Maryland reversed and remanded for a new trial. 316 Md. 551, 560 A.2d 1120 (1989). The Court of Appeals rejected Craig's argument that the Confrontation Clause requires in all cases a face-to-face courtroom encounter between the accused and his accusers, ... but concluded: ... that, "as [it] read *Coy* [v. Iowa, 487 U.S. 1012, 108 S.Ct. 2798, 101 L.Ed.2d 857 (1988)], the showing made by the State was insufficient to reach the high threshold required by that case before § 9–102 may be invoked." Id. 316 Md., at 554–555, 560 A.2d, at 1121 (footnote omitted).

We granted certiorari to resolve the important Confrontation Clause issues raised by this case. 493 U.S. ___, 110 S.Ct. 834, 107 L.Ed.2d 830 (1990).

II

The Confrontation Clause of the Sixth Amendment, made applicable to the States through the Fourteenth Amendment, provides: "In all criminal prosecutions, the accused shall enjoy the right ... to be confronted with the witnesses against him."

We observed in *Coy v. Iowa* that "the Confrontation Clause guarantees the defendant a face-to-face meeting with witnesses appearing before the trier of fact." 487 U.S., at 1016, 108 S.Ct., at 2800 (citing Kentucky v. Stincer), 482 U.S. 730, 748, 749–750, 107 S.Ct. 2658, 2668–2669, 2669, 96 L.Ed.2d 631 (1987) ... This interpretation derives not only from the literal text of the Clause, but also from our understanding of its historical roots.

We have never held, however, that the Confrontation Clause guarantees criminal defendants the *absolute* right to a face-to-face meeting with witnesses against them at trial. Indeed, in *Coy v. Iowa,* we expressly "le[ft] for another day ... the question whether any exceptions exist" to the "irreducible literal meaning of the Clause: 'a right to *meet face to face* all those who appear and give evidence at trial.'" 487 U.S., at 1021, 108 S.Ct. at 2802–2803.... The procedure challenged in *Coy* involved the placement of a screen that prevented two child witnesses in a child abuse case from seeing the defendant as they testified against him at trial. See 487 U.S., at 1014–1015, 108 S.Ct., at 2799–2800. In holding that the use of this procedure violated the defendant's right to confront witnesses against him, we suggested that any exception to the right "would surely be allowed only when necessary to further an important public policy"—i.e., only upon a showing of something more than the generalized, "legislatively imposed presumption of trauma" underlying the statute at issue in that case. Id., at 1021, 108 S.Ct. at 2802–2803; see also id., at 1025, 108 S.Ct., at 2804 (concurring opinion). We concluded that "[s]ince there ha[d] been no individualized findings that these particular witnesses needed special protection, the judgment [in the case before us] could not be sustained by any conceivable exception." Id., at 1021, 108 S.Ct., at 2802–2803. Because the trial court in this case made individualized findings that each of the child witnesses needed special protection, this case requires us to decide the question reserved in *Coy.*

The central concern of the Confrontation Clause is to ensure the reliability of the evidence against a criminal defendant by subjecting it to rigorous testing in the context of an adversary proceeding before the trier of fact. The word "confront," after all, also means a clashing of forces of ideas, thus carrying with it the notion of adversariness. As we noted in our earliest case interpreting the Clause:

"The primary object of the constitutional provision in question was to prevent depositions or *ex parte* affidavits, such as were sometimes admitted in civil cases, being used against the prisoner in lieu of a personal examination and cross-examination of the witness in which the accused has an opportunity, not only of testing the recollection and sifting the conscience of the witness, but of compelling him to stand face to face with the jury in order that they may look at him, and judge by his demeanor upon the stand and the manner in which he gives his testimony whether he is worthy of belief." [Mattox v. United States, 156 U.S. 237, 242–43, 15 S.Ct. 337, 339–40, 39 L.Ed. 409 (1895).]

As this description indicates, the right guaranteed by the Confrontation Clause includes not only a "personal examination," id., at 242, 15 S.Ct., at 339, but also "(1) insures that the witness will give his statements under oath—thus impressing him with the seriousness of the matter and guarding against the lie by the possibility of a penalty for perjury; (2) forces the witness to submit to cross-examination, the 'greatest legal engine ever invented for the discovery of truth'; [and] (3) permits the jury that is to decide the defendant's fate to observe the demeanor of the witness in making his statement, thus aiding the jury in assessing his credibility." [California v. Green, 399 U.S. 149, 158, 90 S.Ct. 1930, 1935, 26 L.Ed.2d 489 (1970).]

The combined effect of these elements of confrontation—physical presence, oath, cross-examination, and observation of demeanor by the trier of fact—serves the purposes of the Confrontation Clause by ensuring that evidence admitted against an accused is reliable and subject to the rigorous adversarial testing that is the norm of Anglo–American criminal proceedings. . . .

We have recognized, for example, that face-to-face confrontation enhances the accuracy of factfinding by reducing the risk that a witness will wrongfully implicate an innocent person. See *Coy,* 487 U.S., at 1019–1020, 108 S.Ct., at 2802 ("It is always more difficult to tell a lie about a person 'to his face' than 'behind his back.' . . . That face-to-face presence may, unfortunately, upset the truthful rape victim or abused child; but by the same token it may confound and undo the false accuser, or reveal the child coached by a malevolent adult") . . . We have also noted the strong symbolic purpose served by requiring adverse witnesses at trial to testify in the accused's presence. See *Coy,* supra, 487 U.S., at 1017, 108 S.Ct., at 2800 ("[T]here is something deep in human nature that regards face-to-face confrontation between accused and accuser as 'essential to a fair trial in a criminal prosecution'") (quoting Pointer v. Texas, 380 U.S. 400, 404, 85 S.Ct. 1065, 1068, 13 L.Ed.2d 923 (1965)).

Although face-to-face confrontation forms "the core of the values furthered by the Confrontation Clause," *Green,* supra, 399 U.S., at 157, 90 S.Ct., at 1934, we have nevertheless recognized that it is not the *sine qua non* of the confrontation right. See Delaware v. Fensterer, 474 U.S. 15, 22, 106 S.Ct. 292, 295, 88 L.Ed.2d 15 (1985) (per curiam) ("[T]he Confrontation Clause is generally satisfied when the defense is given a full and fair opportunity to probe and expose [testimonial] infirmities [such as forgetfulness, confusion, or evasion] through cross-examination, thereby calling to the attention of the factfinder the reasons for giving scant weight to the witness' testimony") . . . see also *Stincer,* supra, 482 U.S. at 739–744, 107 S.Ct., at 2664 (confrontation right not violated by exclusion of defendant from competency hearing of child witnesses, where defendant had opportunity for full and effective cross-examination at trial); . . .

For this reason, we have never insisted on an actual face-to-face encounter at trial in *every* instance in which testimony is admitted against a defendant. Instead, we have repeatedly held that the Clause permits, where necessary, the admission of certain hearsay statements against a defendant despite the defendant's inability to confront the declarant at trial. . . . In *Mattox,* for example, we held that the testimony of a government witness at a former trial against the defendant, where the witness was fully cross-examined but had died after the first trial, was admissible in evidence against the defendant at his second trial. See 156 U.S., at 240–244, 15 S.Ct., at 338–340. We explained:

> "There is doubtless reason for saying that . . . if notes of [the witness's] testimony are permitted to be read, [the defendant] is deprived of the advantage of that personal presence of the witness before the jury which the law has designed for his protection. But general rules of law of this kind, however beneficent in their operation and valuable to the accused, must occasionally give way to considerations of public policy and the necessities of the case. To say that a criminal, after having once been convicted by the testimony of a certain witness, should go scot free simply because death has closed the mouth of that witness, would be carrying his constitutional protection to an unwarrantable extent. The law in its wisdom declares that the rights of the public shall not be wholly sacrificed in order that an incidental benefit may be preserved to the accused." Id., at 243, 15 S.Ct., at 339–340.

We have accordingly stated that a literal reading of the Confrontation Clause would "abrogate virtually every hearsay exception, a result long rejected as unintended and too extreme." [Ohio v. Roberts, 448 U.S. 56, 63, 100 S.Ct. 2531, 2537, 65 L.Ed.2d 597 (1980).] Thus, in certain narrow circumstances, "competing interests, if 'closely examined,' may warrant dispensing with confrontation at trial." Id., at 64, 100 S.Ct., at 2538 (quoting Chambers v. Mississippi, 410 U.S. 284, 295, 93 S.Ct. 1038, 1045, 35 L.Ed.2d 297 (1973), and citing *Mattox,* supra). We have recently held, for example, that hearsay statements of nontestifying co-conspirators may be admitted against a defendant despite the lack of any face-to-face encounter with the accused. See Bourjaily v. United States, 483 U.S. 171, 107 S.Ct. 2775, 97 L.Ed.2d 144 (1987); United States v. Inadi, 475 U.S. 387, 106 S.Ct. 1121, 89 L.Ed.2d 390 (1986). Given our hearsay cases, the word "confront," as used in the Confrontation Clause, cannot simply mean face-to-face confrontation, for the Clause would then, contrary to our cases, prohibit the admission of any accusatory hearsay statement made by an absent declarant—a declarant who is undoubtedly as much a "witness against" a defendant as one who actually testifies at trial.

In sum, our precedents establish that "the Confrontation Clause reflects a *preference* for face-to-face confrontation at trial," *Roberts,* supra, 448 U.S., at 63, 100 S.Ct., at 2537 (emphasis added; footnote omitted), a preference that "must occasionally give way to considerations of public policy and the necessities of the case," *Mattox,* supra, 156 U.S., at 243, 15 S.Ct., at 339–340. "[W]e have attempted to harmonize the goal of the Clause—placing limits on the kind of evidence that may be received against a defendant—with a societal interest in accurate factfinding, which may require consideration of out-of-court statements." *Bourjaily,* supra, 483 U.S., at 182, 107 S.Ct., at 2782. We have accordingly interpreted the Confrontation Clause in a manner sensitive to its purposes and sensitive to the necessities of trial and the adversary process. ...Thus, though we reaffirm the importance of face-to-face confrontation with witnesses appearing at trial, we cannot say that such confrontation is an indispensable element of the Sixth Amendment's guarantee of the right to confront one's accusers. ...

This interpretation of the Confrontation Clause is consistent with our cases holding that other Sixth Amendment rights must also be interpreted in the context of the necessities of trial and the adversary process. See, e.g., Illinois v. Allen, 397 U.S. 337, 342–343, 90 S.Ct. 1057, 1060, 25 L.Ed.2d 353 (1970) (right to be present at trial not violated where trial judge removed defendant for disruptive behavior); ... Taylor v. United States, 484 U.S. 400, 410–416, 108 S.Ct. 646, 653–656, 98 L.Ed.2d 798 (1988) (right to compulsory process not violated where trial judge precluded testimony of a surprise defense witness); Perry v. Leeke, 488 U.S. 272, 280–285, 109 S.Ct. 594, ___, 102 L.Ed.2d 624 (1989) (right to effective assistance of counsel not violated where trial judge prevented testifying defendant from conferring with counsel during a short break in testimony). We see no reason to treat the face-to-face component of the confrontation right any differently, and indeed we think it would be anomalous to do so.

That the face-to-face confrontation requirement is not absolute does not, of course, mean that it may easily be dispensed with. As we suggested in *Coy,* our precedents confirm that a defendant's right to confront accusatory witnesses may be satisfied absent a physical, face-to-face confrontation at trial only where denial of such confrontation is necessary to further an important public policy and only where the reliability of the testimony is otherwise assured. See *Coy,* 487 U.S., at 1021, 108 S.Ct., at 2802–2803....

III

Maryland's statutory procedure, when invoked, prevents a child witness from seeing the defendant as he or she testifies against the defendant at trial. We find it significant, however, that Maryland's procedure preserves all of the other elements of the confrontation right: the child witness must be competent to testify and must testify under oath; the defendant retains full opportunity for contemporaneous cross-examination; and the judge, jury, and defendant are able to view (albeit by video monitor) the demeanor (and body) of the witness as he or she testifies. Although we are mindful of the many subtle effects face-to-face confrontation may have on an adversary criminal proceeding, the presence of these other elements of confrontation—oath, cross-examination, and observation of the witness' demeanor—adequately ensures that the testimony is both reliable and subject to rigorous adversarial testing in a manner functionally equivalent to that accorded live, in-person testimony. These safeguards of reliability and adversariness render the use of such a procedure a far cry from the undisputed prohibition of the Confrontation Clause: trial by *ex parte* affidavit or inquisition, see *Mattox,* 156 U.S., at 242, 15 S.Ct., at 389; see also *Green,* 399 U.S., at 179, 90 S.Ct., at 1946 (Harlan, J., concurring) ("[T]he Confrontation Clause was meant to constitutionalize a barrier against flagrant abuses, trials by anonymous accusers, and absentee witnesses"). Rather, we think these elements of effective confrontation not only permit a defendant to "confound and undo the false accuser, or reveal the child coached by a malevolent adult," *Coy,* 487 U.S., at 1020, 108 S.Ct., at 2802, but may well aid a defendant in eliciting favorable testimony from the child witness. Indeed, to the extent the child witness' testimony may be said to be technically given out-of-court (though we do not so hold), these assurances of reliability and adversariness are far greater than those required for admission of hearsay testimony under the Confrontation Clause. . . . We are therefore confident that use of the one-way closed-circuit television procedure, where necessary to further an important state interest, does not impinge upon the truth-seeking or symbolic purposes of the Confrontation Clause.

The critical inquiry in this case, therefore, is whether use of the procedure is necessary to further an important state interest. The State contends that it has a substantial interest in protecting children who are allegedly victims of child abuse from the trauma of testifying against the alleged perpetrator and that its statutory procedure for receiving testimony from such witnesses is necessary to further that interest.

We have of course recognized that a State's interest in "the protection of minor victims of sex crimes from further trauma and embarrassment" is a "compelling" one. . . . "[W]e have sustained legislation aimed at protecting the physical and emotional well-being of youth even when the laws have operated in the sensitive area of constitutionally protected rights." [New York v. Ferber, 458 U.S. 747, 756–757, 102 S.Ct. 3348, 3354, 73 L.Ed.2d 1113 (1982).] In *Globe Newspaper,* for example, we held that a State's interest in the physical and psychological well-being of a minor victim was sufficiently weighty to justify depriving the press and public of their constitutional right to attend criminal trials, where the trial court makes a case-specific finding that closure of the trial is necessary to protect the welfare of the minor. [Globe Newspaper Co. v. Superior Court, 457 U.S. 596, 608–609, 102 S.Ct. 2613, 2620–2621, 73 L.Ed.2d 248 (1982).] This Term, in Osborne v. Ohio, 495 U.S. ___, 110 S.Ct. 1691, 109 L.Ed.2d 98 (1990), we upheld a state statute that proscribed the possession and viewing of child pornography, reaffirming that " '[i]t is evident beyond the need for elaboration that a State's interest in "safeguarding the physical and psychological well-being of a minor" is "compelling." ' " . . .

We likewise conclude today that a State's interest in the physical and psychological well-being of child abuse victims may be sufficiently important to outweigh, at least in some cases, a defendant's right to face his or her accusers in court. That a significant majority of States has enacted statutes to protect child witnesses from the trauma of giving testimony in child abuse cases attests to the widespread belief in the importance of such a public policy. ...Thirty-seven States, for example, permit the use of videotaped testimony of sexually abused children; 24 States have authorized the use of one-way closed circuit television testimony in child abuse cases; and 8 States authorize the use of a two-way system in which the child-witness is permitted to see the courtroom and the defendant on a video monitor and in which the jury and judge is permitted to view the child during the testimony.

The statute at issue in this case, for example, was specifically intended "to safeguard the physical and psychological well-being of child victims by avoiding, or at least minimizing, the emotional trauma produced by testifying." Wildermuth v. State, 310 Md. 496, 518, 530 A.2d 275, 286 (1987). The *Wildermuth* court noted:

> " ... This would both protect the child and enhance the public interest by encouraging effective prosecution of the alleged abuser." Id., at 517, 530 A.2d, at 285.

Given the State's traditional and " 'transcendent interest in protecting the welfare of children,' " [Ginsberg v. New York, 390 U.S. 629, 640, 88 S.Ct. 1274, 1281, 20 L.Ed.2d 195 (1968)] and buttressed by the growing body of academic literature documenting the psychological trauma suffered by child abuse victims who must testify in court, ... we will not second-guess the considered judgment of the Maryland Legislature regarding the importance of its interest in protecting child abuse victims from the emotional trauma of testifying. Accordingly, we hold that, if the State makes an adequate showing of necessity, the state interest in protecting child witnesses from the trauma of testifying in a child abuse case is sufficiently important to justify the use of a special procedure that permits a child witness in such cases to testify at trial against a defendant in the absence of face-to-face confrontation with the defendant.

The requisite finding of necessity must of course be a case-specific one: the trial court must hear evidence and determine whether use of the one-way closed circuit television procedure is necessary to protect the welfare of the particular child witness who seeks to testify. ...The trial court must also find that the child witness would be traumatized, not by the courtroom generally, but by the presence of the defendant. ...Denial of face-to-face confrontation is not needed to further the state interest in protecting the child witness from trauma unless it is the presence of the defendant that causes the trauma. In other words, if the state interest were merely the interest in protecting child witnesses from courtroom trauma generally, denial of face-to-face confrontation would be unnecessary because the child could be permitted to testify in less intimidating surroundings, albeit with the defendant present. Finally, the trial court must find that the emotional distress suffered by the child witness in the presence of the defendant is more than *de minimis*, i.e., more than "mere nervousness or excitement or some reluctance to testify," *Wildermuth*, 310 Md., at 524, 530 A.2d, at 289; see also State v. Mannion, 19 Utah 505, 511–512, 57 P. 542, 543–544 (1899). We need not decide the minimum showing of emotional trauma required for use of the special procedure, however, because the Maryland statute, which requires a determination that the child witness will suffer "serious emotional distress such that the child cannot reasonably communicate," § 9–102(a)(1)(ii), clearly suffices to meet constitutional standards.

To be sure, face-to-face confrontation may be said to cause trauma for the very purpose of eliciting truth, cf. *Coy,* supra, 487 U.S., at 1019–1020, 108 S.Ct., at 2802–03, but we think that the use of Maryland's special procedure, where necessary to further the important state interest in preventing trauma to child witnesses in child abuse cases, adequately ensures the accuracy of the testimony and preserves the adversary nature of the trial. . . . Indeed, where face-to-face confrontation causes significant emotional distress in a child witness, there is evidence that such confrontation would in fact *disserve* the Confrontation Clause's truth-seeking goal. See, e.g., *Coy,* supra, 487 U.S., at 1032, 108 S.Ct., at 2809 (Blackmun, J., dissenting) (face-to-face confrontation "may so overwhelm the child as to prevent the possibility of effective testimony, thereby undermining the truth-finding function of the trial itself") . . .

In sum, we conclude that where necessary to protect a child witness from trauma that would be caused by testifying in the physical presence of the defendant, at least where such trauma would impair the child's ability to communicate, the Confrontation Clause does not prohibit use of a procedure that, despite the absence of face-to-face confrontation, ensures the reliability of the evidence by subjecting it to rigorous adversarial testing and thereby preserves the essence of effective confrontation. Because there is no dispute that the child witnesses in this case testified under oath, were subject to full cross-examination, and were able to be observed by the judge, jury, and defendant as they testified, we conclude that, to the extent that a proper finding of necessity has been made, the admission of such testimony would be consonant with the Confrontation Clause.

IV

The Maryland Court of Appeals held, as we do today, that although face-to-face confrontation is not an absolute constitutional requirement, it may be abridged only where there is a " 'case-specific finding of necessity.' " 316 Md., at 564, 560 A.2d, at 1126 (quoting *Coy,* supra, 487 U.S., at 1025, 108 S.Ct., at 2805 (concurring opinion)). Given this latter requirement, the Court of Appeals reasoned that "[t]he question of whether a child is unavailable to testify . . . should not be asked in terms of inability to testify in the ordinary courtroom setting, but in the much narrower terms of the witness's inability to testify in the presence of the accused." 316 Md., at 564, 560 A.2d, at 1126 (footnote omitted). "[T]he determinative inquiry required to preclude face-to-face confrontation is the effect of the presence of the defendant on the witness or the witness's testimony." Id., at 565, 560 A.2d, at 1127. The Court of Appeals accordingly concluded that, as a prerequisite to use of the § 9–102 procedure, the Confrontation Clause requires the trial court to make a specific finding that testimony by the child in the courtroom *in the presence of the defendant* would result in the child suffering serious emotional distress such that the child could not reasonably communicate. Id., at 566, 560 A.2d, at 1127. This conclusion, of course, is consistent with our holding today.

In addition, however, the Court of Appeals interpreted our decision in *Coy* to impose two subsidiary requirements. First, the court held that "§ 9–102 ordinarily cannot be invoked unless the child witness initially is questioned (either in or outside the courtroom) in the defendant's presence." Id., at 566, 560 A.2d, at 1127; see also *Wildermuth*, 310 Md., at 523–524, 530 A.2d, at 289 (personal observation by the judge should be the rule rather than the exception). Second, the court asserted that, before using the one-way television procedure, a trial judge must determine whether a child would suffer "severe emotional distress" if he or she were to testify by *two*-way closed circuit television. 316 Md., at 567, 560 A.2d, at 1128.

Reviewing the evidence presented to the trial court in support of the finding required under § 9–102(a)(1)(ii), the Court of Appeals determined that "the finding of necessity required to limit the defendant's right of confrontation through invocation of § 9–102 . . . was not made here." Id., at 570–571, 560 A.2d, at 1129. . . .

* * *

The Court of Appeals appears to have rested its conclusion at least in part on the trial court's failure to observe the children's behavior in the defendant's presence and its failure to explore less restrictive alternatives to the use of the one-way closed circuit television procedure. See id., at 568–571, 560 A.2d, at 1128–1129. Although we think such evidentiary requirements could strengthen the grounds for use of protective measures, we decline to establish, as a matter of federal constitutional law, any such categorical evidentiary prerequisites for the use of the one-way television procedure. The trial court in this case, for example, could well have found, on the basis of the expert testimony before it, that testimony by the child witnesses in the courtroom in the defendant's presence "will result in [each] child suffering serious emotional distress such that the child cannot reasonably communicate," § 9–102(a)(1)(ii). See id., at 568–569, 560 A.2d, at 1128–1129; see also App. 22–25, 39, 41, 43, 44–45, 54–57. So long as a trial court makes such a case-specific finding of necessity, the Confrontation Clause does not prohibit a State from using a one-way closed circuit television procedure for the receipt of testimony by a child witness in a child abuse case. Because the Court of Appeals held that the trial court had not made the requisite finding of necessity under its interpretation of "the high threshold required by [*Coy*] before § 9–102 may be invoked," 316 Md., at 554–555, 560 A.2d, at 1121 (footnote omitted), we cannot be certain whether the Court of Appeals would reach the same conclusion in light of the legal standard we establish today. We therefore vacate the judgment of the Court of Appeals of Maryland and remand the case for further proceedings not inconsistent with this opinion.

It is so ordered.

■ JUSTICE SCALIA, with whom JUSTICE BRENNAN, JUSTICE MARSHALL, and JUSTICE STEVENS join, dissenting.

Seldom has this Court failed so conspicuously to sustain a categorical guarantee of the Constitution against the tide of prevailing current opinion.

The Sixth Amendment provides, with unmistakable clarity, that "[i]n all criminal prosecutions, the accused shall enjoy the right ... to be confronted with the witnesses against him." The purpose of enshrining this protection in the Constitution was to assure that none of the many policy interests from time to time pursued by statutory law could overcome a defendant's right to face his or her accusers in court. ...

Because of this subordination of explicit constitutional text to currently favored public policy, the following scene can be played out in an American courtroom for the first time in two centuries: A father whose young daughter has been given over to the exclusive custody of his estranged wife, or a mother whose young son has been taken into custody by the State's child welfare department, is sentenced to prison for sexual abuse on the basis of testimony by a child the parent has not seen or spoken to for many months; and the guilty verdict is rendered without giving the parent so much as the opportunity to sit in the presence of the child, and to ask, personally or through counsel, "it is really not true, is it, that I—your father (or mother) whom you see before you—did these terrible things?" Perhaps that is a procedure today's society desires; perhaps (though I doubt it) it is even a fair procedure; but it is assuredly not a procedure permitted by the Constitution.

Because the text of the Sixth Amendment is clear, and because the Constitution is meant to protect against, rather than conform to, current "widespread belief," I respectfully dissent.

I

... It is wrong because the Confrontation Clause does not guarantee reliable evidence; it guarantees specific trial procedures that were thought to assure reliable evidence, undeniably among which was "face-to-face" confrontation. Whatever else it may mean in addition, the defendant's constitutional right "to be confronted with the witnesses against him" means, always and everywhere, at least what it explicitly says: the " 'right to meet face to face all those who appear and give evidence at trial.' " Coy v. Iowa, 487 U.S. 1012, 1016, 108 S.Ct. 2798, 2800, 101 L.Ed.2d 857 (1988), quoting California v. Green, 399 U.S. 149, 175, 90 S.Ct. 1930, 1943–44, 26 L.Ed.2d 489 (1970) (Harlan, J. concurring).

The Court supports its antitextual conclusion by cobbling together scraps of dicta from various cases that have no bearing here. It will suffice to discuss one of them, since they are all of a kind: Quoting Ohio v. Roberts, 448 U.S. 56, 63, 100 S.Ct. 2531, 2537, 65 L.Ed.2d 597 (1980), the Court says that "[i]n sum, our precedents establish that 'the Confrontation Clause reflects a *preference* for face-to-face confrontation at trial,' " ante, (emphasis added by the Court). But *Roberts,* and all the other "precedents" the Court enlists to prove the implausible, dealt with the *implications* of the Confrontation Clause, and not its literal, unavoidable text. When *Roberts* said that the Clause merely "reflects a preference for face-to-face confrontation at trial," what it had in mind as the nonpreferred alternative was not (as the Court implies) the appearance of a witness at trial without confronting the defendant. That has been, until today, not merely "nonpreferred" but utterly unheard-of. What *Roberts* had in mind was the receipt of *other-than-first-hand testimony* from witnesses at trial—that is, witnesses' recounting of hearsay statements by absent parties who, *since they did not appear at trial,* did not have to endure face-to-face confrontation. Rejecting that, I agree, was merely giving effect to an evident constitutional preference; there are, after all, many exceptions to the Confrontation Clause's hearsay rule. But that the defendant should be confronted by the witnesses who appear at trial is not a preference "reflected" by the Confrontation Clause; it is a constitutional right unqualifiedly guaranteed.

The Court claims that its interpretation of the Confrontation Clause "is consistent with our cases holding that other Sixth Amendment rights must also be interpreted in the context of the necessities of trial and the adversary process." Ante, at 3165–3166. I disagree. It is true enough that the "necessities of trial and the adversary process" limit the *manner* in which Sixth Amendment rights may be exercised, and limit the *scope* of Sixth Amendment guarantees to the extent that scope is textually indeterminate. Thus (to describe the cases the Court cites): The right to confront is not the right to confront in a manner that disrupts the trial. Illinois v. Allen, 397 U.S. 337, 90 S.Ct. 1057, 25 L.Ed.2d 353 (1970). The right "to have compulsory process for obtaining witnesses" is not the right to call witnesses in a manner that violates fair and orderly procedures. Taylor v. Illinois, 484 U.S. 400, 108 S.Ct. 646, 98 L.Ed.2d 798 (1988). The scope of the right "to have the assistance of counsel" does not include consultation with counsel at all times during the trial. Perry v. Leeke, 488 U.S. 272, 109 S.Ct. 594, 102 L.Ed.2d 624 (1989). The scope of the right to cross-examine does not include access to the State's investigative files. Pennsylvania v. Ritchie, 480 U.S. 39, 107 S.Ct. 989, 94 L.Ed.2d 40 (1987). But we are not talking here about denying expansive scope to a Sixth Amendment provision whose scope for the purpose at issue is textually unclear; "to confront" plainly means to encounter face-to-face, whatever else it may mean in addition. And we are not talking about the manner of arranging that face-to-face encounter, but about whether it shall occur at all. The "necessities of trial and the adversary process" are irrelevant here, since they cannot alter the constitutional text.

II

Much of the Court's opinion consists of applying to this case the mode of analysis we have used in the admission of hearsay evidence. The Sixth Amendment does not literally contain a prohibition upon such evidence, since it guarantees the defendant only the right to confront "the witnesses against him." ... The phrase obviously refers to those who give testimony against the defendant at trial. We have nonetheless found implicit in the Confrontation Clause some limitation upon hearsay evidence, since otherwise the Government could subvert the confrontation right by putting on witnesses who know nothing except what an absent declarant said. And in determining the scope of that implicit limitation, we have focused upon whether the reliability of the hearsay statements (which are not *expressly* excluded by the Confrontation Clause) "is otherwise assured." Ante. The same test cannot be applied, however, to permit what is explicitly forbidden by the constitutional text; there is simply no room for interpretation with regard to "the irreducible literal meaning of the Clause." *Coy*, supra, 487 U.S., at 1020–1021, 108 S.Ct., at 2803.

Some of the Court's analysis seems to suggest that the children's testimony here was itself hearsay of the sort permissible under our Confrontation Clause cases. ... "In the usual case ..., the prosecution must either produce or demonstrate the unavailability of, the declarant whose statement it wishes to use against the defendant." Ohio v. Roberts, 448 U.S., at 65, 100 S.Ct., at 2538. We have permitted a few exceptions to this general rule—e.g., for co-conspirators' statements, whose effect cannot be replicated by live testimony because they "derive [their] significance from the circumstances in which [they were] made," United States v. Inadi, 475 U.S. 387, 395, 106 S.Ct. 1121, 1126, 89 L.Ed.2d 390 (1986). "Live" closed-circuit television testimony, however—if it can be called hearsay at all—is surely an example of hearsay as "a weaker substitute for live testimony," id., at 394, 106 S.Ct., at 1126, which can be employed only when the genuine article is unavailable. "When two versions of the same evidence are available, longstanding principles of the law of hearsay, applicable as well to Confrontation Clause analysis, favor the better evidence." Ibid. ...

The Court's test today requires unavailability only in the sense that the child is unable to testify in the presence of the defendant. That cannot possibly be the relevant sense. If unconfronted testimony is admissible hearsay when the witness is unable to confront the defendant, then presumably there are other categories of admissible hearsay consisting of unsworn testimony when the witness is unable to risk perjury, uncross-examined testimony when the witness is unable to undergo hostile questioning, etc. California v. Green, 399 U.S. 149, 90 S.Ct. 1930, 26 L.Ed.2d 489 (1970), is not precedent for such a silly system. That case held that the Confrontation Clause does not bar admission of prior testimony when the declarant is sworn as a witness but refuses to answer. But in *Green*, as in most cases of refusal, we could not know *why* the declarant refused to testify. Here, by contrast, we know that it is precisely because the child is unwilling to testify in the presence of the defendant. That unwillingness cannot be a valid excuse under the Confrontation Clause, whose very object is to place the witness under the sometimes hostile glare of the defendant. ...To say that a defendant loses his right to confront a witness when that would cause the witness not to testify is rather like saying that the defendant loses his right to counsel when counsel would save him, or his right to subpoena witnesses when they would exculpate him, or his right not to give testimony against himself when that would prove him guilty.

III

The Court characterizes the State's interest which "outweigh[s]" the explicit text of the Constitution as an "interest in the physical and psychological well-being of child abuse victims," ante, at 3167, an "interest in protecting" such victims "from the emotional trauma of testifying," ante, at 3169. That is not so. A child who meets the Maryland statute's requirement of suffering such "serious emotional distress" from confrontation that he "cannot reasonably communicate" would seem entirely safe. Why would a prosecutor want to call a witness who cannot reasonably communicate? And if he did, it would be the State's own fault. Protection of the child's interest—as far as the Confrontation Clause is concerned[12]—is entirely within Maryland's control. The State's interest here is in fact no more and no less than what the State's interest always is when it seeks to get a class of evidence admitted in criminal proceedings: more convictions of guilty defendants. That is not an unworthy interest, but it should not be dressed up as a humanitarian one.

And the interest on the other side is also what it usually is when the State seeks to get a new class of evidence admitted: fewer convictions of innocent defendants—specifically, in the present context, innocent defendants accused of particularly heinous crimes. The "special" reasons that exist for suspending one of the usual guarantees of reliability in the case of children's testimony are perhaps matched by "special" reasons for being particularly insistent upon it in the case of children's testimony. Some studies show that children are substantially more vulnerable to suggestion than adults, and often unable to separate recollected fantasy (or suggestion) from reality. . . . The injustice their erroneous testimony can produce is evidenced by the tragic Scott County investigations of 1983–1984, which disrupted the lives of many (as far as we know) innocent people in the small town of Jordan, Minnesota. At one stage those investigations were pursuing allegations by at least eight children of multiple murders, but the prosecutions actually initiated charged only sexual abuse. Specifically, 24 adults were charged with molesting 37 children. In the course of the investigations, 25 children were placed in foster homes. Of the 24 indicted defendants, one pleaded guilty, two were acquitted at trial, and the charges against the remaining 21 were voluntarily dismissed. . . . There is no doubt that some sexual abuse took place in Jordan; but there is no reason to believe it was as widespread as charged. A report by the Minnesota Attorney General's office, based on inquiries conducted by the Minnesota Bureau of Criminal Apprehension and the Federal Bureau of Investigation, concluded that there was an "absence of credible testimony and [a] lack of significant corroboration" to support reinstitution of sex-abuse charges, and "no credible evidence of murders." H. Humphrey, report on Scott County Investigation 8, 7 (1985). . . . The value of the confrontation right in guarding against a child's distorted or coerced recollections is dramatically evident with respect to one of the misguided investigative techniques the report cited: some children were told by their foster parents that reunion with their real parents would be hastened by "admission" of their parents' abuse. Id., at 9. Is it difficult to imagine how unconvincing such a testimonial admission might be to a jury that witnessed the child's delight at seeing his parents in the courtroom? Or how devastating it might be if, pursuant to a psychiatric evaluation that "trauma would impair the child's ability to communicate" in front of his parents, the child were permitted to tell his story to the jury on closed-circuit television?

---

12. A different situation would be presented if the defendant sought to call the child. In that event, the State's refusal to compel the child to appear, or its insistence upon a procedure such as that set forth in the Maryland statute as a condition of its compelling him to do so, would call into question—initially, at least, and perhaps exclusively—the scope of the defendant's Sixth Amendment right "to have compulsory process for obtaining witnesses in his favor."

In the last analysis, however, this debate is not an appropriate one. I have no need to defend the value of confrontation, because the Court has no authority to question it. It is not within our charge to speculate that, "where face-to-face confrontation causes significant emotional distress in a child witness," confrontation might "in fact *disserve* the Confrontation Clause's truth-seeking goal." Ante. If so, that is a defect in the Constitution—which should be amended by the procedures provided for such an eventuality, but cannot be corrected by judicial pronouncement that it is archaic, contrary to "widespread belief" and thus null and void. For good or bad, the Sixth Amendment requires confrontation, and we are not at liberty to ignore it. . . .

The Court today has applied "interest-balancing" analysis where the text of the Constitution simply does not permit it. We are not free to conduct a cost-benefit analysis of clear and explicit constitutional guarantees, and then to adjust their meaning to comport with our findings. The Court has convincingly proved that the Maryland procedure serves a valid interest, and gives the defendant virtually everything the Confrontation Clause guarantees (everything, that is, except confrontation). I am persuaded, therefore, that the Maryland procedure is virtually constitutional. Since it is not, however, actually constitutional I would affirm the judgment of the Maryland Court of Appeals reversing the judgment of conviction.

NOTES

1. **Accusatory confessions.** In Bruton v. United States, 391 U.S. 123, 88 S.Ct. 1620, 20 L.Ed.2d 476, (1968), there was a joint trial of the petitioner and a codefendant upon a charge of armed postal robbery. A postal inspector testified that the codefendant, Evans, had confessed to him that Evans and the petitioner had committed the robbery. This evidence was, concededly, wholly inadmissible against the petitioner. Evans did not testify. Although the trial judge instructed the jury to disregard the evidence of Evans' confession in considering the question of the petitioner's guilt, the Supreme Court reversed the petitioner's conviction. The primary focus of the Court's opinion in *Bruton* was upon the issue of whether the jury in the circumstances presented could reasonably be expected to have followed the trial judge's instructions. The Court found that the risk of prejudice in petitioner's case was unacceptable when "the powerfully incriminating extrajudicial statements of a codefendant, who stands accused side-by-side with the defendant, are deliberately spread before the jury in a joint trial." 391 U.S. at 135–36, 88 S.Ct. at 1628, 20 L.Ed.2d 485. Accordingly, the Court held that "in the context of a joint trial we cannot accept limiting instructions as an adequate substitute for petitioner's constitutional right of cross-examination." 391 U.S. at 137, 88 S.Ct. at 1628, 20 L.Ed.2d at 485.

2. **Interlocking confessions.** Lee v. Illinois, 476 U.S. 530, 106 S.Ct. 2056, 90 L.Ed.2d 514 (1986) also involved a co-defendant's confession. Lee and her boyfriend, Thomas, were jointly tried for two murders. Lee had confessed to police that after her boyfriend had killed one of the persons she confronted the other, her aunt, who brandished a knife, whereupon Lee stabbed her to death. Thomas' confession was similar to Lee's but added that they had earlier planned both killings. Both were tried before the court without a jury, and neither testified. Both confessions were introduced into evidence. Lee took the position that, in accordance with her confession, she had nothing to do with the death of the second person and that with respect to her aunt's death, it was either self-defense or at least voluntary man-

slaughter upon a sudden provocation. The trial court rejected all these contentions, basing his conclusions explicitly upon the accusations in Thomas' statement as to Lee's knowledge and behavior. She was convicted of two counts of murder and upon appeal the Illinois Court of Appeals affirmed on the ground that her confession and Thomas' were so similar—"interlocking"—that her right of confrontation was not violated by the use against her of Thomas' statements. The United States Supreme Court, in an opinion by Justice Brennan, reversed. The basic Confrontation Clause principle is that "when one person accuses another of a crime under circumstances in which the declarant stands to gain by inculpating another, the accusation is presumptively suspect and must be subjected to the scrutiny of cross-examination." 476 U.S. at 541, 106 S.Ct. at 2062, 90 L.Ed.2d at 526. The fact that the confessions "interlock" at certain points does not change the situation:

> [A] codefendant's confession is presumptively unreliable as to the passages detailing the defendant's conduct or culpability because those passages may well be the product of the codefendant's desire to shift or spread blame, curry favor, avenge himself, or divert attention to another. If those portions of the codefendant's purportedly "interlocking" statement which bear to any significant degree on the defendant's participation in the crime are not thoroughly substantiated by the defendant's own confession, the admission of the statement poses too serious a threat to the accuracy of the verdict to be countenanced by the Sixth Amendment.

476 U.S. at 545, 106 S.Ct. at 2064, 90 L.Ed.2d at 529. The Court concluded that there were not sufficient indicia of reliability from the circumstances surrounding the making of the confession or its "interlocking" character to overcome the presumption against admission. Justice Blackmun, joined by Chief Justice Burger, Justice Powell and Justice Rehnquist, dissented on the ground that there were indicia of reliability of Thomas' statement, primarily that his statement was adverse to his own penal interest. Indeed, his own statement tended to incriminate himself more than did the statement of Lee. Further, there was corroboration for the statement, principally Lee's confession. Although Lee's confession was not identical to Thomas', it did not contradict it either, that is, Lee in her statement did not deny that the planning activity recounted in Thomas' statement occurred.

The Court again addressed the question of interlocking confessions in Cruz v. New York, 481 U.S. 186, 107 S.Ct. 1714, 95 L.Ed.2d 162 (1987). Eulogio Cruz and his brother, Benjamin, were on trial for killing a person during a gas station robbery. At the trial, Benjamin's videotaped confession was admitted, which incriminated Eulogio as well as himself. A state's witness testified that both Eulogio and Benjamin confessed to him before they were apprehended that they had killed the gas station attendant. This testimony was impeached by evidence that the witness believed that Eulogio and Benjamin had killed his brother and thus presented his testimony in revenge. The trial court instructed the jury that neither defendant's confession could be used against the other. Eulogio's conviction was affirmed by the New York Court of Appeals, but the United States Supreme Court, in an opinion by Justice Scalia, reversed. The Court rejected the reasoning of previous plurality opinions that the devastating effects of a codefendant's confession, as condemned by *Bruton*, see note 1, are not present when the defendant has also confessed, the so-called interlocking confessions exception to *Bruton:*

> "[I]nterlocking" bears a positively inverse relationship to devastation. A codefendant's confession will be relatively harmless if the incriminating story it tells is different from that which the defendant himself is alleged to have told, but enormously damaging if it confirms, in all essential respects, the defendant's alleged confession. It might be otherwise if the defendant were *standing by* his confession, in which case it could be said that the codefendant's confession does

no more than support the defendant's very own case. But in the real world of criminal litigation, the defendant is seeking to *avoid* his confession—on the ground that it was not accurately reported, or that it was not really true when made. ... Quite obviously, what the "interlocking" nature of the codefendant's confession pertains to is not its *harmfulness* but rather its *reliability:* If it confirms essentially the same facts as the defendant's own confession it is more likely to be true. Its reliability, however, may be relevant to whether the confession should (despite the lack of opportunity for cross-examination) be *admitted as evidence* against the defendant, ... but cannot conceivably be relevant to whether, assuming it cannot be admitted, the jury is likely to obey the instruction to disregard it, or the jury's failure to obey is likely to be inconsequential. The law cannot command respect if such an inexplicable exception to a supposed constitutional imperative is adopted. Having decided *Bruton,* we must face the honest consequences of what it holds.

481 U.S. at 192–93, 107 S.Ct. at 1718–19, 95 L.Ed.2d at 171. The Court held that

where a nontestifying codefendant's confession incriminating the defendant is not directly admissible against the defendant, ... the Confrontation Clause bars its admission at their joint trial, even if the jury is instructed not to consider it against the defendant, and even if the defendant's own confession is admitted against him. Of course, the defendant's confession may be considered at trial in assessing whether his codefendant's statements are supported by sufficient "indicia of reliability" to be directly admissible against him [under Lee v. Illinois] and may be considered on appeal in assessing whether any Confrontation Clause violation was harmless.

481 U.S. at 193–94, 107 S.Ct. at 1719, 95 L.Ed.2d at 172. Justice White, joined by The Chief Justice, and Justices Powell and O'Connor, dissented.

3. **Testimony at a prior hearing.** In Ohio v. Roberts, 448 U.S. 56, 100 S.Ct. 2531, 65 L.Ed.2d 597 (1980), Roberts was arrested for forgery of a check in the name of Bernard Isaacs. At his preliminary examination, he called as a defense witness Anita Isaacs, daughter of the complainant, in an effort to show that she had given him the checkbook with the assurance that it was permissible for him to use it. She denied doing so. Roberts was indicted and his case was set for trial on four different dates. Anita failed to respond to the court's subpoena on each occasion. On the fifth try, the case was presented to a jury and Roberts testified that he had been given permission by Anita to use the checkbook. In rebuttal, the state was permitted to read a transcript of Anita's preliminary examination testimony to the jury over respondent's objection that his rights of confrontation were being violated. Anita's mother testified at the trial that Anita had run away from home shortly after the preliminary examination and she did not know her whereabouts. The Ohio Supreme Court reversed the conviction on the ground that Roberts' confrontation rights were violated. The Supreme Court, by a vote of 6–3, reversed. Justice Blackmun's opinion for the Court attempted to distill from the Court's earlier decisions a standard for determining when admission of hearsay violates the Sixth Amendment:

[W]hen a hearsay declarant is not present for cross-examination at trial, the Confrontation Clause normally requires a showing that he is unavailable. Even then, his statement is admissible only if it bears adequate "indicia of reliability." Reliability can be inferred without more in a case where the evidence falls within a firmly rooted hearsay exception. In other cases, the evidence must be excluded, at least absent a showing of particularized guarantees of trustworthiness.

448 U.S. at 66, 100 S.Ct. at 2539, 65 L.Ed.2d at 608. Here, the Court concluded that Anita's testimony fell within the traditional hearsay exception for testimony at a

prior hearing. Since defense counsel had subjected her to the equivalent of full cross examination, the Court found no need to consider whether the mere unexercised opportunity for cross examination (or *de minimis* questioning) at the prior hearing would suffice. Since the case came within a "firmly rooted hearsay exception," no particularized search for "indicia of reliability" was necessary. Moreover, the evidence of the state's efforts to locate Anita and the absence of knowledge concerning her location sufficed to establish unavailability. Justice Brennan, joined by Justices Marshall and Stevens, dissented on the ground that the state had failed to adequately follow up certain leads to Anita's location and therefore had not made an adequate showing of unavailability.

4. **Statements of a co-conspirator.** In United States v. Inadi, 475 U.S. 387, 106 S.Ct. 1121, 89 L.Ed.2d 390 (1986), respondent was convicted of drug conspiracy in a trial in which the recorded statements of a co-conspirator were admitted into evidence over his objection that the Confrontation Clause as interpreted in Ohio v. Roberts required a showing of unavailability of the declarant as a predicate to admission. The Court of Appeals reversed the conviction on that ground but the United States Supreme Court, in an opinion by Justice Powell, reversed the Court of Appeals. *Roberts* dealt with the admissibility of prior testimony and the requirement of unavailability of the witness is a traditional and sound requirement for that category of evidence for if the witness is available then the jury ought to hear his testimony from the witness stand. With respect to co-conspirator's statements, however, their evidentiary value derives from the fact that they are made in furtherance of the conspiracy:

> When the Government—as here—offers the statement of one drug dealer to another in furtherance of an illegal conspiracy, the statement often will derive its significance from the circumstances in which it was made. Conspirators are likely to speak differently when talking to each other in furtherance of their illegal aims than when testifying on the witness stand.

475 U.S. at 395, 106 S.Ct. at 1126, 89 L.Ed.2d at 398. Justice Marshall, joined by Justice Brennan, dissented.

5. **Statements to a physician by a child.** In a companion case to Maryland v. Craig, also involving child abuse, Idaho v. Wright, 497 U.S. 805, 110 S.Ct. 3139, 111 L.Ed.2d 638 (1990), the Court considered whether there were sufficient indicia of reliability in hearsay statements offered by the examining physician. Respondent Wright was charged with sexual abuse of her two daughters, 5½ and 2½ years old. Dr. Jambura, an experienced pediatrician, found physical evidence of sexual abuse. At trial, the judge determined the younger girl was not capable of communicating to the jury. The judge then admitted Dr. Jambura's testimony concerning statements the child had made in an interview with him. This ruling was based on Idaho's "residual hearsay exception" under which hearsay was admissible despite witness availability so long as it met a three-part test for trustworthiness: (A) offered as evidence of a material fact; (B) more probative than any other evidence which can be procured through reasonable efforts; and (C) in the interests of justice. Respondent was convicted on both counts. She appealed the conviction involving the younger daughter. The Idaho Supreme Court reversed, finding Dr. Jambura's testimony inadmissible because his interview technique lacked adequate procedural safeguards: the interview was not recorded; the doctor asked "blatantly leading questions"; and he had "a preconceived idea of what the child should be disclosing."

The United States Supreme Court in an opinion by Justice O'Connor affirmed. The Court assumed for purposes of the opinion that the child was an "unavailable witness" and proceeded to the "indicia of reliability" test from Ohio v. Roberts, supra. Because no "firmly rooted hearsay exception" applied, the inquiry focused on the other *Roberts* alternative—whether the statements were supported by "a showing of particularized guarantees of trustworthiness." In holding that this requirement was not met, the Court held:

> We think the "particularized guarantees of trustworthiness" required for admission under the Confrontation Clause must [like the firmly rooted hearsay exceptions] be drawn from the totality of circumstances that surround the making of the statement . . . [And likewise the] evidence admitted . . . must . . . be so trustworthy that adversarial testing would add little to its reliability . . . Thus, unless an affirmative reason, arising from the circumstances in which the statement was made, provides a basis for rebutting the presumption that a hearsay statement is not worthy of reliance at trial, the Confrontation Clause requires exclusion of the out-of-court statement.

497 U.S. at 820–21, 110 S.Ct. at 3149–50, 111 L.Ed.2d at 655–56.

The Court announced that consideration of corroborating evidence for this analysis would improperly bootstrap and frustrate the rule that the hearsay be so reliable as to render cross-examination "of marginal utility." The majority concluded that corroboration more properly would go to harmless error analysis if at all. The Court concluded:

> Of the factors the trial court found relevant, only two relate to circumstances surrounding the making of the statements: whether the child had a motive to "make up a story of this nature," and whether, given the child's age, the statements are of the type "that one would expect a child to fabricate." . . . The other factors . . . such as the . . . physical evidence of abuse, the opportunity of the respondent to commit the offense, and the older daughter's corroborating identification . . . are irrelevant . . .

> We think the Supreme Court of Idaho properly focused on the presumptive unreliability of the out-of-court statements and on the suggestive manner in which Dr. Jambura conducted the interview. Viewing the totality of the circumstances . . . we agree with the court below that the State has failed to show that the younger daughter's incriminating statements to the pediatrician possessed sufficient "particularized guarantees of trustworthiness" under the Confrontation Clause to overcome that presumption.

497 U.S. at 826–27, 110 S.Ct. at 3152–53, 111 L.Ed.2d at 659–60.

Justice Kennedy, joined by the Chief Justice and Justices White and Blackmun, dissented:

> The Court's apparent misgivings about the weight to be given corroborating evidence may or may not be correct, but those misgivings do not justify wholesale elimination of this evidence from consideration, in derogation of an overwhelming judicial and legislative consensus to the contrary.

497 U.S. at 829–30, 110 S.Ct. at 3154, 111 L.Ed.2d at 661–62.

Justice Kennedy insisted that "[t]he Court in *Lee* was unanimous in its recognition of corroboration as a legitimate indicator of reliability . . . "and that the Court in *Cruz* had unequivocally rejected the suggestion that corroboration goes more to harmless error than to reliability when it said:

> "Quite obviously, what the 'interlocking' nature of the codefendant's confession pertains to is not its *harmfulness* but rather its *reliability*: If it confirms essentially the same facts as the defendant's own confession it is more likely to be true." Cruz v. New York, 481 U.S. 186, 192, 1j07 S.Ct. 1714, 1719, 95 L.Ed.2d 162 (1987) (emphasis in original).

497 U.S. at 832, 110 S.Ct. at 3155, 111 L.Ed.2d at 6630.

6. **Outcry evidence.** The Petitioner in White v. Illinois, 502 U.S. 346, 112 S.Ct. 736, 116 L.Ed.2d 848 (1992) was seen exiting the bedroom of a four-year old girl by her babysitter who was awakened by the girl's screams. The babysitter recognized the petitioner as a friend of the girl's mother. The girl told the babysitter that petitioner had engaged in sexual contact with her. About 30 minutes later, she told her mother the same story and about 45 minutes after the alleged assault, she told the same story to a police officer. About 4 hours after the alleged assault she told the same story first to a nurse and then to a doctor at a local hospital.

Statements by the babysitter, mother, police officer, nurse and doctor were admitted into evidence over hearsay and confrontation objections. The girl was called as a witness but did not testify. Petitioner was convicted of various offenses. The Supreme Court, in an opinion by The Chief Justice, affirmed the convictions.

The Court rejected as coming too late in history the *amicus curiae* arguments of the United States Government that the Confrontation Clause should be restricted to efforts to prove criminal charges by ex parte affidavits, that is, "where the circumstances surrounding the out-of-court statement's utterance suggest that the statement has been made for the principal purpose of accusing or incriminating the defendant." In this case, the girl's statements to her babysitter, mother and the police officer came within the traditional exception to the hearsay rule for spontaneous declarations while the last two statements came within the traditional exception for statements made in the course of receiving medical treatment:

> A statement that has been offered in a moment of excitement—without the opportunity to reflect on the consequences of one's exclamation—may justifiably carry more weight with a trier of fact than a similar statement offered in the relative calm of the courtroom. Similarly, a statement made in the course of procuring medical services, where the declarant knows that a false statement may cause misdiagnosis or mistreatment, carries special guarantees of credibility that a trier of fact may not think replicated by courtroom testimony.

502 U.S. at 356, 112 S.Ct. at 742–43, 116 L.Ed.2d at 859. The Court concluded that "where proffered hearsay has sufficient guarantees of reliability to come within a firmly rooted exception to the hearsay rule, the Confrontation Clause is satisfied." 502 U.S. at 356, 112 S.Ct. at 743, 116 L.Ed.2d at 859.

Contrary to petitioner's contention, the Court said that Coy v. Iowa and Maryland v. Craig do not require any showing of necessity for the statements at issue to be admitted in this case. Those cases "involved only the question of what *in-court* procedures are constitutionally required to guarantee a defendant's confrontation right once a witness is testifying. Such a question is quite separate from that of what requirements the Confrontation Clause imposes as a predicate for the introduction of out-of-court declarations." 502 U.S. at 358, 112 S.Ct. at 743–44, 116 L.Ed.2d at 860.

Justice Thomas, joined by Justice Scalia, concurred in the judgment. He would hold that

> the Confrontation Clause is implicated by extrajudicial statements only insofar as they are contained in formalized testimonial materials, such as affidavits, depositions, prior testimony, or confessions. It was this discrete category of testimonial materials that was historically abused by prosecutors as a means to depriving criminal defendants of the benefit of the adversary process, and under this approach, the Confrontation Clause would not be construed to extend beyond the historical evil to which it was directed.

502 U.S. at 365, 112 S.Ct. at 747, 116 L.Ed.2d at 865.

7. **Right of defendant to be present during trial.** Included within a defendant's right of confrontation is the right to be present in the courtroom. Under what circumstances can a constitutionally-valid conviction result from a trial which the defendant declines to attend? In Taylor v. United States, 414 U.S. 17, 94 S.Ct. 194, 38 L.Ed.2d 174 (1973) (per curiam), the defendant Taylor, after a noon recess, failed to return to his trial for sale of cocaine. Relying upon the then-effective provisions of Fed.R.Crim.P. 43, that in a noncapital case "the defendant's voluntary absence after the trial has been commenced in his presence shall not prevent continuing the trial to and including the return of the verdict," the trial judge directed the trial to continue. The jury was admonished that no inference of guilt could be drawn from his absence; it returned a verdict of guilty. After being arrested, Taylor was sentenced. He challenged his conviction on the ground that it violated his Sixth Amendment right to confront witnesses. The Supreme Court found no merit in the challenge. Rule 43, it noted, reflects a long-recognized rule that voluntary absence from a trial operates as a waiver of the right to be present and permits the court to proceed as if the defendant were present. Taylor never challenged the voluntariness of his absence; both the trial court and the lower appellate court had concluded that his absence was voluntary. Taylor, however, urged that he could lose his Sixth Amendment confrontation right only by a waiver constituting an intentional relinquishment of a known right, and that no such waiver could be found in the absence of evidence that he knew or had been expressly warned that trial would continue if he were to be absent. The Court rejected this, noting that Taylor was questioned at sentencing about his flight and never contended that he was unaware that if he fled the trial would continue. Further, the Court reasoned:

> The right at issue is the right to be present, and the question becomes whether that right was effectively waived by [Taylor's] voluntary absence.
>
> It is wholly incredible to suggest that [Taylor] ... entertained any doubts about his right to be present at every stage of the trial. It seems equally incredible to us, as it did to the Court of Appeals, "that a defendant who flees from a courtroom in the midst of a trial—where judge, jury, witnesses and lawyers are present and ready to continue—would not know that as a consequence the trial could continue in his absence."

414 U.S. at 20, 94 S.Ct. at 196, 38 L.Ed.2d at 177–78. Does this mean that if, on the facts of another case, a trial judge was convinced that a defendant tried *in absentia* under the rule was actually unaware that trial would continue in his absence, the continuation of that trial was in violation of the defendant's Sixth Amendment rights?

The relevant portions of Rule 43 of the Federal Rules of Criminal Procedure now provide:

> (a) Presence Required. The defendant shall be present at the arraignment, at the time of the plea, at every stage of the trial including the impaneling of the jury and the return of the verdict, and at the imposition of sentence, except as otherwise provided by this rule.
>
> (b) Continued Presence Not Required. The further progress of the trial to and including the return of the verdict, and the imposition of sentence, will not be prevented and the defendant will be considered to have waived the right to be present whenever a defendant, initially present at trial, or having pleaded guilty or nolo contendere,
>
> > (1) is voluntarily absent after the trial has commenced (whether or not the defendant has been informed by the court of the obligation to remain during the trial),

(2) in a noncapital case, is voluntarily absent at the imposition of sentence, or

(3) after being warned by the court that disruptive conduct will cause the removal of the defendant from the courtroom, persists in conduct which is such as to justify exclusion from the courtroom.

Whether a defendant's failure to appear at trial for reasons of financial hardship amounts to a knowing and intelligent waiver of the right to be present is "primarily a factual issue" for the trial court, noted the Supreme Court in a per curiam dismissal of a writ of certiorari in Tacon v. Arizona, 410 U.S. 351, 352, 35 S.Ct. 998, 999, 35 L.Ed.2d 346, 348 (1973).

8. **Right to be present when trial begins.** Whether a federal criminal trial can begin under Rule 43 if the accused does not appear was presented in Crosby v. United States, 506 U.S. 255, 113 S.Ct. 748, 122 L.Ed.2d 25 (1993). Crosby failed to appear for trial, although his attorney and three codefendants were present. After several days of searching failed to turn him up, the district judge began trial without him. He was convicted. Six months later he was apprehended in another state and brought back to the trial court for sentencing. Under Rule 43, the Supreme Court ruled, the trial court erred in beginning Crosby's trial without him present. "The language, history, and logic of Rule 43," it reasoned, "support a straightforward interpretation that prohibits the trial *in absentia* of a defendant who is not present at the beginning of trial." In explanation, Justice Blackmun offered for the Court:

[W]e do not find the distinction between pretrial and midtrial flight so far-fetched as to convince us that Rule 43 cannot mean what it says. As a general matter, the costs of suspending a proceeding already under way will be greater than the cost of postponing a trial not yet begun. If a clear line is to be drawn marking the point at which the costs of delay are likely to outweigh the interests of the defendant and society in having the defendant present, the commencement of trial is at least a plausible place at which to draw that line. . . .

There are additional practical reasons for distinguishing between flight before and flight during a trial. * * * [T]he Rule treats midtrial flight as a knowing and voluntary waiver of the right to be present. Whether or not the right constitutionally may be waived in other circumstances—and we express no opinion here on that subject—the defendant's initial presence serves to assure that any waiver is indeed knowing. "Since the notion that trial may be commenced in absentia still seems to shock most lawyers, it would hardly seem appropriate to impute knowledge that this will occur to their clients." Starkey, Trial in Absentia, 54 N.Y.St.B.J. 30, 34, n. 28 (1982). It is unlikely, on the other hand, " 'that a defendant who flees from a courtroom in the midst of a trial—where judge, jury, witnesses and lawyers are present and ready to continue—would not know that as a consequence the trial could continue in his absence.' " Taylor v. United States, 414 U.S. 17, 20, 94 S.Ct. 194, 196, 38 L.Ed.2d 174 (1973), quoting from Chief Judge Coffin's opinion, 478 F.2d 689, 691 (C.A.1 1973), for the Court of Appeals in that case. Moreover, a rule that allows an ongoing trial to continue when a defendant disappears deprives the defendant of the option of gambling on an acquittal knowing that he can terminate the trial if it seems that the verdict will go against him—an option that might otherwise appear preferable to the costly, perhaps unnecessary, path of becoming a fugitive from the outset.

506 U.S. at 261–62, 113 S.Ct. at 752–53, 122 L.Ed.2d at 32. Having thus resolved the case, the Court emphasized that it was not reaching Crosby's claim that his trial *in absentia* was prohibited by the United States Constitution. 506 U.S. at 262, 113 S.Ct. at 753, 122 L.Ed.2d at 33.

10. **Presence during capital trials.** Is the Sixth Amendment rule any different in capital cases? Should it be? Does the Constitution protect a defendant from being convicted in absentia in a capital case? Even if his absence is voluntary? In Drope v. Missouri, 420 U.S. 162, 182, 95 S.Ct. 896, 909, 43 L.Ed.2d 103, 119 (1975), the Court was able to side-step this issue where defendant inflicted a gunshot wound upon himself, and thus was absent during a portion of his trial for an offense for which death was a possible penalty.

11. **Conferences in chambers.** The Court expanded further on the extent of a defendant's right to be present at all stages of his criminal trial in United States v. Gagnon, 470 U.S. 522, 105 S.Ct. 1482, 84 L.Ed.2d 486 (1985). Gagnon and three other respondents were jointly being tried for drug offenses when a juror contacted the trial judge to express concern over Gagnon's sketching portraits of the jurors "because of what could happen afterwards." The trial judge interviewed the juror in chambers with Gagnon's attorney and a court reporter. She explained that Gagnon was an artist and that the portraits had been confiscated. She also determined that the juror was not prejudiced by the sketching and the trial proceeded without objection by any of the respondents as to the interviewing of the juror with only Gagnon's counsel present. On appeal from convictions, however, each respondent claimed that rights to an impartial jury and to presence under Rule 43 had been violated by the in chambers examination. The Ninth Circuit reversed the convictions under Rule 43 and the due process clause of the Fifth Amendment. The Supreme Court, in a *per curiam* opinion, reversed. While the Court acknowledged that due process includes a right to presence even when a witness is not being confronted under the Sixth Amendment, it disposed of the claim with the comment that due process is not violated by an ex parte conversation between a trial judge and a juror and that "the defense has no constitutional right to be present at every interaction between a judge and a juror, nor is there a constitutional right to have a court reporter transcribe every such communication." The Court also held that the respondents had waived any claim they might have under Rule 43 to presence "at every stage of the trial.... " because they knew about the proposed conference with the juror in chambers and failed to assert a right to be present.

12. **Ejection for disruptive conduct.** The right to be present may also be lost by disruptive conduct in the courtroom, as was recognized in Illinois v. Allen, 397 U.S. 337, 90 S.Ct. 1057, 25 L.Ed.2d 353 (1970). Allen had been ejected from his trial for robbery after he interrupted the proceedings, tore up a file, and threatened the judge. He was permitted to return but was again removed when he repeated his disruptive conduct. In later federal habeas corpus proceedings attacking the resulting conviction, the Court of Appeals held that Allen's absolute right to be present had been violated. The Supreme Court reversed:

> [W]e explicitly hold ... that a defendant can lose his right to be present at trial if, after he has been warned by the judge that he will be removed if he continues his disruptive behavior, he nevertheless insists on conducting himself in a manner so disorderly, disruptive, and disrespectful of the court that his trial cannot be carried on with him in the courtroom. Once lost, the right to be present can, of course, be reclaimed as soon as the defendant is willing to conduct himself consistently with the decorum and respect inherent in the concept of courts and judicial proceedings.

It is essential to the proper administration of criminal justice that dignity, order, and decorum be the hallmarks of all court proceedings in our country.

The flagrant disregard in the courtroom of elementary standards of proper conduct should not and cannot be tolerated. We believe trial judges confronted with disruptive, contumacious, stubbornly defiant defendants must be given sufficient discretion to meet the circumstances of each case. No one formula for maintaining the appropriate courtroom atmosphere will be best in all situations. We think there are at least three constitutionally permissible ways for a trial judge to handle an obstreperous defendant like Allen: (1) bind and gag him, thereby keeping him present; (2) cite him for contempt; (3) take him out of the courtroom until he promises to conduct himself properly.

397 U.S. at 343–44, 90 S.Ct. at 1060–61, 25 L.Ed.2d at 359. Addressing the exercise of the discretion it recognized in the trial judge, the Court continued:

Trying a defendant for a crime while he sits bound and gagged before the judge and jury would to an extent comply with that part of the Sixth Amendment's purposes that accords the defendant an opportunity to confront the witnesses at the trial. But even to contemplate such a technique, much less see it, arouses a feeling that no person should be tried while shackled and gagged except as a last resort. Not only is it possible that the sight of shackles and gags might have a significant effect on the jury's feelings about the defendant, but the use of this technique is itself something of an affront to the very dignity and decorum of judicial proceedings that the judge is seeking to uphold. Moreover, one of the defendant's primary advantages of being present at the trial, his ability to communicate with his counsel, is greatly reduced when the defendant is in a condition of total physical restraint. It is in part because of these inherent disadvantages and limitations in this method of dealing with disorderly defendants that we decline to hold with the Court of Appeals that a defendant cannot under any possible circumstances be deprived of his right to be present at trial. However, in some situations which we need not attempt to foresee, binding and gagging might possibly be the fairest and most reasonable way to handle a defendant who acts as Allen did here.

* * *

[C]iting or threatening to cite a contumacious defendant for criminal contempt might in itself be sufficient to make a defendant stop interrupting a trial. If so, the problem would be solved easily, and the defendant could remain in the courtroom. Of course, if the defendant is determined to prevent *any* trial, then a court in attempting to try the defendant for contempt is still confronted with the identical dilemma that the Illinois court faced in this case. And criminal contempt has obvious limitations as a sanction when the defendant is charged with a crime so serious that a very severe sentence such as death or life imprisonment is likely to be imposed. In such a case the defendant might not be affected by a mere contempt sentence when he ultimately faces a far more serious sanction. Nevertheless, the contempt remedy should be borne in mind by a judge in the circumstances of this case.

Another aspect of the contempt remedy is the judge's power, when exercised consistently with state and federal law, to imprison an unruly defendant such as Allen for civil contempt and discontinue the trial until such time as the defendant promises to behave himself. This procedure is consistent with the defendant's right to be present at trial, and yet it avoids the serious shortcomings of the use of shackles and gags. It must be recognized, however, that a defendant might conceivably, as a matter of calculated strategy, elect to spend a prolonged period in confinement for contempt in the hope that adverse witnesses might be unavailable after a lapse of time. A court must guard against allowing a defendant to profit from his own wrong in this way.

397 U.S. at 344–45, 90 S.Ct. at 1061–62, 25 L.Ed.2d at 359–60.

2. CROSS-EXAMINATION AND COMPULSORY PROCESS TO OBTAIN WITNESSES

As the opinions in the previous section indicate, confrontation and cross-examination are interrelated. Indeed a major purpose behind the right of confrontation is cross-examination. In addition, the Sixth Amendment explicitly provides that the accused is "to have compulsory process for obtaining witnesses in his favor." The principal case in this section combines all of these procedural rights.

Chambers v. Mississippi

Supreme Court of the United States, 1973.
410 U.S. 284, 93 S.Ct. 1038, 35 L.Ed.2d 297.

■ MR. JUSTICE POWELL delivered the opinion of the Court.

Petitioner, Leon Chambers, was tried by a jury in a Mississippi trial court and convicted of murdering a policeman. The jury assessed punishment at life imprisonment and the Mississippi Supreme Court affirmed, one justice dissenting. . . . Subsequently the petition for certiorari was granted to consider whether petitioner's trial was conducted in accord with principles of due process under the Fourteenth Amendment. We conclude that it was not.

* * *

II.

Chambers filed a pretrial motion requesting the court to order McDonald to appear. Chambers also sought a ruling at that time that, if the State chose not to call McDonald itself, he be allowed to call him as an adverse witness. Attached to the motion were copies of McDonald's sworn confession and of the transcript of his preliminary hearing at which he repudiated that confession. The trial court granted the motion requiring McDonald to appear but reserved ruling on the adverse witness motion. At trial, after the State failed to put McDonald on the stand, Chambers called McDonald, laid a predicate for the introduction of his sworn out-of-court confession, had it admitted into evidence, and read it to the jury. The State, upon cross-examination, elicited from McDonald the fact that he had rejected his prior confession. McDonald further testified, as he had at the preliminary hearing, that he did not shoot Liberty, and that he confessed to the crime only on the promise of Reverend Stokes that he would not go to jail and would share in a sizable tort recovery from the town. He also retold his own story of his actions on the evening of the shooting. . . .

At the conclusion of the State's cross-examination, Chambers renewed his motion to examine McDonald as an adverse witness. The trial court denied the motion, stating: "He may be hostile, but he is not adverse in the sense of the word, so your request will be overruled." On appeal, the State Supreme Court upheld the trial court's ruling, finding that "McDonald's testimony was not adverse to appellant" because "[n]owhere did he point the finger at Chambers."

Defeated in his attempt to challenge directly McDonald's renunciation of his prior confession, Chambers sought to introduce the testimony of the three witnesses to whom McDonald had admitted that he shot the officer. The first of these, Sam Hardin, would have testified that, on the night of the shooting, he spent the late evening hours with McDonald at a friend's house after their return from the hospital and that, while driving McDonald home later that night, McDonald stated that he shot Liberty. The State objected to the admission of this testimony on the ground that it was hearsay. The trial court sustained the objection.

Berkley Turner, the friend with whom McDonald said he was drinking beer when the shooting occurred, was then called to testify. In the jury's presence, and without objection, he testified that he had not been in the cafe that Saturday and had not had any beers with McDonald. The jury was then excused. In the absence of the jury, Turner recounted his conversations with McDonald while they were riding with James Williams to take Chambers to the hospital. When asked whether McDonald said anything regarding the shooting of Liberty, Turner testified that McDonald told him that he "shot him." Turner further stated that one week later, when he met McDonald at a friend's house, McDonald reminded him of their prior conversation and urged Turner not to "mess him up." Petitioner argued to the court that, especially where there was other proof in the case that was corroborative of these out-of-court statements, Turner's testimony as to McDonald's self-incriminating remarks should have been admitted as an exception to the hearsay rule. Again, the trial court sustained the State's objection.

The third witness, Albert Carter, was McDonald's neighbor. They had been friends for about 25 years. Although Carter had not been in Woodville on the evening of the shooting, he stated that he learned about it the next morning from McDonald. That same day he and McDonald walked out to a well near McDonald's house and there McDonald told him that he was the one who shot Officer Liberty. Carter testified that McDonald also told him that he had disposed of the .22–caliber revolver later that night. He further testified that several weeks after the shooting he accompanied McDonald to Natchez where McDonald purchased another .22 pistol to replace the one he had discarded. The jury was not allowed to hear Carter's testimony. Chambers urged that these statements were admissible, the State objected, and the court sustained the objection. On appeal, the State Supreme Court approved the lower court's exclusion of these witnesses' testimony on hearsay grounds. 252 So.2d, at 220.

In sum, then, this was Chambers' predicament. As a consequence of the combination of Mississippi's "party witness" or "voucher" rule and its hearsay rule, he was unable either to cross-examine McDonald or to present witnesses in his own behalf who would have discredited McDonald's repudiation and demonstrated his complicity. Chambers had, however, chipped away at the fringes of McDonald's story by introducing admissible testimony from other sources indicating that he had not been seen in the cafe where he says he was when the shooting started, that he had not been having beer with Turner, and that he possessed a .22 pistol at the time of the crime. But all that remained from McDonald's own testimony was a single written confession countered by an arguably acceptable renunciation. Chambers' defense was far less persuasive than it might have been had he been given an opportunity to subject McDonald's statements to cross-examination or had the other confessions been admitted.

III.

The right of an accused in a criminal trial to due process is, in essence, the right to a fair opportunity to defend against the State's accusations. The rights to confront and cross-examine witnesses and to call witnesses in one's own behalf have long been recognized as essential to due process. ...

A.

Chambers was denied an opportunity to subject McDonald's damning repudiation and alibi to cross-examination. He was not allowed to test the witness' recollection, to probe into the details of his alibi, or to "sift" his conscience so that the jury might judge for itself whether McDonald's testimony was worthy of belief. The right of cross-examination is more than a desirable rule of trial procedure. It is implicit in the constitutional right of confrontation, and helps assure the "accuracy of the truth-determining process." Dutton v. Evans, 400 U.S. 74, 89, 91 S.Ct. 210, 220, 27 L.Ed.2d 213 (1970).... Of course, the right to confront and to cross-examine is not absolute and may, in appropriate cases, bow to accommodate other legitimate interests in the criminal trial process. But its denial or significant diminution calls into question the ultimate "integrity of the fact-finding process" and requires that the competing interest be closely examined.

* * *

The argument that McDonald's testimony was not "adverse" to, or "against," Chambers is not convincing. The State's proof at trial excluded the theory that more than one person participated in the shooting of Liberty. To the extent that McDonald's sworn confession tended to incriminate him, it tended also to exculpate Chambers. And, in the circumstances of this case, McDonald's retraction inculpated Chambers to the same extent that it exculpated McDonald. It can hardly be disputed that McDonald's testimony was in fact seriously adverse to Chambers. The availability of the right to confront and to cross-examine those who give damaging testimony against the accused has never been held to depend on whether the witness was initially put on the stand by the accused or by the State. We reject the notion that a right of such substance in the criminal process may be governed by that technicality or by any narrow and unrealistic definition of the word "against." The "voucher" rule, as applied in this case, plainly interfered with Chambers' right to defend against the State's charges.

B.

We need not decide, however, whether this error alone would occasion reversal since Chambers' claimed denial of due process rests on the ultimate impact of that error when viewed in conjunction with the trial court's refusal to permit him to call other witnesses. The trial court refused to allow him to introduce the testimony of Hardin, Turner and Carter. Each would have testified to the statements purportedly made by Mc-Donald, on three separate occasions shortly after the crime, naming himself as the murderer. The State Supreme Court approved the exclusion of this evidence on the ground that it was hearsay.

The hearsay rule, which has long been recognized and respected by virtually every State, is based on experience and grounded in the notion that untrustworthy evidence should not be presented to the triers of fact. Out-of-court statements are traditionally excluded because they lack the conventional indicia of reliability: they are usually not made under oath or other circumstances that impress the speaker with the solemnity of his statements; the declarant's word is not subject to cross-examination; and he is not available in order that his demeanor and credibility may be assessed by the jury. California v. Green, 399 U.S. 149, 158, 90 S.Ct. 1930, 1935, 26 L.Ed.2d 489 (1970). . . .

* * *

The hearsay statements involved in this case were originally made and subsequently offered at trial under circumstances that provided considerable assurance of their reliability. First, each of McDonald's confessions was made spontaneously to a close acquaintance shortly after the murder had occurred. Second, each one was corroborated by some other evidence in the case—McDonald's sworn confession, the testimony of an eyewitness to the shooting, the testimony that McDonald was seen with a gun immediately after the shooting, and proof of his prior ownership of a .22–caliber revolver and subsequent purchase of a new weapon. The sheer number of independent confessions provided additional corroboration for each. Third, whatever may be the parameters of the penal-interest rationale[13] each confession here was in a very real sense self-incriminatory and unquestionably against interest. McDonald stood to benefit nothing by disclosing his role in the shooting to any of his three friends and he must have been aware of the possibility that disclosure would lead to criminal prosecution. Indeed, after telling Turner of his involvement, he subsequently urged Turner not to "mess him up." Finally, if there was any question about the truthfulness of the extrajudicial statements, McDonald was present in the courtroom and had been under oath. He could have been cross-examined by the State, and his demeanor and responses weighed by the jury. See California v. Green, 399 U.S. 149, 90 S.Ct. 1930, 26 L.Ed.2d 489 (1970). The availability of McDonald significantly distinguishes this case from the prior Mississippi

---

13. The Mississippi case which refused to adopt a hearsay exception for declarations against penal interest concerned an out-of-court declarant who purportedly stated that he had committed the murder with which his brother had been charged. The Mississippi Supreme Court believed that the declarant may have been motivated by a desire to free his brother rather than by any compulsion of guilt. The Court also noted that the declarant had fled, was unavailable for cross-examination, and may well have known at the time he made the statement that he would not suffer for it. Brown v. State, 99 Miss. 719, 55 So. 961 (1911). There is, in the present case, no such basis for doubting McDonald's statements. See Note, 43 Miss.L.J. 122, 127–129 (1972).

precedent, Brown v. State, supra, and from the *Donnelly*-type situation, since in both cases the declarant was unavailable at the time of trial.[14]

Few rights are more fundamental than that of an accused to present witnesses in his own defense. In the exercise of this right, the accused, as is required of the State, must comply with established rules of procedure and evidence designed to assure both fairness and reliability in the ascertainment of guilt and innocence. Although perhaps no rule of evidence has been more respected or more frequently applied in jury trials than that applicable to the exclusion of hearsay, exceptions tailored to allow the introduction of evidence which in fact is likely to be trustworthy have long existed. The testimony rejected by the trial court here bore persuasive assurances of trustworthiness and thus was well within the basic rationale of the exception for declarations against interest. That testimony also was critical to Chambers' defense. In these circumstances, where constitutional rights directly affecting the ascertainment of guilt are implicated, the hearsay rule may not be applied mechanistically to defeat the ends of justice.

We conclude that the exclusion of this critical evidence, coupled with the State's refusal to permit Chambers to cross-examine McDonald, denied him a trial in accord with traditional and fundamental standards of due process. In reaching this judgment we establish no new principles of constitutional law. Nor does our holding signal any diminution in the respect traditionally accorded to the States in the establishment and implementation of their own criminal trial rules and procedures. Rather, we hold quite simply that under the facts and circumstances of this case the rulings of the trial court deprived Chambers of a fair trial.

The judgment is reversed and the case is remanded to the Supreme Court of Mississippi for further proceedings not inconsistent with this opinion.

It is so ordered.

Reversed and remanded.

NOTES

1. **Governmental restrictions on cross-examination for bias.** The Sixth Amendment restricts the states' ability to place limits upon the nature and extent

---

14. McDonald's presence also deprives the State's argument for retention of the penal-interest rule of much of its force. In claiming that "[t]o change the rule would work a travesty of justice," the State posited the following hypothetical:

"If the rule were changed, A could be charged with the crime; B could tell C and D that he committed the crime; *B could go into hiding* and at A's trial C and D would testify as to B's admission of guilt; A could be acquitted and B would return to stand trial; B could then provide several witnesses to testify as to his whereabouts at the time of the crime.

The testimony of those witnesses along with A's statement that he really committed the crime would result in B's acquittal. A would be barred from further prosecution because of the protection against double jeopardy. No one could be convicted of perjury as A did not testify at his first trial, B did not lie under oath, and C and D were truthful in their testimony." Respondent's Brief, at 7 n. 3 (emphasis supplied).

Obviously, "B's" absence at trial is critical to the success of the justice-subverting ploy.

of cross-examination. In Davis v. Alaska, 415 U.S. 308, 94 S.Ct. 1105, 39 L.Ed.2d 347 (1974), the Supreme Court reversed a conviction in a case where the trial court had barred defense cross-examination of a witness to show that he was on juvenile probation which could be revoked unless he assisted the state. Because "the exposure of a witness' motivation in testifying is a proper and important function of the constitutionally protected right of cross-examination," 415 U.S. at 316, 94 S.Ct. at 1110, 39 L.Ed.2d at 354, the Supreme Court concluded that this right is "paramount to the State's policy of protecting a juvenile offender." 415 U.S. at 319, 94 S.Ct. at 1112, 39 L.Ed. at 355.

However, a violation of the defendant's right to confront and cross-examine witnesses may be harmless error. In Delaware v. Van Arsdall, 475 U.S. 673, 106 S.Ct. 1431, 89 L.Ed.2d 674 (1986), the defendant, on trial for murder, was prohibited from cross-examining a State's witness to elicit evidence of bias arising out of a prior plea bargaining arrangement. The Supreme Court reversed the conviction:

> [A] criminal defendant states a violation of the Confrontation Clause by showing that he was prohibited from engaging in otherwise appropriate cross-examination designed to show a prototypical form of bias on the part of the witness, and thereby "to expose to the jury the facts from which jurors ... could appropriately draw inferences relating to the reliability of the witness." Davis v. Alaska. Respondent has met that burden here: A reasonable jury might have received a significantly different impression of [the witness'] credibility had respondent's counsel been permitted to pursue his proposed line of cross-examination.

475 U.S. at 680, 106 S.Ct. at 1436, 89 L.Ed.2d at 684. But the Court remanded the case for harmless error analysis under Chapman v. California (discussed in Chapter 26):

> The correct inquiry is whether, assuming that the damaging potential of the cross-examination were fully realized, a reviewing court might nonetheless say that the error was harmless beyond a reasonable doubt. Whether such an error is harmless in a particular case depends upon a host of factors ... includ[ing] the importance of the witness' testimony in the prosecution's case, whether the testimony was cumulative, the presence or absence of evidence corroborating or contradicting the testimony of the witness on material points, the extent of cross-examination otherwise permitted, and, of course, the overall strength of the prosecution's case.

475 U.S. at 684, 106 S.Ct. at 1438, 89 L.Ed.2d at 686–87.

The petitioner in Olden v. Kentucky, 488 U.S. 227, 109 S.Ct. 480, 102 L.Ed.2d 513 (1988) was convicted of forcible sodomy on the basis of the testimony of the complaining witness, Matthews, whose testimony was corroborated by one Russell, who had seen her exiting the car of petitioner's co-defendant, Harris, the night in question. Petitioner's defense was consent. On cross-examination, he attempted to show that at the time of the alleged offense the complaining witness and Russell, although married to others, were having an affair with each other and that at the time of trial they were living with each other. Thus, petitioner's theory was that when Russell saw the complainant exit the co-defendant's car, she fabricated the rape charge to avoid jeopardizing her relationship with Russell. The trial court refused to admit this evidence on the ground that since the complainant was white and Russell and petitioner were black the evidence would be more prejudicial to the State than probative for the defense. The Kentucky Court of Appeals affirmed the conviction, but the Supreme Court reversed in a per curiam opinion. The Court concluded that the trial court violated the right to confrontation and that the error was not harmless:

Here, Matthews' testimony was central, indeed crucial, to the prosecution's case. Her story, which was directly contradicted by that of petitioner and Harris, was corroborated only by the largely derivative testimony of Russell, whose impartiality would also have been somewhat impugned by revelation of his relationship with Matthews. Finally ... the State's case against petitioner was far from overwhelming. In sum, considering the relevant *Van Arsdall* factors within the context of this case, we find it impossible to conclude "beyond a reasonable doubt" that the restriction on petitioner's right to confrontation was harmless.

488 U.S. at 233, 109 S.Ct. at 484, 102 L.Ed.2d at 520–21.

2. **Pretrial discovery of investigatory files for cross-examination.** The defendant in Pennsylvania v. Ritchie, 480 U.S. 39, 107 S.Ct. 989, 94 L.Ed.2d 40 (1987) was prosecuted for sexual abuse of his 13–year–old child. He demanded and was refused pretrial discovery of the file maintained by the governmental agency that investigated the child abuse case against him. State law made that material privileged, but defendant claimed that under Davis v. Alaska that privilege had to yield to his right of confrontation, a position accepted by the Pennsylvania Supreme Court. A plurality of the United States Supreme Court rejected that interpretation of *Davis:*

The Pennsylvania Supreme Court apparently interpreted our decision in *Davis* to mean that a statutory privilege cannot be maintained when a defendant asserts a need, prior to trial, for the protected information that might be used at trial to impeach or otherwise undermine a witness' testimony....

If we were to accept this broad interpretation of *Davis,* the effect would be to transform the Confrontation Clause into a constitutionally-compelled rule of pretrial discovery. Nothing in the case law supports such a view. The opinions of this Court show that the right of confrontation is a *trial* right, designed to prevent improper restrictions on the types of questions that defense counsel may ask during cross-examination. The ability to question adverse witnesses, however, does not include the power to require the pretrial disclosure of any and all information that might be useful in contradicting unfavorable testimony.

480 U.S. at 52–53, 107 S.Ct. at 998–99, 94 L.Ed.2d at 54. The Court also rejected defendant's claim that the right of compulsory process requires disclosure of the file to enable the defense to identify and subpoena possible favorable witnesses. The Court held that such a claim should be analyzed under the due process standards of the Brady v. Maryland line of cases (supra) rather than under the compulsory process clause of the Sixth Amendment. Applying those standards, the Court decided that the Pennsylvania court was incorrect in holding that Ritchie's attorney had the right to examine the file to determine whether it contained useful material because that would interfere with the confidentiality interests that were recognized by state law. Further, it held that defendant's interests would be fully protected by requiring the trial court to examine the entire file *in camera* and to disclose to the attorneys information that is material under the *Brady* line of cases.

3. **Compulsory production of witnesses.** As *Chambers* makes clear, the Sixth Amendment also protects an accused's right to produce testimony. The leading case developing this aspect of the provision is Washington v. Texas, 388 U.S. 14, 87 S.Ct. 1920, 18 L.Ed.2d 1019 (1967). Washington was charged with murder and the state's evidence indicated that either Washington or one Fuller fired the fatal shot. Fuller had already been convicted of murder on the basis of the shooting. Washington sought to call Fuller to testify that Washington tried to persuade Fuller to leave the scene before the killing and ran off before Fuller fired the fatal shot. Fuller's testimony was excluded pursuant to a Texas statute which provided that

persons charged or convicted as coparticipants in a crime could not testify for one another. Reviewing Washington's conviction, the Supreme Court noted that the effect of the state statute was not to refuse to compel the attendance of Washington's witness but to bar his testimony whether he was present or not. "We are thus called upon to decide," it stated, "whether the Sixth Amendment guarantees a defendant the right under any circumstances to put his witnesses on the stand, as well as the right to compel their attendance in court." 388 U.S. at 19, 87 S.Ct. at 1923, 18 L.Ed.2d at 1023. The Texas statute, it observed, was a remnant of a common law rule that disqualified many witnesses, including codefendants, from testifying on the basis of interest. This rule was based on the fear that if codefendants were permitted to testify for each other, each would lie in an effort to exonerate his companion. The Court noted that under the Texas statute accused accomplices can be called as witnesses by the prosecution and by the defense after acquittal at their own trials. In both situations, it reasoned, the accomplice has a significant incentive to commit perjury, perhaps greater than in the situations in which his testimony is barred under the statute. The Texas statute, therefore, arbitrarily selected a class of witnesses whose testimony would be unavailable to criminal defendants, and this violated the Sixth Amendment:

> [Washington] was denied his right to have compulsory process for obtaining witnesses in his favor because the State arbitrarily denied him the right to put on the stand a witness who was physically and mentally capable of testifying to events that he had personally observed, and whose testimony would have been relevant and material to the defense. The Framers of the Constitution did not intend to commit the futile act of giving to a defendant the right to secure the attendance of witnesses whose testimony he had no right to use.

388 U.S. at 23, 87 S.Ct. at 1925, 18 L.Ed.2d at 1025.

What result if the government deports a potential witness for the defense in connection with the same criminal activity that led to the defendant's arrest? In United States v. Valenzuela–Bernal, 458 U.S. 858, 102 S.Ct. 3440, 73 L.Ed.2d 1193 (1982), the Supreme Court concluded, in an opinion by Justice Rehnquist: "The mere fact that the Government deports such [illegal alien] witness is not sufficient to establish a violation of the Compulsory Process Clause of the Sixth Amendment or the Due Process Clause of the Fourteenth Amendment. A violation of these provisions requires some showing that the evidence lost would be both material and favorable to the defense." 458 U.S. at 872–73, 102 S.Ct. at 3449, 73 L.Ed.2d at 1206.

4. **Hypnotically-enhanced testimony by defendant.** Petitioner in Rock v. Arkansas, 483 U.S. 44, 107 S.Ct. 2704, 97 L.Ed.2d 37 (1987), was charged with the shooting death of her husband. She told police she acted in self-defense and gave a sketchy version of the events leading to the killing. As part of defense preparation for trial, she was placed under hypnosis and questioned about the events. For the first time, she recalled that her finger was on the hammer of the handgun, not the trigger, and that the weapon had discharged when her husband grabbed her arm. Later defense-ordered examination of the handgun showed that it was defective and was prone to fire when hit or dropped without the trigger's being pulled. The trial court prohibited the petitioner from testifying to any facts she recalled as a result of the hypnosis but she was permitted to testify as to her pre-hypnotic recall, which did not include the placement of the weapon in her hand or her husband's grabbing her arm. Her conviction for manslaughter over her interposed claim of self-defense was affirmed by the Arkansas Supreme Court in an opinion which prohibited any use of hypnotically-induced testimony. The United States Supreme Court, in an opinion by Justice Blackmun, vacated that decision. The Court found that a defendant's right to testify is based on the due process, compulsory process and self-incrimination clauses. Further, "restrictions of a defendant's right to testify may

not be arbitrary or disproportionate to the purposes they are designed to serve. In applying its evidentiary rules a State must evaluate whether the interests served by a rule justify the limitation imposed on the defendant's constitutional right to testify." 483 U.S. at 55–56, 107 S.Ct. at 2711, 97 L.Ed.2d at 49. Justice Blackmun then reviewed the current status of hypnosis and the risk of inaccuracy it poses:

> Hypnosis by trained physicians or psychologists has been recognized as a valid therapeutic technique since 1958,.... The use of hypnosis in criminal investigations, however, is controversial, and the current medical and legal view of its appropriate role is unsettled.

> * * *

> The inaccuracies the process introduces can be reduced, although perhaps not eliminated, by the use of procedural safeguards. . . .

> The more traditional means of assessing accuracy of testimony also remain applicable in the case of a previously hypnotized defendant. Certain information recalled as a result of hypnosis may be verified as highly accurate by corroborating evidence. Cross-examination, even in the face of a confident defendant, is an effective tool for revealing inconsistencies. Moreover, a jury can be educated to the risks of hypnosis through expert testimony and cautionary instructions....

> We are not now prepared to endorse without qualifications the use of hypnosis as an investigative tool; . . . But [the state] has not shown that hypnotically enhanced testimony is always so untrustworthy and so immune to the traditional means of evaluating credibility that it should disable a defendant from presenting her version of the events for which she is on trial.

483 U.S. at 58–61, 107 S.Ct. at 2712–14, 97 L.Ed.2d at 51–52. The Chief Justice, joined by Justices White, O'Connor and Scalia, dissented on the ground that "until there is a much more general consensus on the use of hypnosis than there is now, the Constitution does not warrant this Court's mandating its own view of how to deal with the issue." 483 U.S. at 65, 107 S.Ct. at 2716, 97 L.Ed.2d at 55.

D.   EXERCISE AT TRIAL OF THE PRIVILEGE AGAINST COMPELLED SELF-INCRIMINATION

The essence of the Fifth Amendment's self-incrimination clause—"No person shall be ... compelled in any criminal case to be a witness against himself.... "—is obviously that during a criminal trial the prosecution cannot call the defendant as a witness. But the constitutional privilege has much greater ramifications, some of which are developed in this Section. First, the inferences that can be drawn from a defendant's failure to testify are explored. Second, attention is turned to a defendant's ability to waive the privilege by testifying in his own behalf and the ramifications of a decision to so waive the privilege.

1.   COMMENT UPON AND INFERENCES FROM THE FAILURE TO TESTIFY

There are many reasons why a defendant might choose not to testify at the trial. The decision, to testify or not, is personal to the defendant. But certainly the silence of the one whose conduct is under scrutiny may cause jurors to draw inferences about the defendant's failure to testify. Accordingly, defense counsel's strategy and advice on this decision is often very problematic. At issue in the following case is what instruction, if any, should be given a jury under these circumstances.

Carter v. Kentucky

Supreme Court of the United States, 1981.
450 U.S. 288, 101 S.Ct. 1112, 67 L.Ed.2d 241.

■ JUSTICE STEWART delivered the opinion of the Court.

* * *

The petitioner was ... indicted for third-degree burglary of Young's Hardware Store. The indictment also charged him with being a persistent felony offender,.... The prosecutor's opening statement recounted the evidence expected to be introduced against the petitioner. The opening statement of defense counsel began as follows:

> "Let me tell you a little bit about how this system works. If you listened to Mr. Ruff [the prosecutor] you are probably ready to put Lonnie Joe in the penitentiary. He read you a ... true bill that was issued by the Grand Jury. ...[T]he defendant is ... not allowed to present any of his testimony before this group of people. The only thing that the Grand Jury hears is the prosecution's proof.... I suppose that most of you would issue a true bill if Mr. Ruff told you what he has just told you and you didn't have a chance to hear what the defendant had to say for himself. Now, that is just completely contrary to our system of law. A man, as the Judge has already told you, ... is innocent until ... proved guilty.... "

The prosecution rested after calling Officers Ellison, Davis, another officer, and the owner of Young's Hardware Store.

* * *

... [T]he petitioner's counsel advised the court that there would be no testimony introduced on behalf of the defense.[15] He then requested that the following instruction be given to the jury:

> "The defendant is not compelled to testify and the fact that he does not cannot be used as an inference of guilt and should not prejudice him in any way."

The trial court refused the request.

The prosecutor began his summation by stating that he intended to review the evidence "that we were privileged to hear,".... The prosecutor continued that if there was a reasonable explanation why the petitioner ran when he saw the police, it was "not in the record."[16]

---

15. Defense counsel summarized his private conversation with his client for the record, observing "that the advice of counsel to Mr. Carter was that in plain terms he was between a rock and hard place.... " If the petitioner testified he would be impeached and "if he didn't testify the jury, ... would probably use that against him."

16. Defense counsel began his closing argument as follows:

The jury found the petitioner guilty, recommending a sentence of two years. The recidivist phase of the trial followed. The prosecutor presented evidence of the previous felony convictions that had been listed in the indictment. The defense presented no evidence, and the jury found the petitioner guilty as a persistent offender, sentencing him to the maximum term of 20 years in prison.

Upon appeal, the Kentucky Supreme Court rejected the argument that the Fifth and Fourteenth Amendments to the United States Constitution require that a criminal trial judge give the jury an instruction such as was requested here. ...[17]

* * *

[This] Court had held that the Fifth Amendment command that no person "shall be compelled in any criminal case to be a witness against himself" is applicable against the States through the Fourteenth Amendment. Malloy v. Hogan, 378 U.S. 1, 84 S.Ct. 1489, 12 L.Ed.2d 653. In *Griffin,* the Court considered the question whether it is a violation of the Fifth and Fourteenth Amendments to invite a jury in a state criminal trial to draw an unfavorable inference from a defendant's failure to testify. Griffin v. California, 380 U.S. 609, 85 S.Ct. 1229, 14 L.Ed.2d 106. The trial judge had there instructed the jury "that a defendant has a constitutional right not to testify," and that the defendant's exercise of that right "does not create a presumption of guilt or by itself warrant an inference of guilt" nor "relieve the prosecution of any of its burden of proof." But the instruction additionally permitted the jury to "take that failure into consideration as tending to indicate the truth of [the State's] evidence and as indicating that among the inferences that may be reasonably drawn therefrom those unfavorable to the defendant are the more probable." Id., at 610, 85 S.Ct., at 1230.

This Court set aside Griffin's conviction because "the Fifth Amendment ... forbids either comment by the prosecution on the accused's silence or instructions by the Court that such silence is evidence of guilt." Id., at 615, 85 S.Ct., at 1233.[18] It condemned adverse comment on a defendant's failure to testify as reminiscent of the "inquisitorial system of criminal justice," and concluded that such comment effected a court-

"Ladies and Gentlemen of the jury, I am sure you all right now are wondering well what has happened? Why didn't Mr. Carter take the stand and testify? Let me tell you. The judge just read to you that the man is presumed innocent and that it is up to the prosecution to prove him guilty beyond a reasonable doubt. He doesn't have to take the stand in his own behalf. He doesn't have to do anything."

17. Kentucky is one of at least five States that prohibit giving such an instruction to the jury. Others are Minnesota, ... Nevada, Oklahoma and Wyoming. A few States have a statutory requirement that such an instruction be given to the jury unless the defendant objects. See, e.g., Conn. Gen.Stat.Ann. § 54–84 (West 1958). The majority of the States, by judicial pronouncement, require that a defense request for such a jury instruction be honored. See, e.g., Woodard v. State, 234 Ga. 901, 218 S.E.2d 629.

18. The Court in the *Griffin* case expressly reserved decision "on whether an accused can require ... that the jury be instructed that his silence be disregarded." 380 U.S., at 615, n. 6, 85 S.Ct., at 1233, n. 6.

imposed penalty upon the defendant that was unacceptable because "[i]t cuts down on the privilege by making its assertion costly."

The Court returned to a consideration of the Fifth Amendment and jury instructions in Lakeside v. Oregon, 435 U.S. 333, 98 S.Ct. 1091, 55 L.Ed.2d 319, where the question was whether the giving of a "no-inference" instruction over defense objection violates the Constitution. Despite trial counsel's complaint that his strategy was to avoid any mention of his client's failure to testify, a no inference instruction[19] was given by the trial judge. The petitioner contended that when a trial judge in any way draws the jury's attention to a defendant's failure to testify, unless the defendant acquiesces, the court invades the defendant's privilege against compulsory self-incrimination. This argument was rejected.

The *Lakeside* Court reasoned that the Fifth and Fourteenth Amendments bar only *adverse* comment on a defendant's failure to testify, and that "a judge's instruction that the jury must draw *no* adverse inferences of any kind from the defendant's exercise of his privilege not to testify is 'comment' of an entirely different order." 435 U.S., at 339, 98 S.Ct., at 1094. The purpose of such an instruction, the Court stated, "is to remove from the jury's deliberations any influence of unspoken adverse inferences," and "cannot provide the pressure on a defendant found impermissible in *Griffin*." Ibid.

The Court observed in *Lakeside* that the petitioner's argument there rested on "two very doubtful assumptions:"

> First, that the jurors have not noticed that the defendant did not testify and will not, therefore, draw adverse inferences on their own. Second, that the jurors will totally disregard the instruction, and affirmatively give weight to what they have been told not to consider at all. Federal constitutional law cannot rest on speculative assumptions so dubious as these." 435 U.S., at 340, 98 S.Ct., at 1095 (footnote omitted).

Finally, the Court stressed that "the very purpose" of a jury instruction is to direct the jurors' attention to important legal concepts "that must not be misunderstood, such as reasonable doubt and burden of proof," and emphasized that instruction "in the meaning of the privilege against compulsory self-incrimination is no different." Ibid.

* * *

... The principles enunciated in our cases construing this privilege,[20] against both statutory and constitutional backdrops, lead unmistakably to

---

19. The *Lakewood* trial judge gave the following instruction to the jury:

> "Under the laws of this State a defendant has the option to take the witness stand in his or her own behalf. If a defendant chooses not to testify, such a circumstance gives rise to no inference or presumption against the defendant, and this must not be considered by you in determining the question of guilt or in-

nocence." 435 U.S., at 335, 98 S.Ct., at 1092.

20. The Court has recognized that there are many reasons unrelated to guilt or innocence for declining to testify:

> "It is not every one who can safely venture on the witness stand though entirely innocent of the charge against him. Excessive timidity, nervousness when facing others and attempting to explain

the conclusion that the Fifth Amendment requires that a criminal trial judge must give a "no adverse inference" jury instruction when requested by a defendant to do so.

* * *

The *Griffin* case stands for the proposition that a defendant must pay no court-imposed price for the exercise of his constitutional privilege not to testify. The penalty was exacted in *Griffin* by adverse comment on the defendant's silence; the penalty may be just as severe when there is no adverse comment, but when the jury is left to roam at large with only its untutored instincts to guide it, to draw from the defendant's silence broad inferences of guilt. Even without adverse comment, the members of a jury, unless instructed otherwise, may well draw adverse inferences from a defendant's silence.[21]

The significance of a cautionary instruction was forcefully acknowledged in *Lakeside,* where the Court found no constitutional error even when a no-inference instruction was given over a defendant's objection. The salutary purpose of the instruction, "to remove from the jury's deliberations any influence of unspoken adverse inferences," was deemed so important that it there outweighed the defendant's own preferred tactics.[22]

* * *

A trial judge has a powerful tool at his disposal to protect the constitutional privilege—the jury instruction—and he has an affirmative constitutional obligation to use that tool when a defendant seeks its employment. No judge can prevent jurors from speculating about why a defendant stands mute in the face of a criminal accusation, but a judge can,

transactions of a suspicious character, and offences charged against him, will often confuse and embarrass him to such a degree as to increase rather than remove prejudices against him. It is not every one, however honest, who would, therefore, willingly be placed on the witness stand." Wilson v. United States, 149 U.S. 60, 66, 13 S.Ct. 765, 766, 37 L.Ed. 650.

Other reasons include the fear of impeachment by prior convictions (the petitioner's fear in the present case), or by other damaging information not necessarily relevant to the charge being tried, *Griffin,* 380 U.S., at 615, 85 S.Ct., at 1233, and reluctance to "incriminate others whom [defendants] either love or fear," *Lakeside,* 435 U.S., at 344, n. 2, 98 S.Ct., at 1097, n. 2 (dissenting opinion).

21. Indeed, the dissenting opinion in *Griffin* suggested that more harm may flow from the lack of guidance to the jury on the meaning of the Fifth Amendment privilege than from reasonable comment upon the exercise of that privilege. With specific reference to decisions from Kentucky and one other State, the dissenters observed that "[w]ithout limiting instructions, the danger exists that the inferences drawn by the jury may be unfairly broad." The Court in *Griffin* indicated no disagreement with this view.

22. It has been almost universally thought that juries notice a defendant's failure to testify. "[T]he jury will of course realize this quite evident fact, even though the choice goes unmentioned.... [It is] a fact inescapably impressed on the jury's consciousness." *Griffin,* 380 U.S., at 621, 622, 85 S.Ct., at 1237 (dissenting opinion). In *Lakeside* the Court cited an acknowledged authority's statement that "[t]he layman's natural first suggestion would probably be that the resort to privilege in each instance is a clear confession of crime." 435 U.S., at 340, n. 10, 85 S.Ct., at 1095, n. 10, quoting 8 Wigmore, Evidence § 2272, p. 426 (McNaughton rev. ed. 1961).

and must, if requested to do so, use the unique power of the jury instruction to reduce that speculation to a minimum.[23]

The only state interest advanced by Kentucky in refusing a request for such a jury instruction is protection of the defendant: "the requested 'no inference' instruction ... would have been direct comment by the court and would have emphasized the fact that the accused had not testified in his own behalf." Green v. Commonwealth, Ky., 488 S.W.2d 339–341. This purported justification was specifically rejected in the *Lakeside* case, where the Court noted that "[i]t would be strange indeed to conclude that this cautionary instruction violates the very constitutional provision it is intended to protect." 435 U.S., at 339, 98 S.Ct., at 1094.

* * *

While it is arguable that a refusal to give an instruction similar to the one that was requested here can never be harmless, we decline to reach the issue, because it was not presented to or considered by the Supreme Court of Kentucky.

... [T]he failure to limit the jurors' speculation on the meaning of that silence, when the defendant makes a timely request that a prophylactic instruction be given, exacts an impermissible toll on the full and free exercise of the privilege. Accordingly, we hold that a state trial judge has the constitutional obligation, upon proper request, to minimize the danger that the jury will give evidentiary weight to a defendant's failure to testify.

For the reasons stated, the judgment is reversed, and the case is remanded to the Supreme Court of Kentucky for further proceedings not inconsistent with this opinion.

It is so ordered.

■ JUSTICE POWELL, concurring.

* * *

The one person who usually knows most about the critical facts is the accused. For reasons deeply rooted in the history we share with England, the Bill of Rights included the self-incrimination Clause, which enables a defendant in a criminal trial to elect to make no contribution to the factfinding process. But nothing in the Clause requires that jurors not draw logical inferences when a defendant chooses not to explain incriminating circumstances. Jurors have been instructed that the defendant is presumed to be innocent and that this presumption can be overridden only by evidence beyond a reasonable doubt. California Chief Justice Traynor commented that judges and prosecutors should be able to explain that "a jury [may] draw unfavorable inferences from the defendant's failure to explain or refute evidence when he could reasonably be expected to do so. Such comment would not be evidence and would do no more than make clear to the jury the extent of its freedom in drawing inferences." Traynor,

---

23. The importance of a no-inference instruction is underscored by a recent national public opinion survey conducted for the National Center for State Courts, revealing that 37% of those interviewed believed that it is the responsibility of the accused to prove his innocence. 64 ABAJ 653 (1978).

The Devils of Due Process in Criminal Detection, Detention, and Trial, 33 U.Chi.L.Rev. 657, 677 (1966).

I therefore would have joined JUSTICES STEWART and WHITE in dissent in *Griffin*. But *Griffin* is now the law, and based on that case the present petitioner was entitled to the jury instruction that he requested. I therefore join the opinion of the Court.

■ JUSTICE STEVENS, with whom JUSTICE BRENNAN joins, concurring.

While I join the Court's opinion, I add this comment to emphasize that today's holding is limited to cases in which the defendant has requested that the jury be instructed not to draw an inference of guilt from the defendant's failure to testify. I remain convinced that the question whether such an instruction should be given in any specific case—like the question whether the defendant should testify on his own behalf—should be answered by the defendant and his lawyer, not by the State.

NOTES

1. **Comment on failure to testify in response to defense argument.** Defense counsel in United States v. Robinson, 485 U.S. 25, 108 S.Ct. 864, 99 L.Ed.2d 23 (1988) had argued to the jury that the government had breached its duty to play fair in its handling of his client's mail fraud case in that his client had not been given the opportunity to explain the charges. After a conference at the bench in which the trial court stated that he interpreted counsel's argument to refer to his client's opportunity to testify at trial as well as to offer explanations during the investigatory stage of the case, the prosecutor was permitted in rebuttal argument to state that the defendant "could have taken the stand and explained it to you, anything he wanted to." Defense counsel did not dispute the trial court's characterization of his argument or object to the prosecutor's argument. The Court of Appeals reversed the conviction on the grounds that Griffin v. California had been violated.

The United States Supreme Court, in an opinion authored by The Chief Justice, reversed. While defense counsel's argument was ambiguous as it appears in the printed record, the trial court in the bench conference interpreted it to refer to the defendant's opportunity to testify at trial as well as to his opportunity to explain his position to investigators. Since defense counsel did not dispute that characterization with the trial court and did not object to the prosecutor's argument, the Court accepted the trial court's interpretation of the defense argument. *Griffin* does not control this case:

> "[The] central purpose of a criminal trial is to decide the factual question of the defendant's guilt or innocence".... To this end it is important that both the defendant and the prosecutor have the opportunity to meet fairly the evidence and arguments of one another.... It is one thing to hold, as we did in *Griffin,* that the prosecutor may not treat a defendant's exercise of his right to remain silent at trial as substantive evidence of guilt; it is quite another to urge, as defendant does here, that the same reasoning would forbid the prosecutor from fairly responding to an argument of the defendant by adverting to that silence.

485 U.S. at 33–34, 108 S.Ct. at 869–70, 99 L.Ed.2d at 32. Justice Marshall, joined by Justice Brennan, dissented on the ground that the Court's departure from the "bright-line rules of *Griffin* ... is unsettling and unwarranted." Justice Blackmun, concurring in part and dissenting in part, expressed concern with whether the

Supreme Court had properly formulated a plain error doctrine to guide lower courts reviewing cases of unobjected to error.

2. **Self-incriminatory acts of production.** The potential breadth of the self incrimination protection as well as its limitations are exemplified by its attempted application under the unusual facts of Baltimore City Dept. of Social Serv. v. Bouknight, 493 U.S. 549, 110 S.Ct. 900, 107 L.Ed.2d 992 (1990). In *Bouknight,* a juvenile court ordered a child, whose whereabouts were unexplained and subject to a homicide investigation, taken from his mother's custody and placed in foster care. The court cited the mother, Bouknight, for contempt and directed that she be imprisoned until she purged herself of contempt by either producing her son, Maurice, or revealing to the court his exact whereabouts. Bouknight argued that the juvenile court's order violated her privilege against self incrimination.

Justice O'Connor, writing for the majority, stated that the act of producing the child might be testimonial in nature, operating as an "implicit communication of control over Maurice at the moment of production," but:

> The possibility that a production order will compel testimonial assertions that may prove incriminating does not, in all contexts, justify invoking the privilege to resist production ... Even assuming that this limited testimonial assertion is sufficiently incriminating and "sufficiently testimonial," ... Bouknight may not invoke the privilege to resist the production order because she has assumed custodial duties related to production and because production is required as part of a noncriminal regulatory regime.

493 U.S. at 555–56, 110 S.Ct. at 905, 107 L.Ed.2d at 1000.

The Court cited its authority in Shapiro v. United States, 335 U.S. 1, 68 S.Ct. 1375, 92 L.Ed. 1787 (1948) (required records exception to Fifth Amendment privilege); In re Harris, 221 U.S. 274, 279, 31 S.Ct. 557, 55 L.Ed. 732 (1911) (Fifth Amendment not applicable to surrender of property (account books) which defendant was no longer entitled to keep); and California v. Byers, 402 U.S. 424, 91 S.Ct. 1535, 29 L.Ed.2d 9 (1971) (ability to invoke the privilege may be greatly diminished when invocation would interfere with the effective operation of a generally applicable civil regulatory requirement directed at the public at large—privilege not applicable to drivers involved in accidents who are required by statute to stop and provide their names and addresses). According to the Court, by agreeing to the terms of an initial protective order, Bouknight had impliedly agreed to "permit inspection" of Maurice who, like certain books and public records, was the object of legitimate State regulatory interests. The Court also noted that the juvenile court's demand for production of the child did not single out the parent as a person suspected of criminal activity, but merely promoted concern for the child's safety. The Court suggested that some limitations might be placed upon the State's power to use Bouknight's "testimony" in a future criminal proceeding, but declined to rule on that issue.

Justice Marshall, in a dissent joined by Justice Brennan, observed that because Bouknight could face criminal abuse and neglect or even homicide charges, the threat of self incrimination was more significant than the majority recognized. Justice Marshall also took exception to the Court's analogies. A mother is not similar to a custodian of records, he argued. And the child custody statute employed in this case was, unlike the hit and run statute in *Byers,* linked to a related criminal statute (covering child abuse).

2.   WAIVER

In a variety of situations, defendant faces the hard choice of whether to testify. The choice is hard because some advantages are given up by testifying. For example, if a defense motion for acquittal at the end of the Government's case is denied, the defendant must decide whether to stand on his motion or put up a defense—which may include his taking the stand—with the unintended but possible result that the Government's case may be strengthened sufficiently to justify a guilty verdict. In addition, a defendant who takes the stand may be impeached by highly prejudicial evidence that would not otherwise be admissible, including some kinds of unconstitutionally obtained evidence.

Of immediate concern here is the extent to which a defendant who chooses to testify in his own defense waives his privilege against self-incrimination.

United States v. Hearst

United States Court of Appeals, Ninth Circuit, 1977.
563 F.2d 1331.

■ Before BROWNING, TRASK, and WALLANCE, CIRCUIT JUDGES.

PER CURIAM:

Appellant was tried under a two-count indictment charging her with armed robbery of a San Francisco bank [the Hibernia Bank].... The government introduced photographs and testimony descriptive of appellant's role in the robbery. Appellant raised the defense of duress, contending her co-participants[, members of the Symbionese Liberation Army, who had kidnapped her,] compelled her to engage in the criminal activity. [To rebut this defense, the government was permitted to introduce evidence tending to show that appellant voluntarily participated in various revolutionary activities of her captors. Some of this evidence tended to show that appellant fired with an automatic weapon upon a clerk at Mel's Sporting Goods when the clerk attempted to arrest two of appellant's captors—Bill and Emily Harris—for shoplifting. Editors.] The jury found appellant guilty....

Appellant argues that the trial judge erred ... in ruling on appellant's privilege against self-incrimination....

During the trial appellant elected to testify in her own behalf. She described in exhaustive detail the events immediately following her kidnapping of February 4, 1974. These included physical and sexual abuses by members of the Symbionese Liberation Army (SLA), extensive interrogations, forced tape recordings and written communications designed to convince her family that she had become a revolutionary, and training in guerrilla welfare. She next described how the SLA compelled her under threat of death to participate in the robbery of the Hibernia Bank on April 15, 1974, and to identify herself by reading a revolutionary speech. She explained that by the time the group moved to Los Angeles, the SLA had convinced her that they would kill her if she tried to escape and that the Federal Bureau of Investigation also desired to murder her. Appellant added that the SLA required her to make various post-robbery admissions about her voluntary role in the crime.

Appellant's story continued by describing her participation one month after the robbery in the disturbance at Mel's Sporting Goods Store. She claimed that her reaction in firing at the store resulted from fear of the SLA, as did her admission to Thomas Matthews of complicity in the bank robbery. She then told how she, the Harrises, and Jack Scott traveled from Los Angeles to Berkeley, then to New York, to Pennsylvania, and finally to Las Vegas in September of 1974. Again, she emphasized that she was an unwilling companion of the group. After mentioning her arrival in Las Vegas, her testimony jumped a year to the time of her arrest in San Francisco on September 18, 1975.

On cross-examination, appellant refused to answer most questions concerning the period between her arrival in Las Vegas and her arrest in San Francisco.[24] In response to questions about her activities, residences, and association with other suspected members of the SLA during this year, she invoked the Fifth Amendment privilege against self-incrimination 42 times.

Prior to government questioning, appellant had moved for an order limiting the scope of the cross-examination so as to avoid the necessity of invoking the Fifth Amendment in response to questions implicating her in other crimes for which she was not on trial. Finding that appellant had waived her privilege against self-incrimination as to all relevant matters by testifying in her own behalf, the court denied this motion and allowed the government to ask her questions which resulted in her assertion of the Fifth Amendment. United States v. Hearst, 412 F.Supp. 885 (N.D.Cal. 1976). Appellant now offers five separate grounds for finding that the court committed reversible error in making this ruling.

1. The Fifth Amendment provides that "[n]o person ... shall be compelled in any criminal case to be a witness against himself." But it is also true, as the trial court stressed, that a defendant who testifies in his own behalf waives his privilege against self-incrimination with respect to the relevant matters covered by his direct testimony and subjects himself to cross-examination by the government. Brown v. United States, 356 U.S. 148, 154–55, 78 S.Ct. 622, 2 L.Ed.2d 589 (1958). Appellant contends that she "did not voluntarily waive her Fifth Amendment privilege by testifying because her testimony was compelled by the introduction of certain evidence, i.e., post-crime conduct, which was challenged as inadmissible and highly prejudicial." Reply Brief for Appellant at 7. She pleads that she was caught between the "rock and the whirlpool" when forced to decide whether to testify or allow the evidence to stand unrebutted.

The validity of this argument depends largely on appellant's assumption that evidence of her post-robbery behavior was admitted erroneously, and that she had no choice but to respond to this inadmissible evidence. We

---

24. Appellant did answer some of the government's questions about her activities during this period, but she refused to answer questions which she or her counsel perceived as incriminating. Thus, she answered questions about the membership of James Kilgore, Stephen Soliah, and Cathleen Soliah in a subversive organization, the New World Liberation Front. R.T. 1826–27. However, she refused to discuss her relationship with these individuals. She also discussed her August 12, 1975 visit to a dermatologist. R.T. 1827–29.

have concluded previously, however, that the trial court determined correctly that this evidence was relevant and admissible. Thus, appellant's attempt to compare her situation to that involved in Harrison v. United States, 392 U.S. 219, 88 S.Ct. 2008, 20 L.Ed.2d 1047 (1968), where the defendant had to testify in order to overcome the impact of prior confessions which had been illegally obtained and introduced, is unconvincing. In the present case, neither the trial court nor we found that any illegal, inadmissible evidence forced appellant to testify.

Appellant also suggests it is sufficient that she *thought* she was being compelled to testify in response to the admission of evidence which she *perceived* as prejudicial, inadmissible, and damaging to her defense. We refuse to hold that a defendant's subjective impressions of what he is "forced" to do during his trial are enough to render his testimony involuntary. A defendant often will view evidence as incriminating and inadmissible, and feel that he must take the witness stand in order to save his case. This is an inherent feature of our criminal justice system, however:

> The defendant in a criminal trial is frequently forced to testify himself and to call other witnesses in an effort to reduce the risk of conviction. When he presents his witnesses, he must reveal their identity and submit them to cross-examination which in itself may prove incriminating or which may furnish the State with leads to incriminating rebuttal evidence. That the defendant faces such a dilemma demanding a choice between complete silence and presenting a defense has never been thought an invasion of the privilege against compelled self-incrimination.

Williams v. Florida, 399 U.S. 78, 83–84, 90 S.Ct. 1893, 1897, 26 L.Ed.2d 446 (1970). In *Williams,* the Supreme Court found that the defendant had a free choice between giving notice of his alibi defense, as required by a Florida statute, and refraining from presenting this defense. Similarly, in our case, we find that appellant freely elected to testify in her own behalf.

2.   Appellant also argues that she did not waive her privilege against self-incrimination because her testimony was limited to the collateral issue of the voluntariness of certain statements (i.e., the admissions of willing participation in the bank robbery) made by her and introduced into evidence over her objection. She contends that since her testimony did not address the merits of the case, the government should not have been allowed to ask questions which attempted to prove her guilt. She refers us to Calloway v. Wainwright, 409 F.2d 59, 66 (5th Cir.), cert. denied, 395 U.S. 909, 89 S.Ct. 1752, 23 L.Ed.2d 222 (1969), which stated: "[t]hat appellant took the stand for the sole purpose of testifying upon the credibility of the voluntariness of his [earlier] confession should not be taken as a complete waiver of his constitutional privilege against self-incrimination."

Appellant's assumption about the nature of her testimony is completely erroneous. The central theme of her lengthy testimony was that from the moment of her kidnapping to the time of her arrest she was an unwilling victim of the SLA who acted under continual threats of death. She tried to show, not merely that she made her admissions involuntarily, but that she acted under duress in robbing the Hibernia Bank, firing at the sporting goods store, and traveling with the Harrises for over one year. She disputed the main element of the government's case: that she had the necessary criminal intent when she participated in the bank robbery. Thus, her reliance on *Calloway* is misplaced, for that case dealt with the much narrower situation in which a defendant takes the witness stand solely to deny the voluntariness of his confession. Calloway v. Wainwright, supra, 409 F.2d at 66.

3. Appellant next claims that even if she did waive her privilege against self-incrimination by testifying in her own behalf, the waiver did not extend to the period between her arrival in Las Vegas and her arrest in San Francisco. She argues that since she did not testify concerning her activities during this "lost year," the government had no right or reason to ask any questions about it. She would confine the proper scope of cross-examination to the events which she specifically discussed during her direct testimony.

We find that appellant misinterprets the controlling case law on waiver and the permissible limits of the cross-examination of a testifying defendant. The Supreme Court has stated that when a defendant takes the witness stand, "his credibility may be impeached and his testimony assailed like that of any other witness, and the breadth of his waiver is determined by the scope of relevant cross-examination." Brown v. United States, supra, 356 U.S. at 154–55, 78 S.Ct. at 626. "[A] defendant who takes the stand in his own behalf cannot then claim the privilege against cross-examination on matters reasonably related to the subject matter of his direct examination." McGautha v. California, 402 U.S. 183, 215, 91 S.Ct. 1454, 1471, 28 L.Ed.2d 711 (1971). This rule is premised on basic goals of fairness and ascertainment of the truth:

> The witness himself, certainly if he is a party, determines the area of disclosure and therefore of inquiry. Such witness has the choice, after weighing the advantage of the privilege against self-incrimination against the advantage of putting forward his version of the facts and his reliability as a witness, not to testify at all. He cannot reasonably claim that the Fifth Amendment gives him not only this choice but, if he elects to testify, an immunity from cross-examination on the matters he has himself put in dispute.

Brown v. United States, supra, 356 U.S. at 155–56, 78 S.Ct. at 627. Nowhere in this rule is there even a suggestion that the waiver and the permissible cross-examination are to be determined by what the defendant actually discussed during his direct testimony. Rather, the focus is on whether the government's questions are "reasonably related" to the subjects covered by the defendant's testimony.

Applying this principle to the present case, we conclude that the trial court did not abuse its broad discretion, ... in allowing the government to ask questions about the year which appellant failed to cover in her direct testimony. As we have already concluded, appellant's testimony was not limited to disputing the voluntariness of her post-robbery admissions. Instead, she attempted to show that from her kidnapping until her arrest she acted exactly as her captors directed.[25] She tried to persuade the jury

---

25. Appellant's counsel, Mr. Bailey, indicated very directly his desire to show that appellant had been threatened, abused, and coerced by the SLA for almost two years.

that her post-robbery conduct and feelings of fear, dependence, and obedience proved that she had also acted involuntarily and without criminal intent in robbing the Hibernia Bank.

We agree with the trial court's conclusion that appellant's testimony placed in issue her behavior during the entire period from abduction to arrest, and gave the government a right to question her about the "lost year." See United States v. Hearst, supra, 412 F.Supp. at 887. Although appellant did not discuss this year, the natural inference from her other testimony, if believed, was that she had acted involuntarily during this period. Having offered selective evidence of the nature of her behavior for the whole period, appellant had no valid objection to the government's attempt to show that her conduct during the omitted year belied her story and proved that she was a willing member of the SLA. Since appellant's direct testimony raised an issue about the nature of her conduct during the entire one and one-half years prior to her arrest, the government's questions about her activities, associations, and residences during the interim year were more than "reasonably related" to the subject matter of her prior testimony. That answers to these questions might have implicated appellant in crimes for which she was not on trial had no bearing on the questions' relevancy or relationship to her direct testimony.

4.   Appellant argues that even if she had no right to refuse to answer the government's questions, the court erred in allowing the prosecution to continue to ask questions which it knew would elicit repeated assertions of the privilege against self-incrimination. We find that appellant's authorities do not support her proposition. Her cases involve situations in which the government or the defendant questioned a witness or a co-defendant, knowing that a valid, unwaived Fifth Amendment privilege would be asserted. ...She fails to offer support relating to the very different problem, present in our case, in which the government attempts to cross-examine a witness-defendant who has previously waived his privilege against self-incrimination.

In determining whether it is improper for the government to ask a defendant questions which will result in an assertion of the privilege against self-incrimination, the central consideration is whether the defendant has waived his privilege as to the propounded questions. When a witness or a defendant has a valid Fifth Amendment privilege, government questions designed to elicit this privilege present to the jury information that is misleading, irrelevant to the issue of the witness's or the defendant's credibility, and not subject to examination by defense counsel. ...Therefore, we do not allow this form of questioning.

But when a defendant has voluntarily waived his Fifth Amendment privilege by testifying in his own behalf, the rationale for prohibiting privilege-invoking queries on cross-examination does not apply. The defen-

When he sought to gain admission into evidence of a portion of her testimony, he stated: "She has been threatened by them [the Harrises] for two years, Your Honor." R.T. 1416. He termed her testimony "a rebuttal to the notion that Mr. Browning [the United States Attorney] wishes to sell this jury that she had no actual fear of the Harrises." R.T. 1418.

dant has chosen to make an issue of his credibility; he has elected to take his case to the jury in the most direct fashion. The government, accordingly, has a right to challenge the defendant's story on cross-examination. . . . The government may impeach the defendant by developing inconsistencies in his testimony; the government may also successfully impeach him by asking questions which he refuses to answer. If the refusals could not be put before the jury, the defendant would have the unusual and grossly unfair ability to insulate himself from challenges merely by declining to answer embarrassing questions. He alone could control the presentation of evidence to the jury.

Our view finds support in decisions construing the propriety of judicial and prosecutorial comment upon a defendant's refusal to testify. Griffin v. California, 380 U.S. 609, 615, 85 S.Ct. 1229, 14 L.Ed.2d 106 (1965), held that neither the government nor the court may comment on an accused's exercise of his Fifth Amendment privilege by refusing to testify. But it has long been established that comment is allowed when a defendant fails to explain evidence against him after first waiving his privilege by taking the witness stand. Caminetti v. United States, 242 U.S. 470, 492–95, 37 S.Ct. 192, 61 L.Ed. 442 (1917).[26] Since the offering of questions designed to elicit invocations of the Fifth Amendment is really only a form of comment upon the defendant's failure to testify, intended to present to the jury the government's interpretation of his credibility, we believe that the rule of *Caminetti* should apply to the present case.

We have concluded that appellant waived her privilege against self-incrimination with respect to her activities during the interval between her arrival in Las Vegas and her arrest in San Francisco. Therefore, it was permissible for the government to ask questions about this period, even though they led to 42 assertions of the Fifth Amendment.

* * *

NOTES

1. **Privileges of defendants and witnesses.** McCormick on Evidence distinguishes two "branches" of the privilege against compelled self-incrimination: the privilege of an accused in a criminal proceeding and the privilege of a witness:

> A criminal accused ordinarily need not affirmatively "invoke" his privilege, as he is even entitled not to be called as a witness at all. A non-accused who appears as a witness, in contrast, will ordinarily invoke the privilege as a response to particular questions asked on direct or cross-examination.

1 Kenneth S. Broun, et al., McCormick on Evidence § 118 (5th ed. 1999). There is a similar difference in regard to when persons in the two statuses have "waived" the privilege. A witness "waives" the privilege only by actually disclosing incriminating information such that further testimony would not significantly increase the risk of incrimination. Id. § 134. But, as the principal case holds, an accused waives the privilege by testifying in his own behalf. Id. § 129.

---

26. The indication in Brown v. United States, supra, 356 U.S. at 154–55, 78 S.Ct. 622, that a defendant retains a privilege against self-incrimination as to subjects not related to his direct testimony suggests that the prosecution may not comment upon the defendant's silence on matters beyond the scope of his direct examination.

2. **Scope of cross-examination.** The scope of permitted cross-examination varies from jurisdiction to jurisdiction. At one end of the spectrum stands the English rule, also in force in a number of American states, which permits the cross-examiner to ask about any facts relevant to any issue in the case. At the opposite end stand the federal and most state courts: Cross-examination is limited to matters brought out on direct. Not surprisingly, there are in between positions. The one sub-rule shared by all jurisdictions is that cross-examination conducted solely to impeach is not restricted to matters brought out on direct.

The question of importance at this point is not the relative merits of those rules, but whether the federal constitutional rights of a defendant in one state ought to vary from the rights of a defendant in another state according to the accident of which cross-examination rule the state has. One writer has advanced the position that as a practical matter, the limited scope of the federal cross-examination rule leaves "a portion of the privilege intact." He then argues, from the reasoning in cases like Malloy v. Hogan, that the first, fourth and sixth amendment protections should be the same in scope whether the action complained of was that of the federal or a state government, that the waiver by taking the stand might well be limited in scope to that which would occur in a federal case. See Note, 45 N.C.L.Rev. 1030 (1967).

3. **Using inadmissible evidence to cross-examine.** A defendant who testifies in his own behalf also loses the right to have certain evidence totally excluded because of the way in which it was obtained. Thus a confession elicited in violation of Miranda v. Arizona, 384 U.S. 436, 86 S.Ct. 1602, 16 L.Ed.2d 694 (1966), can be used for otherwise permissible impeachment of a testifying defendant, Harris v. New York, 401 U.S. 222, 91 S.Ct. 643, 28 L.Ed.2d 1 (1971), as may evidence obtained in an unreasonable search or seizure, United States v. Havens, 446 U.S. 620, 100 S.Ct. 1912, 64 L.Ed.2d 559 (1980). Coercion in obtaining a confession, however, casts doubt upon the confession's reliability and thus precludes its use even for impeachment. Mincey v. Arizona, 437 U.S. 385, 98 S.Ct. 2408, 57 L.Ed.2d 290 (1978). In *Havens,* the Court also held that the prosecution could use otherwise inadmissible evidence to impeach statements made by a testifying defendant during cross examination as well as in the course of direct examination, as long as those statements made during cross examination were "reasonably suggested by the defendant's direct examination." 446 U.S. at 627, 100 S.Ct. at 1917, 64 L.Ed.2d at 566. The Court explained:

> We have repeatedly insisted that when defendants testify, they must testify truthfully or suffer the consequences. This is true even though a defendant is compelled to testify against his will. It is essential, therefore, to the proper functioning of the adversary system that when a defendant takes the stand, the government be permitted proper and effective cross-examination in an attempt to elicit the truth. The defendant's obligation to testify truthfully is fully binding on him when he is cross-examined. His privilege against self-incrimination does not shield him from proper questioning. He would unquestionably be subject to a perjury prosecution if he knowingly lies on cross-examination. In terms of impeaching a defendant's seemingly false statements with his prior inconsistent utterances or with other reliable evidence available to the government, we see no difference of constitutional magnitude between the defendant's statements on direct examination and his answers to questions put to him on cross-examination that are plainly within the scope of the defendant's direct examination. Without this opportunity, the normal function of cross-examination would be severely impeded.

446 U.S. at 626–27, 100 S.Ct. at 1916–17, 64 L.Ed.2d at 565–66.

CHAPTER 24

EFFECTIVE ASSISTANCE OF COUNSEL

Analysis

The major traditional issue in applying the Sixth Amendment's right to representation by counsel has been the prosecutions to which it applies. Betts v. Brady, 316 U.S. 455, 62 S.Ct. 1252, 86 L.Ed. 1595 (1942), held that failure to appoint counsel for an indigent defendant in a state felony prosecution violated the right to counsel only if, considering all the circumstances, the absence of representation was a denial of fundamental fairness. This approach was abandoned in Gideon v. Wainwright, 372 U.S. 335, 83 S.Ct. 792, 9 L.Ed.2d 799 (1963), in which the Supreme Court held that all indigent state defendants charged with serious crimes are entitled to state-provided representation. The Court reasoned that "in our adversary system of criminal justice, any person haled into court, who is too poor to hire a lawyer, cannot be assured of a fair trial unless counsel is provided for him." 372 U.S. at 344, 83 S.Ct. at 796, 9 L.Ed.2d at 805. Argersinger v. Hamlin, 407 U.S. 25, 92 S.Ct. 2006, 32 L.Ed.2d 530 (1972), held that an indigent defendant tried and convicted of the misdemeanor of carrying a concealed weapon and sentenced to 90 days in jail was denied the right to counsel when he made no waiver of the right to representation and no lawyer was provided at state expense. But in Scott v. Illinois, 440 U.S. 367, 99 S.Ct. 1158, 59 L.Ed.2d 383 (1979), the Court declined to require state-provided representation for indigent defendants charged with misdemeanors carrying possible jail sentences but whose actual sentence did not include a period of confinement. In explaining the holding that the Sixth and Fourteenth Amendments require only that no indigent defendant be sentenced to a term of imprisonment unless the state has offered access to appointed counsel, Justice Rehnquist stated:

> [A]ctual imprisonment as the line defining the constitutional right to appointment of counsel ... has proved reasonably workable, whereas any extension would create confusion and impose unpredictable, but substantial costs on 50 quite diverse States.

440 U.S. at 373, 99 S.Ct. at 1162, 59 L.Ed.2d at 389. Flexibility in the *Argersinger-Scott* standard appeared in Middendorf v. Henry, 425 U.S. 25, 96 S.Ct. 1281, 47 L.Ed.2d 556 (1976), where the Court held that given the unique characteristics of the military community, a military summary court-martial is not a "criminal proceeding" within the meaning of the Sixth Amendment. Consequently, imposition of thirty days' confinement at hard labor upon a soldier by such a proceeding, without providing access to representation, did not violate the Sixth Amendment.

The two major issues presented by the Sixth and Fourteenth Amendments' right to representation are developed in the two sections of this Chapter. First, the requirement that counsel be effective is explored. Second, defendants' right to self-representation and the related matter of waiver of this right and the right to representation by counsel is presented.

A.   THE RIGHT TO HAVE COUNSEL BE "EFFECTIVE"

There has long been general agreement that the right to counsel involves the right to have counsel actually perform effectively. However, there had been widespread disagreement concerning the standard that must be applied to determine whether the performance of counsel was so deficient as to deny the defendant the Sixth and Fourteenth Amendments' right to representation. As late as 1978 Justice White chastised the Court for failing to grant certiorari to address the issue in Maryland v. Marzullo, 435 U.S. 1011, 98 S.Ct. 1885, 56 L.Ed.2d 394 (1978).

A number of lower courts had traditionally distinguished between retained and publicly provided lawyers for purposes of Sixth Amendment analysis. But this approach was apparently rejected by the Supreme Court in Cuyler v. Sullivan, 446 U.S. 335, 100 S.Ct. 1708, 64 L.Ed.2d 333 (1980). Responding to the argument that a conflict of interest on the part of Sullivan's retained counsel did not violate the Sixth Amendment because the conduct of such an attorney involved no state action, the Court explained:

> A proper respect for the Sixth Amendment disarms [the] contention that defendants who retain their own lawyers are entitled to less protection than defendants for whom the State appoints counsel. ...Since the State's conduct of a criminal trial itself implicates the State in the defendant's conviction, we see no basis for drawing a distinction between retained and appointed counsel that would deny equal justice to defendants who must choose their own lawyers.

446 U.S. at 344–45, 100 S.Ct. at 1716, 64 L.Ed.2d at 344.

United States v. Cronic

Supreme Court of the United States, 1984.
466 U.S. 648, 104 S.Ct. 2039, 80 L.Ed.2d 657.

■ JUSTICE STEVENS delivered the opinion of the Court.

Respondent and two associates were indicted on mail fraud charges. ...Shortly before the scheduled trial date, respondent's retained counsel withdrew. The court appointed a young lawyer with a real estate practice to represent respondent, but allowed him only 25 days for pretrial preparation, even though it had taken the Government over four and one-half years to investigate the case and it had reviewed thousands of documents during that investigation. The two codefendants agreed to testify for the Government; respondent was convicted on 11 of the 13 counts in the indictment and received a 25–year sentence.

The Court of Appeals reversed the conviction because it concluded that respondent did not "have the Assistance of Counsel for his defence" that is guaranteed by the Sixth Amendment to the Constitution. This conclusion was not supported by a determination that respondent's trial counsel had made any specified errors, that his actual performance had prejudiced the defense, or that he failed to exercise "the skill, judgment, and diligence of a reasonably competent defense attorney"; instead the conclusion rested on the premise that no such showing is necessary "when circumstances hamper a given lawyer's preparation of a defendant's case." The question presented by the Government's petition for certiorari is whether the Court of Appeals has correctly interpreted the Sixth Amendment.

I

The indictment alleged a "check kiting" scheme. At the direction of respondent, his codefendant Cummings opened a bank account in the name of Skyproof Manufacturing, Inc. (Skyproof), at a bank in Tampa, Florida, and codefendant Merritt opened two accounts, one in his own name and one in the name of Skyproof, at banks in Norman, Oklahoma. ...By "kiting" insufficient funds checks between the banks in those two cities, defendants allegedly created false or inflated balances in the accounts. ...

At trial the Government proved that Skyproof's checks were issued and deposited at the times and places, and in the amounts, described in the indictment. Having made plea bargains with defendants Cummings and Merritt, who had actually handled the issuance and delivery of the relevant written instruments, the Government proved through their testimony that respondent had conceived and directed the entire scheme, ...

After the District Court ruled that a prior conviction could be used to impeach his testimony, respondent decided not to testify. Counsel put on no defense. By cross-examination of Government witnesses, however, he established that Skyproof was not merely a sham, but actually was an operating company with a significant cash flow, though its revenues were not sufficient to justify as large a "float" as the record disclosed. Cross-examination also established the absence of written evidence that respondent had any control over Skyproof, or personally participated in the withdrawals or deposits.

The four-day jury trial ended on July 17, 1980, and respondent was sentenced on August 28, 1980. His counsel perfected a timely appeal, which was docketed on September 11, 1980. Two months later respondent filed a motion to substitute a new attorney in the Court of Appeals, and also filed a motion in the District Court seeking to vacate his conviction on the ground that he had newly discovered evidence ... and ... he also challenged the competence of his trial counsel.[1] The District Court refused to entertain the motion while the appeal was pending. ...

The Court of Appeals reversed the conviction because it inferred that respondent's constitutional right to the effective assistance of counsel had been violated. That inference was based on its use of five criteria: "(1) [T]he time afforded for investigation and preparation; (2) the experience of counsel; (3) the gravity of the charge; (4) the complexity of possible defenses; and (5) the accessibility of witnesses to counsel." United States v. Cronic, 675 F.2d 1126, 1129 (C.A.10 1982) (quoting United States v. Golub, 638 F.2d 185, 189 (C.A.10 1980)). Under the test employed by the Court of Appeals, reversal is required even if the lawyer's actual performance was flawless. By utilizing this inferential approach, the Court of Appeals erred.

II

An accused's right to be represented by counsel is a fundamental component of our criminal justice system. Lawyers in criminal cases "are necessities, not luxuries." Their presence is essential because they are the means through which the other rights of the person on trial are secured. Without counsel, the right to a trial itself would be "of little avail," as this Court has recognized repeatedly. "Of all the rights that an accused person has, the right to be represented by counsel is by far the most precious, for it affects his ability to assert any other right he may have."

The special value of the right to the assistance of counsel explains why "[i]t has long been recognized that the right to counsel is the right to the effective assistance of counsel." McMann v. Richardson, 397 U.S. 759, 771, n. 14, 90 S.Ct. 1441, 1449, 25 L.Ed.2d 763 (1970). The text of the Sixth Amendment itself suggests as much. The amendment requires not merely the provision counsel to the accused, but "Assistance," which is to be "for his defence." Thus, "the core purpose of the counsel guarantee was to assure 'Assistance' at trial, when the accused was confronted with both the intricacies of the law and the advocacy of the prosecutor." United States v. Ash, 413 U.S. 300, 309, 93 S.Ct. 2568, 2573, 37 L.Ed.2d 619 (1973). If no actual "Assistance" "for" the accused's "defence" is provided, then the constitutional guarantee has been violated. To hold otherwise

> "could convert the appointment of counsel into nothing more than a formal compliance with the Constitution's requirement that an accused be given the assistance of counsel. The Constitution's guarantee of assistance of counsel cannot be satisfied by mere formal appointment." Avery v. Alabama, 308 U.S. 444, 446, 60 S.Ct. 321, 322, 84 L.Ed. 377 (1940) (footnote omitted).

Thus, in *McMann* the Court indicated that the accused is entitled to "a reasonably competent attorney," 397 U.S., at 770, 90 S.Ct., at 1448, whose advice is "within the range of competence demanded of attorneys in

---

1. During trial, in response to questions from the bench, respondent expressed his satisfaction with counsel's performance. However, in his motion for new trial, respondent attacked counsel's performance and ex- plained his prior praise of counsel through an affidavit of a psychologist who indicated that he had advised respondent to praise trial counsel in order to ameliorate the lawyer's apparent lack of self-confidence.

criminal cases." In Cuyler v. Sullivan, 446 U.S. 335, 100 S.Ct. 1708, 64 L.Ed.2d 333 (1980), we held that the Constitution guarantees an accused "adequate legal assistance." And in Engle v. Isaac, 456 U.S. 107, 102 S.Ct. 1558, 71 L.Ed.2d 783 (1982), the Court referred to the criminal defendant's constitutional guarantee of "a fair trial and a competent attorney."

The substance of the Constitution's guarantee of the effective assistance of counsel is illuminated by reference to its underlying purpose. "Truth," Lord Eldon said, "is best discovered by powerful statements on both sides of the question." This dictum describes the unique strength of our system of criminal justice. "The very premise of our adversary system of criminal justice is that partisan advocacy on both sides of a case will best promote the ultimate objective that the guilty be convicted and the innocent go free." Herring v. New York, 422 U.S. 853, 862, 95 S.Ct. 2550, 2555, 45 L.Ed.2d 593 (1975). It is that "very premise" that underlies and gives meaning to the Sixth Amendment. It "is meant to assure fairness in the adversary criminal process." United States v. Morrison, 449 U.S. 361, 364, 101 S.Ct. 665, 667, 66 L.Ed.2d 564 (1981). Unless the accused receives the effective assistance of counsel, "a serious risk of error infects the trial itself." Cuyler v. Sullivan, 446 U.S., at 343, 100 S.Ct., at 1715.

Thus, the adversarial process protected by the Sixth Amendment requires that the accused have "counsel acting in the role of an advocate," Anders v. California, 386 U.S. 738, 743, 87 S.Ct. 1396, 1399, 18 L.Ed.2d 493 (1967). The right to the effective assistance of counsel is thus the right of the accused to require the prosecution's case to survive the crucible of meaningful adversarial testing. When a true adversarial criminal trial has been conducted—even if defense counsel may have made demonstrable errors—the kind of testing envisioned by the Sixth Amendment has occurred. But if the process loses its character as a confrontation between adversaries, the constitutional guarantee is violated. As Judge Wyzanski has written: "While a criminal trial is not a game in which the participants are expected to enter the ring with a near match in skills, neither is it a sacrifice of unarmed prisoners to gladiators." United States ex rel. Williams v. Twomey, 510 F.2d 634, 640 (CA7), cert. denied, 423 U.S. 876, 96 S.Ct. 148, 46 L.Ed.2d 109 (1975).[2]

III

While the Court of Appeals purported to apply a standard of reasonable competence, it did not indicate that there had been an actual breakdown of the adversarial process during the trial of this case. Instead it concluded that the circumstances surrounding the representation of respondent mandated an inference that counsel was unable to discharge his duties.

---

2. Thus, the appropriate inquiry focuses on the adversarial process, not on the accused's relationship with his lawyer as such. If counsel is a reasonably effective advocate, he meets constitutional standards irrespective of his client's evaluation of his performance. See Jones v. Barnes, 463 U.S. [475], 103 S.Ct. 3308, 77 L.Ed.2d 987 (1983); Morris v. Slappy, 461 U.S. 1, 103 S.Ct. 1610, 75 L.Ed.2d 610 (1983). It is for this reason that we attach no weight to either respondent's expression of satisfaction with counsel's performance at the time of his trial, or to his later expression of dissatisfaction.

In our evaluation of that conclusion, we begin by recognizing that the right to the effective assistance of counsel is recognized not for its own sake, but because of the effect it has on the ability of the accused to receive a fair trial. Absent some effect of challenged conduct on the reliability of the trial process, the Sixth Amendment guarantee is generally not implicated. . . . Moreover, because we presume that the lawyer is competent to provide the guiding hand that the defendant needs, . . . the burden rests on the accused to demonstrate a constitutional violation. There are, however, circumstances that are so likely to prejudice the accused that the cost of litigating their effect in a particular case is unjustified.

Most obvious, of course, is the complete denial of counsel. The presumption that counsel's assistance is essential requires us to conclude that a trial is unfair if the accused is denied counsel at a critical stage of his trial. Similarly, if counsel entirely fails to subject the prosecution's case to meaningful adversarial testing, then there has been a denial of Sixth Amendment rights that makes the adversary process itself presumptively unreliable. No specific showing of prejudice was required in Davis v. Alaska, 415 U.S. 308, 94 S.Ct. 1105, 39 L.Ed.2d 347 (1974) because the petitioner had been "denied the right of effective cross-examination" which " 'would be constitutional error of the first magnitude and no amount of showing of want of prejudice would cure it.' " Id., at 318, 94 S.Ct., at 1111 (citing Smith v. Illinois, 390 U.S. 129, 131, 88 S.Ct. 748, 749, 19 L.Ed.2d 956 (1968), and Brookhart v. Janis, 384 U.S. 1, 3, 86 S.Ct. 1245, 1246, 16 L.Ed.2d 314 (1966)).

Circumstances of that magnitude may be present on some occasions when although counsel is available to assist the accused during trial, the likelihood that any lawyer, even a fully competent one, could provide effective assistance is so small that a presumption of prejudice is appropriate without inquiry into the actual conduct of the trial. Powell v. Alabama, 287 U.S. 45, 53 S.Ct. 55, 77 L.Ed. 158 (1932), was such a case.

The defendants had been indicted for a highly publicized capital offense. Six days before trial, the trial judge appointed "all the members of the bar" for purposes of arraignment. "Whether they would represent the defendants thereafter if no counsel appeared in their behalf, was a matter of speculation only, or, as the judge indicated, of mere anticipation on the part of the court." Id., 287 U.S., at 56, 53 S.Ct., at 59. On the day of trial, a lawyer from Tennessee appeared on behalf of persons "interested" in the defendants, but stated that he had not had an opportunity to prepare the case or to familiarize himself with local procedure, and therefore was unwilling to represent the defendants on such short notice. The problem was resolved when the court decided that the Tennessee lawyer would represent the defendants, with whatever help the local bar could provide.

> "The defendants, young, ignorant, illiterate, surrounded by hostile sentiment, haled back and forth under guard of soldiers, charged with an atrocious crime regarded with special horror in the community where they were to be tried, were thus put in peril of their lives within a few moments after counsel for the first time charged with any degree of responsibility began to represent them." Id., at 58–59, 53 S.Ct., at 60.

This Court held that "such designation of counsel as was attempted here was either so indefinite or so close upon the trial as to amount to a denial of effective and substantial aid in that regard." Id., at 53, 53 S.Ct., at 58. The Court did not examine the actual performance of counsel at trial, but instead concluded that under these circumstances the likelihood that counsel could have performed as an effective adversary was so remote as to have made the trial inherently unfair. *Powell* was thus a case in which the surrounding circumstances made it so unlikely that any lawyer could provide effective assistance that ineffectiveness was properly presumed without inquiry into actual performance at trial.

But every refusal to postpone a criminal trial will not give rise to such a presumption. In Avery v. Alabama, 308 U.S. 444, 60 S.Ct. 321, 84 L.Ed. 377 (1940), counsel was appointed in a capital case only three days before trial, and the trial court denied counsel's request for additional time to prepare. Nevertheless, the Court held that since evidence and witnesses were easily accessible to defense counsel, the circumstances did not make it unreasonable to expect that counsel could adequately prepare for trial during that period of time. Similarly, in Chambers v. Maroney, 399 U.S. 42, 90 S.Ct. 1975, 26 L.Ed.2d 419 (1970), the Court refused "to fashion a *per se* rule requiring reversal of every conviction following tardy appointment of counsel." Thus, only when surrounding circumstances justify a presumption of ineffectiveness can a Sixth Amendment claim be sufficient without inquiry into counsel's actual performance at trial.[3]

The Court of Appeals did not find that respondent was denied the presence of counsel at a critical stage of the prosecution. Nor did it find, based on the actual conduct of the trial, that there was a breakdown in the adversarial process that would justify a presumption that respondent's conviction was insufficiently reliable to satisfy the Constitution. The dispositive question in this case therefore is whether the circumstances surrounding respondent's representation—and in particular the five criteria identified by the Court of Appeals—justified such a presumption.

3. The Government suggests that a presumption of prejudice is justified when counsel is subject to "external constraints" on his performance. In this case the Court of Appeals identified an "external" constraint—the District Court's decision to give counsel only 25 days to prepare for trial. The fact that the accused can attribute a deficiency in his representation to a source external to trial counsel does not make it any more or less likely that he received the type of trial envisioned by the Sixth Amendment, nor does it justify reversal of his conviction absent an actual effect on the trial process or the likelihood of such an effect. Cf. United States v. Agurs, 427 U.S. 97, 110, 96 S.Ct. 2392, 2400, 49 L.Ed.2d 342 (1976) (prosecutorial misconduct should be evaluated not on the basis of culpability but by its effect on the fairness of the trial). That is made clear by *Chambers* and *Avery*. Both cases involved "external constraints" on counsel in the form of court-imposed limitations on the length of pretrial preparation, yet in neither did the Court presume that the "constraint" had an effect on the fairness of the trial. In fact, only last Term we made it clear that with respect to a trial court's refusal to grant the defense additional time to prepare for trial, an "external constraint" on counsel, great deference must be shown to trial courts, because of the scheduling problems they face. See Morris v. Slappy, 461 U.S. 1, 11, 103 S.Ct. 1610, 1616, 75 L.Ed.2d 610 (1983). Conversely, we have presumed prejudice when counsel labors under an actual conflict of interest, despite the fact that the constraints on counsel in that context are entirely self-imposed. See Cuyler v. Sullivan, 446 U.S. 335, 100 S.Ct. 1708, 64 L.Ed.2d 333 (1980).

IV

The five factors listed in the Court of Appeals' opinion are relevant to an evaluation of a lawyer's effectiveness in a particular case, but neither separately nor in combination do they provide a basis for concluding that competent counsel was not able to provide this respondent with the guiding hand that the Constitution guarantees.

Respondent places special stress on the disparity between the duration of the Government's investigation and the period the District Court allowed to newly appointed counsel for trial preparation. . . .

Neither the period of time that the Government spent investigating the case, nor the number of documents that its agents reviewed during that investigation, is necessarily relevant to the question whether a competent lawyer could prepare to defend the case in 25 days. The Government's task of finding and assembling admissible evidence that will carry its burden of proving guilt beyond a reasonable doubt is entirely different from the defendant's task in preparing to deny or rebut a criminal charge. Of course, in some cases the rebuttal may be equally burdensome and time consuming, but there is no necessary correlation between the two. In this case, the time devoted by the Government to the assembly, organization, and summarization of the thousands of written records evidencing the two streams of checks flowing between the banks in Florida and Oklahoma unquestionably simplified the work of defense counsel in identifying and understanding the basic character of the defendants' scheme. When a series of repetitious transactions fit into a single mold, the number of written exhibits that are needed to define the pattern may be unrelated to the time that is needed to understand it.

The significance of counsel's preparation time is further reduced by the nature of the charges against respondent. Most of the Government's case consisted merely of establishing the transactions between the two banks. A competent attorney would have no reason to question the authenticity, accuracy or relevance of this evidence—there could be no dispute that these transactions actually occurred. As respondent appears to recognize, the only *bona fide* jury issue open to competent defense counsel on these facts was whether respondent acted with intent to defraud. When there is no reason to dispute the underlying historical facts, the period of 25 days to consider the question whether those facts justify an inference of criminal intent is not so short that it even arguably justifies a presumption that no lawyer could provide the respondent with the effective assistance of counsel required by the Constitution.

That conclusion is not undermined by the fact that respondent's lawyer was young, that his principal practice was in real estate, or that this was his first jury trial. Every experienced criminal defense attorney once tried his first criminal case. Moreover, a lawyer's experience with real estate transactions might be more useful in preparing to try a criminal case involving financial transactions than would prior experience in handling, for example, armed robbery prosecutions. The character of a particular lawyer's experience may shed light in an evaluation of his actual performance, but it does not justify a presumption of ineffectiveness in the absence of such an evaluation.

The three other criteria—the gravity of the charge, the complexity of the case, and the accessibility of witnesses—are all matters that may affect what a reasonably competent attorney could be expected to have done under the circumstances, but none identifies circumstances that in themselves make it unlikely that respondent received the effective assistance of counsel.

V

This case is not one in which the surrounding circumstances make it unlikely that the defendant could have received the effective assistance of counsel. The criteria used by the Court of Appeals do not demonstrate that counsel failed to function in any meaningful sense as the Government's adversary. Respondent can therefore make out a claim of ineffective assistance only by pointing to specific errors made by trial counsel. In this Court, respondent's present counsel argues that the record would support such an attack, but we leave that claim—as well as the other alleged trial errors raised by respondent which were not passed upon by the Court of Appeals—for the consideration of the Court of Appeals on remand.

The judgment is reversed and the case is remanded for further proceedings consistent with this opinion.

It is so ordered.

■ JUSTICE MARSHALL concurs in the judgment.

NOTES

1. **External constraints on effectiveness.** A number of aspects of trial procedure have been scrutinized and sometimes condemned on the basis of government interference with the right to counsel. In Ferguson v. Georgia, 365 U.S. 570, 81 S.Ct. 756, 5 L.Ed.2d 783 (1961), for example, Georgia procedure permitted a defendant to make an unsworn statement—but no more—before the jury. Because this denied a defendant the right to have his attorney question him before the jury to elicit his version of the events, the Court found the procedure a denial of the right to "the guiding hand of counsel as is guaranteed by due process." In Brooks v. Tennessee, 406 U.S. 605, 92 S.Ct. 1891, 32 L.Ed.2d 358 (1972), a Tennessee requirement that a defendant who wishes to testify in his own behalf do so before any other defense witness testifies was found to suffer the same defect. By Herring v. New York, 422 U.S. 853, 95 S.Ct. 2550, 45 L.Ed.2d 593 (1975), the Court stated, "The right to the assistance of counsel has . . . been given a meaning that ensures to the defense in a criminal trial the opportunity to participate fully and fairly in the adversary factfinding process." 422 U.S. at 858, 95 S.Ct. at 2553, 45 L.Ed.2d at 598. In *Herring,* the Court held that complete denial to defense counsel of any opportunity, in a bench trial, to make closing or summary argument violated the right to counsel. "[N]o aspect of . . . advocacy could be more important than the opportunity finally to marshall the evidence for each side before submission of the case to judgment." 422 U.S. at 862, 95 S.Ct. at 2555, 45 L.Ed.2d at 600. Geders v. United States, 425 U.S. 80, 96 S.Ct. 1330, 47 L.Ed.2d 592 (1976) involved a trial judge's order that during a 17–hour overnight recess, between the defendant's testimony on direct and his cross examination the next day, the defendant not consult with his attorney "about anything." Stressing the existence of alternative methods of dealing with the potential problem of "coaching" a witness, the Supreme Court found the defendant's Sixth Amendment right infringed. But the trend was re-

versed in Lakeside v. Oregon, 435 U.S. 333, 98 S.Ct. 1091, 55 L.Ed.2d 319 (1978). After losing his argument that an instruction to the jury that no inference could be drawn from the defendant's failure to testify violated his Fifth Amendment rights, Lakeside urged that the instruction interfered with defense counsel's strategy and thus violated the right to counsel. Rejecting this "ingenious" argument, the Court reasoned that the Sixth Amendment has never been read as giving defense counsel the right to veto otherwise permissible actions of a trial judge. "To hold otherwise," it continued, "would mean that the constitutional right to counsel would be implicated in almost every wholly permissible ruling of a trial judge, if it is made over the objection of the defendant's lawyer." 435 U.S. at 341, 98 S.Ct. at 1096, 55 L.Ed.2d at 326.

In Morris v. Slappy, 461 U.S. 1, 103 S.Ct. 1610, 75 L.Ed.2d 610 (1983) defendant, charged with several felonies, was assigned a deputy public defender to represent him. A week before trial that attorney was hospitalized for emergency surgery and another deputy public defender was assigned to the case. Respondent made several requests for a continuance of his trial to permit the hospitalized defender to represent him. The trial court refused the motions for continuances on the assurance of the replacement that he was prepared to try the case. The United States Court of Appeals found that the trial court's action denied respondent's Sixth Amendment right to counsel because it denied respondent "a meaningful attorney-client relationship." The Court, in an opinion by the Chief Justice, reversed:

> The Court of Appeals' conclusion that the Sixth Amendment right to counsel "would be without substance if it did not include the right to a *meaningful attorney-client relationship*," . . . is without basis in the law. . . . No court could possibly guarantee that a defendant will develop the kind of rapport with his attorney—privately retained or provided by the public—that the Court of Appeals thought part of the Sixth Amendment guarantee of counsel. Accordingly, we reject the claim that the Sixth Amendment guarantees a "meaningful relationship" between an accused and his counsel.

461 U.S. at 13–14, 103 S.Ct. at 1617, 75 L.Ed.2d at 621.

The Court returned to the issue raised in *Geders,* supra, in Perry v. Leeke, 488 U.S. 272, 109 S.Ct. 594, 102 L.Ed.2d 624 (1989). The Court held that an order prohibiting contact between defendant and his attorney during a fifteen minute recess between defendant's direct and cross-examination did not violate the right to counsel. The Court surmised that only the defendant's impending cross-examination would be discussed during such a break, whereas during the overnight recess in *Geders* a variety of matters not involving testimony could be expected to be discussed.

> [W]hen he assumes the role of a witness, the rules that generally apply to other witnesses . . . are generally applicable to him as well.

* * *

> [I]t is simply an empirical predicate of our system of adversary rather than inquisitorial justice that cross-examination of a witness who is uncounseled between direct examination and cross-examination is more likely to lead to discovery of truth.

488 U.S. at 282, 109 S.Ct. at 600–01, 102 L.Ed.2d at 634–35.

2. **Forfeiture of assets intended as attorney's fees.** Federal drug and racketeering statutes permit forfeiture to the government of all property derived from illegal activities. Do the Fifth and Sixth Amendments place restrictions upon forfeitures of property used or intended to be used by an accused to pay the legal fees of defense counsel? In Caplin & Drysdale, Chartered v. United States, 491 U.S.

617, 109 S.Ct. 2646, 105 L.Ed.2d 528 (1989), one Reckmeyer was charged with drug offenses. After conviction, an order was entered forfeiting specified assets to the government. Petitioner, a law firm representing Reckmeyer, intervened to claim $17,000 of those funds for legal fees. The Supreme Court, in an opinion by The Chief Justice, held that the forfeiture statutes were not intended by Congress to exempt attorneys' fees from their reach. As to the claim that the Sixth Amendment prohibits such a forfeiture, the Court said

> Whatever the full extent of the Sixth Amendment's protection of one's right to retain counsel of his choosing, that protection does not go beyond "the individual's right to spend his own money to obtain the advice and assistance of . . . counsel." A defendant has no Sixth Amendment right to spend another person's money for services rendered by an attorney, even if those funds are the only way that that defendant will be able to retain the attorney of his choice. A robbery suspect, for example, has no Sixth Amendment right to use funds he has stolen from a bank to retain an attorney to defend him if he is apprehended. The money, though in his possession, is not rightfully his; the government does not violate the Sixth Amendment if it seizes the robbery proceeds, and refuses to permit the defendant to use them to pay for his defense.

491 U.S. at 626, 109 S.Ct. at 2652–53, 105 L.Ed.2d at 541–42. As to petitioner's Fifth Amendment claim, that this use of the forfeiture statute would upset the balance of forces between the accused and his accuser, because a prosecutor could use the forfeiture provisions deliberately to deprive the defendant of the opportunity to retain especially effective counsel, the Court responded that

> The Constitution does not forbid the imposition of an otherwise permissible criminal sanction, such as forfeiture, merely because in some cases prosecutors may abuse the processes available to them, e.g., by attempting to impose them on persons who should not be subjected to that punishment. . . . Cases involving particular abuses can be dealt with individually by the lower courts, when (and if) any such cases arise.

491 U.S. at 634–35, 109 S.Ct. at 2657, 105 L.Ed.2d at 547. Justice Blackmun, joined by Justices Brennan, Marshall and Stevens, dissented.

In the companion case of United States v. Monsanto, 491 U.S. 600, 109 S.Ct. 2657, 105 L.Ed.2d 512 (1989), the Court held that a trial court may enter a pretrial order freezing assets based on a finding of probable cause that the assets are forfeitable and that such an order can reach assets intended by the defendant to pay his attorney.

Strickland v. Washington

Supreme Court of the United States, 1984.
466 U.S. 668, 104 S.Ct. 2052, 80 L.Ed.2d 674.

■ JUSTICE O'CONNOR delivered the opinion of the Court.

This case requires us to consider the proper standards for judging a criminal defendant's contention that the Constitution requires a conviction or death sentence to be set aside because counsel's assistance at the trial or sentencing was ineffective.

I

A

During a ten-day period in September 1976, respondent planned and committed three groups of crimes, which included three brutal stabbing murders, torture, kidnapping, severe assaults, attempted murders, attempted extortion, and theft. After his two accomplices were arrested, respondent surrendered to police and voluntarily gave a lengthy statement confessing to the third of the criminal episodes. The State of Florida indicted respondent for kidnapping and murder and appointed an experienced criminal lawyer to represent him.

Counsel actively pursued pretrial motions and discovery. He cut his efforts short, however, and he experienced a sense of hopelessness about the case, when he learned that, against his specific advice, respondent had also confessed to the first two murders. By the date set for trial, respondent was subject to indictment for three counts of first degree murder and multiple counts of robbery, kidnapping for ransom, breaking and entering and assault, attempted murder, and conspiracy to commit robbery. Respondent waived his right to a jury trial, again acting against counsel's advice, and pleaded guilty to all charges, including the three capital murder charges.

In the plea colloquy, respondent told the trial judge that, although he had committed a string of burglaries, he had no significant prior criminal record and that at the time of his criminal spree he was under extreme stress caused by his inability to support his family. He also stated, however, that he accepted responsibility for the crimes. The trial judge told respondent that he had "a great deal of respect for people who are willing to step forward and admit their responsibility" but that he was making no statement at all about his likely sentencing decision.

Counsel advised respondent to invoke his right under Florida law to an advisory jury at his capital sentencing hearing. Respondent rejected the advice and waived the right. He chose instead to be sentenced by the trial judge without a jury recommendation.

In preparing for the sentencing hearing, counsel spoke with respondent about his background. He also spoke on the telephone with respondent's wife and mother, though he did not follow up on the one unsuccessful effort to meet with them. He did not otherwise seek out character witnesses for respondent. Nor did he request a psychiatric examination, since his conversations with his client gave no indication that respondent had psychological problems.

Counsel decided not to present and hence not to look further for evidence concerning respondent's character and emotional state. That decision reflected trial counsel's sense of hopelessness about overcoming the evidentiary effect of respondent's confessions to the gruesome crimes. It also reflected the judgment that it was advisable to rely on the plea colloquy for evidence about respondent's background and about his claim of emotional stress: the plea colloquy communicated sufficient information about these subjects, and by foregoing the opportunity to present new evidence on these subjects, counsel prevented the State from cross-examining respondent on his claim and from putting on psychiatric evidence of its own.

Counsel also excluded from the sentencing hearing other evidence he thought was potentially damaging. He successfully moved to exclude respondent's "rap sheet." Because he judged that a presentence report might prove more detrimental than helpful, as it would have included respondent's criminal history and thereby undermined the claim of no significant history of criminal activity, he did not request that one be prepared.

At the sentencing hearing, counsel's strategy was based primarily on the trial judge's remarks at the plea colloquy as well as on his reputation as a sentencing judge who thought it important for a convicted defendant to own up to his crime. Counsel argued that respondent's remorse and acceptance of responsibility justified sparing him from the death penalty. Counsel also argued that respondent had no history of criminal activity and that respondent committed the crimes under extreme mental or emotional disturbance, thus coming within the statutory list of mitigating circumstances. He further argued that respondent should be spared death because he had surrendered, confessed, and offered to testify against a co-defendant and because respondent was fundamentally a good person who had briefly gone badly wrong in extremely stressful circumstances. The State put on evidence and witnesses largely for the purpose of describing the details of the crimes. Counsel did not cross-examine the medical experts who testified about the manner of death of respondent's victims.

The trial judge found several aggravating circumstances with respect to each of the three murders. He found that all three murders were especially heinous, atrocious, and cruel, all involving repeated stabbings. All three murders were committed in the course of at least one other dangerous and violent felony, and since all involved robbery, the murders were for pecuniary gain. All three murders were committed to avoid arrest for the accompanying crimes and to hinder law enforcement. In the course of one of the murders, respondent knowingly subjected numerous persons to a grave risk of death by deliberately stabbing and shooting the murder victim's sisters-in-law, who sustained severe—in one case, ultimately fatal—injuries.

With respect to mitigating circumstances, the trial judge made the same findings for all three capital murders. First, although there was no admitted evidence of prior convictions, respondent had stated that he had engaged in a course of stealing. In any case, even if respondent had no significant history of criminal activity, the aggravating circumstances "would still clearly far outweigh" that mitigating factor. Second, the judge found that, during all three crimes, respondent was not suffering from extreme mental or emotional disturbance and could appreciate the criminality of his acts. Third, none of the victims was a participant in, or consented to, respondent's conduct. Fourth, respondent's participation in the crimes was neither minor nor the result of duress or domination by an accomplice. Finally, respondent's age (26) could not be considered a factor in mitigation, especially when viewed in light of respondent's planning of the crimes and disposition of the proceeds of the various accompanying thefts.

In short, the trial judge found numerous aggravating circumstances and no (or a single comparatively insignificant) mitigating circumstance. With respect to each of the three convictions for capital murder, the trial judge concluded: "A careful consideration of all matters presented to the court impels the conclusion that there are insufficient mitigating circumstances ...to outweigh the aggravating circumstances. ..." See Washington v. State, 362 So.2d 658, 663–664 (Fla.1978), cert. denied, 441 U.S. 937, 99 S.Ct. 2063, 60 L.Ed.2d 666 (1979) (quoting trial court findings). He therefore sentenced respondent to death on each of the three counts of murder and to prison terms for the other crimes. The Florida Supreme Court upheld the convictions and sentences on direct appeal.

B

Respondent subsequently sought collateral relief in state court on numerous grounds, among them that counsel had rendered ineffective assistance at the sentencing proceeding. Respondent challenged counsel's assistance in six respects. He asserted that counsel was ineffective because he failed to move for a continuance to prepare for sentencing, to request a psychiatric report, to investigate and present character witnesses, to seek a presentence investigation report, to present meaningful arguments to the sentencing judge, and to investigate the medical examiner's reports or cross-examine the medical experts. In support of the claim, respondent submitted fourteen affidavits from friends, neighbors, and relatives stating that they would have testified if asked to do so. He also submitted one psychiatric report and one psychological report stating that respondent, though not under the influence of extreme mental or emotional disturbance, was "chronically frustrated and depressed because of his economic dilemma" at the time of his crimes.

The trial court denied relief without an evidentiary hearing, finding that the record evidence conclusively showed that the ineffectiveness claim was meritless. ...

* * *

The Florida Supreme Court affirmed the denial of relief. Washington v. State, 397 So.2d 285 (Fla.1981). ...

C

...[T]he United States District Court for the Southern District of Florida ...denied the petition for a writ of habeas corpus.

On appeal, a panel of the United States Court of Appeals for the Fifth Circuit affirmed in part, vacated in part, and remanded ...The panel decision was itself vacated when ...the Eleventh Circuit, decided to rehear the case en banc. 679 F.2d 23 (1982). The full Court of Appeals developed its own framework for analyzing ineffective assistance claims and reversed the judgment of the District Court and remanded the case for new factfinding under the newly announced standards. 693 F.2d 1243 (1982).

* * *

D

Petitioners, who are officials of the State of Florida, filed a petition for a writ of certiorari seeking review of the decision of the Court of Appeals. ...

In assessing attorney performance, all the Federal Courts of Appeals and all but a few state courts have now adopted the "reasonably effective assistance" standard in one formulation or another. . . . Yet this Court has not had occasion squarely to decide whether that is the proper standard. With respect to the prejudice that a defendant must show from deficient attorney performance, the lower courts have adopted tests that purport to differ in more than formulation. . . .

For these reasons, we granted certiorari to consider the standards by which to judge a contention that the Constitution requires that a criminal judgment be overturned because of the actual ineffective assistance of counsel. . . .

II

* * *

. . . Government violates the right to effective assistance when it interferes in certain ways with the ability of counsel to make independent decisions about how to conduct the defense. See, e.g., Geders v. United States, 425 U.S. 80, 96 S.Ct. 1330, 47 L.Ed.2d 592 (1976) (bar on attorney-client consultation during overnight recess); Herring v. New York, 422 U.S. 853, 95 S.Ct. 2550, 45 L.Ed.2d 593 (1975) (bar on summation at bench trial); Brooks v. Tennessee, 406 U.S. 605, 612–613, 92 S.Ct. 1891, 1895, 32 L.Ed.2d 358 (1972) (requirement that defendant be first defense witness); Ferguson v. Georgia, 365 U.S. 570, 593–596, 81 S.Ct. 756, 768–770, 5 L.Ed.2d 783 (1961) (bar on direct examination of defendant). Counsel, however, can also deprive a defendant of the right to effective assistance, simply by failing to render "adequate legal assistance," Cuyler v. Sullivan, supra, 446 U.S., at 344, 100 S.Ct., at 1716. Id., at 345–350, 100 S.Ct., at 1716–1719 (actual conflict of interest adversely affecting lawyer's performance renders assistance ineffective).

The Court has not elaborated on the meaning of the constitutional requirement of effective assistance in the latter class of cases—that is, those presenting claims of "actual ineffectiveness." In giving meaning to the requirement, however, we must take its purpose—to ensure a fair trial—as the guide. The benchmark for judging any claim of ineffectiveness must be whether counsel's conduct so undermined the proper functioning of the adversarial process that the trial cannot be relied on as having produced a just result.

The same principle applies to a capital sentencing proceeding such as that provided by Florida law. We need not consider the role of counsel in an ordinary sentencing, which may involve informal proceedings and standardless discretion in the sentencer, and hence may require a different approach to the definition of constitutionally effective assistance. A capital sentencing proceeding like the one involved in this case, however, is sufficiently like a trial in its adversarial format and in the existence of standards for decision, . . . that counsel's role in the proceeding is comparable to counsel's role at trial—to ensure that the adversarial testing process works to produce a just result under the standards governing decision. For purposes of describing counsel's duties, therefore, Florida's capital sentencing proceeding need not be distinguished from an ordinary trial.

III

A convicted defendant's claim that counsel's assistance was so defective as to require reversal of a conviction or death sentence has two components. First, the defendant must show that counsel's performance was deficient. This requires showing that counsel made errors so serious that counsel was not functioning as the "counsel" guaranteed the defendant by the Sixth Amendment. Second, the defendant must show that the deficient performance prejudiced the defense. This requires showing that counsel's errors were so serious as to deprive the defendant of a fair trial, a trial whose result is reliable. Unless a defendant makes both showings, it cannot be said that the conviction or death sentence resulted from a breakdown in the adversary process that renders the result unreliable.

A

As all the Federal Courts of Appeals have now held, the proper standard for attorney performance is that of reasonably effective assistance. The Court indirectly recognized as much when it stated in McMann v. Richardson, supra, 397 U.S., at 770, 771, 90 S.Ct., at 1448, 1449, that a guilty plea cannot be attacked as based on inadequate legal advice unless counsel was not "a reasonably competent attorney" and the advice was not "within the range of competence demanded of attorneys in criminal cases." When a convicted defendant complains of the ineffectiveness of counsel's assistance, the defendant must show that counsel's representation fell below an objective standard of reasonableness.

More specific guidelines are not appropriate. The Sixth Amendment refers simply to "counsel," not specifying particular requirements of effective assistance. It relies instead on the legal profession's maintenance of standards sufficient to justify the law's presumption that counsel will fulfill the role in the adversary process that the Amendment envisions. The proper measure of attorney performance remains simply reasonableness under prevailing professional norms.

Representation of a criminal defendant entails certain basic duties. Counsel's function is to assist the defendant, and hence counsel owes the client a duty of loyalty, a duty to avoid conflicts of interest. From counsel's function as assistant to the defendant derive the overarching duty to advocate the defendant's cause and the more particular duties to consult with the defendant on important decisions and to keep the defendant informed of important developments in the course of the prosecution. Counsel also has a duty to bring to bear such skill and knowledge as will render the trial a reliable adversarial testing process.

These basic duties neither exhaustively define the obligations of counsel nor form a checklist for judicial evaluation of attorney performance. In any case presenting an ineffectiveness claim, the performance inquiry must be whether counsel's assistance was reasonable considering all the circumstances. Prevailing norms of practice as reflected in American Bar Association standards and the like, e.g., ABA Standards for Criminal Justice 4–1.1

to 4–8.6 (2d ed. 1980) ("The Defense Function"), are guides to determining what is reasonable, but they are only guides. No particular set of detailed rules for counsel's conduct can satisfactorily take account of the variety of circumstances faced by defense counsel or the range of legitimate decisions regarding how best to represent a criminal defendant. Any such set of rules would interfere with the constitutionally protected independence of counsel and restrict the wide latitude counsel must have in making tactical decisions. Indeed, the existence of detailed guidelines for representation could distract counsel from the overriding mission of vigorous advocacy of the defendant's cause. Moreover, the purpose of the effective assistance guarantee of the Sixth Amendment is not to improve the quality of legal representation, although that is a goal of considerable importance to the legal system. The purpose is simply to ensure that criminal defendants receive a fair trial.

Judicial scrutiny of counsel's performance must be highly deferential. It is all too tempting for a defendant to second-guess counsel's assistance after conviction or adverse sentence, and it is all too easy for a court, examining counsel's defense after it has proved unsuccessful, to conclude that a particular act or omission of counsel was unreasonable. A fair assessment of attorney performance requires that every effort be made to eliminate the distorting effects of hindsight, to reconstruct the circumstances of counsel's challenged conduct, and to evaluate the conduct from counsel's perspective at the time. Because of the difficulties inherent in making the evaluation, a court must indulge a strong presumption that counsel's conduct falls within the wide range of reasonable professional assistance; that is, the defendant must overcome the presumption that, under the circumstances, the challenged action "might be considered sound trial strategy." There are countless ways to provide effective assistance in any given case. Even the best criminal defense attorneys would not defend a particular client in the same way.

The availability of intrusive post-trial inquiry into attorney performance or of detailed guidelines for its evaluation would encourage the proliferation of ineffectiveness challenges. Criminal trials resolved unfavorably to the defendant would increasingly come to be followed by a second trial, this one of counsel's unsuccessful defense. Counsel's performance and even willingness to serve could be adversely affected. Intensive scrutiny of counsel and rigid requirements for acceptable assistance could dampen the ardor and impair the independence of defense counsel, discourage the acceptance of assigned cases, and undermine the trust between attorney and client.

Thus, a court deciding an actual ineffectiveness claim must judge the reasonableness of counsel's challenged conduct on the facts of the particular case, viewed as of the time of counsel's conduct. A convicted defendant making a claim of ineffective assistance must identify the acts or omissions of counsel that are alleged not to have been the result of reasonable professional judgment. The court must then determine whether, in light of all the circumstances, the identified acts or omissions were outside the wide range of professionally competent assistance. In making that determination, the court should keep in mind that counsel's function, as elaborated in prevailing professional norms, is to make the adversarial testing process work in the particular case. At the same time, the court should recognize that counsel is strongly presumed to have rendered adequate assistance and made all significant decisions in the exercise of reasonable professional judgment.

These standards require no special amplification in order to define counsel's duty to investigate, the duty at issue in this case. As the Court of Appeals concluded, strategic choices made after thorough investigation of law and facts relevant to plausible options are virtually unchallengeable; and strategic choices made after less than complete investigation are reasonable precisely to the extent that reasonable professional judgments support the limitations on investigation. In other words, counsel has a duty to make reasonable investigations or to make a reasonable decision that makes particular investigations unnecessary. In any ineffectiveness case, a particular decision not to investigate must be directly assessed for reasonableness in all the circumstances, applying a heavy measure of deference to counsel's judgments.

The reasonableness of counsel's actions may be determined or substantially influenced by the defendant's own statements or actions. Counsel's actions are usually based, quite properly, on informed strategic choices made by the defendant and on information supplied by the defendant. In particular, what investigation decisions are reasonable depends critically on such information. For example, when the facts that support a certain potential line of defense are generally known to counsel because of what the defendant has said, the need for further investigation may be considerably diminished or eliminated altogether. And when a defendant has given counsel reason to believe that pursuing certain investigations would be fruitless or even harmful, counsel's failure to pursue those investigations may not later be challenged as unreasonable. In short, inquiry into counsel's conversations with the defendant may be critical to a proper assessment of counsel's investigation decisions, just as it may be critical to a proper assessment of counsel's other litigation decisions.

B

An error by counsel, even if professionally unreasonable, does not warrant setting aside the judgment of a criminal proceeding if the error had no effect on the judgment. The purpose of the Sixth Amendment guarantee of counsel is to ensure that a defendant has the assistance necessary to justify reliance on the outcome of the proceeding. Accordingly, any deficiencies in counsel's performance must be prejudicial to the defense in order to constitute ineffective assistance under the Constitution.

In certain Sixth Amendment contexts, prejudice is presumed. Actual or constructive denial of the assistance of counsel altogether is legally presumed to result in prejudice. So are various kinds of state interference with counsel's assistance. Prejudice in these circumstances is so likely that case by case inquiry into prejudice is not worth the cost. Moreover, such circumstances involve impairments of the Sixth Amendment right that are easy to identify and, for that reason and because the prosecution is directly responsible, easy for the government to prevent.

One type of actual ineffectiveness claim warrants a similar, though more limited, presumption of prejudice. In Cuyler v. Sullivan, 446 U.S., at 345–350, 90 S.Ct., at 1716–1719, the Court held that prejudice is presumed when counsel is burdened by an actual conflict of interest. In those circumstances, counsel breaches the duty of loyalty, perhaps the most basic of counsel's duties. Moreover, it is difficult to measure the precise effect on the defense of representation corrupted by conflicting interests. Given the obligation of counsel to avoid conflicts of interest and the ability of trial courts to make early inquiry in certain situations likely to give rise to conflicts, see, e.g., Fed.Rule Crim.Proc. 44(c), it is reasonable for the criminal justice system to maintain a fairly rigid rule of presumed prejudice for conflicts of interest. Even so, the rule is not quite the *per se* rule of prejudice that exists for the Sixth Amendment claims mentioned above. Prejudice is presumed only if the defendant demonstrates that counsel "actively represented conflicting interests" and "that an actual conflict of interest adversely affected his lawyer's performance."

Conflict of interest claims aside, actual ineffectiveness claims alleging a deficiency in attorney performance are subject to a general requirement that the defendant affirmatively prove prejudice. The government is not responsible for, and hence not able to prevent, attorney errors that will result in reversal of a conviction or sentence. Attorney errors come in an infinite variety and are as likely to be utterly harmless in a particular case as they are to be prejudicial. They cannot be classified according to likelihood of causing prejudice. Nor can they be defined with sufficient precision to inform defense attorneys correctly just what conduct to avoid. Representation is an art, and an act or omission that is unprofessional in one case may be sound or even brilliant in another. Even if a defendant shows that particular errors of counsel were unreasonable, therefore, the defendant must show that they actually had an adverse effect on the defense.

It is not enough for the defendant to show that the errors had some conceivable effect on the outcome of the proceeding. Virtually every act or omission of counsel would meet that test, and not every error that conceivably could have influenced the outcome undermines the reliability of the result of the proceeding. Respondent suggests requiring a showing that the errors "impaired the presentation of the defense." That standard, however, provides no workable principle. Since any error, if it is indeed an error, "impairs" the presentation of the defense, the proposed standard is inadequate because it provides no way of deciding what impairments are sufficiently serious to warrant setting aside the outcome of the proceeding.

On the other hand, we believe that a defendant need not show that counsel's deficient conduct more likely than not altered the outcome in the case. This outcome-determinative standard has several strengths. It defines the relevant inquiry in a way familiar to courts, though the inquiry, as is inevitable, is anything but precise. The standard also reflects the profound importance of finality in criminal proceedings. Moreover, it comports with the widely used standard for assessing motions for new trial based on newly discovered evidence. Nevertheless, the standard is not quite appropriate.

Even when the specified attorney error results in the omission of certain evidence, the newly discovered evidence standard is not an apt source from which to draw a prejudice standard for ineffectiveness claims. The high standard for newly discovered evidence claims presupposes that all the essential elements of a presumptively accurate and fair proceeding were present in the proceeding whose result is challenged. An ineffective assistance claim asserts the absence of one of the crucial assurances that the result of the proceeding is reliable, so finality concerns are somewhat weaker and the appropriate standard of prejudice should be somewhat lower. The result of a proceeding can be rendered unreliable, and hence the proceeding itself unfair, even if the errors of counsel cannot be shown by a preponderance of the evidence to have determined the outcome.

Accordingly, the appropriate test for prejudice finds its roots in the test for materiality of exculpatory information not disclosed to the defense by the prosecution, United States v. Agurs, 427 U.S., at 104, 112–113, 96 S.Ct., at 2397, 2401–2402, and in the test for materiality of testimony made unavailable to the defense by Government deportation of a witness, United States v. Valenzuela–Bernal, 458 U.S., at 872–874, 102 S.Ct., at 3449–3450. The defendant must show that there is a reasonable probability that, but for counsel's unprofessional errors, the result of the proceeding would have been different. A reasonable probability is a probability sufficient to undermine confidence in the outcome.

* * *

The governing legal standard plays a critical role in defining the question to be asked in assessing the prejudice from counsel's errors. When a defendant challenges a conviction, the question is whether there is a reasonable probability that, absent the errors, the factfinder would have had a reasonable doubt respecting guilt. When a defendant challenges a death sentence such as the one at issue in this case, the question is whether there is a reasonable probability that, absent the errors, the sentencer—including an appellate court, to the extent it independently reweighs the evidence—would have concluded that the balance of aggravating and mitigating circumstances did not warrant death.

* * *

IV

...Although those principles should guide the process of decision, the ultimate focus of inquiry must be on the fundamental fairness of the proceeding whose result is being challenged. In every case the court should be concerned with whether, despite the strong presumption of reliability, the result of the particular proceeding is unreliable because of a breakdown in the adversarial process that our system counts on to produce just results.

To the extent that this has already been the guiding inquiry in the lower courts, the standards articulated today do not require reconsideration of ineffectiveness claims rejected under different standards. ...In particular, the minor differences in the lower court's precise formulations of the performance standard are insignificant: the different formulations are mere variations of the overarching reasonableness standard. ...

Although we have discussed the performance component of an ineffectiveness claim prior to the prejudice component, there is no reason for a court deciding an ineffective assistance claim to approach the inquiry in the same order or even to address both components of the inquiry if the defendant makes an insufficient showing on one. In particular, a court need not determine whether counsel's performance was deficient before examining the prejudice suffered by the defendant as a result of the alleged deficiencies. The object of an ineffectiveness claim is not to grade counsel's performance. If it is easier to dispose of an ineffectiveness claim on the ground of lack of sufficient prejudice, which we expect will often be so, that course should be followed. Courts should strive to ensure that ineffectiveness claims not become so burdensome to defense counsel that the entire criminal justice system suffers as a result.

The principles governing ineffectiveness claims should apply in federal collateral proceedings as they do on direct appeal or in motions for a new trial.

* * *

V

Having articulated general standards for judging ineffectiveness claims, we think it useful to apply those standards to the facts of this case in order to illustrate the meaning of the general principles. . . .

Application of the governing principles is not difficult in this case. The facts as described above make clear that the conduct of respondent's counsel at and before respondent's sentencing proceeding cannot be found unreasonable. They also make clear that, even assuming the challenged conduct of counsel was unreasonable, respondent suffered insufficient prejudice to warrant setting aside his death sentence.

With respect to the performance component, the record shows that respondent's counsel made a strategic choice to argue for the extreme emotional distress mitigating circumstance and to rely as fully as possible on respondent's acceptance of responsibility for his crimes. Although counsel understandably felt hopeless about respondent's prospects, nothing in the record indicates, as one possible reading of the District Court's opinion suggests, that counsel's sense of hopelessness distorted his professional judgment. Counsel's strategy choice was well within the range of professionally reasonable judgments, and the decision not to seek more character or psychological evidence than was already in hand was likewise reasonable.

The trial judge's views on the importance of owning up to one's crimes were well known to counsel. The aggravating circumstances were utterly overwhelming. Trial counsel could reasonably surmise from his conversations with respondent that character and psychological evidence would be of little help. Respondent had already been able to mention at the plea colloquy the substance of what there was to know about his financial and emotional troubles. Restricting testimony on respondent's character to what had come in at the plea colloquy ensured that contrary character and psychological evidence and respondent's criminal history, which counsel had successfully moved to exclude, would not come in. On these facts, there can be little question, even without application of the presumption of adequate performance, that trial counsel's defense, though unsuccessful, was the result of reasonable professional judgment.

With respect to the prejudice component, the lack of merit of respondent's claim is even more stark. The evidence that respondent says his trial counsel should have offered at the sentencing hearing would barely have altered the sentencing profile presented to the sentencing judge. As the state courts and District Court found, at most this evidence shows that numerous people who knew respondent thought he was generally a good person and that a psychiatrist and a psychologist believed he was under considerable emotional stress that did not rise to the level of extreme disturbance. Given the overwhelming aggravating factors, there is no reasonable probability that the omitted evidence would have changed the conclusion that the aggravating circumstances outweighed the mitigating circumstances and, hence, the sentence imposed. Indeed, admission of the evidence respondent now offers might even have been harmful to his case: his "rap sheet" would probably have been admitted into evidence, and the psychological reports would have directly contradicted respondent's claim that the mitigating circumstances of extreme emotional disturbance applied to his case.

* * *

Failure to make the required showing of either deficient performance or sufficient prejudice defeats the ineffectiveness claim. Here there is a double failure. More generally, respondent has made no showing that the justice of his sentence was rendered unreliable by a breakdown in the adversary process caused by deficiencies in counsel's assistance. Respondent's sentencing proceeding was not fundamentally unfair.

We conclude, therefore, that the District Court properly declined to issue a writ of habeas corpus. The judgment of the Court of Appeals is accordingly reversed.

■ JUSTICE BRENNAN, concurring in part and dissenting in part [omitted].

■ JUSTICE MARSHALL, dissenting.

* * *

My objection to the performance standard adopted by the Court is that it is so malleable that, in practice, it will either have no grip at all or will yield excessive variation in the manner in which the Sixth Amendment is interpreted and applied by different courts. To tell lawyers and the lower courts that counsel for a criminal defendant must behave "reasonably" and must act like "a reasonably competent attorney," is to tell them almost nothing. In essence, the majority has instructed judges called upon to assess claims of ineffective assistance of counsel to advert to their own intuitions regarding what constitutes "professional" representation, and has discouraged them from trying to develop more detailed standards governing the performance of defense counsel. In my view, the Court has thereby not only abdicated its own responsibility to interpret the Constitution, but also impaired the ability of the lower courts to exercise theirs.

* * *

...It is an unfortunate but undeniable fact that a person of means, by selecting a lawyer and paying him enough to ensure he prepares thoroughly, usually can obtain better representation than that available to an indigent defendant, who must rely on appointed counsel, who, in turn, has limited time and resources to devote to a given case. Is a "reasonably competent attorney" a reasonably competent adequately paid retained lawyer or a reasonably competent appointed attorney? It is also a fact that the quality of representation available to ordinary defendants in different parts of the country varies significantly. Should the standard of performance mandated by the Sixth Amendment vary by locale? The majority offers no clues as to the proper responses to these questions.

* * *

...I agree that counsel must be afforded "wide latitude" when making "tactical decisions" regarding trial strategy, but many aspects of the job of a criminal defense attorney are more amenable to judicial oversight. For example, much of the work involved in preparing for a trial, applying for bail, conferring with one's client, making timely objections to significant, arguably erroneous rulings of the trial judge, and filing a notice of appeal if there are colorable grounds therefor could profitably be made the subject of uniform standards.

* * *

I object to the prejudice standard adopted by the Court for two independent reasons. First, ...The difficulties of estimating prejudice after the fact are exacerbated by the possibility that evidence of injury to the defendant may be missing from the record precisely because of the incompetence of defense counsel. [I]t seems to me senseless to impose on a defendant whose lawyer has been shown to have been incompetent the burden of demonstrating prejudice.

Second and more fundamentally, the assumption on which the Court's holding rests is that the only purpose of the constitutional guarantee of effective assistance of counsel is to reduce the chance that innocent persons will be convicted. In my view, the guarantee also functions to ensure that convictions are obtained only through fundamentally fair procedures. The majority contends that the Sixth Amendment is not violated when a manifestly guilty defendant is convicted after a trial in which he was represented by a manifestly ineffective attorney. I cannot agree. Every defendant is entitled to a trial in which his interests are vigorously and conscientiously advocated by an able lawyer. A proceeding in which the defendant does not receive meaningful assistance in meeting the forces of the state does not, in my opinion, constitute due process.

In Chapman v. California, 386 U.S. 18, 23, 87 S.Ct. 824, 827, 17 L.Ed.2d 705 (1967), we acknowledged that certain constitutional rights are "so basic to a fair trial that their infraction can never be treated as harmless error." Among these rights is "the right to the assistance of counsel at trial." Id., at 23, n. 8, 87 S.Ct., at 827, n. 8; see Gideon v. Wainwright, 372 U.S. 335, 83 S.Ct. 792, 9 L.Ed.2d 799 (1963). In my view, the right to *effective* assistance of counsel is entailed by the right to counsel, and abridgment of the former is equivalent to abridgment of the latter. I would thus hold that a showing that the performance of a defendant's lawyer departed from constitutionally prescribed standards requires a new trial regardless of whether the defendant suffered demonstrable prejudice thereby.

* * *

NOTES

1. **Proving prejudice.** Justice Stevens, in his opinion in *Cronic,* supra, stated that some circumstances so clearly indicate a denial of effective assistance of counsel and are so likely to prejudice the defendant that no specific showing of prejudice is required. The most obvious example is complete denial of counsel. Yet in some instances counsel may be present but render such minimal assistance that prejudice will be presumed.

However, the fact that defense counsel suffered from a rare sleep disorder, causing him to occasionally doze off during trial for as much as 30 seconds each time, did not result in reversal in a 1984 California federal district court case. The defendant was unable to specify exactly how many or when the naps occurred. He said he awakened counsel quickly because his snoring was embarrassing. Following an evidentiary hearing on effectiveness of counsel, Judge Garcia, explicitly applying *Strickland,* refused to grant a retrial because the defendant had failed to prove that his defense was prejudiced by counsel's conduct. Sacramento Bee, Nov. 7, 1984, at B1.

Strickland's test was developed—perhaps only for very unusual situations—in Lockhart v. Fretwell, 506 U.S. 364, 113 S.Ct. 838, 122 L.Ed.2d 180 (1993). In 1985, upon proof that he killed the victim in the course of a robbery, Fretwell was convicted of capital felony murder in an Arkansas court. At the penalty stage, the State sought the death penalty and argued that the facts showed two aggravating circumstances: (a) that the murder was committed for pecuniary gain; and (b) that the murder was committed to facilitate Fretwell's escape. Shortly before the trial, the Eighth Circuit Court of Appeals had held in Collins v. Lockhart, 754 F.2d 258 (8th Cir.), cert. denied, 474 U.S. 1013, 106 S.Ct. 546, 88 L.Ed.2d 475 (1985) that a death sentence in a felony murder case was unconstitutional if it was based upon an aggravating factor that duplicated an underlying element of the felony. Fretwell's lawyer did not object to the trial judge's submission to the jury of the first aggravating circumstance urged by the State, even though reliance upon it was almost certainly contrary to *Collins.* The jury found the first aggravating circumstance to have been proved and sentenced Fretwell to death.

In later federal habeas corpus proceedings, Fretwell argued that he had been denied the effective assistance of counsel because defense counsel had not raised *Collins* in connection with the sentencing proceeding. By this time, however, *Collins* had been overruled as inconsistent with an intervening decision of the Supreme Court. Thus Fretwell challenged his counsel's performance on the basis of counsel's failure to raise an argument that was "good law" at the time of trial but at the time of his attack was recognized as without ultimate legal merit. The lower federal courts granted Fretwell relief. Counsel's failure to invoke *Collins* constituted deficient performance under *Strickland.* If counsel had invoked *Collins,* the trial judge would not have permitted the State to rely upon their first proffered aggravating circumstance, the jury would not have found the other circumstance shown by the evidence, and the jury would not have sentenced Fretwell to death. Thus Fretwell had established prejudice under *Strickland.*

The Supreme Court reversed, concluding that the lower federal courts had erred in finding that Fretwell showed prejudice. Defendants are afforded the Sixth Amendment right to counsel, Chief Justice Rehnquist explained for the majority, to protect their right to a fair—that is, reliable—trial. *Strickland's* test reflects this concern with reliability.

> Thus, an analysis focusing solely on mere outcome determination, without attention to whether the result of the proceeding was fundamentally unfair or unreliable, is defective. To set aside a conviction or sentence solely because the outcome would have been different but for counsel's error may grant the defendant a windfall to which the law does not entitle him.

* * *

> The result of the sentencing proceeding in the present case was neither unfair nor unreliable.

506 U.S. at 369–71, 113 S.Ct. at 842–43, 122 L.Ed.2d at 189–90.

Under *Strickland,* the Court agreed, whether counsel performed acceptably is to be viewed as of the time of the conduct challenged. Whether a defendant was prejudiced, however, is not to be determined under such a "rule of contemporary assessment." If counsel's ineffectiveness does not deprive a defendant of any substantive or procedural right to which the law—as it is later or ultimately known to be—entitles the defendant, no unreliability or unfairness results and there has been no prejudice. Since Fretwell is now known not to have been entitled to have the trial judge follow *Collins,* he suffered no prejudice from counsel's deficiency in failing to argue *Collins.* 506 U.S. at 371, 113 S.Ct. at 844, 122 L.Ed.2d at 191.

Justice O'Connor concurred to suggest that the Court's holding will affect only the unusual situations where defendants attempt "to demonstrate prejudice based on considerations that, as a matter of law, ought not inform the inquiry." In the vast majority of cases, she added, the Court's decision will have no effect on the prejudice inquiry under *Strickland.* 506 U.S. at 373, 113 S.Ct. at 845, 122 L.Ed.2d at 192 (O'Connor, J., concurring).

Justice Stevens, joined by Justice Blackmun, dissented, arguing that ineffective assistance of counsel claims should be evaluated under the law as it stood at the time of trial:

> Hindsight has no place in a Sixth Amendment jurisprudence that focuses, quite rightly, on protecting the adversarial balance at trial. * * * [A]s it happened, counsel's failure to object came at a time when it signified a breakdown in the adversarial process. A *post hoc* vision of what would have been the case years later has no bearing on the force of this showing.

506 U.S. at 381, 113 S.Ct. at 849, 122 L.Ed.2d at 197 (Stevens, J., dissenting).

2. **Advice by counsel.** The Supreme Court applied Strickland v. Washington to advice by counsel at the plea-bargaining stage in Hill v. Lockhart, 474 U.S. 52, 106 S.Ct. 366, 88 L.Ed.2d 203 (1985). The Court, through Justice Rehnquist, stated:

> In the present case the claimed error of counsel is erroneous advice as to eligibility for parole under the sentence agreed to in the plea bargain. We find it unnecessary to determine whether there may be circumstances under which erroneous advice by counsel as to parole eligibility may be deemed constitutionally ineffective assistance of counsel, because in the present case we conclude that petitioner's allegations are insufficient to satisfy the *Strickland v. Wash-*

ington requirement of "prejudice." Petitioner did not allege in his habeas petition that, had counsel correctly informed him about his parole eligibility date, he would have pleaded not guilty and insisted on going to trial. He alleged no special circumstances that might support the conclusion that he placed particular emphasis on his parole eligibility in deciding whether or not to plead guilty. Indeed, petitioner's mistaken belief that he would become eligible for parole after serving one-third of his sentence would seem to have affected not only his calculation of the time he likely would serve if sentenced pursuant to the proposed plea agreement, but also his calculation of the time he likely would serve if he went to trial and were convicted.

> Because petitioner in this case failed to allege the kind of "prejudice" necessary to satisfy the second half of the *Strickland v. Washington* test, the District Court did not err in declining to hold a hearing on petitioner's ineffective assistance of counsel claim.

474 U.S. at 60, 106 S.Ct. at 371, 88 L.Ed.2d at 211. Justice White, joined by Justice Stevens, concurred in the judgment on the ground petitioner had not alleged his attorney knew of the prior conviction which altered his parole eligibility period but failed to advise petitioner of the correct parole eligibility term despite that knowledge.

3. **Duty not to tolerate perjury.** A lawyer's duty when he knows or suspects that a client or witness will testify falsely may involve more than ethical considerations. Those decisions may lead to claims of ineffective assistance of counsel.

In State v. Lee, 142 Ariz. 210, 689 P.2d 153 (1984), defense counsel gave in to his client's demand that he call two witnesses whose testimony defense counsel believed would be perjurious. Counsel let the witnesses give narrative accounts on the stand. He then told the judge in chambers that he believed the witnesses were lying; but after much "mental wrestling" he believed that he could not interfere with the defendant's constitutional right to present testimony on his own behalf. Under the circumstances, he felt his ethical duty required waiver of closing argument. The defendant was then convicted and received the maximum sentence.

The Arizona Supreme Court found ineffective assistance of counsel under the *Strickland* test, holding that the first prong of the test, deficient performance of counsel, had been met and remanding for a determination of prejudice. Counsel should have either refused to call the witnesses (as this was a tactical choice to be left to the attorney), or made a closing argument omitting any reference to the perjured testimony.

In Nix v. Whiteside, 475 U.S. 157, 106 S.Ct. 988, 89 L.Ed.2d 123 (1986), the defense attorney feared that the defendant himself intended to give perjured testimony. After stating in earlier interviews that he failed to see a gun in the hand of the victim, Whiteside told his attorney immediately before trial that he then recalled seeing something "metallic" in the victim's hand and commented, "If I don't say I saw a gun I'm dead." His attorney informed Whiteside that he would not allow him to commit perjury, that if he did so he would inform the trial court, would withdraw from the case and would be allowed to impeach that testimony. Whiteside testified without mentioning the metallic object and was convicted. Writing for the Court, Chief Justice Burger stated that the attorney's conduct in this case was not ineffective assistance under *Strickland*. Justice Burger reviewed the various bar association statements of professional responsibility and concluded,

> Considering [the defense attorney's] representation of respondent in light of these accepted norms of professional conduct, we discern no failure to adhere to reasonable professional standards that would in any sense make out a

deprivation of the Sixth Amendment right to counsel. Whether [the attorney's] conduct is seen as a successful attempt to dissuade his client from committing the crime of perjury, or whether seen as a "threat" to withdraw from representation and disclose the illegal scheme, [his] representation of Whiteside falls well within accepted standards of professional conduct and the range of reasonable professional conduct acceptable under *Strickland*.

475 U.S. at 171, 106 S.Ct. at 996, 89 L.Ed.2d at 137. The Court also held that as a matter of law respondent could not have been prejudiced under *Strickland* because his attorney kept him from committing perjury. Justice Brennan concurred in the judgment but characterized Justice Burger's "essay regarding what constitutes the correct response to a criminal client's suggestion that he will perjure himself" as "pure discourse without force of law." 475 U.S. at 177, 106 S.Ct. at 999, 89 L.Ed.2d at 141. Justice Blackmun, joined by Justices Brennan, Marshall and Stevens, concurring in the judgment, found that Whiteside had failed to show prejudice under *Strickland* and would not have reached the question of whether counsel's conduct was in some manner deficient. Justice Stevens, concurring in the judgment, commented on the difficulties facing trial counsel in this situation:

A lawyer's certainty that a change in his client's recollection is a harbinger of intended perjury—as well as judicial review of such apparent certainty—should be tempered by the realization that, after reflection, the most honest witness may recall (or sincerely believe he recalls) details that he previously overlooked. Similarly, the post-trial review of a lawyer's pretrial threat to expose perjury that had not yet been committed—and, indeed, may have been prevented by the threat—is by no means the same as review of the way in which such a threat may actually have been carried out. Thus, one can be convinced—as I am—that this lawyer's actions were a proper way to provide his client with effective representation without confronting the much more difficult questions of what a lawyer must, should, or may do after his client has given testimony that the lawyer does not believe.

475 U.S. at 190–91, 106 S.Ct. at 1006, 89 L.Ed.2d at 150.

4. **Joint representation.** Joint representation—representation of several co-defendants by a single lawyer (or possibly, by a single law firm), Burger v. Kemp, 483 U.S. 776, 107 S.Ct. 3114, 97 L.Ed.2d 638 (1987)—raises special Sixth Amendment problems. It has long been clear that while joint representation is not a *per se* violation of each defendant's right to counsel, joint representation by one lawyer of codefendants whose interests conflict *may* violate that right. Glasser v. United States, 315 U.S. 60, 62 S.Ct. 457, 86 L.Ed. 680 (1942).

In Cuyler v. Sullivan, 446 U.S. 335, 100 S.Ct. 1708, 64 L.Ed.2d 333 (1980), the Court reasoned:

In order to establish a violation of the Sixth Amendment, a defendant who raised no objection at trial must demonstrate that an actual conflict of interest adversely affected his lawyer's performance. . . . [A] defendant who shows that a conflict of interests actually affected the adequacy of his representation need not demonstrate prejudice in order to obtain relief. But until a defendant shows that his counsel actively represented conflicting interest, he has not established the constitutional predicate for this claim of ineffective assistance.

446 U.S. at 348–50, 100 S.Ct. at 1718–19, 64 L.Ed.2d at 346–47. In Glasser v. United States, supra, the Court found a conflict of interests shown by evidence that counsel failed to cross-examine a critical Government witness and to challenge arguably inadmissible evidence because of a desire to diminish the jury's perception of the guilt of Glasser's co-defendant.

Fed.R.Crim.P. 44 provides:

Rule 44. Right to and Assignment of Counsel

* * *

(c) *Joint Representation.* Whenever two or more defendants have been jointly charged pursuant to Rule 8(b) or have been joined for trial pursuant to Rule 13, and are represented by the same retained or assigned counsel or by retained or assigned counsel who are associated in the practice of law, the court shall promptly inquire with respect to such joint representation and shall personally advise each defendant of his right to the effective assistance of counsel, including separate representation. Unless it appears that there is good cause to believe no conflict of interest is likely to arise, the court shall take such measures as may be appropriate to protect each defendant's right to counsel.

5. **Conflicts created by fee arrangements.** Wood v. Georgia, 450 U.S. 261, 101 S.Ct. 1097, 67 L.Ed.2d 220 (1981), involved another type of conflict of interests. When a criminal defendant is represented by a lawyer hired and paid by a third party, there are inherent dangers that are increased when the third party is the operator of the alleged criminal enterprise. In such a case, involving the prosecution of adult bookstore employees, the Court stated:

> One risk is that the lawyer will prevent his client from obtaining leniency by preventing the client from offering testimony against his former employer or from taking other actions contrary to the employer's interest. Another kind of risk is present where ... the party paying the fees may have had a long-range interest in establishing a legal precedent and could do so only if the interests of the defendants themselves were sacrificed.

450 U.S. at 269–70, 101 S.Ct. at 1102–03, 67 L.Ed.2d at 229.

6. **Civil liability for ineffective assistance.** To what extent is a suit for damages against a defense attorney who has rendered ineffective assistance a useful method of setting and enforcing professional standards? Such cases are relatively rare. In Ferri v. Ackerman, 444 U.S. 193, 100 S.Ct. 402, 62 L.Ed.2d 355 (1979), an attorney appointed by a federal judge to represent an indigent defendant in a federal criminal prosecution was sued for malpractice in state court. Lower courts had sustained the attorney's claim that under federal law he was entitled to absolute immunity from suit, but the Supreme Court reversed on the ground that the role of the defense attorney is such that there is no need for conferring upon him the same immunity that is given to judges and prosecutors. Thus, the door to potential liability—and the setting of standards—was opened; however, in Polk County v. Dodson, 454 U.S. 312, 102 S.Ct. 445, 70 L.Ed.2d 509 (1981), the federal courthouse door was closed to some such cases. Respondent had sued his former state public defender in federal court in a civil rights action under 42 U.S.C.A. § 1983. The Supreme Court, in an opinion by Justice Powell, held that the public defender was not acting under color of state law and, therefore, could not be sued under Section 1983. The Court stressed that the duties of the public defender or appointed attorney are the same as privately-retained counsel and that those duties do not involve serving the public except as a by-product of participation on behalf of the client in the adversary process:

> Within the context of our legal system, the duties of a defense lawyer are those of a personal counselor and advocate. ...[The adversary system] posits that a defense lawyer best serves the public, not by acting on behalf of the State or in concert with it, but rather by advancing "the undivided interests of his client." This is essentially a private function, traditionally filled by retained counsel, for which state office and authority are not needed.

454 U.S. at 318–19, 102 S.Ct. at 450, 70 L.Ed.2d at 516–17.

7. **Expert and investigative assistance for counsel.** To what extent should, or must, an indigent be entitled to public funding for expert and investigational assistance? Statutory provision for such aid is quite frequent. 18 U.S.C.A. § 3006A, "Adequate Representation of Defendants ...", provides:

(e) Services Other Than Counsel.

(1) Upon request.—Counsel for a person who is financially unable to obtain investigative, expert, or other services necessary for adequate representation may request them in an ex parte application. Upon finding, after appropriate inquiry in an ex parte proceeding, that the services are necessary and that the person is financially unable to obtain them, the court, or the United States magistrate if the services are required in connection with a matter over which he has jurisdiction, shall authorize counsel to obtain the services.

(2) Without prior request.—(A) Counsel appointed under this section may obtain, subject to later review, investigative, expert, and other services without prior authorization if necessary for adequate representation. Except as provided in subparagraph (B) of this paragraph, the total cost of services obtained without prior authorization may not exceed $300 and expenses reasonably incurred.

(B) The court, or the United States magistrate (if the services were rendered in a case disposed of entirely before the United States magistrate), may, in the interest of justice, and upon the finding that timely procurement of necessary services could not await prior authorization, approve payment for such services after they have been obtained, even if the cost of such services exceeds $300.

(3) Maximum amounts.—Compensation to be paid to a person for services rendered by him to a person under this subsection, or to be paid to an organization for services rendered by an employee thereof, shall not exceed $1,000, exclusive of reimbursement for expenses reasonably incurred, unless payment in excess of that limit is certified by the court, or by the United States magistrate if the services were rendered in connection with a case disposed of entirely before him, as necessary to provide fair compensation for services of an unusual character or duration, and the amount of the excess payment is approved by the chief judge of the circuit. The chief judge of the circuit may delegate such approval authority to an active circuit judge.

(4) Disclosure of fees.—The amounts paid under this subsection for services in any case shall be made available to the public.

The standard for determining whether requested assistance is "necessary" under these statutes, however, is not entirely clear. In United States v. Bass, 477 F.2d 723, 725 (9th Cir.1973), quoted with approval in United States v. Sims, 617 F.2d 1371, 1375 (9th Cir.1980), the court held:

> The statute requires the district judge to authorize defense services when the defense attorney makes a timely request in circumstances in which a reasonable attorney would engage such services for a client having the independent financial means to pay for them.

But defendants have frequently experienced great difficulty convincing appellate courts that a trial court's refusal to authorize expenditures under these statutes is reversible error. In *Sims,* for example, the court noted that even an erroneous refusal to appoint the requested expert on eyewitness testimony would require reversal only if the defendant showed prejudice.

But in a few cases failure to provide assistance to counsel has been held reversible error on constitutional grounds. [T]he Supreme Court found a deprivation of due process and reversed a death sentence in Ake v. Oklahoma, 470 U.S. 68, 105 S.Ct. 1087, 84 L.Ed.2d 53 (1985). Justice Marshall wrote:

> This Court has long recognized that when a State brings its judicial power to bear on an indigent defendant in a criminal proceeding, it must take steps to assure that the defendant has a fair opportunity to present his defense. This elementary principle, grounded in significant part on the Fourteenth Amendment's due process guarantee of fundamental fairness, derives from the belief that justice cannot be equal where, simply as a result of his poverty, a defendant is denied the opportunity to participate meaningfully in a judicial proceeding in which his liberty is at stake.

> * * *

> Meaningful access to justice has been the consistent theme of these cases. We recognized long ago that mere access to the courthouse doors does not by itself assure a proper functioning of the adversary process, and that a criminal trial is fundamentally unfair if the State proceeds against an indigent defendant without making certain that he has access to the raw materials integral to the building of an effective defense. Thus, while the Court has not held that a State must purchase for the indigent defendant all the assistance that his wealthier counterpart might buy, see Ross v. Moffitt, 417 U.S. 600, 94 S.Ct. 2437, 41 L.Ed.2d 341 (1974), it has often reaffirmed that fundamental fairness entitles indigent defendants to "an adequate opportunity to present their claims fairly within the adversary system," id., at 612, 94 S.Ct., at 2444. To implement this principle, we have focused on identifying the "basic tools of an adequate defense or appeal," Britt v. North Carolina, 404 U.S. 226, 227, 92 S.Ct. 431, 433, 30 L.Ed.2d 400 (1971), and we have required that such tools be provided to those defendants who cannot afford to pay for them.

> * * *

> Three factors are relevant to this determination. The first is the private interest that will be affected by the action of the State. The second is the governmental interest that will be affected if the safeguard is to be provided. The third is the probable value of the additional or substitute procedural safeguards that are sought, and the risk of an erroneous deprivation of the affected interest if those safeguards are not provided.

> * * *

> We therefore hold that when a defendant demonstrates to the trial judge that his sanity at the time of the offense is to be a significant factor at trial, the State must, at a minimum, assure the defendant access to a competent psychiatrist who will conduct an appropriate examination and assist in evaluation, preparation, and presentation of the defense. This is not to say, of course, that the indigent defendant has a constitutional right to choose a psychiatrist of his personal liking or to receive funds to hire his own. Our concern is that the indigent defendant have access to a competent psychiatrist for the purpose we have discussed, and as in the case of the provision of counsel we leave to the State the decision on how to implement this right.

470 U.S. at 76–83, 105 S.Ct. at 1092–96, 84 L.Ed.2d at 61–66.

B. SELF-REPRESENTATION AND WAIVER OF SIXTH AMENDMENT RIGHTS

The constitutional right to counsel is not so absolute that it cannot be waived. Most instances in which courts have confronted the issue have involved indigents, but it is clear that non-indigents have the same right to waive counsel. As a practical matter, some non-indigents may try to waive counsel merely because they do not choose to spend money for representation. This may be done simply because the non-indigent intends to plead guilty and if so it approximates a "pure waiver" situation. In addition, both indigents and non-indigents may also try to waive counsel because (1) they wish to stand trial, and believe that some unusual features of their cases can best be brought out if they have full control over the conduct of that trial, or (2) they have a general distrust of the bar, or (3) they are less concerned about the result of their cases than they are about using the court as a forum for exposure of political views.

These three situations represent a combination of the waiver problem with the problem of whether there is a right to act for one's self; if there is, whether it is statutory or constitutional in dimension; whether it must be asserted at any particular time; and under what circumstances it can be limited or lost. Whether the cases in this section dealing with self-representation by indigents are fully applicable to efforts of non-indigents to represent themselves should be considered.

The test for waiver of counsel most often stated is found in Johnson v. Zerbst, 304 U.S. 458, 58 S.Ct. 1019, 82 L.Ed. 1461 (1938). It requires that the waiver be intelligent and competent, a standard which must be particularized by the facts and circumstances of the case, " ... including the background, experience, and conduct of the accused." 304 U.S. at 464, 59 S.Ct. at 1023, 82 L.Ed. at 1466.

In Von Moltke v. Gillies, 332 U.S. 708, 68 S.Ct. 316, 92 L.Ed. 309 (1948), Mr. Justice Black laid down a more exacting standard:

> We have said: "The constitutional right of an accused to be represented by counsel invokes, of itself, the protection of a trial court, in which the accused—whose life or liberty is at stake—is without counsel. This protecting duty imposes the serious and weighty responsibility upon the trial judge of determining whether there is an intelligent and competent waiver by the accused." To discharge this duty properly in light of the strong presumption against waiver of the constitutional right to counsel, a judge must investigate as long and as thoroughly as the circumstances of the case before him demand. The fact that an accused may tell him that he is informed of his right to counsel and desires to waive this right does not automatically end the judge's responsibility. To be valid such waiver must be made with an apprehension of the nature of the charges, the statutory offenses included within them, the range of allowable punishments thereunder, possible defenses to the charges and circumstances in mitigation thereof, and all other facts essential to a broad understanding of the whole matter. A judge can make certain that an accused's professed waiver of counsel is understandingly and wisely made only from a penetrating and comprehensive examination of all the circumstances under which such a plea is tendered.

> This case graphically illustrates that a mere routine inquiry—the asking of several standard questions followed by the signing of a standard written waiver of counsel—may leave a judge entirely un-

aware of the facts essential to an informed decision that an accused has executed a valid waiver of his right to counsel.

332 U.S. at 723–24, 68 S.Ct. at 323, 92 L.Ed. at 320–21 (plurality opinion).

Ascertaining the validity of purported waivers of Sixth Amendment rights is further complicated by the principal case in this section, which establishes a constitutional right to self-representation. To the extent that a defendant must select either representation by counsel (and, if indigent, by court-provided counsel) or self-representation, is the process better conceptualized as one of "choice" rather than "waiver?" If so, does this make any difference?

Faretta v. California

Supreme Court of the United States, 1975.
422 U.S. 806, 95 S.Ct. 2525, 45 L.Ed.2d 562.

■ MR. JUSTICE STEWART delivered the opinion of the Court.

The Sixth and Fourteenth Amendments of our Constitution guarantee that a person brought to trial in any state or federal court must be afforded the right to the assistance of counsel before he can be validly convicted and punished by imprisonment. This clear constitutional rule has emerged from a series of cases decided here over the last 50 years. The question before us now is whether a defendant in a state criminal trial has a constitutional right to proceed *without* counsel when he voluntarily and intelligently elects to do so. Stated another way, the question is whether a State may constitutionally hail a person into its criminal courts and there force a lawyer upon him, even when he insists that he wants to conduct his own defense. It is not an easy question, but we have concluded that a State may not constitutionally do so.

I.

Anthony Faretta was charged with grand theft in an information filed in the Superior Court of Los Angeles County, California. At the arraignment, the Superior Court Judge assigned to preside at the trial appointed the public defender to represent Faretta. Well before the date of trial, however, Faretta requested that he be permitted to represent himself. Questioning by the judge revealed that Faretta had once represented himself in a criminal prosecution, that he had a high school education, and that he did not want to be represented by the public defender because he believed that that office was "very loaded down with . . . a heavy case load." The judge responded that he believed Faretta was "making a mistake" and emphasized that in further proceedings Faretta would receive no special favors. Nevertheless, after establishing that Faretta wanted to represent himself and did not want a lawyer, the judge, in a "preliminary ruling," accepted Faretta's waiver of the assistance of counsel. The judge indicated, however, that he might reverse this ruling if it later appeared that Faretta was unable adequately to represent himself.

Several weeks thereafter, but still prior to trial, the judge *sua sponte* held a hearing to inquire into Faretta's ability to conduct his own defense, and questioned him specifically about both the hearsay rule and the state law governing the challenge of potential jurors.[4] After consideration of

4. The colloquy was as follows:

"THE COURT: In the Faretta matter, I brought you back down here to do some reconsideration as to whether or not you should continue to represent yourself.

"How have you been getting along on your research?

"THE DEFENDANT: Not bad, your Honor.

"Last night I put in the mail a 995 motion and it should be with the Clerk within the next day or two.

"THE COURT: Have you been preparing yourself for the intricacies of the trial of the matter?

"THE DEFENDANT: Well, your Honor, I was hoping that the case could possibly be disposed of on the 995.

"Mrs. Ayers informed me yesterday that it was the Court's policy to hear the pretrial motions at the time of trial. If possible, your Honor, I would like a date set as soon as the Court deems adequate after they receive the motion, sometime before trial.

"THE COURT: Let's see how you have been doing on your research.

"How many exceptions are there to the hearsay rule?

"THE DEFENDANT: Well, the hearsay rule would, I guess, be called the best evidence rule, your Honor. And there are several exceptions in case law, but in actual statutory law, I don't feel there is none.

"THE COURT: What are the challenges to the jury for cause?

"THE DEFENDANT: Well, there is twelve peremptory challenges.

"THE COURT: And how many for cause?

"THE DEFENDANT: Well, as many as the Court deems valid.

"THE COURT: And what are they? What are the grounds for challenging a juror for cause?

"THE DEFENDANT: Well, numerous grounds to challenge a witness—I mean, a juror, your Honor, one being the juror is perhaps suffered, was a victim of the same type of offense, might be prejudice toward the defendant. Any substantial

ground that might make the juror prejudice toward the defendant.

"THE COURT: Anything else?

"THE DEFENDANT: Well, a relative perhaps of the victim.

"THE COURT: Have you taken a look at that code section to see what it is?

"THE DEFENDANT: Challenge a juror?

"THE COURT: Yes.

"THE DEFENDANT: Yes, your Honor. I have done—

"THE COURT: What is the code section?

"THE DEFENDANT: On voir diring a jury, your Honor?

"THE COURT: Yes.

"THE DEFENDANT: I am not aware of the section right offhand.

"THE COURT: What code is it in?

"THE DEFENDANT: Well, the research I have done on challenging would be in Witkins Jurisprudence.

"THE COURT: Have you looked at any of the codes to see where these various things are taken up?

"THE DEFENDANT: No, your Honor, I haven't.

"THE COURT: Have you looked in any of the California Codes with reference to trial procedure?

"THE DEFENDANT: Yes, your Honor.

"THE COURT: What codes?

"THE DEFENDANT: I have done extensive research in the Penal Code, your Honor, and the Civil Code.

"THE COURT: If you have done extensive research into it, then tell me about it.

"THE DEFENDANT: On empaneling a jury, your Honor?

"THE COURT: Yes.

"THE DEFENDANT: Well, the District Attorney and the defendant, defense counsel, has both the right to 12 peremptory challenges of a jury. These 12 challenges are undisputable. Any reason that the defense or prosecution should feel that a juror would be inadequate to try the case or to rule on a case, they may then discharge that juror.

Faretta's answers, and observation of his demeanor, the judge ruled that Faretta had not made an intelligent and knowing waiver of his right to the assistance of counsel, and also ruled that Faretta had no constitutional right to conduct his own defense. The judge accordingly reversed his earlier ruling permitting self-representation and again appointed the public defender to represent Faretta. Faretta's subsequent request for leave to act as cocounsel was rejected, as were his efforts to make certain motions on his own behalf. Throughout the subsequent trial, the judge required that Faretta's defense be conducted only through the appointed lawyer from the public defender's office. At the conclusion of the trial, the jury found Faretta guilty as charged, and the judge sentenced him to prison.

The California Court of Appeal, relying upon a then recent California Supreme Court decision that had expressly decided the issue, affirmed the trial judge's ruling that Faretta had no federal or state constitutional right to represent himself. Accordingly, the appellate court affirmed Faretta's conviction. A petition for rehearing was denied without opinion, and the California Supreme Court denied review.[5] We granted certiorari. 415 U.S. 975, 94 S.Ct. 1559, 39 L.Ed.2d 870.

II.

In the federal courts, the right of self-representation has been protected by statute since the beginnings of our Nation. Section 35 of the Judiciary Act of 1789, 1 Stat. 73, 92 . . . The right is currently codified in 28 U.S.C.A. § 1654.

With few exceptions, each of the several States also accords a defendant the right to represent himself in any criminal case. The constitutions of 36 States explicitly confer that right.[6] Moreover, many state courts have expressed the view that the right is also supported by the Constitution of the United States.

This Court has more than once indicated the same view. In Adams v. United States ex rel. McCann, 317 U.S. 269, 279, 63 S.Ct. 236, 241, 87 L.Ed. 268, the Court . . . did recognize, albeit in dictum, an affirmative right of self-representation:

"But if there is a valid challenge due to grounds of prejudice or some other grounds, that these aren't considered in the 12 peremptory challenges. There are numerous and the defendant, the defense and the prosecution both have the right to make any inquiry to the jury as to their feelings toward the case."

5. The California courts' conclusion that Faretta had no constitutional right to represent himself was made in the context of the following not unusual rules of California criminal procedure: An indigent criminal defendant has no right to appointed counsel of his choice. . . . The appointed counsel manages the lawsuit and has the final say in all but a few matters of trial strategy. . . . A California conviction will not be reversed on grounds of ineffective assistance of counsel except in the extreme case where the quality of representation was so poor as to render the trial a "farce and a sham."

6. Some States grant the accused the right to be heard, or to defend, in person *and* by counsel . . . . .

Others grant the right to defend in person *or* by counsel. . . .

Still others provide the accused the right to defend either by himself, by counsel, or both. . . .

"The right to assistance of counsel and the *correlative right to dispense with a lawyer's help* are not legal formalisms. They rest on considerations that go to the substance of an accused's position before the law. . . .

"What were contrived as protections for the accused should not be turned into fetters. . . . To deny an accused a choice of procedure in circumstances where he, though a layman, is as capable as any lawyer of making an intelligent choice, is to impair the worth of great Constitutional safeguards by treating them as empty verbalisms.

" . . . When the administration of the criminal law . . . is hedged about as it is by the Constitutional safeguards for the protection of an accused, to deny him in the exercise of his free choice the right to dispense with some of these safeguards . . . is to imprison a man in his privileges and call it the Constitution." Id., at 279–280, 63 S.Ct., at 241–242 (emphasis added).

* * *

The United States Courts of Appeals have repeatedly held that the right of self-representation is protected by the Bill of Rights. . . .

This Court's past recognition of the right of self-representation, the federal court authority holding the right to be of constitutional dimension, and the state constitutions pointing to the right's fundamental nature form a consensus not easily ignored. "[T]he fact that a path is a beaten one," Mr. Justice Jackson once observed, "is a persuasive reason for following it." We confront here a nearly universal conviction, on the part of our people as well as our courts, that forcing a lawyer upon an unwilling defendant is contrary to his basic right to defend himself if he truly wants to do so.

III.

This consensus is soundly premised. The right of self-representation finds support in the structure of the Sixth Amendment as well as in the English and colonial jurisprudence from which the Amendment emerged.

A.

The Sixth Amendment includes a compact statement of the rights necessary to a full defense:

"In all criminal prosecutions, the accused shall enjoy the right . . . to be informed of the nature and cause of the accusation; to be confronted with the witnesses against him; to have compulsory process for obtaining witnesses in his favor, and to have the Assistance of Counsel for his defence."

* * *

The Sixth Amendment does not provide merely that a defense shall be made for the accused; it grants to the accused personally the right to make his defense. It is the accused, not counsel, who must be "informed of the nature and cause of the accusation," who must be "confronted with witnesses against him," and who must be accorded "compulsory process for obtaining witnesses in his favor." Although not stated in the Amendment in so many words, the right to self-representation—to make one's own defense personally—is thus necessarily implied by the structure of the Amendment. The right to defend is given directly to the accused; for it is he who suffers the consequences if the defense fails.

The counsel provision supplements this design. It speaks of the "assistance" of counsel, and an assistant, however expert, is still an assistant. The language and spirit of the Sixth Amendment contemplate that counsel like the other defense tools guaranteed by the Amendment, shall be an aid to a willing defendant—not an organ of the State interposed between an unwilling defendant and his right to defend himself personally. To thrust counsel upon the accused, against his considered wish, thus violates the logic of the Amendment. In such a case, counsel is not an assistant, but a master; and the right to make a defense is stripped of the personal character upon which the Amendment insists. It is true that when a defendant chooses to have a lawyer manage and present his case, law and tradition may allocate to the counsel the power to make binding decisions of trial strategy in many areas. . . . This allocation can only be justified, however, by the defendant's consent, at the outset, to accept counsel as his representative. An unwanted counsel "represents" the defendant only through a tenuous and unacceptable legal fiction. Unless the accused has acquiesced in such representation, the defense presented is not the defense guaranteed him by the Constitution, for, in a very real sense, it is not his defense.

B.

The Sixth Amendment, when naturally read, thus implies a right of self-representation. This reading is reinforced by the Amendment's roots in English legal history.

In the long history of British criminal jurisprudence, there was only one tribunal that ever adopted a practice of forcing counsel upon an unwilling defendant in a criminal proceeding. The tribunal was the Star Chamber. That curious institution, which flourished in the late 16th and early 17th centuries, was of mixed executive and judicial character, and characteristically departed from common-law traditions. . . .

The Star Chamber was swept away in 1641 by the revolutionary fervor of the Long Parliament. The notion of obligatory counsel disappeared with it.

By the common law of that time, it was not representation by counsel but self-representation that was the practice in prosecutions for serious crime. At one time, every litigant was required to "appear before the court in his own person and conduct his own cause in his own words." While a right to counsel developed early in civil cases and in cases of misdemeanor, a prohibition against the assistance of counsel continued for centuries in prosecutions for felony or treason. Thus, in the 16th and 17th centuries the accused felon or traitor stood alone, with neither counsel nor the benefit of other rights—to notice, confrontation and compulsory process—that we now associate with a genuinely fair adversary proceeding. The trial was merely a "long argument between the prisoner and the counsel for the

Crown." As harsh as this now seems, at least "the prisoner was allowed to make what statements he liked. . . . Obviously this public oral trial presented many more opportunities to a prisoner than the secret enquiry based on written depositions, which, on the continent had taken the place of a trial. . . ."

With the Treason Act of 1695, there began a long and important era of reform in English criminal procedure. The 1695 statute granted to the accused traitor the rights to a copy of the indictment, to have his witnesses testify under oath, and "to make . . . full defense, by counsel learned in the law." It also provided for court appointment of counsel, *but only if the accused so desired.* Thus, as new rights developed, the accused retained his established right "to make what statements he liked." The right to counsel was viewed as guaranteeing a choice between representation by counsel and the traditional practice of self-representation. The ban on counsel in felony cases, which had been substantially eroded in the courts, was finally eliminated by statute in 1836. In more recent years, Parliament has provided for court appointment of counsel in serious criminal cases, but only at the accused's request. At no point in this process of reform in England was counsel ever forced upon the defendant. . . .

C.

In the American colonies the insistence upon a right of self-representation was, if anything, more fervent than in England.

The colonists brought with them an appreciation of the virtues of self-reliance and a traditional distrust of lawyers. When the Colonies were first settled, "the lawyer was synonymous with the cringing Attorneys–General and Solicitors–General of the Crown and the arbitrary Justices of the King's Court, all bent on the conviction of those who opposed the King's prerogatives, and twisting the law to secure convictions." This prejudice gained strength in the colonies where "distrust of lawyers became an institution." Several Colonies prohibited pleading for hire in the 17th century. The prejudice persisted into the 18th century as "the lower classes came to identify lawyers with the upper class." The years of Revolution and Confederation saw an upsurge of anti-lawyer sentiment, a "sudden revival, after the War of the Revolution of the old dislike and distrust of lawyers as a class." In the heat of these sentiments the Constitution was forged.

This is not to say that the Colonies were slow to recognize the value of counsel in criminal cases. Colonial judges soon departed from ancient English practice and allowed accused felons the aid of counsel for their defense. At the same time, however, the basic right of self-representation was never questioned. We have found no instance where a colonial court required a defendant in a criminal case to accept as his representative an unwanted lawyer. Indeed, even where counsel was permitted, the general practice continued to be self-representation.

The right of self-representation was guaranteed in many colonial charters and declarations of rights. These early documents establish that the "right to counsel" meant to the colonists a right to choose between pleading through a lawyer and representing oneself. After the Declaration of Independence, the right of self-representation, along with other rights basic to the making of a defense, entered the new state constitutions in wholesale fashion. The right to counsel was clearly thought to supplement the primary right of the accused to defend himself, utilizing his personal rights to notice, confrontation and compulsory process. And when the Colonies or newly independent States provided by statute rather than by constitution for court appointment of counsel in criminal cases, they also meticulously preserved the right of the accused to defend himself personally.

The recognition of the right of self-representation was not limited to the state lawmakers. As we have noted, § 35 of the Judiciary Act of 1789, signed one day before the Sixth Amendment was proposed, guaranteed in the federal courts the right of all parties "to plead and manage their own cause personally or by the assistance of . . . counsel." See 1 Stat. 92 (1789) as amended, 28 U.S.C.A. § 1654 (1970). . . . No State or Colony had ever forced counsel upon an accused; no spokesman had ever suggested that such a practice would be tolerable, much less advisable. If anyone had thought that the Sixth Amendment, as drafted, failed to protect the long-respected right of self-representation, there would undoubtedly have been some debate or comment on the issue. But there was none.

In sum, there is no evidence that the colonists and the Framers ever doubted the right of self-representation, or imagined that this right might be considered inferior to the right of assistance of counsel. To the contrary, the colonists and the Framers, as well as their English ancestors, always conceived of the right to counsel as an "assistance" for the accused, to be used at his option, in defending himself. The Framers selected in the Sixth Amendment a form of words that necessarily implies the right of self-representation. That conclusion is supported by centuries of consistent history.

IV.

There can be no blinking the fact that the right of an accused to conduct his own defense seems to cut against the grain of this Court's decisions holding that the Constitution requires that no accused can be convicted and imprisoned unless he has been accorded the right to the assistance of counsel. See Powell v. Alabama, 287 U.S. 45, 53 S.Ct. 55, 77 L.Ed. 158; Johnson v. Zerbst, 304 U.S. 458, 58 S.Ct. 1019, 82 L.Ed. 1461; Gideon v. Wainwright, 372 U.S. 335, 83 S.Ct. 792, 9 L.Ed.2d 799; Argersinger v. Hamlin, 407 U.S. 25, 92 S.Ct. 2006, 32 L.Ed.2d 530. For it is surely true that the basic thesis of those decisions is that the help of a lawyer is essential to assure the defendant a fair trial. And a strong argument can surely be made that the whole thrust of those decisions must inevitably lead to the conclusion that a State may constitutionally impose a lawyer upon even an unwilling defendant.

But it is one thing to hold that every defendant, rich or poor, has the right to the assistance of counsel, and quite another to say that a State may compel a defendant to accept a lawyer he does not want. The value of state-appointed counsel was not unappreciated by the Founders, yet the notion of compulsory counsel was utterly foreign to them. And whatever else may be said of those who wrote the Bill of Rights, surely there can be no doubt that they understood the inestimable worth of free choice.

It is undeniable that in most criminal prosecutions defendants could better defend with counsel's guidance than by their own unskilled efforts. But where the defendant will not voluntarily accept representation by counsel, the potential advantage of a lawyer's training and experience can be realized, if at all, only imperfectly. To force a lawyer on a defendant can only lead him to believe that the law contrives against him. Moreover, it is not inconceivable that in some rare instances, the defendant might in fact present his case more effectively by conducting his own defense. Personal liberties are not rooted in the law of averages. The right to defend is personal. The defendant, and not his lawyer or the State, will bear the personal consequence of a conviction. It is the defendant, therefore, who must be free personally to decide whether in his particular case counsel is to his advantage. And although he may conduct his own defense ultimately to his own detriment, his choice must be honored out of "that respect for the individual which is the lifeblood of the law." Illinois v. Allen, 397 U.S. 337, 350–351, 90 S.Ct. 1057, 1064, 25 L.Ed.2d 353 (concurring opinion of Brennan, J.).[7]

V.

When an accused manages his own defense, he relinquishes, as a purely factual matter, many of the traditional benefits associated with the right to counsel. For this reason, in order to represent himself, the accused must "knowingly and intelligently" forego those relinquished benefits. Johnson v. Zerbst, 304 U.S. 458, 464–465, 58 S.Ct. 1019, 1023, 82 L.Ed. 1461. . . .Although a defendant need not himself have the skill and experience of a lawyer in order competently and intelligently to choose self-representation, he should be made aware of the dangers and disadvantages of self-representation, so that the record will establish that "he knows what he is doing and his choice is made with eyes open." Adams v. United States ex rel. McCann, 317 U.S. 269, 270, 63 S.Ct. 236, 242, 87 L.Ed. 268.

Here, weeks before trial, Faretta clearly and unequivocally declared to the trial judge that he wanted to represent himself and did not want counsel. The record affirmatively shows that Faretta was literate, competent, and understanding, and that he was voluntarily exercising his in-

7. We are told that many criminal defendants representing themselves may use the courtroom for deliberate disruption of their trials. But the right of self-representation has been recognized from our beginnings by federal law and by most of the States, and no such result has thereby occurred. Moreover, the trial judge may terminate self-representation by a defendant who deliberately engages in serious and obstructionist misconduct. See Illinois v. Allen, 397 U.S. 337, 90 S.Ct. 1057, 25 L.Ed.2d 353. Of course, a State may—even over objection by the accused—appoint a "standby counsel" to aid the accused if and when the accused requests help, and to be available to represent the accused in the event that termination of the defendant's self-representation is necessary. See United States v. Dougherty, 154 U.S.App. D.C. 76, 473 F.2d 1113, 1124–1126.

The right of self-representation is not a license to abuse the dignity of the courtroom. Neither is it a license not to comply with relevant rules of procedural and substantive law. Thus, whatever else may or may not be open to him on appeal, a defendant who elects to represent himself cannot thereafter complain that the quality of his own defense amounted to a denial of "effective assistance of counsel."

formed free will. The trial judge had warned Faretta that he thought it was a mistake not to accept the assistance of counsel, and that Faretta would be required to follow all the "ground rules" of trial procedure. We need make no assessment of how well or poorly Faretta had mastered the intricacies of the hearsay rule and the California code provisions that govern challenges of potential jurors on *voir dire*. For his technical legal knowledge, as such, was not relevant to an assessment of his knowing exercise of the right to defend himself.

In forcing Faretta, under these circumstances, to accept against his will a state-appointed public defender, the California courts deprived him of his constitutional right to conduct his own defense. Accordingly, the judgment before us is vacated, and the case is remanded for further proceedings not inconsistent with this opinion.

It is so ordered.

■ MR. CHIEF JUSTICE BURGER, with whom MR. JUSTICE BLACKMUN and MR. JUSTICE REHNQUIST join, dissenting.

...[T]here is nothing desirable or useful in permitting every accused person, even the most uneducated and inexperienced, to insist upon conducting his own defense to criminal charges. Moreover, there is no constitutional basis for the Court's holding and it can only add to the problems of an already malfunctioning criminal justice system. I therefore dissent.

...Its ultimate assertion that such a right is tucked between the lines of the Sixth Amendment is contradicted by the Amendment's language and its consistent judicial interpretation. ...[T]his Court's decisions have consistently included the right to counsel as an integral part of the bundle making up the larger "right to a defense as we know it." ...[I]n all but an extraordinarily small number of cases an accused will lose whatever defense he may have if he undertakes to conduct the trial himself.

* * *

In short, both the "spirit and the logic" of the Sixth Amendment are that every person accused of crime shall receive the fullest possible defense; in the vast majority of cases this command can be honored only by means of the expressly-guaranteed right to counsel, and the trial judge is in the best position to determine whether the accused is capable of conducting his defense. True freedom of choice and society's interest in seeing that justice is achieved can be vindicated only if the trial court retains discretion to reject any attempted waiver of counsel and insist that the accused be tried according to the Constitution. This discretion is as critical an element of basic fairness as a trial judge's discretion to decline to accept a plea of guilty. See Santobello v. New York, 404 U.S. 257, 262, 92 S.Ct. 495, 498–499, 30 L.Ed.2d 427 (1971).

[The dissent further argued that the judge and prosecutor are charged with the duty of insuring that justice, "in the broadest sense of that term," is achieved in every criminal trial, and that objective is ill-served "when an easy conviction is obtained due to the defendant's ill-advised decision to waive counsel."

The dissenters also argued that the majority's assumption that the accused who has elected to defend himself will not be heard to complain of it later ignores the role of appellate review, with the result that "many expensive and good-faith prosecutions will be nullified on appeal for reasons that trial courts are now deprived of the power to prevent." Editors.]

[Justice Blackmun's separate dissent, in which the Chief Justice and Justice Rehnquist joined, is omitted.]

NOTE

Standby counsel. In *Faretta,* the majority said in a footnote that "a State may—even over objection by the accused—appoint a 'standby counsel' to aid the accused if and when the accused requests help." Is it always impermissible, as the language from *Faretta* suggests, for standby counsel to interject himself into a trial without a request from the defendant? The Court dealt with this question in McKaskle v. Wiggins, 465 U.S. 168, 104 S.Ct. 944, 79 L.Ed.2d 122 (1984). Wiggins was permitted by the trial court to represent himself, but two standby attorneys were appointed to assist him. At various points in the trial, one or the other of the standby attorneys participated in the proceedings without specific invitation by Wiggins. Sometimes Wiggins approved of the participation and sometimes he did not. At some points in the trial, standby counsel participated at the specific request of Wiggins. Wiggins was convicted and, after exhausting state remedies, filed a federal petition for writ of habeas corpus claiming that the uninvited participation by standby counsel in his trial deprived him of his right to pro se representation under *Faretta.* The Fifth Circuit held for Wiggins on the ground that standby counsel is "to be seen, but not heard" unless and to the extent specifically requested by the *pro se* defendant. Wiggins v. Estelle, 681 F.2d 266 (5th Cir.1982). The Supreme Court granted the State of Texas' petition for writ of certiorari and, in an opinion authored by Justice O'Connor, reversed.

The Court specifically rejected the position of the Fifth Circuit. Instead, it adopted a two part test: a defendant's right of *pro se* representation is not violated if he maintains actual control over the defense and if counsel's participation does not destroy the jury's perception that the defendant is representing himself:

First, the *pro se* defendant is entitled to preserve actual control over the case he chooses to present to the jury. This is the core of the *Faretta* right. If standby counsel's participation over the defendant's objection effectively allows counsel to make or substantially interfere with any significant tactical decisions, or to control the questioning of witnesses, or to speak *instead* of the defendant on any matter of importance, the *Faretta* right is eroded.

Second, participation by standby counsel without the defendant's consent should not be allowed to destroy the jury's perception that the defendant is representing himself. The defendant's appearance in the status of one conducting his own defense is important in a criminal trial, since the right to appear *pro se* exists to affirm the accused's individual dignity and autonomy....From the jury's perspective, the message conveyed by the defense may depend as much on the messenger as on the message itself. From the defendant's own point of view, the right to appear *pro se* can lose much of its importance if only the lawyers in the courtroom know that the right is being exercised.

465 U.S. at 178–79, 104 S.Ct. at 951, 79 L.Ed.2d at 133–34. The Court then examined counsel's uninvited participation in those portions of the trial that occurred outside the presence or hearing of the jury. It found no violation of the actual control standard, since Wiggins was given ample opportunity to participate in

all matters under discussion, the trial court repeatedly informed Wiggins that his tactical decisions, not those of standby counsel, would control, and in all instances of conflict the wishes of Wiggins were honored.

The Court characterized counsel's participation in front of the jury as "more problematic." At times, Wiggins invited counsel to participate in front of the jury, at times counsel participated without specific invitation and Wiggins appeared to approve, and at times Wiggins specifically disapproved of counsel's uninvited participation. The Court thought Wiggins' various positions were significant:

> *Faretta* does not require a trial judge to permit "hybrid" representation of the type Wiggins was actually allowed. But if a defendant is given the opportunity and elects to have counsel appear before the court or jury, his complaints concerning counsel's subsequent unsolicited participation lose much of their force. A defendant does not have a constitutional right to choreograph special appearances by counsel. Once a *pro se* defendant invites or agrees to any substantial participation by counsel, subsequent appearances by counsel must be presumed to be with the defendant's acquiescence, at least until the defendant expressly and unambiguously renews his request that standby counsel be silenced.

465 U.S. at 183, 104 S.Ct. at 953, 79 L.Ed.2d at 136.

The Court isolated standby counsel's role in assisting the defendant in understanding trial procedure and to achieve his own goals, such as by showing him how to get testimony or objects admitted into evidence, and explicitly approved of that role without any requirement of invitation by the defendant: "Participation by counsel to steer a defendant through the basic procedures of trial is permissible even in the unlikely event that it somewhat undermines the *pro se* defendant's appearance of control over his own defense." 465 U.S. at 184, 104 S.Ct. at 954, 79 L.Ed.2d at 137. Counsel's other unsolicited activities in front of the jury, while not "a model for future trials," were not so extensive as to undermine the jury's perception that Wiggins was representing himself.

Justice White, joined by Justices Brennan and Marshall, dissenting, criticized the majority for providing inadequate guidance to lower courts on the question of when standby counsel has gone too far. The dissent concluded that the actions of standby counsel in this case,

> distracted Wiggins and usurped his prerogatives, altered the tenor of the defense, disrupted the trial, undermined Wiggins' perception that he controlled his own fate, induced a belief—most assuredly unfounded, but sincerely held nevertheless—that "the law contrive[d] against him," and undoubtedly reduced Wiggins' credibility and prejudiced him in the eyes of the jury.

465 U.S. at 195–96, 104 S.Ct. at 960, 79 L.Ed.2d at 144.

CHAPTER 25

SENTENCING

Analysis

Sentencing in a narrow sense is that stage of the criminal justice process involving decisions about what to do initially with convicted criminal offenders. Later decisions may also be involved, of course, and may be made by a variety of decisionmakers, including parole authorities. In a broader sense, however, the entire criminal justice process has sentencing implications for the suspect or defendant even if he is not prosecuted or convicted. Thus pre-trial diversion can be regarded as essentially a "sentencing" decision made at a very early stage of the process, sometimes by the police.

Sentencing in both senses has been the subject of a great deal of recent concern and law revision. Perhaps the most controversial recent development is the federal Sentencing Reform Act of 1984, considered at several places in this chapter. See Breyer, "The Federal Sentencing Guidelines and the Key Compromises Upon Which They Rest," 17 Hofstra L.Rev. 1 (1988); and von Hirsch, "Federal Sentencing Guidelines: The United States and Canadian Schemes Compared," IV Occasional Papers From The Center for Research in Crime and Justice at N.Y.U. School of Law (1988).

This chapter is an introduction to the major legal issues that touch upon sentencing. It lists the goals that might be pursued in the sentencing process, describes the manner in which the sentencing process might be structured, and explores several procedural issues concerning the carrying out of the sentencing task. The chapter then provides an introduction to some alternatives and supplements to sentences of imprisonment.

A. SENTENCING GOALS

Underlying the sentencing process are various ideas of what sentencing might accomplish. These ideas have given rise to several commonly recognized philosophies which can be applied in sentencing tasks. Some are complementary; some are mutually exclusive. One or more of these philosophies is implicit in every sentencing decision, including legislative decisions as to how to structure sentencing systems.

BURNS AND MATTINA, SENTENCING 1–5 (1978)*

JUDICIAL PHILOSOPHIES OF SENTENCING

Judges ...will necessarily be expressing their personal philosophy of the ends of the criminal law, whether they realize it or not. ...

...[W]e can identify four basic ends which a sentencing judge may consider.

I. Deterrence:

Deterrence ...is customarily looked at from two perspectives. One, commonly referred to as "specific" or "individual" deterrence, rests on the notion that the sentence imposed will deter the individual defendant from repetition of the behavior that brought him before the court in the first instance. ...

The second perspective is that of "general" deterrence. This rests on the notion that by the sentence imposed on an individual defendant, and by communication of that sentence to others who might commit similar crimes, the latter will forego their projected criminal behavior out of fear they will suffer the same or similar sentence.

* * *

...One may argue ...that general deterrence is more class-specific than crime-specific.

Consideration of the effectiveness of general deterrence also requires an evaluation of the means and extent of communicating sentencing information to the group of persons sought to be deterred. ...

* * *

[I]f the criminal behavior involved is impulsive, tends to occur in the presence of high emotion and with little time for reflection (as, for example, most family homicides), the general deterrent rationale for sentencing may not apply or may apply only minimally. By contrast, where the criminal behavior is carefully planned and carried out over an extended period (such as certain criminal frauds, embezzlement, and the like), the very fact of a period for reflection by the criminal ought to make the general deterrent purpose more available.

II. Separation:

...This end is sometimes referred to as incapacitation or neutralization. Normally, separation is considered appropriate in the case of crimes that involve a grave risk to the personal peace and safety of members of the community. ...The separation rationale assumes that the conduct in these crimes is so serious and the chance of repetition so great that the judge, acting for society, must conclude that protection of the public is the primary objective. ...In a sense, imposition of a death sentence is based in part upon separation rationale.

*Published by The National Judicial   Reno, Nevada.
College located at The University of Nevada,

Even apart from homicides, in most jurisdictions armed robbery, rape, serious physical assault, residential burglary, and other similar crimes, carry lengthy maximum sentences. In these cases there has been an initial legislative determination that persons who commit such acts should be separated (or considered for separation) from society through imprisonment for a lengthy period of time. . . .

III. Rehabilitation:

. . . [I]f rehabilitation is the prime consideration, total confinement in a large central prison is rare . . .

Customarily, rehabilitation is . . . [the goal of] probation, either with no confinement involved or with a limited period of partial confinement. Partial confinement (a limited period of time in a county jail, work release, or other community treatment center) coupled with probation will usually be selected in cases where the judge believes that the primary goal of the sentence is to promote rehabilitation of the defendant. . . .

IV. Retribution:

The fourth major purpose of sentencing is frequently referred to as retribution (sometimes "punishment;" sometimes "vengeance"). . . . This notion incorporates a basic human feeling. . . . If law lacks a sanction, the argument runs, no reason exists for the law-abiding to obey the law when they see that those who violate it do not have to "pay." . . . The criminal offender has acted in violation of societal rules and must be "punished" in order that he or she receives "just deserts." This ingrained concept of punishment or retribution is the product of thousands of years of history, culture, tradition, religion and other societal forces.

To be valid as a principle of sentencing, retribution must be proportional. . . . Initially, the legislature, by fixing a maximum (e.g., five years for car theft) expresses societal estimation of the maximum retribution to be demanded. Thereafter, it is for the sentencing judge to decide how much the offender ought to "pay" in a given case, where retribution is either the primary, or a significant goal.

V. The Choice of Sentence:

. . . Frequently, the judge is faced with the dilemma of knowing that if he imposes a particular type of sentence to achieve one purpose, he thereby frustrates the likelihood of achieving another. . . .

B.   STRUCTURING THE SENTENCING SYSTEM

The major issues presented by the need for a sentencing system are the amount of discretion that should exist and, to the extent that discretion is appropriate, upon whom the authority to exercise it should be conferred, and how it should be exercised and controlled. A partial historical perspective was provided by Chief Justice Burger in United States v. Grayson, 438 U.S. 41, 98 S.Ct. 2610, 57 L.Ed.2d 582 (1978):

In the early days of the Republic, when imprisonment had only recently emerged as an alternative to the death penalty, confinement in public stocks, or whipping in the town square, the period of incarceration was generally prescribed with specificity by the legislature. Each crime had its defined punishment. ...The "excessive rigidity of the [mandatory or fixed sentence] system" soon gave way in some jurisdictions, however, to a scheme permitting the sentencing judge— or jury—to consider aggravating and mitigating circumstances surrounding an offense, and, on that basis, to select a sentence within a *range* defined by the legislature. Tappan, Sentencing Under the Model Penal Code, 23 Law & Contemp.Prob. 528, 529 (1958). Nevertheless, the focus remained on the crime: Each particular offense was to be punished in proportion to the social harm caused by it and according to the offender's culpability. ...The purpose of incarceration remained, primarily, retribution and punishment.

Approximately a century ago, a reform movement asserting that the purpose of incarceration, and therefore the guiding consideration in sentencing, should be rehabilitation of the offender, dramatically altered the approach to sentencing. A fundamental proposal of this movement was a flexible sentencing system permitting judges and correctional personnel, particularly the latter, to set the release date of prisoners according to informed judgments concerning their potential for, or actual, rehabilitation and their likely recidivism. Indeed, the most extreme formulations of the emerging rehabilitation model, with its "reformatory sentence," posited that "convicts [regardless of the nature of their crime] can never be rightfully imprisoned except upon proof that it is unsafe for themselves and for society to leave them free, and when confined can never be rightfully released until they show themselves fit for membership in a free community." Lewis, The Indeterminate Sentence, 9 Yale L.J. 17, 27 (1899).

This extreme formulation, although influential, was not adopted unmodified by any jurisdiction. ..."The influences of legalism and realism were powerful enough ...to prevent the enactment of this form of indeterminate sentencing. Concern for personal liberty, skepticism concerning administrative decisions about prisoner reformation and readiness for release, insistence upon the preservation of some measure of deterrent emphasis, and other such factors, undoubtedly, led, instead, to a system—indeed, a complex of systems—in which maximum terms were generally employed." Id., at 530. ...To an unspecified degree, the sentencing judge is obligated to make his decision on the basis, among others, of predictions regarding the convicted defendant's potential, or lack of potential, for rehabilitation.

Indeterminate sentencing under the rehabilitation model presented sentencing judges with a serious practical problem: how rationally to make the required predictions so as to avoid capricious and arbitrary sentences, which the newly conferred and broad discretion placed within the realm of possibility. ...

438 U.S. at 45–48, 98 S.Ct. at 2613–14, 57 L.Ed.2d at 586–88. Obviously, parole authorities were presented with similar problems in exercising their role in traditional indeterminate sentencing.

Whether this discretion in sentencing judges and parole authorities is desirable and can be adequately regulated is, of course, a major concern. This section first addresses the nature of this sentencing discretion and then turns to its regulation by relatively traditional legal devices. Attention is then directed to recent proposals and reforms that substantially reduce and further structure the exercise of discretion in sentencing and release from imprisonment.

1.   THE PROBLEM OF DISCRETION IN SENTENCING

The indeterminate sentencing structure described by Chief Justice Burger in *Grayson* provides for substantial discretion in the sentencing judge and/or parole boards. Indeed, this discretion is seen as a major attribute of that structure. But is it reasonable to expect that this discretion will be exercised wisely? Effectively? Are legal controls on it desirable? Are they feasible? The present subsection places these issues in the judicial sentencing context existing prior to current reform efforts.

Frankel, Lawlessness in Sentencing

41 Cincinnati Law Review 1, 4–10 (1972).

The common form of criminal penalty provision confers upon the sentencing judge an enormous range of choice. . . .

The statutes granting such powers characteristically say nothing about the factors to be weighed in moving to either end of the spectrum or to some place between. . . . Even the most basic sentencing principles are not prescribed or stated with persuasive authority. There is, to be sure, a familiar litany in the literature of sentencing "purposes": retribution, deterrence ("special" and "general"), "denunciation," incapacitation, rehabilitation. Nothing tells us, however, when or whether any of these several goals are to be sought, or how to resolve such evident conflicts as that likely to arise in the effort to punish and rehabilitate all at once. . . .

. . . [W]e have no structure of rules, or even guidelines, affecting other elements arguably pertinent to the nature or severity of the sentence. Should it be a mitigating factor that the defendant is being sentenced upon a plea of guilty rather than a verdict against him? Should it count in his favor that he spared the public "trouble" and expense by waiving a jury? Should the sentence be more severe because the judge is convinced that the defendant perjured himself on the witness stand? Should churchgoing be considered to reflect favorably? Consistently with the first amendment, should it be considered at all? What factors should be assessed—and where, if anywhere, are comparisons to be sought—in gauging the relative seriousness of the specific offense and offender as against the spectrum of offenses by others in the same legal category? The list of such questions could be lengthened. Each is capable of being answered, and is answered by sentencing judges, in contradictory or conflicting, or at least differing, ways. There is no controlling requirement that any particular view be followed on any such subject by the sentencing judge.

With the delegation of power so unchanneled, it is surely no overstatement to say that "the new penology has resulted in vesting in judges and parole and probation agencies the greatest degree of uncontrolled power over the liberty of human beings that one can find in the legal system." The process would be totally unruly even if judges were superbly and uniformly trained for the solemn work of sentencing. As everyone knows, however, they are not trained at all. . . .

Viewed as a group, the people who enter upon service as trial judges are somewhat elderly, more experienced than most lawyers in litigation, almost totally unencumbered by learning or experience relevant to sentencing, and inclined by temperament and circumstance toward the major orthodoxies. Nothing they studied in law school touched our subject more than remotely. Probably a large majority had no contact, or trivial contact, with criminal proceedings of any kind during their years of practice. Those who had such exposure worked preponderantly on the prosecution side. Whether or not this produces a troublesome bias, the best that can be said is that prosecutors tend generally either to refrain altogether from taking positions on sentencing or to deal with the subject at a bargaining level somewhat removed from the plane of penological ideals.

Thus qualified, the new judge may be discovered within days or weeks fashioning judgments of imprisonment for long years. No training, formal or informal, precedes the first of these awesome pronouncements. Such formal and intentional education, other than from the job itself, as may happen along the way is likely to be fleeting, random, anecdotal, and essentially trivial. Shop talk with fellow judges—at least in my experience on a court where the judges are numerous, convivial, and likely to talk shop in the court lunchroom and other gathering places—rarely lights on problems of sentencing. Because the sentence is not appealable except on rare and extraordinary grounds, there is little occasion for the kind of relatively organized reflection instigated by the reading of advance sheets. The experienced trial judge, then, is one who has imposed many sentences, improving, we would hope, from a course of solitary brooding and conversations with probation officers, consulting in the end himself as the final authority, and perhaps sinking deeper each year the footings of premises that have never been tested by detached scrutiny or by open debate.

Given the sure combination of substantially unbounded discretion and decision-makers unrestrained by shared professional standards, it is not astonishing that the commonplace worry in any discussion of sentencing concerns "disparity." The factual basis for the worry is clear and huge; nobody doubts that essentially similar people in large numbers receive widely divergent sentences for essentially similar or identical crimes. The causes of the problem are equally clear: judges vary widely in their explicit views and "principles" affecting sentencing; they vary, too, in the accidents of birth and biography generating the guilts, the fears, and the rages that affect almost all of us at times and in ways we often cannot know. The judge who reports there is no surge of emotion when he imposes a stiff sentence is likely to be mistaken, unperceptive, or a person of alarmingly flat affect. It is unnecessary, though not irrelevant, to frighten ourselves with the statistical probability and direct personal knowledge that some percentage of judges may be psychotic. It is disturbing enough that a charged encounter like the sentencing proceeding, while it is the gravest of legal matters, should turn so arbitrarily upon the variegated passions and prejudices of individual judges.

* * *

But at least in one critical respect our training, our habits, and our accomplishments ought to be pertinent: we are taught and qualified to seek and formulate rules—that is, law. We are steeped in a tradition of hostility to unruliness, the condition we condemn when we denounce the arbitrary and the capricious. If we have not followed the tradition in sentencing, it may be because the effort is hopeless. Or it may be that we have not tried hard enough despite all the professions of concern. I join with many others in the belief that a much nearer approach to law and order in sentencing is possible as well as desirable.

* * *

There is no ... requirement [to give reasons] in the announcement of a prison sentence. Sometimes judges give reasons anyway, or reveal in colloquy the springs of their action. The explanations or revelations sometimes disclose reasoning so perverse or mistaken that the sentence, normally unreviewable, must be invalidated on appeal. Most trial judges (to my impressionistic and conversational knowledge, at least) say little or nothing, certainly far less than a connected "explanation" or rationale of the sentence. Many, aware of their unreviewable powers, and sharing a common aversion to being reversed, are perhaps motivated by the view (not unknown on trial benches) that there is safety in silence. It is likely that the judge, not expected to explain, has never organized a full and coherent explanation even for himself. Some judges use the occasion of sentencing to flaunt or justify themselves by moral pronunciamentos and excoriations of the defendant. This has no relation to the serious and substantial idea that the community's "denunciation" is a—possibly the—chief aim of sentencing. It is, in any event, not kin to the reasoned decisions for which judges are commissioned.

The judge's failure to explain is part of a more pervasive silence that makes sentencing and its sequelae so much a shadowland of doubt, ignorance, and fragmented responsibility. ...

2. CONTROLLING SENTENCING DISCRETION BY APPELLATE REVIEW

If the existence of substantial discretion in the sentencing judge is in fact a matter of serious concern, one response is to attempt to regulate that discretion by traditional means such as appellate review. This subsection addresses such efforts, first by judicial review of a sentencing judges' consideration of specific matters, and, second, by judicial review of the final sentence imposed by the sentencing judge.

a.   APPELLATE REVIEW OF SENTENCING CONSIDERATIONS

Among the legal controls that might be placed upon sentencing discretion is review of a sentencing judge's decision to consider certain information in imposing sentence. The principal case deals with the appropriateness of consideration in sentencing of what the judge believes was the defendant's false trial testimony. If it is determined that at least in some circumstances certain factors should not be considered, it is then necessary to consider whether judicial review of the sentencing decision is an effective method of preventing their consideration.

United States v. Grayson

Supreme Court of the United States, 1978.
438 U.S. 41, 98 S.Ct. 2610, 57 L.Ed.2d 582.

■ MR. CHIEF JUSTICE BURGER delivered the opinion of the Court.

We granted certiorari to review a holding of the Court of Appeals that it was improper for a sentencing judge, in fixing the sentence within the statutory limits, to give consideration to the defendant's false testimony observed by the judge during the trial.

In August 1975, respondent Grayson was confined in a federal prison camp under a conviction for distributing a controlled substance. . . . [H]e escaped but was apprehended. . . . He was indicted for prison escape. . . .

Grayson testified in his own defense. . . .

Grayson's version of the facts was contradicted by the Government's rebuttal evidence and by cross-examination on crucial aspects of his story.
. . .

The jury returned a guilty verdict, whereupon the District Judge ordered the United States Probation Office to prepare a presentence report. At the sentencing hearing, the judge stated:

> "I'm going to give my reasons for sentencing in this case with clarity, because one of the reasons may well be considered by a Court of Appeals to be impermissible; and although I could come into this Court Room and sentence this Defendant to a five-year prison term without any explanation at all, I think it is fair that I give the reasons so that if the Court of Appeals feels that one of the reasons which I am about to enunciate is an improper consideration for a trial judge, then the Court will be in a position to reverse this court and send the case back for resentencing.

> "In my view a prison sentence is indicated, and the sentence that the Court is going to impose is to deter you, Mr. Grayson, and others who are similarly situated. Secondly, *it is my view that your defense was a complete fabrication without the slightest merit whatsoever. I feel it is proper for me to consider that fact in the sentencing, and I will do so.*" (Emphasis added.)

He then sentenced Grayson to a term of two years' imprisonment, consecutive to his unexpired sentence.

On appeal, a divided panel of the Court of Appeals for the Third Circuit directed that Grayson's sentence be vacated and that he be resentenced by the District Court without consideration of false testimony. . . .

We granted certiorari to resolve conflicts between holdings of the Courts of Appeals. . . .We reverse.

* * *

A defendant's truthfulness or mendacity while testifying on his own behalf, almost without exception, has been deemed probative of his attitudes toward society and prospects for rehabilitation and hence relevant to sentencing. . . .Judge Marvin Frankel's analysis for the Second Circuit is persuasive:

> "The effort to appraise 'character' is, to be sure, a parlous one, and not necessarily an enterprise for which judges are notably equipped by prior training. Yet it is in our existing scheme of sentencing one clue to the rational exercise of discretion. If the notion of 'repentence' is out of fashion today, the fact remains that a manipulative defiance of the law is not a cheerful datum for the prognosis a sentencing judge undertakes. . . .Impressions about an individual being sentenced—the likelihood that he will transgress no more, the hope that he may respond to rehabilitative efforts to assist with a lawful future career, the degree to which he does or does not deem himself at war with his society—are, for better or worse, central factors to be appraised under our theory of 'individualized' sentencing. The theory has its critics. While it lasts, however, a fact like the defendant's readiness to lie under oath before the judge who will sentence him would seem to be among the more precise and concrete of the available indicia." United States v. Hendrix, 505 F.2d 1233, 1236 (1974).

Only one Circuit has directly rejected the probative value of the defendant's false testimony in his own defense. In Scott v. United States, 135 U.S.App.D.C. 377, 382, 419 F.2d 264, 269 (1969), the court argued that

> "the peculiar pressures placed upon a defendant threatened with jail and the stigma of conviction make his willingness to deny the crime an unpromising test of his prospects for rehabilitation if guilty. It is indeed unlikely that many men who commit serious offenses would balk on principle from lying in their own defense. The guilty man may quite sincerely repent his crime but yet, driven by the urge to remain free, may protest his innocence in a court of law."

. . .The *Scott* rationale rests not only on the realism of the psychological pressures on a defendant in the dock—which we can grant—but also on a deterministic view of human conduct that is inconsistent with the underlying precepts of our criminal justice system. A "universal and persistent" foundation stone in our system of law, and particularly in our approach to punishment, sentencing and incarceration, is the "belief in freedom of the human will and a consequent ability and duty of the normal individual to choose between good and evil." Morissette v. United States, 342 U.S. 246, 250, 72 S.Ct. 240, 243, 96 L.Ed. 288 (1952). . . .Given that long accepted view of the "ability and duty of the normal individual to choose," we must conclude that the defendant's readiness to lie under oath—especially when, as here, the trial court finds the lie to be flagrant—may be deemed probative of his prospects for rehabilitation.

* * *

...The right guaranteed by law to a defendant is narrowly the right to testify truthfully in accordance with the oath—unless we are to say that the oath is mere ritual without meaning. This view of the right involved is confirmed by the unquestioned constitutionality of perjury statutes, which punish those who willfully give false testimony. ...Further support for this is found in an important limitation on a defendant's right to the assistance of counsel: Counsel ethically cannot assist his client in presenting what the attorney has reason to believe is false testimony. ...Assuming, *arguendo,* that the sentencing judge's consideration of defendants' untruthfulness in testifying has any chilling effect on a defendant's decision to testify falsely, that effect is entirely permissible. There is no protected right to commit perjury.

...Nothing we say today requires a sentencing judge to enhance, in some wooden or reflex fashion, the sentences of all defendants whose testimony is deemed false. Rather, we are reaffirming the authority of a sentencing judge to evaluate carefully a defendant's testimony on the stand, determine—with a consciousness of the frailty of human judgment—whether that testimony contained willful and material falsehoods, and, if so, assess in light of all the other knowledge gained about the defendant the meaning of that conduct with respect to his prospects for rehabilitation and restoration to a useful place in society. Awareness of such a process realistically cannot be deemed to affect the decision of an accused but unconvicted defendant to testify truthfully in his own behalf.

Accordingly, we reverse the judgment of the Court of Appeals and remand for reinstatement of the sentence of the District Court.

Reversed and remanded.

■ Mr. Justice Stewart, with whom Mr. Justice Brennan and Mr. Justice Marshall join, dissenting.

The Court begins its consideration of this case with the assumption that the respondent gave false testimony at his trial. But there has been no determination that his testimony was false. This respondent was given a greater sentence than he would otherwise have received—how much greater we have no way of knowing—solely because a single judge *thought* that he had not testified truthfully. In essence, the Court holds today that *whenever* a defendant testifies in his own behalf and is found guilty, he opens himself to the possibility of an enhanced sentence. Such a sentence is nothing more nor less than a penalty imposed on the defendant's exercise of his constitutional and statutory rights to plead not guilty and to testify in his own behalf.

* * *

NOTES

1. **Accepting responsibility as a sentencing criterion.** Section 3C1.1 of the Federal Sentencing Guidelines provides an increased penalty if the defendant

has "willfully impeded or obstructed, or attempted to impede or obstruct the administration of justice during the investigation or prosecution...." The Commentary to that section lists "testifying untruthfully" as conduct which "may provide a basis for applying this adjustment." However, section 3E1.1 provides for a reduction in penalty if "the defendant clearly demonstrates a recognition and affirmative acceptance of personal responsibility for the offense...."

In United States v. Gonzalez, 897 F.2d 1018 (9th Cir.1990), a United States Court of Appeals rejected Fifth and Sixth Amendment challenges to application of section 3E1.1. Gonzales argued that the reduction in sentence for acceptance of responsibility was effectively unavailable to those defendants who exercise their right to have a jury trial instead of pleading guilty, unless they also sacrifice their Fifth Amendment privilege against self-incrimination. The court agreed that a defendant who protests innocence throughout trial may have difficulty in later accepting responsibility for the crime "without appearing to contradict his previous stance." But this difficulty does not encourage perjury in violation of the Fifth Amendment; and the Sixth Amendment right to a jury trial is not sacrificed by the provision because a defendant "may manifest sincere contrition despite the exercise of his right to go to trial—as when he goes to trial to assert and preserve issues unrelated to factual guilt...." 897 F.2d at 1021.

2. **Perjurious testimony.** United States v. Dunnigan, 507 U.S. 87, 113 S.Ct. 1111, 122 L.Ed.2d 445 (1993) raised the question of increasing punishment under the Sentencing Guidelines because the trial judge believed the defendant committed perjury in her trial testimony. Five witnesses testified for the Government as to defendant's involvement in cocaine trafficking. Defendant testified on her own behalf and denied any involvement. Following conviction, the trial judge increased the punishment under § C1.1 of the Guidelines because he believed she committed perjury at trial. The Court of Appeals set aside the sentence, distinguishing United States v. Grayson (Casebook p. 1147) on the ground that Grayson was based on the greater need for rehabilitation demonstrated by a defendant's committing perjury, while the Sentencing Guidelines base enhancement on punishment considerations. Also, the Court of Appeals believed that Grayson did not support the rigid enhancement imposed by the Guidelines.

The Supreme Court, in an opinion by Justice Kennedy for a unanimous Court, reversed. Grayson did not state that rehabilitation is the only justification for increasing a sentence because the defendant committed perjury. There are other considerations:

> [A] defendant who commits a crime and then perjures herself in an unlawful attempt to avoid responsibility is more threatening to society and less deserving of leniency than a defendant who does not so defy the trial process. The perjuring defendant's willingness to frustrate judicial proceedings to avoid criminal liability suggests the need for incapacitation and retribution is heightened as compared with the defendant charged with the same crime who allows judicial proceedings to progress without resorting to perjury.

507 U.S. at 97–98, 113 S.Ct. at 1118, 122 L.Ed.2d at 455. Just because a defendant testifies in his own defense and is convicted does not mean his testimony was perjurious:

> [A]n accused may give inaccurate testimony due to confusion, mistake or faulty memory. In other instances, an accused may testify to matters such as lack of capacity, insanity, duress or self-defense. Her testimony may be truthful, but the jury may nonetheless find the testimony insufficient to excuse criminal liability or prove lack of intent. For these reasons, if a defendant objects to a sentence enhancement resulting from her trial testimony, a district court must review the evidence and make independent findings necessary to establish a

willful impediment to or obstruction of justice, or an attempt to do the same
* * *.

507 U.S. at 95, 113 S.Ct. at 1117, 122 L.Ed.2d at 454.

3. **Refusing to cooperate with law enforcement authorities.** That cooperation with the police may result in a more lenient sentence for the criminal defendant is well established. But should a refusal to cooperate be considered in imposing a harsher sentence than would otherwise be the case? In Roberts v. United States, 445 U.S. 552, 100 S.Ct. 1358, 63 L.Ed.2d 622 (1980), the defendant had confessed his involvement in a conspiracy to distribute heroin but refused to name other dealers in his community in exchange for a favorable disposition of his case. The District Court imposed consecutive rather than concurrent terms and gave as one of its reasons the defendant's refusal to name names. Upholding consideration of this factor as proper, the Supreme Court observed that "gross indifference to the duty to report known criminal behavior remains a badge of irresponsible citizenship" and that the defendant had "rejected an 'obligation of community life' that should be recognized before rehabilitation can begin." It brushed aside the defendant's claim that his refusal was motivated by fear of retaliation and self-incrimination because these explanations were never offered to the sentencing court.

4. **Right to remain silent at sentencing.** Does a defendant who enters a plea of guilty waive his right to remain silent at the sentencing phase of the case? The defendant in Mitchell v. United States, 526 U.S. 314, 119 S.Ct. 1307, 143 L.Ed.2d 424 (1999) entered a plea of guilty to four drug distribution counts, the punishment for which depended upon the quantity of drugs she distributed and could have been as short as one year or as long as life. She reserved her right to contest at sentencing the amount of drugs she distributed. At sentencing, there was testimony from accomplices as to the amount of drugs she normally distributed over a period of time as part of the conspiracy. Based upon that testimony, the District Court concluded it was required to impose a sentence of at least ten years and imposed a ten year sentence. At sentencing, the court stated that he "held it against" the defendant that she did not testify at sentencing to minimize the quantity of drugs she distributed. The Court of Appeals upheld the sentence but the Supreme Court, in an opinion by Justice Kennedy, reversed. The Court held that neither the entry of a plea of guilty nor the colloquy that accompanies such a plea is a waiver of the defendant's right not to incriminate herself at sentencing. Justice Kennedy commented that accepting the Government's contrary position would mean

> prosecutors could indict without specifying the quantity of drugs involved, obtain a guilty plea, and then put the defendant on the stand at sentencing to fill in the drug quantity. The result would be to enlist the defendant as an instrument in his or her own condemnation, undermining the long tradition and vital principle that criminal proceedings rely on accusations proved by the Government, not on inquisitions conducted to enhance its own prosecutorial power.

526 U.S. at ___, 119 S.Ct. at 1313.

The Court also ruled that the Fifth Amendment prohibits the trial court from drawing an adverse inference from the defendant's silence at sentencing:

> The concerns which mandate the rule against negative inferences at a criminal trial apply with equal force at sentencing. Without question, the stakes are high: Here, the inference drawn by the District Court from petitioner's silence may have resulted in decades of added imprisonment. The Government often has a motive to demand a severe sentence, so the central purpose of the

privilege—to protect a defendant from being the unwilling instrument of his or her own condemnation—remains of vital importance.

526 U.S. at ___, 119 S.Ct. at 1315. Justice Scalia, joined by The Chief Justice and Justices O'Connor and Thomas, dissented, taking the position that the defendant still retained a privilege against self-incrimination at sentencing but that the Fifth Amendment was not violated by the District Court drawing an adverse inference from her assertion of that right. Justice Thomas, dissenting separately, called for a re-examination of Griffin v. California and its progeny, which established the no adverse inference rule for the guilt/innocence phase of trials.

5. **Imposing a more severe sentence following appellate reversal.** In North Carolina v. Pearce, 395 U.S. 711, 89 S.Ct. 2072, 23 L.Ed.2d 656 (1969), the Supreme Court held:

> Neither the double jeopardy provision nor the Equal Protection Clause imposes an absolute bar to a more severe sentence upon reconviction [following reversal of a conviction on appeal]. A trial judge is not constitutionally precluded, in other words, from imposing a new sentence, whether greater or less than the original sentence, in the light of events subsequent to the first trial that may have thrown new light upon defendant's "life, health, habits, conduct, and mental and moral propensities." Williams v. New York, 337 U.S. 241, 245, 69 S.Ct. 1079, 1082, 93 L.Ed. 1337 (1949). Such information may come to the judge's attention from evidence adduced at the second trial itself, from a new presentence investigation, from the defendant's prison record, or possibly from other sources. The freedom of a sentencing judge to consider the defendant's conduct subsequent to the first conviction in imposing a new sentence is no more than consonant with the principle, fully approved in Williams v. New York, supra, that a State may adopt the "prevalent modern philosophy of penology that the punishment should fit the offender and not merely the crime." . . .

395 U.S. at 723, 89 S.Ct. at 2079–80, 23 L.Ed.2d at 668.

The Court, however, went on to state:

> This Court has never held that the States are required to establish avenues of appellate review, but it is now fundamental that, once established, these avenues must be kept free of unreasoned distinctions that can only impede open and equal access to the courts. . . .

> Due process of law, then, requires that vindictiveness against a defendant for having successfully attacked his first conviction must play no part in the sentence he receives after a new trial. And since the fear of such vindictiveness may unconstitutionally deter a defendant's exercise of the right to appeal or collaterally attack his first conviction, due process also requires that a defendant be freed of apprehension of such a retaliatory motivation on the part of the sentencing judge.

> In order to assure the absence of such a motivation, we have concluded that whenever a judge imposes a more severe sentence upon a defendant after a new trial, the reasons for his doing so must affirmatively appear. Those reasons must be based upon objective information concerning identifiable conduct on the part of the defendant occurring after the time of the original sentencing proceeding. And the factual data upon which the increased sentence is based must be made part of the record, so that the constitutional legitimacy of the increased sentence may be fully reviewed on appeal.

395 U.S. at 724–26, 89 S.Ct. at 2080–81, 23 L.Ed.2d at 669–70.

In Wasman v. United States, 468 U.S. 559, 104 S.Ct. 3217, 82 L.Ed.2d 424 (1984), the Court considered the question whether *Pearce* was violated. Petitioner had been convicted of a criminal offense and received a sentence of six months' imprisonment to be followed by three years' probation. At the time of sentencing, petitioner had another charge pending against him. The sentencing judge stated he did not take the pending charge into account in fixing the sentence. Petitioner appealed his conviction and received a new trial. In the meantime, he was convicted on the pending charge and received two years' probation. Upon re-conviction for the first offense, the same trial judge sentenced petitioner to two years' imprisonment, stating he was taking into account the conviction which occurred between the first and second trials of the case. The Supreme Court, in an opinion by The Chief Justice, held these events did not violate *Pearce:*

> Consideration of a criminal conviction obtained in the interim between an original sentencing and a sentencing after retrial is manifestly legitimate. This amply rebuts any presumption of vindictiveness. Here, the trial judge's justification is plain even from the record of petitioner's first sentencing proceeding; the judge informed the parties that, although he did not consider pending *charges* when sentencing a defendant, he always took into account prior criminal *convictions*. This, of course, was proper; indeed, failure to do so would have been inappropriate.

468 U.S. at 569–70, 104 S.Ct. at 3224, 82 L.Ed.2d at 434.

6. **Imposing a more severe sentence following trial court granting of a new trial.** In Texas v. McCullough, 475 U.S. 134, 106 S.Ct. 976, 89 L.Ed.2d 104 (1986), the respondent was convicted of murder and sentenced by the jury to 20 years' imprisonment. He filed a motion for new trial on the basis of prosecutorial misconduct, which was granted by the trial judge. In the second trial, respondent elected to be sentenced by the trial judge. He was again convicted of murder and the trial judge sentenced him to 50 years' imprisonment. The trial judge justified the sentence on the ground that two witnesses had testified during the second trial who had not testified during the first and had stated that respondent, rather than his accomplice, had slashed the throat of the victim, and that during the second trial the trial judge learned for the first time that respondent had been released from prison only four months before the offense was committed. The trial judge also stated that had she been the sentencer after the first trial she would have imposed more than the 20 years assessed by the jury. The Texas appellate courts set aside the sentence on the ground it violated North Carolina v. Pearce, but the Supreme Court in an opinion authored by Chief Justice Burger reversed.

The majority concluded that because the trial judge, rather than an appellate court, set aside the first conviction there should be no presumption that she acted vindictively in selecting the second sentence. The majority also concluded that the presumption is inapplicable because a different sentencer was involved in the second trial than the first—that there can be no claim she imposed a harsher sentence after the first conviction was set aside than she imposed before. The majority also concluded that if the presumption of vindictiveness of *Pearce* were applicable, it was sufficiently rebutted in this case. *Pearce* was not intended to restrict the sentencer to taking into account conduct of the defendant that occurred after the first conviction was set aside. Rather, it permits consideration of any objective information justifying the increased sentence. The trial testimony of the two new witnesses and the new information about McCullough's criminal history amply rebut any presumption of vindictiveness that might be present. Justice Brennan concurred in the judgment on the ground that the *Pearce* presumption should not apply here where it was the trial judge herself who granted the new trial. Justice Marshall, joined by Justices Blackmun and Stevens, dissented.

7. **Change from plea to trial following reversal.** Should it make a difference under North Carolina v. Pearce if the conviction that was set aside was based on a plea of guilty while the second conviction was based on a trial? In Alabama v. Smith, 490 U.S. 794, 109 S.Ct. 2201, 104 L.Ed.2d 865 (1989), respondent was charged with burglary, rape and sodomy. He plead guilty to burglary and rape and the State dismissed the sodomy charge. He was sentenced to 30 years' imprisonment on each offense to run concurrently. Later, he succeeded in vacating the pleas on the ground the trial court had improperly admonished him. The sodomy charge was reinstated and respondent went to trial on all three charges. He was convicted of all three and the same trial judge who presided at the first trial imposed concurrent life sentences on the burglary and sodomy convictions and a consecutive 150 year sentence on the rape conviction. The Supreme Court, in an opinion by The Chief Justice, held this sequence of events did not violate North Carolina v. Pearce. Information was presented during the trial of the case, not presented when the guilty pleas were accepted, that respondent repeatedly raped and sodomized the victim at knife point for over an hour in her own bedroom next to the bedroom where her three small children were sleeping. The Court concluded

> that when a greater penalty is imposed after trial than was imposed after a prior guilty plea, the increase in sentence is not more likely than not attributable to the vindictiveness on the part of the sentencing judge. Even when the same judge imposes both sentences, the relevant sentencing information available to the judge after the plea will usually be considerably less than that available after a trial. ...[I]n the course of the proof at trial the judge may gather a fuller appreciation of the nature and extent of the crimes charged. The defendant's conduct during trial may give the judge insights into his moral character and suitability for rehabilitation....Finally, after trial, the factors that may have indicated leniency as consideration for the guilty plea are no longer present.

490 U.S. at 801, 109 S.Ct. at 2205–06, 104 L.Ed.2d at 873–74. Justice Marshall dissented on the ground that any increase in punishment following re-conviction is a violation of double jeopardy guarantees. What implications, if any, does the majority's reasoning have on the appropriateness of post plea bargain sentences?

b.   APPELLATE REVIEW OF THE SENTENCES IMPOSED

Sentencing discretion might also be controlled or regulated by judicial review of the sentence ultimately imposed. The National Academy of Science commented that "in virtually all common law jurisdictions except the United States, appellate review of sentences has been the principal method used to develop principles for and achieve consistency in sentencing." National Academy of Science Panel on Sentencing Research, I Research on Sentencing: The Search for Reform 141 (1983). Over half of American jurisdictions permit appellate review of sentences that are within statutory limits. IV American Bar Association Standards for Criminal Justice 20.7 (1980). The standards for review, however, vary tremendously and are often quite limited. Some jurisdictions authorize modification by the appellate court of sentences simply found to be "excessive." But in others no relief is available on appeal unless the sentence is found "manifestly excessive," "clearly erroneous," or an "abuse of discretion." See Zalman, Appellate Review of Sentences and the Antinomy of Law Reform, 1983 Det.C.L.Rev. 1513, 1513–14.

As the principal case in this subsection indicates, appellate review can also be accomplished as a matter of federal constitutional law.

Can appellate review be realistically accomplished, given that the appellate courts do not have first hand opportunities to observe witnesses and the defendant himself? If appellate review is provided, what standard of review should be used? Are the criteria applied in the principal case appropriate?

Solem v. Helm

Supreme Court of the United States, 1983.
463 U.S. 277, 103 S.Ct. 3001, 77 L.Ed.2d 637.

■ JUSTICE POWELL delivered the opinion of the Court.

The issue presented is whether the Eighth Amendment proscribes a life sentence without possibility of parole for a seventh nonviolent felony.

I

By 1975 the State of South Dakota had convicted respondent Jerry Helm of six nonviolent felonies. In 1964, 1966, and 1969 Helm was convicted of third-degree burglary. In 1972 he was convicted of obtaining money under false pretenses. In 1973 he was convicted of grand larceny. And in 1975 he was convicted of third-offense driving while intoxicated. . . . [A]lcohol was a contributing factor in each case.

In 1979 Helm was charged with uttering a "no account" check for $100. . . . Helm pleaded guilty.

Ordinarily the maximum punishment for uttering a "no account" check would have been five years imprisonment in the state penitentiary and a $5,000 fine. . . . As a result of his criminal record, however, Helm was subject to South Dakota's recidivist statute:

"When a defendant has been convicted of at least three prior convictions [*sic*] in addition to the principal felony, the sentence for the principal felony shall be enhanced to the sentence for a Class 1 felony."

. . .

The maximum penalty for a "Class 1 felony" was life imprisonment in the state penitentiary and a $25,000 fine. . . . Moreover, South Dakota law explicitly provides that parole is unavailable: . . .

Immediately after accepting Helm's guilty plea, the South Dakota Circuit Court sentenced Helm to life imprisonment. . . . The court explained:

" 'I think you certainly earned this sentence and certainly proven that you're an habitual criminal and the record would indicate that you're beyond rehabilitation and that the only prudent thing to do is to lock you up for the rest of your natural life, so you won't have further victims of your crimes, just be coming back before Courts. You'll have plenty of time to think this one over.' " . . .

The South Dakota Supreme Court, in a 3–2 decision, affirmed the sentence despite Helm's argument that it violated the Eighth Amendment.

* * *

In November 1981, Helm sought habeas relief in the United States District Court for the District of South Dakota. Helm argued, among other things, that his sentence constituted cruel and unusual punishment under the Eighth and Fourteenth Amendments. Although the District Court recognized that the sentence was harsh, it concluded that this Court's recent decision in Rummel v. Estelle, 445 U.S. 263, 100 S.Ct. 1133, 63 L.Ed.2d 382 (1980), was dispositive. It therefore denied the writ.

The United States Court of Appeals for the Eighth Circuit reversed. 684 F.2d 582 (1982). The Court of Appeals noted that Rummel v. Estelle was distinguishable. Helm's sentence of life without parole was qualitatively different from Rummel's life sentence with the prospect of parole because South Dakota has rejected rehabilitation as a goal of the criminal justice system. The Court of Appeals examined the nature of Helm's offenses, the nature of his sentence, and the sentence he could have received in other States for the same offense. It concluded, on the basis of this examination, that Helm's sentence was "grossly disproportionate to the nature of the offense." 684 F.2d, at 587. It therefore directed the District Court to issue the writ unless the State resentenced Helm. Ibid.

We granted certiorari to consider the Eighth Amendment question presented by this case. 459 U.S. 986, 103 S.Ct. 339, 74 L.Ed.2d 381 (1982). We now affirm.

II

The Eighth Amendment declares: "Excessive bail shall not be required, nor excessive fines imposed, nor cruel and unusual punishments inflicted." The final clause prohibits not only barbaric punishments, but also sentences that are disproportionate to the crime committed.

A

The principle that a punishment should be proportionate to the crime is deeply rooted and frequently repeated in common-law jurisprudence. . . .

* * *

B

The constitutional principle of proportionality has been recognized explicitly in this Court for almost a century. In the leading case of Weems v. United States, 217 U.S. 349, 30 S.Ct. 544, 54 L.Ed. 793 (1910), the defendant had been convicted of falsifying a public document and sentenced to 15 years of "cadena temporal," a form of imprisonment that included hard labor in chains and permanent civil disabilities. . . . The Court endorsed the principle of proportionality as a constitutional standard, see, e.g., id., at 372–373, 30 S.Ct., at 551, and determined that the sentence before it was "cruel in its excess of imprisonment," id., at 377, 30 S.Ct., at 553, as well as in its shackles and restrictions.

The Court next applied the principle to invalidate a criminal sentence in Robinson v. California, 370 U.S. 660, 82 S.Ct. 1417, 8 L.Ed.2d 758 (1962). A 90–day sentence was found to be excessive for the crime of being " 'addicted to the use of narcotics.' . . . Even one day in prison would be a cruel and unusual punishment for the 'crime' of having a common cold." Ibid.

Most recently, the Court has applied the principle of proportionality to hold capital punishment excessive in certain circumstances. Enmund v. Florida, 458 U.S. 782, 102 S.Ct. 3368, 73 L.Ed.2d 1140 (1982) (death penalty excessive for felony murder when defendant did not take life, attempt to take life, or intend that a life be taken or that lethal force be used); Coker v. Georgia, 433 U.S. 584, 592, 97 S.Ct. 2861, 2866, 53 L.Ed.2d 982 (1977) (plurality opinion) ("sentence of death is grossly disproportionate and excessive punishment for the crime of rape"); id., at 601, 97 S.Ct., at 2870 (Powell, J., concurring in the judgment in part and dissenting in part) ("ordinarily death is disproportionate punishment for the crime of raping an adult woman"). . . .

C

* * *

. . . It is true that the "penalty of death differs from all other forms of criminal punishment, not in degree but in kind." Furman v. Georgia, 408 U.S. 238, 306, 92 S.Ct. 2726, 2760, 33 L.Ed.2d 346 (1972) (Stewart, J., concurring). As a result, "our decisions [in] capital cases are of limited assistance in deciding the constitutionality of the punishment" in a noncapital case. Rummel v. Estelle, 445 U.S., at 272, 100 S.Ct., at 1138. We agree, therefore, that, "[o]utside the context of capital punishment, *successful* challenges to the proportionality of particular sentences [will be] exceedingly rare," ibid. (emphasis added); see Hutto v. Davis, 454 U.S., at 374, 102 S.Ct., at 705. This does not mean, however, that proportionality analysis is entirely inapplicable in noncapital cases.

In sum, we hold as a matter of principle that a criminal sentence must be proportionate to the crime for which the defendant has been convicted. Reviewing courts, of course, should grant substantial deference to the broad authority that legislatures necessarily possess in determining the types and limits of punishments for crimes, as well as to the discretion that trial courts possess in sentencing convicted criminals. But no penalty is *per se* constitutional. As the Court noted in Robinson v. California, 370 U.S., at 667, 82 S.Ct., at 1420, a single day in prison may be unconstitutional in some circumstances.

III

A

When sentences are reviewed under the Eighth Amendment, courts should be guided by objective factors that our cases have recognized. First, we look to the gravity of the offense and the harshness of the penalty. . . .

Second, it may be helpful to compare the sentences imposed on other criminals in the same jurisdiction. If more serious crimes are subject to the same penalty, or to less serious penalties, that is some indication that the punishment at issue may be excessive. . . .

Third, courts may find it useful to compare the sentences imposed for commission of the same crime in other jurisdictions. . . .

* * *

B

Application of these factors assumes that courts are competent to judge the gravity of an offense, at least on a relative scale. . . . Comparisons can be made in light of the harm caused or threatened to the victim or society, and the culpability of the offender. . . . For example, as the criminal laws make clear, nonviolent crimes are less serious than crimes marked by violence or the threat of violence. . . .

There are other accepted principles that courts may apply in measuring the harm caused or threatened to the victim or society. The absolute magnitude of the crime may be relevant. Stealing a million dollars is viewed as more serious than stealing a hundred dollars—a point recognized in statutes distinguishing petty theft from grand theft. . . . Few would dispute that a lesser included offense should not be punished more severely than the greater offense. . . . It also is generally recognized that attempts are less serious than completed crimes. . . . Similarly, an accessory after the fact should not be subject to a higher penalty than the principal.

Turning to the culpability of the offender, there are again clear distinctions that courts may recognize and apply. In *Enmund* the Court looked at the petitioner's lack of intent to kill in determining that he was less culpable than his accomplices. Most would agree that negligent conduct is less serious than intentional conduct. . . . A court, of course, is entitled to look at a defendant's motive in committing a crime. Thus a murder may be viewed as more serious when committed pursuant to a contract. . . .

This list is by no means exhaustive. It simply illustrates that there are generally accepted criteria for comparing the severity of different crimes on a broad scale, despite the difficulties courts face in attempting to draw distinctions between similar crimes.

C

Application of the factors that we identify also assumes that courts are able to compare different sentences. This assumption, too, is justified. The easiest comparison, of course, is between capital punishment and noncapital punishments, for the death penalty is different from other punishments in kind rather than degree. For sentences of imprisonment, the problem is not so much one of ordering, but one of line-drawing. It is clear that a 25–year sentence generally is more severe than a 15–year sentence, but in most cases it would be difficult to decide that the former violates the Eighth Amendment while the latter does not. Decisions of this kind, although troubling, are not unique to this area. . . .

* * *

IV

It remains to apply the analytical framework established by our prior decisions to the case before us. We first consider the relevant criteria, viewing Helm's sentence as life imprisonment without possibility of parole. We then consider the State's argument that the possibility of commutation is sufficient to save an otherwise unconstitutional sentence.

A

Helm's crime was "one of the most passive felonies a person could commit." State v. Helm, 287 N.W.2d, at 501 (Henderson, J., dissenting). It involved neither violence nor threat of violence to any person. The $100 face value of Helm's "no account" check was not trivial, but neither was it a large amount. One hundred dollars was less than half the amount South Dakota required for a felonious theft. It is easy to see why such a crime is viewed by society as among the less serious offenses. . . .

Helm, of course, was not charged simply with uttering a "no account" check, but also with being an habitual offender.[1] And a State is justified in punishing a recidivist more severely than it punishes a first offender. Helm's status, however, cannot be considered in the abstract. His prior offenses, although classified as felonies, were all relatively minor. All were nonviolent and none was a crime against a person. Indeed, there was no minimum amount in either the burglary or the false pretenses statutes, and the minimum amount covered by the grand larceny statute was fairly small.

Helm's present sentence is life imprisonment without possibility of parole. Barring executive clemency, . . ., Helm will spend the rest of his life in the state penitentiary. This sentence is far more severe than the life sentence we considered in Rummel v. Estelle. Rummel was likely to have been eligible for parole within 12 years of his initial confinement, a fact on which the Court relied heavily. . . .Helm's sentence is the most severe punishment that the State could have imposed on any criminal for any crime. Only capital punishment, a penalty not authorized in South Dakota when Helm was sentenced, exceeds it.

* * *

In sum, there were a handful of crimes that were necessarily punished by life imprisonment: murder, and, on a second or third offense, treason, first degree manslaughter, first degree arson, and kidnapping. There was a larger group for which life imprisonment was authorized in the discretion of the sentencing judge, including: treason, first degree manslaughter, first degree arson, and kidnapping; attempted murder, placing an explosive device on an aircraft, and first degree rape on a second or third offense; and any felony after three prior offenses. Finally, there was a large group of

---

1. Helm, who was 36 years old when he was sentenced, is not a professional criminal. The record indicates an addiction to alcohol, and a consequent difficulty in holding a job. His record involves no instance of violence of any kind. Incarcerating him for life without possibility of parole is unlikely to advance the goals of our criminal justice system in any substantial way. Neither Helm nor the State will have an incentive to pursue clearly needed treatment for his alcohol problem, or any other program of rehabilitation.

very serious offenses for which life imprisonment was not authorized, including a third offense of heroin dealing or aggravated assault.

Criminals committing any of these offenses ordinarily would be thought more deserving of punishment than one uttering a "no account" check—even when the bad-check writer had already committed six minor felonies. Moreover, there is no indication in the record that any habitual offender other than Helm has ever been given the maximum sentence on the basis of comparable crimes. It is more likely that the possibility of life imprisonment under § 22-7-8 generally is reserved for criminals such as fourth-time heroin dealers, while habitual bad-check writers receive more lenient treatment.[2] In any event, Helm has been treated in the same manner as, or more severely than, criminals who have committed far more serious crimes.

Finally, we compare the sentences imposed for commission of the same crime in other jurisdictions. . . . it is clear that Helm could not have received such a severe sentence in 48 of the 50 States. . . . even under Nevada law, a life sentence without possibility of parole is merely authorized in these circumstances. See Nev.Rev.Stat. § 207.010(2) (1981). We are not advised that any defendant such as Helm, whose prior offenses were so minor, actually has received the maximum penalty in Nevada. It appears that Helm was treated more severely than he would have been in any other State.

B

The State argues that the present case is essentially the same as Rummel v. Estelle, for the possibility of parole in that case is matched by the possibility of executive clemency here. The State reasons that the Governor could commute Helm's sentence to a term of years. We conclude, however, that the South Dakota commutation system is fundamentally different from the parole system that was before us in *Rummel*.

As a matter of law, parole and commutation are different concepts, despite some surface similarities. Parole is a regular part of the rehabilitative process. Assuming good behavior, it is the normal expectation in the vast majority of cases. The law generally specifies when a prisoner will be eligible to be considered for parole, and details the standards and procedures applicable at that time. . . . Thus it is possible to predict, at least to some extent, when parole might be granted. Commutation, on the other hand, is an *ad hoc* exercise of executive clemency. A Governor may commute a sentence at any time for any reason without reference to any standards.

* * *

2. The State contends that § 22-7-8 is more lenient than the Texas habitual offender statute in *Rummel*, for life imprisonment under § 22-7-8 is discretionary rather than mandatory. Brief for Petitioner 22. Helm, however, has challenged only his own sentence. No one suggests that § 22-7-8 may not be applied constitutionally to fourth-time heroin dealers or other violent criminals. Thus we do not question the legislature's judgment. Unlike in *Rummel*, a lesser sentence here could have been entirely consistent with both the statute and the Eighth Amendment. See Note, Disproportionality in Sentences of Imprisonment, 79 Colum.L.Rev. 1119, 1160 (1979).

The Texas and South Dakota systems in particular are very different. In *Rummel,* the Court did not rely simply on the existence of some system of parole. Rather it looked to the provisions of the system presented, ...Thus Rummel ...could have expected to become eligible, in the normal course of events, in only 12 years.

In South Dakota commutation is more difficult to obtain than parole. ...In fact, no life sentence has been commuted in over eight years, ...while parole—where authorized—has been granted regularly during that period,... .Furthermore, even if Helm's sentence were commuted, he merely would be eligible to be considered for parole. Not only is there no guarantee that he would be paroled, but the South Dakota parole system is far more stringent than the one before us in *Rummel.* ...[3]

The possibility of commutation is nothing more than a hope for "an *ad hoc* exercise of clemency." It is little different from the possibility of executive clemency that exists in every case in which a defendant challenges his sentence under the Eighth Amendment. Recognition of such a bare possibility would make judicial review under the Eighth Amendment meaningless.

V

The Constitution requires us to examine Helm's sentence to determine if it is proportionate to his crime. Applying objective criteria, we find that Helm has received the penultimate sentence for relatively minor criminal conduct. He has been treated more harshly than other criminals in the State who have committed more serious crimes. He has been treated more harshly than he would have been in any other jurisdiction, with the possible exception of a single State. We conclude that his sentence is significantly disproportionate to his crime, and is therefore prohibited by the Eighth Amendment. The judgment of the Court of Appeals is accordingly

Affirmed.

■ CHIEF JUSTICE BURGER, with whom JUSTICE WHITE, JUSTICE REHNQUIST, and JUSTICE O'CONNOR join, dissenting.

The controlling law governing this case is crystal clear, but today the Court blithely discards any concept of *stare decisis,* trespasses gravely on the authority of the States, and distorts the concept of proportionality of punishment by tearing it from its moorings in capital cases. Only two Terms ago, we held in Rummel v. Estelle, 445 U.S. 263, 100 S.Ct. 1133, 63 L.Ed.2d 382 (1980), that a life sentence imposed after only a *third* nonviolent felony conviction did not constitute cruel and unusual punishment under the Eighth Amendment. Today, the Court ignores its recent precedent and holds that a life sentence imposed after a *seventh* felony convic-

---

3. Assume, for example, that in 1979 the Governor had commuted Helm's sentence to a term of 40 years (his approximate life expectancy). Even if Helm were a model prisoner, he would not have been eligible for parole until he had served over 21 years— more than twice the *Rummel* minimum. And this comparison is generous to South Dakota's position. If Rummel had been sentenced to 40 years rather than life, he could have been eligible for parole in less than 7 years.

tion constitutes cruel and unusual punishment under the Eighth Amendment. Moreover, I reject the fiction that all Helm's crimes were innocuous or nonviolent. Among his felonies were three burglaries and a third conviction for drunk driving. By comparison Rummel was a relatively "model citizen." Although today's holding cannot rationally be reconciled with *Rummel*, the Court does not purport to overrule *Rummel*. I therefore dissent.

I

A

...What the Court means is that a sentence is unconstitutional if it is more severe than five justices think appropriate. In short, all sentences of imprisonment are subject to appellate scrutiny....

* * *

...This analysis is completely at odds with the reasoning of our recent holding in *Rummel,* in which, of course, Justice Powell dissented.

B

The facts in *Rummel* bear repeating. Rummel was convicted in 1964 of fraudulent use of a credit card; in 1969, he was convicted of passing a forged check; finally, in 1973 Rummel was charged with obtaining money by false pretenses, which is also a felony under Texas law. These three offenses were indeed nonviolent. Under Texas' recidivist statute, which provides for a mandatory life sentence upon conviction for a third felony, the trial judge imposed a life sentence as he was obliged to do after the jury returned a verdict of guilty of felony theft.

Rummel, in this Court, advanced precisely the same arguments that respondent advances here; we rejected those arguments notwithstanding that his case was stronger than respondent's. The test in *Rummel* which we rejected would have required us to determine on an abstract moral scale whether Rummel had received his "just desserts" for his crimes. We declined that invitation; today the Court accepts it. Will the Court now recall Rummel's case so five justices will not be parties to "disproportionate" criminal justice?

...[E]ven a cursory review of our cases shows that this type of proportionality review has been carried out only in a very limited category of cases, and never before in a case involving solely a sentence of imprisonment. ...

* * *

...In language quoted incompletely by the Court, ante, at 3009, n. 14, the *Rummel* Court stated:

> "Given the *unique nature* of the punishments considered in *Weems* and in the death penalty cases, one could argue without fear of contradiction by any decision of this Court that for crimes concededly classified and classifiable as felonies, that is, as punishable by significant terms of imprisonment in a state penitentiary, the *length of the*

sentence actually imposed is purely a matter of legislative prerogative."
445 U.S., at 274, 100 S.Ct., at 1139. (Emphasis added.)

Five Justices joined this clear and precise limiting language.

. . . [T]he *Rummel* Court emphasized that drawing lines between different sentences of imprisonment would thrust the Court inevitably "into the basic line-drawing process that is pre-eminently the province of the legislature" and produce judgments that were no more than the visceral reactions of individual Justices. Ibid.

The *Rummel* Court categorically rejected the very analysis adopted by the Court today. . . .

First, it rejected the distinctions Rummel tried to draw between violent and nonviolent offenses, noting that "the absence of violence does not always affect the strength of society's interest in deterring a particular crime or in punishing a particular individual." Ibid. Similarly, distinctions based on the amount of money stolen are purely "subjective" matters of line drawing. Id., at 275–276, 100 S.Ct., at 1140.

Second, the Court squarely rejected Rummel's attempt to compare his sentence with the sentence he would have received in other States—an argument that the Court today accepts. The *Rummel* Court explained that such comparisons are flawed for several reasons. . . . Perhaps most important, such comparisons trample on fundamental concepts of federalism. Different states surely may view particular crimes as more or less severe than other states. Stealing a horse in Texas may have different consequences and warrant different punishment than stealing a horse in Rhode Island or Washington, D.C. . . .

Finally, we flatly rejected Rummel's suggestion that we measure his sentence against the sentences imposed by Texas for other crimes: . . .

Rather, we held that the severity of punishment to be accorded different crimes was peculiarly a matter of legislative policy. Ibid.

In short, *Rummel* held that the length of a sentence of imprisonment is a matter of legislative discretion; this is so particularly for recidivist statutes. I simply cannot understand how the Court can square *Rummel* with its holding that "a criminal sentence must be proportionate to the crime for which the defendant has been convicted."[4]

If there were any doubts as to the meaning of *Rummel,* they were laid to rest last Term in Hutto v. Davis, 454 U.S. 370, 102 S.Ct. 703, 70 L.Ed.2d 556 (1982) *(per curiam).* There a United States District Court held that a 40–year sentence for the possession of nine ounces of marijuana violated the Eighth Amendment. The District Court applied almost exactly the same analysis adopted today by the Court. . . .

. . . We reversed in a brief *per curiam* opinion, holding that *Rummel* had disapproved each of the "objective" factors on which the District Court

4. Although Rummel v. Estelle, 445 U.S. 263, 274, n. 11, 100 S.Ct. 1133, 1139, n. 11, 63 L.Ed.2d 382 (1980), conceded that "a proportionality principle [might] come into play . . . if a legislature made overtime parking a felony punishable by life imprisonment," the majority has not suggested that respondent's crimes are comparable to overtime parking. Respondent's seven felonies are far more severe than Rummel's three.

and *en banc* Court of Appeals purported to rely. 454 U.S., at 373, 102 S.Ct., at 704. It was therefore clear error for the District Court to have been guided by these factors, which, paradoxically, the Court adopts today.

...*Hutto* makes crystal clear that under *Rummel* it is error for appellate courts to second-guess legislatures as to whether a given sentence of imprisonment is excessive in relation to the crime, as the Court does today.

...While the doctrine of *stare decisis* does not absolutely bind the Court to its prior opinions, a decent regard for the orderly development of the law and the administration of justice requires that directly controlling cases be either followed or candidly overruled.[5] Especially is this so with respect to two key holdings only three years old.

II

Although historians and scholars have disagreed about the Framers' original intentions, the more common view seems to be that the Framers viewed the Cruel and Unusual Punishments Clause as prohibiting the kind of torture meted out during the reign of the Stuarts. Moreover, it is clear that until 1892, over 100 years after the ratification of the Bill of Rights, not a single Justice of this Court even asserted the doctrine adopted for the first time by the Court today. The prevailing view up to now has been that the Eighth Amendment reaches only the *mode* of punishment and not the length of a sentence of imprisonment. In light of this history, it is disingenuous for the Court blandly to assert that "[t]he constitutional principle of proportionality has been recognized explicitly in this Court for almost a century." That statement seriously distorts history and our cases.

* * *

By asserting the power to review sentences of imprisonment for excessiveness the Court launches into uncharted and unchartable waters. Today it holds that a sentence of life imprisonment, without the possibility of parole, is excessive punishment for a seventh allegedly "nonviolent" felony. How about the eighth "nonviolent" felony? The ninth? The twelfth? Suppose one offense was a simple assault? Or selling liquor to a minor? Or

---

5. I do not read the Court's opinion as arguing that respondent's sentence of life imprisonment without possibility of parole is so different from Rummel's sentence of life imprisonment with the possibility of parole as to permit it to apply the proportionality review used in the death penalty cases, e.g., Coker v. Georgia, 433 U.S. 584, 97 S.Ct. 2861, 53 L.Ed.2d 982 (1977), to the former although not the latter. Nor would such an argument be tenable. As was noted in Woodson v. North Carolina, 428 U.S. 280, 305, 96 S.Ct. 2978, 2991, 49 L.Ed.2d 944 (1976) (opinion of Justice Stewart, Justice Powell, and Justice Stevens),

"[T]he penalty of death is qualitatively different from a sentence of imprisonment. Death, in its finality, differs more from life imprisonment than a 100–year prison term differs from one of only a year or two. Because of that qualitative difference, there is a corresponding difference in the need for reliability in the determination that death is the appropriate punishment in a specific case."

The greater need for reliability in death penalty cases cannot support a distinction between a sentence of life imprisonment with possibility of parole and a sentence of life imprisonment without possibility of parole, especially when an executive commutation is permitted as in South Dakota.

statutory rape? Or price-fixing? The permutations are endless and the Court's opinion is bankrupt of realistic guiding principles. Instead, it casually lists several allegedly "objective" factors and arbitrarily asserts that they show respondent's sentence to be "significantly disproportionate" to his crimes. Must all these factors be present in order to hold a sentence excessive under the Eighth Amendment? How are they to be weighed against each other? Suppose several States punish severely a crime that the Court views as trivial or petty? I can see no limiting principle in the Court's holding.

There is a real risk that this holding will flood the appellate courts with cases in which equally arbitrary lines must be drawn. It is no answer to say that appellate courts must review criminal convictions in any event; up to now, that review has been on the validity of the judgment, not the sentence. The vast majority of criminal cases are disposed of by pleas of guilty, and ordinarily there is no appellate review in such cases. To require appellate review of all sentences of imprisonment—as the Court's opinion necessarily does—will "administer the *coupe de grace* to the courts of appeal as we know them." H. Friendly, Federal Jurisdiction: A General View 36 (1973). This is judicial usurpation with a vengeance; Congress has pondered for decades the concept of appellate review of sentences and has hesitated to act.

* * *

NOTES

1. **Cruel and unusual punishment for drug possession.** The Supreme Court re-visited the Solem v. Helm issue in Harmelin v. Michigan, 501 U.S. 957, 111 S.Ct. 2680, 115 L.Ed.2d 836 (1991). Petitioner was convicted of possessing 672 grams of cocaine and sentenced to a mandatory term of life imprisonment without possibility of parole. He contended the sentence violated Eighth Amendment because it was disproportionate to the crime and because it was mandatory. The Supreme Court upheld petitioner's sentence and in doing so delivered five different opinions. Justice Scalia announced the judgment of the Court and delivered an opinion. In Part V of that opinion, joined by Chief Justice Rehnquist and Justices O'Connor, Kennedy and Souter, the Court rejects the argument that the sentence in this case was cruel and unusual because it was mandatory and, therefore, precluded the sentencer from taking mitigating circumstances into account. "Severe, mandatory penalties may be cruel, but they are not unusual in the constitutional sense, having been employed in various forms throughout our Nation's history." It is true that a requirement of individualization of sentence has been imposed in death penalty cases but there is a "qualitative difference between death and all other penalties."

> It is true that petitioner's sentence is unique in that it is the second most severe known to the law; but life imprisonment *with* possibility of parole is also unique in that it is the third most severe. And if petitioner's sentence forecloses some "flexible techniques" for later reducing his sentence, * * * it does not foreclose all of them, since there remain the possibilities of retroactive legislative reduction and executive clemency. In some cases, moreover, there will be negligible difference between life without parole and other sentences of imprisonment—for example, a life sentence with eligibility for parole after 20 years, or even a lengthy term sentence without eligibility, given to a 65-year-old man.

But even where the difference is the greatest, it cannot be compared with death.

501 U.S. at 996, 111 S.Ct. at 2702, 115 L.Ed.2d at 865. Justice Scalia, writing for himself and Chief Justice Rehnquist, contended that the Eighth Amendment does not prescribe a constitutional requirement of proportionality of penalty to offense and argued that *Solem* should be overruled. Justice Kennedy, joined by Justices O'Connor and Souter, rejected Justice Scalia's view of the Eighth Amendment and contended that "*stare decisis* counsels our adherence to the narrow proportionality principle that has existed in our Eighth Amendment jurisprudence for 80 years." He then compared the seriousness of petitioner's offense with that of Solem. The cocaine possessed in this case would produce between 32,500 and 65,000 doses. Petitioner's "crime threatened to cause grave harm to society:"

> Studies * * * demonstrate a direct nexus between illegal drugs and crimes of violence * * *. 57 percent of a national sample of males arrested in 1989 for homicide tested positive for illegal drugs * * *. The comparable statistics for assault, robbery, and weapons arrests were 55, 73 and 63 percent, respectively * * *. In Detroit, Michigan in 1988, 68 percent of a sample of male arrestees and 81 percent of a sample of female arrestees tested positive for illegal drugs * * *. And last year an estimated 60 percent of the homicides in Detroit were drug-related, primarily cocaine-related.

501 U.S. at 1003, 111 S.Ct. at 2706, 115 L.Ed.2d at 870. Since petitioner's punishment is not disproportionate to his offense, there is no need to perform an analysis comparing his sentence to those imposed on others. As to the mandatory feature of the Michigan sentencing scheme,

> The scheme provides clear notice of the severe consequences that attach to possession of drugs in wholesale amounts, thereby giving force to one of the first purposes of criminal law—deterrence. In this sense, the Michigan scheme may be as fair, if not more so, than other sentencing systems in which the sentencer's discretion or the complexity of the scheme obscures the possible sanction for a crime, resulting in a shock to the offender who learns the severity of his sentence only after he commits the crime.

501 U.S. at 1008, 111 S.Ct. at 2708, 115 L.Ed.2d at 873.

Justice White, joined by Justices Blackmun and Stevens, dissented, emphasizing the fact that this was petitioner's first criminal conviction. Examining the case in light of the factors in *Solem*, he would have found the sentence to violate the Eighth Amendment. Justice Marshall agreed with Justice White's opinion, except that portion asserting that the Eighth Amendment does not proscribe the death penalty. Justice Stevens, joined by Justice Blackmun, also agreed with Justice White's opinion but added that life without parole cannot purport to serve a rehabilitative purpose and that "no jurisdiction except Michigan has concluded that the offense belongs in a category where reform and rehabilitation are considered totally unattainable."

2. **Capital cases.** The argument that federal constitutional considerations require "proportionality review" of a somewhat different sort in death penalty cases was rejected in Pulley v. Harris, 465 U.S. 37, 104 S.Ct. 871, 79 L.Ed.2d 29 (1984). Because under then-prevailing capital sentencing schemes the death penalty was being imposed discriminatorily, wantonly and freakishly, and infrequently, the Court in Furman v. Georgia, 408 U.S. 238, 92 S.Ct. 2726, 33 L.Ed.2d 346 (1972), held that any given death sentence was cruel and unusual within the meaning of the Eighth Amendment. In 1976, however, the Court upheld death penalties imposed under several procedures developed after *Furman*. Gregg v. Georgia, 428 U.S. 153, 96 S.Ct. 2909, 49 L.Ed.2d 859 (1976); Proffitt v. Florida, 428 U.S. 242, 96

S.Ct. 2960, 49 L.Ed.2d 913 (1976); Jurek v. Texas, 428 U.S. 262, 96 S.Ct. 2950, 49 L.Ed.2d 929 (1976). In *Harris*, the argument was made that a capital sentencing scheme sufficiently assures against arbitrary application of the death penalty to meet *Furman's* Eighth Amendment standards only if the scheme requires that an appellate court consider whether the death penalty is unacceptable in each case because it is disproportionate to the punishment imposed upon others convicted of the same or similar offenses.

But the Court found "no basis in our cases for holding that comparative proportionality review by an appellate court is required in every case in which the death penalty is imposed and the defendant requests it." 465 U.S. at 50–51, 104 S.Ct. at 879, 79 L.Ed.2d at 40. Assuming that some capital sentencing schemes might be so lacking in checks on arbitrariness that comparative proportionality review would be necessary to meet constitutional requirements, the majority concluded that the California sentencing scheme was not of that sort. Whether or not to impose the death penalty is addressed only if the defendant is convicted of first degree murder and the jury finds that the state has proven at least one "special circumstance." At a penalty hearing, additional evidence is taken and the jury is given a list of factors relevant to the sentencing decision. The jury is to determine whether life imprisonment or death is to be imposed. If death is imposed, the trial judge reviews the matter and makes an independent determination as to whether the "weight of the evidence" supports the jury's determination. Reasons for the judge's conclusions are to be placed in the record. Appeal is automatic and the appellate court must consider whether the evidence relied upon by the trial judge is sufficient. Despite the absence of a requirement that the appellate tribunal engage in proportionality review, the Court concluded, the California procedure—on its face—cannot be said to contain constitutionally insufficient protection against the defects found in *Furman*. 465 U.S. at 53, 104 S.Ct. at 881, 79 L.Ed.2d at 42.

3. **Effectiveness of appellate review of sentences.** Generally speaking, the evaluations of appellate review of sentences have not been overwhelmingly favorable. A major concern has been that appellate tribunals are so reluctant to override sentencing judges' discretionary decisions that review is seldom meaningful. One commentator who reviewed thirty years of appellate review of sentences in Arizona concluded:

> Despite the incorporation into the formal legal framework of an authorization for appellate supervision of the sentencing process, the participants in the process (the appellate judges as well as the trial bench and bar) rejected the underlying assumptions of the proposal: (a) that scientific sentencing was possible; (b) that a body of relatively precise rules for the conduct of judicial sentencing could be developed; and (c) that the appellate judiciary was the appropriate agency to supervise reform of the sentencing process. Given the failure of the participants to accept the underlying assumptions, the attempt to achieve reform by revision of the legal framework was destined to fail from the beginning.

Dix, Judicial Review of Sentences: Implications for Individual Disposition, 1969 Law and the Social Order 369, 405. See also, Zeisel and Diamond, Search for Sentencing Equality: Sentence Review in Massachusetts and Connecticut, 4 Am.Bar Foundation Research J. 881 (1977).

3. REDUCING DISCRETION BY "DETERMINATE" SENTENCING

Another response to what might be perceived as the serious problems posed by discretion under traditional "indeterminate" sentencing schemes is, of course, to alter the basic structure of the sentencing process. Many jurisdictions have undertaken to do this. Among them is 1984 legislation dramatically altering the sentencing and correctional process in the federal criminal justice system.

a.   STATE REFORMS

Hussey and Lagoy, The Impact of Determinate Sentencing Structures

17 Criminal Law Bulletin 197–203 (1981).*

The intensity of recent intellectual and legislative activity relative to the sentencing of criminal offenders suggests that a broad and fundamental change in sentencing policy—and perhaps even in underlying ideologies of criminal justice—is taking place. Frustrated by the criminal justice system's inability to rehabilitate criminals, sentencing reformers of many types, including radical criminologists, more traditional academicians, blue-ribbon commissions, and the federal judiciary, have endorsed proposals for broad-brush changes in criminal sentencing which focus on the crime committed rather than the rehabilitative needs of the criminal. . . .

Since the turn of the century, most jurisdictions at each level of government have embraced the rehabilitative ideal, a criminological theory which perceives crime as a pathology and has as its objective the effecting of a cure in the afflicted offender. The rehabilitative ideal was expressed in the use of indeterminate sentencing systems and parole. Indeterminate sentences are perhaps best described as a . . . process involving discretionary legislative, judicial, and administrative decisions. Characteristically, the legislature established broad ranges of prison time for each offense or class of offense within which convicted criminals could be sentenced. The potential ranges increased according to the severity of the particular offense. The actual determination of sentence within these ranges was the province of the judge who was required to select both a minimum term, which had to be served, and a maximum term. The portion of the term to be served in excess of the minimum term, and which could extend until the maximum was served, was left to the parole board or other administrative body which made its decision ostensibly based on the perceived rehabilitation of the offender.

Now, in several states the indeterminate sentence, with its wide ranges of minimum and maximum sentences, has been replaced by sentences which, theoretically at least, are much more specific in nature. As testimony to the extent of this shift, it was recently reported that seven states had altered radically their sentencing systems "resulting in more predictable and definite lengths of prison terms." There is little doubt that legislative bodies which have altered their sentencing structures have done so with the objectives of limiting discretion in sentencing both at the judicial and administrative level, decreasing disparity of sentences among similar offenders who have committed similar offenses, and increasing the overall definiteness or determinacy of prison terms.

* * *

The first criminal code that appeared to bring greater determinacy to sentencing was enacted in Maine in 1976. The passage of Maine's new code brought to fruition sentencing reform efforts begun in the 1960s, before most literature on determinate sentencing appeared. Maine's sentencing code resulted in two notable features. First, sentences to incarceration were for a specific number of years and, essentially, could be reduced only through the operation of good time. Second, Maine abolished not only the parole board but also post-sentence supervision for offenders sentenced under the new code. It did not follow the prescription for presumptive sentences . . .; nor was there any formal mechanism for the consideration of aggravating and mitigating factors. Furthermore, the code provided for only maximum sentences for the five classes of crime; no minimums were specified. . . .

The second state to implement reform was California, and it chose to adopt a presumptive sentencing system. Under that approach, felony offenses, except for murder, were placed into one of four classes of crime and for each class three terms were specified: a presumptive term which was to be imposed absent aggravating or mitigating circumstances, a lower term which could be selected if mitigating factors predominated, and an upper term which could be imposed in cases in which aggravating factors were predominant. Offenders are released at the expiration of their term, less good time earned which may range up to four months per year or a 33 percent reduction. Once released, offenders serve a three-year "parole" period. Inasmuch as the power to release from prison does not lie with a parole board and the three-year parole period does not fall within a maximum term, the parole period might more legitimately be seen as a post-incarceration "add-on." However, the California code still labels this as a parole period.

Indiana followed California in implementing what has been called a hybrid approach to determinate sentencing. Indiana adopted the mechanics of presumptive sentencing but also specified very wide ranges for sentences in mitigation and aggravation. For example, in California the sentencing range for rape is three to eight years,[a] while in Indiana it is six to fifty years. These potentially long sentences can be greatly modified by the provision of good time which ranges between zero good time and day-for-day good time, amounting to a 50 percent reduction in sentence. An offender is released on parole at the completion of the determinate term (reduced by good time) and undergoes parole supervision for the remainder of the term. The offender, however, must be discharged after one year if parole has not been revoked.

Illinois was the last of the "pioneer" states to adopt determinate sentencing. Illinois does not specify presumptive sentences but does define

a. In order to reduce disparity, under California's Determinate Sentence Law *as originally enacted*, all sentence ranges were 2 years. For example, rape was 3, 4, or 5 years before any enhancements.

a range for various crime classes within which a determinate sentence must be selected. Offenders are released at the expiration of sentence and must serve one, two, or three years on parole. The length of the parole period is related to the class of crime committed. As in each of the other determinate sentencing states, good time may reduce a term of incarceration up to 50 percent (day-for-day good time).

NOTES

1. **Formal sentencing criteria.** California's Determinate Sentence law required, for the first time, "rules providing criteria for the consideration of the trial judge at the time of sentencing." Cal.Pen.Code § 1170.3. Criteria for selecting one of three base prison terms possible for most California crimes are set out here. Among the other rules promulgated are those for enhancing base terms and imposing consecutive terms. Factors to be considered for the crucial probation decision are set out in that section, infra.

CALIFORNIA JUDICIAL COUNCIL, SENTENCING RULES FOR THE SUPERIOR COURTS (1990)

Rule 421. Circumstances in Aggravation [Upper Term]

Circumstances in aggravation include:

(a) Facts relating to the crime, including the fact that:

(1) The crime involved great violence, great bodily harm, threat of great bodily harm, or other acts disclosing a high degree of cruelty, viciousness or callousness, whether or not charged or chargeable as an enhancement under section 12022.7.

(2) The defendant was armed with or used a weapon at the time of the commission of the crime, whether or not charged or chargeable as an enhancement under section 12022 or 12022.5.

(3) The victim was particularly vulnerable.

(4) The crime involved multiple victims.

(5) The defendant induced others to participate in the commission of the crime or occupied a position of leadership or dominance of other participants in its commission.

(6) The defendant threatened witnesses, unlawfully prevented or dissuaded witnesses from testifying, suborned perjury, or in any other way illegally interfered with the judicial process.

(7) The defendant was convicted of other crimes for which consecutive sentences could have been imposed but for which concurrent sentences are being imposed.

(8) The planning, sophistication or professionalism with which the crime was carried out, or other facts, indicate premeditation.

(9) The defendant used or involved minors in the commission of the crime.

(10) The crime involved an attempted or actual taking or damage of great monetary value, whether or not charged or chargeable as an enhancement under section 12022.6.

(11) The crime involved a large quantity of contraband.

(12) The defendant took advantage of a position of trust or confidence to commit the offense.

(b) Facts relating to the defendant, including the fact that:

(1) He has engaged in a pattern of violent conduct which indicates a serious danger to society.

(2) The defendant's prior convictions as an adult or adjudications of commission of crimes as a juvenile are numerous or of increasing seriousness.

(3) The defendant has served prior prison terms whether or not charged or chargeable as an enhancement under section 667.5.

(4) The defendant was on probation or parole when he committed the crime.

(5) The defendant's prior performance on probation or parole was unsatisfactory.

Rule 423. Circumstances in Mitigation [Lower Term]

Circumstances in mitigation include:

(a) Facts relating to the crime, including the fact that:

(1) The defendant was a passive participant or played a minor role in the crime.

(2) The victim was an initiator, willing participant, aggressor or provoker of the incident.

(3) The crime was committed because of an unusual circumstance, such as great provocation, which is unlikely to recur.

(4) The defendant participated in the crime under circumstances of coercion or duress, or his conduct was partially excusable for some other reason not amounting to a defense.

(5) A defendant with no apparent predisposition to do so was induced by others to participate in the crime.

(6) The defendant exercised caution to avoid harm to persons or damage to property, or the amounts of money or property taken were deliberately small, or no harm was done or threatened against the victim.

(7) The defendant believed he had a claim or right to the property taken, or for other reasons mistakenly believed his conduct was legal.

(8) The defendant was motivated by a desire to provide necessities for his family or himself.

(b) Facts relating to the defendant, including the fact that:

(1) He has no prior record or an insignificant record of criminal conduct considering the recency and frequency of prior crimes.

(2) The defendant was suffering from a mental or physical condition that significantly reduced his culpability for the crime.

(3) The defendant voluntarily acknowledged wrongdoing prior to arrest or at an early stage of the criminal process.

(4) The defendant is ineligible for probation and but for that ineligibility would have been granted probation.

(5) The defendant made restitution to the victim.

(6) The defendant's prior performance on probation or parole was good.

2. **Abolishing parole.** Also consider the following approach to sentencing disparity embodied in Section 1170 of the West's Ann. California Penal Code:

(a)(1) The Legislature finds and declares that the purpose of imprisonment for crime is punishment. This purpose is best served by terms proportionate to the seriousness of the offense with provision for uniformity in the sentences of offenders committing the same offense under similar circumstances. The Legislature further finds and declares that the elimination of disparity and the provision of uniformity of sentences can best be achieved by determinate sentences fixed by statute in proportion to the seriousness of the offense as determined by the Legislature to be imposed by the court with specified discretion.

* * *

(d) When a defendant ... has been sentenced to be imprisoned in the state prison and has been committed to the custody of the Director of Corrections, the court may, within 120 days of the date of commitment on its own motion, or at any time upon the recommendation of the Director of Corrections or the Board of Prison Terms, recall the sentence and commitment previously ordered and resentence the defendant in the same manner as if he had not previously been sentenced, provided the new sentence, if any, is no greater than the initial sentence. The resentence under this subdivision shall apply the sentencing rules of the Judicial Council so as to eliminate disparity of sentences and to promote uniformity of sentencing. Credit shall be given for time served.

* * *

(f)(1) Within one year after the commencement of the term of imprisonment, the Board of Prison Terms shall review the sentence to determine whether the sentence is disparate in comparison with the sentences to be imposed in similar cases. If the Board of Prison Terms determines that the sentence is disparate, the board shall notify the judge, the district attorney, the defense attorney, the defendant, and the Judicial Council. The notification shall include a statement of the reasons for finding the sentence disparate.

Within 120 days of receipt of this information, the sentencing court shall schedule a hearing and may recall the sentence and commitment previously ordered and resentence the defendant in the same manner as if the defendant had not been sentenced previously, provided the new sentence is no greater than the initial sentence. In resentencing under this subdivision the court shall apply the sentencing rules of the Judicial Council and shall consider the information provided by the Board of Prison Terms.

3. **Sentencing grids.** Many jurisdictions adopted systems involving sentencing commissions. Minnesota, for example, created a sentencing commission and directed it to develop guidelines. Minn.Stat.Ann. § 244.09. Its guideline development resulted in the following grid:

CRIMINAL HISTORY SCORE

SEVERITY LEVELS OF CONVICTION OFFENSE		0	1	2	3	4	5	6 or more
Unauthorized Use of Motor Vehicle Possession of Marijuana	I	12*	12*	12*	13	15	17	19 18-20
Theft Related Crimes ($250-$2500) Aggravated Forgery ($250-$2500)	II	12*	12*	13	15	17	19	21 20-22
Theft Crimes ($250-$2500)	III	12*	13	15	17	19 18-20	22 21-23	25 24-26
Nonresidential Burglary Theft Crimes (over $2500)	IV	12*	15	18	21	25 24-26	32 30-34	41 37-45
Residential Burglary Simple Robbery	V	18	23	27	30 29-31	38 36-40	46 43-49	54 50-58
Criminal Sexual Conduct. 2nd Degree (a) & (b)	VI	21	26	30	34 33-35	44 42-46	54 50-58	65 60-70
Aggravated Robbery	VII	24 23-25	32 30-34	41 38-44	49 45-53	65 60-70	81 75-87	97 90-104
Criminal Sexual Conduct 1st Degree Assault, 1st Degree	VIII	43 41-45	54 50-58	65 60-70	76 71-81	95 89-101	113 106-120	132 124-140
Murder, 3rd Degree Murder, 2nd Degree (felony murder)	IX	105 102-108	119 116-122	127 124-130	149 143-155	176 168-184	205 195-215	230 218-242
Murder, 2nd Degree (with intent)	X	120 116-124	140 133-147	162 153-171	203 192-214	243 231-255	284 270-298	324 309-339

The guideline sentence (expressed in months) is found by determining the offense severity and criminal history score and then looking to the grid cell in the appropriate row and column. Cells below the heavy black line contain sentences of imprisonment in a state prison system; cells above the line refer to probated sentences. First degree murder carries a mandatory life sentence and is exempted from the guidelines.

A number of rules govern the calculation of a defendant's criminal history score. For each prior felony conviction, one point is assigned. One additional point is assigned if the defendant was on probation or parole, jailed or imprisoned, or released pending sentence at the time the offense was committed. One "unit" is assigned for each misdemeanor conviction, unless the misdemeanor was a "gross" or serious one, in which case two units are assigned; four "units" equal one point. A further point is assigned if the defendant committed two offenses as a juvenile (after his sixteenth birthday) that would have been felonies if committed by an adult.

b. FEDERAL REFORM: THE SENTENCING REFORM ACT OF 1984

The Sentencing Reform Act of 1984, Chapter II of the Comprehensive Crime Control Act of 1984 and codified primarily as 18 U.S.C.A. §§ 3551–

3580, dramatically changed the framework for sentencing persons convicted of criminal offenses in federal courts. Its progress through Congress was lengthy and troubled. It finally became effective November 1, 1987. But court challenges to many of its provisions are numerous and ongoing. For example, prior to the decision in the principal case, which follows, "158 U.S. district courts had ruled that the guidelines were unconstitutional, while 116 others had upheld them. Two U.S. Circuit Courts of Appeals were also in conflict—the 9th Circuit striking the guidelines down, by a 2-to-1 vote, and the 3rd Circuit upholding them, also by a 2-to-1 vote." 20 Crim.J.Newsletter No. 3, February 1, 1989, p. 1.

The principal case is the first to be decided by the Supreme Court. It provides an outline of some of the main points of the Act while addressing the constitutionality of the Sentencing Commission created by the Act. More detailed descriptions and other provisions of the statute are presented elsewhere in this chapter.

Mistretta v. United States

Supreme Court of the United States, 1989.
488 U.S. 361, 109 S.Ct. 647, 102 L.Ed.2d 714.

■ Justice Blackmun delivered the opinion of the Court.

In this litigation, we granted certiorari before judgment in the United States Court of Appeals for the Eighth Circuit in order to consider the constitutionality of the Sentencing Guidelines promulgated by the United States Sentencing Commission. The Commission is a body created under the Sentencing Reform Act of 1984, as amended (Act), 18 U.S.C. § 3551 et seq. (1982 ed., Supp. IV), and 28 U.S.C. §§ 991–998 (1982 ed., Supp. IV). The United States District Court for the Western District of Missouri ruled that the Guidelines were constitutional. United States v. Johnson, 682 F.Supp. 1033 (W.D.Mo.1988).

I

A

Background

For almost a century, the Federal Government employed in criminal cases a system of indeterminate sentencing. Statutes specified the penalties for crimes but nearly always gave the sentencing judge wide discretion to decide whether the offender should be incarcerated and for how long, whether he should be fined and how much, and whether some lesser restraint, such as probation, should be imposed instead of imprisonment or fine. This indeterminate-sentencing system was supplemented by the utilization of parole, by which an offender was returned to society under the "guidance and control" of a parole officer.

Both indeterminate sentencing and parole were based on concepts of the offender's possible, indeed probable, rehabilitation, a view that it was realistic to attempt to rehabilitate the inmate and thereby to minimize the risk that he would resume criminal activity upon his return to society. It obviously required the judge and the parole officer to make their respective sentencing and release decisions upon their own assessments of the offender's amendability to rehabilitation. As a result, the court and the officer were in positions to exercise, and usually did exercise, very broad discretion. This led almost inevitably to the conclusion on the part of a reviewing court that the sentencing judge "sees more and senses more" than the appellate court; thus, the judge enjoyed the "superiority of his nether position," for that court's determination as to what sentence was appropriate met with virtually unconditional deference on appeal. The decision whether to parole was also "predictive and discretionary." The correction official possessed almost absolute discretion over the parole decision.

Historically, federal sentencing—the function of determining the scope and extent of punishment—never has been thought to be assigned by the Constitution to the exclusive jurisdiction of any one of the three Branches of government. Congress, of course, has the power to fix the sentence for a federal crime, and the scope of judicial discretion with respect to a sentence is subject to congressional control. Congress early abandoned fixed-sentence rigidity, however, and put in place a system of ranges within which the sentencer could choose the precise punishment. Congress delegated almost unfettered discretion to the sentencing judge to determine what the sentence should be within the customarily wide range so selected. This broad discretion was further enhanced by the power later granted the judge to suspend the sentence and by the resulting growth of an elaborate probation system. Also, with the advent of parole, Congress moved toward a "three-way sharing" of sentencing responsibility by granting correction personnel in the Executive Branch the discretion to release a prisoner before the expiration of the sentence imposed by the judge. Thus, under the indeterminate-sentence system, Congress defined the maximum, the judge imposed a sentence within the statutory range (which it usually could replace with probation), and the Executive Branch's parole official eventually determined the actual duration of imprisonment. . . .

Serious disparities in sentences, however, were common. Rehabilitation as a sound penalogical theory came to be questioned and, in any event, was regarded by some as an unattainable goal for most cases. See N. Morris, The Future of Imprisonment, 24–43 (1974); F. Allen, The Decline of the Rehabilitative Ideal (1981). . . .

. . . Congress had wrestled with the problem for more than a decade when, in 1984, it enacted the sweeping reforms that are at issue here.

* * *

Before settling on a mandatory-guideline system, Congress considered other competing proposals for sentencing reform. It rejected strict determinate sentencing because it concluded that a guideline system would be successful in reducing sentence disparities while retaining the flexibility needed to adjust for unanticipated factors arising in a particular case. . . . The Judiciary Committee rejected a proposal that would have made the sentencing guidelines only advisory. . . .

B

The Act

The Act, as adopted, revises the old sentencing process in several ways:

1. It rejects imprisonment as a means of promoting rehabilitation, 28 U.S.C. § 994(k), and it states that punishment should serve retributive, educational, deterrent, and incapacitative goals, 18 U.S.C. § 3553(a)(2).

2. It consolidates the power that had been exercised by the sentencing judge and the Parole Commission to decide what punishment an offender should suffer. This is done by creating the United States Sentencing Commission, directing that Commission to devise guidelines to be used for sentencing, and prospectively abolishing the Parole Commission. 28 U.S.C. §§ 991, 994, and 995(a)(1).

3. It makes all sentences basically determinate. A prisoner is to be released at the completion of his sentence reduced only by any credit earned by good behavior while in custody. 18 U.S.C. §§ 3624(a) and (b).

4. It makes the Sentencing Commission's guidelines binding on the courts, although it preserves for the judge the discretion to depart from the guideline applicable to a particular case if the judge finds an aggravating or mitigating factor present that the Commission did not adequately consider when formulating guidelines. §§ 3553(a) and (b). The Act also requires the court to state its reasons for the sentence imposed and to give "the specific reason" for imposing a sentence different from that described in the guideline. § 3553(c).

5. It authorizes limited appellate review of the sentence. It permits a defendant to appeal a sentence that is above the defined range, and it permits the Government to appeal a sentence that is below that range. It also permits either side to appeal an incorrect application of the guideline. §§ 3742(a) and (b).

* * *

C

The Sentencing Commission

The Commission is established "as an independent commission in the judicial branch of the United States." § 991(a). It has seven voting members (one of whom is the Chairman) appointed by the President "by and with the advice and consent of the Senate." "At least three of the members shall be Federal judges selected after considering a list of six judges recommended to the President by the Judicial Conference of the United States." Ibid. No more than four members of the Commission shall be members of the same political party. The Attorney General, or his designee, is an ex officio nonvoting member. The Chairman and other members of the Commission are subject to removal by the President "only for neglect of duty or malfeasance in office or for other good cause shown." § 991(a). Except for initial staggering of terms, a voting member serves for six years and may not serve more than two full terms. §§ 992(a) and (b).

D

The Responsibilities of the Commission

In addition to the duty the Commission has to promulgate determinative-sentence guidelines, it is under an obligation periodically to "review and revise" the guidelines. § 994(*o*). It is to "consult with authorities on, and individual and institutional representatives of, various aspects of the Federal criminal justice system." Ibid. It must report to Congress "any amendments of the guidelines." § 994(p). It is to make recommendations to Congress whether the grades or maximum penalties should be modified. § 994(r). It must submit to Congress at least annually an analysis of the operation of the guidelines. § 994(w). It is to issue "general policy statements" regarding their application. § 994(a)(2). And it has the power to "establish general policies . . . as are necessary to carry out the purposes" of the legislation, § 995(a)(1); to "monitor the performance of probation officers" with respect to the guidelines, § 995(a)(9); to "devise and conduct periodic training programs of instruction in sentencing techniques for judicial and probation personnel" and others, § 995(a)(18); and to "perform such other functions as are required to permit Federal courts to meet their responsibilities" as to sentencing, § 995(a)(22).

We note, in passing, that the monitoring function is not without its burden. Every year, with respect to each of more than 40,000 sentences, the federal courts must forward, and the Commission must review, the presentence report, the guideline worksheets, the tribunal's sentencing statement, and any written plea agreement.

II

This Litigation

On Dec. 10, 1987, John M. Mistretta (petitioner) and another were indicted in the United States District Court for the Western District of Missouri on three counts centering in a cocaine sale. Mistretta moved to have the promulgated Guidelines ruled unconstitutional on the grounds that the Sentencing Commission was constituted in violation of the established doctrine of separation of powers, and that Congress delegated excessive authority to the Commission to structure the Guidelines. As has been noted, the District Court was not persuaded by these contentions.

The District Court rejected petitioner's delegation argument on the ground that, despite the language of the statute, the Sentencing Commission "should be judicially characterized as having Executive Branch status," and that the Guidelines are similar to substantive rules promulgated by other agencies. The court also rejected petitioner's claim that the Act is unconstitutional because it requires Article III federal judges to serve on the Commission. . . .

Petitioner then pleaded guilty to the first count of his indictment (conspiracy and agreement to distribute cocaine, in violation of 21 U.S.C. §§ 846 and 841(b)(1)(B)). The Government thereupon moved to dismiss the remaining counts. That motion was granted. Petitioner was sentenced under the Guidelines to 18 months' imprisonment, to be followed by a 3–

year term of supervised release. The court also imposed a $1,000 fine and a $50 special assessment.

Petitioner filed a notice of appeal to the Eighth Circuit, but both petitioner and the United States, pursuant to this Court's Rule 18, petitioned for certiorari before judgment. Because of the "imperative public importance" of the issue, as prescribed by the Rule, and because of the disarray among the Federal District Courts, we granted those petitions.

III

Delegation of Power

Petitioner argues that in delegating the power to promulgate sentencing guidelines for every federal criminal offense to an independent Sentencing Commission, Congress has granted the Commission excessive legislative discretion in violation of the constitutionally based nondelegation doctrine. We do not agree.

The nondelegation doctrine is rooted in the principle of separation of powers that underlies our tripartite system of government. The Constitution provides that "[a]ll legislative Powers herein granted shall be vested in a Congress of the United States," U.S. Const., Art. I, § 1, and we long have insisted that "the integrity and maintenance of the system of government ordained by the Constitution," mandate that Congress generally cannot delegate its legislative power to another Branch. Field v. Clark, 143 U.S. 649, 692, 12 S.Ct. 495, 504, 36 L.Ed. 294 (1892). We also have recognized, however, that the separation-of-powers principle, and the non-delegation doctrine in particular, do not prevent Congress from obtaining the assistance of its coordinate Branches. . . .

. . . Accordingly, this Court has deemed it "constitutionally sufficient if Congress clearly delineates the general policy, the public agency which is to apply it, and the boundaries of this delegated authority." American Power & Light Co. v. SEC, 329 U.S. 90, 105, 67 S.Ct. 133, 142, 91 L.Ed. 103 (1946).

* * *

In light of our approval of these broad delegations, we harbor no doubt that Congress' delegation of authority to the Sentencing Commission is sufficiently specific and detailed to meet constitutional requirements. Congress charged the Commission with three goals: to "assure the meeting of the purposes of sentencing as set forth" in the Act; to "provide certainty and fairness in meeting the purposes of sentencing, avoiding unwarranted sentencing disparities among defendants with similar records . . . while maintaining sufficient flexibility to permit individualized sentences," where appropriate; and to "reflect to the extent practicable, advancement in knowledge of human behavior as it relates to the criminal justice process." 28 U.S.C. § 991(b)(1). Congress further specified four "purposes" of sentencing that the Commission must pursue in carrying out its mandate: "to reflect the seriousness of the offense, to promote respect for the law, and to provide just punishment for the offense"; "to afford adequate deterrence to criminal conduct"; "to protect the public from further crimes of the defendant"; and "to provide the defendant with needed ... correctional treatment." 18 U.S.C. § 3553(a)(2).

In addition, Congress prescribed the specific tool—the guidelines system—for the Commission to use in regulating sentencing. More particularly, Congress directed the Commission to develop a system of "sentencing ranges" applicable "for each category of offense involving each category of defendant." 28 U.S.C. § 994(b).[6] Congress instructed the Commission that these sentencing ranges must be consistent with pertinent provisions of Title 18 of the United States Code and could not include sentences in excess of the statutory maximum. Congress also required that for sentences of imprisonment, "the maximum of the range established for such a term shall not exceed the minimum of that range by more than the greater of 25 percent or 6 months, except that, if the minimum term of the range is 30 years or more, the maximum may be life imprisonment." § 994(b)(2). Moreover, Congress directed the Commission to use current average sentences "as a starting point" for its structuring of the sentencing ranges. § 994(m).

To guide the Commission in its formulation of offense categories, Congress directed it to consider seven factors: the grade of the offense; the aggravating and mitigating circumstances of the crime; the nature and degree of the harm caused by the crime; the community view of the gravity of the offense; the public concern generated by the crime; the deterrent effect that a particular sentence may have on others; and the current incidence of the offense. § 994(c)(1)–(7). Congress set forth 11 factors for the Commission to consider in establishing categories of defendants. These include the offender's age, education, vocational skills, mental and emotional condition, physical condition (including drug dependence), previous employment record, family ties and responsibilities, community ties, role in the offense, criminal history, and degree of dependence upon crime for a livelihood. § 994(d)(1)–(11). Congress also prohibited the Commission from considering the "race, sex, national origin, creed, and socio-economic status of offenders," § 994(d), and instructed that the guidelines should reflect the "general inappropriateness" of considering certain other factors, such as current unemployment, that might serve as proxies for forbidden factors, § 994(e).

In addition to these overarching constraints, Congress provided even more detailed guidance to the Commission about categories of offenses and offender characteristics. Congress directed that guidelines require a term of confinement at or near the statutory maximum for certain crimes of

6. Congress mandated that the guidelines include:

"(A) a determination whether to impose a sentence to probation, a fine, or a term of imprisonment;

"(B) a determination as to the appropriate amount of a fine or the appropriate length of a term of probation or a term of imprisonment;

"(C) a determination whether a sentence to a term of imprisonment should include a requirement that the defendant be placed on a term of supervised release after imprisonment, and, if so, the appropriate length of such a term; and

"(D) a determination whether multiple sentences to terms of imprisonment should be ordered to run concurrently or consecutively." 28 U.S.C. § 994(a)(1).

violence and for drug offenses, particularly when committed by recidivists. § 994(h). Congress further directed that the Commission assure a substantial term of imprisonment for an offense constituting a third felony conviction, for a career felon, for one convicted of a managerial role in a racketeering enterprise, for a crime of violence by an offender on release from a prior felony conviction, and for an offense involving a substantial quantity of narcotics. § 994(i). Congress also instructed "that the guidelines reflect . . . the general appropriateness of imposing a term of imprisonment" for a crime of violence that resulted in serious bodily injury. On the other hand, Congress directed that guidelines reflect the general inappropriateness of imposing a sentence of imprisonment "in cases in which the defendant is a first offender who has not been convicted of a crime of violence or an otherwise serious offense." § 994(j). Congress also enumerated various aggravating and mitigating circumstances, such as, respectively, multiple offenses or substantial assistance to the Government, to be reflected in the guidelines. §§ 994(*l*) and (n). In other words, although Congress granted the Commission substantial discretion in formulating guidelines, in actuality it legislated a full hierarchy of punishment—from near maximum imprisonment, to substantial imprisonment, to some imprisonment, to alternatives—and stipulated the most important offense and offender characteristics to place defendants within these categories.

We cannot dispute petitioner's contention that the Commission enjoys significant discretion in formulating guidelines. The Commission does have discretionary authority to determine the relative severity of federal crimes and to assess the relative weight of the offender characteristics that Congress listed for the Commission to consider. See §§ 994(c) and (d) (Commission instructed to consider enumerated factors as it deems them to be relevant). The Commission also has significant discretion to determine which crimes have been punished too leniently, and which too severely. § 994(m). Congress has called upon the Commission to exercise its judgment about which types of crimes and which types of criminals are to be considered similar for the purposes of sentencing.[7]

* * *

Developing proportionate penalties for hundreds of different crimes by a virtually limitless array of offenders is precisely the sort of intricate,

---

7. Petitioner argues that the excessive breadth of Congress' delegation to the Commission is particularly apparent in the Commission's considering whether to "reinstate" the death penalty for some or all of those crimes for which capital punishment is still authorized in the Federal Criminal Code. Whether, in fact, the Act confers upon the Commission the power to develop guidelines and procedures to bring current death penalty provisions into line with decisions of this Court is a matter of intense debate between the Executive Branch and some members of Congress, including the Chairman of the Senate Judiciary Committee. We assume, without deciding, that the Commission was assigned the power to effectuate the death penalty provisions of the Criminal Code. That the Commission may have this authority (but has not exercised it) does not affect our analysis. Congress did not authorize the Commission to enact a federal death penalty for any offense. As for every other offense within the Commission's jurisdiction, the Commission could include the death penalty within the guidelines only if that punishment was authorized in the first instance by Congress and only if such inclusion comported with the substantial guidance Congress gave the Commission in fulfilling its assignments. Justice Brennan does not join this footnote.

labor-intensive task for which delegation to an expert body is especially appropriate. Although Congress has delegated significant discretion to the Commission to draw judgments from its analysis of existing sentencing practice and alternative sentencing models, "Congress is not confined to that method of executing its policy which involves the least possible delegation of discretion to administrative officers." Yakus v. United States, 321 U.S., at 425–426, 64 S.Ct., at 668. We have no doubt that in the hands of the Commission "the criteria which Congress has supplied are wholly adequate for carrying out the general policy and purpose" of the Act. Sunshine Coal Co. v. Adkins, 310 U.S. 381, 398, 60 S.Ct. 907, 915, 84 L.Ed. 1263 (1940).

IV

Separation of Powers

Having determined that Congress has set forth sufficient standards for the exercise of the Commission's delegated authority, we turn to Mistretta's claim that the Act violates the constitutional principle of separation of powers.

* * *

In sum, since substantive judgment in the field of sentencing has been and remains appropriate to the Judicial Branch, and the methodology of rulemaking has been and remains appropriate to that Branch, Congress' considered decision to combine these functions in an independent Sentencing Commission and to locate that Commission within the Judicial Branch does not violate the principle of separation of powers.

* * *

V

We conclude that in creating the Sentencing Commission—an unusual hybrid in structure and authority—Congress neither delegated excessive legislative power nor upset the constitutionally mandated balance of powers among the coordinate Branches. The Constitution's structural protections do not prohibit Congress from delegating to an expert body located within the Judicial Branch the intricate task of formulating sentencing guidelines consistent with such significant statutory direction as is present here. Nor does our system of checked and balanced authority prohibit Congress from calling upon the accumulated wisdom and experience of the Judicial Branch in creating policy on a matter uniquely within the ken of judges. Accordingly, we hold that the Act is constitutional.

The judgment of the United States District Court for the Western District of Missouri is affirmed.

It is so ordered.

■ JUSTICE SCALIA, dissenting [omitted].

NOTES

1. **Congressional directives.** In the legislation, Congress has provided a number of additional directives concerning the substance of the guidelines that the

Commission is to develop. 28 U.S.C.A. § 994(b)–(m). For example, the Commission is directed to assure that the guidelines will specify a sentence to "a substantial term of imprisonment" for categories of defendants in which the defendant has a history of two or more prior felony convictions for offenses committed on different occasions. 28 U.S.C.A. § 944(i)(1).

In addition, the Commission is to promulgate general policy statements regarding application of the guidelines and other aspects of sentencing or sentencing implementation.

2. **Statutory sentencing criteria.** The legislation directs the court, in selecting a sentence, to consider:

(1) the nature and circumstances of the offense and the history and characteristics of the defendant;

(2) the need for the sentence imposed—

(A) to reflect the seriousness of the offense, to promote respect for the law, and to provide just punishment for the offense;

(B) to afford adequate deterrence to criminal conduct;

(C) to protect the public from further crimes of the defendant; and

(D) to provide the defendant with needed education or vocational training, medical care, or other correctional treatment in the most effective manner;

(3) the kinds of sentences available;

(4) the kinds of sentences and the sentencing range established for the applicable category of offense committed by the applicable category of defendant as set forth in the guidelines that are issued by the Sentencing Commission . . . ;

(5) any pertinent policy statement issued by the Sentencing Commission . . . ;

(6) the need to avoid unwarranted sentence disparities among defendants with similar records who have been found guilty of similar conduct; and

(7) the need to provide restitution to any victims of the offense.

18 U.S.C.A. § 3553(a). The sentence is to be "sufficient, but not greater than necessary, to comply with the purposes set forth in paragraph (2). . . ." Id.

With regard to the Sentencing Commission's guidelines, the statute provides:

The court shall impose a sentence of the kind and within the range, [of the guidelines issued by the Sentencing Commission] unless the court finds that an aggravating or mitigating circumstance exists that was not adequately taken into consideration by the Sentencing Commission in formulating the guidelines and that should result in a sentence different from that described.

18 U.S.C.A. § 3553(b).

At the time of sentencing, the court "shall state in open court the reasons for the imposition of the particular sentence. . . ." 18 U.S.C.A. § 3553(c). If the sentence is not of the kind, or outside the range, provided for in the Commission's guidelines, the court is also to state the specific reason for the imposition of a sentence different from that indicated by the guidelines. Id.

3. **Elimination of parole.** The legislation abolishes parole as it has traditionally been administered in the federal system and in many states. A convicted defendant sentenced to imprisonment is to be released on the expiration of his sentence, less any time credited to him for "satisfactory behavior." 18 U.S.C.A.

§ 3624(a). Within 15 days of the end of each year of a prison term, a defendant is to receive—in addition to credit for time actually served—credit for 54 more days unless the Bureau of Prisons determines that during the year the defendant has not satisfactorily complied with institutional disciplinary regulations. Once such additional time has been credited to a defendant, it "vests" and cannot be withdrawn for later misbehavior. 18 U.S.C.A. § 3624(b). This, of course, means that a defendant's actual release date is no longer determined as a discretionary matter by a parole authority.

Nevertheless, a defendant may not, upon completion of his term of imprisonment, be entitled to absolute discharge. A sentencing court is authorized to impose upon a convicted defendant, in addition to a term of imprisonment, a requirement that the defendant be placed on a term of "supervised release" after imprisonment. 18 U.S.C.A. § 3583. The length of the term of supervised release which the court is authorized to impose ranges from one to five years, depending upon the crime of which the defendant has been convicted. Conditions may be imposed upon this release. If a term of supervised release has been imposed by the sentencing court, the defendant—upon release from imprisonment—is to be supervised by a probation officer "to the degree warranted by the conditions specified by the sentencing court." 18 U.S.C.A. § 3624(e). The term of supervised release is subject to revocation upon a showing by a preponderance of the evidence that the defendant has violated its terms. No credit for time served on supervised release will be given upon revocation. 18 U.S.C.A. § 3583(e)(3).

During service of a term of imprisonment, efforts are to be made to prepare the prisoner for transition from prison to community life. The Bureau of Prisons is directed "to the extent practicable" to assure that a prisoner spends a portion of the last part of his term of imprisonment "under conditions that will afford the prisoner a reasonable opportunity to adjust to and prepare for his re-entry into the community." 18 U.S.C.A. § 3624(c).

4. **Appellate review.** A defendant is authorized to appeal from a sentence on the ground that it was imposed in violation of law or as a result of an incorrect application of the Sentencing Commission's guidelines, or that it was greater than is provided for in the guidelines or in a plea agreement. 18 U.S.C.A. §§ 3742(a) and 3742(c)(1). The Government may appeal on similar grounds, although its case would, of course, be based on the proposition that the sentence was less severe than that provided for in the guidelines. 18 U.S.C.A. §§ 3742(b) and 3742(c)(2).

The Court of Appeals is to "give due regard to the opportunity of the district court to judge the credibility of the witnesses." It is to accept the findings of fact by the district court unless they are clearly erroneous. 18 U.S.C.A. § 3742(d). The appellate tribunal is authorized to remand a case for either the imposition of a lesser or more severe sentence or for further sentencing proceedings. It is also permitted to itself impose a lesser or greater sentence. 18 U.S.C.A. § 3742(e).

The Government in Koon v. United States, 518 U.S. 81, 116 S.Ct. 2035, 135 L.Ed.2d 392 (1996) argued that appellate courts should apply a *de novo* review to sentences to determine there compliance with the guidelines. The Supreme Court, in an opinion by Justice Kennedy, rejected this contention. An appellate court must in most instances grant deference to the district court's sentencing findings:

> That the district court retains much of its traditional discretion does not mean appellate review is an empty exercise. Congress directed courts of appeals to "give due deference to the district court's application of the guidelines to the facts." 18 U.S.C. § 3742(e)(4). The deference that is due depends on the nature of the question presented. The district court may be owed no deference, for instance, when the claim on appeal is that it made some sort of mathematical error in applying the Guidelines; under these circumstances, the appellate court

will be in as good a position to consider the question as the district court was in the first instance.

A district court's decision to depart from the Guidelines, by contrast, will in most cases be due substantial deference, for it embodies the traditional exercise of discretion by a sentencing court.

518 U.S. at 98, 116 S.Ct. at 2046, 135 L.Ed.2d at 412–13.

Koon involved the federal prosecution to Los Angeles police officers for violating the civil rights of Rodney King by beating him after stopping him during a high-speed chase. The incident was videotaped by a by-stander. Defendants had previously been tried and acquitted in state court. They were then tried and convicted of civil rights violations in federal court. The federal district court determined that the offense level was 27, which would have yielded a sentence of 70 to 87 months. However, the court granted a five-level downward departure because it determined that King's wrongful conduct contributed significantly to provoking the offense. It also granted a three-level downward departure because defendants were particularly likely to be the object of abuse in prison, would be terminated from their jobs as police officers, had been significantly burdened by having to defend successive state and federal prosecutions for the same conduct, and were unlikely to recidivate. Thus, it concluded the modified offense level was 19, which resulted in a sentence range of 30 to 37 months. The district court imposed a 30 year sentence.

The Supreme Court held that the district court did not abuse its discretion in departing five levels because of King's misconduct. With respect to the three-level departure, the Court concluded that the sole issue is whether the Sentencing Commission has proscribed the use of any particular sentencing factor. "If the answer to the question is no—as it will be most of the time—the sentencing court must determine whether the factor, as occurring in the particular circumstances, takes the case outside the heartland of the applicable Guideline." 518 U.S. at 109, 116 S.Ct. at 2051, 135 L.Ed.2d at 419. The defendants' career loss was inappropriately used to justify departure because the nature of a civil rights act violation—an intentional violation of another's civil rights—means that loss of public employment would not be unusual as a consequence of being convicted of such an offense. The unlikelihood of recidivism was also inappropriately taken into account because that was already taken into account in the criminal history portion of the matrix. The susceptibility to abuse in prison was based on the notoriousness of this offense and was, therefore, sufficiently unusual to justify downward departure. Finally, the successive state and federal prosecutions were sufficiently unusually burdensome to justify downward departure.

5. **Downward departures for substantial assistance to the government.** Federal law authorizes a District Court to impose a sentence below a statutory or guidelines minimum if the Government has filed a motion stating the defendant has provided substantial assistance in the investigation or prosecution of another person. The petitioner in Wade v. United States, 504 U.S. 181, 112 S.Ct. 1840, 118 L.Ed.2d 524 (1992) pleaded guilty to an offense that carried a 10 year minimum sentence. At sentencing he asked the District Court to impose a sentence less than 10 years on the ground he had provided substantial assistance. The District Court refused, taking the position it lacked that power without a motion from the Government. The United States Supreme Court, in an opinion for a unanimous Court by Justice Souter, upheld this decision. A District Court lacks power to impose a sentence lower than a statutory minimum or the minimum provided by guidelines unless the Government has filed a substantial assistance motion or unless the defendant can show that its failure to do so was based upon an unconstitutional motive, such as race or religion. This is the same standard that governs judicial review of prosecutorial charging decisions. Wade made no claim of

unconstitutional motive. Wade also did not claim that the Government's failure to file a substantial assistance motion was a breach of a plea agreement.

6. **Sentencing Commission policy statements and commentaries.** In addition to guidelines, the United States Sentencing Commission publishes policy statements and commentaries. What weight should courts give to those "lesser" declarations from the Commission? In Williams v. United States, 503 U.S. 193, 112 S.Ct. 1112, 117 L.Ed.2d 341 (1992), the petitioner was convicted of possession of a firearm by a convicted felon. The District Court imposed a longer sentence than normally authorized by the sentencing guidelines on the basis of the petitioner's arrest record. While such action was not specifically prohibited by guidelines, it was done contrary to a policy statement that records of arrests for unadjudicated offenses can not be taken into account in this manner. The Supreme Court, in an opinion by Justice O'Connor, held that "[w]here ... a policy statement prohibits a district court from taking a specified action, the statement is an authoritative guide to the meaning of the applicable guideline. An error in interpreting such a policy statement could lead to an incorrect determination that a departure was appropriate." 503 U.S. at 201, 112 S.Ct. at 1119, 117 L.Ed.2d at 353. The Court vacated sentence and remanded for a determination whether the sentence was a result of the "error in interpreting" the policy statement or of authorized considerations in the case. Justice White, joined by Justice Kennedy, dissented.

The weight to be given to Commission commentaries was considered by the Court in Stinson v. United States, 508 U.S. 36, 113 S.Ct. 1913, 123 L.Ed.2d 598 (1993). Petitioner was also convicted of possession of a firearm by a convicted felon. The District Court sentenced him as a career offender based on a finding that the offense of possession of a firearm by a convicted felon is a "crime of violence" justifying that upward departure. Later, the Commission promulgated a commentary to the guidelines stating explicitly that possession of a firearm by a convicted felon is not a crime of violence under the career offender guidelines. The Supreme Court, in a unanimous opinion by Justice Kennedy, held that guidelines should be given a weight akin to an administrative agency's interpretation of its own legislative rules. "[P]rovided an agency's interpretation of its own regulations does not violate the Constitution or a federal statute, it must be given 'controlling weight unless it is plainly erroneous or inconsistent with the regulation.' " 508 U.S. at 45, 113 S.Ct. at 1919, 123 L.Ed.2d at 608. The Court also addressed the relationship between amendments in the commentary, as occurred in this case, and prior inconsistent appellate court interpretations of the underlying guideline:

> Although amendments to guidelines provisions are one method of incorporating revisions, another method open to the Commission is amendment of the commentary, if the guideline which the commentary interprets will bear the construction. Amended commentary is binding on the federal courts even though it is not reviewed by Congress, and prior judicial constructions of a particular guideline cannot prevent the Commission from adopting a conflicting interpretation that satisfies the standard we set forth today.

508 U.S. at 46, 113 S.Ct. at 1919, 123 L.Ed.2d at 608–09. The Court remanded the case to the Court of Appeals for it to determine what effect, if any, the amended commentary should be given in petitioner's case.

C. PROCEDURAL ISSUES IN SENTENCING

Traditionally the procedures employed in gathering information and making the initial decision as to sentence have been comparatively informal. A sentencing hearing may be held at which witnesses are placed under oath and testimony and evidence is taken. But the procedure may be far less formal. The sentencing judge may obtain information in many ways. Suggestions and arguments are frequently offered by counsel for both sides and perhaps the defendant as well. Letters and phone calls may also have been the source of information to the judge from the probation officer, an examining psychiatrist, or other interested party. Most commonly, however, the court's probation officer will have been directed to conduct an investigation into the circumstances of the offense and the defendant's background. The written product, often made available to the judge before the hearing, is usually called the presentence report (or presentence investigation report [PSI]). The dominance of guilty pleas and the trend toward determinate sentencing have resulted in increased attention upon the sentencing process. This subsection considers some of the practices and issues concerning information used in sentencing and the parts played at this stage by opposing counsel.

1.   DEVELOPMENT OF SENTENCING INFORMATION

Presentence reports play an integral part in sentencing and correctional decisions in the federal system and in many states. Therefore, the data contained in these reports is vital. This subsection focuses upon the content of the report, disclosure and challenge of these contents, and the manner in which the data is collected, presented and used.

Fennell and Hall, Due Process at Sentencing: An Empirical and Legal Analysis of the Disclosure of Presentence Reports in Federal Courts

93 Harvard L.Rev. 1613, 1627–30 (1980).

C.   Importance of the Presentence Report

The presentence report serves two essential functions in the sentencing process. First, because an overwhelming majority of defendants plead guilty and therefore forgo trial, the report often substitutes for the trial itself as a mechanism through which facts are found in a criminal case. In those cases, the report provides the sentencing judge with his only knowledge of the offense and the defendant, other than the minimal facts necessary to support the acceptance of a guilty plea.[8] . . .

---

8. . . . In several districts, the report also plays an important role in the plea bargaining process. For example, in one district the probation office initiates the investigation prior to arraignment. After the report is completed, the probation office recommendation for disposition is voted on at a staff meeting, with each probation officer and the chief judge casting one vote. The resulting recommendation and the information from the investigation are conveyed to the Assistant United States Attorney on the case. He uses these as the basis for his negotiations with the defense attorney. If he strays too far from the recommendation, the judge will refuse to accept the negotiated sentence. After negotiations, the defendant is arraigned—and in this district, 95% of the defendants plead guilty at arraignment.

A second district has a presentence conference that includes a magistrate, prosecutor, and defense attorney. The magistrate is supplied with the probation office recommendation and copies of the report's prior-record section. He gives the

After sentencing, the presentence report continues to function as the central document in the correctional process. If the defendant is placed on probation, the report helps the probation officer determine an appropriate treatment program and level of supervision. If incarceration is necessary, the report is used in determining both the proper institution and the defendant's classification within the institution. The report also plays a crucial role in parole decisions and in aiding parole supervision when the defendant returns to the community. . . .

D. Problems Associated with the Presentence Report

The principal problem inherent in the use of the presentence report is its potential for introducing inaccurate or misleading information into the sentencing decision. Because of the report's importance in the sentencing and later correctional processes, any misinformation or misleading statements it contains often have a multiple impact—affecting not only the severity of the sentence, but also the offender's classification in prison, his ability to obtain furloughs and work release, and the likelihood of his early parole. . . .

The opportunity for inclusion of misinformation is particularly acute after the guilty plea, when the probation officer engages in a new investigation of the offense without the use of traditional adversarial and evidentiary safeguards for ensuring fairness and accuracy. Similarly, when a probation officer attempts to determine whether an offender was represented by counsel at a conviction,[9] a significant possibility of error exists because the recordkeeping practices of local courts are often inadequate.

Misleading information in the presentence report, in the form of subtle distortions resulting from incompleteness, innuendo, or ambiguity, can also adversely affect the defendant's treatment. For example, one presentence report stated that a sex offender "had a knife" when he committed the offense; the knife proved to be merely a pocketknife that the defendant customarily carried but did not use in the commission of the crime. Computerized data may often be deceptive in that information is often transmitted in the form of a categorical, often pejorative, label such as "major drug supplier" or "organized crime member." Without further substantiation, the reliability of these labels cannot be tested. Even clinical information, though valuable in portraying the defendant's character and criminal motivation, has a tendency both to categorize the individual and to negate the impact of equally important, but less authoritative, data. Moreover, clinical evaluations are generally unverifiable without knowledge of the expert's credentials and the basis for his assessment of the defendant.

prior-record section to the attorneys but retains the recommendation. Negotiations then commence. In the past, the magistrate acted as a referee, nodding his head when the attorneys got "warm" and grimacing when they strayed too far from the recommended sentence. Now, because of concern over the implications of this practice for judicial participation in plea bargaining, the magistrate presides silently over the proceeding and gives no indication of the court's position.

9. It is unconstitutional for uncounseled convictions to be used as the basis for imposing sentence. United States v. Tucker, 404 U.S. 443, 447–49 (1972).

Concerns such as these led to the eventual amendment of rule 32(c)(3) to require disclosure of the presentence report and to permit the defendant to comment upon it. The policy of the new rule, as stated in the Advisory Committee Note, is that "[t]he best way of insuring accuracy is disclosure with an opportunity for the defendant and counsel to point out to the court information thought to be inaccurate, incomplete, or otherwise misleading."

* * *

FEDERAL RULES OF CRIMINAL PROCEDURE RULE 32 SENTENCE AND JUDGMENT

* * *

(c) Presentence Investigation.

(1) When Made. A probation officer shall make a presentence investigation and report to the court before the imposition of sentence unless the court finds that there is in the record information sufficient to enable the meaningful exercise of sentencing authority pursuant to 18 U.S.C. 3553, and the court explains this finding on the record.

Except with the written consent of the defendant, the report shall not be submitted to the court or its contents disclosed to anyone unless the defendant has pleaded guilty or nolo contendere or has been found guilty.

(2) Report. The report of the presentence investigation shall contain—

(A) information about the history and characteristics of the defendant, including prior criminal record, if any, financial condition, and any circumstances affecting the defendant's behavior that may be helpful in imposing sentence or in the correctional treatment of the defendant.

(B) the classification of the offense and of the defendant under the categories established by the Sentencing Commission ...; the kinds of sentence and the sentencing range suggested for such a category of offense committed by such a category of defendant as set forth in the guidelines issued by the Sentencing Commission ...; and an explanation by the probation officer of any factors that may indicate that a sentence of a different kind or of a different length than one within the applicable guideline would be more appropriate under all the circumstances;

(C) any pertinent policy statement issued by the Sentencing Commission ...;

(D) verified information stated in a nonargumentative style containing an assessment of the financial, social, psychological, and medical impact upon, and cost to, any individual against whom the offense has been committed;

(E) unless the court orders otherwise, information concerning the nature and extent of nonprison programs and resources available for the defendant; and

(F) such other information as may be required by the court.

(3) Disclosure.

(A) At least 10 days before imposing sentence, unless this minimum period is waived by the defendant, the court shall provide the defendant and the defendant's counsel with a copy of the report of the presentence investigation including the information required by subdivision (c)(2) and not including any final recommendation as to sentence, and not to the extent that in the opinion of the court the report contains diagnostic opinions which if disclosed, might seriously disrupt a program of rehabilitation; or sources of information obtained upon a promise of confidentiality; or any other information which, if disclosed, might result in harm, physical or otherwise, to the defendant or other persons. The court shall afford the defendant and his counsel an opportunity to comment on the report and, in the discretion of the court, to introduce testimony or other information relating to any alleged factual inaccuracy contained in it.

(B) If the court is of the view that there is information in the presentence report which should not be disclosed under subdivision (c)(3)(A) of this rule, the court in lieu of making the report or part thereof available shall state orally or in writing a summary of the factual information contained therein to be relied on in determining sentence, and shall give the defendant and the defendant's counsel an opportunity to comment thereon. The statement may be made to the parties in camera.

(C) Any material which may be disclosed to the defendant and the defendant's counsel shall be disclosed to the attorney for the government.

(D) If the comments of the defendant and the defendant's counsel or testimony or other information introduced by them allege any factual inaccuracy in the presentence investigation report or the summary of the report or part thereof, the court shall, as to each matter controverted, make (i) a finding as to the allegation, or (ii) a determination that no such finding is necessary because the matter controverted will not be taken into account in sentencing. A written record of such findings and determinations shall be appended to and accompany any copy of the presentence investigation report thereafter made available to the Bureau of Prisons.

* * *

Gardner v. Florida

Supreme Court of the United States, 1977.
430 U.S. 349, 97 S.Ct. 1197, 51 L.Ed.2d 393.

■ MR. JUSTICE STEVENS announced the judgment of the Court and delivered an opinion, in which MR. JUSTICE STEWART and MR. JUSTICE POWELL joined.

Petitioner was convicted of first-degree murder and sentenced to death. When the trial judge imposed the death sentence he stated that he was relying in part on information in a presentence investigation report. Portions of the report were not disclosed to counsel for the parties. Without reviewing the confidential portion of the presentence report, the Supreme Court of Florida, over the dissent of two justices, affirmed the death sentence. 313 So.2d 675 (1975). We conclude that this procedure does not satisfy the constitutional command that no person shall be deprived of life without due process of law.

I.

On June 30, 1973, the petitioner assaulted his wife with a blunt instrument, causing her death. On January 10, 1974, after a trial in the Circuit Court of Citrus County, Fla., a jury found him guilty of first-degree murder.

The separate sentencing hearing required by Florida law in capital cases was held later on the same day. The State merely introduced two photographs of the decedent, otherwise relying on the trial testimony. That testimony, if credited, was sufficient to support a finding of one of the statutory aggravating circumstances, that the felony committed by petitioner "was especially heinous, atrocious, or cruel."

In mitigation petitioner testified that he had consumed a vast quantity of alcohol during a day-long drinking spree which preceded the crime, and professed to have almost no recollection of the assault itself. His testimony, if credited, was sufficient to support a finding of at least one of the statutory mitigating circumstances.[10]

After hearing this evidence the jury was instructed to determine by a majority vote (1) whether the State had proved one of the aggravating circumstances defined by statute, (2) whether mitigating circumstances outweighed any such aggravating circumstance, and (3) based on that determination, whether the defendant should be sentenced to life or death.

After the jury retired to deliberate, the judge announced that he was going to order a presentence investigation of petitioner. Twenty-five minutes later the jury returned its advisory verdict. It expressly found that the mitigating circumstances outweighed the aggravating circumstances and advised the court to impose a life sentence.

The presentence investigation report was completed by the Florida Parole and Probation Commission on January 28, 1974. On January 30, 1974, the trial judge entered findings of fact and a judgment sentencing petitioner to death. His ultimate finding was that the felony "was especially heinous, atrocious or cruel; and that such aggravating circumstances outweighs the mitigating circumstance, to-wit: none." As a preface to that ultimate finding, he recited that his conclusion was based on the evidence presented at both stages of the bifurcated proceeding, the arguments of counsel, and his review of "the factual information contained in said presentence investigation."

10. The statute provides, in part:
"(6) Mitigating circumstances.—Mitigating circumstances shall be the following:
"(b) The capital felony was committed while the defendant was under the influence of extreme mental or emotional disturbance.

"(f) The capacity of the defendant to appreciate the criminality of his conduct or to conform his conduct to the requirements of law was substantially impaired." Fla.Stat.Ann. §§ 921.141(6)(b), (f) (Supp.1976).

* * *

There is no dispute about the fact that the presentence investigation report contained a confidential portion which was not disclosed to defense counsel. Although the judge noted in his findings of fact that the State and petitioner's counsel had been given "a copy of that portion [of the report] to which they are entitled," counsel made no request to examine the full report or to be apprised of the contents of the confidential portion. The trial judge did not comment on the contents of the confidential portion. His findings do not indicate that there was anything of special importance in the undisclosed portion, or that there was any reason other than customary practice for not disclosing the entire report to the parties.

* * *

II.

The State places its primary reliance on this Court's landmark decision in Williams v. New York, 337 U.S. 241, 69 S.Ct. 1079, 93 L.Ed. 1337 [(1949)]. In that case, as in this, the trial judge rejected the jury's recommendation of mercy and imposed the death sentence in reliance, at least in part, on material contained in a report prepared by the court's probation department. The New York Court of Appeals had affirmed the sentence, rejecting the contention that it was a denial of due process to rely on information supplied by witnesses whom the accused could neither confront nor cross-examine.

This Court referred to appellant's claim as a "narrow contention," id., at 243, 69 S.Ct., at 1081, and characterized the case as one which

> "presents a serious and difficult question . . . relat[ing] to the rules of evidence applicable to the manner in which a judge may obtain information to guide him in the imposition of sentence upon an already convicted defendant." Id., at 244, 69 S.Ct., at 1082.

The conviction and sentence were affirmed, over the dissent of two Justices.

Mr. Justice Black's opinion for the Court persuasively reasons why material developed in a presentence investigation may be useful to a sentencing judge, and why it may not be unfair to a defendant to rely on such information even if it would not be admissible in a normal adversary proceeding in open court. We consider the relevance of that reasoning to this case in Part III of this opinion. Preliminarily, however, we note two comments by Mr. Justice Black that make it clear that the *holding* of *Williams* is not directly applicable to this case.

It is first significant that in *Williams* the material facts concerning the defendant's background which were contained in the presentence report were described in detail by the trial judge in open court. Referring to this material, Mr. Justice Black noted:

> "The accuracy of the statements made by the judge as to appellant's background and past practices was not challenged by appellant or his counsel, nor was the judge asked to disregard any of them or to afford appellant a chance to refute or discredit any of them by cross-examination or otherwise." Ibid.

In contrast, in the case before us, the trial judge did not state on the record the substance of any information in the confidential portion of the presentence report that he might have considered material. There was, accordingly, no similar opportunity for petitioner's counsel to challenge the accuracy or materiality of any such information.

It is also significant that Mr. Justice Black's opinion recognized that the passage of time justifies a re-examination of capital-sentencing procedures. As he pointed out:

> "This whole country has traveled far from the period in which the death sentence was an automatic and commonplace result of convictions—even for offenses today deemed trivial." Id., at 247–248, 69 S.Ct., at 1083.

Since that sentence was written almost 30 years ago, this Court has acknowledged its obligation to re-examine capital-sentencing procedures against evolving standards of procedural fairness in a civilized society.

III.

In 1949, when the *Williams* case was decided, no significant constitutional difference between the death penalty and lesser punishments for crime had been expressly recognized by this Court. At that time the Court assumed that after a defendant was convicted of a capital offense, like any other offense, a trial judge had complete discretion to impose any sentence within the limits prescribed by the legislature. As long as the judge stayed within those limits, his sentencing discretion was essentially unreviewable and the possibility of error was remote, if, indeed, it existed at all. In the intervening years there have been two constitutional developments which require us to scrutinize a State's capital-sentencing procedures more closely than was necessary in 1949.

First, five Members of the Court have now expressly recognized that death is a different kind of punishment from any other which may be imposed in this country. . . . From the point of view of the defendant, it is different in both its severity and its finality. From the point of view of society, the action of the sovereign in taking the life of one of its citizens also differs dramatically from any other legitimate state action. It is of vital importance to the defendant and to the community that any decision to impose the death sentence be, and appear to be, based on reason rather than caprice or emotion.

Second, it is now clear that the sentencing process, as well as the trial itself, must satisfy the requirements of the Due Process Clause. Even though the defendant has no substantive right to a particular sentence within the range authorized by statute, the sentencing is a critical stage of the criminal proceeding at which he is entitled to the effective assistance of counsel. Mempa v. Rhay, 389 U.S. 128, 88 S.Ct. 254, 19 L.Ed.2d 336; Specht v. Patterson, 386 U.S. 605, 87 S.Ct. 1209, 18 L.Ed.2d 326. The defendant has a legitimate interest in the character of the procedure which leads to the imposition of sentence even if he may have no right to object to a particular result of the sentencing process. . . . [11]

---

11. The fact that due process applies does not, of course, implicate the entire panoply of criminal trial procedural rights.

"Once it is determined that due process applies, the question remains what pro-

In the light of these developments we consider the justifications offered by the State for a capital-sentencing procedure which permits a trial judge to impose the death sentence on the basis of confidential information which is not disclosed to the defendant or his counsel.

The State first argues that an assurance of confidentiality to potential sources of information is essential to enable investigators to obtain relevant but sensitive disclosures from persons unwilling to comment publicly about a defendant's background or character. The availability of such information, it is argued, provides the person who prepares the report with greater detail on which to base a sentencing recommendation and, in turn, provides the judge with a better basis for his sentencing decision. But consideration must be given to the quality, as well as the quantity, of the information on which the sentencing judge may rely. Assurances of secrecy are conducive to the transmission of confidences which may bear no closer relation to fact than the average rumor or item of gossip, and may imply a pledge not to attempt independent verification of the information received. The risk that some of the information accepted in confidence may be erroneous, or may be misinterpreted, by the investigator or by the sentencing judge, is manifest.

If, as the State argues, it is important to use such information in the sentencing process, we must assume that in some cases it will be decisive in the judge's choice between a life sentence and a death sentence. If it tends to tip the scales in favor of life, presumably the information would be favorable and there would be no reason why it should not be disclosed. On the other hand, if it is the basis for a death sentence, the interest in reliability plainly outweighs the State's interest in preserving the availability of comparable information in other cases.

The State also suggests that full disclosure of the presentence report will unnecessarily delay the proceeding. We think the likelihood of significant delay is overstated because we must presume that reports prepared by professional probation officers, as the Florida procedure requires, are generally reliable. In those cases in which the accuracy of a report is contested, the trial judge can avoid delay by disregarding the disputed material. Or if the disputed matter is of critical importance, the time invested in ascertaining the truth would surely be well spent if it makes the difference between life and death.

The State further urges that full disclosure of presentence reports, which often include psychiatric and psychological evaluations, will occasionally disrupt the process of rehabilitation. The argument, if valid, would hardly justify withholding the report from defense counsel. Moreover, whatever force that argument may have in non-capital cases, it has abso-

cess is due. It has been said so often by this Court and others as not to require citation of authority that due process is flexible and calls for such procedural protections as the particular situation demands. ...Its flexibility is in its scope once it has been determined that some process is due; it is a recognition that not all situations calling for procedural safeguards call for the same kind of procedure." Morrissey v. Brewer, 408 U.S. 471, 481, 92 S.Ct. 2593, 2600, 33 L.Ed.2d 484.

lutely no merit in a case in which the judge has decided to sentence the defendant to death. Indeed, the extinction of all possibility of rehabilitation is one of the aspects of the death sentence that makes it different in kind from any other sentence a State may legitimately impose.

Finally, Florida argues that trial judges can be trusted to exercise their discretion in a responsible manner, even though they may base their decisions on secret information. However acceptable that argument might have been before Furman v. Georgia, it is now clearly foreclosed. Moreover, the argument rests on the erroneous premise that the participation of counsel is superfluous to the process of evaluating the relevance and significance of aggravating and mitigating facts. Our belief that debate between adversaries is often essential to the truth-seeking function of trials requires us also to recognize the importance of giving counsel an opportunity to comment on facts which may influence the sentencing decision in capital cases.

* * *

We conclude that petitioner was denied due process of law when the death sentence was imposed, at least in part, on the basis of information which he had no opportunity to deny or explain.

IV.

There remains only the question of what disposition is now proper. Petitioner's conviction, of course, is not tainted by the error in the sentencing procedure. The State argues that we should merely remand the case to the Florida Supreme Court with directions to have the entire presentence report made a part of the record to enable that court to complete its reviewing function. That procedure, however, could not fully correct the error. For it is possible that full disclosure, followed by explanation or argument by defense counsel, would have caused the trial judge to accept the jury's advisory verdict. Accordingly, the death sentence is vacated, and the case is remanded to the Florida Supreme Court with directions to order further proceedings at the trial court level not inconsistent with this opinion.

Vacated and remanded.

■ THE CHIEF JUSTICE concurs in the judgment.

[The opinions of Justice White and Justice Blackmun, concurring in the judgment, the separate opinion of Justice Brennan, and the dissenting opinions of Justice Marshall and Justice Rehnquist, are omitted].

NOTES

1. **Defense access to report.** In United States v. Rone, 743 F.2d 1169 (7th Cir.1984), the Seventh Circuit held that the district court's failure to assure defendant access to his presentence report at a reasonable time before the sentencing hearing required vacation of sentence and remand for new sentencing. In reaching this decision, the court stated that all defendants have a due process right to a fair sentencing procedure which includes the right to be sentenced on the basis of accurate information, but that the trial court at the sentencing hearing need

directly ask defendant only three questions: whether he has had an opportunity to read the presentence report; whether defendant and defense counsel have discussed the report; and whether defendant wishes to challenge any facts in the report. A sentence must be set aside, the court said, where defendant can demonstrate that false information formed part of the basis for the sentence.

2. **Constitutionality of using presentence reports.** In Williams v. New York, 337 U.S. 241, 69 S.Ct. 1079, 93 L.Ed. 1337 (1949), distinguished in *Gardner,* supra, on the issue of nondisclosure, the Court also held that the Due Process Clause of the Fourteenth Amendment did not require a judge to have hearings and to give a convicted person an opportunity to participate in those hearings when he came to determine the sentence to be imposed. Justice Black stated:

> Under the practice of individualizing punishments, investigational techniques have been given an important role. Probation workers making reports of their investigations have not been trained to prosecute but to aid offenders. Their reports have been given a high value by conscientious judges who want to sentence persons on the best available information rather than on guesswork and inadequate information. To deprive sentencing judges of this kind of information would undermine modern penological procedural policies that have been cautiously adopted throughout the nation after careful consideration and experimentation. We must recognize that most of the information now relied upon by judges to guide them in the intelligent imposition of sentences would be unavailable if information were restricted to that given in open court by witnesses subject to cross-examination. And the modern probation report draws on information concerning every aspect of a defendant's life. The type and extent of this information make totally impractical if not impossible open court testimony with cross-examination. Such a procedure could endlessly delay criminal administration in a retrial of collateral issues. . . .

337 U.S. at 249–50, 69 S.Ct. at 1084, 93 L.Ed. at 1343.

How viable is *Williams* after *Gardner?*

3. **Required findings of fact.** Specht v. Patterson, 386 U.S. 605, 87 S.Ct. 1209, 18 L.Ed.2d 326 (1967), had earlier distinguished *Williams* in a different kind of sentencing situation.

Mr. Justice Douglas delivered the opinion of the Court.

> The question is whether the rule of the *Williams* case applies to this Colorado case where petitioner, having been convicted for indecent liberties under one Colorado statute that carries a maximum sentence of 10 years . . . but not sentenced under it, may be sentenced under the Sex Offenders Act . . . for an indeterminate term of from one day to life without notice and full hearing. The Colorado Supreme Court approved the procedure, ... The case is here on a petition for certiorari. . . .

* * *

> We adhere to Williams v. People of State of New York, supra; but we decline the invitation to extend it to this radically different situation. . . . We hold that the requirements of due process were not satisfied here. . . .

> The Sex Offenders Act does not make the commission of a specified crime the basis for sentencing. It makes one conviction the basis for commencing another proceeding under another Act to determine whether a person constitutes a threat of bodily harm to the public, or is an habitual offender and mentally ill. That is a new finding of fact . . . that was not an ingredient of the offense charged. The punishment under the second Act is criminal punishment

even though it is designed not so much as retribution as it is to keep individuals from inflicting future harm. ...

... Under Colorado's criminal procedure, here challenged, the invocation of the Sex Offenders Act means the making of a new charge leading to criminal punishment. The case is not unlike those under recidivist statutes where an habitual criminal issue is "a distinct issue" ...on which a defendant "must receive reasonable notice and an opportunity to be heard." ...Due process, in other words, requires that he be present with counsel, have an opportunity to be heard, be confronted with witnesses against him, have the right to cross-examine, and to offer evidence of his own. And there must be findings adequate to make meaningful any appeal that is allowed. ...None of these procedural safeguards we have mentioned is present under Colorado's Sex Offenders Act. We therefore hold that it is deficient in due process as measured by the requirements of the Fourteenth Amendment. ...

386 U.S. at 607–11, 87 S.Ct. at 1211–13, 18 L.Ed.2d at 328–31.

4. **Freedom of Information Act.** In United States Department of Justice v. Julian, 486 U.S. 1, 108 S.Ct. 1606, 100 L.Ed.2d 1 (1988), the Court was faced with the question of whether an inmate could compel disclosure of his presentence investigation report under the Freedom of Information Act from the Bureau of Prisons or the Parole Commission. The Court, through The Chief Justice, held that disclosure was required by the Freedom of Information Act, subject to the same three restrictions of Federal Rules of Criminal Procedure Rule 32(c)(3)(A) [supra] for diagnostic opinions, confidential sources of information, or harmful material.

2. DEFENSE COUNSEL'S ROLE

In most cases the guilt-innocence question is resolved by the defendants' pleas of guilty. If defense counsel has little opportunity to challenge the prosecution's ability to prove the defendant guilty, counsel's primary opportunity to serve the defendant involves sentencing. How this might best be done is addressed in this subsection. Various ethical dilemmas in defense counsel's sentencing role are also touched upon.

Mempa v. Rhay

Supreme Court of the United States, 1967.
389 U.S. 128, 88 S.Ct. 254, 19 L.Ed.2d 336.

■ MR. JUSTICE MARSHALL delivered the opinion of the Court.

These consolidated cases raise the question of the extent of the right to counsel at the time of sentencing where the sentencing has been deferred subject to probation.

Petitioner Jerry Douglas Mempa was convicted in the Spokane County Superior Court on June 17, 1959, of the offense of "joyriding," Wash.Rev. Code § 9.54.020. This conviction was based on his plea of guilty entered with the advice of court-appointed counsel. He was then placed on probation for two years on the condition, *inter alia,* that he first spend 30 days in the county jail, and the imposition of sentence was deferred pursuant to Wash.Rev.Code §§ 9.95.200, 9.95.210.

About four months later the Spokane County prosecuting attorney moved to have petitioner's probation revoked on the ground that he had been involved in a burglary on September 15, 1959. A hearing was held in the Spokane County Superior Court on October 23, 1959. Petitioner Mempa, who was 17 years old at the time, was accompanied to the hearing by his stepfather. He was not represented by counsel and was not asked whether he wished to have counsel appointed for him. Nor was any inquiry made concerning the appointed counsel who had previously represented him.

At the hearing Mempa was asked if it was true that he had been involved in the alleged burglary and he answered in the affirmative. A probation officer testified without cross-examination that according to his information petitioner had been involved in the burglary and had previously denied participation in it. Without asking petitioner if he had anything to say or any evidence to supply, the court immediately entered an order revoking petitioner's probation and then sentenced him to 10 years in the penitentiary, but stated that it would recommend to the parole board that Mempa be required to serve only a year.

* * *

In 1948 this Court held in Townsend v. Burke, 334 U.S. 736, 68 S.Ct. 1252, 92 L.Ed. 1690, that the absence of counsel during sentencing after a plea of guilty coupled with "assumptions concerning his criminal record which were materially untrue" deprived the defendant in that case of due process. Mr. Justice Jackson there stated in conclusion, "In this case, counsel might not have changed the sentence, but he could have taken steps to see that the conviction and sentence were not predicated on misinformation or misreading of court records, a requirement of fair play which absence of counsel withheld from this prisoner." . . .

. . . Townsend v. Burke, supra, illustrates the critical nature of sentencing in a criminal case and might well be considered to support by itself a holding that the right to counsel applies at sentencing. . . .

. . . It is true that sentencing in Washington offers fewer opportunities for the exercise of judicial discretion than in many other jurisdictions. Obviously to the extent . . . recommendations [by the judge to the Parole Board which determines the length of imprisonment] are influential in determining the resulting sentence, the necessity for the aid of counsel in marshaling the facts, introducing evidence of mitigating circumstances and in general aiding and assisting the defendant to present his case as to sentence is apparent.

Even more important . . . is the fact that certain legal rights may be lost if not exercised at this stage. For one, . . . absence of counsel . . . might well result in loss of the right to appeal. While ordinarily appeals from a plea of guilty are less frequent than those following a trial on the merits, the incidence of improperly obtained guilty pleas is not so slight as to be capable of being characterized as *de minimis*. . . .

Likewise the Washington statutes provide that a plea of guilty can be withdrawn at any time prior to the imposition of sentence . . . if the trial judge in his discretion finds that the ends of justice will be served. . . . An uncounseled defendant might very likely be unaware of this opportunity.

The two foregoing factors assume increased significance when it is considered that, as happened in these two cases, the eventual imposition of sentence on the prior plea of guilty is based on the alleged commission of offenses for which the accused is never tried.

In sum, we do not question the authority of the State of Washington to provide for a deferred sentencing procedure coupled with its probation provisions. Indeed, it appears to be an enlightened step forward. All we decide here is that a lawyer must be afforded at this proceeding whether it be labeled a revocation of probation or a deferred sentencing. We assume that counsel appointed for the purpose of the trial or guilty plea would not be unduly burdened by being requested to follow through at the deferred sentencing stage of the proceeding.

NOTES

1. **Functions of counsel.** While discussing the important functions counsel could have performed in the Washington probation revocation proceedings, was it by oversight that Mr. Justice Marshall failed to mention the functions of counsel (1) in litigating the issue whether probation was violated and, (2) if the trial court concluded it was, in representing his client in an attempt to persuade the judge to exercise his discretion not to revoke probation? How do these functions of counsel compare in importance with those discussed in the opinion?

2. **Right to hearing and counsel.** In Gagnon v. Scarpelli, 411 U.S. 778, 93 S.Ct. 1756, 36 L.Ed.2d 656 (1973), the case presented "the related questions whether a previously sentenced probationer [unlike *Mempa*] is entitled to a hearing when his probation is revoked and, if so, whether he is entitled to be represented by appointed counsel at such a hearing." The court stated:

> Probation revocation, like parole revocation, is not a stage of a criminal prosecution, but does result in a loss of liberty. Accordingly, we hold that a probationer, like a parolee, is entitled to a preliminary and a final revocation hearing, under the conditions specified in Morrissey v. Brewer, [408 U.S. 471, 92 S.Ct. 2593, 33 L.Ed.2d 484 (1972)].

* * *

> The second, and more difficult, question posed by this case is whether an indigent probationer or parolee has a due process right to be represented by appointed counsel at these hearings. In answering that question, we draw heavily on the opinion in *Morrissey*.

* * *

> At the preliminary hearing, a probationer or parolee is entitled to notice of the alleged violations of probation or parole, an opportunity to appear and to present evidence in his own behalf, a conditional right to confront adverse witnesses, an independent decisionmaker, and a written report of the hearing. ...The final hearing is a less summary one because the decision under consideration is the ultimate decision to revoke rather than a mere determination of probable cause, but the "minimum requirements of due process" include very similar elements:

> > "(a) written notice of the claimed violations of [probation or] parole; (b) disclosure to the [probationer or] parolee of evidence against him; (c) opportunity to be heard in person and to present witnesses and documentary evidence; (d) the right to confront and cross-examine adverse witnesses

(unless the hearing officer specifically finds good cause for not allowing confrontation); (e) a 'neutral and detached' hearing body such as a traditional parole board, members of which need not be judicial officers or lawyers; and (f) a written statement by the fact-finders as to the evidence relied on and reasons for revoking [probation or] parole." Morrissey v. Brewer, supra, 408 U.S., at 489, 92 S.Ct., at 2604.

These requirements in themselves serve as substantial protection against ill-considered revocation, . . . [but] may in some circumstances depend on the use of skills which the probationer or parolee is unlikely to possess.

. . . We think, . . . that the decision as to the need for counsel must be made on a case-by-case basis in the exercise of a sound discretion by the state authority charged with responsibility for administering the probation and parole system. Although the presence and participation of counsel will probably be both undesirable and constitutionally unnecessary in most revocation hearings, there will remain certain cases in which fundamental fairness—the touchstone of due process—will require that the State provide at its expense counsel for indigent probationers or parolees.

* * *

Presumptively, it may be said that counsel should be provided in cases where, after being informed of his right to request counsel, the probationer or parolee makes such a request, based on a timely and colorable claim (i) that he has not committed the alleged violation of the conditions upon which he is at liberty; or (ii) that, even if the violation is a matter of public record or is uncontested, there are substantial reasons which justified or mitigated the violation and make revocation inappropriate and that the reasons are complex or otherwise difficult to develop or present. In passing on a request for the appointment of counsel, the responsible agency also should consider, especially in doubtful cases, whether the probationer appears to be capable of speaking effectively for himself. In every case in which a request for counsel at a preliminary or final hearing is refused, the grounds for refusal should be stated succinctly in the record.

411 U.S. at 782–91, 93 S.Ct. at 1759–64, 36 L.Ed.2d at 661–67.

3. **Sentencing functions before the sentencing hearing.** According to Kuh, Defense Counsel's Role in Sentencing, 14 Criminal Law Bulletin 433 (1978), counsel's role begins at the first client meeting with information gathering and advice on the subsequent attitude and conduct of the defendant. The possibility of a preplea investigation and social report to provide an early sentence reading is the next step, followed by counsel's discreet but protective presence at the presentence investigation, examination of the presentence report, defense sentencing memorandum, and in-court statement. See also Feit, "Before Sentence is Pronounced . . .": A Guide to Defense Counsel on the Exercise of his Post–Conviction Responsibilities, 9 Criminal Law Bulletin 140 (1973), which provides a sentencing checklist.

4. **Defense advocacy strategies at sentencing.** Commentary, ABA Standards Relating to Sentencing Alternatives and Procedures, Approved Draft (1968), § 5.3 states:

[T]he lawyer should . . . assume the same position of advocacy that is his duty at the trial. While the lawyer is indeed obligated at trial to make for the defendant the "best possible defense," there are obvious limits which in concrete cases require the lawyer on the spot to draw some tough ethical lines. The "best possible defense," for example, clearly does not include the knowing use of perjured testimony: while this may be "best" from the point of view of the client, the lawyer owes a much larger duty to the court and to the system not to participate in such a scheme. By analogy, there will be limits to the representations that the lawyer can and should make on the sentencing issue. The lawyer should not be expected to argue probation for a rape-murder by a sixth offender by submitting that his record is clean and the offense only minor. At the same time, such a defendant—to the same extent that he deserves "the best possible defense" on guilt, and for the same reasons—deserves the best possible statement of his point of view at the sentencing proceeding. In concrete terms, what this means is that the defense attorney must make a judgment about what sentences are realistically possible, and use the facts at his disposal to do the best he can for the interests of his client.

* * *

Just as the lawyer would not think of pleading him guilty without consultation, he should not ignore the wishes of the client at the sentencing stage. In extreme cases, this may force the attorney to the conclusion that he cannot in conscience pursue the course demanded of him by his client. The difficulty of this position is paralleled by the possibility of its occurrence at the guilt stage as well. The point, in other words, is that the relationship of lawyer to client should not be very much different just because of the arrival of a different stage of the proceeding. And it should be recognized by the lawyer that for many convicted defendants, the sentence will be the most important and the only really difficult issue in the case.

An explanation by the lawyer of the sentencing alternatives and their consequences can also serve a collateral purpose. As was observed in a slightly different context:

> [T]he actual consequences of any sentence for a defendant and his family are usually more complex than expressed by the recitation of statutory sentencing provisions. In some instances there are civil consequences of conviction, such as loss of a license, which are not usually mentioned by the court. Some sentences, for certain sex offenders for example, are predicated on the existence of treatment facilities while in other situations no specific therapy is provided. The nature of imprisonment, the conditions of probation, eligibility for release, and the consequences of these for himself and for his family are all primary concerns of the defendant. In practice, these matters are explained to the defendant by his defense counsel, if they are explained at all. Neither the judge nor the prosecutor usually feels called upon to go into specific, individual consequences of conviction and sentencing; they rely on counsel to relate these details to his client and to his client's family.

Newman, Conviction: The Determination of Guilt or Innocence without Trial 209 (1966).

A defendant who understands what is happening to him is much more likely to respond favorably to the ultimate sentence which is imposed. There is thus a significant correctional objective served by leaving the client with the impression that he has been fairly dealt with. It takes very little effort by the lawyer to convince the average client that he has been railroaded.

There is also a third objective which can be served by a conference between an informed lawyer and his client. That the lawyer can play a significant role in the rehabilitation of his client is often lost in the zeal to procure an expedient sentence. The attorney should not so readily assume that the "best deal" for the client is the lightest possible sentence. There may well be particular correctional services available which will better suit his long-run needs. The lawyer should be aware of these possibilities, and be prepared to recommend their consideration to his client.

* * *

In addition to the fact that the defendant normally must desire such a . . . disposition in order for it to work, the lawyer can find himself in an embarrassing position if his client openly disagrees with a recommendation to the court on his behalf. Most importantly, however, it is not the lawyer's function to decide what is the best disposition for his client. The lawyer is a representative and an advisor, and when he suggests that a . . . disposition is desirable he ought to be doing so with the consent of his client.

A more "collaborative" or "educational" role for defense counsel at sentencing is put forward by Judge Cooper in the context of a real case. Cooper, United States v. Unterman: The Role of Counsel at Sentencing, 13 Criminal Law Bulletin 101 (1977).

Also see Dash, The Defense Lawyers Role At The Sentencing Stage of a Criminal Case, 54 F.R.D. 315 (1972), for a more detailed consideration of the complex ethical issues involved.

3.   PROSECUTOR'S ROLE

The prosecutor's role at sentencing is the subject of broad disagreement, even among prosecutors themselves. The following survey provides the range of possibilities and their rationales.

Teitelbaum, The Prosecutor's Role in the Sentencing Process: A National Survey

1 American Journal of Criminal Law 75 (1972).

[T]he vast majority of district attorney's offices do participate in the sentencing process in some fashion. Though a significant minority of offices indicate that as a general policy they abstain from participation, some do intervene in the case of certain major crimes.

The majority of offices taking part in the sentencing process participate in three distinct ways: (1) the prosecutor presents arguments concerning the nature and severity of the crime and the criminal history of the defendant; (2) the prosecutor expresses his position concerning the desirability of an award of probation; and (3) the prosecutor makes a specific sentence recommendation. The next largest group of offices employs only method (3), and the third largest group makes use solely of method (1).

* * *

The survey inquired into the philosophy of the offices that take part in the sentencing process. . . . A slight plurality selected what might be called a "quasi-judicial" position—the prosecutor should recommend exactly the same sentence that he would impose were he the judge. The others favored what might be called an "advocate" philosophy: the job of the prosecutor is to suggest aggravating factors to counterbalance the mitigating factors presented by the defense. . . .

The twenty-six offices that do not participate in the sentencing process are scattered throughout the nation with no regional or geographical pattern. A number of these offices maintained that it would be improper for prosecutors to tender sentence recommendations to the court and they suggested a number of reasons for this view. Most pointed out that the court has the assistance of a probation department or similar agency to assist it in determining the appropriate sentence; they also suggested that sentence determination is a judicial prerogative which should not be lightly invaded. The most startling comment came from Canton, Ohio: sentence recommendations by the prosecutor would "inhibit the system, develop difficulties between the court and the district attorney's office, and make plea bargaining more difficult."

* * *

Most of the offices that usually abstain from the sentencing process abandon that policy in certain cases. ...The sorts of crime that cause prosecutors to abandon their usual policy of nonparticipation in the sentencing process cover a wide range of activity.

The most frequently listed exception came in cases involving organized crime. Only three other exceptions were listed by more than one office: sex crimes involving children, assaults on police officers, and cases involving defendants with no serious prior record who had cooperated with the police.

* * *

Most district attorney's offices expend the energy to formulate sentence recommendations, yet how often do the courts follow this advice? A plurality of the offices participating in the sentencing process believe that their recommendations are followed "almost all the time." A substantial percentage, however, believe that the courts accept their sentence recommendations only "more than half the time." A small percentage of offices report that their recommendations are followed "less than half the time."

Neither the presence of a probation department nor a difference in prosecutorial philosophy substantially affects the prosecutor's self-perceived success in persuading the court to concur with his recommendations. District attorneys in jurisdictions with a probation office and those with a preference for the "advocate theory" of sentencing see their proposals followed slightly less often than do other prosecutors.

* * *

Prosecutorial sentence recommendations do provide the court with additional information for the decision-making process. Certainly an abundant informational input contributes to thoughtful deliberation; however, rational results depend not merely on quantity of information but also on its relevance. The ultimate question then becomes: Do prosecutorial sentence recommendations provide information helpful to a judge trying to determine an appropriate sentence?

Those district attorney's offices that do make sentence recommendations justify their practice by claiming (in order of importance) that their sentence recommendations provide the court with (1) a law enforcement viewpoint regarding the appropriate sentence, (2) the victim's viewpoint concerning the appropriate sentence, (3) pressure necessary to restrain some judges' propensity for leniency, and (4) information based on greater experience than many judges themselves have had.

* * *

The survey reveals that most district attorney's offices actively take part in the sentencing process. Though prosecutors generally believe that their participation contributes to the effectiveness of the criminal justice system, the value of their contribution remains questionable. . . .

No evidence suggests that the quality of justice suffers in those areas where the prosecutor refrains from actively participating in the sentencing process. . . .

D. ALTERNATIVES OR SUPPLEMENTS TO INCARCERATION

Despite record rates of incarceration, a high level of public concern about crime continues. Overcrowded institutions, many thus subject to constitutional challenge, are the result. Given these circumstances, there is an urgent need for dispositions or penalties that may be imposed as alternatives to any incarceration or, in some situations at least, in addition. The present section describes some of these alternatives or supplements— probation, fines, and restitution. It also deals with methods of extending periods of incarceration by civil commitment proceedings or by recidivist statutes.

1. PROBATION

A defendant sentenced to probation is placed under the supervision of a probation officer and must comply with various conditions of probation. Upon a showing that the defendant has violated these conditions, the sentencing court is generally authorized—but not required—to "revoke" the probation and sentence the defendant to a term of incarceration.

Initially, probation was reserved largely for offenders who had committed relatively minor crimes. But in 1973, the National Advisory Commission on Criminal Justice Standards and Goals stated:

> The Commission believes that the most hopeful move towards effective corrections is to continue and strengthen the trend away from confining people in institutions and towards supervising them in the community. . . . The thrust of the Commission's *Report on Corrections* is that probation, which is now the largest community-based program, will become the standard sentence in criminal cases, with confinement retained chiefly for those offenders who cannot safely be supervised in the community.

* * *

There are compelling reasons to continue the move away from institutions. First, State institutions consume more than three-fourths of all expenditures for corrections while dealing with less than one-third of all offenders. Second, as a whole they do not deal with those offenders effectively. There is no evidence that prisons reduce the amount of crime.

A National Strategy to Reduce Crime 121 (1973).

But, as the material in this subsection indicates, there was substantial later concern that probation may be overused. Insofar as it is used, there is also concern that the heavier caseloads may result in offenders being actually given little supervision.

Among the major issues raised by the availability of probation are the circumstances in which it is desirable, the conditions which can or should be imposed upon it, and when revocation is appropriate. These are addressed in the present subsection.

NATIONAL ADVISORY COMMISSION ON CRIMINAL JUSTICE STANDARDS AND GOALS, CORRECTIONS 150 (1973)

Standard 5.2 Sentencing the Nondangerous Offender

Criteria should be established for sentencing offenders. Such criteria should include:

1. A requirement that the least drastic sentencing alternative be imposed that is consistent with public safety. The court should impose the first of the following alternatives that will reasonably protect the public safety:

   a. Unconditional release.

   b. Conditional release.

   c. A fine.

   d. Release under supervision in the community.

   e. Sentence to a halfway house or other residential facility located in the community.

   f. Sentence to partial confinement with liberty to work or participate in training or education during all but leisure time.

   g. Total confinement in a correctional facility.

2. A provision against the use of confinement as an appropriate disposition unless affirmative justification is shown on the record. Factors that would justify confinement may include:

   a. There is undue risk that the offender will commit another crime if not confined.

   b. The offender is in need of correctional services that can be provided effectively only in an institutional setting, and such services are reasonably available.

   c. Any other alternative will depreciate the seriousness of the offense.

3. Weighting of the following in favor of withholding a disposition of incarceration:

a. The offender's criminal conduct neither caused nor actually threatened serious harm.

b. The offender did not contemplate or intend that his criminal conduct would cause or threaten serious harm.

c. The offender acted under strong provocation.

d. There were substantial grounds tending to excuse or justify the offender's criminal conduct, though failing to establish defense.

e. The offender had led a law-abiding life for a substantial period of time before commission of the present crime.

f. The offender is likely to respond affirmatively to probationary or other community supervision.

g. The victim of the crime induced or facilitated its commission.

h. The offender has made or will make restitution or reparation to the victim of his crime for the damage or injury which was sustained.

i. The offender's conduct was the result of circumstances unlikely to recur.

j. The character, history, and attitudes of the offender indicate that he is unlikely to commit another crime.

k. Imprisonment of the offender would entail undue hardship to dependents.

l. The offender is elderly or in poor health.

m. The correctional programs within the institutions to which the offender would be sent are inappropriate to his particular needs or would not likely be of benefit to him.

CALIFORNIA JUDICIAL COUNCIL, SENTENCING RULES FOR THE SUPERIOR COURTS (1990)

Rule 414. Criteria Affecting Probation

Criteria affecting the decision to grant or deny probation include:

(a) Statutory provisions authorizing, limiting or prohibiting the grant of probation.

(b) The likelihood that if not imprisoned the defendant will be a danger to others.

(c) Facts relating to the crime, including:

(1) The nature, seriousness and circumstances of the crime.

(2) The vulnerability of the victim and the degree of harm or loss to the victim.

(3) Whether the defendant was armed with or used a weapon.

(4) Whether the defendant inflicted bodily injury.

(5) Whether the defendant planned the commission of the crime, whether he instigated it or was solicited by others to participate, and whether he was an active or passive participant.

(6) Whether the crime was committed because of an unusual circumstance, such as great provocation, which is unlikely to recur.

(7) Whether the manner in which the crime was carried out demonstrated criminal sophistication or professionalism on the part of the defendant.

(8) Whether the defendant took advantage of a position of trust or confidence to commit the crime.

(d) Facts relating to the defendant, including:

(1) Prior record of criminal conduct, including the recency and frequency of prior crimes, age at which first convicted as an adult or adjudicated to have committed a crime as a juvenile, age at which first confined for prior crimes, and whether the record indicates a pattern of regular or increasingly serious criminal conduct.

(2) Prior performance on probation or parole and present probation or parole status.

(3) Willingness and ability to comply with the terms of probation.

(4) Age, education, health, mental faculties, and family background and ties.

(5) Employment history, military service history, and financial condition.

(6) Danger of addiction to or abuse of alcohol, narcotics, dangerous drugs, or other mood or consciousness-altering substances.

(7) The likely effect of imprisonment on the defendant and his dependents.

(8) The possible effects on the defendant's life of a felony record.

(9) Whether the defendant is remorseful.

(10) Whether a financially able defendant refuses to make restitution to the victim.

18 U.S.C.A.

§ 3563.   Conditions of Probation

(a) Mandatory Conditions.—The court shall provide, as an explicit condition of a sentence of probation—

(1) for a felony, a misdemeanor, or an infraction, that the defendant not commit another Federal, State, or local crime during the term of probation;

(2) for a felony, that the defendant also abide by at least one condition set forth in subsection (b)(2), (b)(3), or (b)(13), unless the court finds on the record that extraordinary circumstances exist that would make such a condition plainly unreasonable, in which event the court shall impose one or more of the other conditions set forth under subsection (b); and

(3) for a felony, a misdemeanor, or an infraction, that the defendant not possess illegal controlled substances.

If the court has imposed and ordered execution of a fine and placed the defendant on probation, payment of the fine or adherence to the court-established installment schedule shall be a condition of the probation.

(b) Discretionary Conditions.—The court may provide, as further conditions of a sentence of probation, to the extent that such conditions are reasonably related to the factors set forth in section 3553(a)(1) and (a)(2) and to the extent that such conditions involve only such deprivations of liberty or property as are reasonably necessary for the purposes indicated in section 3553(a)(2), that the defendant—

(1) support his dependents and meet other family responsibilities;

(2) pay a fine . . . ;

(3) make restitution to a victim of the offense . . . ;

(4) give [notice and explanation] to the victims of [fraud] . . . ;

(5) work conscientiously at suitable employment or pursue conscientiously a course of study or vocational training that will equip him for suitable employment;

(6) refrain, in the case of an individual, from engaging in a specified occupation, business, or profession bearing a reasonably direct relationship to the conduct constituting the offense, or engage in such a specified occupation, business, or profession only to a stated degree or under stated circumstances;

(7) refrain from frequenting specified kinds of places or from associating unnecessarily with specified persons;

(8) refrain from excessive use of alcohol, or any use of a narcotic drug or other controlled substance, as defined in section 102 of the Controlled Substances Act (21 U.S.C. 802), without a prescription by a licensed medical practitioner;

(9) refrain from possessing a firearm, destructive device, or other dangerous weapon;

(10) undergo available medical, psychiatric, or psychological treatment, including treatment for drug or alcohol dependency, as specified by the court, and remain in a specified institution if required for that purpose;

(11) remain in the custody of the Bureau of Prisons during nights, weekends, or other intervals of time, totaling no more than the lesser of one year or the term of imprisonment authorized for the offense in section 3581(b), during the first year of the term of probation;

(12) reside at, or participate in the program of, a community corrections facility . . . for all or part of the term of probation;

(13) work in community service as directed by the court;

(14) reside in a specified place or area, or refrain from residing in a specified place or area;

(15) remain within the jurisdiction of the court, unless granted permission to leave by the court or a probation officer;

(16) report to a probation officer as directed by the court or the probation officer;

(17) permit a probation officer to visit him at his home or elsewhere as specified by the court;

(18) answer inquiries by a probation officer and notify the probation officer promptly of any change in address or employment;

(19) notify the probation officer promptly if arrested or questioned by a law enforcement officer;

(20) remain at his place of residence during nonworking hours and, if the court finds it appropriate, that compliance with this condition be monitored by telephonic or electronic signaling devices, except that a condition under this paragraph may be imposed only as an alternative to incarceration; or

(21) satisfy such other conditions as the court may impose.

(c) Modifications of Conditions.—The court may modify, reduce, or enlarge the conditions of a sentence of probation at any time ...

(d) Written Statement of Conditions.—The court shall direct that the probation officer provide the defendant with a written statement that sets forth all the conditions to which the sentence is subject, and that is sufficiently clear and specific to serve as a guide for the defendant's conduct and for such supervision as is required.

NOTES

1. **Validity of probation conditions.** When a defendant is eligible for probation, judges have almost limitless discretion in setting probation conditions. People v. Lent, 15 Cal.3d 481, 541 P.2d 545, 124 Cal.Rptr. 905 (1975), set forth the traditional circumstances in which a probation condition will be found invalid:

> The Legislature has placed in trial judges a broad discretion in the sentencing process, including the determination as to whether probation is appropriate and, if so, the conditions thereof. A condition of probation will not be held invalid unless it "(1) has no relationship to the crime of which the offender was convicted, (2) relates to conduct which is not in itself criminal, and (3) requires or forbids conduct which is not reasonably related to future criminality...." (People v. Dominguez (1967) 256 Cal.App.2d 623, 627, 64 Cal.Rptr. 290, 293.) Conversely, a condition of probation which requires or forbids conduct which is not itself criminal is valid if, that conduct is reasonably related to the crime of which the defendant was convicted or to future criminality.

15 Cal.3d at 486, 541 P.2d at 548, 124 Cal.Rptr. at 908.

2. **Relationship of condition to crime.** In People v. Higgins, 22 Mich.App. 479, 177 N.W.2d 716 (1970), the defendant pleaded guilty to burglary. He was placed on probation. In addition to the usual conditions of probation, the court imposed a special condition stating: "No varsity or professional basketball during probation unless permitted by the Court." A state statute authorized the trial court to impose "such other lawful conditions of probation ... as the circumstances of the

case may require or warrant, or as in its judgment may be meet and proper." The defendant was a college basketball player "of no small ability" and was in school on an athletic scholarship which he would lose if he were not permitted to play. Although seven months after defendant was placed on probation the trial judge permitted him to play varsity ball, the appellate court held the special condition was invalid:

> The trial judge stated no reason for the restriction, nor have the people explained how this restriction might be related to the defendant's rehabilitation. On the other hand, the defendant has persuasively shown that the restriction on playing basketball is more likely to impede than to promote his rehabilitation. As no rational reason has been suggested in justification and as it appears that the restriction is more likely to impede rehabilitation than promote it, we conclude that it is not a 'lawful provision' within the meaning of the statute.

22 Mich.App. at 482, 177 N.W.2d at 718. The dissenting judge commented: "It is not for an appellate court to . . . try to second guess the rehabilitation efforts of the trial judge. In fact, from what has been disclosed, the efforts of the trial judge have been successful. The defendant, to the knowledge of this writer, has in fact lived up to all the conditions of probation and may now realize that his former behavior will not lead to the type of career which he hopes to pursue at the end of his educational endeavors." 22 Mich.App. at 482, 177 N.W.2d at 719.

3. **Searches of probationers.** "Searches" of the property of convicted persons who have been placed on probation were held subject to significantly relaxed Fourth Amendment standards in Griffin v. Wisconsin, 483 U.S. 868, 107 S.Ct. 3164, 97 L.Ed.2d 709 (1987). Probation officials received "information" from a police detective that "there were or might be" guns in Griffin's apartment. A Wisconsin administrative regulation permits a probation officer to search a probationer's home without a search warrant if there are "reasonable grounds" to believe that contraband is in the home and a probation department supervisor approves the search. Pursuant to this regulation, Griffin's apartment was searched and a handgun found. The demands of a state's probation system, Justice Scalia reasoned for the 5 person majority, include effective supervision. "The search of Griffin's home satisfied the demands of the Fourth Amendment because it was carried out pursuant to a regulation that itself satisfies the Fourth Amendment's reasonableness requirement . . . [This] is a 'special need' of the State permitting a degree of impingement upon privacy that would not be constitutional if applied to the public at large." 483 U.S. at 873–75, 107 S.Ct. at 3168–69, 97 L.Ed.2d at 718. See Chapter 5.

In a much earlier case, an otherwise illegal search was held to be permissible where the person searched was a probationer subject to the following conditions: "submit his person, place of residence, vehicle, to search and seizure at any time of the day or night, with or without a search warrant, whenever requested to do so by the Probation Officer or any law enforcement officer." People v. Mason, 5 Cal.3d 759, 97 Cal.Rptr. 302, 488 P.2d 630 (1971), *cert. denied* 405 U.S. 1016, 92 S.Ct. 1289, 31 L.Ed.2d 478 (1972).

4. **Jail as a probation condition.** Although a jail term may be the court's complete sentence, jail time is also frequently ordered as a condition of misdemeanor or felony probation. A probationary period of incarceration and non-incarceration is sometimes referred to as a split sentence.

5. **Restitution.** Payment of restitution is a very common condition of probation. (See also the section on restitution infra.) There is no doubt that the willingness and ability of the defendant to make restitution payments is a factor weighing heavily in his favor in being placed on probation in the first place. To the

extent that financial ability to make restitution (or pay other court orders) influences the decision to grant or deny probation is the probation system in violation of equal protection of the laws? When practicable, some courts regularly require probationers to pay the costs of prosecution and probation supervision as a condition of probation and some courts require the probationer to pay a fee to his court-appointed counsel.

6. **Reimbursement for the costs of appointed counsel.** In Fuller v. Oregon, 417 U.S. 40, 94 S.Ct. 2116, 40 L.Ed.2d 642 (1974), the Supreme Court held that a state may impose, as a condition of probation or as part of the sentence of a convicted person, the repayment of the cost of state-appointed defense counsel. Such a condition is permissible only if the convicted person is or will be able to pay the costs. Repayment is "quite clearly directed only at those convicted defendants who are indigent at the time of the criminal proceedings against them, but who subsequently gain the ability to pay the expenses of legal representation." 417 U.S. at 45, 94 S.Ct. at 2121, 40 L.Ed.2d at 647.

7. **Support of dependents.** If the probationer has a history of failure to support his family, the court is very likely to require payment of family support as a condition of probation; the order often requires the probationer to make periodic payments to the probation department which in turn pays his dependents. The frequency with which financial orders are made conditions of probation and the very substantial role which collecting payments from probationers plays in the supervision process has led to criticism of the probation system as a glorified collection agency.

Black v. Romano

Supreme Court of the United States, 1985.
471 U.S. 606, 105 S.Ct. 2254, 85 L.Ed.2d 636.

■ JUSTICE O'CONNOR delivered the opinion of the Court.

In this case we consider whether the Due Process Clause of the Fourteenth Amendment generally requires a sentencing court to indicate that it has considered alternatives to incarceration before revoking probation. After a hearing, a state judge found that respondent had violated his probation conditions by committing a felony shortly after his original prison sentences were suspended. The judge revoked probation and ordered respondent to begin serving the previously imposed sentences. Nearly six years later, the District Court for the Eastern District of Missouri held that respondent had been denied due process because the record of the revocation hearing did not expressly indicate that the state judge had considered alternatives to imprisonment. The District Court granted a writ of habeas corpus and ordered respondent unconditionally released from custody. ...The Court of Appeals for the Eighth Circuit affirmed. ...We granted certiorari, ...and we now reverse.

I

On November 15, 1976, respondent Nicholas Romano pleaded guilty in the Circuit Court of Laclede County, State of Missouri, to two counts of transferring and selling a controlled substance. ...Romano's attorney urged the court to order probation. He argued that the offenses had not involved any victim, that Romano had no previous felony convictions, and that, except for running a stop sign, he had not violated the law after his arrest on the controlled substance charges. ... Both the Probation Department and the prosecutor opposed probation. ... The trial judge nonetheless concluded that probation was appropriate because the underlying charges did not involve an offense against the person. ...

The judge imposed concurrent sentences of twenty years on each count, suspended execution of the sentences, and placed Romano on probation for five years. ... The trial judge observed that Romano appeared to "have an uphill run on this probation," ... given the presentence report and the fact that his "past track record [was] not too good." ... The trial judge warned that if any of the conditions of probation were violated, he would revoke probation and order Romano imprisoned under the terms of the suspended sentence. ... Only two months after being placed on probation, Romano was arrested for leaving the scene of an automobile accident. ... he was charged with ... a felony punishable by up to five years' imprisonment. ...

On July 18, 1977, the judge who had sentenced Romano on the controlled substance charges held a probation revocation hearing. Several witnesses gave testimony. ... Romano offered no explanation of his involvement in the accident. Instead, his counsel challenged the credibility of the witnesses, argued that the evidence did not justify a finding that Romano had violated his probation conditions, and requested the court to continue the defendant's probation. ... Neither Romano nor his two lawyers otherwise proposed or requested alternatives to incarceration. The judge found that Romano had violated his probation conditions by leaving the scene of an accident, revoked probation, and ordered execution of the previously imposed sentence. ... Although the judge prepared a memorandum of his findings, ... he did not expressly indicate that he had considered alternatives to revoking probation. On October 12, 1977, the State filed an amended information reducing the charges arising from the automobile accident to the misdemeanor of reckless and careless driving. ... Romano was convicted on the reduced charges and ordered to pay a $100 fine. ...

Romano was incarcerated in state prison following the revocation of his probation. ...

II

The Due Process Clause of the Fourteenth Amendment imposes procedural and substantive limits on the revocation of the conditional liberty created by probation. ...

A

In identifying the procedural requirements of due process, we have observed that the decision to revoke probation typically involves two distinct components: (1) a retrospective factual question whether the probationer has violated a condition of probation; and (2) a discretionary determination by the sentencing authority whether violation of a condition warrants revocation of probation. ... Probationers have an obvious interest in retaining their conditional liberty, and the State also has an interest in assuring that revocation proceedings are based on accurate findings of fact and, where appropriate, the informed exercise of discretion. ... Our previous cases have sought to accommodate these interests while avoiding the imposition of rigid requirements that would threaten the informal nature of probation revocation proceedings or interfere with exercise of discretion by the sentencing authority.

. . . One point relevant to the present case is immediately evident from a review of the minimum procedures set forth in some detail in *Gagnon* and *Morrissey:* the specified procedures do not include an express statement by the factfinder that alternatives to incarceration were considered and rejected.

. . . Where such discretion [to order incarceration] exists, however, the parolee or probationer is entitled to an opportunity to show not only that he did not violate the conditions, but also that there was a justifiable excuse for any violation or that revocation is not the appropriate disposition. . . . This Court has not held that a defendant who is afforded these opportunities is also entitled to an explicit statement by the factfinder explaining why alternatives to incarceration were not selected.

We do not question the desirability of considering possible alternatives to imprisonment before probation is revoked. . . . Nonetheless, incarceration for violation of a probation condition is not constitutionally limited to circumstances where that sanction represents the only means of promoting the State's interest in punishment and deterrence. The decision to revoke probation is generally predictive and subjective in nature, *Gagnon,* 411 U.S., at 787, 93 S.Ct., at 1762, and the fairness guaranteed by due process does not require a reviewing court to second-guess the factfinder's discretionary decision as to the appropriate sanction. Accordingly, our precedents have sought to preserve the flexible, informal nature of the revocation hearing, which does not require the full panoply of procedural safeguards associated with a criminal trial. . . . We believe that a general requirement that the factfinder elaborate upon the reasons for a course not taken would unduly burden the revocation proceeding without significantly advancing the interests of the probationer. . . .

The procedures already afforded by *Gagnon* and *Morrissey* protect the defendant against revocation of probation in a constitutionally unfair manner. . . . Cf. Douglas v. Buder, 412 U.S. 430, 93 S.Ct. 2199, 37 L.Ed.2d 52 (1973) (per curiam) (revocation invalid under Due Process Clause where there was no evidentiary support for finding that probation conditions were violated). . . .

B

The Court's decision in Bearden v. Georgia [461 U.S. 660, 103 S.Ct. 2064, 76 L.Ed.2d 221 (1983)] recognized that in certain circumstances, fundamental fairness requires consideration of alternatives to incarceration prior to the revocation of probation. Where a fine or restitution is imposed as a condition of probation, and "the probationer has made all reasonable efforts to pay . . . yet cannot do so through no fault of his own, it is fundamentally unfair to revoke probation automatically without considering whether adequate alternative methods of punishing the defendant are available." 461 U.S., at 668–669, 103 S.Ct., at 2070, 2071 . . . *Bearden* acknowledged this Court's sensitivity to the treatment of indigents in our criminal justice system . . .

We need not decide today whether concerns for fundamental fairness would preclude the automatic revocation of probation in circumstances other than those involved in *Bearden*. . . . Under Missouri law, the determination to revoke probation was at the discretion of the trial judge, who was obligated to make independent findings and conclusions apart from any recommendation of the probation officer. . . . We must presume that the state judge followed Missouri law and, without expressly so declaring, recognized his discretionary power to either revoke or continue probation. . . .

III

. . . Romano does not dispute that he had a full opportunity to present mitigating factors to the sentencing judge and to propose alternatives to incarceration. The procedures required by the Due Process Clause of the Fourteenth Amendment were afforded in this case, even though the state judge did not explain on the record his consideration and rejection of alternatives to incarceration.

As a substantive ground for challenging the action of the state court, Romano argues that because the offense of leaving the scene of an accident was unrelated to his prior conviction for the controlled substance offenses, revocation of his probation was arbitrary and contrary to due process. This argument also lacks merit. The revocation of probation did not rest on a relatively innocuous violation of the terms and conditions of probation, but instead resulted from a finding that Romano had committed a felony involving injury to another person only two months after receiving his suspended sentence. The Fourteenth Amendment assuredly does not bar a State from revoking probation merely because the new offense is unrelated to the original offense. Nor is our conclusion in this regard affected by the fact that after the revocation proceeding, the charges arising from the automobile accident were reduced to reckless and careless driving.

. . . The judgment of the Court of Appeals is reversed.

It is so ordered.

■ JUSTICE POWELL took no part in the consideration or decision of this case.

■ JUSTICE MARSHALL, with whom JUSTICE BRENNAN joins, concurring. [Omitted.]

* * *

Petersilia, Turner, Kahan, and Peterson
GRANTING FELONS PROBATION V–XIII (1985)

Summary

* * *

Although the data used in our study are limited to California, we believe our findings have significance for other states as well. California's probation system is the largest in the nation, was once regarded as the most innovative, and has suffered the most severe budget cuts. Consequently, its experiences should prove instructive to other states.

* * *

Major Findings and Conclusions

In our opinion, felons granted probation present a serious threat to public safety. During the 40–month follow-up period of our study, 65 percent of the probationers in our subsample were rearrested, 51 percent were reconvicted, 18 percent were reconvicted of serious violent crimes, and 34 percent were reincarcerated. Moreover, 75 percent of the official charges filed against our subsample involved burglary/theft, robbery, and other violent crimes—the crimes most threatening to public safety.

The performance of felony probationers raises questions about the sentencing criteria the courts use in the prison/probation decision. There is a high correlation between sentencing to prison and offenders' "basic factors" (i.e., having two or more conviction counts, having two or more prior convictions, being on parole or probation at the time of arrest, being drug addicts, being armed, using a weapon, or seriously injuring the victim). For all offenses except assault, offenders having three or more of these characteristics had an 80 percent probability of going to prison in California, regardless of the type of crime of which they were currently convicted. The factors identified by our statistical models as significant in the prison/probation decision are quite consistent with those that the California Penal Code (Sec. 1203) states should be weighed prior to granting probation in felony cases.

After controlling for these basic factors, we performed analyses to determine whether the manner in which the case was officially processed by the courts made a difference in the prison/probation decision. The analyses revealed that having a private attorney could reduce a defendant's chances of imprisonment for all six offenses. For drugs and forgery cases, whether the defendant was represented by a public or court-appointed attorney was not significant. For all six of the crimes we considered, obtaining pretrial release lessened the probability of going to prison, whereas going to trial (except for forgery) increased that probability. ...

...These data suggest that many offenders who are granted felony probation are indistinguishable in terms of their crimes or criminal record from those who are imprisoned.

...In our subsample, 78 percent of those who were granted probation when our models predicted imprisonment were eventually rearrested. The recidivism rate for felons for whom our model had predicted a probation sentence was considerably lower—55 percent.

These findings indicate that the factors specified by law as appropriate considerations in the prison/probation decision appear, in practice, to strongly influence that decision. Moreover, these indicators probably should be used more consistently in sentencing, since they are also related to probationer recidivism. However, our findings also suggest that, *given the information now routinely provided to the court,* the ability to predict which felons will succeed on probation probably cannot be vastly improved.

To determine which factors were associated with rearrests, reconvictions, and reconvictions for violent crime, we created a hierarchy of levels of information similar to the hierarchy the court uses in the prison/probation decision. Through regression analysis, we found that the following factors predicted recidivism: type of conviction crime (property offenders recidivated most often); number of prior juvenile and adult convictions (the greater the number, the greater the recidivism); income at arrest (some income was associated with lower recidivism); and whether the offender was living with spouse and/or children (if yes, recidivism was lower). After controlling for these factors, we found no effects for factors such as drug abuse, prior probation revocations, or education level.

But how accurately were we able to predict which offenders would recidivate and which would not? ...We predicted subsequent convictions with 64 percent accuracy, and violent crime convictions with 71 percent accuracy.

* * *

...Sixty-three percent of those recommended for probation in the PSI report were subsequently rearrested, as compared with 67 percent of those recommended for prison. ...[V]ery few adults convicted of felonies in Los Angeles and Alameda counties are good candidates for probation, as it is now administered.

We believe that the criminal justice system needs an alternative, intermediate form of punishment for those offenders who are too antisocial for the relative freedom that probation now offers, but not so seriously criminal as to require imprisonment. A sanction is needed that would impose intensive surveillance, coupled with substantial community service and restitution. It should be structured to satisfy public demands that the punishment fit the crime, to show criminals that crime really does not pay, and to control potential recidivists.

What might such a sentencing alternative look like, and how could the courts identify appropriate candidates? Several states have experimental programs in place which indicate that an intensive surveillance program (ISP) should have intensive monitoring and supervision; real constraints on movement and action; employment; added requirements of community service, education, counseling, and therapy programs; and mechanisms for immediately punishing probationers who commit infractions. Early evaluations of programs in New York and Wisconsin offer hope that intensive surveillance may reduce the recidivism rates of high-risk offenders.

We believe that ISPs will be one of the most significant criminal justice experiments in the next decade. If ISPs prove successful, they will restore probation's credibility and reduce imprisonment rates without increasing crime. Most important, they may offer the prospect of rehabilitating some of the offenders who participate.

* * *

2. FINES

Fines, of course, serve to impose upon an offender a financial penalty payable to the government. When does a fine serve legitimate sentencing purposes? What considerations might militate against the imposition of a fine? What limits exist—or should exist—upon imposition or enforcement of a fine? These issues are addressed in the present subsection.

AMERICAN LAW INSTITUTE, MODEL PENAL CODE AND COMMENTARIES (Official Draft and Revised Comments) 1985*

Section 7.02 Criteria for Imposing Fines.

(1) The Court shall not sentence a defendant only to pay a fine, when any other disposition is authorized by law, unless having regard to the nature and circumstances of the crime and to the history and character of the defendant, it is of the opinion that the fine alone suffices for protection of the public.

(2) The Court shall not sentence a defendant to pay a fine in addition to a sentence of imprisonment or probation unless:

(a) the defendant has derived a pecuniary gain from the crime; or

(b) the Court is of opinion that a fine is specially adapted to deterrence of the crime involved or to the correction of the offender.

(3) The Court shall not sentence a defendant to pay a fine unless:

(a) the defendant is or will be able to pay the fine; and

(b) the fine will not prevent the defendant from making restitution or reparation to the victim of the crime.

(4) In determining the amount and method of payment of a fine, the Court shall take into account the financial resources of the defendant and the nature of the burden that its payment will impose.

18 U.S.C.A.

§ 3572. Imposition of a sentence of fine and related matters

(a) **Factors to be considered.**—In determining whether to impose a fine, and the amount, time for payment, and method of payment of fine, the court shall consider, in addition to the factors set forth in section 3553(a)—

(1) the defendant's income, earning capacity, and financial resources;

(2) the burden that the fine will impose upon the defendant, any person who is financially dependent on the defendant, or any other person (including a government) that would be responsible for the welfare of any person financially dependent on the defendant, relative to the burden that alternative punishments would impose;

(3) any pecuniary loss inflicted upon others as a result of the offense;

(4) whether restitution is ordered or made and the amount of such restitution;

(5) the need to deprive the defendant of illegally obtained gains from the offense;

(6) the expected costs to the government of any imprisonment, supervised release, or probation component of the sentence;

(7) whether the defendant can pass on to consumers or other persons the expense of the fine; and

(8) if the defendant is an organization, the size of the organization and any measure taken by the organization to discipline any officer, director, employee, or agent of the organization responsible for the offense and to prevent a recurrence of such an offense.

(b) **Fine not to impair ability to make restitution.**—If, as a result of a conviction, the defendant has the obligation to make restitution to a victim of the offense, the court shall impose a fine or other monetary penalty only to the extent that such fine or penalty will not impair the ability of the defendant to make restitution.

NOTES

1. **Use of fines in Europe.** Harris and Dunbaugh, Premise for a Sensible Sentencing Debate: Giving Up Imprisonment, 7 Hofstra L.R. 417, 451-2 (1979):

Motivated by the strong belief that imprisonment should be used only as a last resort and then only in small increments, Dutch sentencing practices rely heavily on fines, even for serious offenses. In 1975, fines constituted 43.4% of all penalties imposed for serious offenses. An additional 20.7% of the penalties consisted of fines combined with suspended incarcerative sentences.

Use of money fines as a criminal penalty could be expanded considerably in the United States. Fines could be graded according to ability to pay; in addition, installment payments could be permitted and other nonincarcerative penalties instituted if payment is not made. The Swedish "day fine" system offers a model worth emulating. The theory underlying the day-fine system is that "a monetary penalty should be equally burdensome for both rich and poor." The amount of a fine is based on (1) the seriousness of the offense and (2) the offender's financial resources. Offense severity is ranked on a scale of "day fines" from 1 to 120. The offender's financial worth is reduced to a per diem income, generally formulated at one-tenth of one percent of annual income. For example, drunk driving might be assigned a value of 50 "day fines." An offender earning $20,000, would have a per diem figure of $20. Thus, the penalty set for this offender would be 50 multiplied by $20 or $1000. For an offender who earned $10,000 annually, the penalty would be half as much.

Although imprisonment for unpaid fines is possible in Sweden, strenuous efforts are made to avoid it. By considering ability to pay, allowing extensions of time and installment payments, and enforcing payment, the number of persons actually imprisoned for nonpayment is kept between 100 and 200 persons per year. Given that about 250,000 persons are punished with fines each year, nonincarcerative methods of enforcement clearly predominate.

2. **Imprisonment for failure to pay fines.** Under what circumstances may a state imprison an indigent criminal defendant for failure to pay a fine?

In Williams v. Illinois, 399 U.S. 235, 90 S.Ct. 2018, 26 L.Ed.2d 586 (1970), the defendant was given the maximum sentence for petty theft provided by state law: one year imprisonment and a $500 fine. The judgment directed that if the fine and court costs had not been paid by the time the year was up, defendant was to remain in jail to "work it off" at the rate of $5 per day. The result was to permit imprisonment of indigent defendants beyond the statutory maximum. Calling this practice impermissible discrimination based on ability to pay, the Court vacated the judgment on Equal Protection grounds.

In Tate v. Short, 401 U.S. 395, 91 S.Ct. 668, 28 L.Ed.2d 130 (1971), the petitioner was imprisoned because he was unable due to indigency to pay $425 in accumulated traffic fines. Under state law, the offenses of which Tate was convicted were punishable by fine only. The Court held that Tate's imprisonment was unconstitutional under Williams v. Illinois. Justice Brennan, writing in the Court's opinion of alternative methods of enforcing payment of fines, such as permitting payment in installments, concluded with this statement: "Nor is our decision to be understood as precluding imprisonment as an enforcement method when alternative means are unsuccessful despite the defendant's reasonable efforts to satisfy the fines by those means; the determination of the constitutionality of imprisonment in that circumstance must await the presentation of a concrete case." Id. at 400–01, 91 S.Ct. at 672, 28 L.Ed.2d at 134.

In Wood v. Georgia, 450 U.S. 261, 101 S.Ct. 1097, 67 L.Ed.2d 220 (1981), the Court was faced with the issue of whether *Tate* would govern a situation where the defendant's probation was revoked and jail ordered when monthly fine installments were not paid. However, the court vacated and remanded on other grounds.

As pointed out in *Romano,* supra, the court surveyed another ramification of the defendant's failure to pay a fine in Bearden v. Georgia, 461 U.S. 660, 103 S.Ct. 2064, 76 L.Ed.2d 221 (1983). There, the defendant was sentenced to probation on the condition that he pay a $500 fine. The defendant paid $200, but then was laid off his job and could not find other employment. Consequently the defendant did not pay the fine on time. The court held that the trial court had erred in automatically revoking probation because of failure to pay the fine. Before revocation for failure to pay a fine, a court must determine that the probationer has not made "sufficient bona fide efforts to pay or that adequate alternative forms of punishment [do] not exist." 461 U.S. at 662, 103 S.Ct. at 2067, 76 L.Ed.2d at 226.

3. RESTITUTION

Most criminal sanctions do little to address the plight of the victim of the crime. Restitution is an exception. When a court orders restitution, the defendant is ordered to give the victim either money, property, or services as reparation for personal or property damages caused by the crime. In the past, American courts made little use of restitution. Almost incidentally, restitution was sometimes directed as a condition of probation. But recent emphasis upon the rights of crime victims has resulted in increased attention being paid to restitution. This subsection illustrates how restitution functions as a sentence and some of the problems caused by the quasi-criminal nature of restitutionary damages.

18 U.S.C.A.

§ 3663. Order of restitution

(a)(1)(A) The court, when sentencing a defendant convicted of an offense . . . may order, in addition to or, in the case of a misdemeanor, in lieu of any other penalty authorized by law, that the defendant make restitution to any victim of such offense, or if the victim is deceased, to the victim's estate. The court may also order, if agreed to by the parties in a plea agreement, restitution to persons other than the victim of the offense.

(B)(i) The court, in determining whether to order restitution under this section, shall consider—

(I) the amount of the loss sustained by each victim as a result of the offense; and

(II) the financial resources of the defendant, the financial needs and earning ability of the defendant and the defendant's dependents, and such other factors as the court deems appropriate.

(ii) To the extent that the court determines that the complication and prolongation of the sentencing process resulting from the fashioning of an order of restitution under this section outweighs the need to provide restitution to any victims, the court may decline to make such an order.

(2) For the purposes of this section, the term "victim" means a person directly and proximately harmed as a result of the commission of an offense for which restitution may be ordered including, in the case of an offense that involves as an element a scheme, conspiracy, or pattern of criminal activity, any person directly harmed by the defendant's criminal conduct in the course of the scheme, conspiracy, or pattern. In the case of a victim who is under 18 years of age, incompetent, incapacitated, or deceased, the legal guardian of the victim or representative of the victim's estate, another family member, or

any other person appointed as suitable by the court, may assume the victim's rights under this section, but in no event shall the defendant be named as such representative or guardian.

(3) The court may also order restitution in any criminal case to the extent agreed to by the parties in a plea agreement.

(b) The order may require that such defendant—

(1) in the case of an offense resulting in damage to or loss or destruction of property of a victim of the offense—

(A) return the property to the owner of the property or someone designated by the owner; or

(B) if return of the property under subparagraph (A) is impossible, impractical, or inadequate, pay an amount equal to the greater of—

(i) the value of the property on the date of the damage, loss, or destruction, or

(ii) the value of the property on the date of sentencing, less the value (as of the date the property is returned) of any part of the property that is returned;

(2) in the case of an offense resulting in bodily injury to a victim including an offense under chapter 109A or chapter 110—

(A) pay an amount equal to the cost of necessary medical and related professional services and devices relating to physical, psychiatric, and psychological care, including nonmedical care and treatment rendered in accordance with a method of healing recognized by the law of the place of treatment;

(B) pay an amount equal to the cost of necessary physical and occupational therapy and rehabilitation; and

(C) reimburse the victim for income lost by such victim as a result of such offense;

(3) in the case of an offense resulting in bodily injury also results in the death of a victim, pay an amount equal to the cost of necessary funeral and related services;

(4) in any case, reimburse the victim for lost income and necessary child care, transportation, and other expenses related to participation in the investigation or prosecution of the offense or attendance at proceedings related to the offense; and

(5) in any case, if the victim (or if the victim is deceased, the victim's estate) consents, make restitution in services in lieu of money, or make restitution to a person or organization designated by the victim or the estate.

(c)(1) Notwithstanding any other provision of law (but subject to the provisions of subsections (a)(1)(B)(i)(II) and (ii)), when sentencing a defendant convicted of an offense described in section 401, 408(a), 409, 416, 420, or 422(a) of the Controlled Substances Act (§ 21 U.S.C. 841, § 848(a), § 849, § 856, § 861, § 863), in which there is no identifiable victim, the court may order that the defendant make restitution in accordance with this subsection.

(2)(A) An order of restitution under this subsection shall be based on the amount of public harm caused by the offense, as determined by the court in accordance with guidelines promulgated by the United States Sentencing Commission.

(B) In no case shall the amount of restitution ordered under this subsection exceed the amount of the fine ordered for the offense charged in the case.

(3) Restitution under this subsection shall be distributed as follows:

(A) 65 percent of the total amount of restitution shall be paid to the State entity designated to administer crime victim assistance in the State in which the crime occurred.

(B) 35 percent of the total amount of restitution shall be paid to the State entity designated to receive Federal substance abuse block grant funds.

(4) The court shall not make an award under this subsection if it appears likely that such award would interfere with a forfeiture under chapter 46 or chapter 96 of this title or under the Controlled Substances Act (21 U.S.C. 801 et seq.).

(5) Notwithstanding section 3612(c) or any other provision of law, a penalty assessment under section 3013 or a fine under subchapter C of

chapter 227 shall take precedence over an order of restitution under this subsection.

(6) Requests for community restitution under this subsection may be considered in all plea agreements negotiated by the United States.

(7)(A) The United States Sentencing Commission shall promulgate guidelines to assist courts in determining the amount of restitution that may be ordered under this subsection.

(B) No restitution shall be ordered under this subsection until such time as the Sentencing Commission promulgates guidelines pursuant to this paragraph.

(d) An order of restitution made pursuant to this section shall be issued and enforced in accordance with section 3664.

§ 3664. Procedure for issuance and enforcement of order of restitution

(a) For orders of restitution under this title, the court shall order the probation officer to obtain and include in its presentence report, or in a separate report, as the court may direct, information sufficient for the court to exercise its discretion in fashioning a restitution order. The report shall include, to the extent practicable, a complete accounting of the losses to each victim, any restitution owed pursuant to a plea agreement, and information relating to the economic circumstances of each defendant. If the number or identity of victims cannot be reasonably ascertained, or other circumstances exist that make this requirement clearly impracticable, the probation officer shall so inform the court.

(b) The court shall disclose to both the defendant and the attorney for the Government all portions of the presentence or other report pertaining to the matters described in subsection (a) of this section.

(c) The provisions of this chapter, chapter 227, and Rule 32(c) of the Federal Rules of Criminal Procedure shall be the only rules applicable to proceedings under this section.

(d)(1) Upon the request of the probation officer, but not later than 60 days prior to the date initially set for sentencing, the attorney for the Government, after consulting, to the extent practicable, with all identified victims, shall promptly provide the probation officer with a listing of the amounts subject to restitution.

(2) The probation officer shall, prior to submitting the presentence report under subsection (a), to the extent practicable—

(A) provide notice to all identified victims of—

(i) the offense or offenses of which the defendant was convicted;

(ii) the amounts subject to restitution submitted to the probation officer;

(iii) the opportunity of the victim to submit information to the probation officer concerning the amount of the victim's losses;

(iv) the scheduled date, time, and place of the sentencing hearing;

(v) the availability of a lien in favor of the victim pursuant to subsection (m)(1)(B); and

(vi) the opportunity of the victim to file with the probation officer a separate affidavit relating to the amount of the victim's losses subject to restitution; and

(B) provide the victim with an affidavit form to submit pursuant to subparagraph (A)(vi).

(3) Each defendant shall prepare and file with the probation officer an affidavit fully describing the financial resources of the defendant, including a complete listing of all assets owned or controlled by the defendant as of the date on which the defendant was arrested, the financial needs and earning ability of the defendant and the defendant's dependents, and such other information that the court requires relating to such other factors as the court deems appropriate.

(4) After reviewing the report of the probation officer, the court may require additional documentation or hear testimony. The privacy of any records filed, or testimony heard, pursuant to this section shall be maintained to the greatest extent possible, and such records may be filed or testimony heard in camera.

(5) If the victim's losses are not ascertainable by the date that is 10 days prior to sentencing, the attorney for the Government or the probation officer shall so inform the court, and the court shall set a date for the final determination of the victim's losses, not to exceed 90 days after sentencing. If the victim subsequently discovers further losses, the victim shall have 60 days after discovery of those losses in which to petition the court for an amended restitution order. Such order may be granted only upon a showing of good cause for the failure to include such losses in the initial claim for restitutionary relief.

(6) The court may refer any issue arising in connection with a proposed order of restitution to a magistrate judge or special master for proposed findings of fact and recommendations as to disposition, subject to a de novo determination of the issue by the court.

(e) Any dispute as to the proper amount or type of restitution shall be resolved by the court by the preponderance of the evidence. The burden of demonstrating the amount of the loss sustained by a victim as a result of the offense shall be on the attorney for the Government. The burden of demonstrating the financial resources of the defendant and the financial needs of the defendant's dependents, shall be on the defendant. The burden of demonstrating such other matters as the court deems appropriate shall be upon the party designated by the court as justice requires.

(f)(1)(A) In each order of restitution, the court shall order restitution to each victim in the full amount of each victim's losses as determined by the court and without consideration of the economic circumstances of the defendant.

(B) In no case shall the fact that a victim has received or is entitled to receive compensation with respect to a loss from insurance or any other source be considered in determining the amount of restitution.

(2) Upon determination of the amount of restitution owed to each victim, the court shall, pursuant to section 3572, specify in the restitution order the manner in which, and the schedule according to which, the restitution is to be paid, in consideration of—

(A) the financial resources and other assets of the defendant, including whether any of these assets are jointly controlled;

(B) projected earnings and other income of the defendant; and

(C) any financial obligations of the defendant; including obligations to dependents.

(3)(A) A restitution order may direct the defendant to make a single, lump-sum payment, partial payments at specified intervals, in-kind payments, or a combination of payments at specified intervals and in-kind payments.

(B) A restitution order may direct the defendant to make nominal periodic payments if the court finds from facts on the record that the economic circumstances of the defendant do not allow the payment of any amount of a restitution order, and do not allow for the payment of the full amount of a restitution order in the foreseeable future under any reasonable schedule of payments.

(4) An in-kind payment described in paragraph (3) may be in the form of—

(A) return of property;

(B) replacement of property; or

(C) if the victim agrees, services rendered to the victim or a person or organization other than the victim.

(g)(1) No victim shall be required to participate in any phase of a restitution order.

(2) A victim may at any time assign the victim's interest in restitution payments to the Crime Victims Fund in the Treasury without in any way impairing the obligation of the defendant to make such payments.

(h) If the court finds that more than 1 defendant has contributed to the loss of a victim, the court may make each defendant liable for payment of the full amount of restitution or may apportion liability among the defendants to reflect the level of contribution to the victim's loss and economic circumstances of each defendant.

(i) If the court finds that more than 1 victim has sustained a loss requiring restitution by a defendant, the court may provide for a different payment schedule for each victim based on the type and amount of each victim's loss and accounting for the economic circumstances of each victim. In any case in which the United States is a victim, the court shall ensure that all other victims receive full restitution before the United States receives any restitution.

(j)(1) If a victim has received compensation from insurance or any other source with respect to a loss, the court shall order that restitution be paid to the person who provided or is obligated to provide the compensation, but the restitution order shall provide that all restitution of victims required by the order be paid to the victims before any restitution is paid to such a provider of compensation.

(2) Any amount paid to a victim under an order of restitution shall be reduced by any amount later recovered as compensatory damages for the same loss by the victim in—

(A) any Federal civil proceeding; and

(B) any State civil proceeding, to the extent provided by the law of the State.

(k) A restitution order shall provide that the defendant shall notify the court and the Attorney General of any material change in the defendant's economic circumstances that might affect the defendant's ability to pay restitution. The court may also accept notification of a material change in the defendant's economic circumstances from the United States or from the victim. The Attorney General shall certify to the court that the victim or victims owed restitution by the defendant have been notified of the change in circumstances. Upon receipt of the notification, the court may, on its own motion, or the motion of any party, including the victim, adjust the payment schedule, or require immediate payment in full, as the interests of justice require.

(*l*) A conviction of a defendant for an offense involving the act giving rise to an order of restitution shall estop the defendant from denying the essential allegations of that offense in any subsequent Federal civil proceeding or State civil proceeding, to the extent consistent with State law, brought by the victim.

(m)(1)(A)(i) An order of restitution may be enforced by the United States in the manner provided for in subchapter C of chapter 227 and subchapter B of chapter 229 of this title; or

(ii) by all other available and reasonable means.

(B) At the request of a victim named in a restitution order, the clerk of the court shall issue an abstract of judgment certifying that a judgment has been entered in favor of such victim in the amount specified in the restitution order. Upon registering, recording, docketing, or indexing such abstract in accordance with the rules and requirements relating to judgments of the court of the State where the district court is located, the abstract of judgment shall be a lien on the property of the defendant located in such State in the same manner and to the same extent and under the same conditions as a judgment of a court of general jurisdiction in that State.

(2) An order of in-kind restitution in the form of services shall be enforced by the probation officer.

(n) If a person obligated to provide restitution, or pay a fine, receives substantial resources from any source, including inheritance, settlement, or other judgment, during a period of incarceration, such person shall be required to apply the value of such resources to any restitution or fine still owed.

* * *

Hughey v. United States

Supreme Court of the United States, 1990.
495 U.S. 411, 110 S.Ct. 1979, 109 L.Ed.2d 408.

■ JUSTICE MARSHALL delivered the opinion of the Court.

The restitution provisions of the Victim and Witness Protection Act of 1982 (VWPA), 18 U.S.C. §§ 3579, 3580 (1982 ed. and Supp. IV), authorize federal courts, when sentencing defendants convicted of certain offenses, to order, "in addition to or in lieu of any other penalty authorized by law, that the defendant make restitution to any victim of such offense." 18 U.S.C. § 3579(a)(1) (1982 ed., Supp. IV). We must decide whether these provisions allow a court to order a defendant who is charged with multiple offenses but who is convicted of only one offense to make restitution for losses related to the other alleged offenses. We hold that the language and structure of the Act make plain Congress' intent to authorize an award of restitution only for the loss caused by the specific conduct that is the basis of the offense of conviction.[12]

I

In 1986, petitioner Frasiel L. Hughey was indicted for three counts of theft by a United States Postal Service employee and three counts of use of unauthorized credit cards. Petitioner pleaded guilty to count four of the indictment in exchange for the Government's agreement to dismiss the remaining counts and to forgo prosecution "for any other offense arising in the Western District of Texas as part of the scheme alleged in the indictment." App. 7. Count four charged "[t]hat on or about October 18, 1985, ...[petitioner] did knowingly and with intent to defraud use an unauthorized [MBank Mastercard credit card] issued to Hershey Godfrey, ...and by such conduct did obtain things of value aggregating more than $1,000...." Id., at 5. During the plea proceeding and as part of the factual basis of petitioner's plea, the Government proffered evidence that petitioner had stolen not only Godfrey's card, but also at least fifteen other cards. Id., at 10. Petitioner's counsel informed the court at that time that petitioner's plea was confined to the allegations in count four and that petitioner did "not mak[e] admissions to anything other than the facts pertaining to count four." Id., at 11.

After the plea hearing but before sentencing, the Government notified petitioner that it would propose that he be ordered to pay restitution of $147,646.89. The Government calculated that figure by adding the losses of several financial institutions, including MBank, that resulted from petitioner's alleged theft and use of approximately 30 credit cards. Petitioner objected to the proposed restitution order on the ground that the proposed figure was unauthorized because it "exceed[ed] the losses of any victims of the offense of which the Defendant was convicted." Id., at 13. The Government then submitted a revised restitution figure of $90,431, the total of

---

12. The restitution provisions in effect at the time of petitioner's sentencing were recodified, effective November 1, 1987, pursuant to the Sentencing Reform Act of 1984, 98 Stat.1987. Thus, 18 U.S.C. § 3579 now appears as 18 U.S.C. § 3663, and 18 U.S.C. § 3580 appears as 18 U.S.C. § 3664. We will refer to the provisions as they were codified at the time of petitioner's sentencing in April 1987. See 18 U.S.C. §§ 3579–3580 (1982 ed.).

MBank's losses relating to petitioner's alleged theft and use of 21 cards from various MBank cardholders. Petitioner countered that the appropriate restitution figure should be $10,412, the losses MBank sustained as a result of all unauthorized uses of the Godfrey credit card identified in the count for which he was convicted.

The District Court ordered petitioner to make restitution to MBank in the amount of $90,431. Id., at 78. Petitioner moved to reduce and correct his sentence under Federal Rule of Criminal Procedure 35, arguing that the District Court had exceeded its authority in ordering restitution for offenses other than the offense of conviction. The District Court denied the motion. Id., at 82–85. The Court of Appeals for the Fifth Circuit affirmed, holding that "VWPA permits a court to require restitution beyond that amount involved in the offense of conviction when there is a significant connection between the crime of conviction and similar actions justifying restitution." 877 F.2d 1256, 1264 (1989).

The courts of appeals have reached varying conclusions regarding a court's ability under VWPA to require an offender to pay restitution for acts other than those underlying the offense of conviction. We granted certiorari to resolve this split in authority. 493 U.S. ___, 110 S.Ct. 716, 107 L.Ed.2d 736 (1990).

II

A

As in all cases involving statutory interpretation, we look first to the language of the statute itself. . . . Given that the ordinary meaning of "restitution" is restoring someone to a position he occupied before a particular event, see, e.g., Webster's Third New International Dictionary 1936 (1986); Black's Law Dictionary 1180 (5th ed. 1979), the repeated focus in § 3579 on the offense of which the defendant was convicted suggests strongly that restitution as authorized by the statute is intended to compensate victims only for losses caused by the conduct underlying the offense of conviction.

The Government argues, however, that § 3579 answers only the question of who may receive restitution and offers no guidance as to how much restitution a court may order the defendant to pay. In the Government's view, § 3579(a) indicates merely that to receive restitution, a victim must be a victim of the offense of conviction. Once such a victim is identified, the Government maintains, the amount of restitution is calculated in accordance with 18 U.S.C. § 3580(a) (1982 ed.), which provides:

> "The court, in determining whether to order restitution under section 3579 of this title and the amount of such restitution, shall consider the amount of the loss sustained by any victim as a result of the offense, the financial resources of the defendant, the financial needs and earning ability of the defendant and the defendant's dependents, and such other factors as the court deems appropriate."

Specifically, the Government contends that the catchall phrase of § 3580(a), which directs courts to consider "such other factors as the court deems appropriate," authorizes courts to include in their restitution calculus losses resulting from offenses other than the offense of conviction.

The Government's reading of §§ 3579 and 3580 is unconvincing. . . .

. . . The Government's argument ignores this Court's commitment to "giving effect to the meaning and placement of the words chosen by Congress." Adams Fruit Co. v. Barrett, 494 U.S. ___, ___, 110 S.Ct. 1384, 1388, 108 L.Ed.2d 585 (1990). . . .

. . . Indeed, had Congress intended to permit a victim to recover for losses stemming from all conduct attributable to the defendant, including conduct unrelated to the offense of conviction, Congress would likely have chosen language other than "the offense," which refers without question to the offense of conviction. . . .

The remaining considerations preceding the catchall phrase also are designed to limit, rather than to expand, the scope of any order of restitution. These factors—"the financial resources of the defendant" and "the financial needs and earning ability of the defendant's dependents"—provide grounds for awarding less than full restitution under the statute. Congress plainly did not intend that wealthy defendants pay more in "restitution" than otherwise warranted because they have significant financial resources, nor did it intend a defendant's dependents to be forced to bear the burden of a restitution obligation because they have great "earning ability." In light of the principle of *ejusdem generis*—that a general statutory term should be understood in light of the specific terms that surround it—the catchall phrase should not be read to introduce into the restitution calculus losses that would expand a defendant's liability beyond the offense of conviction. . . .

B

The Government endeavors to buttress its interpretation of the statute by invoking the expansive declaration of purpose accompanying VWPA, see, e.g., § 2(b)(2), note following 18 U.S.C. § 1512 (one purpose of the Act is "to ensure that the Federal Government does all that is possible within limits of available resources to assist victims . . . without infringing on the constitutional rights of the defendant"), and by referring to portions of the legislative history that reflect Congress' goal of ensuring "that Federal crime victims receive the fullest possible restitution from criminal wrongdoers," 128 Cong.Rec. 27391 (Oct. 1, 1982) (remarks of Rep. Rodino). The Government also emphasizes policy considerations that purportedly support court-ordered restitution for acts outside the offense of conviction. Without such authority, the Government insists, in many cases courts cannot compensate victims for the full losses they suffered as a result of a defendant's conduct. The potential for undercompensation is heightened by prosecutorial discretion in charging a defendant, the argument goes, because prosecutors often frame their indictments with a view to success at trial rather than to a victim's interest in full compensation. See, e.g., United States v. Hill, 798 F.2d 402, 405 (C.A.10 1986). Finally, the Government maintains that the extensive practice of plea bargaining would, as a practical matter, wholly undermine victims' ability to recover fully for their losses because prosecutors often drop charges of which a defendant may be guilty in exchange for a plea to one or more of the other charges. See, e.g., United States v. Berrios, 869 F.2d 25, 30 (C.A.2 1989).

These concerns are not insignificant ones, but neither are they unique to the issue of victim compensation. If a prosecutor chooses to charge fewer than the maximum possible number of crimes, the potential recovery of victims of crime is undoubtedly limited, but so too is the potential sentence that may be imposed on a defendant. And although a plea agreement does operate to limit the acts for which a court may order the defendant to pay restitution, it also ensures that restitution will be ordered as to the count or counts to which the defendant pleads guilty pursuant to the agreement. The essence of a plea agreement is that both the prosecution and the defense make concessions to avoid potential losses. Nothing in the statute suggests that Congress intended to exempt victims of crime from the effects of such a bargaining process.

C

...Even were the statutory language regarding the scope of a court's authority to order restitution ambiguous, longstanding principles of lenity, which demand resolution of ambiguities in criminal statutes in favor of the defendant, ...preclude our resolution of the ambiguity against petitioner on the basis of general declarations of policy in the statute and legislative history.

III

The plain language of VWPA makes clear that the District Court's restitution order in this case was unauthorized. Petitioner pleaded guilty only to the charge that he fraudulently used the credit card of Hershey Godfrey. Because the restitution order encompassed losses stemming from alleged fraudulent uses of cards issued to persons other than Godfrey, such portions of the order are invalid. Accordingly, the decision of the Court of Appeals is reversed and the case is remanded for further proceedings consistent with this opinion.

It is so ordered.

NOTES

1. **Civil or criminal sanction?** A sentence of restitution resembles an award of damages in a civil action. This has led to some confusion in the federal courts about whether restitution is a criminal or civil penalty. In United States v. Welden, 568 F.Supp. 516 (N.D.Ala.1983), the court found the federal restitution provisions unconstitutional. The Act, said the court, "turns a restitution order into a civil judgment", 568 F.Supp. at 534, because it provides for civil enforcement and collateral estoppel. The Act failed to provide the defendant with a civil jury to determine the amount of restitution, and thus violated the defendant's Seventh Amendment right to a jury in a suit at common law. The Act was also said to run afoul of equal protection and due process.

Welden was reversed on appeal in United States v. Satterfield, 743 F.2d 827 (11th Cir.1984). The Court of Appeals said that " ...Congress made clear in both the language of the statute and its accompanying legislative history that victim restitution would be imposed as a criminal, rather than civil, penalty."

743 F.2d at 836. Since the restitution or sentencing hearing is not a civil action at common law, there is no Seventh Amendment right to a jury. A similar conclusion was reached in United States v. Brown, 744 F.2d 905 (2d Cir.1984).

2. **Determining a restitution amount.** The amount of restitution is often determined by reference to the presentence report, which under Fed.R.Crim.P. 32(c)(2)(D) includes a victim impact statement. The presentence report draws on various sources, many of which constitute hearsay, to present a comprehensive background for sentencing. One court has ruled that the presentence report alone does not meet the government's burden of proof as to the extent of the victim's injuries. United States v. Watchman, 749 F.2d 616 (10th Cir.1984).

3. **Inability to pay restitution.** What happens if the defendant is unable to pay the restitution ordered? This question was treated briefly in dicta in *Satterfield,* supra. The court reasoned that, since restitution automatically becomes a condition of probation or parole, *Bearden,* supra, should apply. Therefore, before deciding to revoke probation or parole for failure to pay restitution, the court should consider " ...whether the defendant has made a bona fide effort to pay; and if he has done so and still cannot comply, whether alternative measures of punishment are available." 743 F.2d at 842. What is the remedy for failure to pay restitution when restitution is ordered independent of probation?

4. **Restitution orders when there are multiple defendants.** The nuances of restitution by multiple defendants under the federal provisions have not yet been fully explored. One case, United States v. Wyzynski, 581 F.Supp. 1550 (E.D.Penn. 1984), refused to reduce one defendant's restitutionary sentence to the same level as his co-defendant. The defendant claimed that he was less culpable than his co-defendant; he cooperated with the authorities while his co-defendant did not; and he was unemployed; yet he had been ordered to pay $25,000 restitution while his co-defendant was ordered to pay only $10,000. In refusing to reduce the restitution order, the court pointed out that the appropriate amount of restitution does not depend upon the relative culpabilities of the defendants, rather, the amount of restitution is calculated to make the victim whole.

4. INVOLUNTARY COMMITMENT OF "SEXUAL PREDATORS"

Kansas v. Hendricks
Supreme Court of the United States, 1997.
521 U.S. 346, 117 S.Ct. 2072, 138 L.Ed.2d 501.

■ JUSTICE THOMAS delivered the opinion of the Court.

In 1994, Kansas enacted the Sexually Violent Predator Act, which establishes procedures for the civil commitment of persons who, due to a "mental abnormality" or a "personality disorder," are likely to engage in "predatory acts of sexual violence." Kan. Stat. Ann. § 59–29a01 et seq. (1994). The State invoked the Act for the first time to commit Leroy Hendricks, an inmate who had a long history of sexually molesting children, and who was scheduled for release from prison shortly after the Act became law. Hendricks challenged his commitment on, inter alia, "substantive" due process, double jeopardy, and ex post facto grounds. The Kansas Supreme Court invalidated the Act, holding that its pre-commitment condition of a "mental abnormality" did not satisfy what the court perceived to be the "substantive" due process requirement that involuntary civil commitment must be predicated on a finding of "mental illness." In re

Hendricks, 259 Kan. 246, 261, 912 P.2d 129, 138 (1996). The State of Kansas petitioned for certiorari. Hendricks subsequently filed a cross-petition in which he reasserted his federal double jeopardy and ex post facto claims. We granted certiorari on both the petition and the cross-petition, 518 U.S. 1004, 116 S.Ct. 2522, 135 L.Ed.2d 1047 (1996), and now reverse the judgment below.

I

A

The Kansas Legislature enacted the Sexually Violent Predator Act (Act) in 1994 to grapple with the problem of managing repeat sexual offenders. Although Kansas already had a statute addressing the involuntary commitment of those defined as "mentally ill," the legislature determined that existing civil commitment procedures were inadequate to confront the risks presented by "sexually violent predators." In the Act's preamble, the legislature explained:

> "[A] small but extremely dangerous group of sexually violent predators exist who do not have a mental disease or defect that renders them appropriate for involuntary treatment pursuant to the [general involuntary civil commitment statute]. . . . In contrast to persons appropriate for civil commitment under the [general involuntary civil commitment statute], sexually violent predators generally have anti-social personality features which are unamenable to existing mental illness treatment modalities and those features render them likely to engage in sexually violent behavior. The legislature further finds that sexually violent predators' likelihood of engaging in repeat acts of predatory sexual violence is high. The existing involuntary commitment procedure . . . is inadequate to address the risk these sexually violent predators pose to society. The legislature further finds that the prognosis for rehabilitating sexually violent predators in a prison setting is poor, the treatment needs of this population are very long term and the treatment modalities for this population are very different than the traditional treatment modalities for people appropriate for commitment under the [general involuntary civil commitment statute]." Kan. Stat. Ann. § 59–29a01 (1994).

As a result, the Legislature found it necessary to establish "a civil commitment procedure for the long-term care and treatment of the sexually violent predator." Ibid. The Act defined a "sexually violent predator" as:

> "any person who has been convicted of or charged with a sexually violent offense and who suffers from a mental abnormality or personality disorder which makes the person likely to engage in the predatory acts of sexual violence."

§ 59–29a02(a).

A "mental abnormality" was defined, in turn, as a "congenital or acquired condition affecting the emotional or volitional capacity which predisposes the person to commit sexually violent offenses in a degree constituting such person a menace to the health and safety of others." § 59–29a02(b).

As originally structured, the Act's civil commitment procedures pertained to: (1) a presently confined person who, like Hendricks, "has been convicted of a sexually violent offense" and is scheduled for release; (2) a person who has been "charged with a sexually violent offense" but has been found incompetent to stand trial; (3) a person who has been found "not guilty by reason of insanity of a sexually violent offense"; and (4) a person found "not guilty" of a sexually violent offense because of a mental disease or defect. § 59–29a03(a), § 22–3221 (1995).

The initial version of the Act, as applied to a currently confined person such as Hendricks, was designed to initiate a specific series of procedures. The custodial agency was required to notify the local prosecutor 60 days before the anticipated release of a person who might have met the Act's criteria. § 59–29a03. The prosecutor was then obligated, within 45 days, to decide whether to file a petition in state court seeking the person's involuntary commitment. § 59–29a04. If such a petition were filed, the court was to determine whether "probable cause" existed to support a finding that the person was a "sexually violent predator" and thus eligible for civil commitment. Upon such a determination, transfer of the individual to a secure facility for professional evaluation would occur. § 59–29a05. After that evaluation, a trial would be held to determine beyond a reasonable doubt whether the individual was a sexually violent predator. If that determination were made, the person would then be transferred to the custody of the Secretary of Social and Rehabilitation Services (Secretary) for "control, care and treatment until such time as the person's mental abnormality or personality disorder has so changed that the person is safe to be at large." § 59–29a07(a).

In addition to placing the burden of proof upon the State, the Act afforded the individual a number of other procedural safeguards. In the case of an indigent person, the State was required to provide, at public expense, the assistance of counsel and an examination by mental health care professionals. § 59–29a06. The individual also received the right to present and cross-examine witnesses, and the opportunity to review documentary evidence presented by the State. § 59–29a07.

Once an individual was confined, the Act required that "[t]he involuntary detention or commitment . . . shall conform to constitutional requirements for care and treatment." § 59–29a09. Confined persons were afforded three different avenues of review: First, the committing court was obligated to conduct an annual review to determine whether continued detention was warranted. § 59–29a08. Second, the Secretary was permitted, at any time, to decide that the confined individual's condition had so changed that release was appropriate, and could then authorize the person to petition for release. § 59–29a10. Finally, even without the Secretary's permission, the confined person could at any time file a release petition. § 59–29a11. If the court found that the State could no longer satisfy its burden under the initial commitment standard, the individual would be freed from confinement.

B

In 1984, Hendricks was convicted of taking "indecent liberties" with two 13–year-old boys. After serving nearly 10 years of his sentence, he was slated for release to a halfway house. Shortly before his scheduled release, however, the State filed a petition in state court seeking Hendricks' civil confinement as a sexually violent predator. On August 19, 1994, Hendricks appeared before the court with counsel and moved to dismiss the petition on the grounds that the Act violated various federal constitutional provisions. Although the court reserved ruling on the Act's constitutionality, it concluded that there was probable cause to support a finding that Hendricks was a sexually violent predator, and therefore ordered that he be evaluated at the Larned State Security Hospital.

Hendricks subsequently requested a jury trial to determine whether he qualified as a sexually violent predator. During that trial, Hendricks' own testimony revealed a chilling history of repeated child sexual molestation and abuse, beginning in 1955 when he exposed his genitals to two young girls. At that time, he pleaded guilty to indecent exposure. Then, in 1957, he was convicted of lewdness involving a young girl and received a brief jail sentence. In 1960, he molested two young boys while he worked for a carnival. After serving two years in prison for that offense, he was paroled, only to be rearrested for molesting a 7–year-old girl. Attempts were made to treat him for his sexual deviance, and in 1965 he was considered "safe to be at large," and was discharged from a state psychiatric hospital. App. 139–144.

Shortly thereafter, however, Hendricks sexually assaulted another young boy and girl—he performed oral sex on the 8–year-old girl and fondled the 11–year-old boy. He was again imprisoned in 1967, but refused to participate in a sex offender treatment program, and thus remained incarcerated until his parole in 1972. Diagnosed as a pedophile, Hendricks entered into, but then abandoned, a treatment program. He testified that despite having received professional help for his pedophilia, he continued to harbor sexual desires for children. Indeed, soon after his 1972 parole, Hendricks began to abuse his own stepdaughter and stepson. He forced the children to engage in sexual activity with him over a period of approximately four years. Then, as noted above, Hendricks was convicted of "taking indecent liberties" with two adolescent boys after he attempted to fondle them. As a result of that conviction, he was once again imprisoned, and was serving that sentence when he reached his conditional release date in September 1994.

Hendricks admitted that he had repeatedly abused children whenever he was not confined. He explained that when he "get[s] stressed out," he "can't control the urge" to molest children. Id., 172. Although Hendricks recognized that his behavior harms children, and he hoped he would not sexually molest children again, he stated that the only sure way he could keep from sexually abusing children in the future was "to die." Id., at 190. Hendricks readily agreed with the state physician's diagnosis that he suffers from pedophilia and that he is not cured of the condition; indeed, he told the physician that "treatment is bull——." Id., at 153, 190.

The jury unanimously found beyond a reasonable doubt that Hendricks was a sexually violent predator. The trial court subsequently determined, as a matter of state law, that pedophilia qualifies as a "mental abnormality" as defined by the Act, and thus ordered Hendricks committed to the Secretary's custody.

Hendricks appealed, claiming, among other things, that application of the Act to him violated the Federal Constitution's Due Process, Double Jeopardy, and Ex Post Facto Clauses. The Kansas Supreme Court accepted Hendricks' due process claim. In re Hendricks, 259 Kan., at 261, 912 P.2d, at 138. The court declared that in order to commit a person involuntarily in a civil proceeding, a State is required by "substantive" due process to prove by clear and convincing evidence that the person is both (1) mentally ill, and (2) a danger to himself or to others. Id., at 259, 912 P.2d, at 137. The court then determined that the Act's definition of "mental abnormality" did not satisfy what it perceived to be this Court's "mental illness" requirement in the civil commitment context. As a result, the court held that "the Act violates Hendricks' substantive due process rights." Id., at 261, 912 P.2d, at 138.

The majority did not address Hendricks' ex post facto or double jeopardy claims. The dissent, however, considered each of Hendricks' constitutional arguments and rejected them. Id., at 264–294, 912 P.2d, at 140–156 (Larson, J., dissenting).

II

A

Kansas argues that the Act's definition of "mental abnormality" satisfies "substantive" due process requirements. We agree. Although freedom from physical restraint "has always been at the core of the liberty protected by the Due Process Clause from arbitrary governmental action," Foucha v. Louisiana, 504 U.S. 71, 80, 112 S.Ct. 1780, 1785, 118 L.Ed.2d 437 (1992), that liberty interest is not absolute. The Court has recognized that an individual's constitutionally protected interest in avoiding physical restraint may be overridden even in the civil context:

> "[T]he liberty secured by the Constitution of the United States to every person within its jurisdiction does not import an absolute right in each person to be, at all times and in all circumstances, wholly free from restraint. There are manifold restraints to which every person is necessarily subject for the common good. On any other basis organized society could not exist with safety to its members."

Jacobson v. Massachusetts, 197 U.S. 11, 26, 25 S.Ct. 358, 361, 49 L.Ed. 643 (1905).

Accordingly, States have in certain narrow circumstances provided for the forcible civil detainment of people who are unable to control their behavior and who thereby pose a danger to the public health and safety. See, e.g., 1788 N.Y. Laws, ch. 31 (Feb. 9, 1788) (permitting confinement of the "furiously mad"); see also A. Deutsch, The Mentally Ill in America (1949) (tracing history of civil commitment in the 18th and 19th centuries); G. Grob, Mental Institutions in America: Social Policy to 1875 (1973) (discussing colonial and early American civil commitment statutes). We have consistently upheld such involuntary commitment statutes provided the confinement takes place pursuant to proper procedures and evidentiary standards. See Foucha, supra, at 80, 112 S.Ct., at 1785–1786; Addington v. Texas, 441 U.S. 418, 426–427, 99 S.Ct. 1804, 1809–1810, 60 L.Ed.2d 323 (1979). It thus cannot be said that the involuntary civil confinement of a limited subclass of dangerous persons is contrary to our understanding of ordered liberty. Cf. id., at 426, 99 S.Ct., at 1809–1810.

The challenged Act unambiguously requires a finding of dangerousness either to one's self or to others as a prerequisite to involuntary confinement. Commitment proceedings can be initiated only when a person "has been convicted of or charged with a sexually violent offense," and "suffers from a mental abnormality or personality disorder which makes the person likely to engage in the predatory acts of sexual violence." Kan. Stat. Ann. § 59–29a02(a) (1994). The statute thus requires proof of more than a mere predisposition to violence; rather, it requires evidence of past sexually violent behavior and a present mental condition that creates a likelihood of such conduct in the future if the person is not incapacitated. As we have recognized, "[p]revious instances of violent behavior are an important indicator of future violent tendencies." Heller v. Doe, 509 U.S. 312, 323, 113 S.Ct. 2637, 2644, 125 L.Ed.2d 257 (1993); see also Schall v. Martin, 467 U.S. 253, 278, 104 S.Ct. 2403, 2417, 81 L.Ed.2d 207 (1984) (explaining that "from a legal point of view there is nothing inherently unattainable about a prediction of future criminal conduct").

A finding of dangerousness, standing alone, is ordinarily not a sufficient ground upon which to justify indefinite involuntary commitment. We have sustained civil commitment statutes when they have coupled proof of dangerousness with the proof of some additional factor, such as a "mental illness" or "mental abnormality." See, e.g., Heller, supra, 314–315, 113 S.Ct., at 2639–2640 (Kentucky statute permitting commitment of "mentally retarded" or "mentally ill" and dangerous individual); Allen v. Illinois, 478 U.S. 364, 366, 106 S.Ct. 2988, 2990–2991, 92 L.Ed.2d 296 (1986) (Illinois statute permitting commitment of "mentally ill" and dangerous individual); Minnesota ex rel. Pearson v. Probate Court of Ramsey Cty., 309 U.S. 270, 271–272, 60 S.Ct. 523, 524–525, 84 L.Ed. 744 (1940) (Minnesota statute permitting commitment of dangerous individual with "psychopathic personality"). These added statutory requirements serve to limit involuntary civil confinement to those who suffer from a volitional impairment rendering them dangerous beyond their control. The Kansas Act is plainly of a kind with these other civil commitment statutes: It requires a finding of future dangerousness, and then links that finding to the existence of a "mental abnormality" or "personality disorder" that makes it difficult, if not impossible, for the person to control his dangerous behavior. Kan. Stat. Ann. § 59–29a02(b) (1994). The precommitment requirement of a "mental abnormality" or "personality disorder" is consistent with the requirements of these other statutes that we have upheld in that it narrows the class of persons eligible for confinement to those who are unable to control their dangerousness.

Hendricks nonetheless argues that our earlier cases dictate a finding of "mental illness" as a prerequisite for civil commitment, citing Foucha, and Addington. He then asserts that a "mental abnormality" is not equivalent to a "mental illness" because it is a term coined by the Kansas Legislature, rather than by the psychiatric community. Contrary to Hendricks' assertion, the term "mental illness" is devoid of any talismanic significance. Not only do "psychiatrists disagree widely and frequently on what constitutes mental illness," Ake v. Oklahoma, 470 U.S. 68, 81, 105 S.Ct. 1087, 1095, 84 L.Ed.2d 53 (1985), but the Court itself has used a variety of expressions to describe the mental condition of those properly subject to civil confinement. See, e.g., Addington, 441 U.S., at 425–426, 99 S.Ct., at 1808–1810 (using the terms "emotionally disturbed" and "mentally ill"); Jackson, 406 U.S., at 732, 737, 92 S.Ct., at 1855, 1857–1858 (using the terms "incompetency" and "insanity"); cf. Foucha, 504 U.S., at 88, 112 S.Ct., at 1789–1790 (O'CONNOR, J., concurring in part and concurring in judgment) (acknowledging State's authority to commit a person when there is "some medical justification for doing so").

Indeed, we have never required State legislatures to adopt any particular nomenclature in drafting civil commitment statutes. Rather, we have traditionally left to legislators the task of defining terms of a medical nature that have legal significance. Cf. Jones v. United States, 463 U.S. 354, 365, n. 13, 103 S.Ct. 3043, 3050, n. 13, 77 L.Ed.2d 694 (1983). As a consequence, the States have, over the years, developed numerous specialized terms to define mental health concepts. Often, those definitions do not fit precisely with the definitions employed by the medical community. The legal definitions of "insanity" and "competency," for example, vary substantially from their psychiatric counterparts. See, e.g., Gerard, The Usefulness of the Medical Model to the Legal System, 39 Rutgers L.Rev. 377, 391–394 (1987) (discussing differing purposes of legal system and the medical profession in recognizing mental illness). Legal definitions, however, which must "take into account such issues as individual responsibility . . . and competency," need not mirror those advanced by the medical profession. American Psychiatric Association, Diagnostic and Statistical Manual of Mental Disorders xxiii, xxvii (4th ed. 1994).

To the extent that the civil commitment statutes we have considered set forth criteria relating to an individual's inability to control his dangerousness, the Kansas Act sets forth comparable criteria and Hendricks' condition doubtless satisfies those criteria. The mental health professionals who evaluated Hendricks diagnosed him as suffering from pedophilia, a condition the psychiatric profession itself classifies as a serious mental disorder. See, e.g., id., at 524–525, 527–528; 1 American Psychiatric Association, Treatments of Psychiatric Disorders, 617–633 (1989); Abel & Rouleau, Male Sex Offenders, in Handbook of Outpatient Treatment of Adults 271 (M. Thase, B. Edelstein, & M. Hersen, eds. 1990). Hendricks even conceded that, when he becomes "stressed out," he cannot "control the urge" to molest children. App. 172. This admitted lack of volitional control, coupled with a prediction of future dangerousness, adequately distinguishes Hendricks from other dangerous persons who are perhaps more properly dealt with exclusively through criminal proceedings. Hendricks' diagnosis as a pedophile, which qualifies as a "mental abnormality" under the Act, thus plainly suffices for due process purposes.

B

We granted Hendricks' cross-petition to determine whether the Act violates the Constitution's double jeopardy prohibition or its ban on ex post facto lawmaking. The thrust of Hendricks' argument is that the Act establishes criminal proceedings; hence confinement under it necessarily constitutes punishment. He contends that where, as here, newly enacted "punishment" is predicated upon past conduct for which he has already been convicted and forced to serve a prison sentence, the Constitution's Double Jeopardy and Ex Post Facto Clauses are violated. We are unpersuaded by Hendricks' argument that Kansas has established criminal proceedings.

The categorization of a particular proceeding as civil or criminal "is first of all a question of statutory construction." Allen, 478 U.S., at 368, 106 S.Ct., at 2992. We must initially ascertain whether the legislature meant the statute to establish "civil" proceedings. If so, we ordinarily defer to the legislature's stated intent. Here, Kansas' objective to create a civil proceeding is evidenced by its placement of the Sexually Violent Predator Act within the Kansas probate code, instead of the criminal code, as well as its description of the Act as creating a "civil commitment procedure." Kan. Stat. Ann., Article 29 (1994) ("Care and Treatment for Mentally Ill Persons"), § 59–29a01 (emphasis added). Nothing on the face of the statute suggests that the legislature sought to create anything other than a civil commitment scheme designed to protect the public from harm.

Although we recognize that a "civil label is not always dispositive," Allen, supra, at 369, 106 S.Ct., at 2992, we will reject the legislature's manifest intent only where a party challenging the statute provides "the clearest proof" that "the statutory scheme [is] so punitive either in purpose or effect as to negate [the State's] intention" to deem it "civil." United States v. Ward, 448 U.S. 242, 248–249, 100 S.Ct. 2636, 2641, 65 L.Ed.2d 742 (1980). In those limited circumstances, we will consider the statute to have established criminal proceedings for constitutional purposes. Hendricks, however, has failed to satisfy this heavy burden.

As a threshold matter, commitment under the Act does not implicate either of the two primary objectives of criminal punishment: retribution or deterrence. The Act's purpose is not retributive because it does not affix culpability for prior criminal conduct. Instead, such conduct is used solely for evidentiary purposes, either to demonstrate that a "mental abnormality" exists or to support a finding of future dangerousness. We have previously concluded that an Illinois statute was nonpunitive even though it was triggered by the commission of a sexual assault, explaining that evidence of the prior criminal conduct was "received not to punish past misdeeds, but primarily to show the accused's mental condition and to predict future behavior." Allen, supra, at 371, 106 S.Ct., at 2993. In addition, the Kansas Act does not make a criminal conviction a prerequisite for commitment—persons absolved of criminal responsibility may nonetheless be subject to confinement under the Act. See Kan. Stat. Ann. § 59–29a03(a) (1994). An absence of the necessary criminal responsibility suggests that the State is not seeking retribution for a past misdeed. Thus, the fact that the Act may be "tied to criminal activity" is "insufficient to render the statut[e] punitive." United States v. Ursery, 518 U.S. 267, 291, 116 S.Ct. 2135, 2149, 135 L.Ed.2d 549 (1996).

Moreover, unlike a criminal statute, no finding of scienter is required to commit an individual who is found to be a sexually violent predator; instead, the commitment determination is made based on a "mental abnormality" or "personality disorder" rather than on one's criminal intent. The existence of a scienter requirement is customarily an important element in distinguishing criminal from civil statutes. See Kennedy v. Mendoza–Martinez, 372 U.S. 144, 168, 83 S.Ct. 554, 567–568, 9 L.Ed.2d 644 (1963). The absence of such a requirement here is evidence that confinement under the statute is not intended to be retributive.

Nor can it be said that the legislature intended the Act to function as a deterrent. Those persons committed under the Act are, by definition, suffering from a "mental abnormality" or a "personality disorder" that prevents them from exercising adequate control over their behavior. Such persons are therefore unlikely to be deterred by the threat of confinement. And the conditions surrounding that confinement do not suggest a punitive purpose on the State's part. The State has represented that an individual confined under the Act is not subject to the more restrictive conditions placed on state prisoners, but instead experiences essentially the same conditions as any involuntarily committed patient in the state mental institution. App. 50–56, 59–60. Because none of the parties argues that people institutionalized under the Kansas general civil commitment statute are subject to punitive conditions, even though they may be involuntarily confined, it is difficult to conclude that persons confined under this Act are being "punished."

Although the civil commitment scheme at issue here does involve an affirmative restraint, "the mere fact that a person is detained does not inexorably lead to the conclusion that the government has imposed punishment." United States v. Salerno, 481 U.S. 739, 746, 107 S.Ct. 2095, 2101, 95 L.Ed.2d 697 (1987). The State may take measures to restrict the freedom of the dangerously mentally ill. This is a legitimate non-punitive governmental objective and has been historically so regarded. Cf. id., at 747, 107 S.Ct., at 2101–2102. The Court has, in fact, cited the confinement of "mentally unstable individuals who present a danger to the public" as one classic example of nonpunitive detention. Id., at 748–749, 107 S.Ct., at 2102–2103. If detention for the purpose of protecting the community from harm necessarily constituted punishment, then all involuntary civil commitments would have to be considered punishment. But we have never so held.

Hendricks focuses on his confinement's potentially indefinite duration as evidence of the State's punitive intent. That focus, however, is misplaced. Far from any punitive objective, the confinement's duration is instead linked to the stated purposes of the commitment, namely, to hold the person until his mental abnormality no longer causes him to be a threat to others. Cf. Jones, 463 U.S., at 368, 103 S.Ct., at 3051–3052 (noting with approval that "because it is impossible to predict how long it will take for any given individual to recover [from insanity]—or indeed whether he will ever recover—Congress has chosen ...to leave the length of commitment indeterminate, subject to periodic review of the patients's suitability for release"). If, at any time, the confined person is adjudged "safe to be at large," he is statutorily entitled to immediate release. Kan. Stat. Ann. § 59–29a07 (1994).

Furthermore, commitment under the Act is only potentially indefinite. The maximum amount of time an individual can be incapacitated pursuant to a single judicial proceeding is one year. § 59–29a08. If Kansas seeks to continue the detention beyond that year, a court must once again determine beyond a reasonable doubt that the detainee satisfies the same standards as required for the initial confinement. Ibid. This requirement again demonstrates that Kansas does not intend an individual committed pursuant to the Act to remain confined any longer than he suffers from a mental abnormality rendering him unable to control his dangerousness.

Hendricks next contends that the State's use of procedural safeguards traditionally found in criminal trials makes the proceedings here criminal rather than civil. In Allen, we confronted a similar argument. There, the petitioner "place[d] great reliance on the fact that proceedings under the Act are accompanied by procedural safeguards usually found in criminal trials" to argue that the proceedings were civil in name only. 478 U.S., at 371, 106 S.Ct., at 2993. We rejected that argument, however, explaining that the State's decision "to provide some of the safeguards applicable in criminal trials cannot itself turn these proceedings into criminal prosecutions." Id., at 372, 106 S.Ct., at 2993. The numerous procedural and evidentiary protections afforded here demonstrate that the Kansas Legislature has taken great care to confine only a narrow class of particularly dangerous individuals, and then only after meeting the strictest procedural standards. That Kansas chose to afford such procedural protections does not transform a civil commitment proceeding into a criminal prosecution.

Finally, Hendricks argues that the Act is necessarily punitive because it fails to offer any legitimate "treatment." Without such treatment, Hendricks asserts, confinement under the Act amounts to little more than disguised punishment. Hendricks' argument assumes that treatment for his condition is available, but that the State has failed (or refused) to provide it. The Kansas Supreme Court, however, apparently rejected this assumption, explaining:

> "It is clear that the overriding concern of the legislature is to continue the segregation of sexually violent offenders from the public. Treatment with the goal of reintegrating them into society is incidental, at best. The record reflects that treatment for sexually violent predators is all but nonexistent. The legislature concedes that sexually violent predators are not amenable to treatment under [the existing Kansas involuntary commitment statute]. If there is nothing to treat under [that statute], then there is no mental illness. In that light, the provisions of the Act for treatment appear somewhat disingenuous."

259 Kan., at 258, 912 P.2d, at 136.

It is possible to read this passage as a determination that Hendricks' condition was untreatable under the existing Kansas civil commitment statute, and thus the Act's sole purpose was incapacitation. Absent a treatable mental illness, the Kansas court concluded, Hendricks could not be detained against his will.

Accepting the Kansas court's apparent determination that treatment is not possible for this category of individuals does not obligate us to adopt its legal conclusions. We have already observed that, under the appropriate circumstances and when accompanied by proper procedures, incapacitation may be a legitimate end of the civil law. See Allen, supra, at 373, 106 S.Ct., at 2994; Salerno, 481 U.S., at 748–749, 107 S.Ct., at 2102–2103. Accordingly, the Kansas court's determination that the Act's "overriding concern" was the continued "segregation of sexually violent offenders" is consistent with our conclusion that the Act establishes civil proceedings, 259 Kan., at 258, 912 P.2d, at 136, especially when that concern is coupled with the State's ancillary goal of providing treatment to those offenders, if such is possible. While we have upheld state civil commitment statutes that aim both to incapacitate and to treat, see Allen, supra, we have never held that the Constitution prevents a State from civilly detaining those for whom no treatment is available, but who nevertheless pose a danger to others. A State could hardly be seen as furthering a "punitive" purpose by involuntarily confining persons afflicted with an untreatable, highly contagious disease. Accord Compagnie Francaise de Navigation a Vapeur v. Louisiana Bd. of Health, 186 U.S. 380, 22 S.Ct. 811, 46 L.Ed. 1209 (1902) (permitting involuntary quarantine of persons suffering from communicable diseases). Similarly, it would be of little value to require treatment as a precondition for civil confinement of the dangerously insane when no acceptable treatment existed. To conclude otherwise would obligate a State to release certain confined individuals who were both mentally ill and dangerous simply because they could not be successfully treated for their afflictions. Cf. Greenwood v. United States, 350 U.S. 366, 375, 76 S.Ct. 410, 415, 100 L.Ed. 412 (1956) ("The fact that at present there may be little likelihood of recovery does not defeat federal power to make this initial commitment of the petitioner"); O'Connor v. Donaldson, 422 U.S. 563, 584, 95 S.Ct. 2486, 2498, 45 L.Ed.2d 396 (1975) (Burger, C. J., concurring) ("[I]t remains a stubborn fact that there are many forms of mental illness which are not understood, some which are untreatable in the sense that no effective therapy has yet been discovered for them, and that rates of 'cure' are generally low").

Alternatively, the Kansas Supreme Court's opinion can be read to conclude that Hendricks' condition is treatable, but that treatment was not the State's "overriding concern," and that no treatment was being provided (at least at the time Hendricks was committed). 259 Kan., at 258, 912 P.2d, at 136. See also ibid. ("It is clear that the primary objective of the Act is to continue incarceration and not to provide treatment"). Even if we accept this determination that the provision of treatment was not the Kansas Legislature's "overriding" or "primary" purpose in passing the Act, this does not rule out the possibility that an ancillary purpose of the Act was to provide treatment, and it does not require us to conclude that the Act is punitive. Indeed, critical language in the Act itself demonstrates that the Secretary of Social and Rehabilitation Services, under whose custody sexually violent predators are committed, has an obligation to provide treatment to individuals like Hendricks. § 59–29a07(a) ("If the court or jury determines that the person is a sexually violent predator, the person shall be committed to the custody of the secretary of social and rehabilitation services for control, care and treatment until such time as the person's mental abnormality or personality disorder has so changed that the person is safe to be at large" (emphasis added)). Other of the Act's sections echo this obligation to provide treatment for committed persons. See, e.g., § 59–29a01 (establishing civil commitment procedure "for the long-term care and treatment of the sexually violent predator"); § 59–29a09 (requiring the confinement to "conform to constitutional requirements for care and treatment"). Thus, as in Allen, "the State has a statutory obligation to provide 'care and treatment for [persons adjudged sexually dangerous] designed to effect recovery,'" 478 U.S., at 369, 106 S.Ct., at 2992 (quoting Ill.Rev.Stat., ch. 38, ¶ 105–8 (1985)), and we may therefore conclude that "the State has . . . provided for the treatment of those it commits." 478 U.S., at 370, 106 S.Ct., at 2992.

Although the treatment program initially offered Hendricks may have seemed somewhat meager, it must be remembered that he was the first person committed under the Act. That the State did not have all of its treatment procedures in place is thus not surprising. What is significant, however, is that Hendricks was placed under the supervision of the Kansas Department of Health and Social and Rehabilitative Services, housed in a unit segregated from the general prison population and operated not by employees of the Department of Corrections, but by other trained individuals. And, before this Court, Kansas declared "[a]bsolutely" that persons committed under the Act are now receiving in the neighborhood of "31.5 hours of treatment per week." Tr. of Oral Arg. 14–15, 16.[13]

Where the State has "disavowed any punitive intent"; limited confinement to a small segment of particularly dangerous individuals; provided strict procedural safeguards; directed that confined persons be segregated from the general prison population and afforded the same status as others who have been civilly committed; recommended treatment if such is possible; and permitted immediate release upon a showing that the individual is no longer dangerous or mentally impaired, we cannot say that it acted with punitive intent. We therefore hold that the Act does not establish criminal proceedings and that involuntary confinement pursuant to the Act is not punitive. Our conclusion that the Act is nonpunitive thus removes an essential prerequisite for both Hendricks' double jeopardy and ex post facto claims.

1

The Double Jeopardy Clause provides: "[N]or shall any person be subject for the same offence to be twice put in jeopardy of life or limb." Although generally understood to preclude a second prosecution for the

---

13. Indeed, we have been informed that an August 28, 1995, hearing on Hendricks' petition for state habeas corpus relief, the trial court, over admittedly conflicting testimony, ruled that: "[T]he allegation that no treatment is being provided to any of the petitioners or other persons committed to the program designated as a sexual predator treatment program is not true. I find that they are receiving treatment." App. 453–454. Thus, to the extent that treatment is available for Hendricks' condition, the State now appears to be providing it. By furnishing such treatment, the Kansas Legislature has indicated that treatment, if possible, is at least an ancillary goal of the Act, which easily satisfies any test for determining that the Act is not punitive.

same offense, the Court has also interpreted this prohibition to prevent the State from "punishing twice, or attempting a second time to punish criminally, for the same offense." Witte v. United States, 515 U.S. 389, 396, 115 S.Ct. 2199, 2204, 132 L.Ed.2d 351 (1995) (emphasis and internal quotation marks omitted). Hendricks argues that, as applied to him, the Act violates double jeopardy principles because his confinement under the Act, imposed after a conviction and a term of incarceration, amounted to both a second prosecution and a second punishment for the same offense. We disagree.

Because we have determined that the Kansas Act is civil in nature, initiation of its commitment proceedings does not constitute a second prosecution. Cf. Jones v. United States, 463 U.S. 354, 103 S.Ct. 3043, 77 L.Ed.2d 694 (1983) (permitting involuntary civil commitment after verdict of not guilty by reason of insanity). Moreover, as commitment under the Act is not tantamount to "punishment," Hendricks' involuntary detention does not violate the Double Jeopardy Clause, even though that confinement may follow a prison term. Indeed, in Baxstrom v. Herold, 383 U.S. 107, 86 S.Ct. 760, 15 L.Ed.2d 620 (1966), we expressly recognized that civil commitment could follow the expiration of a prison term without offending double jeopardy principles. We reasoned that "there is no conceivable basis for distinguishing the commitment of a person who is nearing the end of a penal term from all other civil commitments." Id., at 111–112, 86 S.Ct., at 763. If an individual otherwise meets the requirements for involuntary civil commitment, the State is under no obligation to release that individual simply because the detention would follow a period of incarceration.

Hendricks also argues that even if the Act survives the "multiple punishments" test, it nevertheless fails the "same elements" test of Blockburger v. United States, 284 U.S. 299, 52 S.Ct. 180, 76 L.Ed. 306 (1932). Under Blockburger, "where the same act or transaction constitutes a violation of two distinct statutory provisions, the test to be applied to determine whether there are two offenses or only one, is whether each provision requires proof of a fact which the other does not." Id., at 304, 52 S.Ct., at 182. The Blockburger test, however, simply does not apply outside of the successive prosecution context. A proceeding under the Act does not define an "offense," the elements of which can be compared to the elements of an offense for which the person may previously have been convicted. Nor does the Act make the commission of a specified "offense" the basis for invoking the commitment proceedings. Instead, it uses a prior conviction (or previously charged conduct) for evidentiary purposes to determine whether a person suffers from a "mental abnormality" or "personality disorder" and also poses a threat to the public. Accordingly, we are unpersuaded by Hendricks' novel application of the Blockburger test and conclude that the Act does not violate the Double Jeopardy Clause.

2

Hendricks' ex post facto claim is similarly flawed. The Ex Post Facto Clause, which " 'forbids the application of any new punitive measure to a crime already consummated,' " has been interpreted to pertain exclusively to penal statutes. California Dept. of Corrections v. Morales, 514 U.S. 499,

505, 115 S.Ct. 1597, 1601, 131 L.Ed.2d 588 (1995) (quoting Lindsey v. Washington, 301 U.S. 397, 401, 57 S.Ct. 797, 799, 81 L.Ed. 1182 (1937)). As we have previously determined, the Act does not impose punishment; thus, its application does not raise ex post facto concerns. Moreover, the Act clearly does not have retroactive effect. Rather, the Act permits involuntary confinement based upon a determination that the person currently both suffers from a "mental abnormality" or "personality disorder" and is likely to pose a future danger to the public. To the extent that past behavior is taken into account, it is used, as noted above, solely for evidentiary purposes. Because the Act does not criminalize conduct legal before its enactment, nor deprive Hendricks of any defense that was available to him at the time of his crimes, the Act does not violate the Ex Post Facto Clause.

III

We hold that the Kansas Sexually Violent Predator Act comports with due process requirements and neither runs afoul of double jeopardy principles nor constitutes an exercise in impermissible ex post facto lawmaking. Accordingly, the judgment of the Kansas Supreme Court is reversed.

It is so ordered.

■ JUSTICE KENNEDY, concurring.

I join the opinion of the Court in full and add these additional comments.

Though other issues were argued to us, as the case has matured it turns on whether the Kansas statute is an ex post facto law. A law enacted after commission of the offense and which punishes the offense by extending the term of confinement is a textbook example of an ex post facto law. If the object or purpose of the Kansas law had been to provide treatment but the treatment provisions were adopted as a sham or mere pretext, there would have been an indication of the forbidden purpose to punish. The Court's opinion gives a full and complete explanation why an ex post facto challenge based on this contention cannot succeed in the case before us. All this, however, concerns Hendricks alone. My brief, further comment is to caution against dangers inherent when a civil confinement law is used in conjunction with the criminal process, whether or not the law is given retroactive application.

On the record before us, the Kansas civil statute conforms to our precedents. If, however, civil confinement were to become a mechanism for retribution or general deterrence, or if it were shown that mental abnormality is too imprecise a category to offer a solid basis for concluding that civil detention is justified, our precedents would not suffice to validate it.

■ JUSTICE BREYER, with whom JUSTICES STEVENS and SOUTER join, and with whom JUSTICE GINSBURG joins as to Parts II and III, dissenting.

* * *

II

Kansas' 1994 Act violates the Federal Constitution's prohibition of "any . . . ex post facto Law" if it "inflicts" upon Hendricks "a greater punishment" than did the law "annexed to" his "crime[s]" when he "committed" those crimes in 1984. Calder v. Bull, 3 Dall. 386, 390, 1 L.Ed. 648 (1798) (opinion of Chase, J.); U.S. Const., Art. I, § 10. The majority agrees that the Clause " 'forbids the application of any new punitive measure to a crime already consummated.' " California Dept. of Corrections v. Morales, 514 U.S. 499, 504, 115 S.Ct. 1597, 1601, 131 L.Ed.2d 588 (1995) (citation omitted; emphasis added). Ante, at ___. But it finds the Act is not "punitive." With respect to that basic question, I disagree with the majority.

* * *

III

To find that the confinement the Act imposes upon Hendricks is "punishment" is to find a violation of the Ex Post Facto Clause. Kansas does not deny that the 1994 Act changed the legal consequences that attached to Hendricks' earlier crimes, and in a way that significantly "disadvantage[d] the offender," Weaver v. Graham, 450 U.S. 24, 29, 101 S.Ct. 960, 964, 67 L.Ed.2d 17 (1981). See Brief for Respondent State of Kansas 37–39.

To find a violation of that Clause here, however, is not to hold that the Clause prevents Kansas, or other States, from enacting dangerous sexual offender statutes. A statute that operates prospectively, for example, does not offend the Ex Post Facto Clause. Weaver, 450 U.S., supra, at 29, 101 S.Ct., at 964–965. Neither does it offend the Ex Post Facto Clause for a State to sentence offenders to the fully authorized sentence, to seek consecutive, rather than concurrent, sentences, or to invoke recidivism statutes to lengthen imprisonment. Moreover, a statute that operates retroactively, like Kansas' statute, nonetheless does not offend the Clause if the confinement that it imposes is not punishment—if, that is to say, the legislature does not simply add a later criminal punishment to an earlier one. Ibid.

The statutory provisions before us do amount to punishment primarily because, as I have said, the legislature did not tailor the statute to fit the nonpunitive civil aim of treatment, which it concedes exists in Hendricks' case. The Clause in these circumstances does not stand as an obstacle to achieving important protections for the public's safety; rather it provides an assurance that, where so significant a restriction of an individual's basic freedoms is at issue, a State cannot cut corners. Rather, the legislature must hew to the Constitution's liberty-protecting line. See The Federalist, No. 78, p. 466 (C. Rossiter ed. 1961) (A. Hamilton).

I therefore would affirm the judgment below.

5. ENHANCED PUNISHMENT UNDER RECIDIVIST PROVISIONS

Almendarez-Torres v. United States

Supreme Court of the United States, 1998.
523 U.S. 224, 118 S.Ct. 1219, 140 L.Ed.2d 350.

■ JUSTICE BREYER delivered the opinion of the Court.

Subsection (a) of 8 U.S.C. § 1326 defines a crime. It forbids an alien who once was deported to return to the United States without special permission, and it authorizes a prison term of up to, but no more than, two years. Subsection (b)(2) of the same section authorizes a prison term of up to, but no more than, 20 years for "any alien described" in subsection (a), if the initial "deportation was subsequent to a conviction for commission of an aggravated felony." § 1326(b)(2). The question before us is whether this latter provision defines a separate crime or simply authorizes an enhanced penalty. If the former, i.e., if it constitutes a separate crime, then the Government must write an indictment that mentions the additional element, namely a prior aggravated felony conviction. If the latter, i.e., if the provision simply authorizes an enhanced sentence when an offender also has an earlier conviction, then the indictment need not mention that fact, for the fact of an earlier conviction is not an element of the present crime.

We conclude that the subsection is a penalty provision, which simply authorizes a court to increase the sentence for a recidivist. It does not define a separate crime. Consequently, neither the statute nor the Constitution require the Government to charge the factor that it mentions, an earlier conviction, in the indictment.

I

In September 1995, a federal grand jury returned an indictment charging petitioner, Hugo Almendarez–Torres, with having been "found in the United States ...after being deported" without the "permission and consent of the Attorney General" in "violation of ...Section 1326." App. 3. In December 1995, Almendarez–Torres entered a plea of guilty. At a hearing, before the District Court accepted his plea, Almendarez–Torres admitted that he had been deported, that he had later unlawfully returned to the United States, and that the earlier deportation had taken place "pursuant to" three earlier "convictions" for aggravated felonies. Id., at 10–14.

In March 1996, the District Court held a sentencing hearing. Almendarez–Torres pointed out that an indictment must set forth all the elements of a crime. See Hamling v. United States, 418 U.S. 87, 117, 94 S.Ct. 2887, 2907–2908, 41 L.Ed.2d 590 (1974). He added that his indictment had not mentioned his earlier aggravated felony convictions. And he argued that, consequently, the court could not sentence him to more than two years imprisonment, the maximum authorized for an offender without an earlier conviction. The District Court rejected this argument. It found applicable a Sentencing Guideline range of 77 to 96 months, see United States Sentencing Commission, Guidelines Manual § 2L1.2; ch. 5, pt. A (sentencing table) (Nov. 1995) (USSG), and it imposed a sentence of 85 months' imprisonment. App. 17.

On appeal the Fifth Circuit also rejected petitioner's argument. 113 F.3d 515 (1996). Like seven other Circuits, it has held that subsection (b)(2) is a penalty provision which simply permits a sentencing judge to impose a higher sentence when the unlawfully returning alien also has a record of prior convictions....The Ninth Circuit, however, has reached the opposite conclusion. . . .We granted certiorari to resolve this difference among the Circuits.

II

An indictment must set forth each element of the crime that it charges. Hamling v. United States, supra, at 117, 94 S.Ct., at 2907–2908. But it need not set forth factors relevant only to the sentencing of an offender found guilty of the charged crime. Within limits, see McMillan v. Pennsylvania, 477 U.S. 79, 84–91, 106 S.Ct. 2411, 2415–2419, 91 L.Ed.2d 67 (1986), the question of which factors are which is normally a matter for Congress. See Staples v. United States, 511 U.S. 600, 604, 114 S.Ct. 1793, 1796, 128 L.Ed.2d 608 (1994) (definition of a criminal offense entrusted to the legislature, " 'particularly in the case of federal crimes, which are solely creatures of statute' ") (quoting Liparota v. United States, 471 U.S. 419, 424, 105 S.Ct. 2084, 2087, 85 L.Ed.2d 434 (1985)). We therefore look to the statute before us and ask what Congress intended. Did it intend the factor that the statute mentions, the prior aggravated felony conviction, to help define a separate crime? Or did it intend the presence of an earlier conviction as a sentencing factor, a factor that a sentencing court might use to increase punishment? In answering this question, we look to the statute's language, structure, subject matter, context, and history—factors that typically help courts determine a statute's objectives and thereby illuminate its text. See, e.g., United States v. Wells, 519 U.S. 482, __, 117 S.Ct. 921, __, 137 L.Ed.2d 107 (1997); Garrett v. United States, 471 U.S. 773, 779, 105 S.Ct. 2407, 2411–2412, 85 L.Ed.2d 764 (1985).

The directly relevant portions of the statute as it existed at the time of petitioner's conviction included subsection (a), which Congress had enacted in 1952, and subsection (b), which Congress added in 1988. See 8 U.S.C. § 1326 (1952 ed.) (as enacted June 27, 1952, § 276, 66 Stat. 229); 8 U.S.C. § 1326 (1988 ed.) (reflecting amendments made by § 7345(a), 102 Stat. 4471). We print those portions of text below:

"§ 1326. Reentry of deported alien; criminal penalties for reentry of certain deported aliens.

"(a) Subject to subsection (b) of this section, any alien who—

"(1) has been . . .deported . . . , and thereafter

"(2) enters . . . , or is at any time found in, the United States [without the Attorney General's consent or the legal equivalent], "shall be fined under title 18, or imprisoned not more than 2 years, or both.

"(b) Notwithstanding subsection (a) of this section, in the case of any alien described in such subsection—

"(1) whose deportation was subsequent to a conviction for commission of [certain misdemeanors], or a felony (other than an aggravated felony), such alien shall be fined under title 18, imprisoned not more than 10 years, or both; or

"(2) whose deportation was subsequent to a conviction for commission of an aggravated felony, such alien shall be fined under such title, imprisoned not more than 20 years, or both." 8 U.S.C. § 1326.

[In Sections A and B of Part II, the Court concluded that Congress intended its amendment to be a sentencing provision, not an element of the offense.]

III

Invoking several of the Court's precedents, petitioner claims that the Constitution requires Congress to treat recidivism as an element of the offense—irrespective of Congress' contrary intent. Moreover, petitioner says, that requirement carries with it three subsidiary requirements that the Constitution mandates in respect to ordinary, legislatively intended, elements of crimes. The indictment must state the "element." See, e.g., Hamling v. United States, 418 U.S., at 117, 94 S.Ct., at 2907–2908. The Government must prove that "element" to a jury. See, e.g., Duncan v. Louisiana, 391 U.S. 145, 149, 88 S.Ct. 1444, 1447, 20 L.Ed.2d 491 (1968). And the Government must prove the "element" beyond a reasonable doubt. See, e.g., Patterson v. New York, 432 U.S. 197, 210, 97 S.Ct. 2319, 2327, 53 L.Ed.2d 281 (1977). We cannot find sufficient support, however, in our precedents or elsewhere, for petitioner's claim.

This Court has explicitly held that the Constitution's Due Process Clause "protects the accused against conviction except upon proof beyond a reasonable doubt of every fact necessary to constitute the crime with which he is charged." In re Winship, 397 U.S. 358, 364, 90 S.Ct. 1068, 1073, 25 L.Ed.2d 368 (1970). But Winship, the case in which the Court set forth this proposition of constitutional law, does not decide this case. It said that the Constitution entitles juveniles, like adults, to the benefit of proof beyond a reasonable doubt in respect to the elements of the crime. It did not consider whether, or when, the Constitution requires the Government to treat a particular fact as an element, i.e., as a "fact necessary to constitute the crime," even where the crime-defining statute does not do so.

Mullaney v. Wilbur, 421 U.S. 684, 95 S.Ct. 1881, 44 L.Ed.2d 508 (1975), provides petitioner with stronger support. The Court there struck down a state homicide statute under which the State presumed that all homicides were committed with "malice," punishable by life imprisonment, unless the defendant proved that he had acted in the heat of passion. Id., at 688, 95 S.Ct., at 1884. The Court wrote that "if Winship were limited to those facts that constitute a crime as defined by state law, a State could undermine many of the interests that decision sought to protect" just by redefining "the elements that constitut[ed] different crimes, characterizing them as factors that bear solely on the extent of punishment." Id., at 698, 95 S.Ct., at 1889. It simultaneously held that the prosecution must establish "beyond a reasonable doubt" the nonexistence of "heat of passion"— the fact that, under the State's statutory scheme, distinguished a homicide punishable by a life sentence from a homicide punishable by a maximum of 20 years. Id., at 704, 95 S.Ct., at 1892. Read literally, this language, we concede, suggests that Congress cannot permit judges to increase a sentence in light of recidivism, or any other factor, not set forth in an indictment and proved to a jury beyond a reasonable doubt.

This Court's later case, Patterson v. New York, supra, however, makes absolutely clear that such a reading of Mullaney is wrong. The Court, in Patterson, pointed out that the State in Mullaney made the critical fact— the absence of "heat of passion"—not simply a potential sentencing factor, but also a critical part of the definition of "malice aforethought," which was itself in turn "part of" the statute's definition of "homicide," the crime in question. Patterson, 432 U.S., at 215–216, 97 S.Ct., at 2329–2330. (The Maine Supreme Court, in defining the crime, had said that "malice" was "presumed" unless "rebutted" by the defendant's showing of "heat of passion." Id., at 216, 97 S.Ct., at 2330.) The Court found this circumstance extremely important. It said that Mullaney had considered (and held "impermissible") the shifting of a burden of proof "with respect to a fact which the State deems so important that it must be either proved or presumed." 432 U.S., at 215, 97 S.Ct., at 2329 (emphasis added). And the Court then held that similar burden-shifting was permissible with respect to New York's homicide-related sentencing factor "extreme emotional disturbance." Id., at 205–206, 97 S.Ct., at 2324–2325. That factor was not a factor that the state statute had deemed "so important" in relation to the crime that it must be either "proved or presumed." Id., 205–206, 215, 97 S.Ct., at 2324–2325, 2329.

The upshot is that Mullaney's language, if read literally, suggests that the Constitution requires that most, if not all, sentencing factors be treated as elements. But Patterson suggests the exact opposite, namely that the Constitution requires scarcely any sentencing factors to be treated in that way. The cases, taken together, cannot significantly help the petitioner, for the statute here involves a sentencing factor—the prior commission of an aggravated felony—that is neither "presumed" to be present, nor need be "proved" to be present, in order to prove the commission of the relevant crime. See 8 U.S.C. § 1326(a) (defining offense elements). Indeed, as we have said, it involves one of the most frequently found factors that effects sentencing—recidivism.

Nor does Specht v. Patterson, 386 U.S. 605, 87 S.Ct. 1209, 18 L.Ed.2d 326 (1967), which petitioner cites, provide significant additional help, for Specht was decided before Patterson (indeed before Winship); it did not consider the kind of matter here at issue; and, as this Court later noted, the Colorado defendant in Specht was "confronted with 'a radically different situation' from the usual sentencing proceeding." McMillan v. Pennsylvania, 477 U.S., at 89, 106 S.Ct., at 2417. At most, petitioner might read all these cases, taken together, for the broad proposition that sometimes the Constitution does require (though sometimes it does not require) the State to treat a sentencing factor as an element. But we do not see how they can help petitioner more than that.

We turn then to the case upon which petitioner must primarily rely, McMillan v. Pennsylvania, supra. The Court there considered a Pennsylvania statute that set forth a sentencing factor—"visibly possessing a firearm"—the presence of which required the judge to impose a minimum prison term of five years. The Court held that the Constitution did not require the State to treat the factor as an element of the crime. In so holding, the Court said that the State's "link[ing] the 'severity of punishment' to 'the presence or absence of an identified fact' " did not automatically make of that fact an "element." 477 U.S., at 84, 106 S.Ct., at 2415 (quoting Patterson v. New York, supra, at 214, 97 S.Ct., at 2329). It said, citing Patterson, that "the state legislature's definition of the elements of the offense is usually dispositive." 477 U.S., at 85, 106 S.Ct., at 2415. It said that it would not "define precisely the constitutional limits" of a legislature's power to define the elements of an offense. Id., at 86, 106 S.Ct., at 2416. And it held that, whatever those limits might be, the State had not exceeded them. Ibid. Petitioner must therefore concede that "firearm possession" (in respect to a mandatory minimum sentence) does not violate those limits. And he must argue that, nonetheless, "recidivism" (in respect to an authorized maximum) does violate those limits.

In assessing petitioner's claim, we have examined McMillan to determine the various features of the case upon which the Court's conclusion arguably turned. The McMillan Court pointed out: (1) that the statute plainly "does not transgress the limits expressly set out in Patterson," id., at 86, 106 S.Ct., at 2416; (2) that the defendant (unlike Mullaney 's defendant) did not face " 'a differential in sentencing ranging from a nominal fine to a mandatory life sentence,' " 477 U.S., at 87, 106 S.Ct., at 2417 (quoting Mullaney, 421 U.S., at 700, 95 S.Ct., at 1890); (3) that the statute did not "alte[r] the maximum penalty for the crime" but "operates solely to limit the sentencing court's discretion in selecting a penalty within the range already available to it," 477 U.S., at 87–88, 106 S.Ct., at 2417; (4) that the statute did not "creat[e] a separate offense calling for a separate penalty," id., at 88, 106 S.Ct., at 2417; and (5) that the statute gave "no impression of having been tailored to permit the visible possession finding to be a tail which wags the dog of the substantive offense," but, to the contrary, "simply took one factor that has always been considered by sentencing courts to bear on punishment . . . and dictated the precise weight to be given that factor," id., at 88, 89–90, 106 S.Ct., at 2417, 2418.

This case resembles McMillan in respect to most of these factors. But it is different in respect to the third factor, for it does "alte[r] the maximum penalty for the crime," 477 U.S., at 87, 106 S.Ct., at 2417; and, it also creates a wider range of appropriate punishments than did the statute in McMillan. We nonetheless conclude that these differences do not change the constitutional outcome for several basic reasons.

First, the sentencing factor at issue here—recidivism—is a traditional, if not the most traditional, basis for a sentencing court's increasing an offender's sentence. See, e.g., Parke v. Raley, 506 U.S. 20, 26, 113 S.Ct. 517, 521–522, 121 L.Ed.2d 391 (1992) (Recidivism laws "have a long tradition in this country that dates back to colonial times" and currently are in effect in all 50 States); U.S. Dept. of Justice, Office of Justice Programs, Statutes Requiring the Use of Criminal History Record Information 17–41 (June 1991) (50–state survey); USSG §§ 4A1.1, 4A1.2 (Nov. 1997) (requiring sentencing court to consider defendant's prior record in every case). Consistent with this tradition, the Court said long ago that a State need not allege a defendant's prior conviction in the indictment or information which alleges the elements of an underlying crime, even though the conviction was "necessary to bring the case within the statute." Graham v. West

Virginia, 224 U.S. 616, 624, 32 S.Ct. 583, 585–86, 56 L.Ed. 917 (1912). That conclusion followed, the Court said, from "the distinct nature of the issue," and the fact that recidivism "does not relate to the commission of the offense, but goes to the punishment only, and therefore . . . may be subsequently decided." Id., at 629, 32 S.Ct., at 588 (emphasis added). The Court has not deviated from this view. See Oyler v. Boles, 368 U.S. 448, 452, 82 S.Ct. 501, 503–504, 7 L.Ed.2d 446 (1962) (due process does not require advance notice that trial for substantive offense will be followed by accusation that the defendant is an habitual offender); Parke, supra, at 27, 113 S.Ct., at 522 ("[A] charge under a recidivism statute does not state a separate offense, but goes to punishment only"). And, as we said before, infra, at 5–6, Congress, reflecting this tradition, has never, to our knowledge, made a defendant's recidivism an element of an offense where the conduct proscribed is otherwise unlawful. See United States v. Jackson, 824 F.2d 21, 25, and n. 6 (C.A.D.C.1987) (R. Ginsburg, J.) (referring to fact that few, if any, federal statutes make "prior criminal convictions . . . elements of another criminal offense to be proved before the jury"). Although these precedents do not foreclose petitioner's claim (because, for example, the state statute at issue in Graham and Oyler provided for a jury determination of disputed prior convictions), to hold that the Constitution requires that recidivism be deemed an "element" of petitioner's offense would mark an abrupt departure from a longstanding tradition of treating recidivism as "go[ing] to the punishment only." Graham, supra, at 629, 32 S.Ct., at 587–588.

Second, the major difference between this case and McMillan consists of the circumstance that the sentencing factor at issue here (the prior conviction) triggers an increase in the maximum permissive sentence, while the sentencing factor at issue in McMillan triggered a mandatory minimum sentence. Yet that difference—between a permissive maximum and a mandatory minimum—does not systematically, or normally, work to the disadvantage of a criminal defendant. To the contrary, a statutory minimum binds a sentencing judge; a statutory maximum does not. A mandatory minimum can, as Justice STEVENS dissenting in McMillan pointed out, "mandate a minimum sentence of imprisonment more than twice as severe as the maximum the trial judge would otherwise have imposed." McMillan, supra, at 95, 106 S.Ct., at 2421. It can eliminate a sentencing judge's discretion in its entirety. See, e.g., 18 U.S.C. § 2241(c) (authorizing maximum term of life imprisonment for sexual abuse of children; mandating life imprisonment for second offense). And it can produce unfairly disproportionate impacts on certain kinds of offenders. See United States Sentencing Commission, Mandatory Minimum Penalties in the Federal Criminal Justice System 26–34 (Aug. 1991) (discussing "tariff" and "cliff" effects of mandatory minimums). In sum, the risk of unfairness to a particular defendant is no less, and may well be greater, when a mandatory minimum sentence, rather than a permissive maximum sentence, is at issue.

Although McMillan pointed to a difference between mandatory minimums and higher authorized maximums, it neither, "rested its judgment" on that difference, nor "rejected" the above analysis, as the dissent contends, post, at 1236. Rather, McMillan said that the petitioners' argument in that case would have had "more *superficial* appeal" if the sentencing fact "exposed them to greater or additional punishment." 477 U.S., at 88, 106 S.Ct., at 2417 (emphasis added). For the reasons just given, and in light of the particular sentencing factor at issue in this case—recidivism—we should take McMillan's statement to mean no more that it said, and therefore not to make a determinative difference here.

Third, the statute's broad permissive sentencing range does not itself create significantly greater unfairness. Judges (and parole boards) have typically exercised their discretion within broad statutory ranges. See, e.g., supra, at 1224, 1226 (statutory examples); National Institute of Justice, Sentencing Reform in the United States (Aug. 1985) (survey of sentencing laws in the 50 States); L. Friedman, Crime and Punishment in American History 159–163 (1993) (history of indeterminate sentencing). And the Sentencing Guidelines have recently sought to channel that discretion using "sentencing factors" which no one here claims that the Constitution thereby makes "elements" of a crime.

Finally, the remaining McMillan factors support the conclusion that Congress has the constitutional power to treat the feature before us—prior conviction of an aggravated felony—as a sentencing factor for this particular offense (illegal entry after deportation). The relevant statutory provisions do not change a pre-existing definition of a well-established crime, nor is there any more reason here, than in McMillan, to think Congress intended to "evade" the Constitution, either by "presuming" guilt or "restructuring" the elements of an offense. Cf. McMillan, supra, at 86–87, 89–90, 106 S.Ct., at 2416–2417, 2417–2418.

For these reasons, we cannot find in McMillan (a case holding that the Constitution permits a legislature to require a longer sentence for gun possession) significant support for the proposition that the Constitution forbids a legislature to authorize a longer sentence for recidivism.

Petitioner makes two basic additional arguments in response. He points to what he calls a different "tradition"—that of courts having treated recidivism as an element of the related crime. See, e.g., Massey v. United States, 281 F. 293, 297–298 (C.A.8 1922); Singer v. United States, 278 F. 415, 420 (C.A.3 1922); People v. Sickles, 156 N.Y. 541, 51 N.E. 288, 289 (N.Y.1898); see also post, at 9–10 (citing authority). We do not find this claim convincing, however, for any such tradition is not uniform. See Spencer v. Texas, 385 U.S., at 566, 87 S.Ct., at 654–55 ("The method for determining prior convictions . . . varies between jurisdictions affording a jury trial on this issue . . . and those leaving that question to the court"); Note, Recidivist Procedures, 40 N.Y.U.L.Rev. 332, 347 (1965) (as of 1965, eight States' recidivism statutes provide for determination of prior convictions by judge, not jury). Nor does it appear modern. Compare State v. Thorne, 129 Wash.2d 736, 776–784, 921 P.2d 514, 533–538 (1996) (upholding state recidivism law against federal constitutional challenge) with State v. Furth, 5 Wash.2d 1, 11–19, 104 P.2d 925, 930–933 (1940). And it nowhere (to our knowledge) rested upon a federal constitutional guarantee. See, e.g., Massey v. United States, supra, at 297 (applying federal law, noting jury determination of prior offense applied "unless the statute designates a different mode of procedure").

Petitioner also argues, in essence, that this Court should simply adopt a rule that any significant increase in a statutory maximum sentence would trigger a Constitutional "elements" requirement. We have explained why we believe the Constitution, as interpreted in McMillan and earlier cases, does not impose that requirement. We add that such a rule would seem anomalous in light of existing case law that permits a judge, rather than a jury, to determine the existence of factors that can make a defendant eligible for the death penalty, a punishment far more severe than that faced by petitioner here. See Walton v. Arizona, 497 U.S. 639, 647, 110 S.Ct. 3047, 3053–3054, 111 L.Ed.2d 511 (1990) (rejecting capital defendant's argument that every finding of fact underlying death sentence must be made by a jury); Hildwin v. Florida, 490 U.S. 638, 640–641, 109 S.Ct. 2055, 2056–2057, 104 L.Ed.2d 728 (1989) (per curiam) (judge may impose death penalty based on his finding of aggravating factor because such factor is not element of offense to be determined by jury); Spaziano v. Florida, 468 U.S. 447, 465, 104 S.Ct. 3154, 3164–3165, 82 L.Ed.2d 340 (1984) (same). And we would also find it difficult to reconcile any such rule with our precedent holding that the sentencing-related circumstances of recidivism are not part of the definition of the offense for double jeopardy purposes. Graham, 224 U.S., at 623–624, 32 S.Ct., at 585–586.

For these reasons, we reject petitioner's constitutional claim that his recidivism must be treated as an element of his offense.

IV

We mention one final point. Petitioner makes no separate, subsidiary, standard of proof claims with respect to his sentencing, perhaps because he admitted his recidivism at the time he pleaded guilty and would therefore find it difficult to show that the standard of proof could have made a difference to his case. Accordingly, we express no view on whether some heightened standard of proof might apply to sentencing determinations which bear significantly on the severity of sentence. Cf. United States v. Watts, 519 U.S. 148, ___ and n. 2, 117 S.Ct. 633, 637–638 and n. 2, 136 L.Ed.2d 554 (1997) (per curiam) (acknowledging, but not resolving, "divergence of opinion among the Circuits" as to proper standard for determining the existence of "relevant conduct" that would lead to an increase in sentence).

The judgment of the Court of Appeals is

Affirmed.

■ JUSTICE SCALIA, with whom JUSTICE STEVENS, JUSTICE SOUTER, and JUSTICE GINSBURG join, dissenting.

Because Hugo Roman Almendarez–Torres illegally re-entered the United States after having been convicted of an aggravated felony, he was subject to a maximum possible sentence of 20 years imprisonment. See 8 U.S.C. § 1326(b)(2). Had he not been convicted of that felony, he would have been subject to a maximum of only two years. See 8 U.S.C. § 1326(a). The Court today holds that § 1326(b)(2) does not set forth a separate offense, and that conviction of a prior felony is merely a sentencing enhancement for the offense set forth in § 1326(a). This causes the Court to confront the difficult question whether the Constitution requires a fact which substantially increases the maximum permissible punishment for a crime to be treated as an element of that crime—to be charged in the indictment, and found beyond a reasonable doubt by a jury. Until the Court said so, it was far from obvious that the answer to this question was no; on the basis of our prior law, in fact, the answer was considerably doubtful.

In all our prior cases bearing upon the issue, however, we confronted a criminal statute or state-court criminal ruling that unambiguously relieved the prosecution of the burden of proving a critical fact to the jury beyond a reasonable doubt. In McMillan v. Pennsylvania, 477 U.S. 79, 106 S.Ct. 2411, 91 L.Ed.2d 67 (1986), the statute provided that " 'visibl[e] possess[ion][of] a firearm' " " 'shall not be an element of the crime[,]' " but shall be determined at sentencing by " '[t]he court . . . by a preponderance of the evidence,' " id., at 81, n. 1, 106 S.Ct., at 2413, n. 1 (quoting 42 Pa. Cons.Stat. § 9712 (1982)). In In re Winship, 397 U.S. 358, 90 S.Ct. 1068, 25 L.Ed.2d 368 (1970), it provided that determinations of criminal action in juvenile cases " 'must be based on a preponderance of the evidence,' " id., at 360, 90 S.Ct., at 1070 (quoting N.Y. Family Court Act § 744(b)). In Patterson v. New York, 432 U.S. 197, 97 S.Ct. 2319, 53 L.Ed.2d 281 (1977), the statute provided that extreme emotional disturbance " 'is an affirmative defense,' " id., at 198, n. 2, 97 S.Ct., at 2321, n. 2 (quoting N.Y. Penal Law § 125.25 (McKinney 1975)). And in Mullaney v. Wilbur, 421 U.S. 684, 95 S.Ct. 1881, 44 L.Ed.2d 508 (1975), Maine's highest court had held that in murder cases malice aforethought was presumed and had to be negated by the defendant, id., at 689, 95 S.Ct., at 1884–1885 (citing State v. Lafferty, 309 A.2d 647 (1973)).

In contrast to the provisions involved in these cases, 8 U.S.C. § 1326 does not, on its face, place the constitutional issue before us: it does not say that subsection (b)(2) is merely a sentencing enhancement. The text of the statute supports, if it does not indeed demand, the conclusion that subsection (b)(2) is a separate offense that includes the violation described in subsection (a) but adds the additional element of prior felony conviction. I therefore do not reach the difficult constitutional issue in this case because I adopt, as I think our cases require, that reasonable interpretation of § 1326 which avoids the problem. Illegal re-entry simpliciter (§ 1326(a)) and illegal reentry after conviction of an aggravated felony (§ 1326(b)(2)) are separate criminal offenses. Prior conviction of an aggravated felony being an element of the latter offense, it must be charged in the indictment. Since it was not, petitioner's sentence must be set aside.

[The balance of Justice Scalia's dissenting opinion is omitted.]

CHAPTER 26

APPEAL AND COLLATERAL ATTACK

Analysis

This final chapter follows up the prior materials about trial court proceedings with an introduction to some general principles governing post-trial proceedings. There are some post-trial matters that have already been addressed in this book. Chapter 22 covered two. One is the extent to which failure to comply with procedural requirements for the taking of guilty pleas justifies disturbing a conviction on appeal or in collateral proceedings. The other is the degree to which various other issues continue to exist despite a guilty plea, allowing them to be addressed on collateral attack. In addition, Chapter 25 addressed appellate review of sentences.

In order to conceptualize post-trial proceedings in a practical manner, this chapter distinguishes post-trial proceedings that involve direct appeal from those that consist of so-called "collateral" attacks upon a conviction or sentence. But first, the 1990 Report of the Federal Courts Study Committee, which immediately follows, highlights the tension between providing for post-conviction relief and court congestion.

A. THE CONTEXT: TENSION BETWEEN APPELLATE CASELOAD AND POST CONVICTION REMEDIES

REPORT OF THE FEDERAL COURTS STUDY COMMITTEE, 109–110
  (APRIL 2, 1990)

Chapter 6

Dealing with the Appellate Caseload Crisis

However people may view other aspects of the federal judiciary, few deny that its appellate courts are in a "crisis of volume" that has transformed them from the institutions they were even a generation ago. Further and more fundamental change to the appellate courts would seem to be inevitable unless there is a halt to the climb in appellate workload. While it is impossible to read the future, we see little reason to anticipate such a halt.

If growth continues, the nation must ask how further changes in the appellate courts will occur. Will they be insidious and unplanned; will oral argument and reasoned opinions simply fade away, for example? Or will Congress and the courts fashion new structures and procedures specifically designed to preserve the hallmarks of our judiciary? Those hallmarks include that the judges do much of their own work, grant oral argument in cases that need it, decide cases with sufficient thought, and produce opinions in cases of precedential importance with the care they deserve, including independent, constructive insight and criticism from judges on the court and the panel other than the judge writing the opinion. These conditions are essential to a carefully crafted case law. Modern society requires no less.

Today's federal appellate courts have been able to provide these conditions only through increases in productivity that seem to be approaching their limit. Further attempts to raise productivity by the most commonly suggested and employed means, such as increases in staff and reducing opportunity for oral argument, could threaten the integrity of the process.
. . .

. . . The crisis is caused partly by an increase in district court cases but mainly by a heightened proclivity to appeal district court terminations. In 1945, litigants appealed about one of every forty district court terminations; they now appeal about one in eight. As a result, appellate filings have risen nearly fifteen-fold. . . . The number of appellate judges, however, has increased since 1945 by a factor of less than three, from 59 to 168. Consequently, the caseload per judge has multiplied by nearly six over the same period. . . .

To date, the courts of appeals have managed to avoid the worst effects of this growth. There has been no systemic breakdown in the quality of the courts' work. . . . But the appellate courts have avoided major deterioration only by pushing productivity to maximum levels and by adopting truncated procedures that probably have reached the limits of their utility without compromising the quality of the process.

The appellate caseload explosion, moreover, threatens not only the courts of appeals as we know them. It also threatens the Supreme Court's role as the enunciator of national law. The Court is unable to give full review to more than about 150 cases per year. As court of appeals decisions increase in number, there is a corresponding decline in the percentage of those decisions that the Supreme Court reviews, thus making the thirteen intermediate appellate courts more and more the nation's courts of last resort. . . .

B. APPEAL

EDITORS' INTRODUCTION: STRUCTURES FOR DIRECT APPEAL

Statutes and court rules governing criminal procedure generally provide for convicted defendants to have access to one or more appellate tribunals to review actions by the trial court that contributed to the conviction. In the federal system, for example, a defendant convicted in federal District Court may appeal, as a matter of right, to the appropriate United States Court of Appeals. 28 U.S.C.A. § 1291. If denied relief at this level, the defendant may seek further review by the United States Supreme Court by application for a writ of certiorari. 28 U.S.C.A. § 1254. The Supreme Court's rules indicate that it will exercise its discretion to review a decision only where "special and important reasons" exist. Among the reasons suggesting that the Court will review a Court of Appeals decision are a split among the Court of Appeals on the issue involved, the presentation of an important and undecided question of federal law that should be settled, and determination of a federal question by the Court of Appeals in a way conflicting with Supreme Court precedent. Sup.Ct.R. 17.

Although the Supreme Court has never held that federal constitutional considerations require states to provide convicted defendants with appellate review, see Abney v. United States, 431 U.S. 651, 656, 97 S.Ct. 2034, 2038, 52 L.Ed.2d 651, 657–58 (1977), the states have generally provided for appeals from convictions. A large number of states have patterned appellate review after the federal system, with only limited (if any) review as of right beyond the first of several levels of appellate courts. Appeal by a defendant from an intermediate Court of Appeals to the state's highest court is generally discretionary. In cases involving a penalty of death or life imprisonment, appeal is often directly to the state's highest court.

A state criminal defendant can seek review by the United States Supreme Court of a decision of the highest court of the state to which he has access under state law. This review is by means of application for the writ of certiorari. See 28 U.S.C.A. § 1257. The Supreme Court has indicated that it will exercise its discretionary authority to review state court decisions on certiorari pursuant to the same sort of guidelines used to determine whether to review decisions of the United States Courts of Appeal. Sup.Ct.R. 17.

Appellate review is generally "on the record." This means that the reviewing court considers only the formal record compiled in the trial court. This record consists of the original papers and exhibits (including physical or "real" evidence) filed in the trial court, a transcription of the proceedings (usually a typed version of the court reporter's notes), and a copy of the trial court's docket entries related to the case. See Fed.R.App.Pro. 10. The reviewing court considers claims that the trial court erred in the proceeding. Generally, an appellate court will consider only matters that were brought to the attention of the trial court. But certain types of errors will be reviewed even if raised for the first time on appeal. Fed.R.Crim.P. 52(b) ("Plain errors" or "defects affecting substantial rights" may be considered on appeal even though not called to attention of trial court). Appellate relief to the defendant, if it is granted, may take any of a number of forms, depending upon the defect found in the trial proceeding and the procedural posture of the matter. For example, the appellate court may direct that the trial court hold a new trial, dismiss the charges, or enter judgment of acquittal for the defendant.

But certain errors, even if established, may be too insubstantial to warrant any relief at all. Thus F.R.Crim.P. 52(a), titled "Harmless Error," directs that on appeal "any error, defect, irregularity, or variance which does not affect substantial rights shall be disregarded." In ruling upon a contention that an error of federal constitutional dimensions is "harmless," i.e., does not require granting relief, the Supreme Court has directed that an especially stringent standard be used. In Chapman v. California, 386 U.S. 18, 87 S.Ct. 824, 17 L.Ed.2d 705 (1967), the Court observed that some federal constitutional errors may well be of such a nature as to preclude a finding that they are harmless. It held, however, that comments upon the defendant's failure to testify at trial could be regarded as harmless, but only if the prosecution convinced the appellate court beyond a reasonable doubt that the comments "did not contribute to the ... convictions." 386 U.S. at 26, 87 S.Ct. at 829, 17 L.Ed.2d at 711.

The United States Supreme Court held in Brecht v. Abrahamson, 507 U.S. 619, 113 S.Ct. 1710, 123 L.Ed.2d 353 (1993) that when review is obtained in federal habeas corpus proceedings the proper harmless error standard is the less onerous one of Kotteakos v. United States, 328 U.S. 750, 66 S.Ct. 1239, 90 L.Ed. 1557 (1946)—whether the constitutional violation "had substantial and injurious effect or influence in determining the jury's verdict"—rather than the *Chapman* standard that is applied on direct appeal.

Provisions are also made—albeit less frequently—for the prosecution to have access to appellate review. Considerations of Double Jeopardy limit the ability of an appellate court to give the prosecution relief; these matters are considered in detail in Chapter 20. The 1970 revision of the applicable federal statute, 18 U.S.C.A. § 3731, has been construed as intended to permit the Government to appeal in any situation where appeal is not barred by Double Jeopardy. See United States v. Wilson, 420 U.S. 332, 337–39, 95 S.Ct. 1013, 1018–19, 43 L.Ed.2d 232, 238–39 (1975). As a general rule, interlocutory appeals have not been favorably regarded in criminal litigation. But some provisions for such appeals exist, especially in situations where only such a procedure can enable the prosecution to be given access to appellate review without violation of defendants' Double Jeopardy rights. Interlocutory appeals by the prosecution from rulings on pretrial motions are considered in Chapter 21, and by the defense on a claim of former jeopardy in Chapter 20. That no general federal constitutional right to interlocutory appeals exists, however, was strongly suggested by United States v. MacDonald, 435 U.S. 850, 98 S.Ct. 1547, 56 L.Ed.2d 18 (1978), involving a speedy trial claim, suggests, however, that there is no general federal constitutional right to interlocutory appeals.

Ross v. Moffitt

Supreme Court of the United States, 1974.
417 U.S. 600, 94 S.Ct. 2437, 41 L.Ed.2d 341.

■ MR. JUSTICE REHNQUIST delivered the opinion of the Court.

I.

* * *

[In federal habeas corpus litigation, the Fourth Circuit Court of Appeals held that respondent's federal constitutional rights had been violated by the refusal of North Carolina to provide him with court-appointed counsel in seeking discretionary review by the state and U.S. Supreme courts. Editors.]

II.

This Court, in the past 20 years, has given extensive consideration to the rights of indigent persons on appeal. In Griffin v. Illinois, 351 U.S. 12, 76 S.Ct. 585, 100 L.Ed. 891 (1956), the first of the pertinent cases, the Court had before it an Illinois rule allowing a convicted criminal defendant to present claims of trial error to the Supreme Court of Illinois only if he procured a transcript of the testimony adduced at his trial. No exception was made for the indigent defendant, and thus one who was unable to pay the cost of obtaining such a transcript was precluded from obtaining appellate review of asserted trial error. . . . The Court in *Griffin* held that this discrimination violated the Fourteenth Amendment.

Succeeding cases invalidated similar financial barriers to the appellate process, at the same time reaffirming the traditional principle that a State is not obliged to provide any appeal at all for criminal defendants. . . .

The decisions . . . stand for the proposition that a State cannot arbitrarily cut off appeal rights for indigents while leaving open avenues of appeal for more affluent persons. In Douglas v. California, 372 U.S. 353, 83 S.Ct. 814, 9 L.Ed.2d 811 (1963), however, . . . the Court departed somewhat from the limited doctrine of the transcript and fee cases and undertook an examination of whether an indigent's access to the appellate system was adequate. The Court in *Douglas* concluded that a State does not fulfill its responsibility toward indigent defendants merely by waiving its own requirements that a convicted defendant procure a transcript or pay a fee in order to appeal, and held that the State must go further and provide counsel for the indigent on his first appeal as of right. It is this decision we are asked to extend today.

* * *

The precise rationale for the *Griffin* and *Douglas* lines of cases has never been explicitly stated, some support being derived from the Equal Protection Clause of the Fourteenth Amendment, and some from the Due Process Clause of that Amendment. Neither Clause by itself provides an entirely satisfactory basis for the result reached, each depending on a different inquiry which emphasizes the different factors. "Due process" emphasizes fairness between the State and the individual dealing with the State, regardless of how other individuals in the same situation may be treated. "Equal protection," on the other hand, emphasizes disparity in treatment by a State between classes of individuals whose situations are arguably indistinguishable. We will address these issues separately in the succeeding sections.

III.

* * *

We do not believe that the Due Process Clause requires North Carolina to provide respondent with counsel on his discretionary appeal to the State Supreme Court. At the trial stage of a criminal proceeding, the right of an indigent defendant to counsel is fundamental and binding upon the States by virtue of the Sixth and Fourteenth Amendments. Gideon v. Wainwright, 372 U.S. 335, 83 S.Ct. 792, 9 L.Ed.2d 799 (1963). But there are significant differences between the trial and appellate stages of a criminal proceeding. The purpose of the trial stage from the State's point of view is to convert a criminal defendant from a person presumed innocent to one found guilty beyond a reasonable doubt. To accomplish this purpose, the State employs a prosecuting attorney who presents evidence to the court, challenges any witnesses offered by the defendant, argues rulings of the court, and makes direct arguments to the court and jury seeking to persuade them of the defendant's guilt. Under these circumstances "reason and reflection require us to recognize that in our adversary system of criminal justice, any person haled into court, who is too poor to hire a lawyer, cannot be assured a fair trial unless counsel is provided for him." Id., at 344, 83 S.Ct., at 796.

By contrast, it is ordinarily the defendant, rather than the State, who initiates the appellate process, seeking not to fend off the efforts of the State's prosecutor but rather to overturn a finding of guilt made by a judge or a jury below. The defendant needs an attorney on appeal not as a shield to protect him against being "haled into court" by the State and stripped of his presumption of innocence, but rather as a sword to upset the prior determination of guilt. This difference is significant for, while no one would agree that the State may simply dispense with the trial stage of proceedings without a criminal defendant's consent, it is clear that the State need not provide any appeal at all. McKane v. Durston, 153 U.S. 684, 14 S.Ct. 913, 38 L.Ed. 867 (1894). The fact that an appeal *has* been provided does not automatically mean that a State then acts unfairly by refusing to provide counsel to indigent defendants at every stage of the way. Douglas v. California, supra. Unfairness results only if indigents are singled out by the State and denied meaningful access to the appellate system because of their poverty. That question is more profitably considered under an equal protection analysis.

IV.

* * *

In this case we do not believe that the Equal Protection Clause, when interpreted in the context of these cases, requires North Carolina to provide free counsel for indigent defendants seeking to take discretionary appeals to the North Carolina Supreme Court, or to file petitions for certiorari in this Court.

* * *

The facts show that respondent ...received the benefit of counsel in examining the record of his trial and in preparing an appellate brief on his behalf for the state Court of Appeals. Thus, prior to his seeking discretionary review in the State Supreme Court, his claims had "once been presented by a lawyer and passed upon by an appellate court." Douglas v. California, 372 U.S., at 356, 83 S.Ct., at 816. We do not believe that it can be said, therefore, that a defendant in respondent's circumstances is denied meaningful access to the North Carolina Supreme Court simply because the State does not appoint counsel to aid him in seeking review in that court. At that stage he will have, at the very least, a transcript or other record of trial proceedings, a brief on his behalf in the Court of Appeals setting forth his claims of error, and in many cases an opinion by the Court of Appeals disposing of his case. These materials, supplemented by whatever submission respondent may make *pro se,* would appear to provide the Supreme Court of North Carolina with an adequate basis for its decision to grant or deny review.

V.

Much of the discussion in the preceding section is equally relevant to the question of whether a State must provide counsel for a defendant seeking review of his conviction in this Court. ...

* * *

Reversed.

■ MR. JUSTICE DOUGLAS, with whom MR. JUSTICE BRENNAN and MR. JUSTICE MARSHALL concur, dissenting.

* * *

NOTES

1. **Effective assistance in first appeal of right.** Although a defendant does not have a right to counsel on a discretionary appeal under *Ross,* the Supreme Court has found a due process right to the effective assistance of counsel on the defendant's first appeal as of right. In Evitts v. Lucey, 469 U.S. 387, 105 S.Ct. 830, 83 L.Ed.2d 821 (1985), defendant's appeal had been dismissed by the Kentucky Court of Appeals when his counsel failed to file the required statement of appeal:

> [N]ominal representation on an appeal as of right—like nominal representation at trial—does not suffice to render the proceedings constitutionally adequate; a

party whose counsel is unable to provide effective representation is in no better position than one who has no counsel at all.

469 U.S. at 396, 105 S.Ct. at 836, 83 L.Ed.2d at 830.

Chief Justice Burger and Justice Rehnquist vigorously dissented, Chief Justice Burger on the grounds that the decision "adds another barrier to finality and one that offers no real contribution to fairer justice." 469 U.S. at 406, 105 S.Ct. at 841, 83 L.Ed.2d at 836.

2. **Ineffective assistance is discretionary review proceedings.** The respondent in Wainwright v. Torna, 455 U.S. 586, 102 S.Ct. 1300, 71 L.Ed.2d 475 (1982) was represented at trial and on appeal by retained counsel. After losing his state appeal, his attorney agreed to present a petition for discretionary review to the Florida Supreme Court. Because of a mistake by a secretary in the attorney's office, the petition was filed one day late. The Florida court dismissed it because it was untimely filed. In federal habeas, an out-of-time appeal was ordered on the ground respondent did not receive the effective assistance of counsel. The Supreme Court reversed in a per curiam opinion. The majority concluded that since under Ross v. Moffitt, supra, there was no Sixth Amendment right to counsel to petition for discretionary review before the state supreme court, there could be no ineffective assistance of counsel either. Further, there was no due process violation since the fault lay with retained counsel, not the state. Justice Marshall, dissenting, took the position that

when a defendant can show that he reasonably relied on his attorney's promise to seek discretionary review, due process requires the State to consider his application, even when the application is untimely. To deny the right to seek discretionary review simply because of counsel's error is fundamentally unfair. Requiring the state courts to consider untimely applications when a defendant can show that he reasonably relied on his counsel will not impose a heavy burden. The State is not required to grant the application; it is simply barred from dismissing the application on the ground that it was not timely filed.

455 U.S. at 589, 102 S.Ct. at 1302, 71 L.Ed.2d at 479. If Justice Marshall's position were adopted and applied elsewhere in the criminal process, what effect would it have on numerous time requirements in the process?

3. **Is counsel obliged to brief all claims?** In Jones v. Barnes, 463 U.S. 745, 103 S.Ct. 3308, 77 L.Ed.2d 987 (1983), respondent wished his appointed counsel to present on appeal certain claims but counsel refused to do so, concentrating instead on other claims he believed had more merit. After his conviction was affirmed on direct appeal, respondent obtained federal relief on the ground that his attorney appointed for appeal had rendered ineffective assistance and denied respondent the equal protection of the laws. The Supreme Court, in an opinion by the Chief Justice, reversed. The lower federal court had granted relief on the basis of Anders v. California, 386 U.S. 738, 87 S.Ct. 1396, 18 L.Ed.2d 493 (1967), in which the Court had held that appointed counsel who determines that an appeal is frivolous is not permitted simply to refuse to brief and argue the case. He is required to present to the appellate court a brief referring to anything in the record that might arguably support the appeal no matter what counsel's professional opinion of the merits of those claims may be. The Chief Justice distinguished *Anders* on the ground that "experienced advocates since time beyond memory have emphasized the importance of winnowing out weaker arguments on appeal and focusing on one central issue if possible, or at most on a few key issues." 463 U.S. at 751–52, 103 S.Ct. at 3313, 77 L.Ed.2d at 994. Indeed, the Chief Justice concluded that *Anders* supported the Court's decision in this case:

Anders recognized that the role of the advocate "requires that he support his client's appeal to the best of his ability." . . . Here the appointed counsel did just that. For judges to second-guess reasonable professional judgments and impose on appointed counsel a duty to raise every "colorable" claim suggested by a client would disserve the very goal of vigorous and effective advocacy that underlies *Anders*.

463 U.S. at 754, 103 S.Ct. at 3314, 77 L.Ed.2d at 995. Justice Brennan, joined by Justice Marshall, dissented, taking the position that *Anders* and Faretta v. California, (Chapter 24) require counsel on appeal to honor the wishes of his client as to which nonfrivolous issues to pursue:

I cannot accept the notion that lawyers are one of the punishments a person receives merely for being accused of a crime. Clients, if they wish, are capable of making informed judgments about which issues to appeal, and when they exercise that prerogative their choices should be respected unless they would require lawyers to violate their consciences, the law, or their duties to the court.

463 U.S. at 764, 103 S.Ct. at 3319, 77 L.Ed.2d at 1001–02.

The Court further considered the obligations of an attorney appointed for appeal in McCoy v. Court of Appeals of Wisconsin, 486 U.S. 429, 108 S.Ct. 1895, 100 L.Ed.2d 440 (1988). The Wisconsin Supreme Court had adopted a rule requiring an appointed attorney who concludes that an appeal lacks arguable merit to file a brief that complies with *Anders* and that also contains a "discussion of why the issue lacks merit." Counsel for appellant concluded that the appeal lacked merit and filed a brief complying with *Anders*. He specifically refused to comply with the rule requiring a discussion of why the issue lacked merit on the grounds such a requirement was contrary to *Anders*, and that compliance would violate his client's right to counsel and would be unethical conduct. The Court of Appeals ordered the appellant's brief stricken and that a brief complying with the rule be filed. Appellant filed an original action in the Wisconsin Supreme Court seeking a declaration that its rule was unconstitutional. When the Wisconsin Supreme Court upheld its rule, he appealed to the United States Supreme Court. The Court, in an opinion by Justice Stevens, affirmed the Wisconsin Supreme Court. The Court noted that the basis of appellant's claim is that the rule discriminates against the indigent. It observed that an attorney, whether appointed or retained, is under an ethical obligation to refuse to proceed with a frivolous appeal. To the extent the rule requires counsel to inform an appellate court of law contrary to the arguments he is making, it places no obligation on counsel that the rules of legal ethics do not already impose. To the extent the rule requires counsel to disclose to the appellate court his thinking about why the appeal lacks merit, the rule furthers, rather than frustrates, the interests advanced in *Anders*:

Because counsel may discover previously unrecognized aspects of the law in the process of preparing a written explanation for his or her conclusion, the discussion requirement provides an additional safeguard against mistaken conclusions by counsel that the strongest arguments he or she can find are frivolous. Just like the references to favorable aspects of the record required by *Anders*, the discussion requirement may forestall some motions to withdraw and will assist the court in passing on the soundness of the lawyer's conclusion that the appeal is frivolous.

486 U.S. at 442, 108 S.Ct. at 1904, 100 L.Ed.2d at 456. Justice Brennan, joined by Justices Marshall and Blackmun, dissented on the ground that the Wisconsin requirement is inconsistent with counsel's obligations as advocate for his client.

The United States Supreme Court in Pennsylvania v. Finley, 481 U.S. 551, 107 S.Ct. 1990, 95 L.Ed.2d 539 (1987), rejected the position that the United States Constitution requires that the procedural steps set out in *Anders* must be followed when appointed counsel concludes that other state post-conviction proceedings are frivolous. All that is required is for counsel to satisfy the appointing court that he should be permitted to withdraw from the appointment because there are no meritorious grounds of relief to present.

4. **Frivolous certiorari petitions.** In a series of decisions, the Court has issued orders prospectively denying *in forma pauperis* status to pro se litigants who have repeatedly filed frivolous petitions in the United States Supreme Court. See In re McDonald, 489 U.S. 180, 109 S.Ct. 993, 103 L.Ed.2d 158 (1989) (73 filings with the Supreme Court since 1971); In re Sindram, 498 U.S. 177, 111 S.Ct. 596, 112 L.Ed.2d 599 (1991) (24 filings with Supreme Court during October 1990 Term); In re Demos, 500 U.S. 16, 111 S.Ct. 1569, 114 L.Ed.2d 20 (1991) (32 filings with the Supreme Court since 1988). These cases culminated in an order amending Rule 39 of the Rules of the Supreme Court of the United States to add Rule 39.8:

> If satisfied that a petition for a writ of certiorari, jurisdictional statement, or petition for an extraordinary writ, as the case may be, is frivolous or malicious, the Court may deny a motion for leave to proceed *in forma pauperis*.

In re Amendment to Rule 39, 500 U.S. 13, 111 S.Ct. 1572, 114 L.Ed.2d 15 (1991). Justice Stevens, joined by Justice Blackmun, dissented. Justice Marshall dissented with the comment,

> This Court once had a great tradition: "All men and women are entitled to their day in Court." That guarantee has now been conditioned on monetary worth. It now will read: "All men and women are entitled to their day in Court only if they have the *means* and the *money*."

500 U.S. at 15, 111 S.Ct. at 1573–74, 114 L.Ed.2d at 18. A denial of *in forma pauperis* status has the effect of requiring the payment of a $300 filing fee and the costs of printing the documents filed.

In In re Anderson, 511 U.S. 364, 114 S.Ct. 1606, 128 L.Ed.2d 332 (1994), the Court, per curiam, invoked Rule 39.8 with respect to the filing of petitions for extraordinary writs. Since the abuse had been limited principally to extraordinary writs, the Court restricted the Rule 39.8 action to extraordinary writs. Justice Stevens, joined by Justice Blackmun, dissented.

5. **Effect of escape on appeal.** In some circumstances, a convicted defendant may lose an otherwise available right of appeal by escaping from custody. In Ortega–Rodriguez v. United States, 507 U.S. 234, 113 S.Ct. 1199, 122 L.Ed.2d 581 (1993), the Supreme Court recounted that it has since 1876 approved of federal courts dismissing appeals of defendants who are fugitives from justice during the pendency of their appeals and has upheld state provisions for dismissal of appeals under similar circumstances. Dismissal is justified in part because any judgments affirming the convictions would be unenforceable. Further, flight or escape can properly be viewed as tantamount to waiver or abandonment of the pending appeal. Dismissal discourages escapes. It also promotes efficient and dignified appellate processes. 507 U.S. at 240–42, 113 S.Ct. at 1203–05, 122 L.Ed.2d at 591–93.

Ortega–Rodriguez, however, had fled after conviction but before sentencing. He was sentenced *in absentia*. Nearly a year later, he was apprehended. The district court granted his motion for resentencing and sentenced him to a somewhat less severe sentence than that imposed while he was a fugitive. When he sought to appeal, the Government moved to dismiss the appeal because he had been a fugitive after his conviction; the Court of Appeals granted the motion. Reversing by a 5-to-4 vote, the Supreme Court held that a federal appellate court cannot dismiss an appeal because the defendant was a fugitive before the appellate process began, unless the appellate court concludes that the defendant's flight significantly interfered with the appellate process.

Such defendants pose no risk that appellate courts' judgments cannot be enforced, Justice Stevens explained for the majority. Nor do they generally interfere with the orderly and efficient operation of the appellate process or affront the dignity of the appellate court. District courts are better equipped to fashion appropriate penalties for escape of defendants while the cases are before those courts; thus dismissal of appeals is not sufficiently necessary to deter pre-appeal escapes. 507 U.S. at 242–49, 113 S.Ct. at 1205–08, 122 L.Ed.2d at 594–97. Dismissal of an appeal is appropriate, however, if on the facts of a particular case an appellate court finds that a defendant's pre-appeal escape actually and substantially interfered with the appellate process. This might occur, for example, if escape prevented the defendant's appeal from being joined with that of his codefendants for expeditious decision together. 507 U.S. at 250, 113 S.Ct. at 1209, 122 L.Ed.2d at 597–98.

Chief Justice Rehnquist, joined by three other justices, argued that dismissal in pre-appeal escape cases was justified as a general rule. Defendants who escape pose a threat to the orderly operation of the appellate process and flout the authority of the judicial process of which the appellate court is an integral part. Moreover, dismissals serve the important interest of discouraging escapes. 507 U.S. at 253–257, 113 S.Ct. at 1211–13, 122 L.Ed.2d at 599–603 (Rehnquist, C.J., dissenting).

Whether *Ortega–Rodriguez* portended federal constitutional limits on fugitive dismissal rules was raised in Goeke v. Branch, 514 U.S. 115, 115 S.Ct. 1275, 131 L.Ed.2d 152 (1995) (per curiam). Branch, a defendant in a Missouri prosecution, had escaped after conviction but before sentencing. She was quickly captured and sentenced. The state appellate court dismissed her attempted appeal based on Missouri's fugitive dismissal rule. Branch sought federal habeas corpus relief and the Eighth Circuit held she was entitled to it. Due process, it reasoned, bars a state from applying a fugitive dismissal rule in a case where the appellant's escape did not delay appellate proceedings, inconvenience the appellate court, or otherwise affect the appellate process. The United States Supreme Court reversed on the ground that any federal constitutional rule barring a state from enforcing its fugitive dismissal rule would be a new rule not enforceable in a federal habeas corpus proceeding. Rejecting Branch's argument that the rule applied by the Eighth Circuit was not a new rule, the Court found no basis for the intermediate court's position in existing or well-settled authority. In *Ortega–Rodriguez,* the Court acknowledged, it had stated "that absent some adverse effect of pre-appeal flight on the appellate process, 'the defendant's former fugitive status may well lack the kind of connection to the appellate process that would justify an appellate sanction of dismissal.' " Nevertheless, the Court explained in *Goeke,* the rationale for *Ortega–Rodriguez* was limited to the Court's supervisory powers and thus did not suggest that dismissal of a fugitive's appeal implicated constitutional principles.

As we explained in Allen v. Georgia, [166 U.S. 138, 140, 17 S.Ct. 525, 526, 41 L.Ed. 949 (1897)], where the Court upheld against constitutional attack the dismissal of the petition of a fugitive whose appeal was pending, "if the Supreme Court of a State has acted in consonance with the constitutional laws of a State and its own procedures, it could only be in very exceptional circumstances that this court would feel justified in saying that there had been a failure of due legal process. We might ourselves have pursued a different course in this case, but that is not the test." The Eighth Circuit converted a rule for the administration of the federal courts into a constitutional one.

514 U.S. at 120, 115 S.Ct. at 1278, 131 L.Ed.2d at 159. The Court emphasized, however, that it was not reaching the merits of Branch's contention that due

process prohibits dismissal of appeals for escapes that do not affect the appellate process.

6. **Retroactive application of new rules.** When a major change or "clarification" in the law is made by judicial decision, should the new law be applied retroactively to cases investigated or litigated before the decision? The Supreme Court's approach to this question of retroactivity was summarized by Justice Brennan:

It is by now uncontroverted that "the Constitution neither prohibits nor requires retrospective effect." [Linkletter v. Walker, 381 U.S. 618, 629, 85 S.Ct. 1731, 1737, 14 L.Ed.2d 601 (1965).] ...[T]hat decision firmly settled that "in appropriate cases the Court may in the interest of justice make the rule prospective ...where the exigencies of the situation require such an application." Id., at 628, 85 S.Ct., at 1737; Johnson v. New Jersey, 384 U.S. 719, 726–727, 86 S.Ct. 1772, 1777, 16 L.Ed.2d 882 (1966).

Similarly, it is clear that resolution of the question of retroactivity does not automatically turn on the particular provision of the Constitution on which the new prescription is based. "Each constitutional rule of criminal procedure has its own distinct functions, its own background of precedent, and its own impact on the administration of justice, and the way in which these factors combine must inevitably vary with the dictate involved." Id., at 728, 86 S.Ct., at 1778. Accordingly, the test consistently employed by the Court to decide whether a new constitutional doctrine should be applied retroactively contemplates the consideration of three criteria: "(a) the purpose to be served by the new standards, (b) the extent of the reliance by law enforcement authorities on the old standards, and (c) the effect on the administration of justice of a retroactive application of the new standards." Stovall v. Denno, 388 U.S. 293, 297, 87 S.Ct. 1967, 1970, 18 L.Ed.2d 1199 (1967).

Moreover, our decisions establish that "[f]oremost among these factors is the purpose to be served by the new constitutional rule," Desist v. United States, 394 U.S. 244, 249, 89 S.Ct. 1030, 1033, 22 L.Ed.2d 248 (1969), and that we will give controlling significance to the measure of reliance and the impact on the administration of justice "only when the purpose of the rule in question [does] not clearly favor either retroactivity or prospectivity." Id., at 251, 89 S.Ct., at 1035. "Where the major purpose of new constitutional doctrine is to overcome an aspect of the criminal trial that substantially impairs its truth-finding function and so raises serious questions about the accuracy of guilty verdicts in past trials, the new rule has been given complete retroactive effect. Neither good-faith reliance by state or federal authorities on prior constitutional law or accepted practice, nor severe impact on the administration of justice has sufficed to require prospective application in these circumstances." Williams v. United States, 401 U.S. 646, 653, 91 S.Ct. 1148, 1152, 28 L.Ed.2d 388 (1971) (plurality opinion of White, J.).

Finally, we have recognized that the extent to which the purpose of a new constitutional rule requires its retroactive application "is necessarily a matter of degree." Johnson v. New Jersey, supra, 384 U.S., at 729, 86 S.Ct., at 1778. Constitutional protections are frequently fashioned to serve multiple ends; while a new standard may marginally implicate the reliability and integrity of the factfinding process, it may have been designed primarily to foster other, equally fundamental values in our system of jurisprudence. Not every rule that "tends incidentally" to avoid unfairness at trial must be accorded retroactive effect. So, too, additional safeguards may already exist that minimize the likelihood of past injustices. In short, "[t]he extent to which a condemned practice infects the integrity of the truth-determining process at trial is a 'question of probabilities.' " Stovall v. Denno, supra, 388 U.S., at 298, 87 S.Ct., at 1970 (quoting Johnson v. New Jersey, supra, 384 U.S., at 729, 86 S.Ct., at 1778). And only when an assessment of those probabilities indicates that the condemned practice casts doubt upon the reliability of the determinations of guilt in past criminal cases must the new procedural rule be applied retroactively.

Brown v. Louisiana, 447 U.S. 323, 327–29, 100 S.Ct. 2214, 2219–20, 65 L.Ed.2d 159, 165–66 (1980).

The Court has been especially reluctant to give retroactive effect to holdings which affect police conduct where such prior conduct had cast no doubt on the accuracy of the convictions or where there was a likelihood of widespread reliance on earlier decisions of the Court. For example, the Court declined to give retroactive effect to the holding in Mapp v. Ohio, 367 U.S. 643, 81 S.Ct. 1684, 6 L.Ed.2d 1081 (1961) (application of exclusionary rule in state courts to evidence obtained in unreasonable search and seizure) in Linkletter v. Walker, supra; Katz v. United States, 389 U.S. 347, 88 S.Ct. 507, 19 L.Ed.2d 576 (1967) (eavesdropping on a private conversation with no physical trespass was a "search" under the Fourth Amendment) in Desist v. United States, supra; or to United States v. Wade, 388 U.S. 218, 87 S.Ct. 1296, 18 L.Ed.2d 1149 (1967) (right to appointed counsel at certain pretrial lineups) in Stovall v. Denno, supra.

Certain holdings relating to the trial process have also been denied retroactivity, such as: Griffin v. California, 380 U.S. 609, 85 S.Ct. 1229, 14 L.Ed.2d 106 (1965) (comment on defendant's failure to testify violates Fifth Amendment) in Tehan v. United States ex rel. Shott, 382 U.S. 406, 86 S.Ct. 459, 15 L.Ed.2d 453 (1966); and cases involving the right to jury trial and the procedures for jury selection (see Daniel v. Louisiana, 420 U.S. 31, 95 S.Ct. 704, 42 L.Ed.2d 790 (1975), DeStefano v. Woods, 392 U.S. 631, 88 S.Ct. 2093, 20 L.Ed.2d 1308 (1968), and Griffith v. Kentucky, 479 U.S. 314, 107 S.Ct. 708, 93 L.Ed.2d 649 (1987).)

On the other hand, the direct and "substantial" relationship between the due process requirement of proof beyond a reasonable doubt and trial accuracy has persuaded the Court to give retroactive effect to its rulings in: Barber v. Page, 390 U.S. 719, 88 S.Ct. 1318, 20 L.Ed.2d 255 (1968) (use of witness' preliminary hearing testimony at trial violates Confrontation Clause unless State has made good faith effort to secure the witness' presence) in Berger v. California, 393 U.S. 314, 89 S.Ct. 540, 21 L.Ed.2d 508 (1969); and Burch v. Louisiana, 441 U.S. 130, 99 S.Ct. 1623, 60 L.Ed.2d 96 (1979) (due process requirement of unanimity in 6–member juries) in Brown v. Louisiana, supra.

In United States v. Johnson, 457 U.S. 537, 102 S.Ct. 2579, 73 L.Ed.2d 202 (1982), the Court adopted a new approach to retroactivity: (1) When an opinion "merely has applied settled precedents to a new and different factual situation" no question of retroactivity is presented since the law has not been altered in any material way. (2) If the opinion is a "clear break with the past" it is to be applied prospectively. (3) Only if the new rule is to the effect that the trial court lacked authority to convict or punish a criminal defendant in the first place, for example, a double jeopardy ruling, is the new rule applied retroactively. In this case the Court concluded that the rule of Payton v. New York (prohibiting warrantless, nonconsensual entry into suspect's home to make routine felony arrest) did not fall into the first, second, or third category and therefore should be applied neither solely prospectively nor fully retroactively. Instead it should be applied to all cases pending on direct review at the time the rule was announced.

In Griffith v. Kentucky, supra, the Court rejected that portion of *Johnson* which mandated prospectivity for "clear break" decisions. Denying retroactive application of such decisions to petitioners on direct review when the decision is announced would improperly depart from the principle that the Court applies current law to cases on direct review and would treat petitioners unequally solely on the fortuity of which case reaches the Court first. "We therefore hold that a new rule for the conduct of criminal prosecution is to be applied ...to all cases, state or federal, pending on direct review or not yet final, with no exception for cases in which the new rule constitutes a 'clear break' with the past." 479 U.S. at 328, 107 S.Ct. at 716, 93 L.Ed.2d at 661. Justice White, joined by The Chief Justice and Justice O'Connor, dissented.

5. **Retroactivity a new rule and the stage of proceedings of the case in which application is sought.** The retroactive application of a new rule of criminal procedure also depends on when it is advanced during the pendency of petitioner's case. Cases on this issue are summarized by Justice Kennedy for the majority in Saffle v. Parks, 494 U.S. 484, 110 S.Ct. 1257, 108 L.Ed.2d 415(1990):

> In Penry v. Lynaugh, 492 U.S. ___, 109 S.Ct. 2934, 106 L.Ed.2d 256 (1989), we held that a new rule of constitutional law will not be applied in cases on collateral review unless the rule comes within one of two narrow exceptions. This limitation on the proper exercise of habeas corpus jurisdiction applies to capital and noncapital cases. See id., at ___, 109 S.Ct. at ___. ...

* * *

> In *Teague,* we defined a new rule as a rule that "breaks new ground," "imposes a new obligation on the States or the Federal Government," or was not "*dictated* by precedent existing at the time the defendant's conviction became final." *Teague,* supra, 489 U.S., at 301, 109 S.Ct., at 1070 (emphasis in original). The explicit overruling of an earlier holding no doubt creates a new rule; it is more difficult, however, to determine whether we announce a new rule when a decision extends the reasoning of our prior cases. As we recognized in Butler v. McKellar, ___ U.S. ___, ___-___, 110 S.Ct. 1212, 1216–1217, [108] L.Ed.2d ___ (1990), the question must be answered by reference to the underlying purposes of the habeas writ. Foremost among these is ensuring that state courts conduct criminal proceedings in accordance with the Constitution as interpreted at the time of the proceedings. See ibid. " '[T]he threat of habeas serves as a necessary additional incentive for trial and appellate courts throughout the land to conduct their proceedings in a manner consistent with established constitutional standards. In order to perform this deterrence function, ...the habeas court need only apply the constitutional standards that prevailed at the time the original proceedings took place.' " *Teague,* supra, 489 U.S., at 306, 109 S.Ct., at 1073 (quoting Desist v. United States), 394 U.S. 244, 262–263, 89 S.Ct. 1030, 1040–1041, 22 L.Ed.2d 248 (1969) (Harlan, J., dissenting). ..."The 'new rule' principle therefore validates reasonable, good-faith interpretations of existing precedents made by state courts even though they are shown to be contrary to later decisions." Butler, supra, ___ U.S., at ___, 110 S.Ct., at 1217. ...

* * *

> ...The first exception permits the retroactive application of a new rule if the rule places a class of private conduct beyond the power of the State to proscribe, see *Teague,* 489 U.S., at 311, 109 S.Ct., at 1075, or addresses a "substantive categorical guarante[e] accorded by the Constitution," such as a rule "prohibiting a certain category of punishment for a class of defendants because of their status or offense." *Penry,* 492 U.S., at ___, 109 S.Ct., at 2953. ...The second exception is for "watershed rules of criminal procedure" implicating the fundamental fairness and accuracy of the criminal proceeding. See *Teague,* supra, 489 U.S., at 311, 109 S.Ct., at 1075; *Butler,* supra, ___ U.S., at

_____-_____, 110 S.Ct., at 1218. ....Although the precise contours of this exception may be difficult to discern, we have usually cited Gideon v. Wainwright, 372 U.S. 335, 83 S.Ct. 792, 9 L.Ed.2d 799 (1963), holding that a defendant has the right to be represented by counsel in all criminal trials for serious offenses, to illustrate the type of rule coming within the exception. . . .

494 U.S. at 486–95, 110 S.Ct. at 1259–64.

In O'Dell v. Netherland, 521 U.S. 151, 117 S.Ct. 1969, 138 L.Ed.2d 351 (1997) the Court held that the rule in Simmons v. South Carolina, 512 U.S. 154, 114 S.Ct. 2187, 129 L.Ed.2d 133 (1994) that a jury in a capital case must be informed if its life sentence verdict alternative is without possibility of parole when dangerousness is argued is a "new rule" which will not be applied to cases that were final when *Simmons* was decided.

C. COLLATERAL ATTACK

EDITORS' INTRODUCTION: STRUCTURES FOR COLLATERAL ATTACK

A collateral attack upon a conviction is an effort to seek relief in a proceeding other than that in which the judgment of conviction was rendered. Thus it is distinguishable from appeal or review by writ of certiorari, both of which are continuations of the original prosecution.

Collateral attacks are different from appeal remedies in at least two important ways. First, they are not subject to stringent time limitations as are appeals. Therefore, a convicted person who has failed to pursue an appeal within the time provided is likely to find collateral attack the only available avenue of further litigation. Second, unlike appeals, collateral attack proceedings are not "on the record" made at the original trial. Therefore, a convicted person may have the opportunity to introduce evidence which was, for whatever reason, not introduced at the original trial proceedings.

A person convicted in a federal District Court can pursue collateral attack only in the federal judicial system. Following a conviction in state court, however, a person may generally seek such relief in state courts, federal courts, or both. Federal and state procedures require separate consideration.

State Procedures

The United States Supreme Court has never held that the states are required by federal constitutional demands to provide persons convicted in their courts with a means for mounting collateral attacks upon those convictions. But as the United States Supreme Court began to develop state defendants' federal constitutional rights and to open federal courts to state defendants' attacks, the states began to develop their own procedures in order to avoid having federal tribunals preempt the area. The tendency was to use familiar vehicles, especially the old common law writs of habeas corpus and, to a lesser extent, coram nobis. Habeas corpus means literally, "you have the body," and was a traditional method of requiring one person holding another in custody to justify that custody. Because of its breadth, the writ was (and still is) used for a variety of purposes other than collateral attacks upon criminal convictions.

Dissatisfaction with procedural problems and technicalities involved in the common law writs led a number of jurisdictions to adopt, by legislation or court rule, fairly comprehensive procedures for postconviction attacks as an alternative to these writs. A major characteristic of many of these procedures is the requirement that the convicted person seek collateral relief in the convicting court rather than in a court with jurisdiction over the geographical area in which the person happens to be confined.

Federal Procedures

Prior to 1948, persons convicted in federal court could attack their convictions collaterally through the use of the writ of habeas corpus. In that year, however, Congress enacted what is now 28 U.S.C.A. § 2255 [infra] providing for collateral attack by a "motion to vacate sentence" filed in the convicting court. Although Article 1, § 9 of the United States Constitution prohibits the suspension of habeas corpus except in situations involving rebellion or invasion, the section 2255 procedure has, for all practical purposes, superseded the writ.

Brown v. Allen, 344 U.S. 443, 73 S.Ct. 397, 97 L.Ed. 469 (1953), made clear that federal constitutional claims of state prisoners are cognizable in federal habeas corpus, that the federal courts are not bound by any disposition of the federal claim that may have been made in state court, and that federal courts may inquire into factual matters related to a state prisoner's federal claim even if those facts were purportedly resolved in the state litigation. The prevailing practice is for a state prisoner to apply for the writ to a federal District Court judge. The judge's action on the application may be appealed by either party to the appropriate Court of Appeals as a matter of right, and the decision of the Court of Appeals is subject to review by the Supreme Court as in other cases.

In Sumner v. Mata, 449 U.S. 539, 101 S.Ct. 764, 66 L.Ed.2d 722 (1981), the Court noted that the enactment of § 2254(d), which follows was intended to alleviate some of the friction between state and federal courts caused by federal courts "refinding" facts related to state defendants' federal constitutional claims. To assure enforcement of Congress' mandate that federal habeas courts not reject state court findings on the basis of the usual "preponderance of the evidence" standard, the Court held that a federal habeas court granting a state prisoner relief on grounds which include rejecting state courts' findings of fact "should include in its opinion ...the reasoning which led it to conclude that any of the first seven factors [specified in § 2254(d)] were present, or the reasoning which led it to conclude that the state finding was 'not fairly supported by the record.' "449 U.S. at 551, 101 S.Ct. at 771, 66 L.Ed.2d at 734.

Another issue with significant federalism implications that is presented by the availability of federal habeas corpus relief is the effect that should or must be given to a state prisoner's failure, during state litigation, to follow state procedures for implementation of federal constitutional rights. This is presented in the principal case in this section.

Federal Habeas Corpus Statutes
(amended as part of the Antiterrorism
and Effective Death Penalty Act of 1996)

28 U.S.C.A. § 2254. State custody; remedies in Federal courts

(a) The Supreme Court, a Justice thereof, a circuit judge, or a district court shall entertain an application for a writ of habeas corpus in behalf of a person in custody pursuant to the judgment of a State court only on the ground that he is in custody in violation of the Constitution or laws or treaties of the United States.

(b) (1) An application for a writ of habeas corpus on behalf of a person in custody pursuant to the judgment of a State court shall not be granted unless it appears that—

(A) the applicant has exhausted the remedies available in the courts of the State; or

(B) (i) there is an absence of available State corrective process; or

(ii) circumstances exist that render such process ineffective to protect the rights of the applicant.

(2) An application for a writ of habeas corpus may be denied on the merits, notwithstanding the failure of the applicant to exhaust the remedies available in the courts of the State.

(3) A State shall not be deemed to have waived the exhaustion requirement or be estopped from reliance upon the requirement unless the State, through counsel, expressly waives the requirement.

(c) An applicant shall not be deemed to have exhausted the remedies available in the courts of the State, within the meaning of this section, if he has the right under the law of the State to raise, by any available procedure, the question presented.

(d) An application for a writ of habeas corpus on behalf of a person in custody pursuant to the judgment of a State court shall not be granted with respect to any claim that was adjudicated on the merits in State court proceedings unless the adjudication of the claim—

(1) resulted in a decision that was contrary to, or involved an unreasonable application of, clearly established Federal law, as determined by the Supreme Court of the United States; or

(2) resulted in a decision that was based on an unreasonable determination of the facts in light of the evidence presented in the State court proceeding.

(e) (1) In a proceeding instituted by an application for a writ of habeas corpus by a person in custody pursuant to the judgment of a State court, a determination of a factual issue made by a State court shall be presumed to be correct. The applicant shall have the burden of rebutting the presumption of correctness by clear and convincing evidence.

(2) If the applicant has failed to develop the factual basis of a claim in State court proceedings, the court shall not hold an evidentiary hearing on the claim unless the applicant shows that—

(A) the claim relies on—

(i) a new rule of constitutional law, made retroactive to cases on collateral review by the Supreme Court, that was previously unavailable; or

(ii) a factual predicate that could not have been previously discovered through the exercise of due diligence; and

(B) the facts underlying the claim would be sufficient to establish by clear and convincing evidence that but for constitutional error, no reasonable factfinder would have found the applicant guilty of the underlying offense.

(f) If the applicant challenges the sufficiency of the evidence adduced in such State court proceeding to support the State court's determination of a factual issue made therein, the applicant, if able, shall produce that part of the record pertinent to a determination of the sufficiency of the evidence to support such determination. If the applicant, because of indigency or other reason is unable to produce such part of the record, then the State shall produce such part of the record and the Federal court shall direct the State to do so by order directed to an appropriate State official. If the State cannot provide such pertinent part of the record, then the court shall determine under the existing facts and circumstances what weight shall be given to the State court's factual determination.

(g) A copy of the official records of the State court, duly certified by the clerk of such court to be a true and correct copy of a finding, judicial opinion, or other reliable written indicia showing such a factual determination by the State court shall be admissible in the Federal court proceeding.

(h) Except as provided in section 408 of the Controlled Substances Act, in all proceedings brought under this section, and any subsequent proceedings on review, the court may appoint counsel for an applicant who is or becomes financially unable to afford counsel, except as provided by a rule promulgated by the Supreme Court pursuant to statutory authority. Appointment of counsel under this section shall be governed by section 3006A of title 18.

(i) The ineffectiveness or incompetence of counsel during Federal or State collateral post-conviction proceedings shall not be a ground for relief in a proceeding arising under section 2254.

28 U.S.C.A. § 2255. Federal custody; remedies on motion attacking sentence

A prisoner in custody under sentence of a court established by Act of Congress claiming the right to be released upon the ground that the sentence was imposed in violation of the Constitution or laws of the United States, or that the court was without jurisdiction to impose such sentence, or that the sentence was in excess of the maximum authorized by law, or is otherwise subject to collateral attack, may move the court which imposed the sentence to vacate, set aside or correct the sentence.

Unless the motion and the files and records of the case conclusively show that the prisoner is entitled to no relief, the court shall cause notice thereof to be served upon the United States attorney, grant a prompt hearing thereon, determine the issues and make findings of fact and conclusions of law with respect thereto. If the court finds that the judgment was rendered without jurisdiction, or that the sentence imposed was not authorized by law or otherwise open to collateral attack, or that there has been such a denial or infringement of the constitutional rights of the prisoner as to render the judgment vulnerable to collateral attack, the court shall vacate and set the judgment aside and shall discharge the prisoner or resentence him or grant a new trial or correct the sentence as may appear appropriate.

A court may entertain and determine such motion without requiring the production of the prisoner at the hearing.

An appeal may be taken to the court of appeals from the order entered on the motion as from a final judgment on application for a writ of habeas corpus.

An application for a writ of habeas corpus in behalf of a prisoner who is authorized to apply for relief by motion pursuant to this section, shall not be entertained if it appears that the applicant has failed to apply for relief, by motion, to the court which sentenced him, or that such court has denied him relief, unless it also appears that the remedy by motion is inadequate or ineffective to test the legality of his detention.

A 1–year period of limitation shall apply to a motion under this section. The limitation period shall run from the latest of—

(1) the date on which the judgment of conviction becomes final;

(2) the date on which the impediment to making a motion created by governmental action in violation of the Constitution or laws of the United States is removed, if the movant was prevented from making a motion by such governmental action;

(3) the date on which the right asserted was initially recognized by the Supreme Court, if that right has been newly recognized by the Supreme Court and made retroactively applicable to cases on collateral review; or

(4) the date on which the facts supporting the claim or claims presented could have been discovered through the exercise of due diligence.

Except as provided in section 408 of the Controlled Substances Act, in all proceedings brought under this section, and any subsequent proceedings on review, the court may appoint counsel, except as provided by a rule promulgated by the Supreme Court pursuant to statutory authority. Appointment of counsel under this section shall be governed by section 3006A of title 18.

A second or successive motion must be certified as provided in section 2244 by a panel of the appropriate court of appeals to contain—

(1) newly discovered evidence that, if proven and viewed in light of the evidence as a whole, would be sufficient to establish by clear and convincing evidence that no reasonable factfinder would have found the movant guilty of the offense; or

(2) a new rule of constitutional law, made retroactive to cases on collateral review by the Supreme Court, that was previously unavailable.

NOTES

1. **Retroactivity of 1996 amendments.** In Lindh v. Murphy, 521 U.S. 320, 117 S.Ct. 2059, 138 L.Ed.2d 481 (1997) the Court, in a 5 to 4 opinion by Justice Souter, held that the standards of Section 2254(d), as amended in 1996, do not apply to federal habeas applications pending on April 24, 1996, the date of enactment.

2. **Exhaustion of state remedies.** The Supreme Court held in O'Sullivan v. Boerckel, 526 U.S. 838, 119 S.Ct. 1728, 144 L.Ed.2d 1 (1999) that the requirement of exhaustion of state remedies in 28 U.S.C. § 2254(b) means that an applicant must present the federal claim to the highest available court of the state even if that court's review is discretionary with it. In this case, the respondent had not included certain federal claims in a petition for discretionary review to the Illinois Supreme Court from a decision of the Illinois Court of Appeals. Thus, he did not exhaust his state remedies and is precluded from raising those issues in federal habeas.

3. **The requirement of custody.** Collateral attacks are available only to persons who are "in custody" as a result of the convictions sought to be attacked. This is specifically provided in the federal statutes, 28 U.S.C.A. §§ 2254, 2255, and is probably a jurisdictional requirement of the traditional writ of habeas corpus. See L. Yackle, Postconviction Remedies § 43 (1981). But the concept of "custody" has been broadly construed. In Jones v. Cunningham, 371 U.S. 236, 83 S.Ct. 373, 9 L.Ed.2d 285 (1963), the Supreme Court held that a state prisoner who had been released on parole was, given the limitations upon the freedom of a parolee, still "in custody" for purposes of federal habeas corpus. A related issue arises if the petitioner is in custody at the time when relief is applied for but is released before a final adjudication of the issues is reached. In Carafas v. LaVallee, 391 U.S. 234, 88 S.Ct. 1556, 20 L.Ed.2d 554 (1968), the Court held that release of a state prisoner would not render his petition for federal habeas corpus moot as long as there were collateral consequences of the conviction which would be affected by a final determination of the issues raised by the petition.

In Maleng v. Cook, 490 U.S. 488, 109 S.Ct. 1923, 104 L.Ed.2d 540 (1989) was a federal prisoner who had been convicted in state court in 1958, but had fully served that sentence. He later received a state court sentence that was enhanced by the earlier state court conviction, but he will not begin serving that sentence until he is released from federal custody. He challenged the 1958 conviction in federal District Court. The District Court dismissed on the ground he was not in custody under the 1958 conviction. The Ninth Circuit reversed and the Supreme Court, in a per curiam opinion, affirmed. The Supreme Court held that he was not in custody under the 1958 conviction because he had fully served that sentence. However, he was in custody under the yet-to-be-begun state sentence because he was in federal custody subject to a detainer filed by the state authorities. Therefore, he was "in custody" for federal habeas purposes, however, the court declined to decide the extent to which he might challenge the 1958 conviction itself.

How should the "in custody" requirement be employed when the petitioner has received consecutive prison sentences? The petitioner in Garlotte v. Fordice, 515 U.S. 39, 115 S.Ct. 1948, 132 L.Ed.2d 36 (1995) received a three year prison sentence on a marijuana charge and two life sentences of murder charges. The life sentences were imposed consecutively to the three year sentence. After serving the three year sentence, but while still incarcerated on the life sentences, petitioner filed a federal habeas petition challenging the validity of the three year sentence. The District Court denied the petition on the merits, but the Fifth Circuit dismissed the petition on the ground he was no longer in custody under the three year sentence. The Supreme Court, in an opinion by Justice Ginsburg, reversed. In Peyton v. Rowe, 391 U.S. 54, 88 S.Ct. 1549, 20 L.Ed.2d 426 (1968), the Court had held that a state prisoner is "in custody" with respect to a consecutive sentence that he had not yet started serving. This case is *Peyton* in reverse. The key feature in this case is that the three year sentence, although already served, continues to postpone petitioner's parole eligibility date on the two life sentences. Since successful challenge of that sentence would advance petitioner's parole eligibility date, he is still in custody under that sentence.

4. **Issues that can be raised.** What issues can be raised in collateral attacks? In early cases, the United States Supreme Court held that only those defects in the proceedings that deprived the trial court of jurisdiction could be considered on habeas corpus. E.g., Ex parte Watkins, 28 U.S. (3 Pet.) 193, 7 L.Ed. 650 (1830). In Waley v. Johnston, 316 U.S. 101, 62 S.Ct. 964, 86 L.Ed. 1302 (1942), however, the Court rejected this jurisdictional standard and held that any issue of federal constitutional dimensions could be raised by federal habeas corpus. But this is no longer strictly accurate. In Stone v. Powell, 428 U.S. 465, 96 S.Ct. 3037, 49 L.Ed.2d 1067 (1976), the Court held that a state prisoner is not entitled to federal habeas corpus relief on the basis that evidence obtained in violation of his Fourth Amendment right to be free from unreasonable searches and seizures was intro- duced at his trial, unless the prisoner also shows that he was denied a full and fair opportunity to litigate his Fourth Amendment claim in state courts. The majority carefully characterized the exclusionary rule which it held could not be enforced in federal habeas proceedings as "a judicially created remedy rather than a personal constitutional right" and emphasized that its decision "is *not* concerned with the scope of the habeas corpus statute as authority for litigating constitutional claims generally." 428 U.S. at 495 n. 37, 96 S.Ct. at 3053 n. 37, 49 L.Ed.2d at 1088 n. 37.

The reach of Stone v. Powell was discussed in Rose v. Mitchell, 443 U.S. 545, 99 S.Ct. 2993, 61 L.Ed.2d 739 (1979), involving a claim of racial discrimination in the selection of a grand jury foreman. A majority of the Court concluded that the defendant had not established a *prima facie* case that such discrimination took place. But in addition, five members of the Court, in an opinion written by Justice Blackmun, rejected the argument—advanced by Justice Powell in dissent—that Stone v. Powell barred a state defendant from raising claims of the sort at issue in federal habeas corpus proceedings. First, Mitchell's claim included allegations that the state judiciary had violated the Fourteenth Amendment; thus the state judiciary could not be relied upon to provide the "full and fair hearing" such a claim requires and a federal forum remains necessary. Second, the claim was of a violation of "the direct command of the Fourteenth Amendment," rather than a judicially created remedy as in *Stone*. Moreover, state judges may, because of their closeness to the alleged problem, be unable to evaluate discrimination claims adequately and thus federal review is likely to produce "great" educative and deterrent effects. Since states remain free to reindict and reconvict defendants who obtain relief in federal proceedings, the costs of federal intervention are less. Finally, the constitutional interests at stake in a claim of racial discrimination involve "fundamental values of our society and our legal system" and are therefore substantially more compelling than those raised in *Stone*. 443 U.S. at 561–64, 99 S.Ct. at 3003–04, 61 L.Ed.2d at 752–55.

In Kimmelman v. Morrison, 477 U.S. 365, 106 S.Ct. 2574, 91 L.Ed.2d 305 (1986), writing for the Court, Justice Brennan held that the failure of trial defense counsel to request pretrial discovery from the State and, therefore, to move to suppress evidence prior to trial as required by New Jersey law, constituted inadequate performance under the first part of the standard of Strickland v. Washington (see chapter 24). He concluded that the Sixth Amendment claim is distinct, although related to, the Fourth Amendment claim barred by Stone v. Powell:

> Although a meritorious Fourth Amendment issue is necessary to the success of a Sixth Amendment claim like respondent's, a good Fourth Amendment claim alone will not earn a prisoner federal habeas relief.

> Only those habeas petitioners who can prove under *Strickland* that they have been denied a fair trial by the gross incompetence of their attorneys will be granted the writ and will be entitled to retrial without the challenged evidence.

477 U.S. at 382, 106 S.Ct. at 2586–87, 91 L.Ed.2d at 324. The Court refused the invitation of the respondent to rule that the record reflected prejudice under *Strickland* and affirmed the decision of the Court of Appeals remanding for that issue. Justice Powell, joined by Chief Justice Burger and Justice Rehnquist, concurred in the judgment on the ground that an error of counsel that results in reliable evidence not being excluded from the trial can never constitute prejudice under the *Strickland* standard because

> the harm suffered by respondent in this case is not the denial of a fair and reliable adjudication of his guilt, but rather the absence of a windfall.

477 U.S. at 396, 106 S.Ct. at 2594, 91 L.Ed.2d at 333.

In Withrow v. Williams, 507 U.S. 680, 113 S.Ct. 1745, 123 L.Ed.2d 407 (1993), by a 5–to–4 vote, the Court held that the *Stone* approach would not be applied when a state defendant sought federal habeas corpus on grounds that a confession obtained in violation of Miranda v. Arizona, 384 U.S. 436, 86 S.Ct. 1602, 16 L.Ed.2d 694 (1966) had been used to convict him. The reasons for not applying *Stone's* approach to *Miranda* claims, Justice Souter explained for the majority, rest in part upon differences between a state defendant's right under Mapp v. Ohio, 367 U.S. 643, 81 S.Ct. 1684, 6 L.Ed.2d 1081 (1961) to have evidence obtained in violation of the Fourth Amendment excluded from trial and *Miranda*. *Mapp* created no personal constitutional right; *Miranda's* requirements, in contrast, safeguard defendants' Fifth Amendment privilege against self-incrimination, "a fundamental *trial* right." *Mapp* protects privacy rights divorced from the correct ascertainment of guilt in criminal trials. *Miranda,* on the other hand "serves to guard against 'the use of unreliable statements at trial' ""[b]y bracing against 'the possibility of unreliable statements in every instance of in-custody interrogation[.]' "

Most importantly, Justice Souter continued, state prisoners barred from raising *Miranda* claims in federal habeas corpus would simply convert those claims into due process claims that involuntary confessions had been used. Federal courts' workload would not be lightened by limiting habeas petitioners' ability to raise *Miranda* claims; federal judges would simply be confronted with due process involuntariness rather than *Miranda* claims. Nor would this change in the form of claims made by state prisoners go far towards reducing tensions between the state and federal judicial systems. "[E]liminating review of *Miranda* claims," Justice Souter concluded, "would not significantly benefit the federal courts in their exercise of habeas jurisdiction, or advance the cause of federalism in any substantial way." 507 U.S. at 693, 113 S.Ct. at 1754, 123 L.Ed.2d at 420. The Chief Justice and Justices O'Connor, Scalia and Thomas dissented. Justice O'Connor explained that when a case is on collateral review, the "marginal" benefits of applying *Miranda* are outweighed by the costs of undercutting finality of state conviction, aggravating tension between state and federal courts, and sometimes requiring reversal of guilty persons' convictions when the passage of time makes reprosecutions impossible.

5. **Claims of evidence insufficiency.** In contrast to *Stone's* reduction of the issues cognizable in federal habeas corpus is Jackson v. Virginia, 443 U.S. 307, 99 S.Ct. 2781, 61 L.Ed.2d 560 (1979), holding that a state prisoner is entitled, in federal habeas corpus proceedings, to some scrutiny by the federal court of the sufficiency of the evidence showing his guilt. The United States Constitution prohibits conviction of a state defendant except upon proof of guilt beyond a reasonable doubt, In re Winship, 397 U.S. 358, 90 S.Ct. 1068, 25 L.Ed.2d 368 (1970), and when a state conviction is challenged in federal habeas corpus proceedings the federal court has a duty to assess the historic facts necessary to determine whether a federal constitutional right was violated. But in performing this task in the context of sufficiency of the evidence, the majority continued, the federal habeas judge should not ask whether he himself believes that the evidence produced at trial established guilt beyond a reasonable doubt:

> Instead, the relevant question is whether, after viewing the evidence in the light most favorable to the prosecution, any rational trier of fact could have found the essential elements of the crime beyond a reasonable doubt.

443 U.S. at 319, 99 S.Ct. at 2789, 61 L.Ed.2d at 573.

6. **Nonconstitutional claims.** There is authority for the proposition that under some collateral attack schemes nonconstitutional errors of limited sorts may be asserted. Sunal v. Large, 332 U.S. 174, 67 S.Ct. 1588, 91 L.Ed. 1982 (1947), is widely read as indicating that a person convicted in federal court cannot use section 2255 as the vehicle for asserting all matters that, if raised on direct appeal, would constitute reversible error. But in Davis v. United States, 417 U.S. 333, 94 S.Ct. 2298, 41 L.Ed.2d 109 (1974), the Supreme Court, noting that section 2255 refers to prisoners claiming their sentences to have been imposed "in violation of the Constitution *or laws* of the United States," refused to limit section 2255 to constitutional claims. Cautioning that "not ...every asserted error of law can be raised on a § 2255 motion," the Court held that the appropriate inquiry to determine whether an issue could be raised in a motion to vacate sentence under section 2255 is:

> whether the claimed error of law was "a fundamental defect which inherently results in a complete miscarriage of justice," and whether "[i]t ...present[s] exceptional circumstances where the need for the remedy afforded by the writ of *habeas corpus* is apparent."

417 U.S. at 346, 94 S.Ct. at 2305, 41 L.Ed.2d at 119.

7. **Claims of innocence.** Is a claim that a person sentenced to death is innocent of the offense for which he was sentenced independently cognizable on federal habeas corpus? The petitioner in Herrera v. Collins, 506 U.S. 390, 113 S.Ct. 853, 122 L.Ed.2d 203 (1993) was convicted of the capital murder of a police officer and was sentenced to death. Later, he plead guilty to the related killing of another police officer. His conviction and sentence were upheld on direct appeal and on state and federal habeas. Under Texas law, motions for new trial based on newly discovered evidence can be made only within 30 days of sentencing. Ten years after his conviction, petitioner urged in state habeas that he was actually innocent of the murders and produced three affidavits from relatives that his now-deceased brother committed the killings. The Supreme Court, in an opinion by The Chief Justice, held that a claim of actual innocence by a state prisoner is not cognizable on federal habeas corpus,

> [I]n state criminal proceedings the trial is the paramount event for determining the guilt or innocence of the defendant. Federal habeas review of state convictions has traditionally been limited to claims of constitutional violations occurring in the course of the underlying state criminal proceedings * * *. History

shows that the traditional remedy for claims of innocence based on new evidence, discovered too late in the day to file a new trial motion, has been executive clemency.

506 U.S. at 416, 113 S.Ct. at 869, 122 L.Ed.2d at 203. The Court acknowledged "for the sake of argument in deciding this case" that "a truly persuasive demonstration of 'actual innocence' made after trial would render the execution of a defendant unconstitutional" but then asserted that the facts in *Herrera* fell far short of such a demonstration. Justice O'Connor, joined by Justice Kennedy, concurred while expressing doubt about the wisdom of the Court's dictum about a truly persuasive demonstration of actual innocence. She then examined all of the evidence in the case, including the affidavits attesting to petitioner's innocence, and concluded that it shows his guilt "overwhelmingly." Justice Scalia, joined by Justice Thomas, concurred with the observation that "[t]here is no basis * * * for finding in the Constitution a right to demand judicial consideration of newly discovered evidence of innocence brought forward after conviction." Justice White concurred on the explicit assumption that the position expressed in argument by the Court that relief would be granted on a persuasive showing of actual innocence would ultimately prevail. Justice Blackmun, joined in part by Justices Stevens and Souter, dissented and would have remanded the case to District Court to give petitioner an opportunity to prove his innocence.

Wainwright v. Sykes

Supreme Court of the United States, 1977.
433 U.S. 72, 97 S.Ct. 2497, 53 L.Ed.2d 594.

■ MR. JUSTICE REHNQUIST delivered the opinion of the Court.

[Respondent Sykes was convicted of murder in a Florida trial court. A confession made by him during police interrogation was offered by the prosecution, no objection was raised by the defense, and it was admitted. Sykes appealed his conviction but no challenge to the propriety of the admission of the confession was made. Then, in state post-conviction proceedings, he urged that his confession had been obtained in violation of Miranda v. Arizona, 384 U.S. 436, 86 S.Ct. 1602, 16 L.Ed.2d 694 (1966), and its use in his prosecution invalidated his conviction. The state courts rejected this claim, apparently on the ground that the state's "contemporaneous objection" rule barred his claim. Under this rule, a failure to object to evidence at the time of its offer by the prosecution precludes a defendant from later complaining of admission of the evidence. He then sought federal habeas corpus relief, and the lower federal courts ruled in his favor. Editors.]

* * *

The simple legal question before the Court calls for a construction of the language of 28 U.S.C.A. § 2254(a), which provides that the federal courts shall entertain an application for a writ of habeas corpus "in behalf of a person in custody pursuant to the judgment of a state court only on the ground that he is in custody in violation of the Constitution or laws or treaties of the United States." ...

[I]t is a well-established principle of federalism that a state decision resting on an adequate foundation of state substantive law is immune from review in the federal courts. The application of this principle in federal habeas corpus proceedings [has resulted in controversy concerning] ...the reviewability of federal claims which the state court had declined to pass on because not presented in the manner prescribed by its *procedural* rules. ...

In Fay v. Noia, [372 U.S. 391, 83 S.Ct. 822, 9 L.Ed.2d 837 (1963)], respondent Noia sought federal habeas to review a claim that his state-court conviction had resulted from the introduction of a coerced confession in violation of the Fifth Amendment to the United States Constitution. While the convictions of his two codefendants were reversed on that ground in collateral proceedings following their appeals, Noia did not appeal and the New York courts ruled that his subsequent *coram nobis* action was barred on account of that failure. This Court held that petitioner was nonetheless entitled to raise the claim in federal habeas....

As a matter of comity but not of federal power, the Court acknowledged "a limited discretion in the federal judge to deny relief ...to an applicant who had deliberately by-passed the orderly procedure of the state courts and in so doing has forfeited his state court remedies." Id., at 438, 83 S.Ct., at 848. In so stating, the Court made clear that the waiver must be knowing and actual—" 'an intentional relinquishment or abandonment of a known right or privilege.' " Johnson v. Zerbst, 304 U.S., at 464, 83 S.Ct., at 862. ...

A decade later we decided Davis v. United States, [411 U.S. 233, 93 S.Ct. 1577, 36 L.Ed.2d 216 (1973)], in which ...we concluded that review of the [federal prisoner's] claim should be barred on habeas, as on direct appeal, absent a showing of cause for the noncompliance and some showing of actual prejudice resulting from the alleged constitutional violation.

Last Term, in Francis v. Henderson, [425 U.S. 536, 96 S.Ct. 1708, 48 L.Ed.2d 149 (1976)], the rule of *Davis* was applied to the parallel case of a state procedural requirement.... As applied to the federal petitions of state convicts, the *Davis* cause-and-prejudice standard was thus incorporated directly into the body of law governing the availability of federal habeas corpus review.

* * *

We thus come to the crux of this case. Shall the rule of Francis v. Henderson, supra, barring federal habeas review absent a showing of "cause" and "prejudice" attendant to a state procedural waiver, be applied to a waived objection to the admission of a confession at trial? We answer that question in the affirmative.

...We leave open for resolution in future decisions the precise definition of the "cause"-and-"prejudice" standard, and note here only that it is narrower than the standard set forth in dicta in Fay v. Noia, 372 U.S. 391, 83 S.Ct. 822, 9 L.Ed.2d 837 (1963), which would make federal habeas review generally available to state convicts absent a knowing and deliberate waiver of the federal constitutional contention. It is the sweeping language of Fay v. Noia, going far beyond the facts of the case eliciting it, which we today reject.[1]

* * *

1. We have no occasion today to consid-   er the *Fay* rule as applied to the facts there

We think that the rule of Fay v. Noia, broadly stated, may encourage "sandbagging" on the part of defense lawyers, who may take their chances on a verdict of not guilty in a state trial court with the intent to raise their constitutional claims in a federal habeas court if their initial gamble does not pay off. The refusal of federal habeas courts to honor contemporaneous-objection rules may also make state courts themselves less stringent in their enforcement. Under the rule of Fay v. Noia, state appellate courts know that a federal constitutional issue raised for the first time in the proceeding before them may well be decided in any event by a federal *habeas* tribunal. Thus, their choice is between addressing the issue notwithstanding the petitioner's failure to timely object, or else face the prospect that the federal habeas court will decide the question without the benefit of their views.

The failure of the federal habeas courts generally to require compliance with a contemporaneous-objection rule tends to detract from the perception of the trial of a criminal case in state court as a decisive and portentous event. . . .

There is nothing in the Constitution or in the language of § 2254 which requires that the state trial on the issue of guilt or innocence be devoted largely to the testimony of fact witnesses directed to the elements of the state crime, while only later will there occur in a federal habeas hearing a full airing of the federal constitutional claims which were not raised in the state proceedings. If a criminal defendant thinks that an action of the state trial court is about to deprive him of a federal constitutional right there is every reason for his following state procedure in making known his objection.

The "cause"-and-"prejudice" exception of the *Francis* rule will afford an adequate guarantee, we think, that the rule will not prevent a federal habeas court from adjudicating for the first time the federal constitutional claim of a defendant who in the absence of such an adjudication will be the victim of a miscarriage of justice. Whatever precise content may be given those terms by later cases, we feel confident in holding without further elaboration that they do not exist here. Respondent has advanced no explanation whatever for his failure to object at trial,[2] and, as the proceeding unfolded, the trial judge is certainly not to be faulted for failing to question the admission of the confession himself. The other evidence of guilt presented at trial, moreover, was substantial to a degree that would negate any possibility of actual prejudice resulting to the respondent from the admission of his inculpatory statement.

We accordingly conclude that the judgment of the Court of Appeals for the Fifth Circuit must be reversed, and the cause remanded to the United

confronting the Court. Whether the *Francis* rule should preclude federal habeas review of claims not made in accordance with state procedure where the criminal defendant has surrendered, other than for reasons of tactical advantage, the right to have all of his claims of trial error considered by a state appellate court, we leave for another day.

2. In Henry v. Mississippi, [379 U.S. 443, 451, 85 S.Ct. 564, 569, 13 L.Ed.2d 408 (1965)] the Court noted that decisions of counsel relating to trial strategy, even when made without the consultation of the defendant, would bar direct federal review of claims thereby forgone, except where "the circumstances are exceptional."

States District Court for the Middle District of Florida with instructions to dismiss respondent's petition for a writ of habeas corpus.

It is so ordered.

[JUSTICE WHITE concurred in the judgment. The separate concurrences of CHIEF JUSTICE BURGER and JUSTICE STEVENS are omitted.]

■ MR. JUSTICE BRENNAN, with whom MR. JUSTICE MARSHALL joins, dissenting.

* * *

[A]ny realistic system of federal habeas corpus jurisdiction must be premised on the reality that the ordinary procedural default is born of the inadvertence, negligence, inexperience, or incompetence of trial counsel. The case under consideration today is typical. The Court makes no effort to identify a tactical motive for the failure of Sykes' attorney to challenge the admissibility or reliability of a highly inculpatory statement. ...[A]ny realistic reading of the record demonstrates that we are faced here with a lawyer's simple error.

Fay's answer to this is plain: the bypass test simply refuses to credit what is essentially a lawyer's mistake as a forfeiture of constitutional rights. I persist in the belief that the interests of Sykes and the State of Florida are best rationalized by adherence to this test....

Florida, of course, can point to a variety of legitimate interests in seeking allegiance to its reasonable procedural requirements, the contemporaneous-objection rule included.

* * *

Punishing a lawyer's unintentional errors by closing the federal courthouse door to his client is both a senseless and misdirected method of deterring the slighting of state rules. It is senseless because unplanned and unintentional action of any kind generally is not subject to deterrence; and, to the extent that it is hoped that a threatened sanction addressed to the defense will induce greater care and caution on the part of trial lawyers, thereby forestalling negligent conduct or error, the potential loss of all valuable state remedies would be sufficient to this end. And it is a misdirected sanction because even if the penalization of incompetence or carelessness will encourage more thorough legal training and trial preparation, the habeas applicant, as opposed to his lawyer, hardly is the proper recipient of such a penalty. Especially, with fundamental constitutional rights at stake, no fictional relationship of principal-agent or the like can justify holding the criminal defendant accountable for the naked errors of his attorney. This is especially true when so many indigent defendants are without any realistic choice in selecting who ultimately represents them at trial. Indeed, if responsibility for error must be apportioned between the parties, it is the State, through its attorney's admissions and certification policies, that is more fairly held to blame for the fact that practicing lawyers too often are ill-prepared or ill-equipped to act carefully and knowledgeably when faced with decisions governed by state procedural requirements.

* * *

In short, I believe that the demands of our criminal justice system warrant visiting the mistakes of a trial attorney on the head of a habeas corpus applicant only when we are convinced that the lawyer actually exercised his expertise and judgment in his client's service, and with his client's knowing and intelligent participation where possible. This, of course, is the precise system of habeas review established by Fay v. Noia.

* * *

NOTES

1. **Cause.** In Engle v. Isaac, 456 U.S. 107, 102 S.Ct. 1558, 71 L.Ed.2d 783 (1982) the Court further explained the meaning of "cause" for failure to comply with state requirements of contemporaneous objection. The respondents were convicted of murder in a trial in which the trial court instructed the jury that the burden of persuasion on the issue of self-defense rested with them. They made no objection to this instruction; it conformed to long-standing Ohio law on the subject. After the trials, the Supreme Court decided Mullaney v. Wilbur (page 1000, supra) in which it held that under some circumstances due process of law is violated when the state seeks to place the burden of persuasion on the defendant in a criminal case. Respondents urged that objection would have been futile since Ohio law on the subject was firmly established against their position and they further argued that they should not be held to have anticipated the Court's decision in *Mullaney*. Writing for the majority, Justice O'Connor stated:

> [T]he futility of presenting an objection to the state courts cannot alone constitute cause for a failure to object at trial. If a defendant perceives a constitutional claim and believes it may find favor in the federal courts, he may not bypass the state courts simply because he thinks they will be unsympathetic to the claim.

* * *

> We need not decide whether the novelty of a constitutional claim ever establishes cause for a failure to object. We might hesitate to adopt a rule that would require trial counsel either to exercise extraordinary vision or to object to every aspect of the proceedings in the hope that some aspect might mask a latent constitutional claim.

456 U.S. at 130–32, 102 S.Ct. at 1572–73, 71 L.Ed.2d at 802. The Court noted that In re Winship (Chapter 23) decided over 4 years before the respondents' trials, could have been used by trial counsel to construct a constitutional claim concerning the burden of persuasion instruction. Some lower courts had decided that *Winship* required the State to shoulder the burden of persuasion for certain defenses:

> Where the basis of a constitutional claim is available, and other defense counsel have perceived and litigated that claim, the demands of comity and finality counsel against labelling alleged unawareness of the objection as cause for a procedural default.

456 U.S. at 134, 102 S.Ct. at 1574, 71 L.Ed.2d at 804.

Two years later the Court in Reed v. Ross, 468 U.S. 1, 104 S.Ct. 2901, 82 L.Ed.2d 1 (1984), addressed the issue. Respondent was tried in state court for murder. The trial court instructed the jury in accordance with long-standing state law that if the jury found that respondent killed intentionally, the burden shifted to him to show self-defense or that he killed in the heat of passion. The trial antedated the Supreme Court's decision in the Winship case. Ultimately, the Fourth Circuit set aside respondent's conviction on the ground the trial court's instruction violated Mullaney v. Wilbur, which the Supreme Court had earlier held to be fully retroactive. The Court of Appeals excused the failure of respondent to make this claim in the trial court on the ground that at that time the claim would have been novel. The Supreme Court, in an opinion by Justice Brennan, affirmed. If counsel had "no reasonable basis" upon which to formulate a constitutional question, that is cause for failure to assert it in a timely fashion:

> Counsel's failure to raise a claim for which there was no reasonable basis in existing law does not seriously implicate any of the concerns that might otherwise require deference to a State's procedural bar. Just as it is reasonable to assume that a competent lawyer will fail to perceive the possibility of raising such a claim, it is also reasonable to assume that a court will similarly fail to appreciate the claim. It is in the nature of our legal system that legal concepts, including constitutional concepts, develop slowly, finding partial acceptance in some courts while meeting rejection in others. Despite the fact that a constitutional concept may ultimately enjoy general acceptance, as the *Mullaney* issue currently does, when the concept is in its embryonic stage, it will, by hypothesis, be rejected by most courts. Consequently, a rule requiring a defendant to raise a truly novel issue is not likely to serve any functional purpose.

468 U.S. at 15, 104 S.Ct. at 2910, 82 L.Ed.2d at 14. Justice Powell concurred; Justice Rehnquist, joined by The Chief Justice and Justices Blackmun and O'Connor, dissented.

In United States v. Frady, 456 U.S. 152, 102 S.Ct. 1584, 71 L.Ed.2d 816 (1982) the Court had also explicated the cause and prejudice standards of Wainwright v. Sykes. Frady was convicted of first degree murder after a jury trial in a United States District Court in the District of Columbia. After his conviction was affirmed on appeal, he filed a petition for post-conviction relief as a federal prisoner under 28 U.S.C.A. § 2255. He contended that the trial court had erroneously instructed the jury in such a way that it was permitted to presume the presence of the element of malice from certain circumstances of the case. Cases decided after Frady's trial and appeal had established that the instructions given were erroneous. Frady's counsel had not objected to the instructions at trial. The Court of Appeals for the District of Columbia Circuit granted post-conviction relief, basing its decision in part on the ground that failure to object at the trial came within the ambit of the "plain error" standard of Rule 52(b) of the Federal Rules of Criminal Procedure. The Supreme Court, in an opinion authored by Justice O'Connor, reversed. It found that the plain error standard was inappropriate for application in a § 2255 proceeding, as opposed to a direct appeal, on the ground that the governmental interest in finality outweighs the defendant's interest in raising a question in a post-conviction proceeding after time for appeal has expired or the appeal has been unsuccessfully taken:

> [T]he Court of Appeals accorded no significance whatever to the existence of a final judgment perfected by appeal. Once the defendant's chance to appeal has been waived or exhausted ...we are entitled to presume he stands fairly and finally convicted, especially when, as here, he already has had a fair opportunity to present his federal claims to a federal forum. Our trial and appellate procedures are not so unreliable that we may not afford their completed operation any binding effect beyond the next in a series of endless post-conviction collateral attacks.

456 U.S. at 165–66, 102 S.Ct. at 1592–93, 71 L.Ed.2d at 828. The majority concluded that the cause and prejudice requirements of Wainwright v. Sykes apply in the § 2255 proceeding. The majority also concluded that whether there may have been "cause" for failure to object at trial, there was no actual prejudice from the erroneous instruction in this case because of the overwhelming evidence of actual malice introduced in the trial.

2. **Cause in an appeal.** The Supreme Court dealt with the question of the meaning of the requirement of cause for procedural defaults in the appeal of criminal convictions raised upon federal habeas corpus in Murray v. Carrier, 477 U.S. 478, 106 S.Ct. 2639, 91 L.Ed.2d 397 (1986). Justice O'Connor held that so long as there is no claim of ineffective assistance of counsel the type of mistake made by counsel has no bearing on whether the cause requirement of Wainwright v. Sykes has been met. Of course, a claim of ineffective assistance can be made in federal habeas, but the petitioner must exhaust state remedies before doing so. Justice O'Connor did recognize an exception to the requirement of a showing of cause for procedural default "in an extraordinary case, where a constitutional violation has probably resulted in the conviction of one who is actually innocent...." 477 U.S. at 496, 106 S.Ct. at 2649, 91 L.Ed.2d at 413. Justice Brennan, joined by Justice Marshall, dissented. Similarly, see also Smith v. Murray, 477 U.S. 527, 106 S.Ct. 2661, 91 L.Ed.2d 434 (1986) in which Justice Stevens, joined by Justices Marshall, Blackmun and Brennan, dissented.

The matter was again considered in Dugger v. Adams, 489 U.S. 401, 109 S.Ct. 1211, 103 L.Ed.2d 435 (1989). Adams argued that where the error concerns capital sentencing an "innocent" defendant is one who does not deserve the death penalty. Rejecting this, the *Adams* majority noted the difficulty of defining defendants who are "actually innocent" of death penalties. But it relied primarily upon its conclusion that the circumstances failed to show that the erroneous jury instruction concerning sentencing responsibilities resulted in a "fundamental miscarriage of justice." 489 U.S. at 410 n. 6, 109 S.Ct. at 1217–18 n. 6, 103 L.Ed.2d at 446 n. 6.

3. **Identifying the basis for state court decision.** In Harris v. Reed, 489 U.S. 255, 109 S.Ct. 1038, 103 L.Ed.2d 308 (1989), a state procedural default to raising a federal constitutional claim does not bar consideration of a claim for federal habeas corpus relief unless the last state court rendering a judgment in the case " 'clearly and expressly' states that its judgment rests on a state procedural bar."

4. **Failing to appeal in state court.** The petitioner in Coleman v. Thompson, 501 U.S. 722, 111 S.Ct. 2546, 115 L.Ed.2d 640 (1991) was convicted in a Virginia state court of murder and given the death penalty. On direct appeal, the Virginia Supreme Court affirmed the conviction and sentence. Coleman then filed a petition for habeas corpus in the state trial court, alleging various additional federal constitutional grounds for relief. The state trial court conducted a two-day evidentiary hearing and denied all relief. Thirty-three days later, Coleman's attorney filed notice of appeal from that decision to the Virginia Supreme Court. On motion of the Commonwealth, that court dismissed the appeal because notice of appeal had not been given within 30 days of the habeas decision. Coleman then filed a petition for habeas corpus in the United States District Court, making the federal claims he had made in his direct appeal and state habeas proceedings. The District Court ruled that Coleman had procedurally defaulted the claims that had been made only in the state habeas proceeding by failing to file a timely notice of appeal; it also considered all the claims on the merits and denied them. This decision was affirmed by the United States Court of Appeals. The Supreme Court, in an opinion by Justice O'Connor, held that Coleman had procedurally defaulted those claims by filing notice of appeal 3 days late. Under the rule of Fay v. Noia, a procedural default

cannot be found except upon a showing petitioner waived the state remedy by deliberately bypassing it and there was no contention the late notice of appeal was deliberate. However, the Court reasoned subsequent cases, primarily Wainwright v. Sykes signal a change in emphasis from *Fay:*

> In all cases in which a state prisoner has defaulted his federal claims in state court pursuant to an independent and adequate state procedural rule, federal habeas review of the claims is barred unless the prisoner can demonstrate cause for the default and actual prejudice as a result of the alleged violation of federal law, or demonstrate that failure to consider the claims will result in a fundamental miscarriage of justice. *Fay* was based on a conception of federal/state relations that undervalued the importance of state procedural rules. The several cases after *Fay* that applied the cause and prejudice standard to a variety of state procedural defaults represent a different view. We now recognize the important interest in finality served by state procedural rules, and the significant harm to the States that results from the failure of federal courts to respect them.

501 U.S. at 750, 111 S.Ct. at 2565, 115 L.Ed.2d at 669. Coleman argued that his counsel was ineffective in filing notice of appeal late and that should be regarded as cause for excusing the procedural default. The Court rejected that argument,

> There is no constitutional right to an attorney in state post-conviction proceedings. Pennsylvania v. Finley, 481 U.S. 551, 107 S.Ct. 1990, 95 L.Ed.2d 539 (1987); Murray v. Giarratano, 492 U.S. 1, 109 S.Ct. 2765, 106 L.Ed.2d 1 (1989) * * *. Consequently, a petitioner cannot claim constitutionally ineffective assistance of counsel in such proceedings * * *. Coleman contends that it was his attorney's error that led to the late filing of his state habeas appeal. This error cannot be constitutionally ineffective, therefore Coleman must "bear the risk of attorney error that results in a procedural default."

501 U.S. at 752, 111 S.Ct. at 2566, 115 L.Ed.2d at 671. Justice Blackmun, joined by Justices Marshall and Stevens, dissented.

In a related opinion, Ylst v. Nunnemaker, 501 U.S. 797, 111 S.Ct. 2590, 115 L.Ed.2d 706 (1991), the Court dealt with the requirement of Harris v. Reed that a state procedural default requires an express statement of reliance on state law as applied to unexplained, memorandum decisions of state courts. Nunnemaker was convicted in a California state court of murder. The California Court of Appeals affirmed his conviction, rejecting a *Miranda* claim on the ground respondent had not raised it in the trial court. The California Supreme Court denied discretionary review. A state habeas petition was denied without opinion, as was a similar petition in the Court of Appeals. Finally, an original state habeas petition was denied by the California Supreme Court by memorandum decision that cited two cases not here relevant. Respondent filed a federal habeas petition alleging the *Miranda* violation, which was rejected by the United States District Court on the ground of state procedural default. The United States Court of Appeals reversed this decision under Harris v. Reed on the ground that since the California Supreme Court decision was not explicitly based on state grounds, it could not be said the decision was not based on federal grounds rather than state procedural requirements. The United States Supreme Court, in an opinion by Justice Scalia, reversed:

> The * * * question presented by the present case * * * is how federal courts in habeas proceedings are to determine whether an unexplained order (by which we mean an order whose text or accompanying opinion does not disclose the reason for the judgment) rests primarily on federal law. The question is not an easy one * * *.

> The problem we face arises * * * because many formulary orders are not meant to convey *anything* as to the reason for the decision. Attributing a reason is therefore both difficult and artificial. We think that the attribution necessary for federal habeas purposes can be facilitated, and sound results more often assured, by applying the following presumption: where there has been one reasoned state judgment rejecting a federal claim, later unexplained orders upholding that judgment or rejecting the same claim rest upon the same ground. If an earlier opinion "fairly appear[s] to rest primarily upon federal law," * * * we will presume that no procedural default has been invoked by a subsequent unexplained order that leaves the judgment or its consequences in place. Similarly where, as here, the last reasoned opinion on the claim explicitly imposes a procedural default, we will presume that a later decision rejecting the claim did not silently disregard that bar and consider the merits.

501 U.S. at 802–03, 111 S.Ct. at 2594, 115 L.Ed.2d at 716–17. While the presumption is rebuttable, it is not rebutted here. Therefore, the memorandum decision of the California Supreme Court did not alter the procedural default ruling of the earlier California Court of Appeals decision and federal habeas relief is barred under Coleman v. Thompson unless respondent can on remand establish cause and prejudice. Justice Blackmun, joined by Justices Marshall and Stevens, dissented.

5. **Total exhaustion.** As 28 U.S.C.A. § 2254(b) makes clear, a state defendant who seeks federal habeas corpus relief must ordinarily exhaust any available state procedure for raising the issue the defendant seeks to raise in the federal forum. This was affirmed in Duckworth v. Serrano, 454 U.S. 1, 102 S.Ct. 18, 70 L.Ed.2d 1 (1981) (per curiam) and in Rose v. Lundy, 455 U.S. 509, 102 S.Ct. 1198, 71 L.Ed.2d 379 (1982), the Court adopted what it termed a requirement of "total exhaustion." A habeas application must be dismissed if it contains any claims which had not been presented to state courts first. This requirement:

> will encourage state prisoners to seek full relief first from the state courts, thus giving those courts the first opportunity to review all claims of constitutional error. As the number of prisoners who exhaust all of their federal claims increases, state courts may become increasingly familiar with and hospitable toward federal constitutional issues. ... Equally as important, federal claims that have been fully exhausted in state courts will more often be accompanied by a complete factual record to aid the federal courts in their review.

455 U.S. at 518–19, 102 S.Ct. at 1203–04, 71 L.Ed.2d at 388. Justice O'Connor then advanced the proposition, concurred in by only three other justices, that a prisoner faced with the dismissal of his application because it contains unexhausted claims could amend it to eliminate those claims but if that course of action is taken "the prisoner would risk forfeiting his unexhausted claims in federal court" under the doctrine of abuse of the writ of habeas corpus by presenting piecemeal claims to the courts. 455 U.S. at 519, 102 S.Ct. at 1204, 71 L.Ed.2d at 389.

In Anderson v. Harless, 459 U.S. 4, 103 S.Ct. 276, 74 L.Ed.2d 3 (1982) the Court further dealt with the requirement of exhaustion of state remedies. Respondent was convicted of murder in a trial in which the jury was instructed in such a way that the burden of persuasion may have been shifted in violation of Sandstrom v. Montana, 442 U.S. 510, 99 S.Ct. 2450, 61 L.Ed.2d 39 (1979). However in state appeals, Respondent simply cited a state case that had dealt with the impropriety of such an instruction under state law. A petition for writ of habeas corpus in federal court was granted and affirmed on appeal. The Supreme Court reversed in a per curiam opinion. The Court noted that "it is not enough that all the facts necessary to support the federal claim were before the state courts ... or that a somewhat similar state-law claim was made. ... [T]he habeas petitioner must have 'fairly presented' to the state courts the 'substance' of his federal habeas corpus claim."

459 U.S. at 6, 103 S.Ct. at 277, 74 L.Ed.2d at 7. See also Castille v. Peoples, 489 U.S. 346, 109 S.Ct. 1056, 103 L.Ed.2d 380 (1989).

6. **State forfeiture of exhaustion claim.** Is the requirement of exhaustion of state remedies waived if the state fails to raise it before the United States District Court? The petitioner in Granberry v. Greer, 481 U.S. 129, 107 S.Ct. 1671, 95 L.Ed.2d 119 (1987), an Illinois prisoner, lost in the District Court on a motion to dismiss for failure to state a claim. He appealed to the Seventh Circuit, where the State of Illinois, for the first time, raised his failure to exhaust state remedies. The Court of Appeals rejected petitioner's argument that the State had waived the exhaustion requirement by failure to raise it before the District Court and, without reaching the merits, remanded the case for dismissal without prejudice. The United States Supreme Court, in an unusual unanimous opinion authored by Justice Stevens, reversed:

> How an appellate court ought to handle a nonexhausted habeas petition when the State has not raised this objection in the district court is a question that might be answered in three different ways. We might treat the State's silence on the matter as a procedural default precluding the State from raising the issue on appeal. At the other extreme, we might treat nonexhaustion as an inflexible bar to consideration of the merits of the petition by the federal court, and therefore require that a petition be dismissed when it appears that there has been a failure to exhaust. Or, third, we might adopt an intermediate approach and direct the courts of appeals to exercise discretion in each case to decide whether the administration of justice would be better served by insisting on exhaustion or by reaching the merits of the petition forthwith.

481 U.S. at 131, 107 S.Ct. at 1673, 95 L.Ed.2d at 123. The Court had previously decided that failure to exhaust does not deprive an appellate court of jurisdiction to consider the federal claim on its merits. Adopting the second position would encourage the state to withhold its exhaustion defense until after a determination on the merits by the District Court, which is "unwise." Eschewing both extremes, the Court adopted the "intermediate approach" and illustrated some of the considerations that should guide courts of appeals in exercising their discretion:

> If . . . the case presents an issue on which an unresolved question of fact or of state law might have an important bearing, both comity and judicial efficiency may make it appropriate for the court to insist on complete exhaustion to make sure that it may ultimately review the issue on a fully informed basis. On the other hand, if it is perfectly clear that the applicant does not raise even a colorable federal claim, the interests of the petitioner, the warden, the state attorney general, the state courts, and the federal courts will all be well served even if the State fails to raise the exhaustion defense, [if] the district court denies the habeas petition, and the court of appeals affirmed the judgment of the district court forthwith.

> Conversely, if a full trial has been held in the district court and it is evident that a miscarriage of justice has occurred, it may also be appropriate for the court of appeals to hold that the nonexhaustion defense has been waived in order to avoid unnecessary delay in granting relief that is plainly warranted.

481 U.S. at 134–35, 107 S.Ct. at 1675–76, 95 L.Ed.2d at 125–26.

7. **Writ abuse.** The subject of abuse of the writ of habeas corpus was addressed in McCleskey v. Zant, 499 U.S. 467, 111 S.Ct. 1454, 113 L.Ed.2d 517 (1991). McCleskey was convicted of murder in a Georgia state court and given the death penalty. After losing appeals, he filed a state habeas corpus petition in which, among other grounds of relief, he claimed a custodial statement had been obtained in violation of Massiah v. United States. Relief was denied. He filed his first federal

habeas petition, in which he made several claims, but not the Massiah claim. Relief was ultimately denied, as was relief on a second state habeas petition. McCleskey then filed his second federal habeas petition, alleging seven grounds of relief, including the Massiah claim missing from the first federal habeas petition. The United States District Court granted relief based on the Massiah claim. It also rejected an argument by the State that McCleskey had abused the federal writ by finding that he had not deliberately abandoned his Massiah claim by failing to raise it in the first federal petition. The United States Court of Appeals reversed the District Court, finding that McCleskey had deliberately abandoned the Massiah claim.

The United States Supreme Court, in an opinion by Justice Kennedy, affirmed the Court of Appeals. It held that a showing of deliberate abandonment was not required for abuse of the writ, that "the same standard [Wainwright v. Sykes] used to determine whether to excuse state procedural defaults should govern the determination of inexcusable neglect in the abuse of the writ context." 499 U.S. at 490, 111 S.Ct. at 1468, 113 L.Ed.2d at 542. The Court then attempted to define a process for resolving questions of writ abuse under this standard:

> When a prisoner files a second or subsequent application, the government bears the burden of pleading abuse of the writ. The government satisfies this burden if, with clarity and particularity, it notes petitioner's prior writ history, identifies the claims that appear for the first time, and alleges that petitioner has abused the writ. The burden to disprove abuse then becomes petitioner's. To excuse his failure to raise the claim earlier, he must show cause for failing to raise it and prejudice therefrom as those concepts have been defined in our procedural default decisions. The petitioner's opportunity to meet the burden of cause and prejudice will not include an evidentiary hearing if the district court determines as a matter of law that petitioner cannot satisfy the standard. If petitioner cannot show cause, the failure to raise the claim in an earlier petition may nonetheless be excused if he or she can show that a fundamental miscarriage of justice would result from a failure to entertain the claim.

499 U.S. at 494–95, 111 S.Ct. at 1470, 113 L.Ed.2d at 545. Finally, the Court concluded that "the requirement of cause * * * is based on the principle that petitioner must conduct a reasonable and diligent investigation aimed at including all relevant claims and grounds for relief in the first federal habeas petition." 499 U.S. at 498, 111 S.Ct. at 1472, 113 L.Ed.2d at 547. Justice Marshall, joined by Justices Blackmun and Stevens, dissented.

Felker v. Turpin

Supreme Court of the United States, 1996.
518 U.S. 651, 116 S.Ct. 2333, 135 L.Ed.2d 827.

■ CHIEF JUSTICE REHNQUIST delivered the opinion of the Court.

Title I of the Antiterrorism and Effective Death Penalty Act of 1996 (Act) works substantial changes to chapter 153 of Title 28 of the United States Code, which authorizes federal courts to grant the writ of habeas corpus. Pub.L. 104–132, 110 Stat. 1217. We hold that the Act does not preclude this Court from entertaining an application for habeas corpus relief, although it does affect the standards governing the granting of such relief. We also conclude that the availability of such relief in this Court obviates any claim by petitioner under the Exceptions Clause of Article III,

§ 2, of the Constitution, and that the operative provisions of the Act do not violate the Suspension Clause of the Constitution, Art. I, § 9.

I

On a night in 1976, petitioner approached Jane W. in his car as she got out of hers. Claiming to be lost and looking for a party nearby, he used a series of deceptions to induce Jane to accompany him to his trailer home in town. Petitioner forcibly subdued her, raped her, and sodomized her. Jane pleaded with petitioner to let her go, but he said he could not because she would notify the police. She escaped later, when petitioner fell asleep. Jane notified the police, and petitioner was eventually convicted of aggravated sodomy and sentenced to 12 years' imprisonment.

Petitioner was paroled four years later. On November 23, 1981, he met Joy Ludlam, a cocktail waitress, at the lounge where she worked. She was interested in changing jobs, and petitioner used a series of deceptions involving offering her a job at "The Leather Shoppe," a business he owned, to induce her to visit him the next day. The last time Joy was seen alive was the evening of the next day. Her dead body was discovered two weeks later in a creek. Forensic analysis established that she had been beaten, raped, and sodomized, and that she had been strangled to death before being left in the creek. Investigators discovered hair resembling petitioner's on Joy's body and clothes, hair resembling Joy's in petitioner's bedroom, and clothing fibers like those in Joy's coat in the hatchback of petitioner's car. One of petitioner's neighbors reported seeing Joy's car at petitioner's house the day she disappeared. A jury convicted petitioner of murder, rape, aggravated sodomy, and false imprisonment. Petitioner was sentenced to death on the murder charge. The Georgia Supreme Court affirmed petitioner's conviction and death sentence, Felker v. State, 252 Ga. 351, 314 S.E.2d 621, and we denied certiorari, 469 U.S. 873, 105 S.Ct. 229, 83 L.Ed.2d 158 (1984). A state trial court denied collateral relief, the Georgia Supreme Court declined to issue a certificate of probable cause to appeal the denial, and we again denied certiorari. Felker v. Zant, 502 U.S. 1064, 112 S.Ct. 950, 117 L.Ed.2d 118 (1992).

Petitioner then filed a petition for a writ of habeas corpus in the United States District Court for the Middle District of Georgia, alleging that (1) the State's evidence was insufficient to convict him; (2) the State withheld exculpatory evidence, in violation of Brady v. Maryland, 373 U.S. 83, 83 S.Ct. 1194, 10 L.Ed.2d 215 (1963); (3) petitioner's counsel rendered ineffective assistance at sentencing; (4) the State improperly used hypnosis to refresh a witness' memory; and (5) the State violated double jeopardy and collateral estoppel principles by using petitioner's crime against Jane W. as evidence at petitioner's trial for crimes against Joy Ludlam. The District Court denied the petition. The United States Court of Appeals for the Eleventh Circuit affirmed, 52 F.3d 907, extended on denial of petition for rehearing, 62 F.3d 342 (1995), and we denied certiorari, 516 U.S. 1133 (1996).

The State scheduled petitioner's execution for the period May 2–9, 1996. On April 29, 1996, petitioner filed a second petition for state collateral relief. The state trial court denied this petition May 1, and the Georgia Supreme Court denied certiorari May 2.

On April 24, 1996, the President signed the Act into law. Title I of this Act contained a series of amendments to existing federal habeas corpus law. The provisions of the Act pertinent to this case concern second or successive habeas corpus applications by state prisoners. Subsections 106(b)(1) and (b)(2) specify the conditions under which claims in second or successive applications must be dismissed, amending 28 U.S.C. § 2244(b) to read:

> (1) A claim presented in a second or successive habeas corpus application under section 2254 that was presented in a prior application shall be dismissed.

> (2) A claim presented in a second or successive habeas corpus application under section 2254 that was not presented in a prior application shall be dismissed unless—

>> (A) the applicant shows that the claim relies on a new rule of constitutional law, made retroactive to cases on collateral review by the Supreme Court, that was previously unavailable; or

>> (B)(i) the factual predicate for the claim could not have been discovered previously through the exercise of due diligence; and

>> (ii) the facts underlying the claim, if proven and viewed in light of the evidence as a whole, would be sufficient to establish by clear and convincing evidence that, but for constitutional error, no reasonable factfinder would have found the applicant guilty of the underlying offense.

110 Stat. 1220–1221.

Subsection 106(b)(3) creates a "gatekeeping" mechanism for the consideration of second or successive applications in district court. The prospective applicant must file in the court of appeals a motion for leave to file a second or successive habeas application in the district court. § 106(b)(3)(A). A three-judge panel has 30 days to determine whether "the application makes a prima facie showing that the application satisfies the requirements of" § 106(b). § 106(b)(3)(C); see §§ 106(b)(3)(B), (D). Section 106(b)(3)(E) specifies that "[t]he grant or denial of an authorization by a court of appeals to file a second or successive application shall not be appealable and shall not be the subject of a petition for rehearing or for a writ of certiorari."

On May 2, 1996, petitioner filed in the United States Court of Appeals for the Eleventh Circuit a motion for stay of execution and a motion for leave to file a second or successive federal habeas corpus petition under § 2254. Petitioner sought to raise two claims in his second petition, the first being that the state trial court violated due process by equating guilt "beyond a reasonable doubt" with "moral certainty" of guilt in voir dire and jury instructions. See Cage v. Louisiana, 498 U.S. 39, 111 S.Ct. 328, 112 L.Ed.2d 339 (1990). He also alleged that qualified experts, reviewing the forensic evidence after his conviction, had established that Joy must have died during a period when petitioner was under police surveillance for Joy's disappearance and thus had a valid alibi. He claimed that the testimony of the State's forensic expert at trial was suspect because he is not a licensed physician, and that the new expert testimony so discredited the State's testimony at trial that petitioner had a colorable claim of factual innocence.

The Court of Appeals denied both motions the day they were filed, concluding that petitioner's claims had not been presented in his first habeas petition, that they did not meet the standards of § 106(b)(2) of the Act, and that they would not have satisfied pre-Act standards for obtaining review on the merits of second or successive claims. 83 F.3d 1303 (C.A.11 1996). Petitioner filed in this Court a pleading styled a "Petition for Writ of Habeas Corpus, for Appellate or Certiorari Review of the Decision of the United States Circuit Court for the Eleventh Circuit, and for Stay of Execution." On May 3, we granted petitioner's stay application and petition for certiorari. We ordered briefing on the extent to which the provisions of Title I of the Act apply to a petition for habeas corpus filed in this Court, whether application of the Act suspended the writ of habeas corpus in this case, and whether Title I of the Act, especially § 106(b)(3)(E), constitutes an unconstitutional restriction on the jurisdiction of this Court. 517 U.S. 1182 (1996).

II

We first consider to what extent the provisions of Title I of the Act apply to petitions for habeas corpus filed as original matters in this Court pursuant to 28 U.S.C. §§ 2241 and 2254. We conclude that although the Act does impose new conditions on our authority to grant relief, it does not deprive this Court of jurisdiction to entertain original habeas petitions.

A

Section 106(b)(3)(E) of the Act prevents this Court from reviewing a court of appeals order denying leave to file a second habeas petition by appeal or by writ of certiorari. More than a century ago, we considered whether a statute barring review by appeal of the judgment of a circuit court in a habeas case also deprived this Court of power to entertain an original habeas petition. Ex parte Yerger, 8 Wall. 85, 19 L.Ed. 332 (1869). We consider the same question here with respect to § 106(b)(3)(E).

Yerger's holding is best understood in the light of the availability of habeas corpus review at that time. Section 14 of the Judiciary Act of 1789 authorized all federal courts, including this Court, to grant the writ of habeas corpus, when prisoners were "in custody, under or by colour of the authority of the United States, or [were] committed for trial before some court of the same." Act of Sept. 24, 1789, ch. 20, § 14, 1 Stat. 82. Congress greatly expanded the scope of federal habeas corpus in 1867, authorizing federal courts to grant the writ, "in addition to the authority already conferred by law," "in all cases where any person may be restrained of his or her liberty in violation of the constitution, or of any treaty or law of the United States." Act of Feb. 5, 1867, ch. 28, 14 Stat. 385. Before the Act of 1867, the only instances in which a federal court could issue the writ to produce a state prisoner were if the prisoner was "necessary to be brought into court to testify," Act of Sept. 24, 1789, ch. 20, § 14, 1 Stat. 82, was "committed . . . for any act done . . . in pursuance of a law of the United States," Act of Mar. 2, 1833, ch. 57, § 7, 4 Stat. 634–635, or was a "subjec[t] or citize[n] of a foreign State, and domiciled therein," and held under state law, Act of Aug. 29, 1842, ch. 257, 5 Stat. 539–540.

The Act of 1867 also expanded our statutory appellate jurisdiction to authorize appeals to this Court from the final decision of any circuit court on a habeas petition. 14 Stat. 386. This enactment changed the result of Barry v. Mercein, 5 How. 103, 12 L.Ed. 70 (1847), in which we had held that the Judiciary Act of 1789 did not authorize this Court to conduct appellate review of circuit court habeas decisions. However, in 1868, Congress revoked the appellate jurisdiction it had given in 1867, repealing "so much of the [Act of 1867] as authorizes an appeal from the judgment of the circuit court to the Supreme Court of the United States." Act of Mar. 27, 1868, ch. 34, § 2, 15 Stat. 44.

In *Yerger,* we considered whether the Act of 1868 deprived us not only of power to hear an appeal from a inferior court's decision on a habeas petition, but also of power to entertain a habeas petition to this Court under § 14 of the Act of 1789. We concluded that the 1868 Act did not affect our power to entertain such habeas petitions. We explained that the 1868 Act's text addressed only jurisdiction over appeals conferred under the Act of 1867, not habeas jurisdiction conferred under the Acts of 1789 and 1867. We rejected the suggestion that the Act of 1867 had repealed our habeas power by implication. *Yerger,* 8 Wall., at 105, 19 L.Ed. 332. Repeals by implication are not favored, we said, and the continued exercise of original habeas jurisdiction was not "repugnant" to a prohibition on review by appeal of circuit court habeas judgments. Ibid.

Turning to the present case, we conclude that Title I of the Act has not repealed our authority to entertain original habeas petitions, for reasons similar to those stated in *Yerger.* No provision of Title I mentions our authority to entertain original habeas petitions; in contrast, § 103 amends the Federal Rules of Appellate Procedure to bar consideration of original habeas petitions in the courts of appeals. Although § 106(b)(3)(E) precludes us from reviewing, by appeal or petition for certiorari, a judgment on an application for leave to file a second habeas petition in district court, it makes no mention of our authority to hear habeas petitions filed as original matters in this Court. As we declined to find a repeal of § 14 of the Judiciary Act of 1789 as applied to this Court by implication then, we decline to find a similar repeal of § 2241 of Title 28—its descendant, n. 1, supra—by implication now.

This conclusion obviates one of the constitutional challenges raised. The critical language of Article III, § 2, of the Constitution provides that, apart from several classes of cases specifically enumerated in this Court's original jurisdiction, "[i]n all the other Cases . . . the supreme Court shall have appellate Jurisdiction, both as to Law and Fact, with such Exceptions, and under such Regulations as the Congress shall make." Previous decisions construing this clause have said that while our appellate powers "are given by the constitution," "they are limited and regulated by the [Judiciary Act of 1789], and by such other acts as have been passed on the subject." Durousseau v. United States, 6 Cranch 307, 314, 3 L.Ed. 232 (1810); see also United States v. More, 3 Cranch 159, 172–173, 2 L.Ed. 397 (1805). The Act does remove our authority to entertain an appeal or a petition for a writ of certiorari to review a decision of a court of appeals exercising its "gatekeeping" function over a second petition. But since it does not repeal our authority to entertain a petition for habeas corpus, there can be no plausible argument that the Act has deprived this Court of appellate jurisdiction in violation of Article III, § 2.

B

We consider next how Title I affects the requirements a state prisoner must satisfy to show he is entitled to a writ of habeas corpus from this Court. Title I of the Act has changed the standards governing our consideration of habeas petitions by imposing new requirements for the granting of relief to state prisoners. Our authority to grant habeas relief to state prisoners is limited by § 2254, which specifies the conditions under which such relief may be granted to "a person in custody pursuant to the judgment of a State court." § 2254(a). Several sections of the Act impose new requirements for the granting of relief under this section, and they therefore inform our authority to grant such relief as well.

Section 106(b) of the Act addresses second or successive habeas petitions. Section 106(b)(3)'s "gatekeeping" system for second petitions does not apply to our consideration of habeas petitions because it applies to applications "filed in the district court." § 106(b)(3)(A). There is no such limitation, however, on the restrictions on repetitive and new claims imposed by subsections 106(b)(1) and (2). These restrictions apply without qualification to any "second or successive habeas corpus application under section 2254." §§ 106(b)(1), (2). Whether or not we are bound by these restrictions, they certainly inform our consideration of original habeas petitions.

III

Next, we consider whether the Act suspends the writ of habeas corpus in violation of Article I, § 9, clause 2, of the Constitution. This clause provides that "[t]he Privilege of the Writ of Habeas Corpus shall not be suspended, unless when in Cases of Rebellion or Invasion the public Safety may require it."

The writ of habeas corpus known to the Framers was quite different from that which exists today. As we explained previously, the first Congress made the writ of habeas corpus available only to prisoners confined under the authority of the United States, not under state authority. Supra, at 6–7; see Ex parte Dorr, 3 How. 103, 11 L.Ed. 514 (1844). The class of judicial actions reviewable by the writ was more restricted as well. In Ex parte Watkins, 3 Pet. 193, 7 L.Ed. 650 (1830), we denied a petition for a writ of habeas corpus from a prisoner "detained in prison by virtue of the judgment of a court, which court possesses general and final jurisdiction in criminal cases." Id., at 202. Reviewing the English common law which informed American courts' understanding of the scope of the writ, we held that "[t]he judgment of the circuit court in a criminal case is of itself evidence of its own legality," and that we could not "usurp that power by the instrumentality of the writ of habeas corpus." Id., at 207.

It was not until 1867 that Congress made the writ generally available in "all cases where any person may be restrained of his or her liberty in violation of the constitution, or of any treaty or law of the United States." Supra, at 6. And it was not until well into this century that this Court interpreted that provision to allow a final judgment of conviction in a state court to be collaterally attacked on habeas. See, e.g., Waley v. Johnston, 316 U.S. 101, 62 S.Ct. 964, 86 L.Ed. 1302 (1942); Brown v. Allen, 344 U.S. 443 (1953). But we assume, for purposes of decision here, that the Suspension Clause of the Constitution refers to the writ as it exists today, rather than as it existed in 1789. See Swain v. Pressley, 430 U.S. 372, 97 S.Ct. 1224, 51 L.Ed.2d 411 (1977); id., at 385 (Burger, C.J., concurring).

The Act requires a habeas petitioner to obtain leave from the court of appeals before filing a second habeas petition in the district court. But this requirement simply transfers from the district court to the court of appeals a screening function which would previously have been performed by the district court as required by 28 U.S.C. § 2254 Rule 9(b). The Act also codifies some of the pre-existing limits on successive petitions, and further restricts the availability of relief to habeas petitioners. But we have long recognized that "the power to award the writ by any of the courts of the United States, must be given by written law," Ex parte Bollman, 4 Cranch 75, 94, 2 L.Ed. 554 (1807), and we have likewise recognized that judgments about the proper scope of the writ are "normally for Congress to make." Lonchar v. Thomas, 517 U.S. 314, ___ (slip op., at 8).

The new restrictions on successive petitions constitute a modified res judicata rule, a restraint on what is called in habeas corpus practice "abuse of the writ." In McCleskey v. Zant, 499 U.S. 467, 111 S.Ct. 1454, 113 L.Ed.2d 517 (1991), we said that "the doctrine of abuse of the writ refers to a complex and evolving body of equitable principles informed and controlled by historical usage, statutory developments, and judicial decisions." Id., at 489. The added restrictions which the Act places on second habeas petitions are well within the compass of this evolutionary process, and we hold that they do not amount to a "suspension" of the writ contrary to Article I, § 9.

IV

We have answered the questions presented by the petition for certiorari in this case, and we now dispose of the petition for an original writ of habeas corpus. Our Rule 20.4(a) delineates the standards under which we grant such writs:

> A petition seeking the issuance of a writ of habeas corpus shall comply with the requirements of 28 U.S.C. §§ 2241 and 2242, and in particular with the provision in the last paragraph of § 2242 requiring a statement of the "reasons for not making application to the district court of the district in which the applicant is held." If the relief sought is from the judgment of a state court, the petition shall set forth specifically how and wherein the petitioner has exhausted available remedies in the state courts or otherwise comes within the provisions

of 28 U.S.C. § 2254(b). To justify the granting of a writ of habeas corpus, the petitioner must show exceptional circumstances warranting the exercise of the Court's discretionary powers and must show that adequate relief cannot be obtained in any other form or from any other court. These writs are rarely granted.

Reviewing petitioner's claims here, they do not materially differ from numerous other claims made by successive habeas petitioners which we have had occasion to review on stay applications to this Court. Neither of them satisfies the requirements of the relevant provisions of the Act, let alone the requirement that there be "exceptional circumstances" justifying the issuance of the writ.

* * *

The petition for writ of certiorari is dismissed for want of jurisdiction. The petition for an original writ of habeas corpus is denied. It is so ordered.

■ JUSTICE STEVENS, with whom JUSTICE SOUTER and JUSTICE BREYER join, concurring [omitted].

■ JUSTICE SOUTER, with whom JUSTICE STEVENS and JUSTICE BREYER join, concurring [omitted].

*

INDEX

References are to Pages

[1]